Praise for *To Obama*

A *DAILY TELEGRAPH* BOOK OF THE YEAR

'A moving and inevitably nostalgic or even elegiac read, redolent of the human grace and statesmanship of the Obama presidency, qualities so brutally absent in the current administration' *Observer*

'*To Obama* gives us a glimpse of a secret and incredibly sweet world within his White House, and paints a portrait of a man deeply concerned with his citizens' problems, struggling to do the right thing … Startling, delicate and immensely readable … Another poignant reminder of what once was' *Daily Telegraph*

'These stories, when you read them all together, tell the American story. It's inspirational, it's frustrating, it's angry, it's grateful, it's resilient' Valerie Jarrett, Senior Advisor to President Barack Obama

'The empathetic, often poetic, polar opposite of the Trump Twitter feed' *Vogue*

'For once, the president is refreshingly not the star of the show. That prize goes to his correspondents, whose loving, joyful, angry and despairing words tell the real story of Obama's America' *Sunday Times*

'Full of lovely details … The insight into America provided by the letters cleverly selected by Laskas is fascinating' *Literary Review*

'The heartbreaking, hope-inducing letters tell the story of a nation' *Elle*

ABOUT THE AUTHOR

JEANNE MARIE LASKAS is the author of eight books, including the *New York Times* bestseller *Concussion,* the basis for the 2015 Golden Globe–nominated film starring Will Smith. She is a contributing writer at the *New York Times Magazine,* a correspondent at *GQ* and a two-time National Magazine Award finalist. Her stories have also appeared in the *New Yorker,* the *Atlantic* and *Esquire.* She serves as Distinguished Professor of English and founding director of the Center for Creativity at the University of Pittsburgh, and lives on a farm in Pennsylvania with her husband and two children.

Jeannemarielaskas.com
@jmlaskas

ALSO BY JEANNE MARIE LASKAS

Concussion

Hidden America

Growing Girls

The Exact Same Moon

Fifty Acres and a Poodle

We Remember

The Balloon Lady and Other People I Know

TO
OBAMA
A PEOPLE'S
HISTORY

JEANNE MARIE LASKAS

BLOOMSBURY PUBLISHING
LONDON · OXFORD · NEW YORK · NEW DELHI · SYDNEY

BLOOMSBURY PUBLISHING
Bloomsbury Publishing Plc
50 Bedford Square, London, WC1B 3DP, UK

BLOOMSBURY, BLOOMSBURY PUBLISHING and the Diana logo are trademarks of
Bloomsbury Publishing Plc

First published in 2018 in the United States by Random House, an imprint
and division of Penguin Random House LLC, New York
First published in Great Britain 2018
This edition published 2019

A catalogue record for this book is available from the British Library

ISBN: HB: 978-1-4088-9452-1; TPB: 978-1-4088-9451-4;
eBook: 978-1-4088-9454-5; PB: 978-1-4088-9450-7

2 4 6 8 10 9 7 5 3 1

Printed and bound in Great Britain by CPI Group (UK) Ltd, Croydon CR0 4YY

To find out more about our authors and books visit
www.bloomsbury.com and sign up for our newsletters

For Anna and Sasha

Contents

TO
OBAMA

Samples, 2008-2009

Gold Hill, OR

November 10, 2008

President-Elect Barack Obama
United States Senate
713 Hart Senate Office Building
Washington DC 20510

Dear President-Elect Obama,

My name is Benjamin Durrett. I am 18 years old. This was my first time voting, and let me tell you it was not a fun experience. I fought with my father over this election so much that I didn't get my ballot filled out till the morning of the election. It was not until that night when the Democrats had a chance to get sixty chairs that I saw some of the things my father was talking about. He showed me how the Democratic Party now has majority control over all branches of the government. He even went as far as to say that we may not have an election in 2012. After he had finished his rant he looked at me, and said "I pray that you are right and I am wrong." Voting for you in this election was truly the first time I have done something that went against my father. I feel that this has been a big step in becoming the person I am meant to become. I truly believe that you are the man who can make this place we call home a great one again. If we are doomed to collapse then so be it, I will look like a fool along with all of my friends, and my father will tell me its okay and that I never could have predicted this. I don't know what you have to do to fix this place we live in. I don't even know if you can. All I ask is that you give it everything you have. If you do that I will know that I made the right choice.

Sincerely,

Benjamin Durrett

38/SAMPLE

MK

June 3, 2009

Dear President Obama,

I saw a report that you take 10 randomly selected letters each day to prepare a response. I hope mine is one of them. I really need to hear from you.

The country I once knew and deeply cared about is disappearing. The capital that I and other generations before me built is being squandered. I have played by the rules thinking my family and I would be secure and that the preparation for old age would be safe in a country that would continue to honor the values of integrity (being a person of your word), fairness (you reap what you sew), self reliance, and discipline(forgoing short term reward for long term gain). All this is crumbling. It started before your watch but is accelerating during your administration. I am saddened.

Let me tell you why I think this way. Like you, I was raised by a single mom of very modest means. My Dad was killed in a plane accident when I was 11. My mom had saved enough to start me in college. I paid for most of it and for all of my MBA which I earned after serving as a US Army Officer. I worked for AT&T/Lucent for 28 years and through a lot of discipline (see definition above) I paid for 2 daughter's undergraduate degrees and helped them with their Masters in Social Work. I have been married for 40 years. I carry no debt except a mortgage. I have served as a church officer, been president of my national fraternity and now tutor, run a business, provide SCORE counseling and serve on a non- profit board. In short I have done my part as a patriotic American and have saved for my retirement without being a burden to my fellow countrymen. I have done all this without government help except for the little I received from the GI bill.

Unfortunately, it appears I have been a sucker. I could be getting transfer payments for being irresponsible i. e. borrowing beyond my means to buy creature comforts, taking extravagant vacations and manipulating the weak to enter agreements they could not afford. I could have avoided the Army. I could have spent all my kid's college money on myself. Instead, I am rewarding this behavior today through my tax dollars and your decisions. Not only that, but I believe the dollar will fail under your wasteful spending and transfer payments to the least productive among us. My savings will be worthless. All my hard work and sacrifice to no avail. All that American capital (moral and physical) from generations past will be spent.

What's more, you make all these decisions knowing that you and your family will never be affected by them. You will always be protected when social unrest and collapse destroys the rest of us.

Here is my request. Reward integrity (people who keep their word), let people reap what they sew (the good and the painful), recognize citizens who have been self reliant and preserve the system that allowed them to become that way, show discipline and demand it of others.

Also, on a personal note, fight against hubris. To be human is to be prone to that condition. I see signs that it is affecting you on the Brian Williams White House report and in your decision to go to NYC on a personal trip using my tax dollars. I think you are probably a decent man but even you can be destroyed by hubris.

I remain a loyal American who at least wrote a letter,

Reply.

Richard A Dexter

Dover, N H

Richard —

THE WHITE HOUSE
WASHINGTON

Thanks for your letter, and for your service to our country. I applaud your life of responsibility, but frankly am puzzled as to why you think I don't share in those values. The only transfer payments we have initiated were to states to prevent wholesale cuts in teachers, police officers, firefighters etc. in the wake of the financial crisis, and short term measures to prevent the banking and auto sectors from collapsing. (over)

You may disagree with some of these policies, but please know that all I want to see is the hard work of individuals like you rewarded.

Again, thank you for your thoughtful note.

Richard A. Dexter

Dover, New Hampshire

JUN 2 2 2009

Jeri LeAnne Harris
Alger, MI

November 5, 2008

President-Elect Barack Obama
John C. Kluczynski Federal Office Building
230 South Dearborn St.
Suite 3900 (39th floor)
Chicago, Illinois 60604

Dear President-Elect Obama,

I'm not quite sure why I am writing to you, but as I feel compelled to do so – here goes! I am a 'dyed in the wool' republican. I didn't vote for you and felt with my whole heart that you should have been defeated (Not the best start for a letter – smile).

HOWEVER, my country didn't agree with me and therefore, you are going to be the 44th President ... my President of these great United States. As of 12pm last night – my heart changed. I wanted to tell you that even though I did not cast my vote for you, I respect the race that you ran and I will commit to you today – that I will pray for you and your presidency each and every day.

I have voted since I was 18 (the last 8 elections) and even, in all my years of voting – I have never made that promise – or written a letter to a President but, as I stated before, I feel compelled. Your acceptance speech was gracious, and showed the makings of a true leader. I, like many others, am part of the fabric of this country and that I am going to be one of your constituents. I am proud to be an American each and every day and I'm proud that we have a due process that spelled out most definitely that America wants Senator Barack Obama as our next President.

I realize you may never receive this, but I hope you do. I hope you know that there are voters – who like you said last night "Didn't vote for you – but you will be our President" – I may have not committed millions to your cause, I may have not supported you before, but as of today, I am committed to serving you as a citizen and to praying for you daily. I can only hope that there are millions more like me – who will make that commitment to you.

Thank you for your honest campaign and as you said last night – May God Bless the United States of America.

Best Regards,

Jeri Harris

Jeri L. Harris

THE WHITE HOUSE

Dear Teri —

Thank you for the wonderful note.
It is most gracious, and please do keep
praying for me, my family, and most importantly,
the country!

Jeri L. Harris
Alger, Michigan

FEB - 2 2009

11/4/2008

DEAR MR. PRESIDENT ELECT:

You HAVE MY SUPPORT
UNTIL I DRAW MY LAST
BREATH.
I GOD BLESS YOU
AND YOURS.

RESPECTFULLY,

[signature]

J. MARTIN BALL
RICHTON PARK IL
USA

Mt

April 6, 2009

Peggy

Spring, TX

Mr. President:

I am an average American woman. I am fifty-five years old. I am a wife, mother and a grandmother of two beautiful little girls, age seven and eleven. I love my country (The USA) and for what it stands.

My husband and I both work very hard to earn our living. Each month we pay our mortgage, bills, TAXES, buy our food and take care of our own business. We are blessed because on top of that we are able to support our local church and various other organizations that feed the hungry, give water to the thirsty and clothe the naked (the simple things that God wants us to do). Please don't make this harder for us to do by reducing our tax deductions.

I also want you to know that life has not always been so easy for me. I was a single mom for several years. Things were hard some of the time, but I say to you that God met my every need and the government never had to "bail me out".

Mr. President, you are to represent the people of this nation. I can honestly say that I DO NOT feel represented by you. I am so disappointed and angry that you and many of the current representatives are trying to lead our nation into socialism. You should know from observing other countries with socialistic governments that this does not work and will not work in the USA.

I, as one of the WE in "WE THE PEOPLE" say to you STOP this terrible debt that you are telling us to take on. This is not the future that I want to leave to my children and my children's children.

Mr. President, as an average citizen of The United States of America, I ask to you STOP what you are doing (NOW), admit that you are on the wrong path and move forward in governing our country with it's original intent and in a way that would be pleasing to God.

Sir, I know that you are very busy, but I feel that if you have not done so in a while you should read the Constitution of the United States and the Bill of Rights. Please remember this is to be a government for the people and by the people.

Thank you for reading my letter.

Sincerely,

Peggy

Reply.

may we never forget what it took & what sacrifices were made to win freedom for our country !!

COPY FROM ORM

Peggy —

THE WHITE HOUSE
WASHINGTON

Thanks for your letter. I wanted to respond briefly.
First, no one is moving the country towards socialism.
I have tried to deal with an unprecedented economic
crisis by increasing government investments in roads,
bridges, schools and other infrastructure to encourage
jobs creation until businesses in the private sector
get back on their feet.

Second, rather than raise taxes, I have actually cut

taxes for 95 percent of working families. I have
proposed to increase taxes on those making over
$250,000 per year to pay for the tax cut for everyone
else, but those increases don't go into effect until
2010, and the rates will still be lower than they
were under Ronald Reagan.

We do need to get control of government spending
over the long term, and I am committing all of my
teams to find places to cut out waste, fraud, and
abuse. But please rest assured that I take my
oath to uphold the Constitution seriously.

Sincerely,

APR 28 2009

CHAPTER 1

The Letters

It felt almost like a secret, the way Shailagh was talking about the letters; she wanted me to know how important they were, and she seemed frustrated, or perhaps just exhausted, like a soldier in some final act of surrender, tossing off the keys to the kingdom right before the village blows up.

This was October 2016. Hurricane Matthew had just rolled out to sea, Samsung phones were abruptly catching fire, and Republican presidential candidate Donald Trump was tweeting—"Nothing ever happened with any of these women. Totally made up nonsense to steal the election. Nobody has more respect for women than me!"— and I suppose Shailagh was feeling as wistful as anyone tumbling inside the gathering awareness of sweeping cultural change in America.

She had served six years in the Obama administration, the past two as a senior advisor, and we were in her office in the West Wing, where she was reaching toward a bookcase filled with thick three-ring binders. Inside the binders were letters to Obama that dated back to the beginning of his administration. They were from constituents. Ordinary Americans writing to their president. "They became a kind of life-force in this place," Shailagh said. She had her shoes off and a woolly sweater wrapped around her; she had a raspy voice and an unfussy Irish look, a person you might sooner find wiping the counter at a pub in Dublin than sitting comfortably across the hall from the Oval Office.

At that point Hillary Clinton was still up by double digits in the national polls, and the unthinkable was still unthinkable. Clinton campaign staffers were jockeying for position in what everyone believed would be the new administration, and Shailagh had no designs on being part of it; two terms in the White House were enough. Her job helping to lead the administration's communications strategy was to act as the gatekeeper between Obama and the people who wrote about him, and it appeared to have taken its toll. "I will not miss the bros," she said. With Obama just a few months away from leaving office, journalists were reaching peak bravado, she said. They wanted exit interviews; they wanted them now; they wanted to be first, biggest, loudest. She was sick of the egos, the same old questions, the lack of imagination, and Trump was tweeting, and it seemed like the world was going haywire.

The letters, she said, served as a kind of respite from all that, and she offered to show some to me. She chose a navy-blue binder, pulled it off the shelf, and opened it, fanning through page after page of letters, some handwritten in cursive on personal letterhead, others block printed on notebook paper and decorated with stickers; there were business letters, emails, faxes, and random photographs of families, soldiers, and pets. "You know, it's this dialogue he's been having with the country that people aren't even aware of," she said, referring to Obama's eight-year habit of corresponding with the American public. "Collectively, you get this kind of American tableau."

Obama had committed to reading ten letters a day when he first took office, becoming the first president to put such a deliberate focus on constituent correspondence. Late each afternoon, around five o'clock, a selection would be sent up from the mailroom to the Oval Office. The "10LADs," as they came to be known—for "ten letters a day"—would circulate among senior staff, and the stack would be added to the back of the briefing book the president took with him to the residence each night. He answered some by hand and wrote notes on others for the writing team to answer, and on some he scribbled, "SAVE."

Everyone on the senior staff knew the importance of the letters, but Shailagh had taken an interest in the story they told in the aggregate, what they said about the country and her boss. She told me she would sometimes put her feet up and devour the material, as if it were a history project and she were a scholar intent on mastery.

"So this is January 23, 2009, right after the inauguration," she said, choosing a letter at random from the binder. "'I'm a seventy-three-year-old owner of a manufacturing company. My husband and I started from nothing . . . put every dime back into the business. We've had no orders or inquiries for over three months now . . . still recovering from open-heart surgery. . . . We've got this house. Our mortgage is nine hundred seventy-nine dollars and seventy-one cents. We still owe a hundred twenty thousand dollars. What are we going to do?'

"You know?" she said. "That kind of stuff. All these signs. Because at that point, it wasn't clear. The job losses hadn't really started yet. There's page after page after page of people venting about the big banks. I mean, that's the other thing: You see the rage. You see the terror. Just the vulnerabilities that people are feeling that so transcend at that point what the fundamentals even looked like. So right at the beginning when Obama took office, he's hearing—he's hearing, like, Larry Summers, the director of his National Economic Council, and then he's hearing, you know, Francis and his wife Collette from Idaho. You know? It's like a running dialogue with the American public.

"You know?" Shailagh said, as if she was pleading with me to *get this.*

I told her I did, or at least I was trying to.

"Did I tell you about the letter from the guy in Mississippi?" she asked.

No, she hadn't.

"Oh my God—"

She stood, headed back to the bookshelf to get a different binder. "Wait till you see this one."

Presidents have dealt with constituent mail differently over the years. Things started simply enough: George Washington opened the mail and answered it. He got about five letters a day. Mail back then was carried by foot or on horseback or in stagecoaches—not super high volume. Then came steamboats, then rail and a modernized postal system, and by the end of the nineteenth century, President William McKinley was overwhelmed. One hundred letters *every day*? He hired someone to help manage the flow, and that was the origin of the Office of Presidential Correspondence. It wasn't until the Great Depression that things got crazy. In his weekly fireside chats, Franklin D. Roosevelt began a tradition of speaking directly to the country, inviting people to write to him and tell him their troubles. About a half million letters came pouring in during the first week, and the White House mailroom became a fire hazard. Constituent mail grew from there, and each succeeding president formed a different relationship with it. By the end of his presidency, Nixon refused to read anything bad anyone said about him. Reagan answered dozens of letters on weekends; he would stop by the mailroom from time to time, and he enjoyed reading the kid mail. Clinton wanted to see a representative stack every few weeks. George W. Bush liked to get a pile of ten already-answered letters on occasion. These, anyway, are the anecdotal memories you get from former White House staff members. Little hard data exists about constituent mail from previous administrations. Historians don't focus on it; presidential libraries don't feature it; the vast majority of it has long since been destroyed.

President Obama was the first to come up with a deliberate practice of reading ten letters every day. If the president was home at the White House (he did not tend to mail when he traveled), he would be reading constituent mail, and everyone knew it, and systems were put in place to make sure it happened. The mail had currency. Some staff members called it "the letter underground." Starting in 2010, all physical mail was scanned and preserved. Starting in 2011, every word of every email factored into the creation of a daily word cloud, its image distributed around the White House so policy makers and staff members alike could get a glimpse at the issues and ideas constituents had on their minds.

In 2009, Natoma Canfield, a cancer survivor from Medina, Ohio, wrote in, detailing her staggering health-insurance premiums in a letter Obama framed and had hung in a corridor between his private study and the Oval Office: "I need your health reform bill to help me!!! I simply can no longer afford to pay for my health care costs!!" It stood in for the tens of thousands of similar letters he got on the healthcare issue alone. They saw spikes in volume after major events like the mass shootings in Newtown, Connecticut, and Charleston, South Carolina; the Paris terrorist attacks; the government shutdown; Benghazi. You could see these spikes in the word clouds. "Jobs" might grow for a time, or "Syria," or "Trayvon," or a cluster like "family-children-fear" or "work-loans-student" or "ISIS-money-war" surrounding a giant "HELP"—the most common word of all. After a gunman opened fire on police officers in Dallas in 2016, the word "police" ballooned, surrounded by "God-guns-black-America" with a tiny "peace" and even tinier "Congress."

At one point during my visit to Shailagh's office that day, there was some commotion out in the hallway, and I followed her to the doorway to see what it was.

"Hey! How you doing?

"Hey, man!

"*This guy!* How you doing?"

"There she is. *How are you?*"

It was Biden. The VP zooming through the West Wing, zooming toward us, flanked by serious-looking men in black suits. "Hey, how you doing?" he said to me in his Joe Biden way. He shook my hand in his Joe Biden way—the net effect is always like you're a neighbor who just won some big bowling tournament, and he's *so pleased*! He gave Shailagh a quick hug and kept on zooming.

"Yeah, I know," Shailagh said when we sat back down in her office. Neither of us even needed to say it out loud. Biden may have been behaving like . . . Biden, but he didn't look like the person we were used to seeing. He looked thin. Brittle. Pale and exhausted. I wondered if perhaps that was just the look of a seventy-three-year-old man who had decided to pass up a lifelong dream to be president.

"I'd say it's more complicated than that," Shailagh said, and for a moment we reminisced.

Biden was how Shailagh and I had become friends in the first place; she was his deputy chief of staff and communications director back in 2013 when I was profiling him for a magazine. She invited me to fly on Air Force Two to Rome for the pope's inauguration, where she and I and a team of patient reporters watched Biden in his aviator sunglasses hobnob with world leaders. I was grateful for the opportunity, but afterward I told Shailagh I didn't really have anything to write about beyond: Here is what it feels like to stand with a bunch of patient reporters watching Biden in his aviator sunglasses hobnob with world leaders. That's how those press trips work. There's a rope: the powerful on one side, the curious on the other, everybody smiling and waving. You couldn't get at how anyone thought, what gave them nightmares, what private moments anybody cherished or even cared about. You couldn't get close.

Shailagh thought about that. "We should go to Wilmington," she said. "Let me ask the VP."

And so that's what we did, the three of us, romping through Biden's Delaware hometown as he relived his childhood there. "It's really muddy back here," Biden said, plowing through the woods to find the old swimming hole, the Secret Service guys trying to keep up. "Shailagh, you will not believe— Come here, Shailagh. I told you about this, didn't I, Shailagh?" He took us past his first girlfriend's house, his second girlfriend's house, his *favorite* girlfriend's house; we stopped at his high school and the hoagie shop he loved, and we sat together on the neighborhood stoop where, as a kid, he'd filled his mouth with rocks, attempting to cure his debilitating stutter. We went to the cemetery where his first wife, Neilia, and his baby Naomi were buried—he didn't want to get too close—and we found ourselves peeking into the front window of his boyhood home so we could see the dining room hutch where his sister, Valerie, used to hide. "Do you see what I'm talking about, Shailagh? Now, if only these people were home, I could show you my room." All day long the two of them laughed and bickered like father and daughter; it was a privilege to witness the tenderness and to begin to see the ways in which a White House operates like a family. Or at least this part of that one did.

I remember asking Shailagh back then if there was a chance Biden would make a run for president in 2016. "Oh, he would never get in the way of Hillary," she said, and that was that—nothing worth talking about. It seemed kind of sad, a guy spending his whole life aiming for the presidency and getting so close but now answering a call to duty that involved shutting up and not mucking up the chance for the country to finally see a woman serve.

That day in her office, after we saw Biden zooming down the hall, Shailagh told me about the toll Beau Biden's brain cancer had taken on everyone; the vice president's son had lost the battle and died at forty-six on May 30, 2015. Shailagh said that was why Biden looked the way he did; she said anyone urging him to launch a presidential bid during his time of grief, as some were doing all the way up through the 2016 primaries, didn't know him or didn't love him.

She let it go at that, like you would if it were your dad suffering.

"God, this early stuff," she said, returning to the letters. She flipped through a red binder. "Oh, I remember this woman. Yeah, we ended up inviting her to a speech."

I suppose nostalgia was the main reason Shailagh thought to tour me through some of the letters that day. The administration ending, everyone getting ready to pack up and leave, all those letters left over. What would become of them? History is . . . big. History is sweeping. History is supposed to be a record of *momentous occasions*, not so much the tiny, insignificant ones.

"These are the voices in the president's head," Shailagh said. And I suppose that got to the heart of the matter. "He internalizes these things. Some of these letters he carries around and stews over. Especially the critical ones. It's a private space he's been able to preserve. Which suits him, you know?"

I got the sense that the letters were kind of Obama's Wilmington. A path toward understanding. A back door swinging open. Here was a chance to get to know Obama in a way most people hadn't. The tiny stories that stuck. The voices that called. The cries and the howls of the people he had pledged to serve. Here was the raw material of the ideas that bounced through his mind as he went about his days in cabinet meetings, bilateral summits, fundraisers, the Situation Room, and to his bed at night.

"Foreclosure, foreclosure, foreclosure," Shailagh said, flipping through some early letters. "I mean, the housing crisis just kind of unfolds in real time in these things. People were coming up against these balloon mortgages that they didn't even know they had. You can see the confluence of the economic crisis and the healthcare crisis happening at the same time. The loss of faith that people have in everything. The banks are collapsing; the Catholic Church is reeling. It's like all these institutions are letting them down. And here's this new president, this person who comes in on a change mandate, that has established a connection with them."

Some of the letter writers would turn into iconic heroes to staffers, Shailagh told me, their stories the stuff of speeches and State of the Union addresses. "As time went on, we often had letter writers at events; letter writers often introduced him. When the president's out traveling around the country, he visits places and has lunch with letter writers. I mean, we didn't want to turn it into a schlocky thing. It's—we tried to be respectful of it. Because it's essentially a series of private relationships he had with these folks. And I think that's what makes them so impactful. The private nature, the vulnerability of these people."

She yanked her glasses off, propped them on her head, stood to get a different binder. "The guy in Mississippi," she said, "I really need to find you that one. He wrote about the calluses on his hands. How the journey of his hands was actually this whole journey of the country at that moment. I'll find it—

"You don't see the cynicism, you know? You don't see the kind of dystopian view of government in these letters that we're so used to seeing. They're almost from another time, like conversations from another era, when people looked to government and to their leaders not just for *stuff* and not just to vent, but because they really wanted the president to understand what their problems were. They really wanted him to understand what their lives were like. And so it's very—you know, against the backdrop of all the polarization and cynicism and negativity and just the onslaught of opposition that we face day to day in the White House, these letters are a constant reminder that some people do view government as essentially a force for good. Or want it to be a force for good, want it to be better at what it does. Want it to serve veterans better, want it to deliver better healthcare.

"So that's been really kind of spiritually uplifting, seriously. In a period, against a backdrop, of just this brutal, you know, day-to-day combat."

I asked her if she thought the letters served a similar purpose for Obama.

"I just think letters suited him," she said. "I mean, the Obamas are, you know, a lot like the Reagans were and the Bushes were, for that matter. They are, like, inherently conservative, normal, traditional people, right? They fully occupy the office. They are as big as the office. They fit it. You know? You know what I mean? It's like the suit fits."

And the letters fit. Like mothballs, and good posture, and proper table manners, and no swearing. "The letters have this kind of otherworldly feel to them that doesn't seem part of the moment that we're in," she said, "even though what people are saying is very much in the moment. But the format feels otherworldly to me. It feels old to me. It feels very . . . Evelyn Waugh."

Like the letter from the guy in Mississippi. She was still looking for it. She had moved on to a green binder. "I know it's here. . . . It was just so well written. It felt like a page falling out of a novel. It's so interesting that people take the time. What compelled him to write that letter, that perfectly crafted little one-page letter?"

I told her that's what I was wondering. Who writes to the president? Not since my Santa Claus days would it have occurred to me to do something like that. Who were all these people? What did they get out of it? Moreover, I wondered about the nature of the experiment itself. Whose idea was it to have Obama read ten letters a day? I wondered what the letters meant to him, and I wondered how, if at all, constituent mail influenced his presidency.

My initial impulse was to meet some of the letter writers, to hear their stories firsthand. And while I would do plenty of that, what I didn't count on was the journey inside the mailroom itself. The people who kept the machine in motion. You couldn't tell one story without the other, an interdependent relationship that serves to tell the story of the Obama administration through the eyes of the people who wrote to him.

Shailagh didn't find the letter she was looking for that day. She promised me she would. The letters came in by the millions, and those in the binders in her office were but a tiny sample, a few thousand of her favorites she liked to occasionally revisit. "You should go to the mailroom if you want the full effect," she said. "Just sit there and read. You'll see what I'm talking about."

I asked her where the mailroom was. She sat back, thought for a moment. "There's a person there who runs it. Her name is Fiona. You'd have to get past her."

I asked if perhaps she could introduce me? She nodded but not convincingly, more as if a scheme was forming in her head.

I made the point that if she could get me on Air Force Two to go to the pope's inauguration with the vice president, surely she could score me a visit to the mailroom.

"You don't know Fiona," she said.

Martha C. Dollarhide

Oxford, MS

MEMPHIS TN 381

16 APR 2009 PM 1 T

President or Mrs. Obama
1600 Pennsylvania Ave.
Washington, D.C. 20500

Bobby Ingram
Oxford, MS.   Reply
APR. 16, 2009

Mister Obama - My President,

In 2007 I was proud of my hands.
They had veneered calluses where my palms
touched my fingers. Cuts and scrapes
were never severe. Splinters and blisters
merely annoyed me. With a vise-like grip
and dextrous touch my hands were heat
tolerant and cold ignorant. I was nimble
when whittling or when sharpening an axe.
I could exfoliate with an open palm when
my wife's back itched or my cat arched for
a rub. My nails were usually stained
after a chore; they were tougher, not cracked,
seldom manicured. My hands defined my
work, passions, my life.

After 23 years as a land surveyor and
nearly 2 years unemployed, I miss my
career and my old hands. I kneel nights
and clutch new hands together, praying we
all can recover what seems lost. May
God guide your hands to mould our future.

Thank you for listening to the Citizen
I am,
        Bobby Ingram

CHAPTER 2

Bobby Ingram,
April 16, 2009

OXFORD, MISSISSIPPI

That last line and the closing are important. Notice the line break in between? That was intentional. Without that you could read it as "Thank you for listening to the citizen *that* I am," which would throw everything off. He didn't mean it that way. He didn't mean to tell the president thank you for listening just to him, Bobby Ingram of Oxford, Mississippi. He wrote "Citizen" with a capital *C* to suggest the citizen in general, the collective—everyone in the United States of America—in a way, he determined, that only a capital *C* could accurately indicate. But is that even a *thing*, grammatically speaking? He stressed over that, sitting there in his den, at that ancient tower computer (we're talking floppy drive) in the old armchair, with Babbitt, his cat, in his lap. *Probably not,* he thought. *That is probably not grammatically a thing.* You can't imagine how many drafts he wrote of that letter. How important it was that he got it just right. This was 2009, sort of at the bottom of things. Yeah, you could say he had hit bottom. He was glad about Obama coming in. Maybe something good would happen. Obama would be a president who would listen to the Citizen. Bobby wanted the president to know he believed that. (He did.) When he'd first conceived of the letter, his plan was that it be the first one Obama got when he reported to work at 8:35 A.M. on

January 21, 2009. He wanted Obama to know: Hey, here's a guy who is not like him, not Ivy League, not from Chicago, not African American. Hey, here's a skinny white guy from rural Mississippi without a super impressive education whose life is pretty terrible at the moment. Here's this guy out here; he's, like, the last kid in the class you'd expect to raise his hand to be called on, but his hand is up for him to say: "Dude, I like you. I want you to do well."

In between drafts (this was over a period of months) and sometimes just to clear his head, Bobby studied the postal route the letter would likely take, and he ticked off days on his calendar, working on the timing so the letter, when he sent it, would have the best chance of being the first thing Obama got when he sat down at his desk. Well, of course he studied the postal route. *You are talking about Bobby Ingram here.* He knows a little bit about everything. More precisely: He knows a lot about everything. That was the way of life his grandfather instilled in him, on his deathbed, when he called the grandbabies in one by one to give them each their personalized goodbye message. "Do everything" was what he told Bobby. "Try it for six months. If you like it, continue."

Anyway, with the whole grammar thing. Martha, his wife, usually gets the final say. They go over most things together. Ethical dilemmas and such. Fortunately, she's loose. Not like her mom, Atomic Betty. Martha understands that being incorrect is not, in itself, always an undesirable outcome. Witness: Michael's deplorable grammar. Michael is Bobby's baby brother, a long-haul trucker who usually writes while waiting his turn for a shower at the Pilot or the Flying J. His letters? You should see his letters. Oddest syntax, misspellings all over the place. The errors have a way of adding nuance to the sentences, Michael's signature *nuance*, that makes you feel his presence on the page. "He's flowing, Martha!" Bobby will say, marveling at the way Michael's letters *move*. The feeling he gets on the page. "He's flowing good now, Martha!" Bobby knows he'll never be the writer Michael is. But it's okay. It's okay.

Letters, Bobby thinks, are important in a man's life. He also writes to his sister, his dad, his friend Brian who's stuck in prison, and to a family of stamp collectors—good people. Letters are emotion on the page. Letters are a gift. When you write to someone, and they write back, you establish a bond. It validates both of you. He likes to throw in big words, but only if they're beautiful. Like when he said "dextrous touch" in the president's letter. Bobby is not sure, to this day, if he nailed that one. A hand can be dextrous, but a touch? Should it have been a "light touch"? But see, that doesn't do it. He needed some syllables. Some rhythm. "Let it go," Martha said. "Let it go." Bobby's favorite word of all, by the way, is "éclaircissement," which means the experience of being enlightened by a subject. See how you got "clarity" as your root word there? That is a hell of a word.

For Bobby, letter writing started with Michael. They began corresponding maybe fifty years ago, back when Bobby went off to basic training. Do you know how hard it is to enlist in the army when you're a Quaker? How many forms, how many *variances*? The army thinks if you're a Quaker, you're a conscientious objector, and you're going to poison the troops. That was not Bobby's intention. He was curious about the concepts he had been protesting along with all those elders in his church marching in antiwar rallies. It started to feel hollow—protesting others doing something you had never even tried. He became curious about war and politics—to say nothing of bugs, spiders, birds, turtles, sign language, antique cars, poetry, kilts, bamboo, bridges, and forestry. Everything. Do everything.

The army sent him to Munich, and he learned how to put rotors on helicopters, and he wrote to Michael to tell him about it. Michael wrote back about converting a Volkswagen to a dune buggy. They never stopped writing after that.

A letter is brotherhood. You start off by extending your hand. That is exactly what Bobby did with the president. *Literally*. He sat at that computer with Babbitt in his lap, and he extended his hand, and he saw how pathetically soft it was, and he needed to explain why. Not to overdramatize, but honestly, the collapse of his entire being, his psyche, his sense of self, his body, and his soul is captured in that image of his hands devoid of calluses.

Maybe you don't think calluses when you think land surveying. You probably don't know about the sledgehammer—eight pounds— and the way to swing it, around and around, bam, bam, just so, banging the stake six inches in. The sledgehammer is his second favorite tool. He bought it in 1983. His first favorite tool is the bush axe. Here again it's the swinging motion; if you stand back, he will demonstrate. Then there is the plumb bob. You hold it like this, and when it stops swinging, it tells you where the center of the earth is. *The center of the earth.* That is an ancient tool. That's just your plumb bob. Between all his tools, he carried eighty pounds of equipment on him every day. Walking through the woods, swamps, all kinds of terrain. He was doing what George Washington did. He was doing what Lewis and Clark did. Land surveying was connecting yourself to somebody from long ago. Getting to know the intent of the landowners. The deeds. You had to read these things and follow. Like that one time he traced the property back to a King George land grant. "Start at the post on the first crest past the water's edge." Well, which water's edge? Which post? "Ride four days by mule to the next corner, head north, sun to your cheek, two days by mule." Well, how fast can a mule walk? He had to figure out the speed of a mule of the size available at the time of King George. And the weather at the time they were surveying it. He figured it out. It was 110 miles. Basically two hours by car. He found that post. Oh, he found it! And then it was just good math to figure out the boundaries of the tract of land. Close the box for that tract of land. Good math. Mind you, when he first started, this was all by slide rule. Tangent. Cosine tables. You looked up the cosine of an angle. Multiplying by *that* would give you *that* tangent distance, and *that's* the angle you need to calculate to match this triangle. Fantastic. Fantastic. Five increments of pi, check it against the radius of the arc. All that stuff, it just meshed with him. He would slop through the swamps with his slide rule doing math and finding hundred-year-old locust posts, and he would think about why the Egyptians, the ones who figured out all this stuff, were of course mystical people.

That's how good land surveying was. It was just *that good.*

Anyway, by now you're probably wondering about that sound. The bark? Then the trill? That is a pileated woodpecker. A lot of people don't pronounce that right. Pi-lee-ay-ted. That's the tallest woodpecker in Mississippi. Eighteen inches. Bark-bark-bark, bark-bark-bark, then too-too-too-too-too-too. His favorite bird is the summer tanager. His favorite tree is the mimosa (a.k.a. Persian silk tree). Martha hates the bamboo down back here. Also, Martha has a spider phobia. Nevertheless, she tolerates his having this spider habitat out here. That's love. The common brown wood spider's web is larger than Bobby's kitchen table. The southern box turtle is also an important species to promote. That turtle on the rock there is named BooHiss. Among the varieties of snakes Bobby promotes are the eastern hognose, the puff adder, and the speckled king. Lizards, of course. This whole yard is about promoting certain species. Indian pink, that's a perennial weed. He's promoting it. Same with swamp irises, chives, lilies, thistles, garlic.

A lot of this knowledge comes from land surveying. You're out there with nature all day, every day.

Until one day they tell you to go home. When the recession hit in December 2007, people all across America lost their jobs. Construction was among the hardest hit industries. No more building, no more properties bought and sold, no more land disputes, no more land surveying.

Bobby was out. He and Martha could get by for a while on Martha's admin work at the university, but that was hardly the point.

He'd lost his purpose. The grief was like if someone had died. Or a divorce. Just any of those big ones that suck all the air from your lungs until you're doubled over. Two years of doubled over. *Two years.* He applied for jobs everywhere, offered to relocate to Texas. He was fifty-two years old. Nobody needed him.

He followed the news. Barack Obama appealed to him. The idea of hope. But the main thing he saw with Obama was, *Wow, this guy is inheriting a shit show. A mess of a country.* He needed help. Everyone needs help. It was like, let's do this together. That's how Bobby started the letter in his mind.

Extending his hand. That was hello. That was: It's me. The guy who used to have the calluses. Middle- to lower-class. Not so much education. That guy. Who is also—this guy. Curious, constantly questioning, a self-taught renaissance man. An enigma. A contradiction. *I'm both guys.* "I am large, I contain multitudes," Walt Whitman said. Don't forget that, Mr. President: multitudes.

Bobby missed the chance at getting his letter to the president on January 21, 2009. He wasn't done writing the letter until April.

After he got it just right, he sat back, exhaled, scooted the cat, and reached for the loose-leaf paper. Printing it in his own hand was paramount. A letter is a part of you. He wanted it to fit on one page, fit exactly, and he wanted it to be block style. It took many attempts. (He has five trash cans in his den.) Then he sent it. Then he forgot about it. Sending it was the main thing. He got it said. In that way, it was like every letter he's ever written. A letter is a prayer.

He came out of his depression shortly after he sent the letter. A switch. *I can't live like this.* Just a switch. Martha needed him. Atomic Betty was dying, which was an incomprehensible concept. The life-force of that woman. He was good with her. Just holding her hand all those days when nobody else could bear it. Then he started with his LOLs. The Little Old Ladies who needed help with daily chores. They needed him. He can soothe people. (He can put a cat to sleep in seconds.) Then of course, BooHiss and all the habitats outside. My God, the birds alone. Pretty soon Jeff was calling. He needed help rebuilding a boat. Everybody needs help! He and Jeff work together now. Jeff does the talking. Bobby can carry six two-by-fours in one go, up a ladder, in the worst heat imaginable.

He's that guy in the background with the bandana, sweating his brains out. You know that guy. But he's this guy too. He's got poetry in his head, and he knows which bird is singing, and he has math equations going on, and now he's trying to solve the hydrology problem down at the lake.

Some months after he sent the letter to the president, he got a response, on a white note card labeled, "The White House."

THE WHITE HOUSE

WASHINGTON

Bobby —

Thanks for the powerful letter. I'm working as hard as I can to make sure that hard working Americans like you have the opportunities you so richly deserve.

He and Martha stood together in the den scrutinizing that thing to determine if it was written in Obama's own hand. Martha said yes, holding it up to the light from the window. He said maybe, squinting over her shoulder. And then he stepped away, and it was like, well, hold on a second there, Martha. The president *writes back*?

Samples, 2009-2010

MK.

reply.

TO: ANYONE WITH ANY COMMON SENSE AT THE WHITE HOUSE,

Bonuses?? BONUSES??? For what? Losing the companies money at a record pace??

A.I.G. ....Freddie Mac....Fannie Mae....Morgan Stanley....Wells Fargo....Merrill Lynch....The list goes on & on!!

I realize I'm not the sharpest knife in the drawer, but for the life of me, I cannot understand what in the world is going on in our business sector! And in our Gov't.!! Can just ONE of you up there please explain to me how in the world this can be justified?? And please, don't start with the "best minds in the biz" routine...heard it all before. If that's the best we got, we're all in a world of hurt!!

Is this what we're teaching our kids to do when they move into the world by themselves...steal? Scam?? All in the name of the almighty dollar??

Since when do we reward incompetance?? Please tell me so I can pass it on to my boss!! Perhaps he's missing something! Since this "recession" showed it's ugly face, I have been cut back to working only 4 days a week. I struggle to pay my bills, gas the car, put food on my table. We watch every dime. I pay my taxes on time and mind my own business, but I now realize I've been doing wrong this whole time. What I really need to do to get ahead in the world is put on a coat & tie, get a wig, and smile like I'm everybodies best friend then SCAM the Hell out of them for all they got!!

And now, not only do you guys give my money away to the greedy ones who made
the very mistakes that put us in this mess, but you GIVE THEM BONUSES?????

I, for one, have had enough. It's time the citizens of this country take back our Gov't. & find someone who will not only tell us the TRUTH, (remember that word??), and who will not reward these idiots because they're the BEST WE GOT!!

BONUSES?? Come on...WAKE UP WASHINGTON!!!!!!

Timothy H. Mullin
LYNCHBURG, VIRGINIA

**COPY FROM
ORM**

THE WHITE HOUSE

WASHINGTON

Tim —

Thanks for your letter. I share your
sentiments, and we are moving as quickly
as we can to restore some common sense
to the financial system.

Mr. Timothy Mullin

Lynchburg, Virginia

APR - 3 2009

#21 11258603 - Linette Jones, In ID: 6858341, Out ID: 6696164

From:
Date: 9/29/2009 10:05:18 AM
Subject:Foreign Affairs

President Obama, I am very disappointed that you believe campaigning for the Olympics to be hosted in your home town is more important than my childs safety in Afghanistan! I did not care for George Bush, but at least I felt safe when he was in office. I cannot say the same now that you are President. I fear for my childs safety serving in the military in Afghanistan, I fear for me and my familys safety here in the United States. Your lack of decision making ability is putting us in jeopardy for attacks from terrorists. Please stop campaigning and do your job!

===== Original Formatted Message Starts Here =====

Date of Msg: September 29, 2009   reply

<APP>CUSTOM
<PREFIX></PREFIX>
<FIRST>Linette</FIRST>
<LAST>Jones</LAST>
<MIDDLE></MIDDLE>
<SUFFIX></SUFFIX>
<ADDR1></ADDR1>
<ADDR2></ADDR2>
<CITY></CITY>   North Yarmouth
<STATE></STATE> ME
<ZIP>   </ZIP>
<COUNTRY></COUNTRY>
<HPHONE></HPHONE>
<WPHONE></WPHONE>
<EMAIL>   </EMAIL>
<ISSUE>W_POTUS</ISSUE>
<ISSUE>W_POL_FA</ISSUE>
<ISSUE></ISSUE>
<MSG>
President Obama, I am very disappointed that you believe campaigning for the Olympics to be hosted in your home town is more important than my childs safety in Afghanistan! I did not care for George Bush, but at least I felt safe when he was in office. I cannot say the same now that you are President. I fear for my childs safety serving in the military in Afghanistan, I fear for me and my familys safety here in the United States. Your lack of decision making ability is putting us in jeopardy for attacks from terrorists. Please stop campaigning and do your job!
</MSG>
</APP>

**COPY FROM
ORM**

THE WHITE HOUSE
WASHINGTON

Dear Linette —

I received your note. I am grateful for your child's service, and have no more important job than keeping America safe. That's why I am puzzled that you would think a one day trip on the Olympics — a trip in which I met with General McCrystal, our commander in Afghanistan, to discuss war strategy — would somehow distract me from my duties as (over)

Commander-in-Chief. You may not like all my policies (that is something you quickly get use to as President), but rest assured that I wake up in the morning and go to bed at night thinking about our soldiers and my responsibilities to them.

Sincerely,

DEC - 9 2009

Pdf emailed to Mike Kelleher
11-30-2009

President Barack Obama
The White House
1600 Pennsylvania Ave, NW
Washington, DC 20500

Dear President Obama;   20/Jan/09

　　　Hello, my name is Michael P. Powers, and I was born in Waukegan, Illinois on July 4, 1954...Enclosed is a picture of my father, and I have carried it for almost 30 years now...His name was Benjamin Maurice Powers Sr. and like me he was born in Waukegan, Illinois on April 1, 1929...Now the reason I have sent you this picture of my father,(You may keep it if you like), is that he smoked 3 packs of cigarettes a day, and on August 21, 1979 at the age of 50 he died from smoking 3 packs a day...I was 25 years old at the time, and since than their has been roughly about one million times that I wanted, and needed to talk to him...I remember watching you on TV in Grant Park when you won, as you walked out I heard one of your daughters almost scream,"Hi Daddy" and at that moment I missed my father more than I think I ever have, because I did the same thing when I was a kid, and he would get home from work...He was and always will be my best friend... If you always want to be there for your girls, than stop smoking NOW! Someday they are going to need you for something,(we all do need our parents for something at sometime or another), and I want you to be there for them, and also I think The United States, and the World need you now more than ever, and I want you to be there for all of us...I just know you are going to do a knockout job for the next eight years, so like Red Skeleton used to say,"Good day and May God Bless"...

Sincerely, Your Friend

Michael P. Powers

THE WHITE HOUSE

Michael —
Thanks so much for the wonderful
letter, and the good advice. I am
returning the picture, since it must be
important to you, but I will remember
your dad's memory.

Barack Obama

From: Ali Hazzah
   Hobe Sound, Florida
   September 16, 2009

I lost my job in 2001, after the tech meltdown. Was a senior IT manager for an Internet company in NY that went belly up. I applied to hundreds of jobs, after this disastrous event - nothing. I was never able to get a full time job, I guess due to my age (I am now 58), but got by on my considerable savings, and some minor real estate transactions. Of course I hade to take out private insurance. I was assured by the sales agent that rates rarely went up. Since 2001, my insurance premiums have gone up exactly one hundred per cent - and i have never had a serious illness of any sort. In the last 8 years, I have paid almost ONE HUNDRED THOUSAND DOLLARS in insurance premiums, for my wife and I, to Blue Cross Blue Shield of Florida. I believed in then Senator Obama, when he said it was time for a change, that yes, he could be the one we could believe in to change things. I was one of the few where I live who put up Obama/Biden election signs (at my own expense, and at some personal risk from Republican goons, who tore them down every night) up and down US1 and did other things (such as contributing $100 to the Senator;s campaign, and working with the local democratic party) to help him get elected - this in a conservative, often bigoted, religion-obsessed county, a place where Rush Limbaugh is actually taken seriously by many. Three month ago, my wife had to have minor arm surgery. Our insurance premium immediately went up 30 per cent, and this is the first claim we have ever put in. I now have to make do without insurance - I can longer afford it - and I am, I repeat, 58 years old, not exactly in my prime. But I guess people like my wife and I dont really matter to you, President Obama, or the rest of the Washington crowd; we are just disposable, powerless losers who will be forced to go through everything we own before we can one day qualify for Medicaid. Thank you, Mr. Obama, thank you so much for reminding me what Washington is really about, and how much my wife and I mean to you. I just have one question: how could you put aside what your own mother had to go through? Sorry for taking up your time. After all, I am nothing but a disposable old fool in your world, right? Good luck getting our vote next time around. I am even going to vote Green or sit out the midterm elections to teach you and your cynical coterie of advisers a very very small lesson about keeping one's promises. You betrayed me, Sir: shame on you. I will never forget it.

THE WHITE HOUSE

WASHINGTON

Dear Ali —

Thanks for your letter. I confess I was confused by the anger directed at the Administration, since we are working every day to get a strong health care bill passed. Of course I wish it would come quickly, but change is never easy. And I am convinced we will get it done before the end of the year.

[signature]

Dear Mr. President,

I was watching your State of the Union address a few nights ago on television. There was a part in your speech where you alluded to the many letters you receive from people throughout the United States. I'm writing because I thought that you might somehow get to read mine.

I am a 21 year old college senior at East Stroudsburg University of Pennsylvania majoring in elementary education. My home is farther South, in the small town of Walnutport. That is where I reside with my family when I am not living at school. My father is in his fifties and has been laid-off from his job as a union construction laborer for many months. He is receiving some money through unemployment, but not nearly as much as he would receive if there were a job available to him. My mother is in her late forties and has a job in a screen printing factory. Her hours are cut frequently without notice. My 18 year old brother graduated from high school last year and has opted to work two jobs, one at a local grocery store, and the other at UPS. I recently had to take a few months off of my jobs as a swim coach for two teams to ensure that I can put all of my energy into student teaching.

The reason I am writing to you is to ask for some advice. I want to help my family. We are lower middle class and very hard-working, especially my mother and father. We are certainly not at the top of the food chain, but we have always been thankful for the things that we do have, knowing there are others with larger needs. My father is used to experiencing temporary lay-offs, as it is typical of the construction industry. Because of that, we have always been an efficient and frugal family. We've also been able to make it through past financial hardships by sticking together and waiting patiently for things to get better. But I'm starting to really worry. My parents have always kept their concerns hidden by telling my brother and me that they were the adults and there were not problems for us to worry about. Well, I am an adult now, so I have a decent idea of what our status is.

Throughout my life, my father has always been positive about everything. He works incredibly hard and is very good at what he does. But since he has been out of work for so long, I can see a marked change. It is mainly in his eyes. They seem much more sullen. He does not laugh nearly as much. He seems smaller somehow. I can tell by the way he acts that he feels responsible for all of our current worries. Will my mom have enough gas to make it to work? Which car will break down this week that he will need to fix? Out of all of the important bills, which is most important to be paid first? How long until his benefits run out? What if one of us gets sick? What groceries will we be able to afford this week? Will he have a pension when he is finally able to retire? The list goes on and on.

I can see it all eating away at him. He can't sleep. And I wonder... if even he is starting to break, what can the rest of us do?

And my mom, she tries hard as well. She stayed home with my brother and me for most of our lives because her job couldn't pay for child care, and she hated the idea of strangers raising us. She went back to work a few years ago. Now, after getting sent home early due to lack of work, I've seen her come inside, a long while after hearing her car park, only to enter the house with red eyes from the tears she just cried to herself in the car.

Please don't get the impression that I am searching for an apology or pity. Those things are never necessary or useful, and there are others who are far worse off than I can imagine. I know action is the only way we can move forward. But I feel so insignificant and helpless. I don't know what I can say or do to help my family. I know the usual answer, "Just wait, things will get better." I have to be honest though, I don't know how much longer we can wait. I don't know how much longer I can bear to look into my father's eyes and see the deep-seeded sadness that has replaced his positive demeanor and posture. I don't know how much longer I can watch them be told to "just wait, it will be ok," just to see their hopes be smashed again and again. I don't know how much longer I can listen to the subtle note of defeat that is invading my mother's words. And I don't know how much longer I can deal with the guilt of putting additional financial strain on my family by trying to be the first of us to attend and graduate college. And now, I am realizing that the chances of me being able to get an honest job as a teacher is more like a fairy tale than a reality.

I guess the advice I am searching for is "What do I do?" I know that as the president, you have a lot of expectations placed on you. A lot of the things that people are expecting of you are not even things you have direct control over. I also understand that all of the things contributing to our country's problems will not and cannot be fixed overnight, or even over four years. It's not your job to respond to me, or even to read this letter. But for some reason, I felt that I needed to try. Maybe my mind finds comfort in the fact that I took some sort of an action.

Anyway, I don't care about having enough money to buy a new car, or a laptop, or a smartphone. I just want to be able to walk back into my home and see my mom smile the way she used to, or hear my dad laugh without it sounding like it is coming from someone else. I miss that more than anything.

Name withheld
Walnutport, Pennsylvania
March 17, 2010

nfl

29 U

Ellen F. Crain, MD, PhD
Professor, Pediatrics and
Emergency Medicine
Network Director,

Reply.

January 23, 2009

The Honorable Barack H. Obama
President of the United States
The White House
1600 Pennsylvania Avenue NW
Washington, D.C. 20500

Dear President Obama:

I want to share with you a story from our pediatric emergency department which demonstrates the impact of your Presidency on our young people in a way that might not otherwise be apparent. Both the patient and her mother have given me permission to share this story with you as well as their names and address.

On January 21, 13-year-old   was brought to our pediatric emergency room by her mother,   , after being punched in the face by other youths on her way home from school. She had two lacerations just below her right eye that needed suturing, but she was crying and trembling so much that we couldn't treat the wounds without risking injury to her eye. Nothing anyone said could calm her down. Then I asked if she had watched the inauguration and President Obama's speech. She said yes, and I asked her, "What would President Obama want us to do right now?" She replied, "He would want us to do what we have to do and do our best." She took a deep breath and became still, and we were able to successfully and close her wounds. I told her President Obama would be very proud of her, and she beamed. I know she would treasure a communication from your office. Her address is below:

Ms.

More impressive than the many remarks we heard from citizens about your inauguration's meaning to them was to see how your election and inaugural remarks could give a young person the strength to successfully deal with a personally frightening situation.

Sincerely,

Ellen Crain

Ellen F. Crain, MD, PhD
Medical Director,

THE WHITE HOUSE
WASHINGTON

Your doctor, Ellen Crain, told me about your recent difficulty. I'm proud of how you handled things, and have confidence you will do great things in the future.

Be well!

MAR 17 2009

COPY FROM ORM

THE WHITE HOUSE

WASHINGTON

Dr. Crain —

Thanks for the note. I wrote to Ms. ████, and appreciate your interest!

Dr. Ellen F. Crain
Medical Director

MAR 17 2009

11/25/09
MR

Reply

Support 2

Kenny Jops

Chicago, IL

Dear President Obama,

I heard that you are good at correcting homework.
I was wondering if you could take a look at
this (particularly the highlighted portion on the
back). How did I do?

Thank you,
Kenny Jops, Beaubien School
Chicago, IL

Kenny Jobs

- wants you to look
  at his homework

Send back with the
vocabulary list.

Kenny Jops
Beaubien

Vocab Lesson 2

1	dubious	c	d	precariously	c
2	vacillate	a	c	qualms	c
3	qualm	d	b	conclusively	a
4	precarious	d	c	unequivocally	b
5	indeterminate	b	d	apprehensiveness	d
6	apprehensive	c	b	tentatively	c
7	tentative	a	b	categorically	d
→8	categorical	d	d	dubiously	d
→9	unequivical	d	c	indeterminate	c
10	conclusive	b	b	vacillation	d
11		c	F		
12			T		
13			T		

- apprehensive, anxious, uneasy, Bill was apprehensive about sky diving.
- categorial, absolute, Her categorial boycott of Cheese Flavored Cheese Snacks left her yearning for cheese.
- conclusive, decisive, ending uncertainty, His colclusive report on cells changed the science world.
- dubious, unsure, This report left no one dubious.
- indeterminate, vague, Even slightly inde terminate state ments made by the president seemed to fascinate FOX news.
- precarious, dangerous, This puts Obama in a precarious position.
- qualm, a sense of doubt, He is probably in a qualm as to why this is happening.
- tentative, uncertain or provisional, FOX is probably tentative as to what to do when he makes good decisions.
- unequivocal, perfectly clear, Some believe that it is unequivocal that during this scenario FOX will run around like a headless chicken and scream death panels.
- vacillate, to switch opinions, They always seem to vacillate drastically so as to disagree with him.

THE WHITE HOUSE

WASHINGTON

Kenny—

Nice job on the homework. I caught only two words misspelled on the vocabulary list. Dream big dream.

**COPY FROM
ORM**

Kenny Jops

Chicago, Illinois

✳ Encl. Original homework
vocab list.

DEC 14

June M. Lipsky

East Meadow, NY

March 4, 2009

Dear President Obama:

I have not been able to contain myself over the news I have been hearing in the last few days.

I voted for you in the last election and I was very excited about the change you promised. I watched the presidential debates. I remember hearing you say that you would stop the special pork that has plagued every bill passed in Washington for the last several years. I remember you saying that your presidency will be marked by putting an end to special interest groups. I was so excited about the prospect of these changes.

Newsday reported this week that Lobbyists are gearing themselves to help special groups to seek the distribution of the billions of dollars that the Stimulus Package and the Proposed Budget make available contrary to what you promised for CHANGE.

You have nominated and sworn individuals who have been part of the problem in Washington for many years, and while you indicated in your speeches before being elected that you will   CHANGE. It sounds like more of the same.

I am a Democrat and I have always voted with the Democratic Party.   I am a regular citizen, part of the middle class. I have worked all of my life, living within my means. Never collected unemployment insurance, never applied for Medicaid, never asked for financial assistance. My mortgage is paid off.   I have been saving regularly for my retirement and invested to have a comfortable retirement.

I hear that your program will serve the needs of many taxpayers that earn less than $250,000, that I will receive a sum of money $800 if I remember correctly.

Frankly, I am very disappointed. The $800 will hardly do me any good. You have provided bail out money for large companies who have a history of failing, continue to fail, and you continue to bail them out. Typically the automobile manufacturers, the insurance companies like AIG, the banks, who by the way are licensed to steal money from hard working folk like myself.

If my business had failed, I would have gone bankrupt without credit and without a helping hand such as the one your government is providing these large companies.

Where is the fairness?. I have lived within my means all of my life. I sent my children to school without public assistance, paid my taxes and penalties when required.
In the meanwhile some of the people you appointed are known to have failed to pay their fair share. Even in Congress, Mr. Rangel, head of the Ways and Means Committee has been accused of failing to pay his fair share among other pending accusations that the Ethics committee has failed to investigate. Yet, Mr. Rangel continues to serve.

How would you like me to react when I see that manufacturers, banks, insurance companies, and individuals who have acted irresponsibly are being rewarded while people like me are not reaping the reward of having acted responsibly.

Is this what our sense of justice is?

Thieves such as Bernard Madoff, who have been indicted for stealing 50 billion dollars from hard working folk as well as rich companies, pension plans, rich individuals, retirees, has the gall of requesting that 62 million dollars in his wife's name not be used to compensate the victims of his fraud. Where did a middle class person from Laurelton, Queens, NY get to accumulate such as vast sum of money? Now he wants his wife to keep the reward of this Ponzi scheme to keep it while he serves out his time in jail? How do you expect honest working people to feel when we see so much injustice being committed.

No, Mr. President it is not about republicans or democrats, it is about fairness. We the middle class have been denied the opportunities by previous administrations. We have been holding the bag while banks and powerful politicians in Washington continue to steal our hopes and dreams.

You, Mrs. Pelosi and Mr. Reed are not really trying to work in a bipartisan way, and in the process we the hard working middle class is paying for your vendetta against each other.

Mr. President, it is time to stop the bickering. Your stimulus package and your present budget proposal have violated the promises you have made during the presidential debates and continue to reward a sector of society that hardly contributes to the wealth of this nation.

Wall Street is reacting to the insecurity exhibited by your appointees and by your failure to keep your promises. If you want us to trust you, you must keep the promises you made. You are serving the same interests you spoke against during the presidential campaign, and like in the past, went the same as many other politicians. This, for the Americans is a policy of NO CHANGE!

Like always, in Washington business is as usual, and so far you have not CHANGED anything. Please restore the faith and trust I put in you when I voted for you in

November. When I argued with my friends and yes, even my father and my children, that things would be different if you got into office. So far, they were right and I was wrong. Nothing has changed.

Sincerely,

June M. Lipsky

THE WHITE HOUSE
WASHINGTON

June —

Thanks for the letter. Please know that the only thing I spend my days thinking about is how to help hard-working Americans like you. I share your outrage about the big banks, and the only reason we are helping them is to make sure that the whole banking system doesn't collapse and result in even more hardship for ordinary Americans.

As for my keeping promises, the budget I've outlined only gives tax breaks to middle class folks, and moves us in the direction of health care reform and energy independence. That's what I campaigned on, and that's what I intend to deliver.

I understand your frustrations; I'm frustrated too. But don't give up hope — we will get this done!

Sincerely,

Ms. June M. Lipsky
East Meadow, New York

MAR 17 2009

мK

1.28.2009

Dear President Obama,

 I am in 6 graid, I am a girl, I am elevin years old, I am the only child.

I live with my mom in   and my dad livs in

I am a artist, I draw cartoons. my dad werks on the boats, and my mom werks at the marina. somtimes I pick up trash at the beach.

my contry is the u.s.a, and its fine. my contry is grait be cawse we all are safe, my contry is beautiful, we all runto the beatch and pick up sheals, I run to the beatch with my dog rozi. I want to cainch my contry into...somthing thats in the future in 3001.

me and my mom are homeless. I want a circle house with a bedroom upstears, my mom and me would live thear. the kitchen is supposed to be big. the house neads to be in the forest near a big lake.

ail, see you laiter!

sincerely,

E

THE WHITE HOUSE
WASHINGTON

E▓▓▓▓

Thanks for the beautiful letter, and the great cartoons!

I will be working hard so that all families have a nice place to live, and I will keep you and your family close to my heart.

8/9/2009

Subject: Health Care

Dear President Obama -

I am very concerned about what I am hearing about your new Health Care Plan. My wife and I care for our only child, an 8 yr. old boy, Mason, who has a form of muscular dystrophy is wheelchair bound, ventilator dependent and feeds through a g-tube. Needless to say he is a very happy little boy and the love of our lives. I work full time and am blessed to have health insurance through my employer. This insurance pays for all of our sons care and the medical equipment we use in the home. Our son requires in home nursing care which is also covered by our health insurances and MediCal. My recent concerns are rumors that I am hearing about our proposed health care plan that would no longer allow children like my son to be cared for in our home and lead to he and children like him being institutionalized in order to contain health care costs. Please help me to alleviate these concerns. I have faith in you as our President and truly appreciate all you do.

Thank you,

Scott, Staceyanne & Mason Fontana

Chico, CA

THE WHITE HOUSE
WASHINGTON

Scott, Stacey anne & Mason —

Thank for your note. I promise — nothing in our health care plan would take away Mason's care. In fact, we are trying to strengthen the system so care will always be there for him.

mple/Hardship

10/29/09
MU

Mr. Barrack Obama
The President
The White House

September 25, 2009

Reply

Dear Mr. President:

Congratulations on your election. It has been very interesting to watch your Administration grow and move forward. I am writing to you today as a concerned citizen from middle class America, because I know I am not alone and I want to enlighten you to what happens in the real world to people who have been working hard to see this country prosper.

Three years ago, my family was living a comfortable life. We had a home, cars, a boat, and were able to pay our bills and still provide the little things for our two growing boys. Then my husband lost his job. While he finally found employment in January 2008, it is at about one third of his previous earnings.

We began to fall behind on our bills and I was forced to draw from my retirement and credit to keep us afloat. All the while, my husband, a highly successful salesperson, was trying to get a job and couldn't even get an interview with a local discount store. To make a long story short, after about a year and a half struggle, the repossessions of a vehicle and a boat, and numerous attempts asking for help from our Mortgage Holder, we lost our home in March of this year. We were too late for your help as much as we desperately wanted it.

So, now we are in a rental unit. We are living paycheck to paycheck. Trying to stay afloat in that two year time frame cost me $80,000 out of my retirement and approximately $200,000.00 of debt from a second mortgage and credit card debts we incurred through that period. Now we can barely pay to put food on our table or clothes on our kids for school. We need to file bankruptcy—it is the only solution. The problem is we cannot file for Bankruptcy protection without $2000.00 to pay for it. If we were able to file, we could make it and start again, but there is no money to file and we have run out of options for loans.

Mr. President, I make a good living and I have been at my job for 14 years. While my husband's income trickles in we have to live off an income that was never designed to be the main income. I just am at a loss as to what to do. We are not buying extras—no new clothes for me in two years, not eating out, and no extra amusements for the kids- and yet we cannot get a leg up. I know there are people out there in worse shape. Recently, when I called the power company for help paying a past due bill to keep the power on at my home, I was directed to a number of charities to ask them for help. I could not bring myself to do it, knowing I make a lot more than most people.

We are not the only people in this situation. We are willing to accept responsibility for our actions and take the hit of filing bankruptcy, but we can't afford to do that and keep a roof over our head, so it seems like a catch 22. I cannot sleep and have developed medical conditions over this. I live in constant fear every morning of waking up to find all the money in my checking account—what little there is—gone from a garnishment from which I cannot defend myself.

After all this, I have a very important question to ask you: What does a person who is trying to recover in this economy supposed to do when they can barely afford to pay their bills and need to file bankruptcy, but they cannot afford to do it? I am not condoning bankruptcy, but it is the only solution for us. Where do we go for help? We did nothing wrong and tried to make good on our obligations, but no one will help us. My husband was even fortunate enough to find some work, but it just isn't enough.

My 13 year old son asked me to write to you. He asked me why you won't do anything to help people who are struggling like us. What do I say to him Mr. President? When he cannot have the new school clothes he needs and I have to explain to him that we cannot afford what we used to take for granted, what do I tell him? No child should worry about money or offer to find a way to work to help his family. But, at 13, he is well aware of the stresses on our family despite our efforts to shield him. How do I prove to him that you are the person and lead an administration that will help us?

I am very interested in your reply. My guess is you will never see this letter and some staffer will respond on some form letter. But, I am trying to show my son that our leaders are hearing our pain and responding. You probably have no way to help us either—I have pretty much given up hope and just hope I don't lose my job because I am in financial danger---you see, I work for Bank of America where associates are held to higher standards and cannot even receive help with Overdraft fees because we should know better. They also hold the second mortgage note that we had to default on, so I just hope I can keep my job. The stress never stops   I just pray a lot and hug my kids a lot and hope we can have a roof over our heads as winter comes.

Thanks for taking the time to read the rambling of a frustrated and scared citizen. I know you have bigger and better fish to fry. If I get a reply I will make sure my son knows it. It is important for kids to respect the President and to know he cares.

I would like to leave you with a quote of inspiration as you plow through the many issues you deal with each day, as it sometimes gets me through my day, "A river cuts through rock, not because of its power, but because of its persistence." (Jim Watkins).

God Bless you and America

THE WHITE HOUSE

WASHINGTON

Dear

I know how tough things are, and I am doing everything in my power to speed up the recovery. The economy took a big hit from the financial crisis, but the steps we have taken have halted the slide into Depression, and I'm confident that if we persist, your family and the country will see brighter days!

God Bless,

DEC - 1

CHAPTER 3

The Mailroom

Fiona was an old lady with a beehive hairdo, tiny glasses at the end of a drooping chain resting on a magnificent bosom, and a bulbous chin sprouting random whiskers that shook as she barked, "No trespassing!" through a brass mail slot from which only darkness and the musty smell of mold spores could be detected.

Or something like that. In my mind I had Fiona out to be a menacing gatekeeper, and so I felt somewhat cheated when she appeared as a perfectly pleasant young woman, early thirties; she had a delicate stature, absorbing dark blue eyes, and the precise diction of a literature professor.

"We will begin with a tour," she said upon welcoming me at the White House security gate on a cool autumn morning. In emails she had said I would have to agree to certain terms before I would be allowed into the mailroom. These mostly had to do with understandable privacy concerns—I couldn't disclose the contents of any letter I read unless it was cleared with its author—but the fortitude with which she announced the rules made the larger point: Fiona cared deeply about people who wrote letters to the president.

It would be some time before I would appreciate the astonishing fullness of Fiona's zeal.

She led me to the loading dock of the Eisenhower Executive Office Building or "EEOB," as people called it, a massive block-long structure that never seems to appear in press photos or cable news backdrops when they show the White House. Which is strange because it's so hard to miss. The EEOB sits just steps away from the door to the West Wing. It's an annex of the most extreme variety, a humongous creation with dramatic pavilions, ornate crestings, elaborate chimney stacks—architecture so exuberant that when it was built back in the late nineteenth century, a lot of people complained that it looked like a big cake. Mark Twain said it was the ugliest building in America; historian Henry Adams called it an "architectural infant asylum." This went on for a while—Truman would later call it "the greatest monstrosity in America"—and its architect, Alfred B. Mullett, would end up killing himself. Nowadays, people take the EEOB for granted, like you would any big old awesome courthouse in a midsize city. It houses more than five hundred government offices, everything from the National Security Council headquarters to the Secret Service locker rooms to the vice president's ceremonial office.

The mailroom was on the ground floor, just off the loading dock. The door says, "Office of Presidential Correspondence." If you send a letter to the president, it ends up here—after having first been screened off-site, at some secret location, to make sure it doesn't contain anything that would blow up or poison people. "So it arrives already opened, flat, the envelope stapled to the back," Fiona told me as she opened the door to an office they called the "hard-mail room." It was a sprawling space that had the tired, unkempt look of a college study hall during finals—paper everywhere, files stacked along walls, bundles under tables, boxes propping up computer monitors dotted with Post-its, cables hanging. Hushed young men in ties and hushed young women in sweater sets and hose—you dress up if you work for the White House—held pencils between their teeth or behind their ears, most of them with their heads bent, reading. There was an equally crowded work space, "the email room," in a satellite office just outside the White House gates on Jackson Place. In total, the Office of Presidential Correspondence—"OPC" was what everyone called it—required the orchestration of fifty staff members, thirty-six interns, and a rotating roster of three hundred volunteers to keep up with about ten thousand letters and messages every day. As the director of the entire operation, Fiona was the one who kept it all humming along.

"Why don't you sit down and read?" she said. It felt more like a command than a question. Ten interns were crowded around two long tables, but there was an extra seat.

Grab a bundle, sit down, and read. It was pretty straightforward: Read.

A girl doesn't want her mom to be deported, and can the president please help? A guy finally admits to his wife that he's gay, and now he would like to tell the president. A car dealer writes to say his bank is shutting him down, and thanks for nothing, Mr. President. A vet who can't stop seeing what he saw in Iraq writes a barely intelligible rant that makes his point all the more intelligible: "Help." An inmate admits to selling crack, but he wants the president to know he is not a lost cause: "I have dreams Mr. President, big dreams." A man can't find a job. A woman can't find a job. A teacher with advanced certification can't find a damn job. A lesbian couple just got married; thank you, Mr. President. A man sends his medical bills; a woman sends her student-loan statements; a child sends her drawing of a cat; a mother sends her teenager's report card—straight As, isn't that awesome, Mr. President?

Dear Mr. President,

. . . YOU, sir, are the PRESIDENT of the United States. YOU, sir, are the one person that IS supposed to HELP the LITTLE PEOPLE like my family and others like us. We are the ones that make this country what it is. You say that jobs are up and spending is up. YOU, sir, need to come to my neck of the woods and see how wrong that is. Because here in Spotsylvania County, it's not. I live in Partlow, a rural community of Spotsylvania, and I tell you what . . . jobs are few and far between. My husband and I just want to be able to live and be able to buy a cake or a present for our kids when it's their birthday or for Christmas. That's another thing—my boys didn't even have a Christmas because we did not have money to buy them

*presents. Have YOU ever had to tell your girls that Santa isn't com-
ing to your house? . . .*

Sincerely,
Bethany Kern
Partlow, Va.

This pile, that pile, another pile over there; pull from the middle if
you want. The narrative was sloppy and urgent, America talking all
at once. No filter. The handwriting, the ink, the choice of letterhead—
every letter was a real object from a real person, and now you were
holding it, and so now you were responsible for it.

Mr. President,

*My wife and I very recently lost our 22-year-old son, David Jr. He
took his life with a handgun that he purchased. Our son was precious to us. He could have done anything he chose to do.*

*I am writing because our son was suffering from mental illness yet
still was able to purchase a gun. He had been involuntarily hospitalized when he was 17, yet Pennsylvania allows people with this on
their record to purchase a gun.*

*The sadness we are feeling is overwhelming us. We are trying to be
strong for our other three sons, but we are breaking down every
day. . . .*

Thank you.
David Costello
Philadelphia

"You'll need a pencil," said a woman seated next to me. She looked
like an intern, but it turned out she was one of Fiona's deputies,
Yena Bae. She was in her midtwenties, and there was a lightness to
her, a welcoming glow, like your first kindergarten teacher. I noticed
Fiona had disappeared; apparently she had passed me off to Yena.

There would be a whole lot of orchestration like that going on during all my time at the White House, somebody always keeping watch.

On a whiteboard at the far end of the room was the countdown: "You have 99 days to make a difference in the life of a letter writer," someone had written, referring to January 19, 2017, the last full day of the Obama administration and the last day for this OPC staff, nearly all of whom were political appointees and would no longer have a job at the White House when the new administration took office. The election was less than a month away. "Our time is, like, ticking," Yena told me. "We want to put our letter writers in good shape for the next administration. We want them to be in good hands.

"Team little people," she said. "That's what we call ourselves." She said the mailroom might seem like the least prestigious place to work in the White House, yet the ethos here was that it held a kind of secret superpower. "You'll see."

Ten letters from this room would, after all, land on the president's desk that night. Part of the work of the mailroom staff was to sift through the thousands of letters that had just come in that morning and pick which ten Obama should see.

"The 10LADs," Yena said, handing me a pencil.

"You have to code," one of the interns said.

The first task in the hard-mail room was to code each letter with a "disposition" on the top left corner (in pencil). What was the person writing about? Gun Violence, Healthcare, Drone Strikes, Domestic Violence, Ukraine, Taxes. Put your initials under the code. Code a stack, then stand to stretch your neck and your legs and take your stack over to "the wall," a tan shelving unit stuffed with paper, shelf after shelf labeled with corresponding dispositions. Gitmo, Mortgage Crisis, Immigration, Bees. (*Bees?*) The codes corresponded to more than a hundred different form-response letters from the president that the OPC writing team, a group of nine, worked to constantly update. In the meantime, all the letters from kids went into a separate bin to be picked up by the kid team upstairs; requests for birthday, anniversary, and baby acknowledgments went to the greetings team; gifts went to the gifts team. A casework team of six across the hall handled letters that required individual attention from a federal agency. Maybe someone needed help getting benefits from the Department of Veterans Affairs, for example; a caseworker could step in and investigate. There were a few more codes to be aware of. Sensitive meant someone was writing to the president about a loss, a sickness, or other personal trauma. Those went over to Jack Cumming, a quiet guy in beige who spent his days reading letter after letter about small and large tragedies suffered by strangers across the country and who often needed a break from the unbearable sadness, and so he liked to hang out in the hard-mail room. "It's nice to come in here and just . . . read," he said.

A lot of people who worked in OPC would tell me that. The hard-mail room was where you went when the rest of your job got difficult, or annoying, or boring. It had a way of re-centering you, reminding you why you were here. Sit down and read. The bins were never empty. America had a lot to say, and without you, there would be no one to listen.

Interns in the hard-mail room were expected to get through three hundred letters a day, and this group had learned to move quickly, everybody scribbling on the corners, distributing into piles.

I told Yena I was still stuck on the first one I'd picked up. A guy in Colorado. He had some problems with heroin. He was writing to the president to say he'd gotten clean.

"Yeah, we get those," Yena said.

He relapsed. He was not comfortable with his own sexuality. His father died. He contemplated suicide. His mom never gave up on him. It was a long letter. The deeper I got into it, the more uncomfortable I felt reading it, as if I were intruding on a private friendship.

"He got clean again," I told Yena. I looked at the stack of letters she had to get through and the piles in front of all the others reading. Were all the letters going to be like this?

"If you want to, you can just go ahead and sample that one," Yena said.

"Sample" was shorthand for: Put the letter in the pile for consideration to be included in the 10LADs, the ten letters that would go to Obama that evening.

I thought about Obama reading about this guy's heroin problem. Should he? Who was I to say? Who were any of these people to say?

"You just write 'Sample' on it," Yena said when I asked her how to sample a letter. You wrote it on the top left corner. In pencil. Small print. (Respect the letter.) You then took it and dropped it in the wooden inbox with a sticker on it that said, "Samples." Fiona would collect them at the end of the day, sift through, and decide. About 2 percent of the total incoming mail, two or three hundred letters a day, ended up in the sample bin.

I tapped my pencil, looked at the letter again. It was typed. The grammar was precise. The guy seemed to have put a lot of time into it. He said he'd been meaning to write for a long time but had wanted to wait until the time was right. He wanted Obama to know he'd been sober a year. Which was great. But did Obama need to know that? Did this stand for something larger? Was someone going to have to prepare a brief asking for more funds for the opioid addiction crisis or something to go along with this letter?

"Don't overthink it," Yena said.

She told me that Fiona kept the bar deliberately low. Does the letter move you in some particular way? Don't overthink it. Sample it. These were *people* writing, and you were a *person* reading, and the president was a *person*. "Just keep remembering that, and you'll be fine," Yena said.

Dear President Obama,

. . . I am an undocumented immigrant. I came to the United States when I was 14 years old. . . . In my mind I am as American as it comes. I still have my first pair of Air Jordans. There are very few pop cultural references I do not understand.

. . . I did not become aware of my status until I was finishing up college and had gotten accepted to medical school and realized I did not qualify for funding.

. . . Until recently with the passing of the Deferred Action for Childhood Arrivals I basically walked on eggshells every day and truly was not sure how safe I was or what path my life would follow. . . .

I would like to say although I did not vote for you . . . mainly because I could not . . . I feel like you voted for me with DACA and all your efforts with the DREAM act. Thank you.

Sincerely yours,
Dare Adewumi, M.D.
Redlands, California

"You get attached," the intern sitting next to me said. Her name was Jamira. She had her hair bundled tightly on top of her head and wore a pretty print top. She said that one time she had opened a letter from a woman who was writing the president to say she had lost a family member to gun violence. "She had enclosed photos. Just blood all over in a car . . ." She tapped her eraser on the table, up and down on the table.

"Everybody has that one letter," Yena said. Letters could take a toll. Unlike most other shops at the White House, OPC offered monthly counseling sessions to anyone who felt the need.

The most important code everyone needed to know about was Red Dot. Red Dots were emergencies. These were from people writing to the president to say they wanted to kill themselves or someone else, or they seemed in some way on the edge. You wrote "Red Dot" on the top of the letter if you got one of those, and then you immediately walked it across the hall and gave it to Lacey Higley, the woman in the back corner more or less in charge of rescuing people.

"Do you need a break?" Yena asked me. "Do you need cookies? We have cookies." She reached for a tub of oatmeal-raisins and slid it over.

I asked her if she had ever red-dotted a letter.

"Oh my," she said. Some two hundred letters a day were red-dotted.

I asked her if she had a letter like Jamira's, one that haunted her.

"It was an email from a mother who missed her son," she said. She pushed her hair behind her ears as if having to prep herself for this one. She said in the email the mom explained that her son had been kidnapped overseas, and at the time the investigation was still under way. Yena read the letter a dozen times, stunned by details in it that, for reasons of OPC confidentiality—and national security—she could not reveal to me. "Everything was hush-hush." She alerted the authorities, then felt helpless because there was nothing more she could do. Weeks later, she was watching CNN, and that was how she learned the son had been killed. It was national news. It was an international incident, and his mom had reached out, and Yena had been on the receiving end of her desperate pleas. And now he was dead.

"I just lost it," she told me. "I sobbed and sobbed and sobbed." It was a Sunday. She came in to the office and sat at her computer. "What if his mom wrote again?" She told me the experience changed the direction of her life and her sense of her place in the world.

Jamira was leaning in to hear Yena tell the story of the mother and the lost son. She had put her pencil down. "It's weird. I'm going to go from this to being back at school," she said. "It's hard to explain all this to my friends."

"You can't," Yena said.

"I never thought about how powerful a letter was."

"Did you even know we had a correspondence office before you came here?" Yena asked her.

"I had no idea."

"You think you're going to be the mail lady or something."

"We're in the mailroom."

"The mailroom."

In the end I didn't sample the letter from the guy who had conquered his heroin problem; I didn't sample any of the ones I read, in part because I wanted to sample all of them and then got overwhelmed by the weight of the responsibility. I surrendered my stack, adding it back in the pile for reconsideration by the group. Later when I saw Fiona, I told her about the guy with the heroin and about some of the other letters I had read, and I wondered if there was something I could do to put my finger on the scale so that if any of them ended up in her daily sample pile, she would give them special attention when she sat down to pick the day's 10LADs.

I learned that pretty much everyone felt that way. You got attached. You became an advocate for your letter. And if yours got picked as one of the 10LADs, it would make your day. And if the president actually wrote back to the person, you felt high. And if something from one of your picks ended up in a speech or a policy decision, well, it was time to throw a party.

When Fiona interviewed people for jobs in OPC, one of the tests she had them do was writing their own letter to the president. Not for her to find out what they had to say. But so they got a chance to know what writing a letter to the president felt like.

The capacity to occupy a stranger's head and heart—that was the key competency needed to land a job in Fiona's mailroom.

Dear President Obama,   January 21, 2009

My name is Thomas J. Meehan III, the father of Colleen Ann Meehan Barkow, age 26, who perished on September 11 2001 at the WTC. Colleen was an employee of Cantor-Fitzgerald, working on the 103rd Floor. Her upper torso was found September 17th, 2001, the date of her first wedding anniversary. In the days and months afterwards there were to be additional discoveries of her, a total of six, which still did not amount to a whole body, but was more than what some other families affected have been given back, Families still speak in terms of body parts found and not found, and what will never be found.

In the past seven years, my wife and I have been committed to the issue of the ashen remains of those lost that day, which have been interred (bulldozed) into the 40 acres of land known as the Fresh Kills landfill on Staten Island, New York. For the one thousand families who did not receive any remains, this is the final resting place, an un-holy, un-consecrated landfill. The lives lost are there with garbage beneath them and construction fill above them, an unbefitting resting place for those we called heroes and took an oath never to forget.

While this issue has been before the courts, and the remains may in fact be permanently interred at the landfill, parents, spouses, siblings, extended family members must live with the knowledge that their loved ones lie in what was the world's largest dump. How we as a society will be judged in the treatment of those lost, only history will record.

My wife and I mourn the continued loss of American lives in the war in Iraq and Afghanistan while we still await the apprehension and trial of those we hold responsible for the death of our daughter and almost 3000 other American and international citizens.

While we understand the reasons for the closure of the detention facility at Guantanamo Bay, we urge you to allow the trials of those defendants charged in connection with the attacks of September 11, 2001, to go forward, and complete the judicial process and give some small measure of Justice to all of the 9/11 family members, while we still await the capture of Osama Bin Laden.

Our lives have been forever changed by the events of September 11,2001, and yet life goes on, we now have two granddaughters, Brett Colleen ,age four an and Ryann Elizabeth, age two ,we hope that their lives will be in a better world that the one which claimed their aunt. And they will have the opportunities to live their lives to the fullest and live in a safer world, free of the threat of terrorism.

I share these facts with you so that you will understand why these issues mean so much to us, and ask that you not forget the promise "Never To Forget", and will bring to justice those responsible for September 11, 2001.

God Bless You and You're Family,
May the Peace of the Lord Be Upon You and Remain With You,

Respectfully,
Thomas J. Meehan III & JoAnn Meehan
Thomas J. Meehan III & JoAnn Meehan

Toms River, New Jersey

CHAPTER 4

Thomas and JoAnn Meehan, January 21, 2009

TOMS RIVER, NEW JERSEY

Thomas Meehan started writing letters soon after the towers came down. He needed an outlet. One of the first letters he wrote was to the navy. He remembers this part so well. A lot of other things are fuzzy. He is seventy-four years old, and the main thing lately is to get everything recorded before his memory goes altogether south.

JoAnn, his wife, lets out a polite chuckle, as you do. But she knows it's true about Tom's memory. The stents, the tranquilizers, the strokes—they've taken a toll.

They're sitting at the dining room table on a hot July morning in their home in Toms River, New Jersey, not far from the ocean and the Pine Barrens. The little dog's name is Chewy. JoAnn has a piece of white marble from Tower 1 she would like to show you. It's from the floor of the lobby, a gift from first responders. "Always remember Colleen. Ground Zero. 9/11/01," they wrote on it. She also would like to show you a piece of window glass they gave her.

"Look how thick," she says. "Maybe an inch thick, for the air pressure."

"It's so thick," Tom says.

One time Colleen took them to watch the fireworks from her

floor. The 103rd floor. You would not believe the elevators. The time it took to get all the way up there. Three separate elevators.

"I was like, 'Where are we going, to heaven?'" JoAnn says.

The whole reason Colleen left college to work in New York was because she got to work in the World Trade Center. That's how JoAnn remembers it. ("Also a romance played a part.") JoAnn was not in favor of Colleen's quitting college; a straight-A student leaving school made no sense. But Colleen told her mother an opportunity like that might never come again. The company needed women. Colleen learned how to read blueprints when they sent her to Ohio to train, and they sent her to London a few times to learn design. She was young and in love and basking in the hustle-bustle. Her job was in facilities. She designed a cafeteria for the 103rd floor of Tower 1 so everyone didn't have to go all the way down all those elevators for lunch. She even made a smoking room with big fans sucking out the smoke. She was extremely proud of that cafeteria.

"We looked *down* at the fireworks," Tom recalls. "That was the whole point. We saw fireworks from the top down."

"The top down!" JoAnn says.

Colleen got married and her husband worked in the city too, and they bought a car. Some days they would drive together into work, and some days they would take the train. Fifty-fifty. If they took the train, they got in early, and if they took the car, they got in late.

So that whole crystal-blue Tuesday morning of September 11, 2001, with all the phones in the region down, and the electricity out in the Carteret, New Jersey, neighborhood where they lived then, and her one neighbor running down the street with that TV from her camper that ran on batteries, JoAnn was pacing on the porch saying, "Please tell me you took the car, please tell me you took the car, please tell me you took the car."

But Colleen had taken the train that day.

Seeing the footage on TV of the smoke, over and over the way they showed it—that alone drove a lot of the families into madness.

"A lot of people forget," Tom says.

The first seventy-two hours was calling hospitals. Nobody knew anything. Nobody had her. By the end of the week, it was evident that she was gone. JoAnn took off work at the school for three months after that. They were extremely understanding, and when she got back, they adapted her position to one-on-one assistance rather than teaching a whole class. She was having bleeding ulcers, and they would get exacerbated by the sight of turbans, which some people did wear at the school.

"Even though they were lovely, nice people," JoAnn says.

"They were Sikhs," Tom says.

"They had nothing to do with 9/11," she says. "Nothing whatsoever."

She would get violently ill when she saw turbans. It wasn't something you could put logic to.

They met other families. A lot of the conversation in the beginning was just about body parts. What you got back. One woman received part of her husband's scalp; the other received a testicle. Some people didn't get anything back; some got a finger. People might say it's gruesome to talk that way. But if it becomes part of your everyday . . . People who got body parts back felt lucky, and people who didn't kept hoping, and so the people who did felt guilt. When they found Colleen's torso, it was among the debris from the north side of the building. The cafeteria was on the north side.

"I think Colleen was in the cafeteria," JoAnn says.

Fresh Kills Landfill on Staten Island was full; it had been officially closed a few months before 9/11, but then the state reopened a section for the sorting of the Twin Tower rubble. Hills 1 and 9 where they did the sorting were adjacent to the neighborhood where Tom and JoAnn lived, just over the river. The mound was like fifty acres. They brought in conveyor belts. And the trucks started coming. For weeks after the attack, the trucks would keep Tom and JoAnn up at night, the engine roars, the backup beeps, the clumping sounds of dumping.

"And the seagulls would attack it, and they would move the body parts," JoAnn says.

"So they put up tents," Tom says.

"The machines would sift it and remove whatever they could, and what was left was bulldozed into the landfill," JoAnn says. "And then on top of that is the fill."

"Industrial."

"Construction fill. Computers. Computer parts. Wires. Concrete."

"I'm sure people would debate, why are you arguing about minuscule elements?" Tom says. "What we are really talking about are bone fragments less than a quarter inch. But for me it doesn't matter the size."

When the sifting was done and they closed Hills 1 and 9 as a crime scene, the people at the sanitation department who ran the landfill would let people in if they wanted to come look, which a lot of families still did. You signed a paper, and a guy would take you to the dump site in a garbage truck.

Eventually, they put up a flagpole.

JoAnn finished out her thirty years with the district, and then she and Tom moved down here to Toms River to be near Daryl and the grandbabies. Daryl is the oldest; then JoAnn had another son who survived only one day, and then she had Colleen. One time when Colleen was two, she was in her crib for a nap, and JoAnn was outside shoveling snow, and suddenly here comes Colleen, fully dressed in her snow gear, out to help.

"I was like, 'What are you doing!'" JoAnn says. "She put all that gear on and figured all that out by herself." Colleen always had pigtails. She would put everything in her mouth. Their house was the one all the kids came to. Sleeping all over the rec room. You never knew who you'd bump into.

Anyway, Tom would like to get back to the letter he wrote to the navy. He says he also wrote to President George W. Bush. Actually, that might have been before the navy.

"No, definitely after," JoAnn says.

It's such a jumble.

Tom wrote to President Bush in anger, asking why he had not sent a note of condolence about Colleen. He figured something like that should have come. Tom got a letter back from the White House explaining that New York kept the list of victims' names, not the White House.

Tom starts wheezing.

"Who was in charge was a big question in the aftermath," JoAnn says, adding that later they did get a sympathy card from Vice President Dick Cheney.

"We have it somewhere here," Tom says. Wheezing is a symptom of chronic obstructive pulmonary disease, which he has, along with diabetes. His computer and the Internet were the keys to his sanity in the aftermath. That was how he managed. He wrote so many letters. The letter to the navy was the first one, definitely among the first. This was, gosh, within days. He was angry and he wanted somebody to do something immediately to get the people who had done this. So he googled, you know, "navy." He picked a ship that was deployed in the Far East. He picked the USS *Carl Vinson*, and he found an email address, and he wrote about Colleen. Within weeks he heard back. Who expects to hear back? The email was from a lieutenant who talked about not forgetting the victims, and he included an attachment. Tom opened the attachment, and it was a photo of a guy in a flight suit leaning over a bomb. "LASER," it said on the bomb. The guy had a pen, and he was writing something on the nose. "COLLEEN ANN MEE—" He was working on the second *E*.

Tom would like to show you the picture.

The *Carl Vinson* had been headed east around the tip of India on September 11, 2001, when, in response to the attacks back home, it abruptly changed course and advanced toward the Arabian Sea. On October 11, 2001, it launched the bomb with Colleen's name on it, one among hundreds the navy dropped in the first air strikes over Afghanistan targeting al-Qaeda and the Taliban in support of Operation Enduring Freedom.

Tom puts the picture of the bomb away and then folds his hands like an obedient schoolboy. JoAnn thinks Chewy is being remarkably quiet. Usually he's bouncing off the walls by now. He's still a puppy.

At the landfill, investigators were able to identify just 300 people (2,753 died in the attacks) out of the 4,257 human remains they recovered. The rest, the remains of more than a thousand victims, have not been identified. "You remember seeing the funerals on television with all those caskets," JoAnn says. "But they were all empty. There was nothing in those caskets."

"People don't remember," Tom says.

People don't know about the way they just covered everything up when they were done. They did not consult the families. They just put dirt and construction debris on top. They did put that flagpole in.

"I know there are parts of my daughter there," JoAnn says.

Tom: "You can argue till doomsday about the legal rights, but the simple fact that they didn't acknowledge it to the families—"

The Ground Zero memorial is a love-hate thing for Tom and JoAnn. It took ten years and $700 million to build. You would think there would be resources set aside for asking the families what they wanted done with the remains of their loved ones. The Office of the Chief Medical Examiner in New York had more than eight thousand body parts they couldn't identify, couldn't complete the DNA on. Somehow the decision had been made to put the body parts in plastic pouches—and then put the pouches in the basement of the museum.

A museum is not a memorial site.

"It costs twenty-four dollars to get into the museum," Tom says.

"Families get in for free," JoAnn says.

"Families are allowed to look in the basement."

"You look through a glass wall. It's a storage facility. It's lockers in rows."

Tom and JoAnn got involved in a lot of activist things with the other families. They got involved with WTC Families for Proper Burial Inc. They got involved in public remembrances, and there were so many nice things people did. Quilts, presents, like this slab of marble and this piece of window from the first responders. In the first few months, Tom wore a badge with Colleen's picture on it. He was in a gift shop, and a woman saw the badge, and she bought him a glass angel in remembrance of Colleen. It's an example. There were poems people wrote. Jewelry people made. Rosaries. Pictures of Colleen people drew. A CD with a song someone wrote. The Flag of Remembrance. Mountains of gifts. "I could start my own mini-museum," JoAnn says. They had to rent a unit at one of those storage places. It's so nice what everyone did.

Every year on the anniversary they have a ceremony at Ground Zero, and they read out the name of every victim. There's a lottery to pick who gets to read. If you get picked, you read twenty names. One year Daryl got picked, and then JoAnn got picked. It's the highest honor to get picked. Now they're talking about doing away with the name reading.

Tom is particularly upset about that one. The whole issue with memory. Tom says there's a saying he's heard veterans use: People die twice. "Once when they leave their physical form and the second time when their name is spoken for the last time."

Now Chewy is acting more like himself. He's skittering around and around the table, and his feet are so tiny the pitter-patter sounds like rain.

"Okay, Chewy," Tom says.

JoAnn is stuck back on a few points she made earlier. "The thought of going to visit where your daughter is buried and you have to call the sanitation department to get an appointment to ride on a garbage truck," she says.

"The issue of the remains and all of that—it's the best kept secret of 9/11," Tom says. "So to speak."

"I do think Colleen was in the cafeteria," JoAnn says.

"People not directly involved in the event have a certain view from the outside of what the families have endured," Tom says.

One day here at the local library, they were putting together a little exhibit, and they asked Tom and JoAnn to contribute mementos of Colleen, and so Tom and JoAnn were arranging the items in the glass cabinet.

Two women walked by. *"Can't these people just get over it?"* the one said.

Clear as day. Tom was ready to pounce. JoAnn gave him the look that said, *Ignore it.*

Tom couldn't.

He came home and wrote a letter. Obama had just gotten elected, so he wrote to him. When he sat down, he thought about what he wanted to say to the new president, and it was the same thing he wanted to say to the lady in the library. In a way the letter was for both. For everybody. Tom wanted everybody to know some of what the families went through. He wanted to say the issue wasn't whether or not the families ever got over it. "The issue was that *you* don't get over it," Tom says.

"But I digress."

"Just the thought of, you have to ride on a garbage truck," JoAnn says.

JoAnn did the proofreading, and Tom mailed the letter, and they were surprised when they heard back just a few weeks later.

Tom would like to show you the letter they got back.

THE WHITE HOUSE
WASHINGTON

Dear Tom & JoAnn —

I am in receipt of your letter, and wanted to respond personally. Your story is heartbreaking, and we will do everything we can to ensure that the process of bringing all those involved in 9/11 is completed.

In the meantime, know that we will never forget Colleen, and that I spend every waking hour in search of ways to make the future brighter for your granddaughters and my daughters.

God Bless,

CHAPTER 5

The Idea

When I asked President Obama how he came up with the idea of reading ten letters a day, he thought a moment, then said, "Pete Rouse." He said it an offhand way, as if this was some easily recognized household name.

"Pete was almost maniacal about correspondence," he went on. "When I first got to the Senate, I was, you know, green behind the ears, and he had been there for a long time. He kind of instilled in me the sense of the power of mail.

"Pete Rouse," he said again.

I kept hearing the name in conversations about the early days of the Obama administration and the origins of its Office of Presidential Correspondence. Shailagh brought him up, and so did David Axelrod, Valerie Jarrett, and Fiona. "There are legions of people around my age who got their start in public service or politics by a conversation with Pete Rouse," Fiona said.

They all talked about him the same way—you know, *Pete!*—more or less disregarding my blank stare.

I came to learn that Pete Rouse was a guy who famously shunned publicity, who never did interviews, who worked hard to stay behind the scenes, and so even though insiders knew him as Obama's right-hand man who sat for years just two doors down from the Oval Office, to people outside the Beltway, he was a stranger.

"I'm not really good at anecdotes," Pete said when I visited him at the Perkins Coie offices in downtown Washington, where he'd worked since retiring from his White House post in 2014. "I don't remember a lot." Then he told me that although he now worked at a law firm, he was not a lawyer, and—he was quick to point out—he was most definitely *not* a lobbyist, and although people regularly asked him if he'd ever write a book about his many years in the White House and on Capitol Hill, "there is not a chance in hell I'll ever write a book."

I wondered about a person choosing to define himself by what he was not and never would be. He was in his early seventies, soft-spoken, amiable, with thick white hair, and he moved like his back hurt, which he volunteered readily that it did. We then veered effortlessly into a discussion of my brother's recent back surgery. I have no idea how we became so familiar so quickly, but within minutes we were talking like friends. Maybe this was why he didn't do interviews. He seemed to have neither guard nor guile.

I told him Obama said he was the one who'd had the idea that the president should read ten constituent letters a day.

"No," he said. "I give him credit for saying he wanted ten letters a day."

I said Obama seemed to think it all went back to him somehow.

"I don't want to sound arrogant," he said. He told me he first met Obama on the 2004 campaign trail. He had already worked in Congress for more than three decades, starting in the 1970s; he had become such a fixture in Washington that people on Capitol Hill referred to him as the "101st senator" during his long tenure as former Senate Majority Leader Tom Daschle's chief of staff. Daschle lost his seat in 2004, the same year Obama was voted into the Senate, leaving Pete, a Hill guru, out of a job. Obama asked Pete to come over to his team, become his chief of staff; Obama said he wanted to hit the ground running, and there was no one in Washington with the breadth of experience that Pete had.

"I said no," Pete told me. "I was in my late fifties. I thought I'd take retirement, do something else."

Obama asked Pete a second time. He wanted the A team. He felt the urgency of the moment, of living up to the expectations he had set when, at the 2004 Democratic National Convention in Boston, he delivered the speech that would catapult him into the national spotlight:

> If there's a child on the South Side of Chicago who can't read, that matters to me, even if it's not my child.
>
> If there's a senior citizen somewhere who can't pay for their prescription and having to choose between medicine and the rent, that makes my life poorer, even if it's not my grandparent.
>
> If there's an Arab American family being rounded up without benefit of an attorney or due process, that threatens my civil liberties.
>
> It is that fundamental belief—it is that fundamental belief—I am my brother's keeper, I am my sister's keeper—that makes this country work.
>
> It's what allows us to pursue our individual dreams, yet still come together as a single American family: E pluribus unum, out of many, one.

Pete said no. Anyone listening to that speech knew that Obama was destined, one day, for a presidential run. Pete was more interested in retirement.

Obama asked a third time. "He said, 'You might have heard I'm thinking about running for president in 2008,'" Pete told me. "He said, 'That is categorically untrue. Maybe at some point in the future, but my wife would never let me do it. My kids are too young. I have no intention of doing that; I just want to get established in the Senate.'

"I thought, *This guy is extraordinarily impressive*," Pete told me.

Pete finally said yes, but only on a temporary basis. "I agreed to get him started, to set up his Senate operation, to get a good team in place, get a good strategic plan in place, get a good structure. I'll lay that foundation. I thought, *I don't have anything else to do right now. I can help set this up for a year and a half. How hard can it be?*"

Less than one year in, Obama, who had made a point to keep a low profile, focusing on local Illinois issues, found himself again in the national news. Hurricane Katrina had just hit, and after touring the devastated Gulf Coast, he made his first appearances on the Sunday morning shows, admonishing the federal government's paltry response, emphasizing not only the racial bias it revealed but also the economic one. "It was a moment I thought I might add a useful perspective to the debate," he told *Time* magazine. "If an issue of justice or equality is at stake," he said, "I will speak out on it." People clamored for more. Speaking invitations were coming in by the hundreds, and that was when Pete, a master strategist almost in spite of himself, drew up a memo:

> It makes sense for you to consider now whether you want to use 2006 to position yourself to run in 2008 if "a perfect storm" of personal and political factors emerges in 2007. If making a run in 2008 is at all a possibility, no matter how remote, it makes sense to begin talking and making decisions about what you should be doing "below the radar" in 2006 to maximize your ability to get in front of this wave should it emerge and should you and your family decide it is worth riding.

It would be nine years after Pete first signed on to set up Obama's Senate office—after a presidential campaign, a presidential transition office, an inauguration (Pete turned down his seat on the inaugural platform, preferring to watch Obama get sworn in on TV at home), a three-month stint pinch-hitting as Obama's chief of staff when Rahm Emanuel left in 2010 ("I said right then, I'm not interested in chief of staff; frankly I don't want the call at three A.M. about the earthquake in Honduras. . . ."), *another* presidential campaign, *another* few years in the White House—before Pete was able to convince Obama that he really meant it, that his assistance was only on a temporary basis, and he was now going to stop, go home, and spend time with his cats.

"Pete said, 'You know, making sure that we've got a good correspondence office that constituents feel that you are hearing them and that you are responding to them, that makes up for a lot of stuff,'" Obama told me, talking about those early days with Pete in his Senate office and about how something as mundane as the mail became a part of the conversation.

"And then during the course of maybe a year and a half of campaigning," Obama said, "every once in a while people would write me a letter. Or they would slip a letter to me on the rope line. And some of them would just be amazing. And they would help shape the stories that I told during the campaign because they weren't abstract.

"You know, this is a mom who's trying to figure out, how do you go back to school and look after her kids at the same time and pay the bills? This is a dad who had lost his job and described how hard it was to feel like he was worth anything.

"And that would . . . orient me."

When Pete talked to me about the origins of the mailroom operation, he was more blunt: "I hate writing letters to friends," he said. "So if someone cares enough to sit down and write a letter, the elected official ought to pay attention to it. It's often the only direct contact that an individual citizen has with his or her elected official. My view has always been that the quality of the communication says something about how the elected official views his or her role in terms of serving the public, regardless of party affiliation or political philosophy."

It was just: Read your mail. It was basic. Like: Tie your shoes. Or perhaps: Say your prayers. It may have seemed painfully obvious. It may have been in Obama's mind all along. But Pete articulated it, and he would continue to articulate it.

"I don't want to overstate it," Pete said. "I mean, I was probably more focused on finding bin Laden than answering an individual letter from Montana. So I'm not suggesting I'm different from anybody else in that regard. But I do think I made a conscious priority to find good people to work in the presidential office of correspondence, and that it was important, and that the president and senior people understood that it was important."

After the inauguration in 2009, Obama's transition team had

arrived to find that the Bush administration had left virtually nothing in terms of guidance about how to set up an Office of Presidential Correspondence. No system in place for sorting mail, no procedure manuals, no templates, no software, no form letters you could simply spit out.

And then came the avalanche. A quarter of a million letters a week to the new president. Boxes of mail stacked to the ceiling and lining the hallways. The Obama team didn't yet have stationery.

Mike Kelleher from Obama's Senate office was the person who stepped up to tackle the mess.

Pete was surprised. He'd figured Mike would want a job like assistant secretary of commerce, something with the oomph and pizzazz befitting a guy of his pedigree. Mike had known Obama since 1999; they were rookies carving careers in politics together—Obama coming from his work as a community organizer and Mike from the Peace Corps. They ran and lost side-by-side campaigns for Congress together, and Mike went on to serve as director of economic development and outreach in Obama's Senate office.

Now Mike said he wanted to do the mail. "It's a challenge, it needs to be done, and I'm willing to do it." He rolled up his sleeves. He carved out the OPC mission statement—"To listen to the American people, to understand their stories and concerns and respond on behalf of the president." He came up with an organizational chart and started interviewing. Candidates would have to pass an elaborate screening process if they wanted to work in OPC. They would have to be willing to volunteer in the mailroom before getting hired; Mike wanted to see how they interacted with one another and with elderly and student volunteers. He looked for compassion. He told them how lucky they would be to be reading mail. They would get to know America better than anyone.

He built the staff, drew up a ten-page strategic plan for the mailroom, wrote algorithms for a mail coding system, set up a casework decision tree, assembled a library of policy-response letters, and developed quality-control manuals. He put in sixteen-hour days, weekends, creating order out of the chaos and assembling an army of empathic mail-reading soldiers, including Fiona.

When I reached out to Mike to ask him about all of this, about building OPC, he said, "I didn't build it. I was there and I managed the people . . . really talented people. . . . I made a couple good decisions in hiring people."

And then he said, "Pete Rouse. Pete Rouse set the tone of what a public servant is for me."

It kept going around like that—Mike crediting Pete, Pete crediting Mike, Pete crediting Obama, Obama crediting Pete.

Say what you will about the Obama administration, but this was not a braggy bunch.

Word came that President Obama wanted to see some of the mail just the day after he took office. Mike got the call from the Oval saying the president wanted to see five letters. Then they called back with a correction. The president wanted to see fifteen letters. They called back one more time. He wanted to see ten that day, and every day.

"By the time I got to the White House and somebody informed me that we were going to get forty thousand or whatever it was pieces of mail a day," Obama told me, "I was trying to figure out, how do I in some way duplicate that experience I had during the campaign?

"Ten a day is what I figured I could do. It was a small gesture, I thought, at least to resist the bubble. It was a way for me to, every day, remember that what I was doing was not about me. It wasn't about the Washington calculus. It wasn't about the political scoreboard. It was about the people who were out there living their lives who were either looking for some help or angry about how I was screwing something up.

"And I, maybe, didn't understand when I first started the practice how meaningful it would end up being to me."

One side benefit of a president asking to read ten letters a day was that it sent a message that reverberated throughout the White House, from the lowest-ranking staffer working the scanners over in the EEOB to speechwriters, policy makers, and senior advisors in the West Wing: Mail was important. And if the mail was important, so were the people handling it. In the early days, Pete would head over to OPC himself, tell everybody in the mailroom how much he appreciated their contribution, tell them that it mattered to the president, that *they* mattered to the president.

"That stuff makes a difference," Pete told me. "Just knowing that your contribution had value and was valued."

He gave me an example, motioned toward a framed photo by the window. It was among a cluster of other photos. It was a picture of him seated at a dinner, the rest of the people in the banquet hall up on their feet giving him a standing ovation and Obama at the lectern. Pete said it was a gift from Obama when Obama had finally given in and let him retire. Obama had thrown Pete a dinner and given him the picture, with a small message at the bottom.

"You can go over and look at that if you want," Pete said.

Pete, there is a city full of people who owe their success to you.
I'm one of them. Thank you, my friend.

"Stuff like that sticks with you," Pete said. He sat up straight, his hands resting gently on his knees.

There was a guitar hanging on the wall near the photo, and it looked like Obama had signed that too. I asked Pete about it, and he got up to come over to admire it. He rocked from side to side as he walked as if to avoid one ache or another.

"A Fender," he said. There was a Senate seal painted on the guitar, an Obama campaign seal, and the presidential seal. Pete said Obama had commissioned it. Another going-away present. "What's it say on here? He wrote on it. It's hard to read."

We leaned toward the guitar, tilting our heads.

"Thanks for . . ." We couldn't read what Obama had written on Pete's guitar.

"So you're a guitarist," I said to Pete.

"No," he said.

Not a guitarist. I paused to recap Pete's résumé. He was not a lawyer, not a lobbyist, not an aspiring author, not a person who lobbied to become Senator Obama's chief of staff, let alone President Obama's chief of staff, and he was not a guitarist. (His job title at Perkins Coie was "senior policy advisor.")

"I'm a Grateful Dead fan," he said, and he smiled. His face was wide, puffy, and the smile lifted all the worry off it. "My two greatest professional accomplishments," he said. "Number two is helping elect the first African American president; number one is reuniting the Grateful Dead."

During the 2008 campaign, the Grateful Dead's Bob Weir had reached out to say he was an Obama supporter. He'd wanted to know if there was anything he could do to help.

"There's one thing," Pete said to Weir. The band had split up in 1995 after lead guitarist Jerry Garcia died; surviving members went on to tour in varying configurations, but never all of them together. "Maybe just one thing . . ."

And so it was that on February 4, 2008, a reunited Grateful Dead played before a sold-out crowd at the Warfield Theatre in San Francisco and then again in October, along with the Allman Brothers Band, before a sold-out crowd at the Bryce Jordan Center in University Park, Pennsylvania, and amid the crowd at both shows, there was Pete Rouse bopping his head to the beat.

"Greatest professional accomplishment," Pete said again.

This reminded him of a related point: Writing thank-you notes to the Grateful Dead and to the Allman Brothers should not be difficult.

Pete expected Obama to gush in the thank-yous. This was *the Grateful Dead*. And this was *the Allman Brothers*.

When it came time to write them, Obama had been on a plane to Hawaii to see his grandmother, who was dying. "That's a long trip," Pete told me. He had sketched out some ideas for the thank-you notes and had sent them with Obama to do on the plane.

"I asked him, 'Please handwrite each one.'" Pete had provided a list of all the band members and some suggested lines so that Obama could personalize each note.

Pete got a call from a staffer on the campaign plane. Obama wanted to know about these thank-you notes. Why couldn't he just write one to the whole Grateful Dead and then one to the whole Allman Brothers Band? Wouldn't that be sufficient?

"Tell him I'm going to quit if he does that," Pete joked to the staffer.

As he relayed this story to me, he underscored the word "joked."

There was no way he would have ever quit on Obama. Pete wanted me to make sure that point was clear and could not be misinterpreted; he was getting antsy. He was not a person who did interviews. He was not good at anecdotes.

"To me it shows that he doesn't have the same sensitivity to this that you or I would," Pete told me. "Which is why he *did* relate to the mail." Expressing heartfelt thanks to famous legends of rock and roll was one kind of communication (pretty basic), answering mail from random folks in Idaho or New Jersey quite another. "When he was responding to individual stories, as opposed to just thanking someone for doing something for him, it became very personal to him. Then he *wanted* to do it."

We went back to the couch, and Pete winced as he sat. He said he had to fly to Chicago in the morning for a meeting, was considering canceling on account of his back. He looked at me, seemed to assess my reaction, as you do when you need a friend to give you permission to bail on something.

"Yeah, you should cancel," I said. "Just walking through the airport—"

"For a two-hour lunch and a dinner," he said. "You know?"

Oh, absolutely.

"Did the surgery help your brother?" he asked.

A hundred percent.

Somehow this led to news of my husband's successful knee replacement.

"Oh, my knees," he said.

Samples, 2010-2012

July 23, 2012

Ms. Emily Nottingham

Tucson AZ

Dear President Obama,

When my son was killed in the Tucson mass murders last year, you asked if there was anything you could do. There is. I am asking you to support some reasonable steps to protect your citizens. Reinstating the ban on assault weapons and extended magazine clips should be a simple step to make our public places more safe for citizens. Our rights of assembly are threatened. I believe that you can be a vigorous supporter of the second amendment and still support modest regulation of weapons of mass murder. If you will not oppose the NRA, then seek out the support of the NRA in this gun safety measure. My son was killed in the mass murder in Tucson. Now it has happened again and more young people have been senselessly murdered by a stranger in a public place armed with weapons designed to kill many people very quickly. Enforcement of existing laws is not a sufficient response; additional steps are necessary to restrict easy access to weapons of mass murder. The Tucson shooter was not diagnosed as mentally ill when he legally purchased these super-lethal weapons; I would not be surprised if the Aurora shooter also had no such diagnosis. We need to look at the weapons themselves.

Please consider being a leader on this issue; others will follow behind you. Thank you for thinking seriously about this and seeking a resolution.

Emily Nottingham

THE WHITE HOUSE

WASHINGTON

Emily —

Thank you for your letter. I can only imagine
the heartbreak you've gone through. I agree with
you about common sense gun control measures, and
although I confess that it is currently challenging to
get Congress to take on the issue, I will do my best to
help move public opinion. Sincerely,

5/9/12 no 4

Contact Us - Civil Rights

Submitted:	May 9, 2012 16:16
Originating Host:	
Remote IP:	
From:	Laura King Ph.D.
Email Address:	
Phone:	
Address (Domestic)	Columbia MO
Topic:	Civil Rights

Back from the OVAL
5/30/12

Message:
I have no idea why you decided to endorse marriage equality today. But I wanted to say thank you, on behalf of myself, my partner, Lisa, and especially our 8 year old son, Sam. In the last few days, I think I had myself convinced that I would be fine if you played the political game and stayed silent on our family's right to exist. I kept telling myself that I "knew" you supported us, even if it didn't make political sense for you to say so. I am a strong supporter of you and your agenda and I had myself convinced that I wanted you to be re-elected more than I needed to hear you say you believe that my family deserves a place at the American table. It turns out I was wrong about that. After hearing about your interview today, I find myself sitting in my office crying and realizing that hearing those words from you means more to me than I ever imagined. I am overwhelmed--touched and surprised and just tremendously grateful that anyone in your position would put principle above politics, would just say the truth about what is right. I admire your courage and character and I am so glad that you are our President. I am proud of you.

My partner's parents live in North Carolina and last night's results were very hurtful to all of us-our son is their only grandchild-as if people could vote away our family. I spent the better part of this morning contemplating what it means to be a member of a tiny minority, so small and dispensable that it seems to be no problem for people to put my civil rights up for a popular vote.

I know from experience that change can only occur when courageous and compassionate straight people take action. To me, the stakes for you seemed impossibly high. I don't know why you decided to take this stand. And I hope that it does not cost you dearly. And I will do all that I can to see that it doesn't. And in the meantime, thank you so much, Mr. President.

Best,

Laura King

Laura A. King, Ph.D.

Columbia MO

February 1, 2010

Pres. Barack Obama
1600 Pensylvania Avenue NW
Washington D.C. 20500

Mr. President:

I operate a small weekly newspaper in Espanola, NM. You visited here in September 2008 when campaigning.

The Rio Grande Sun was started by my parents in 1956. I don't need to tell you the state of newspapers today. It's hard out there for an editor.

My largest expense is payroll. The next is printing. The third is health care.

I have cut other expenses or not replaced employees who have left on their own to avoid layoffs. I will go into reserves to avoid layoffs. Not many newspapers have that luxury.

I have cut pages and "tightened" the newspaper to lower printing costs.

Health care I can do nothing about. I pay all of the premium for my 13 full-time employees. I also pay their deductible and share in their costs to meet the maximum out-of-pocket expenses.

There are two employees on thyroid medication. They both require quarterly blood tests. Insurance doesn't cover the tests. I pay for them. Last year I paid $204 per month, per person. With minimal small insurance claims and no major claims, my rates went up 35 percent this year.

Instead of paying the ransom, I dropped to a plan with a higher deductible, which I will again pay. The employees will have the same coverage. My gamble is that no one will have a catastrophic event and force me to pay the $4,000 deductible. This is how I deal with health insurance.

I did some calculations regarding my old health plan of 1995 when I received my renewal notice last month. In 1995 I paid $112 per person for a great plan: low copay, no deductible, $15 prescription card. That plan today would cost me over $600 per person.

Mr. President, please keep fighting the lobbyists and business-owned right that does not want real reform in this country. Little people like me need you advocating for common sense. Health care reform must happen if we're to move forward as a country.

Sincerely;

Robert B. Trapp

Managing Editor

3/26/10
MK

Dear Mr President
I wrote you and email a few months ago about the health care bill and how I support of what you are doing and ask if congress could please act faster on this bill. I wrote this letter on behalf of my girlfriend Jana Smith On March 18 2010 Jana passed away. Jana had some medical problem. She could not afford to go to the doctors and was waiting to see what would happen with the health care bill. She knew Mr President that you were working on this so all American could receive this much needed health care. I Know that this cannot help My Jana now but I just wanted you to know that We support everything you were doing. Thank you Mr President. I am Retired from the Military and I help Jana through what she was going through. We were going to get married I am very lost right now but I just wanted you to know from me that I want you to keep the great work that you are doing for all American
Thank you for listen to me

SSGT Robert J Doran
U.S. Air Force (Retired)

Reply

≈≈≈≈ Original Formatted Message Starts Here ≈≈≈≈

Date: Mar 23 2010 11:30AM

<PREFIX></PREFIX>
<FIRST>Robert</FIRST>
<LAST>Doran</LAST>

<ADDR2></ADDR2>
<CITY>Gilbertsville</CITY>
<STATE>Kentucky</STATE>

<ISSUE>W_POTUS</ISSUE>

Robert Doran

Gilbertsville, KY

3/25/2010

COPY FROM ORM

THE WHITE HOUSE

WASHINGTON

Robert —

Thank you for your letter. My heart goes out to you for the loss of Tana; but because of the support of people like her, we passed health care reform and can hopefully prevent such hardship for others.   God Bless,

Also, thanks for your service to our country.

Mr. Robert Doran

Berkley Michigan

JUN - 1 2010

Priority Mail

1/3/2010 6:14:28 PM
Desert Hot Springs, California

The unemployment rate in Riverside County, CA, the county in which I live, is over 30%. There are no jobs in sight. Are you going to keep even one campaign promise upon which you built your presidency? I worked for you, I contributed to you and what do I get in return: I'm out of work, I get no cost of living increase on Social Security, and you are going to pay for the new health insurance plan by cutting my Medicare.

Thank you very much.

Respectfully,

Eileen M. Garrish

THE WHITE HOUSE
WASHINGTON

Eileen —

I got your note and wanted to respond.

The day I walked into office, I inherited the worst economic crisis since the Great Depression. And after a very tough year, we have begun to turn the corner, with the economy growing again.

That may be little consolation to you and others that are out of work, and I won't be satisfied

until jobs are being created in Riverside and across the country.

Having said that, I do want to challenge the notion that I haven't kept my campaign promises, or that I have weakened Social Security or Medicare. The existing Social Security formula didn't provide a cost of living increase because prices/inflation went down this year. Nevertheless, I ordered a $250 stimulus check to seniors that made up for it. And contrary to what the Republicans have said, health care reform does not cut Medicare benefits!

Best wishes,

January 8th, 2010

Reply:

Dear Barack Obama,

Hi my name is Rebecca ████.
I am 16 years old, I will be 17 in march, I live in Florida.

I am also in DCF care, which is foster care. I have been in foster care ever since I was 2 years old. I have 3 sisters too. The 2 younger ones names and ages are, B████ she is 15 and J████ she will be 13 on January 10th 2010. My older sister ████████ is 23 years old.

When I turned 6 years old I found a family that wanted to adopt me and my three sisters, so when I turned 7 years old we all was adopted by the ████████. It was a ladie named J████ ████ and a man named D████ ████. Let me tell you a little about them, well I wanted to start a new life so I thought D████ and J████ could be the one's that would help me start that new life but, I guess I thought wrong, because D████ ended up physically and sexually abusing me, and J████ had physically abused me.

J   also new about what D
did to me and she would tell
him not to take it too far or
dont get caught.

                              I also
told D   and J   parents
and they   told me that they would
never do anything like that. I
wouldn't tell my little sisters
what was going on because
they were too young at the time.
they wouldn't understand. so I
went to my older sister and
told her what was going on, so
that night she called the police
and the police came to the house
that night and took me away and
interviewed me, then I was
thrown into foster care. My
little sisters were bribed by the T

to stay, so they did. Then D▓
was arrested over night, then
released the next day, and
nothing happened to J▓. So I
went on through life with
every one thinking that im a
liar. When I left the ▓▓▓▓
house they wouldn't allow me
to talk or see my sisters, so
I ended up getting locked
up, smoking weed, and drinking
liqoor, and running away. Then
the last time I was locked up
which was when I was 16
years old, I told my caseworker
that I need help and that
I can't keep living this life, so
She recomended ▓▓▓▓▓▓
@ ▓▓▓▓▓▓▓
My second day at ▓▓▓ I ended up
attempting to runaway with another
camper. We ended up getting caught,
so they brought us back to
▓▓▓▓▓ ever sense that day I
was a whole new person.

Now it is my 6th month here
and I am a whole new person.
I am a role model\Leader now.
During my 3 month here I found
out that the something that happened
to me happened to them. They
was then put in foster home
with a nice older lady. I have
visits and weekley phone
calls with them. D   is
locked up in prison. We don't
know how much time he
has yet, but I do know that
J   has 2 years of probation.
So now I am back in contact
with my sisters and I am
trying to get in contact with
my biological parents, but the
only problem is that my
biological parents droped there
right towards us, so now they
are struggeling getting
visitations with me.
    I am so happy with
myself I never new I could

be who I am today. Thanks
to _____ when I finish
Highschool I want to go to
college for social services
to be a case worker to work
with other foster kids.

I am so happy to have
a president like you. you
have already changed alot.
I had wrote a letter to George
Bush when I was younger,
but I think one of the
people that works for him
wrote me back. I hope that
didnt happen. so can you
please write me back and
please send pictures to me.
Thanks alot

Sincerely, Rebecca
Rebecca

COPY FROM ORM

THE WHITE HOUSE

WASHINGTON

Rebecca —

Thanks for the moving letter. I am inspired by your courage, and am sure you will succeed if you keep at it.

Best of luck!

Miss Rebecca

MAR - 8 2010

November 18, 2012

Dear President Obama -

My name is Chana Sangkagalo. I came to the United States of America from NortheasternThailand in November of 1988. I remember it being Thanksgiving.

The reason I came to America is because it is a land of opportunity. The United States is known as a country where one can begin with nothing and build it into whatever he wishes and can afford. One's destiny is not pre-determined in the United States - you have the right to become whatever and whoever you wish. You work hard for opportunities for a better life. Hard work and determination can get you much farther in this country than anywhere else in the world - as long as you are working hard enough to do so. I began my work here at Burger King in Rhode Island. Through the years and with education I was able to develop my creativity and open my very own hair salon. I am a successful small business owner in this great country. I am a United States citizen. I have much to be thankful for.

The reason that the United States needs a constant flow of immigrants is because we are the people that have the dream - the desire - the fire inside to do something to better our financial situation. We do not feel entitled to a job or education. We believe in personal responsibility and accountability.

We need new producers in the United States. It's about new blood - new life - new givers - not takers. If you look back through history you will see how new blood has produced and grown our economy.
Immigrants have one thing in common - we work like crazy. We save our money. We open stores and many other businesses. We do not sit around and complain about this - that and the other thing. We do not feel entitled. We are not takers but producers. We need producers and immigrants like myself that provide production. The reasons that so many immigrants came to America are the same reasons that each and every one of us should feel grateful for - freedom - freedom of religion - to escape poverty and oppression - a better future for our families. In short - opportunity.

So Mr Obama - I believe that you are a real person with real beliefs. You have patched many of the holes left by your predecessor and you continue to do so. I applaud your re-election. I believe in you and am excited to see what you can accomplish over the next four years.

God bless you Mr President.

Respectfully -

Chana Sangkagalo
Chana Sangkagalo
Thailand

10/14/1988
10/16/2012

PR Sample
TY LGBT Svc
Gold Star

UNITED STATES NAVAL ACADEMY

Dear MR. President and First Lady.

I want to Thank you for this milestone in my Daughter's life. Signing the bill and Repealing DADT on Sept 20, 2011 changed her life and that of many of her shipmates.

As A parent I Know that there isn't Anything that would stop you from Encouraging your daughters to reach for their dreams. Caitlin went to I-Day, Not under the Radar and I often feared what would happen to her.

You Know what she did? She and 5 others started the Navy spectrum? At the Naval Academy! Nowhere near flying under the Radar. They started the club Because of you!! They only had 5 attend but Now It's 2nd largest club at the Academy. She's my hero and now leaves a legacy at the Naval Academy. She's off to become a pilot after that.

UNITED STATES NAVAL ACADEMY

I just wanted to thank you again on behalf of my daughter, the entire NAVY Spectrum Club and parents around this great nation of children who are gay. THANK you for standing up for them.

With much love and gratitude from one parent of an amazing daughter to another parent of two Awesome DAughters I thank you.

Regina Bryat
Gold STAR Wife
and mom
to an 'icredible daughter!

Go NAVY!

I've made Caitlin a recipe box as part of her graduation gifts. Enclosed you will find a recipe card. If you have an easy, non-fail vegetable or no-meat recipe, please fill it out and we'll include it in her surprise. Bring it to graduation or you can mail it to the address below and I'll add it to her box. You may also email it to

and I will print it out and put it in her box

I know this will be something that she will treasure for years to come.

Caitlin Bryant

c/o R. H. Bryant

Pensacola, Florida.

September 23, 2011

President of the United States
1600 Pennsylvania Ave. NW
Washington, DC. 20500

RE: LETTER BY FEDERAL INMATE JASON HERNANDEZ #07031-078 IN
SUPPORT OF HIS PETITION FOR COMMUTATION OF SENTENCE

Dear Mr. President:

Greetings. My name is Jason Hernandez. I am sure you have no idea
who I am, and probably wondering why on God's earth am I writing to you.
Well, to summarize it as best as I can I am a 34 year old federal inmate
who has served over 14 years on a sentence of life without parole, which
I was given for conspiracy to distribute crack cocaine and other controlled
substances. As a result therof, I have filed a Petition for Commutation
of Sentence with the Pardon Attorney in hopes you determine there is
sufficient cause to grant my request.

As you are aware there has been major support to completely eliminate
the disparity between powder cocaine and crack cocaine. But that is not
what the substance of this letter is about. I'm not going to sit here
and try to downplay the effects crack cocaine or any other drugs have on
our nation. I know first hand the distruction drugs cause on people,
families, and communities.

Nor will I attest that because I didn't kill anyone, commit rape,
or a crime against a child, that I shouldn't be in prison for an excessive
amount of time. Because the simple truth Mr. President is that I was a
drug dealer. And what I didn't know then that I've learned over the years
is that it would not be an overstatement to view my crime as equivalent,
if not more detrimental, than those just stated. I realize this because
I was selling drugs in the community I was born and raised in. I was
selling drugs to people I grew up with, most of whom were either friends
or family. Everybody I came into contact with I was destroying in one
way or another. From the addicts and the families of those addicts, and
the individuals I encouraged to sell drugs that ended up losing years of
their lives in prison; resulting in parents being without a son, wives
without a husband or kids without a father. Now I can see the cycle of
destruction that drugs have caused on my neighborhood and those across
the United States.

I acknowledge that I deserve to be in prison. For how long? I am
in no position to say. I'm sure there are people who could argue either
for or against my current sentence of life without parole. What I can
say for certain Mr. President is that I am a changed man from that boy
who ran those streets over 15-20 years ago. And if I were given a second
at life I would not let you, my family, or society down. I would do
everything I could to right what I have wronged and try to prevent kids
from making the same mistakes I did when I was young.

If you review my Petition for Commutation you will see I have dreams
Mr. President, big dreams. And not just dreams of being free, but dreams
of becoming someone who is going to make a difference in this world. But
to speak of my goals as dreams doesn't do them justice, for I can see
everything I want to accomplish and how I am going to accomplish it as
clear as day. All I need now is for you to give me a chance to turn those
dreams into reality.

I thank you for your time Mr. President, and I hope that after you
read my Petition for Commutation you come to the conclusion that I was not
a bad person growing up, but a person who made bad decisions.

Sincerly,

Jason Hernandez #07031-078
Federal Correctional Institution
Post Office Box 1500
El Reno, Oklahoma. 73036

9/10/12 406

Reply

Sandy Swanson

Merion Station, PA

August 8, 2012

President Barack Obama
The White House
1600 Pennsylvania Avenue, NW
Washington DC 20500

Back from the OVAL
9/11/12

Dear President Obama,

I'm writing to tell you about the $15 my family just donated to your 2012 campaign.

It was $15.

That's really all we could give. My husband is currently a student at Temple University, in the final year of his PhD. Since starting his degree, three years ago, we've been living at several hundred percent below the poverty level (I keep forgetting which percent...does it matter?)

But we aren't complaining. Two healthy daughters– dusty, well-travelled backpacks in the basement – a house full of memories – a future full of hope. We're the lucky ones.

So - we're currently *"poor on money – rich in life"* (as we like to say). It hasn't always been like this. My husband spent most of his life doing what he loved -- playing or coaching basketball. Born in SE Iowa, he was an Academic All-American and once-upon-two-good-knees-ago, the local town hero of his small town – after bringing home the State Championship during his junior year of high school, followed by NJCAA National Championship years later as a coach. Then came a coaching stint in Europe (UK), before returning to the States to coach another small town Division I team. Basketball has been his heart-n-soul; his bread-n-butter for decades. And now, a student again. He hopes to teach one day – to pass on all he's learned coaching here&abroad. His research focus is on leadership – what makes a leader and that sort of thing. He's a big fan of yours by the way...as a player, father and president...not necessary in that order. <wink>

But this really wasn't supposed to be a letter about him.

It's about this year's campaign. It's about wanting to say that $15 means something these days and deserves a moment of pause (and some words on paper) for this girl and her family of Obama fans.

- ❖ $15 is a special pizza dinner at our local pizza stop (Poppy's in Wynnewood).
- ❖ It's 1½ tickets to see the newest film at the old-school cinema we walk our daughter's to.
- ❖ It's getter fresh fruit, instead of frozen; fresh veg, instead of canned.
- ❖ It's tickets to the Franklin Institute in the heart of Philly. (We've never been)

It's all these things to a family like ours.

I've listened with curiosity, mostly frustration, as the nation debates Citizens' United and the string of new laws that now allow the bellowing voices of private interest to drown out the sounds of tiny voices (like ours/mine). Our pebble-in-the-ocean support feels almost pointless. *"Leave the campaigns to the rich,"* I think to myself, *"get your daughters a pizza instead."*

But I refuse to allow new laws to stop us/me from being A PART of this campaign. After all, I will never be a "player" (in the political sense), but I still want to believe I can play a part.

Then, out of the blue, there you are – shooting a jumpshot on my (Facebook) wall– and asking for "players" to join you on your home court. I had to smile, and then I couldn't resist. And so, I have relinquished those $15. Please know that they count. To us. Please stay in Washington. Do, in this second term, what you were not assisted/supported to do during your first term. Get this country moving/working/hoping again. I'm hoping the next pizza will be on you.

Wishes to your brave wife and beautiful daughters from another brave wife with two beautiful daughters.

All good things,

Sandy

Sandy Swanson

p.s. if you're looking for a hard-working, All-American boy from Iowa for your pick-up game, I know a guy...my husband. His name is Steven.

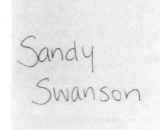

" Code 100" response

THE WHITE HOUSE
WASHINGTON

Sandy —

Your letter inspires me so much.

Thanks,

Ms. Sandy Swanson

Merion Station, Pennsylvania

SEP 19 2012
(Priority w/tracking)

CHAPTER 6

Bill Oliver,
June 20, 2012

UNDISCLOSED LOCATION

Some of this will have to remain vague. Bill Oliver does not want anyone to know where he or his family lives, not the town, not even the state. MS-13, the most violent street gang in the Western Hemisphere, has a presence even in this sleepy city, and if gang members want to find someone, they can.

Needless to say, this has been an education. He is not the person he once was. He just turned eighty.

The reckoning for Bill Oliver began in 2011 when he was on a trip to El Salvador. He had long since retired from teaching, had raised two kids with Sandra, his wife of nearly a half century, and they had fled the Snowbelt for the Sunbelt. He signed up to teach a few courses at the local college to keep his mind active. Taking students on a study abroad trip to Central America was about waking them up. Showing them how the other half lives. "Appreciate what you have." They were international business majors studying things like finance, predictive analytics, and best practices in marketing management strategies. Bill was a lifelong Republican who believed in things like small government, low corporate tax rates, and tight border security.

The dinner the villagers put on was cooked in a big pot boiling over an open flame. Bill wanted his students to see that. The coconut milk came out of the coconuts that they had seen the boys pull off the trees. *Real coconuts.* Before they ate, the local kids challenged Bill's students to a soccer game. Those kids had bare feet. Bill took his students aside. He said, "Now, don't be rude. Make sure you let them win." The local boys completely demolished the American college students. "Well, there you go," Bill said. "*Would you look at that?* Look at that. Look at these people; they have no shoes, they have nothing, and they appear *happy!*"

After dinner, Bill got to know a man who said he was the father of several of the boys. His wife had cooked. Bill and the father stood in the kitchen, and the floor was dirt. The roof was corrugated metal, and the father didn't have a shirt on. He was talking about his six sons, telling Bill all of their names, and he said one of them was not there. That one had just turned seventeen and his name was Quique. Key-kay. The father told Bill about MS-13, about the violence that was rapidly turning El Salvador into the murder capital of the world. He said Quique's school was across the river, a good distance from the village, and that's where the gang was. Gang members had been recruiting Quique, a lonely kid who needed friends and who made the mistake of listening to them. Soon he had found himself caught in a tragic dilemma. Gang members threatened to kill him if he didn't join, and the price of admission was that he murder someone in his own family.

Quique's only hope for survival was to flee. So the father put him on a bus with enough money, he hoped, to pay the coyote to smuggle him across the U.S. border. The father never heard from him again.

Bill is a kind and polite person, and any kind and polite person standing on a dirt floor in El Salvador under a corrugated metal roof with a grieving father would have said the same thing. "Well, if there is anything I can do . . ."

There was nothing Bill could do.

Two weeks after he got home, Bill told Sandra, he said, "Well, I made a promise to the father that I would look for his son." He can't say for sure when or how the notion of a promise kicked in. He hadn't promised anything. His students were finishing the semester, and they would soon move on to MBAs and careers in big banks. Bill was not a busy man, not the way he used to be. If he took a shot at looking for the boy, perhaps he could be the man of honor he believed himself to be.

There was no way he'd be able to find the boy.

Bill started in Texas. He started in Houston. "I'm looking for a boy," he said. Needle in a haystack. He could have stopped there, and his soul would have been at peace because, after all, he did try. He can't say for sure when the compulsion to keep going kicked in, but if he's honest, he'll say at first it was about winning. Like you're doing a crossword puzzle, and this one is not going to beat you. "I'm looking for a boy," he said. "I'm looking for a boy."

By 2012 more than 150,000 kids had been caught crossing the U.S. border, having run from countries in Central America, principally El Salvador, Honduras, and Guatemala, to escape MS-13. They get picked up, detained, and designated as "unaccompanied minors." The Office of Refugee Resettlement, part of the U.S. Department of Health and Human Services, screens the kids for gang ties and holds them in shelters while attempting to place them with relatives or sponsors as they await hearings in immigration court.

New York is where Bill found Quique. The Office of Refugee Resettlement had sent him to a relative of some sort; this part is sketchy. Bill wrote a letter to the district court that Quique had been transferred to. He got no response, so he kept writing. He wrote so many times the judge finally called him. You have to get an attorney and file motions if you want to do anything for the boy, she told him. Bill went online and learned about motions, and he wondered what, exactly, he wanted to do for the boy.

He thought about the father and the metal roof and the dirt floor. The conversation with the father that had been redrawn in Bill's mind as a promise had bloomed into a full-blown test of character. He looked around his house at the display of pots, furs, masks, and other beautiful items crafted by villagers he had met on his various travels to remote parts of the globe. People who came by could see he was a worldly man who knew the taste of food cooked in pots over open flames.

To file the motion in district court, you had to indicate certain things. "I have the means to take care of him," he wrote on the form. *I have means.*

When the motion was granted, they put Quique on a plane, and

Bill went to the airport to pick him up. He recognized Quique because he was brown. Bill is big and round with a white beard, a Santa Claus look, not by choice. Quique went to him, and they walked together to Bill's car. Bill spoke no Spanish, and Quique spoke no English. Bill didn't know if Quique was coming for a day or a month or a year, and neither did Quique. Bill took Quique to a Salvadoran restaurant to make him feel at home. They ate *pupusas,* and the waitress had enormous breasts spilling exquisitely out of her shirt, and that was the only common language, and so that's what they talked about with their eyes and their embarrassed laughter.

There's an app you can get on your phone that translates. You speak English into it, and it comes out Spanish and vice versa, so for weeks at the kitchen table, that's what they did. Bill asked Quique about his journey. In the beginning it had been exhilarating, Quique told Bill. His first time out of El Salvador. On a bus alone to Guatemala. He'd felt like a man. He felt the freedom of someone escaping death. In Mexico, with the strangers, in the back of trucks, he didn't make friends. The Rio Grande was so shallow you could walk the first part. When it got deep, he took off his clothes and held them over his head and swam, and here's where having grown up next to the ocean helped. Some of the others couldn't swim. He put out his arm to help one of them, and that's when he gave up trying to keep his clothes dry. It looked like the coast was clear, but none of them had ever been there before, and so they didn't know where to look. The coast wasn't clear. The person who grabbed him was not rough. He put Quique in a truck. The detention center was clean. You could earn points if you followed the rules. Points bought you candy, toothpaste, and time in the videogame room. He had never seen a videogame. He spent all his remaining points on candy on the last day and then gave it to the other kids because you weren't allowed to take it with you.

Bill told Quique about the promise he had made to Quique's father.

"*Mi papá está muerto,*" Quique said. *My father is dead.*

The news had come from the relative in New York. "*Tu padre está muerto.*" They said it was a heart attack.

"I'm sorry," Bill said.

Bill gave Quique his choice of bedrooms, and Quique picked the one in the corner. Bill said he would have to go to church on Sunday and eat dinner with him and Sandra, and he would have to go to school and learn English. Quique said he didn't want to go to school. At the school Bill told them; he said, "I'm going to be honest with you. He doesn't want to be here, and he's illegal." They said they would figure something out. Bill hired a tutor. Quique discovered the Food Network, and that's what he did after homework. He helped Sandra in the kitchen.

Bill and Sandra decided to adopt Quique. The lawyer said they were too old, and so was Quique. Bill could remain his sponsor until his hearing in immigration court when they decided what to do with him.

Quique got a girlfriend, Rebecca, a sunny, college-bound woman with sleek brown hair who said Quique was so much more mature than American guys. Quique made a lot of friends. He and Rebecca were in the back seat when the other car sped through the intersection. They were wearing their seatbelts. Rebecca was fine. Everybody was fine except Quique, whose bowel was severed by the seatbelt. At the hospital Bill told the ER surgeon; he said, "I'm going to be honest with you: He's illegal." The surgeon said he would figure something out. When the people at church heard about the accident, they said they would figure something out. Rebecca's parents said they would figure something out. It was a community coming together. The question of citizenship, papers, race, who belongs or who doesn't—who is deserving and who isn't—never came into it. It was people helping people, paying for the surgery, nursing Quique back to health.

Bill had no idea where immigration court was or how it worked. He bought Quique a pair of dress pants and a blue shirt. At the hearing Bill made the point that Quique had cost the American taxpayer nothing. People were helping him out. Quique was doing everything right. He had followed the rules. He was in school, and he was learning English. Bill had letters praising Quique's conduct from teachers and from church and even from the mayor, because Bill did know how to pull some strings.

The judge said there was no immunity for a kid who made an illegal crossing on account of MS-13. She said Quique had to go back to El Salvador.

"I'm sorry," Bill's attorney said. Bill told her he was going to appeal. If Quique were to go back to El Salvador, he would have to face the gang he had fled that wanted to kill him and that would almost certainly kill him now.

Bill's attorney hung her head and looked at her shoes. Everyone, she said, appeals. Everyone had the same story.

That same week, on June 15, 2012, President Obama was in the Rose Garden announcing a policy called Deferred Action for Childhood Arrivals (DACA). It allowed certain immigrants to escape deportation and obtain work permits.

Bill was desperate. He was not an Obama supporter. He was the opposite. But he felt like a changed man. Would that make a difference to the president?

Bill reflected on what, exactly, about him had changed. The entire saga could be summed up in one sentence: Bill had gotten to know a person who was in America illegally, and he had grown to love him.

Bill needed his letter to sound important. Just saying "Help!" seemed undignified.

9/27/13
Simple. / Immigration Hardship

June 20, 2012

Back from the OVAL
9/29/13

reply

Can we find out from Ceilia what the best options for this young man might be — does he qualify for deferred action?

President
Barack Obama
1600 Pennsylvania Avenue NW
Washington D.C.
20500

Dear Mr. President:
I have always been a strong Republican. I have disagreed with you on many issues, especially immigration issues.

I believe myself to be an objective person, and because of that I could not understand your tremendous focus on immigration. I disagreed with almost everything you identified.

However my objectiveness "kicked-in;" I decided to personally incorporate some of the immigration beliefs you espoused over and over, identifying your determination in "making things right." Honestly, I didn't believe a difference could be made!

As a retired university provost and chief operating officer, I continue to do adjunct work as a professor ▬▬▬▬▬▬▬▬ I take International Business majors to Central America on a regular basis.

My last trip, while exposing students to a different culture, a life of poverty for many families, I had the opportunity to interact with one family in particular. This is a family of six boys, father, mother, plus another relative. Father's monthly income is about$140.00. They live without the any of the comforts we know, such as electricity and running water. Their "home" has dirt flooring, and corrugated metal walls and roofing. Cooking is done over an open fire and washing clothes in a wash tub.

His letter went on another page and a half, single-spaced; he told Quique's story, and at the end he wrote:

Now what? What can we do? . . .

How can I help the young man of which I speak, and others like him?

He signed it, "William C. Oliver, Ph.D."

At the White House, the OPC machine was in motion, just as it was always in motion. Like probably every other person who wrote a letter to the president, Bill had no idea that interns and staffers with pencils were busily making their marks.

Sample/Immigration Hardship

Bill had no idea that Obama, too, was making his marks.

"Reply," Obama wrote, on the top, in blue ink. And then along the right side he scribbled: "Can we find out from Cecilia what the best options for this young man would be—does he qualify for deferred action?"

. . .

Bill was surprised when he got a personal note back from the president on a white card, handwritten. It's here somewhere. If he finds it, he'll show you. Frankly, the personal note didn't mean nearly as much to him as the phone call he got from a White House staffer who instructed him to call a certain number at a certain time; the person he reached was with U.S. Citizenship and Immigration Services, and she asked Bill questions about Quique's situation.

Among other requirements, to qualify for deferred action, you had to be younger than thirty-one on June 15, 2012, and you had to have come to the United States when you were younger than sixteen, and you had to have lived in the United States since June 15, 2007. The Pew Research Center estimated that as of 2014, up to 1.1 million people were eligible.

Quique wasn't one of them. He was too old, and he hadn't been in the United States nearly long enough. DACA was of no help to Quique.

"I'm sorry to hear that," Bill said.

Bill told Quique to make sure his shirt and dress pants were clean and ironed for whenever the appeal hearing came up, and he called his attorney for an update.

She said something happened. She said Quique's case had been abruptly closed. "Prosecution discretion," she said.

Bill would prefer not to disclose the details of Quique's immigration status, especially given the current climate, but the news is good: "He has the lowest status you can get for someone to stay in this country legally, but he's here legally."

Bill would never know if the ruling had anything to do with his letter to the president; he wondered whom he would even ask. Did it matter? Quique would not have to go back to El Salvador. Quique had a new life. America had given him a second chance. It turned out that finding Quique was about more than finding Quique. For Bill, it was a journey to a whole new kind of patriotism.

Bill took Quique shopping for an engagement ring. Quique and Rebecca got married, and on their honeymoon they watched dolphins swim, and they got back in time to go to church, where Bill was leading the singing.

Bill bought Quique's mom a refrigerator and a microwave, the first in the village.

CHAPTER 7

Fiona Picks the 10LADs

Fiona's office was on the fourth floor of the EEOB, well off the main drag—through a narrow corridor, down a ramp, behind a heavy wooden door. It was a quiet space with a large window too high to reveal anything but a solid cornflower-blue sky, and when I found her there, on a Thursday afternoon, she was perched at the edge of a couch with letters strewn all around her—letters draped like doilies on the couch, letters in piles on the coffee table at her knees, letters on the floor, letters on her lap; the net effect was of the old lady who lived in a shoe with so many children she didn't know what to do.

"It's like a crowd all talking about different things at once," she said. Every day at about four she sat down to do this, cull through the day's samples—about two hundred of them between the letters the hard-mail team set aside and the emails forwarded to her from the email team—and pick which ten the president should read. And no, she didn't want help. "I have to read," she said, bouncing a stack of pages up and down and into order. She was the kind of person who wore her professionalism earnestly: a well-practiced posture, a sensible maroon dress, practical flats. You could imagine her becoming dean of a liberal-arts college one day.

She told me she had never had designs on the kind of life that involved serving a president, although she had grown up in a family loud with conversation about the way government works—her father is the presidential historian Richard Reeves, and her mother, who is no longer living, worked for the United Nations and once ran for the state senate in California. Her mom was the type to decide on a lark that it might be fun for the family to go on a thirty-day trip around the world, and that's what they once did, hopping among sixteen countries, resting on the bank of the Nile, where they studied the clouds. Fiona went to boarding schools, the first of which, on a farm in upstate New York, she still regards as home. "My dad would visit about one weekend a month, and that was different than a lot of other kids, so I felt like my parents were a big part of my life." High school was in England, in the Malvern countryside, and when she came back to the United States to go to Duke, she majored in public policy and African American studies. "I remember my mom really discouraged political science. She said there's no science to politics—it's such a sham. So I was naïve to the process, and I was naïve to the country; I hadn't seen much of it. If President Obama hadn't run for office, I and lots of other people my age wouldn't have dipped a toe in public service."

It was Obama's 2006 book, *The Audacity of Hope*, that first drew her in. Not exactly a self-help book, by not exactly a guru, but something in that direction, especially for the young, the well educated, the dutiful seeking duty.

At the core of the American experience are a set of ideals that continue to stir our collective conscience; a common set of values that bind us together despite our differences; a running thread of hope that makes our improbable experiment in democracy work. These values and ideals find expression not just in the marble slabs of monuments or in the recitation of history books. They remain alive in the hearts and minds of most Americans—and can inspire us to pride, duty, and sacrifice.

As soon as she graduated college, in 2007, she applied for a job on Obama's campaign staff. She eventually landed an interview with Pete Rouse.

She had no idea who he was. "I'm embarrassed by the approach I took. I didn't understand how important he was to Obama. If I'd been more savvy, I would have worked a little harder at seeming smarter or more informed. But I think he must have had so many conversations with folks like me that I like to imagine he doesn't remember how ridiculous I was."

(He doesn't.) He hired her, sent her to New Hampshire to knock on doors.

In almost every successful social movement of the last century, from Gandhi's campaign against British rule to the Solidarity movement in Poland to the antiapartheid movement in South Africa, democracy was the result of a local awakening.

Fiona had the audiobook on a continuous loop on her iTunes. Obama in his own voice, day after day through her earphones. "Of course there's this beautiful cadence, and I would say it to myself again and again while walking down these driveways," she told me. "So he'd say things like 'I ask you to believe in this campaign; I ask you to believe in yourself; I ask you to believe again in the dream that we call America.'

"That middle part about believing in yourself—we all felt that that was the message we were conveying to voters. We didn't realize—folks involved in his campaign and later working in his administration—he was giving that to us.

"It was that idea of courage by necessity being a real gift that he instilled."

She was in Manchester for the 2008 primary, working from the basement in the home of a family who had opened their spare rooms to the team. Obama had won the Iowa caucuses less than a week earlier, and in an ensuing debate, Hillary Clinton had tried to turn his soaring rhetorical skills into a liability. "Making change is not about what you believe; it's not about a speech you make," she had said. "We don't need to be raising false hopes."

"The truth is actually words do inspire," Obama shot back. "Words do help people get involved. . . . Don't discount that power, because when the American people are determined that something is going to happen, then it happens. And if they are disaffected and cynical and fearful and told that it can't be done, then it doesn't. I'm running for president because I want to tell them, yes, we can."

By the eve of the New Hampshire primary, Obama was surging in the state's polls, up by as many as thirteen points. "And it was this feeling of 'The biggest day of my life is tomorrow,'" Fiona told me. "All my high-school girlfriends had come up. None of them were comfortable knocking on doors, but they did a shift. Some of my parents' friends came. My mom reached out and said her friend had told her that my skin wasn't looking well and I needed to take better care of myself. Yeah, thanks, Mom. But you felt like you had been away from friends and family working on this thing that you knew was important, and then really briefly, on election day, you become the center."

Fiona was alone in the Manchester home, cleaning up the kitchen, when the results started coming in. She had the radio on. What she would remember most was the guy on the radio saying how interesting it would be to hear a speaker as powerful as Obama give a speech after a loss.

He lost.

"Yes, we can," Obama said, that night, turning those words into a campaign slogan as he accepted defeat in New Hampshire.

It was a creed written into the founding documents that declared the destiny of a nation: Yes, we can.

It was whispered by slaves and abolitionists as they blazed a trail towards freedom through the darkest of nights: Yes, we can.

It was sung by immigrants as they struck out from distant shores and pioneers who pushed westward against an unforgiving wilderness: Yes, we can.

It was the call of workers who organized, women who reached for the ballot, a president who chose the moon as our new frontier, and a king who took us to the mountaintop and pointed the way to the promised land: Yes, we can, to justice and equality.

Yes, we can, to opportunity and prosperity. Yes, we can heal this nation. Yes, we can repair this world. Yes, we can.

People like Fiona—crowds of already-devoted pollsters and organizers standing out in the cold—listened to those words, felt them in their toes; his words supercharged them. They would commit to working even harder. They would give the next ten months of their lives over to him, and when he was elected president, they moved to Washington, many of them without jobs but knowing they were part of a movement.

"And I remember feeling maybe the landlord wouldn't put me on the lease because there was no proof that I was going to stay," Fiona told me. "The city was so dense with people who worked on the Obama campaign. There were a lot of hang sessions around town."

That was when Fiona met Mike Kelleher, who interviewed her for a job in the fledgling correspondence office. It was not a great interview. She didn't make eye contact. She was painfully shy. She didn't look happy. But Mike saw something. Perhaps it was whatever Pete saw when he hired her to knock on doors. A combination of earnestness, some apparent well of empathy, and the unflappable dedication to the president and his message that so many young Obama devotees had. Courage by necessity. He taught them to believe in themselves.

Cascading emotional chaos—that's how people would remember those early days in OPC. Fiona's first job was as an "analyst," which meant she sat in a cubicle reading constituent mail with a team of other former Obama organizers. They were as overwhelmed by the volume—boxes of mail lining the hallways, *millions* of emails in the inbox—as they were by the content. People telling their stories. Intimate, sad stories. People needing healthcare, people losing businesses, people bankrupted because they couldn't pay student loans, people saying "Help!" Here was the new guy who said he could fix things. It was the getting-to-know-you phase. People told him their problems. They told him to quit smoking. They told him, wow, a black guy in the White House. They told him to get bin Laden. They told him to create jobs. "Let's see if you're as smart as we hope you are." There were threats to the president and first family—about a hundred a day of those alone. In OPC they had to assign one person full-time to deal with nothing but threats. Tea Party protesters flooded the mailroom with tea bags. People sent their credit card bills, showing jumps in interest rates. People sent mortgage foreclosure statements. "HELP!" "DO SOMETHING!" "YOU PROMISED!"

The campaign workers had believed themselves responsible for opening a conduit between the vulnerable and the influential—the powerless and the most powerful man in the world—and now, in the mailroom, they were expected to make good on it.

Youth was the main thing that Annmarie Emmet, a volunteer and a retiree, told me she noticed about the new crop of people coming in to work in OPC under Obama. She had been reading mail, three days a week, since 2001, through most of Bush's two terms in office, and would go on to keep reading through all of Obama's. "I've never been ashamed to say I worked for either administration," she told me.

"When this new group came in, they were maybe twenty years younger than Bush's," she said. "They were very devoted. They were single-minded in making Obama look good."

The tone of the incoming mail was dramatically different, she said. "It was cozier, maybe because of the younger children, watching these girls grow up. With Bush they appreciated the family, but they didn't know it much."

The closeness, she figured, accounted for the personal nature of the letters people wrote to the new president. "With Bush it would be more like 'Why aren't you helping these people as a group or doing more for that group?' as opposed to personal struggles. I would say they felt a more personal connection with the Obamas. Kind of like: 'I'm like you were; I need your help.'

"And then from the beginning the LGBTQ people flocked to him. You never saw that in the Bush administration."

January 2009

Dear Mr. President,

(Because the person I love can be dishonorably discharged for loving me back, even though he is honorably serving his country right now

in Iraq, I have to send this letter anonymously. It pains me to have to do so.)

My partner is currently serving in Iraq, and is in a situation where he is under fire on a daily basis. He's a good soldier, and our country needs him to continue doing the excellent job that he has been recognized for.

The day he deployed, I dropped him off far from his base's main gate, and he walked alone in the dark and the rain to report for duty. Where the rest of his buddies were surrounded by spouses and children at mobilization ceremonies, he stood by himself.

The phone trees don't have my name on them, and base support services don't apply—even though we've been together for 16 years and are raising a beautiful child together. Our communication is self-censored, and we are cruelly unable to nurture each other at the exact moment we both need it the most.

If something were to happen to him, no one from his unit will call me. If, like so many good soldiers before him, he gives that last full measure of devotion, no one will come knock on my door. No one will present me with a flag. It is, and would be, as if the most important thing in his life—his family—never existed.

I am not sure if I can adequately convey the mixture of fear, pride, heartache and hope I feel, all jumbled together, on a daily basis.

Fiona began her career reading letters like that—scanning, coding, sampling—and she gradually took on more responsibility. Mike Kelleher moved on from OPC in 2010, passing the directorship over to Elizabeth Olson, whom both Mike and Fiona would regard as essential in maintaining the stability of the operation, a noble shepherd. Fiona was next, taking the role of director of OPC in 2013. The shy young woman who had interviewed terribly, who could not make eye contact, was now a force.

. . .

"It's a funny channel," Fiona told me that day in her office when she sat on the couch surrounded by letters and worked on figuring out which ten she should give to the president. "Sometimes I think of it as a tray passing under a door."

Curating the 10LADs was a job she regarded as sacrosanct. It was her daily conversation with the president, each package an array of voices she believed most accurately rendered America's mood: *Here's what America is feeling, Mr. President.*

"Well, this one is lovely," she said, holding one letter with her fingertips. "He's a welder. He really paints the scene. A log cabin. A faithful dog. His wife volunteering. 'If you ever need something welded . . .'" She smiled, read it again, considering. "It's largely a support letter, so that's why I'm not sure it will make it." The president needed to hear from more than just supporters, and she was mindful of the mix.

"This one is definitely staying," she said, reaching for another letter. It had pages stapled to it. "She encloses a letter her dad once sent to Roosevelt. I think the president really eats up that historical perspective.

"Oh, and then this one just slays me," she said about another, declining further comment and laying it on her "yes" pile on the couch.

"Then this person is alleging that the Small Business Administration was very present in the disaster recovery immediately in the wake of a flood, but then when the cameras pulled out, so did the resources. I think that's an interesting voice to put before the president, because it's hard for that kind of information to reach him."

Getting a couple hundred letters down to twenty was one kind of challenge, but the real work was getting from twenty to ten. She had to be ruthless. A linear system like subject folders might seem the simplest method: Sort them all by topic, and then give the president one letter about energy, one about healthcare, one about immigration, and so on. "But then letters in each folder would be sort of in competition with each other instead of with the broad group," she said.

I suppose the point was obvious, but it took me a moment to compute the implications. It had to do with fairness and an underlying assumption that the letters represented people, not problems.

"Anyway, a disorderly pile is more honest," she said.

When she had the day's pile down to fifteen, she read through them again, one then the next. Her fingers were long, and her nails were painted shiny red, and she held the pages gently, laying each one down slowly, as if she didn't want to hurt it. "Well, this one has to make it. . . . And then this one—it's hard to follow, but I think even the fact that it's hard to follow is part of the story. . . . And then this. We're getting so many of these long-term legacy reflections. I don't know. . . ." She looked for stories. Not pro-this or anti-that, not screeds, not opinions about what someone heard on NPR. The president needed to hear the stories—that's what he couldn't get himself. "He can't walk down a street and see what it normally looks like," she said. She thought of the letters as a periscope looking outside the bubble, as a way for him to see as he used to see, before Secret Service protection and armored vehicles and a press pool and the world watching.

I asked her if she had a soft spot, a kind of letter or a subject that she might more readily want to put through.

"Inmate mail," she said without hesitation. "Ever since the beginning. It's one of the most extraordinary relationships in letter writing, I suppose because letter writing is more a part of prison culture than the rest of society."

She told me about one of the earliest inmate letters she got. A guy had written in from a prison out west, and he made mosaics. "From candy wrappers," she said. "And he had done a portrait of the president. It was on thick watercolor stock." He had glued tiny pieces of candy wrappers in varying colors to make a convincing likeness. "It was just beautiful," she said, and from the way she averted her eyes, I could tell this story was not going to end well. She said this was back in the early days, when she had just started at OPC. "It was just a support letter explaining that he was excited about this presidency and he wanted to offer this. I remember he also included this detail that for part of his work, he would've liked to have Twix wrappers to capture the color that he was going for. But that there had been an inventory change in the vending machines in his prison, so he had used Rolo wrappers, which he felt didn't convey quite the stroke that he was going for, but it was the best he could do."

She smiled, took a swig from the purple water bottle beside her. She said she had wanted to save that letter and the inmate's gift. "I wondered if I was just allowed to tack it up in my cubicle or something," she said. "But back then you couldn't do things like that—especially not with inmate mail."

There were protocols. Inmate mail didn't get saved. It didn't go to the president. "You would scan it to see if it was a pardon request," she said, "or if the person alleged he was being abused. Those got forwarded as casework. The rest basically went in a box to be shredded."

She took another sip. "It was a policy that had been in place for years and years, and we were just the new guys, you know?"

When Fiona first became director of OPC, one of the first things she did was challenge the policy about inmate mail. Where had it come from? Who had started it? Was it even written down? She credited a plucky intern for encouraging her to look into it. "Well, that doesn't make any sense," the intern had said when she was learning the rules. Surely a president who got his start as a community organizer doling out food to the homeless would want to hear what people stuck in prison had to say.

One day, Fiona wondered what would happen if she simply added a letter from an inmate into a batch of 10LADs. What would Obama do? What would senior staffers do?

Nothing, it turned out. No one said a word about it. So she did it again. And again.

"Well, this is now something we do," Fiona told the staff, and that was how the policy was changed, Fiona-style. Inmate mail got its own code in the hard-mail room, and people were encouraged to sample it along with all the other types of mail.

It was a private triumph, a mailroom coup. "Because there was this feeling like only we knew about it," she said. All those people writing in about sentencing disparities and criminal-justice reform. Not a particularly hot topic in the news. But now the letters made their way to Obama. In 2014, when the administration rolled out a Justice Department program offering executive relief to federal prisoners serving long sentences for nonviolent drug crimes, it surprised no one in the mailroom. The president, they were happy to see, was paying attention to the mail.

There was a similar trajectory with issues around same-sex marriage and repealing the military's "Don't Ask, Don't Tell" policy. Conversations about these things happened in the mail whether or not they happened anywhere else at the White House. Fiona, and Elizabeth before her, and Mike before her made sure to include those voices in the 10LADs. In that way, little by little, voice by voice, the mail could drive actual policy decisions.

The guy who wrote in anonymously in 2009 wrote again in 2014, after "Don't Ask, Don't Tell" was repealed. This time he used his name.

July 4, 2014

Dear Mr. President,

On August 3rd my husband, David Lono Brunstad, will be promoted to Senior Master Sergeant, and I'll be there to hand him his new shirt with the extra stripe on it. I know this is a pretty common occurrence for many military families, but it has special significance for mine—not that long ago our relationship had to remain a secret because of Don't Ask, Don't Tell.

David's deployment to Iraq in 2009 under this misguided policy was [a] dark and lonely time for the both of us. It was common for me not to hear from him for four or five days at a time, and for most families the old axiom "no news is good news" applied. Same-sex partners knew, however, that we weren't on anyone's contact list should something bad happen, so the pressure would just build and build until finally I heard his sweet voice on the other end of the line.

I knew he was under fire on a pretty regular basis and there were times that I struggled with keeping it together at home all by myself. On those days, Mr. President, it was your commitment to end this discriminatory policy that kept me going. I believed you—I trusted you—and I knew that, no matter how bad it got, that there was a light at the end of the tunnel.

My husband will deploy next June, but this time his pack will be a little lighter without the worry of whether or not his family will be taken care of. Sir, I doubt that I will ever be able to thank you in person, so I just need you to know that this military family will always be grateful for all you have done for us.

With Sincere Gratitude,
Darin Konrad Brunstad
Vancouver, Washington

"So we have one, two, three, four," Fiona counted. She was closing in on the finalists. "Nine, ten, and then this one is eleven, so we have to remove one." She read, shook her head. "Okay, okay, I guess." She draped the discard on the far end of the couch. She looked over at it, then reached out to give it a little pat.

She gathered the final ten and began shuffling them, pulling one out, putting it behind another and another in front. I wondered about all the shuffling. "Oh, the order is critical," she said. It was like putting a book of poems together, or a playlist. "The order in which you see stories affects the way you perceive each one," she said. "We sometimes use the term 'sucker punch' in this office, which is brutal, but . . ."

"Ballsy" was the word Yena used to describe Fiona. She did not hesitate to give the president mail brutally critical of his administration, or mail that was disturbing, or mail that was heartbreaking, and when she put the letters in order, it was for maximum impact. She could put three gun-violence pleas back to back. She could set the president up with a letter from someone gushing about the Affordable Care Act and then another from someone on the margin whose life had been made worse because of it. "It's not 'You failed,'" she said. "It's more 'Solutions don't solve things for everyone.'"

She grabbed a pencil. "Sometimes on Friday, particularly on Friday, we'll end with one that's like 'Hey, I like the way you tie your tie.'" She called that a chaser. It could be a comment about the dog or about the president riding his bike, or it could be just "Hey, are you a pancakes or waffles man?"

Dear Mr. President,

I think this country needs more spunk. With all the attack, the Zika virus and the wars, this country is a very sad place. Please do something fun. Wear a tie-dye shirt and shorts to something important. Go on a water-skiing trip in the caribbean. Take your family to disney world. Do something fun and outgoing. Also, please say something that will make everyone calm. You do not know how many polotics worries I have. . . .

Sincerely,
Lily
8 years old

"Okay, this is it," Fiona said, gathering the pages on her lap, smoothing them the way you would pet a cat.

"So I'll open with this one. 'This letter has been in my mind and heart for so many years.'

"And then this person who volunteered on the campaign and has been disappointed with the Affordable Care Act . . . a real personal story.

"Then this notebook paper from a social worker in Texas that talks about trying to make a difference and against a lot.

"And then this letter about a DOJ correction that didn't extend to DHS.

"Right behind the prison comment, I'll have the son with the felony background.

"Then right behind that is this one that's tougher to read but a haunting message from this vet who is haunted by what he's seen.

"And then this reflection on support being temporary after natural disasters.

"And this is one, frankly, I don't have an intuitive place for where it should fit in the batch, but I think I'll have this in here. Dakota Access Pipeline.

"And then the grandson, Jake. His quote: 'I hope Clinton wins.' This little African American boy with two white parents. I'll end with that. That's a powerful line to give the president.

"So that's the order."

She flipped around her pencil and went at the letters with her eraser, removing any and all codes. The president should definitely not see codes. "If a letter takes a turn that is surprising in the text—say, on page three something surprising happens in her life, but the way we've assigned what category it falls into kind of spoils the surprise—then the writer doesn't get to bring the president through her experience in the same way." That was why everybody in the hard-mail room had to use pencil.

Before I left her office that day, I asked Fiona about the candy wrapper mosaic that the inmate made. What ever happened to it? Had it been spared from the shredder?

"It only exists in my memory," she said. "And that just eats at me."

CHAPTER 8

Marnie Hazelton, April 5, 2011

FREEPORT, NEW YORK

She wore a tan jacket and a loose-fitting tangerine blouse. Did she look okay? How about the necklace? Too much? One thing about standing under those insanely hot lights, with gobs of makeup caked on her face, there, in that distinctly American *Who Wants to Be a Millionaire* moment, was that it was very, very hard to think about anything besides *Holy crap, I'm on TV*.

> *[Applause]*
> I'm well. How are you?
> I'm very well. Yes, I mentioned in the introduction that you've had some hard times, got laid off as an educator, even though you are an acclaimed educator, obviously, but you got a letter from the president that gave you confidence.
> Yes.
> And you brought it with you, I noticed, today. So can you read that to us? He really wrote this to you, right?
> Yes. Yes, he did.
> You're not a crazy woman.
> *[Laughter]*
> No, no, no. I had just wanted him to—

It's the official stationery!
Yes. The official White House stationery.
Oooh. Very nice.

She had the letter on the desk in front of her, and she kept her fingertips touching it. It was handwritten in Obama's distinctive swirl (he doesn't cross all his Ts, she had noted) on a white card. The letter had nothing to do with appearing on a game show; it was a private thing, something in her recent past she had happened to mention when they were trying to flesh out her story, make her more TV worthy. They said, "Bring the letter!" Would she read it in front of a live studio audience? (She made a photocopy. There was no way she was going to take the real letter out of her home.)

> Uh. It says, "Marnie." Uh. "Thank you for your dedication to education. I know that things seem discouraging now, but demand for educators and persons with your skills will grow as the economy and state budgets rebound. In the meantime, I'm rooting for you! Barack Obama."
> *[Applause]*
> That is very cool! That is something you keep forever. For sure. Wow. Well, you hold on to that, and keep positive thoughts going about the future in terms of jobs—and the immediate future right here, because you are now going for one hundred thousand dollars. You have forty thousand six hundred dollars in your bank. It is time to play . . . Classic Millionaire!

"I'm rooting for you."

Coming from the president of the United States, those would be powerful words for any one of millions of unemployed people hit by the economic downturn, but for Marnie they were magical. They could transform her. She'd start getting depressed, frustrated, hopeless, and then just thinking, *I'm rooting for you* would turn her back into Marnie again.

Marnie Hazelton!

Marnie Hazelton was not just some unemployed single mom in her forties in a tan jacket and a tangerine blouse trying to win some cash.

. . .

"Get it together, girl," she had told herself back in the day, when she was a young woman just out of college trying to make it as a rapper. (She was selling mixtapes on the street.) "Get it together." It was her dad's voice, her mom's, her grandparents'; backward and backward, all the ancestors telling her the same thing.

Her dad: one of the first black students to integrate Baltimore Polytechnic high school. Her mom: a week in prison after being arrested for trying to integrate a movie theater in Baltimore, then the Peace Corps. A grandfather in World War II, two great-grandfathers in World War I. A great-great-great-grandmother who arrived in the hull of a ship and was sold as a slave. "Get it together, girl." You were part of a continuum. You weren't random. You were the end of a long line of courage and fight, and you had to keep it going. "A life of service," her parents preached. That was her destiny.

"One out of four students in New York cannot read," the ad in the newspaper had said. "What are you going to do about it?" She applied, got the fellowship; in September 2000 she stood for the first time in front of her class of fifth graders at PS 309 in Brooklyn, New York's Bedford-Stuyvesant neighborhood, one of the lowest-performing schools in the state. The fifth graders could neither read nor write. The level of poverty. The stories of violence. "I didn't come from this," she told the students. She did not hold back. She said, My mom went to college, and my dad worked for a large corporation, and I'm telling you there's more to life than what you see at home. (Some of them didn't have homes.) She wanted them to know there was a whole world out there. She showed them photos of her and 50 Cent, Eminem, Public Enemy, from her fangirl days. She showed them maps of all the places she'd seen, said they could see them, too, one day. She taught them their opinions mattered. What did they think of President Bush financing mosquito nets to help all those people in Darfur dying of malaria? They said, "It's great!" She told them, she said, Well, don't tell me. Tell *him*. They wrote to President Bush. He wrote back! With a photo of his dog, Barney! It was a teachable moment. She had become giddy with the idea of teachable moments.

One year later, in 2001, she was in the middle of an English lesson when the first tower of the World Trade Center got hit. They could see it out the window. Then the second tower. Gray smoke turned to black smoke; they could hear people in the street screaming. She told the kids, she said, Everybody stay in your seats; just please stay in your seats, and then the principal came on the loudspeaker telling everyone to remain calm, and teachers ran into the halls asking one another what the hell was going on.

That fellowship in Bed-Stuy was supposed to be for only two years, but she extended it for three more. She had found where she belonged, in the classroom, serving scared kids desperate for heroes.

She rooted for Obama to become president long before any of her friends believed a black man could become president.

In 2011, she listened intently to his second State of the Union address; he was talking to her:

> The biggest impact on a child's success comes from the man or woman at the front of the classroom. In South Korea, teachers are known as "nation builders." Here in America, it's time we treated the people who educate our children with the same level of respect. . . .
>
> . . . To every young person listening tonight who's contemplating their career choice: If you want to make a difference in the life of our nation; if you want to make a difference in the life of a child—become a teacher. Your country needs you.

A nation builder. A patriot. That's what she was.

After Bed-Stuy, in 2005, she accepted a job in another district, the Roosevelt Union Free School District on Long Island—a whole different set of needs, a district so poor and so deeply in debt that the state had to take control of it and put it on a watch list for "fiscal and academic concern." She brought ambition to that school. She won teaching awards, got promoted to an administrative role, to coordinator for elementary education.

It's hard to say exactly how it all unraveled, but after a few years, she could tell something was up. She even went down to the human resources office one day. "Guys, is there something I need to know? Is there something you need to tell me?"

"Nope, everything is fine!"

She came home that same day to a letter waiting for her in the mailbox. "The position has been eliminated . . . budget cuts."

In the mail. *Are you kidding me?* Budget cuts. In the mail.

All right, Marnie, just to recap, you have banked forty thousand six hundred dollars. You are just four questions away from a million dollars, but you have no lifelines left. Here's your question for one hundred thousand dollars—

No lifelines left. This was so pathetic. And let's not even go into how she had to go out and shop for this jacket and this shirt because she had nothing to wear on TV. Did she look fat? Did her eye just twitch? *Holy crap, I'm on TV.* You can't imagine how hard it is to *think* in a situation like that. Put it this way: She'd had to use a lifeline on the question before this one. It was about "Rub-a-Dub-Dub, Three Men in a Tub." Seriously. Here she was, a nation builder, a patriot (she was also by this point two years into a doctorate in educational leadership and policy), and she was stumped by a nursery rhyme.

It was the butcher, the baker, and the what? *The what?* "I think I'll ask the audience, Meredith." *Ninety percent* of the audience (most of whom were probably not two years into a doctorate in educational leadership and policy) knew that, no, there was no *cobbler* in the nursery rhyme.

Four questions away from a million dollars. No lifelines left.

She was at the end of her rope.

She needed the money. She needed to make rent. She was an unemployed single mom in a tangerine blouse, a nation builder with no nation to build.

The night when she got the news *in the mail* about budget cuts, about her position being eliminated—that was probably the lowest point in her life. She needed to do something. She decided what she needed to do was write a letter of complaint to the president. That was who she needed to tell. It takes a certain amount of fury. Sorrow.

The world caving in. Everything you believe in. An entire identity you had carved for yourself. It takes a couple swigs of vodka. Calling your mom, crying your eyes out.

She poured another drink. She called her mom again. She called friends. Crying. Another drink. Look, she's not going to deny she had a lot to drink. "Dear Mr. President."

This was about more than soothing her own ego. This was about soothing cries that went back centuries. The great-grandfathers who had served. The courage and the fight. A great-great-great-grandmother.

April 5, 2011

Dear Mr. President,

My parents represent the very best of America. . . .

My father went on to serve . . .

My mother answered John F. Kennedy's call to serve. . . .

My parents' maternal grandfathers fought together in World War I. . . . My maternal grandfather and great-uncle both fought in World War II. . . .

I followed in my mother's footsteps to become a teacher. . . .

"A nation builder."

Mr. President, I have committed myself to educating America's future and helping them give back to the world when some of them went home at night to homeless shelters. I spent this past February in the Langa Township in South Africa with my five-year-old son, giving school suppl[i]es to students in the township schools.

Mr. President . . . I am sure you receive thousands of letters with the woes of the unemployed and there is very little you can do on an individual basis. But I felt compelled to reach out to you. . . .

I lost my job because the stimulus money to schools has ended and New York Governor Andrew Cuomo took an ax to school aid. My question to you is, if I have dedicated the last eleven years of my life to nation building and educating America's children, how do I now go about providing for my family . . . when the education job market is flooded with thousands of teachers dismissed due to budget cuts?

Carpe diem,
Marnie Hazelton

She was stunned when she got a letter back from the president. She stared at that thing. The official White House stationery. His handwriting is more like drawing. He doesn't cross all his *T*s. She stared at that thing for what felt like hours.

"I'm rooting for you."

No lifelines left. Four questions away from a million dollars. The lights. The makeup. Were her bangs too long? Look, she'd be fine if she didn't win a million dollars. *Fine.* She was thinking a hundred thousand dollars. Walk out with a hundred thousand dollars. A game show. Whatever it takes. Solve the problem. All the résumés she sent out. All the interviews. Nothing. Countless interviews. Nothing happening. Nobody calling back.

Here's your question for one hundred thousand dollars.
[Tense music, blue laser lights beaming in an upward circular motion]
Canada's Simon Fraser University made headlines in 2009 by introducing what educational innovation?

An educational innovation! Well, surely she'd know this one, as an educator two years into a PhD. It was a multiple-choice question, and there were four choices:

A. A major in "everything"
B. A library with no books

C. An all-female football team
D. A grade worse than "F"

Think. A game show is built on the principle that the contestant can disregard these lights and this makeup and *think*. (Or maybe it's not.) On game shows they want you to think out loud so the audience can feel a part of things.

> If I think about innovation, I'm thinking, "Library with no books." Football team, an all-female football team is not innovative. A major in everything . . . Innovation versus motivation . . . I wouldn't say motivation for . . . a grade worse than F.
>
> Well, here's the deal. You do have forty thousand six hundred dollars. You could walk with that, if you choose to, um, but if you get this right, it's worth a hundred thousand dollars. If you were to miss it, you go down to twenty-five thousand dollars.
>
> I came here with nothing.
>
> Heh heh.
>
> *[Tense drum music]*
>
> All right, Meredith, like I said yesterday, I came to win; I'll go with my gut feeling, and . . . I'm going to say a library with no books, *B*, my final answer.
>
> *[Blue laser lights beaming in a downward circular motion]*
>
> It made sense to me, but it was *D*, a grade worse than F.
>
> *[Sorrowful sounds from audience]*

Meredith explained that the correct answer had something to do with a grade for kids who got caught cheating. Something. Something. Something. Her heart. Her stomach. The thud you feel, in your gut. Letting everyone down. Her mom. Her kid. The ancestors. No lifelines. No million dollars. No $100,000. No $40,600. She would be sent home with a consolation prize, $25,000.

> All right, well, I had a wonderful time. I had a wonderful time.
>
> The grade is "FD." It stands for "failed for academic dishonesty."
>
> Oh, a grade worse than F. Okay.

But you know what? As the president said, we are all rooting for you.

[Applause]

Okay.

Meredith leaned in for a kiss, and Marnie obliged and then sauntered off the stage, carrying the letter she had read to the audience, the blue laser lights going around and around.

She got home and took off that stupid jacket and that stupid tangerine shirt and poured some wine and climbed into bed. It took her a moment or two to get it together. To grasp hold of reality. *Wait, I just got handed a check for twenty-five thousand dollars.* It took her a few beats to embrace how lucky a person would be if the clouds suddenly coughed up that kind of cash. But of course she did grasp it.

"I'm rooting for you."

I am Marnie Hazelton!

In the months that followed, she went to more job interviews, and for good luck she carried Obama's letter (the photocopy) with her. She kept it in her purse. It became her talisman. She would pull it out at lunch and after dinner and before breakfast.

Thirteen months after she got laid off, she got a call from the Roosevelt Union Free School District.

They wanted her back. They needed her. *They needed Marnie Hazelton.*

Reinvigorated, reinvented, when she got back into the classroom, she showed her students the note she got from President Obama; it was a teachable moment. She told the kids, she said, "I'm rooting for you." At parent-teacher nights she told the parents she was rooting for them. She told the bigwigs on the school board, teachers, and coaches; she told business leaders in the community (who needed to get it together and *help* that school); she told everybody, "I'm rooting for you!"

She got promoted, she got her PhD, she got promoted a few more times, and then one day in early 2016 she was named superintendent of the Roosevelt Union Free School District.

Superintendent of the school district that had once laid her off.

No longer will you find it on the New York State watch list for fiscal and academic concern. The "Roosevelt Renaissance from

Good to Great!" has begun, with the goal of a 100 percent graduation rate by 2020, and Marnie Hazelton, nation builder, is in charge.

THE WHITE HOUSE
WASHINGTON

Marnie —

Thanks for your dedication to education. I know that things seem discouraging now, but demand for educators and persons with your skills will grow as the economy and state budgets rebound. In the meantime, I'm rooting for you!

July 16, 2016

Dear Mr. President,

. . . The sincerest thanks I can convey to you is a quote by the late Maya Angelou:

"I've learned that people will forget what you said, people will forget what you did, but people will never forget how you made them feel."

Carpe diem,
Marnie Hazelton

Samples, 2013-2014

Contact Us - Other

Submitted:	April 20, 2013 02:10
Originating Host:	
Remote IP:	
From:	Susan Patterson
Email Address:	
Phone:	
Address (Domestic):	
Topic:	

Message:

Dear Mr. President,

I've written and complained about a lot of your policies. I got a response to my opinion on gun control. The response I received I think changed my mind. My concern, one of them, was that mental health seemed over looked. If you do, all you said in the letter, I will support your gun control bills. I also would like to say, I felt very good about the speech you gave last night after the second Boston bomber was captured. I still HATE Obama care, the entire thing. But, the gun stuff could work. Thank you for the response letter, Susan Patterson

From: Erv and Ross Uecker-Walker

Submitted: 11/17/2014 6:35 PM EST

Email:

Phone:

Address: Milwaukee, Wisconsin

Message: We offer our sincere thanks to President Obama and his Administration for their consistent support of civil rights for the LGBT Community and especially for marriage equality. As a result of your efforts, after being in a committed relationship for 57 years, we will be able to be legally married on November 30th at our church, Pilgrim United Church of Christ, Grafton, Wisconsin. It is particularly significant as November 30th is our 57th anniversary. We never thought it would happen. Thank you for the bottom of our hearts.

From: Ms. Melina S

Submitted: 7/15/2013 5:16 PM EDT

Email:

Phone:

Address:

Message: Dear Mr. Presdient,

Today I went to my Kaiser pharmacy to refill my birth control prescription. Automatically I gave my Kaiser ID card and credit card. The pharmacy said to me 'no co-pay' and gave me back my credit card. I slid it back over the counter to the pharmacist and said, 'It's 30 dollars'. She slid it back and said 'you don't have to pay co-pay'. I asked 'why? Since when?' I was puzzled and sure this was a new employee and she was doing something wrong. She said 'it's the new health care provision'. When she said that, it clicked. I have been hearing about it. I knew about it. But here it was in action, and I could not believe it. I kid you not, I felt'emotional'right away. I felt something. Like an injustice, was turned. Like a wrong was, made right. Like when you hear an apology, you know you deserved' I suppose can't describe it very well in an e-mail. But I felt something so strong, that I had to write you right away and say THANK YOU. Thank you for standing up for women. THANK YOU FOR STANDING UP FOR WOMEN! I know it's a small thing' but it's so big to little old me. What it means, and what it stands for; there is a hope. Things can change. Women do have a friend in politics. And I appreciate you so much for doing the right thing. Really, truly' thank you so much!

Sincerely and respectfully,

Melina S

The President
The White House
1600 Pennsylvania Avenue NW
Washington, DC 20500

✓ #043 485
MAY 20 2013

kids support
sample 7/12/13
f. 1

Dear Mr. Obama,

"We are true to our creed when a little girl born into the bleakest poverty knows that she has the same chance to succeed as anybody else, because she is an American, she is free, and she is equal, not just in the eyes of God but also in our own."

Do you recognize this? You said this in your presidential inauguration in January, right around my eighteenth birthday. I wanted you to know how much this impacted me, it made me want to succeed more than ever. I don't want to tell you my whole life's story, but I do want you to know that I was one of those little girls. I was born into horrible poverty, and my parents didn't think that I had much of a chance at a future because of our financial circumstances. I proved them wrong. Every statistic said that I didn't have good chances of getting into a good college. I proved them wrong. I met your wife once, she came to my high school,   and I was one of the lucky few that got to shake her hand. I thought that was the coolest thing that had ever happened to me in my entire life, and it made me realize that I had just as much of a chance getting into a good college as anyone else. I worked harder after that, and when senior year came around I started doubting my future as a college student, through becoming homeless and finding out that I am a lesbian, I got through all of it and here I am. A soon-to- be high school graduate going to   in the fall, and I am telling you all of this so that you know that you had a hand in helping me get where I am today. I heard your inaugural address at school and when you said what you said, I started crying, because I had never had anybody in my entire life tell me that I could succeed just as much as anyone else just because I am an American. People told me that I was crazy, that someone else wrote that speech for you, but I didn't care, I chose to believe your words and I'm happy I did. I just wanted to thank you for saying that, and I wanted to thank your wife for helping me realize that I am equal to everyone else, regardless of how much money I have.

A Hopeful Future College Student,

P.S.: I'm glad you got re-elected☺

From: Matthew Tyrone Pointer
South Gate, California
December 23, 2013

My name is Matthew Tyrone Pointer and I am a varsity basketball player for South Gate high school, located in South Gate, California

This is my first year at South Gate high school. I recently transferred from our town rivals, The South East Jaguars. The reason I transferred was because of basketball. It keeps my grades up and in the long run I know it'll make me a better person as I grow.

The basketball program is great here, we go to many gyms located in many different cities and sometimes even in different counties. I can say the most amazing school/gym I visited was Beverly hills high school, when my team and I were walking around the campus looking for the gym, we all happen to notice this one classroom. The reason for that was because the classroom was filled with ipads, for the students of course. All of us basketball players coming from South Gate high school, were very shocked and just amazed. While we were stuck on talking about how we wished we had the supplies these Beverly Hills students have, a Beverly Hills student walked by and looked at us, we were all in our South Gate attire so that led up to him asking us where South Gate was located, we all replied "by South Central, on Firestone and State St." the student had no idea what we had just said but we all understood why. He just proceeded to wherever he was going.

Well now to express the way I feel on being treated unfairly with equal access of school resources/supplies. Schools like Beverly Hills high school and Redondo Union have great electronic resources and pretty neat school supplies, that us lower class schools like South East, South Gate, and Huntington Park don't have.

I dont know if its because we're a minority as a community or maybe because of our location, but I really feel that school supplies such as computers, classrooms, even pencil and paper should be equally distributed to all schools no matter the district or location. What makes those schools like Beverly Hills and Redondo union better than us? Is it the students? I hope you get the point I'm trying to make Mr.Obama, I just want equality within every community and imm only talking about school wise. To some kids, school is the only thing that can help them make it out of where their stuck in. You want change?, well give us a chance and we'll do our part by doing our job in school.

I dont really care if I get a response back after writing this letter, as long as somebody hears me out and understands im trying to do better for our community.

THE WHITE HOUSE

WASHINGTON

February 11, 2015

Mr. Matthew Tyrone Pointer
Los Angeles, California

Dear Matthew:

I've been meaning to write since I read the letter you sent some time ago. Playing basketball in high school taught me about who I was and what I could do, and I'm glad it's played a positive role in your life as well.

You're right—education is the key to success, and whether students live in Beverly Hills or South Gate, they all should have a world-class education with access to the resources they need to reach for their dreams. Your generation deserves a system worthy of your potential, and every day I'm fighting to make that vision a reality.

Thank you for your message—your passion to lift up your community is admirable. Keep up the hard work, both on and off the court, and know I expect big things from you.

Sincerely,

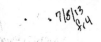

Back from the OVAL
7/9/13

Dear Mr. President,

My name is ▓▓▓▓▓ and I'm from ▓▓▓▓▓
▓▓▓▓▓ a suburb ▓▓▓▓▓ of Boston. I'm a retired Union
Ironworker ▓▓▓▓▓

Enclosed please find my still valid NRA card. I will not be renewing my
membership after today's' disappointing Senate vote.

Reasonable people expect reasonable action to be taken by their elected
officials. That did not happen today. Evidently the NRA's influence is too
intimidating for many people. I no longer feel properly represented by the
NRA and I would be very surprised if there weren't a lot more who share
my opinion.

If you tell the citizens of this country of my actions, I think you'd wind
up with a mailbox full of NRA cards. Background checks are the very least
we can do in light of Sandy Hook ,Aurora, and Arizona, to name a few.
Reasonable people can accept reasonable laws.

Thank you for your time,

Back from the OVAL
10/18/13

Submitted via www.whitehouse.gov/contact

A message from: John Mier

Submitted: 10/16/2013 11:34 AM
Email:
Phone:
Address:

Reply – and save for me.

Leetsdale, Pennsylvania

Message:

Dear President Obama,

My wife and I are signed up for medical insurance due to begin on January 1, 2014 which we bought off of the Healthcare.gov marketplace.

Yes, the website really stank for the first week but it just stank for the next week. Now, it still smells BUT: instead of paying $1600 per month for a group insurance plan of just me and my wife (we are both self-employed and it was the only way we could get coverage) we will have a plan that will only cost us $692 a month - a savings of $900 per month. Once this program gets underway, I would expect the cost to go even lower. And by next year, the website will work like a champ.

You and your team envisioned, put together, and got through a balky Congress this plan. Despite all the histrionics and lies from the Cruz Control, it will be good for America.

Thanks for doing it and thanks for not caving into the idiots.

Best regards to your wonderful wife, Michelle, and to your fine young daughters Talia and Sasha. They have a father to be proud of.

Very Sincerely,

John M. Mier

p.s. In one of the greater acts of hypocritical gall, there are GOP congressmen who want to investigate why the ACA website didn't work very well in those states where Republican governors would cooperate with the program. But they are losers and in '14, not all of them will be coming back for their government job.

Case Number:

THE WHITE HOUSE
WASHINGTON

John —

Thanks for the letter. The website really was a screw up, but I'm glad to hear the actual program is saving you money!

Best wishes,

10/14/14
+1   Sample/Tn/Support/Jauger/au

Jordan Garey

Independence Ky

Dear Mr. President,

I am 7 years old. My name is Jordan. I want to tell you that I am getting adopted on Oct 8, 2014. I have been a foster kid for 6 years, and I have finally found my forever family. I have two dads named Jeremy and Matt that are keeping me forever. I know you can't come to my adoption, but I wanted to tell you thank you for everything that you are doing to keep me safe.

Thank you, Jordan Garey

Jordan Garey

P.S. I wish I could spend the night sometime in your big house.

Th. Daniel F. Jaxin

New York, NY

President Barrack Obama
The White House
1600 Pennsylvania Ave, NW
Washington, D.C. 20500

20500

485 #006

MAR 20 2013

sample/LGBT pol·LGBT
6/25/13
f16

New York, NY

March 6. 2013

President Barrack Obama
The White House
1600 Pennsylvania Avenue NW
Washington, DC 20500.

Dear President Obama,

Martin Luther King, Jr. once said, "Our lives begin to end the day we become silent about things that matter." That statement kept going through my mind as I listened to your inauguration speech. It was a moment that was so surreal …. I never thought I would hear these words in my life from a president:

"We, the people, declare today that the most evident of truths – that all of us are created equal – is the star that guides us still; just as it guided our forebears through Seneca Falls, an Selma, and Stonewall."

My Facebook page got hit like crazy. Family and friends keep calling me on the phone to ask if I heard it. I did, and at first I didn't believe my ears. I thought you must been talking about slavery in Stonewall, Mississippi. I mean after all it was also Martin Luther King, Jr. Day. Then it dawned on me. You were talking about the Stonewall Inn. My Stonewall Inn.   My eyes fill up when I thought back to the first night at the Stonewall Riots when I was a 20 year old gay kid at the bar the night of the raid.

You see Mr. President; I was there for the first 2 nights of the riots. It was like a war zone. I saw garbage cans burning in the streets; bricks being thrown in the air and young silly little gay kids like myself being beaten by police officers and the tactical police force till they bleed. All this violence because we wanted to dance alone and be unseen from a society that did not want us. I was so unaware at the time that I was being denied my right as an American, but I that I was also being denied my basic human right. It is kind of funny when you think about it; my grandfather came to America as an Irish immigrant. He got a job as a laborer assembling the new Stature of Liberty in the New York Harbor. The same one with the mounted plaque that reads "Give me your tired, your poor, your huddled masses yearning to breathe free." I yearn to breathe free Mr. President.

As gay man back then in 1969 I could not serve openly in the military. I could not get a license to practice law or be a hairstylist; if I was trapped doing something "Lewd". I was dammed by almost all religions. The American Psychiatric Association told me that I was mentality ill. I was not allowed to get married, and had to keep my love of another man hidden. I could not adopt children. I was not allowed to receive a legal drink in any bar in New York City with out them loosing their license for serving a "sexual deviant." It was a life that was bleak and filled with one word "NO" and to top it off that night in June 1969, they were now going to tell me I couldn't dance … not even hidden in back of a dark bar.

You made me proud sir when you mentioned that significant part of my life, but it is a battle that is not over yet, and we still have a big fight on our hands. I still have not gotten to dance that dance I started 44 years ago. The big joyous "I Am A Completely Free Gay American Dance" yet, and I so badly want to dance that dance before I meet my maker … not just have spent my life listening to the music.

Thank you for making that dance floor a little bit more accessible and starting to play the music.

Sincerely yours,

Daniel (Danny) Garvin
Stonewall Inn Veteran

THE WHITE HOUSE
WASHINGTON

November 29, 2013

Mr. Daniel Garvin

New York, New York

Dear Daniel:

Thank you for the powerful letter you sent this spring—I read it with interest.

At Stonewall, people joined together and declared they had seen enough injustice. While being beaten down, they stood up and challenged not only how the world saw them, but also how they saw themselves. History shows that once that spirit takes hold, little can stand in its way—so the riots gave way to protests, the protests gave way to a movement, and the movement gave way to a transformation that continues today.

You are right that the dance is unfinished. But as long as I hold this Office, I will keep fighting to open the floor for everyone.

Sincerely,

Contact Us - Economy

Submitted:	August 28, 2013 01:40
Originating Host:	
Remote IP:	
From:	Tom Hoefner
Email Address:	
Phone:	
Address (Domestic):	
Topic:	

Back from the OVAL
9/12/13

reply

Message:
Dear Mr. President,

My wife and I live in Brooklyn. I have a Master's Degree from an Ivy League school. She has one from a CUNY. I haven't been able to find full-time work since 2008. I have six figures of student loans I can't pay, most of which I've defaulted on and are now with private collections agencies. We worry about paying bills from week to week. Yesterday I went over the limit on my Target credit card and had to wait with my 6 year old at customer service figuring out how I could pay for our very modest selection of carefully chosen groceries. I have looked for steady work for five years in my field, education, presumably a stable field that is proving not to be. I send resumes out into the void, never to hear from them again.

I am 34. I will likely never own a home. I will likely never have a retirement pension. My generation was always told that if we worked hard and did well in school and stayed out of trouble we'd have secure futures. We were lied to, or at the very least misled.

We do not have pay-cable channels. We have cell phones, but no landline. We have never taken a vacation.

We get by, day to day. Barely. We will never achieve the American Dream, if it ever existed. We will be silent victims, never suffering enough to be pitied but never succeeding enough to pay off our debts, to be able to live as we were promised.

The system is broken. The middle class is dead. We are its silent victims.

Sincerely,
Tom Hoefner

P.S. - I don't expect a response to this. I'm used to getting form letters as a response, or no response at all. This is just one more thing I needed to shout into the empty void.

THE WHITE HOUSE
WASHINGTON

Tom —

I got your letter. I know things are tough out there right now, and I won't try to pretend that I've got a guaranteed solution to your immediate situation. But the economy is slowly getting better, and we are working every day to push through Congress measures that might help - like student loan forgiveness or mitigation.

I guess what I'm saying is that your President is

thinking about you. And your six year old is undoubtedly lucky to have a dad that cares.

From: **Mr. Bob Melton**

Submitted: 12/18/2014 11:27 PM EST

Email:

Phone:

Address: Morganton, North Carolina

Message: Dear Mr. President,
I thought you would like to know that because of the ACA I went to see a Doctor for the first time in 12 years. I am having pain and the ACA enabled me to at least get examined and now treated. I'm 61 years old and in pretty good shape (At least I think so} but without your help would have had NO insurance. At all. Thank You again Mr. President. You remind me of President Roosevelt. A man was weeping on the street when FDR died. A reporter asked,"Did you know him, you are so upset?" The man replied,"No, I didn't know him. He knew me". I feel that same connection to you Mr. President.

THE WHITE HOUSE
WASHINGTON

December 13, 2016

Mr. Bob Melton
Morganton, North Carolina

Dear Bob:

     I wanted to take a moment to extend my appreciation for the note you sent a few years ago about the difference the Affordable Care Act has made in your life—as you know from my staff's outreach to you, your message moved me and my team deeply.

     Over the course of my Presidency, I've seen in letters like yours the courage, determination, and open-heartedness of our people. "The faith of America" of which President Roosevelt spoke still echoes in every corner of our land—shaped and carried forward by generations. I am confident that it will continue to guide us as long as engaged citizens like you keep speaking out for the ideals that bind us as a Nation and as a people.

     Again, thank you. You have my very best wishes and my gratitude for your steadfast support.

Sincerely,

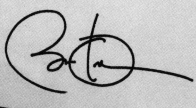

Dear Mr. President,

My name is Gavin Nore. I am a 15 year old young man from Fort Dodge, Iowa. I first met you when I was eight years old. Back in 2007, you gave a speech about your campaign. Once you were done, people were allowed to ask you questions. I got the chance to meet you and I asked, "Would you continue stem cell research?" You told me, you would continue the research. When I turned 14, I was diagnosed with Hodgkins Lymphoma on February 14, 2013. I beat the battle. During the summer of 2013, I was cancer free. Then, in August of last year, I was re-diagnosed. I had to have a stem cell transplant. I beat the battle once again. I would like to thank you very much for continuing the research. If the research haden't continued, I wouldn't be here today. Once again, thank you very much Mr. President!

Sincerely,
Gavin Nore

CHAPTER 9

Barack Obama

THE WHITE HOUSE

I asked Obama if he read the letters in the sequence in which Fiona so carefully arranged them.

"I actually do!" he said. "I'll go through them one at a time. Yeah, I know. You've been rifling through my mail—"

It was a cool autumn afternoon, the trees outside appropriately dropping their leaves, marking the end of a season and, soon, the end of an era. The first African American president. Two terms. Closing.

Obama's Oval Office was decorated with more restraint than many of his predecessors'. He kept a wooden bowl of fresh apples on the coffee table; George Bush usually had an abundant bouquet of roses there. Obama had added striped wallpaper in muted gold tones, and he'd replaced Bush's formal white damask couches with quiet tan ones in soft brushed corduroy. (Clinton had bold, bright stripes. Bush, Sr., had the whole place done up in baby blue and cream.) Red curtains added a pop to Obama's Oval Office; overall the effect was a tailored mid-century modern look.

Soon all that would change to reflect the tastes and the mood of a new leader.

I asked Obama if he typically read the letters there, in the Oval Office—or someplace else? Did he have tea? A brandy, perhaps?

"Usually my habit is to have dinner with my family," he said, "and then I head into the Treaty Room. And I'll have a stack of work. So I'm sitting in my chair, and I've got policy briefings, and I've got decision memos, and I've got, you know, some intelligence report, so it will take me a couple of hours to plow through that. And I usually save the letters for last. And they're in a purple folder. And typically the letter is stapled to the envelope that it came in. Sometimes the packet is sort of bulky and unwieldy, because somebody sent some object along with the letter. The most common would be drawings from kids, or pictures of a family, or some document that shows their interaction with some bank or some bureaucrat that wasn't particularly helpful to them. Every once in a while you'll get some personal artifact that somebody sent, like copies of letters from their dad when he was fighting in World War II or some, you know, personal object that really meant something to them that they wanted me to have."

I don't know why I was surprised by how slowly the president talked. You hear him in public and he sounds so . . . pensive. One on one, he seems even more so, perhaps given your own urge to . . . help, maybe, speed things up? But there is no interrupting; he's in command, plodding forward, each thought a complete sentence with, that is, commas—each word seeming to have come out only after a good amount of consideration. The image I got listening to Obama that day as he sat in the Oval Office courteously contemplating the seemingly mundane matter of his daily mail habit, was that of a conscientious old man putting together a jigsaw puzzle. Some swirly seascape where there is blue, but then there is *blue,* and then there is "blue" and . . . blue! You couldn't argue with it; he's getting it right, and the picture is coming together.

"There have been recurring letters," he went on, "and in that category, I would say, are veterans looking for help, young people with heavy student loan debt trying to figure out whether they qualify for some relief, military personnel or military families who are struggling in some fashion with either a decision or a lack of help from the Department of Defense.

"If there was a letter that particularly moved me, jolted me, saddened me, I got in the habit of asking people to circulate it. So that everyone could take a look at it."

He talked about scribbling notes on letters, asking questions of staff. "Somebody would explain, 'This is what it's like to deal with the federal government on this issue.' Or 'This is how this law has affected me,' regardless of what the theory was." He wanted to know why and what could be done to improve the situation. "And those staff probably didn't always enjoy getting those notes," he said. "But they understood that if I wrote on this letter, I wanted an answer, and I wanted an explanation—that they had to come up with one. Sometimes, you know, you'd hear back from the staff, and they'd say, 'Well, you know, this is why we're doing it this way.' And I'd say, 'Well, that doesn't make any sense. And let's try to change the policy.'

"That would be an interesting exercise, to track the number of initiatives—most of them small, most of them not ones that would get a headline—that we ended up modifying or sparked, at least, a discussion about how we were doing business. It would not be a negligible number.

"And then there have been times where you've seen the reactions to a response," he said. "Probably the most powerful example was we typically have wounded warriors and veterans come in for tours at the White House, and I'll greet them. I remember once meeting a beautiful family, relatively young mom, dad, couple of little kids, and as I came up to shake their hands, the mom started tearing up. And she gave me a big hug, and she said, 'You know, the reason we're here is because of you.' And I said, 'Why is that?' And she said, 'Well, my husband here, who had served, you know, he had pretty severe PTSD, and I was worried that he might not make it, and you had the VA call us directly, and that's what prompted him to get treatment.' You know, and that's when you're reminded that there's something about this office that, when people get a response, they feel that their lives and concerns are important. And that can change in some small way, and maybe in occasionally big ways, how they view their lives."

I asked him how he decides which letters to answer personally. He said that part was easy: "The ones that I usually respond to right then and there are ones that involve somebody having a very personal issue where my sense of what they need is just an affirmation of some sort." I thought of Shelley Muniz from Columbia, California, who had written in 2009 to tell Obama about her teenage son

Micah who had died of leukemia and about the enormous health-care bills facing her grieving family. "It is for families like yours that I am fighting so hard for healthcare reform," Obama wrote to her.

"There have been times I've gotten a letter from, say, a senior, and they'll just go through their budget," he told me. "You know, literally here's what I'm spending per month, and here's what my Social Security check is. You know, 'It's really hard to make it.'

"Sometimes people share letters with me about some sort of transformation they've gone through. There have been a number of letters where somebody talks about how they were raised in a family that was suspicious of people of a different race, or background. The growth that they or a loved one went through in seeing themselves in other people in a way they wouldn't have expected.

"And then there are occasions where the letter is particularly, uh, pointed at what an idiot I am—I feel obliged to respond then and there.

"My correspondence office has always been very clear that if all I'm getting is letters from people saying I'm doing a good job," he told me, "I'm not getting half of the population.

"But, you know, I will tell you that the letters I remember so often are not the ones in the heat of battle that speak directly to an issue that we're in the middle of a fight on, because oftentimes those are fairly predictable. The letters, I think, that matter the most to me are the ones that . . . make a connection, that speak to people's lives and their values and what's important to them."

I resisted the impulse to ask him if he had a favorite letter. I felt it might be like saying, "Hey, who's your favorite American?" And I was more interested to find out which letters, if any, might pop up for him all on their own. Thousands of letters, over an eight-year period, coming to him in the back of his briefing book—would any specific ones come to mind as he looked back on all this?

That day there were three. Three that came up in our casual conversation about the mail and his presidency and the degree to which one influenced the other.

"I remember a father who said, 'I'm very conservative and generally have a very negative view of immigration, but then my son be-friended a young man who, it turned out, was undocumented,'" Obama said, describing the first.

I'd read several letters from conservatives who found themselves changing their minds about immigration, like Bill Oliver's letter about Quique, but I think this one, from Ronn Ohl of Sanford, North Carolina, who wrote to talk about a DREAMer he'd gotten to know, was the one that Obama was referring to that day:

Ronn Ohl

Back from the OVAL
7/3/12

Sanford NC

17 June 2012

TO: President Obama
1600 Pennsylvania Avenue, NW
Washington, DC 20500

Mister President,

Thank you for your leadership in signing the executive order to permit children of illegal aliens to be able to live and work in this country without being deported. You took action where Congress was unable to do the same with the Dream Act. You took bold measures in doing so, even though it was most likely for political purposes. This may be the initial step to resolving the illegal immigration problem and hopefully the next Congress is able to build from this initiative.

I am a descendant of an illegal immigrant into this country. My great-great grandfather was an Irish stow away on a cargo ship of walnuts from England in the late 1800s. I have served in the military for 21 years. I now reside in a community that has a predominate populace of Hispanics. One of my son's friends since middle school is an illegal alien. My son recently graduated from college with a MPA. This friend came to in the United States when he was 4 years old with his parents looking for a better life. That was 21 years ago. He graduated from high school and played varsity soccer. However, he radically found out that he was unable to do other things legally as his other friends. He could not receive a driver's license, could not apply for college, and he could not find legitimate work.

Again, I strongly agree with your decision. I talked to my son's friend this past Christmas about this topic and he thought it would be years before anything would happen to keep him in this country and not being afraid of being deported. For his entire life all he knew was living in the United States as an American. Now he tries to find odd jobs and always on the alert. The illegal immigrants find a way to make a living without being caught and deported. However, many unscrupulous employers and landlords take advantage of this thus abusing and stealing from them.

As I stated in the initial paragraph, I thought this was probably a political tactic. This is the only issue that I agree on your part for the past 31/2 years. I am a Tea Party conservative. I believe in fiscal responsibility with balancing the federal budget. I also believe in limited federal government with certain responsibilities passed to the state governments, such as health care. I do not concur with your notion that the elite rich should pay a little more of their fair share of taxes. That would in line with a rich person paying $4 for a Big Mac sandwich while the poor person is only expected to pay $3.50 for the same. Where is the Liberty and Justice in that?

Respectfully,

RONN OHL

CC: My personal U.S. Congress Representative

Ronn Ohl

Obama sometimes stewed over letters that were critical of him or his administration. This one was particularly confounding. Why was this "Tea Party conservative" so skeptical about the president doing the very thing he was writing to say he thought was commendable?

THE WHITE HOUSE
WASHINGTON

Ronn —

Thanks for the letter. Your cynicism about my motives may be a bit misplaced; I know, and similarly care for, a lot of young people like your son's friend.

I won't try to persuade you about the rest of my agenda, but who knows — maybe we have more common ground than you might think.

Best wishes,

I told Obama I was surprised by how much thought he seemed to put into some of these responses. I mean, one guy in North Carolina doesn't trust the president's motives. Was that really so surprising? And he's going to try to change the guy's mind in a note?

"When you're president, so often you're talking in shorthand," he said. "Almost always you're being reported in shorthand. You can get into habits. You forget that on the other side of any issue is a complex person, or people, or communities that are trying to sort through a whole bunch of stuff that they're dealing with."

So when those sorts of letters landed on his desk, he took special note. "Sometimes I felt as if I was being a little unfair, because I'd sometimes devote more effort and attention to those letters. Because I really wanted them to know that, you know, this isn't just the comments on the Internet. That that's not the function of this. The function is: We're going to engage."

. . .

The second letter Obama mentioned to me that day was one that had stirred up a fuss.

"A letter I received from a woman in Minnesota," he offered. "I actually used her and her family as an example of what was best about America in a State of the Union speech. And if you read the letter, it was just describing, you know, 'Here's what I'm going through.' And 'I'm not looking for a handout or a guarantee for success; I just wish there was something that would maybe make this a little bit easier.'"

It wasn't a particularly exciting letter. It wasn't cute. It wasn't emotional. There were no photos or drawings attached. Even the author of it, Rebekah Erler, told me, when I reached out to her, that she thought it was unremarkable. "I wrote it in like fifteen minutes," she said. "I just wanted him to know what was going on out here."

March 1, 2014

President and Mrs. Obama,

I am writing to you as a voter, a politically involved woman, a wife, and a mother. I want to tell you a little bit about our family. My husband worked in Construction trades from the time he finished high school and I was a college educated administrative professional when we met. . . . If only we had known what was about to happen to the housing and construction market. I was pregnant with our first child.

. . . We decided that in order to survive, we would relocate from my home town of Seattle back to his home town in the midwest and into his parents['] basement with our 6 month old son.

. . . My husband was hired to work as a freight conductor in the railroad industry—a great job with great benefits, but a miserable lifestyle. We had our second son, and I went to a local community college to retrain for a new career as an accountant. I was simultaneously home alone with two kids under 2 years old. I took out very

reasonable student loans. We did everything right. Last October we bought our first house. My husband was able to leave the railroad and return to the remodeling industry. Now he is home for dinner every night, and gets a full night of sleep. It's amazing what you take for granted. It's amazing what you can bounce back from when you have to.

The reason I'm writing to tell you all this is simple. I did what the economy, and you and the country is calling for people to do—go out, retrain, reenter the workforce in a great job with upward mobility.

The cost of our groceries has skyrocketed while we feverishly cut coupons and meal plan. . . . We pay $1900 a month to send our kids to the local preschools while we work. My student loan payments will start in a few months. . . .

The truth is—in America, where two people have done everything they can to succeed and fight back from the brink of financial ruin—through job loss, and retraining, and kids, and credit card debts that are set up to keep you impoverished forever, and the discipline to stop spending any money on yourselves or take a vacation in 5 years—it's virtually impossible to live a simple middle class life. We drive our 10 and 15 year old cars that are too small for our family because they are paid off. When my dad was diagnosed with cancer, he had to pay for the plane tickets for my kids and I to visit because at 35 years old, I can't afford to fly my family to visit their grandfather.

My husband and I can barely afford the basics. Our big splurge is cable TV so we can follow our beloved Minnesota Wild during the hockey season (and watch Team USA in the Olympics!). We don't go out with friends or shop for clothes or toys or anything except at Christmas time or birthdays.

We don't feel like victims of our life—we have a really good life, and we are proud. We have a garden in the back, and we run around

outside in parks and every other free and wonderful thing the Min-
neapolis area has to offer. We are a strong, tight-knit family who has
made it through some very, very hard times in our short 7 years.

I teared up when you were elected President. I took my son to the
voting booth with me in 2012 so when he grows up he can say he
went with me to vote for Barack Obama. . . .

I am just writing to remind you that the silent ones out here, the
ones who are just working as hard as we can to make it, the ones
who voted for you—are out here.

We need childcare to be reasonably priced, or subsidized. Two thou-
sand dollars a month for preschool is an astronomical price to pay
to have your child be safe and taught well while you go to work. . . .
We need food to be affordable. Our wages have not increased in
the last 10 years but the cost of living has multiplied many times
over.

I'm pretty sure this is a silly thing to do—to write a letter to the
President. But on some level—I know that staying silent about what
you see and what needs changing never makes any difference. So
I'm writing you to let you know what it's like for us out here in the
middle of the country. And I hope you will listen.

Thank You, and Best Regards,
Rebekah Erler
Minneapolis, MN

"Everyone was saying the recession is over," Rebekah told me when
I asked her what compelled her to write in 2014. "And I'm like,
'What? No it's not.' And I'm like, 'Surely Obama gets it.' I knew he
wouldn't think that we were just, like, irresponsible. I just thought
that he had been one of us not that long ago. He had student loans.
A regular family. You know, there's that old thing that people would
say Bush didn't know what a gallon of milk cost. Obama struck me
as someone who knew what a gallon of milk cost."

Like almost every other letter writer I talked to, Rebekah hadn't expected the president to read her letter, much less respond to it. But she did get a response, about three months after she sent it. It was a phone call from the White House. "They said, 'The president wants to have lunch with you. He's coming to Minnesota.' I'm like, 'What?'"

Within days, on a Thursday in June 2014, Rebekah was sitting at Matt's Bar in Minneapolis ordering a "Jucy Lucy" (a burger with cheese in the middle), and Obama ordered the same. She was too nervous to eat. He thanked her for her letter. He told her it reminded him of something his mother would have written. He invited her to come with him to a town hall meeting afterward up at Minnehaha Park, and so she rode with him in the motorcade, sat next to him and across from Valerie Jarrett, and they asked her if she'd be able to maybe introduce him the next day, at an economic policy speech he was scheduled to deliver over at Lake Harriet, and so she did that too, brought her family, and when it was over, they all hugged, and Obama said, "Hey, if you're ever in Washington—" and then he was gone.

"And my husband was like, 'What the heck just happened?'"

People in the media were predictably and perhaps appropriately skeptical. The White House featured photos and videos of the visit on its website; they billed it as "a day in the life" of Rebekah. The midterms were coming up, and Obama's approval rating was sitting at just 41 percent. So maybe it was a political stunt. Or maybe, as even staffers readily admitted may have been the case, Obama was just yearning for the old days, when campaigning meant you got to hang out with people outside the bubble and eat burgers.

"People said, 'Oh, he used you,'" Rebekah told me. "'You were a prop.' But I never once felt that way. It just wasn't like that. Even now people ask me, 'What was your impression of him?' And I always tell them he's exactly who I hoped he was when I voted for him. He made me feel like someone was steering the ship. That if we just hung on, we'll be okay. It was like, we've got somebody at the top who cares. And that matters for something."

At Christmastime Rebekah heard from the White House again. Would she and her family like to come to the State of the Union address? When she arrived, she was introduced to people, speechwriters, cabinet members, policy makers of all kinds. She met Fiona. Fiona introduced her to the intern who had been sitting in the hard-mail room the day Rebekah's letter came in. It was among the stack of hundreds he had read that day; it was just one he had sampled, hoping he was doing it right. "I was like, 'Wow, look what you did,'" Rebekah told me. "He was twenty-three or something, and look what he did." She met then–Secretary of Labor Tom Perez. "And he said, 'The president gave every member of the cabinet your letter and said, "Remember who we're working for."'"

At the State of the Union address, she sat between Michelle Obama and Jill Biden. The speech was built around her letter. Obama told Rebekah's story, and he quoted the letter, returning to it like a refrain in the middle and once more at the end.

> I want our actions to tell every child in every neighborhood, your life matters. . . .
>
> I want them to grow up in a country where a young mom can sit down and write a letter to her president with a story that sums up these past six years: "It's amazing what you can bounce back from when you have to. . . . We are a strong, tight-knit family who's made it through some very, very hard times."
>
> My fellow Americans, we, too, are a strong, tight-knit family. We, too, have made it through some hard times. Fifteen years into this new century, we have picked ourselves up, dusted ourselves off, and begun again the work of remaking America. We have laid a new foundation. A brighter future is ours to write. Let's begin this new chapter together—and let's start the work right now.
>
> Thank you. God bless you. God bless this country we love.

There was one more letter Obama brought up that day in the Oval Office when I spoke to him about the mail. It was one that had just crossed his desk, and so it was fresh on his mind. "Somebody just recently wrote me a letter about when they were growing up their mom always used the *N* word and was derogatory about African Americans," he said.

Save File   10/3/16
Logt Version   8/10

Back from the OVAL
10/4/16

From: Mrs. Joelle Graves

Submitted: 9/29/2016 1:25 PM EDT

Email:

Phone:

Reply – nice story!
personally

Address: Medford, Oregon (Valid)

Message: Dear President Obama,
I needed you to hear this story before your last day in the White House. And today's date
reminded me to tell you. My mother-in-law (Peggy) was an Indiana girl; adored Chicago; grew
up in the suburbs; had a job in a dress shop; met her husband to be and moved to California -
the promised land - in the late 40's. Peggy and my father-in-law were life long Republicans.
They were surprisingly prejudiced. They used the N word often! At one point I had to actually
ask them to refrain from saying such harsh things about African Americans in front of their
grandchildren. When my girls were old enough, they asked them that themselves. Fast forward
to today's date seven years ago - the day we buried my mother-in-law at the age of 94. She had
outlived everyone in her family. I took family leave from my work the last 30 days of her life to
provide 12 hours a day of care to save the $7,000 a month it was costing for round the clock
care for her. We were out of money, but didn't want her to know. As I sat with her each of those
30 days, chatting about her life - one day I asked her what was her proudest accomplishment.
She looked at me with a twinkle in her eye and replied, "The day I voted for a black man to be
President of the United States!" She and I both knew that was BIG. She went on to say that she
would go to her grave knowing that finally she had cast a vote that would matter. That she was
part of history. That she was ashamed of the using the N word her entire life. That she never
thought she'd vote for a black man from Chicago! That is was the first time she had voted
Democrat. And that she cried tears of joy during your inauguration. She made me promise to
work hard to be sure you were elected a second term. So when that time arrived my youngest
daughter and I canvassed for you. And we canvassed Peggy's neighborhood. When I
encountered a nay sayer, I told them this story and just asked them to think about it before
casting their vote! She would be so proud of your two terms in office. Somewhere in heaven
she is all dressed up, ready to vote democrat! If only she were here today, right? I just wanted
you to know.
Sincerely,
Joelle Graves

"There are those kinds of letters, I think, that shape your attitudes,"
Obama told me that day. "The individuality and the specificity carries a power that is different than any rational argument that is made
or policy presentation that is made. It carries with it a force that's
different."

I asked him what he thought letters like Joelle's said about the
relationship he'd formed, over the past eight years, with the people
he was elected to serve.

"It says the American people are full of goodness and wisdom,
and you just have to be paying attention," he said. "And sometimes
that's hard to do when you're inside this bubble, but this was a little
portal through which I could remind myself of that every day.

"The letters are beautiful, aren't they?"

CHAPTER 10

Marjorie McKinney,
August 21, 2013

BOONE, NORTH CAROLINA

Marg was in Albany when the incident happened. It might seem like a tiny thing. A run-of-the-mill, everyday thing. But Marg couldn't shake the memory of it, carrying it the way another person carries grief, a feeling of heaviness inside, unmovable and flat.

How do you describe it? Okay. Imagine it's getting dark outside. Cold. Gray. The dreariest dusk, everybody aching to get home for some mashed potatoes and TV. Marg was at the New York State Museum there, doing some work for her husband, Ken, a geologist at the university back home in Boone, North Carolina. Marg helped Ken his whole career; it had been a willing partnership ever since the 1950s when they met in paleontology class. They decided he would get the PhD; she would stay home with the kids. She loved it. They traveled the world together hunting fossils, debating plate tectonics and all the exhilarating implications.

Then Ken had developed muscular dystrophy, and then came the wheelchair, so now Marg, who was in her early seventies, did most of the traveling alone. She's a short woman, compact, with a paper-thin complexion, wire-rimmed glasses, and shaggy white hair she lets fly around naturally. That day she had traveled to Albany to pick up some images of fossils that Ken had requested, and she was headed to her car. (This was 2011, when Ken was still alive. He has since passed.) The plaza outside the museum was huge, a broad quadrangle, acres of concrete reaching toward the horizon, nothing to cut the wind, and the weird thing was not a single person was out there except Marg and one shadowy figure in the distance. Weird because it was a weekday, rush hour, and people should've been storming out of those buildings headed home to their mashed potatoes, shouldn't they?

The person in the distance was a guy, definitely a guy; he was way across the plaza on that parallel sidewalk there. Suddenly he started walking toward Marg. He quickened his pace, came closer. She felt uncomfortable with the way he seemed to be zeroing in on her like that. He looked young. He was black. He was wearing a hoodie. In one swift move, he flipped the hood up and over his head, concealing his face.

I should run, Marg thought. It was more instinct than thought. Her short legs wouldn't take her very far very fast. He kept getting closer. *At what point do I run?* There were no nearby buildings to duck into. She started walking faster, toward the stairwell that led to the parking lot. He did too. She felt hot. She felt a pulse in her toes and on the tips of her ears, a pounding all over saying, "Run like hell."

They both reached the stairwell at the same time. He looked up at her. "Bad wind, isn't it?" he said. Then he told her there was a pedestrian walkway underneath that linked the museum to the parking lot, in case she didn't know. Next time if it's cold out, she might want to take that, he said.

And that was it. He was gone.

It might seem like a tiny thing. A run-of-the-mill, everyday thing. But for Marg it marked a break in who she believed herself to be.

"Why was I afraid of this very pleasant young man? It was just all because I saw he was a black man. I had no reason to be afraid of him. And that just knocked me flat. It wasn't anything I ever expected to feel. It was a turning point in my life, because I realized then, you know, that I was racist. And I had to find a way to get rid of that."

Now, a big part of the problem for Marg was she thought she *had* gotten rid of it. She had made the decision long ago to get rid of it.

For people who grew up in the Deep South, in Birmingham, Alabama, it was a steep climb to work on something like that. It was a decision you had to make, yes or no, if you wanted to learn how to free yourself of racist thinking that had been more or less ingrained in you.

Marg was six when she discovered the white robe and the pointed hood hanging in the neighbor's den on the back of the door. She was playing hide-and-seek with her sister. "What are you doing in here?" the mom said. "You are forbidden to enter this room." She knew what it was. She always wondered who was under those things. He was the town barber. He was so jolly. He and her dad were pals. There were things you didn't talk about.

The black neighborhood was across the street from her school. It was like a separate village you didn't go into. And they didn't come into yours. The buses would come and take the black kids miles away to another school. The public buses had a wooden placard behind the white section. If you were white and got on the bus and there was no place to sit, you pushed the placard back, and those people had to move. And if their section got full, one of them had to get off the bus.

It was normal. It was just the way the world was divided: two types of people. That's why you needed two types of everything: seats, stores, schools, theaters, ball teams. Nobody said anything about it being wrong. She heard about Martin Luther King, Jr., when she was in high school—some of the stuff about the Montgomery bus boycott; she did hear about some of that. At home, when she brought it up, she was told to leave the dinner table and never mention it again. Nothing they should be involved in. It was up to somebody else to get involved.

The first time she ever talked to a black person was when she was in grad school, at the University of North Carolina at Chapel Hill, in the early 1960s. "Well, hello," she said. She had no idea what to expect. "My name is Marg." It was just a normal conversation like she would have with anybody, and that was the thing that jolted her. He was acting like a regular person.

She had a friend, an exchange student from Germany who was considerably older, and at lunch one day, she told him she didn't understand some of the sit-ins and other civil rights demonstrations that students were starting to organize at segregated restaurants and businesses in town. "Black people are satisfied with their lives," she said. "Why stir up a fuss?"

"Where are you hearing this?" her friend said.

"That's how it is back home in Birmingham," she said.

Except of course that's not how it really was back home in Birmingham. That was a polite white girl's dinner table version, where you were told to leave if you brought anything up. In fact, in the 1950s and 1960s, racial segregation was legally required in Birmingham, where just 10 percent of the city's black population was registered to vote, and the unemployment rate for blacks was two and a half times higher than it was for whites; there were no black police officers, firefighters, store clerks, or bus drivers. "Probably the most segregated city in the United States," Martin Luther King, Jr., said about Birmingham.

So there was Marg in grad school, her friend from Germany trying to wake her up from her stupor, explaining racism and bigotry and hate, telling her about his country and his life and about the Hitler Youth. First it had just been a group of little kids. Then other youth groups had to join, church groups, sports leagues. Hitler consolidated them; he outlawed all other youth groups except for the Hitler Youth. It grew to eight million kids. You had to read Nazi books and sing Nazi songs. You could be refused a diploma and a job if you didn't join. Your parents would be hunted down. Two kinds of people, pure or impure, an army enforcing the divide.

Marg would stay friends with the guy from Germany. She would continue to thank him for everything he had explained to her in the lunchroom that day and for setting her life on a new course. "You needed it," he'd say.

In 1963, police dogs were unleashed on black protesters in Birmingham, and then police turned on the fire hoses. King was thrown in jail, and from his cell he wrote an open letter to America. "Injustice anywhere is a threat to justice everywhere," he said.

Marg got involved in the civil rights movement. Throughout her life she tried to see beyond race. Even when she and Ken planned their family. Four kids, they said. One by birth, the rest adopted. So many kids needing love. Two of them were biracial.

So imagine. With all that behind her, all that evolving, a whole life with Ken and the kids. And then she's in Albany, and it's cold and dark, and she finds this pit of ugliness sitting inside her like some dormant worm wriggling to life.

What are you supposed to do with that?

In the background, on the news, the Trayvon Martin tragedy was unfolding. This was now 2012. Trayvon Martin, a seventeen-year-old kid coming back from a run to the store on a February night in Sanford, Florida. He was wearing a black hoodie. George Zimmerman, part of a watch group for the gated community, thought Trayvon Martin looked suspicious, so Zimmerman went after him and after an altercation shot him dead.

Marg heard about it on the radio, at home in Boone, in the house she and Ken had built together, on seventeen acres overlooking the Blue Ridge Mountains. The kids were grown, and Ken was gone, and so it was just her, two goats, a donkey named Rosie who liked Cheetos. Marg was following the Trayvon Martin saga on the radio, thinking about a divided America. She felt complicit. She wondered about Zimmerman. Did he have the same piece in him that she had discovered in herself? Was that what made him do it? Was he surprised to find it, as she was?

Zimmerman walked free for six weeks before he was charged with second-degree murder, provoking protests in Florida and across the country. The trial lasted a month, and when the not-guilty verdict was announced, people took to the streets and social media. "Black lives matter!" became the cry of a new movement.

On July 19, 2013, six days after the Zimmerman verdict, President Obama gave an impromptu speech in the White House press room. "Trayvon Martin could have been me, thirty-five years ago," he said. "I think it's important to recognize that the African American community is looking at this issue through a set of experiences and a history that doesn't go away."

Marg thought it was a gracious speech. She thought Obama was trying to explain the insidious nature of racism by making it personal.

"What I identified with was the complexity of it. I felt that Obama was trying to say, 'You can't just say that this man cold-bloodedly decided to kill Trayvon Martin. There were things going on with him, and with his thinking.'"

That was the way Marg heard it. Things going on in him, like the things she discovered going on in her.

Other people heard it differently. On the radio, conservative commentators and callers were sharply critical of Obama's words. The Zimmerman shooting wasn't about race, they said. It was a scuffle that had ended in tragedy. Nothing more. Obama shouldn't be making it about race, they said. He shouldn't use this tragedy as a way to appease critics decrying him for not doing more during his presidency to address race relations in America.

What is the matter with you people? Marg thought. Of course this was about race. And why wasn't anyone talking about all the other things Obama had to say in that speech that day?

"I think it's going to be important for all of us to do some soul-searching," he had said. "There has been talk about should we convene a conversation on race. I haven't seen that be particularly productive when politicians try to organize conversations. They end up being stilted and politicized, and folks are locked into the positions they already have. On the other hand, in families and churches and workplaces, there's the possibility that people are a little bit more honest, and at least you ask yourself your own questions about, Am I wringing as much bias out of myself as I can? Am I judging people as much as I can based on not the color of their skin, but the content of their character? That would, I think, be an appropriate exercise in the wake of this tragedy."

Marg went to her computer and began typing. She wanted President Obama to know someone was listening. She had never thought of writing to a president before. But this guy needed it. Soon enough she found herself confessing about what had happened in Albany. "I wanted him to know that I had a reason to feel the way I did. I wanted to claim it for myself too. Because I wasn't doing this intellectually; I was doing it from my experience. It was something that was real to me."

"Dear President Obama," she wrote. "As years went by, I thought I had done a pretty good job of shedding the racism in me. . . . Then, came a cold evening in Albany, NY." She told him about the cold and the darkness. "As I pulled a scarf around my neck to cut the wind, I saw the man pull his hoodie up." She told him about the fear that overcame her and how she didn't understand it. "Into my mind popped the notion that he was a black man, had hidden his face (I had, too). . . . I was embarrassed to think that, but it was there."

She thanked the president for his speech about Trayvon Martin, and she said she owed that young man in Albany an apology. "I hope that others who heard your words will be more aware of the fear that lurks within many of us," she said. "It's unreasoned, but there."

GRO- Trayvon Martin
· sample
8/21/13
f · 8

Marjorie McKinney

Back from the OVAL
8/22/13

Boone, NC

Reply

President Barak Obama
The White House
1600 Pennsylvania Avenue, NW
Washington, DC 20500

Dear President Obama,

Thank you for your recent statements after the Zimmerman trial about your own memories of being a young black male. I am a "white" American, born and raised in Birmingham, Alabama where I lived until I moved to North Carolina as a grad student. When I left Alabama, I had the opportunity to know many different people and was impelled to examine the racism in me. I didn't know it existed. I didn't even think about it before.

As years went by, I thought I had done a pretty good job of shedding the racism in me. I had African-American friends, two of my children are bi-racial, I was involved in civil rights issues. Then, came a cold evening in Albany, NY.

I was in Albany for a short visit and was walking in the area between the museum and government buildings. It's a huge plaza with an underground pedestrian area that links the buildings. I had used that to walk to the museum but decided to walk back outside. It was getting dark. The only other person on the plaza was a young black man who was walking parallel to me on the other side. As I pulled a scarf around my neck to cut the wind, I saw the man pull his hoodie up as he changed direction and began walking quickly toward me. Much to my horror, I became afraid and tried to figure why. Into my mind popped the notion that he was a black man, had hidden his face (I had, too), and had suddenly changed direction when he seemed to have looked up and seen me. I was embarrassed to think that, but it was there. I decided to wait and see what happened, fearful all the time. I changed my direction a bit and he seemed to as well. He continued to come directly toward me. As he came near, he looked up and said "Bad wind, isn't it?" and showed me the nearest entry into the pedestrian underground. He was cold as I was and his change of direction was to go into the building close to where I walked. I wish I could have apologized to that fellow. That experience stays with me.

I hope that others who heard your words will be more aware of the fear that lurks within many of us. It's unreasoned, but there. I hope to never forget my walk in Albany and the young man I encountered that cold day. Your candid comments last week meant a lot to me. Thank you.

Sincerely,

Marjorie McKinney

THE WHITE HOUSE

WASHINGTON

Marjorie —

Thanks for your thoughtful letter. Your story is an example of what makes me optimistic about this country!

It was a surprise and a pleasure hearing back from the president. Marg had never expected anything like that. She put the letter in a frame and hung it beside her favorite chair, the blue one with the wooden arms, so she could sit by it. And so that's what she did. She sat by it and did some soul-searching, just as the president had recommended in his speech.

She decided she needed to get out more. Soul-searching, she discovered, goes only so far.

"Convene a conversation on race . . . families and churches and workplaces." Marg thought about some of the other things the president had recommended in his speech. She drove over to Raleigh, attended one of the Moral Mondays civil disobedience protests that were gaining attention there. They were organized by religious leaders like the Rev. Dr. William Barber II, head of the North Carolina chapter of the National Association for the Advancement of Colored People (NAACP). For Marg it was uplifting to be among all those people marching, saying that black lives matter, saying that we have to protect voting rights for all.

She wondered why they didn't do Moral Mondays marches in Boone. (She didn't want to have to keep driving over to Raleigh.) So she got some people together. "Convene a conversation on race." Part of the reason they didn't have Moral Mondays in Boone, she found out, was there was no officially chartered local NAACP chapter in Boone—or anywhere in all of Watauga County, for that matter.

That's when Marg started collecting signatures. "We need a chapter."

On February 15, 2014, three years after her encounter with the kid in Albany, seven months after she'd heard Obama's impromptu speech about Trayvon Martin, the Watauga NAACP branch was officially chartered.

They held meetings. They invited speakers from Appalachian State University. They started seminars, an Unlearning Racism discussion group, a three-part UNpacking (our own) HATE series. They started the Coffee with a Cop series down at the Hospitality House. Hey, cops, they said, come on out and talk to the community that's so scared of you.

Somebody in one of the meetings got the idea about kickball. It's a few years going, the Community Unity Picnic, and of all the things that Marg, now seventy-five, and the newly established Watauga NAACP branch do, that's probably her favorite. They added a dunking pool. Everybody getting dunked—it's so hilarious. Black people, white people, Hispanic people, cops, kids, old people. Everybody likes kickball and getting dunked.

Marg circulates and makes sure people aren't sitting by themselves and also that everyone knows where the food is.

CHAPTER 11
Red Dot

"So I walked over to him, um, barefoot, stepping over all the glass and everything that he had shot. And he was still yelling, and he was still holding the shotgun, and I went to him, and—he was larger than me. My dad was a large man. And immensely strong—I never appreciated how strong he was until that day. But he just started crying and yelling that no one appreciated him and that everybody had forgotten him. And that everybody just shits on him. And that nobody cared. And so I put my arms around him to try to console him, and I guess he took that as a sign of aggression. And he started shooting, and I was trying to restrain him while he was shooting, and he just kept shooting and kept shooting, and at that point—I don't remember screaming. The only reason I know I was screaming is because my brother told me I was. I saw my brother run out of the house. I kind of emotionally shut down. My dad started crying, like sobbing uncontrollably. And I'd never seen my dad cry. As a marine, he put on this façade that he was so strong and that nothing could harm him. I'd never seen him cry. And so his phone was in his pocket, and it started ringing. I took it from him and answered it. It was our neighbor. He said the police were coming. I didn't want my dad to hear because I knew it would just make him even more angry.

So I hung up the phone, and I guided my dad to his room, and on his bed I saw he had laid out every single weapon that he had owned and all the ammunition that he had for those weapons. And I knew what he had planned to do. It was Christmas Eve.

"I was trying to console him and talking very soothingly and reassuring him everything would be okay and nobody was upset with him. I guided him to the front steps, and I got him on the porch. I was trying to push him to go down the steps into the front yard. And it was raining. I saw all of these people surrounding our house. I finally got him into the front yard. And my dad always kept a knife on him, which a lot of marines do. And so they saw the knife, and they told him to drop it. And, um, he wouldn't. So I tried to get it. And he dropped it, and then he tried to lunge for it. So then I tried to push it away, and we were both on the ground at this point when it was raining. And it was muddy. And it was cold. And I'm here, like, with the last amount of strength that I have physically trying to hold him to the ground, yelling for everyone to help me.

"I don't know how many people came to pick him up.

"At the hospital I cried in the hallway on a stretcher until I could no longer cry.

"On Christmas Day my mom, my brother, and I were cleaning up the glass and all the remnants of, um, the fish tank and everything that he had shot up. He shot the flag that was awarded to him when he retired and all of his medals and everything—all the memorabilia associated with the Marine Corps. We cleaned up as much as we could, and then I went upstairs, and I wrote the letter. That's when I wrote the letter. The VA doctors had failed him; his so-called friends had failed him; the Marine Corps had failed him. I didn't know where else to turn. And so I thought, *If the last person that I can think of is the president, and if that's my last resource, then I'm going to give it every single ounce of energy that I have.*"

At the White House, Ashley DeLeon's 2014 letter about the events that occurred at home with her father on Christmas Eve ended up in a pile just like all the others in the OPC hard-mail room. On a cold January afternoon, a staffer named Garrett picked it up. He read through it quickly, as he had done with the letter before it and the letter before that. A few paragraphs in, he slowed down. He rolled his chair back, started from the beginning again, and got to the end. "I need to take a break," he said to an intern nearby.

He took the letter with him on a walk and ended up at the desk of Lacey Higley, whose office was just across the hall from the hard-mail room. "I've been wandering around the hallway," he said.

"Are you okay?" Lacey said.

Lacey was by then used to identifying the various looks people had when they came to her desk. She was the person in charge of Red Dots. A Red Dot was an emergency. Suicide, self-harm, eating disorders, rape, domestic violence, addiction—the flow, as many as four hundred in one day, varied. The rule was that every Red Dot had to be processed within twenty-four hours, assigned to an agency or organization like the Substance Abuse and Mental Health Services Administration or the National Suicide Prevention Lifeline. This rule made more sense with email than it did with hard mail; weeks had already gone by since Christmas, the day Ashley put her letter in the mail.

"We have to figure out what to do," Garrett said, handing Ashley's letter to Lacey.

Lacey began reading Ashley's letter, then slowed down. She started from the beginning again and got to the end. She said she needed a walk, and so she did a lap around the first floor of the EEOB, and Garrett joined her, the two of them talking about what they had read.

Ashley DeLeon
Jacksonville, NC

FAYETTEVILLE NC 283
Coastal Carolina Area
26 DEC 2014 PM 3 ∟

The White House
1600 Pennsylvania Avenue NW
Washington, DC 20500

485
JAN 08 2015 ✓ #031

December 25, 2014

Dear Mr. President,

My father was a United States Marine for 22 years before retiring as a MSgt. As part of the infantry, he deployed on six occasions. Each deployment my father came back less and less like himself. He missed many moments of my life: birthdays, holidays, award ceremonies. He used to love to hunt, to fish, to spend time with my mother, little brother and I. But after he retired, my father was forgotten. You see, when my dad retired he no longer had the brotherhood of fellow marines; no one thanked him for his service; no one called to check on his well being. He was diagnosed with severe PTSD and was medically disabled.

So he drank. And drank. My father's alcoholism stole the man that I had known for 21 years of my life. He could easily spend $100 a night on alcohol. He would drink all night, come back at 6 am, sleep all day, and repeat the cycle.

I am a junior at the University of North Carolina Wilmington. My father never called me to ask how I was, how my classes were, or if I had a good day at work. Everyday I would look in the mirror and see the remnants of him in my facial features. But the man that I resembled so much, the man who constituted half of me, wasn't one that I knew any longer.

Christmas Eve was a rainy day in Jacksonville, NC Mr. President. I was taking a shower upstairs when I heard the first two shots. I knew it was him. As I jumped out of the shower and ran down the stairs in nothing but a towel I could see my father pacing in the living room with a shotgun in his hand and tears in his eyes. He yelled at me, his little girl, "Get the f*** out of my house! GET OUT!" And in that moment I knew that I had two choices: to run and leave my little brother upstairs & my dad with a loaded weapon. Or to stay. I chose the latter. You see, I chose to stay in that room and fight over that gun because I knew that my dad was still in there somewhere. He had to be. As I struggled with my father, he shot. And shot. The small girl who grew up waving the American flag at her daddy's homecomings yelled "NOOOO" from the bottom of her gut. Glass shattered. The dogs barked. And in my peripheral vision I saw my brother run out of the house.

I didn't care if I died Mr. President. I'm 21 years old and I would sacrifice myself without a second thought to save the man who raised me from taking his own life. Because when his country turned their back on him, I was still there. The light has long been gone from his eyes, but he is still my father. I am still his little girl. A little piece of me died that day. I will never be the same. This time of year is one to celebrate with family and to be thankful for the blessings provided to us. Instead I spent Christmas Day sweeping up glass and looking at my home riddled with bullet holes. Like a war zone.

I'm writing to ask for your help. Not for my family Mr. President. My family died that night. I'm asking you to help the others. The little girls and boys who have yet to see their mothers and fathers souls die away. They need help. Get them help. Don't forget about them. They need you. Just like Sasha and Malia need you. They do.

        With hope,
        Ashley De Leon

One thing everyone in OPC learned quickly was that they needed one another. They needed to talk this stuff out. The content of the letters, the constant pleas, the emotions jumping and bouncing off the page. It was impossible to explain to people outside of OPC what it was like to sit all day in the intensity of the material, and that's why so many OPC staffers lived with one another, roommates commuting together, eating dinner together, watching Netflix together. Lacey lived with Vinnie and Steve, then Mitchell, then Heidi. In the office she shared a wall with Yena, and throughout the day they would knock on it, give the signal: *Come over here and read this one, please. I can't deal.*

Lacey was taller than most of her friends, lanky and unadorned; she moved with a stiffness that suggested her height was a burden. She was just twenty-three, and if you asked her to describe herself, she would say she was timid. Perhaps the last person you'd imagine being able to handle a portfolio as emotionally challenging as Red Dots. She had started at OPC as an intern while still in college. Walking to the EEOB that first day, she had felt like a bird falling too soon out of the nest. She got lost, called her dad in tears. "Help me." She believed she was too anxious to make it in the real world, her voice too thin, her throat too tight, air not moving. She would never make it in the real world. She thought there was something wrong with her, and surely one of the people at the White House would discover she had no business being among them. She had no background in government; she would not be able to participate in conversations about policy or policy making; unlike the others she had not worked on Obama's campaign—or anyone's campaign. She was a nobody who would never belong.

"One voice can change a room." If she had a favorite speech of Obama's, it was that one, an old one, inspired by a woman with a gold tooth. The woman with the gold tooth was in Greenwood, South Carolina, at a rally for Obama in 2007. The rally was a bust, no one there but a small gathering of local folks needing something to do. Obama was looking out at the emptiness. "Fired up, ready to go!" the woman with the gold tooth abruptly shouted. And as if on cue, the people around her repeated her words, began to chant, and in an instant the rally went from dismal to glorious.

"It shows you what one voice can do. That one voice can change a room," Obama said at a campaign rally over a year later, recounting the story. "And if a voice can change a room, it can change a city. And if it can change a city, it can change a state. And if it can change a state, it can change a nation. And if it can change a nation, it can change the world."

If you asked Lacey about her evolution from scared intern to the warrior who could handle hundreds of Red Dots every day, she would say it had to do with Obama and those words. One voice. One letter. One intern. Everybody matters.

"You will cry," she would tell each class of new interns that came under her charge, now that she was the person manning the Red Dot desk. "It's normal. You will see me cry at least twice while you're here. This work is intense. This work is hard. If you need to go home, you can go home."

. . .

When she finished her walk with Garrett that day, Lacey ran Ashley's letter through the scanner and forwarded the scan to the VA's crisis unit. She wondered about the idea of sampling the letter; what would happen if the president had a chance to read Ashley's story? It was not something people did. Red Dots were special cases that required emergency assistance, and taking the time to run them by the president could only bog down the effort, so they were never sampled. That bothered Lacey. She had herself recently begun treatment for depression and anxiety, and she knew all too well the damaging effects of the stigma surrounding mental health issues. Perhaps she was in a unique position to help raise the voices of people who were so often suffering in silence.

She saw Fiona in the hall. "The president needs to see this," Lacey said, handing Fiona Ashley's letter. *"He needs to see this."*

Everyone in OPC had one letter that defined his or her work, and for Lacey it would be Ashley's. She made a photocopy of it and taped it to the wall above her desk. She took a pink highlighter and marked the last paragraph.

> *I'm writing to ask for your help. Not for my family, Mr. President. My family died that night. I'm asking you to help the others. The little girls and boys who have yet to see their mother's and father's souls die away. They need help. Get them help. Don't forget about them. They need you. Just like Sasha and Malia need you. They do.*

"I hold on to it as my guidepost for what I'm doing and why I'm here," she would later say.

That afternoon, Fiona included Ashley's letter in the stack of 10LADs that went to the president.

The letter didn't come back in the next batch marked, "Back from the OVAL." It didn't come back in the batch after that either. Some letters the president sat on.

It would be more than a week before Obama had a response ready for Ashley.

THE WHITE HOUSE
WASHINGTON

Ashley —

I was so moved by your letter. As a father, I can only imagine how heartbreaking the situation must be, and I'm inspired by the strength and perspective you possess at such a young age.

I am asking the VA to reach out to your family to provide any support that you need. And please know that beneath the pain, your father still loves his daughter, and is surely proud of her.

Sincerely,

[signature]

"I received a manila envelope from the White House. And inside was a note—it was a small note, and it was handwritten by the president. I was completely taken aback. I didn't expect anyone to read it, much less respond to it. And it basically said to stay strong.

"They called me, and they put me in contact with the VA, and they were trying to get my dad resources that could help with his addictions and with his depression. But by that time I wasn't in contact with my father because I didn't feel safe around him to be honest. He went to FOCUS, a marine rehabilitation program, I believe.

"My mom tried so hard to try to get us to be closer again. That's my biggest regret—that I believed so much in the future, that I would have time to heal."

The conversation about Ashley and her dad didn't end with the president's response, or with the assistance from the VA to get him into a rehab program, or, for that matter, with Lacey's decision to hang the letter over her desk. Every letter that came into OPC was in essence a potential conversation starter that could zig and zag and meander throughout the White House and Congress and to people watching on TV.

When people in the West Wing talked about "the letter underground," this is part of what they meant. This whole thing was just supposed to be about the president getting ten letters a day, but it grew into something else; letters informed policy proposals and speeches, and they affected people personally.

Just seven weeks after Ashley sent her letter, on February 12, 2015, in the East Room, Obama signed the Clay Hunt SAV Act into law. "And SAV stands for Suicide Prevention for American Veterans," he said in his remarks, and it didn't take long to figure out whom he was talking about in the speech.

I think of the college student who recently wrote me a letter on Christmas Day. This is as tough a letter as I've received since I've been president. She talked about her father, who's a retired marine, and told me about how her dad used to love to hunt and fish and spend time with her and her little brother. But gripped with post-traumatic stress, he became less and less like himself and withdrew from the family. And yet, despite these struggles, she wrote, "I knew that my dad was still in there somewhere. . . . He is still my father. And I am still his little girl." And she was writing, she said, to ask for help—help her father find his way back—"not for my family, Mr. President," she said. "I'm asking you to help the others"—other families like hers. And she said, "Don't forget about them."

And that's really what today is about: Don't forget. . . . If you are hurting, know this: You are not forgotten. You are not alone.

You are never alone. We are here for you. America is here for you—all of us. And we will not stop doing everything in our power to get you the care and support you need to stay strong and keep serving this country we love. We need you. We need you. You make our country better.

So I thank all of you. God bless our troops, our veterans, our military families. God bless the United States of America.

"I was sitting on campus, I remember, by myself. I was streaming the video. And it was more towards the end of the remarks. They had asked my permission. I agreed, if they omitted my identification. I didn't know how my letter was going to be interpreted or if it was going to be misconstrued in some way. I just had all these thoughts racing through my mind. And then I heard it, and I started crying because he said that it was one of the hardest letters that he's had to read.

"We have this idea that the president is so much larger than us and that he's this other type of person. But he's exactly like we are.

"And so for him to read my letter and for me to see his reaction— that he was able to use it on a platform to help other people, that was powerful for me.

"My mom said that when my dad was watching the remarks, he cried. And he kept repeating that he was sorry."

Lacey hadn't heard the speech, so she didn't know why her Black-Berry was buzzing the way it was—emails from coworkers using exclamation points. People knew how important Ashley's letter was to Lacey. It was the first of many Red Dots to make it to the president's desk, and here was the president talking about it as he signed a bill into law. Lacey read Obama's remarks. She was so easily moved to tears; that part of her had not changed. Maybe this was as good as it gets for a letter, she thought. A person suffering, making a call for action, and the president hearing—and acting.

She would later decide to pursue a career helping veterans.

. . .

Months passed, and still Ashley had not talked to her father. She needed distance. She buried herself in schoolwork, began to feel strong for taking charge of her life.

"And then in May, I was intending on taking summer classes, so I was living on campus. I was getting ready for work, and I got the call around six A.M. And it was from our neighbor. And it was from my mom's phone, which I thought was odd. So I knew immediately something was wrong. He said, 'You have to come to Greenville. There's been an accident.'

"When I got to the ICU, they had someone come talk to me. And they were like, 'We're doing everything we can.' I asked all the questions I could. I'm the type of person that likes to know everything as soon as possible, and I like to have control of situations. And my dad was the exact same way. And so this, for me, was torture, because I didn't have control of anything. And they said they were doing everything they could do but that they didn't know. That's what they kept telling us—that they didn't know if he would make it. They didn't know if he would be normal if he did make it. They didn't know.

"He was in the first room on the left. And as I entered the double doors, I saw him. But it wasn't him. It was a completely different thing. It wasn't a person. I collapsed. I started yelling, 'No!' Just like I did when he was shooting. And I just kept yelling no. And they said that the main problem was that when my dad was on the motorcycle, he hit, um, an SUV at an intersection going fifty miles per hour. And when he inhaled, he inhaled all of the fumes. So that was burning his lungs. And they said you can't fix that. They said that there wasn't anything that anyone could do to fix that.

"They said, 'No, ma'am, we can't save him. You have to tell us what you want us to do.'

"I went through denial that it wasn't happening, that he was deployed and that he was coming back. Just like he was when I was little. That if I waited long enough, he would come back."

Samples, 2015

Ms. Alisa Bowman

Submitted via whitehouse.gov
6/27/2015 2:33 PM

Dear President Obama,

I've been voting Democrat since age 18, and I voted for you three times
(including in the primary against Clinton). Throughout your Presidency, I've
rooted for you and cheered for you and celebrated you. But last week, when
you said "Shame on you" to Jennicet Gutierrez, I felt chilled and
disappointed. You are a living example of civil rights progress. I've always
seen you as someone who gets the plight of marginalized and discriminated
against people. In that moment, I realized that I was wrong. You don't seem
to get it. Jennicet was not heckling you. She was merely trying to get your
attention -- on an important issue that affects a nearly invisible class of
people. I understand she may have done it in a rude way, but you are in a
position of great power and she is in a position of being marginalized. You've
so many times demonstrated your ability to be the big person -- the mature
person, the right person, the intelligent person. In this case, you stumbled,
and I forgive you for it. But please, make it right. I am not trans, but I am
raising a transgender child. This world terrifies me -- how it brutalizes,
openly discriminates against, and shames trans people. Gay marriage was a
big step, but only one step. You are in a position to take many more steps
before your last day in office. Please invite Jennicet to the White House and
hear her out. Please look into the injustices happening to trans women--
especially trans women of color. Please ask the attorney general to do the
same. Please listen to their voices rather than shaming them. That is all I ask.

THE WHITE HOUSE
WASHINGTON

Alisa —

Thanks for the letter, and the support.

I've got to disagree with you on my handling of the
heckler awhile back. This wasn't a public event;
she had been invited. We fully support the trans
community agenda, which is why they were so well
represented at the event. Rather than start shouting,
all she needed to do was talk to the numerous White

House staff who were there and already working with
the LGBT community on a wide range of issues.

So... there's a need sometimes to shout to be heard.
I'm an old community organizer, and have organized
disruptive actions myself.

That wasn't the time.

But I really appreciate your thoughtfulness and
compassion.

Simple/ TY Prayers

1 .. 7/9/15
f. 1

President Barak Obama
The White House
1600 Pennsylvania Avenue NW
Washington, DC 20500

Back from the OVAL
7/10/15

Reply

Dear Mr. President:

I am writing to tell you how my heart went out to you the other day when you announce
that you have to make too many announcements about violent episodes in this country
At that moment, I felt a deep kinship with you, albeit a rather sad one. You see I am the
pastor of a small church in Newbern, Virginia. Each time one of these horrors occurs I
know that on Sunday morning my little flock will be expecting their pastor to have
something meaningful to say to them – something that will help them make some
semblance of sense out of it all and offer them some comfort and hope. Frankly, Mr.
President, I have grown bone weary at this repeated responsibility and I have only
twenty souls in my care. Your congregation is so much larger.

I hope it is helpful to you to know there is a pastor in southwestern Virginia who
understands something of what you are going through and is keeping you in her
prayers.

Shalom, Mr. President,

Christine G. Reisman

Rev. Christine G. Reisman,
Newbern Christian Church

Christiansburg, VA

July 1, 2015

President Barack Obama
The White House
1600 Pennsylvania Avenue NW
Washington, DC 20500

Dear Mr. President,

As we approach Independence Day, and after I heard you sing Amazing Grace at my fellow Pastor's funeral, I wanted to share with you my story.

I grew up in a white, military, Christian, right wing family. I have always towed the republican line. I have never voted for a democrat in my life. I worked against your election and reelection, not that the republican candidates were so great, I just knew that democrats were "bad for America". But inside I was facing a struggle, a struggle I'd been dealing with since I was 6 years old.

I grew up, married a wonderful woman, helped create two awesome kids and have lived my life as a conservative Baptist minister. In December, my struggle nearly brought me to the point of ending my life and on December 7, 2014, I finally admitted to myself that I was gay AND that God made me that way. I shared this with my wife and it has been rough these 6 months. I am also looking for another job as this information would be grounds for dismissal in my church if it were discovered.

I write all this to tell you, thank you for being my President. After December 7th my outward perspective reflected the man within and your presidency changed in my eyes. You have done a remarkable job in spite of incredible opposition. From health care, immigration, marriage equality to normalization of relations with Cuba, your presidency will go down as historic. You have brought social justice to so many.

I see our flag in a new light now. To me it always stood for American power in the world, but today for me it stands for liberty and equality for everyone, no more second class citizens.

Thank you for being the first President of ALL the people. I am so proud of you, Mr. President. You have been so good for America and in fulfilling the vision for a truly free republic for everyone.

From the depths of my heart, thank you, Sir.

Cordially,

 REINVENTING
ReEntry

Scottsdale, AZ

Sue Ellen Allen, Founder

May 11, 2015

President Barack Obama
The White House
1600 Pennsylvania Ave
NW Washington, DC 20500

Dear President Obama:

You get a lot of mail. I hope this reaches your file, particularly in the light of the deep-seated rage that is exploding in our country. I'm sad, I'm privileged, and I care.

10 reasons why I'm privileged
1. White
2. College educated
3. Mother & Father who believed in me.
4. Taught in very underprivileged schools.
5. Worked in corporate America.
6. Served time in prison late in life with advanced breast cancer. Found my life purpose there.
7. Upon release six years ago, co-founded a 501(c)3 organization to bring educational programs into women's prison. Our success rate is an unprecedented 6%.
8. After AHA moment, founded a new nonprofit with a mission to educate and reshape society's perception of former inmates because Nothing will change unless the perception changes.
9. Am a Tigger in an Eyore world. I never give up.
10. Am aware that I'm privileged.

3 reasons why I'm not privileged
1. I'm old. Definitely a woman of a certain age.
2. I'm poor. I don't look or feel poor but legally I live below the official poverty line.
3. I'm a felon. I will have a prison number **forever**.

You know the recidivism rate. Imagine if Mayo Clinic or Apple with their budgets had a business plan with a 60% failure rate (through death or product returns). That business plan would be unacceptable. So why is our prison business plan with a 60% failure rate acceptable in our country?

School failures; dropout rates; marginalized, disenfranchised. Add to that the complete distrust of our police force. We have a problem. **Remember, I'm privileged.** I was taught to believe the police were my friends, lawyers never lied, and judges were fair and honest. **I was wrong.**

Mission: To educate and reshape our society's perception of former inmates so they may successfully reintegrate and be given a fair chance for employment, housing, education and entrepreneurial opportunities.

If you had told me what I would see and experience in prison, I would have said, "Not in our country. We don't treat people that way." **I was wrong**. Seven years in prison for securities fraud gave me my life purpose. The treatment inside is draconian; the preparation for re-entry is laughable.

Now that I'm out and have created two useful organizations, the judgement and treatment continue in myriad humiliating ways (like a decent place to live for starters). **Remember, I'm privileged.** How much harder is it for a poor Black or Latino man or woman?

How about a task force? Not one full of law enforcement, prison officials and academics. Consider former inmates who have from 5 to 30 years experience inside, mothers willing to chase their sons down the street during a riot, people sent down because they are mentally ill, women and men who are making a difference because of and despite their records. Real prison experts at the table. There are many of us who would be honored to serve. Then add some of the "officials."

The primary reason for this letter is to once again encourage you to visit a prison, not a sanitized Presidential visit (OK, that might not be possible), but a real one, talking to inmates and seeing their cells, eating real prison food. This would be a powerful message to the 2.3 million incarcerated Americans. Most attorneys and judges have never been inside a prison except in the sanitized visitation room. No president has ever visited. You have no idea of the horror inside.

President Obama, you are my president. I admire your approach, your intellectual style, your dignity and your sense of humor. Believe it or not, I've only been disappointed about your approach to racism. I think you should be tougher. The conservatives won't like it, but they don't like anything you do so why worry? The progressives would love it and there are a lot of us just waiting for this part of your leadership. This task force of former felons would be a great start, especially if someone listens. Currently, we are invisible and voiceless. Please see us and be our voice.

Sincerely,

Sue Ellen Allen
Founder

PS: I know your staff seems to chose letters for your folder that are handwritten but I wrote with a golf pencil for a long time and swore I'd never do that again.

Mission: To educate and reshape our society's perception of former inmates so they may successfully reintegrate and be given a fair chance for employment, housing, education and entrepreneurial opportunities.

From: **Yolanda**

Submitted: 10/16/2015 4:08 AM EDT

Email:

Phone:

Address:

Message: Dear Mr. President and First Lady Obama,
This is Yolanda   and it is with a grateful heart that I write this letter to you. I wrote previously a couple of years ago, telling you about my status as a veteran who is disabled and was living out of my car and constantly having nightmares from sexual trauma that occurred while I was in the Navy. You and your cabinet made a national declaration to all states to work on ending homelessness. I let you know about my silent prayer of wanting to be a productive member of society, able to live, pay rent, and contribute. I did not want to die on the side of the road like a piece of trash.

It is with grateful tears that I am able to tell you that today, I signed a lease to Veterans Village for a 1 bedroom apartment. I am able to pay for it with my OWN money. The application process was rigorous and I was fearful that I would not be able to obtain one as there were 2000 other applicants whom I am sure had more money than me. It was my last hope. I had no other game plan left, I thought my car would be my grave.

Today, I cried tears of joys. I was so proud to be able to give them the money order for rent. It made me feel good that I have a budget and that I am making a productive move. It is all thanks to you, your administration, your staff, and your followers. I am not a number, I am not a piece of dirt that people spit on, I am not forgotten, and I am not unworthy of anything.

God bless you Mr. President and First Lady. I wish I could give you a hug or shake your hand. Something to express these tears of joy that will not stop flowing. I am literally 10 minutes away from my church where I do a lot of volunteer work with the youth and young adults. I am living!!! I am being productive!!!! I NOW have a place to live, a place I can call HOME. How can I express this gratitude that keeps me smiling and my eyes glistening? I Love you and all that work with you!!! Please communicate with them, that I do not take this lightly, I will live up to this graceful gift that has been given to me.THANK YOU!!!! I will make a photobook of my apartment and send it to you so that you can see what all your work as the President and First Lady has done. I will tell all who will listen. I pray God blesses you, your family, your administration, your staff and all whom honor is due.

Sincerely, Yolanda

6/30/15
fr 8

From: Mary Susan Sanders
Submitted: 6/27/2015 12:02 PM EDT

Reply personally — and copy.

Email:
Phone:
Address: Kansas City, Missouri

Message: Mr. President, I was deeply touched by your Eulogy in Charleston. After wiping the tears from my face, I got my paint brush and paint and went to the lawn jockey on my deck. It represented my heritage: a white, privileged woman from Nashville, Tennessee. I had great uncles who fought for the Confederacy during the Civil War. Now I live in Kansas City. I always told myself this black lawn jockey, like the Conferate flag, was a relic of history. But your words : "that Confederate flag represents more than one history", finally resonated. I began to cry. With all the pain in that Church, with all those families grieving, I made a decision. I went to that lawn jockey and painted him Caucasian. I never want to be the cause, directly or indirectly, to anyone's suffering. Thank you, Mr. President. I believe you are one of the Greatest Presidents our USA has ever had.
Because I'm also gay, I now feel I am a bonafide American.
Respectfully submitted,
Mary Susan Sanders

THE WHITE HOUSE
WASHINGTON

Mary Susan —
    Thanks for your letter. It's good hearted
people like you that always make me
optimistic about this country.

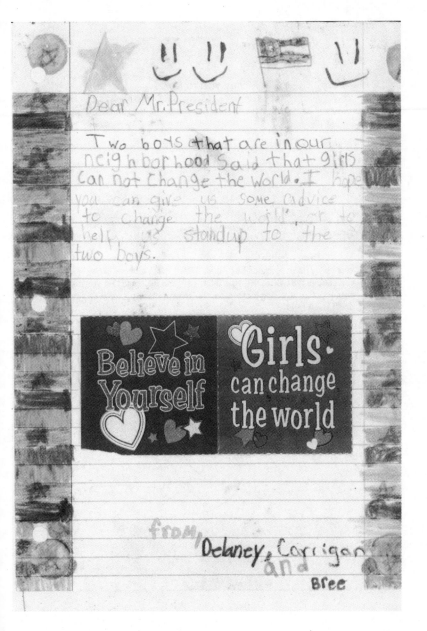

Dear Mr. President

Two boys that are in our neighborhood said that girls can not change the world. I hope you can give us some advice to change the world, or to help us standup to the two boys.

Believe in Yourself

Girls. can change the world

from Delaney, Corrigan and Bree

THE WHITE HOUSE
WASHINGTON

December 8, 2015

Dear Delaney:

Thanks for writing to me with your friends to let me know what was going on in your neighborhood. Don't listen to those boys—girls can change the world, and your letter gave me the sense that you are a strong group of young ladies who will always speak up when things don't seem right.

In the years ahead, remember nothing is beyond your reach as long as you set your sights high and stay involved in issues that matter to you. Know that our Nation is one where everyone can pursue their dreams and that with hard work, you can accomplish anything you can imagine. I'm confident all three of you have bright futures ahead—and if any boys tell you otherwise, let them know their President said they better start recognizing that girls change the world every day.

Your friend,

GPCL

Gretchen Elhassani

Wilmington, Delaware

5/1/2015

Dear Sir:

So many things happening in the world, and I feel selfish encased in my own skin, in my own dreams and aspirations. This isn't a political letter. It isn't a fan letter. It's just a letter, maybe a diary, something that I didn't want to put on the internet, and I didn't want to say to anyone I know. Maybe I choose you because I know you'll never read this, but I can put a stamp on it and drop it in the mailbox, and relieve myself of the burden of carrying these feelings around inside.

I am a writer. Not a successful writer, a struggling writer. See there, that was a sentence fragment.

I wrote a screenplay and entered it into a contest and I did not win. So I am sad. That's it. Thank you for reading.

Gretchen Elhassani

Registered Democrat
Non profit secretary
Mother

THE WHITE HOUSE

WASHINGTON

July 10, 2015

Ms. Gretchen Elhassani
Wilmington, Delaware

Dear Gretchen:

I am glad you trusted me with your letter, and I want you to know it was read.

I write a lot, too, and it seems we both know the challenges and disappointments it can bring. You shouldn't be afraid of those, though, and you don't have to worry about whether or not what you write will be considered good. I hope you'll keep working at your writing and reaching for your goals—that's the resolve that pushes America forward.

I appreciate the courage it took to send your note. Don't give up—have faith in yourself and hold on to the dreams that have brought you this far.

Sincerely,

Adam Apo

Chicago, IL.

Mr. President,

As the year nears its close, I realize my list of chores would not be complete without first offering you my humblest gratitude for the great honor and cherished experience you gave to me a few months ago. I am a gay teacher and librarian in a Catholic high school in Chicago; and in early September, I wrote you the first letter I had ever written to a President. I asked that as you meet the Holy Father, Pope Francis, in September, that you keep in mind my fellow gay brothers and sisters and the legal, cultural, and moral equality we continue to fight for in our daily lives. I wrote about hardships and discrimination I have faced as a gay man and as a teacher in a Chicago Catholic high school.

A few days after I sent this letter, I received a call from Max Sgro in your Office of Presidential Correspondence; and I was honored to hear that you had read my letter and that I was invited to the South Lawn for Pope Francis' arrival ceremony. I cried during the call. The privilege of such an occasion was unmatched in my life. And despite many travel complications, Max worked diligently to see to my arrival. He even went so far as to meet me outside the White House perimeter in the early morning hours of the event to hand me my ticket personally. His hospitality was remarkable, and the experience of a member of the federal government working directly for me during those moments humbled me and breathed new air into my love for my country. Furthermore, that night he led me in a tour of the West Wing. In one of the hallways I saw a photograph of the North Portico illuminated in rainbow colors following the *Obergefell v. Hodges* decision. This was an emotional moment I will cherish forever. As a boy in Hawaii, I never thought I'd have the strength to embrace my identity, yet there I stood, personally invited to the White House, having walked the halls of the administration that fought to secure my legal right to marry. I was filled with overwhelming pride for my President, my country, and myself.

Unfortunately, I was asked by my school to withhold the news of my letter entirely. This terrific example of how an ordinary citizen, by the written word, can excel his cause to the highest office in the land, and earn the momentary ear of the President of the United States—will never reach the students who need to hear it. It was snuffed because I am gay, and because it was presumed that people in my community are not yet ready to accept that one of their teachers is gay. And while I've successfully kept my name off the growing list of gay teachers fired from schools, it does not come without pain. It makes me weary, but I have hope. And I remember the surprise and gratitude I felt when standing in the West Wing and I saw that photograph proudly hung.

Thank you, Mr. President, for all that you do, all that you've done, and all that you will do to change our history and arc it toward a greater equality for all.

With highest regards,

Adam Apo

PS: I can't wait to see your Presidential Library in Chicago! Looking for a librarian?

124-
Sample
immigration
hardship
4/1/15
fr 1

March 14, 2015

Dear President Obama,

The year was 2000, we had a small apple orchard in Eastern WA, a bright eyed 4 year old came into my house. Her family was picking apples outside and I was going to read to her in my house. She looked around and asked "what do you do with all these rooms." I told her just my husband and I lived here, but my daughter would come visit and she could have a room. I fell in love with that little 4 year old and have followed her life since that day. Attending her Cincenera and high school graduation and other milestones in her life.

Yesterday she called me sobbing that her dad had been taken away. His crime, he was trying to work. Now please understand I have known this family of 4 plus their extended family since 2000. All I can tell you about them is they came to work from Mexico. Her father said, I came to make a better life for my children. Some have graduated from colleges and hold respectable jobs. Her father's immigration papers have been a problem. Her mom has always worked and just excitedly told me her "papers" will be finalized by July.

I am aware you have worked so hard with congress to get a bill passed to assist persons living in our country without proper papers, but this has been difficult for congress to complete.

I feel such sadness, like I have lost one of my sons, but the grief this family, mom, sister, brother are feeling is immeasurable. I ask that you could please do anything in your power to assist the people of our country who are here undocumented who are just looking to make a better life and work become legal citizens.

Most sincerely,

Sheryl L Cousineau

Sheryl Cousineau

Kennewick, WA

THE WHITE HOUSE
WASHINGTON

September 15, 2015

Mrs. Sheryl Cousineau
Kennewick, Washington

Dear Sheryl:

Thank you for taking the time to write me a letter. This country's immigration system has been broken for a very long time, and stories like yours underscore the hardships created by this system. It's clear you care deeply about fixing it.

America is not a nation that kicks out hardworking people who strive to earn a piece of the American dream. We're a nation that finds a way to welcome them and to harness their talents so we can make the future brighter for everybody—that's the legacy we need to leave to the next generation.

Again, thank you for writing. In the months ahead, I will keep your letter in mind as I continue to do everything in my power to ensure America remains a place where all of us have the chance to live up to our fullest potential, and where we celebrate the diverse contributions of immigrants across our great Nation.

Sincerely,

November /21/2015

President Barack Obama

I am a Syrian girl. I am 17. I want to start by my life in Syria.

Before the War, my life was perfect. I used to make a small party with my friends every Friday. I lived in Idleb, in a small Town is called Taftanaz. My school was good. I liked my friends and my teachers. I was a little child. That made my life perfect.

When the War started, the Syrian army attacked our town. Its tanks destroyed my school and some of my house. I heard much of the sounds of bombing. Because of that, we crossed into Turkey. We found a house and we rented it. There, a Syrian man established a school for all Syrian children. It was very nice choice. I met a lot of girls from other cities of Syria. I learnt many things. My little sister sufferes from autism, we requested to come here because we could not find choices to go to the Turkesh Collages. For tunnnately, your organization accepted our request and we did come.

America is nice country. People here respect us. The School is good. Your curreculm is easy. I like it. I want to be a dotctor in the future

The helpings you give us are good. My language is not full yet, but I'm learning. I don't have any idea about your universities. I need that in order to forget every thing I saw in Syria. I am Thankful, I thank you from my heart because every thing is nice. My teachers at School here are helpful. They are trying to help me as they can. That makes me better. I edored math. I like the American Pizza and pickle. Very nice food. The most important thing is that I'm free and living in peace with my family.

  Best wishes,

Heba Hallak

THE WHITE HOUSE

WASHINGTON

May 9, 2016

Heba Hallak
Short Hills, New Jersey

Dear Heba:

Your letter reached my desk, and I wanted to thank you for writing to share your story with me.

I know it must have been difficult to leave your life behind in Syria and make new friends here, but I am glad to hear you are enjoying school—and the pizza—in the United States. Despite all you have been through, I want you to know that America will always be a place where brave young women like you and your sister can come to learn, thrive, and find a sense of belonging.

The optimism and determination of families like yours are what help set our country apart. I trust you'll keep working hard in school and reaching for your dreams—as long as you do, I'm confident there are no limits to what you can achieve.

Sincerely,

From: **Mr. Dane Jorgensen**

Submitted: 10/11/2015 12:52 AM EDT

Email:

Phone:

Address: Salt Lake City, Utah

Message: Mr. President, thank you.

In 2008, I couldn't afford to go to college. I tried to get student loans and was rejected. Later, because of actions taken by you, in 2009, I was eligible for and received a Pell grant and a student loan which allowed me to attend college. With federal student aid I could afford to attend college, and in May of 2015, I graduated with my bachelor's degree in Accounting. Before 2009 I had spent two years trying save enough money to attend school but, the cost of attending was always beyond the reach of my savings. Mr. President, I don't know you but; when your actions made it possible for me to pursue a college education; it felt like you knew me. It felt as if you knew how desperately I wanted to be able to afford a college education and YOU, Mr. President, decided I deserved a chance. I now earn a good wage working as an accountant at a property management firm. God bless you Mr. Obama. I will always regard you as my President because; you were the President who believed in me.

Your friend,

Dane Jorgensen

CHAPTER 12

Friends of the Mail

And why should the president be the only one reading ten letters a day? What about everyone else in the West Wing? Surely Obama's advisors and senior staff could benefit from seeing this material. "We're all kind of obsessed with this idea that this is where government is at," Yena told me. "This is the juice." Advancing the mail's reach would become an overarching OPC mission. Fiona and her team began to see it as their obligation to the letter writers, and their obligation to policy makers, and, if you got them talking about it long enough, their obligation to America: Be a megaphone for these voices. Open all the channels, full blast.

"Basically, I just started spamming people," Fiona told me. She developed a distribution list, kept adding to it. Letters to the president, dozens of them, just popping into people's inboxes. Why not? And not just 10LADs but also others from the sample piles. "We send out batches of letters we think are striking," she said. At first she worried about being an annoyance, but then she got bold. "I hope people read them; that's why I spam them. But I mean, they don't *have* to read them."

They did. Soon, people started asking why they *weren't* on the distribution list. "I remember Valerie Jarrett's assistant reached out and said that Valerie wanted to be added," Fiona said. "She had been perceived as so senior that we were not spamming her." They put her on the list. Soon the people in OPC came to know which people in the West Wing were particularly tuned in to the letters. The OPC staff came to regard these people as special agents, ambassadors, and they had a name for them: Friends of the Mail.

Shailagh, of course, was a Friend of the Mail. She told me that the constant flow of letters into the West Wing was part of the regular morning conversation among senior staff. "We'd receive them by email, and then different people would distribute specific letters that caught their eye. The chief of staff, Denis McDonough, would often distribute letters at our senior staff meetings. Just flagging things that were interesting to him or that he found especially poignant. Everybody had a different definition of what they thought was a great letter. For me, a great letter was one that would make me feel confused about issues and expand my understanding of the implications of what we were doing."

Dear Mr. President,

I have never had more conflicting emotions about a public figure. I was deeply discouraged when I heard about the ICE raids. But, you . . . have also fought hard to change the criminal justice system. There are many people in my social network that were unjustly criminalized because of their drug addictions. However, the consequences that drug convictions have on immigrants . . . remain inhumane under your administration.

. . . I have been very disappointed in you. I have also never been more proud of a president before you. . . .

Lisa K. Okamoto
South Pasadena, CA

Valerie Jarrett, Obama's longest serving senior advisor, became a Friend of the Mail. For her, the letters were a kind of nourishment. "When you're having a really bad day in Washington, there's nothing like picking up a letter from a citizen," she told me. Sometimes she would be so moved by a letter she would pick up the phone and call the person. "I want to just emphasize: Washington is so impersonal," she said. "Imagine your worst impression of what it would be like and then magnify that. It's removed. It's *physically* removed. You get caught up in the sausage making." She believed that the administration's emphasis on continued contact with constituents was a reflection of Obama's own struggles with that separation. "He did not enjoy the isolation. He spoke about it often. That human interaction—he craved it.

"What I remember is an overarching request that the president gave to us to ensure that we had regular interaction with the American people," she said. "And it began with what his wife did the day after Inauguration Day, when she opened up the White House to the American people and said, 'Please, come in. This is your house. This is the people's house.'"

And so picking up the phone and calling a letter writer seemed to her like a perfectly natural thing to do, like checking in with a neighbor. "I'd ask people what motivated them to write, and more times than not, they would say they wrote out of a feeling of frustration or desperation or inspiration, love."

Love, frustration, desperation—that was the stuff you couldn't get if you were caught up in the sausage making. The letters were access. The letters were emotion, context, and narrative.

I reached out to other Friends of the Mail and found ideas like that emerging and reemerging, going back to the earliest days of the administration and the days of the campaign. David Axelrod, who served for years as Obama's senior advisor and chief strategist on both his presidential campaigns, said the letters were Obama's lifeline from the start. "They were more than a kind of ceremonial nod to, you know, to the grassroots," he said. "Remember, you have a guy here who four years before—a little more than four years before—was a state senator. Basically representing some communities on the South Side of Chicago. And his habit was to travel that district and interact with people. And so to go from that experience in four years to being the president of the United States is, you know—it only accentuates the loss of contact.

"I was impressed by how faithful he was to the practice," he said, about the 10LADs ritual. "I saw him go back to his residence with—I mean, ultimately it was carried over there because it was such a load for him to put on the elevator. It always impressed me that he made the time for the letters.

"But, I mean, look, you serve in the White House. Everyone who's worked there and everyone who's sat in that Oval Office has served the people. So I don't mean to make invidious comparisons and suggest that somehow he was more virtuous than others. But the regularized communication he had with people seemed to me to be pretty extraordinary."

One thing I noticed about all of the Friends of the Mail I reached out to was they were delighted to learn that people in OPC thought of them as Friends of the Mail—"Oh, it's so true!"—and they readily volunteered names of others I should know about. There were recognizable names like Illinois senator Dick Durbin, White House press secretary Robert Gibbs, and speechwriter Jon Favreau, as well as plenty of people I'd never heard of, and the names kept multiplying—two more here, six more there, and then each of *those* people had more names. It got so I started wondering, *Is anybody over there in the West Wing* not *a Friend of the Mail?*

Probably not, Chris Lu told me. He served as deputy secretary of labor for the administration and White House cabinet secretary; before that he was in the trenches with Pete Rouse on the transition team and in Obama's senate office. Chris talked about getting "steeped in the ethos of how we do mail in Obama world" as a kind of credentialing. "It's one of the things that was really kind of ingrained in us," he said. If you didn't appreciate the mail, you wouldn't have lasted. In Obama world, letters were part of the deal.

"The president would say, 'Send this to Secretary Vilsack, and I want to know what his response is,'" he told me. "And believe me, those letters went. I would send it to, in this case, to the Department of Agriculture. And they understood. A fire was lit under those agencies to respond.

"I think it's all part of the broader spirit of transparency," he said. "The idea is that government works best when people can participate in that government. And look, obviously when you're in a country of three hundred million, it's hard to do that. But people express their views not only by voting; people express their views by writing letters."

Like so many others, Chris Lu told me that Obama carried letters around with him. If not the actual paper they were written on, which he sometimes would, then the stories they told. It was, he said, simply the way Obama thought. Stories were how he bracketed ideas. Stories had protagonists. The protagonists were the *point*. The letters would provide an ongoing supply of material. A ready inventory of parables.

Speechwriter Cody Keenan (Friend of the Mail) said the letters were constant fodder for speeches. "The president will just call me upstairs and say, you know, 'Read this letter; this is awesome; let's work this into something,'" he told me. "I remember when we were embroiled in a debate with Congress about extending unemployment insurance. And we got this letter from a woman named Misty DeMars in Chicago. She was just like your totally average American, and she and her husband had just bought a house. She got laid off because of budget cuts, and she was like, 'We are the face of the unemployment crisis.' Whereas the Republicans then were casting it as, like, you know, these greedy minorities trying to game the system. POTUS was like, 'Boom! Misty DeMars. This is exactly what we're talking about.'" Cody built the 2014 State of the Union address around her story.

> Misty DeMars is a mother of two young boys. She'd been steadily employed since she was a teenager. She put herself through college. She'd never collected unemployment benefits. In May, she and her husband used their life savings to buy their first home. A week later, budget cuts claimed the job she loved. Last month, when their unemployment insurance was cut off, she sat down and wrote me a letter—the kind I get every day. "We are the face of the unemployment crisis," she wrote. "I am not dependent on the government. . . . Our country depends on people like us who build careers, contribute to society . . . care about our neighbors. . . . I am confident that in time I will find a job. . . . I will pay my taxes, and we will raise our children in their own home in the community we love. Please give us this chance."

Misty attended the State of the Union address, sat next to Michelle Obama, and clapped on cue. The tradition of "stacking the First Lady's box" with constituents had started under President Reagan. Over the years, presidents would use the practice as a way of illustrating certain policy issues or to honor heroes. For Obama's team, stacking the First Lady's box was a simple matter of digging into the mail.

"If there was a way to make every letter he got for eight years a piece of data somehow," Cody said, "put all that data together, that would tell a pretty great story. Whether it was love finally recognized. Or despair and fear turned around. Or hopes unfulfilled. Or fear unaddressed. Or prayers answered. I mean, if there was some way to quantify that into trend lines, it would tell a pretty big story of America."

He said the letters helped inform Obama's attitudes about ending his two terms in office. "You know, he'll close a speech by saying, 'My faith in America is stronger than ever,'" Cody told me. "And people say: 'How can you say that when the country looks poised to elect some demagogue?' But it is true. And I think it has to do with these letters. He sees the unvarnished, unedited dramas of the American people every day—in a way that most people don't. We all go to our curated Twitter feeds and to our Fox or MSNBC corners and kind of wrap ourselves in our own worldviews, with people who think exactly like we do. And we assume the worst in the other side. But he sees the mail. You know? Fiona's good about giving him a really representative sample. Some are like, 'You're an asshole, and I can't wait till you lose.' But most are at least kind, even in their disagreement. One of the letters he told me to put in the convention speech this year was—there was a conservative, from, I think, Texas, who basically wrote to say: I disagree with you on absolutely everything, I'm opposed to almost everything you stand for, but I appreciate that you've been a good dad. He loves that letter."

Dear Mr. President,

As the father of three daughters, I am touched to see President Obama with his girls. Politically it would be hard to find someone further apart, I am a rabidly pro-gun libertarian, but I appreciate the

sacrifices you make to serve our country and the stress on your fam-
ily. I am always happy to see you as a father. I just saw your visit to
central park and wanted to take the small chan[c]e you['d] see this
message. Long after your term as president is done, your job as a
father will continue and all accounts suggest you are doing a great
job. It is also encouraging that if the leader of the United States can
take the time to walk in the park with his family, the rest of us should
take the time to do the same.

God bless you.
Dr. Joshua Racca
Flower Mound, TX

"I've always looked at the letters as hopeful," Cody added finally. "It's
even—no matter how painful or upset your letter might be, there's
still something hopeful about sitting down and thinking that maybe
somebody will see this. There's a hope that the system will work.
Even if you're sitting down to write, 'Dear Shit-for-Brains,' there's a
chance that someone might read it, you know?

"There was one letter, one of the best ever, was just this guy who
was broke, and screwed, and completely out of luck, and then he got
a job as a dishwasher and said it's the best thing to ever happen to
him. And he completely credited Barack Obama for it, even though
I can't think of anything we did to help him get a job as a dishwasher."

Hey Mr. President Barack Obama

I just want to write to you from Richmond, Virginia and let you
know my life is getting better. A few years ago I didn't have a job and
my whole family was scrambling to make ends meet. I prayed daily
that something would happen positive for this young man on the
brink of a nervous breakdown.

I was at home watching television and the phone rang. I was sure it
was a bill collector. Turns out it was a hotel in need of a dishwasher.
I was so happy. To make a long story short I got the job and I have
been there for two (2) years now. I [at]tribute my job finding to the

Obama Administrations relentless work to turning the economy around. I am a witness and now instead of visiting the food closet at our local church, me and my family can donate three (3) or four (4) cans a week so someone else experiencing hard times can eat. Thank you Mr. Obama!

[Name withheld]

And why did that guy think to write to Obama? That was the question that Shailagh would continually get stuck on. "You know, just going back to this notion of, like, Who are you going to tell this story to? *Well, I think I'll write to the president of the United States.* I mean, that's a powerful insight into how people view leadership and kind of still idealize it, even though they may pretend not to."

For Shailagh the letters became a resource for study, a sociology project, a history lesson. "I started looking back through letters chronologically, to get a different version of the presidency," she told me. "Establishing the public trajectory of the presidency as opposed to the legislative one or the policy calendar. This was the outside looking in."

One of the things she found was confirmation that these voices provided a kind of emotional nudge to decision-makers.

"It's apparent through these letters alone," she said, "even despite the political risk of doing a partisan healthcare bill, for example, why we stuck to that and saw it through, even at a pretty heavy political cost in the midterm elections. The raw terms that were revealed, time and time again, in letter after letter after letter, of people up against these incredible headwinds," Shailagh said, "and the one thing we could do for them was create at least a foundation of health-care coverage where they were going to get . . . *something.* It's a totally different perspective on decisions like that. You think, *Oh, that was naïve of Obama to try to pass that healthcare bill with just Democratic votes. Didn't he realize he was going to lose Congress over that?* Well, if you're reading ten people a day, eight people a day, dealing with health-insurance problems and huge COBRA payments after having lost their jobs—it's a totally different perspective on it."

Senior staff could have, after all, opted to synthesize the voices coming out of the mailroom. They could have made charts indicating trends. "Imagine if Obama received them and we digested them for him," Shailagh said. "Just summaries of the letters, for instance. Any of these letters you could condense into a couple sentences, get the point across, without the texture and the voice and the color. And he would certainly be able to track what people were concerned about, you know? But you wouldn't have those Bobby Ingram voices; the depth; the personal, plaintive cries; and the stories as vignettes. All those things would be lost."

The human side of the story, the ideas you can't squeeze into a briefing memo or translate into bar graphs or dots on a chart. The voices of letter writers were a constant chorus in the background, pop songs you couldn't get out of your head, the tunes that defined a culture.

"I think it's the absence of that," Shailagh said, "that produces a different outcome."

CHAPTER 13

Shane Darby,
February 2, 2016

KILLEN, ALABAMA

Shane Darby does not remember anything about what he wrote to the president or when he wrote it. If you're telling him it was February 2, 2016, well, he'll have to believe you, but that is surprising. That would have been just three days after everything happened. So whatever he put in the email must have been pretty terrible. Just, like, anger. That is the only thing he remembers. But why he would have written to President Obama about it, he has no idea. He's almost embarrassed to look now.

Please don't bother Stephanie with this. It has destroyed her. The person she was on the day before January 30, 2016, will never be seen again. She's doing well, given what happened.

Stephanie is sitting over by the corner hutch, listening. Not really moving, as she tends not to these days. Shane is a big guy. Thick goatee, wire-frame glasses, dressed in a black T-shirt with Mickey Mouse on it.

They bought this house two months after the funeral. It was a way of keeping Stephanie distracted. Looking at houses. The idea of decorating. And just getting away from Crissy's room and all the memories. Her door squeaked. You would not believe. He used to say good night, then shut the door super slow, let the squeak go on and on, until Crissy would say, *"Dad!"* Every night. And if she was in a crappy teenage mood (which she hardly ever was), she couldn't maintain it if the squeak went on. Every time. *"Dad!"* She was so funny. Nothing embarrassed her. Imagine a teenager choosing to go to dinner with her family over her friends. And, like, excited to go on vacation with them. A teenager loving her parents the way she did. Father's Day, taking him to see the Superman movie, showing up dressed all in Superman gear, including socks. Those socks had capes sticking out the back. Little red capes. He was like, "I can't believe you."

Crissy and Stephanie—they were like twins. They might as well have been twins. Same sense of humor. Best friends. Texting all the time. Crissy was *happy.* Honestly, there were no signs. Not one. Of course then you get into: Was he paying attention? Could he have seen something if he was paying closer attention? That is basically what every parent who has ever suffered through something like this thinks. That is where you are stuck and will be stuck for the rest of your life.

So.

It's crazy he wrote to Obama. First of all, he's a Republican. But not political. Well, he tried getting into politics; like in 2000 he paid attention to George Bush and Al Gore arguing, but after a while he quit. Nothing people in Washington, D.C., did had any effect on his life. It was better to just leave it be. So why he would have gone to the computer and typed an email to the president of the United States—it makes no sense. He doesn't even hardly use the computer. He's an iPad and iPhone guy.

Stephanie would like to put the dog to bed now. He's a golden-doodle. Yeah, pretty chill. Stephanie guides the dog to the crate, goes back to her spot by the hutch.

This house is spotless, the way Stephanie keeps it. It's like a museum. Nothing moves. He does his part. She chose the pink for the under-chair rail part. All the white wood in the kitchen. Everything is spotless, and the lawn outside is carpet smooth, and the bushes they put in are the kind that hardly grow, so you don't have to do anything.

Shane manages a paint store. Stephanie is a mail carrier. Cassie is the youngest daughter. The Cassie part is a whole thing he would like to redo. She was seven at the time. In the back seat, just sitting there. Stephanie out in the parking lot with the phone, collapsing. Him throwing up. Cassie sitting there watching this. Seven years old.

One thing that happens when someone in your family dies is people bring you food. He used to think that was the dumbest thing. Like, a roast beef is going to help? Turns out it does. Like, deeply helpful. All of that outpouring. Plus him and Stephanie had stopped eating. Stopped going to work. Mostly he just sat in his room.

The military doesn't tell you anything. There's a number you call where they're supposed to tell you things. But that guy was a robot. "No information at this time." Same thing, over and over, to the point where you're like, *"Can't somebody go bust her door down?"*

Maybe they already had and they weren't allowed to say. Maybe. The whole way they handled it—

That sound? Okay, believe it or not, it's the clock, like a cuckoo clock, but not. Just listen. It's playing "Hey Jude." The batteries are low, so it doesn't play the whole thing. At Christmas they switch it, and it plays Christmas carols. They're big on Christmas. You can see in this picture they're all dressed like elves. Even Crissy. Imagine a teenager wanting to do something like that. She was bubbly. She had that long blond hair. You see her military portrait, and it's unrecognizable.

An eighteen-year-old should make her own decisions. That's why he didn't go with her to the recruiter. But *the military?* Crissy? The girl in tie-dyed shorts and mismatched socks and Vans? She always had to have her Vans, even on those rare occasions you could get her to wear a dress. It did seem out of the blue, her wanting to be military. He thought she would be more suited to something where you use your people skills to cheer people up. When she was seventeen, she got a job at Shoney's. You know how they have that big dancing bear in the parking lot waving to people? She was the bear. Which is funny considering all her life she was terrified of anybody in costume. Like at Disney she would not go near Mickey or Minnie.

When Stephanie was Crissy's age, she did serve for a short time with the marines. So that may have been a part of it. But even that. Stephanie busted up her ankle, and they let her go or however the military does that. She didn't last long, and it's not like she was the type of person walking around like, "Oh, I hope my girls will grow up to be soldiers!" Nothing like that.

The air force recruiter must have been pretty convincing is all he can think. Germany was one place Crissy came home excited about going to. Paris. Japan. She was excited about the military sending her out to see the world. She always did like Epcot. Where you walk from country to country? That could have factored in too.

Special enforcement was her job. Military police. She worked the gates at Lackland Air Force Base. She said it was boring. He told her, "That's what it is being an adult; you have to do a lot of boring things." He was trying to instill values.

Lackland is fourteen hours away from Killen. So she couldn't just drive home. She would facetime Stephanie at least once a day. Usually a lot more. That one time she facetimed to show her mom a flame. Just a big flame on the stove. They were like, "Crissy, throw some baking soda on it!" But she left the iPad there in front of the flame, not saying anything. Maybe she thought it was funny. She didn't know how to cook.

So.

The first time she got DNA'd he didn't know what it meant. She was home on leave, and she said it casual. DNA means Do Not Arm. It means they take your weapons away for like a week because you said something that made them think you wanted to hurt yourself or someone else. She made it sound stupid, like they were being so ridiculous, like she was a kid getting caught chewing gum. So he didn't think much of it.

By the way, those figurines next to Stephanie are all Disney. All the princesses. There are more on the mantel. Then this candleholder is decorated with flowers from the funeral. That's a service you can get, making candleholders with flowers from the funeral. Yeah, he didn't know they did that either.

There was a relationship Crissy got in. Long distance. Crissy was air force, and the girl was army, and there's a thing—if you're married, they station you close together. So they got married. They didn't have a wedding. It was just quick. They got an apartment right outside Lackland. Him and Stephanie had different opinions on the relationship. But, look, this was Crissy. She could have loved a tree, and it wouldn't make no matter.

The second time she got DNA'd he probably should have thought more of it. Look, he had no experience with the military. They would give her somebody to talk to if it was serious, wouldn't they? She was fourteen hours away. They owned her. Here's where the anger comes out. He tries to keep it in. You would think they would want to protect their investment. Because that's what she was to them. An investment. But you don't have to protect your investment when you've got a busload of soldiers coming the next night. And the next night and the next. You don't have to care about any one person. If you're the commander at Lackland, you sit behind your desk watching them roll in, knowing they can be replaced.

The last Christmas Crissy ever had was in 2015. She saved up all her vacation so she could come home and go with them to Disney. His parents, Stephanie's parents, cousins—eighteen of them total. The fireworks over the castle were probably the biggest thing. They did the Bippity Boppity Boo breakfast. Crissy bit into the strawberry pancakes, and he looked over at her. "Crissy, are you *crying*?"

"It's just so . . . good," she said.

After that trip to Disney, she did not want to go back to the military. She said she wanted out. She was willing to accept dishonorable discharge in order to get out. Him and Stephanie were trying to keep her in. Stephanie has a ton of guilt over that. Being nineteen, you try to get them to follow through with their commitments to set them up for their future. But he should have just run off and brought her home. Let them do whatever court case they had to do with her. He could live with his child having a piece of paper that said they left the military. Hell, he'd *frame* that piece of paper.

The call came one month and four days after Disney. January 30, 2016. Him, Stephanie, and Cassie were shopping in Nashville, like two hours away. Good stores. Something to do. And at some point Courtney, their oldest daughter, in Texas, called to say, "I can't reach Crissy. Something feels weird."

And then it was just tiny bits of information. Basically nothing. They were shopping. They were starting to get worried. It was hours later, in the car headed home, that Stephanie got the Facebook message. "I'm so sorry about what happened to Crissy. I wish I could have done more."

What? What happened to Crissy?

They pulled the car over into a parking lot. A mall. They called everywhere. "No additional information at this time." They called the Red Cross. "Can you get us information?" They kept calling the military. "No additional information at this time."

Stephanie gets up, leaves the room.

He finally got on Twitter. He found Crissy's Twitter name. He found her partner's Twitter name. He tweeted. "Please call us. If you know what's going on, please call us, because no one will give us any information." Five minutes later the partner calls. Stephanie answers. Shane knew just by her face. Then she collapsed. Him calling the military again. "No information at this time." Stephanie talking to Crissy's partner. They weren't together anymore. She was the one who found Crissy. Stephanie collapsing. Him throwing up. Cassie in the back seat watching all this.

He doesn't remember driving home. He remembers the airman coming to the door. He felt sorry for that airman. Nobody should have to do that job. He remembers sitting in his room all alone. Roast beef. No one he felt he could talk to. He's not a person who talks to people, not like that, not about pain. And ugliness inside you.

Why she did this makes no sense. If she left a note even. If she had said something. They took her weapons away. Did they even talk to her? They treated it like it was the flu. She's in their hands. You would think they would want to protect their investment.

Greetings Mr. President and First Lady,

I know my letter will 99.9999% never get read by either of you, but I feel like for the first time in my adult life I must reach out to someone. My 19 year old daughter is dead. She took her own life Jan 30th at Lackland Air Force Base. She left home in 2014 the most happy girl you'd ever meet. If I could attach photos I'd show you a smile that would melt your hearts. I feel like the military failed her on many levels. She had made comments that screamed "get me help" and yet all they did was DNA'd her twice (took weapons away) for like two weeks at a time.

They advised her to get some help but low and behold her "amazing" military insurance would not cover the costs of speaking with

someone weekly, if it had my daughter may still be able to pick up a
phone and call home, but instead she's laying in Lackland, waiting
on a plane ticket home in a casket. Like I said I understand you wont
get this, or be able to personally reply to me, I'm sure I'll get an au-
tomatic reply, because what's my daughters life worth to anyone
who isn't her family? Nothing. She isn't a priority to anyone in
Washington DC, but if it was your family member laying in a casket
you'd be upset to. I did not vote for you, I didn't vote for anyone, but
I believe your family is the best, and most truth worthy family that's
been in the White House since our founding fathers. I believe you all
have tried very hard to correct the wrongs in our country and with-
out hidden agenda. I don't care about oil, immigration, or any of
that stuff. What I care about is another family doesn't get a knock
on their front door letting them know our Military Failed to help
their own. We send our babies to you, and you sometimes send them
back to us in a casket. Mr. President, and First Lady, I thank you for
your time if by any chance you see this.

—*Cristina's Dad*

Reading that now, he's surprised. It's not a good letter. He wishes he would've been angrier. If he wrote it now, it would have been angrier.

She had her weapons back. She wasn't DNA'd anymore. But she didn't use a weapon. That's not how she did it. That's where you think, *Well, was she just staging something to get someone's attention, and then . . . slipped?* You come up with all kinds of explanations. If she left a note. A clue. Something.

They waited for the military to send Crissy's body back. The waiting was a lot of extra pain. Over a week. That's too long to make a family wait to bury a child. "We'll call you when we know when we're sending her back."

They sent a video of a memorial they did at Lackland. The main guy over at the base talking about Crissy. Stephanie watched it. She told Shane, "Don't watch it." She said the video implied that a person who resorted to killing herself was maybe somebody who was weak. She said, "Don't watch it," and so he hasn't. He doesn't want to put himself in a situation where he would go down to Lackland and confront a man with that much power. It would not end well. Shane would end up in jail.

The military preys on people who don't know what the military is. That's how they do it. If you're wondering how they do it, that's how they do it.

He doesn't blame President Obama, which maybe is odd. If anything, he felt like Obama would be on his side. It's weird to think about. He felt the Obamas were human beings, at least. He did not know he felt this. It's weird to discover. You're alone in your room, numb. You're not a guy to talk, but you need to talk. You pick the president of the United States to talk to?

Maybe father to father, is what he felt. He never uses that computer. He doesn't know what compelled him. He doesn't remember hitting send.

The military did an investigation into what exactly happened. They haven't sent the report yet. It's been two years, and they still haven't sent anything. She wasn't DNA'd anymore. That's not how she did it. There were no signs. She spent the two days before cleaning her car. Playing with the dog. Just out of the blue. She wrote something on Twitter about missing her mom.

The recruiter who told Crissy about Germany, about Paris and Japan, he never said anything. He lives like fifteen minutes away, and he never called to say he was sorry to hear that Crissy killed herself.

August 5, 2016

Dear Shane:

Thank you for your heartfelt email. I was deeply saddened to learn of the loss of your daughter, Airman First Class Cristina Silvers, USAF. As the father of two daughters, I am profoundly and personally saddened by your loss.

Too many Americans suffer from depression, and our service members are no exception. Cristina's suicide is tragic and a powerful reminder of why we must continuously work to improve access to mental healthcare. It is still not a perfect system and we are working every day to close the gaps so we can move toward a future where other military families are spared the pain suicide has brought them. I will continue doing everything in my power to help ensure other families do not have to endure the terrible loss you suffered.

At this difficult time, Michelle and I hope cherished memories of your time with Cristina help temper your grief. You and your family will remain in our thoughts and prayers.

Sincerely,
Barack Obama

Shane put the letter away. It wasn't like he showed it around. The main thing he took from it was Obama spelled "Cristina" right. Most people put the *h* in there. The guy that has more power than anyone. More responsibility than anyone. For that brief moment, he's thinking about you and your family. Your daughter is in his thoughts.

Samples, 2015–2016

3/25/16
8:4

3/29/16

Reply personally

From: **Mr. Patrick Allen Holbrook**

Submitted: 1/14/2016 10:37 PM EST

Email:

Phone:

Address: Honolulu, Hawaii

Message: Dear, Mr. President

It's late in the evening here on Oahu, and the sun will soon be sinking behind the horizon into the ocean. I sight that gives me comfort when times are confusing, and peace at the end of a long day. Sir, I was injured in Afghanistan in 2011 it was my first deployment, and my last. I was medically retired from the US Army, and after some discussion with my family moved here to help heal the wounds-- it is slow in coming, but I remain hopeful. I started college when I arrived here it has been a difficult experience, but this summer God willing; I will be a college graduate. It's a funny thing fear, I wasn't afraid in Afghanistan, but I am horrified at thought of my future. I want to serve my country, make a difference, and live up to the potential my family sees in me. I am scared I think, because I have no plan on what employment to pursue. It is something that is extremely difficult to me, and with my family leaving the island soon; I am truly lost. Sir, all my life I've tried to find what a Good man is, and be that man, but I release now life is more difficult for some. I'm not sure where I am going, and it is something that I can not shake. P.S. I watched your final State of the Union, and I thought it was well spoken. I too dream of a sustainable future for the next generation.

Sincerely,

Patrick A. Holbrook

THE WHITE HOUSE
WASHINGTON

Patrick —

Thank you for your thoughtful letter, and more importantly for your service and sacrifice. I can tell from your letter you are already a good man; you just need to find the calling that will express that goodness — or it will find you. So trust yourself, and remember that your Commander-in-Chief didn't know what he would do with his life till he was in his thirties!

From: **Mrs. Kelli McDermott**
Submitted: 9/14/2016 12.37 AM EDT
Email:
Phone:
Address:
                    Levittown, Pennsylvania

Message: Dear Mr. President Obama,

My grandfathers have been shamed, exiled, and ridiculed most of their young lives. What made it more difficult for them is that they were an interracial couple. They do not like to be in the spotlight, but I wanted to share our story.

My grandfather Richard and Vietnam Veteran Grandfather Al have been together for 35 years. I have grown up knowing that there relationship was perfectly normal. Surrounded by friends and classmates who would ridicule and even bully me whenever I spoke up about the LGBTQ community. To me, there was nothing wrong with love and my grandfathers truly love each other. They have been waiting patiently in Georgia to get married and I was so happy to see their wait was over. On June 26, 2015, Richard and Al finally married. However, a month late my Grandpa Richard was diagnosed with pancreatic cancer. He passed on November 22, just five months after they finally tied the knot.

With a sad heart, I can live on knowing that my Grandfathers were able to make their dream reality. They were able to share their bond legally. My family and I miss him dearly, but it helps to know that Grandpa Richard passed as a married man to the love of his life. I wanted thank you, President Obama and all the politicians involved that made marriage equality leg from the very bottom of my heart. You truly changed the world for the better for my family I. Thank you.

With the Deepest Appreciation,
Kelli McDermott

William Johnson 961072
S.C.C.I
295 Justice Blvd
Griffin, Ga 30224

ATLANTA METRO 300

05 JUL 2016 PM 5 L

FOREVER
USA

White House
President OBAMA
1800 Pennsylvania Ave N.W
Washington DC 20500

485

JUL 15 2016

20500-

✓#035

485

JUL 15 2016

QC✓#028

9/19/16
f.b

Sample
HR

Dear Mr President

My Name is William Johnson. Im In
a Georgia prison serving a Five year Sentence
For Failing a Urain test. I Was self Medi-
cating Because I did Not have any Medical
Insurance And I dont qualify For the tax
Break For Me to afford Obama Care.
   I have been IN and out of Jails and
prison My whole Life All Because of My
Drug use. Without Regulations on the
Drugs I have to get on the Street the
quality of the drugs Very and so does
the potency. Whitch Makes for a Vary
dangerous Combination. Here is My point
and Why Im Writing you. When I was
Working and had Medical Insurance I
Had No problems With Law Enforcement.
When I Lost My Job and Insurance, I
started Buying Illegal Drugs on the Street
For Depresion I use Cocaine and Meth
for My Back pains I Buy pain pills on
the Street to. As Soon as I got Caught
With these types of Drugs I Was put
In Jail and then put on probation
the probation Department tells Me I
Cant Do any Drugs unless given to Me
From a doctor. Here Lies the problem.
No Doctor Will See Me Without Insurance.

And I Cant Afford Insurance. the prison System is full of people Just Like Me When I get out the State Will give Me a fresh Set of Clothes and 25 dollars. With No Medical Help. Letting Drug users out of prison Without ACCsess to Doctors is a huge problem they Will go Back to Self Medicating As Soon as they feel Sick. and then they Will Be Back In prison. In Georgia you Can Beat Someone to death and get food Stamps But IF you get Caught With an once of pot you Cant. I think the Affordable Care Act Should Include people Coming out of prison. you Want to Lower the Repeat Drug offenders this is a Clear Choice. the Working Poor Can Not Afford Medical Insurance even With the Tax Break Most Jobs are keeping there Employee's under 40 hrs. So they dont have to pay there Insurance that Loop Hole Needs to be Closed. More and More people are buying Street Drugs Because of these problems.

thank You
Can you please   William Johnson
Reply Back with A photo   /2016

THE WHITE HOUSE
WASHINGTON

January 13, 2017

Mr. William Johnson
Griffin, Georgia

Dear William:

Thank you for sharing your story with me. It's clear you've faced great challenges, and I want you to know I'm listening.

I believe that all people, even people who have made mistakes, have the capacity to make the right choices and to have a positive impact on those around them. Your story shows that improving our justice system will require broadening access to health care and public services, including for those who have been incarcerated. That is why I've worked to support reentry programming for adults with substance use disorders and improve the provision of treatment options. This includes the Affordable Care Act's provision to extend Medicaid to all low-income adults in all States. However, because of a Supreme Court ruling in 2012, each State must choose whether to expand Medicaid. As a result, Republican resistance in some States—like Georgia—has stood in the way of affordable coverage being extended to people like you, even though the Federal Government would cover virtually all of the costs. My Administration has been encouraging States like yours to expand Medicaid so more of our citizens can get the care they deserve, and your message drives us in that effort.

Thank you, again, for your letter. If you have faith in yourself and work hard to pursue a productive path, you can affect not only your own life but also the lives of those close to you. Your story will remain on my mind in the years ahead.

Sincerely,

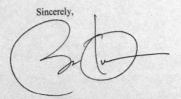

From: Ms. Yvonne Arnetta Wingard

Submitted: 7/9/2016 3:21 PM EDT

Email:

Phone:

Address: Augusta, Georgia

Message: Dear President Obama,

My name is Yvonne Wingard, and I am an 18-year-old, African American female. With all of the recent events occurring around this country, many people are scared. Many people are concerned. They are afraid and don't know what to do or where to turn. What is even worse, is that many who share the same skin color as me are the most fearful.

I am terrified for my life. As a black youth, it is painful and heartbreaking seeing so many posts and hearing so many news reports of people killed or severely hurt because someone automatically saw them as a threat for being black. It should not be illegal to be black in this country, nor should it warrant suspicion or excessive force.

I am simply asking for change and reform. I am asking that all of the leaders of this nation look at all of the news and terror occurring everywhere and realize that something needs to be done to reform our broken system.

I have the utmost respect for our officers. They risk their lives every day to serve their communities and apprehend those who deserve to face the consequences of their crimes. We need to keep cops armed in case of dangerous situations, but we also need to find ways to train them to know the correct measures of protocol in situations where bullets are not needed to calm the situation.

I have to live my life in fear that an officer will try to kill me simply because he sees me as a threat. I have to fear that someone will think I'm a criminal or thug or thief simply because I'm walking down the street. I have to fear even attending protests or marches because I'm afraid someone will try to shoot me or hurt me simply because they don't want to see me and my people fighting and crying out for justice.

My people are hurting. We are scared. We are afraid to be in our own skin. I am asking simply for our leaders in power to come together and find ways to improve our police and criminal justice system. Thank you for your time and consideration, and I hope that you will find it in your heart to do what is truly best for your constituents, and this nation, as a whole.

Thank You,
Yvonne Wingard

Anne ▪▪▪▪ Bunting

Submitted via whitehouse.gov
11/13/2016 7:10 PM

Dear Mr. President,
Thank you for saving my life. My name is Anne ▪▪▪▪ Bunting. In 2008, I
was diagnosed with Heart Failure (HF) and had a pacemaker implanted. I was
in the final stages of HF. I did well until 2012 when my heart began to fail
again. By July, 2013, I was once more in the final stages of HF. I was told I
needed a heart transplant and was put on the list. That's when we discovered
that my individual insurance policy (I was self-employed) did not cover a
heart transplant.
The only way to save my life was to implant a Left Ventricular Assist Device
(LVAD - like Dick Cheney). A few hours after that surgery, the doctors
realized the right side of my heart was dying. So they went back in and
implanted a VAD on the right side of my heart. I was the first person at that
hospital to survive this surgery and go home.
My heart was powered by 2 pumps run by computers and batteries which
were attached to me at all times. I lived with those pumps for 9 months.
Then in 2014, the Affordable Care Act came into being and abolished the
restriction on pre-existing conditions. I was able to get an insurance policy
that covered heart transplants and was put back on the list. 10 days later, I
received the gift of life through a heart transplant. So, I tell everyone that you
saved my life and I truly believe that.
You and the First Lady have both been wonderful leaders. Thank you both
for what you have done for our country and its people.
And thank you again for saving my life.
Anne Bunting

THE WHITE HOUSE

WASHINGTON

December 9, 2016

Ms. Anne   Bunting

Dear Anne:

Thank you for your kind words and for taking the time to share your moving story with me. It's clear you have faced tremendous challenges over the last few years, and I am glad to hear the Affordable Care Act helped you to get a heart transplant when you needed it most. Your story highlights how the Affordable Care Act has been life-changing for so many Americans. And in some cases, even life-saving. As a result of so many more people having coverage, we're avoiding an estimated 24,000 deaths annually. And countless other Americans are living better lives because they're receiving the care they need and deserve. It is why I worked so hard to pass health reform in the first place.

Again, thank you for writing and for your support. Michelle and I send our very best.

Sincerely,

08, 21, 2010

Dear President obama,
Remember the boy who was
picked up by the ambulance- in
Syria? Can you please go get
him and bring him to

Park in the driveway or
on the street and we'll be wai-
-ting for you guys with flags
flowers and balloons. We
~~will~~ will ~~give~~ give him a
family and he will be our
brother. Catherine, my little
sister will be collect-
-ing butterflies and fireflies
for him. In my school I have
a friend from Syria, Omar, and
I will introduce him to Omar and

We can all Play together.
We can invite him to birthday
Parties and he will teach us anoth
-er language. We can teach him Eng
-lish too, Just like we taught my
friend Aoto from Japan. Please tell him
that his brother will be Alex
Who is a very kind boy, Just like
him. Since he won't bring toys and
doesn't have toys Catherine will
Share her big blue Stripy white
bunny. And I Will Share my
bikke and I Will teach him
how to ride it. I Will teach
him additions and Subtraction
in math. and he Smell Catherine
's lip gloss Penguin which is

green. She doesn't let anyone touch it.

Thank you very much! I can't wait for you to come!

Alex
6 years old

Donald W. Molloy
United States District Judge

August 4, 2016

President Barack Obama
The White House
1600 Pennsylvania Avenue NW
Washington, DC 20500

      RE: Douglas George Jensen
              Cause No. CR 03-27-M-DWM

Dear Mr. President:

     I assume there is little chance that you will personally see this letter.
Even so, I want to express my gratitude and appreciation to you for
commuting the sentence of Douglas Jensen. On August 16, 2016, I will have
reached my 20th Anniversary as a federal district judge. The life sentence I
imposed on Douglas Jensen has haunted me for more than half of that time.
Your commutation of his sentence finally eases my conscience and the
struggle within me that was caused by following the law even when it was
unjust. Thank you.

                    With great respect,

                    Donald W. Molloy
                    U.S. District Judge

Address:
Email:

From: Ms. Dawn Benefiel

Submitted: 8/12/2016 9:30 AM EDT

Email:

Phone:

Address: Indianapolis, Indiana

Message: Dear Mr. President, I am a 44 year old woman who moved back to her hometown of Indianapolis IN from Southern California three years ago. I come from a mixed race blended family that began back in the late 70's. I was the only white child that walked to school. Back in the day, Indianapolis Public Schools had huge bussing campaigns to comply with desegregation. I was teased by the white kids since I didn't take the bus and I was beaten up by the black kids on the way home from school for that same reason. I still remember my 4th grade teacher who let me stay after school and sing with her until all the kids left. She knew I was tormented. She also had me sing in front of our class. All those kids that did not like me. I sang "The Greatest Love of All". This was long before Whitney Houston recorded the song. But it was my favorite song. I closed my eyes and sang that song with everything I had. For that few minutes, I forgot all the hatred in those staring eyes. I imagine that being the leader of the western world feels a lot like that. I told you that story because it bears reference to something I am about to say. Eight years ago, I worked on your campaign in Orange County CA. Not much, just worked the phone banks, went out to voter registration tables and talked to people about Barack Obama. You spoke to that 9 year old girl in me. You made me believe there is hope for our flawed country. You reminded a very jaded generation x that it is OK to hope, to believe in the good. You were our JFK. After 8 years, you still inspire. You and your wife remind me every day. You did what you set out to do. I just wanted to thank you for leading with grace and dignity. For closing your eyes and ignoring the hate and doing what you felt was right for our Nation. No one knew when you were elected, what we were about to face as a nation. No one knew how badly we needed someone that could ignite and inspire and stand tall. I don't believe there was anyone else who could have done it better. With all of the ugly things you may hear, I just wanted you to know that you have made a difference. Tears filling my eyes right now because I am sure I am not expressing exactly what I set out to. I suppose just to say, thank you for speaking to that little girl who faced so much hate and prejudice and giving her someone to believe in. With much respect and admiration, Dawn Benefiel.

\ //

From: Mrs. Heather Wells

Submitted: 9/21/2016 2:37 PM EDT

Email:

Phone:

Address: Kokomo, Indiana

Message: Dear Mr. President as you are coming to the end of your second term I wanted to share with you a story about the night you were elected. I am a nurse at an Indiana hospital. Due to being short staffed I was called and asked to work on election night. I agreed to come in as long as I could vote first. Late that night I received an admission from the ER. The patient arrived to the floor and I went in to see him. He was a black man who was about my age that was HIV positive and no longer responding to treatment. When I walked in to greet him he had the election coverage pulled up on the television. I introduced myself and noticed his Obama shirt right away. I asked if he had the opportunity to vote and he said that he refused to come to the hospital before he did. I laughed and pointed to my "I Voted" sticker and told him I said the same thing. I proceeded to pull open my scrub jacket and showed him my "Obama Mama" t-shirt and told him not to worry he was in good hands. We had a laugh and I proceeded to admit him. There weren't a lot of patients on the floor so I was able to spend a little more time just talking to him. He told me that he contracted HIV from IV drug use and that he had lived a rough life. He had two daughters at home and worried about their future. We discussed how much it meant to us for you to win the election. He shared how it gave him hope that his daughters might be able to grow up in a world where it didn't matter what race or background you came from, and that maybe one day they would have an opportunity to be president. We both laughed at that, because who would ever think a woman would get that opportunity (Boy I wish he could be here today to witness the possibility!) We spent most of that night laughing and sharing stories while we watched the votes roll in. When the final votes were tallied and the official announcement was made I am proud to say that I sat in that room with him and we held each other and cried tears of joy. Your election meant so much to me, because I truly believe in you. Your election however meant so much more to him. It meant hope, a promise that his daughters would be ok, security for their future. We spent the rest of the night celebrating he passed away 2 days later. I like to think that the moment we shared was one of his last good times on this earth. I will forever be grateful to that man for all of the hope he instilled in me for the future. Thank you Mr. President for being a part of that.

9/26/16
8.1

From: Mrs. Myriah Lynn Johnson

Submitted: 9/22/2016 2:21 PM EDT

Email:

Phone:

Address: Lakeland, Florida ▓▓▓▓ (valid)

Message: 22 September 2016

Mr. President,

I feel compelled to write you as I sit and watch a great tragedy unfold. You see, I am the one thing no parent wants to be, a Gold Star Mom. On July 12th of this year I lost my son, SPC Alexander Johnson, to a self-inflicted gunshot wound. All I'm left with is to wonder why. He was a bright and talented young man with a beautiful fiancé and a large & loving group of family and friends. Alex, however, didn't want to address the fact he was suffering from depression. I don't and won't ever know what prevented him from seeking help, but I do know one thing. He was afraid of the stigma around mental illness. He was afraid he would lose something that has been his lifelong dream. That he should just be "Army Strong". To "be a man" and just "suck it up". All of these pressures prevented him from seeking treatment. Treatment which could have saved his life.

I have since been inundated with staggering statistics, that more of the young men and women in our armed forces are taken by suicide than in combat. Numbers range from 18 to 22 per day. 18 to 22 families that are shattered. 18 to 22 parents who lose a child, fiancés and spouses who lose their partner, children who lose their parent, brothers & sisters their siblings. What is worse is I have seen story after story of soldiers & sailors sent away from VA treatment facilities for any number of reasons. This has to stop. We need to destigmatize mental illness. Seeking help is not weakness, it is a show of strength.

As a parent I beg you to consider finding a way to allow both active duty and veterans to seek low or no cost mental health treatment at any available facility, not just a VA facility. If it could save even one family from going through what we are it would be worth it.

Thank you for your time.

Sincerely,

Myriah L. Johnson
Gold Star Mom and Proud American

8/26/16

August 4, 2016

Dear President Obama,

Eight years ago, you came to UNC-Chapel Hill to speak —
you weren't president yet, but, after hearing you speak, we all
knew you would be soon. I want to thank you for that day.
You were running a campaign based on hope rather than fear,
and I want you to know that, for the 12-year-old-girl whose
father had died suddenly just one week before your speech,
your message was invaluable. I can't pretend to have
understood, at the time, everything you said — nor can I tell
you that I remember all of it. But the message — that we,
as Americans, have a disposition that tends uniquely toward
a hope that the future can look better — has stayed with
me, from that day when I needed most to hear it all the
way to the present.

I'm 20 now, and I'm actually a student at UNC-Chapel
Hill. Sometimes, when I'm walking across campus, I still
think of your visit. This November marks the first presidential
election for which I can vote, and it's certainly shaping up to
be an unusual one. I wish, of course, that I could vote for
you, but instead I'll vote with your message in mind.
Some of the popular political rhetoric right now is bent
on using fear to create divisions and suggest that the
narrative of hope is not worth striving for, and I just
wanted to be sure that you heard from at least one
more member of my generation that these fear-based
strategies are ineffective. One of the reasons for the failure
of fear (for us, anyway) is that we got to grow up
listening to you.

I hope you never have days where you feel
discouraged or ineffectual, but just in case you do,
please know — you've done something remarkable for
my generation. You helped show us that there exists
far more power in hope than there does in fear. We

learned that from you, and that knowledge and belief cannot be taken away. (And even if I can't speak for all my peers, I can speak for the 12-year-old girl who saw you that night one April. I haven't forgotten.) I don't know what's coming next or what my generation will one day have to accomplish, but I think you've prepared us well for it. We're not throwing away our shot.

Congratulations on all you've accomplished these past eight years. It means so much, in so many ways. Thankyou.

Best,
Nell Ovitt

Chapel Hill, NC

Message: Dear President Barack Obama,

I am Noor Abdelfattah. Born in Chicago in November of 97', I was blessed enough to grow up on Chicago's North Shore. Growing up as child of a Muslim immigrant, I truly realize how privileged I am to live in the greatest country in the world. My grandfather left his homeland in 1951, the year my father was born, in search of his American dream. My father would not meet his own father until he was sixteen years old. Coming to this country with very little, my father was unable to attend college. However, he would spend long hours working low-paid jobs in order to provide for his family. Both my parents and five older brothers faced many difficulties before I was born.

At age seven, my oldest brother was caught in a Chicago gang fight where he took a bullet in the face. Today, that same brother is thirty-three years old and a graduate of University of Michigan Law School. The sacrifices my parents endured for their kids allowed us to prosper within our educational careers. Together, the educational institutions we have attended include University of Illinois-Urbana Champaign, Northwestern University, University of Michigan, and Loyola University Chicago.

Growing up, my parents have always taught us to treat everyone with respect. Although I grew up Muslim, my parents sent my siblings and I to Catholic high schools that placed us in an environment different than our own. Being the only Muslim in my class, I was allowed to interact with people who were raised different than myself. The opportunities my parents have given me allowed me to enter college open minded. I have met people I consider friends from all over the world.

However, with the hostile attitude some people carry towards Muslims, I believe that it is important that we remain together as a nation. I believe that the tradition of hosting an Iftar Dinner at the White House during the month of Ramadan is one tradition that shows the diversity our country holds. We, as Americans, are accepted for what we practice and how we look. On behalf of the Muslims living in the land of the free and home of the brave, I want to thank you for standing firmly with us in rejection of those who are hoping to limit our rights. Additionally, as your term comes to an end, I want to thank you for all the hard work you have done for all Americans and the rest of the world these past eight years as the President of the United States.

All the best,

Noor Abdelfattah

From: Ms. Madison Sky Drago

Submitted: 2/15/2016 7:43 PM EST

Email:

Phone:

Address: Holbrook, New York

Message: I am 13. I am American and I would like to peirce my nose to express myself. My parents disagree with my situation but I feel as I am my own person, I am American and i want to peirce my face. It is my face to show and it represents me and I feel as nobody should have a say against it. What happened to the land of the free? You only live once...who knows when my time will come and I want to make the best of my years.

 **Verizon** 12:31 PM 93%

Done **Samantha Frashier incoming.pdf**

Ms. Samantha Lauren Frashier
Cincinnati, Ohio

Submitted via whitehouse.gov
7/20/2016 10:03 AM

Dear Mr. President,

I know this is a long shot, but I being optimistic and I'm trying. I want to make a change. I may be one person but I've already changed the lives of others. I am 29 years old, the mother of 7 month old twin boys and have almost 3 years clean from using heroin. I have been contacting my local officials and sharing my story of hope with others. I am helping start a non profit recovery home here in Warren County, Ohio by Cincinnati. We have nothing. I spent hours on the phone trying to find a place for a friend. I am watching my friends around me die. And I can't help them because the only option is to send them to Florida, New York, California ect. I remember hearing you speak about putting in some funding into substance abuse and I am curious what it went to? I am also interested in figuring out the best way to help addicts. Prison is not helping and the laws are crazy with this involuntary manslaughter charges. Prison is not the answer. I urge you to please contact me, I have sooo many things I would love to speak with you about. I know it may not be possible, but a girl can dream! Thank you!!

Done   **Samantha Frashier.pdf**

THE WHITE HOUSE
WASHINGTON

August 4, 2016

Ms. Samantha Lauren Frashier
Cincinnati, Ohio

Dear Samantha:

Thank you for writing and for sharing your story. Every day, I am inspired by resilient Americans like you who summon extraordinary courage and strength to live healthy and productive lives in recovery.

Too many Americans are affected by the prescription opioid and heroin epidemic. My Administration has been doing everything we can to increase access to treatment, but it won't be enough without more resources from Congress. That's why I have called on Congress to provide $1.1 billion in new funding to help ensure that all Americans who want treatment for an opioid use disorder can get the help they need. Unfortunately, Congress has repeatedly failed to provide these resources. Congress needs to act quickly because lives are at stake.

My Administration is committed to promoting evidence-based strategies to combat substance use disorders, and to reforming the criminal justice system to address unfair sentencing disparities and provide alternatives to incarceration for nonviolent, justice-involved individuals with substance use disorders. Recovery can transform individuals, families, and communities.

Thank you, again, for taking the time to write. With access to treatment and other supports, recovery is possible for American with substance use disorders, and I will continue to work alongside you until we achieve this reality.

Sincerely,

CHAPTER 14

The Writing Team

"Back from the OVAL" was what the stamp said on the letters Obama had read. They were returned in batches to OPC, and most had some kind of notation in the margins. "What's going on here?" the president may have written, which meant he was requesting a follow-up memo from staff with some broader context—say, in response to a teenager dealing with a trend he didn't understand. He might write, "DOJ, can we help?" which meant he wanted the staff to reach out to the Justice Department to look into the situation by doing something like making sure an inmate was getting the medications he needed. Or he could simply write "REPLY," and if he did that, he would offer notes in the margins for the writing team to use as guidelines for how to respond in his name.

The writing team was not easy to find. They worked in the attic, up on the fifth floor of the EEOB—where most of the elevators didn't go; you had to take a back staircase. It was a tight space with low, slanted ceilings; tiny windows set back in alcoves; people tucked into corners staring into glowing screens. "Even people in the White House don't know this office exists," one of the writers said to me.

They were the elves of the operation. Every thank-you note, gift acknowledgment, condolence letter, congratulations greeting—every piece of typed correspondence with the president's signature on it (the notes in longhand were authored by the president himself) came from the writing team, nine people in all. Perhaps the heaviest lift for the shop was composing the form letters that were sent automatically and in accordance with the way incoming mail was coded. All the form responses the team wrote—more than a hundred of them dealing with specific subject areas like immigration, race relations, climate change—had to be continually updated in accordance with the news cycle, policy changes, topics covered in presidential speeches. Each week a group would comb through and revise the letters, while another, the "conditional language tech team," constantly tweaked algorithms they had designed to allow for personal touches. So, for example, a teacher writing about immigration reform would get the immigration letter, with an added thank-you for his or her service to students; a recent retiree writing about climate change would get the climate change letter and a "best wishes on your retirement." The algorithms allowed for hundreds of combinations.

The goal was to make sure that everyone who wrote a letter to the president got something of substance back. If people believed in this president enough to write to him, that belief needed to be nurtured. The underlying assumption for the writing team was that this president *did* care. If you didn't hold that notion at your core, you wouldn't last. Fiona was at the helm, maintaining quality control and constantly singing her song: This matters. She tracked reader responses to the form letters, organized those into "smile" and "frown" files so the team could gauge its own success rate. "So if someone writes, 'Thank you for the acknowledgment of the death of my mother; your letter really meant a lot,' that goes into the smile file," she told me. "Then another person may write to say, 'Your letter about Syria didn't answer my concern.' That's a frown."

Nobody wanted a frown. Everybody wanted a smile. Everything needed to be perfect. The formatting, the margins, avoiding extra paragraph breaks and random periods, the address label, the printing—it all fell on the writing team, and no detail was too small. This may have been a form letter, but this was a form letter *from the president*. This would be one citizen's proof. It might end up in a frame, hung on someone's wall—passed down to children and to grandchildren. This was an artifact, a piece of American history.

. . .

Kolbie Blume was the person on the writing team in charge of answering the 10LADs. If Obama wrote "REPLY" and scrawled notes in the margins of a letter, that meant a personal response had to be created, and those all went to her.

She had a separate office. "I'm *not* the youngest person here," she said when she got up to greet me, as if to preempt an all-too-familiar conversation. She had the clean, unadorned look of an adolescent: a neat, short bob; a buttoned-up top with pearls. She was twenty-three. "This is my first job out of college," she said. "I mean, it's a lot of pressure." She'd been at it for two years already.

It took me a moment to do the calculations. Kolbie would not even have been eligible to vote when Obama was first elected; she would have been in high school. "Basically, my job is to channel the leader of the free world," she said. "I'm doing my best to be . . . him," she said, adding, appropriately I thought, "um."

I asked her how she'd learned to write in President Obama's voice.

"Listening to speeches, mostly," she said, sitting down at her desk and motioning for me to take a seat too. She said Obama's speeches were a *thing* for her, ever since she was a kid back in Utah, standing in front of the living room TV. "The way he could master words, the way he phrased ideas . . ." She had never bothered listening to a politician before. Those blah-blah talking heads were for her parents or for other people, not her. But this guy was different. *He's talking to me.* She wanted to learn about him, began reading his books. He was somewhat dangerous: a Democrat. The novelty factor alone could have been part of the appeal. Had she ever met a Democrat before? Did Utah even have any? She fell for the cadence and rhythm of his sentences. "The way he could so eloquently, so powerfully, and so poignantly say something and move people to tears." She became a closet Democrat, then an out one.

"I was so excited to vote for the first time in 2012," she told me. "And I remember my boyfriend was like, 'Why? What good is it going to do?' It struck such a chord with me. Something that I'd been so excited for, and here there were so many people so jaded; they didn't think one vote was going to make a difference.

"I mean, you could argue that my one vote in 2012 didn't really help anything. One Democrat in a totally Republican district. Well, it helped *me*. Because I felt empowered. I remember getting the sticker. 'I voted.' I put it on the back of my phone case, I was so proud of it."

The sticker had barely worn off by the time she arrived at the White House two months later, just before Obama's second inauguration, having secured an internship through Utah State, where she was majoring in literary studies. "And I just remember my phone case was still all gummy—"

I was still trying to catch up with the fact that a person this young was the one who wrote all the personal letters that went out with the president's signature on them.

"I love my job," she said.

It turned out that a steady diet of Obama's speeches made you especially talented at this sort of work. "You listen to so many speeches, you just have a running commentary in your head," she said. OPC interns with ambition and drive would routinely apply for staff openings once their internships were completed; Kolbie was just one of many following that path. Fiona recognized her knack early on, hired her to be part of the writing team, and soon put her in charge of the 10LADs portfolio.

"When I draft a letter, I'll sit and read it out loud," she said, trying to explain her methodology. "I'll hear what kind of inflections the president would have. If it sounds like him, I know it's right. If it doesn't, then I'll try to make it so it does.

"I wish I could tell you exactly how to do that, but . . . I just do it every day."

She gave me an example. A letter from a woman in Tulsa sitting on top of her day's to-do pile. "So my job is to take what the president wanted to say to this person," she said, holding it up, "and turn it into the custom response that every letter writer deserves but that the president wanted this particular constituent to have." The letter was about a shooting—a white cop had fatally shot an unarmed black man who, according to the letter, was seen raising his hands above his head in videos released after the shooting. The woman was outraged; she wanted to know why Obama wasn't doing more to repair the growing tensions between police and people in African American communities.

Fiona had chosen it as one of the 10LADs, and the president had read it. He wrote "REPLY" on top, and down one margin he wrote, "I'm mad, too." He underlined various sentences, added exclamation points in the margin, various squiggles, and a few other brief comments.

"See?" Kolbie said, pointing to one of Obama's exclamation points. "See this right here? And this over here—" The markings Obama had scrawled on the letter may have been sparse, but Kolbie understood the code.

She turned to her computer, pulled up a draft of the response she had been working on. It was a Word doc with an array of annotations in rainbow colors running down the side. Footnote everything—that was Kolbie's motto. If she was quoting Obama verbatim from his scrawling on the letter, she would indicate it; if she had borrowed language from a speech he had given on the topic, or another letter on the topic, or a town-hall conversation about the topic, she would indicate those things. She had made it her habit to constantly search through the archives on Whitehouse.gov to gather bits of Obama's language to use in letters. In the end, crafting the responses in his name was one part deciphering, one part collating, and one megadose of confidence that you were just the person to inhabit the mind of the leader of the free world and put this thing together right.

I asked her where she got the confidence.

She grabbed her pearls and twirled them. "It's so easy to think linearly," she said. "Like, okay, here's a person who wrote about climate change, so let's just plunk in some language about climate change here." She said those attempts were all duds. Fiona, the grand pooh-bah of quality control, would toss those right back to her, saying, "No," and "Try again," and "You're not nailing this." Fiona needed to remind Kolbie that this was a *person* she was writing to. And the president was a *person*.

"And I vividly remember, almost like an epiphany," Kolbie told me. "It was like one day I just got it." Every letter coming from the president was ultimately a variation on the same theme, she realized. "It's: 'Look, I hear you. You exist, and you're important, and I care about your voice.'"

I thought about how that underlying message, not cynical, not fancy, not loaded—no baggage—was perhaps best kept in the protective arms of a person not far from childhood.

Kolbie flipped through the pile of letters she needed to get through that afternoon, about fifteen in all. Back from the OVAL, Back from the OVAL, Back from the OVAL, REPLY, REPLY, REPLY. "A few of these will be easy," she said, pulling out one. A person was writing to give advice to the president on what he should do after he retires. "'Ride a bike daily. Volunteer. Don't be afraid to day-drink. Go out to lunch as often as possible with Mrs. Obama.'" The president had written little more than "Thanks for the great advice!" in his comments. "I'll probably flesh that out a little," Kolbie said. "I remember recently he joked about wanting to take three or four months to sleep; maybe I'll incorporate some of that language—"

She pulled out another letter. A woman was writing to apologize; she had first written to Obama years earlier accusing him of being anti-Christian. Now she was writing again, having had a change of heart, and saying she was sorry. Obama wrote "REPLY" on top, and along the side: "Thanks for being thoughtful and open to ideas. I'm sure you will do well."

"I have not drafted this one yet," Kolbie said. "But it won't be much more than what he said here. It just needs . . . what he said there." She put it back in the stack, fanned through some of the others. "And you know, the vast majority of these start by people saying, 'I know my letter will never reach you,'" she said. "Or 'I'm sure some staffer will just toss this letter in the trash.' So for me, knowing that the person is going to get a response, knowing that their cynicism or their disillusionment is going to be chipped away just a little bit— that feels like a victory."

I thought about some of the letter writers I had met and what getting a personal letter back from Obama meant to them.

I thought about Shane Darby, who wrote to howl in the aftermath of his daughter's suicide; the thing that soothed him about the president's response was seeing the president spell Cristina's name right. "Most people put the *h* in there."

I thought about Donna Coltharp, an attorney in San Antonio, Texas, who wrote a letter of thanks to the president for commuting the two life sentences of her client. What moved Donna was that the president thought to thank her for her service as a public defender. "No one ever thanks us."

I thought of Bob Melton, a guy in North Carolina who wrote in 2014 to thank Obama for the Affordable Care Act; it enabled him to see a doctor for the first time in twelve years. The president wrote back, and Bob Melton showed the letter to everyone. "I couldn't believe it! I immediately jumped in the car and went down to Walmart and bought a frame." He got invited to the Burke County, North Carolina, Democratic Party meeting to come read President Obama's letter out loud, and everyone clapped, and so now other local groups are asking him to come read it for them too. "I'm just overwhelmed by the whole situation. I mean, little old me, you know? Down here in North Carolina. You know? I never thought I'd get any kind of applause." Because of that letter, Bob Melton will tell you, he now walks as a tall man.

I thought, finally, about Patty Ries, a woman in Dallas, Texas, whom I'd recently gotten to know. She wrote in 2016 because she wanted Obama to see one of her own family heirlooms, a letter her father had once written to President Roosevelt, in 1943.

> I have meant to write to you for some time. Now I am concerned whether this letter will reach you before you leave office. . . . I am deeply concerned about Donald Trump running for President. I sincerely hope that he doesn't win. I fear that our country will go back in time if this comes to pass. . . . My father was born in Germany and came to the United States when he was eighteen. My father desperately wanted to become a United States citizen so that he could join the US army and fight against the Germans during WWII. . . . He was sworn in as a US citizen at two in the morning by a Justice of the Peace after this letter was received in Washington. If Donald Trump was the President, my father probably would not have been allowed in the United States let alone been sworn in as a US citizen. . . . When the war ended he did find his mother who had been a prisoner at the concentration camp Theresienstadt. She too was able to come to the United States after the war and lived almost fifty years in the US before her death at age 99! Unfortunately I did not get to meet my grandfather. He was killed in Auschwitz concentration camp.

THE WHITE HOUSE

WASHINGTON

January 13, 2017

Ms. Patty Ries
Dallas, Texas

Dear Patty:

Your letter reached my desk, and I wanted to thank you for sharing your family's story with me. I was deeply moved by it and by the letter your father wrote to President Roosevelt—what a powerful piece of history.

It's clear you come from a long line of people committed to building a more inclusive, more just future, and your pride in that legacy came through in every word. I hear your concerns about our country's politics. I know it may sometimes seem as if the loudest and angriest among us drive our national conversation, but I firmly believe that the most thoughtful and compassionate voices will ultimately win out and shape the stronger America we all deserve. Hearing from folks like you only reaffirms my optimism for our country's future.

Again, thank you for writing to me, and for your father's dedication to our country. It's been a tremendous privilege to serve as your President these past eight years, and your words—as well as your father's and grandfather's—will stay with me.

All the best,

I remembered how proud Patty was of that letter from the president, like Bob Melton, like so many of the others. She put it in a brown frame and hung it over her computer, prime real estate, a new family heirloom to add to a collection that dated back to her grandfather's imprisonment and murder in Auschwitz.

I suppose Kolbie was the one who actually wrote that letter to Patty, and the letters to Shane Darby, Bob Melton, and Donna Coltharp, and so many of the other typewritten responses I had read. I didn't ask Kolbie about any of those letters specifically. This was inching way too deep into Santa Claus territory. I remember Yena telling me that one of the reasons she and other people in OPC didn't like talking about their work to outsiders was because they felt a responsibility to preserve the illusion. Like the magician's pledge— thou shalt not reveal the tricks of the trade. Your silence was your gift.

"Every day I just can't believe that (a) I'm here," Kolbie told me that afternoon, "and (b) that the president cares so much about these letters."

It was impossible not to root for Kolbie. The more time I spent with her, the more I thought there was probably nobody I'd rather see be in charge of the magic than a woman with a tender heart whose still-burgeoning belief in a hero had not been tainted.

I asked Kolbie what she needed to do to finish the letter to the woman in Tulsa who wrote about the shooting, and she went back to her computer, scrolled up, then down.

"Okay, so what I've done here is break down the sections of his thoughts," she said, tapping the screen. "See? It's 'I'm mad, too.' And 'My administration can't intervene in individual cases.' And 'But this is what we are doing.' And 'No one should have to fear being profiled.' And then he ends with 'This is what you need to do.'

"Basically, POTUS has given me topic sentences, and I'm filling in the blanks," she said with a shrug. "I'm an English major. It's what we do."

The final version, including all the annotations, would go to Fiona, who would inspect and edit it, then forward it to the interns who manned the printer. Fiona would inspect the printed version, the margins, the consistency of the ink—no random dots or splotches—before finally sending it back to Obama for his signature. Then the letter would be out the door, destined for a mailbox in Tulsa and, likely, a frame on a wall.

"If my job didn't exist, so many people would have unanswered letters; you know what I mean?" Kolbie said. "They wouldn't know that the president cares. They wouldn't know that their voice does matter. They just wouldn't *know*."

I asked her if she'd ever had a chance to talk to Obama about what it was like to channel his voice.

"I've never met him, no," she said. "I mean, he hand signs these letters, and he knows that they don't just come out of nowhere, so he knows my job exists."

But that was as close as he was to knowing her. She told me that would soon change, however. Every White House staffer was due to get a departure photo taken with the president during his final months in office, and Kolbie's appointed time was just a few weeks away.

"I'm trying to mentally prepare," she said. "It's bigger than anything that's ever happened to me. Sometimes I spaz out in front of people, so I'm trying to prepare.

"I'm going to shake his hand. I'm going to make sure he knows who I am. I'm going to say, 'My name is Kolbie, and I'm your voice.'"

CHAPTER 15

Donna Coltharp and Billy Ennis, August 4, 2016

EL PASO, TEXAS

Billy was fifteen the first time he got kidnapped. It was a Saturday morning, back in the 1980s, in Anthony, New Mexico, just north of El Paso, Texas, where the family moved after they got rich. Billy was asleep in his room. He was a skinny kid who loved motocross and who lived by the rules his parents taught him: If you're hit, hit back harder, and don't go bothering your parents about it. Take care of your own problems.

So this one morning the doorbell rings, and Billy answers it, and the guy asks for Billy's dad. "He's not home," Billy says, and the guy leaves only to return an hour later with more guys who grab Billy by the hair, drag him across the yard, and stuff him in the trunk of a car. Next thing Billy knows he's handcuffed to a bed frame in a house somewhere in Mexico, and everybody's calling him Chester.

"My name is Billy," Billy says.

Chester was his brother, a few years older.

They got the wrong kid. Ransom-wise, a firstborn was worth more. Billy learned a lot just listening. This situation clearly had something to do with his dad's booming drug business, the extent of which Billy was only beginning to grasp. It had always been more of a vague thing. A lot of garbage bags moving into and out of his parents' bedroom, put it that way. After three days with the kidnappers and no ransom coming, Billy escaped in the middle of the night—he tricked the guy with the key to the handcuffs—and ran for his life through the desert. With the help of the Mexican police (who knew Billy's dad), he was deposited at the border, and his dad picked him up.

A few weeks later, Billy got kidnapped again, only this time they took both him and Chester. They came in the middle of the night, and they shot up the house, and they bashed his mom's head in with the butt of a machine gun because she wouldn't stop screaming. They again stuffed Billy into the trunk of a car, which was much more crowded with Chester jammed in there too. Again the kidnappers drove to Mexico. This time they hog-tied Billy and put him face-down on a couch. The guy who had been in charge of the handcuff key beat Billy repeatedly saying he shouldn't have tricked him like that. "You would have done it too," Billy told him. "I wasn't doing anything a normal person wouldn't do." They were so much meaner this time. They threatened to kill Billy's mom, and they beat him and Chester. The rescue, days later, by the Mexican police (who knew Billy's dad), came after a shoot-out.

Nothing was the same after that. Billy was so angry he got kidnapped twice and so was Chester. They wanted retribution. They got guns. They believed they knew who was behind the kidnappings, and they said they were going to go get him. Their dad pleaded with them not to do this. Their mom said, "Well, I'm not letting you kids go alone," so she got her .44 and got in the car with them, and so then their dad got in too—the four of them, off to go get even.

It did not go well. The guy they were after was not home, and so Billy and his parents and Chester took the wife, a maid, and two kids hostage. They took them to a hotel room. "I was an asshole," Billy would later remark, looking back on how he treated them. He did buy them food, though, and toothbrushes. It was a fiasco. Everybody was terrified. In the end, Billy's family locked the hostages in a U-Haul and turned themselves in. His dad worked the deal. Everybody was part of the drug trade. Everybody. Nobody pressed charges. Everyone walked away.

· · ·

"I found out later it wasn't a normal childhood," Billy was telling Donna Coltharp in 2002. He was now thirty-three.

It was the first time Donna had ever talked to her client. Billy was calling from the Florence Federal Correctional Institute, a medium-security prison in Colorado; she was a newly appointed federal public defender in the Western District of Texas, and she had been assigned his appeal.

"Nice to meet you," she had said after he introduced himself. "How was your morning?"

Billy told her that his dad was his cellmate, and that his dad snored, so they were moving him.

Donna asked Billy how he ended up in prison with his dad, and Billy was trying to summarize. He explained about the kidnappings, and he told her that by the time he turned sixteen, he was homeless. His dad had been busted—"with ten tons of marijuana," as Billy recalled it—and went to prison. Chester also went to prison, but it was for gang stuff he got involved in. Billy's mom couldn't afford the house, so she took off. She did not take Billy with her. "I was an asshole," Billy said, defending his mom. Billy found a spot under a bridge to live in. The school told him he couldn't come back because he no longer had an address in the district. (He did not tell them about the bridge.) He broke into a vacant trailer and lived there for a while. He stole groceries for food. He met a guy who said there was a better way. It took Billy just a few hours to sell a kilo of coke. He made twelve thousand dollars that first day. From then on it was party central.

Billy put his story on fast-forward and told Donna about the two convictions that had led up to his current situation. He said his teenage cocaine business was wildly successful. When he got busted, in his early twenties, he was full of fury, until he figured out it was the best thing that could have happened to him. In prison he learned about normal childhoods. He got clean. Drug dealing, he discovered, led to one of two possible outcomes: prison or death. He tested the theory when he got out; it took him another round of prison for the point to stick. It was after finishing his second prison sentence that he got it together. He got a job. He had a son.

Billy wouldn't snitch on anybody; that could be part of why the cops got so mad when they came and raided his house in 2002.

They didn't find any drugs. They found diapers and baby toys, and Billy told them to take their hands off his son.

Billy's father was the one they wanted. He'd been free for a few years and had opened a print shop with Billy's mom. Billy suspected his dad was up to no good, but he wouldn't give any information to the cops. When the cops finally busted his dad and a neighbor as part of an organized crime investigation called Operation Power Play, they wrapped Billy into the arrest.

"I had nothing to do with it," Billy said. He confessed to having dealt weed—his occasional freelance work when he needed to make rent. That much he did do. He told them, you can have me for that, but not for this.

They tried three of them at once: Billy, his dad, and the neighbor. The jury came back with a guilty verdict for all but Billy. On his case, they reached an impasse. The judge instructed the jury to continue deliberating. In the end, the jury found Billy guilty, and because of his priors and the "three strikes" law imposing mandatory prison time for repeat offenders, the judge handed him two concurrent life sentences.

"For a drug conviction," Donna said that day on the phone. Two life sentences for a drug conviction was the kind of thing that drove Donna crazy. She was the type of person who thought a lot about mercy and the power of imagination. Warehousing nonviolent offenders was doing nothing to help society.

"Well, let's get to work," Donna said.

Over the years, Donna and Billy grew close, even though they never met in person. Everything they did was by phone. That's pretty typical when you are talking federal appeals court. They chatted about their sons; they both had toddlers. When Donna's son started preschool, so did Billy's. Both boys learned how to tie their shoes and started sports. Donna and Billy would compare notes, as parents do. They became the kind of friends that parents become, sharing transitions. Donna knew that for Billy the transitions were theoretical. She could feel the passage of time in a way Billy could not, and the disparity would eat at her.

Billy's appeal came down to a black-and-white box. At trial, police had testified that they had aerial surveillance of Billy carrying a box into his dad's house. Thirty kilograms of cocaine had been found in a box. Specifically, a Gateway computer box. Gateway was an iconic brand in those days. Its mascot was a Holstein cow, and all its boxes had large black cow splotches on them. Did the guy in the helicopter see the splotches? He should have been able to, the defense said. Could he have instead seen any number of other boxes Billy may have taken over to his dad's? In deliberations at the first trial, the jury was hung up on the question of the box. No fingerprints or other physical evidence had connected Billy to it, just the aerial surveillance. The jury asked to see the box. "Sorry," they were told. The box had been inadvertently destroyed by courthouse cleaning personnel.

Donna thought the missing evidence should have cleared Billy then and that it should clear Billy on appeal.

It didn't.

It was 2005. She called Billy with the news. The denied appeal was three years in the making.

"I'm so sorry," she said.

Billy said he wanted to keep fighting. There had to be *something* they could do.

Donna was out of ideas. She told him, well, we can always appeal to the president of the United States to grant clemency—that's how out of ideas she was.

Unlike presidents before him, Obama had not made use of his pardon power. People said he had pardoned more turkeys than people. In fact, he wouldn't commute a single sentence until 2011, and even then it was just one.

A pardon is forgiveness of a crime, wiping out the conviction entirely, while a commutation leaves the conviction intact but wipes out the punishment.

The idea of the president commuting Billy's sentence was, Donna knew, a fantasy. It was like hoping for the tooth fairy to be real. But it was all that was left. So she prepared the plea, told Billy's story, and contacted a commutation attorney to file it.

It wasn't until late into his second term that the dam burst open for Obama on the issue of commutations. On July 14, 2015, he gave his first major criminal justice speech at the NAACP convention in Philadelphia. "Mass incarceration makes our country worse off, and we need to do something about it," he said. "I'm going to shine a spotlight on this issue, because while the people in our prisons have made some mistakes—and sometimes big mistakes—they are also Americans, and we have to make sure that as they do their time and pay back their debt to society that we are increasing the possibility that they can turn their lives around."

Obama followed the speech with a visit to the El Reno Federal Correctional Institution in Oklahoma two days later. "When they describe their youth, these are young people who made mistakes that aren't that different from the mistakes I made and the mistakes that a lot of you guys made," he said there. "The difference is that they did not have the kind of support structures, the second chances, the resources that would allow them to survive those mistakes."

He was the first sitting president to visit a federal prison. His presidency was coming to an end, and he had certain things he wanted to accomplish; he would use his power of commutation as a form of criminal-justice reform.

Obama granted 46 commutations in the summer of 2015, another 78 in December 2016, and then hundreds more, including 330 on January 19, 2017, his last full day in office. In total, he would grant executive clemency to 1,927 people convicted of federal crimes, more than the past thirteen presidents combined.

. . .

U.S. Department of Justice

Office of the Pardon Attorney

Washington, D.C. 20530

August 3, 2016

FLORENCE
Warden
Florence FCI
5880 State Highway 67
Florence, CO 81226-9791

        Re: William Edward Ennis
              Reg. No. 62601-080
              Recipient of commutation of sentence

Dear Warden:

    Please find enclosed a certified copy of the warrant by which President Barack Obama
has commuted the prison sentence of William Edward Ennis, Reg. No. 62601-080. Please
deliver the enclosed warrant to the inmate and ensure he has completed the enclosed receipt
acknowledging that he has received the warrant. The receipt should be returned to this office via
email to USPardon.Attorney@usdoj.gov. Thank you for your assistance.

                        Sincerely,

                        Robert A. Zauzmer
                        Acting Pardon Attorney

Enclosures

Donna had never wanted to be an attorney. She wanted to be a literature professor. She wanted to teach *Moby-Dick*. Law school was more her mom's idea.

She was in her office when she got the voicemail from Billy. He was weeping. She called him back right away but couldn't reach him. She checked her email and found the list of new commutations there, and she scrolled up and down to make sure what she was seeing was really there.

• William Ennis—El Paso, Tex.
Commutation Grant: Prison sentence commuted to expire on December 1, 2016.

She forwarded the news to everyone in the office, to everyone in the district, to everyone she knew. She couldn't sit still. She kept trying to reach Billy. For a couple of hours, she tried to work, then drove home. She wanted her husband to take her out to dinner. She couldn't sit still. She wondered if Obama knew how commutations affected people. She wondered why he had done it. He would get no political capital for a thing like this. She wondered if anybody in the press would say it was the right thing to do. What an odd, quaint thing to have in America, she thought, the idea that politicians could step outside of the system and say, "Enough is enough." All of these ideas were racing through her mind, and her husband wasn't home yet to take her to dinner, so she was going to just pour herself a drink to calm herself down, but instead she got the idea to open her laptop. She drafted the email, slept on it, edited it the next morning. She wanted to get it just right.

She wondered if anybody ever bothered to thank the president. When a person in a position of power does a powerful thing, the focus tends to be on the thing, not the person who did it.

. . .

19/16
8/5

From: **Donna Coltharp**

Submitted: 8/4/2016 12:14 PM EDT

Email:

Phone:

Address: San Antonio, Texas

Message: Dear Mr. President

Yesterday, you announced the commutation of the three-life sentences one of my first clients as a federal public defender is serving. His name is William (Billy) Ennis. No one I have ever represented is more deserving of a second chance. In fact, for this reason, I referred Billy's case to a commutation lawyer a year before our national commutation projects began.

Billy grew up with parents who trafficked in drugs at the border. At one point, when he was a child, he was actually kidnaped by people who were seeking to collect drug debts from his parents. For awhile, as a child, Billy lived under a bridge. It was not surprising that, as a young adult, he picked up two drug convictions -- one relatively minor. Then, he went straight. Quit using drugs. He had a son. But, he got pulled back into his parents' dealings and performed a role in a drug transaction. And, the drug laws put him away for three lifetimes. His son, whom he had custody of, was just a baby.

I lost Billy's direct appeal. But, I have remained in touch with him for the past 14 years. We talk at least once a month. So much has changed. His son now plays high school football in El Paso! His mother passed away a few years after he was sentenced. Billy has participated in every prison program available to him and has the respect of prison staff and inmates alike.

Billy deserved a second chance. But not many people would have given it to him. I am profoundly grateful that you have the courage to look at people whom society has decided are not worth looking at and see an opportunity for redemption rather than just a criminal. Yesterday, the day I heard about Billy's commutation, is the single best day I've had as a criminal defense attorney. I've seen clients walk free because of my representation (not many!), but I have never seen a client handed the gift of grace that you gave Billy.

Billy called me in tears yesterday. I may never hear from him again, but I will never forget him or that call. Please keep him in your prayers as he tries to find a way forward to a better life.

Billy has never met Donna in person. Today she's in El Paso for some kind of meeting, and that's why he's finally getting to meet her. He imagines her with dark hair, probably about fifty. He knows he's put on weight, and he wishes he still had hair. In a few minutes he'll be ready to head out, but first you can look around if you want.

As you can see, the house needs work. When Billy first walked in a few months ago, the cobwebs were like *The Addams Family*. He's tackling the plumbing and the electric first. It's weird being forty-seven and coming back to the house you grew up in. Billy lived here until he was thirteen, back before everything went haywire. His grandmother owned it. When she died, she left the house to Billy, even though he was serving two life sentences. Not three, as Donna says in her letter to Obama. When it comes to multiple life sentences, it's easy to lose track.

Over the years, while the house sat vacant, people came through and trashed the place. But that's okay. As you can see, they left the family photos. Here's one from a vacation at Knott's Berry Farm in about 1980. Billy is maybe ten here. He and Chester and a cousin, Billy's mom and dad, all dressed like cowboys at one of those booths where you get to wear historic costumes. That's Billy's dad with the sheriff badge. Everyone in this picture besides Billy is either dead or in prison.

He's glad he has a house to live in. He's been able to see his son, William, a few times. William is tall and super involved in church and school, so he's busy. He got Billy a dog. They named him Zeus.

Billy's job is in roofing. Metal roofs. He appreciates the guy giving him a chance. After just months on the job, he's already been promoted to supervisor. He sometimes feels like Rip Van Winkle. Everyone now is so obsessed with their phones. When he left for prison fifteen years ago, it was still the flip phone. Billy does not yet quite understand texting. He recently went to his first Starbucks. Also, he recently got a girlfriend. They met in the supermarket.

"Don't I know you?" she said.

"My name is Billy," he said.

"Ennis!" she said.

They recognized each other from seventh grade, before everything happened.

Dear Donna:

Thank you for taking the time to write to me last August. I read your message personally, and it meant a lot to hear your perspective on

Billy's case. People who have made mistakes deserve opportunities to earn second chances, and stories like his underscore why we need to make our criminal justice system fairer and more effective, particularly when it comes to nonviolent drug offenses.

I firmly believe that exercising my power as President to commute the sentences of deserving men and women is an important step toward restoring the fundamental ideals of justice and fairness. Still, there is more work to do, and your experience speaks to the responsibility we have to make sure people who learn from their mistakes are able to continue to be a part of our American family.

Again, thank you for your inspiring message. I am tremendously grateful for your years of service as a public defender, and your message will stay with me.

Sincerely,
Barack Obama

When Billy gets to the office in El Paso, Donna is eating birthday cake. It's awkward. They can hardly make eye contact. She offers him cake. She says there's quesadillas in the back. She finds that she really wants to feed him.

"How is your son?" she asks.

"How is your son?" he asks.

They exchange updates and soon begin showing pictures.

"He looks just like you!"

"I got fat."

"You look fantastic."

He tells her about getting promoted to supervisor on the job; $17.50 an hour is pretty good for El Paso. She tells him she got promoted to supervisor, too, to deputy federal public defender. "It's weird. But I guess it's worth it—"

"Definitely."

"Right."

"Anyway—"

It's hard to find words sometimes.

"I want you to know I appreciate everything you've done for me," he says finally.

"You kept me optimistic," she says, and she opens her arms.

"I'm sorry," he says about crying, and she holds him.

"I'm sorry," she says.

It turns into more of a laugh-cry for both of them.

"It's hard to believe life can be so good sometimes," she says.

CHAPTER 16

Election Day

On Election Day, Hillary Clinton had an 85 percent chance of becoming the next president of the United States, according to The Upshot in *The New York Times*. "Mrs. Clinton's chance of losing is about the same as the probability that an N.F.L. kicker misses a 37-yard field goal," the *Times* reported. Over at FiveThirtyEight, she had a 71 percent chance of winning, and she was predicted to take 302 electoral votes.

Yena and others on the OPC staff were headed over to Lacey's apartment, where they would watch the election results together. There would be champagne. It would be a celebration, albeit a bittersweet one. The last full day of the Obama administration, January 19, 2017, would be the last day for this OPC staff. They could apply for positions under the new administration, but there were no guarantees of anything; this team was breaking up, and everyone knew it.

Much of the focus over the past month had been on preparing transition materials. Fiona remembered 2009 all too well; the Bush OPC staff had left the Obama team virtually nothing in the way of guidance. No procedure manuals, no letter templates, no software, no hardware, no computer, no telephones . . . no paper. Mike Kelleher had had to start from scratch to create the foundation for what would turn into this OPC empire, and Fiona was determined to hand it to the new folks intact—with detailed manuals. She had instructed her staff to document everything: Break down every beat of every process, sorting, sampling (in pencil), dispositions, Red Dots, policy letters, casework referrals, inmate mail, kid mail, condolence letters, emerging issues meetings, the conditional language tech team, algorithms. If they prepared the materials properly, it would be plug and play for the new administration. She organized the materials into binders, and when the transition team came in, as they were scheduled to do sometime soon after the election, she would hand the material over to them and let them know she was available for questions, for training sessions, anything at all.

Fiona wasn't going to Lacey's party. She wanted to watch the results in the quiet of her home with her husband. The next morning was going to be nuts, she warned me. She had readied the staff: Nobody should even bother going to the hard-mail room. She would need everyone, all the interns, all the volunteers, all hands on deck in the email room. Major national events, like State of the Union addresses, always generated massive amounts of email, and this one—the first woman ever to be elected president, the first black president handing the reins over to the first woman president—was sure to blow the circuits.

Cody Keenan was watching the election results at his apartment with his wife and his friends Ben Rhodes and Dan Pfeiffer. His phone rang at about 2:30 A.M.

It was Obama. "You know we're going to need to rewrite this statement for tomorrow," he said.

"Yeah, I know," Cody said, and he turned off the TV.

He scrapped the remarks he had begun drafting for Obama to deliver in the Rose Garden on the day after the election congratulating Hillary Clinton for her historic win.

Donald Trump had won the presidency, and Cody wondered what in the world Obama should now say to America from the Rose Garden.

At six in the morning, Cody sent Obama his revisions.

"A little too dark," Obama told him.

"Yeah, I know," Cody said.

It was raining on the morning after the election, and I arrived at the White House gates early. No one at the main OPC office on the fourth floor of the EEOB was in yet except for Fiona, who was shuffling through papers as I sat on the other side of her desk.

"Well," she said, looking up. Her face held the vague puffiness of a morning after little sleep.

"Well," she started again, bouncing a stack of pages up and down and into order. She was having trouble making eye contact. The sky outside her window was a flat steel gray. I could hear the distant whirr of a printer revving up. There was a wet umbrella at my feet.

"Well, your hair looks great," she said.

I told her, no, her hair did.

"Oh, it's just—" She shook her head to make a swish. We discussed my bangs.

Hair talk is a refuge.

"I'm sorry," she said finally, dropping back in her chair. "It's just that you're the first person I've talked to."

"Same," I said.

We muttered awkwardly about greeting the security guys out at the gate, and did that count? No, yeah, no.

I suppose a lot of people will always remember where they were when the sun came up. The first person you talked to. What you said. The implications, one by one, hitting you. *Wait, what? This wasn't supposed to happen.* How strange it was to feel that reality had gotten ahead of you and now you had to race to catch up. If you even wanted to catch up. The lethargy of not wanting to join the new reality would increasingly feel like a flu spreading.

The email room was in another building, in the satellite office over on Jackson Place, and soon Fiona and I would head over and join the staff and the voices from all the people all over America who had awakened that morning to the results and had the thought: *Today I need to write to President Obama.*

From: Sam K-G
Submitted: 11/9/2016 8:20 AM EST
Address: Granville, Ohio
Message:

Dear Mr. President,

I'm not really the "writing a letter to the president" type. It seems like more of an idealistic gesture than anything else. But this morning, I am frightened for the future of our country. As, I am sure, are you. As any reasonable person would be. What I ask is this: Please please do whatever you can to curtail Trump. Anything you can do to mitigate this catastrophe that is underway.

I'm sorry your presidency has to end like this.
Sam

P.S. To the volunteer reading this: must be a crazy day in there. Keep up the good work

Fiona finally broke down in tears that morning in her office. It was only a matter of time, and now she was getting it over with. "I'm sorry," she said, her head hanging. She talked about her husband, Chris. They were newly married. She reminded me that Chris had worked at OPC and that was where they met; they had trained together, eight hours a day reading hard mail together. An experience like that bonds you, she said.

"I'm sorry," she said again.

So many people throughout my time at OPC talked about the bond. It reminded me of the way soldiers talk, or coal miners: groups of people on the front line of something most people never witness. The mailroom. Who would think something like that would happen in a mailroom?

"You ready to head over?" Fiona said, and we both grabbed our umbrellas and our coats.

I saw Kolbie on the way out; she was leaning against a wall with another staffer who seemed to be consoling her. She was looking down at her shoes, biting the nail on her thumb.

. . .

Jackson Place is the street across from the White House that forms the western border of Lafayette Square. It's lined with cherry trees and stately brick townhouses that were built in the nineteenth century. They were the homes of diplomats and dignitaries, including Henry Reed Rathbone, the military officer who was sitting in the President's Box at Ford's Theatre next to Abraham Lincoln when Lincoln was assassinated; Rathbone never recovered from the trauma—he went mad and lived out his days in an insane asylum. President Theodore Roosevelt and his family also lived in one of the townhouses on Jackson Place while the White House underwent renovations in 1902. The federal government acquired the properties in the 1950s with the idea of tearing them down and putting up a federal office building. In 1962, First Lady Jacqueline Kennedy intervened, said, don't destroy those beautiful old buildings, and the project was canceled. Now the townhouses hold an array of federal offices that feel homey and interesting and full of intrigue.

The email room was on the third floor of 726 Jackson Place; it was a wide open space that could have once been a formal parlor. The ceilings were high, and the windows were encased in ornate moldings, and there were deep window seats. Otherwise it was cubicle after cubicle after cubicle with computer monitors flickering and maybe fifty people jammed in; at either end of the room, the staffers in charge had their computers propped up on boxes so they could stand while they worked.

One of the staffers in charge I'll call John, even though that's not his real name. The weird thing that happened the morning after the election was some people in OPC started to ask me not to use their real names. That had not once happened before. It was as if everyone had been under the protective shield of Fiona, of Shailagh, of Obama; it was as if OPC was a collective, and what was good for one was good for all.

But now there was a feeling of a free fall, every man for himself. People had futures to worry about—jobs—and political affiliations would matter.

John stood to address the packed room of staffers and interns to give them a pep talk. "We're seeing a lot of people in meltdown mode," he said. He was a young guy with a neat appearance and jet-black hair. "Look, the president is counting on us to do this. So let's do this. This is our thing. It's why we're here. It might just be a little weirder today . . ."

He told them if the mail was getting to them, they should go take a walk. He told them to keep the TV off. "It's not helpful. It's not helpful to say, if this person would have run or did this or that. *It's not helpful.*

"Look, we are all processing this."

People leaned their heads away from the rows of screens to listen. There were tissues. People were crying. Extra office chairs had been rolled in, along with donuts, juice, power bars, and when John finished his pep talk, the staffers and interns went back to reading, and talking, and reading, and trying to console one another.

"We just have to go into duty versus feeling."

"Here's one from a fourteen-year-old girl. 'Dear Mr. President, Please help me understand what to do.'"

"Here's two women who got married four years ago and are going to have a baby this week and are terrified to bring a baby into the world now."

"Last night we were watching, and we were like, 'Fine, fine, whoa. Whoa!' We didn't talk at all. At the end someone was like, 'What are we going to tell our letter writers? What are we going to do with the mail tomorrow?' And we all just lost it."

"I was like, 'I need to go see the mail.'"

"It gives you purpose. It all feels hopeless, but this is something proactive."

"It's that sense of responsibility, that we still need to be there for the people who want to reach out to the president."

"I don't know what we're going to tell all these people. But we're going to have to tell them something. . . ."

"I'm seeing fear. Mostly fear."

"I haven't seen anybody saying, 'I'm happy.'"

"It was about twenty of us. A bottle of wine. We cleared out so much vodka."

"It's not even about the results. It's looking at what used to be."

"It's looking at what we see as progress and to have it, in one day, all of a sudden you're saying, Is this even real, or will it still exist?"

. . .

People had questions for John; they were getting confused about how to proceed. Email was the same as hard mail: Each post had to be coded. Immigration. Israel. Economy. The codes corresponded with the policy-response letters that the writing team had ready to go and that the algorithms were set to personalize. But on this day staffers had had to come up with all new codes: Election Pro, Election Con, and Legacy.

"So Election Pro is like, 'Donald Trump is the best, and this is a great day for America,'" John told the group. "And then Election Con is going to be like, 'I'm scared,'" he went on. He was standing in the middle of the room, and you could tell he was not used to having to make his voice carry.

"So, like, 'I don't know what to do. I have a disability. I'm an LGBT family. I don't know what's going on anymore.' That's Election Con.

"Then Legacy is going be 'You know, I was really disappointed about last night; your family is amazing; I think you did great things'—that's Legacy. Some of these things will be a little vague, and I know it's going to be hard, but feel free to ask questions as we're going through this, and let's try to make sure you're being as specific as possible."

"What about people talking about election recounts and fraud and rigging?" one intern asked.

"Election fraud? Just close those out—"

"What about people writing before the results were out?" asked another. "Like people writing in to say, 'I'm looking forward to President Clinton,' but it's clearly obvious that that's . . . not."

"Yeah. We can close those. We can close those out."

"What if they're saying, 'I'm nervous about the election. I don't know what I'll do'?"

"Election Con."

"'Do we need to call up the military?'"

"Election Con."

"'My wife is undocumented; I have three children; I've never been so scared in my life.'"

"Election Con."

" 'I'm disabled; I have seizures. Will I still have healthcare?' "

"Election Con."

" 'Is he going to void my marriage? Am I going to still be with the person I love?' "

Con. Con. Con.

The writing team would have to figure out a response to the election email later that day. What, exactly, should Obama say to all these people?

Three elderly women in pastel blouses came barging in, asking to turn on the TV. "Are you watching Hillary's concession speech?" one of them asked.

"I wasn't sure where you're from?" an OPC staffer said politely.

"FLOTUS! We're volunteers from FLOTUS! Can we watch the speech?"

But the TV wasn't on. Perhaps the polite thing to do was to turn it on. Sure, they would turn it on. But did they have to? There was hemming and hawing, and they put the TV on with the sound down while Wolf Blitzer waited for Clinton and the crawl beneath brought updated margins from Pennsylvania, and Ohio, and Michigan, and most of the people in the email room went back to their screens, to the email and America in meltdown mode.

From: Mr. Martin A. Gleason
Submitted: 11/9/2016 8:07 AM EST
Address: Chicago, Illinois
Message:

Mr. President—I am sorry I let you down.

I know I could only vote once, and that I could not call every unde-cided voter, or fund every down ballot Democrat. Where I, and every other college educated white male who voted for you in '08 and '12[,] failed you, is in our inability or unwillingness to address the struc-tural racism that has given birth to President-Elect Trump.

I have not spoken up—to family, friends, and neighbors—about rac-ism.

I have not fought hard enough for my fellow Americans.

I have not called out, or called in, other white people enough.

In order for the country to heal, well meaning whites like me need to "take the gun away" from white supremacists. Not only did we literally give white supremacists the gun (and the bomb), we also gutted the safety net that you t[ri]ed to repair.

I am sorry. We let you down.

When you leave office, and return to civilian life, I will join you in whatever task you undertake. I will do whatever it takes to keep your legacy intact.

With love and respect,
Martin Gleason

At the end of the day, Fiona had to pick the 10LADs from the email that had come flying in, and a guy on the writing team who sat not far from Kolbie's office was in charge of composing the response to America in meltdown mode.

"I haven't gotten very far," he said, sitting in front of a blank screen. He didn't want me to use his name. He had been up all night, at his parents' house in Ohio, where he'd been knocking on doors to get out the vote, and then he flew back to work, and he had never expected to have to write a letter like this.

"Personally, the worst thing is that it feels like a rebuke of the connection we're trying to make between the president and the people," he said. "Like, if our responsibility in this office is to connect the president to the people, I'm asking myself, 'Did we fail?'"

He looked at me, expecting something.

"And I don't understand it, because he's read more mail than any president in history," he said. "He seems more connected to the people than any president in history."

I felt compelled to remind him that Obama hadn't been running for reelection. Clinton was the one who had lost.

"The bargaining stage of grief," he mumbled.

Some hours later, he would show me the letter he had composed on behalf of President Obama to America in meltdown mode.

Thank you for writing. I understand the feelings of uncertainty many Americans have had lately. But one thing I am certain of is that America remains the greatest nation on earth. What sets us apart is not simply our economic and military power, but also the principles upon which our Union was founded: pluralism and openness, the rule of law, civil liberties, and the self-evident truth—expanded with each generation—that we are all created equal.

One election does not change who we are as a people. The America I know is clear-eyed and big-hearted—full of courage and ingenuity. Although politics can significantly affect our lives, our success has always been rooted in the willingness of our people to look out for one another and help each other through tough times. More than my Presidency, or any Presidency, it is the optimism and hard work of people like you that have changed our country for the better and that will continue to give us the strength we need to persevere.

Progress doesn't come easily, and it hasn't always followed a straight line, but I firmly believe that history ultimately moves in the direction of justice, prosperity, freedom, and inclusion—not because it is inevitable, but because people like you speak out and hold our country accountable to our highest ideals. That's why I hope you continue to stay engaged. And I want you to know Michelle and I will be right there with you.

Again, thank you for writing. Whatever challenges we may face, there is no greater form of patriotism than the belief that America is not yet finished and a brighter future lies ahead.

Sincerely,

Barack Obama

I could hear Yena outside in the hall, laughing and joking with some other people on the writing team; the discrepancy was palpable. Yena was the kind of person you would want at your mother's funeral. She was trying to put a positive spin on the situation.

"Isn't it so cool?" she was saying. "I think we have a real opportunity to hone in on the president's message. But more than that, like, this is friggin' America. Which is like, what an opportunity. Like, what an honor. You know what I mean? Like, woo! What an honor! Like, what? I lived my life!"

She told me about her work helping Fiona assemble the transition materials, said she was determined to feel optimistic about the new team continuing their work on behalf of letter writers.

"It's like, the Obama administration did all this to hear people's stories," Yena said. "How could they possibly not meet us and grow it further?"

I asked her what she thought she'd do after she left this place. She said she was applying to grad school; she wanted to learn about hostage negotiations. It was because of her time in OPC. That letter she told me about when I first met her, about the mother and the kidnapped son—it had changed her. Lacey had had a similar awakening; she was planning to forge a career working with veterans. Ever since the letter from Ashley about her dad and the guns and the shooting. Kolbie wasn't sure what she'd do next. Something with language, something with children and the power of language. Fiona said she wanted to focus on being married for a while.

I stopped by Fiona's office to see how she was coming with the 10LADs. She was already on the couch with her choices on her lap. "I had some rice pudding," she said, managing a smile. The emails had been printed, and she was flipping through the pages considering the sequence. "I think it will hit him like it hit us, a pile of voices that don't follow a tight narrative." She spoke quietly as she sorted, mostly to herself. "People concerned for others," she said, holding a few out. "People concerned for themselves," she said about another group, and when she was finished, she sat up straight.

"Okay, so this is the first one," she said, showing it to me. The writer was cheering Trump's victory. He recommended a fire into which Obama could put all of his executive orders and, together with the rest of the ruinous liberals, watch them burn.

"It's an introduction, because it sort of feels like the day began," Fiona said, and I could tell she had no interest in defending her choice.

"And then I like the personal nature of this one for the second," she said, going through her choices with the satisfaction of an author reading her final draft. "She's married to someone who voted differently from her. But they will continue to be a family. I think it's nice to have something so passionate and uplifting closer to the front.

"Then this is one where I felt it was moving; he isn't sharing his own personal stake; he's saying this is what I hope you'll do with the power you hold right now for others.

"Then behind him this is someone who is in dire financial straits. I felt that was someone whose voice really matters right now.

"Then this is someone with disabilities, a community that has self-identified as vulnerable.

"Then this one is incredible. What a guy. 'I will join you in whatever task you undertake.'

"Then this is a Trump supporter who is making his case. . . . Obviously there are difficult parts of this. But he is someone who volunteers, and he wants to share who he is and why he wanted this outcome. And he also is really frustrated by the presence of immigrants in the U.S.

"Behind him, this is someone who works on tech that he thinks could be dangerous.

"Then a deferred action recipient.

"Then I'll end with this. Because I think so many people are thinking, *What do we tell our daughters today?*"

She gathered the letters. She checked her phone. She jiggled the lid on the glass water bottle that always accompanied her. "So I'm going to hand them off. And they'll get scanned and sent around."

Some weeks later, Fiona got a call from Rob Porter, the person who had been hired to become White House staff secretary for President-Elect Donald Trump. He wanted a meeting, so Fiona went. He asked about the mailroom, how it worked, and Fiona told him about the transition materials, the binders, and she did her best to summarize.

"Ten letters a day," she said, as if that would simply be the normal order of business. The president would be *expected* to read his mail and answer it. Rob took notes. The meeting was maybe twenty minutes. He said someone would be getting back to her for more information.

No one did.

Samples, 2016

11/9/16
fr 2

From: james

Submitted: 11/9/2016 12:12 PM EST

Email:

Phone:

Address:

Message: Start packing ! Get ready to watch a big bonfire, maybe in the vegetable garden, where Trump will burn the AFA and most of your executive orders. You can watch it from your new residence with all the other liberals who have been trying to destroy the country.

From: **Alessandra Shurina**

Submitted: 11/9/2016 8:08 AM EST

Email:

Phone:

Address: Tallahassee, Florida

Message: President Obama -
My heart is broken this morning. It is so, seemingly irreparably broken. I am trying hard not to wallow in the hurt that I feel and instead trying to channel my outrage in grief into something productive. I have a five month old daughter and this is not the world I want her to grow up in - please tell me there is something I can do to help remedy this situation? To lessen the blow? How can I get involved? What do you recommend that I do to ensure that at the VERY most we only have four years of a fascist demagogue as president? I'm willing to devote my life to volunteering for a cause or a candidate with the promise of defeating not only Trump but the hateful principles that he was elected on. This has been a wake up call for me. I can't just vote. I must DO. Please, President Obama tell me, what do I do?

From: Amanda Bott

Submitted: 11/9/2016 2:29 AM EST

Email:

Phone:

Address: Rochester, Washington

Message: November 8, 2016

Dear President Obama,

Eight years ago on election night I wrote a letter to my unborn children telling them how proud I was to be one of the millions of Americans who voted for you. On that night I cried tears of joy and pride and happiness. Tonight I'm crying tears of sorrow. I'm crying for my beautiful country with its beautiful ideals. I can't see a way through four years of a hatemonger in the oval office. For the first time in my life I am terrified for my country. Terrified. I have two beautiful daughters. I have a two year old and a five year old and they deserve to have a future and I'm honestly and genuinely scared that there may not be a future with this man in office. He has the ability to deploy nuclear weapons and he has said he would use them.

How did we fall so far? How did this happen? Eight years ago we voted for hope and tonight we voted for hate. How is that possible? Eight years ago I voted for you to be my leader. I'm asking you to lead me now. Please Mr. President, tell us what we can do as a nation now? Tell me what to do as a citizen and a mother. Now that this person is Commander in Chief of the largest, most powerful military on earth what can I do? Do I have to write letters to world leaders apologizing and explaining that we really don't want a nuclear holocaust? Should I write to the heads of state of every nation on earth and apologize for the next four years and beg them to realize that this hatemonger does not speak for us? But, doesn't he?

We elected him. We elected him to speak for us. We heard the hate and prejudice and anger and bigotry. We saw him mock the handicapped and prisoners of war and gold star families - things both republicans and democrats alike always treated as sacred, and yet we voted for him. God help us we voted for him. God help us all.

From: **Ms. Nicole Davis**

nitted: 11/9/2016 12:37 AM EST

Email:

'hone:

dress: Tobyhanna, Pennsylvania

sage: Hello President Obama, thank you for all you've done for our country. During your terms you've made me feel safe, and safe to raise my daughter. Now I am entering a stage where I am terrified to survive with Trump. I am a disabled individual as I have seizures. Trumps comments about those who are disabled have turned individuals against those like me. I am afraid he will hurt individuals like myself, is this a rationalized fear? I'm just afraid and would appreciate any type of reassurance he can not hurt me for my sickness. Thank you so much.

2016

From: ████████████

Submitted: 11/9/2016 12:01 AM EST

Email: ████████████

Phone: ████████████

Address: ████████████

Message: Mr President,

First and foremost, thank you for all you've done. I am so proud to call you my president. I have such a tremendous amount of respect for you as a husband and a father. As I'm watching election results, I'm literally in tears. My wife is undocumented. I have three children. I have never been so scared in my life. I know there is very little you can do now for immigration reform, but thank you so much for trying. We've been working on adjusting her status, but I do not know what will happen now. There is now a very good chance I'll be separated from my family and that is terrifying to me. I know you've done all you can do and I thank you for that. I have been so proud of you over the last 8 years and I wish you the best for the future.

Sincerely,

████████████

From:

Submitted: 11/9/2016 2:17 PM EST

Email:

Phone:

Address: Santiago de los Caballeros,

Message: Dear President Obama,

My name is _____. I am not from the United States and do not live there.

I know that there is a big chance that you will not read this letter, but there are some things that I would like you to know.

Growing up as a gay man in a country where everything about being homosexual is wrong and embarrassing is hard. Death threats from parents, bullying at school, or just simple "Gay jokes" that make someone of our sexual orientation or with an open mind feel bad.

You gave me hope, reading about everything you did for our people in your country made me realize that, maybe, the world is not as bad as it seems, maybe there is more than being scared and hiding all the time. You inspired me to move on, to be better and to be the change that I want to see in the world, hoping that one day I would live in the United States so that I could have a normal life.

It is heartbreaking knowing that your presidency is coming to an end, and that the LGBT community will suffer a huge impact,

Thank you, Mr. President for 8 years of hope, for helping me growing up and for a doing a great job, not only for America, but for the rest of the world too,

From:

mitted: 11/9/2016 9:13 AM EST

Email:

Phone:

ldress:

ssage: Dear Mr. President,

I woke up this morning in a state of disbelief. Partly because I only slept 4 hours after drinking down a whole bottle of Jagermeister, but mostly because Donald Trump is President Elect.

My family has been in this country a long time. My earliest family came to this country on the Mayflower. They struggled and worked hard for "The American Dream" and the fruits of their labor was shown through their achievements. Most notably would be ▓▓▓▓▓▓ signer of the Articles of Confederation ▓▓▓▓▓▓ delegate to the Continental Congress and ▓▓▓▓▓▓

My dreams for what would be a happy and prosperous America are dimmer today. I took a walk this morning to take in the air and just experience the day. I live in ▓▓▓▓ and I heard no birds chirping. Here ▓▓▓▓▓▓ it was raining, very fitting in my opinion, because it feels like the world is crying. I keep in touch with pen pals overseas in the U.K. and they're all in disbelief as well.

I just find it hard to believe that we can "Make America Great Again" through the path that Trump is providing. The America he speaks of is a divided America. An America that wouldn't let women and African Americans vote, an America that would have me separated in schools and offices and bathrooms... I feel like I'm playing the 'Trumped up' version of a board game and we had to "Go back 5 spaces".

I never one-hundred percent agreed with everything you said. But I firmly believe that you're going to go down in history as one of the country's greatest Presidents. You've done so much for civil rights and upholding justice. Keeping Americans as healthy as you could. Honestly, my heart is breaking for you and Michelle and your family. I'm so sorry that for the next four years, you have to watch an angry Oompa Loompa with thin wisps of hair attempt to make America "Go back 5 spaces".

Wishing you all the best,

From: Mrs. Katie Lowden Bahr

Submitted: 11/9/2016 10:20 AM EST

Email:

Phone:

Address:
Madison, Wisconsin

Message: Dear Mr. President,

Eight years ago, when you won the presidential election I was elated. I was hopeful. I watched in awe as you took the stage with your wife and daughters. It felt amazing. Four years later, when you won once again, I was relieved. I had welcomed my first daughter two months earlier. A daughter born with a heart defect. A daughter who will forever have a pre-existing condition. Last night I watched in disbelief, as our country elected Donald Trump. I have another daughter now, and I'm sure as the father to two young women yourself, you feel the disgust over Mr. Trumps treatment of women as well.

I'm writing you this morning out of fear. This election was won on fear. Fear of the other, fear of the unknown. Fear of race, sexual orientation, gender, religion. Fear bred of ignorance. And now I too am afraid. I'm afraid of how this will change our country, and the world, in the next four years. You have always given me hope as a leader, and I could use a little of that right about now.

This morning I ask one thing of you; make these next two months count. As much as you possibly can. Secure the next four years for our country. For the American people that don't even realize what a grave mistake they have made. Do what you can to secure health care, foreign policy, immigration, education, the environment, jobs, and all of the other important issues we all know Mr. Trump is hoping to unravel.

Thank you for the last eight years. You will go down in history as one of the greatest leaders our country has known. Your accomplishments and grace under pressure has been a gift to us all.

Gratefully,
Katie Lowden Bahr

11/9/17
#1   Dec 20, 2016

Dear President Obama,

For five years I was a
home health nurse in your old
hometown of Chicago. My
territory included Rogers Park
and south Evanston, one of
the most diverse neighborhoods
in this wonderful country of
ours.

I've been in more homes
than most people, and I
want you to know, that every
African American home I
entered had a picture of you
in it. Usually it was the
entire beautiful Obama
family. You have meant
so much to so many
people - your grace,
intelligence and integrity
will be so missed.

Like so many other
people I am horrified
and anxious about the
results of the election. I
hope you continue to speak
out and work for the
values we hold so dear -
the democratic process, and
the equality of all people.

You and your family
are truly beautiful, and
will be so sorely missed.
I certainly don't blame you
for wanting to take a break,
but this country continues
to desperately need you.
I hope to continue to see
you on the world stage,
fighting for good.

             Much Love,
             Tracy LaRock

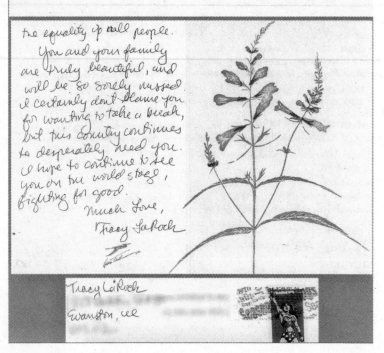

Tracy LaRock

Evanston, IL

November 20, 2016

Dear President Obama:

In January of 2009, in the absence of ability, time or energy (or all three) to travel to DC for your swearing in, our close-knit group of friends and neighbors decided to throw our own inaugural ball in your honor. We cleared out a living room, dressed to the nines, drank champagne and danced all night. Parents, kids, everyone. Several weeks prior to Christmas, I had been in DC for a visit (I am a DC native) and as I walked through Union Station, I saw Barack Obama in a gift store and knew I had found the perfect "party favor" for our ball. At the party, we hung the American flag from my father's funeral on the living room wall (he fought in the South Pacific in WWII), and stood O up in front of it (see small picture in the enclosed; that's me with you) and party guests "had their picture taken with the President". My father would have been so proud to be a part of this.

On November 13 this year, we had a post-election potluck. Alas, we had anticipated it being a celebration, but reality intervened. We considered cancelling, but quickly realized that gathering our friends around us was what we, and they, needed even more. We brought O down from the attic, and posted a board for all of us to "teach 'em how to say goodbye." (I am obsessed with "Hamilton".) Enclosed are photos of what we want to say to you.

I believe strongly that we will get through this, and that we will come out better on the other side, but it will be difficult, enraging and in many ways sad. Your influence in our lives and in the lives of our children was incalculable. My daughter is a NC Teaching Fellow, and she is in her third year teaching sixth grade math at a Title 1 school in Durham: she can tell by their behavior when her kids return from a school break who had food in their home during the break and who didn't. She recently did a successful GoFundMe campaign and raised money to buy new desks for her classroom: the old ones were falling apart right in front of the children. But she and her ridiculously dedicated teaching peers are the future of this country. (And I know she would welcome a presidential visit to her classroom, should you have future spare time...). We will get through this, in part due to the dedication of people like Millie and her fellow teachers.

Thank you for all that you did. Thank you for your kindness. Thank you for sharing your wonderful family with us. Thank you for being the president our children really knew first, and will always hold as the hallmark of what a president should be. I have your first acceptance speech taped to my home office wall, and read it periodically for inspiration. Your hair may be a little grayer now, but you can be sure that those gray hairs were honestly earned. Thank you.

Maureen Dolan Rosen,

Chapel Hill NC

BARACK OBAMA

April 26, 2017

Ms. Maureen Dolan Rosen
Chapel Hill, North Carolina

Dear Maureen:

Thank you for the very kind note and for passing along the thoughtful messages from those who attended your potluck. Your optimism is inspiring, and I share your hope for our country's future.

Remember that the long sweep of America is defined by forward motion. And although it sometimes seems like we take one step back for every two steps forward, I am confident that so long as engaged and passionate citizens like you keep speaking out and working in earnest to defend the values that make us who we are, our progress will continue.

Thanks again for thinking of me. Serving as your President was the greatest honor of my life—it was worth every gray hair! Please tell Millie I'm proud of her service in the classroom. I wish you and your loved ones the very best.

Sincerely,

4/18/17
s16

December 6, 2016
Jaconita, New Mexico

Dear President Obama,

I heard your speech from Florida today and was comforted. I wondered what you did the day after the election to salve your wounds. I baked an apple-cranberry crumb pie and ate half of it that very day. Two friends of mine went out for a salsa lesson. A neighbor down the road read "Hillbilly Elegy" until first light and then threw herself into putting her garden to bed for the winter. A retired teacher friend in D.C. went to her scheduled piano lesson, stopping on the way home for a bottle of bourbon. (She usually drinks a little port at twilight)

At first I swore off watching the news. Then I decided that if I were going to hell in a handbasket

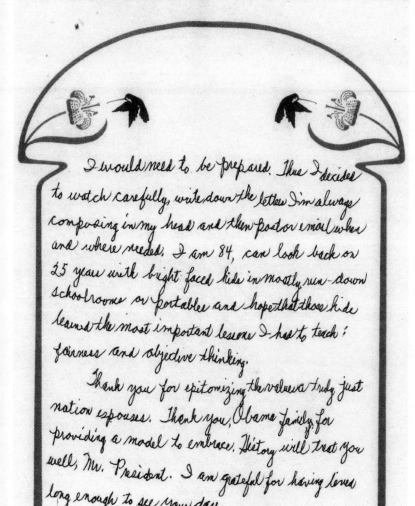

I would need to be prepared. Thus I decided to watch carefully, write down the letters I'm always composing in my head and then post or email when and where needed. I am 84, can look back on 25 years with bright faced kids in mostly run-down schoolrooms or portables and hope that those kids learned the most important lessons I had to teach: fairness and objective thinking.

Thank you for epitomizing the values a truly just nation espouses. Thank you, Obama family, for providing a model to embrace. History will treat you well, Mr. President. I am grateful for having lived long enough to see your day.

Sincerely yours,
Roberta Fine

Michaela

602

12 NOV 2016 PM 4 1

President Barack Obama
The White House
1600 Pennsylvania Avenue NW
Washington, DC 20500

20500—

QC✓#020

✓#034

"RECEIVED DAMAGED"
488

NOV 17 2016

1/9/17
p.3

Dear Mr. President,

I am writing to you on the morning after the election after a restless night and two hours of sleep. I remember today going very differently eight years ago, when it was announced that you had been elected. I was in my first year at community college, walking through an icy quad in my snow boots with a big, dumb grin on my face, every closed door before me suddenly opening up, like magic. There was so much hope in that moment. It would be another four years before the DACA program would change my life.

I was born in the Philippines to two hardworking, college-educated parents. We lived in Manila, had a house, two cars, a dog I loved more than anything. We'd vacation in Chicago every few years. One of those early trips involved a rare April snow when I was four. One of my first memories was scooping some up in my mitten'd hand and taking it inside, only to watch it melt not two minutes later. It was my first snow. That might have been the moment I fell in love with this place.

When my father was forced into early retirement and unable to find work, my parents spent a year trying to make it on his severance and my mother's secretary salary. In 2000, they decided to leave everything behind and try to make it here. Though we were petitioned as a family through my maternal grandparents, the broken immigration system and extreme backlogs caused all three of us to become undocumented after overstaying our Visas. What followed were 16 of the hardest years of our lives. Countless lost jobs and missed opportunities, the university I never got to attend, the job offers I had to decline, days of staying indoors with nothing to do but wait and worry, depression and anxiety, the isolation of being friendless by choice (too many questions), losing our health insurance and deciding to go without to save money, the foreclosure of our home, my parents' eventual divorce. The pain of those years is still so palpable and raw that I doubt I'll ever be able to let it go.

I was amazed at how fast the transition was for me from "illegal alien" to "real person". Within 2 months of DACA approval I had a social security number, learned how to drive (properly, at 23), got a license and a part time job. Within a year I had landed a full time position _____ at a firm I still work for today (but never did let go of that weekend job). I started making friends again. I made plans for a future that included furthering my education and skillset _____. I happily paid rent, taxes and bills. I jokingly complained about, but secretly enjoyed, being tired from working seven days a week. I enjoyed the minutiae of my daily life. I was a real person, with the luxury of mundane, real person problems. I did not squander this gift. I have savored every last bit of it.

For the past four years, the road for me had been become quiet and predictable. But today, I am terrified. As an early DACA recipient, who has since renewed twice, everything I have worked for is in jeopardy. I grew up here. This has and always will be my home. But today I woke up feeling like I couldn't trust anyone, and have barely been able to eat or speak. It's been very hard to stay positive, but the more I look around, the more I see a community of support building, and with it, there is hope. Struggle has imbued us immigrants (documented or not) with a magic and a fire that cannot be quelled. We are here. Please don't give up on us.

Before I close this, I want you to know that regardless of what happens, _____
_____ I am grateful for everything the DACA program brought into my life. I would not have had the courage, nor the will to go on after this election were it not for the confidence this program, my education and experience has given me. Someday I'll teach my future child about the value of compassion, sacrifice and hard work in the face of adversity. And who knows, maybe someday she'll be President.

With great admiration and respect,

Michaela _____

Darin M. Reffitt

Wilmington, DE

President Barack Obama
c/o Fiona Reeves
Office of Presidential Correspondence
Room 412
Eisenhower Executive Office Building
1650 Pennsylvania Avenue, NW
Washington, DC 20502

November 9, 2016

Mr. President:

I wrote you on this same day eight years ago, which seems to have passed far too quickly and yet feels like a lifetime ago. I wrote the day after the 2008 elections, and was honored to learn recently that my letter was selected as one of the ten that you are given each day to read.

With everything that has happened in the intervening years, I do not expect that you would remember my letter or my specific situation. But on that day I congratulated you on your victory, and explained how—while my heart had soared with pride at you being elected as our 44th President—I awoke that next morning to news of passed ballot measures that had stripped or codified the removal of rights for my LGBT brothers and sisters in California, Florida, Arizona, and Arkansas. I then shared with you the story of my partner's car accident, and how the lack of same sex marriage had impacted us so dramatically as we dealt with everything from insurance companies to cell phone companies to hospitals. I poured my heart out about the frustrations I had faced at repeatedly hearing that I had no rights as his partner, hoping that my story could help you understand why the issue was so tremendously important.

And now, knowing that you actually read my letter within the first month of your presidency, I hope that it in some small way helped to ignite within you the understanding that led to your change of heart on marriage equality, and that my story had something to do with your decision to not defend the Defense of Marriage Act. I cling to that hope today, because the only thing keeping me from brink of despair at the outcome of last night's election is the hope that one person can indeed make a difference.

Because I will be fighting on and I do plan to make a difference.

But this letter isn't about me. It's about you. I am writing today to thank you. To thank you for so many things that you've done over the past eight years, and for the integrity, dignity, and class that you brought to the office of the President. To thank you because you validated every bit of faith that I had in you in 2008, and made me proud that I had been an advocate and volunteer during your campaign.

It hasn't been an easy eight years for those of us who supported you. First, we had to defend you to the people who were sure that you were going to take their guns, turn us into a socialist state, and destroy our economy. Instead, you shored up our economy, pulled us out of the worst financial disaster since the great depression, and fought for people who were less fortunate. Under your leadership, we were able to insure millions of less fortunate people who lacked access to healthcare, we saw the Dow soar to record levels, and we experienced the longest period of job growth on record.

But then, we also had to defend you to our own, to people who voted for you but then didn't think you did enough; people who either don't understand that a President isn't all powerful or who saw you trying to work across the aisle and viewed compromising and negotiation as weakness, instead of an integral part of how things were designed to work by our founding fathers. We had to explain that incremental change is better than no change; that sometimes you don't get perfect, but you accept better and go from there.

We had to watch in horror as Republicans in Congress blocked every initiative, brought us to the brink of defaulting on our debt, and refused to address the growing epidemic of gun violence in our nation. We cried with you as you spoke following shooting after shooting, even as those who opposed you failed to accept that you were expressing genuine sorrow, to our shock and dismay.

They vilified you at every turn, but we loved you through it all, knowing that you would keep fighting for what was right, and just, and fair for even the least fortunate of our citizens.

And through it all, you brought honor and dignity to the White House.

I have many friends in other countries, people who could attest first-hand to me how much you and your team—Secretary Clinton especially—had done to rebuild the reputation of our great nation overseas. I recall a trip we took to Italy in 2003 where our group of Americans was shunned because of the situation in Iraq, so much so that I began telling people we were Canadian to avoid being overcharged and snubbed. But you repaired all of that, and you brought us back to being a nation respected the world over.

And somehow you always stayed positive. You never sank to the level of some people who feel they need to respond to every personal attacks and perceived slight. And that's perhaps the most amazing thing of all.

I cannot remotely fathom what it must be like to see yourself and your family attacked in the vicious ways I've witnessed yours being assaulted online and in social media. I'm sure as a loving father you did your best to shield your daughters from being exposed to the hateful rhetoric lobbed against your family. But I know that at some point they inevitably became aware of it, and I can only imagine the heart wrenching pain it must have caused you to see them hurting as you explained that there are people who simply hate; how they would need to fight against that discrimination for the rest of their lives; and how even becoming the most powerful man in the world can't overcome it or matter to some people—people who will never accept that a man isn't inferior because of the color of his skin.

It wasn't until your wife—a paragon of grace and class as our First Lady—shared the mantra "When they go low, we go high," during the Democratic Convention, that I realized how you kept your beautiful daughters smiling throughout it all: you led by example. It's my fervent hope that they will someday follow in your footsteps and take a role in our great democracy. But whatever they do, I'm sure that they will succeed, inspired by the passion and determination of their father.

But it's not just them that you've inspired.

I'm sure that today you fear for your legacy; that, over the next four years, you will see so much of what you accomplished in the last eight years destroyed. I share your fear.

In Lin-Manuel Miranda's *Hamilton*, Alexander Hamilton asks, "What is a legacy? It's planting seeds in a garden you never get to see." Shortly thereafter, Thomas Jefferson states, "I'll give him this: his financial system is a work of genius. I couldn't undo it if I tried. And I tried."

The coming administration may work to reverse the progress you made. But they cannot undo the secondary impact of those accomplishments, nor the memory of the country as it is today.

Since I last wrote you, I'm pleased to share that my now-husband and I were joined in a civil union in August of 2012, which became a legal marriage in 2013 when Delaware became the 11th state to approve same-sex marriage. We now share full rights and privileges, at least for the time being. But 55% of Americans now support same-sex marriage, and will no longer buy into the hateful rhetoric that it will destroy society or hurt children. That's part of your legacy too. The changes in attitudes and values that your policies instilled won't just vanish overnight.

And unlike Mr. Hamilton, you are still here, still able to plant more seeds.

I have to believe in the basic goodness of Americans, that common sense will eventually prevail. I am sure that you and Secretary Clinton, and others like you, will find ways to bring some good out of what has happened. Whether it's convincing the 33% of eligible Americans who aren't registered to vote to do so, or getting more people engaged in the political process at local levels, or just enabling us to better understand the things that drove us to where we are, we know it's not over.

I had the great pleasure of hearing President Clinton speak at a conference in 2014. One of the things he said that inspired me was this (roughly paraphrased): "I travel all over the world, and one thing is consistently true: in places where people are focused on what they have in common, instead of on what divides them, great things are happening; in places where people are focused on what separates them, instead of what brings them together, great things aren't possible." I was proud to meet him and shake his hand that day, and I hope one day to meet you and shake your hand similarly.

In the meantime, I can only hope that the vast majority of Americans will soon realize how much our next President has driven us to focus on what divides us, and will recognize that we can't survive as a nation and do great things as long as that's the case.

And until then, we will continue to fight for the ideals you put forth eight years ago. We can afford to do no less. And I promise that I'll be here to support you and fight with you when the time comes to do so in the future.

So thank you, again. I've learned so much from you over the past 8 years. You've inspired me to care more and to be a better American.

I remain proud to call you my President.

Sincerely,

Darin M. Reffitt

CHAPTER 17

Vicki Shearer,
November 9, 2016

RENTON, WASHINGTON

> *Submitted: 11/9/2016 12:11 PM EST*
> *Message:*
> *You said that the sun would shine tomorrow. Sir, I live in Seattle WA and the sun is not shining. In fact it's raining. I am so upset with the election outcome, on all levels. But, the hardest of all is the division I feel in my own family now. My oldest son is gay. My younger son is married to a legal Mexican immigrant. Their newborn daughter was born just weeks ago. My husband, their father, voted for [T]rump. Yes, as he keeps telling me, his vote is his right. I do get it. But, in my heart, he voted against our family. He could have written in a name or left it blank like George W. Bush supposedly did. I have felt so safe and confident my family was being looked after and accepted by your Presidency. I don't have those feelings now. . . .*

Vicki has lived in this small ranch house for the past seventeen years and all her life in Renton, south of Seattle. The hanging pots are mostly petunias, and as you can see, she doesn't care about a color scheme. It's just: color! An explosion of color. Tim put in an automatic watering system last year, and that's the reason they look this good. Gardening is her exercise. That plus her morning walk around the neighborhood, just seeing what's going on.

Before everyone gets here, Vicki, who is in her early sixties, soft and round with a dark pixie cut, would like to say a few words about Tim.

"Tim is a gentleman. Of course he loves our kids and our family. He has a better way of turning things off. He's more logical, and I'm more emotional."

She would like to let Tim speak for himself about why he voted the way he did. "He's explained it to me a hundred times, and I still can't hear it."

Vicki and Tim have been married for forty-one years. They met right when she got out of high school on a summer afternoon. She always tells people how impressed he was with her brand-new car. ("It was a Volkswagen Rabbit," Tim will say. He was not impressed with that car.) They got to talking. They went to the Space Needle. They talked and talked. "You're the first person to hear what I'm saying," he said. "Who doesn't like to hear that?" she said.

Vicki has heard of couples divorcing in the aftermath of the 2016 election. Of families split apart. Sisters avoiding brothers, cousins disinvited, in-laws going silent or into hiding. Vicki doesn't think that kind of thing could happen to her family, but she acknowledges it's been a strain.

"That night was sad and depressing and gray and dark and not happy."

She and Tim were home, tuned in to news. Remember this is the West Coast, so everything is three hours earlier. Both of them were pretty bitter at that point. They missed Bernie. That whole thing with Bernie disappearing the way he did—that had them both raging against the Democratic Party. Which is sad because they were lifers. For example, on Election Night 2008, Vicki had baked an Obama pie. (She is known for her theme pies. "Pies are happy food.") It was strawberry-blueberry. She had tried to carve a likeness of Barack into the crust, but she kind of messed up the chin—"too wide!" Everyone joked that Michelle would have appreciated the big ears because they knew Michelle liked to tease Barack about those ears. Everyone in the family referred to the president as "Barack."

On Election Night 2016, Vicki had no interest in making a pie. She planned to watch Hillary Clinton win and get it over with; she was not a fan. She was disappointed in herself for getting caught up with every twist and turn of the campaign. What a waste of time. It was all so ugly. It took her out of the garden. Tim would be at work at the asphalt plant. A lot of those guys on the crew are Republicans, so maybe that contributed to it.

But really, she has no idea how it happened. One day she looked up, and she was married to a Trump voter. An alien in her own home. *How could something like that have happened?*

She had found out Tim was a Trump voter a few weeks before Election Day when—get this—he filled out an absentee ballot, and—seriously, get this—she was the one making the run to the post office that day. That's what makes this whole thing doubly and triply hard. *She had it in her hand.* She stood in front of that mailbox hemming and hawing. She didn't have to drop it in. Tim would never have known. She thought about secrets. She thought about the boys. The boat. Fishing and hiking and all the love. The happiest life she could have hoped for. She pulled open the mailbox and closed her eyes, and with a flick of a wrist, it was done.

A vote against her family. A vote against her as a woman. Against Neil, a gay man. Against Nick and his wife, Dani, from Mexico. Against Isla too. Against the dog if they'd still had one. How does a family absorb something like that? How does a country? Factions forming, betrayal happening, suspicion and hate popping up.

Forgetting the whole mess would need to happen. That was how Vicki thought about it on Election Night when she sat there watching the results with Tim. Hillary Clinton would win, and Trump would be out of the picture, and the forgetting could begin.

But then of course blue states started going red, and Vicki couldn't believe it, and she went to bed. Pulled the covers over her head. Tim came in later. She has no idea when.

One thing about this house is there's no TV in the living room. That's always been the rule. A living room is for conversation and being together. It's small, just off the kitchen, soft beige wall-to-wall carpet and couches coming together to form an L around an end table.

Most of the decorations are Vicki's crafts, framed embroidery, pots of dried flowers; Tim nailed up that narrow shelf so Vicki could display a row of adorable miniature houses, barns, and churches—a cheerful little town.

Neil, the older son, is first to arrive. He's thirty-eight, tall, with a full beard, a gray cap, the same smile as his mom's. He knows what he wants to accomplish today in the living room. He wants to be forthright. Six months have passed since Election Day, and he wants his dad to know his vote still hurts. "That there was something he would choose that superseded *me*," Neil says. "And I know that's just ego talking. It doesn't mean it's right or wrong. It just means that it hurt."

Neil has always been good at explaining things. It's why he loves his job working with customers at the insurance company. (Even policy language has nuance.) Explaining things is about more than imparting knowledge; it's about having compassion for those who don't yet understand. Neil learned that one the hard way, just after college, when he was struggling with how to come out to his parents. It was not a smooth transition. Out of nowhere a postcard arrived in the mail from a friend, the message referring to some guy Neil thought was cute. His mom happened upon it. *Wait, what?* And should she discuss the matter with Tim? A lot of hush-hush, confusion, and shame.

Neil grew distant, eventually moved away to Olympia. He was determined to live an honest life, whether his parents understood it or not. Soon he came to miss them. He wondered if that part would fade with time. Apparently not. After about six years, he couldn't bear it anymore, and he made the decision to reunite with his parents. His gestures were grand at first—fancy dinners, evenings on the town—one more awkward than the next.

Eventually, Neil decided to just come home, here, to the living room, once a week. Every Friday, no matter what, no matter how the conversation had gone the week before or how they left it. There would always be another Friday. It took the pressure off. They got to know one another again. That was maybe ten years ago. It seems ridiculous now to think there was ever a problem.

. . .

Nick and Dani are next to arrive. Nick works with Tim at the asphalt plant. When Nick was little, he played with G.I. Joe. "He's all boy!" his grandma would say. (Neil had a Raggedy Ann doll.) People still say Nick and Neil look like twins, right down to the matching dimples on their chins, except now Nick has a totally shaved head and no hat, so you can see it comes to a point.

Nick and Dani got married last year. Dani does almost all of the talking, which Nick loves. She has added so much pizzazz to this family. For example, no one else in the family curses. ("She can light it up," Tim says.) Dani was twelve when she and her family left Mexico. They had been selling CDs on the street to buy groceries. It took them fifteen years to become U.S. citizens. "They put us through hell." She's a husky woman with thick, dark hair swept to the side and an easy laugh, and she's here on the couch holding Isla, the baby, who's eight months old now. Isla has Nick's complexion—fair, almost translucent skin. When Dani first laid eyes on her, she said she was glad Isla came out that way. Light. It would make her life easier. Vicki can hardly listen to talk like that.

Tim is the last to enter the room. He's a rounder version of Neil and Nick, bald on top, white tufts on the sides. He's any guy you'd see at Home Depot. He's the guy who would let you go ahead of him in line because you only have a few things. When he retires in a few years, Tim wants to stay right here in this house and in this beautiful part of the country. All the outdoors, all the activities. He'll be able to do things during the workweek. No lines. This entire area has become jammed with people and money and huge houses. It was good for the asphalt business, though.

Anyway, it's time to deal with it. The fact of Tim's vote and the pain it has caused. A family has to deal with it. America has to deal with it.

Vicki pulls up a chair so she has a good view of everybody gathered together on the couches. They ordered a fish plate from the local deli—smoked salmon, cheese, crackers—which should be here soon.

"You know, I felt it was a vote against our family," Vicki starts, turning to Tim. It's not the first time she's uttered these words. "I was like, Who am I married to?"

"I know there are people who voted in the sense of, like, trolling," Neil offers, looking over at his dad. " 'The election is broken. Let's break it further and *vote for a reality TV star!* ' "

"He was against everything that we are as a family," Dani says, the pile-on continuing without interruption.

"What upset me was that Trump *didn't* upset you. He doesn't upset you!"

"He gave permission to people who were on the fence about being racist. He gave them the green light. You see now, like, holy shit, it's still alive and kicking."

"That cynicism—Trump is such a cynical choice. And I don't believe that you are cynical, Dad."

"He's a con man. He conned America. Some people think that makes him a great businessman. He's a con man and a bully. I think you're smarter—I *know* you're smarter."

Tim has his arms folded tight, his gazed fixed on a spot on the carpet.

"I realize I'm the bad guy here," he says. "But somehow this has got to stop."

Nick would like to take a moment to address a related topic. He would like to offer an image of the hell that was his and Dani's house on Election Night.

"Dani's mom was staying with us, and those two got in a big argument," Nick says.

"Huge argument," Dani says. She is happy to tell the story, as many times as necessary if it will help her . . . deal. "So we're watching TV," she says, "and my mom comes into the room. My dad's there too. And I'm like, 'I can't believe this asshole won.' And she's like, 'Well, we voted for him.'

"And I just went, *'What?!'*"

She takes a gulp of air, slides forward on the couch as if needing the proper position from which to gather and emit a high volume of hot steam. Isla, for her part, does not stir. Isla appears prepared to snooze on through her mother in revved-up mode.

"Because up until that point, it was all about *this* family," Dani goes on. She talks fast, a patter that draws people in. "This entire time I was like, *I still can't believe Nick's dad voted for Trump. His entire family is what Trump's trying to fight.* So for my parents to tell me that they had voted for him, to me it was like, *What are you doing? He doesn't want us here!* My brother's not a citizen yet. When he was younger, he got in some trouble with an ex-girlfriend. So I'm telling my mom, 'Do you realize that the president you voted into the White House is probably going to want to deport your son?' I could see the lightbulb going on in her head. I was like, *'This guy's going to deport your son!'* And she said, 'Well, I never thought of it that way.' *Well, what do you think he's been up to this entire time?* Two years we've been hearing Mexican people are rapists. We're criminals. We're drug dealers. We're everything. *What do you think he's going to do?* And she's like, 'I just thought he was a good businessman.' And I'm like, 'Please elaborate.' I just went, like—I couldn't believe it. Even my dad was like, 'Should we leave?' Even Nick was like, 'You need to go easy.'"

"It was pretty rough," Nick says.

"I worry about my brother constantly," Dani goes on. "I'm always telling him, 'You need to have a backup plan.' Go to Canada or Belgium. And now when my mom talks to me about politics, like, 'Did you see what Trump said or what he did?' I'm like, 'Don't even talk to me about it. You have no right to talk shit about him; it's *your* fault. People like you who are uneducated about the candidates basically made this asshole president.'"

"It's still pretty rough," Nick says.

The doorbell rings. It's the guy with the fish. Everybody gets a break, bags opening, plates clanking. Vicki fixes the spread so it looks pretty, the lemon-pepper-smoked fillets fanning down the sides, candy-smoked and alder-smoked in the middle, a ring of rosemary and sesame crackers around the edge.

On the far wall in the living room, off in a corner, inside a frame, hangs the letter Vicki got back from Obama in response to the note she wrote to him on the morning after the election. "Remember that although politics can significantly affect our lives," reads the letter, typed on White House stationery, "our success has always been rooted in the willingness of our people to look out for one another and help each other through tough times—rain or shine."

"To get a personal response," Vicki says. "I felt light. I felt heard. It made me feel: There's still goodness out there. That he made it a part of his day. That there was a place for me . . ."

This in contrast to the way her husband made her feel in the aftermath of the election, a point lost on no one.

"A former president writing a letter, though," Tim says, motioning toward it. "He's acting like I don't even live here. It makes it a little tough."

Vicki shoots him a warning glance: *Leave Barack out of this.*

This has nothing to do with Barack. This is about Trump.

"You can't have a conversation about the presidential race without including the people who were in it," Tim announces firmly. "You can't have that conversation with me without acknowledging the fact of who he was running against."

This is not about Trump. This is about Hillary.

"Well, I'm pro-Hillary," Neil says, "which I think is not a common stance in this room."

Definitely not a common stance in the room. Both Nick and Dani voted for Hillary reluctantly, and Vicki, who determined that neither candidate was worthy, did not vote at all. She knows her decision not to go to the polls makes her voice weak. Everybody knows it, but nobody, not even Tim—who could certainly use some firepower—brings it up. *Respect your mother* is the subtext in this house.

"I'm so done with the Democratic Party," Tim says. "I should have been more vocal about that. The reason I voted the way I did was to stop somebody else. It was a protest against the Democratic candidate. That's what it was—that's exactly what it was."

Tim thinks that should be the end of it. What more is there to say? A protest vote. Can't that be the end of it? Why is everyone still so upset about this? Another person might storm off. *You people are being ridiculous. I said my piece. Deal with it.*

"Do you think if we had been a swing state," Nick asks his dad, "you'd have thought about it differently?" If this were Ohio, or Florida, or Pennsylvania, surely his dad would have voted more . . . responsibly.

"No," Tim says. "Not with Hillary Clinton. I thought her story was way outdated, and she doesn't represent—she only represents herself."

"But so does Trump," Dani says.

"Both of them are exactly the same in that respect to me," Tim says.

"That's really fascinating," Neil says. "So like—her experience doing that job, being a politician, doesn't count for anything?"

"It was a direction I didn't want to go in," Tim says. "It doesn't matter how fast you're going if you're going the wrong way."

"Trump's complete lack of experience—did that also not count?" Neil asks him.

"The only requirement is to be a citizen in this country," Tim says. "I disagree that career politicians mean that they're more qualified to represent me."

"I'm just trying to understand," Neil says. "So Trump's plan for the country was the better plan?"

"I felt that he would be pretty irrelevant," Tim says. "But not more of the same; I was not interested in more of the same."

"So it's like you're driving your car," Neil says, leaning to the edge of the couch. His arms bounce up and down as he offers this metaphor, one, two, three: *Get this straight. This is what you're saying, Dad.* "You're driving your car, and you see that you're almost out of gas, so you crash your car into the wall and say, 'Well, now I don't need to get gas because I stopped!'"

"I'm sorry this upsets you at the level that it does," his father replies.

"I think about when Mount St. Helens blew up," Vicki says.

Isla awakens, kicks her legs out.

"Does anybody want more fish?" Nobody wants any more fish.

Perhaps Tim just needs to apologize, admit he made a horrible mistake. Because here's Vicki mad, and Neil working overtime on a metaphor, and Nick throwing out lifelines, and Dani offended. How do you clean this up? Perhaps independent voters across America just need to apologize, whether they think they did anything wrong or not.

Isla clamps her fist around her mother's thumb, pulls it back and forth. Dani jiggles her knee—"Whee!"—while the others look on.

"The thing that's interesting to me is our current state of politics is absolutely against the sense of community," Tim says. "It's separated all things right and left."

"Voting for someone doesn't equal all our problems getting solved," Neil offers. "We start at the wrong end. Even if Sanders had been elected, that's just getting one person in power."

It's one thing, besides Isla, that everyone in the room can agree on. You need a starting point. "My analogy has been we have this big ship, and it has this really small rudder," Tim says. "Turn it all the way one way, it's just going to move a little bit. The presidency only has a certain amount of power."

"I do believe that if Hillary was in power right now and she were involved with the Russians, that it would be ten times the clamor," Neil says.

"She would be out on her ass right now," Dani says. "She would be impeached already."

"So the waste of time would've been comparable," Neil says.

Everyone's trying to make this be okay. Trump is a waste of time. Hillary would have been a waste of time.

Maybe?

"What did Barack say to you?" Tim says to Vicki, motioning again toward the letter. "It's going to be all right. He believes it; I believe it too. Democracy is messy. It's loud."

Maybe.

"What about the *Access Hollywood* tapes?" Vicki says. It's the one thing she'll never get past. "What did you think when you heard that statement?" she asks Tim. "When he said that about women?"

"To hear he's got those kind of standards didn't surprise me a bit," he says.

"But what he said against *women*," Vicki repeats. "It upset me so much." Does that not matter to him?

"This is a really bad thing to say out loud," Tim says. "But there's a certain kind of language some people on the East Coast have. They seem to be— Howard Stern is really welcome there. It's more typical and more common in New York than it is out here. Their culture's different. I never gave it much thought."

"I just know how much you respect women and how polite you are," Vicki says. "And I would have thought that that would have offended you."

"It most certainly did," Tim says. "The guy's a pig."

This declaration seems to break much of the tension in the room.

"Remember we had the Women's March on TV?" Vicki says as if to verify the fact that Tim thinks Trump is a pig. "I saw one sign that I would have been so happy if you carried it. It said: 'Stop Pissing Off My Wife.'"

"I'd be happy to carry that sign," Tim says.

Well, this is all such a relief. Tim is still the Tim they know and love.

Except, wait, Tim voted for a pig *on purpose*?

What the hell is the matter with him?

Isla screams abruptly.

"She's hungry," Nick says.

"She needs to be changed," Dani says, standing, hauling Isla to the back bedroom, the scream losing volume as they head down the hall. "Niiiiick!" Dani shouts then, and so Nick jumps to his feet, and so does Vicki, both of them heading back to help.

Alone together in the living room, baby clamor in the distance, Neil and his dad lean back on the couch, their heads at the exact same height, underneath the shelf with the row of little houses. They both have their legs crossed the same way, as if one is copying the other. It's like all those Fridays again. Here in the living room. Every Friday, no matter what, no matter how the conversation had gone the week before or how they left it. They got to know each other again.

"I respect you and I love you," Neil says finally. "But there's still, like— That moment, that choice, I wasn't there. And I wonder about that. I trust how intelligent you are and how caring you are and sharing and giving. But can you see where I would just have that moment of, like, *How?*"

"So did Dani," Tim says. "So did your mom. All you guys did."

"Well, I think it's brave of you to be able to talk about how you voted," Neil says. "Like, there's no malice in there. I get that."

"I don't put the weight on it that you guys do, and I never will. And I'm not going to change about that."

"I'm interested in the fact that people who didn't feel heard now feel heard," Neil offers. "And what that means for them."

This is not about Barack, not about Trump, not about Hillary. This, now, is about rebuilding.

"I didn't know that they didn't feel heard," Neil continues. "It wasn't that I wasn't interested. I was maybe oblivious, but I didn't know."

"All these people are vocal now, and none of these people were vocal a year ago," Tim says. "Hopefully good people will stand up, find leadership that makes some sense."

"I'm glad we've gotten to a place where we can continue to discuss ideas," Neil says. "This election changed me. I don't even know if I was prepared for how different I would feel. I do feel differently in this modern world."

By the time Dani comes marching back in, with a cleaned-up Isla and the others trailing behind, the mood in the room has completed its shift. Like an eclipse happened. But it's not just the Earth routinely spinning on its axis. It's all human effort. "For people who are so disappointed," Neil says to the group, "or confused by family members' votes, or the way they're talking about politics right now, I think we all have to listen to each other and admit when we don't understand. I think everyone wants to be heard right now. I even think Trump wants that. I think he just wants someone to say, 'You are the president!' To acknowledge that he *did* that. As a human to a human, I can have compassion for needing to be heard."

"Yay! I agree with you," Dani says. "I love you."

"I have this silly phrase that I like," Neil says. " 'Forgiveness equals fun.' The more forgiveness I can have, the more I get to enjoy things, because I'm not so caught up. Like, the point of contention doesn't have to be where we stop. It's where something new starts."

"Well, I told Nick," Dani says. "I said, 'You need to apologize to your dad.' We need to be more understanding. We've all got to move on. And I feel like we did. I feel like we did a good job. I think we moved on, right?"

"I think so," Vicki says.

"We're still angry," Dani says. "But, like, not at each other."

"I'm not mad at anybody in this room," Vicki says. "But I'm mad at the situation."

"Conflict is a way of demonstrating love," Neil says. "As long as you keep at it. You have to keep the work up."

"I thought that was a pretty gloves-off letter you wrote," Tim says to Vicki, after everyone has gone. "Am I the only person you throw under the bus when writing emails?"

"I didn't write anybody else," she says. "I just wrote to Barack. It was a factual statement. I was telling him that you voted against our family as though he were sitting across from me. It was like a friend thing."

CHAPTER 18

Obama in Jeans

Fiona told me she was nervous, and when I asked her why, she let out a burst of laughter, like, *What a stupid question.* It was a windy day in March 2018, and we were in my hotel room, about to head over to meet with Obama in the postpresidency office he maintains in Washington.

Since leaving the White House, Fiona had become a mom. She and her husband, Chris, whom she had met in her earliest days working in OPC (he was the person assigned to handle mail containing threats to the president), had named the baby Grace.

The fact that Obama had agreed to a postpresidency conversation said more than probably anything he was about to put into words that day. He'd been largely absent from public life since he left office, working on his foundation and his book, offering no comment on the cascading tumult that characterized America's new political landscape. Like Bush before him, Obama had been careful to step off the presidential stage, no matter how weird things got, no matter how destructive the new administration may have been to the accomplishments of the old, no matter how many of his supporters clamored for him to jump in and somehow rescue America from what they came to see as the grip of a tyrant.

At that point in his postpresidency, well over a year in, he had done just three interviews: one about his early days as a community organizer, another that brought David Letterman out of retirement, and a third with Prince Harry.

And now he would do one more: a conversation about the mailroom.

The mailroom, with the mail lady.

It's not as if he and Fiona were pals, not by a long stretch. The divide between a president and the person running the mailroom was, well, a metaphor all on its own. A king and a servant, a rock star and a roadie, a president and the mail lady. If Fiona and Obama had any kind of relationship, it was largely a silent one, restricted to a purple folder in the back of his daily briefing book, an archived sample of voices, a smattering of responses scribbled in margins: REPLY, REPLY, REPLY. I remembered what Fiona had said: It was like passing a tray under a door.

She and Obama had met a few times previously, mostly for photo ops, and he had called her over to the Oval Office during the last days of his presidency to thank her for her service. She told me she had been nervous for that meeting too. "I thought a lot about how I wanted to thank him, and then you walk in, and he completely throws you off, and you don't remember what you were going to say. He gave me a letter. He had folded it, and that's not normal. We don't fold his letters.

"He talked about the unglamorous part of the White House, the idea of service at its core." Then he gave her a hug. "He's a hugger," she said.

I asked her about a letter she had once written to him. It came out of a session at an OPC staff retreat as part of an "empathy-building exercise." The prompt was, "If you wrote to the president, what would you say?" The staff broke into small groups and shared their letters with one another. The point wasn't for the president to ever get those letters. Fiona had thrown hers in a folder, and that was the end of it.

Maybe she wanted to give it to him today?

"Oh, he doesn't need that," she said brusquely, and then she busied herself with her coat and marched toward the door, and she took in a deep gulp of air, let it out slowly.

Again I asked her why she was nervous. "What's the worst thing that could happen? You'll be speechless? You'll say something you'll regret?"

She stood still for a moment, looked at me. I'd forgotten how big and round her eyes were; a person could climb inside those eyes.

"I'll cry?" she said. She reached into her coat pocket, showed me the wads of rolled-up toilet paper she had thought to arm herself with before she left the house.

"Oh, for God's sake." I grabbed a fistful of proper tissues from the bathroom, folded them, and handed them to her.

The suite was bright, airy, and colorful. Large images of the Pacific Ocean adorned the waiting area, along with knickknacks of distinction—the set of Muhammad Ali boxing gloves he used to have on display in the Oval Office dining room, a replica Vince Lombardi Trophy. Heading down the wide center hall toward Obama's office brought you steadily closer to a photograph of Martin Luther King, Jr., featured prominently at the end. The image was of King's back as he stood before a crowd—the point of view of the speaker, not the listener.

Many of the staffers, about twelve in all, had worked for Obama in the White House, and most of them knew Fiona; people stepped out of their offices to greet her: "How's Chris? *How's the baby?*" And Obama appeared just like the rest of them, like any old worker taking a break; suddenly he was with us, smiling wide, saying he had just finished filling out his March Madness brackets and was feeling good about them, really good. You don't realize just how lanky he is until you see him in person, a long, flat physique; he looked fit, even youthful, his hair cut super short so that all the new gray he'd famously acquired during his presidency was less pronounced. He walked up to Fiona with his arms outstretched and asked about her family, and she sheepishly stepped in for a hug.

"I'm great. She's great. We're just great. . . ."

"Well, we've got babies popping out," Obama said, referring to a staffer who was due to deliver any day. "It's the best thing. I've got all these staff who started with me when they were like twenty. And now suddenly it's like they've got kids everywhere. It's sweet. And a bunch of them, you know, a number of them met on the campaign or at the White House. But nobody yet has named a child Barack—"

"A lot of letter writers did," Fiona offered, perhaps too quietly for him to hear.

"I'm a little frustrated about that," Obama continued with a laugh. "I'm like, 'Come on, people!'"

We followed him into his office. It was a wide space done in shades of tan and brown, earthy, warm, and welcoming. Zero razzle-dazzle. He offered us a seat on the couch, and he sunk into the chair at the end. He was in jeans and a light blue shirt unbuttoned at the top. He put his feet up on the coffee table, crossed his legs at the ankles; overall this was the portrait of one relaxed man. Pete Souza's book of photographs was on the coffee table; family pictures were everywhere, on end tables, on the walls; and Obama's expansive desk on the other side of the room was covered in paper, piles, books— a place of activity. He mentioned the book he's been working on, said it was . . . difficult. "Writing is just so hard. Painful. It's—everybody thinks it's, you know. But it's work. It's like having homework all the time. Yeah, it's hard.

"I should mention to you, by the way, Fiona," he said, as we were getting settled, "we're still getting like two hundred fifty thousand letters a year. It's a lot—"

"I was really excited when Emily told me that you were going to keep getting mail after you were president," Fiona said. "Because people weren't just writing to you as president—as sort of like this guy who got elected, so now my problems are his problems. Like, I think people thought that you might *believe in them*. And so I'm not shocked that they're continuing to write."

I thought Fiona was masking her jitters remarkably well, or else they had already dissipated. She wasn't the mail lady. He wasn't a king. I told Obama about Fiona's image of a tray passing under a door, asked him if he ever had that same sense of a kind of silent relationship with the strangers over there in OPC.

"One of the things I learned fairly early on about the presidency is that people change around you," he said. "They're constantly watching you and measuring your responses, and—you can tilt the field. And so I actually liked the fact that Fiona and the other people in the office were not inhibited or constrained by trying to think about *What would he like?* or *What would he want?* But rather they were in some ways helping to channel, through all the sifting that was going on, something that was representative of the mood of the moment, the emotions that were bubbling up through all the mail that was coming in."

I noticed that over by his desk, on a wall, he had hung the same framed letter he used to have displayed in the corridor between his private study and the Oval Office. Natoma Canfield, a cancer survivor from Medina, Ohio, had written in 2009 about her ballooning health-insurance premiums; Obama had said she reminded him of his mom, who died at age fifty-two of a similar cancer. The letter had stood as a reminder to him of his commitment to healthcare reform.

"The only instruction I gave was that I wanted every packet to be representative," he continued. "And understanding that it wouldn't be perfect. It didn't mean that, you know, out of every ten letters, there had to be two positive and two negative and three neutral and one funny. It wasn't formulaic like that. But that was the one thing I insisted on—that this is not useful to me if all I'm getting are, you know, happy birthday wishes. And I think they did a wonderful job of channeling the American people in that way."

"It wasn't just me," Fiona said. "It was this big group. And folks in the office came from different backgrounds. We had our volunteer workforce. And there were some old people in the mix too. So we had a lot of people putting stuff forward for you, a lot of people interpreting what 'representative' meant."

"I will say this does also have to do with a culture that we tried to develop early on in the campaign," he said. "Which was putting a lot of confidence in a bunch of young people to fairly, meaningfully, and passionately reflect the people they were interacting with. Whether that was on a campaign and they were out there organizing or in the office."

That would be a theme that would come up repeatedly during our time together that day. The continuum. The values established in the earliest days of campaigning, maintained and carried forward in the hands of people like Fiona, who may not even have understood, when they first got started, what drew them in.

.   .   .

"So this is Marnie," I said, placing a file on the coffee table and reaching inside. The folder was filled with some of the letters I hoped to talk about, along with photographs taken during visits with letter writers.

"I reviewed the letters and the responses in preparation for this meeting," Obama said. "I didn't memorize them. . . ." I wondered how to tell him it was okay he didn't memorize them. (Memorize them?) Here was a guy committed to excellence in homework.

I reached for a photo and handed it to him. "Marnie Hazelton," I said. He studied it closely, leaning in. In the photo Marnie was seated behind her big, impressive desk at the Roosevelt Union Free School District administration offices, looking every bit the superintendent.

"She's an example of someone who was writing to you for help," I said. "And your response, the words 'I'm rooting for you'—she carried them everywhere. She read them out loud to Meredith Vieira on *Who Wants to Be a Millionaire*."

"I didn't hear that!" he said. "That's cool."

"But she choked. She missed a question. It was 'Rub-a-Dub-Dub—'"

"Oh."

"But now she's the *superintendent* of the entire school district!"

"That's pretty cool!"

"I wonder if you have any sense of the power of your responses to these folks," I said.

"I think I understood that if somebody writes a letter and they get any kind of response, that there's a sense of . . . being heard," he said, carefully considering my simple question. I knew enough by then to not be surprised by Obama's exceedingly slow delivery, but that didn't stop me from continuing to marvel at it. He's a ponderous man; he is a person who ruminates. It's not the sort of blathering a person does to hear his own voice or to fulfill some need to command the room; he's not a mansplainer. He is, rather, thoughtful to the extreme. A person who would memorize homework. His words are precise, and the sentences are . . . dense. It's like you could add water to them, and they'd keep expanding.

"And so often, especially back in 2009, 2010, 2011, a lot of people were going through a lot of hardship," he said. "And a lot of them felt alone in that hardship. They were losing their homes, or they're dealing with somebody at the bank and the bank saying, 'There's nothing we can do. You're going to lose your house.' Or they've got a pink slip, and they've lost their job, and they're going to interview after interview after interview. Over time, I think it's easy for folks to feel a little invisible, as if nobody's paying attention. And so I did, I think, understand that if I could at least let them know that I saw them and I heard them, maybe they'd feel a little bit less lonely in those struggles."

I wondered if this might be the sort of stuff that made Fiona reach for the tissues. The raw kindness. It's wonderful to behold it in anyone, let alone to hear that it was a value at the core of a president.

"Certainly what I learned during the presidency was that the office of the president itself carries enormous weight," Obama went on. "And, sadly, probably where I learned that best was in moments of tragedy where you'd visit with grieving families. Sometimes they were in places where—I think it's fair to say—I didn't get a whole lot of votes. You know, after a tornado or a flood or a shooting. And what was clear was that my presence there signified to those families that they were important. Their loved ones were important. The grief they were feeling was important. That it had been seen and acknowledged.

"That was fairly consistent throughout my presidency," he said.

I thought about President George W. Bush and the ways in which he'd botched that particular presidential duty in the aftermath of Hurricane Katrina and how damaging his perceived lack of compassion for flood victims was to his entire presidency. I thought about the ways in which Bill Clinton was the opposite; there was a president who glopped it on thick. "I feel your pain," he'd say, and he did that little bite of his bottom lip. People came to mock him for it, or at least distrust it. Maybe he wasn't being sincere. Maybe there was nothing behind it. For Clinton, the "maybe" took over.

I don't think that happened for Obama. Whatever people thought of his presidency, I think he was given credit for being a man who brought a solid well of empathy to the office.

But since when did empathy become a requisite trait for a president? Sympathy, the capacity to feel compassion for others, is perhaps the baseline expectation we have of any good neighbor, let alone leader. Obama was the first modern president to explicitly and repeatedly raise that bar. Empathy, he said, in *The Audacity of Hope*, "is at the heart of my moral code, and it is how I understand the Golden Rule—not simply as a call to sympathy or charity, but as something more demanding, a call to stand in somebody else's shoes and see through their eyes."

In his presidency he would demand it of himself—what was the 10LADs experiment if not a daily reminder to experience the world as others did?—and his expectation seemed to be that a call for empathy would trickle down to those who served in his administration.

"That notion of being heard," I said about his response to Marnie's cry for help. "That message that you matter. It seemed to be embedded throughout all of this." I told him that Pete Rouse had talked about it, about how it spread through the staff. If the mail mattered, the people reading it mattered. I told Obama it was the message that so many people, so many letter writers and Friends of the Mail, kept hitting when I talked to them. "You matter."

"I still believe it," he said.

It's hard to argue with empathy. It's a deeply admirable trait. It's Pope Francis. It's a tenet of Christianity. It's a mindset religious leaders throughout the world have sought and taught followers to seek.

It made you a good person. But a good president? Obama had been criticized bitterly by conservatives, in 2009, for perhaps taking the call for empathy too far when he said it was the thing he was looking for in a U.S. Supreme Court justice. "I view that quality of empathy, of understanding and identifying . . . people's hopes and struggles as an essential ingredient for arriving at just decisions and outcomes." Conservatives had called it "the empathy standard"— Obama's personal litmus test—and said it was an awfully "touchy-feely" reason for choosing Supreme Court Justice Sonia Sotomayor. "Empathy," said Utah senator Orrin Hatch, was "a code word for an activist judge." They said relying on personal experience would lead judges to reach subjective interpretations of U.S. laws. We're supposed to have impartial judges sworn to provide equality under the law, independent of the whims of personal preference. The word "empathy" does not appear in the U.S. Constitution.

Moreover, Obama's empathy, you could argue, was what begot Trumpism. Its opposite. We now had a president who seemed to go out of his way to remind us how little he cared about the struggles of the less fortunate.

Was this simply a style issue? A caring, thoughtful president versus a wild and oafish one? Perhaps leadership styles fell on a continuum, and people oscillated between a preference for one or the other. It's hard to imagine, though. We don't want a president who cares about people?

"Where does this even come from?" I asked Obama—that focus on empathy as a core value for a president.

"I think this whole letter-writing process and its importance reflected a more fundamental vision of what we were trying to do in the campaign and what I was trying to do with the presidency and my political philosophy," he said. "The foundational theory, it probably connects to my early days organizing. Just going around and listening to people. Asking them about their lives, and what was important to them. And how did they come to believe what they believe? And what are they trying to pass on to their children?"

When he talked like that, starting to dig in deep, he didn't make eye contact. He looked straight ahead, at a spot somewhere near his feet propped up on the coffee table, brown leather boots, like the desert boots the boys I knew in seventh grade used to wear.

"I learned in that process that if you listen hard enough, everybody's got a sacred story," he said. "An organizing story. Of who they are and what their place in the world is. And they're willing to share it with you if they feel as if you actually care about it. And that ends up being the glue around which relationships are formed, and trust is formed, and communities are formed. And ultimately—my theory was, at least—that's the glue around which democracies work."

"Listening," I said.

"Yeah," he said, and he looked up at me, into my eyes, as if he were coming up for air.

"I don't want to suggest that I would have necessarily described it in a sort of a straight line from when I started running," he said. "But I do think that that was pretty embedded in our campaign philosophy. I think that's how we won Iowa, was having a bunch of young kids form those relationships because they were listening to people. It wasn't us selling a policy manifesto, and it wasn't even because we were selling *me*. It was because some young person in a town they've never been to went around and talked to people, and listened to them, and saw them. And created the kinds of bonds that made people want to then try to work together."

I could tell he was talking about Fiona and all the people like her who knocked on doors. I looked over. She had her eyebrows up. I wanted to say, "So how does that make you feel?" I don't know how it was that we got tiptoeing toward therapy.

I referred back to the picture of Marnie on the table. She was wearing a black suit, and her hands were folded neatly on a desk covered in piles of paperwork, Post-it notes, files—a place of work not unlike Obama's desk on the other side of the room. Next to the photo was a copy of Obama's response to her. "I'm rooting for you."

"When I think about somebody like Marnie in particular," he said, "it was important, because based on what she had written, I felt fairly confident that this would be a temporary rather than permanent circumstance."

As he continued talking about his correspondence with Marnie, I came to realize that what he zeroed in on was not "I'm rooting for you"—which to me, and to Marnie, and to Meredith, and to a live studio audience and all the folks back home was the important part. No, what Obama was focused on was the blah-blah-blah part, the what-a-president-*should*-say part in his response to Marnie.

I know that things seem discouraging now, but demand for educators and persons with your skills will grow as the economy and state budgets rebound.

"Part of what happened during the early parts of this Great Recession," Obama said, "was state and local governments were seeing their budgets hemorrhage. And a big part of the Recovery Act was getting money to states and school districts so that they would not lay off massive numbers of teachers, firefighters, and cops. And given what Marnie was describing, I felt as if, if she could stay at it, that, like in school districts across the country, there'd be the opportunity for her to be rehired at some point."

The Recovery Act. That note about rooting for Marnie was about the American Recovery and Reinvestment Act? In his mind apparently it was. It wasn't just "I hear you," or "I feel your pain," or even "I'm rooting for you." It was, "Hang in there; I've got this."

"It's the power of empathy not as an end-all, be-all," he said. "Because even after you've listened to somebody or seen them, they still have a concrete problem. They've lost their house. They've lost their job. They disagree with you on abortion. They think that you're pulling troops out of Afghanistan too soon and, you know, potentially betraying the sacrifices that have been made by the fallen. There are all these concrete issues that are real. And there are real conflicts and real choices.

"But what this form of story sharing and empathy and listening does is it creates the conditions around which we can then have a meaningful conversation and sort through our differences and our challenges," he said, "and arrive at better decisions because we've been able to hear everybody. Everybody feels heard so that even if a decision's made that they don't completely agree with, then at least they feel like, *Okay, I was part of this. This wasn't just dumped on me.*"

"Well, now you sound just like Neil," I said.

He had no idea who Neil was, of course. Neil's mom, Vicki Shearer, had not used his name in her letter to the president.

I pulled out Vicki's letter. Here was a family trying to keep it together after the 2016 election when one of them, the father, had voted for Trump against the perceived interests of the rest of the family. I had a photo of the group gathered around the couch in their living room. "Here's Neil," I said, pointing. I told Obama that the whole Shearer family were supporters of his to the core. "In fact, when you won in 2008, Vicki baked an Obama pie."

I had a picture of the pie too.

"Oh, that's a good pie," Obama said, reaching for the picture. "That's excellent. Thanks for the ears there—"

"Yeah, Vicki thought Michelle would appreciate the ears."

"She got it just right."

I read him some of the things Neil had said about the transformative power of listening.

348 | Jeanne Marie Laskas

For people who are so disappointed or confused by family members' votes, or the way they're talking about politics right now, I think we all have to listen to each other and admit when we don't understand. I think everyone wants to be heard right now. I even think Trump wants that. I think he just wants someone to say, "You are the president!" To acknowledge that he *did* that. As a human to a human, I can have compassion for needing to be heard.

"Exactly," Obama said. (He offered no comment on the part about Trump needing validation.) "Which is why I wanted to offer that corrective to the idea that, you know, empathy—putting yourself in somebody's shoes—somehow solves all the divisions and conflicts we have in the country. That's wishful thinking. But what *is* true is that if a person is recognized, and how they're feeling is validated as being true for them, then they are more prone to engage. And open up to the possibilities of other people's perspectives and maybe even at some point say, 'Hmm. I didn't think of that. Maybe I'm going to rethink how I think about certain things.'

"I will tell you—and Fiona will recall this—some of my favorite letters were actually to people who violently disagreed with me. So, okay, you want to call me an idiot. Well, I want you to know there's a person at the other end of this thing who's listening to you, and here's why, actually, I did what I did. And I can see why you're thinking this way, but here are some countervailing facts for you to consider.

"Those letters I always hoped got into circulation. Right? That there were entire communities or families or schools where people looked at that and they said, 'Huh. I still disagree with the guy, but the fact that he bothered to write back—that's interesting to me.' And maybe then it starts breaking open some new possibilities. Maybe not immediately. Maybe it's in the future. Maybe it's a kid notices that, and they say, 'Huh, there's actually this human who's in the White House. And if you have something to say, he's supposed to listen to you.'"

"I think that worked often," Fiona chimed in. "And sometimes it got back to you, and you personally got a follow-up where, after you sent a handwritten letter to someone who disagreed with you, they wrote back either saying, 'I still disagree and here's why' or 'You know what? I'd like to rescind my earlier statement.' And in other cases where it didn't make its way back to you, we got word in our office that, you know, a letter had been put up in a faculty lounge or sort of small conversations started out of something that began with a pretty angry late-night email."

"It goes both ways, right?" Obama said. "I want to emphasize the degree to which this was important and useful to me doing my job.

"There was a sizeable percentage of the letters where, if they were critical, I'd read them and say, 'Well, that's not fair. I don't think that's true. They obviously don't know this.' But there were times where somebody would write a letter, and I'd say, 'I can see their point.' And I'd circle it, and I'd write it on the margins: 'Is this true?' or 'Can you explain why this is?' or 'Why don't we fix this?'"

We talked about two other letters that day, and both pointed him in that same direction—the degree to which the letters helped him do his job. The emphasis surprised me, although I suppose it shouldn't have. I remembered that he had brought it up the last time we had talked, when he was still in the White House. We'd been discussing some of the mail he got in the wake of the 2016 election. "There was a lot of anxiety and sadness I had to respond to," he said that day. "I remember one that said, 'Pack up your bags because, thank goodness, we're about to undo everything you've done; it couldn't have come a moment too soon,' something along those lines. I don't think I responded to that one. . . ."

I remember that I had asked him then how he might advise President-Elect Donald Trump on what to do with the mail.

He had laughed. I think it was more out of awkwardness than because of any sort of image the question may have conjured, but I can't say for sure.

"But, um, it, ah," he said about the idea of President-Elect Trump reading the mail. "You know what, this is a great habit. I think it worked for me because it wasn't something I did for anyone else. I did it because, as you said, it sustained me. So maybe it will sustain others in the future. Okay?"

Okay. But I never used the word "sustained." I remember wondering how that word had popped up.

"I can tick off the bills and the policies and the accomplishments," he said. "But I tell you one of the things I'm proud of about having been in this office is that I don't feel like I've . . . lost myself."

Like everything else, that thought came out slowly. But I suppose not losing yourself is a big thing to think about quickly.

"I feel as if—even if my skin is thicker from, you know, public criticism, and I'm wiser about the workings of government, I haven't become . . . cynical, and I haven't become calloused, and I would like to think that these letters have something to do with that," he said.

The letters as sustenance was the same idea he came around to when we talked about the letter from Donna Coltharp. "She's the attorney who wrote to thank you for commuting her client's two life sentences," I said, handing him a picture.

"Is this Billy here?" he asked.

"That's Billy!" I said. "And there's Donna. They had never met in person before this. They had this really wonderful Oprah moment."

"Is that right?" he said, looking deeper into the photo, smiling wide. "How *cool* is that?"

I told him Billy was doing great. He got a job as a roofer. He got promoted to supervisor. He got a girlfriend. Obama's action had given Billy a second chance at life, and he was determined to make the most of it.

"That's wonderful," Obama said. "That means a lot."

I told him the reason Donna had told me she wrote. She'd wanted to acknowledge that there was a human being behind all those last-minute sentence commutations; forgiveness was, after all, a personal act. "She wanted to thank you."

"That means a lot," he said. "I will say, selfishly, that the number of people who would write letters acknowledging the meaningful difference that a policy had made in their lives—making it real as opposed to abstract—was sustaining.

"The numbers are telling you twenty million people got healthcare through the ACA," he said. "But that's not the same as a mom writing a letter saying, 'My son got insurance. He got his first physical in a decade. They caught a tumor. It's out. He's fine.' And you go, *Okay*, that *is the work we're doing.*

"And the same is true in this circumstance. You read not only that Billy had contacted Donna to say thank you to her but that he's rebuilding his life."

"When you wrote back to Donna, you thanked her for her service," I said. "That was what meant so much to her. She's like, 'No one ever thanks us.'"

"Well, she was deserving," he said. "It was a little lovefest."

"A thank-you loop."

"A loop!"

He could see another photo popping out of my file folder. He tilted his head up as if to peek.

"That's Marg," I said, handing the photo to him.

"Marjorie? Look at Marg! Marg is pretty cute. I love the pictures behind Marg too. And the little dolls—"

"She was writing to tell you that she was listening to you."

"It's a beautiful letter."

She was writing about trying to expel the racism she believed was lodged like some kind of poison in her heart. She had discovered it and wanted to get rid of it.

"And now here's Marg starting a chapter of the NAACP in her town," I said.

"What a great story."

"She went for it. She wanted to tell you that."

"It makes me proud," he said. "My grandmother, who loved me more than anyone, had an initial reaction like Marg to young black men approaching."

He sat for a moment before finishing his thought, his gaze going back to the spot in front of him occupied by his shoes. He had told the story about his grandmother publicly back in the earliest days of the presidential campaign, in a speech during the 2008 primary against Hillary Clinton. Afterward, he had been criticized for his candor about a topic as sensitive as unconscious bias. In a radio interview later, he tried to explain what he had meant, which made it only more controversial. "The point I was making," he said to the host, "was not that Grandmother harbors any racial animosity. She doesn't. But she is a typical white person, who, if she sees somebody on the street that she doesn't know, you know, there's a reaction that's been bred in our experiences that don't go away and that sometimes come out in the wrong way, and that's just the nature of race in our society."

"Typical white person." You're not supposed to say stuff like that, especially not as the first black candidate ever to run for the office. The Clinton campaign pounced. Obama was clearly new at this game.

As he sat in silence and thought that day with me and Fiona, the room felt static, like we weren't supposed to move. Behind him was a large window with wooden shades blocking some of the light. Behind that the March winds were whooshing; you could hear them. I thought about how people talk about a person having the wind at his back, and they talk about having it in front, fighting it. But here was a man with neither. Here was a person set apart from a current violently streaming by. The world out there in tumult. The calmness in here.

All that listening he'd been talking about—eight years of it—was just history. All those letters he'd received during his presidency, millions of them, had been shipped off to the National Archives. I was glad that he, or someone in his administration, had thought to save them. They'll live on, artifacts for a museum exhibit someday. Here are the voices of America, from 2009 to 2017. This is *us* during the Obama years, surviving an economic crisis, a healthcare overhaul, a couple of wars, mass shootings, a government shutdown, heartache at our borders, hurricanes, the ravages of climate change, and all the rest of it. This is who we were, and there is an innocence about it, as there is always an innocence when you look back at yourself. Get too close, and it hurts, depending on your point of comparison.

Wallowing in the sorrow of what's lost is always a temptation.

But the letters offer more. They reignite the imagination. They remind you that kindness matters (seriously, we can all use a palate cleanser on that one alone), whether it's in style or, as it may appear to be under the Trump administration, it's out. They remind you that government *can* work and that people committed to public service really do exist. Moreover, there is the deepening discovery of what used to be. All that was right under your nose that maybe you hadn't noticed. I'd had no idea, not until the last few months of Obama's presidency, that a place like the mailroom even existed. I had never known that all those quiet conversations between the president and his constituents were going on, that there were all those random people believing they had the president's ear or believing that they could have it by simply jotting him a note. I'd had no idea that there was an entire army of caretakers reporting to duty each day to make sure the conversation kept going.

A discovery like that can give you hope. We *had* this, which means we can have it again. "And, you know, right now," Obama said to me, finally looking up from his shoe trance and meeting my eyes, "a lot of people who have worked with me in the past or supported me or voted for me, you know, can get discouraged by the news day to day. And that's understandable. I always have to be careful in not sounding as if I am Pollyannaish about the future."

The future. I hadn't said the word out loud. But it was, of course, the elephant in the room. America was not, as of late, aging gracefully. Did he feel responsible? Did he want to get back to it?

"A better future is earned," he said. "It's hard work. And democracy in a country this big, with such a diverse population, is especially hard. And complicated. And there are times in our history where we've had bad, ugly stretches. And so it's important not to ever forget and to recognize that the ideals and the best version of America isn't preordained.

"But I do think that when you hear someone like Marjorie, at her age, just take a leap of faith like that, then you can't help but feel as if it is worth the effort.

"If we duplicate enough of those moments, enough of those interactions, enough of those shared stories, over time we get better at this thing called democracy. And that is something that all of us have the capacity to do. That's not the job of the president. That's not the job of a bunch of professional policy makers. It's the job of citizens."

Over to you, citizens.

. . .

"You didn't cry," I said to Fiona afterward.

"I welled up," she said.

I asked her when. And why?

"The parallels between knocking on doors and answering letters," she said. "This idea that first we're going to ask something of you, and then you're going to ask something of us."

She said that part cut deep. "That he draws that connection on his own. We were a bunch of young people who had never worked in government. We were given the gift of his signature and trusted to know what we were doing. And we were winging it to some extent, just watching what he did and mirroring those values without hearing him expound on them. We only had the behavior to watch. Not some process document. So then hearing the 'why' behind it and hoping that the whys that were implied and the ones we implemented more broadly were not so off base.

"Treating empathy as a starting point," she said. "Not letting empathy be the end game. His take on the idea that our hearts were in the right place. And the idea of that being something worthy of being proud of in and of itself."

I told her I still wished she had read her letter to him or that at least she had given it to him.

"Oh, he doesn't need that," she said.

Dear President Obama,

Toward the end of my time in college, when I had no plan and no pull in any direction, my mother sent me Kurt Vonnegut's book "A Man Without a Country" with a note in it that said 'You and your generation have a lot of fixing up work to do!' I felt totally at a loss as to how I or even my generation could live up to that kind of task, and I thought that was such a classic mom move to put such an impossible ball in my court.

A few months later, I found myself walking down long New Hampshire driveways to interrupt family meals, first on hot days and later on snowy ones. As I walked by myself, I would repeat a few lines in my best imitation of your voice, which is a horrible imitation but made me laugh to myself and also somehow fortified me. I dreaded every unwelcome interaction, beginning with 'the primary isn't for 8 months' and moving into 'you've already been here too many times,' but I was able to keep going because I felt like I was part of a broader team, a team you understood, needed, and cared about, and a team that made me better than I had been without them. The people who came together for you in New Hampshire and in every state I went on to see made me so much better and stronger, and the road you sent me down taught me, among other things, just how emboldening a clipboard can be.

When your early state organizers fanned out for Super Tuesday and the later primaries, I found myself feeling flanked by your organization even when there were no other organizers in sight. When I stood on a garbage can at Delaware State University to let everyone lined up know there was no more room to see Michelle Obama but I really needed them to write down their contact information and sign up for canvassing shifts, I was able to draw on courage I didn't have but had seen in a Merrimack mom who, on a very rainy Saturday 6 months prior, had put garbage bags over herself and her son so they could spend the day canvassing their neighborhood. She had told me "there's always a reason not to," and she had canvassed every Saturday between that one and the New Hampshire primary. When I felt out of my depth speaking from a pulpit in Akron about the Ohio primary, and later felt like the ultimate enemy of fun while pleading with a group of Alphas hosting a Ted Kennedy speech to stop letting all the beautiful women circumvent the sign-in process, I knew I could do whatever needed to be done because kids like me were in over their heads for you in places all across America, and we owed it to one another to give it our all.

I was just one of many, but that was kind of the wonderful part. Together, we could really do something that mattered. One time before one of my mom's brain surgeries, you called her to wish her luck, and you told her a lie—you told her I was one of the best you had in the field. That wasn't true by a longshot, but man did it mean a lot to her. Thanks for telling her that, and thanks for building a movement that really wasn't about who was the best but rather what we were together. There were these pink and blue-haired teenagers who joined me to make phone calls one afternoon in Fond Du Lac, Wisconsin—they didn't get through many calls, in fact I have to admit they ended up making posters, but their presence reminded me what I was part of on a day when I needed it. They kept me going, like so many other people along the way.

that lowest of volunteer tasks

When I interviewed the person who most recently started in my office, which of course is your office, she told me a familiar story I get the feeling a lot of people have told over the years since you first declared your candidacy. She described the experience of working on the 2012 convention, and the reasons it had felt right for her rang so true for me and should make you feel so proud. She said that it wasn't the work itself that made the job fulfilling, but rather working alongside the people who came together around your presidency and your campaign—people who felt passionate about what they were working toward and who wanted to play a part in making things better. I felt so lucky to know what she meant. *exactly*

Thank you for letting me have that experience too, and for letting me make so many people a part of it. Thank you for connecting with so many of us and connecting us with one another, and thank you for reconnecting me with our country and its promise. And most of all, thank you for making me and so many others like me feel like we could really be a part of the fixing up work my mom demanded of us.

Sincerely,

Samples, 2016-2017

Zoe E. Ruff
Bath, ME

Mr. President
1600 Pennsylvania Ave. NW
Washington DC
20500

485
DEC 07 2016

✓#016 900#/OO

1/12/17
LH 4

Sample

Tuesday, November 29th, 2016

Dear President Obama,

Hello! My name is Zoe Ruff. I am thirteen years old, and I live in Bath, Maine. I wrote you this poem to show you that people care about this election. I think, in the end, it all comes down to pride. Whether someone voting for Donald Trump or for Hillary Clinton, or for someone else, how you take the results is as vital as the results themselves. As an extremely opinionated liberal myself, I believe the citizens of America should be proud. Not that we elected Donald J. Trump into the White House, but that we got to live under the name Obama. That, in and of itself, is an honor. You have taught love and kindness to this country, and that's not something our future president can take away from us. We can make it through the next four years if we can keep our heads up, and not let anyone tell us we should act one way, believe in a certain god, or be threatened because of color. Because if we do, he's really won. And we cannot let anyone as afraid as him win. We have gained too much to go back now.

I wanted to thank you for everything you've done for my home, and more. You have been honest, kind, and smart as our leader, and I couldn't be prouder to be American.

Yours Sincerely,

Zoe Ruff
age 13
grade 8

Election Results
An Abecedarian

A shuffle of slippers awakes me. I arise from my
bed. Mom looks at me through tearstained cheeks. "Honey, she lost.
Clinton lost." I squeeze my eyes shut. I can't even pretend to suppress the
dry sob that
echoes in my throat. Someone
fear-driven will be the head of this
glorious nation, my
home country. How could we have done this?
I convince myself to get up. The days are now numbered until
January 20th, that dreaded day when our true leader is
kicked out, no
longer in the position to
make our country the place we
need it to be. Right now,
only Obama can make me feel better, so I
press the *Home* button on my iPad to watch his speeches.
Quiet tears leak down my face, a whispered
reminder: my Mexican, Asian, and Muslim friends may
soon be leaving me, all because of
Trump, who can't even begin to
understand the rest of the world's point of
view. I thought I
would be angry. Instead, I'm sad that he's brainwashed America with his
xenophobia-ridden lies. I turn back to Obama,
yearning for everything and nothing at the same time. I tell myself,
"Zoe. We can get through this."

—ZOE RUFF

This is an abecedarian. what makes an abecedarian special
is that the first letter of each line follows the alphabet.

BARACK OBAMA

May 31, 2017

Ms. Zoe Ruff
Bath, Maine

Dear Zoe:

   Thank you for writing to me and for sharing your thoughtful poem. In the letters I receive from young people like you, I see the creativity and patriotism of your generation, and in particular, your reflections on the election and your outlook for the future give me tremendous hope for what lies ahead.

   I know it sometimes seems like for every two steps forward, we take one step back. But remember that the course our country takes from here will be charted by engaged citizens like you who step forward and speak out for what they believe in. And I'm confident that as long as you stay focused on your education, set your sights high, and seek out new challenges, you can help shape a brighter future and effect positive change in your community and in the lives of those around you.

   Thank you, again, for your kind note. Know that I'm rooting for you in all you do, and I wish you the very best.

Your friend,

Little Passports
A GLOBAL ADVENTURE
STUDENTS/118

im 8 Years old
(min of thy kids)
Your my
Favorite
President.
1/31/17
817

Dear president

obama I Know we
don't want Donald
trump to be
president there is
one reason I don't
want him to be president
www.littlepassports.com

because he hates a kid in
muslims and I am a muslim from the united states

white house
1600 pennsylvania
Ave Nw,
washington, Dc 20500

FOREVER

From: Jamie Snyder

Submitted: 1/12/2017 11:24 PM EST

Email:

Phone:

Address: Los Angeles, California

Message: Mr. President and Mrs. Obama, I am currently VERY pregnant with my second child (and first girl). My husband and I were thrilled to find out that her scheduled due date would be on what we thought would be HRC's historical Inauguration Day. We quickly became distraught knowing that she is now due to come into the world on the day that Trump takes office. After speaking truthfully with my angel of an OB, she rescheduled the c-section to happen on Thursday, January 19th. So my sweet girl will be born on the last day of your amazing presidency! The Snyder Family has the utmost admiration and respect for you both, and we hope to become a fraction of the superb parents you have been to your beautiful and brilliant girls. We thank you for your service and unwavering dedication to our country, and we will miss you dearly. We are excited to think that our daughter will be a small reminder of your legacy. Thank you for everything. Jamie Snyder

BARACK OBAMA

June 14, 2017

Mrs. Jamie Snyder
Los Angeles, California

Dear Jamie:

      I read the email you sent just a few days before the birth of your daughter, and I wanted to congratulate you and your husband and let you know how moved I was by your message. Your love for and pride in your children is abundantly clear—a feeling I know quite well—and your kind words meant a great deal to Michelle and me. We hope your family has been able to enjoy some precious time together these last few months.

      I know that now remains a time of great uncertainty for many. But I'm confident that so long as parents like you and your husband continue striving to instill in their children the same values, selflessness, and sense of common purpose that came through in your email, the future will be bright. As your son and daughter continue to learn and grow, know that Michelle and I wish the very best for all of you.

      Thank you, again—for everything.

Sincerely,

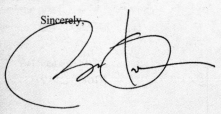

11/19/17
f.g.

7:44 am
15 Dec 2016
Marietta, GA

Dear President Obama,
    I'm writing this at the proverbial kitchen table, after sending my two boys (13, 16 y.o) off to school. I haven't written a letter to a president for 10 years, since I was 7 years old and living in Alabama. I wrote to Jimmy Carter then, excited that a man my parents had taken me to visit on the campaign trail was in the White House. He seemed so kind and my little girl self had so many important things to share with him. And miracle of miracles, he wrote me back. Maybe that made me less cynical* over the years - or a lifelong Democrat,** which got hard in a state like Alabama. I'm picking up a pen to write another president – you – because I'm profoundly thankful for your service to our country and I

*about government and the good it can represent

** #proud

felt it was important for you to
know what good your presidency
did in the lives of just one
family living in Marietta, Georgia.

and for me to say in writing

When you were first running for
office, in 2008, my husband was
laid off, with his whole department,
from CNN. This was in the spring and
we had no idea that the whole
economy was tanking. I was working
as a teacher (and still do — college)
and he got unemployment, which was
thankfully extended for almost a
year. It was scary — those lean times,
but your win and presidency and
your personal kindness and decency
made us know that times would
get better. We were able to put our
youngest son in free pre-k, economize,
and keep our house. (we always
paid the mortgage first) My husband
eventually got a job, until the company
folded, went on unemployment again
(thankfully that safety net was still there)
Finally, he got a good job in 2011, and

and has worked ever since. Your steady leadership through the recession gave us hope (not just a slogan to us!) and I was thankful every day that my boys grew up with you in the white House,* with you as the model of a president. Our family is in a much better place than it was when you took office — two good jobs, a nest egg** for retirement, and kids who have known a president with a good heart and a work ethic and vision that made their lives better. To say that dealing with such push-back (from Congress) wasn't easy is, I'm sure, an understatement, but we've all felt that you've put the people first and done tangible things to make our lives better. Thank you. Thank you. Thank you.

I'm not sure I can love two presidents as much as I love you and Jimmy Carter, but I hope all who follow can do as much good as you have.

Respectfully,
Lynn Murray Luxemburger

*and Michelle too!

**your steady economic policies made this happen

→ my actual tears :'(
(of gratitude)

BARACK OBAMA

June 19, 2017

Ms. Lynn Murray Luxemburger
Marietta, Georgia

Dear Lynn:

Thank you for sitting down and taking the time to write me a note after sending your two boys off to school this past December. I read it on the final night of my Presidency and just wanted to let you know how much your story moved me.

It's folks like you and your husband who were on my mind every single day that I was President. You're right that "hope" is more than just a slogan, but rather what got so many through such difficult times. It certainly kept me going, and knowing our actions helped so many hardworking families like yours means so much. I'm glad to hear things are looking up.

From my family to yours, thank you—for everything. You have our very best wishes.

Sincerely,

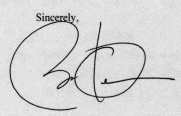

11/6/17
FS

12-05-2016

DEAR PRESIDENT OBAMA,

I OWE YOU AN APOLOGY.

THERE IS NO QUESTIONS THAT WE ARE AT
DIFFERENT PLACES ON THE POLITICAL SPECTRUM. THERE
FEW THINGS THAT WE AGREE ON WHEN IT COMES TO
POLICY AND THE DIRECTION OF OUR GOVERNMENT.

HERE'S WHERE I WENT WRONG. I LET MY
DISAGREEMENTS WITH YOU TAINT THE WAY I VIEWED
YOU AS A PERSON. I HELD YOU IN CONTEMPT AND
SHARED MY POOR OPINION OF YOU.

BUT THAT WAS WRONG, AND UNCHRISTIAN. AS
THE YEARS HAVE GONE BYE I HAVE TAKEN A CLOSER
LOOK. MY OPINION WAS WAY OFF. WE STILL DISAGREE
ON A VAST NUMBER OF THINGS. BUT YOU, SIR, ARE
A PATRIOT. I HAVE COME TO ADMIRE YOU AS A MAN
OF PRINCIPLE, A MAN WITH A GOOD HEART, A MAN WITH
A TREMENDOUS SENSE OF HUMOR, A FAMILY MAN,
A MAN OF FAITH AND A MAN WHO LOVES THIS COUNTRY.
I HAVE SEEN AND READ ABOUT HOW YOU TREAT OUR MILITARY
AND THE SECRET SERVICE WITH RESPECT. I HAVE SEEN YOUR
GENUINE HUMILITY (AS MUCH AS ONE CAN SEE IN A POLITICIAN).

I DO STRONGLY AGREE WITH YOUR OPENNESS TO CUBA.
I APPLAUDE YOUR CANCER INITIATIVE. SO WE CAN AGREE
ON SOME THINGS.

YOU WILL NEVER MEET ME. YOU PROBABLY WON'T EVER EVEN SEE THIS LETTER. BUT I JUDGED YOU WRONGLY AND HARSHLY. MY FAITH AND MY MOTHER RAISED ME TO ADMIT WHEN I AM WRONG AND MAKE AMENDS TO THE PERSON I'VE OFFENDED. SO I THOUGHT THIS THE BEST WAY TO ATTEMPT THAT; A HANDWRITTEN APOLOGY.

So THERE IT IS. I WANT TO THANK YOU. THANK YOU FOR YOUR EXAMPLE OF FATHERHOOD, AS A HUSBAND AND A MAN. THANK YOU, MR PRESIDENT, FOR YOUR SERVICE TO THIS GREAT COUNTRY.

I PRAY THAT GOD MAY BLESS YOU AND YOUR FAMILY ALWAYS AND IN ALL WAYS.

SINCERELY,

Patrick J. O'Connor

PATRICK J. O'CONNOR

AKRON, OH

Rust Eddy.
Canton, NY

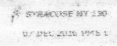

STOREHOUSE NY 130

07 DEC 2016 PM 6 1

The President of the United
                              States
The White House   of America
1600 Pennsylvania Ave NW
Washington, DC 20500

485
DEC 15 2016
✓ #039

Hope is a thing with feathers.
                    E. Dickinson
11/9/17
8:5
Dear Mr. President,

Borders seem to be all the
rage these days, mostly strengthening
and reinforcing them. It has
been a gift of my life to live
it across borders. I am a
white man married to a black
woman for 26 years. We live
in a small town in far
northern NY, Canton. My wife,
Dr. Sheryl Scales, teaches
Literacy in the School of
Education at SUNY Potsdam.
My life drifts between the two
worlds of Hillary and Trump;

Sheryl's circle of academia,
and the local small town
friends and acquaintances
who are the perfect microcosm
of Trump voters. Needless to
say living across that border has
caused me more than a little
difficulty in recent days, sometimes
feeling more like a curse than a
gift.

Please know that your example
of strength and compassion,
resolve and empathy, intellectual
curiosity and sense of wonder,
have inspired us throughout
your presidency, and more
importantly will resonate in
your legacy, continuing to
inspire us to persevere.
            Thank You Sir
            Russ Eddy and Sheryl Scales

Sample 11/4/19
f.4

Charlotte Blome

Crystal Lake, IL

18 November 2016

President Barack Obama
The White House
1600 Pennsylvania Avenue NW
Washington, DC 20500

Dear Mr. President,

In this time of uncertainty, I would like to share with you a small, but bright spot that I am sure in not an isolated one.

We are a mixed race family that lives in the reddest county in Chicagoland. I am white. My adopted son Noah is black. His school is overwhelmingly white. Last year, his 7th grade elected him the most likely to become President of the United States, in spite of the fact that he reminded them he is Ethiopian by birth. They did not care. This year, he ran for student council president and won.

It may seem like a small thing on the surface, but I do not think that 20 years ago this would have happened at your typical 98% white school. Noah is likely the first black student council president at his Jr. High, but my impression is it is so normal for him and his fellow students, that it has not even been mentioned! He has experienced quite a bit of racial bias in his 13 years, but never from his peers. Even in a conservative county like ours. I attribute this largely to you. (He gets some credit, too, for being a good, hard-working guy!)

So, I thank you and the First Lady for setting us on the right course. We sure are going to miss you.

With profound gratitude and respect,

Charlotte Blome

BARACK OBAMA

May 4, 2017

Ms. Charlotte Blome
Crystal Lake, Illinois

Dear Charlotte:

Thanks for your note. It's clear you've raised a wonderful young man, and I can tell how proud you are of Noah.

Noah's accomplishments reflect an idea at the heart of our nation's promise: that in America, all people should be able to make of their lives what they will—no matter the color of their skin or the country they are from. The story you shared of his experience in school gives me tremendous hope for our country's future.

Thanks again. You and your family have my very best.

Sincerely,

BARACK OBAMA

May 4, 2017

Mr. Noah Blome
Crystal Lake, Illinois

Dear Noah:

Your mother wrote to tell me about all you've achieved in school—congratulations on being elected Student Council President! It's clear your mom is very proud of you, and I want you to know that I am, too.

In the face of challenges, I hope you'll remember that there are no limits to what you can achieve. As long as you hold on to the passion and determination that have brought you this far and keep dreaming big dreams, you can help effect positive change—in your school, across your community, and throughout our nation.

Again, congratulations—and good luck with your new responsibilities. I'm rooting for you and wish you the very best.

Sincerely,

From: Mr. Joshua David Hofer

Submitted:

Email:

Phone:

Address:

Bloomington, Nebraska

Message:
Honorable President Barack Obama,

Dear Mr President I appreciate how hard you work and as a former veteran I understand how things you believe get twisted against you by the military. That most saddest thing I see is the hatred towards the Muslim world and the separation our country is going towards. I feel your President Abraham Lincoln and Im watching history repeat itself against color of skin. I served in the military at a young age and being from Nebraska I learned their is no such thing as race. The people who still look out for me today are of different color. I think america is sheltered and needs to see what veterans have seen since the war on Terrorism began. We need more commercials that teach lessons and give other point of views like South Korea does in order to maintain their social customs for their younger youth. I truly believe in what you do buy because I served I saw were the money went to support Pakistan (Terrorism) and Iran. I believe america when you do a presidential speech need to see what life is like when you live in a country that is at war. I have photos of a one girl who reminded me of my sister as I was losing my mind in 2003 in Iraq. I never will leave me but I wanted to change lives for them. Their country has oppressed them to where they were starving. I gave her chocolate and all kinds of stuff but I realized the error in my ways. As I would try to help her out predators because she was a female made an example. As we were leaving I saw that an older child saw what I have done. She cared for her younger brother as well. He was stomped to death and she was being dragged down the street. I care her picture with me to this day. I didnt see Muslim or Christian, I saw human. When you oppress someone and kill their family, they grow up in a world of hate. I believe I have many more things to offer my country then retired veteran but in this new world where your born into privilege it is hard for a veteran who cries from his nightmares to separate. This country is filled with so much hate it kills me. I dont see black and white I see my brothers. I have been wronged and you are the only one who could help me move on. Like people that are angry I feel I was wronged but by leaders in my military service.

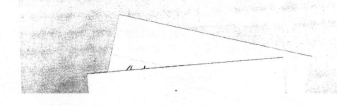

From: **Mr. larry wright**

Submitted: 1/11/2017 7:17 AM EST

Email:

Phone:

Address: Greensboro, North Carolina

Message: Mr President

For 8 years you were loved, hated, mistreated and berated. For 8 years you sung, danced cried and amazing graced us when racism and hatred came knocking at God's door. You was a Muslim, Terrorist, half bread, African but never American. You help two industries that were on the verge of collapse and pulled this country out of its worse recession in years. We seen you go from dark hair to gray hair, we seen your kids grow and become beautiful young ladies and your wife is the woman most admired by many women around the globe. I credit your wife for restoring pride in all women especially black women. You gave people the opportunity to be insured and feel safe when it came to the safety of this country. I'm sure there are things that you are not proud of and wish you could go back and fix them, but we all have things we would love to fix in our lives as well. In closing I would like to say this. There may never be another face like your in the white house, there may never be another family like your in the white house and there may never be a husband and wife team like you and your wife that lived a scandal free campaign in the white house. The one thing that will be missed when you close that door behind you will be Mr. Barack Obama our 44th President of the United States.

From: **Marjan Schneider Carasik**

Submitted: 12/24/2016 12:36 PM EST

Email:

Phone:

Address: Ithaca, New York

Message: Dear Mr President,

Thank you for standing up for the rights of Palestinians as well as Israelis. Answers to all questions lie somewhere in the middle.

I am the child and grandchild of Jewish refugees who suffered greatly before coming to America. It causes me much pain to see Palestinians sometimes being mistreated as my family members were mistreated before arriving on these shores.

I am grateful to you for your courage in standing where you do. This does not make you an anti-Semite, but rather pro-All Human Beings.

With Much Admiration and Affection, and Thanks,

Marjan S. Carasik

Ithaca, N.Y.

Mr. President and Mrs. Obama,   1/10/17
                                 f. 20

I cannot tell you how much I have loved and appreciated your work in the White House for the last 8 years.

As a daughter of immigrants and a woman of color, your actions in office have given me so much hope. Thank you for leading an America that was inclusive and that craved justice.

I got to attend your inauguration in 2008. I still have a lot of the cheesy keepsakes Pepsi was handing out that week. I remember that it was freezing. and that it hurt to cry because of that. I remember being stranded at the Air and Space Museum for 4 hours while we waited for our charter bus. I was interviewed like 3 times that week by LatinAmerican news stations. I cried in all three as I explained that your presidency validated my dreams.

As you transition out of the presidency, I want you to know it was worth it. It was worth all the Fox news attacks. It was worth it to honor and respect Muslims. It was worth it to champion the rights of women. To cry out against injustice. To mourn the loss of black lives at the hands of law enforcement.

Your courage and humility in leadership will be sorely missed. But not forgotten. All the voices you've pulled out of silence — we're all in unison and ready to rally for justice, unity, and equality.

So when you move out of the White House, go on vacation. Drink some margaritas for me. We'll be here fighting the good fight till you get back.

                So much love,
                Mary-Beth Johnson

MILWAUKIE, OR

BARACK OBAMA

June 14, 2017

Mrs. Mary-Beth Johnson
Milwaukie, Oregon

Dear Mary-Beth:

Thanks for sharing your reflections on the last eight years, including my first inauguration, in the letter you sent me—I agree; it was all worth it.

I was moved by your kind words, and I am inspired by your commitment to continue stepping forward, speaking out, and working to defend the values that make us who we are. As you do, please know Michelle and I will be standing right alongside you, as we always have been, fighting for the America we both know is possible.

Thanks again for writing—you, Benjamin, and Estel have my very best.

Sincerely,

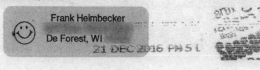

Preardent Barack +
Frest Lady Michelle Obama
The White House
1600 Pennsylvania Ave
NW, Washington, D.C.
20500

President Barack & 1/19/17
First Lady Michelle, fr10

This modest card probably
will not get to you. I want to
thank you for the last eight years.
It has been a honor. You started
out with a part of my heart, and
you leave with the whole thing.

Frank Heunbecker
DeForest WI

BARACK OBAMA

June 19, 2017

Mr. Frank Heimbecker
DeForest, Wisconsin

Dear Frank:

On the final night of my Presidency, I read the handwritten card you sent me, and I wanted to reach out to thank you. Your kind words were deeply moving, and while I appreciate your thinking of me, please know the honor was all mine—it was the privilege of my life to serve as your President.

There are certainly milestone moments we will always remember from the past eight years, but for me, it was hearing from people like you that kept me going every single day. My heart has been touched time and again by the daily acts of kindness that embody the American people at their core, and as I take some time now to rest and reflect on all we achieved together, know that your thoughtful gesture will stay with me.

Sincerely,

Epilogue

Benjamin Durrett (page 4), twenty-eight, is married and living in Oregon. He works as an office administrator for a water company, and is not registered with a political party.

Despite their differing views of government, Richard Dexter (page 5) treasured Obama's response to his letter, and plans to pass it on to his daughters.

Jeri Harris (page 7) kept her promise to pray for Obama every day of his two terms. His letter hangs inside a frame on a wall in her living room. She wrote a letter to President Trump after the 2016 election, saying she would pray for him too.

J. Martin Ball (page 9) died in 2011. His daughter, Natasha, remembers the day her father wrote to Obama—it was her son's eighteen-month birthday. Her father was overjoyed knowing that his grandson would grow up knowing a black president.

Shailagh Murray (page 12) is not writing as many letters as she believes she should. She thinks often of Bobby Ingram and the thousands of Americans whose stories lived in binders in her West Wing office, and whose voices and conviction were her guiding force.

Every day at about three o'clock, Bobby Ingram (page 23) watches his cat, Purdy, step out on the back porch, hop onto the railing, and begin nudging morsels of cat food off of it. The food drops into the yard below where BooHiss, the fat turtle, awaits with contentment. "Purdy is just fascinated by that," Bobby reports.

Linette Jones (page 34) is glad she shot her angry email to Obama, and would do it again; his response was comforting. Her daughter Sophia, who was stationed in Kabul when Linette wrote to the president, is safely home, living close to her mom in Florida.

Michael Powers (page 36) allowed White House staff to share his letter publicly, along with Obama's reply. The letters showed up on a conservative blog where Obama's handwritten response earned a place as one of the top ten gaffes he made during his first six months in office. (He misspelled "advice," or at least didn't properly curve the "c.")

Kenny Jops (page 48), twenty-two, graduated from Northwestern University in 2018 with a double major in math and environmental studies.

Fiona Reeves (page 64) works for a Democratic communications firm, and her husband, Chris Liddell-Westefeld, collects oral histories for the Barack Obama Presidential Library. Their daughter, Grace, has a letter from Obama framed on her bedroom wall. Her parents report that Grace goes canvassing with them every chance she gets.

Yena Bae (page 67) is pursuing a graduate degree in international security studies at Columbia University. She is a frequent host of wine nights, potlucks, and get-togethers where stories of #teamlittle-people continue to be shared.

Thomas and JoAnn Meehan's (page 74) son, Daryl, named one of his three daughters after Colleen.

Pete Rouse (page 83) delights in watching the young people who came of age under "the Obama experience" continue to contribute to civic engagement. He's enjoying quality time with Buster, his Maine Coon cat, who now weighs twenty-seven pounds so Pete's putting him on a diet.

Mike Kelleher (page 88) works in the United Nations liaison office at the World Bank in Washington, D.C. He also composes, arranges, and performs music professionally; his 2015 jazz album, *Mélange*, is a collaboration with his wife, Karin, a classical violinist.

Laura King (page 96) is now legally married to Lisa.

Robert B. Trapp (page 97) is still the managing editor of *The Rio Grande Sun*.

Retired U.S. Air Force Staff Sergeant Robert Doran (page 98) discovered that his fiancée, Jana', had not been taking her blood pressure medication before she died; she was unable to afford it. SSgt Doran gave Obama's reply to his letter to Jana''s daughters.

Chana Sangkagalo (page 108) enjoys continued success at his popular hair salon in Rhode Island.

Regina Bryant (page 109) received a recipe from Michelle Obama for a vegetarian bean dip. "Some serious spices!" Her letter and the Obamas' reply are saved in an album for her daughter, Caitlin.

Jason Hernandez's (page 112) life sentence for a drug conviction was commuted by President Obama on December 19, 2013. He lives in Dallas, where he is writing a book about the justice system and where he assists federal inmates serving life sentences with clemency petitions.

A campaign staffer was so moved by Sandy Swanson's (page 113) letter that she sent the family a pizza, and then President Obama called her from Air Force One to thank her.

Bill Oliver (page 116) and his wife, Sandra, host a weekly philosophy study group at their home. Quique plans to go to culinary school. Quique's wife, Rebecca, is a premed student in college. Bill and Quique talk daily.

In July 2016, Darin Konrad Brunstad's (pages 129 and 134) husband, Senior Master Sergeant and two-time Airman of the Year awardee David Lono Brunstad, retired from the military after twenty-two years of service. Darin and David rode on an F-15 fighter jet to celebrate. They are now foster parents.

Marnie Hazelton (page 138) is starting her fourth school year as superintendent of the Roosevelt Union Free School District. In 2018, she shared her letter to President Obama with a third-grade class to demonstrate the importance of writing well.

Erv and Ross Uecker-Walker (page 151) will celebrate sixty-one years together and four years of marriage on November 30, 2018.

Jordan Garey (page 160) lived in eleven foster homes before his two dads adopted him. He got invited to the White House for its 2015 Easter Egg Roll, and met the First Lady.

In June 2014, Danny Garvin (page 162) was invited to attend a White House reception celebrating LGBT Pride Month. Obama asked for a picture taken beside him. Danny died in 2015. He was honored by several publications for his activism and his demonstration at the Stonewall Inn.

Tom Hoefner (page 164) is a stay-at-home dad looking after his two girls. He works weekends at a residential facility for disabled people, and is drafting the second volume of a serialized adventure/comedy book series, *The Unlikely Adventures of Race & Cookie McCloud*. He is still looking for full-time work in his field.

Bob Melton (page 166) continues to read his letter from President Obama at the monthly Tuesday meetings of the Burke County, North Carolina, Democratic Party. He lives with his wife, Tammy, in their home of twenty-five years, where they ride and maintain dune buggies.

Shelley Muniz (page 171) is the author of *Eagle Feathers and Angel Wings: Micah's Story*, which chronicles her son's illness and struggles with healthcare coverage.

Since Ronn Ohl (page 173) wrote his letter to Obama, his son's friend, now thirty-four, was granted DACA status, allowing him to obtain a green card, get a driver's license, attend college, and land a full-time job.

Joelle Graves (page 180) became email buddies with an OPC staffer, who relayed to her that Obama was so moved by her letter that he read it to his family in the White House residence. Joelle went on to write a letter to the queen of England, who also responded personally.

Marjorie McKinney (page 181) renovated her house to welcome her daughter Rachel and granddaughter Kirby, who now live with her. She has begun attending a church in Janaluska, one of the region's oldest historically black neighborhoods.

Ashley DeLeon (page 191) got engaged to be married in May 2018, on the same day she graduated from the University of North Carolina Wilmington with a master's degree in marine biology. She gets her love of the ocean from her dad.

Lacey Higley (page 192) works for the United States Digital Service at the Department of Veterans Affairs, building and modernizing digital tools that enable veterans to discover, apply for, and track the benefits they've earned.

A year after sending her 2015 letter to Obama, Alisa Bowman (page 204) and her transgender son addressed their local school board in support of trans students. In 2017, Alisa was elected to the board, which went on to pass a comprehensive nondiscrimination policy that protects students' gender identity. Alisa wrote another letter to Obama in 2018, saying she was "embarrassed" by the anger in her first one. "You gave me the courage to put an end to living small," she told him.

Rev. Christine G. Reisman (page 206), the pastor of Newbern Christian Church in Newbern, Virginia, and her husband moved into a new condo on November 9, 2016, the day after the presidential election. The mover who packed her framed letter from Obama wrote "**Fragile! Historical artifact! Letter from Obama!**" many times on the box.

As a result of her letter to Obama, Sue Ellen Allen (page 208) was invited to attend the 2016 State of the Union address as a guest in the First Lady's box, where she met Attorney General Loretta Lynch. Sue Ellen told the attorney general about her efforts back home to reform the culture of incarceration. "Can you imagine, I'm a felon meeting with Loretta Lynch?"

Mary Susan Sanders (page 211) is the author of three books, including *Solo,* about losing her late partner, artist and wood carver Kathy Ruth Neal. Mary Susan used Kathy's paints to paint her lawn jockey.

Delaney (page 213) wrote a thank-you note back to President Obama with a sticker on top that said "My Fave Person."

Gretchen Elhassani (page 215) is a screenwriter for Georgia Film Company.

Sheryl Cousineau's (page 218) neighbor who helped in the orchard remains in Mexico after his deportation. He drives a taxi. His daughter, Janitza, works near Sheryl at a real estate company.

Heba Hallak (page 220), twenty, is studying biochemistry at Drew University. She plans to become a pediatrician.

Cody Keenan (page 228) is helping President Obama prepare his next book.

In May 2018, Shane Darby (page 233) received a mysterious package in the mail. It was from an anonymous airman who had served with Cristina. Inside the package were an American flag, a hat, and a patch with Cristina's name on it, along with a certificate from the 494th Expeditionary Fighter Squadron of the U.S. Air Force dated May 4, 2018—her birthday. "This flag was proudly flown in an F-15 E Strike Eagle on a combat sortie over Syria and Iraq in support of OPERATION INHERENT RESOLVE. Flown in memory of: Cristina Danielle Silvers. For her smile was strong and true."

William Johnson (page 248) was released from prison on parole. He has a handyman business with his sons.

Yvonne Wingard (page 251) is a junior at Brown University, where she studies public health, serves on the student council, and works as a peer counselor.

Anne Bunting (page 252) shared President Obama's letter with her heart-transplant surgeons. Now, four years after her operation, she enjoys hiking and traveling.

Alex Myteberi (page 254), eight, has a LEGO White House in his bedroom that he will not let anyone touch. He is learning to play the piano.

Myriah Johnson (page 260) continues to raise awareness about veteran suicide in memory of her son, U.S. Army Specialist Alexander Johnson.

Noor Abdelfattah (page 263) was invited to a White House dinner celebrating Muslim Americans as well as Eid al-Fitr, the holiday marking the end of Ramadan.

Madison Drago (page 264), sixteen, received a reply from President Obama advising her to listen to her parents. She got her nose pierced anyway. "And a lot more," her mom reports.

Kolbie Blume (page 269) works in media relations at the Association of International Educators, the world's largest nonprofit dedicated to international education and exchange. She made a present for Fiona Reeves's baby, Grace: a framed calligraphy drawing quoting the speech Hillary Clinton gave on November 9, 2016. "To all the little girls: Never doubt that you are valuable and powerful and deserving of every chance and opportunity in the world to pursue and achieve your own dreams." It hangs on the wall near Grace's crib, next to the letter Obama wrote to Grace.

Patty Ries (page 273) suffered a house fire in January 2018, losing almost everything. But a few of her father's photos and writings, along with his army discharge papers, were found intact in the rubble. Patty felt it was a miracle, the work of her long lost grandmother. "I survived a concentration camp; you'll get through this," she imagined her grandmother saying.

Billy Ennis (page 277) got another raise at his roofing job. He is still with his girlfriend, the woman he recognized from seventh grade in the supermarket. He talks to his dad, who is still in prison, weekly. When Billy watched his teenage son take fourth place in discus at the state track and field meet, he broke down in tears. His son called him a big baby.

Since receiving President Obama's message to "stay engaged," Alessandra Shurina (page 305) went back to school at Florida State University, graduated, and began a master's program in political science and public policy.

"At the risk of sounding hokey, this whole thing has rejuvenated my faith in people and in this country," Maureen Dolan Rosen (page 313) said of receiving a personal response to her letter from President Obama.

Roberta Fine (page 316) enjoys planting flowers and maintaining her vegetable garden. She is the proud great-grandmother of two.

Vicki and Tim Shearer (page 324) bought an RV and frequently go camping together.

Joshua Hofer (page 377) served in the military for ten years. He recalls busting up human trafficking operations in South Korea. He has struggled with the effects of traumatic brain injury.

Mary-Beth Johnson (page 380) keeps Obama's letter framed next to her bed, beside a hand-lettered print that says "I am with you always," a quote from the Book of Matthew. She enjoys writing *Heart of Celebration,* her food blog.

President Obama still receives five thousand letters a week.

Acknowledgments

To Obama grew out of a story for *The New York Times Magazine* that my longtime editor and friend Mike Benoist encouraged me to pursue. My thanks to Mike for his early belief in the wisdom of the mailroom, to Jake Silverstein for his support and willingness to showcase it, and to President Obama for his generous response to the article, for taking the time to meet with me—and for allowing me to keep digging through his mail.

This book was an entirely collaborative effort. Fiona Reeves was its guiding light from the outset; she inspired me with her quiet and determined service to the president and to the country, and my gratitude to her lead is boundless. Researcher Rachel Wilkinson was on the case from beginning to end, and I could not have written the book without her. Her compassion and intelligence are all through these pages, and I'm deeply grateful to her. My thanks also to audio producer Erin Anderson, who along with Rachel trekked across the country talking to people about their letters and whose wisdom guided so many editorial decisions, and to the rest of the people at Cement City Productions—Tim Maddocks, Erin Kello, Tyler McCloskey, Rachel Mabe, Rachel Brickner—whose efforts kept the engines

humming. In addition, I would like to thank Michael Lewis for helping me find the courage to take on this book project.

I would like to thank Eric Schultz, Obama's postpresidency senior advisor, for his trust and support and for being so much fun to
work with; communications director Katie Hill for her kindness and
persistence in providing materials; Mike Kelleher for his insight and
generosity; Shailagh Murray for her vision and guidance; and all the
people in the mailroom who shared their stories of extraordinary
service and who helped track down letter writers from all over the
country. Every effort was made to remove all identifying information
from any letter whose author requested anonymity and from those
whose authors were unreachable; samples from the archives at
obamawhitehouse.archives.gov were cleared prior to appearing in
this book, and I'm indebted to these letter writers (especially Emily,
whose letter is featured on the back cover of this book) who contributed their words and stories to Obama's legacy and to the embrace
of history.

My agent, Elyse Cheney, was a ferocious advocate for the book.
My ongoing thanks to her and everyone at the agency, especially
Alex Jacobs, Alice Whitwham, Claire Gillespie, and Natasha Fair-
weather.

Andy Ward, at Random House, is the kind of editor every writer
dreams of having; he's a writing partner who demands more and
makes everything better than you knew it could be. He has shaped
my books and articles over the long arc of my career, and as always I
can't find words big enough to adequately express my gratitude. I
would like to thank the entire team at Random House for their support, notably Susan Kamil and Tom Perry, and the heroic production
efforts of Chayenne Skeete and Loren Noveck, Anna Bauer for the
beautiful cover, Debbie Glasserman for the interior design, Matthew
Martin for protecting the work, and Cindy Murray for her creativity
in spreading the word.

I get tremendous support from the people at the University of
Pittsburgh, and I would like to say a special thanks to them for the
work they do. Pat Gallagher, chancellor of the university, offered
helpful insights into this project, and Provost and Senior Vice Chancellor Patty Beeson, along with Executive Vice Provost Dave DeJong,
provided especially helpful encouragement and care. John Cooper,

deputy vice chancellor for research, remains an enthusiastic supporter; my sincere thanks to him and to Kathy Blee, dean of the Dietrich School of Arts and Sciences, and Don Bialostosky, chair of the department of English, for their ongoing kindness and generous patronage. I'm grateful to my colleagues in the writing program, notably Peter Trachtenberg, Michael Meyer, and Maggie Jones for filling in the gaps while I took leave, and I would like to extend a special thanks to Kit Ayars, my longtime friend, who guided the ship at the Center for Creativity while I took the time to write this book.

I would like to thank my husband, Alex, whose love and support makes all this work possible, and my daughters, Anna and Sasha, who endured my absence during all that time back in the hole.

Finally, I offer my ongoing gratitude to all of the letter writers who gave permission to reprint their letters, and who allowed me the privilege of hearing and sharing their remarkable stories.

Permission Credits

Replies from President Obama written after his presidency are reprinted by permission of the Office of President Obama. Samples from the archives at obamawhitehouse. archives.gov were cleared prior to appearing in this book.

Letter written by Dare Adewumi reprinted by permission of Dare A. Adewumi, M.D.
Letter written by Sue Ellen Allen reprinted by permission of Sue Ellen Allen.
Letter written by Adam Apo reprinted by permission of Adam Y. Apo.
Letter written by J. Martin Ball reprinted by permission of Natasha Ball-Madkins.
Letter written by Dawn Benefiel reprinted by permission of Dawn Marie Benefiel.
Letter written by Charlotte Blome reprinted by permission of Charlotte J. Blome.
Letter written by Amanda Bott reprinted by permission of Amanda Bott.
Letter written by Alisa Bowman reprinted by permission of Alisa Bowman.
Letters written by Darin Konrad Brunstad reprinted by permission of Darin Konrad Brunstad.
Letter written by Regina Bryant reprinted by permission Regina Bryant.
Letter written by Anne Bunting reprinted by permission of Anne Bunting.
Letter written by Marjan Carasik reprinted by permission of Marjan S. Carasik.
Letter written by Donna Coltharp reprinted by permission of Donna F. Coltharp.
Letter written by Sheryl Cousineau reprinted by permission of Sheryl L. Cousineau.
Letter written by Ellen Crain reprinted by permission of Ellen F. Crain, MD, PhD.
Letter written by Shane Darby reprinted by permission of Shane Darby.
Letter written by Nicole Davis reprinted by permission of Nicole M. Davis.
Letter written by Madison Drago reprinted by permission of Madison Drago and Susan Drago.

THE SELECTED LETTERS OF

TENNESSEE
WILLIAMS

VOLUME II • 1945–1957

BY TENNESSEE WILLIAMS

Tennessee Williams, ca. 1956

THE SELECTED LETTERS OF

TENNESSEE

WILLIAMS

VOLUME II ◆ 1945–1957

EDITED BY ALBERT J. DEVLIN

CO-EDITED BY NANCY M. TISCHLER

A NEW DIRECTIONS BOOK

In memory of
Lyle Leverich, Dick Leavitt, and Jordan Massee
friends of Tennessee

The Selected Letters of Tennessee Williams, Volume II, is published by arrangement with
The University of the South, Sewanee, Tennessee.

Design by Sylvia Frezzolini Severance

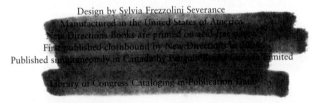

Manufactured in the United States of America
New Directions Books are printed on acid-free paper
First published clothbound by New Directions in 2004
Published simultaneously in Canada by Penguin Books Canada Limited

Library of Congress Cataloging-in-Publication Data

Williams, Tennessee, 1911-1983.
  [Correspondence. Selections]
  The selected letters of Tennessee Williams / edited by Albert J. Devlin
  co-edited by Nancy M. Tischler.
    p. cm.
  Includes index.
  Contents: v. 2. 1945-1957
  ISBN 0-8112-1600-4 (alk. paper)
  1. Williams, Tennessee, 1911-1983—Correspondence. 2. Dramatists,
American—20th century—Correspondence. I. Devlin, Albert J.
II. Tischler, Nancy Marie Patterson. III. Title.
  PS3545.I5365 Z48 2000
  812'.54—dc21
  [B]   99-087398

New Directions books are published for James Laughlin
by New Directions Publishing Corporation,
80 Eighth Avenue, New York, NY 10011

CONTENTS

LIST OF ILLUSTRATIONS

INTRODUCTION

Of the 800 collected letters, notes, and telegrams that fall into the years of Volume II, nearly 350 appear in *The Selected Letters of Tennessee Williams*. They begin in May 1945 as a restless playwright, beset by fame, prepares to leave for Mexico City. They end a dozen years later as a dejected playwright, still mulling the hazards of Broadway, prepares to sail for the Far East after the failure of *Orpheus Descending* (1957). If Volume I of *The Selected Letters* was "a manual of survival," of timely escape from "'two-by-four situations,'" Volume II is an account of the rising odds against escape in the years of Tennessee Williams's maturity. In both cases, escape was intended to refresh the imagination and to keep the threat of being "peddled" at bay, but the deft, intuitive maneuvers of youth have become ponderous and deliberate and aided by addictions. Nothing better evokes the altered mood of Volume II than the beleaguered closing of a letter to Audrey Wood: "This is the end of a long, hard day, and the end of a long, hard summer, and I suppose it is the beginning of a long, hard Fall, but what the hell, we are still with it!" (September 28, 1951).

Six major Broadway shows—each preceded by tedious, nerve-wracking negotiations and followed by tour, film, and revival—fill the calendar of Volume II. They confirm Williams's view of playwriting as the most "exhausting" of art forms: "It literally takes the strength of an ox . . . to carry a play from conception all the way through to its opening night on Broadway." Policing the regime were the "hard-boiled critics" (March 21, 1951) who demanded instant and repeated success, especially from Tennessee Williams, whose aura of self-interest and sexual difference did little to soften his critical reception. These and other pressures form the refrain of Volume II: one of exhaustion, of being written out, used up, dismissed from the theatre, whose economic order Williams had failed to uphold. "It's awful," he warned Carson McCullers, "how quickly a theatrical reputation declines on the market. A few years ago and I could have anything I wanted in the theatre, now I have to go begging. Two plays that didn't make money and, brother, you're on the skids!" (August 1952).

As the letters indicate, the "recessive periods" of Volume II were painful and prolonged and not easily separated from the fame of *Streetcar* (1947), whose daunting effect Williams described to Elia Kazan: "I have been floundering around most of the time since Streetcar, flapping my arms in the air as if they were wings" (July 29, 1952). But the "flapping," however futile it may have seemed at the time, was not without point or direction, nor would the plays that initially failed to "make money"—*Summer and Smoke* (1948) and *The Rose Tattoo* (1951)—lack successful revival. Williams absorbed their sharp lessons and went on to challenge the realistic tenets of Broadway with *Camino Real* (1953), an imaginative farrago whose brief run further greased the "skids" of his career. Underlying the frantic pace of production, and the acute addiction to writing, was a challenge to Broadway that Williams issued in 1949 and then repeated following mixed notices for *The Rose Tattoo*. He claimed for dramatists the same latitude given to painters and poets, arguing that it usually "takes ten years of a man's life to grow into a new major attitude toward . . . the world he exists in" (March 21, 1951). However quixotic the calculation, Williams gradually developed a new "attitude" in the years of Volume II, one shaped by the "world" as he came to know it and brilliantly deployed in *Cat on a Hot Roof* (1955).

Volume I bristled with international disorder, but for Williams the parochial tenor of St. Louis and the conventional ties of family and home were far more disturbing. Their unhappy influence he moderated by taking brief sanctuary in such bohemian quarters as New Orleans, Laguna Beach, and Key West. In Volume II Williams no longer traveled on a budget, nor were the post-war years so overtly beset with danger; but as an artist of achievement and accrued sensitivity, he felt, and annually fled, the pressures of living in America. Its repressive culture, epitomized by Senator Joseph McCarthy, remanded political dissidents and homosexuals to the margins of national life. Williams was publicly accused of Communist leanings and covertly investigated by Naval Intelligence as a sexual deviant. *Time* magazine considered him a dissolute writer, as did Francis Cardinal Spellman, who enjoined the faithful from seeing *Baby Doll* (1956) "under pain of sin." Paris, Rome, Barcelona, and Tangier replaced the American enclaves in Williams's ceaseless travel, adding materially to the distant, broken rhythms of Volume II. These and other public pressures formed a new "attitude" which is first evident in *Cat on a Hot Tin Roof*. The intense inwardness

of Williams's earlier theatre—nostalgia, retrospection, resignation, idealism, despair—would not suffice in *Cat*, which is driven instead by prophecy: "Mendacity is a system that we live in."

Elia Kazan understood this truth, both as a subject of congressional investigation in 1952 and as Williams's friend and favored director. Volume II contains twenty letters addressed to Kazan and as such it represents the first major infusion of this correspondence into the record. (Some eighty additional letters, notes, and telegrams written by Tennessee Williams are held by the Wesleyan University Cinema Archives. The Kazan side of the exchange is less well represented.) To read the extensive Williams correspondence is to appreciate the complexity of the relationship and to withhold categorical judgment. During the years of Volume II, Williams depended heavily upon the magic of Kazan's staging to bring out the latent drama of his plays. Kazan often resisted such importuning by delay, demand for revision, and reluctant refusal. His creative will no doubt blurred the distinction between authorship and direction, but the initial drafts submitted to Kazan—which are documented in the annotations— were often so rushed or fragmentary as to invite elaborate notes for revision. Especially intriguing is the way that each checked the other's lapses in taste or judgment. Kazan declined to film Williams's "cornball" additions to *Streetcar*, while Williams lectured his northern friend on the logic of race in the Mississippi Delta. Most importantly, the selected letters follow the controversial production of *Cat*, revealing Williams's critique of the play in the tryout stage and his efforts to supply motivation for Brick without violating the mysterious origins of his passivity.

The Audrey Wood letters, the largest gathering in Volume II, mark the busy intersection of art and commerce that followed the production of *Streetcar*. Wood astutely managed this enterprise and remained the playwright's first and most trusted reader. But the perils of management are evident in Williams's oddly conjoined fears of being "peddled" unduly and mismanaged financially, perhaps with excessive self-interest on the part of his agent and her husband, Bill Liebling. Their repeated attempts to draw Williams into a production partnership, if only to avoid such abrasive managers as Irene Selznick, stimulated the client's penchant for suspicion and led to the abrupt dissolution of a company formed to produce *Orpheus Descending*. Perhaps the most tender moment in Volume II is to be found in Wood's reassurance of Williams as he painfully tried new

themes following *Streetcar*: "Know that I love you dearly as a man and admire you as much as always as a writer" (March 5, 1950).

Williams's identity as a writer was formed among his "own kind of vague, indefinite folks" (Volume I, October 21, 1939) in the dreaded "City of St. Pollution." Family correspondence in Volume I accounts for one-third of the collection and as such it preserves both the lyrical core of memory and the domestic base upon which Tennessee Williams's theatre was founded. Family letters are greatly reduced in the sequel, a reflection of events which ended any semblance of shared living in St. Louis: the mental illness and hospitalization of Rose, the death of "Grand," Dakin's military service, the final separation of Cornelius and Edwina, and especially the older son's liberating success in *The Glass Menagerie* (1945). Never were the ties of family broken, but they are significantly loosened in Volume II and replaced in part by alternative bonds. By Maria Britneva, the Lady St. Just, a new friend and traveling companion, whose protective gestures both served and irritated the playwright; by Carson McCullers, another new friend and correspondent, with whom Williams briefly considered a scheme to live and work together, which Audrey Wood deemed "pure madness"; especially by intimate relationships with Pancho Rodriguez and Frank Merlo. The latter began in the fall of 1948 and persisted until Merlo's death in 1963. From the beginning the union was volatile, troubling, and marked by strategic separation and sexual leeway. The stock view of the relationship, which casts Tennessee Williams as the restless, promiscuous partner and Merlo as the staunch *bourgeois*, requires second thought in light of the letters and journal entries published in Volume II. At the same time, Merlo adjusted more smoothly to Williams's public-professional life than did Rodriguez, and he was undoubtedly more reliable in crises which affected the playwright. In special moments of physical need and emotional intensity, Williams acknowledged that "my 'Horse' is my little world" (*Journal*, December 30, 1953).

It is fitting that Volume II end with Tennessee Williams and Elia Kazan in conversation. Of their friendship, Kazan wrote many years later that he and Williams were quite similar: "We both felt vulnerable to the depredations of an unsympathetic world, distrustful of the success we'd had, suspicious of those in favor, anticipating put-downs, expecting insufficient appreciation and reward." Kazan's "most loyal and understanding friend" following the debacle in Washington "was Tennessee Williams" (Kazan, *A*

Life, p. 495). So annealing was their sympathy that they collaborated on four major productions in less than a decade. Each derived fame and a measure of wealth from their legendary collaboration, whose seesaw rhythm—volatility and patience, candor and reserve, trust and suspicion—is happily preserved in letters of uncommon length, detail, and self-revelation. In closing, Williams adds a grace note to the collection, as it were, lamenting the failure of *Orpheus Descending*, whose proper "'key'" Kazan would surely have found, and expressing guarded optimism for the future, which is the story of Volume III. What has changed from Williams's earlier proclamations is not the sacred nature of art—its redemptive effect—but the exceedingly high cost of its service.

Albert J. Devlin
Columbia, Missouri
September 2004

EDITORIAL NOTE

Volume II of *The Selected Letters of Tennessee Williams* is intended to provide complete, accurate texts and to preserve as many authorial conventions as publication will allow. Each heading begins with a reference number followed by the correspondent's name, the letter's place of origin and date of composition, and a bibliographical description of the original source, including its present location.

Marked SH (Stationery Headed) is the stationery of hotels, clubs, ships, railways, and other organizations—evidence of Tennessee Williams's relentless travel and incessant composition. Williams's own notations of address and date have also been preserved, but they are often supplemented with data placed in brackets. Bracketed too is the editorial dating of correspondence which is undated in part or whole. When available, postmarked envelopes (PM) are cited to approximate the time of composition. Dating evidence is also drawn from concurrent and recipient letters and especially from the journal, which begins in 1936 and continues, with lapses, through the years of Volume II. Information pertinent to composition, dating, or manuscript provenance may often be found in the final paragraph of the annotations.

The selected letters are transcribed from original sources held by institutions and individual cited in the Key to Collections. The few exceptions to this rule are noted in the heading. The great majority of letters is also published here for the first time. Those few printed in *Remember Me to Tom* (1963), Edwina Dakin Williams's memoir, have been transcribed from original manuscript sources. Williams typed most of his correspondence in block form with double spacing used to mark paragraph breaks. Economy requires that the indented form of his autograph letters be used in Volume II. Closings and signatures are also printed on one line and their punctuation regularized. Salutations remain unedited.

Tennessee Williams's erratic spelling has not been corrected, save in the case of mechanical or inadvertent error, nor has capitalization or punctuation been standardized. The intrusive convention [*sic*] is not used. Rough syntax has occasionally been smoothed with the insertion, in brackets, of

elements needed to create a readable text. In no case has an addition been made where the author's intention is not reasonably clear. Brackets are also used to enclose a description of the state of the manuscript: [*end of letter missing*]. Strikeovers are retained when they are decipherable and significant. Ellipsis is Williams's own practice and is used primarily for emphasis or punctuation rather than to indicate omission.

Bracketed annotations follow nearly every letter and are not keyed to a footnote or other visual system of identification. The intent, as in Volume I, is to discourage the usual discontinuous practice of letter reading, one which occasions undue editorial intrusion into the text and invites the reader to break its pace and mood to consult a language of explication. The annotations are not, however, without design. Some few, especially those which open a unit of letters or summarize a phase of travel, begin with a statement of orientation before taking up specific items mentioned in the letter. Items selected for annotation are paragraphed to follow the letter's internal order of composition. Occasionally an annotation will be delayed until the item of interest has been developed in successive or closely related letters. Sources used in drafting the annotations include material drawn from letters of Williams not chosen for publication (usually because of their repetitive and/or perfunctory nature), from the unpublished journal, and related correspondence. These and many other documentary sources are identified and may be consulted by readers who wish to supplement the annotations. Dates for Williams's extensive works are given parenthetically in the annotations, according to the following practice: Non-dramatic texts are dated by their first appearance in print or, if unpublished, by their manuscript date and provenance. Dramatic texts are dated by their first major performance unless otherwise noted. To keep the reader apprized of Williams's complex body of writing, the dating of texts is repeated with the first mention of each in the six parts of Volume II.

The great majority of persons, events, and texts mentioned in the letters has been identified to the extent warranted by importance. A brief biographical statement, including life dates, usually accompanies the first appearance of each of TW's correspondents.

ACKNOWLEDGMENTS

Grateful acknowledgment is made to leading scholar-critics for their basic research on Tennessee Williams: the late Lyle Leverich, Williams's authorized biographer, and Donald Spoto, an earlier writer; Andreas "Andy" Brown, who was instrumental in forming the Williams collection at the Humanities Research Center, Austin, Texas; Drewey Wayne Gunn, who published the first major description of the Williams canon, and George W. Crandell, who gave it definitive bibliographical form. Acknowledgment is also due Brian Parker and Sarah Boyd Johns for pioneering genetic study of the plays; Brenda Murphy for incisive performance history; and Allean Hale, Kenneth Holditch, and Philip Kolin for long devotion to Williams scholarship.

Valuable information, as well as engaging correspondence, may be found in two earlier collections: *Tennessee Williams' Letters to Donald Windham, 1940-1965*, and *Five O'Clock Angel: Letters of Tennessee Williams to Maria St. Just, 1948-1982*. Edited, respectively, by Donald Windham and Maria St. Just, the volumes often provide a revealing counterpoint to letters included in the present collection. The unpublished journal of Tennessee Williams, forthcoming under the editorship of Margaret Thornton, is quoted by special arrangement with Yale University Press. Special thanks are due Margaret Thornton for generous support of the "Letters" project.

The preponderance of letters in Volume II is drawn from the seminal Williams collection at the Harry Ransom Humanities Research Center, University of Texas at Austin. *The Selected Letters* could not have been undertaken in the present form without the support of this exemplary institution. Very special thanks and admiration are reserved for Tara Wenger, Pat Fox, and Elizabeth L. Garver. Their competence, friendliness, and timely assistance ably represent the cultural and intellectual virtues of the HRC.

Thanks are also due for the support and courtesy of other major collectors of Williams correspondence: Billy Rose Theatre Collection, New York Public Library for the Performing Arts (Robert Taylor); Butler

Library, Columbia University (Bernard R. Crystal); Harvard Theatre Collection (Fredric Woodbridge Wilson); Houghton Library, Harvard University (Leslie Morris); Wesleyan University Cinema Archives (Leith Johnson and Joan Miller). The many other collectors, institutional and private, who kindly supplied letters or research material are listed in the Key to Collections.

Four years of preparation have revealed special friends and benefactors of *The Selected Letters*. None is more appreciated than the estate of Elia Kazan, which gave permission to examine the Kazan archive at Wesleyan University (Middletown, Connecticut) and to publish a selection of Williams's correspondence with his close friend and collaborator. Dakin Williams, the only surviving member of the playwright's immediate family, has also given access to important papers and answered questions which no one else could presume to address. Jordan Massee, recently deceased, also gave valuable papers and photographs and astutely answered questions about his friendship with Williams and Paul Bigelow. Before his death, Richard F. Leavitt, compiler of *The World of Tennessee Williams*, offered valuable advice on the selection of photographs. The biographers of Williams's correspondents and friends—especially Virginia Spencer Carr (Carson McCullers), Gerald Clarke (Truman Capote), Fred Kaplan (Gore Vidal), Helen Sheehy (Margo Jones), and Ralph Voss (William Inge)—have greatly facilitated research for Volume II. So have Stephanie Womack and Sean Battles, who joined the "Letters" project through the Undergraduate Mentorship Program at the University of Missouri. Thanks are due Stephanie Womack for research on the production and reception history of *A Streetcar Named Desire*. Sean Battles has served with uncommon energy and intelligence as the primary research assistant for Volume II. No doubt his talents, and good nature, will grace journalism as noticeably as they have literary scholarship. Matthew Alofs, who first joined the project though the MU Mentorship Program, has prepared the main indexes of Volume II with typical efficiency and skill. Richard Kramer, a Williams scholar in his own right, has provided valuable liaison with libraries and collectors in New York, while Travis Pittman has provided the same service in Austin. Finally, to a diverse group of readers—Elizabeth Garver, Heather Moulaison, Joan Smith, Nicholas Moschovakis, and Steve Lawson—who gave valuable advice on the manuscript sincere thanks are given.

Professor Devlin's research was supported by several grants and a

research leave funded by the University of Missouri Research Board and Research Council. Generous assistance was supplied by reference and special collections librarians at the University of Missouri: Anne Barker, Anne Edwards, Margaret Howell, Hunter Kevil, and Michael Muchow, as well as an Interlibrary Loan staff headed by Marilyn Voegele. To the University of the South, copyright holder of the works of Tennessee Williams, grateful acknowledgment is made for permission to edit and publish the playwright's correspondence. Peggy Fox, president of New Directions, Thomas Keith, editor, and Sylvia Frezzolini Severance, book designer, deserve praise for their good care and perseverance. Finally, Jennifer Zarrelli transcribed the letters with her typical competence and good cheer.

The following librarians, research assistants, and other friends and informants have provided valuable help in preparing Volume II: Hilary Aid, Columbia, Missouri, Beth Alvarez, University of Maryland; Pamela Arceneaux, Williams Research Center, New Orleans; Annie Armour, University of the South; Lisa Aronson, New York; Fred Bauman, Library of Congress; Andrea Beauchamp, University of Michigan; Robert Bray, Middle Tennessee SU; Linda Briscoe, Humanities Research Center; Jackson Bryer, University of Maryland; Alison Carrick, Washington University; Ruth Carruth, Yale University; Kay Cattarulla, Dallas Museum of Art; Mark Cave, Williams Research Center, New Orleans; Erin Chase, Huntington Library; Cathy Cherbosque, Huntington Library; William Bedford Clark, Texas A&M University; Lynda Claassen, University of California, San Diego; Robert Collins, University of Missouri; April Cunningham, Huntington Library; Sharon DeLano, *The New Yorker*; Luke Dennis, Harvard Theatre Collection; Mitch Douglas, International Creative Management, New York; Elizabeth Dunn, Duke University; William Eigelsback, University of Tennessee; Pamela Evans, Mission, Texas; Annette Fern, Harvard Theatre Collection; Jack Frick, Canton, North Carolina; Michelle Gachette, Harvard University; Kim Gallon, University of Pennsylvania; Cara Gilgenbach, Kent State University; Julie Grob, University of Houston; Barbara Hall, Margaret Herrick Library; Susan Halpert, Houghton Library, Harvard University; Christopher Harter, Indiana University; Cathy Henderson, Humanities Research Center; Noah Heringman, University of Missouri; Robert Hines, Canton, North Carolina; Howard Hinkel, University of Missouri; Sue Hodson, Huntington Library; Tom Hyry, Yale University; Dan Isaac, New York;

Russell James, Columbus-Lowndes Public Library, Columbus, Mississippi; Kirsten Jensen, University of Arizona; J.C. Johnson, Boston University; Fred Kaplan, New York; Nathaniel Keller, Columbia, Missouri; David Kessler, University of California, Berkeley; John Kirkpatrick; Humanities Research Center; Suzanne Marrs, Millsaps College; Edwin Matthias, Library of Congress; Rebecca Melvin, University of Delaware; Janie Morris, Duke University; Timothy Murray, University of Delaware; Sean Noel, Boston University; Carol Meszaros, University of Michigan; Nita Murphy, Taos Historic Museums; Nathaniel Parks, Boston University; Margaret Sayers Peden, University of Missouri; Bridget Pieschel, Mississippi University for Women; Sue Presnell, University of Indiana; Thomas Richardson, Mississippi University for Women; Carol Roark, Dallas Public Library; Jenny Romero, Margaret Herrick Library; Myrtle Rosen, Taos, New Mexico; Donald Share, Harvard University; Nancy Shawcross, University of Pennsylvania; Ellen Shea, Radcliffe Institute; Kathy Smith, Indiana University; Fred Todd, San Antonio; Carol Turley, UCLA; James and Catherine Wallace, Columbia, Missouri; Rick Watson, Humanities Research Center; Raymond Wemmlinger, Hampden-Booth Theatre Library, New York; Shawn Wilson, Kinsey Institute, Indiana University.

ABBREVIATIONS

ALS	Autograph letter signed
APCS	Autograph postcard signed
ca.	about
Carr	Virginia Spencer Carr, *The Lonely Hunter: A Biography of Carson McCullers*. New York: Doubleday & Company, 1975.
Collected Stories	Tennessee Williams, *Collected Stories*. New York: New Directions, 1985.
Conversations	*Conversations with Tennessee Williams*. Ed. Albert J. Devlin. Jackson, MS: University Press of Mississippi, 1986.
Journal	The unpublished journal of Tennessee Williams. Forthcoming from Yale University Press. Ed. Margaret Thornton.
Kazan	Elia Kazan, *Elia Kazan: A Life*. New York: Alfred A. Knopf, 1988.
Leverich	Lyle Leverich, *Tom: The Unknown Tennessee Williams*. New York: Crown Publishers, 1995.
Memoirs	Tennessee Williams, *Memoirs*. New York: Doubleday & Company, 1975.
n.d.	no date of publication
PM	Postmarked
qtd.	quoted
rpt.	reprinted
SH	Stationery headed
Spoto	Donald Spoto, *The Kindness of Strangers: The Life of Tennessee Williams*. Boston: Little, Brown and Company, 1985.

St. Just	*Five O'Clock Angel: Letters of Tennessee Williams to Maria St. Just, 1948-1982*. Ed. Maria St. Just. New York: Alfred A. Knopf, 1990.
TL	Typewritten letter unsigned
TLS	Typewritten letter signed
TLSx	Typewritten letter signed copy
TLx	Typewritten letter unsigned copy
TW	Tennessee Williams
Where I Live	Tennessee Williams, *Where I Live: Selected Essays*. Ed. Christine R. Day and Bob Woods. New York: New Directions, 1978.
Windham	*Tennessee Williams' Letters to Donald Windham, 1940-1965*. Ed. Donald Windham. New York: Holt, Rinehart and Winston, 1977.

KEY TO COLLECTIONS

Beinecke	Beinecke Rare Book and Manuscript Library, Yale University
Boston U	Howard Gotlieb Archival Research Center, Mugar Memorial Library, Boston University
BRTC	Billy Rose Theatre Collection, The New York Public Library for the Performing Arts, Lincoln Center
Columbia U	Rare Book and Manuscript Library, Columbia University
Dallas Public Library	Texas/Dallas History and Archives Library Division, Dallas Public Library
Duke U	Special Collections Library, Duke University
Herrick	Margaret Herrick Library, Center for Motion Picture Study, Academy of Motion Picture Arts and Sciences, Beverly Hills, California
Houghton	Houghton Library, Harvard University
HRC	Harry Ransom Humanities Research Center, University of Texas at Austin
HTC	Harvard Theatre Collection, Houghton Library, Harvard University
Huntington	Manuscripts Department, Huntington Library, San Marino, California
Kent State U	Department of Special Collections and Archives, Kent State University Libraries
Kinsey Institute	Kinsey Institute Library and Special Collections, Indiana University
Leavitt	*The World of Tennessee Williams*. Ed. Richard F. Leavitt. New York: G.P. Putnam's Sons, 1978.
Library of Congress	Manuscript Division, The Library of Congress, Washington, D.C.

Massee Collection   Private collection of Jordan Massee, Macon, Georgia

Northwestern U   McCormick Library of Special Collections,
                     Northwestern University

Princeton U   Department of Rare Books and Special Collections,
                     Princeton University

Rendell   Kenneth W. Rendell Gallery, New York

SHS of Wisconsin   State Historical Society of Wisconsin, Madison,
                     Wisconsin

Smith Collection   Private collection of Jane Lawrence Smith, New York

Southern Illinois U Special Collections, Morris Library,
                     Southern Illinois University

St. Just   *Five O'Clock Angel: Letters of Tennessee Williams
                     to Maria St. Just, 1948-1982*. Ed. Maria St. Just.
                     New York: Alfred A. Knopf, 1990.

Todd Collection   Fred W. Todd Collection, Williams Research Center,
                     Historic New Orleans Collection, New Orleans

UCLA   Department of Special Collections, Research Library,
                     University of California, Los Angeles

U of Chicago   Department of Special Collections, University of
                     Chicago Library

U of Delaware   Special Collections, Hugh H. Morris Library,
                     University of Delaware

U of Houston   Special Collections and Archives, University of
                     Houston Libraries

U of Pennsylvania   Annenberg Rare Book & Manuscript Library,
                     University of Pennsylvania Library

Windham   *Tennessee Williams' Letters to Donald Windham,
                     1940-1965*. Ed. Donald Windham. New York: Holt,
                     Rinehart and Winston, 1977.

WUCA   Wesleyan University Cinema Archives, Middletown,
                     Connecticut

PART I
1945-1947

1. To Eddie Dowling

[Dallas, Texas]
[May 30, 1945]
[TLx, 2 pp. HRC]

Dear Eddie:

I am very grateful for your letter and the understanding in it. What a delicate operation we performed together, all of us, and what a strong bond it should be and I think is - now that it's worked out so well! Artists are peculiar creatures - no one is more guiltily aware of this than I! - the strain we work under, so much greater than that of all the mundane occupations - makes us touchy, difficult even for each other always to understand - but we have such a great community of interest that the differences are relatively slight and unimportant, at least they should be.

I am leaving early tomorrow morning for Mexico after a week here with Margo - catching a plane, which always makes me nervous - I am not a good flyer. I hope to settle down at some quiet place and devote myself to work - much neglected since last Fall - for the next two months.

I have met nearly everyone connected with Margo's Dallas Theatre and I feel that the outlook is really wonderful. I attended a meeting of the executive board. They are a very capable, serious and progressive bunch, completely earnest about what they're doing, and determined to push it through. Margo has dedicated herself to this thing heart and soul and, knowing her, and having met her co-workers, I'm fairly certain that something very important to all of us is going to happen down here. I think it will be valuable to theatre all over the country.

For me personally, it means a place to experiment and clarify. I have no interest at this time in more Broadway productions, for I feel that my problem is getting work done, not produced, - which takes so much time from the other and more important struggle. This is not really selfish, since I can make no important contribution without a great deal of solitary labor. But a theatre like Margo's is an excellent place to remain in touch with stage while at the same time escaping the exhausting responsibilities of Broadway - a proving ground for things I'm not sure of. "Battle" is a case in point. I still have no script that is really definitive of that play but feel that one might come out of a production down here, so it is tentatively our plan to do it here sometime next season. Naturally I hope this trial will

interest you, if it comes off. I can think of no one in the theatre to whom a theatre like Margo's would offer more interest than to you, because of your peculiar devotion to theatrical frontiers, so we both are hoping you will watch what goes on here.

Now that a road-company of "Menagerie" is being organized I think the matter of its direction ought to be taken up. I have talked with Margo about this and know that she is eager to undertake it. Of course it should be as close a duplication of what was done with the original company as possible, and so it seems to me that Margo would be the only right person. You are busy as an actor and producer so I am sure you would need another's assistance on this job. There will be just as many problems with this company as there were with the original production - possibly even more - and we don't want it to fall short, in any respect, of the best that could be offered. I don't think this is anything that I have [to] "sell" you on, for you know how faithful Margo is to whatever she undertakes, and her deep "family" interest in the "Menagerie" which no one else could match.

Please let me hear from you while I am in Mexico. My love to Laurette, Julie, Tony - Randy, Bill, Jean and all of the company.

Ever,

[Eddie Dowling (1894-1976) produced and directed *The Glass Menagerie* (1945) and played Tom Wingfield to Laurette Taylor's incomparable Amanda. He recently answered TW's conciliatory letter of May 17 with thanks for having written "a beautiful play" and regret that the "shoddy" (May 19, 1945, HRC) tactics of his co-producer and backer, Louis J. Singer, had added to the "strain" of production. TW deferred an offer to restage *Battle of Angels* (1940), a notorious failure in Boston, with a tribute to Dowling's innovative presence on Broadway.

From Mexico City TW informed his family that Dallas had been "terribly hot" (June 6, 1945, HTC) and gregarious and that he had disappointed his host, Margo Jones, by remaining only a week. He did, however, join the "board" of Theatre '45 and began to revise *Battle of Angels* for the relaxed "proving ground" of Dallas. Conceived as an antidote to Broadway, Jones's experiment in decentralized theatre would shun recent hits, revive a few classics each season, and develop the talent of such gifted new playwrights as TW.

Jones, Dowling's co-director in the "original company" of *The Glass Menagerie*, would not direct the tour production.]

2. To Guthrie McClintic

SH: Hotel Geneve
7a. De Londres 130
Mexico City, Mexico
Friday [June 1, 1945]
[TLS, 2 pp. HRC]

Dear Guthrie:

I flew down here yesterday from Dallas. I have never liked flying and did not spend a comfortable moment in the plane, but was so exhausted by Dallas that the quickest way of getting furthest seemed best.

I'm sorry I missed your call but the long wire was very heartening and I am happy over Katharine Willard being Emmie. I have not yet had a chance to pick up my mail at Wells-Fargo, will do that this morning, and I hope you've thought of some people for me to meet. I have loads of names given me in Dallas by various sweet old ladies, which would only bring me in contact with more sweet old ladies. My seclusion in the Dallas hotel room was enjoyed very briefly and the stay turned into a social whirl-wind. I met Ida Camp and all her crowd, which correspond roughly to the 'horsey set on Long Island', although one or two of the women are fabulously and crazily amusing - if only you could have a concealed dictaphone when they are talking! All the energy and color seems to have gone into the Dallas females and the poor husbands look as if they had donated entirely too much blood and to the wrong cause. They just sit around holding glasses with a look which is far away but not dreamy, while the women rock and roar in one continual effusion.

One thing I didn't count on - in reference to Margo's project - is the vitality of these women. It is really out of the world, and if Margo can get them on her side - miracles may happen! Of course they don't have any real discrimination, these women, but they are snobs and in my opinion you can do almost anything with snobs if you handle them carefully. I suspect they will embrace almost anything if it is presented to them as having "smartness". They suck up all the "new books" like vacuum cleaners, in fact I don't see how it is possible to read that much and that fast. Of course they are still gabbing about 'Forever Amber'. But some of them have even been reading Richard Wright. When they get a few drinks under their girdles, their talk becomes right down lascivious, and that is another good sign for "The Project". All it needs to have is something phallic about it.

And as a matter of fact that something may be the title! At any rate, they are all very interested in it, though Ida Camp said she wasn't sure that she was "behind it".

Margo wants to open her season with "Battle of Angels" and I think it might be a good thing. There is a lot of material in that play that is worth salvaging, and I have never prepared a definitive script of it, and this would be a good chance to. She wants to get Bobby Jones down here to design it and music by Bowles.

This hotel I am in is impossible so will not be my address. Must find a place where there is swimming and a balcony or patio where I can work in the sun and privacy. As usual I feel a terrible desolation in Mexico, but I must grit my teeth for a week or so until it wears off. The electric signs here are lovely! They are the color of soft drinks and much livelier than the ones on Broadway.

I will go, now, and pick up the letters you mention and let you know where I am when I settle.

Tenn.

[Guthrie McClintic (1893-1961) was the producer/director of more than fifty original Broadway plays and revivals, many starring his wife, the distinguished Katharine Cornell. He rejected *You Touched Me!* in 1943, but the work had gained stature following the success of *The Glass Menagerie* and was now being cast for a late-September opening on Broadway. Katherine Willard, as indicated, would play one of the leads.

The women of Dallas were "still gabbing about" *Forever Amber* (1944), Kathleen Winsor's *succès de scandale* set in Restoration England. Richard Wright's autobiography, *Black Boy* (1945), was number two on national bestseller lists when TW visited Dallas in May.]

3. To Audrey Wood

[Mexico City]
6/20/45
[TLS, 1 p. HRC]

Dear Child of God:

I wrote you a very gloomy letter the last time for I had swallowed one of those Mexican bugs that prey on American tourists and I was feeling

very low indeed. But I found a little Mexican doctor who gave me shots and pills, enough to kill a horse with - but I survived the treatment and have been feeling exceptionally well ever since.

Disregard the instructions affecting prize money in last Memo. Won't need it as I have wired Chase Natl. to let me draw $500. through Banco de Commercio in Mexico. This will, I hope, see me through the Mexican junket and perhaps even back to the wilds of Texas and New York.

I have met the following here: Leonard Bernstein, Dolores Del Rio, Rosa Covarrubias, Norman Foster (Now directing Mexican films), Romney Brent's sister, Balanchine, Chavez, and many lesser notables of the International Set (!) all of whom have invited me places. But it is not like Chicago and New York, that is, the society is not at all exhausting and I have plenty of time to work. And I love Mexico, I think it is really and truly my native land! I will stay here till it is almost time to go back for "YTM".

Guthrie has sent me several wires about casting and I also got a wire from Katharine Cornell (Signed Kit) saying she had seen "Menagerie" and wanted me to write her one. And today - having pinched myself, I know I am wide awake! - I received a letter from Lawrence Stanislavsky Langner, the one who operates that famous Art Theatre on E. 56th Street - saying that he still has the scenery of "Battle" stored at Westport and has a new director in mind for it! This was profoundly touching, but also a little funny I thought - so I am mentioning it to you and Liebling!

One cannot help loving people who make you laugh! And I think the Guild has been favored by the Gods because their serious antics have even gotten a chuckle out of Cothurnus! - Imagine enticing us with the news that that horrible old brown set, probably all webbed and molded, was waiting for us in a store-room at Westport! Of course my instinct is to wire Lawrence, "You should have stood in Miami!" But instead I shall write him one of my nicest testimonials of affection, for this last communication has completed the cycle, often observed in life, from deepest tragedy to lightest farce!

Love - 10.

[Audrey Wood (1905-1985) represented TW from 1939 until their parting thirty-two years later.

"Prize money" of $1,500 accompanied the Sidney Howard Award announced on June 5. The citation lauded TW as "a vigorous new talent" who "has the sense

*Tennessee Williams with Bill Liebling and Audrey Wood: "A very small and dainty woman with . . . a look of cool perspicacity in her eyes" (*Memoirs*).*

of poetry and of character of which great drama is made." Earlier selection of *The Glass Menagerie* by the Drama Critics' Circle gave TW two of three major awards for the past season. Mary Chase won the Pulitzer for *Harvey* (1944).

Leonard Bernstein seemed harsh and egotistical, although TW later described him as a "true" (*Memoirs*, p. 94) revolutionary in social expression. The ballet master George Balanchine disliked Mexico City and feared that his "girls," as TW mocked, were "sick with sumzings" (qtd. in Windham, p. 173) in New York. Dolores Del Rio, a veteran of silent films and Hollywood musicals of the 1930s, had returned to her native Mexico to restore a fading career in the cinema. TW met her at the home of Rosa Covarrubias, an American-born dancer married to the painter and writer Miguel Covarrubias.

Guthrie McClintic's "wires" brought a terse reply from TW: "Clift has more experience and charm Brown has more foxy upstart quality I have dysentery You decide" (telegram, June 9, 1945, HRC). Montgomery Clift played the role of Hadrian in *You Touched Me!*

Ever cautious, Wood instructed TW to "be quiet" (July 5, 1945, HRC) about writing a play for Katharine Cornell, lest he restrict her ability to sell it.

Lawrence Langner and Theresa Helburn, co-directors of the Theatre Guild, supervised the first professional staging of a TW play, *Battle of Angels*. Langner wrote

earlier to congratulate TW on the success of *The Glass Menagerie* and to propose that the Guild offer *Battle* once again. Even "Cothurnus," stern image of tragedy, would be amused, TW thought, by the "antics" of the venerable Theatre Guild.]

4. To Lawrence Langner

[Mexico City]
6/20/45
[TLS, 1 p. Beinecke]

Dear Lawrence:

A whole pile of my mail, tied up somewhere on the trail between New York, Dallas and Mexico City, finally overtook me this morning, including the particularly welcome letter from you.

The statement in PM was sincerely meant. There are times, especially in the theatre, when it is only fair to judge by intentions and not by results, and God knows you and Terry had every intention of making "Battle" a good show. It was not quite in the book, nor in the stars, and our plans "ganged aft agley". As for the re-write, I was in no condition at the time to straighten things out, for I had gone through the most disturbing experience of my life. I solved a few dramaturgic problems by augmenting the physical action in the last half, but the more serious problem of expressing a violent theme in terms that were acceptably controlled and measured, of clarifying my ideas and characters - my state of mind at the time was by no means equal to!

But there are bolts of lightning in the script which may still be harnessed and put to work for the theatre, so it may interest you and Terry to know that Margo Jones is planning to try it out at her Dallas Theatre, perhaps as an opening production and perhaps designed by Robert Edmond Jones. With this in mind, I have prepared another version of the script with the use of whatever new restraint and technical knowledge I may have picked up along the years since Boston, 1940. The prologue and epilogue have been eliminated, also the fire phobia and the rather pompous stuff about the boy's book. My stake in this is a purely abstract one. I don't want another Broadway production, perhaps not for four or five years, for it is too nervously exhausting and takes too much time from my essential business, for I have done such a microscopic part of what I wanted to do in everything I've undertaken, and life is a tiny peep-hole at this big show!

You and Terry are so closely bound up with my first years in the theatre, and in a way that was finally so helpful, that I feel you are definitely a part of my professional family and I part of yours.

Cordially, Tennessee.

[Audrey Wood may have prompted the "statement in PM" to counter recent charges by TW that the Theatre Guild had "messed up" *Battle of Angels*. Lawrence Langner (1890-1962) could not "agree" that the Boston production had been "'superb'" (June 6, 1945, HRC), as TW now maintained, but he thanked him nonetheless and allowed the earlier criticism to pass.

Although factually flawed, the interview in *PM Magazine* (rpt. in *Conversations*, pp. 12-19) is notable for TW's guarded reference to his sister Rose, whose charm and beauty are cited but not her chronic mental illness or hospitalization in Missouri.

The latest revision of *Battle of Angels* concerns Val Xavier's mortal fear of fire and the portentous book which he is writing.

This letter bears a reception date of July 3, 1945.]

5. To Margaret "Margo" Jones

SH: Hotel Lincoln
Revillagigedo 24, Mexico. D.F.
[Mexico City]
June 25, 1945.
[TLS, 2 pp. HRC]

Dear Margo:

It must be three or four in the morning but I am not a bit sleepy so will try writing a letter which is a usually effective narcotic.

The correspondance got here after about ten days - God knows why it takes so long to get my mail across the border, I think they must be making a special study of it. I always try to put in something I think will be interesting for the censor, which is perhaps a mistaken policy.

I am dying to know how you came out on the new building deal. And just why it was necessary. And all about Milzener's plans. Was it a serious crisis? I do hope you got it all straightened out by now.

My nerves always get tied up in knots about the middle of the summer, due to heavy work or some emotional cycle that moves with the seasons - whatever it is - this summer is no worse than usual, perhaps somewhat

better - but the last few days I've been about to jump out of my skin, and though I've finally made loads of acquaintances, I don't feel like seeing anybody. Society here is nice, though. I am dancing a lot for the first time since I left college and there are two or three little Indians who take me around sight-seeing, Etc. And I am crazy about the bull-fights and have joined a Y which has a lovely out-door pool, only two blocks from my hotel. Mexico is full of accidental beauty, like passing an archway, right in a city block and seeing a big white rooster staring imperially back at you, blind beggars led along the street by tiny, tiny, dirty, dirty white dogs, things like that. I am trying to work some of them into a fantasy of several scenes, on which I alternate with the long play begun in Chicago. - I have met Dolores Del Rio and Norman Foster, and perhaps if I come back here next year, I may try to do some work on a Mexican film. Not having the Hayes office, their art films can be very exciting. Photographically, plastically - they are far superior to nearly all American pictures. I am picking up bits of the language constantly, though I havn't tried to. - Love it!

I'm glad I have that lovely picture of you, you look so strong and idealistic in it! Not that you <u>ain't</u>, Baby! But everybody notices it and says, 'Muy bonita!'

Just gotten and immediately <u>lost</u> a letter from little Bob Carter, the kid you met in Chicago. I hadn't let him know I'd left New York and he is now there and doesn't know a soul and of course is utterly wretched. I can't think of a soul to tell him to see. As a matter of fact I don't have one N.Y. associate - Don being on Nantuckett island - that I think would be a safe and advantageous contact for such a youngster - Do you? And besides I have lost the letter, now, and don't have his address. Must write by way of Chicago. The very young really break my heart, though God knows youth's an advantage! But, oh - ! The years, the years - !

That rooster I saw in the archway is lifting his voice - Me Voy! A Duerme! Is that correct?

If anything important comes up, call me long-distance. - I haven't heard one note out of Mother since I left New York. Do you suppose she is angry I didn't stop in St. Louis - or what? McClintic is trying to get Robert Fleming out of the British army for Hadrian, but Clift and Phil Brown are still in the running.

With love, 10.

[Margo Jones (1911-1955) met a shy, impoverished TW in New York in 1942 and became enamored of the man and his work. Her staging of *You Touched Me!* (1943) and "The Purification" (1944) in regional theatres sealed their friendship and led TW to recommend that she assist Eddie Dowling in directing *The Glass Menagerie*.

Jo Mielziner, acclaimed set designer of *The Glass Menagerie*, was asked by Jones to evaluate a theatre building in Dallas, which he found "impractical" (qtd. in Windham, p. 175).

Work on *A Streetcar Named Desire* (1947) and *Camino Real* (1953)—the "long play" and the "fantasy"—would occupy TW through the following winter in New Orleans.

Hollywood producers established the "Hayes office" in 1921 to forestall external censorship of the film industry. The first director, Will H. Hays, was followed by Joseph Breen, whose hand was strengthened by the censorship crusades of the 1930s and fell heavily upon the filming of TW's theatre, beginning with *The Glass Menagerie*.

"Little Bob Carter," one of the "university kids" (qtd. in Windham, p. 159) whom TW met during tryouts of *The Glass Menagerie*, later thanked TW for the gift of a sweater and added that it "fits perfectly. I can't <u>imagine</u> how you ever found out my size so well" (March 28, 1945, Private Collection). TW inscribed an early draft of *Streetcar* to Carter "in return for the Key to Chicago" ("Electric Avenue," n.d., HRC).]

6. To Margaret "Margo" Jones

[Guadalajara, Mexico]
[early-July 1945]
[TLS w/ autograph marginalia
and enclosure, 2 pp. HRC]

Dear Margo:

The original of this article, which was probably somewhat better put together, was lost in the departure from Mexico [City]. I had to reproduce it here in Guadalajara from memory. I had meant to mail it the same evening I wrote it, in accordance to my wire, as I know you want it quickly, but your wire came in the middle of my pulling up stakes which as you know is always a soul-shaking experience for me. There has only been a delay, however, of about 24 hours and I hope they get it through the censors quickly. I am <u>crazy</u> about this part of Mexico. The air and the scenery are like around Taos, and Guadalajara is clean and lovely. The plaza at night is really like a dream. White lamp-posts all along the walks with

fivebranch lamps on them. In the middle a band-stand, octagonal, with graceful loops and Victorian flourishes, all traced with lights and a big chandelier in the middle. The cathedral and old government buildings around it. My hotel has a big out-door spring-water swimming pool and the view from my room, (the bed has inner-spring mattress and 4 pillows) is across a wide pale green plain to a range of green and purple mountains. It is only eight pesos a day (about $1.50 American money), yellow tile and cream-colored walls, everything immaculate. Visiting Chapala for a few days tomorrow: it is the big lake where Lawrence wrote 'The Plumed Serpent'. I am writing a play about a were-wolf - Cabeza de Lobo - inspired by a Mexican painting of one. It will be a bit longer than Purification and I hope it may finally be good enough to use on a program with it. It is full of horror, so after working on it I have to sleep with my light on.

Will see you around the fifteenth in Dallas. Wire you exact time of arrival so you can do something about a place for me.

Has the Project blown up yet?

Love, Tennessee.

[TW joined the select company of Katharine Cornell and Robert Edmond Jones in publicizing Theatre '45. He praised Margo Jones's vision and drive and renewed his criticism of Broadway for ignoring "the real theatrical needs" of the country. That "a true art theatre" had now emerged in the South did not surprise TW, endowed as the region was with the "emotional richness and vitality" of its heritage. In a patriotic closing he urged local patrons to support the "vast cargo of heart-hungry youth" returning from war: "You've got to give them a richer life than they went away from" (*Dallas Morning News*, July 22, 1945, sec. 4, pp. 1-2).

TW later drafted a preface for the "fantasy" begun in Mexico City and given strong new impetus by his trip to Guadalajara. From this "dream-like" journey arose the principal characters of *Camino Real:* Marguerite Gautier, the ill-fated Dame aux Camélias, and Kilroy, the "poor man's Don Quixote." Their "juxtaposition" formed a "new congruity of incongruities," which required a text "less written than painted" ("Foreword," May 1946, HRC).

In Cabeza de Lobo the Gypsy describes a legendary werewolf which takes "the form of a beautiful virgin" at each full moon and "descends to the village" to claim a lover, who is allowed "to lift" (n.d., HRC) her veil. The roles of the Gypsy and her daughter, Esmeralda, as well as a major scene with Kilroy, are evident in this early source for *Camino Real*. TW later used "Cabeza de Lobo" as fictional shield for the Barcelona scenes in *Suddenly Last Summer* (1958).

Penned in the left-hand margin of page 1 is the notation "billiard & ping pong tables on veranda - noiseless at night." Enclosed was "A Playwright's Statement" (July 1945, HRC), which appeared in the *Dallas Morning News*.]

7. *To Robert Penn Warren*

SH: "Gran Hotel"
Guadalajara, Jal., Mex.
July 16, 1945.
[TLS, 2 pp. Beinecke]

Dear Mr. Warren:

I was confined to the hospital for an eye operation the two weeks before I left the States and nearly all the events of that period are somewhat shadowy, but I believe that among them was the especially dream-like reading to me of a letter of invitation to record some of my verse for the collection at the library of Congress. It seems like a paranoiac fantasy invented to compensate for critical reactions to my verse, but as I am not ordinarily subject to these, I am recklessly assuming that it has some basis in fact. - I am going to be in Washington early in September when a play of mine will be tried out in that city. If the invitation is actual and still holds good, I will be happy and proud to say a piece for you at that time. I have heard the recordings of poets at Harvard, including the one of Joyce which is really a treasure. But what a pity it seems to me that nobody ever got Hart Crane's voice, when so many of the canaries, finches, and sparrows have been shrilling their pipes off - there is not one peep from the nightingale!

I hope you feel the same way about him, for otherwise this comment will be mistakenly construed as impolite to the others - all I mean is I could not like them half so well if I didn't love Crane more!

Cordially, Tenn. Williams

[Robert Penn Warren (1905-1989) succeeded his friend and former Fugitive-Agrarian confederate Allen Tate as Consultant in Poetry of the Library of Congress (1944-1945). His "invitation" to TW was part of an ambitious plan to record both older and younger poets reading from their selected work. The Library of Congress holds no such recording by TW—some in the series have not survived—nor have the editors found any evidence that he followed through on his promise to read.

TW once cast himself as a "frail ghost-brother" of Hart Crane and asked that the poet "guide" (*Journal*, August 23, 1942) his uncertain career. TW found inspiration, sources, and titles for his own work in *The Collected Poems of Hart Crane* (1933), a volume which he "appropriated" from Washington University in St. Louis and often packed for travel.

The eye operation performed in New York in early-May was TW's fourth since 1941, the result of "a childhood game of considerable violence" (*Memoirs*, p. 74). TW would describe the "shadowy" period of the latest surgery as one which gave peace and protection to a writer disillusioned by the success of *The Glass Menagerie* (see "On a Streetcar Named Success," 1947; rpt. in *Where I Live*, pp. 15-22).]

8. To Audrey Wood

SH: Western Union
Laredo Tex
1945 Jul 28 AM 4 50
[Telegram, 1 p. HRC]

AUDREY WOOD=

MANUSCRIPTS HELD FOR INSPECTION AT BORDER REMAINING TILL CLEARED PLEASE WIRE HUNDRED DOLLARS HOTEL HAMILTON LAREDO=

TENNESSEE WILLIAMS.

["Certainly feel your manuscripts worth hundred dollars of anybodys money," Audrey Wood replied, and cabled the "vast amount" (July 28, 1945, HRC) to her stranded client. Donald Windham learned the outcome of TW's conflict with U.S. Customs following the apparent seizure of "One Arm" (1948). The missing script had not been confiscated but typically mislaid by TW "beneath a pile of dirty shirts" (qtd. in Windham, p. 176). He concealed the discovery from Customs, allowing the story of a mutilated gay prostitute to enter the States unexamined. TW quickly passed through Dallas and returned to New York in time for rehearsals of *You Touched Me!*]

9. *To Burton Rascoe*

SH: Shelton Hotel
Lexington Avenue
48th to 49th Streets
New York
August 11, 1945
[TLS, 4 pp. U of Pennsylvania]

Dear Burton Rascoe:

During my peaceful retreat into Mexico I received a letter from a New York friend that contained the news that you had attacked the printed versions of my plays in your column. And so I was very agreeably surprised when I returned to town this week to discover these articles, which I read for the first time, were not attacks at all but really quite fair and reasonable and in some respects more charitable than I myself would be inclined to speak of them. You have a command of irony and a wit that could make the object squirm, as Mr. Nathan has frequently done, but there is a distinct difference in that your motives are obviously more humanitarian. You don't feel that an effective attack is necessarily a savage one. You made several excellent points against me in these columns, and they are made so fairly or cleanly that I must say - <u>Touché</u>! I have worked very hard with nerves that are usually ragged and now and then I have let myself explode into ill-considered and sophomoric bursts of rhetoric. It is quite possible that some of the things I said in the preface to 'Battle' were in that category, certainly they were put in a way that was over-emphatic. It is always darkest just before daybreak, and even as recently as those remarks came off my feverish portable - (the present red ink is just because the ribbon is upside down!) - I was right behind the 8-ball, my most familiar location! I was outwardly calm but inwardly boiling and I suppose it was inevitable that some of this should escape in angry writing.

However I would like to clarify my feelings about the commercial theatre.

It is not that I am <u>against</u> something as much as that I am intensely <u>for</u> something else. - For the past two years I have been terribly concerned, with Margo Jones, in the establishment all over the States of professional theatres [which] are not of a strictly commercial kind. I've just come back from the scene of such an enterprise which is THEATRE '45 now being organized in Dallas, Texas. And so when the chance is offered, I try to

point out the advantages such a plan has for creative workers in theatre, the advantage it has over theatres run primarily for profit. When you are for something you have to make negative comments on whatever it is you would like to see revised or improved on.

As you point out, the commercial theatre has always and will always exist. And why not? All I feel is that it is inadequate and unsuitable to the entire needs of artists working in the theatre. Only recently one of the greatest of these, Alla Nazimova, died in California after being off the stage - how many years? - at least ten, I believe. It is the possibility of such talent as hers having no place to hang its hat that makes me feel so passionately that there must be these other kinds of theatre in America than the kind which must look to its pocket before its heart.

I have been luckier than I deserve but that ought not to blind a person to privations and disappointments elsewhere. I know of fine actors who are so devoted to the theatre that they are willing to serve it in backstage obscurity if they are lucky enough to serve it at all, and I know of at least one playwright with considerably more talent than some of us who are successful ones - who at last reports was working in the kitchen of a Hollywood night-club. If there were theatre capitals such as the one now being formed in Dallas all over the States - theatres that are subsidized and ardently supported by their own communities - not little or amateur theatres but full-fledged professional ones that employ theatre-workers as a permanent family group - giving them security in place of the gradually wearing-out process of fear and privation, attention in place of neglect, action and release in place of repression and dissipating idleness, fellowship in place of embittering loneliness and isolation - If there were such theatres as commonly as there are state universities and civic orchestras, wherever the community is large enough to support them - Think what a happy difference it would make for all of us and what we might be inspired to do and be!

Then you may feel like beating the drum with more influence and eloquence than any of us now beating it! I can't think of anyone associated with the stage - even the down-right gold-prospectors - who don't have more to gain than to lose by the catching on of such an idea, for all it means is that the theatre will be a thousand times as great and powerful as it now is in this country! If it starts out well in Dallas - and God grant that it may!

- it will spread like a grass-fire and multiply like rabbits! - There will be a tremendously increased demand for all of these items - plays, actors, designers, stage-hands, producers, directors, singers, dancers, clowns, acrobats - and even the circulation of Mr. Nathan's books will undoubtedly increase!

I don't think that art is a weapon but I think it is certainly an instrument and was there ever a time when a new and powerful instrument was needed to work on human society more than the present? Millions of home-coming young men are bringing keyed-up nerves and pentup emotions and new ideas and - most of all! - a terrific restless urge to create and express instead of merely to defend and struggle and destroy! They deserve these new avenues of self-realization that a resurgent nation-wide professional theatre can give them! Deserve them and truly need them.

Long live Broadway, and all the brave individuals in it who have held it valiantly above the level of mere profit-making - the national theatres we dream of might well be dedicated to the Eddie Dowlings of this Broadway, the Guthrie McClintics, Theatre Guilds and Group Theatres, that have striven usually against the tide to keep truth and poetry flowing through the wings and across the footlights. It is these islands that I have hopped across to my present footing and it is to them that my devoir is due. You may call them the commercial theatre if you want to be technical about it - but I call them The Theatre! And the seeds of a so much greater Theatre to come.

This is a long, long letter but I know you have been a good friend of the Wingfields and I feel that I can talk to you without constraint.

I will be in town here for about a month and if you would like to have a drink with me - and maybe Audrey - I wish you would call me sometime.

Cordially, Tennessee Williams

[Burton Rascoe (1892-1957), drama critic for the *New York World-Telegram*, qualified his initial praise of *The Glass Menagerie* by implying that superb production values had obscured the play's faulty structure (June 11)—a slighting strategy devised by George Jean Nathan, whom TW considered a nemesis. Publication of the book in July revealed the incompatible roles of author and director and led to a further qualification of praise. The written defense of Tom's survival had been converted by Eddie Dowling's "Catholic" conscience into "another evasion" of duty. The "humanitarian feelings" (July 30) of the audience were aptly served and the character of Tom given the sympathy which it lacked.

Rascoe's column of June 16 drew TW's closest attention and reply. Quoting the

author's preface to *Battle of Angels*, Rascoe chastised TW for having bitten the hand which was feeding him royalties of $1,500 per week. (He probably did not know that TW had given half of the profits of *The Glass Menagerie* to his mother, Edwina.) Most offensive was TW's comparison of entrusting the theatre arts to "business men and gamblers" and "the conduct of worship" to "a herd of water-buffalos" ("The History of a Play," *Pharos*, 1945, p. 113). Rascoe concluded that TW "owes much" to the "'commercial' genius" of Dowling and to the "gambling chance" of the backer, Louis J. Singer, for having "turned a faulty play into a smash hit."]

10. To the Williams Family

SH: Shelton Hotel
Lexington Ave. & 49th St.
New York 17, N.Y.
[August 15, 1945]
[TLS, 2 pp. HRC]

Dear Folks:

I plan to write each of you individually but at present am lucky to sandwich in one letter to all, what with "You Touched Me" in rehearsal and Aunt Ella in town and the phone ringing just about every three minutes. I am disappointed, too, that I couldn't get through Saint Louis. It looked as if I was going to be stranded in Dallas for another week, as there were no train reservations to be had on account of the transfer of troops going on. Then I wangled a plane reservation through the Braniffs who own one of the big air-lines and managed to get back just in time for the start of rehearsals. Everything looks very favorable. We have one of the finest casts ever assembled, particularly Edmund Gwenn, the English character actor, in the role of the old Captain. We are going to open in Boston in about three weeks.

Aunt Ella seems to be fine. I took her and Lucy Pearce out to dinner at a lovely Penthouse restaurant a few nights ago and today am taking them to lunch in the garden restaurant at the Ritz-Carlton. Lucy took us all, including two of her sons to dinner and the theatre - to see Harvey - and a little excitement was added when she lost her diamond watch-bracelet. Then found it still lying under the table at the restaurant where we had dinner - several hours later. Cousin Lucy is very peculiar, really a character, she admits that she gets everything she wants from the black market regardless of cost. But I like her a lot now that I have seen her several times.

Mary Hunter is rehearsing a show, too. Hers opens in Boston the same time ours does. Hers is an all-negro musical show starring Katharine Dunham. I'm afraid Mary is pretty hard up now so I am praying that it will be a hit. I had brought a lovely silver compact back from Mexico with me which I was intending to give you, Mother - but I didn't get through Saint Louis. When I saw poor Mary, she was so nervous and depressed that I decided to give her the compact because I thought you would prefer her to have it. It seemed to cheer her up considerably.

I have not seen 'Menagerie' since I came back but I visited the cast back-stage. Laurette is behaving herself marvellously and the show is still the biggest hit in town. They are now planning a London company, as announced in this morning's paper. Guthrie is also intending to have a London company of "You Touched Me" so I may have two shows in England before long. When that happens I think we should go there!

The book has come out of 'Menagerie' and Audrey has several copies at her office. I told her to send them to you all. Laughlin is in town and is preparing to bring out a book of my one-act plays.

I hope Congress revises the tax situation soon enough to help us pre-serve some funds.

We open in New York September 17th - Mother, if you are coming up for the opening - and I think you should - you had better make your reser-vations now. Why don't you fly up this time?

Give me Dakin's address. I want to congratulate him on his commission.

With much love to you all, Tom.

[Not scarcity of "reservations" but fear of his father, Cornelius, kept TW from vis-iting St. Louis at this time. Such estrangement did not, however, prevent his con-tributing to the support of "Aunt Ella," Cornelius's sister, who was visiting from Knoxville.

The parallel fortunes of Mary Hunter and TW may have seemed poignant to each and were perhaps the underlying reason for the latter's impulsive gift. Hunter, a founder of the American Actors Company (1938-1944), was TW's first choice to produce You Touched Me!, but the sounder financial management of Guthrie McClintic had prevailed. Hunter's new play, Carib Song (1945), closed after thirty-six performances on Broadway.

Plans for "a London company" of The Glass Menagerie were announced in the New York Times on August 15, 1945, the source for dating this letter.]

11. *To Margaret "Margo" Jones*

[Shelton Hotel, New York]
[early-September 1945]
[TLS w/ autograph postscript, 1 p. HRC]

Look, baby, I haven't time to write much right now. Not only rehearsals, incessant phone calls and pleasures and pains too innumerable to mention - but an old maid Aunt is in town, and though on my father's side, she is such a sweet old thing that I cannot neglect her!

I had lunch yesterday with a friend and emissary of Bill Inge and I gave him a good talking to. I think I have sold them on the absolute necessity of having an off-Broadway production of Bill's play. I will take an option on it myself - if necessary - provided some arrangement is made by which the advances are repaid to me in the usual fashion out of the play's royalties. That is between you and Bill and the Dramatist Guild - except that I will advance the money provided Dallas has not yet come through with it.

I have discussed with Audrey the question of making this gift to the Project and she is not at all in favor of it - I mean the $1500. It is the only money I have which is tax-exempt and I believe I have told you that she and my lawyer have calculated that I will have about one thousand left at the end of the year when taxes and living-expenses are deducted. Also, confidentially, 'Menagerie' advance sales at this point are only $30,000. which is hardly congruous with the idea that we will run for years! Until I know where I stand financially it would be rather foolish to make any large disbursals, even to anything so important. I may seem stingy to you and the girls in the little pink stucco cottage - but surely you can imagine how I feel, that it is necessary to protect myself and my work - primarily the latter - from what would be the final blow of finding myself broke again. - The volume of money coming into my hands at the present time means nothing except to the government. And I don't even <u>like</u> the <u>Truman</u> administration! - The Mirror says in its editorial page that we 'are making giant strides toward Traditional Americanism with Truman!' - URP! (If we can work out any way of making contribution - will do.)

I cannot materially affect the success of your undertaking except by such means as I have already used. Give unto Caesar the things which are Caesar's may be a somewhat misfit quotation but it contains the germ of

an idea relative to my feelings. Your problem is Dallas, I wish I could help you with it, - you know that! But I have tilted at wind-mills, too, and sometimes thrown them over. It can be done. You will do it. But in the meantime let us be understanding and realistic!

We have a swell cast for "YTM" - Gwenn, Clift, and Willard are doing great jobs but I think the real surprise is going to be our ingenue, Marianne Stewart, who played the Annabella role in "Jacobowsky" in her only previous Broadway appearance. She has the shape of a pin-up girl and the talent of a first-rate emotional actress. If she plays as she is developing now, she will be a sensation! - And Guthrie has a very sound instinct as a director, particularly of this script.

The London Menagerie is Dowling bull. As far as I can make out.

Love - 10.

P.S. We go to Boston Sunday. Open here 25th - hope you come up.

[*You Touched Me!* was put into rehearsal on August 14, with tryouts set for Boston in September.

William Inge met and interviewed TW shortly before *The Glass Menagerie* opened in Chicago (rpt. in *Conversations*, pp. 6-8). Inge's own domestic comedy, *Farther Off from Heaven* (1947), would not be immediately staged on Broadway—the apparent mission of the "emissary"—but produced as the initial offering of Margo Jones's Theatre '47. Revised and renamed, it became the Broadway hit *The Dark at the Top of the Stairs* (1957). TW introduced Inge to Audrey Wood, who became his agent and who guided the friends through sharp competition in the 1950s.

Jones apparently asked TW to contribute $1,500 to "the Project" as he passed through Dallas en route to New York. The "girls" were assistants Joanna Albus, Rebecca Hargis, and June Moll, who worked in a guesthouse on the Burford estate which served as temporary headquarters. The original Burford home is now a fashionable restaurant known as The Mansion.

Marianne Stewart played the "ingenue," Matilda Rockley, in *You Touched Me!* She was last seen on Broadway in S.N. Behrman's comedy *Jacobowsky and the Colonel* (1944), with direction by Elia Kazan and music by Paul Bowles, close friends and collaborators of TW.

"Dowling bull" refers to Eddie Dowling's announcement in the *New York Times* (August 15, 1945) of plans for a London production of *The Glass Menagerie*.

TW probably wrote this letter in the week of September 2, 1945, before traveling to Boston for the opening of *You Touched Me!* The two-week tryout

(September 11-22) produced solid reviews for the play and excellent notices for
Edmund Gwenn as the rollicking Captain Rockley.]

12. *To Walter Edwin Dakin*

SH: Hotel Algonquin
West 44th Street
New York 18, N.Y.
Sept. 28, 1945
[ALS, 4 pp. Columbia U]

Dear Grandfather -

I am happy that you have gotten away from home and the unpleasant
situation there. I am sure it must be a relief to you, as it always was to me,
to be removed from a certain party's vicinity. His behavior has always been
shocking and incomprehensible - I can only suppose, charitably as possible,
that he is not quite sane.

The play opened Tuesday night. The notices were "mixed" - that is,
they ranged from excellent to poor. Not as good reviews as "The
Menagerie" received but nevertheless business at the box-office is lively and
the audiences seem to love it. We are hopeful of having a good run.

I am planning to spend the winter in the South, probably New Orleans.
So I thought I might join you in Memphis and we could go to Columbus
together for a visit. I expect I'll leave here in about a month as I can work
better out of New York.

I am sending a checque which I hope you will use to have a good time.
Mother is going around very socially. And to the theatre nearly every night.
She is flying back to Saint Louis Tuesday.

Everyone who met you here last Spring regrets that you didn't come
back this time. You seem to have made a vivid and favorable impression on
all of them!

Much love, Tom.

[Cornelius Williams caused the "unpleasantness" by heavy drinking and rude treat-
ment of his father-in-law, Walter Dakin (1857-1954), long retired from the active
Episcopal ministry and living periodically at his daughter Edwina's home in
Clayton, Missouri, a well-to-do suburb of St. Louis.

You Touched Me! opened on September 25 to mixed reviews and unfavorable

comparisons with *The Glass Menagerie*, to which it bears a passing resemblance. TW and his collaborator Donald Windham had transformed D.H. Lawrence's ruthless wartime story (1922) into a quaint romantic comedy with an updated World War II setting. The action transpires in a "shut-down" pottery plant in rural England to which the bibulous Cornelius Rockley, a former sea captain, has retired after grounding his last commission. He flouts the strict decorum of his old-maid sister, Emmie, vigilant guardian of his delicate daughter Matilda's virginity. Into this sterile world comes Hadrian, once a foster child who lived with this family, now a Royal Canadian Air Force bombardier, who seeks to awaken Matilda's sexuality and take her back with him to Canada. The battle lines are drawn between the sexes, with a prissy Anglican priest joining Miss Emmie's campaign for celibacy.

Audrey Wood read the mood of the critics on opening night, as TW related in *Memoirs*: "As I filed out of the theatre with crestfallen Windham, my collaborator, she said in a sort of crooked-mouth whisper, 'Mixed notices, dear'" (p. 96). *You Touched Me!* closed on January 5, 1946, after 109 performances.]

13. To Kenneth Thorpe Rowe

SH: Shelton Hotel
Lexington Ave. & 49th St.
New York 17, N.Y.
November 4, 1945
[TLS, 1 p. Beinecke]

Dear Mr. Rowe:

The Theatre Guild is now in such a pre-eminent position, with such a distinguished record behind it and with so much continuing force and vitality still evident through its successful venture into the new field of light opera, that I would not be surprised to see it undertake now and then a production that would correspond to what the major film studios occasionally turn out called a 'prestige film'. As you know, that is one in which more than the usual or routine degree of artistry is invested, a film which is aimed not simply at success but to show the world how much can be accomplished in the amateur spirit and with the professional and highest professional facilities. It is perhaps too rarely that the single artist working alone is possessed by this ideal of perfection, to do not only what is successful and expedient but what is the fullest and highest realization. But it is ever so much more rarely that this impulse really takes hold of a company, and when a company has a set number of things to do in a limited

time and only so much alloted to each, the ideal of perfection when it occurs cannot be very freely or easily indulged. Nevertheless it should be, just for the pure joy and catharsis of doing it.

I wrote Mr. Langner last summer that I was in no haste to have "Battle" done again. The reason is that I am waiting until some producer is moved to approach this script in the amateur spirit (with the highest professional skill) that I have mentioned above, to make a 'prestige' production out of it of the highest order. Maybe that is what Lawrence has in mind, for certainly no managers in New York are in a position more favorable to such an undertaking, and of course I would be very happy to talk to him about it any time he wishes.

Cordially - Tenn. Williams

[Kenneth Rowe (1900-1988) was on leave from the University of Michigan to direct the annual playwriting seminar of the Theatre Guild. Apparently he revived the past summer's discussion of *Battle of Angels*. Apropos of such interest, Audrey Wood had regaled TW with news of Theresa Helburn's blithe proposal to do a "season of plays formerly ruined by the Theatre Guild," adding that "on such a list your play would get their very best second-rate attention" (July 5, 1945, HRC).

The light operas to which TW refers are *Oklahoma!* (1943) and *Carousel* (1945). Massive hits by Richard Rodgers and Oscar Hammerstein II, they helped to modernize the musical stage and to make the Theatre Guild "resoundingly rich."

The "amateur spirit" was a constant ideal in TW's lifelong critique of Broadway. In "Something Wild" (1948), TW recalls the innocence and dynamism of the St. Louis Mummers, a community theatre group which staged two of his apprentice plays in the late 1930s. Theirs was a "kind of excessive romanticism" (*Where I Live*, p. 9) which he seldom found in theatres run for profit.]

14. To James "Jay" Laughlin

SH: Hotel Touraine, Boston
Wed. A.M. (3:30) [November 14, 1945]
[ALS, 3 pp. Houghton]

Dear Jay -

I'd hoped we'd have more time and less company last night. There was a lot I <u>wanted</u> to talk over with you, mainly my work. I have a childish need, right now, for reassurance about it - more than usual - and that is why I

started reading things to you. It was not out of vanity but out of self-distrust. I have become suspicious of myself and what I've been doing - perhaps because of the vast alteration (improvement???) in my manner of living.

You are my literary conscience - the only one outside of myself - so I am over-awed by you and it isn't easy to talk to you.

I am disturbed by your apparently real dissatisfaction with your own life. I would be glad to have you tell me more about it if you think I am able to advise or help in any way.

We should have had 2 or 3 bottles of champagne last night and talked a lot more. So let me know when you have another evening in New York.

Ever, Tennessee.

(The reading has not yet occured. I have a room. Oliver is prowling the streets.)

[As TW's "literary conscience," James Laughlin (1914-1997) cared less for profit than for quality and most of all for writing that was adventurous and new. His bold venture in publishing, New Directions, would issue some forty separate titles by TW during the next six decades.

Oliver Evans, a friend who joined TW for the "reading" at Harvard, is cast here, and later in fiction, as a tireless gay cruiser.]

15. To James "Jay" Laughlin

[Shelton Hotel, New York]
Monday - [November/December 1945]
[TLS w/ autograph marginalia
and postscript, 2 pp. Houghton]

Dear Jay:

Your letter meant a lot to me! Immediately I felt a resurgence of vitality and went back to work on the play with such vigor that I worked out a brand new climax and ending which I think makes it definitely a solid thing in my hands.

The work on ONE ARM was so long-drawn-out and tormented by my inability to fuse matter with style and the sensational with the valid, that I was unable to read it myself with a clear perception, but what you say about it - if you are not just being kind - indicates that I have done the second thing

James Laughlin, founder of New Directions Publishing Corporation: "<u>You</u> are my literary <u>conscience</u>."

at least acceptably. That gives me a wonderful feeling! All of my good things, the few of them, have emerged through this sort of tortured going over and over - "Battle", "Menagerie", the few good stories. "YTM" is an example of one that <u>didn't</u> work out, not with any amount of struggle, though it was (the labor) pretty terrific. But always when I look back on the incredible messiness of original trials I am amazed that it comes out as clean as it does.

In one way the Boston reading went off pretty well. I was not scared of the audience as I thought I would be and they all said that I read so everybody could hear me. But I made the terrible mistake of trying to read "Dos Ranchos". It went all to pieces while I was reading it. It began to sound like shit. My voice became loud and expressionless and I kept going on, hoping to find a passage suitable to close with. I really murdered it! As I did not give them a synopsis to begin with or select in advance the parts that could be offered out of context. However I closed with a couple of

very bawdy folk-poems which at least put them back in a fairly pleasant humor. I kept looking at poor Mr. Mathieson on the front row. He was squirming in his seat the whole time and looked much more unhappy than I was, like a school-boy about to suffer some awful punishment. However he was wonderfully nice about it and I liked him best of anyone there. Oliver says that he is the most erudite man in America! There was an English faculty tea preceding the reading. I had told Mr. Spencer that it would be necessary for me to have a stiff drink on the platform just to give me moral support, even if I didn't drink it. But he demurred over this, said he didn't think there was any opaque glasses and if I drank anything on the platform it would have to be something that looked like water, such as straight gin or vodka. All I had with me was a pint of yellow brandy, so I poured a stiff shot of it in my tea at the faculty thing, and I think they were all shocked and apprehensive over it, though very polite. All except a professor named Sterling Lanier. I told him that my middle name was Lanier and that we must be related and he raised his eyebrows and said 'The ramifications of the Lanier family are immense and appalling!' I was just drunk enough (I was cold sober soon as I got on the platform) to be just as saucy as he was and we engaged in a verbal tilt over our tea, in which I, having the stronger tea, did not come out unimpressively.

The next day I made some recordings. They said the records could be offered for public distribution provided they were subsidized so I gave them a cheque for $142. to subsidize them. If they are all sold I will get back royalties amounting almost to that sum. Anyway it seemed to please them a great deal, as it was the first time a poet had done such a thing. Ought to make them suspicious of the poetry!

See you Wednesday.

Tenn.

Would you like to see "5 folders of Crane material, including penny arcade photo of him" - ? A Mr. Jack Birss in Brooklyn has invited me to inspect them any evening.

[Drafting of *Summer and Smoke* (1948), the play in progress, began in New York in the preceding spring. Its "climax and ending" never ceased to plague TW and led to multiple experiments.

James Laughlin recently encouraged TW to "write another story as good as One Arm" (Saturday {November, 17, 1945} Houghton). Drafts dated May 1942 and August 1945 (HRC) reveal that the story had doubled in length during its "tortured" composition, perhaps with some blurring of the pure, instinctive morality of Oliver Winemiller, the one-armed gay hustler. TW worked on the later script in Mexico and completed it in Dallas after the harrowing passage through Customs.

TW's reading at Harvard on November 14 was arranged by Theodore Spencer, a kindly scholar-poet whom Laughlin and many other Harvard students considered their favorite professor. F.O. Matthiessen is the "squirming" author of *American Renaissance: Art and Expression in the Age of Emerson and Whitman* (1941). Sterling Lanier, the Harvard "professor" with whom TW jousted, was actually a teaching fellow at work on a doctorate in American literature. He died in 1974.

TW read the verse play "Dos Ranchos or, The Purification," a meditation on incest written in the dark poetic style of Lorca and published in *New Directions Eight* (1944). TW's recording of seven briefer poems is preserved in the Woodberry Poetry Room, Harvard College Library.

TW wrote this letter between November 19 and December 3, 1945, and probably mailed it later in December from New Orleans, as a notation penned in the upper margin of page 1 suggests: "Dear Jay - wrote this in N.Y. - just found it among my papers."]

16. *To Donald Windham*

SH: The Pontchartrain Apartment Hotel
New Orleans 12, La.
[December 26, 1945]
[TLS, 2 pp. HTC]

Dear Don:

The lovely wind-instrument just reached me and I want to tell you at once how enchanted I am by it, as you must have known I would be. In spite of its extreme fragility it arrived altogether intact, not a bit displaced or broken, and I have been wandering around my room with it, unable to set it down, as it tinkles and jingles. It will go in the brightest spot of my new Apartment which I move into tonight or tomorrow and which is a dream, all the windows being shuttered doors twelve feet high and with a balcony looking out on the negro convent and the back of St. Louis cathedral, easy sanctuary in times of duress. I also loved your card, "The Peaceable Kingdom", although Miss Lion looks as if she were about to start something.

I was going home for Xmas but fortunately all north-bound planes were grounded, which heaven-sent dispensation kept me here. Christmas day was one of those exquisitely soft balmy days that occur here between the rains in winter, felt like an angel's kiss. I spent it in the Quarter in the apartment I am going to occupy as the present tenant, moving out this week, was almost as fortuitious a discovery as the apartment itself. It was so warm that we had dinner in a patio and wore skivvy shirts and dungarees. This present tenant has an aged grandmother who is the all-time high in southern ladies innocence. She entered our room this morning at a very early and most inopportune moment and as she strolled by the bed she remarked, "You boys must be cold, I am going to shut these doors."

I would like to know if Jane got a job in the Hamilton show. Received a little hand-painted picture from Neil Fitzgerald with a cross note about hating to go on tour, so it must mean that "YTM" is taking to the road. I don't imagine any of them are very happy about it as they do not seem like the sort of little group that would find each other terribly stimulating on long train-rides. Just imagine Mr. Fitzgerald and Miss Whozit who plays Matilda at breakfast in a diner! One can sometimes be happier thinking of the things one has missed than those one has had. But they were all rather sweet, especially when you consider the rather disheartening circumstances at the Booth.

Audrey sent me a clipping from Montreal that contained a withering attack on Miss Hopkins and Louis J. Singer. The latter delighted me, but I was sorry for Miriam.

My coffee has come up and I must get to work, though it is hard to take my eyes off the wind-instrument.

I have ordered you a copy of "Goodbye to Berlin" when it comes from New Directions press. I know you've read it but I thought you'd like one to keep.

Best wishes for the New Year, and love,

Tennessee

[TW's arrival in New Orleans in 1938 was antidote to the stagnant, "dangerously cornered" feeling of life in St. Louis: "Here surely is the place that I was made for if any place on this funny old world" (*Journal*, October 16 and December 28, 1938). The present return (ca. December 12) followed a similar period of exile in

New York: "Broadway seems like some revolting sickness, that involves vomiting and eating and shitting all at once" (qtd. in Windham, p. 178). TW "put up" at the Pontchartrain, a "plush hotel" (*Memoirs*, p. 99) near the Garden District which bespoke his new affluence. By late-December he was living in the "heterogeneous" Vieux Carré once again.

TW met Donald Windham (b. 1920) in New York in 1940. Their friendship would be strained by collaboration on *You Touched Me!* and further tested by myriad slights and wrongs, real or imagined, as TW's fame grew in the 1940s. Nonetheless TW wrote some of his finest letters to Windham, who published a collection in 1977.

Earlier in December TW prepared the "Folks" for his own fervently desired absence at Christmas: "It is impossible to get a train reservation at this time but I have my name at several plane companies and they are going to call me if any cancellation comes in" (Tuesday {December 18, 1945} HTC).

Jane Smith has informed the editors that she is not familiar with the "Hamilton show"—probably *Angel Street* (1941)—nor does she know to which theatrical "job" her friend TW may have been referring.

TW imagined a tense scene on tour between Neil Fitzgerald, the effete Reverend Guildford Melton, and Marianne Stewart, the decorative Matilda, in *You Touched Me!*

In 1946 New Directions issued the *Berlin Stories*, a reprint of Christopher Isherwood's autobiographical tales (1935/1939) of pre-war Germany. TW ranked them with Chekhov.

TW later informed Windham that this letter was lost in moving and not mailed.]

17. To Audrey Wood

710 Orleans St.
[New Orleans, Louisiana]
Jan. 3, 1946.
[TLS w/ autograph postscript, 1 p. HRC]

Dear Audrey:

If you can imagine how a cat would feel in a cream-puff factory you can imagine my joy at being back in the Quarter. It was always my particular milieu but I was never here before with money! Now I can afford a place where the windows are all doors twelve feet-high with shutters, and a balcony looking out on the negro convent and the back of the cathedral. I never put on a shirt, just a leather jacket, I go unshaven for days and nobody says, Look at that bum, they say, That is the fellow who wrote The

Glass Menagerie! Droit de Seigneur, Noblesse Oblige and Honi Soit Qui Mal Y Pense, all rolled into one! I make my own coffee, have breakfast cream you have to dip out with a spoon, no telephone to ring, three friends who are all Mexicans and no more, a swimming club in the neighborhood, and long unbroken days to work in.

So far I have no servant to clean the place but I have been promised a negro girl to come in. She had better hurry!

I was very happy over the cigarette case, it being one of the only two gifts I received, more than I deserved for I didn't even send cards to my friends and I broke my promise to come home for Xmas on the thin excuse of planes being grounded. Conditions at home must be worse than terrible, for my father has retired from business, is at home all the time so poor grandfather has to stay in his room all the time. They can't stand the sight of each other! I will have to do something for Grandfather, but I don't know what. Perhaps bring him down here.

Please call the Shelton and give them my forwarding address, 710 Orleans. I have a short script for you and a more exciting longer one may come on soon.

Love to you and Liebling, Tenn.

Send me <u>Story</u>, please. Unobtainable here.

[A draft version of this letter found TW mulling his estate with little "joy." The simpler life of New Orleans had occasioned "a bad spell of self-examination and castigation," whose only "refuge is work." "Poets," however, "cannot forget time. A certain amount is in you and you have got to use it as well and as prudently as you can so that when the iceman cometh there will be some stuff worth keeping in the ice-box" (n.d., Private Collection).

The forthcoming production of *The Iceman Cometh* (O'Neill, 1946) was well known at this time and may have influenced TW's imagery. The same colloquial expression appears in a draft of *Streetcar*, which is partially typed on stationery of the Pontchartrain Hotel: "Who's been getting it all this summer? The ice man?" (n.d., HRC), asks a frustrated George (Mitch) of Blanche DuBois in a study of Scene Nine.

TW recalls that he could "see in the garden behind the cathedral the great stone statue of Christ, his arms outstretched as if to invite the suffering world to come to Him" (*Memoirs*, p. 99). The "convent" of the Sisters of the Holy Family, a religious order of "negro" nuns, was a place of charitable and educational work from 1881 to 1964. The building now houses the Bourbon Orleans Hotel.

The "short script" is "The Unsatisfactory Supper" (1946), a somber companion of the one-act play "27 Wagons Full of Cotton" (1945). The "more exciting" work in progress is *Streetcar*.

"The Important Thing," an early story of sexual discovery, appeared in the current number of *Story* magazine (November-December 1945). The editor, Whit Burnett, first published TW in 1939 and was probably mindful of his recent success.

Partially canceled in the letterhead is the imprint of the Pontchartrain Hotel in New Orleans.]

18. To William Carlos Williams

710 Orleans
[New Orleans, Louisiana]
[January 1946]
[TLS w/ autograph marginalia, 1 p. Beinecke]

Dear W.C. Williams:

I don't know why you should have felt any hesitation whatsoever about writing me about your play. My God, if there is no willingness among poets to be of any help they can to each other - what in hell have we! (Alas, we know!) But so far I have always enjoyed being helpful when I can be at all.

Audrey is peculiar little girl (of 40). My suggestion is that you <u>talk</u> to her, for she will do so much more out of personal interest and she is a soft enough person, in spite of years in the hardest racket, to want to do more for those whom she genuinely likes and she is still capable of genuine liking. So go and talk to her and in the meantime I will explain to her your position in the world of letters, that side of it which she has little opportunity to know. The chances are that she has heard of your name, at least, and I think you are the honest type of person she goes for.

Don't send me the play. I want to read it but I am entirely too negligent about mailing things back and this is especially true when I am working hard as I am now. I rarely mail the letters I write - I trust this will be an exception. Besides you will know better than anyone else can tell you whether or not you have done with this play what you wanted, and Audrey is the one to judge its saleability - no agent is infallible in this respect, however.

Best of luck to you, Tenn.

[William Carlos Williams (1883-1963) was advised by his friend and publisher James Laughlin to ask if TW's "hot shot agent" might represent his new play, *A Dream of Love* (1949). He later paid special tribute to poems by TW appearing in *New Directions Nine* (1946): "Camino Real," "Recuerdo," and "Lady, Anemone" (see *William Carlos Williams and James Laughlin: Selected Letters*, ed. Witemeyer, 1989, pp. 124-125).

Penned in the lower margin and keyed to the second paragraph is the notation "as your play is probably highly eclectic by her standards explain about it to her."

TW wrote this letter between January 3 and 15, 1946, as related correspondence indicates. Partially canceled in the letterhead is the imprint of the Pontchartrain Hotel in New Orleans.]

19. To the Williams Family

710 Orleans
[New Orleans, Louisiana]
[mid-January 1946]
[ALS, 3 pp. HTC]

Dear folks -

I got a wire from Laurette asking me to call her long distance as she had something to tell me "very important". I called her yesterday - it seems that "Menagerie" is going to give a "command performance" for the President and Washington dignitaries in Washington on Jan 27th. Laurette insists that I must come up for it. If Audrey approves, I shall - as it is unquestionably a big occasion. I will arrange either to go or return by way of Saint Louis so I can combine the two trips. If Grandfather feels able to go I would be happy to give him the trip as a Xmas present. I suppose we would meet the President and there may be a White House dinner, according to Laurette. She was very thrilled over it, but sorry it was Truman instead of Roosevelt.

I am busy as can be, working on a long script and hate to leave off even for a short trip.

It is ideal conditions here. Though I still haven't secured a maid to clean up my apt. and it is beginning to look it.

Much love - Tom.

[The "'command performance'" of *The Glass Menagerie* was scheduled for January 27 to inaugurate the "Roosevelt Birthday Celebration." TW and Laurette Taylor

were ardent admirers of the deceased president, if not of Truman, his successor from Missouri.

Partially canceled in the letterhead is the imprint of the New Orleans Athletic Club.]

20. To Audrey Wood

<u>710 Orleans</u>.
[New Orleans, Louisiana]
Jan. 15, 1946.
[TLS, 2 pp. HRC]

Dear Audrey:

I don't know what to do about Washington. Have you any advice to give me? Laurette wired me to call her and I did. She informed me of the honor and seems to expect me to come up for it. Do you think it justifies the trip? As you know I am not very much excited by social occasions but at the same time I want to do what is expected of me. What would go on there? Would there be a dinner at the White House? That might be too important to pass up.

I am afraid I will have to do something immediately about Grandfather. Got the most awful letter this morning from Mother. Dad retired from business at New Years and subsequently retired to his bedroom with the bottle. Does nothing but stay home and drink. When sufficiently drunk I think he is dangerous. Mother says that he talks threateningly and abusively to my grandfather, and I have received a letter from grandfather virtually imploring me to take him to New Orleans with me. I don't think I could have grandfather in this small apartment with me and get much work done, but I am hoping that I can find a suitable boarding-house for him here, am working on that. These are the last few years of his life and he should not be allowed to spend them in such hellish circumstances as those now prevailing at home. As for Mother, she embodies all the errors and mistakes and misunderstandings that her time and background could produce, she is so full of them that she is virtually a monument of them, nor has she out-grown a single one of them - her mental horizon has apparently never expanded one inch - I'm sure I could never live with her again! - but I respect her endurance, a sort of tragic magnitude she does seem to have! - <u>society</u> should be <u>scourged</u> for producing such

"Christian martyrs"! - such monuments of misapprehension! - undoubtedly she once had the makings of an awfully fine woman.

I am switching back and forth between two long plays, the one about the sisters started in Chicago and one about a Spinster begun in New York. Right now I am doing more with the sisters, it is now set in New Orleans and is called "A Street-car Named Desire" - there is one by that title that runs close by my apartment, and proceding in the other direction down the next street is one called "Cemetaries". In spite of this I am not really in a very morbid state of mind, as this might suggest.

Were you disappointed in the one-act? Your silence about it offers that impression. It was the first one-act I've done in quite a while. Perhaps it lacks something that I used to have in my earlier one-act plays. The tragic intensity in a small sphere, such as 'This Property', was partly out of my own desperation at the time it was done and now that I am on better terms with existence - some of that may be lost. I hope not too much of it and I hope I can go on drawing new perceptions out of experience, but all that I can actively do is to go on working and hoping that my wish to do something new will not take me outside of what is communicable to a large enough audience.

Have you heard of William Carlos Williams? Laughlin wants me to read one of his plays and recommend it to you for marketing. I wrote Williams not to send me the play but to give it to you directly, as I always forget to send things back to people. He is one of the top three or four American poets [and] has immense prestige in his field, but his work in drama may not be anything for Broadway. You can tell. His address is Dr. W. C. Williams, 9 Ridge Road, Rutherford, New Jersey. He is a fine fellow, and I am flattered that Laughlin thought of us both in this connection.

Ever, Tenn.

[Audrey Wood advised TW that the command performance of *The Glass Menagerie* could not "be treated too lightly" from "a good business standpoint." She also urged that he "do something about" his grandfather, bullied as he was by Cornelius, and promised to be as "helpful" (January 19, 1946, HRC) as possible.

The "long plays" in progress are *A Streetcar Named Desire* and *Summer and Smoke*. TW experimented with Chicago and Atlanta as settings for *Streetcar* before deciding upon New Orleans. He also arrived at the famous title after testing at least eight alternatives.

Wood informed TW that she was "tremendously" moved by the "very frailty" of his new one-act, "The Unsatisfactory Supper" (January 19, 1946, HRC). It shares with "27 Wagons Full of Cotton" a Mississippi Delta setting and much the same cast of characters, if with variant names and roles. Their antics, rife with venality, pathos, and humor, would be recast in *Baby Doll* (1956).

A Dream of Love was not "Broadway material," Wood advised William Carlos Williams, and urged that he "clarify the story in dramatic terms" (May 7, 1946, HRC). The play was published by New Directions in 1948 and performed the following year by an off-Broadway company. It was not Williams's first or last foray into theatre.]

21. To Oliver Evans

[710 Orleans Street
New Orleans, Louisiana]
[mid-January 1946]
[TLS, 1 p. HRC]

My dear Daughter:

I have been turning things over in my mind, which is where I also turn things over sometimes, and have come to the conclusion that it is time for you to be brought out in society. Your term with the Sisters has taught you many useful things, such as your needle-work, your dancing and your singing of those charming French songs. You have acquired many graces for the drawing-room, but it is time that you learned there are rooms to a house, besides the music room, the drawing room, the library and the kitchen. In short I think it is time that you were brought into association with a select number of your mother's friends' children, so that you may experience a little of the harmless gaiety which is suitable to one of your years and station in society. As a matter of fact, I am writing the Sisters at once in regard to this view and suggesting that you be prepared and equipped for emergence from the convent. I have suggested a few purchases for your wardrobe, six or seven changes of light-weight underwear, one taffeta with a train and one without a train, a small, girlish hat with some discreet kind of paper flower on it - no plumes are worn by the younger girls this season, though matrons of your mother's standing sometimes display them in the afternoons. I do not know if your figure requires a corset, for I have not seen you lately and a girl's figure undergoes rapid changes at

your time of life, but it would be good to have one just in case! I am sorry it will be necessary for you to travel alone - that is, if a suitable duenna cannot be provided from the convent. However the Sisters will surely instruct the conductor to look out for you and see that you are [not] engaged in conversation by strangers, for that is something your mother knows only too well may lead to serious misapprehensions if not real compromise.

I have a delightful small furnished apartment at 710 Orleans, half a block from the cathedral. Three big rooms, a small study and a balcony that faces the negro convent. The streets are teeming with ambulatory vistas, the small dark kind that are barely contained by their buttons and while I know that you will grieve for the Sisters left behind you, I have no doubt that certain errands of piety and mercy may draw you occasionally out upon the streets.

I did like the poem, though it is perhaps more like a collection of sharp and vivid notes for an essay than a lyric. But that is your particular style. I hope to hear of you writing more prose also.

Ever, Tenn.

[Oliver Evans (1915-1981) and TW met in the early 1940s and became close friends and traveling companions. The New Orleans-born poet and critic taught at several universities after taking a master's degree at the University of Tennessee in 1941.

TW's satire was inspired no doubt by the propinquity of his apartment to the "negro convent," once a festive ballroom and reportedly the site of the famous quadroon balls of antebellum New Orleans. TW's allusion to a delicate, cloistered sexuality led Evans to recall a much coarser trade at the Shelton Hotel in New York, where TW lived during the staging of *You Touched Me!* Writing as "Olivia," Evans wishes her "sainted Mother" a "safe and speedy return" to services at the "Shelton Cathedral": "I have even gone so far as to make a special offering at the shrine of Our Lady of the Steam Room." Olivia herself planned to "linger yet awhile" in New York, "surrounded by the pious Sisters of our beloved Order of St. Vaseline" (n.d., HRC).

This letter is tentatively dated on the basis of stationery and typography which resemble TW's correspondence of January 15, 1946, to Audrey Wood.]

22. To James "Jay" Laughlin

["enroute to Washington D.C."]
Jan. 25, 1946.
[TLS w/ autograph postscript, 2 pp. Houghton]

Dear Jay:

We are passing through Hattiesburg Mississippi enroute to Washington D.C. for the "command performance" of "Menagerie". I had decided not to go up for it as I have so fallen in love with N.O. LA that I was unwilling to part with it for even a week-end, but a young lady friend of mine thought differently and bought my ticket and poured me on the train more or less forcibly. She is along too and that may be why she was firm about it. In fact I am going through quite an experience with this young lady. She is one of these people with a passion for lost causes, is beautiful enough to have anybody she wanted but is apparently attracted only by the line of most resistance. So she came down here from New York and so far the most complete and graphic candor on my part has not convinced her that propinquity will not conquer all. I have always been more or less overlooked by goodlooking women and once upon a time I sometimes suffered acutely from the fact, so the novelty of the situation makes it all the more impossible to cope with. I dare say you have had infinitely more experience in the matter and at any rate are infinitely more resourceful, so let us exchange fatherly advices. No, I don't want to be "saved", I don't think anyone has ever been happier with his external circumstances than I have learned how to be, and as for my internal circumstances, only I can affect them. So is there anything to be gained from the complicating entrance of a lady? I would like to arrange for you to meet her, for she is a delectable article for anyone on the market. Or are you still engaged by the dark lady of the sonnets in New York? I do hope you will come to New Orleans with her, and if Sylvia - yes, that is her name - is still down here - she threatens to get a job here - something very interesting might develop for you. At any rate you will love New Orleans and it is a grand place to take anybody you are in love with as it rains so much but always clears up after while. - Your poem about the girl and her lost husband - like the one about Baudelaire - has a richness of texture ~~and feeling~~ that you don't always indulge in. Incidentally I received a letter of lavish praise from Bigelow about your book of poems. I hope I have saved it for you. Bigelow is my brightest friend, too. He is a fascinating personality that

I hope you may get to know. A bit like Isherwood's Mr. Norris, - that is, in the mysteries of his origin Etc. - but much deeper and warmer I think. I think he is a bit supernatural, a sort of very wonderful 'witch!'

I got all the books and am delighted with "27 Wagons", it is perfectly gotten out. Bob's jacket is a dream! I hope the critics don't make you suffer for it. Some of the characters are a bit peculiar and the author does not come thru as a terribly wholesome individual. I wrote Audrey at once about W.C.W'S play - I hope she will feel inclined to do something about it. She will if it appears at all marketable.

In spite of what you say about my prose I think it is pretty awkward and I think I can get my best effects, with good directors and actors, on the stage when there is so much besides verbal values to work with - except when there is a subject like "One Arm" that you can't put on the stage as it now exists. - If you have a chance to - see a picture with the awful name of "Fallen Angel". I think it's extraordinary in some respects. It could almost be happening, the characters come as close to life as any the screen has ever touched and some of the scenes - the psychological suggestions, perhaps undeliberate - are really haunting.

I hope that this new girl will continue to give you interest if not happiness in New York. Or Vermont.

Ever, Tenn.

P.S. I am so shy with this girl Sylvia that I suffer acutely when alone in a room with her. Have you ever felt that way with anyone? I have told her I feel that way - she makes it worse by enquiring every few minutes, 'Am I making you uncomfortable? Do you want me to go out now? Is it all right if I sit here? Don't talk to me unless you want to, Etc.' Then she sits there with her brilliant eyes taking in every embarassed change of expression as if she were conducting some marvelous experiment in a lab so that I don't know where to look, let alone what to say. Exactly like Lillian Gish or at best Harold Lloyd in an old silent film. What are women made of?!

In a week or so I am going to send you a 30 or 35 p. Ms. of a "work for the Plastic Theatre" with Mexican backgrd. & characters that include Oliver Winemiller, Baron de Charlus, and Don Quixote! I want it produced on a program with Dos Ranchos.

["Sylvia" has not been identified, but TW apparently told his mother of her presence in New Orleans, and of her encumbered condition. "I can't imagine," Edwina replied, that "you are doing much work with a distracting lady on hand. How come she has 'nothing to do' when she has two children?" (February 16, 1946, Private Collection).

His friend Paul Bigelow, TW thought, resembled the title character of Christopher Isherwood's novella *The Last of Mr. Norris* (1935; rpt. by New Directions, 1946). Norris is a charming voluptuary of mysterious origin and illicit means of support who epitomizes the disordered life of pre-war Berlin.

New Directions published *27 Wagons Full of Cotton and Other One-Act Plays* on December 27, 1945. The cover art, which derives from the title play, shows a long thin plume of smoke rising from a burning gin. The *New York Times* reviewer was typical of others in finding TW's characters so peculiar as to be outside "the boundaries of credibility and unfeigned sympathy" (February 24, 1946).

The melodramatic plot of *Fallen Angel* (1945) turns upon the murder of Stella (Linda Darnell), a small-town waitress, whose dark, alluring beauty haunts the drifter, Eric Stanton (Dana Andrews). *Fallen Angel* was considered a disappointing sequel to Otto Preminger's direction of *Laura* in 1944.

TW intended the latest draft of *Camino Real*, subtitled "A Work for the Plastic Theatre" (n.d., HRC), to be performed with "Dos Ranchos" ("The Purification"). Oliver Winemiller, the vagrant hustler of "One Arm," would soon be renamed Kilroy. TW advocated "a new, plastic theatre which must take the place of the exhausted theatre of realistic conventions" ("Production Notes," *The Glass Menagerie*, 1945). The emphasis would fall upon visual and aural rather than literary effects and would require innovative "subtleties" of direction and stage design.]

23. To Neil Fitzgerald

[710 Orleans Street
New Orleans, Louisiana]
[February 1946]
[TLS, 2 pp. HRC]

Dear Neil:

You see I am faithful to the Shelton, at least to their stationary!

Of course I was inexpressibly sad about what happened to our play. I also feel that it needn't have happened, and that's what makes it hurt so. I am now in a position to write a play about a mother's sorrow for the death of an invalid child, for I felt exactly that way about it. I so wanted it to live!

Nobody writes me from New York except Donnie and poor Windham

lives in such a world of his own that I don't get much news out of him. When you have time I would appreciate some account of things there. How did Antigone fare with the press? I have only read one notice, THE SUN, which corresponds to what I felt about the play when I read it. I can't understand how Cornell or even McClintic could be so obtuse about a silly script.

I have a lovely apartment here in the French Quarter. Ceilings about 12-feet high and a balcony that looks out on the back-yard of the Cathedral. The atmosphere and life is tranquil and I have been working continually. Two long scripts are in progress and a short-long play Mexican fantasy with music and dancing is finished: it is only about 55 pages long, however, and I won't know how good it is till I've let it set for a while. The speeches are frighteningly long!

Neil, your work in "YTM" and our association is one of my very happiest memories in the theatre: not just a memory but a lasting experience I am sure. I hope it will be your fortune to find an excellent part.

Any change in the Shelton management must be an improvement! When I'm coming back I will wire you in the hope you can get me another suite there, however. I had a good time in spite of the bitches at the desk! - and that old white-headed bull-dog - is he still patroling the lobby?

Love, Tenn

[Neil Fitzgerald (1893-1982)—the Rev. Guildford Melton in *You Touched Me!*—apparently lived at the Shelton Hotel in New York, whose stationery TW playfully used for this letter. News of a "change" in hotel management may have reminded TW of the former manager's warning note: "It has been called to our attention you have been in the habit of doing considerable entertaining in your room 1832" (November 23, 1945, Private Collection). TW's "chicken run" and Oliver Evans's "raids on the steam room and the bar" (qtd. in Windham, p. 179) were observed no doubt by the "white-headed bull-dog" who patrolled the lobby.

The Cornell-McClintic production of *Antigone* opened to mixed reviews on February 18. Ward Morehouse, writing in the *New York Sun*, granted the boldness of the experiment—based upon Anouilh's wartime adaptation (1943)—but he and other reviewers found the updated Sophocles to be jarring in effect and not "very stimulating theater" (February 19, 1946).]

24. *To Audrey Wood*

SH: Western Union
New Orleans La
1946 FEB 26 PM 1 18
[Telegram, 1 p. HRC]

AUDREY WOOD=

IF USE OF UNDERSTUDY IS DAMAGING PLAY PLEASE INVOKE ANY LEGAL RIGHTS I MAY HAVE TO CLOSE TILL TAYLOR RESUMES PART OR STAR REPLACEMENT IF SHE DOES NOT. LOVE=

TENNESSEE.

[Audrey Wood cabled TW and later wrote in detail about Laurette Taylor's severe laryngitis and absence from the cast of *The Glass Menagerie*. To Wood's dismay—and Taylor's also—the play continued to run with the understudy taking the role of Amanda. Wood viewed this decision as yet another skirmish in the "Dowling-Taylor Civil War" and confirmation that the backer, Louis J. Singer, "loves money more than art" (to TW, February 26, 1946, HRC). She urged TW to "send very strong wires" stating his "concern for Taylor's health" and instructing that the play be closed during her illness to avert "possible damage" (telegram, February 25, 1946, HRC) to the property itself.

Taylor, nearing sixty-two, had been continuously in rehearsal or performance of *The Glass Menagerie* for fifteen months. Because she recovered from similar throat problems during the Chicago run, there probably seemed little cause for alarm. In retrospect her declining health can be dated from this episode.]

25. *To Paul Bigelow*

710 Orleans.
[New Orleans, Louisiana]
PM: New Orleans, February 27, 1946
[ALS, 4 pp. Columbia U]

Dear Paul -

If only you had sent me that "Bundle of letters" a little earlier in my career. It is much too late for me to learn the efficacy of the sponge bath and the advisability of bathing my "sacred inner organs" - and when I think of the times that I have been "drugged and stupefied by unscrupulous men" I could scream!

I have been having quite a hectic time of it - living with a little Mexican

full of tricks, for about two months. I didn't mind her bringing in trade as long as she saved a little of her energy for my own entertainment but recently she started falling asleep as soon as her trade departed. So I kicked her out of bed and sent her out on the streets. She is a pretty thing - She took refuge with a Creole belle who had wanted her badly while she was staying with me but was considerably disconcerted to have her altogether on his hands. I wrote her a mildly affectionate note of farewell which she mistakenly interpreted as a plea to return. So back she came tonight with her 2 shirts, alarm clock and perfume. When I left the apartment she was singing gaily in the bathtub and no doubt I will return to find her coiled snake-like around at least 2 more sailors. These Mexicans are charming little things - if you can live through them! I wonder how Miss Maxwell would handle the situation! Alas, I have never been able to scream very convincingly about my beautiful body!

I have been hard at work in spite of distracting circumstances - completed a Mexican fantasy and am plowing through a New Orleans play - more gradually.

Don't plan to leave here till it's finished - maybe not for three or four months.

I love it here, though society isn't much. I have been going out to some of the debutante parties but no balls - I don't have a tux and don't want to bother with one.

Let me hear from you. Love to you both!

Tenn.

[Paul Bigelow (1905-1988) was variously a journalist, raconteur, aspiring playwright, and production assistant to the Theatre Guild and Cheryl Crawford. In 1939 he and his friend Jordan Massee moved from Georgia to New York, where they met TW.

Pancho Rodriguez, the new companion, "occupied the center" of TW's life "from the late fall of {1945} till at least half a year later" (*Memoirs*, p. 99). "Miss Maxwell" is Gilbert Maxwell, poet, friend, and informal biographer of TW.]

26. To Audrey Wood

[710 Orleans Street
New Orleans, Louisiana]
March 12, 1946
[TLS, 1 p. HRC]

Dear Audrey:

I have read over Camino Real and I don't think it ought to be typed up in its present form. In this version the only good scene is the one at the Gypsy's. I don't see anything objectionably coarse in that. Kilroy is the name that you see written in public places nowadays. "Kilroy was here", "Kilroy is here", Etc. is the favorite inscription on walls of bars, stations, cheap hotel rooms, fences. So in writing about him I wanted to catch the atmosphere of the world he lived in, bars, stations, cheap hotel-rooms. An atmosphere of the American comic-strip transposed into a sort of rough, colloquial poetry. Comic-strip bar-room idyll, the common young transient's affair with longing and disappointment, a very rough sort of tenderness mixed with cynicism. Touches of coarseness were necessary to get that effect. Of course the veil-lifting was symbolic of something more intimate, but since visually it [is] only a veillifting, I don't see why it should be offensive. It was a mistake to identify the couple as ~~Jacques~~ Casanova and Camille. Better to call them "Actor & Actress" or "He and She". And their long scene together should be cut down to include only the street-cleaners and the long monologue commencing "This dusty plaza with its dried up fountain." The Baron should be eliminated and the play begin with Kilroy's entrance. That will make it a lot shorter but clearer and stronger. I will prepare this version when I can take the time off my longer script. I think it is worth doing as the Kilroy sections and the ending have charm. And if I make a good script of it, it will go nicely with "Dos Ranchos".

I am getting back on "The Street-car Named Desire". I hope reading it over will not be as shocking as "Camino". I sometimes wonder if any professional (?) writer can write as badly as I.

I want to buy an inexpensive second-hand car to knock about in, the weather is becoming so nice here. Do you think I can afford to? Taylor and movie-sale are both so uncertain that I cannot feel any economic security.

With love, Tenn.

[A call from Audrey Wood instructing TW to "'put it away, don't let anybody see it'" (qtd. in *Memoirs*, p. 101), was reportedly her first acknowledgment of *Camino Real*. The "only good scene" refers to Block Seven, where Kilroy unveils Esmeralda in a coy simulation of sex that Wood apparently found "coarse." Much later TW observed that agents "are sometimes very obtuse in their recognition of an original and striking piece of work in its early stages" (*Memoirs*, p. 101).

Casanova and Camille were listed in the Broadway credits of *Camino Real* as "Gentleman of Fortune" and "Lady of Legend." TW retained the Baron de Charlus, Proust's aging homosexual, but as initially staged in New York, the play began with the entrance of the Survivor, rather than Kilroy.

Later in March TW learned that Cary Grant was considering an independent film production of *The Glass Menagerie*, in which he would take the "star role" and "an effort" would be made "to secure Laurette Taylor" (telegram, Vincent to Wood, March 22, 1946, HRC). In reply Wood stated "that Tennessee Williams has evolved a way of avoiding an unhappy ending" (telegram, to Vincent, April 5, 1946, HRC), should this be a commercial consideration.]

27. To Audrey Wood

SH: Adler Hotel
75 Linden near Main
Memphis, Tenn.
April 21, 1946.
[TLS, 2 pp. HRC]

Dear Audrey:

I would like to have this story typed up and one copy sent to <u>Laughlin</u> (500 5th Ave.). I know that you may not like it and so I am not suggesting that you send it to anyone else. If you should like it, you may use your own discretion, which is always best, about sending it other places. But send one copy to me as I want sometime to make a short (maybe two act) play out of it, in which case the title might be changed to "Some of God's Creatures". That might make a good over-all title for a group of my short plays. (will send address later)

I have bought a super-jalopy (a 1937 model convertible Packard roadster) and am proceding gradually toward home. The car is still beautiful in spite of its age, all black and shiny silver, and very gracefully designed with leather seats that smell wonderful in the sun, although the stuffing is beginning to come out of them. However the radiator is cracked so that it has to

be filled with water about every ten miles and the tires have blown out with the regularity of percussion instruments in a Shostakovitch symphony. I have had to buy a complete set of new ones, including tubes, between here and Baton Rouge. But I have learned how to use an hydraulic jack and a lug-wrench, which is really a milestone in my life! The car has unlimited speed, eight cylinders! I intend to have it over-hauled in Saint Louis, and then pro-cede West, probably to Taos, N.M. It will be wonderful for the desert!

I have not gotten as far along with either of the long plays as I intend-ed. The last few weeks in New Orleans were awfully hectic. I had dis-agreements with the owner of the apartment-building and was put out of my nice apartment and could not find another that was at all agreeable. When I get to another stopping place (Taos?) I hope to surround myself with acres of uninhabited terrain and concentrate on an active singular existence. Let come of it what may!

Somebody named Perlmutter has written me a couple of times asking that I endorse a drive against cancer. I've lost his letter so don't know where to answer. If you can get in touch with him, please tell him that I am com-pletely against it, the disease.

I am going to leave here this afternoon for Saint Louis.

With love, Tennessee.

P.S. I have stored a trunk containing papers and other belongings at a warehouse called Gallagher's in New Orleans.

[Audrey Wood may have surprised TW by cabling that she liked his new story, "The Night of the Iguana," a "great deal" (May 17, 1946, HRC). It shares with the later play (1961) a setting at the Hotel Costa Verde near Acapulco and scenes between Miss Jelkes and a male protagonist who, like the tethered creature of the title, is "helpless." The first draft of the story, however, is openly gay in design. An older and a younger writer reveal their sexual tension in caustic discussions of the prying Miss Jelkes and of "homolectuals" who must either turn "vicious" or "crack" (April 1946, HRC).

TW withheld a more provocative story from Wood entitled "Desire and the Black Masseur" (1948). He knew that this tale of a bi-racial sado-masochistic affair ending in cannibalism would have given her "fits!" (to Laughlin, April 23, 1946, Houghton).

TW's abrupt departure from New Orleans continued his perennial battle with

landlords, usually a result of such colorful guests as Oliver Evans, who had joined the ménage at 710 Orleans. For Evans's "amazingly frequent convenience" (qtd. in Windham, p. 184), TW placed a mattress on the floor.

Herbert Perlmutter asked many prominent Americans, including TW, to lobby Congress on behalf of a massive government program aimed at finding a cure for cancer.

TW last visited his family in March 1945, before *The Glass Menagerie* was transferred to New York.]

28. To Amado "Pancho" Rodriguez y Gonzalez

[53 Arundel Place
Clayton, Missouri]
[late-April 1946]
[TLS, 1 p. HRC]

Dear Pancho:

I am sorry I couldn't talk to you much on the phone. We have two phones, one upstairs and one down and Mother usually listens at the other phone. I was terrified that you would say something. She had already opened and read your telegram and they are full of conjecture and suspicion occasioned by that. It will be a little embarassing to tell them now that I am going to Taos. I should have warned you more about my home situation. But don't worry about it.

I wanted to ask you all kinds of things but had to cut the conversation as short as possible because of the eavesdropping. Why did you leave N.O. so suddenly? I hoped you would wait till I had finished my stay here - I have to stay here about a week - and then I might have picked you up somewhere on the road. It is unfortunate that you have to arrive there not knowing anybody. Though I am sure Spud will be nice to you. Had you met him in New Orleans? Oh, yes, in the Bourbon house. I've just gotten here and am not functioning mentally after the terrific grind on the road.

I will wire you some money tonight. Can't send much at the present as my funds were badly depleted by tire-purchases and unexpected costs on the road. Have to draw on my N.Y. bank this week. When that comes in can wire you some more. I wish you would write me immediately but please be extremely careful what you put in any communication addressed here. Make the letter very casual but tell me where you are staying in Taos, how

you like it - do you think you'll be happy there? Is there anything you can do? Staying with me you would not need much money but knowing you, I am afraid you will be restless without something in the way of an occupation. I shall be writing awfully hard during the days and there is not society of the sort in New Orleans - although I consider that to be an advantage.

However the important thing is that I shall see you very soon! I plan to leave here in exactly a week. It ought not to take me more than four days on the road, as I shall get the car in good condition while here. We can talk about everything when I arrive.

Stay out in the sun, rest, relax! Don't worry about anything. You may not like the desert at first but it will grow on you if you give it a chance. I hope you will look up Dorothy Brett and also Mrs. Lawrence if she is around Taos. Give them all my regards and particularly Spud. I am glad you have met him and I appreciate any help he's giving you - I'm sure you must have felt pretty lost when you first hit there.

Will you look around for a small (2 or three room) house, if any such thing is available around Taos. Spud might know. Mrs. Rendall mentioned some apartments in the Haworth foundation. Love -

Tennessee.

[A report that TW met Pancho Rodriguez (1921-1995) at Taos—presumably when he last visited the city in 1943—is not documented, nor is it supported by correspondence (see Spoto, pp. 121-122). TW later placed their meeting in New York in June 1946, discreetly removing the principals from New Orleans, where they probably met in late 1945 (see *Memoirs*, p. 99). Pancho's family roots were in southwest Texas (Eagle Pass) near the Mexican border.

By March 1946 TW found New Orleans and the "Mexican affair" a "bit miasmic" (qtd. in Windham, p. 184) and availed himself of travel once again. Probably sensing evasion, Pancho quit his job and preceded TW to Taos. His telegram and repeated calls for money raised suspicions at home and led TW to surmise that "the cat is all but out of the bag." Dakin, "home from India," was grinning "foxily" (qtd. in Windham, p. 188) at his brother's sexual proclivity.

TW met "Spud" Johnson, writer, publisher, and secretary to Mabel Dodge Luhan, and Dorothy Brett, painter and devotee of D.H. Lawrence, during his first visit to Taos in 1939. He and Brett became sympathetic friends after a meeting in her rented room, which was reached by an Indian ladder: "One day a young man came climbing up my ladder, he had been told to come and see me, I think about Lawrence. He said he wanted to be a playwrite, that he was determined to be one.

That he was called Tennessee Williams, the Tennessee a nickname given him at school because he came from Tennessee. He was so young and ambitious, and sure of himself. He certainly carried out his ambitions" (Brett, unpublished autobiography, n.d., Northwestern U).]

29. To the Williams Family

[Holy Cross Hospital
Taos, New Mexico]
May 23, 1946
[TLS, 2 pp. HTC]

Dear Folks:

I am leaving the hospital today and considering that I have had a major operation I am feeling remarkably well. I shall have to take it easy for about three weeks and am going up to Frieda Lawrence's place to rest and recuperate. I shall spend most of the time lying out-doors in a hammock.

The experiences since I left Saint Louis have been so unpleasant that I don't even like to write about them. I took sick the first day on the road, started having sharp pains. I was immediately afraid of appendicitis and [so] I called in a doctor that evening when I arrived at Springfield, Mo. He said it was just cramps from nervousness, so I went on the next day. Fortunately the bearings burnt-out which compelled me to stop in Alva, Okla. I saw another doctor who thought I had a kidney stone and advised me to take the train up to Wichita to see a specialist there, which I did. He put me in a hospital for a couple of days. I had X-rays and while nothing seemed to be revealed the doctor there diagnosed it as low-grade appendix but dismissed me from the hospital thinking an operation was not necessary. I had to leave the car as it would not be ready for several weeks, parts being difficult to replace. So I went on to Taos by bus, continuing to suffer. When I got here I had a fever and a blood-count of 18,000 which indicated a serious infection. The doctors here put me right in the hospital. The pains had suddenly stopped so they suspected the appendix had burst. Naturally I was quite alarmed at this news. They decided they had better operate immediately, and did that evening. According to the doctors (there were two of them) the appendicitis was a lucky accident, for when they made the incision they discovered another acute condition which might not otherwise have been suspected. Something called "Meccles diverticulum"

(phonetic spelling) which is attached to the small intestine was seriously infected and at the point of rupture which would have caused peritonitis. Had to be removed. Also appendix. I was on the table about two hours as they had to talk things over. They are very young doctors, the surgeon being just 31, and recently out of the army, but they seem to be quite modern and capable. They told me there was nothing malignant in the condition. I don't suppose they would tell me if it was, so I thought it might be a good idea for Dr. Alexander to call or write them for a fuller account of their findings. If it was anything more serious than they represented to me, it might be better for me to go to New York where the best treatment is available. Up till the day I left Saint Louis I had had no pain or sickness whatsoever, had been unusually well all winter in New Orleans, not a sign of any intestinal trouble and putting on weight. Well, life is full of surprises! I must have an excellent constitution for I was sitting up the second day after the operation and walking around the fifth. I feel a bit weak and shaky now but otherwise pretty good. Have started working again on my plays. Everyone here has been wonderful, I am never alone, my room is full of flowers. Mabel Dodge Luhan, the local social dictator, paid me a call, Frieda and Brett have called nearly every day and my Mexican friend Pancho has served as Secretary and kept me with books and a radio. The people around here are the kindest I have met, and the country is indescribably beautiful. Frieda's ranch is the nicest part of it!

Audrey writes that she has sold a couple of my stories, one to Madamoiselle for four hundred dollars, and one to Town & Country which is also one of the highest paying mags. I hope these will cover my sickness expenses. I should have had hospital insurance!

I hope you have not been worried. These things happen to all of us now and then and you have to take them philosophically.

I will write you again in a short time.

With love, Tom.

[TW was attended at Holy Cross Hospital by Drs. Albert Rosen and Ashley Pond. The aftermath of the operation (ca. May 15) was probably more complicated than the procedure itself, which the surgeon's widow, Myrtle Rosen, has described as "fairly simple." Legend has it that Pancho Rodriguez caused a post-operative row by scaling a balcony and making his way into TW's bed. The nuns who found them

together had "a fit," as Mrs. Rosen recalled with a grin. Polish nuns of the order of the Holy Family of Nazareth arrived in 1937 to staff the new hospital, unprepared as they were for ministry to TW.

TW planned to convalesce at Kiowa Ranch, the "place" in the mountains where Frieda Lawrence and her husband had briefly lived in the 1920s. TW thought it "the dreamiest spot on earth" and hoped that D.H. Lawrence's lingering "spirit" would "animate" (to Wood, n.d., HRC) his own. The ascent on May 23 was marked by liberal toasting of wine, sudden "breathlessness," and a "wild" return to the hospital with Frieda driving her car like "a firetruck" (*Memoirs*, p. 104). Her friendship with TW led to the present invitation, as it had to her support for earlier literary projects related to Lawrence.

On June 2 TW wired Audrey Wood from Albuquerque that he and Pancho were "driving East" (June 2, 1946, HRC) and planned to spend the summer at Woodstock, New York, with Oliver Evans. Neither health related fears nor an early departure from Taos had deterred TW from preparing "a revised and abridged version of 'Camino Real'" (to Wood, n.d., HRC).]

Tennessee Williams and Pancho Rodriquez, New Orleans: "My Mexican friend Pancho."

30. To Audrey Wood

[31 Pine Street
Nantucket, Massachusetts]
[June 1946]
[TLS, 2 pp. HRC]

Dear Audrey:

I meant to see you again before I left New York but the visit there tired me so I wasn't fit to see anyone. I decided on Nantucket and here I am. Have engaged a little house for the season. Pancho is with me, doing the cooking and housework while I resume work on a play. I detest the "Olde Antique Shoppe" atmosphere of the island and the old ladies on it, but the swimming is good and I shall make every effort to tie myself down. Perhaps I am all right now, as the doctors tell me, but I feel very unsettled inside, as if hung together by a few loose strings, so I want to get as much work done as quickly as I can.

I don't believe I told you about my car. It is still at the Ford garage in Alva, Okla. The owner of the garage was a perfect bastard about it. He wired me to call for it but when we arrived in Alva it still wasn't ready. We hung around that horrid place for a week waiting for it. It had been there for over a month. But they kept stalling and finally told me that one of the new parts, something called an "insert", didn't fit and it would take ten more days to get a new one. Then I said I would have to leave the car as I couldn't wait around any longer. The manager was extremely snotty. Said he would just stop work entirely on the car if I left town. Now I have about a thousand dollars invested in the car - the motor having been almost completely rebuilt - so I don't want to throw it away. I wonder if Eddie Cohen could not write the man, assuring him that I will pay for the repairs if and when completed and that I have a friend who will call for the car and drive it East for me. (Jane Lawrence's husband, Tony, has offered to do this.) In any case, I don't think it is legal for the garage owner to refuse to complete a job and thus make it impossible to remove a car that he has agreed to repair. I don't know what legal action could be taken if he persists in that attitude, but since he is agent for the Ford Motor company, perhaps some pressure could be exerted through the Detroit headquarters. The car is a '37 Packard convertible - the bearings had burnt out and the bill for labor and replacements (which I have not yet paid but will when work is

completed) was $137.85. There were two people in Alva interested in buying the car if the repairs were completed. And I would like to have it myself. Could Eddie do anything about this? Garage owner is Mr. Davis, Ford Garage Alva, Oklahoma. - Sorry to worry you with it.

I saw Wycherly. All but first three scenes - I got in a bit late. I thought she was doing a reasonably good job but it seemed just a substitution. She does not have Taylor's humor. That was the big deficiency. And Taylor's little insertions which only she could put over sounded pretty incongrous coming from Wycherly. I don't think she is really right for the part. Hope you'll find someone better, if a road company is organized. Of course this opinion is only based on her performance in the last three scenes the night I was there.

I wish Taylor and Wycherly both would get a certain line right: It's the one about Tom taking a service-car home from the office. Taylor and Wycherly both say "Station-wagon" which is of course fantastic! The wonderful thing about Taylor is that she can get away with anything, even that!

I didn't see her or call her - or Dowling either - while I was in New York, so perhaps it is better not to let either know I was there.

My address here is 31 Pine Street, Nantucket, Mass.

With love, 10.

[A fragment of TW's journal, apparently the first preserved entry since late 1943, records a depressing trip to Alva, Oklahoma, to reclaim the Packard, abandoned a month earlier and still not repaired. "Been here three days with Pancho - we have both descended into a nearly speechless gloom and apathy. . . . I wonder how much more I can take. If the operation had not knocked me out nervously I would bear up better. As it is I'm a quivering mass of anxieties" (June 5, 1946). TW later confirmed the decisive effect of his illness: it had made a "zombie" of him, "a man infected with creeping death," who "felt himself excused from emotional participation with anything but the people he could create in his work" (qtd. in Windham, pp. 298-299).

TW and Pancho visited New York before settling on Nantucket Island, rather than Woodstock, for the remainder of the summer. On June 24 TW approved a request from Gilmor Brown that *Stairs to the Roof* (1945) be restaged at the Pasadena Playhouse in 1947. He also wanted Brown, the supervising director, "to see" *Camino Real* after he had "brooded over it a while longer" (June 24, 1946, Huntington). TW probably resumed work on *Summer and Smoke*.

Margaret Wycherly replaced Laurette Taylor during her vacation in June.

Transfer of *The Glass Menagerie* to a new theatre and a cut in the top from $4.20 to $3.60 were planned to coincide with Taylor's return to the cast on July 1—in hopes of reversing a decline in business.

The anachronism cited by TW occurs in Scene Six of *The Glass Menagerie*, where Amanda says to Laura, "I gave your brother a little extra change so he and Mr. O'Connor could take the service car home." A former resident of St. Louis has described the service car as "a cross between the streetcar and a taxi. It made regular stops, cost a quarter (more than streetcar fare), and reached a destination quicker and perhaps more safely."

Penned in the upper margin of page 1 is a probable filing date of July 1946. A retyped excerpt (paragraph #2) held by the HRC bears a reception date of June 24, 1946, indicating that the letter was probably written in the week of June 16.]

31. To Frieda Lawrence

31 Pine St.
Nantucket Mass!
June 25, 1946.
[TLS, 1 p. HRC]

Dear Frieda:

We have finally come to rest, after weeks of exhausting travel, here on Nantucket Island. It is nothing like as nice as Taos and Pancho and I both are sad about being unable to stay there. It would have been heavenly. I am a bit disgusted with myself for the cowardly retreat, for after all it would be better to die at a place like your ranch than to live on Nantucket Island. Everything here is very Antique Shoppe in atmosphere, full of aggresive propriety. We went to a tea-party yesterday that cured me of all such social occasions. The old ladies and gentlemen all sat around in a circle and stared at me and Pancho till I became so nervous that my tea-cup rattled like castanets. Fortunately the swimming is good. That is the only good thing. I spend half the day writing, furiously to make up for lost time, and the rest on the beach. And I am still full of uneasiness and apprehension of a vague, continual sort. I am afraid those doctors and nervous nuns must have cut out a large piece of my guts! How I would like to talk to you and Lawrence for an evening in front of the ranch stove. (When I talked to you I always seemed to be talking to Lawrence also.)

Do you know our car is still in Oklahoma? They kept us waiting

around in that awful dust-bowl town for a week while they fooled around, doing practically nothing. Then told us some of the new parts didn't fit and we'd have to wait another ten days. So we gave up and left the car there and came East by train. It is still there and I don't think they have any intention of repairing it. Horrible people!

Thank you so much for sending the book I left there. We have the picture of you and the cartoon of Lawrence on the mantal of our little house here which we have taken for the season. Did I tell you that I have acquired an original letter of Lawrence's? Thornton Wilder presented it to me last fall at the Boston opening of You Touched Me. It was nicely mounted by Wilder and inscribed underneath. Wilder was crazy about "Y.T.M." - saw it three times. He is here on Nantucket but I haven't seen him yet as his mother is very sick right now.

Pancho is cooking and getting better at it all the time. I am writing. That seems to be the whole story.

Please give Brett our affectionate greetings, and the same to the Vanderbilts and Mrs. Luhan and Spud. And Angelino!

With God's permission a reverdici!

Ever, Tennessee.

[Vivid and endearing memories of Frieda Lawrence (1879-1956) date from TW's first visit to Taos in 1939, when she befriended the young writer and approved his plan to write a play about her husband's life in New Mexico. During a second visit in 1943, TW described Frieda to James Laughlin as a lusty "Valkyrie," the "only exciting woman I've known!"

Mabel Dodge Luhan, patron of artists and writers, urged the Lawrences to settle at Taos in the early 1920s. Contrary to reports, the present meeting with Luhan was TW's first.

"Angelino" is Frieda's companion, Angelo Ravagli, an officer whom she met in Italy in 1925 and married many years later.

The address and date of this letter appear to be in Pancho Rodriquez's hand.]

32. To James "Jay" Laughlin

[31 Pine Street
Nantucket, Massachusetts]
[mid-July 1946]
[TLS w/ enclosures, 2 pp. Houghton]

Dear Jay:

It is good to know that you still think of me. I have been having a bad time of it and have felt dissociated from almost everything else. The physical machine in a state of collapse and what may politely be called the spiritual element, crouching in the corner with both hands clapped to its eyes.

I was on my way to New Mexico in an ancient Packard convertible which I bought in New Orleans when I took suddenly and without any warning quite ill. Had to have an emergency operation in Taos, performed by an almost amateur doctor and some nervous Nuns. They thought it was acute appendix but it turned out to be an acute 'Meccles diverticulum' which they say is a section of the small intestine. It was cut out and I have been in a prolonged state of shock ever since. The day after the operation one of the good Sisters of the Holy Cross came into my room and advised me to make my peace with the Lord as whatever improvement I showed would only be temporary. Ever since then, and despite the assurances of the doctors, I have been expecting to die, which is something I have never really looked forward to at all. So I gave up my plan of remaining in Taos for the summer and rushed East and took a house on Nantucket - and tried to forget my apprehensions in hard work on a long play. But it is not so easy. I had x-ray pictures taken last week which they told me did not show anything wrong but even if this is quite true, I will probably remain in a state of morbid alertness for a long time. Consequence of having nerves! - "Oh, for a robust conscience and the Viking spirit in life!"

I am interested to hear you are going to Europe. I am planning (if I don't die!) to go to Spain next year. And Constantinople, Greece, and Russia. My Mexican friend, Pancho, is still with me and wants to go to Europe, too. Perhaps we can make a party of it.

I got the typed story. The Masseur does not eat the bones. It is clearly stated that he puts them in a sack which he drops in the lake at the end of the car-line. So the story is all right on the realistic level.

I am sending two more. Have the "Saint" one typed for me, it's the

original only copy. The long one gets a bit too preachy toward the end as I started thinking of it as a one-act or two-act play. It would be good theatre if one could get it produced, I think.

Audrey read this long one and showed it to my kid brother, just out of the CBI air-force, when he visited New York while I was out West. She asked him if she ought to show it to anybody and he said 'Yes'. But right afterwards wrote me a letter saying I was going to come to an end like Edgar Allan Poe, if not worse. On the whole, a sympathetic letter, however. He is a bright kid, though not at all like me. Has a law-degree. I want him to practise law in New York so he could take a hand in my affairs (theatrical). I think they have been bungled. "The Menagerie" has not been sold to the movies and it is slowly dying at the box-office - should have been sold in the very beginning when it was hot! But I am kept in the dark about such matters and never really know how things stand. Not even what I have in the bank!

Have you read Carson McCuller's new book? I think it's superb.

Ever, Tenn.

P.S. I wrote this some time ago. Just discovered I hadn't mailed it. Damned gloomy letter! Ought to tear it up as I am feeling more cheerful now. Carson McCullers is here, visiting me as the result of a brief correspondance. The minute I met her she seemed like one of my oldest and best friends! We are planning to collaborate on a dramatization of her last book soon as I get my present play finished. I think this play will be last effort to write for Broadway. From now on I shall write for a nonexistant art-theatre.

I am enclosing the two 'myths' which belong with the one about the 'Masseur'. Will you have these typed for me, as you did with the other? Either send me a bill for them or deduct the typing cost from royalties. And send me copies. I read them to Carson and she seemed very pleased with them. - Tell Lowry I think his story in ND #9 is magnificent!

[TW spent the week of July 7 in New York hoping to relieve a mind "full of hypochondriacal anxieties." He informed his mother that Elizabeth Curtis, a wealthy socialite whom he met through Oliver Evans, had provided lodging "just off Park avenue" and made the "arrangements" (n.d., HTC) for his medical testing.

Apropos of "morbid alertness" and "nerves," TW quotes a favorite passage from *The Master Builder* (Ibsen, 1892): "Oh, for a robust conscience and the Viking spirit in life!" (Act Three).

Stories cited by TW are "Desire and the Black Masseur," which James Laughlin has apparently misconstrued, and two other recent works, "Chronicle of a Demise" (1948) and "The Night of the Iguana." At least seven "quality" magazines would reject "Iguana" before it first appeared in TW's collection, *One Arm* (1948).

TW wrote this letter in the week of July 14, while the postscript was written, and the letter presumably mailed, later in the month—after Carson McCullers had reached Nantucket. Accounts which place her on the island before mid-July are not confirmed by TW's summer correspondence or itinerary. McCullers's "new book," *The Member of the Wedding*, was published on March 19, 1946, and was generally well received. TW read and admired her first novel, *The Heart Is a Lonely Hunter*, when it was published in 1940.

The "'myths'" probably belong to an unpublished gathering of stories entitled "Three Myths and A Malediction" (n.d., HRC). Listed on the title page are "Blue Roses and the Polar Star," "Desire and the Black Masseur," "The Myth," and "The Malediction" (1945)—a forerunner of *One Arm*.

Robert Lowry's story "Layover in El Paso" (*New Directions Nine*, 1946) concerns a young soldier on leave who forsakes visiting his family to court an aging floozy whom he meets on the train. The story may have reminded TW of his own "layover" in El Paso, where he was stranded in 1939 amid "choking" dust and "sterile" mountain scenery.]

33. To Katharine "Kit" Cornell

[31 Pine Street
Nantucket, Massachusetts]
July 31, 1946.
[TLS, 1 p. HRC]

Dear Kit:

Forgive me for not answering your wire sooner. I have been in a quandary about the play. Almost immediately after I wrote you about it, I really read it through for the first time and as always happens at a first reading, I was profoundly depressed to find it was so different from what I thought I was writing. My impulse was to throw it into the ocean, but instead I went back to work on it. I conceived a new ending, much lighter than the one before and yet not at all violating the play's quality. However

it made a lot of the earlier material unsuitable and reduced the play's length to about 60 pages. Out of eight scenes there are now about four that are reasonably readable. I will bring it over to Martha's Vineyard and read you, or let you read, as much as I dare, however embarassing it may be to us both.

Right now Carson McCullers - you probably know of her novels - is visiting me here in Nantucket. She is planning to dramatize her wonderful book, "The Member of the Wedding", and we are sort of working together. I advising her, and she me.

She'll be leaving here in about a week. She is terrified of journeys and I may accompany her to the mainland and I thought perhaps we could stop off at Martha's Vineyard and spend an evening with you, at which time you could look at what I've done on the play. "Portrait With A Parasol". That's the new title. The heroine carries a yellow silk parasol. Eventually it should be good, but you must not expect anything now.

You will love Carson! Probably the sweetest person in the literary world! I felt immediately that you should know each other.

Ever, Tennessee.

[TW assured "Kit" Cornell (1893-1974) that he was "feverishly" writing a play for her and would send a copy "in a week or two." The "plot is slight," he added: "A Mississippi spinster tells the story of her luckless romance with 'the wild boy of the town.'" The present ending apparently replaced a "tragic" conclusion in which Alma's suicide was relieved by a "fantasy" (to Cornell, July 10, 1946, HRC) of life everlasting in a good-time house. This early draft stage of *Summer and Smoke* appears to exist only in fragmentary scenes and passages of dialogue.

TW mentioned to Paul Bigelow his delight in reading *The Member of the Wedding*, only to discover—or recall—that Bigelow's friend, Jordan Massee, was Carson McCullers's third cousin. TW presumably used this contact to invite McCullers to visit Nantucket, where she worked on a dramatic version of her novel, and he continued to revise *Summer and Smoke*. To Audrey Wood he described McCullers as "a strange girl" with "a phobia that she is going to faint in public and be put in jail!" ({July 29, 1946} HRC). She planned to leave the island in early-August, after a visit of nearly three weeks. (TW's letter to Wood is misdated August 29, 1946; the editors have assigned a date of composition one month earlier.)

Virginia Spencer Carr, McCullers's biographer, remarks that a tipsy Carson introduced herself to Miss Cornell by asking for a sanitary napkin.]

34. To Amado "Pancho" Rodriguez y Gonzalez

[31 Pine Street
Nantucket, Massachusetts]
[July/August 1946]
[TLS, 1 p. HRC]

Dear Pancho:

Perhaps I have not made certain things clear to you, and just in that case I will put them down in black and white.

1. As you ought to know, I have no one else in my emotional life and have no desire for anyone else.

2. I have never thought of you as being employed by me. That is all an invention of your own. If we were man and woman, it would be very clear and simple, we would be married and simply sharing our lives and whatever we have with each other. That is what I had thought we were actually doing. When I say 'Pancho is doing the cooking and house-work' I am only saying that Pancho is being kind enough to help me, and know-ing me as you do, you should realize that that is the only way in which I could possibly mean it.

3. This is a dark, uncertain period that we are passing through and a time when we ought to stand beside each other with faith and courage and the belief that we have the power in us to come back out in the light.

4. I love you as I have never loved anyone else in my life.

5. You are not only my love but also my luck. For 3 months I have lived in a dark world of anxiety, inexpressible even to you, which has made me seem different - You may not have guessed this, but you are about the only thing that has kept me above the water.

10.

[Pancho Rodriguez kept house for TW and Carson McCullers, but by late-July he was in "a mysterious Mexican rage" and had "packed his trunk" (to Wood, {July 29, 1946} HRC) to leave the island—resentful, TW surmised, of his and Carson's friendship and his own subservient role. Pancho remained on Nantucket, reconciled perhaps by TW's appeal.]

35. *To Audrey Wood*

31 Pine Street,
Nantucket. [Massachusetts]
August 29, 1946.
[TLS w/ autograph postscript, 1 p. HRC]

Dear Audrey:

I had gone down to W.U. to wire you to hold the scripts for revision when they handed me your wire. I think you are probably right about with-olding them for a while. I made the mistake of promising them too early to Cornell and I hated to let her down as she seemed so eager to get an idea of what I was doing. Also I've felt so insecure about the play that I needed strongly someone else's interest and advice. Sometimes the solitary struggle of writing is almost too solitary for endurance! I am sure I would work better and easier if I could feel more casually about it but I get so tied up in the things emotionally that it hinders me. I hope that you were able to feel in the play a sort of Gothic quality - spiritually romantic - which I wanted to create. It is hard for you to use such stuff in a modern play for a modern audience, but I feel it is valid. But requires awfully careful treatment. It would be infinitely easier to do it on the screen. I am going to send you the silent film sequences which I think should accompany the script whether or not they are to be incorporated in a stage production. Incidentally, if you could interest a movie producer in the play as a screen story I would be eager to work on a screen adaptation of it prior to a stage production. (If a stage production isn't possible now). I also hope you will feel that it might be practicable to actually combine the silent film sequences (perhaps 16 MM.) with the stage scenes. I will send you at the same time a rewrite of Scene V, which is the most incomplete scene in the script you now have. The best place I can think of for an entirely additional scene is between scenes three and four - leading up to Alma's first visit to John's office. Of course if the film sequences are admissible, no more material will be necessary as they round out the story quite completely. - Of course Cornell is not the only ultimate possibility. If it is worked out well enough it might be a vehicle for a star team like Hepburn and Tracy.

I dread making another trip - it takes all day to get from here to New York except by air, and I don't think I can afford air-travel under the present indefinite circumstances. However I will wire you or call you about the

Pittsburgh trip a few days in advance. - Will you please ask Eddie Colton to send my brother (Officer's Mail Section, Lowry Field, Denver) all the titles, Etc. that I sent him for my Packard? Dakin is going to take possession of the car. - With love.

Tennessee

P.S. Please mail me a copy of typed script.

[TW's "solitary struggle" produced the "first reading version" of *Summer and Smoke*. The epigraph from Rilke—"Who, if I were to cry out, would hear me among the angelic orders?"—bespeaks the frustration of Alma Winemiller, a young woman who has been placed in the conservative culture of the Delta and tempted by the sexual freedom afforded to the men whom she knows. The "Gothic quality" to which TW refers is conveyed by the Episcopal manse, Alma's spiritual setting, which reinforces both her moral idealism and cloistered condition. A stone fountain in the form of an angel, one of four staging areas, marks the perennial conflict of spirit and flesh. "Her name," Alma explains, "is Eternity and her body is stone and her blood is - mineral water . . ." ("Summer and Smoke," August 1946, HRC).

A typical film sequence begins with "Alma lying sleepless in bed," dissolves to the notorious Moon Lake Casino, and ends with her "knocking" ("Silent Screen Interludes," n.d., HRC) on the door of John Richardson's (later Buchanan) office. Audrey Wood claimed that she was open to the use of "motion picture techniques" (to TW, September 6, 1946, HRC) in *Summer and Smoke* and awaited further information. TW later described his plan to use "stage and screen in combo" as a "lunatic notion."

The closing of *The Glass Menagerie* (August 3, 1946) and the delayed sale of film rights made TW's finances seem "indefinite." TW confided to Edwina that "the play could have run another year if Laurette and Dowling had stayed on good terms and the show had been properly managed" (n.d., HRC). Taylor's declining health, seemingly overlooked by TW, may have hastened the play's closing after 561 performances.

The tour of *The Glass Menagerie* was set to open in Pittsburgh on September 2, 1946, with Pauline Lord playing Amanda and Eddie Dowling directing the new company. None of the original players entered the cast.]

36. To Katharine "Kit" Cornell

31 Pine Street
Nantucket [Massachusetts]
September 5, 1946
[TLS, 1 p. HRC]

Dear Kit:

I haven't known what to say to you about the play so I have put off writing. I took it into New York to have it typed up about two weeks ago. I had the copies delivered to Audrey as she naturally insists on reading my work first. Then I received, after returning to the island, a long wire from her in which she said she thought it would be unwise to show it in the present form. She thought you and Guthrie might be "sufficiently disappointed to make other plans". To tell you the truth, this only confirmed my own feeling, or suspicion. I felt terribly insecure about it, as you probably understood when I visited you. I don't think Audrey is altogether gloomy about it. At least she said it "had many things to recommend it" but needed a good deal of building. The typed manuscript turned out to be only about 80 pages. It would have been full length if I had not scrapped two original ideas, one being narration and the other silent film sequences. I still think the silent film sequences was a good idea, if at all practicable. Some of the best material in the story could only be shown on the screen. And I think the combination of screen and stage has an exciting value as something new in the American theatre. (It has been tried in Europe). I will include the film sequences in the next typed version. (As something tentative).

I'm leaving the island about Sept. 15th and I hope by that time Audrey may feel that I have done enough to show you. It is a hard play to write and of course the important thing for all concerned (if any beside myself) is to do the best possible job regardless of time. If it takes unreasonably long, I naturally won't expect you to wait for it but I'll do all I can to urge it along rapidly. Illness and anxiety were a great impediment in the early stages.

I visited Carson McCullers in Nyack to see how she was coming along with her dramatization. That is taking longer than expected, too. It's her first attempt at theatre and it's a bit hard for her to think in theatrical terms. She has the delicate novelist's suspicion of dramatic effects. Meeting you was good for her. Made a deep impression and greatly increased her respect for theatre.

With love and best wishes, Tennessee

["Narration" and "film sequences" were attractive devices for a playwright who struggled with exposition, as did TW. Alma's opening lines in an early draft of *Summer and Smoke*—"I was twenty-nine the summer that I met him, and I felt this to be the last summer of my youth" ("The Water Is Cool," n.d., HRC)—are sharply reminiscent of Tom's prologue in *The Glass Menagerie*.

TW's interest in "film sequences" recalls a similar plan to use "magic-lantern slides" in *The Glass Menagerie*. Both projects reveal a playwright's fascination with film, perhaps stimulated by TW's early relation with the director Erwin Piscator, who often used documentary footage (and narrators) to historicize his "epic theatre."

TW visited Carson McCullers in late-August, when he returned to New York to deliver the latest draft of *Summer and Smoke*.]

37. *To Walter Edwin Dakin*

SH: Nantucket Island, Massachusetts
Sept. 9, 1946
[TLS, 2 pp. HRC]

Dear Grandfather:

I just now heard through Audrey that you had been ill. Mother hadn't mentioned it to me. In fact I haven't heard from her in about a month and I haven't known exactly where you were, although I knew it was in Ohio. I have wanted to write to you all summer but have been uncertain of the address. I hope you realize that I have been thinking of you and am very unhappy over the fact we couldn't be together somewhere. As you know I was very sick last Spring and for quite a while after the operation. I just had to throw myself down on the beach here for a couple of months and forget everything else. I got so behind with my work that when I was able to resume it I had to devote myself to it all the time, trying to finish a long play for Katharine Cornell in time for her to read it and make her plans for the Fall. It still isn't finished and she hasn't seen it yet but the worst is over. It has a Mississippi delta background like most of my other plays. I shall really have to go back South pretty soon and renew my acquaintance with some of our old home-towns such as Columbus if I am going to continue to write about them. Do you remember Marion Wise who lived near us in Columbus and played with Rose? He was here in Nantucket this summer and we met each other. Of course I didn't remember him but he did me. He is living in New York and has an excellent job with an advertising firm. If I return South this Fall or winter, as I am planning to do, I hope I can spend

a little while in Columbus. It would probably help me to add some authentic background to the new play.

Audrey says you are better now. I know how you love to be up and around but you must take your time about it. I suspect that you have not paid enough deference to your years and have tried to go out too much in society this summer.

The road company of "The Glass Menagerie" has opened in Pittsburgh and got very good notices. Audrey went over to see it. She reported the road company to be quite good so the royalty checks will start rolling in again I trust.

I am going back to New York city the sixteenth of this month. It is difficult for me to work there so I probably won't remain more than a week. Then will return somewhere in the South to finish up the new play. Let me know if there is anything I can do for you. And take the best care of yourself!

                                        With much love, Tom

[Edwina and Audrey Wood apparently conspired to shield TW from news that his grandfather had suffered a "severe heart attack" at the Friends Boarding Home in Waynesville, Ohio. "He is much better now," Wood later informed TW, explaining that just as Edwina was preparing to go to her father, she received a letter "saying, 'Don't come. Will send for you when I need you'" (September 6, 1946, HRC). The Friends Home in Waynesville—Walter Dakin's birthplace—was founded by local Quakers to provide "rooms for the elderly, retired teachers, and transients."

Wood saw *The Glass Menagerie* in Pittsburgh and reported that Pauline Lord "will be quite good when she finally has conquered the part," although "she will never be as good as Taylor" (to TW, September 6, 1946, HRC). The part of Tom (Richard Jones) was well played, she thought, but the Gentleman Caller (Edward Andrews) and Laura (Jeanne Shepherd) were disappointing. Nonetheless the Pittsburgh critics wrote of the play's "soaring beauty" and business was good.]

38. *To Audrey Wood*
                              SH: Nantucket Island, Massachusetts
                                              [ca. September 9, 1946]
                                              [TLS, 2 pp. HRC]

Dear Audrey:

Thank you for your long and helpful letter. I am sorry I couldn't get to Pittsburgh. I had hoped to but my digestion got out of order again. I

haven't been able to eat a regular meal in about a week. I am disgusted with myself thoroughly, and thoroughly baffled, for it is not like me to be so pusillanimous. This play is something I should
be able to handle with perfect ease for it is the sort of material I've always handled best but either nervous or physical fatigue is making it absurdly difficult for me. I have been making some progress on a second draft but the real flowering must wait for a better psychological period than I am in at the moment or simply till I am feeling a bit better.

Carson phoned me that she is coming up here tomorrow with her husband, bringing the finished first draft of her dramatization. I suspect it will need a good deal more work, too. Her theatrical eye is not yet fully developed, of course. I'll suggest that she have you read what she's done.

The fiction editor of the New Yorker, William Maxwell, was on the island and wrote me a note. I asked him over - he says they'd be happy to use some of my short stories if I have any suitable. You or Laughlin may have something, though I can't think what it would be. Laughlin is talking about bringing out a book of them, perhaps privately, at $5 a copy.

Pancho and I are leaving the Island the 16th or 17th, and I will be in New York for a few days before continuing South. If you happen to know of procurable hotel space (a double room) I wish you'd reserve it for the night of the 16th. The Lawrences are getting thrown out of their apartment - Squatters rights don't work in the U.S.A. - so we can't stay with them.

The International outlook is becoming quite fearful. Don't you think there ought to be an organized movement in the Theatre to insist upon a clarification of U.S. foreign policy? It appears to me that Byrnes and the administration have formulated a policy of their own in line with the most reactionary elements in the country and they are taking the shortest cut to world destruction through their inflammatory meddling in Europe. This is without the understanding or sanction of the vast body of Americans who, like everybody else, will go down the drain if we're drawn into war with Russia. I think there ought to be popular demonstrations of all kinds in protest against it. The theatre could start such a program.

The news of Grandfather's illness is horribly upsetting. I wired mother and she answered that he was much improved and I have written him. The human situation - God!

With love, Tenn

[Audrey Wood's "helpful letter" bore advice but no statement of enthusiasm for *Summer and Smoke*. Wood suggested that TW expand the roles of Alma's mother and aunt and that he treat small-town rituals of courtship and marriage with greater authenticity. The death of John Richardson's father revealed a more serious and finally intractable flaw. The climactic event not only lacked detail but its redemptive effect upon the son, whom Alma silently loves, had been stated rather than dramatized: "There is no indication what happens to father except Alma's speech, 'Your father's dying in order for you to redeem yourself' etc." (September 6, 1946, HRC).

The New Yorker published only one story by TW: "Three Players of a Summer Game" (1952).

One Arm and Other Stories, the collection planned by James Laughlin, would require a limited edition as well as selective distribution and review. "Tenn's Broadway reputation should not be compromised" (September 5, 1946, Houghton), Laughlin assured Wood, in earlier remarks meant to disarm her.

Discussion of Cold War politics may have been provoked by *Time* magazine, where TW often found his news. The report that Secretary of State Byrnes had made "the great American decision" (September 9, 1946) to keep Germany from entering the Soviet Union is perhaps the "inflammatory meddling" to which TW refers.

This letter bears an incomplete reception date of "9/ /46."]

39. To Guthrie McClintic

[New York]
[September 1946]
[TLS, 1 p. HRC]

Dear Guthrie:

I can't tell you what it means to me to have the continuing interest of yourself and Kit in the play that I have promised and delayed so often. The trouble is entirely in myself: it is ailing because I am. It is the sort of material that I use best but there is simply a lack of physical energy, which with me is creative energy, to get it over the hurdles except by slow stages. Progress is being made, though. I hope that Audrey will agree that enough has been done to show you before I leave town. I am going South, at my doctor's advice. He says the rat-race of New York is too much for me. I had gotten so I simply could not eat anything. After a few days in the hospital that condition has passed but I must be careful to avoid a recurrence.

My love to both you and Kit, and be assured of my best efforts to make you a play.

Ever, Tennessee

["Am I dying?" TW wrote, as he prepared to leave Nantucket by ferry on September 14. By noon he felt "a bit better" and described his progress to the mainland: "I have a little private state room, procured from a kind lady by Pancho. I do not think much. Brain really seems sort of anesthetized. Carson is with me {McCullers had returned to Nantucket for a brief second visit} and she has been an angel. Though I have only really felt like seeing Pancho. He has not been an angel . . . but I think we love one another" (*Journal*, September 14, 1946).

An undated journal entry reveals the cause of TW's persistent illness: "Today I have entered St. Luke's hospital for purgation of a tape worm. A rugged ordeal tomorrow salts and medicines all day." Donald Windham found TW "regally withdrawn" when he visited St. Luke's and concluded that their "lives had gone different directions" (Windham, p. 192).

TW was hospitalized in the week of September 15, 1946. Precisely when he was released and left with Pancho for New Orleans is unclear.]

40. To Audrey Wood

[632 ½ St. Peter Street
New Orleans, Louisiana]
[early-October 1946]
[TLS, 2 pp. HRC]

Dear Audrey:

I am very well situated here in a furnished apartment on the nicest street in the Quarter, only $75. a month. It has a huge front room with a grand piano and furniture that belongs to an antique dealer!

I have been feeling well since I got here and Miss Alma is making progress. In fact I now think the play may run over the usual playing length. I am developing several new ideas which means more time but the result will be worth it. For one thing I am building up Mrs. Winemiller, as you suggested. I have a new comedy idea. Her sister Albertine eloped with a fraudulent promotor, a man who built something called a Mechanical Museum and got all the Winemillers friends to invest in it. It was a collection of mechanical marvels and "a big snake", sort of a side-show that travelled about the country. Albertine was deserted and died, Mr. Forsythe

the promoter, landed in jail. At every opportunity Mrs. Winemiller, who is obsessed with clearing her sister's and Mr. Forsythe's name of connection with the scandal, refers to the Musee Mecanique and describes the marvels as if it were still going on under prosperous circumstances. Perhaps if it is built up sufficiently it would make a part for Laurette! - Tell Guthrie that I am expanding the play in this way and ask him to be patient about it.

I received a heart-breaking letter from Grandfather. He is just waiting to die in that Quaker home in Ohio! Speaks of it with resignation and beautiful courage but I can't think of it without wanting to bat my head against a brick wall. I am going to send him a checque. Of course there is nothing that money or anything else could do. It seems such a pity he had to wait for it, that it couldn't just have come quietly, without any warning as nobody who ever lived deserved an easy way out as much as he does!

Pancho returned here with me and is resuming his old job at the best department store.

I hope MGM offers a good price for the one-act. I had never thought of expanding it and don't think I ever would. But I think we should retain the right to produce it in its present form in a program of one-acts.

With love, Tennessee.

I hope you have sent "The Angel in the Alcove" to the typist. A copy should go to Laughlin. Carson says that she thinks <u>Madamoiselle</u> would take it. I am sending you another little story I found in the Bigelow box - to be typed up.

[Once settled in the Quarter, TW reverted to old rites of authorship: "I would rise early, have my black coffee and go straight to work" (*Memoirs*, p. 109). Further revision produced a second draft of *Summer and Smoke* dated November 1946 and entitled "A Chart of Anatomy" (HRC). The variant title refers to a "lecture" in Scene Eleven in which young Dr. John Buchanan affirms only the appetites and the finality of death and corruption.

TW developed Mrs. Winemiller in relation to her sister Albertine and the whimsical "Musee Mecanique." Mrs. Winemiller's "breakdown," a consequence of her sister's death "in a good-time house" in New Orleans, created a burden of care for Alma and her clerical father as well as the town's polite disapproval. TW no doubt saw and perhaps visited the Musée Méchanique which operated at 523

Royal Street during his visit to New Orleans in early 1939. Kenneth Holditch has identified the curious landmark and noted that it was moved to San Francisco for the Golden Gate Exposition, which TW visited in July 1939.

MGM's interest in "This Property is Condemned" (1941) led Audrey Wood to set film rights at "fifty thousand dollars" and to add deceptively that TW "had always considered possibility making three act play" (telegram, to Freed, October 12, 1946, HRC).

Rejected by *Mademoiselle* and *Town and Country*, "The Angel in the Alcove" first appeared in *One Arm and Other Stories* in 1948. The "Angel" refers to TW's maternal grandmother, Rosina Otte Dakin ("Grand"), whose ghostly figure casts "a gentle, unquestioning look" upon her grandson's sexual difference. TW later wrote that "'Grand' was all that we knew of God in our lives!" ("Grand," 1964).

This letter, which is written on stationery of the Shelton Hotel in New York, bears a reception date of October 8, 1946.]

41. To Walter Edwin Dakin

632½ St. Peter Street
New Orleans, La.
PM: New Orleans, October 10, 1946
[TLS, 2 pp. HTC]

Dear Grandfather:

I have returned to my winter quarters in New Orleans and was lucky enough to get an apartment almost as soon as I arrived, a very lovely one, furnished by an antique dealer with his own things. A huge living room with four double windows, the size of two large rooms. Two bedrooms, one of which I am using for a study, a kitchen and a bath with automatic heater. I was planning to stay in New York for a while but it is so crowded there that it was not possible for anybody to get me even a hotel room for more than one night. I was sick when I arrived in New York, so I went straight into the hospital and stayed there till I could get space on a plane to New Orleans. I had been over-working and it had affected my stomach. I couldn't eat anything solid for about a week. That condition has now cleared up and I am feeling well again. I am still working on the play for Miss Cornell. Have been working on it for about a year now and it is just getting into shape. But I still haven't shown it to her. I wanted it to be as good as possible before she sees it. I think it will eventually be an excellent play for her. Or somebody else.

I am glad that you are taking a calm and philosophical attitude toward your present illness. That always helps you to recover. I have had heart-trouble for ten years now and I am not afraid of it anymore. By the calendar I am somewhat younger than you, but only by the calendar which is an unimportant thing. You are one of the youngest people I have ever known, and incidentally one of the two people I have most loved and admired in this world. You know who the other one was and still is.

The Menagerie seems to be doing well on the road. It made over $24,000. one week in Saint Louis. So Mother and I are getting our royalty checks again. I am enclosing a check for you in case there is a little extra something you may want or need. When you are able to come South I want you to remember that I have a room for you here and that I would love having you with me for the winter.

All of the seasons debutantes are coming to my apartment a week from this Saturday. One of them is the niece of a friend of mine and he is using my apartment to entertain them. The social life down here is always very pleasant and I have more nice friends here than anywhere else.

Don't worry! Take care of yourself!

With much love to you, Tom

[TW's authorized biographer, the late Lyle Leverich, states that "Tennessee believed all his life, despite repeated diagnoses to the contrary, that his 'defective heart' was an organic condition" rather than one subject to passing "emotional and physical stress" (Leverich, p. 148).

The tour of *The Glass Menagerie* in St. Louis "was completely sold out for all performances" and "very well" received, as Dakin Williams, on military leave at the time, informed his brother. Eddie Dowling's "absence" from the cast he thought "a tremendous improvement" (October 6, 1946, HRC).

In the preceding winter TW and Pancho entertained "society beaux" following a debutante party, but their "whirl in high society" ended abruptly with gossip about the homosexual ménage at 710 Orleans. "I am told that my name is now mentioned only in whispers in mixed company" (qtd. in Windham, pp. 181-182). This event or another like it was embellished in *Memoirs* and given a salacious finale (pp. 100-101).

Partially canceled in the letterhead is the imprint of the New Orleans Athletic Club. Penned on back of the envelope in Walter Dakin's hand is the notation "A dear precious letter I value it highly."]

42. To Walter Dakin Williams

632 ½ St. Peter St.
N.O., LA.
Oct. 11, 1946
[TLS, 1 p. HTC]

Dear Dakin:

Awfully sorry you've had all this trouble with the car. About the title: Louisiana is one of the few states where a bill of sale is equivalent to a title. They didn't give me anything but the papers Colton sent you. Nothing was lost. I found out in Alva, Okla. that these papers were inadequate outside of La. I will go to the place where I bought the car and see if I can get a title or something that will satisfy a Denver buyer. Perhaps it would be simpler for me to just transfer the car to your legal ownership. Would it? - If the car is now in good running condition and you have any use for it, why don't you just keep it? But do whatever you think best. I would like to have a car but think I'll wait till I can get a new one. I hope that you will take some steps against the bastard Davis in Alva. At least write the Ford headquarters in Detroit about his chicanery. I think he is already in their bad graces and he should have his dealer's license revoked. He did everything possible to take advantage of us both.

I have given up all thought of a musical career and will be happy to surrender my title to the guitar without compensation.

I had planned to stay in New York for a while, till my new play is finished but it was impossible to get even a hotel room there, so I flew South almost immediately and have now gotten a lovely apartment in New Orleans. It is a better place for me to work. I'm afraid Miss Cornell is getting pretty impatient for the play. She still hasn't read any version of it. The more I do on it, the more there seems yet to be done, but the final result should be gratifying.

I'm awfully distressed over Grandfather's condition. He wrote me a pretty blue letter. I sent him a checque for a hundred dollars and have been writing him. I really think Mother ought to go up there. It's awful to think of him being without any close relatives and apparently likely to die at any time.

Audrey just wired me that she has received an offer of $150,000. and ten

percent of Picture gross over one million and something for the screen rights to "Menagerie". I wired her back the terms were okay. Of course they are considerably less than the original prospects but since the show has closed on Broadway one cannot expect much. When you get out of the army I think you should try to connect with a law-firm in the East. Then you could protect my financial interests. The Menagerie was badly handled all the way around. I am sure Audrey did what she thought was best but it was a mistake not to accept a moderately good price in the beginning. I am including a movie scenario in the script of my new play and I hope that I can sell the screen rights simultaneous with the play when it is finally finished.

Love - Tom.

[The saga of the Packard continued with Dakin Williams (b. 1919) seeking title clearance to sell the car, which TW provided.

On October 16 Audrey Wood cabled TW that Charles Feldman had "officially" bought film rights of *The Glass Menagerie*. She added that the columnist Louella Parsons reported an initial payment of $500,000, "which I wish were true," Wood lamented, and went on to explain that "bad business" (October 16, 1946, HRC) in San Francisco had convinced her to sell rights at this time. TW replied that he was "very happy over deal" (October 18, 1946, HRC). Laurette Taylor's prolonged illness and inability to tour nationally or to star in a London production may have helped to depress the value of film rights.

Charles Abramson, Feldman's astute assistant, reported that dealing with Wood and her attorney had been "a very difficult business." Their proposal for an initial payment of $350,000 and a predetermined release agreement bespoke fears, he thought, that the "gossamer" play may fail as a film, or that TW, a lucky novice, "may never write another successful property" (to Feldman, February 4, 1946, HRC).]

43. *To Margaret "Margo" Jones*

[632 ½ St. Peter Street
New Orleans, Louisiana]
Oct. 17, 1946
[TLS, 1 p. HRC]

Dear Margo:

I have been extraordinarily lucky here. Got a lovely furnished apartment my second day, owned and furnished by an antique dealer with real

good taste. A huge living room with the sort of work-table in it I've always wanted, about half a block long! With a sky-light directly over it. Also a Grand piano and some old Italian pieces. (You can have them, baby!) And I have been feeling well and getting a lot of work done. Miss Alma and her wild young doctor are coming to life in their native climate. For a while the silent film sequences were only tentative and I was careful to keep the main body of the play independant of them, but now I'm going whole hog and making them an integral part of the script. I know it can be done, the question is - Will anybody do it? (Don't mention this to anyone till the play is finished). Working is life, the only real true life, the rest is incidental. People are shadows except when I am trying to put them on paper. So I am a bastard, and have been ever since I started writing.

I sent Pancho home to visit his folks as he had not seen them since he got in the army. He served two and a half years in the South Pacific, right in the thick of it, and then was let out of the army without an honorable discharge simply because he had a spell of confusion and talked too trustingly to an officer about it. So he has nothing to show for what he went through, and none of the G.I. compensations, which I think is an outrage. I think something should be done about it in Washington. He is coming back here to resume his old job at a department store.

I am afraid the 29th is too early for me to make another trip. But if I find that I can, I'll wire you. Of course I could not get too clear an impression of the script from that scattered reading in your hotel room, but I can see you have a tough job on your hands. However that has never dismayed you.

I certainly want to work with you again on something. You feel about work as I do, though it doesn't traumatize your social character so badly. I would like to start on the West coast with a play and bring it all the way across the country for two or three months before going into New York. (Wouldn't it really be easier to cast and just as easy to stage a production out there?)

With love to you and Joanna and wishes for your success!

Tenn.

[Pancho Rodriguez may have received a Section VIII discharge for "undesirable habits or traits of character." During World War II the majority of such legal

separations from military service were "honorable," the discharge without honor reserved for aggravated cases involving "psychopathic behavior, chronic alcoholism, or sexual perversion."

Margo Jones was currently on leave from Theatre '46 to direct *Joan of Lorraine* (1946), the new Maxwell Anderson play starring Ingrid Bergman. "Tough job" would not adequately describe her experience.]

44. *To Margaret "Margo" Jones*

632 ½ St. Peter Street
[New Orleans, Louisiana]
Tuesday Morning. [November 19, 1946]
[TLS, 1 p. HRC]

Dearest Margo:

I've just heard a flash over my radio about the brilliant success of your opening. If the news reaches New Orleans before noon the next day you know it must be something! This puts you publicly in the top rank of New York directors and I'm more happy about it than I can say. I could tell from the brief glance I took that it was an extremely tricky play to put on and I'm sure more than usual credit will go to the direction. <u>Mil</u> <u>felicidades</u>!

I am working on a final draft of "A Chart of Anatomy" and it looks like the commitment with Cornell is out. Guthrie and Audrey got together over the second draft and decided it was not right for her. Guthrie wired me enthusiastically about the play and Audrey says they are "thinking in terms of a younger Helen Hayes" and he took the script to England. But I would not make any commitment with Guthrie as I don't think the play is the sort of thing for him, as I told you. I want <u>you</u> to see the final draft first. The second ran to 174 pages and the remaining work is mostly weeding out inessential material and I think I can eliminate the silent film sequences, all but maybe one. I'm afraid they would break the poetic unity. The part I meant for Cornell is a terrifically demanding role. It is a young part, about 27, but I can't think of any younger actress who could handle it except perhaps Hepburn. The male part is almost as big but much more easily cast.

Are you coming South now?

With much love, Tenn.

P.S. The Lorca play was thrilling to me, and also to Pancho whose Spanish background gave it special appeal. Our thanks and affectionate greetings to Joanna.

[Maxwell Anderson and Ingrid Bergman reportedly lost confidence in Margo Jones's relaxed style of direction and doubted her ability to bring *Joan of Lorraine* to New York. Apparently unbeknown to TW, she had been fired during tryouts in Washington and replaced by Sam Wanamaker. The "tricky" play reached Broadway on November 18, 1946, won positive reviews, and ran for nearly 200 performances. Jones was fully credited as director and paid all of her contractual fees, as her agent, Audrey Wood, had doubtless arranged.

Kit Cornell's withdrawal from *Summer and Smoke* surprised and disappointed TW. Wood, however, thought it inevitable that the commanding actress, last seen on Broadway as Antigone, would balk at the role of a woman dominated by parents, church, and "a man she loves but who doesn't love her" (to TW, November 18, 1946, HRC).

Lorca's play *La Casa de Bernarda Alba* (1945) was "the best thing" which TW had read "lately" (n.d., Houghton), as he observed to James Laughlin in the new year.

Partially canceled in the letterhead is the imprint of the Pontchartrain Hotel in New Orleans.]

45. To Audrey Wood

[632 ½ St. Peter Street
New Orleans, Louisiana]
Nov. 22, 1946.
[TLS w/ enclosure, 2 pp. HRC]

Dear Audrey:

Your long letter about the play was gratefully received. I am so anxious for this play to turn out right, almost absurdly so!

I feel that the relationship between John and Alma is entirely valid, even her offering herself to him in their last scene together as it is continually stressed that she is going through a profound change, having lived up till then by standards which were not natural to her, but this offer can be played and directed delicately enough to avoid a shock.

I am taking all the film sequences out. But they should be kept as the basis for a film scenario.

You are entirely right about the phony effect of the epidemic. I think if it is established that his father was engaged in that work immediately prior to his death (was in the fever district rather than attending medical convention) it will seem believable that John, after his father's death, continued the father's work and developed the serum which redeems him in the public eye.

As for Nellie, her infatuation with John is established in the first ~~two~~ scenes of the play. I felt that a brief scene between her and John - post-redemption - would be enough to prepare for their ultimate marriage. He remarks that he had told her to keep their plans secret and it should be established that the ceremony is to be simple, semi-private one. My mother's marriage in Columbus, Miss. came as an almost complete surprise to nearly all her friends in the town: it was performed in the church but privately and was a shocking surprise to the congregation as my father was considered "too fast" for a minister's daughter.

You are also entirely right about the original last scene being better. I always thought that was the best scene in the play but that it continued the play's action too long after what was its actual culmination in Alma's final loss of John. I think I have worked out a good solution in the pages enclosed, which brings John and Nellie back into the play through a dual scene at the very end and also makes clearer John's feeling for Alma. A rather complicated feeling but one that is totally understandable to me and I think with proper handling can be made so to even a Broadway audience. John is sincere when he says "he felt a hunger for her which wasn't a physical hunger". She represented certain ideals - principles - ineffable qualities - which he was running away from and even after assuming adult responsibility, he was still repelled (as much as attracted) by her kind of intensity.

My objection to the casino set is mainly for physical reasons. I think this play has to move with the same fluidity as Menagerie in order to hold attention. There should be no curtain except at intermission and a shifting of light should move it smoothly and swiftly from scene to scene. Also I like to keep the poetic unity of the three permanent sets, the two interiors and the elevated out-door fountain-set. The only value in the casino set I mind sacrificing is that of Serio's appearance which somewhat prepared for his use in the old doctor's death. I dislike all the talk about "honor" and "plumes" and I think that can be dispensed with. Having a long last scene there is plenty of cutting which I can now afford to do. In a play of such

romantic intensity, you are continually stepping on eggs and have to make sure that you step lightly. Some are bound to be broken here and there, no matter how lightly you step on them!

I am glad to hear that Margo has made good with the Bergman show as I feel that Margo and I, working together, could do more on this play than any other director. Margo likes intensely romantic material and I think she knows how to handle it, and she believes in fidelity to the author's intention. Also she spares no effort in giving a thing the best physical support, while Guthrie is inclined to "cut corners" financially as well as artistically. I don't think a typical, hard-boiled Broadway director could feel sincerely enough about this script to direct it sincerely. - How do you feel about The Playwrights' Company? Do you think they might consider a play by a non-member? I have had some correspondance with Robert Sherwood. He wired me about the Washington race-discrimination deal and I added my name to the protest and he has since written a very friendly letter of thanks, enclosing clippings. - I think their set-up is ideal for a playwright. His own choice in all matters. - After them, I would consider the Theatre Guild providing it is understood they will give sufficient license and control to author. I am not afraid of them anymore.

As for my health, that has been ever since the operation a disturbing problem, in fact a constant shadow. I don't have the severe attacks of pain that I had just before the operation, but keep on having discomfiting symptoms and a general weakness which continually remind me of it. The doctor here, like the ones in New York, tell me that I do not have a malignant condition but there is a certain ambiguity in their attitude which does not reassure me and I don't know what to make of it. And my nature is not bold enough to be sure that I want to. I have never had a particle of physical courage about anything!

Has Laughlin misplaced or lost the stories? I trust not. I have an idea for a lovely long story about a sad little Mexican who repairs watches - called 'Joy Rio'. I hope I can write it when I've finished this play. There are so many things I want to do, no end of them!

Love - Tenn.

P.S. I <u>can</u> get this last version ready, at least roughly, in about a week.

If I feel well enough, I might venture to New York <u>with</u> it for a week, provided I could be assured of a hotel room. Do you approve of this idea?

[Audrey Wood cited a second major flaw after reading the latest version of *Summer and Smoke*. Women might accept the relationship of Alma and John, but she feared that "most men won't quite understand why John, who has all the freedom in the world sexually, should remain so fascinated by a woman like Alma for such a long period of time" (to TW, November 18, 1946, HRC).

The "original" ending of *Summer and Smoke* is set in the rectory, a house of ill repute since the death of Alma's father, and consists mainly of verbal foreplay between Alma and Floyd Kramer, a "slightly paunchy" salesman whom she has met at the train station. As the play ends he kisses Alma "with clumsy, middle-aged passion" ("Summer and Smoke," August 1946, HRC).

TW realized the seriousness of Wood's criticism and enclosed "a dual scene" written to validate John's attraction to Alma. John and Nellie play their marital discord, and John his longing for Alma, against Alma's interlude with Kramer, in houses adjacent to each other. "How pitiful for you both that you made the mistake of taking me instead," Nellie says, to which John replies, "She had - too much of something . . ." (Revision of Original Ending, n.d., HRC).

The Playwrights' Company which produced *Joan of Lorraine* did not publicly announce the firing of Margo Jones, nor perhaps did Wood broach the subject to TW at this time.

The story about "a sad little Mexican who repairs watches" is entitled "The Mysteries of the Joy Rio" (1954).

This letter bears a reception date of November 23, 1946.]

46. To Edwina Dakin Williams

SH: New Orleans Athletic Club
New Orleans 16, La.
Dec. 3, 1946
[ALS, 4 pp. HTC]

Dear Mother -

Surprised and happy to get the box of gifts, presumably for Xmas, though there was only a Santa Claus seal to indicate it.

Haven't heard from you in so long was afraid you might be ill.

I have been absorbed in work, as usual. Had to rewrite my latest play a couple of times and am still applying some final touches.

Audrey is peculiarly taciturn about the picture sale of "Menagerie".

She wired me about it a month ago but I have received no further confirmation.

Margo passes through here this week for a short visit on her way to Dallas after directing Ingrid Bergman in the hit play "Joan of Lorraine."

I know you're happy to have Dakin home. The check he sent me was incorrectly made out for two dollars instead of $200. I hope this was a slip of the pen. I think he should take a commission for the sale, so deduct about $25. when you make out another check.

Tell Grandfather I am looking forward to his visit and I think I can put him up comfortably - there is a long flight of stairs to my apartment which is on third floor. Otherwise it should suit him perfectly - I hope he is feeling well.

Love to you all, Tom.

[Correspondence between TW and Edwina (1884-1980) is sharply reduced in volume 2 of *The Selected Letters*. Disagreement over Rose's care and Edwina's apparent coolness toward Pancho Rodriguez (see letter #52) may have contributed to the "sad distance" (*Journal*, June 6, 1954) which came to separate them.

The contract for film rights of *The Glass Menagerie* had been refined in the preceding month and was "ready" (HRC) for signing, as Audrey Wood informed TW on December 13. She had shielded her suspicious client from a tedious legal process that would have baffled and distracted him.

Margo Jones's visit to New Orleans occasioned a reading of "Paper Lantern," a variant title of *Streetcar*, and "Chart of Anatomy." Blanche DuBois was impressive, Jones thought, but she was "completely obsessed" by "Chart." Her letter of thanks ends with familiar praise for TW: "There is nobody living who can write like you do" (January 7, 1947, HRC). Jones may have informed TW at this time of her embarrassing experience with *Joan of Lorraine*.

Walter Dakin was "most unhappy" living with Edwina "because of the unfriendly attitude of Dad" (December 3, 1946, HRC), TW reported to Wood.]

47. *To Audrey Wood*

SH: Western Union
New Orleans La
1946 Dec 10 AM 11 11
[Telegram, 1 p. HRC]

AUDREY WOOD=

INEXPRESSIBLY SHOCKED AND GRIEVED WIRED YOU SUNDAY BUT
WIRE RETURNED. WILL TRY TO WRITE ARTICLE. LOVE=

TENNESSEE.

[Laurette Taylor suffered a heart attack and died on December 7, 1946, at the age
of sixty-two. TW did not attend the service in New York but wrote a poignant
"appreciation" of Taylor's career: "In this unfathomable experience of ours there
are sometimes hints of something that lies outside the flesh and its mortality. I suppose these intuitions come to many people in their religious vocations, but I have
sensed them more clearly in the work of artists and most clearly of all in the art of
Laurette Taylor. There was a radiance about her art which I can compare only to
the greatest lines of poetry, and which gave me the same shock of revelation as if
the air about us had been momentarily broken through by light from some clear
space beyond us" ("An Appreciation," *New York Times*, December 15, 1946, sec.
2, p. 4).
    John Buchanan's admission that "a vaporous something" may give "value" to
"this unfathomable experience of ours" ("A Chart of Anatomy") became in effect
the final line which TW wrote for Laurette Taylor.]

48. *To Audrey Wood*

SH: New Orleans Athletic Club
New Orleans 16, La.
1/9/47
[TLS, 2 pp. HRC]

Dear Audrey:

    Grandfather just arrived today and I have been extremely busy preparing
for him. I thought it would be better to get him a room close to my apartment
as I don't have much space, but no rooms were available so I had to make a
place for him here. Luckily we had a small extra room but it was practically
unfurnished. The only nice room in the house, the big front room with the
skylight, is the one in which I work. As Grandfather is now unable to read

his only diversion is listening to the radio. I do hope that I can settle him comfortably and happily somewhere in Florida. We are driving down there soon as the weather clears up, perhaps in a day or two.

Concerning "Chart": I agree with you that the remaining movie sequence should be left out. As for the ending, I deliberated a great deal about that and finally I felt that the shorter and simpler ending was prefer-able. The long one is more theatrical and better in itself but it is like the beginning of another play and is not as true to the play as a whole. The short ending by the fountain contains all the implications of the longer one and I feel there is poetic rightness in returning to the stone angel in the last scene. I think we should keep that other ending in reserve but have the Ms. typed up with this one. I do think the script should be typed up now, in its present form, as I do not feel it would be wise for me to continue work on it now. My interest has shifted to the other long play which I hope will turn out stronger. Somehow or other, for a complex of psychological reasons, I did not do as well with "Chart" as I should have. I shall have to read it over when it has been typed up and a little time has elapsed before I can form a clear impression of it myself. I do know there is too much material, particularly in the beginning. It needs a tighter development, perhaps the complete elimination of one or two early scenes. I hate tedium above all else and I am afraid there is a tedium in that part of the play. As for actress-es, I have wondered if it would interest the English actress Celia Johnson who was so remarkable in Coward's film "Brief Encounter". Perhaps it could be done first in England.

The problems of the other play are totally different. It is relatively short, 94 pages, structurally very compact, one set, about six characters and rather harsh, violent and melodramatic with some pretty rough char-acters: a relief after the rectory.

Here is a brief account of my living expenses. As the play has a New Orleans background it can be said that my residence here is for profes-sional purposes. Apartment: $150 a month. Food and incidental living expenses about the same amount a week. Then I have regular medical expenses which you are acquainted with. Garage: $20 a month. During the Spring and summer, Pancho travelled with me as my secretary-companion and general assistant, due to my ill health. As you know we travelled exten-sively, to New Mexico, back from there to New York, then to Nantucket

where we maintained a house for the season. Then back to New York where I was a week in a hospital. Then South to New Orleans where I resumed work on my New Orleans play. I now have my grandfather as a dependant and have been helping him financially for some time. I bought a car here for $1400. The maintenance of this car should also be included and the cost of my operation in Taos which you can check on. I do not remember figures very clearly: I am afraid you will have to approximate the travelling expenses for the two of us and let us allow Pancho a monthly salary of $200, which he is easily worth. If this is not detailed enough, wire me. In other details why not follow last year's?

Happiness and good fortune! With love,

Tenn.

[Walter Dakin arrived in New Orleans three months shy of his ninetieth birthday.

The preferred ending of "'Chart'" is set in the park and cast with a younger, slimmer version of the original traveling salesman. Archie Kramer accepts a "merciful" tablet from Alma and obeys her invitation to "sit down beside me, stranger." She then "inclines her head" to his shoulder and asks wearily, "Do you - mind?" (November 1946, HRC). The brief scene was intended to confirm Alma's loss of John Buchanan and to end the play on a note of tender resignation. In later revision TW roused the players and supplied the upbeat ending used on Broadway and published thereafter: Alma and Archie hail a taxi and depart for the pleasures of Moon Lake Casino.

In the preceding December TW returned to *Streetcar*, whose prospects for a "harsh" ending had also led to experiments with uplift. Eddie Zawadzki—an early version of Mitch named for a St. Louis friend of TW—forgives Blanche her lies and promiscuity at the urging of his sick mother, who has "suffered" herself and "wants to know" ("Electric Avenue") this vulnerable woman. The play ends with a near promise of marriage. A tougher, more cynical Blanche who secretly desires Ralph (Stanley) radically changed the ground of experimentation. By dismissing her rape in a hard-boiled morning-after scene—"I am really surprised the walls are still standing"—Blanche confirms her sensuality and resilience and earns the faint respect of her antagonist. The scene ends with Blanche preparing to go "away somewhere" in search of "life" (n.d., HRC). TW was still "experimenting with different endings" in the new year, as he informed Audrey Wood, but "otherwise" the play was "complete" (January 3, 1947, HRC).

TW closes the letter, which bears a reception date of January 10, 1947, with a hopeful list of income tax deductions.]

49. To Amado "Pancho" Rodriguez y Gonzalez

SH: Hotel La Concha
Key West, Florida
[ca. January 31, 1947]
[TLS w/ autograph postscript, 2 pp. HRC]

Dear Pancho:

We got here 2 days after I left New Orleans, made the entire trip from outskirts of Tampa to Miami in about eight hours, came on to Key West the next morning. Trip was swell except for the last ten miles when the water boiled out of the radiator and a tire blew out at the same time. I had no tools for changing the tire and was scared to put sea-water in the radiator so we were stranded quite a while till a negro truck-driver came along and put us together again. They had a couple of nice rooms for us here with connecting bath. Grandfather made friends with the Episcopal minister and has had a nice time socially. We spend the afternoons on the beach and I have been doing a lot of work in the mornings. The Poker Night is developing into a strong play, I believe, and I am hopeful about it. I think the change was good for me, physically, but I miss being with you all the time. We must take the next trip together. From my sixth floor window I can see the ocean almost all around the island and a breeze comes through all the time. It would be an excellent place to live permanently, that is, to have a small home - and a boat! Grandfather has bought a pith helmet and a pair of swimming trunks covered with palm-trees - you cannot imagine what a fantastic sight he is! Everyone smiles at us on the street, we are such an odd-looking couple, I suppose. Yesterday he walked in a fruit-store and said, "I want a dozen California oranges!" And it takes him half an hour to order a meal because he really wants everything on the menu. I have to read it to him all the way through several times shouting like a circus-barker. But he is enjoying himself and that is really the object of the trip. I dread having to drive all the way back over the same road. Maybe we'll make it a bit longer and go up the East coast instead. I think we'll leave here not later than Feb. 5th.

I have just noticed that "Menagerie" is supposed to open in Washington for two weeks Feb. 3rd. As you know, I signed a pledge, with practically all other important playwrights, not to have a show in Washington while negros are being kept out of Washington theatres. This creates a most embarassing situation. I had no idea they were bringing the

show into Washington and now I must wire Audrey to do what she can to stop it. Heaven knows what! Will probably also wire Dramatist Guild for advice about legal steps to prevent opening. Very upsetting!

Have you gone back to work? How are things? You promised to write me!

With love, Tennessee.

Please give this check to real estate co. Also one for Catharine.

[TW replaced the Packard with a "snow-white secondhand Pontiac convertible" (*Memoirs*, p. 112) which also gave trouble on the road. Nonetheless the trip to Key West was a bracing, productive experience: "Not till Grandfather came and you escaped with him to Florida did you really seem to catch hold of life again - and wrote 'Streetcar' all in about 6 weeks. . . . You recovered your lost manhood!" (*Journal*, October 27, 1947).

Walter Dakin enjoyed meeting Miriam Hopkins and her husband at Ernest Hemingway's former house on Whitehead Street. They "are stopping at the finest hotel in Key West," he informed Edwina, "we are not" (February 10, 1947, Columbia U). Hopkins starred in *Battle of Angels* and had endeared herself to TW by staunchly defending the play against the Boston censors.

"The Poker Night," a variant title of *Streetcar*, remained in strong contention through the spring. Audrey Wood thought it "suggested a Western action novel" and urged that the now famous title be used instead.

TW's report of progress on *Streetcar* led to a prescient thought, as Pancho Rodriguez awaited TW's return to New Orleans: "I have sometimes felt that I was hampering him and that he could not write with me around. I will hate leaving him but it is the best way out" (Rodriguez to Jones and Albus, February 13, 1947, HRC).

To his friend Donald Windham TW recommended room #602 in the Hotel La Concha for its "clean sweep of the sea that covers the bones of Crane" (qtd. in Windham, p. 193).]

50. *To Audrey Wood*

Western Union
Key West Flo
1947 Jan 31 PM 3 19
[Telegram, 1 p. HRC]

AUDREY WOOD=

JUST NOTIFIED PLAY BOOKED INTO WASHINGTON NEXT WEEK. CON-TRARY TO MY PLEDGE WITH ALL OTHER PLAYWRIGHTS TO BOYCOTT

WASHINGTON THEATRES WHICH BAR NEGROES. THINK IT DISGRACE-
FUL TO VIOLATE PLEDGE WILL WIRE DRAMATISTS GUILD UNLESS YOU
ADVISE OTHER ACTION TODAY. LOVE=

TENNESSEE.

[TW's apology appeared in the *New York Times* on February 3, 1947, opening
night of *The Glass Menagerie* at Washington's National Theatre: "I want to state
that I have protested bringing 'The Glass Menagerie' into Washington, but have no
legal power to prevent it. I can only express my humiliation that a play of mine
should be denied to Negroes in the nation's capital. Any future contract I make will
contain a clause to keep the show out of Washington while this undemocratic practice continues" (p. 23). The *Menagerie's* co-producer, Louis J. Singer, was quoted in
the same article as feeling "badly" himself but holding that "the contracts were
signed nine months ago and there is nothing one can do now."

The National, the only legitimate theatre in Washington at the time, was the
focus of racial protest which grew in 1947 to include the support of Actors Equity,
the Dramatists' Guild, and some forty-odd active playwrights. TW had been contacted in 1946 by Robert Sherwood, a protest leader, and joined the first group of
writers to support the "boycott." Marcus Heiman, lessee of the National, was not
unsympathetic, but he resented "the guinea pig aspect of the case" and claimed that
he was following the social customs of Washington and, implicitly, of the theatre
itself.]

51. To Audrey Wood

Western Union
Jacksonville Flo
1947 Feb 19 PM 12 41
[Telegram, 1 p. HRC]

AUDREY WOOD=

THANKS FOR YOUR GOOD OFFICES. CAR AND I RELEASED. PLEASE
WIRE GRANDFATHER FIFTY DOLLARS AT NEW ORLEANS ADDRESS. HE
IS NOW THERE AND MAY BE DESTITUTE. LOVE=

TENNESSEE.

[The Highway Patrol stopped TW near Jacksonville, Florida, as he returned to New
Orleans. Dakin Williams recounts the episode in *Tennessee Williams: An Intimate
Biography* (1983): "He had no taillights, something he hadn't thought to check.
They asked him for his driver's license, and he didn't have that either. The police

were convinced he must be either criminal or crazy, and handcuffed his wrist to his ankle. He was thrown into jail, spent a night with a crowd of whores, dope addicts and drunks, put up $300 bail and finally had to study for and pass a driving test before he was allowed to move on." The foregoing report is based upon *Memoirs*, where TW includes the piquant detail of "a redheaded youth" (p. 112) picked up while hitchhiking.

Audrey Wood's "good offices" consisted of wiring the Florida Highway Patrol that TW "is a very reputable citizen" and "one of the country's best playwrights" (February 18, 1947, HRC). Walter Dakin had returned to New Orleans by plane.]

52. To Audrey Wood

[632 ½ St. Peter Street
New Orleans, Louisiana]
[late-March 1947]
[TLS, 2 pp. HRC]

Dear Audrey:

You are so much closer to the whole situation than I am that I think it would [be] foolish and presumptuous of me to tell you what to do about the English rights. I always prefer to follow my heart - or my instinct - in matters wherever that is at all practical, and my heart and my instinct prefer to work with Randy and Bill simply because they are young, struggling, and definitely in the class of "right guys". We know what Dowling is like and personally I have never wanted any part of Singer (except his millions, which I can't get). Also I am deeply indignant over their - particularly Dowling's - cynical attitude toward the road-company. It is really a travesty of the play, mainly because of the glaring, stupefying incompetence of one member of the cast, Eddie Andrews. I think if they had really respected the play, even just as a commodity, they would not have allowed it to drag about the country in this disgraceful condition when all they had to do was fire or buy out one intolerable actor to make a creditable company of it. Of course I realize that Singer probably does not know a bad from a good actor but Dowling certainly does and he should have paid some attention. For these reasons I feel an instinctive reluctance to continue with them. On the other hand I am sure that you have considered the situation from all angles and are in a much better position to make a decision in the matter, and therefore I would rather you made up your own mind about it.

My dislike of Singer is premised, that is - originates - from his attempt to make me sabotage the play in Chicago with fantastic "happy" endings and other tripe, and his arrogant, bullying attitude up till the time the play was proven a commercial success. Perhaps he has redeemed himself since then. I am still afraid of him, though. Finally, I don't particularly care, at this point, whether there is a London production or not. You decide!

(I hope all this does not sound ill-humored, as I am in a very reasonable humor tonight).

Grandfather suddenly insisted on leaving. I think Mother gave him the idea that I was not altogether fitting company for a clergyman to keep. I doubt if he subscribes to her ideas in the matter, he is much too liberal for that, but evidently she talked him into going, which was a real sorrow to me as I had grown so attached to him and it was such a joy having him with me. He broke down and cried as I left him at the train. I felt heartsick about the old man venturing forth again by himself, for he is really more dependant (visually, Etc.) than he appears. However he has many friends in Memphis who will look out for him to a great extent, and I have told him to rejoin me for the summer if he wants to. I don't know <u>where</u> I shall go. Do you think anything will be done about "Poker Night" this summer? I hope the production can be arranged for early Fall. I want to take a very active part in it, particularly casting, and I am wondering whether that would be done more likely on the East or West Coast. This sounds as though I were quite certain it <u>will</u> be produced. Actually I am only hoping so, very strongly. Would appreciate your advice as to which Coast I should go to. I don't want to move around more than necessary. To my mind the play should open a long way from Broadway, and any contract should stipulate a minimum of six weeks on the road. - Do you think Blanche at all right for Bankhead? My fear is that Bankhead would not be sympathetic enough in the softer aspects of the character. But she would certainly be thrilling in the big scenes.

Windham has sent me a bunch of his stories. One long one is truly superb and I want you to see it. I am writing a foreword.

With love, Tenn

Please do advise me about where to go!

*Pancho Rodriguez,
Margo Jones, and
Walter Dakin, New
Orleans, 1947:
"I wish Tom would
marry her" (letter,
Walter Dakin to
Edwina, March 19,
1947).*

[TW's failure to consult Audrey Wood on "English rights" of *The Glass Menagerie*
put her in a "difficult situation" (to TW, March 26, 1947, HRC) once again. The
contract which she reluctantly drew gave Will Gould and Randy Echols, stage managers in the original company, one week to form a partnership with Eddie Dowling
and Louis J. Singer. The American managers had no legal rights, Wood informed
TW, but at this time she favored their inclusion as ballast to an inexperienced production team.

Harsh criticism of Eddie Andrews, the touring Gentleman Caller, was a
byproduct of TW's recent trip to Boston to evaluate Pauline Lord for the London
production of *The Glass Menagerie*.

Walter Dakin's departure for Memphis was well planned and probably not—
as TW suspected—the result of Edwina's moralistic prompting. There was, however, an undercurrent of family criticism regarding Pancho Rodriguez. Dakin
Williams wrote earlier in March to assure TW of Edwina's safe return following her
visit to New Orleans. He noted that "Mother knows nothing of my reasons for dis-
liking P. Though she shares my opinion of him in general." Pancho, he advised, is
not "an asset to you socially" and "has all the attributes of . . . well . . . you know
what" (March 8, 1947, HRC). When Dakin visited New Orleans in April, he was
apparently propositioned by Pancho, an episode which he reported to TW with further advice and indignation regarding his brother's indiscreet life (see *Tennessee
Williams: An Intimate Biography*, pp. 141-142).

This letter bears a reception date of April 1, 1947.]

53. To Audrey Wood

Western Union
New Orleans La
1947 Apr 8 PM 3 02
[Telegram, 1 p. HRC]

AUDREY WOOD=

MY TRAIN LEAVES 5:30 WEDNESDAY EVENING ARRIVES 8:15 THURSDAY
EVENING. THIS WOMAN HAD BETTER BE GOOD=

TENNESSEE.

[Irene Selznick, Audrey Wood's choice to produce *A Streetcar Named Desire*, awaited TW's arrival and inspection in Charleston, South Carolina: "She is supposed to
have 16 million dollars *and* good taste. I am dubious" (qtd. in Windham, p. 198).
Selznick recalls meeting a shy, taciturn author with a cast in his "cloudy" left eye
who oddly turned away whenever she spoke to him. TW quickly accepted her as

*Tennessee Williams
and Irene Selznick:
"This woman had
better be good."*

producer and signed the contracts with little sentiment or ceremony. Selznick wired her assistant, Irving Schneider, with a coded report of success: "'Blanche has come to live with us. Hooray and love'" (qtd. in Selznick, *A Private View*, 1983, p. 297).]

54. To James "Jay" Laughlin

632 ½ St. Peter,
New Orleans, La.
April 9, 1947
[TLS w/ enclosure, 2 pp. Houghton]

Dear Jay:

I was afraid you had decided that I was "Derriere garde" and crossed me off your list.

The heat and dampness are descending on New Orleans and it is like a Turkish bath only not as socially inspiring. So I am wondering whether to go East or West. From the looks of things generally, one would do well to get clear out of the country and stay out for at least the opening stages of "The American Century". I have a feeling that if we survive the next ten years, there will be a great purgation, and this country will once more have the cleanest air on earth, but right now there seems to be an unspeakable foulness. All the people at the controls are opportunists or gangsters. The sweetness of reason died out of our public life with FDR. There doesn't even seem to be a normal intelligence at work in the affairs of the nation. Aren't you frightened by it?!

I have done a lot of work, finished two long plays. One of them, laid in New Orleans, A STREETCAR CALLED DESIRE, turned out quite well. It is a strong play, closer to "Battle of Angels" than any of my other work, but is not what critics call "pleasant". In fact, it is pretty unpleasant. But Audrey is enthusiastic about it and we already have a producer "in the bag". A lady named Irene Selznick (estranged wife of David Selznick and a daughter of Louis B. Mayer). Her chief apparent advantage is that she seems to have millions. Audrey says that she also has good taste. Of course I am skeptical. But I am going half-way to meet her. She is flying down to Charleston and I up and we are to have a meeting-conference tomorrow evening at the Hotel Fort Sumter. This is all Audrey's idea. I recognize the danger of working with a Female Moneybags from Hollywood but Audrey claims the woman is "safe" and will give an "all-out" production, which is

what the play requires to put it over. Unfortunately we have fallen out with Dowling and the main problem is to find a really strong but fastidious director. (And a good female star).

The other play, which I worked on all last summer, intended for Miss Cornell, was a disappointment and a pretty bad one. In fact, I was so depressed over it that I am surprised that I was able to go on working. Margo does not feel that way about it and she is planning to try it out this summer in Dallas. Eventually something might work out of it. The basic conception was very pure and different from anything else I have tried. It was built around an argument over the existence of a "human soul" but that got pretty thoroughly lost in a narrative that somehow slipped to the level of magazine fiction, or worse.

Donnie (Windham) sent me a group of his short-stories and I am happy to report that they are excellent, especially a long one called "The Starless Air" which I want you to read. I think it is the finest portrait I have seen of middle-class southern society. It makes KAP seem "cute". I am to write a foreword before Donnie submits them to publishers. It is a difficult job as the qualities I like in the stories are so difficult to define. Except in such vague and cliche terms as "organic" "pure" "honest" Etc. But then I could never write criticism anyhow.

I am becoming infected with your passion for Kafka, since reading "The Burrow". It is so like our State Department, or any neurotic personality. Except that of course the little animal in the burrow devoured the "smaller fry" for much more sympathetic motives, and his apprehension was more sensible.

Audrey says she sent you a bunch of stories. Which ones do you lack? Check with the enclosed list and let me know or notify Audrey. I am glad you still want to do the volume, and I hope you still want to do it privately so we can include the best ones.

Ever, Tennessee

[Henry Luce, influential founder of *Time* and *Life* magazines, foresaw an American "powerhouse" defeating Nazi Germany and spreading its unique democratic ideals around the world, creating in effect "the 20th Century—our Century" ("The American Century," *Life,* February 17, 1941). Luce's jingoism, it seemed to TW, had hardened into a risky Cold War policy of containing Communism, as recently

formulated by the Truman Doctrine. Intertwined with this aggressive foreign policy were signs of growing intolerance and repression at home.

Donald Windham's family reminiscence, "The Starless Air," was dramatized and produced in 1953, with direction by TW. The story was later collected in *The Warm Country* (1962), with a brief introduction by E.M. Forster.

Fear of a great unknown "enemy" assails the rodent-speaker in Franz Kafka's late story "The Burrow" (1931).

Of sixteen stories on "the enclosed list," eleven appeared in the collection *One Arm*.]

55. *To Amado "Pancho" Rodriguez y Gonzalez*

[The Royalton, New York]
Tuesday - [April 15, 1947]
[ALS, 4 pp. HRC]

Dear Pancho -

It looks like I may either be tied up here several days longer or <u>else</u> have to make another trip up here before going west. I think it is definitely better to get everything ironed out now as I see no point in taking the trip twice.

I signed contract with Irene in Charleston but they insisted I come up to see the designer and select a director. We are now engaged in these problems which are very involved. I still may get away tomorrow (Wednesday) night. Otherwise may have to stay through Thursday or Friday. I sent you a money-order last night.

Irene thinks my presence in California would be more valuable as she expects most of the casting will be done at that end. So we can get started out there soon as I return from New York.

All my time here is taken up with interviews and conferences. Irene is nice but overwhelmingly energetic and a real slave-driver - But I think she is determined to give the show the best of everything that money can buy. She will be in California this summer, too.

This is a tough job, baby, but a great deal - in fact, everything - depends on it. I just hope the old Toro will stand up under pressure!

In Calif. we must get in a quiet, restful place so I can reserve some energy. You can help me a lot if you want to.

Will see you in a few days - sorry it took this long.

Yours - 10.

P. S. Planning to leave Thursday night. (tomorrow)

[The "old Toro" remained in New Orleans while TW traveled to Charleston and New York. Audrey Wood sternly enforced this rule, stating "twice on the phone" that he "should come '*alone!*'" The "Princess was inconsolable" (qtd. in Windham, p. 198), TW reported to Donald Windham.]

56. To Elia "Gadge" Kazan

[632 ½ St. Peter Street
New Orleans, Louisiana]
April 19, 1947
[TLS, 2 pp. WUCA]

Dear Gadge:

I am bitterly disappointed that you and Mrs. Selznick did not come to an agreement. I am wondering what was the primary trouble - the script itself or your unwillingness to tie up with another producer. Frankly I did not know that you were now in the producing field. Working outside of New York has many advantages but a disadvantage is that you lack information about such things. I have known you only in the capacity of actor and director.

I am sure that you must also have had reservations about the script. I will try to clarify my intentions in this play. I think its best quality is its authenticity or its fidelity to life. There are no "good" or "bad" people. Some are a little better or a little worse but all are activated more by misunderstanding than malice. A blindness to what is going on in each other's hearts. Stanley sees Blanche not as a desperate, driven creature backed into a last corner to make a last desperate stand - but as a calculating bitch with "round heels". Mitch accepts first her own false projection of herself as a refined young virgin, saving herself for the one eventual mate - then jumps way over to Stanley's conception of her. Nobody sees anybody <u>truly</u>, but all through the flaws of their own ego. That is the way we all see each other in life. Vanity, fear, desire, competition - all such distortions within our own egos - condition our vision of those in relation to us. Add to those distortions in our <u>own</u> egos, the corresponding distortions in the egos of the <u>others</u> - and you see how cloudy the glass must become through which we look at each other. That's how it is in all living relationships except when there is that

rare case of two people who love intensely enough to burn through all those layers of opacity and see each others naked hearts. Such a case seems purely theoretical to me.

However in creative fiction and drama, if the aim is fidelity, people are shown as we never <u>see</u> them in life but as they <u>are</u>. Quite impartially, without any ego-flaws in the eye of the beholder. We see from <u>outside</u> what could not be seen <u>within</u>, and the truth of the tragic dilemma becomes apparent. It was not that one person was bad or good, one right or wrong, but that all judged falsely concerning each other, what seemed black to one and white to the other is actually grey - a perception that could occur only through the detached eye of art. (As if a ghost sat over the affairs of men and made a true record of them) Naturally a play of this kind does not exactly present a theme or score a point, unless it be the point or theme of human misunderstanding. When you begin to arrange the action of a play to score a certain point the fidelity to life may suffer. I don't say it always does. Things may be selected to score a point clearly without any contrivance toward that end, but I am afraid it happens rarely.

Finding a director aside from yourself who can bring this play to life exactly as if it were happening in life is going to be a problem. But that is the kind of direction it has to have. (I don't necessarily mean "realism": sometimes a living quality is caught better by expressionism than what is supposed to be realistic treatment.)

I remember you asked me what should an audience feel for Blanche. Certainly pity. It is a tragedy with the classic aim of producing a katharsis of pity and terror, and in order to do that Blanche must finally have the understanding and compassion of the audience. This without creating a black-dyed villain in Stanley. It is a thing (misunderstanding) not a person (Stanley) that destroys her in the end. In the end you should feel - "If only they all had <u>known</u> about each other!" - But there was always the paper lantern or the naked bulb!

(Incidentally, at the close of the play, I think Stanley should remove the paper lantern from the bulb - after Blanche is carried out and as he goes to resume the game.)

I have written all this out in case you were primarily troubled over my intention in the play. Please don't regard this as "pressure". A wire from Irene and a letter from Audrey indicate that both of them feel you have

definitely withdrawn yourself from association with us and that we must find someone else. I don't want to accept this necessity without exploring the nature and degree of the differences between us. (Especially as they are now talking about someone I have never heard of, an Englishman named Tyrone Guthrie - sounds like some frightening kind of hybrid! - don't, please, mention any of this to anybody but Molly!)

Sincerely, Tennessee.

P.S. And also because I would want to be certain that we were in full accord and understanding about the play's intention.

[TW saw *All My Sons* (1947) while in New York and immediately opened a correspondence with Elia Kazan (1909-2003). He wrote that the play "'tops any direction I have seen on Broadway,'" adding that he would send "'congratulations'" to Arthur Miller and a copy of his own work to Kazan. "'It may not be the sort of play that interests you but I hope so'" (qtd. in Kazan, pp. 326-327). Kazan recalled that he did not "rush to read" *Streetcar* and wondered if he and TW "were the same kind of theatre animal—Miller seemed more my kind" (Kazan, p. 327).

The present letter follows a breakdown in early negotiations with Kazan as TW returned to New Orleans on April 17. Audrey Wood informed him of Kazan's abrupt withdrawal of interest and surmised that it was meant "either to unnerve us, frighten us, or make him seem harder to get and therefore increase his bargaining power later on" (April 18, 1947, HRC). TW urged her "to keep Irene partly immobilized" until he could return to New York and added that he had "not given up on Kazan" (April 21, 1947, HRC). Restored negotiations with Kazan would identify artistic control and billing, rather than script, as the chief obstacles to his direction of *Streetcar*.

Tyrone Guthrie's stage credits were numerous but almost exclusively English. His only recent direction on Broadway was a Theatre Guild revival of *He Who Gets Slapped* (1946), which was not well received.

Typed in the upper margin of p. 1 is TW's return address "C/o Audrey Wood, 551 Fifth Ave., N.Y."]

57. *To Irene Mayer Selznick*

[632 ½ St. Peter Street
New Orleans, Louisiana]
April 21, 1947
[TLS, 1 p. Private Collection]

Dear Irene:

I am shocked by Kazan's behavior. As for myself, I don't care how a director or actor treats me as long as he does a good job. He could spit in my face every morning and if he was the right man for the job, I'd wipe it off and say, Thank you! But I do not at all like his discourtesy to you and I find it particularly baffling after our conversations at dinner and on the phone, as on both occasions I had the distinct impression that he felt a genuine interest and even enthusiasm. This would not be worth bothering over except for the fact that it leaves us with so few names we can dare to consider.

John Huston comes next on my list. He is the only one mentioned who has a record that would indicate he would know how to handle such a "special" and "difficult" assignment as this one. As for Tyrone Guthrie, he is English. This is an American play with a peculiarly local or provincial color. And I remember "Piccadilly Peg's" bewilderment over Mississippi. We flew down there so she could absorb it in 48 hours.

Logan? Well, he belongs with Kauffman and Kanin in a group of directors who function brilliantly with a certain type of very slick Broadway product. "On Borrowed Time" comes closest to being a similar type of play, but even that is not really similar. It would be sheer speculation, as far as I can see. These men know Broadway, but the rest of the world is a fog. And I am not articulate enough to help them. I have a feeling that Huston knows more than Broadway and Hollywood. At least he has a literary acquaintance with the outside world and is sensitive to poetic values which unfortunately anyone who directs my work has to deal with if the work is to survive at all. - That is what makes the problem so difficult. - I will not mention Margo Jones to you, now, for you have already expressed your feeling about a woman-director. But the hour may come when the word is torn from my lips! (Margo and I together did the only good production of "You Touched Me" at Pasadena. Her advantage is that she and I have a hand-in-glove understanding of each other as persons and workers.)

I leave here tomorrow or Wednesday. I am driving and am a liesurely driver so I cannot say the definite day I'll get in New York but I will wire you and Audrey along the road of my progress. I want to get a place on the water near enough to New York so that we can be easily accessible to each other and yet I can have "tranquillity". I hope you and Audrey will get together a complete list of directors who are available so we can go through them exhaustively when I get to New York.

Ever, Tennessee.

[Irene Selznick (1907-1990) was seldom at a loss for words, but Audrey Wood's invitation to produce *Streetcar* had left her nearly speechless: "All I could say was, why? I reminded her that I was not only a novice, I had just had a failure," which closed in Philadelphia. Wood's reply, "'Find me someone else'" (qtd. in *A Private View*, pp. 294-295), bespoke a theatre establishment which lacked fresh production talent and respect for the author's intention. These qualities Wood foresaw in Selznick, as well as a sizeable bankroll and extensive Hollywood connections. "I truly felt," she later explained, "that after what Williams had been through in the past, he had to have complete protection, artistically as well as financially" (*Represented by Audrey Wood*, 1981, p. 151).

TW considered John Huston's screenplay for *The Maltese Falcon* (1941) "one of the finest pieces of dramatic writing ever produced." Huston's recent staging of *No Exit* (1946) received sharply mixed reviews and closed after thirty-one performances on Broadway. Paul Bowles adapted the original Sartre play.

Annie Get Your Gun (1946) was the latest of several hit musicals directed by Joshua Logan, who was Selznick's early choice to stage *Streetcar*. He made his directorial debut on Broadway in Paul Osborn's bittersweet comedy *On Borrowed Time* (1938).]

58. To Elia "Gadge" Kazan

SH: The Park Central
Seventh Avenue · 55 to 56 Street
New York City 19, N.Y.
May 1, 1947
[TLS, 4 pp. WUCA]

Dear Gadge:

I was immensely pleased to find your letter waiting for me here and to learn that there is no real impasse in the situation. I only got here last night after a full week on the road driving up from New Orleans. I talked

immediately to Audrey and Bill. They are 100% in agreement with me in feeling that you are the man we want, the only one that we would feel really secure with. This afternoon I saw Irene. "Saw" is putting it mildly. "Heard" is closer but not by any means an adequate statement! It was one of those three-or-four-hour audiences that you have already experienced. It is funny. No matter how intelligent these people are, one thing they can't understand and that is how downright brutal it is to make anyone who is doing creative work go through these awful, interminable "consultations". They wear you down, debilitate you, finally suck you dry - if you let them! I cannot tell you how fully I sympathize with your allergy to all the peripheral involvements, complications, arguments and discussions that go with the usual play production. We have only so much energy to give, even to our most cherished work - it is all too quickly depleted - so it is certainly a sad thing that so much of it must be dissipated in all the incidental "fuss" that goes with a production. It almost makes you wish you'd never shown the play to anybody! - This is not directed at Irene but at producers in general. The freshness of vision and energy of attack are wastefully spent in arguments over things that should be simply and immediately decided by one or two people. - I am glad you use the word <u>fusion</u>. It is diffusion that seems to be the basic fault in so many productions. The various elements simply don't form a congruous whole. It is certainly not deprecating the plastic elements of the theatre (I think that exciting theatre is half a plastic art) to insist that they be dominated by the unifying influence of the script-and-director. If those two elements are in accord at the outset, so closely that they really constitute a single unit of two complementary parts, everything in the production should take shape under them and in that way fuse all the elements into a single artistic conception. I am getting all wound up in words, but you understand me. - Then something is created, whether it be a success or failure, something is brought to <u>be</u>. A living thing not just a hunk of formless matter. That is what we are interested in doing, making something <u>live</u>, - <u>Basta</u>!

I am going to put things as clearly and frankly as possible. - Irene still considers you the best director but she is now somewhat afraid of you. She thinks you are likely to be tyrannical or autocratic. I believe she visualizes herself being bodily ejected from the theatre and me writing new scenes with a bayonet at my ribs! (That's over-stating it a bit.) But I think what is

needed to straighten things out, if you want to direct this show half as much as I want you to - is to give her a bit of reassurance along that line. After all she is primarily in this for fun, and her fun - I suppose - will come from feeling that she is somehow <u>participating</u>. If this could be managed without exposing yourself to undue interference - I feel it could be.

Irene says you think the play needs considerable re-writing. As you never said this, or intimated it, in our talk or your letter, I don't take this seriously, but I think it is only fair to tell you that I don't expect to do any more <u>important</u> work on the script. I spent a long time on it and the present script is a distillation of many earlier trials. It certainly isn't as good as it could be but it's as good as I am now able to make it. - I have never been at all difficult about cuts and incidental line-changes but I'm not going to do anything to alter the basic structure - with one exception. For the last scene, where Blanche is forcibly removed from the stage - I have an alternative ending, physically quieter, which could be substituted if the present ending proves too difficult to stage. That's about all the important change I could promise any director, and only that if the director finds the other unworkable.

If you are content with this understanding about the script - then I can just say - "Irene, I want Gadge and won't take anyone else." AUDREY and Bill would back me up, and I think could run interference for you all the way down the field.

I guess that's about all. Except I think we are anticipating more trouble with Irene than is really likely. I think we are dealing with a woman of sincerity and ethical principles, as well as considerable sense and taste, who is right now over-compensating nervously for some emotional shock. I suspect this producing adventure is partly a kind of occupational therapy for her, and once we show her a certain warmth and deference she will have the good sense to stay in her own corner except when called for.

I think it will work out, in fact I'm sure it will, if we are firm but gentle!

Ever, Tennessee.

Write me c/o Audrey Wood, 551 Fifth Ave., as I will retreat to the country soon as I find a place. All I really want to know is your willingness to accept the script as it now stands.

[TW returned to New York in late-April to monitor negotiations between Irene Selznick and Elia Kazan, the latter now at work in California. Kazan reportedly told TW during his earlier visit that he would direct *Streetcar* only if Selznick were fired as producer. As further incentive he framed an alarming picture of her father, Louis B. Mayer, and her estranged husband, David O. Selznick, "sitting in the front row during rehearsals" (*A Private View*, p. 299). Selznick apparently had similar fears that Kazan would be "tyrannical or autocratic" and usurp her authority as producer.

Kazan wired TW that he had not "put bayonet in an author's ribs for a heck of a time" and promised to accept *Streetcar* "exactly as is." He also suggested that Selznick check his references. "There are an awful lot of people I've worked with whom I didn't terrify" (May 5, 1947, HRC).]

59. To Irene Mayer Selznick

SH: The Park Central
Seventh Avenue · 55 to 56 Street
New York City 19, N.Y.
Friday Night [May 1947]
[TLS, 2 pp. Private Collection]

Dear Irene:

Just had a talk over phone with Audrey. I am leaving early tomorrow morning for the Cape.

Audrey told me Gadge's terms and I must admit - though I have no idea what directors ordinarily receive - that these seem pretty stiff.

Irene, I don't think you have yet given sufficient consideration to the idea of direction by <u>myself</u> <u>and</u> Margo Jones. I know and appreciate your aversion to direction by a woman. However this would actually be direction by the author <u>through</u> a woman who is the only one who has a thorough interpretative understanding of his work. Also I think you must have observed how much direction is actually incorporated in the script itself. In writing a play I see each scene, in fact every movement and inflection, as vividly as if it were occuring right in front of me. However I could not direct by myself as I am insufficiently articulate. However with Margo I <u>could</u>. We have a sort of mental short-hand or Morse code, we are so used to each other and each other's work, and with Margo it would be a labor of love. Love cannot be discounted, even in a hardboiled profession, as one of the magic factors in success. I have a profound conviction that the two

of us, working on this script, with you and Audrey and Liebling as a supporting team - could do something a little better with the play than any other single director, including Gadge. I felt that all along but pressed for Gadge because I felt at the outset that you were irrevocably prejudiced against another woman-director. Well, there is only one woman director and that's Margo. Regardless of what anyone says, I know she has the stuff - and her shortcomings are exactly what I am able to supply. With her I could also continue to function as a writer, during the rehearsals, but with any other - perhaps even Gadge - I don't think I would be able to achieve much more. I mean we have a way of stimulating each other.

Irene, this is not to be construed as pressure. I just thought - in view of the stiff terms offered by Kazan - that you should know that there is an alternative and it is in fact an alternative which I think is even preferable. Needless to say my direction would be gratuitous and Margo's terms would be negligible compared to the others.

I hope you will think about this. See you next week.

Love, Tennessee.

[Elia Kazan's "stiff" terms for directing *Streetcar* stipulated his billing as co-producer and a twenty-percent share of the profits, in addition to the "usual fee and top percentage of the gross." Irene Selznick threatened "to step aside" rather than "knuckle under" to such "an ultimatum" (*A Private View*, pp. 299-300).

TW informed Margo Jones at this time that he had originally recommended three directors to Selznick: Jones, Kazan, and John Huston. Selznick, he claimed, was still smarting over the failed "woman-director" of "Heartsong," the Laurents play which closed in Philadelphia, and "swore that she would take another 'over her dead body.'" Presumably Kazan was the beneficiary of Selznick's "aversion to direction by a woman" (n.d., HRC).

Related correspondence indicates that TW wrote this letter on May 9, 1947, shortly before he and Pancho Rodriguez left for Provincetown.]

60. To Elia "Gadge" Kazan

[Peter Nyholm House
Provincetown, Massachusetts]
[May 1947]
[TLS, 2 pp. WUCA]

Dear Gadge:

I sincerely hope by the time you get this everything will be straightened out among the lawyers. When I pulled out of town they were still in a huddle and the fur was flying. There was nothing I could do except stand pat, so I did - and removed myself to the Cape. I have taken a little house right on the water and about a mile out of town and my friend Pancho and I are now busy painting everything red, white, yellow and green to counteract the grey weather. When you get back to this Coast, I hope you will come up here for a week-end. It might be the best place to go over the script. Needless to say, I am eager for your ideas. I think this play has some excellent playing scenes but there are also some weak passages and some corny touches. I am determined to weed these out as much as possible before we go into rehearsal. You and I may not agree about exactly which and where these are but I am sure a lot of good will come out of consultation between us. The cloudy dreamer type which I must admit to being needs the complementary eye of the more objective and dynamic worker. I believe you are also a dreamer. There are dreamy touches in your direction which are vastly provocative, but you have a dynamism that my work needs to be translated into exciting theatre. I don't think "Pulling the punches" will benefit this show. It should be controlled but violent. - I went to see "All My Sons" again. I was more impressed than ever, the way lightning was infused into all the relationships, everything charged with feeling, nothing, even the trivial exchanges, allowed to sag into passivity. Yes, I think you can try new things in my play. In that sense it might be good for you, and it will certainly be good for me. It is a <u>working</u> script. I think we can learn and grow with it and possibly we can make something beautiful and alive whether everyone understands it or not. People are willing to live and die without understanding exactly what life is about but they must sometimes know exactly what a play is about. I hope we can show them what it is about but since I cannot say exactly what it is about, that is just a hope. But maybe if we succeed in our first

objective of making it <u>alive</u> on the stage, the meaning will be apparent.

On second visit to "Sons", I decided that Malden <u>was</u> right for Mitch. I hope you agree. The face is comical but the man has a dignified simplicity and he is a great actor. I also met Burt Lancaster. Was favorably impressed. He has more force and quickness than I expected from the rather plegmatic type he portrayed in The Killers. He also seemed like a man who would work well under good direction.

Let me know if you can come down here or would rather work with me in New York. We have a guest room here and it would be a pleasure to have you with us. - I want to absorb your ideas as early as possible so that I will have plenty of time to chew them over by myself and extract what is helpful.

Ever, Tennessee

[TW hoped to find "tranquillity" at Provincetown as the "<u>working</u> script" of *Streetcar* was revised and the production assembled. He had summered there in the early 1940s with some of the same friends who now reappeared on the Cape: Fritz Bultman and family, David Gregory, a New York friend and aspiring writer, Donald Windham and Sandy Campbell, the artist Buffie Johnson, and Jane Lawrence and Tony Smith.

Karl Malden played the supporting role of George Deever in *All My Sons*. His character attempts to restore a father's honor following an unfair wartime conviction. Malden would play Mitch in *Streetcar*. Burt Lancaster appeared as Alvaro in the film version of *The Rose Tattoo* (1955).]

61. To Margaret "Margo" Jones

[The Royalton, New York]
Friday, May 23, 1947.
[ALS, 3 pp. HRC]

Dearest Margo -

I have taken a little house in Provincetown for the summer but immediately after moving in, I had to return to N.Y. and thrash out the director-problem with Mrs. Selznick. Well, she has finally signed Kazan, virtually on her own terms. He wanted to be co-producer but she beat him down on that. You know how I hate fighting, uncertainty, Etc. It has been hell, and has made me sick again. This morning I had a very disquieting experience.

My mouth suddenly filled with blood. Pancho called the doctor and he has put me to bed for a couple of days. I hope I will be able to go back to Provincetown early this week (next) as I cannot - obviously - take the strenuous life anymore. Honey, I pray to God I can come to Dallas in July. Somehow I am <u>more eager</u> to see <u>your production</u> [of] "S. & S." ~~even~~ than "Streetcar." If I don't make it - and I am <u>planning</u> <u>to</u> make it - you must know it is simply a matter of <u>impossibility</u> that prevents me. But I shall do everything I can to make it possible for me to make the trip.

Of course you <u>will</u> have first option on this script - as <u>director-producer</u>. That is a promise.

I don't want it brought into N.Y., however, too <u>soon</u> after "<u>Streetcar</u>". It would not be fair to either play. Nor would I be in any condition to go - <u>immediately</u> - through <u>another</u> production. It is something that takes so much out of you. I would prefer to hold it at least until after Christmas. And perhaps I will be able to make some <u>good</u> <u>changes</u> before it is produced <u>up</u> <u>here</u>. The <u>conception</u> is so much better than the script as it now stands. Eventually - perhaps soon - a lot could be done to strengthen it.

I am delighted with your report (and brochure) of the company. How I would love to see <u>all</u> the plays, especially the beautiful Inge play. I know Carol will be thrilling in it.

See Chaplin's new film. It is a brilliant piece, in its unity of style and delicacy. Real Cinematic art.

I look forward to seeing you and Joanna. Incidentally, if you have extra copies of those lovely photographs in the brochure, I would love a copy of you both, to put up in the summer cottage, until I see you again.

Sorry to write such a dull letter but I have taken a seconal tablet and am nearly asleep.

Love, love, love! Tennessee.

[Irene Selznick refused to share authority as producer, but she agreed to a compromise billing: "Irene M. Selznick presents Elia Kazan's Production of *A Streetcar Named Desire*." She also gave Kazan twenty percent of the show, reducing her own share and that of the investors accordingly.

Pancho Rodriguez added to "the strenuous life" of New York by shredding TW's clothes and books, although not his manuscripts, and publicly denouncing two of his friends as the "'biggest whores on Broadway'" (qtd. in *Memoirs*, p. 106). TW apologized to Donald Windham, a victim of Pancho's misplaced jealousy, and

admitted that he foresaw no "happy ending" to the "impossible situation" (qtd. in Windham, p. 200).

TW's view of *Summer and Smoke* had not changed appreciably since the preceding December, when he termed the play "an unhappy cross between Dr. Faustus and a radio soap-opera!" (to Wood, December 3, 1946, HRC). He now repeated a promise to Margo Jones that she would bring the show to New York, if it proved to be "Broadway material" (n.d., HRC). *Summer and Smoke* was set for a July 8 premiere at Theatre '47 in Dallas.

Charlie Chaplin played a witty bluebeard in his "new film," *Monsieur Verdoux* (1947).

The "seconal tablet" is TW's first reference in letters to this particular drug, a barbiturate prescribed as a sedative and hypnotic.]

62. To Audrey Wood

[Peter Nyholm House
Provincetown, Massachusetts]
[mid-June 1947]
[TLS w/ autograph postscript, 1 p. HRC]

Dear Audrey:

Margo is already yelping for me to show in Dallas but I shall remain here through June. I expect I'll pass through New York, say, about June 30th, and spend that day there, proceding the next to Dallas. May have to make it a couple days earlier, depending on length of trip. You'll know definitely early next week. I don't think much publicity about me is wise until the play has opened successfully. Neither my political sentiments nor my unconventional mode of living would make a favorable impression from what I can observe of public opinion. Of course a profile in "LIFE", which Irene mentioned, would be difficult to resist if obtainable: usually their treatment is more impersonal.

As for Mother investing: if the show costs about $100,000. I don't suppose there would be any return on investment until that amount has been paid off. Is this right? There are several things to consider. Coming recession, prissy moral attitudes of the N.Y. press, but mostly the casting of Blanche. I would not recommend investment in this show to any friend until that part has been satisfactorily cast. By satisfactorily I mean with a really powerful dramatic actress in the part. Sullavan is strictly compromise on that score. She is the sort of actress that would get "excellent personal

notices" but do the play no good: unless she has more on the ball than we derived from her readings. Right now Tandy is the only one who looks good to me and I am waiting till I see her and hear her. Could you leave a piece ($5000.) open until Blanche is cast? Then I'll know whether or not Mother ought to invest.

Another question: will Tandy be in New York this summer? Could she come East for inspection here? If she was the Blanche we dream of, then I could dispense with the Coast trip which I dread making, as I would probably have to travel alone, and when I got there, would probably be subjected to intense pressure for script changes: the best I can do for this production is to stay in good shape for rehearsals. There isn't much in the script that should be altered until we know the exact limitations of the Blanche selected and hear the lines spoken. I will do a lot of cutting then. The rewrite on Scene V does not read as well as original but I think it will play better and is more sympathetic for Blanche. (Makes Mitch more important to her). - Francine Larrimore wants to read for Blanche!

Love, Tenn.

Expect me in N.Y. about June 27.

[A "profile" of TW appeared in *Life* magazine on February 16, 1948.

Audrey Wood suggested that Edwina invest in *Streetcar* as a "way of setting up a trust fund" (to TW, June 11, 1947, HRC) for Rose.

Margaret Sullavan, a veteran actor who had won major awards in theatre and film, was apparently Irene Selznick's choice to play Blanche. TW could not, however, "see her purging the emotions with anything stronger than pathos" (to Selznick, June 13, 1947, Private Collection). His judgment may have been shaded by the many popular films in which Sullavan played ingenue or leading lady to Jimmy Stewart, Fredric March, and Charles Boyer.

In the preceding January Hume Cronyn directed Jessica Tandy in "Portrait of a Madonna" (1945), a one-act play with strong intimations of *Streetcar*. He advised Wood of his wife's "fine" performance and now claimed that "Tandy is the only person in the world who can play Blanche" (Wood to TW, June 6, 1947, HRC). Wood informed TW that film work—ironically, *Forever Amber* (1947)—would keep Tandy on the Coast and that his own presence there was unavoidable (June 19, 1947, HRC).

As Scene Five of *Streetcar* evolved, TW replaced Blanche's disdainful criticism of Mitch with a more subtle analysis of their social and intellectual differences. Her

strong antipathy to marrying Mitch was also softened, both to gain sympathy for Blanche and to prepare for her discovery that his protection is needed.

This letter bears a reception date of June 16, 1947.]

63. To Margaret "Margo" Jones

SH: Santa Fe Super Chief
[early-July 1947]
[TLS, 2 pp. HRC]

Dearest Margo:

It breaks my heart to miss the rehearsal period in Dallas. I know you don't need me but I would have so loved being there. However I had an imperative summons from Mme. Selznick. She said Tandy and others could not wait any longer for a decision about casting as they had other offers and commitments. I could not approve casting without seeing them so there was nothing to do but go out there immediately. I do hope Tandy is right. We heard two actresses in N.Y., Pamela Brown and Margaret Sullavan, both disappointing. Sullavan would do but she lacked any of the fragility Blanche should have and Pamela was cold. I did not realize it was going to be so terrifically hard to cast. If the right one doesn't turn up I will not go on with the production. With the wrong actress this would repeat the experience with "Battle". I am still working on the last scene as I think that is the weak point in the script.

I shall leave the Coast the moment it is possible, that is, when some decision is reached about Blanche. It should not take more than a week to explore everything there and I shall then come back through Dallas. I feel very hopeful about "Summer & Smoke". I would not if anyone else were doing it. It is such a romantic play that I think it really expresses you more than it does me. When it is done in a real theatre, design will add a great deal. See the picture of "Stairs to the Roof" in Theatre Arts. I think Summer should be performed against a sky like that. Practically no walls.

Jo's designs for Streetcar are almost the best I've ever seen. The back wall of the interior is translucent with a stylized panorama showing through it of the railroad yards and the city (when lighted behind). It will add immensely to the poetic quality. He must also do Summer.

I hope Balfour is working out. You must work mostly against

monotony in that part, the same as on Blanche. If an interpretation is too exageratted it becomes monotonous.

Liebling sent someone over to see me whom he said would make a perfect John in Summer. He looked like Mickey Rooney, only a little taller.

David Gregory is on the train with me as he is also called West on business. Pancho is along, too. I felt he would make the trip easier for me, and I dreaded making it alone. We are going to stay in a guest-house on the estate of George Cukor. - I will call or wire you in a few days. My address is c/o Irene Selznick, 1050 Summit Drive, Beverly Hills. (at present). - David is finishing a straight play! - Haven't read it yet but the idea sounds great. - Will you come East after the summer work-out? Or do you intend to enter a sanitarium with Blanche?

Ever with love, 10.

[TW wired Audrey Wood to arrange for his and Pancho's trip to the West Coast on June 30. Margo Jones held out hope that he would attend the premiere of *Summer and Smoke*, but "Mme. Selznick" proved a greater force of nature than the "Texas Tornado."

The English actor Pamela Brown made her Broadway debut in recent Theatre Guild productions of *The Importance of Being Earnest* (Wilde, 1895) and *Love for Love* (Congreve, 1695).

Reprinted in *Theatre Arts* (July 1947) was a still from the recent Pasadena Playhouse production of *Stairs to the Roof* (February 26-March 9, 1947).

Irene Selznick accepted Jo Mielziner's "high terms" for designing *Streetcar* because he claimed that it would be "the best job he's ever done!" (April 18, 1947, HRC). At the time, Wood may have shared this information with TW to soften Kazan's apparent withdrawal and to calm a nervous author by touting Selznick's production.

Katharine Balfour rather than Margaret Phillips played Alma in the Dallas production of *Summer and Smoke*. In the preceding spring TW advised Jones "to eliminate the play" from her repertory if Phillips were unavailable. Only she "would justify a summer production" (April 17, 1947, HRC). In effect TW repeated Wood's advice that he could no longer afford to "have a play casually tried out" (to TW, April 2, 1947, HRC).]

64. To Helen Hayes

[c/o Irene Selznick
1050 Summit Drive
Beverly Hills, California]
July 23, 1947
[TLS, 1 p. Private Collection]

Dear Miss Hayes:

Charlie Feldman who owns the picture rights to "Menagerie" has told me that there is a chance you might be induced to play in the film when it is made. I do hope there is reason to entertain such a hope, as I cannot think of any actress now living who would portray Amanda more beautifully on the screen. Charlie showed me the screen treatment of the play and I was genuinely enthusiastic over the work done on it. It is in very good taste and structurally it shows an improvement over the original. He has asked me to do a little additional work on it, and I am taking the script back East for that purpose. I feel that if it is properly cast it will be a picture of distinction and I am most eager to know how you feel about it.

Cordially, Tenn. Williams

[Helen Hayes would play Amanda in the London stage production of *The Glass Menagerie* (1948) but not in the 1950 film version.]

65. To George Cukor

SH: The Stoneleigh
Dallas, Texas
August 3, 1947.
[TLS w/ autograph marginalia, 2 pp. Herrick]

Dear George:

I don't know what awful thing we did in L.A. to be sent to Dallas! You cannot conceive of how hot it is. If you could just lie still it would be endurable but there is a great deal of entertainment going on.

I suppose seeing the play was worth it, as Margo had done a remarkably good job under the limitations of her tiny theatre. The play has a living quality which Margo always gets in her productions and to my surprise it seems to have a strong popular appeal. Two hundred people were turned

away from last night's performance and it has been like that right along. We have been talking about doing it in New York. I think a better plan would be to open on the West Coast and do L.A. and Frisco and Chicago for as long as possible and then come into New York in the early Spring, as I don't want to follow "Streetcar" too close. How do you feel about opening a play on the West Coast? I would like rehearsing out there. The life agrees with me, and now I feel at home there, having made so many friends. I don't think I have ever felt so close to anybody in such a short time as I did to you, George. You have a wonderful gift for dissolving the walls between people which I have always suffered from, being usually unable to do anything about it. You were kindness itself, taking us in so cordially and giving us the hospitality of your heavenly place. I have never been treated like that before, anywhere, and I will not soon forget it. Irene had praised you lavishly but for once I feel the lady was guilty of understatement.

Perhaps more than anything else, even the play, a letter waiting for me here gave me happiness. It was from the one friend to whom I was afraid to show "Streetcar". Donald Windham, who worked with me on "You Touched Me." He is occupying the house during my absence. He found a copy of the play lying around and read it and pronounced it superior to "Menagerie". I had been so afraid of his judgement! He is a merciless critic. (And I think he is going to be one of the literary landmarks some day - for his stories which are extraordinary.) I also found a letter from Carson McCullers who is now in Paris. Do you know her work? I think all of her books, especially the last one, "Member of the Wedding", would make great films.

You promised to give me G.G'S phone number or address in N.Y. Will you send it to me care of Audrey?

Affectionately, Tennessee.

[Many gay celebrities found a haven at George Cuckor's lavish estate in Hollywood, including TW, whose week-long stay was arranged by Irene Selznick. It was probably through Cukor (1899-1983), who directed Greta Garbo in *Camille* (1937), that TW met the reclusive star, writing to Donald Windham that she goes by the name of Harriet Brown and "is really hermaphroditic, almost as flat as a boy" (qtd. in Windham, p. 201).

Margo Jones opened Theatre '47 in June with a repertory of five plays, including *Farther Off from Heaven*, by William Inge, and *Summer and Smoke*, as it was

now firmly entitled. The building which she selected in cramped, post-war Dallas sat only 200 and required the expedient of staging in the round. The *Times* critic Brooks Atkinson admired TW's "rueful idyll" of the South, but he warned that its transfer to New York would involve "a calculated risk": "For the magic of the informal staging in Theatre '47 has completely unpacked the heart of Mr. Williams' poignant narrative. The Broadway style is seldom that sensitive" (*New York Times*, August 10, 1947).

TW wrote to Atkinson from Provincetown, beginning a long and friendly correspondence. Atkinson briefly replied how "very much interested" he and his wife were in the playwright's "experience" (August 25, 1947, Private Collection) with *Summer and Smoke*.

Penned in the upper margin of page 1 is the notation "Provincetown, Mass. Gen. Del."]

66. To Margaret "Margo" Jones

[Peter Nyholm House
Provincetown, Massachusetts]
August 15, 1947
[TLS, 1 p. HRC]

Dearest Margo:

The day I left New York Audrey told me she was having our lawyer make out a contract for "Summer and Smoke". Please let me hear from you about this contract when you receive it, your complete reaction. I do not know what the terms in it will be as I did not discuss it with Audrey. If it is unsatisfactory in any respect contact me directly before you do Audrey. I know that Liebling (and probably Audrey) thinks you should have a co-producer. What is your feeling about this? Would a co-producer relieve you of some business details and simplify the production? Audrey seemed to feel that it would. My own feeling is that I want to avoid any and all complications: in other words, a total autonomy between the two of us with no outside pressure and interference. I don't know if you are ready to assume that much responsibility so I would like to have your own direct and explicit reaction. Speak as freely as possible as anything you have to say will be just between the two of us. I feel that this play should be financed fully before "Streetcar" comes in, to provide against the possibility "Streetcar" might fail and it would then be more difficult to raise backing. Also I think it would strengthen my bargaining position if we kept as quiet

as possible about our agreements until after "Streetcar" has opened in N.Y.
I mean if Selznick Etc. know that my next play is sewed up they will be less
anxious to stay in my good graces. It is nasty but sometimes necessary to
think in such terms. (That is one of the things I want to avoid in the future).

We are back at Provincetown. Buffie Johnson is also in town.
Otherwise nothing interesting. I started working on another long play
today: just the opening shot. But I shall not push it hard until after
"Streetcar" is in. I call it Quebrada, meaning The Cliff. The scene is a hotel
at Acapulco built on a cliff over the Pacific which will be used symbolically as the social and moral precipice of our times, the characters some intellectual derelicts: will be able to use Mexican music!

When are you coming East? Our phone number is Provincetown 973
M if you want to call me. Address General delivery.

Love from myself and Pancho, Tennessee.

[TW and Pancho Rodriguez planned to return to Provincetown ca. August 8.

Margo Jones rejected the "idea of a co-producer" (to TW, August 20, 1947,
Private Collection) for the Broadway production of *Summer and Smoke*. The
"autonomy" which TW preferred is a near restatement of Elia Kazan's formula for
directing *Streetcar*: "'I work best in single collaboration with the author. I'll never
go back to working for a producer when it means consulting with him (her) on
every point as well as with administrators, executives, production committees,
agents, backers and various and sundry personal associates'" (to TW, qtd. in Kazan,
p. 329).

"Quebrada" appears to be a dramatic adaptation of the story "The Night of
the Iguana."]

67. To Audrey Wood

[Peter Nyholm House
Provincetown, Massachusetts]
August 25, 1947
[TLS, 3 pp. HRC]

Dear Audrey:

A good many things have happened to upset and disturb me in connection with the management of "Streetcar" and I am sure you would want
me to tell you frankly about them. In the first place, the new last scene of

the play, the crucial scene upon which the success or failure of the play may very well depend, has either been lost or deliberately withheld for it is not in the new scripts, one of which Irving has just now delivered to me. I worked on various versions of this scene the whole time I was on the Coast and in Dallas and on the train coming to New York. I delivered it to a typist at the Selznick office together with the other (less important) revisions with the clearly stated and unmistakable direction that all of these revisions were to be incorporated in a new script. I did this so that Gadge would have the new script, and particularly the new last scene, to read and consider when he went into his Connecticutt retreat. It now turns out that Gadge has never seen my revision of the last scene. He told me this on the phone. Weeks are passing at a period when every day counts, without any exchange of views on this all-important last scene. A mystery is made about it. Nobody even seems to know where my original copy of it is? Now this is the sort of high-handed, officious and arbitrary treatment that seems to characterize the Selznick company. My work is too important to me, in fact it has always been and is now even more so - for me to accept this sort of treatment from a company that has only produced one failure which closed out of town. I suppose this sounds as if I were gnashing my teeth with rage. I admit that is true. I <u>am</u>. I am willing to accept the bungling of the Garfield deal and the nerve-wracking battle that was waged to secure the right director, but when arbitrary action is taken interfering with my irreductible rights as an author, I'm not going to take it. This is not a sudden display of peevishness on my part. I entered the agreement with Selznick because we were led to believe that we would have what we wanted in every respect and that there were great advantages to be derived from her management in casting due to her Hollywood connections. These advantages have not materialized. In fact the casting has been just about the biggest headache I've had in my theatrical experience - outside of Boston. I am not alone in this opinion, as you must know if you have talked to Kazan. It was bad management that announced Garfield in the papers before he was signed and I strongly suspect that good management would have signed him. The play has already been damaged and compromised before it has even gone into rehearsals.

I am getting this off my chest now in order to clear the atmosphere and so you will understand that if it is necessary for me to take a strong

independant stand at any point in my future dealings with the Selznick company that you will see I am not doing it capriciously but with a feeling of justification. I am not going to lose this play because of poor management and I am going to see to it that it is protected in every possible and reasonable way because that is what I have a right to expect as the one who has given most and who has the most at stake. A play is my life's blood.

I also want you to know that my personal feelings toward everyone involved are sincerely and perfectly friendly. I like Irene as a person. I just feel that I am being asked to gamble, to take more of a risk, than is equitable for a playwright who is now in a position, after much effort and travail, to make choices and decisions for himself and to give his work the maximum protection.

So much for my state of being, at this point.

The actor George Beban was flown out here from the Coast and read for me this morning. This actor has had summer stock experience and has chased a stage coach in a Grade B Western. It was his first time on a horse. He is more adventuresome than I. I don't want to put my play under him. He gave a fair reading. He is of medium height with a rather tough and virile quality but he was monotonous, there was no gradation to his reading, no apparent humor or dexterity which comes from experience and from natural acting ability. He read one scene on his feet and his body movements were stiff and self-conscious with none of the animal grace and vitality (When I say grace I mean a virile grace) which the part calls for and it made me more bitterly conscious than ever of how good Garfield would have been. I think it was a brutal experience for this actor, and I do regard actors as being human beings some of them just as sensitive and capable of disappointment and suffering as I am. I don't understand why he was put through this ordeal with no more apparent attributes than he showed this morning. Of course it was a great strategic error, if the Selznick office hoped to interest me in this actor, to accompany him with the new scripts, for when I saw that my final scene had been left out I was somewhat distracted from anything else. I am sure, however, that I gave the actor a pretty fair appraisal, notwithstanding this factor. None of us, Gadge, Irene or I, were at all impressed by the screen-tests we saw of him on the Coast.

That leaves us with Marlon Brando, of the ones that have been mentioned to date. I am very anxious to see and hear him as soon as I can. He

is going to read for Gadge and if Gadge likes him I would like to have a look at him. I also think it would be a good idea for someone outside the Selznick office to explore the Garfield situation. I should like to know if there are terms he would accept, at this point. And precisely what those terms are so that I myself can judge whether or not they were reasonable and practicable for this production. I don't think it would be wise, now, to let him sign for less than a full season - that is, till May - but I think he should be sounded out for his financial terms under that consideration. Gadge thinks any other management would have signed him and I am inclined to go along with Gadge's opinion as he knows Garfield better than the rest of us.

I think at this point we must avoid all unnecessary friction with the Selznick office but be prepared to take decisive action. Irene should not know that I have talked things over with Gadge and that he has expressed these opinions, for it would only make trouble between them which would further complicate our position.

I am aware of the possibility that Gadge and I both may perhaps have judged Irene mistakenly in her conduct of the Garfield affair.

Please tell Colton, for me - I'll write him myself a bit later - that I want a contract drawn up with Margo that will leave the date of production to our joint discretion, and that whether or not we have an associate producer should also be at our joint discretion, to be discussed and decided when we are ready to put that play in production. I now regard Margo with absolute reverence, because I know that in any dealings with her I would know exactly what was going on all the time and there would be a real autonomy of management and artistic control.

Affectionately yours, Tennessee

[Audrey Wood answered TW on August 27, typing the letter herself to insure confidentiality. The latest revisions of *Streetcar* had not been "lost" or "withheld" but sent first to Irene Selznick's office in California, as per usual practice. They were now on their way to Elia Kazan (August 27, 1947, HRC).

Selznick recalls that revision of the last scene of *Streetcar* was "confined to Blanche's departure, which was not only over-long but too harrowing" (*A Private View*, p. 301). TW attempted to soften the original "Poker Night" sequence by removing Blanche's more extreme symptoms—catatonic and hallucinatory—as well as her sedation with a hypodermic needle and departure in a straitjacket.

In July Hume Cronyn re-staged "Portrait of a Madonna" at the Actors' Lab to coincide with TW's visit to the West Coast. Tandy's portrayal of the delusional Miss Collins made it "instantly apparent" that "Jessica was Blanche" (*Memoirs*, p. 132), and she was signed.

John Garfield and Elia Kazan were friends and former members of the Group Theatre (1931-1941), but Garfield's loyalty, protests aside, was to a flourishing career in Hollywood. His "signing" to play Stanley was announced on August 1 but by the 18th plans had begun to unravel, as reported in the *New York Times*. A "very disturbed" TW cabled Wood for "complete details on Garfield situation and advance notice of any new terms offered him" (August 18, 1847, HRC). Garfield reportedly sought a limited run of four months and a guarantee of the film role, which Selznick rejected.]

68. To Audrey Wood

[Peter Nyholm House
Provincetown, Massachusetts]
August 29, 1947.
[TLS, 2 pp. HRC]

Dear Audrey:

I am grateful for your hand-made letter which was eloquent and moving, all the more so because of the technical difficulties. My rage is pacified and in spite of all the gnashing my teeth including the new bridge-work are still in place. The last scene arrived from the Coast. I do not know why it went there (exclusively) but since it has returned in good shape I am willing to surrender all suspicion of caballistic intentions. There is perhaps a touch of paranoia in my mind lately: I am like Mother Wingfield, I am not paranoiac but my life is paranoia.

I can't tell you what a relief it is that we have found such a God-sent Stanley in the person of Brando. It had not occured to me before what an excellent value would come through casting a very young actor in this part. It humanizes the character of Stanley in that it becomes the brutality or callousness of youth rather than a vicious older man. I don't want to focus guilt or blame particularly on any one character but to have it a tragedy of misunderstandings and insensitivity to others. A new value came out of Brando's reading which was by far the best reading I have ever heard. He seemed to have already created a dimensional character, of the sort that the war has produced among young veterans. This is a value beyond any that

Garfield could have contributed, and in addition to his gifts as an actor he has great physical appeal and sensuality, at least as much as Burt Lancaster. When Brando is signed I think we will have a really remarkable 4-star cast, as exciting as any that could possibly be assembled and worth all the trouble that we have gone through. Having him instead of a Hollywood star will create a highly favorable impression as it will remove the Hollywood stigma that seemed to be attached to the production. Please use all your influence to oppose any move on the part of Irene's office to reconsider or delay signing the boy, in case she doesn't take to him. I hope he will be signed before she shows in New York.

We had a full house this week, Joanna, Margo and Marlon in addition to Pancho and I. Things were so badly arranged that Margo and Brando had to sleep in the same room - on twin cots. I believe they behaved themselves - the fools! We had fixed a double-decker bunk for Margo and Joanna to occupy but when Margo climbed into her upper bunk several of the slats refused to support her. Also the plumbing went bad so we had to go out in the bushes. I had a violent quarrel with the plumber over the phone so he would not come out. Also the electric wiring broke down and "plunged us into everlasting darkness" like the Wingfields at supper. All this at once! Oh, and the kitchen was flooded! Marlon arrived in the middle of this domestic cataclysm and set everything straight. That, however, is not what determined me to give him the part. It was all too much for Pancho. He packed up and said he was going back to Eagle Pass. However he changed his mind, as usual. I am hoping that he will go home, at least to New Orleans, while the play is in rehearsal, until December. He is not a calm person. In spite of his temperamental difficulties he is very lovable and I have grown to depend on his affection and companionship but he is too capricious and excitable for New York especially when I have a play in rehearsal. I hope it can be worked out to keep him in the South for that period or at least occupied with a job. That would make things easier for me. I think it would also help a lot if I could find a small furnished apartment. Hotels are never restful enough. Are you having any luck with that problem? Perhaps some real estate agent would find one for me. I will stay on here until needed for casting.

Wherever it is possible I want to have my professional connections with persons I know, understand and am fond of, reciprocally, so I know

you will understand my wish to publish through Laughlin and produce "Summer & Smoke" through Margo. I think such action gives a meaning to life: that is, sharing faith and keeping loyalties. Sometimes there is a conflict with professional interests, but unless that conflict is really important, I think it is better to sacrifice a little of the material advantage. I am not delivering a sermon to you on this subject as it is one on which we have no difference of opinion whatsoever, I am only putting this down to clarify my reasons for sometimes asking you to disregard what you, as my representative, feel always obliged to protect. I would not make commitments with any friend that would <u>seriously</u> imperil my work, as that always comes first, and in both these instances I feel there is actually no material <u>disad</u>vantage and very likely an advantage. So this is not being terribly noble, after all . . .

With love, Tennessee.

["Finding a Stanley," Elia Kazan recalls, "proved almost as simple—once we forgot about movie stars (the natural place for Irene to look)—as finding Blanche" (Kazan, p. 341). Marlon Brando's reading so impressed a visiting Margo Jones that she "jumped up and let out a 'Texas Tornado' shout." It was "'the greatest reading'" that she had "'ever heard—in or outside of Texas!'" (qtd. in *Memoirs*, p. 131). The twenty-three-year-old Brando had two promising Broadway seasons to his credit and was well known to Kazan for his supporting role in *Truckline Café* (1946), a play of little merit by Maxwell Anderson which Harold Clurman and Kazan had co-produced.

"Not a calm person" refers to another violent episode with Pancho, who reportedly tried to run down TW with the Pontiac and then subjected Margo Jones and Joanna Albus to "a night of horror" (*Memoirs*, p. 134). His apparent provocation was TW's meeting of a young man at the Atlantic House and their subsequent idyll in the sand dunes. Frank Merlo, "a youth of Sicilian extraction," would become TW's "closest, most long-lasting companion" (*Memoirs*, p. 132), when they met again in New York.]

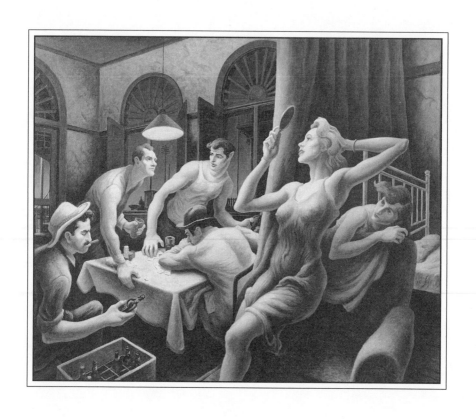

PART II
1947-1948

Overleaf: Thomas Hart Benton, The Poker Night *(from* A Streetcar Named Desire*).*

69. To Irene Mayer Selznick

SH: Provincetown, Massachusetts
Sept. 8, 1947
[TLS, 3 pp. Private Collection]

Dear Irene:

I hope you will forgive me for stealing another week on the Cape. The Indian summer here is too glorious to miss altogether: a mellow golden light suffuses everything and the lingering warmth is much sweeter. Now that the tourists have gone the real salty character of the fishing community emerges. - I talked to Gadge and he said he wouldnt need me till the fifteenth. I plan to return to New York by then. As the four principals have been cast (and very happily), I don't think there is anything very urgent or immediate for me to do in New York right now. I do want to check with Lehmann on the music. I have not heard from him since our meeting last month. I would like to have a hand in the selection of Eunice. But I am sure that you all can weed out the field and let me look over the final contestants. As for the poker players: I am sure Gadge will do a good job on them. ~~I don't think it will hurt to cast the Mexican for comedy. A plump~~ There is the Mexican and Steve Hubbs in addition to Mitch and Stanley. Steve should be a big beefy guy. The Mexican is called a "Greaseball". Might be cast accordingly. I would say all men around Stanley's age, or a bit older. Eunice is a coarse and healthy character. The nurse is a bit sinister: a large and masculine type. I don't know whether or not you want to use the Mexican woman selling the tin flowers. Check with Gadge on that. If not her speeches can be easily deleted from the script.

As for the last scene, I will give it another work-out. I feel that my last revision on it is the best to date. It has not as much "plus-quality" in the writing as I would like. However I think it will play well. Where it lacks most is the dialogue between Stella and Eunice: there is still something too cut-and-dried in the necessary exposition between them. I will try (but can't promise) to improve on that. I would like your opinion about the relative sympathetic treatment of the doctor. It may soften too much. We mustn't lose the effect of terror: everybody agrees about that.

I have talked to Irving and Audrey about getting Joanna into the company. I don't believe you have met her, which is unfortunate as she is a very rare person. She is not quite right for any part in the play but could understudy Eunice and the nurse, not that she is their type but is an excellent actress

who could play anything in a pinch. However her real value would be in backstage relations. She would take an intense personal interest in everything connected with the play and would serve in countless ways in addition to "holding the book". She is one of those miracles of general competence! Every show needs somebody like that to hold things together behind the scenes. My idea was that she could be engaged as promptress and understudy for a couple of the women. It would mean a great deal to her for personal reasons. She was not at all happy last summer at Dallas. Margo wants her back there but Joanna definitely wants to stay with a New York show and particularly this one which she is crazy about.

It seems that I <u>will</u> have an Apartment when I arrive in N.Y. Expect me on the 15th.

With love, Tennessee.

[Selection of Kim Hunter and Karl Malden completed the principal cast of *A Streetcar Named Desire* (1947). Finding a Stella was uncertain and prolonged. Only by chance did Irene Selznick "spot three lines in *Variety* mentioning that Kim was touring in a small stock company upstate. . . . I dared to propose her." Hunter would make a difficult adjustment to the role in her first appearance on Broadway. Malden, by contrast, was "the first and last" to read for the part of Mitch and "was wonderful" (Selznick, *A Private View*, 1983, p. 303).

Elements of jazz and the blues in Alex North's score were intended to "fit," as Elia Kazan put it, the respective violence and desperation of Stanley and Blanche. Lehman Engle, musical director, supervised the four-piece band tucked away in the Ethel Barrymore Theatre.

The "exposition" between Stella and Eunice in Scene Eleven of *Streetcar* reveals that Stella has settled for the self-preserving lie, denying that Stanley raped her sister.

Joanna Albus served as an uncredited staff assistant in the *Streetcar* company.]

70. To Walter Dakin Williams

[Hotel Algonquin, New York]
PM: New York, September 20, 1947
[TLS, 1 p. HRC]

Dear Dakin:

I am sorry we didn't get together on your trip East. You came a little too late to visit me in Provincetown as I was leaving the day after I got your wire.

Is it true that you are entering a law-firm in St. Louis? Audrey got that

impression. Are you sure this will suit you better? I wish you had made some legal connection in New York, for I would then be able to put you in charge of my financial and legal affairs. I am not happy over having them entirely under one control as they now are, as my lawyer is also the Lieblings lawyer. I think it is best to separate the two. Perhaps after "Streetcar" opens I can make some different arrangement, for then my business affairs will be too complicated for me to watch over carefully. I don't feel that I have realized as much, financially, from the last play as I should have and I want to be more careful about the new ones. If you come to New York for the opening of "Streetcar", we can talk that over.

I am moving into a small apartment the first of October. It is just one room with a kitchenette and bath but it's the best available. It is right off Park avenue on 36th street, one of the few blocks in New York that have real trees. Living at the Algonquin is a strain as the place is infested with actors looking for jobs. It is impossible to get from the door to the elevator, a fairly short distance, without being snagged by one.

Have they found anyone to take Rose around? And where is Grandfather planning to go after Sewanee?

With love, Tom.

[Discharged from the Army Air Corps as a captain, Dakin Williams briefly taught law at St. Louis University before joining the local firm of Martin, Peper & Martin.

Rose Williams was beginning her eleventh year as a patient at Farmington State Hospital in southeastern Missouri. Visits by TW were rare, and painful, and perhaps discouraged by Edwina, who feared that they would unnerve her son. TW had recommended to the superintendent that a companion be found to accompany Rose on brief trips away from the hospital.]

71. To Amado "Pancho" Rodriguez y Gonzalez

108 E. 36th Street [New York]
Oct. 1947.
[TLS w/ autograph marginalia
and postscript, 2 pp. HRC]

Dear Pancho:

I was awfully happy to get your letter this morning with the account of your day with the nephews. They seem to take after their uncle in some respects.

This is the first I have heard from you about the garage's offer for the car. Perhaps you wrote about it before and the letter didn't reach me. It seems like a good offer. I will look through my papers for the registration card you want. Is that all that will be necessary to make the transaction?

I wish I could write you an equally amusing letter but I don't have any little nephews to supply me with comic material. I feel very sober and dull. And when I get home at night, after a day at the disposal of the Selznick company and the Liebling-Wood Corporation, I barely have the strength to hit the typewriter keys. You must try and forgive me for being so stupid and do write me whenever you can. It does me good to hear about your peaceful family life in New Orleans where I would much prefer to be. However I have now moved into my apartment. It can hardly be called that as it is really just one room with little kitchenette and bathroom. No one has learned the phone number so I have a feeling of privacy which is a comfort after the Algonquin. Jo Healy has been taking me to all the openings. She gets tickets through the agency she works for. There has only been one hit so far this season and it is a war-play which the public may not support long. We start rehearsals Monday. Gadge is full of vitality and optimism. Miss Tandy has arrived in town looking very pretty with her new blond hair and all the script changes have been approved and finally typed up.

Today I got a notice to call the Athletic Club so perhaps it has been arranged for me to join there. I have been swimming daily at the "Y", walking a good deal, and have managed to lose seven pounds. I also had to give up potatoes - which I love. But when I saw my new photographs - with a face like a full moon only not nearly so bright - I knew that something must be done about it. I had other pictures taken after I lost the 7 pounds and the new ones are quite nice. I'll send you one.

Grandfather wrote me a long letter from the Wm. Len hotel in Memphis. He says he is waiting for me to come South again. Dear old man, he is so brave and wonderful, going along by himself at the age of ninety! I sent him a nice check, for I doubt that Mother had provided for him sufficiently.

I also got a note from Oliver who has gone to teach at Nebraska. No news in it.

Buffie is furious with me because I stood her up at a cocktail party. When I last saw her she was entertaining a woman whom she introduced

to me as "The Countess Hamilton". A plain-looking woman with bulging blue eyes and seedy looking out-fit - but anyhow she was a countess so Buffie was nearly bursting with pride. She told me that I was not fit to associate with well-mannered people! I agreed with her and left. She is now in her house but only one room is reasonably finished. And Irene is about to have kittens.

Jane Lawrence is back in town. Her hair is light golden red but she looked awfully tired the day I saw her. She helped me pack my things and move over here and I am going to do what I can to help her find a singing job in a show. However the chances are not good as the theatrical season seems to be unusually bad. Few shows opening and those of doubtful quality.

I took Celeste Holm (musical star) to hear your niece, Carmen, sing. She liked her and may interest other people. Jo Healy invited Carmen to lunch but Carmen did not even acknowledge the invitation. I can't imagine why. Jo lives with Gypsy Rose Lee and has many theatrical contacts. She took quite a friendly interest in Carmen because of me.

Take care of yourself. Be good, be good, be good! And take your nephews to the zoo. I expect to see you in a couple of months. You might enquire at the Pontalba if the lady Mrs. Vacarro knows could get me an apartment there. That is, if, if, if!

Your loving friend, Tenn.

P.S. Will mail papers this week-end. Please wire collect name of buyer and garage.

[Pancho Rodriguez was persuaded—perhaps by Irene Selznick—to rejoin his family in New Orleans shortly after he and TW arrived in New York on September 14. In seeking title clearance, he was following TW's advice to sell the Pontiac should repairs prove costly.

Rehearsals of *Streetcar* afforded TW no relief from dullness: "This was a lost day. I went to bed at 9 a.m. and got up when it was getting dark and did nothing but attend rehearsals. Tonight I made the mistake of drinking coffee. My belly aches a bit in a dull way and my mind seems to imitate that feeling." The journal passage ends with the admission that "today I was particularly aware of missing Pancho" (Monday {October 1947}).

The "war-play" *Command Decision* (1947), by William W. Haines, closed after 408 performances on Broadway. TW's escort appears to have been Jo Healy, a Theatre Guild friend from the early 1940s who would serve at times as a companion for Rose.

TW closes with a litany of family, friends, and celebrities, including Celeste Holm, the original Ado Annie of *Oklahoma!* (1943) fame. He would be joined by Pancho much sooner than expected or seemingly desired.

TW wrote this letter before rehearsals of *Streetcar* began on October 6, 1947. Keyed to the fifth paragraph is a marginal reference to Walter Dakin, "Send him a card!"]

72. To Margaret "Margo" Jones

> [108 East 36th Street, New York]
> [October 1947]
> [TLS, 2 pp. HRC]

Dearest Margo:

I am commencing the Sabbath at three P.M. with a stiff slug of Scotch, about three fingers, with a little faucet water, being too nervous to get out the ice-cubes. This sounds like things are going badly. Actually I believe they are going pretty good. I cannot find words to tell you how wonderful Jessica and Gadge are, and what a superb combination their talents appear to be. I have never seen two people, except maybe you, work as hard on anything. Or have as much respect for each other, which is so important. Gadge's method is to stage one new scene each day and to go over all the preceding scenes in sequence. Tomorrow, Monday, he will stage the final, eleventh scene, which I think is the crucial one. We have not come into conflict on any point. Occasionally I have to suggest a little less realistic treatment of things, to which he always accedes. His great gift is infusing everything with vitality. Sometimes in his desire to do this he neglects to dwell sufficiently upon a lyric moment. However this is not through failure to comprehend them, and he is always eager for my advice. Everybody is working out fine with the possible exception of Kim Hunter. She was very bad at first, is now improving but will, I am afraid, always be the lame duck in the line-up. She too is working like a fire-horse but is not a very gifted actress, and shows up badly in contrast to one as emotionally and technically rich as Jessica. You should see Joanna! She is everybody's darling! The Selznick office possesses her body and soul and they consider her the pearl beyond price! (Which she undoubtedly is). I have not had a chance to talk to her since the production started.

Honey, you don't know what a wonderful gift that pressed wood was!

My fire is my big comfort here. And that pressed wood is miraculous, the way it starts blazing right up and keeps at it! Every time I light a fire with it, I think about Margo whose gift to the world is fire, the fire of belief and devotion in comparison to which everything else in this universe is a heap of dead ashes.

Here is a bit of news for you. The Mexican problem returned to Manhattan a couple of days ago, quite unexpectedly, and is now sharing the one-room apartment with me. Manana he will look for a job. (Always Manana). I don't know what has happened but something has flown out the window, maybe never to return. Sympathy is not enough. There must be respect and understanding on both sides. I wish I could talk to you about this. I am terribly troubled. I don't think I am acting kindly, and that is what I hate above all else.

Please send me a little bulletin, just a few lines, on the Project.

With love, 10.

[Kim Hunter recalls that TW would silently advise Elia Kazan by tucking a note into his "coat pocket." Kazan, TW confirms, "was one of those rare directors who wanted the playwright around at all rehearsals. . . . Once in a while he would call me up on stage to demonstrate how I felt a certain bit should be played. I suspect he did this only to flatter me for he never had the least uncertainty in his work" (*Memoirs*, p. 135). Uncertainty was the lot of Irene Selznick, who feared that Marlon Brando's Stanley would never overcome his legendary mumbling.

TW ambivalently recorded Pancho's return to New York: "My feeling for P. has more or less definitely fallen from desire to custom though my affection is not lost. I don't think it was time or repetition. It was partly that but other things, a spiritual disappointment was the more important factor. He is incapable of reason. Violence belongs to his nature as completely as it is abhorrent to mine. Most of all, I want and now must have - simple peace. The problem is to act kindly and still strongly, for now I know that my manhood is sacrificed in submitting to such a relationship. Oh, well - it will work out somehow" (*Journal*, October 27, 1947).

Margo Jones assured TW that he was "incapable of acting unkindly" toward Pancho and urged that he not allow his "huge responsibility to the world" to be affected by this "dangerous" relationship. She advised that he "take a definite stand once and for all" (Tuesday night {October 1947} HRC).

TW may have written this letter on Sunday, October 19, 1947, after Pancho's return to New York.]

73. *To Amado "Pancho" Rodriguez y Gonzalez*

SH: The Ritz-Carlton, Boston
[November 1947]
[TLS, 3 pp. HRC]

Dear Pancho:

I expect I'll see you in New York early this week, and I sincerely hope that I'll find you in a pleasant and reasonable state of mind. I myself am so tired that it is impossible for me right now to cope with unreasonable moods. In my life there has been so much <u>real</u> tragedy, things that I cannot speak about and hardly dare to remember, from the time of my childhood and all the way through the years in between that I lack patience with people who are spoiled and think that they are entitled to go through life without effort and without sacrifice and without disappointment. Life is hard. As Amanda said, "It calls for Spartan endurance." But more than that, it calls for understanding, one person understanding another person, and for some measure of sacrifice, too. Very few people learn until late in life how much courage it takes to live, but if you learn it in the beginning, it will be easier for you. Excuse me for preaching. I am not a good preacher and perhaps I have no right to. But I feel concerned for you, worried over your lack of purpose. You have so much more than I have in so many ways. Your youth, your health and energy, your many social graces which I do not have. Life can hold a great deal for you, it can be very rich and abundant if you are willing to make some effort and to stop thinking and acting altogether selfishly. In this world the key to happiness is through giving, more than getting. For instance when you see that someone needs peace more than anything else, needs quietness and a sense of security, you cannot expect to involve that person in continual turmoil and tension and anxiety and still have him cherishing your companionship all the time. No, for his own protection if he wishes to go on living and working, he must withdraw sometime from these exhausting conditions. One does not suffer alone. It is nearly always two who suffer, but sometimes one places all the blame on the other.

Of all the people I have known you have the greatest and warmest heart but you also unfortunately have a devil in you that is constantly working against you, filling you with insane suspicions and jealousies and ideas that are so preposterous that one does not know how to answer them.

It is a terrifying thing. You must face it and make a determined effort to master it now before it becomes too well-established. Try to understand all those whom you get these foolish prejudices against. If you know them you'll see how wrong you are and laugh at yourself. Most of all - get busy at something. Then you will regain your self-confidence and independance and you will take a man's place in the world.

You know that my affection for you and my loyalty to you as a friend remains unalterable and that while I am alive you will have my true friendship always with you.

Ever, Tennessee.

[Notices for the Boston tryout of *Streetcar* (November 3-15, 1947) were generally positive, if qualified by moral concerns and "second thoughts" regarding the play's stature as tragedy. Especially flattering were reviews of Jessica Tandy's performance, which was deemed "superb, imaginative and illuminating." Notices for Marlon Brando, while strong, did not justify the fear that he would dominate Tandy and make the play his own. The Boston censor tried, without success, to have the rape scene struck.

TW probably wrote this letter before Pancho Rodriguez made a "surprise visit" to Boston and burst into his room at the Ritz-Carlton. He was pacified and removed by Irene Selznick, whose suite was nearby. TW wrote in *Memoirs* that "it was years" (p. 137) before he saw Pancho again.]

74. To Amado "Pancho" Rodriguez y Gonzalez

[108 East 36th Street, New York]
[ca. late-November 1947]
[TLS, 1 p. HRC]

Dear Pancho:

There are some things I feel I ought to try to say to you and since you don't apparently want me to talk to you I will try to write them. If I had not cared for you deeply you would not have hurt me and if you had not hurt me I would not have "blown my top" as I did. I spoke and acted in a blind rage. Maybe you don't know what provoked it and maybe I don't either. It just happened, as I told you it might happen at lunch that day, when I said I thought it would be safer for us to live separately. There was a tight coil of emotion in me as a result of the two preceding incidents -

which any little thing could set off. And it did. If you search your heart you will understand these things. I have never said an untrue thing to you all the times that I have been with you except in those few blind panicky moments when it seemed, perhaps unreasonably, that you had never cared for me at all and that I had been just a matter of convenience for whom you held contempt. To explain those things you have to go back through the entire history of a life, all its loneliness, its disappointments, its hunger for understanding and love. ~~And perhaps even you get only a~~ No, there is no point in talking about it any further. I don't ask anything of you, Pancho, this is not to ask anything, not even your pardon. I only want to tell you that I am your friend and will remain so regardless of how you may feel toward me. I offered you more of my heart than I have anybody in the last five years, which you may not have wanted and may now despise but believe me it is still full of the truest affection for you. Wherever you are I want you to have happiness - salud, amor y pesados!

10.

[The dating of this letter is speculative in light of the ceaseless turmoil and periodic ruptures of TW's relationship with Pancho Rodriguez. Nonetheless its summary character may indicate the final decisive break during the tryout period of *Streetcar*.]

75. *To Edwina Dakin Williams*

SH: Liebling-Wood
Authors' Representatives
551 Fifth Avenue
New York 17, N.Y.
[late-November 1947]
[TLS, 1 p. HTC]

Dear Mother:

I am just in town for the day and am borrowing Audrey's office to get off a few letters. I am glad you and Dakin have decided to come up for the opening. Forewarned is forearmed so you will be prepared for a rugged evening in the theatre. Most of the ladies seem to enjoy the play a great deal and one of the Boston Cabots, a lady of great refinement, wrote me that she was "inexpressibly delighted" by the street-car ride I gave her in Boston.

I shall not listen to any moral homilies and dissertations so please leave them at home, but do bring a Spanish shawl with you, one of those that Grandfather purchased in Italy. We have been trying to get one for the play and have had no luck as they are no longer fashionable. I will see that Madame Selznick gives you several times the purchase price for it. I love to spend her money. I have been staying in luxurious suites at the best hotels on the road, as it is all out of her fifteen million dollars and I think she needs every possible assistance in reducing that all but intolerable burden.

How about the Catholic priest? Is he coming to the play, too? Wouldn't you rather stay at one of the hotels on the park such as the Plaza or the St. Moritz? I think reservations could be arranged. What do you hear from Grandfather, and is anything being done for Rose? If this play goes over I am going to establish a fund to provide for her somewhat better.

I shall be terribly busy till after opening night but I can meet your train if you let me know when you arrive on Monday.

With love, Tom.

[TW was in and out of "town" while attending the final tryout of *Streetcar* in Philadelphia (November 17-29, 1947), where it did excellent business and received the strongest notices to date. It "is bound to linger long in the memory, vividly and vitally, after most of the facile and ephemeral footlight offerings . . . have been forgotten," predicted one astute reviewer.

TW informed his grandfather at this time that Edwina and Dakin planned to attend the New York opening, although he doubted that "Mother will approve of this play: it is a little too colorful for her Presbyterian tastes. You'd like it better" (n.d., HTC). Edwina later proclaimed *Streetcar* TW's "greatest" work and added that "sons have such trouble understanding mothers!" (Edwina Dakin Williams, *Remember Me to Tom*, 1963, p. 188).]

76. To James "Jay" Laughlin

[108 East 36th Street, New York]
[December 4, 1947]
[TLS w/ enclosures, 1 p. Houghton]

Streetcar opened last night to tumultuous approval. Never witnessed such an exciting evening. So much better than New Haven you wdn't believe it; N.H. was just a reading of the play. Much more warmth, range,

intelligence, interpretation, etc. - a lot of it because of better details in direction, timing. Packed house, of the usual first-night decorations, - Cecil B'ton, Valentina, D. Parker, the Selznicks, the others and so on, - and with a slow warm-up for first act, and comments like "Well, of course, it isn't a play," the second act (it's in 3 now) sent the audience zowing to mad heights, and the final one left them - and me - wilted, gasping, weak, befoozled, drained (see reviews for more words) and then an uproar of applause which went on and on. Almost no one rose from a seat till many curtains went up on whole cast, the 4 principles, then Tandy, who was greeted by a great howl of "BRavo!" from truly all over the house. Then repeat of the whole curtain schedule to Tandy again and finally . . . . 10 Wms crept on stage, after calls of Author! and took bows with Tandy. All was great, great, GREAT! As you can see by the reviews enclosed. Will send from evening papers tomorrow. 20th-Century Fox has already called for a copy. I want to go to play again! Bielenson is printing it this minute and shd be bound and ready next week. E says that [there] are many many orders already, and with the success, we think we shd bind all 5000. What do you? Pauper will hold type for re-print if necessary, but cdn't possibly know now.

Do you want to see the poesie I have to select, or shd I just add one or two. None are longer than 1 type (single) page. Still think you really ought to print the nurse-actor story, though. That fits with ND 10.

T. Williams

[No reviewer was more aware of the dramatic integrity of *Streetcar* than Louis Kronenberger. The play, he wrote, "carries us into the only part of the theater that really counts—not the most obviously successful part, but the part where, though people frequently blunder they seldom compromise; where imagination is seated higher than photography; and where the playwright seems to have a certain genuine interest in pleasing himself" (*PM Magazine*, December 5, 1947). James Laughlin published the book in late-December 1947, while the play went on to win the Drama Critics' Circle and the Pulitzer prizes and to amass 855 performances on Broadway. Warner Brothers would release the first film version in 1951.]

The principal Broadway cast of A Streetcar Named Desire *(1947): Karl Malden, Marlon Brando, Jessica Tandy, and Kim Hunter. "Streetcar opened last night to tumultuous approval."*

77. To John van Druten

SH: Hotel Woodrow
West 64th Street, New York
December 7, 1947
[TLS, 2 pp. BRTC]

Dear John:

Your letter is the most honest and beautiful that has come to me in connection with any of my writing. I think it is a fine "human document" and I don't want to lose it. As I shall be travelling around a good deal this year, I have given to my friend and agent Audrey Wood to keep for me. There will be times when I will want to read it again. I don't feel able, at the moment, to answer you properly but the letter has left me with a feeling of companionship. We have shared like experiences. You have weathered a great deal more success than I and I hope that I wear it as well, for your

humanity is not depleted. This is amply testified in your work also by those who know you and particularly by this letter.

I think we must face the fact that there are some problems for which no perfect solution exists and popular success, the dislocation it brings, is one of those problems. However it is helped by facing it squarely. A grave illness such as you mention, anything that brings one close to fundamentals, is also a great help as I have discovered. It brings out the Chinaman in your soul and values slip back into a more natural allignment. You say that you are tempted to write a play about this problem. Why don't you? I know that "The Mermaids Sing" touched upon it, but I feel too superficially. Incidentally, "The Druid Circle" is a far, far better play and I found it more touching than "Voice of the Turtle". No one is better able than you to examine searchingly the problems of popular success in the theatre, its impact on the artist, and I think you can do it without repeating anything in your earlier work. But I, too, am faced with a problem of themes and material. There is always something but it is difficult to keep it away from stuff you have explored in the past. I don't think, for instance, I could get away with another southern play about a woman. I must try something different now. And I must not be afraid of failure. It is more a part of growth than success is.

I am hiding out temporarily in this flea-bag. Someone out of the past is making trouble. Have you ever had that? It is one of the ugly and sordid details coincident with a success. I don't want this known, but I am sailing on the 30th for Europe. If you are in town during the holidays, let us do, by all means, get together, you and Walter and I. I hope I will be back in my apartment by then and I have a basket of fine (1937) French champagne that Mme. Selznick gave me as an opening present. We will uncork one, and it will be better than that synthetic stuff I gave you at the Shelton - remember?

The best to you, John, and many, many thanks for your beautiful letter.

Ever, Tenn.

[*The Voice of the Turtle* (1943) and *I Remember Mama* (1944) illustrate the varied and successful career of the London-born playwright John van Druten (1901-1957). The plays ran for 1557 and 714 performances, respectively, the latter giving Marlon Brando his first important role on Broadway.

Van Druten wrote to applaud *Streetcar* but especially to underscore TW's

recent article in the *New York Times*, "On a Streetcar Named Success" (November 30, 1947). "You have told things that I have never read in print before, yet long know to be a part of me. The turning away from people; the sense that every conversation is like a Victrola record; the mistrust of sincerity; the involuntary rudeness, cold-shouldering and neglect towards old friends; the ever-accompanying sense of a fictitious personage, bearing one's own name, who inhibits your freedom of action; and lastly, the hatred of one's own work" (December 4, 1947, BRTC). TW had used his own remarks on the "catastrophe" of success—the depression and isolation which followed the opening of *The Glass Menagerie* (1945) in New York—as a timely advertisement for *Streetcar*.

"Plush days" at the Hotel Woodrow, an old haunt of TW, were fondly recalled in a journal entry: "The portable victrola by my bed and always money enough to eat or smoke or fuck" (ca. October 20, 1941). The "someone" making "trouble" is Pancho Rodriguez.]

78. To Justin Brooks Atkinson

Liebling-Wood Inc.
551 - 5 Ave. [New York]
Monday Dec. 15, 1947.
[TLS, 1 p. BRTC]

Dear Brooks:

At last a criticism which connects directly with the essence of what I thought was the play! I mean your Sunday article which I have just read with the deepest satisfaction of any the play's success has given me. So many of the others, saying 'alcoholic', 'nymphomaniac', 'prostitute', 'boozy' and so forth seemed - though stirred by the play - to be completely off the track, or nearly so. I wanted to show that people are not definable in such terms but are things of multiple facets and all but endless complexity that they do not fit "any convenient label" and are seldom more than partially visible even to those who live just on the other side of "the portieres".

You have also touched on my main problem: expanding my material and my interests. I can't answer that question. I know it and fear it and can only make more effort to extend my "feelers" beyond what I've felt so far. Thank you, Brooks. I am leaving for Europe soon. I will get in touch with you and Orianne before I sail.

Yours, Tenn.

[Atkinson (1894-1984) shunned categorical terms and described *Streetcar* as "a work of art" which "arrives at no general moral conclusions." Instead TW has exposed a desperate woman to "an alien environment that brutally wears on her nerves." The playwright takes "no sides in the conflict" and knows how "right" it is for each character to survive the impending "disaster." The article ends with a friendly, if serious, warning that the "uniformity" shown to date in the "choice of characters and in the attitude toward life . . . may limit the range of Mr. Williams' career as a playwright" (*New York Times*, December 14, 1947).]

79. To James "Jay" Laughlin

SH: Liebling-Wood
Authors' Representatives
551 Fifth Avenue
New York 17, N.Y.
December 29, 1947
[TLS, 1 p. Houghton]

Dear Jay:

I sail for Europe tomorrow afternoon on the "America", and I will go directly to Paris where I am stopping at the hotel GEORGE V. I don't know anybody there, I just have a bunch of letters to people, so I do hope you will [be] in Paris now and then. I will probably travel around a bit, to Italy wherever it is warm and there is some swimming.

My first reaction to the book cover was adverse. I think it was the color more than the design. It's a sort of shocking pink which reminds me of a violet scented lozenge. However, everything else about the book is very fine and I have only myself to blame for not paying more attention when it was being planned. I don't need to tell you what a deep satisfaction it is to have you bring it out, so forget about the cover. The design was original and striking. I hope you will like SUMMER AND SMOKE, when it is ready to be seen well enough to bring it out too.

I'm glad you liked the article. You bet I meant every word of it, and you of all people should know that. Get in touch with me when I arrive. I will be lonesome as hell I expect. Poor Carson McCullers is over here half paralyzed due to nervous shock over a lousy dramatization of her book, but she is slowly recovering. I will arrive about January 7th. Warmest regards.

As ever, Tenn

P.S. I am nervous over the advertising on ONE ARM. I don't think the book should be publicized and sold through the usual channels. We agreed to have it sold on a subscription basis. This is mostly because of consideration for my family, and because only a few of us will understand and like it, and it is bound to be violently attacked by the rest.

TW:ew

["At the end of that December, no longer able to cope with the unremitting publicity in New York, I sailed for Europe" (*Memoirs*, p. 139).

The "shocking pink" cover of *Streetcar* depicts two abstract female forms dominated by a third, a centered male, who holds one figure in willing embrace and the other in attempted flight. James Laughlin agreed to change the background color, but he hesitated to "abandon" the cover entirely, as Audrey Wood had requested. Alvin Lustig's designs sparked controversy and sold more books "than conventional ones" (to Wood, January 17 {1948} HRC). Lustig would design the jacket of each of TW's succeeding books published by New Directions, until his death in 1955.

The "article" to which Laughlin refers is probably "On a Streetcar Named Success."

Carson McCullers socialized, drank heavily, and did little if any serious work during 1947, when she and her husband, Reeves, lived in France. She suffered paralyzing strokes and was further weakened by the stress of a collaborative relation suggested by the Theatre Guild, which had conditionally agreed to produce *The Member of the Wedding* (1946). McCullers returned to the States in December, received neurological treatment at Columbia Presbyterian Hospital, and convalesced at her mother's home in Nyack, New York. TW visited McCullers before sailing for Europe.

Laughlin reassured Wood that the forthcoming publication of *One Arm and Other Stories* (1948) would involve "no advertising" and "no review copies." "You may be sure," he added, "that I don't want any scandal any more than you do" (January 17 {1948} HRC).]

80. To Margaret "Margo" Jones

[*America*]
12/31/47.
[TLS w/ autograph marginalia, 2 pp. HRC]

Dearest Margo:

I am writing you on the new typewriter delivered by Monty Clift. It is an adorable little Swiss machine called Hermes Baby, is as light as a feather,

almost pocket-size, and yet has everything on it the big ones have. It also has charm and humor which other machines don't have and I enjoy using it. Oddly enough I had been shopping for a new typewriter that very morning but had not found any to suit me and given up because I had so little time. Your idea was really psychic and I was deeply moved and touched by it. You will also be pleased to know that I gave my old one to Donnie. Donnie's had been stolen just a short while ago and he is still working on his novel so he needed one badly.

I am one day out on the ocean, travelling first class so that I can use the large swimming pool. That's the only agreeable feature. The first class passengers are a mess. All lousey rich and falling to pieces with age, refinement, and so forth. The assistant purser is the only one I've seen who interests me. So I am staying in my stateroom to avoid fraternization. Fortunately I have a good supply of books, mostly on physics. I have developed a great interest in atomic and cosmic science and the books on those subjects are fascinating. But I am so stupid I have to read each page twice and sometimes twice again before I absorb the content. Even so it is better than prevailing trends in fiction. I also have Dostoevsky's The Idiot, a parting gift from Donnie, my Crane and Lorca's poems.

I had a packing-bee the morning of my departure. About six people came over to pack me, as I had put it off till the last minute. Gadge brought champagne: the others drank while Joanna did all the packing, and she did a beautiful job of it. You know I always liked Joanna but the more I see of her the more I am impressed by the real beauty of her nature. She is blossoming out in New York. I think it is good for her to create her own little world as she is now doing. I think she is having many new experiences and assimilating them into new values, so it has all worked out for the best. I shall miss her in Europe, in fact I shall miss all of my friends. There are a few people I value dearly. Now that I am living alone I have felt much closer to them. Poor Pancho made such a barrier! He is now living in Miami Beach and has a job at Saks store down there. He writes me that he has a crew haircut and a deep tan and is "looking terrific"! Enclosed a snapshot to verify the statement. Also that he has met the Walter Chrysler Jr's and been entertained on their yacht: his dream factory is still working.

I had a good talk with Jo about Summer. I told him it should be designed completely away from Streetcar and Glass, using very pure colors an almost abstract design with Gothic effects and sky, sky, sky! He thinks

he will have to get a really good sculptor to execute the angel: I think that is justified for we shall have to depend on the best of poetic effects. I strongly feel we should open in Chicago and play there for a couple of months, some place that hasn't seen Streetcar for the comparison will not be helpful. It takes a long out-of-town period for my stuff to catch on. Jo also thinks we should find out about Margaret Phillips availability: see what her plans are for the late summer and Fall. I think the ideal time to commence would be in August. I am thinking of giving this play to my sister so that she will have independant means if it is successful. I doubt that I could keep any money from it anyhow so it is no sacrifice.

Gadge wants to know if you would be interested in heading the Drama department at Bennington College. He was asked to take the job but he recommended you as he is too restless. It is close to New York and an important artistic center. Of course I am hoping that some day you will be at the head of ANTA when it has a real nation-wide importance. There is nothing more hopeful for the theatre than this idea of government charter and support.

I don't know whether it's the accumulated fatigue of months or the cradle rocking of the vessel but I feel sleepy all the time. My nights have been wild and wonderful in Manhattan, lasting always till five in the morning, seldom getting more than four or five hours sleep. I need this rest and I have a lot to remember.

I do hope Manning's play was a distinguished and popular success. Joanna thought it should be.

With much, much love, Tenn (at sea)

[Margo Jones directed the fall season of Theatre '47 in Dallas, including a program of one-acts by TW, and continued to plan the Broadway premiere of *Summer and Smoke* (1948). Jo Mielziner would design the set and Margaret Phillips, unavailable for the earlier production in Dallas, was signed to play Alma Winemiller.

Jones apparently rejected the offer from Bennington College. Her unhappy experience at the University of Texas in the early 1940s made her wary of another academic appointment.

Chartered by Congress in 1935, ANTA (American National Theatre and Academy) had recently launched a membership drive to achieve its goal of bringing "the best in the theatre to every State." Its programs, although far ranging and varied, were centered in New York and thus differed fundamentally from Jones's idea of a national theatre with resident companies scattered throughout "this big country

of ours." Nonetheless Jones was active in ANTA and served on the board of directors. On November 30, 1947, ANTA and the National Broadcasting Company sponsored the first televised performance of a TW play, "The Last of My Solid Gold Watches" (1943).

Dallas politely received Manning Gurian's comedy, *Lemple's Old Man* (1947). Gurian was Jones's business manager and romantic interest—their intimate relationship perhaps unknown to TW.

Penned in the upper margin of page 1 is the notation "Hotel George V Paris, France (for a while)."]

81. *To Paul Bigelow*

SH: Hotel George V
31, Avenue George V, Paris
<u>1/7/48</u>
[TLS, 3 pp. Columbia U]

Dear Paul:

How I enjoyed your candy! Altogether too much, for a curvacious figure has to be watchful or it gets out of bounds. If you have seen any of my recent pictures I am sure you know what I mean. Austerity in Europe may be useful.

I arrived here yesterday after a quiet and restful crossing. I spent it mostly lying down, the accumulated fatigue of months. It was luxurious to just sleep, and sleep. I was put at the Captain's table but he was such a drip that I never showed up after the first meal. I had the others in my quarters.

Margo sent me this damned Swiss machine as a parting gift. It is about the size of a highschool geography book, but a thing of infinite complexity and caprice. Every little gadget on it seems to have a dual or triple purpose. Some day I will touch something in the wrong place and it will bite my nose off and make cocktail sausages.

This hotel is a mess, only one advantage which will please you. The bathroom has a bidet with hot and cold water! Also they serve real Brazilian coffee. But it is full of sleek women with chows. I will probably move to one of the little places in the Latin Quarter if I remain in Paris. The town has changed since I was here at sixteen. Plenty of time to do so, as you will observe. However I remember it as being so light and lively at night. Now the streets are rather dim and murky. Today and yesterday there was continual rain. However it still has charm. I will stay here a

while, then probably move south to Rome and Tangiers where Paul Bowles is staying. I wonder if Gide was right about those little natives?

Pancho and I have separated, I guess you know that. He could not adjust himself to New York and the increasing involvement of my professional life. He behaved pretty badly, more than I could finally put up with, but it wasn't his fault. I am not a good person to live with. Being alone again is both a relief and a sorrow. At any rate it gives me more time with my old friends.

Paul dear, I am distressed to hear that you are still troubled with the jaw and that you must have an operation on it. I wish I could be with you during that ordeal as you were with me during the miserable times I had with my eye.

Maxwell broke his hip, gave up his job - in the opposite sequence - and is now "visiting some dear old friend" in Tampa Florida. He has a slight limp and carries a cane but is otherwise the same, quite the same, only nobody has recently mistaken him for a boy at Princeton. Donnie has finished one draft of his novel. It was turned down by Random House and he is writing it over. It needs at least another year's work but I think it has a quality that is original and striking. It is about Butch's early life in Atlanta.

Mother is finally getting a legal separation from my father. She gets the house and part of the shoe stock and he returns to Knoxville to live with his old maid sister, God help her. And God help them both. This deal was to be consummated around Christmas, in time I hope for a happy holiday. It means that my ancient grandfather, ninety years old, can return home and spend the rest of his days with Mother. I hope it may also mean that my sister can visit home, and of course that I can. So a tragic situation works itself out, a little too late, but better than never at all. As for the old man, he has probably suffered as much as anyone, possibly even more, and I am afraid it will be a lonely and bitter end to his blind and selfish life.

When you come to New York for the operation, let Audrey know. Also let me hear from you, care of her.

I am reading a lovely book that you would enjoy, "The Mysterious Universe" by Sir James Jeans - Physics!

Love - Tenn.

[TW's first night in Paris was not auspicious: "I explored the town by myself and was nearly murdered, not by Frenchmen but by a bunch of drunken GI's who 'did

not like my looks'" (to Laughlin, January 7, 1948, Houghton). He soon informed Elia Kazan that all "you really need in Europe is one suit, two shirts, and a pocket full of prophylactics" (January 25, 1948, WUCA).

TW noted that reading "Miss Gide" was a "bit dry" for his own "fruity tastes," although he envied "the length and felicity of her days" (*Journal*, October 27, 1947). Several Arab boys whom André Gide met in North Africa as a young man had revealed the nature of his "propensities."

Paul Bigelow's jaw, reportedly broken in 1941 in a mugging, became chronically infected (osteomyelitis) and required surgery. At forty-three TW's friend Gilbert Maxwell was comically vain about his age and appearance and universally referred to as "Miss." Donald Windham dedicated his novel *The Dog Star* (1950) to Fred "Butch" Melton, his former companion.

Edwina traces the "legal separation" to an ultimatum that her father could no longer live with them in Clayton. "I said to Cornelius, 'I cannot allow my father to be put out on the street. You'll have to make up your mind whether you want to go or stay'" (qtd. in *Remember Me to Tom*, p. 199). Dakin Williams, who arranged his parents' separation and division of property, has reported that no divorce decree was sought and that Edwina and Cornelius never met again after nearly forty years of marriage.

The British mathematician Sir James Jeans wrote a series of popular books on astronomy including *The Mysterious Universe* (1930). When the *Saturday Review* queried TW on his "current reading" (March 6, 1948), he included Jeans's book and *The Theory of Relativity* by Albert Einstein.]

82. To Elizabeth "Tiz" Schauffler and Audrey Wood

L'Hotel Lutetia
42, Blvd. Raspail, Room 411-12
Paris, January ?, 1948
[TLS, 2 pp. HRC]

Dear Taudrey:

(THIS IS A CORPORATE FORM OF ADDRESS FOR TIZ AND AUDREY)

First of all, could you send me <u>air-mail</u> some cans of condensed <u>milk</u>? I have been having to drink <u>black</u> Brazilian coffee here which <u>may</u> (peut-etre) be good for my writing but is bad for my excitable heart!

Just three or four cans would turn the trick, as I will probably find my way eventually to the right black-marketeer who can supply me.

My impressions of Paris are mixed notices. The people seem terribly greedy, in fact avaricious, and while they like Americans, I think they like

them in the way that a bird likes worms. You go to bed with fifty thousand francs and wake up with twenty-five if you are lucky! Don't ask me how you spend money in your sleep but apparently you manage it somehow. . . .

The George V was comfortable but in the bourgeois part of town. So I moved over here. When I took these two rooms the price marked on the door was about 750 francs. Next time I looked at the card it had mysterious[ly] changed to 1250 francs. Today there is no heat so I stayed in bed till about 4 PM, receiving visitors under a quilt - that is, I was! They sat in their overcoats. I probably have a stronger constitution than I usually imagine but even so if I get off this continent in better shape than Carson McCullers you will know that my good angels are still with me.

The day I sailed a bunch of people from the show came to see me off, shortly after you all departed, Gadge, Jessica, Kim, Peg, Rudy Bond and Vito Cristi - they brought me a shower of presents, a dozen fine white shirts, a cashmere sweater and a bottle of Scotch! Which proves that actors can be angels. I was really very much touched by it. I imagine it was mainly Gadge's idea but it was damned sweet of them all. Whiskey is virtually unobtainable here. I am still drinking the Scotch as a warming libation when I get out of bed and the shirts were a God send as I had practically no white ones. I wish you would mention how pleased I was with these things for I may forget to write about it.

I feel that the theatre here is 20 years behind Broadway, incredible as that may seem. This is a somewhat premature judgement as I haven't seen much. But the hamming, mugging, and the prevailingly chi-chi quality of the material, the corruption of the critics, the arrogance of the stars is really shameful. Last night I saw Louis Jouvet as Don Juan (the Moliere play). Only the decor was good. M. Jouvet preened himself like an old peacock, never spoke directly to any of the supporting cast but only to the audience or the scenery.

Mr. Rothschild intimated that I only had about 80,000 francs here. If that is so, then I think we should make other connections, for that is a sum which corresponds to something like $500. And the theatre was not a particularly good one. He seems nice but is by no means prominent. Nobody seems to have ever heard of him here. I have become acquainted with the editor of the two leading newspapers, France-Soir and L'Intransigeant through his daughter who was on the boat and he is making enquiries about Rothschild and the conduct of the production. In the meantime I am

being complete[ly] non-committal. It may be entirely possible - if we think a Paris production is advisable - to function independantly without Rothschild, but that would require careful investigation on my part and talks with many people in the theatre to get a knowledge of the local conditions which are so different from ours. Here the thing of main importance is the theatre itself. The manager is really the man who owns the theatre. And the star system is infinitely more powerful than in the U.S.

Beaumont has cabled me about a London production of one-acts. I cabled back that I was taking a vacation from the theatre but would visit London in the Spring and would then be happy to discuss such a production provided the best talent was available. Badly done the one-acts would have a destructive influence on our London market. I am enclosing a rave-notice from an Englishman who is supposed to be "the George Jean Nathan of England" - I hope he deserves a better appelation. It appeared in the Evening Standard in London. Please send it on to Mother when you have read it. It would be particularly pleasing to Grandfather.

Would you mind writing Doctor Hoctor, State Hospital #4, Farmington Mo. - Enquiring why he has not answered my letter relative to getting a companion for my sister to take her out walking, Etc. And possibilities of improving her general situation. I want to keep after them till something definite is done.

I suppose you want to know how the food is! Well, it is good for my figure. You can figure that one out for yourselves. . . .

Much, much love and all thanks! Tenn

[Elizabeth Schauffler, a staff assistant at Liebling-Wood, played a minor role in efforts to improve the care of Rose Williams.

TW soon moved to the Hotel Lutétia, less staid and imposing than the George V, his first destination in Paris, but without "heat." The radiators, he informed Donald Windham, "are about as warm as Mary Hunter's left tit!" (qtd. in Windham, p. 205). He wrote a more courtly note to his grandfather, recalling their European tour of 1928: "Paris does not seem the same without you and the ladies from Mississippi" (postmarked Paris, January 17, 1948, Columbia U).

Adolf Rothschild's agency supervised the Paris production of *The Glass Menagerie* in May 1947.

Hugh "Binkie" Beaumont, managing director of H.M. Tennent Ltd., hoped to gain English rights of *The Glass Menagerie* and *Streetcar*, as well as TW's one-act plays. Wood cabled TW that she had offered the *Menagerie* to Beaumont for a spring production, with some haste, she indicated, for the Gould-Echols contract had

"lapsed" and the now unwanted Louis J. Singer was planning to intervene. Beaumont, she added, was the "best producer" (January 29, 1948, HRC) in England.

Dr. Emmett Hoctor, superintendent of Missouri State Hospital No. 4, informed Wood that "there is nothing particular" which TW "could do" to improve his sister's "condition" (January 27, 1948, HRC). "What do you suggest is the next move on this?" (February 2, 1948, HRC), Wood asked in a following letter to TW.

TW wrote this letter in the week of January 11, 1948, after moving to the Hotel Lutétia on the Left Bank.]

83. To Carson McCullers

SH: Hotel Lutétia
43, Boulevard Raspail, Paris
[mid-January 1948]
[ALS, 6 pp. Duke U]

Dearest Carson -

I am laid up in bed, too! I think it is the vile food here and the absolute lack of any milk which I have depended on so much in the States. Also the noxious stuff they call coffee. I drink 3 or 4 cups and feel no stimulation, only nausea, so it is difficult to work after breakfast. Just now some mysterious Samaritan left at my door a can of <u>powdered</u> milk - no name, no message, just the can of white granules which the <u>maitre d'hotel</u>, whom I summoned to explain, says is dehydrated milk and should be mixed with hot water and he has taken it out for the mixing. Not a pleasant idea but if it turns out to be anything even remotely like milk I shall know that the anonymous donor was directly from God. Isn't it absurd how such a small comfort as a cup of milk can be so important when not accessible!

I have been here about a week, spent in getting settled, packing and unpacking. The first two hotels I tried, on the right bank, were incompatible. This one, on the left, is pleasant in every respect but heating. My two rooms are not heated at all. So I have not yet had a chance to form a good impression of the city. No place seems heavenly when you are chilled and nauseous - so I am waiting! I left all your letters of introduction in New York - <u>but</u> every one of them was sent on to me and I now have them all with me. I am so glad to have the one to Bob Myers; in case I am not better tomorrow I shall call him.

Your letter reached me today - I have read it over and over for company as I lie here in bed feeling sorry for myself.

What a relief it is to know they will not push your play into production! Believe me, Carson, it would have been disastrous. You and I cannot take such experiences without being smashed on the rocks. By next Fall the production can mature gracefully, and you can feel confident of the script being ready. Now <u>rest</u>! Let everything go like a piece of loose thread!

As for the other emotional difficulties, perhaps now is not the right time to think about them. On the other hand, whatever troubles and disturbs you deeply has to be removed because being a great artist you must save and protect yourself continually. It may seem selfish, but actually <u>not</u> to do so is finally <u>more</u> selfish. I had to act ruthlessly to save myself from Pancho. I had to lock the doors and windows of my apartment, the last time he came to New York, and hear him screaming through them and trying to hammer them down with his fists. And know that instead of helping him the two years we gave each other may have been his destruction, and not able to explain or do anything but brutally lock myself away and refuse to see or write - but otherwise I could not have survived. Now you have never wasted your love on anyone who could not understand you or it, or been forced to imitate the implacability of a stone in order to free yourself of an impossible alliance. But when such a thing is necessary - because your life and your work require it - then you must carry it out relentlessly. I am a vulnerable person, but it frightens me to see how even <u>more</u> vulnerable <u>you</u> are. Is there no way you can defend and spare yourself, learn how to live not so acutely, and still be yourself and an artist? I have been so careful of myself physically because I have to - to live - but you are quite heedless about keeping yourself physically well - when you get up again you must promise all who love you to treat yourself with all the tenderness and wisdom that your work deserves from you. Think only of restoration.

Wherever I see a bookstand here I see translations of your work, more than any other American writer.

I shall write you again when I am back on my feet - these times of "error" don't usually last long. Then I shall get to know all your friends and write you news of them.

Did Audrey give you the framed Dufy print? I did not have a chance to deliver it myself.

My love to Reeves and your wonderful Mother -

Much, much to you, Tennessee.

[One of the "letters of introduction" supplied by Carson McCullers would lead TW to Dr. Robert Myers. McCullers became infatuated with Myers after he treated her at the American Hospital in Neuilly in 1947.

Production of McCullers's play *The Member of the Wedding* had been delayed, but the Theatre Guild was "confused," as Audrey Wood informed TW, "about the next step it must take" (February 2, 1948, HRC).

McCullers wrote to TW of "intense emotional strain" and the realization that her marriage with Reeves had failed: "I can no longer be his wife and share my inner life with him. . . . He is so dependent on me in every way that he will suffer; I cannot bear to think of how he will manage. But Tenn, another year like the last one would blunt my soul. . . . It would mean that I would have to accustom myself to lies, dishonesty and that I cannot do" (January 11, 1948, HRC).

TW cites recent French translations of *The Heart Is a Lonely Hunter* (1940) and *Reflections in a Golden Eye* (1941).]

84. To Audrey Wood

[Hotel Lutétia, Paris]
1/17/48
[TLS w/ autograph marginalia,
addendum and enclosure, 3 pp. HRC]

Dear Audrey:

I have been laid up in bed two or three days with a gastric disturbance attributable mainly, I think, to the bad diet here, so as soon as I am up again, I will probably pack - God help me! - and head South, probably to Italy where I hear it is easier to obtain a bland diet of the sort I depend on. Here, for instance, only babies can get milk, and milk is essential for me despite my relatively mature age.

I am sorry to give you such an unfavorable report on Adolf Rothschild but I dislike him and I have heard nothing to indicate he is of any value to us. The earnings of the Menagerie were less than I told you originally. In fact only 62,000 francs. I don't think there is any dishonesty but just bad management and ineptitude. However I have still not succeded in obtaining this money. We have gone twice, Rothschild and I, to the authors society. The first time we found it closed. The second time Mr. Rothschild was apparently greatly surprised to learn that the money had been transferred in some way - I cannot explain how - and would not be available for about a week or more. By that time I shall probably have left France for Italy or the Mediterranean so it is unlikely that I shall get to use it. Now I

have a very good and influential friend here, a Mme. Lazareff. She is editor of an enormously popular magazine named ELLE and her husband is editor of the two leading daily newspapers. Their connections are the best. She has introduced me to the actor-manager, Louis Jouvet. I have seen his screen performances in America, and you may have also. He is the top-notch manager in Paris. At Mme. Lazareff's and his request I wired for a copy of the play to submit to him. He has the best theatres at his disposal. You see it is unnecessary to use Rothschild and from what I hear, a disadvantage, for he is not known here in theatrical circles. I would like your opinion of this for you may feel that there is some commitment to Rothschild. For one thing, he gave Duhamel the translator exactly the same royalty that I received. Ordinarily the author gets ten and the translator five. We each got six percent and Bowles only got 1 percent and the leading actors were paid about six dollars a night and the director got 10,000 francs which amounts to about thirty dollars (for entire job). You can judge for yourself, from these figures, the sort of management that Rothschild was associated with and how lucky we were to get off with good notices and an "artistic success". Fortunately Claude Maritz (who has a low opinion of Rothschild) was a good and sincere director. I personally cannot forgive the man R. for dragging me twice to that damned society when I was not feeling well - and neither time accomplishing anything when he could so easily have ascertained beforehand whether or not the place was open or the money accessible. I wish you would give Mme. Tallant a full report on all this and explain my unwillingness to have any connection with Rothschild concerning Streetcar.

I don't think it fair to keep Feldman on the string any longer. It seems psychologically impossible for me to revert to that script. Especially knowing that the original conception must be weakened or distorted in some way. I cannot work without enthusiasm and I cannot feel enthusiasm over such a project. I don't think Feldman has ~~a grain of~~ enough taste and it would be better for him to sell his rights to someone who has, and let that producer hire a good writer to prepare a screen treatment that would not violate the quality and meaning of the play. The film must be honest to be any good. If I were quite well, full of vigor and there seemed an unbroken expanse of time and energy in which to do all the things I want so much to do, I would undertake the job gladly, but as it is I feel I must conserve what I have for what I have not yet done. Could Feldman understand this? I am sure that you can. If he must have his $2500 back, give it to him - but I

think I did that much work on the stuff in Provincetown. I want as much as you do to see a good picture come out of it, but I can't force myself back to it now.

Hugh Beaumont has wired about doing a program of one-acts. Strikes me as an excellent idea and I have written him for further information. He mentioned the Lyric Hammerstein theatre in London.

Carson's doctor in Paris came to see me today and prescribed some powders. They are so unpalatable that I spit them right out. His report on Carson was very depressing. He doesn't think she will be able to walk again and that she has some incurable vascular disease which is likely to be progressive and result in other attacks. I don't take his word for this, however, and I hope that no one has told Carson anything of this nature. It is too awful to believe! Don't talk about it.

I will cable you when I have decided where to go in my search for better living conditions.

With love, Tenn.

P.S. Have just gotten your long letter and it has relieved my depression to hear from home which I think of your office as being. Of course I would love to have the Menagerie done in Germany and perhaps later I can accept their invitation there, when the weather is milder. Re: "nigger-peckerwood" dispute. The last time I saw Gadge he told me that numerous colored persons had assured him Walter White was all wet and that nigger in this context and from such a character was totally inoffensive. I always had a ~~profound~~ conviction that it was. Gadge wanted to revert to "nigger" so I said okay. I think old farmer is all right if you alternate it with "old peckerwood" in the next reference during the story. - I cannot at this moment recall name of the garage but it is on Royal street in the Quarter, and is the only garage along there. Why not call Dick Orme long distance, ask him name of garage and also tell him I cannot resume tenancy of the apartment? Margo removed practically all my stuff (papers) from apartment and Dick could store the rest for me. His name is Richard M. Orme, 632 St. Peter and you could best reach him about noon when he is just waking up. Assure him I would have loved to return to New Orleans but the pressure of circum-stances made it impossible and would he please continue our present arrangement of subleasing the place in my name. I will enclose a note to

him myself. Yes, it is better to conduct sale of car without Pancho's intervention. The less connection I maintain with him the better, since I am unable to really help him in any basic way.

Thanks for everything, and so much!

Sometimes I must seem to take all your help for granted, but that is because I have lived in such turmoil. I am infinitely obliged for everything you and Bill and Tiz did to make the trip easy for me.

T.

[Ninon Tallon, an associate of the Rothschild agency, arranged the Paris production of *La Ménagerie de Verre*. She described the play as "a sensational hit from the young intellectual point of view" and added that a majority of the French critics were also "on the positive side" (to Wood, May 10, 1947, HRC).

Audrey Wood assured TW that she could "maneuver {her} way out of the whole situation" (January 21, 1948, HRC) with Adolph Rothschild. She had also "airmailed" a copy of *Streetcar* for Louis Jouvet's consideration, warning TW not to "close any deal until advising terms and setup" (telegram, January 17, 1948, HRC). A leading figure in the French theatre, Jouvet would not have a hand in the Paris production of *Streetcar* (1949).

Charles Feldman, owner of film rights of *The Glass Menagerie*, learned in the preceding July that TW was apparently "thrilled" with the screenplay and willing to do some additional "polishing" (to Abramson, July 7, 1947, HRC), for which he would receive $5,000. Revision begun in Provincetown in August 1947 had evidently dampened TW's enthusiasm for the adaptation by Peter Berneis.

Walter White, secretary of the NAACP, criticized gratuitous use of "the word 'nigger'" (to Selznick, December 10, 1947, HRC) in Scene Three of *Streetcar*. He soon thanked TW for agreeing to substitute "'farmer'" in the off-color joke, adding that he was "sorry it took this kind of an episode to cause us to meet" (December 16, 1947, HRC). Elia Kazan's restoration of "nigger" brought "telephone complaints daily" (January 6, 1948, HRC), as Wood informed TW, who finally decided to use "peckerwood" instead. "Nigger" appeared in the first four American printings of the book (1947-1948).

As TW prepared to leave Paris after two dreary weeks, Wood sought to tie up the loose ends of his far-flung, disorderly life: an unneeded apartment in New Orleans, the everlasting sale of the Pontiac, and the threat of Pancho Rodriguez's return.

Penned in the upper margin of page 1 is the notation "via '<u>Air Mail</u>.'"]

85. To Carson McCullers

[Auberge de la Colombe d'Or
St. Paul de Vence, France]
[late-January 1948]
[TLS w/ autograph marginalia, 1 p. Duke U]

Dear Carson:

This is to assure you that I am feeling a lot better and am about to set out for Rome, soon as my Italian visa is ready which will be tomorrow. I left Paris soon as I got out of the hospital where I was for two or three wretched days. Honey, I did not like that doctor of yours one bit! I don't know what was the matter with me, some kind of toxic condition. I felt like I couldn't stay awake and I couldn't eat anything. I think it was brought on by the poisonous liquor and food I had to consume in Paris and the depressing weather which never let up. Myers said I was threatened with a couple of awful sounding things like Scylla and Charybdis but I didn't like him or the hospital so I got out of bed and left town. I went down here to this little place in the Alpes Maritimes where I know a lovely girl of 18 who is a tubercular patient. It has been dull here, still raining continually and a lot of dirty white doves flopping around in the orange trees to give a quaint atmosphere, but the rest and the excellent food has done me a world of good and if I finally catch up with the sun in Rome, I shall be all right. If you know anybody there, drop me a line care of American Express in that city. I remember it as a place of misty gold light and cypresses and ruins and public fountains and some wonderful things by Michelangelo that Frankie and her new friend, Mary, would love. I shall probably remain in the South of Europe until the nasty winter is through with, and then return to Paris and take up residence at that hotel which you recommended on the right bank. Honey, they have now stabilized the franc at a wonderful figure for Americans. It is officially three hundred and something for the dollar and of course the black market has gone up even higher. I shall live like an Oriental potentate when I return from Italy! By that time you and Reeves may be ready to come back. Donald Windham is also planning to come abroad this Spring and my friend, Oliver Evans - I am sure you have heard me speak of him often, and of his prodigious energy outside academic pursuits - is going to teach English this summer at the university in Athens, so it will be like old home-week over here. I wish it were already Spring. It is silly to be in Europe in the winter, isn't it? In this place I do almost

nothing but read and eat. I read a good book by Jean Paul Sartre which is called <u>The Age of Reason</u>. Get that. It is badly written, in a way, but there is a terrifyingly keen analysis of mental processes and emotions or lack of emotions. Do you like physics? I am reading a lot about astronomical physics and relativity and so forth as it really exercises the mind and the imagination to think about those things, such as curved space and the electrical particles that matter is made of, all of them dashing around at the rate of thousands of miles a second, and everything being made of them - <u>fancy that</u>! as Professor Tesman would say. Well -

You will also be pleased to hear that I have acquired a taste for Bach, out of desperation: there was nothing else to play on the victrola here. I love the <u>Toccato and Fugue</u> which I never could stand before.

Do you have a good victrola at home? I left a swell one in the States that I would love for you to use, an electric changer and all, if you don't have one - let Audrey Wood know. Will write from Rome - Love!

Tenn.

[A week's rest in the south of France allowed TW to slip by the medical perils of "Scylla and Charybdis"—hepatitis and mononucleosis—as diagnosed by Dr. Robert Myers, whom TW had come to regard as "a thoroughly disagreeable and cold-blooded young man" (to Bigelow, n.d., Massee Collection). McCullers later assured TW that her infatuation with Myers had ended: "I could not love anyone you do not even like" (Valentine day {February 14, 1948} Duke U).

"Frankie" dreams of traveling abroad with "her new friend, Mary," in the upbeat conclusion of *The Member of the Wedding*. With "<u>Fancy that</u>!" TW alludes to a second, less bracing text, *Hedda Gabler* (Ibsen, 1890), which ends with the suicide of a desperate wife—prefiguring in effect McCullers's own attempt in the following March.

Probably written in the week of January 25, 1948, this letter was forwarded to McCullers by Audrey Wood, whose apology for a "coffee stain - discourtesy Audrey Wood - " appears in the upper margin.]

86. *To Oliver Evans*

[Albergo Palazzo-Ambasciatori, Rome]
Jan 31, 1948.
[TLS, 2 pp. HRC]

Cher:

I have only been in Rome three days but I am already established. It is really the capitol of my heart! In Paris it rained all but continually, the food was abominable and served with disgusting flourishes, no milk except powdered, no coffee except that Brazilian stuff that blew you right out from under your beret. It all made me ill and I spent the last two days in the American hospital and a week afterwards resting at St. Paul de Vence in the Alpes Maritimes. But Rome has already made up for all the vicissitudes of the North. My first night on the Boulevard I met a young Neapolotan who is a professional lightweight boxer. How I thought of you! Thick glossy black hair and a small but imperial torso! The nightingales busted their larynx! And Miss Keats swooned in her grave! I can hardly wait for you to come over this Spring: by that time my address book will probably be running into the tricentennial edition in gold and scarlet morocco with illustrations hand-painted. I wish I could tell you more about this boxer, details, positions, amiabilities - but this pale blue paper would blush! Besides such confidences are only meant to be whispered in the bed-chamber. Orally! The tongue has inflections which the typewriter wants!

I received yesterday the copy of Voices and was delighted with the three poems, especially the one about the cow-boys. It has been so long since I have written a good poem, even a bad one, that I am humbly amazed at your lyric out-put in volume and always increasing force and quality of line, and the material, or content, is so far superior to the contrived interests of the moiety.

Well, I have much to tell you. First of all, living in Europe is inexpensive when you have learned the ropes. And in Italy there is an abundance of everything if you can afford to buy it. American cigarettes are sold on every corner for about seventy cents a package. You can live well here on $200. a month which you can't in the States. Paris - no! You can live cheaply, but bad food, lack of heat, a certain wolfish attitude in the people makes it not worth it. I doubt if I will return to Paris before late Spring when I may pass through going to England. I hear that Palermo, Sicily is the place for romance! I contemplate a visit. Write me at Rome c/o

American Express. I rub the turquoise and wish you happiness and good fortune and an early arrival on these shores! With love

Tennessee.

["As soon as I crossed the Italian border my health and life seemed to be magically restored. There was the sun and there were the smiling Italians" (*Memoirs*, p. 141). TW stayed briefly at the Ambassador on via Veneto before moving to a nearby apartment. Both were located in central Rome in a tourist area dominated by grand hotels and smart shops and cafés. TW soon bought an "old jeep" with a defective muffler in which he raced "drunk as hell" around the fountains of St. Peter's in a pre-dawn ritual of sobering up, confident that "an *Americano* could get away with a whole lot" (*Memoirs*, p. 146) in 1948.

"Rodeo," the Oliver Evans poem admired by TW, ends with a wistful appeal to the young "gladiators" of the "arena": "My lariat love lies empty at your feet" (*Voices*, January 1948).]

Tennessee Williams and Gore Vidal, Rome, 1948.
"An Americano *could get away with a whole lot" (*Memoirs*).

87. To Margaret "Margo" Jones

SH: Albergo Palazzo-Ambasciatori, Roma
Feb 3, 1948
[TLS w/ autograph marginalia, 4 pp. HRC]

Dearest Margo:

I have now settled down more or less in Rome which is the first city I've been over here that I really and truly like very much. Paris was cold and wet and the people had a wolfish air about them. The food and liquor was so bad it made me ill. Then I went down to the Riviera and it was raining constantly there, too, but for the week I've been here, the city has been bathed in mellow golden light and is a dream of loveliness. I have a room with a big balcony right over Via Venuto which is the Fifth avenue of Rome and I keep it filled with fresh flowers, violets and all shades of carnations, which are sold in huge bunches on almost every street-corner. For about a hundred a week you can live the life of Tiberius in this town! Everything is available - for a little dinero! Friday I am taking a plane to Sicily for a few days to watch the making of a film down there, in which no actors, only Native Sicilians, are employed, and it is being directed by the man who directed "Zoo di Vetro" over here (Dago for Glass Menagerie). I hope to show you some of the stills from this picture, "The Earth Shall Tremble," the best most moving photography and lighting I've seen ever! I have met many people here, in fact too many. The phone is beginning to ring too much.

I have not yet gotten down seriously to work, but have been pecking away at Summer & Smoke in an effort to tighten it up and provide some sort of reliable climax. In the latter I think I am working out some improvement. You ask me why I think this play should not cover the same territory as "Streetcar" in try-outs. Honey, it is only because I am dead certain that Streetcar is a much, much better play. I know how you feel about "Summer" and how Joanna does - you are both especially equipped by nature, with sensitive hearts and responsive souls, to get things that are only half stated and to understand the unrealized intentions, but to me "Summer" was a devastating failure in comparison to what I meant it to be, and one of the bitterest I have had. I am talking about the script, you understand, and this is only for you to read. Since we are going to produce it we must not share my misgivings with the world at this point. In conception it was by far my best play but something happened to me during the work on it, I froze up or went dead on it and everything turned to

powder which should have been alive and flashing. Only at scattered moments does it have the pure and tremulous candle-like glow that I meant it to have all the way through. I think it was the despair that I felt over Summer that enabled me to put such violence and passion into Streetcar in spite of my physical exhaustion at the time of writing. However I am continuing to work on it. Perhaps there will be a period of illumination, though so far there has been only an effort of will. I am concentrating on Scene 9, the one that ends with the shooting of the doctor, and I am enlarging the part of Jessie who is now a Mexican girl named Rosa. I think the Serios should be Mexican and perhaps the town should be in Texas. How does that strike you? This scene is the only one that can serve as a real climax. If I get this right, I shall attack the next weakest spot which is the scene after the doctor's death and in which John returns home a hero. That is altogether too fortuitous and adventitious. It seems to pop out of nowhere and I am afraid Yankee critics would never let us get away with it. It must be given more body and reason: somehow integrated with the line of the story. Do not be discouraged by my frank confession of failure in this play: all of my plays have been failures in some respect relative to their conceptions, for the simple reason that I have so little craftsmanship to rely on. If Milzener does a beautiful job and we get the right players we can surely create some beauty. But if we stay in the East, we will have to go over that old Hangman's Trail - New Haven, Boston, Philly. Washington is apparently still ruled out. It is a murderous routine. Each opening is a little hell to go through bare-footed! It ravages the nerves and breaks the spirit, and long before you come into New York, everyone knows whether or not you are a success or failure. The verdict is sealed already. If we opened at the Coronet in Los Angeles, say, or any good theatre in Chicago - no comparison, good or bad, could be made to "Streetcar" - we could count on three or four weeks in one-place to get the show working smoothly without everybody including Howard Rineheimer breathing down our necks. I think four weeks is long enough out of town. It proved just about right for "S.C." Well, we need not come to any decision about this for several months, in which time I will have completed my work on the script. I will certainly not discuss going to Chicago or other places with anybody: the less we talk about any of our plans the better.

It is so lovely here, it is difficult to remain indoors. I specially like riding out in the fiacres, the open horse-drawn carriages, around the

Colisseum and the Appian way. Trouble is it gets even lovelier in the Spring! The Italians are like <u>good</u> Mexicans. Much love -

Tenn.

[Luchino Visconti's production of *The Glass Menagerie* premiered in Rome on December 13, 1946, and was restaged in Florence and Milan the following year. Visconti regarded TW as a writer of avant-garde, if not revolutionary, tendencies and in the post-war years produced his work along with that of Erskine Caldwell, Hemingway, Cocteau, and Sartre.

TW informed Irene Selznick that he was "trying to put more iron" into *Summer and Smoke* but doubted that he would succeed "till I myself have a more metallic vibration" (January 14, 1948, Boston U). Margo Jones's unbounded enthusiasm for a faulty play did little to convince TW of her status as a major director.

TW added flair to "Scene 9" of *Summer and Smoke* by dressing Rosa Gonzales in a flamenco costume and developing her sensuality in bouts of merriment and lovemaking with John Buchanan. Poised against his dissipation and despair is Alma's chaste idealism, her attraction made evident as John is drawn mysteriously from his father's house to appear by her side in the rectory. The "enormous silence" is broken as Alma "sinks onto a love seat" and John "buries his face in her lap": "Eternity and Miss Alma have such cool hands!" (March 1948, HRC), he intones. Revision of Scene Nine was intended to add "body and reason" to the reformation of John Buchanan, which follows the murder of his father.

The New York attorney Howard E. Reinheimer represented Irene Selznick and was a financial backer—apparently overbearing—of *Streetcar*.

Penned in the upper margin of page 1 is the notation "Address = c/o American Express, Rome."]

88. *To Carson McCullers*

[Sicily/Naples]
2/8/48
[TLS, 2 pp. Duke U]

Dearest Carson:

First let me say you must not talk this foolishness about being wicked and punished for it. If I had never known or seen you your work alone would assure me that you are a Saintly person. It is the only modern work that gives me such an assurance of Saintliness in the writer, even more than one feels in Chekhov or Doestoevsky or in the letters of Vincent Van Gogh to his brother Theo to depart a little from the field of professional literature.

There is no evil in you at all, anywhere, so this idea is positive lunacy and is perhaps hindering your recovery so don't allow it to remain in your mind.

Then let me remind you that I decided to come to Europe because you were here and I thought would stay here and after my life with Pancho broke up in disgrace and horror, you were the only person I wanted to be with. Whenever you are strong enough you must come back here and join me. I say here in Europe for I feel that this is the place for us both, especially here in Italy, this place of soft weather and golden light and of great bunches of violets and carnations sold on every corner and the Greek ideal surviving so tangibly in the grace and beauty of the people and the antique sculpture as well. I cannot write very coherently about Rome as I love it so much! But I can see that you think of me far, far too charitably. You must remember all the bad things about me, my sensuality and license and neurotic moodiness at times - all the irregularities of my life and nature - I cannot put all of those things into a letter! - and then ask yourself if you could really endure a close association or would I perhaps add to your worries and your emotional strains. But perhaps you have already considered all these obvious defects and still believe, as I do, that being near each other would give a mutual tranquillity we both need so much. I am thinking of your work and of mine, as well, as of our lives. - Sometime will you send me "Ballad of the Sad Cafe" which I have still never read and which would perhaps make a good one-act play or two-acts - this is parenthetical indeed! - I just now thought of it.

I am glad you wrote me this about Bob Myers. He is the first doctor I have ever disliked and distrusted instinctively and I felt he was altogether lacking in common humanity. When he put me in the hospital, at my own suggestion, he did not even bother to give them any instructions about my diet or treatment. I had to instruct them myself. He told me that in a few days my skin and eyes would turn yellow and that glands under my arms would swell up, so naturally I thought I had the black plague. None of these things happened. My eyes and skin are perfectly clear and nothing is swollen. I decided to pay no attention to him and I left the hospital and went South. Incidentally, he wanted me to pay him thirty dollars instead of the (much smaller) amount in French money for his one visit to the hotel, but that is unimportant. I sent him a check and wrote a very catty letter, really quite sarcastic, praising him for his treatment and his great "human

warmth which is so much more important" but probably he thought I meant it. He does not seem modest enough to suspect otherwise.

Well, Carson, as we grow older we stop blaming anybody for anything, don't we? We talk very crossly about their bad conduct but we don't really feel any bitterness against them, and that is much better. It is all so understandable, the distortions and falsities that the world creates in us all. - Audrey writes that Pancho has sold my car in New Orleans, after swearing under oath that it belonged to him and is now in California and "some mysterious person" in Hollywood has seen a number of producers and claimed to be Tennessee Williams and demanded $500. advance for certain story ideas or manuscripts, for film production! Do you suppose that could be Pancho? <u>HA*HA</u>!!

If you send the play to me c/o American Express in Rome I will surely receive it and give it my closest and most loving attention. Are you feeling better? Are you resting and eating properly and <u>not</u> <u>worrying</u>? I feel that we are always very close to each other: the ocean is nothing between us! I think of you each day and I pray for your happiness which I <u>know</u> is coming! Otherwise I would not believe in God, and I do most truly believe in Him.

With much love, Tennessee.

In my next letter I will try to tell you more about people and places. If parts of this letter seem silly, it may be because I have been travel[ling] around so much by myself that I have become a little bit touched in the head. I talk out loud to myself nearly all the time now!

[Carson McCullers began the new year by recalling their "moments at Nantucket" and anticipating "other dear times in the future" (January 11, 1948, HRC) with TW. Did he think they could "travel and have a house together" (Valentine day {February 14, 1948} Duke U), she wrote in answer to the present correspondence. Audrey Wood deemed such an arrangement "pure madness" (to TW, March 12, 1948, HRC).

McCullers's novella *The Ballad of the Sad Café* first appeared in *Harper's Bazaar* in August 1943.

Wood recently informed TW that Pancho Rodriguez had sold the Pontiac and kept the profits after swearing that he was the car's legal owner. More alarming news concerned an impostor in California who had solicited a producer for "a five hundred dollar advance" (February 5, 1948, HRC) in TW's name.

A reference in McCullers's correspondence indicates that this letter was mailed in Naples although it may have been written before TW left Sicily.]

89. *To Audrey Wood*

[Naples]
February 1948
[TLS w/ enclosures, 1 p. HRC]

Dear Audrey:

I have delayed writing because I do not like writing letters that sound like the outraged clucking of a wet hen, and the news that Colton had paid $30,000. income tax for last year put me into a most terrible and despondent humor - You know that I think of money only in terms of what it does for you. But that money could have done a whole lot, and not just for me but for several others. The productive years of an artist are pitifully few! His capital must be conserved, not only for himself but his worthy friends, dependants and beneficiaries. I am not lecturing you on this subject, you know that, but I think Colton ought to take his responsibilities more seriously and not arrange matters so that a big sum comes in at one time and the appalling amount of sixty thousand - thirty from me and thirty from mother! - has to be paid out as if we made that much every year of our lives on the black market! Spilt milk is spilt milk, and the government is a dreadfully implacable force for us poor mortals to mess with - However tell Colton, and very forcibly, that nothing is to be done in the future that would expose me to that sort of income tax! In other words when Streetcar is sold, it must be sold so that small amounts are paid over a period of ten years. That is GOT TO BE!

I was also distressed over the news that Gould-Echols contract had lapsed as just before I left New York I gave Maggie Gould my solemn promise that they could keep it. That was while Bill was in the hospital with a virus pneumonia. In the rush of departure I probably did not talk to you about this, and now I am afraid it makes me look like a bigger heel than I already actually am. Can you adjust it some way so that they will not regard it as a betrayal of trust on my part? I really would never have taken it away from them.

I am enclosing the long, long-delayed article for Leonard Lyons. It is about my trip to Sicily from which I am just returning. It is probably too long for his column. If so perhaps the TIMES would use it, or Harper's Bazaar. It is to be typed up before it goes out, and a copy sent back to me, as Visconti and Downes want to see it. Also please send me an up-to-date script or book of "Streetcar" for the Roman producers - same ones that did

Menagerie and the only progressive crowd in Italy. I am enclosing an article that came out in the Communist paper. They also had a terrifying picture of me with a caption that called me "Maggiore scrittore da Sinistra". Which means a major Communist writer! I wonder if I will be let back into the States. . . .

I am now in Naples at a hotel which is half in ruins. Will go on tomorrow, back to my room at the Ambassador in Rome. Address remains American Express in Rome. Never got the coffee and canned milk. They are probably enjoying it at the Lutetia in Paris, that horrible place where you had to stay in the bathtub all day to keep warm - I fell asleep in it and nearly drowned.

Much love, Tennessee.

[The hefty income tax paid by TW and Edwina, co-owners of *The Glass Menagerie*, reflects the sale of film rights in the preceding year. Audrey Wood quickly pacified her client with a plan to ask one million dollars for rights of *Streetcar*, with payments to be spread over ten years. She also defended the attorney Edward Colton and reminded TW that his own poor record keeping had not improved the "tax situation" (March 1, 1948, HRC), which placed him in the seventy-five percent bracket.

Wood also reminded TW that the "Gould-Echols contract" had "lapsed" after more than a year of fruitless search for funding. She advised that the last two option payments be returned to "adjust" (March 1, 1948, HRC) an awkward situation with friends. TW instructed Wood to "consummate deal with Beaumont" (telegram, February 12, 1948, HRC) to stage the *Menagerie* in London.

The enclosed "article" circulated to numerous magazines, including *The New Yorker*, whose editors considered the piece "unbelievably bad" and rejected it. "A Movie Named *La Terra Trema*" finally appeared in *'48 Magazine* (June 1948, pp.102-104, 111-113). TW admired the "tenderness toward life" which he observed in the villagers recruited by Visconti. The director himself had "a look of inflammable repose."

Fabio Coen, Wood's representative in Italy, received a copy of *Streetcar* for delivery to Campagnia Italiana di Prosa, Roman producer of *The Glass Menagerie*.

TW probably wrote this letter on February 10, 1948, the day before he returned to Rome.]

90. To Oliver Evans

[Albergo Palazzo-Ambasciatori, Rome]
2/11/48
[TLS w/ enclosure, 2 pp. HRC]

Dear Oliver:

I have just returned from a trip through southern Italy, first to Sicily where I watched the making of an Italian film using Sicilian peasants and their homes and orchards as actors and sets and directed by the man, Count Luchino Visconti, who put on "Zoo di Vetro" in Italy, a very handsome and elegant man of our tastes still in his thirties. Only trouble with Sicily is no bath-tubs which detracts from the charm of the peasants in winter when they don't swim, and I did not even have a bath-tub in my hotel for their use so it was a bit frustrating. Then I went to Naples. I think you would be disappointed in it now. Conditions are frightening, half the population or more living in destitution and bordering on violence. I got some nice little art-objects there, including a copper statue of a boy in Pompeii, which I wrote a poem about. The Galleria is not as you described it so must have changed. The idlers were too shabby and wolfish to bring into a hotel, so I hastened back to Rome, which I find most comfortable and delightful of all the places I've been in Europe. I have a room and balcony on the Via Veneto. Prokosch is also in Rome but I haven't seen him, he is staying at the swankiest hotel across the street from me. The Italians want everything you own but are generally content with what you give them. Do you remember Kimon Friar? He is in Athens, working there and has written and wired me, for permission to do "Streetcar". Has a connection with the Art Theatre in Athens. The letter was discreet - you remember how Miss Friar is! - but between the lines she is obviously having the time of her middle-aged life! Urges me to come there in Spring and go on a trip among the Aegean isles! At the same time they will be doing a revival of Menagerie along with Streetcar at the Art Theatre so I will probably go. When are you coming over? When the Spring term ends? Perhaps I will have found an apartment here in Rome by that time and you can stay with me. The climate here is a little milder than New Orleans in winter.

Audrey writes that Pancho sold my car in New Orleans after swearing under oath that it was his and apparently is now in California trying to sell some manuscripts of mine - so she thinks from a suspicious report that has reached her. Isn't that sad? Don't mention it to anybody! My life with him

now seems like a fantastic dream which turned into a nightmare. Why do I have such abominable luck with romances?! I don't intend to get seriously involved with anyone ever again - life is supportable without it and loneliness is sometimes quite pleasant.

Are things any better in Lincoln?

With love, Tennessee.

[*La terra trema* (1948) was shot on location in Aci Trezza (Sicily) with the villagers serving as cast and helping Luchino Visconti to improvise a script. The slight plot involves a struggle, doomed at the outset, to free local fishermen from exploitive wholesalers and their own traditional culture. The film remains a defining example of Italian neorealism.

"Tennessee had drunk an entire bottle of Scotch and was nearly dead with fear" after a perilous flight from Rome to Sicily. Franco Zeffirelli, assistant to Visconti, went on to describe an engaging, if befuddled, visitor to the set: "When he eventually sobered up, I was charmed by him. He had a childlike naïvety which counterbalanced his rather *louche* life and which made his opinions fresh and interesting" (*The Autobiography of Zeffirelli*, 1986, p. 85). Details of the flight may be recalled in the middle section of *The Roman Spring of Mrs. Stone* (1950).

The "copper statue" led TW to write—and enclose—a lyric entitled "Testa Dell' Effebo" (*Harper's Bazaar*, August 1948).

In 1940 TW was asked to evaluate the "film possibilities" of Frederic Prokosch's novel *Night of the Poor* (1939). It seemed "phoney" to him at the time, but he and Prokosch later became friends and TW an admirer of his work.

TW had been pleased to accept Kimon Friar's invitation to read at the Poetry Center (YMHA) in New York on December 1, 1945. Friar directed the prestigious forum in the 1940s and later became a respected anthologist and translator of Greek poetry.]

91. To Paul Bowles

[45 Via Aurora, Rome]
[mid-February 1948]
[TLS w/ marginalia, 1 p. U of Delaware]

Dear Paul:

I have just moved into an apartment here in Rome. I am so delighted with the town and with the Italians that I shall probably remain here for some time. However sooner or later I shall take the trip to North Africa. I had typhoid and typhus shots before I left New York with that in mind.

There is no reason for me to return to the States before August so there is no hurry.

Paul, I was terribly disappointed that we couldn't get you to write music for Streetcar. I insisted that you should be contacted but you had already departed for Africa. However I hope that you will work with us on "Summer & Smoke" which Margo is going to produce starting about August 16th. Would you have the time or the inclination? The play has many problems. It is not as well-written as Streetcar and will need a brilliant production. Milziner will design: the set and all the plastic and atmospheric elements will be tremendously important and it really needs a musical score like Menagerie had. I would send you a script immediately except that I am still working on it. How much time do you require, that is, if you are able to undertake it? Rehearsals start August 16th but we don't open until about Sept. 5 in Buffalo and will play in Cleveland and Chicago before N.Y. If we can get together at some point on the map of Africa or Europe it would be of great advantage. This damned Swiss machine! It is light as a feather, no ballast, and plays every conceivable trick except actually kicking me in the balls and I'm sure it will eventually manage to do that!

I am very sensitive to changes of water and diet. Would Morocco be troublesome in those respects? What have you done with your house in Tangiers? Audrey showed me a lovely photo you took from a window looking over the Mediterranean.

You are fortunate to have Jane and Denby with you. I am travelling entirely alone, and have actually started talking to myself! Well, I have met a few people in Rome - many strangers! - but it would be good to encounter some old friends. In about two or three weeks I shall have completed my revisions on the script: then let me know where you're staying and I'll either mail you a copy or bring it down with me for a visit.

You remember Carson McCullers? She is paralyzed on one side as the result of a vascular disease and her condition is serious. I saw her before I left New York. We correspond now. It is a great pity! It makes no sense.

Ever - 10

[Their close friendship began in Acapulco in 1940 when a young man wearing a "floppy sombrero" and calling himself "Tennessee" met the perennial travelers, Paul (1910-1999) and Jane Bowles. Paul went on to compose incidental music for

The Glass Menagerie and would soon return to New York—from Tangier—to write the score for *Summer and Smoke*. His failure "to write music" for *Streetcar* may reflect both his absence at the time and the reported dislike of the Kazans for his exotic fiction. The visitor is Edwin Denby, American poet and former dance critic of the *New York Herald Tribune*.

TW's apartment was in a "tawny old" building near via Veneto and within a block of the Borghese Gardens—"favorite resorts for the sort of chance acquaintances that a lonely foreigner is apt to be seeking" (*Memoirs*, p. 141).

Typed in the upper margin is TW's mailing address, "American Express, Rome."]

92. To Paul Bigelow

[45 Via Aurora, Rome]
2/18/48
[TLS w/ autograph marginalia, 3 pp. Duke U]

Dear Paul:

This is the first nasty day we have had in Rome and I am staying in to work and write letters. I now have a two room apartment. It was an impulsive and ill-considered move. I thought it would give me more privacy but exactly the reverse has occured. The apartment is in a pensione which is operated by about six or a dozen very strange women who are never fully or even half-way dressed and their continual attentions and ministrations are nerve-wracking. I go in the bathroom to take a pee. One of them is washing my tub. I go in the bedroom. A couple of them are making my bed. I go in the front room. Three or four of them are re-arranging the furniture. Five or six times before I get up in the morning various ones of them knock to enquire if I am ready for breakfast. Their desperate concern for my comfort is about to drive me insane! But I am sure I will never have the nerve to tell them that I can't stand it and am moving out. I have been under great pains to conceal my love-life from them, waking my over-night guests at dawn and hustling them out before the ladies are stirring. But today I over-slept and so did the guest and all at once the bedroom door pops open - none of the locks work! - and a troop of the women march in serving both of us breakfast in bed and putting the top on the cold cream jar and replacing the towel and even screwing the cap back on the prophylactic tube in the bath-room! After all my secrecy. . . .

That is the charm of Italy!

As for Capri, I have not yet gone there but it is definitely on my itinerary. Old Norman Douglas is still the reigning belle of the island, though she is now in her eighties. She is living with a little boy whom radical opinion holds to be eleven years old and conservatives say is thirteen and will not go anywhere without him. I heard a marvelous story about Douglas which I wish I could repeat just as it was told me by Donald Downes, an American journalist who lives in Rome. It seems that some years ago Douglas' wife, a dope-addict, burned herself to death while smoking in bed. Douglas was expecting a house-guest that week-end. The guest phoned to offer condolences and say that of course she would postpone her visit because of the disaster. But Douglas insisted that she come ahead as planned. The guest thought she would cheer Douglas up by bringing with her an attractive young English belle of artistic pretensions. Miss Douglas received them on a chaise longue and was very laconic and they assumed that her loss had affected her more deeply than she wished to show. The belle made a great effort to be amusing, talked very eloquently about various periods of art, and got nothing out of Douglas but a few exhausted grunts. Until finally, having exhausted other topics, the belle began to talk about Italian cuisine, which was not at all to her liking, especially the way that meat was cooked in the Italian restaurants. For the first time Douglas showed a slight interest and asked the belle how she liked her meat cooked. I like it burned to a crisp on the outside, said the belle, but almost raw in the middle. Well, said Douglas, it is pity you didn't arrive here last Wednesday - You would have loved my wife. . . .

Other people who have been to Capri this season say it has not changed at all. The male population have been "kept men" for centuries and are spoiled but beautiful. The tourists are a conglomeration of faggots and fascists with Mona Williams thrown in for good measure. However I haven't heard anything about it that would keep me away when it gets warm enough for swimming, and I think it is high time that I met the other Miss Williams. For years I have been hearing elegant belles talk about "Mona". Perhaps she is now passe?

Carson and I are exchanging letters by almost every post between the continents. She says she is "unable to eat or sleep" and is in pain. Apparently a great deal of her suffering is mental. She had two unhappy loves in Europe - neither consummated, I take it - and Reeves caused her a great deal of anguish with what she says was deliberate and cunning

persecution. I am relieved to learn, from her last letter, that he is now living in New York city and that she rarely sees him. One must not accept too literally Carson's account of things now. She is in a state of highly inflamed sensibilities. Reeves is also a sick person and a very pitifully maladjusted one who needs help, too. When Carson is better she hopes to join me in Europe and I am also hoping that this could be accomplished. My life is empty except for the "trapeze of flesh" as Crane called it, and it might do me good to have to devote myself to someone who needed and deserved so much care. On the other hand, I wonder if I would be good for her, or would the irregularities of my life and nature - which I know I would not give up - add to her unhappiness? I have talked this over with her in my latest letter. Of course it is very questionable whether she will be able to travel any time soon.

Margo is bound and determined to put on "summer and smoke" though I am most apprehensive about it, following "streetcar". It is by no means as well put together. Consequently I am having to devote most of my energies to re-writing it so it will not show up too badly. In the hands of Kazan - it has great plastic possibilities - it could be made very interesting but I am still skeptical about Margo's gifts as a director as I have really seen so little of her work. There is no doubt about her genius as a manager! She would have a tremendous career if she would concentrate on that end of it and use people like Kazan to do the things requiring brilliant interpretation. However I shall have to eat these words if she puts over "summer and smoke" and when she decides to do a thing nothing that heart and soul can do is left undone! She's a pretty remarkable little woman.

Well, it is time for me to take to the streets!

With love, 10.

[Later correspondence with Margo Jones saw the "pensione" become a "whorehouse" and TW a naive American tourist who belatedly learns its true nature. "At any rate," he quipped, "this is the first place I've ever stayed where I felt my private life was above suspicion and beyond reproach" (postmarked Rome, February 28, 1948, HRC).

The English writer Norman Douglas was seventy-nine and living on Capri with his friend, Kenneth Macpherson. TW's "story" catches the sardonic humor and the devotion to dining for which the author of South Wind (1916) was famous. Douglas was also known to speak bitterly of his former wife after their brief marriage and divorce in 1903.

Mona Harrison Williams rose above modest origins in Kentucky by marrying often and well. She was not "passe," as TW put it, but still a commanding, influential hostess who would entertain him in New York (see Vidal, *Palimpsest*, 1995, pp. 204-205). Her penchant for marriage and imperious manner may have contributed to the role of Mrs. Goforth in *The Milk Train Doesn't Stop Here Anymore* (1963).

Reeves was living in New York and trying to establish himself in a profession apart from being the husband of Carson McCullers. Discharged from the Army in 1946, he had been hampered in efforts to find a job by alcoholism, depression, and goals which surpassed his formal education.

"Yet, to the empty trapeze of your flesh, / O Magdalene, each comes back to die alone." The lines from "National Winter Garden" (1933), by Hart Crane, refer to the poet's loss of spiritual vision and the inevitable "cinch" of the flesh.

Penned in the upper margin of page 1 is the notation "A. Ex. Rome."]

93. *To Carson McCullers*

[45 Via Aurora, Rome]
[March 1, 1948]
[TLS w/ autograph marginalia, 1 p. Duke U]

Dearest Carson:

Sometimes the lamp burns very low indeed! For the past five or six days I have been battering my head against a wall of creative impotence. I have enough strength to do patch-work only on old scripts but I want to start new work. The scenes, the situations, the dialogue do not come to life. The characters remain half in shadow if not in total eclipse. I drink two cups of coffee. Then ring for more. At last my heart starts pounding violently and I have black spots in front of my eyes that grow larger and start to spin. I know I must stop, give up again for a while. So I take to the streets. It is the first day of March, Primavera is already here. A golden haze lies over the whole city as I look down on it from the top of the Piazza di Spagna. I feel comforted somehow. My heart stops hammering so despairingly and I go on to American Express where I find your letter and your story. Then it occurs to me that it is not necessary for me to do and say everything, that there are other writers in the world with souls of more sensibility than mine and greater power. Sometimes that thought is vexatious but today I find it soothing. Yes, individuality is an accidental thing. One being oneself does not imply as much importance and

responsibility as one assumes. Perhaps it is impossible to think, feel and be through any channels other than one's own individual senses, but nevertheless all the others exist all around you. Where you fail, another succeeds. The responsibility is infinitely divided: life is multitudinous: a single wave can be thwarted but not the tide!

I am awfully, <u>awfully</u> glad that you are now in touch with Audrey. She has a deep understanding and a warm and sensitive heart and you will grow to love her as I have and she will have a feeling for your work that no other (merely commercial) agent could have. Joshua Logan was the man that several people wanted to direct "Streetcar". Mrs. Selznick thinks him quite marvelous. I preferred Kazan but next to him I am sure that Logan is excellent. Perhaps for your play even better as Logan used to live in the deep South and he is a man fighting to recapture an artistic position which he somewhat compromised by his work on big musicals like "Annie Get Your Gun". Don't worry anymore, I think your play is now in safe hands. And I do hope you will start on those stories, though perhaps they should wait till you are able to return abroad where we can work in adjoining trances.

Frederic Prokosch and Gore Vidal is here. I met Prokosch for the first time and found him very friendly and unpretentious. Vidal is 23 and a real beauty. His new book "The City and the Pillar" I have just read and while it is not a good book it is absorbing. There is not a really distinguished line in the book and yet a great deal of it has a curiously life-like quality. The end is trashy, alas, murder and suicide both. But you would like the boy as I do: his eyes remind me of yours!

Darling, I shall now go back to bed - the little god kept me awake all night - but I shall take "The Ballad of the Sad Cafe" to bed with me and read it before I go back to sleep. Each day is making you better! It must and it will.

All my love, 10.

[TW confirmed in later correspondence with Elia Kazan that he "started and gave up at least four plays" at this time. "The simple truth," he admitted, "is that I haven't known where to go since Streetcar." To Audrey Wood he observed that it was "frightfully hard to discover a new vein of material," having already "said so much about human relations, especially love" (February 1948, HRC).

Wood was impressed by Joshua Logan's co-writing and staging of the hit

Mister Roberts (1948) and hoped for the same happy result with *The Member of the Wedding*. She asked TW to solicit his interest when Logan visited Rome. Wood was loath, however, to formalize her "handling" (to TW, March 12, 1948, HRC) of Carson McCullers, fearing that it would eventually lead to a conflict of interest with TW.

Sir Harold Acton, observer of the expatriate community, wrote that TW, Frederic Prokosch, and Gore Vidal "created a bohemian annexe to the American Academy," while viewing "Classical and Romantic Rome" as "no more . . . than a picturesque background." He considered TW the "mildest" of the group and noted that this "moustached little man . . . wandered as a lost soul among the guests he assembled in an apartment which might have been in New York, for it contained nothing suggestive of Rome" (*More Memoirs of an Aesthete*, 1970, p. 211).

TW was unaware that McCullers had suffered a setback in late-February which alarmed her family and doctors.

Penned in the upper margin is the notation "Address 'Member' c/o American Exp."]

94. *To Audrey Wood*

[45 Via Aurora, Rome]
[March 1948]
[TLS, 1 p. HRC]

Dear Audrey:

Yesterday I mailed a revision of story "Night of the Iguana". I did not have a copy of the story so I am not sure exactly where this new material should be attached to the original. It replaces the long didactic speech of the writer and makes a new ending which I think is more harmonious with the rest. Please have Tiz or Creekmore, preferably Tiz, find the point at which this material connects and have the story re-typed accordingly and published this way. Tiz sent various questions from Creekmore. Please tell him the story title is not "Field of Blue <u>Chickens</u>". Title is "Field of Blue <u>Children</u>" and was published in STORY magazine sometime in 1939 or 1940. "The Important Thing" was also published in STORY. I believe in 1945. He can get both stories through Whit Burnett if you don't have them. "Something About Him" appeared in Madamoiselle a couple of springs ago. These stories must go into volume. "Bobo" is now called "The Yellow Bird". The complete and final text is the one that was published in "Town & Country." Creekmore must get copy of magazine and use their title and text for volume.

Perhaps with the new ending "Night of the Iguana" would be acceptable

to "Harper's Bazaar". Please send them a copy of it in present form, which I think is shorter. Just before I left New York they wanted almost anything I had to give them - greater love hath no publisher!

Please tell Carson that I am utterly and truly entranced by her story "The Ballad of the Sad Cafe" which she recently sent me. I think it is wonderful material for a film-fantasy similar to Cocteau's film, "The Beauty and the Beast" and perhaps she and I together could work out a film treatment of it. I will write her about this idea this week.

The young (23 years old) novelist Gore Vidal is now in Rome. He and Frederic Prokosch. I see them every day. Vidal is awfully nice and his shocking new book is on the best-seller list in the States. I will see if I can get him for you! I am sure he is going to have a long and successful career.

How are you and Bill? My love to you both.

Tennessee

P.S. TIZ FORWARDED A VALENTINE GREETING FROM PANCHO IN WHICH HE SAID THAT HE WAS ENTERING "CHARITY HOSPITAL" (New Orleans) FOR A MONTH. HE GAVE NO REASON. WOULD YOU PLEASE CALL THE HOSPITAL LONG DISTANCE TO VERIFY THIS STATEMENT AND ENQUIRE ABOUT HIS CONDITION? ANONYMOUSLY IF POSSIBLE. MANY THANKS FOR YOUR LONG LETTER JUST NOW RECEIVED. I WILL HAVE TO ANSWER IT UNDER "SEPARATE COVER". CONDUCT THE GOULD-ECHOLS DEAL ACCORDING TO YOUR DISCRETION.

[Of the stories cited by TW, only "Something About Him" would not appear in *One Arm*.

Audrey Wood's cable—"Important know immediately your present attitude Jones directing" (March 11, 1948, HRC)—was prompted by Margo Jones's request that contracts for *Summer and Smoke* be drawn before her arrival in New York to cast the show. It was a final effort by Wood to deter TW from a course which she knew to be based upon personal rather than professional considerations. She was later "shocked" to learn that Jones was using her own casting agents in addition to Liebling-Wood. "This makes it a rat race as to who gets actor on phone first" (telegram, to Jones, March 25, 1948, HRC).

Pancho Rodriguez sent TW a "Valentine greeting" with news that he was entering a "charity hospital" (TW to Wood, 3/48, HRC) in New Orleans. Wood's staff could not verify the report.

TW wrote this letter, which bears a reception date of March 19, 1948, late in the week of March 7 before leaving for Amalfi, in company with Gore Vidal.]

95. To Carson McCullers

[45 Via Aurora, Rome]
[March 1948]
[TLS w/ autograph postscript, 1 p. Duke U]

Dearest Carson:

A friend of mine, Paul Moor, has just sent me a clipping of your letter about me to LIFE. Nobody has ever said such things about me and nobody but you has ever thought such things about me! Bless you for it! I am a little embarassed for the most I can ever do is approximate virtue and only that at intervals but it is deeply moving to learn that anybody could see me in such a light and perhaps it will encourage me to improve.

I have been a little worried about you as I haven't heard from you in some time, and I have not received the play that you were going to send me.

For three nights last week I read "The Ballad of the Sad Cafe" and they were the loveliest nights I have had in Europe. The story of Miss Amelia and the hunchback is in my opinion the most beautiful story in all American fiction. I wrote Audrey that I thought it would make a film. Perhaps she has called you about it. When that happy day comes when we are working together, that can be one of our projects if you like.

It is really Prima Vera here in Rome. A succession of perfectly radiant days, and I have bought a Jeep, an old one that still runs well, so that I can spend a lot of time outdoors. I finished my rewrite of "Summer and Smoke". It has been difficult for me to get started on the new play, so I am leaving it for a while and trying to improve my general condition by a lot of out-door life. Gore Vidal the young (23 year old) novelist is here. He is interesting but is infected with that awful competitive spirit and seems to be continually haunted over the successes or achievements of other writers such as Truman Capote. He is positively obsessed with poor little Truman Capote. You would think they were running neck and neck for some fabulous gold prize! I don't like that attitude and spirit in young writers. But of course it is a result of insecurity. Prokosch is also here. He is suffering from jaundice and his skin and eyes are bright yellow but his nature is healthier than Vidal's. He is sort of a hedonist, I don't like his social and political principles, but he is quite modest and friendly and has a good sense of humor. You will like him, I think, if you can ignore his social views - which are pretty reactionary and classical and all that. There is not an awful lot to choose from in the

way of American society here, but that does not matter as the city and the weather and the natives are all you need.

I shall be [at] Amalfi for a few days this week (coming) to enjoy some swimming. I will write you from there. Let me hear from you as often as you feel like writing and know that my love is with you all of the time.

Tenn.

(Just got your letter, thank heavens! So happy you wrote story!)

[Carson McCullers praised author and subject of TW's profile in *Life* magazine (February 16, 1948): "Tennessee Williams is not only an extraordinarily great artist, a genius, he is also one of the wholly beautiful human beings I have ever known" (*Life*, March 8, 1948, p. 14). The author, Lincoln Barnett, closely followed the evolving Williams legend of an idyllic southern childhood, hard times in St. Louis, and long-delayed success on Broadway. Rose was cast as the "closest companion" of TW's youth, but neither her medical history nor the unhappy state of the family was mentioned in the profile.

The controversial novels of Gore Vidal and Truman Capote—*The City and the Pillar* and *Other Voices, Other Rooms*—were published within days of each other in January 1948. Capote's prose won critical honors and the notorious dust jacket the fiercely waged publicity battle. McCullers was no doubt hurt by a reviewer who ranked Capote as "a minor imitation of a very talented minor writer, Carson McCullers" (Elizabeth Hardwick, *Partisan Review*, March 1948).

TW had acquired one of the "natives," Rafaello, as discreetly named in *Memoirs*. A suggestive reference to this "'*giovane*'" in a newspaper article "launched {TW} upon a long period of personal notoriety in Rome" (*Memoirs*, p. 145), as later events would confirm.

Composition of this letter late in the week of March 7, 1948, is coincident with McCullers's reported suicide attempt. She was hospitalized in New York and by April 10 was "feeling better" (Wood to TW, April 10, 1948, HRC).]

96. To Justin Brooks Atkinson

[45 Via Aurora, Rome]
March 29, 1948
[TLS, 2 pp. BRTC]

Dear Brooks:

I have been living in Rome for two months now and would like to stay on indefinitely but, alas, it looks as if the political situation will make it

most uncomfortable for foreigners, especially those from the States. Most of my American friends here are making plans to pull out before the elections which are April 18th. Frederic Prokosch has been living here and I met him for the first time and was surprised to find him quite simple and friendly, which is certainly not the impression you get from the austere pictures of him that usually appear on the back of his books. He is driving his Lincoln Continental across the French border this week. Another and more precocious American writer, Gore Vidal, is also here and he is flying to Cairo. Various others are scattering to various other places. I have not yet made any plans and the way that I drift along here, time flows almost imperceptibly although so swiftly, I doubt that I will make any move until the last moment. As I do not live at all conspicuously, and drive a second-hand Jeep, perhaps the Communists will overlook [me] completely if they come into power! Orson Welles is in Rome. I have not met him but I have seen him sitting in front of Doney's which is the fashionable sidewalk cafe in front of the fashionable hotel Excelsior where he is staying. He was reading a book called <u>DECADENCE</u>. I have been told that he has taken a house here for two years, so perhaps Orson is politically invulnerable. Most of the people I've talked to think that Togliatti will win. The trouble is that none of the other parties have put up candidates that appeal to the people. There is a terrific reaction here against the church particularly since Monsignor Scippio skipped off with a vast amount of money. When you mention de Gasperi to the Italian-in-the-streets he makes a wry face and says 'Prete!' Nothing at all has apparently been done by the native government, as it now exists, to relieve the really appalling social conditions. It honestly looks as if seventy percent of the Italian population are mendicants and prostitutes, families are living in the roofless shells of buildings in the bombed cities such as Naples. I feel that if we had made really sacrificial efforts to relieve the distress of Europe the Communists would have no appeal. As it is, the people in their really dire circumstances, bewildered by vacillating and make-shift puppet governments headed by weak and blandly opportunistic figures, rooted in no defined party or policy or philosophy, are a natural and easy prey to extremists. What a tragedy it is, that America, our nation, at the one great moment of destiny, suddenly lost the man, Roosevelt, who was apparently the one leader in the Western World who could see realistically and think idealistically and feel humanely enough to get us all through this interval of panic without a catastrophe

which now seems to be coming. What it really took was simple human understanding which somehow seems to be lacking in the present leadership. No, of course it takes more than that, but with that as a basis I believe we might have kept the world in the hands of liberals and moderates and so kept going. - Well, a miracle may happen. - Speaking of miracles I was out at St. Peters on Good Friday and [saw] a most amusing spectacle. A dignitary of the church, in scarlet robes and cap - apparently a cardinal - was seated in a little fenced enclosure with a narrow gate at either side. There was a line of people, easily half a mile long, moving at a slow trot through one gate and out the other, for all the world like a sheep-dip, while the Cardinal sitting on his ornate throne, cracked them over the head as they went by him with a very long stick, like a black board pointer. He was apparently in a vile humor for he hit some of them so smartly that they winced with pain. One old lady was dazed by the blow he gave her and started to trot back in the opposite direction, against the current and he gave her a second crack even harder than the first which seemed to set her straight again. There was a young American priest alongside me, as irreverent as myself, and when I asked him what this ceremony was about he told me that everybody who got cracked over the head with the stick had 300 days knocked off his sentence in Purgatory!

Purgatory indeed! What most of these people needed was a bar of soap, a clean shirt and a good square meal. The Italians are a beautiful and very lovable people, I like them even better than Mexicans. I don't think Communism is really their dish but we have got to offer them a more inspiring number of alternatives if we want to keep their faith. They do not hate Americans at all, in fact the whole time I've been here I haven't had an unfriendly word or look from any of them.

I hope the theatrical season has picked up. I understand from Kazan that MR. ROBERTS is a grand play and likely to win the prizes. Joshua Logan is in Italy and has written me and I expect we will meet in Rome.

I am working pretty well here, although Primavera is even more distracting than Spring, one pure golden day after another. I sometimes suspect that I died at the American hospital in Paris and went to heaven! That is, when I think and feel selfishly which is, of course, most of the time.

My best greetings to you and to your wife,

Ever, Tennessee.

[The Christian Democrat party of Premier Alcide de Gasperi defeated the Communist-led Popular Front of Palmiro Togliatti and kept control of the government. Cold War competition of East and West had intensified the election, with the future of the Marshall Plan an issue of debate. Little violence accompanied the campaign and serious post-election disturbances did not immediately occur.

Orson Welles lived in Rome during the filming of *Black Magic* (1949). TW's remark that Welles would be "invulnerable" to a Communist government echoes charges stateside that he was "'red as a firecracker.'" He was probably reading *Decadence: A Philosophic Inquiry* (1948), by C.E.M. Joad.

Streetcar, rather than *Mister Roberts*, swept the "prizes" for the current season, winning the Drama Critics' Circle Award and the Pulitzer by wide margins. *Streetcar* was only the second play in the history of the awards to claim both—the first *The Time of Your Life* (1939) by William Saroyan.]

97. To Audrey Wood

[45 Via Aurora, Rome]
4/2/48
[TLS, 1 p. HRC]

Dear Audrey:

This must be telegraphic as I am worn out from working.

I suppose Margo will be arriving in New York this week. Do by all means put all possible (humane) pressure to assure that Summer and Smoke does not rush into New York. I think a West Coast opening would be ideal but if that is not feasible, concentrate on the subject of Chicago. If you want to (<u>dare</u> to) bring up the subject of Kazan directing, do so, but I doubt that you will get anywhere with it as our girl Jones unquestionably regards herself as the American Stanislavsky which it is still faintly possible that she may be however much we may doubt it. Also please make sure that no one is definitely signed before I return sometime in the middle of summer, probably not the end of July or early in August. While still on the subject, ask Eddie if it possible (legally) for me to give half of this play (Summer) to my sister, so that if it is moderately successful there will no longer be any question of there being money enough to do something for her? Also please thank Eddie for his letter which I will answer as soon as I can get around to it.

I loved your long letter and especially the part about the afternoon at McCullers! I never knew you had such a gift for graphic and lively narrative!

It is among the letters I will keep with me. I don't understand what you mean about not wanting to handle Carson, however, because of possible collision between her interests and mine. I don't see how that could happen, as she is a basically wise and sensible girl and I myself am not hysterical enough to ever want to bring out a joint volume with any other writer, let alone one who would make my work appear so pale in comparison as hers would! Frederic Prokosch has just read her "Ballad of a Sad Cafe" and pronounces it the finest piece of American (poetic) fiction. He is going to write her about it.

I am a bit worried over Windham and his friend Campbell coming over here. I don't want any unnecessary responsibilities right now and I'm afraid that is going to turn into one, especially with political crises developing all over the continent, focussing particularly on Rome. Would it be possible to get an advance, for Windham, on his novel? Otherwise I will almost certainly have to take care of him over here! - Don't mention this but please investigate the chances with the "League of Authors" Etc. His published and unpublished stories are certainly good enough to get him a fellowship or loan or advance of some kind.

I may have to leave Italy if the elections go far to the left, as probably all Americans would be in a hazardous position. I have heard from Fabio Coen, the man you mentioned, and I plan to see him. You have no idea how time flies here! The American colony is desperately gregarious and you can only work by bolting doors and shutters. Yes, some of them even climb in the window if they suspect you have a little cognac on the place!

Love - 10.

P.S. I have just met Fabio and like him extremely. We are going to collect my 30,000 lire on Friday.

[Eddie Colton advised TW that a trust fund would be the safest way "to give half" of *Summer and Smoke* to his sister Rose. He went on to pose "difficult" (April 30, 1948, HRC) legal questions which probably baffled TW.

The "afternoon at McCullers" (March 6) reminded Audrey Wood of "a Tennessee Williams story." Carson "was in bed in little boy's pink woolen pajamas" surrounded by adoring mother, sister, husband, and friends. "The only thing she could discuss over and over again was MEMBER OF THE WEDDING — and Tennessee Williams! The climax of the afternoon came when with adoration in her

eyes she asked us whether we wanted to hear you recite a poem on a record. . . . It began and though I listened as hard as I ever have in my life not one word was understandable. As this monotonous noise droned on, McCullers leaned forward with great ecstasy and . . . said, 'Isn't that the most beautiful poem you have ever heard?'" (March 12, 1948, HRC).

TW would soon devise a more biting parody of McCullers in correspondence with Paul Bigelow (see letter #170).]

98. To Margaret "Margo" Jones

[45 Via Aurora, Rome]
[mid-April 1948]
[TLS, 1 p. HRC]

Dearest Girl:

I am so happy that you can really come over for a while! Also over the news that you think Margaret Phillips is available. Has the script arrived yet? I mailed it to Audrey, air mail registered, about five days ago and it certainly should have reached her by this time.

I am anxious to know Milzener's reactions. I think I have made my idea of the set, at last, quite explicit and I hope he will find it stimulating for so much depends on what he is going to give us, far more than in any other work, for this play deals with intangibles which need plastic expression far more than verbal. The knowledge that you and I and he will be working together all by ourselves is a happy one. I am sure that Audrey and Bill will also give us every possible support and altogether we should come through with colors not drooping.

Don't dismiss Todd until you're quite sure that you have someone really better. Remember the boy must be <u>attractive</u>! If you can get that <u>and</u> real ability as an actor, we will be in luck. Anyone you consider very seriously, please send me a picture air-mail. I am particularly anxious that the part of Nellie should be well-played as she has to sustain some of the weaker scenes in the play. The doctor's part has been greatly reduced with the elimination of his long scene with Alma and I think in scene eight he should not be lighted except as a silhouette, to give him an impersonal quality. The face never visible. For it is too late in the play to introduce a new character. In eight the light only on Rosa Gonzales (formerly the Serio girl). In costuming this play I think Lucinda Ballard would be marvelous.

Why don't you talk with her and see if she is willing to adapt herself to the budget? I think the period and style of the play would fit her talents which are highly interpretive as well as pictorial. Her one drawback is temperament but that is also part of her value, and she is a great person. Jo always wants her which is an excellent sign. - For God's sake get some good kids for the prologue. The play must get off to a good start. Have an understanding with everyone (except perhaps Phillips) that they are not finally cast until after the first five days of rehearsal, or rather till I have seen and heard them.

Such a sad letter from Carson McCullers. Do not mention this, but not long ago she slashed her wrist in an attempt at suicide and has recently been in a psychiatric clinic. She still has the paralytic condition of the left side and perhaps suspects that it is permanent. If I were not sure that Pancho would pounce on me, I would come back to the States. That is going to be a big problem when I do return, as he is almost certain to learn where I am and to reappear.

Helen Hayes is sailing for England early in June to do the Menagerie in London, opening I think about July fifteenth. I do hope you can stay over till then. We will spend some time here, then fly to Paris and see what is going on there, then wind up in England for the opening of Hayes. I think you should have a real vacation over here, so give yourself plenty of time. The way things look at the moment I don't think the Communists are powerful enough to make much trouble in Italy.

Love - 10.

[TW's production notes for *Summer and Smoke* were so precise and revealing, Jo Mielziner wrote, that "it would be truly difficult to design a setting for this play that was poor in concept. It might be inadequate in execution, but the extraordinarily knowledgeable and sensitive eye of the dramatist created a picture that even a mediocre designer could not spoil" (*Designing for the Theatre*, 1965, p. 153).

Tod Andrews played young John Buchanan in the Dallas and Broadway productions of *Summer and Smoke*, as well as on tour.

Lucinda Ballard designed the costumes for *Streetcar* but not for *Summer and Smoke*.

Carson McCullers was released from Payne Whitney Psychiatric Clinic in mid-April and soon began revising *The Member of the Wedding*. A draft sent to TW brought the encouraging reply, "'Script a thousand times better'" (qtd. in Carr, p. 305).]

Jo Mielziner, full set design for Summer and Smoke *(1948).*

99. *To Audrey Wood*

[45 Via Aurora, Rome]
4/19/48
[TLS, 2 pp. HRC]

Dear Audrey:

I have been very scatter-brained and unbusiness-like in my recent communications with the home-front and I have left undone all those things
which ought to have been done. (Erred and strayed from thy ways like lost
sheep! Followed too much the devices and desires of my own heart, Etc.)

It is now the day after election, a day of reckoning. I must sit down and
make a few important emendations.

First off, do not send Richard Orme anymore money for that G.D.
apartment of his. I can't afford (or get tax exemption) for maintaining two
residences and I wrote him last January from Paris that he would have to
keep the girls in the place or sublet it to someone else. I signed that lease as
a friendly accomodation to him with the clear understanding that it was to
be sub-let until and if I wanted it back. Now of course since I have broken
up with Pancho under such distressing circumstances I could not return to
New Orleans where he and his family live. Do not please state this in the letter to Orme who is a terrible and vicious gossip and a rather cruel person.

Second, please see what you can do to either stop publication of Moor's article for Harper's or see that we get final corrected proofs before it is published. It is direct contradiction of most of the known facts about me, worst of all it is terribly dull. I have written Moor to get a postponement and he has wired that is impossible. Please see, at least, that either the usual date of 1914 is given for my birth or the painful subject is altogether avoided. The article is a mass of inaccuracies and misinterpretations due to the fact that I have never really had an interview only friendly (and very laconic) meetings with Moor on three or four occasions.

Send me any good books on the frontier days (colorful anecdotal atmospheric) about the frontier days of the Texas oil-industry as that is the background of my latest attempt at a comedy. I've started three or four different plays but this is perhaps the most promising.

My masseur-gym instructor has arrived and I have to get to work. Perhaps I will think of some more jobs for you later.

With love, Tennessee.

RE: Tito Guerini. I have not yet had the heart to tell him that you think his story is bad. He refers to it as his "Seule et derniere espoir!" (We have to converse in French as my Italian remains a bit inadequate.) As a matter of fact, I think it is a good slice of Italian life, this story, but perhaps the translation is still bad. Send it to New Directions, please, if no where else - along with my account of the author. These Italians break my heart, or what's left of it. They are such lovable and pitiful people, and up against such a blank wall, politically, economically, almost every conceivable way. I hate to make friends among them - easy as that is! - because I shall feel so badly when I leave them here with the sort of future that seems to be inevitable.

If our state department could think of Europe in terms of human beings rather than parties, governments, then perhaps a world-disaster could be side-stepped.

Logan is here and also Carson's script has arrived. The script is better and I shall call Logan today. I hope he will work on it with her.

Yes, please have Tiz's father investigate Rose's circumstances. Soon as I come back [to] the States I shall find another place for her. Perhaps that could even be done before my return. She has been in that goddam place

for twelve years now! I can't hardly believe it. If God has forgotten her there, we have got to remember. I have been much too preoccupied with my self.

Along with the (one good) book on Texas oil development please send me the <u>new</u> biography of Hart Crane, not the old one by Philip Horton which I have read. I have read, finally, Capote's book. One third of it is brilliant. The rest falls flat and is terribly derivative of Faulkner and Carson McCullers. But he has the finest writing style of any of the new novelists.

For some reason my health in Italy has been exceptionally good, absolutely no gastric disturbances since I got here, but I have not done much work. One story, one poem, and only the beginnings of several plays which have lovely conceptions but no second act complications (plots!).

Statement for Theatre Arts? Say I was pleased to get it! What more can be said about that?

[Penitential lines from *The Book of Common Prayer* were easily and accurately quoted by the grandson of an Episcopal priest.

In 1938 TW lowered his age by three years to qualify for a Group Theatre contest (see Vol. I, letter #86). Paul Moor skirted the deception by vaguely placing TW's birth "a little before the first world war" ("A Mississippian Named Tennessee," *Harper's Magazine*, July 1948).

TW's request for books about the "oil-industry" pertains to a work-in-progress entitled "The Big Time Operators." An outline tentatively identifies the "Operators" as an "Oil corporation?" (n.d., HRC) and reveals the play to be a partial study of *Sweet Bird of Youth* (1956/1959).

Tito Guerrini asked TW for help in placing a story of his, probably "My Maternal Aunt" (*New Directions Twelve*, 1949).

"Tiz" Schauffler's father, a Kansas City physician, learned that Rose Williams had shown "some improvement" following recent insulin and electric shock treatment but her prognosis was "poor" (Hoctor to Robert Schauffler, n.d., HRC). Dr. Schauffler advised that "there does not seem to be much equity in removing Miss Williams to a private hospital and physician" (to Elizabeth Schauffler, May 8, 1948, HRC).

Theatre Arts had asked TW to comment on the Drama Critics' Circle Award given to *Streetcar*.]

100. To Audrey Wood

[45 Via Aurora, Rome]
4/24/48
[TLS, 2 pp. HRC]

Dear Audrey:

I hope I remember all these things you have asked me!

First about Singer: I have no idea why he is supposed to get one percent of the London show but I hope you will do everything in your power to prevent it as you know my opinion of that [mind] and all his works. It was my understanding that we were now completely free of any legal connection with him. His influence on "Menagerie" was solely negative and came near being destructive.

Cast for London production: I do think Ross is definitely too old. His age was only acceptable when coupled with Dowling's. Also he has many other problems which make him precarious. With Hayes as the mother I think he would seem definitely too old, and I say this in spite of liking him and his performance.

Directors: Harold Clurman has just written me expressing his eagerness to direct the play in London. I have a profound respect and liking for Clurman as a director and person and would be delighted to have him if he is acceptable to Miss Hayes. Joshua Logan who is now in Rome has also told me he would like to do the show in London. My fear about him is that he goes overboard on farcical effects. I get that impression from his detailed account of <u>Mr. Roberts</u> as well as from the really awful job he did on Hayes show which has just closed. He seems to delight in tricks and gags of the most obvious nature. On the other hand, I find him likeable as a person. He has worked with Hayes and they seem to like each other - according to him! - I am not at all keen about Gielgud. It would quite probably be like Margaret Webster directing Battle of Angels. He is too English, too stylish, too removed from the subject and spirit of the script. I would much prefer Logan of those two - Incidentally Logan is going to England and he expressed his desire to direct "Menagerie" in a letter which reached me a few days ago in Florence, where I had gone to meet Windham, so he is obviously serious about it. I suggest that you talk to Hayes, very confidentially, about Logan and see if she thinks he can be trusted to avoid broad comedy devices - without letting her know that I personally have expressed that concern about him.

My first choice is still Clurman but I realize that I may meet with too strong opposition from all quarters on that score, which is a pity for Clurman represents the things I most value in theatre.

In any case will you please call Clurman and assure him that I have written you in recommendation of him?

I like Phil Brown for either Gentleman Caller or Tom. Awfully sorry about Monty. How about Bill Eyethe? He is supposed to be wonderful and would look good with Hayes and I like him personally.

Tell Irene I have no ideas about costumes. I can't cable replies to things like that as I cannot send cables collect and they cost enormously. I still think of myself as a poor man and I will until Colton has figured out someway to rescue me from the tax collectors. I am writing Colton this week.

On reading over Guerini's story, I still like it, but I see that it has been very awkwardly translated. I will think more about that.

I will also <u>consider</u> restoring scene in Summer & Smoke. I felt it did not advance the plot to any appreciable extent and that it gave the audience more time in which to get tired of Miss Alma. If Phillips is really good we can throw it back in. Windham says Clift would like to play John. What do you and Margo think about that? Originally he seemed a little lacking in vitality but perhaps he has changed in that respect. He has the looks and other qualifications for the part.

I was surprised to find that the acting edition of Menagerie contained ~~practically all~~ of the little vulgarisms which Babs and I spent practically a whole day weeding out. How did they get back in? I particularly detest that closing line * * "And this is where the play ends and your imagination begins". - Other respects show improvement.

I think the connection with Theatre Guild is regrettable because of their scandalous treatment of Guild and Equity members. Hate to seem to be sanctioning such behavior. - Carson's script is better but confidentially it is still not right. I must think of something! Logan is on the fence - very cagey about it -

Love - 10.

[*The Glass Menagerie* was set to open in London in the following July with Tennent Ltd. as managing concern. Louis J. Singer demanded one percent of TW's royalty as compensation for an option which he charged that Audrey Wood had terminated unfairly. She later advised payment to avoid lengthy arbitration.

Helen Hayes reluctantly agreed to play Amanda in London. She and Wood favored Anthony Ross, who originated the role of the Gentleman Caller, but his age and drinking worried TW.

Wood advised TW that "British labor policy" (telegram, April 21, 1948, HRC) might preclude use of an American director in staging *The Glass Menagerie*. Harold Clurman, a founder of the Group Theatre (1931-1941), would eventually direct *The Member of the Wedding* (1950). Joshua Logan received mixed rather than "awful" reviews for his direction of Hayes in *Happy Birthday* (1946). TW feared that John Gielgud would repeat the problems which Margaret Webster had brought to *Battle of Angels* (1940): both were "too English, too stylish," to direct plays "soaked in American provincialism."

Apparently Irene Selznick consulted TW about costumes for a British production of *Streetcar* which she and Hugh Beaumont were planning.

Cut in the latest version of *Summer and Smoke* was a long expository scene (Scene Two) between Alma and the elder Buchanan. The new scene opens in the rectory, rather than the doctor's office, and features a telephone call in which Alma flirtatiously reminds young John Buchanan of a promised automobile ride: "I was just reprimanding you, sir! Castigating you verbally! Ha-ha!" (March 1948, HRC). Echoes of *The Glass Menagerie* and *Streetcar* are unmistakable.

The line detested by TW—"And there my memory ends and your imagination begins"—appears in the acting edition of *The Glass Menagerie* (Dramatists Play Service, 1948), but not in the first American edition published by Random House (1945). Eddie Dowling's dissatisfaction with the final lines reportedly led to the addition.

Actors Equity recently suspended a Theatre Guild manager for harassing cast members of the musical *Allegro* (1947). TW objected in turn to the Guild's co-producing *The Glass Menagerie*, but Wood explained that it was only a "courtesy" (May 5, 1948, HRC) billing to thank the Guild for its help in casting Miss Hayes.

This letter bears a reception date of May 1, 1948.]

101. To Gore Vidal

[45 Via Aurora, Rome]
[ca. April 25, 1948]
[TLS, 2 pp. Houghton]

Bright eyes!

This is glorious news about the play! Glorious plays are not usually written in such a short time, but Saroyan did it so why not you. I imagine that you will read it over after a while and decide it is slightly less glorious than you originally supposed in the first flush of exultation. That is nearly always the unhappy case. However there is no reason why it should not be

the beginning of a glorious play, anyhow. And I am hoping it is and will be. By all means do send it to me. When a thing goes that quickly it is a good sign, for it means that the impulse was vital and the vision was clear. Don't be surprised if it takes you several months more to make it as good as you first thought it was.

Windham and Sandy Campbell have come to Italy. I met them in Florence and we came down to Rome together and they are now putting up at the Inglaterra and are simply wild about Rome. Both of them think it is glorious. I hope it doesn't break up their happy marriage. We are looking at apartments this afternoon. If we find the right one we will set up housekeeping, the four of us. Yes, my mouse is still with me and swishing his little tail about as usual. Diretto! Destra! Sinistra! There has been a terrific influx of dikes. Mostly journalistic ones. Flanner (Janet) and her girl-friend came down to cover the election. Yesterday we all went to a private screening of a film called Berlin Anno Zero by the man who made Open City & Shoe Shine. When we arrived Janet said, "The ladies will sit in the front row and the gentlemen in the rear." And Esther, the biggest one of the Dikes who looks like Wallace Beery in drag, said, "Ah-ha! Sex discrimination!" They are a jolly bunch and the social life is considerably better than when there was just us girls, sunning ourselves like a bunch of lizards on the walk in front of Doney's. No word from Fritz and Russell who went off together. The French actor is still around but I haven't seen him. Poor La Traube! He has the clap now, the only one of us to be stricken, just when he was getting over the crabs. Afflictions, mortal afflictions! Especially those of love, how troublesome they are. I am glad you did not have carnal associations in Cairo, not only because it would have interfered with the glorious work but because I kept thinking, If Gore is not careful he will catch one of those things from the dirty Egyptians.

Franco Brusatti just now climbed in my window but has now climbed back out again. I told him I was working. There was no liquor, but he drank what was left of my coffee. With a threat to return. A gold filling has come out. The litany of my sorrows is now complete.

The sky is serenely blue, the light is golden. It is the sort of Roman day that we will remember all of these days being when we are back in the States.

I have one more letter to write, to Helen Hayes, who is going to do the Menagerie in London. Then to the Jeep!

I close now with an affectionate and mildly libidinous kiss on your soft under lip which I never kissed.

Ever fondly, Tennessee

Lesbia passed through Rome, heavily veiled. No sign of Willard. No word. Only a whisper of silk and a few rose leaves floating after. The scent of frangi-pangi. A few days later a gilt-edged card, saying "Sorry!" Post-marked Istanbul, dictated, unsigned. With Lesbia one is never certain, such a thin line, so easily crossed over! - Nerves . . .

[Gore Vidal (b. 1925) and TW met at a party given by the composer Samuel Barber for visiting Americans in Rome. " 'I particularly like New York on hot summer nights when all the . . . uh, superfluous people are off the streets'" (qtd. in Vidal, *Palimpsest*, p. 149). So apparently began TW's first conversation with Vidal, giving a wry, conspiratorial tone to their friendship and marking the streets of Rome as erotic. "We walked—cruised—a lot in the golden age," Vidal added many years later.

TW soon pronounced the "glorious" new play "'the worst . . . he'd read in some time,'" and Vidal, for the moment, "'solemnly abandoned playwriting for good'" (qtd. in Kaplan, *Gore Vidal: A Biography*, 1999, p. 273).

Franca Danesi was Janet Flanner's liaison and assistant in reporting the recent Italian elections for *The New Yorker*. Natalia Danesi Murray, Franca's older sister, was Flanner's intimate companion. Roberto Rossellini directed *Germania, anno zero* (1947) and *Open City* (1945) but not *Shoeshine* (1946), a film by Vittorio de Sica.

Internal evidence reveals that TW wrote this letter ca. April 25, 1948.]

102. *To Helen Hayes*

[45 Via Aurora, Rome]
4/25/48
[TLS, 2 pp. Private Collection]

Dear Helen Hayes:

I hope that my wire conveyed something of my exultation over the tentative news, now confirmed. I did not dare to believe it was actually going to happen, but apparently it has, and I am so very happy!

Now every care must be taken to see that you have the very best direction and supporting cast that can be obtained. I have written Audrey a few suggestions, all of which are of course entirely contingent upon your approval.

I do not much like the idea of Gielgud as a director unless no American is available, and that does not seem to be the case. Joshua Logan is now in Rome. How do you feel about him? He wrote me (while I was in Florence) expressing his willingness to direct you in London if you so wished. I met him here for the first time and liked him tremendously. In complete confidence, I must say that I have a suspicion that he is inclined to lean a bit too heavily on broad comedy effects in his direction. This I gathered from his detailed account of "Mr. Roberts" which I have not seen, and the other comedies which I have. What he would do with a play requiring a delicate and finely balanced touch is a matter of faith and speculation which you are better able to judge than I am, for I have seen and known so little of him and his work, but I would unhesitatingly prefer him to Gielgud or any other Englishman.

Harold Clurman has written me saying he would love to direct the play. There is a man I would love to work with! He represents everything I most value and respect in the theatre, for his seriousness, his sensitivity, his humility and his rare intelligence. I know some people think he is too highbrow or literary but that I doubt and I think he is needing some encouragement now and deserves it certainly.

Jessica Tandy has wired me suggesting her husband Hume Cronyn. Hume I know is a good director from his work on "Portrait of a Madonna" with Jessica at the Actors' Lab in Hollywood.

My feeling against Gielgud is primarily that he is British and I think there is an inherent incapacity in the British to interpret a play that is soaked in American provincialism. The body would be there, but some indefinite but immensely important thing would be missing. Then I wonder if he is not a little bit cold and dry and too dependant on theatrical effects and devices, especially for an artist like you whose instrument is so much of the heart. Warmth and humanity is what we want above everything else and that has seemed to be lacking in the directorial work of his I have seen, however much I admire him as a technical master.

Actors? I thought Clift would be swell but now I hear he is not available. Phil Brown is about equally gifted. How about Bill Eythe who is doing a West coast production now? You and Audrey will manage all that, however.

You must satisfy yourself completely in all these matters. I am only suggesting. I do think any British actors would be a big mistake! But it

would be hard to make a mistake big enough to seriously impair the effect of your Amanda which I look forward to almost as much as if it were the first time - not forgetting.

Sincerely, Tennessee.

[Audrey Wood pulled "every possible wire, string, and cobweb to lure Miss Hayes into the City of London" (to TW, April 13, 1948, HRC). Probably more telling was a promise which Laurette Taylor had secured from Hayes (1900-1993)—who regarded the older actor as her "guiding star"—to bring *The Glass Menagerie* to London if she herself could not. Hayes later wrote that meeting Edwina in London helped to explain why she felt "uneasy" playing Amanda. She realized the kind of unhappy family "memories" upon which TW had drawn and concluded that Edwina "was everything I disliked in an aging Southern belle" (*My Life in Three Acts*, 1990, p. 168).

Wood reported earlier that Hayes and Hugh Beaumont were "interested" in John Gielgud's direction of *The Glass Menagerie* and asked TW if he were "agreeable" (telegram, April 21, 1948, HRC). Gielgud was named director as TW wrote in reply or shortly thereafter. Phil Brown played the part of Tom Wingfield.]

103. *To Walter Edwin Dakin*

[45 Via Aurora, Rome]
May 17, 1948
[TLS, 2 pp. HTC]

Dear Grandfather:

Your letter made me feel quite sad for you. I hope you are not more than temporarily depressed, for that is not like you. I am not at all pleased with your apparent decision to stay in America. I would so much rather you came over with Mother and Dakin for I don't think there is anyone in the world who enjoys travelling as much as you do. Please think it over, reconsider, and let me <u>and</u> Audrey know. Audrey has wonderful connections with travel agencies and she can make all the arrangements for your passage by ship or by air. If you are really afraid of an ocean voyage, then why not let Audrey buy you a round-trip plane ticket which is not more expensive and which only takes about 18 hours. Mother says you are not going because you are "afraid of being buried at sea". Now that is ridiculous! In the first place you would not die. In the second place we would make sure that you were returned to Grand's side in Ohio. So put that silly idea out of your mind,

and take this holiday which is due you after the long winter in Saint Louis. It will make me, personally, ever so much happier to have you there in London. I don't like the English and I am only going out of duty. It is difficult to tear myself away from Italy which is the nearest to heaven that I have ever been, the people so friendly, gentle and gracious and the days so tranquil and sunny. I have an old Jeep that I travel around in. Perhaps I shall drive it to London. Margo is flying to Rome. She will join me here on the 26th and we will go North together, either in the Jeep or by train. You and she could have some nice card-games as you did in New Orleans while I am at rehearsals. Perhaps we could all get a nice apartment together.

So if you feel you really might enjoy the trip, write Audrey a note or have Mother call her long-distance. The trip will be with my compliments, of course, and Audrey will buy the tickets and make the reservations whichever way you decide.

                                   With much love to all of you, Tom.

[The "long winter in Saint Louis" may have led Walter Dakin to travel next to Clarksdale, Mississippi, rather than to London with his daughter and grandson.
    This letter was first published in Edwina Dakin Williams's memoir, *Remember Me to Tom*, pp. 224-225.]

104. To James "Jay" Laughlin

[45 Via Aurora, Rome]
May 18, 1948.
[TLS w/ marginalia, 2 pp. Houghton]

Dear Jay:

These days the melancholy task of collecting the wildly scattered papers, letters, manuscripts begun and abandoned, sorting out, throwing away or packing: the sad and exhausting business that always puts a long-drawn period to my stay in a place: wondering if anything is worth keeping except a few letters from friends but not quite daring to obey the impulse to make a bonfire of it all. This stay in Rome has been relatively felicitous. Sunny. Peaceful. I have made some good friends here such as Frederic Prokosch and that unhappy young egotist Gore Vidal who is now in Paris and a great number of ephemeral bird-like Italians, sweet but immaterial, like cotton-candy: I shall remember all of them like one person

who was very pleasant, sometimes even delightful, but like a figure met in a dream, insubstantial, not even leaving behind the memory of a conversation: the intimacies somehow less enduring than the memory of a conversation, at least seeming that way now, but possibly later invested with more reality: ghosts in the present: afterwards putting on flesh, unlike the usual way. Anyhow, Italy has been a real experience, a psychic adventure of a rather profound sort which I shall be able to define in retrospect only. I also have a feeling it is a real caesura: pause: parenthesis in my life: that it marks a division between two very different parts which I leave behind me with trepidation. The old continuity seems broken off now, by more than just travel and time. I have an insecure feeling more acute than usual. It is certainly not a good point at which to return to Broadway, but that is what I must do after a brief period in London for the Helen Hayes production of "Menagerie". Right after that, in July, I must return to New York for rehearsals of "Summer & Smoke", which is an uncertain quantity.

How right you are about the prizes! They mean nothing to me except that they make the play more profitable. Even so I shall probably not make much out of it. All I made out of "Menagerie" - after taxes and living expenses - was $30,000. If Streetcar had not been a success I would have been broke again in two years. It is evident that I have not been well-managed financially, but there is nothing that I can do about it without devoting my life to personal care of my earnings. It bothers me mostly because there are people I want to help and am not able to as much as I should. - Oh! While I'm on the subject of Streetcar - I thought the first format was infinitely preferable to the second: would it be possible to revert to it if there is another edition? All that I didn't like about the first was the color. The design was quite wonderful. The present is the worst I've ever seen on a New Directions book! I am afraid there must have been a total misunderstanding between Audrey and Creekmore. Unfortunately I was too busy at the time to make my own reactions clear to him.

About the stories: there is one very important change I want to make: the cutting of a certain passage in the story ONE ARM. Windham and I both feel that it cheapens the story, it is the #5 of my typed manuscript with the sentence: "They gave him half a tumbler of whiskey to loosen his tongue" and it ends on page seven with phrase: "assured the youth's conviction and doomed him to the chair". It was put into the story later and can be removed without affecting the continuity. Please make sure this

deletion is made on the proofs. It concerns the blue-movie which was made on the broker's yacht and it really cheapens the story.

I suggest that you send me the proofs c/o Hugh Beaumont, H.M. Tennant Ltd., London. (Address is Globe Theatre, I believe.) I am afraid they might not reach me here before I start north in my Jeep with Margo who is arriving on the twenty-sixth. I may even start before she arrives and have her meet me in Paris or London. There is to be a congress of Gypsies near Arles on the 24th of May and I should like very much to see it, as well as the town where Van Gogh wrote and painted the fiercest expressions ever made of this world's terrible glory. I wish that God would allow me to write a play like one of his pictures, but that is asking too much. I am too diffuse, too "morbido" - that wonderful Italian word for soft!

You must get Carson's Ballad for your anthology, but I do not quite know how to get the manuscript for you immediately. Joshua Logan who was to direct her play borrowed it and promised to return it by mail from Florence. As yet he has not done so. Surely there are other copies! It was published twice, first in Harper's Bazaar and again in a collection of stories selected by authors as the story they would like to have written. Kay Boyle selected Carsons. If you want to use one of mine, use "Desire & The Black Masseur" which is probably the best.

Carson and I exchange letters continually and we talk about making a home together. I doubt however that we could agree upon a location. She likes places near New York: I could not live anywhere that close to Broadway and continue to function as anything loosely resembling an artist.

Windham's novel is the finest thing, in some respects, that I have read in American letters: the quality is totally original. I wish that you were in a position to make him the necessary advance: he would need about a thousand dollars: for it is a book which only New Directions should publish, no one else. It is literature of the first order, the order of angels! However Audrey is sending it around to publishers like Dodd-Mead who have no idea what it is worth artistically, now and to be. I am afraid he will settle with them simply because he needs money. I am lending him some but naturally he is reluctant to take it and anything of that sort is deleterious to a friendship. I am afraid of the book being mutilated by uncomprehending suggestions and demands from a commercial house. I have never quite understood your lack of excitement over Don as a writer. (apparent.) I do

understand the difficulty of advancing money, however, when one is not a commercial publisher. That I do understand thoroughly. I am one of those who feel that New Directions has been a notably altruistic concern, the only one that exists. I also feel, however, that Windham's novel would be a sound investment financially as well as artistically if it is handled by an understanding house. Windham is now in Rome [*text obscured*] you will see him here or in Europe.

Ever - 10.

[Audrey Wood informed TW on January 21—when he was ill and in transit—that James Laughlin had agreed to change both the color and design of the *Streetcar* jacket. The second and third printings—"the worst" TW had seen—dispensed with the Lustig design and used brown lettering on a pale green background. With the fourth printing the original abstract design was reproduced on a red background, to the author's apparent satisfaction.

Canceling the passage in "One Arm" cited by TW would have removed all reference to "the blue-movie" made on the broker's yacht, as well as Oliver Winemiller's first exposure to such pornography while a sailor on leave in Marseille. Only the Marseille scene, which occurs in a brothel, and snatches of dialogue from "the blue-movie" were cut in the 1948 edition of *One Arm*—some twenty-eight lines in all.

The *New Republic* would harshly review Laughlin's forthcoming "anthology" (*New Directions Ten,* 1948), with "Desire and the Black Masseur," a story which ends in cannibalism, affording the critic a clever insult: "This little parable is delivered from a straight face, but it would be underrating Williams' showmanship to deny him the neat accomplishment here of providing an antidote to himself" (December 20, 1948).

Reviewers of *The Dog Star*, Donald Windham's first novel, were appreciative but far less enthusiastic than TW.

Typed in the upper margin of page 1 is the notation "Please bill me for 5 copies of your poems: inscribed to myself, Carson, Windham, Margo, Joanna Albus, and mail c/o Audrey Wood or Tennant Ltd in London."]

105. *To Audrey Wood*

Western Union
Roma
1948 May 21 PM 3 47
[Telegram, 1 p. HRC]

=HEARTILY APPROVE NEGRO COMPANY MENAGERIE TELL MARGO I
WILL MEET HER AT AIRPORT LOVE=

=TENNESSEE.

[The "all Negro company" planned to visit "schools and colleges" in the South.
There was "little money in this," Audrey Wood observed, but it would set a "fine
precedent" (telegram, to TW, May 14, 1948, HRC) for *The Glass Menagerie* and
other successful Broadway plays.

Margo Jones was due to arrive in Rome on May 26, 1948.]

106. *To Carson McCullers*

["on the Orient Express"]
June 8, 1948
[TLS w/ autograph marginalia, 1 p. Duke U]

Dearest Carson:

We are on the Orient Express, Margo Jones and I, travelling North to
Paris, then on to London. The very thought of packing and arranging this
trip had overwhelmed me but Margo with her amazing feminine competence
took over and managed everything for me. All I had to do was collect my
papers and letters. (That in itself was job enough for one person). Do you
think people like us would ever go <u>anywhere</u> if we didn't have people like
Margo pushing and pulling? I shall be in Paris for only two days but I shall
finally use some of your letters of introductions which I have kept in my
trunk. My first time there I was too ill for society. This time I may be too
nervous. I am still as nervous as a cat! Will continue more or less in that
condition until I get back to work. Until then the unused energy is a dozen
wildcats under the skin. I used to think a lot of sex would release it, but
somehow it doesn't at all. But I must settle somewhere to really get down
to work in a satisfactory way. Trips and visitors, a continual procession,
have kept me distracted and keyed up the last two months in Rome.

Honey, the news of Pancho is terrifying! He is in New York with some

mysterious travelling companion staying at a very expensive hotel on Central Park, has called Audrey and everybody to inform them that he is sailing for Europe June 11th, the day I arrive in England. He lands at Liverpool and presumably will come directly to London to look me up. It gives one a feeling of inescapable doom!

How I envy your retreat to the quiet place in Florida. Only retreat is the wrong word for it. It is a wonderful progress. If I have to remain in America next year, I think Key West might be a suitable place? Do you think you would like it there? It is the least commercial of the Florida resorts and the swimming is incomparable, better even than Capri. There is a small and really nice little society of artists and many pleasant little frame houses like the one in Nantucket. Oh, I'm so glad you didn't move into that Connecticutt barn! It is much too close to Broadway for one to ever feel away.

Audrey is so proud and happy that she has secured you this contract with the New Yorker and I am crazy to read the stories. Harper's Bazaar decided not to publish mine but they took a little poem I had written in Italy, almost the only thing that I finished there.

This country is like one continual Watteau rolling past. Now and then a flash of Van Gogh, but rarely quite that intense. I guess his country was mostly in his own crazy head. To get out of one's own crazy head: wouldn't it be nice to know how?

Please be happy and well! (I feel now that you will be.)

Much love - Tenn.

["I have news for you!" Audrey Wood wrote, informing TW that "Pancho is in town!" (June 1, 1948, HRC) and planning to sail for Liverpool on June 11 with an unidentified companion. Carson McCullers also knew of his return to New York and urged TW not to worry: "You have rejected the disorder and fatigue of a Pancho existence" (n.d., Private Collection).

McCullers's plan for a Florida "retreat" did not materialize. With the exception of several brief trips, McCullers remained in Nyack through the spring and summer of 1948. She and Reeves were beginning to reconcile and spend weekends together.

Wood arranged a potentially lucrative contract for McCullers which gave The New Yorker "the first reading option" (to TW, May 5, 1948, HRC) on her work for one year. The "little poem" by TW is "Testa Dell' Effebo."

Penned in the upper margin is TW's interim mailing address, "American Express, London, England."]

107. To Audrey Wood

[Cumberland Hotel, London]
[June 13, 1948]
[TL, 2 pp. HRC]

Dear Audrey:

I guess England is about the most unpleasant, uncomfortable and expensive place in the world you could be right now, and this is especially true on a Sunday which seems to be regulated by the society of Scotch Protestants who made such a fuss over Princess Elizabeth's scandalous day in Paris. When I finished work, in my usual state of nerves, I went downstairs to find a bar and a drink. It was ten after two and there wasn't a drink to be had in all of London until seven. I had to take a couple of barbital tablets instead. - Binkie Beaumont is not in town, Helen has not yet arrived but I have met Gielgud and the prospective gentleman caller. He is a big fellow, about 35 I should guess, with a rather weak-looking mouth but otherwise looks okay. I thought his speech was distinctly British but the British thought it was distinctly American, so there you are. Where are you? I feel quite unnecessary here. I was not asked to hear the young man read but was told that he would rehearse with us starting Tuesday and if found unsatisfactory could be replaced. I suggested that it might be diplomatic to allow Miss Hayes to feel that she was having some part in the selection as she is accustomed to some authority of that kind and it was agreed that this might indeed be a more flattering procedure. When I arrived in town there was no word of message and there was reserved for me at the Cumberland the barest and ugliest single room that I've ever seen outside of a YMCA. There wasn't even a bed-lamp. The hotel is like a Statler except there is no laundry or valet service in less than a week's time. When Margo and I called on Gielgud he announced that Josh Logan was in town and that he was consulting him "about the original production" which he hoped not to duplicate in any way. He seemed to ignore the fact that Margo had been co-director of the original show. He seems a frightfully nervous high-handed prima donna type of person, like Guthrie, and I don't feel that I could possibly control or influence him in anyway. Perhaps Helen can. I shall stay around for the first week of rehearsal if Helen wishes, but after that I think I may as well quietly withdraw. I take it the management is not paying my expenses here. Has the advance gone to the States? I heard no more about it since signing the papers. For me it is going to be an enormously

expensive trip for the exchange is unfavorable and everything high as a cat's back. - I am glad I am going to get this monthly bank statement from now on as I can keep better track of what I am spending. Please keep them informed at the bank of my address. I still have about a thousand left on my five thousand dollar letter of credit but I doubt it will last me until I leave Europe, not at the rate that money dissolves around here and I am quite incapable of learning the relative values of all these crazy coins, bobs, half crowns, ten shillings, quids, Etc. When Margo deserts me I shall be in total chaos!

What shall I do about the letter of credit when it runs out? Can I get another one from the bank? Can I draw from Tennent? What will Tennent do with my royalties when the show opens? Etc. Etc. Etc.

How much money, in the way of outright gifts to friends such as Windham, is deductible from taxes, when they are used for creative purposes? Please get Colton's statement on this, the exact or approximate amount that I can give away with exemption. I want to help my indigent friends as much as possible now while I have a lot of money coming in.

DID PANCHO SAIL ON THE MEDEA? Please cable me if he did so I can put on a fright wig and a set of whiskers. I'm afraid I would just drop dead at the sight of that character!!

Have seen Irene. She's the only one here who was really particularly pleasant to us, especially Margo.

With love,

[TW and Margo Jones arrived in London late in the week of June 6 after touring Capri and Ischia and spending several days in Paris. Audrey Wood placed TW under strict orders to attend rehearsals of *The Glass Menagerie*: "Helen Hayes is making a tremendous gesture towards you as a writer" (June 1, 1948, HRC). Following a two-week tryout in Brighton, the play was set to open in London on July 28 with a cast of three Americans and one Canadian.

Wood cabled TW on June 16 that his unsatisfactory hotel would be changed and that Pancho Rodriguez was still in New York. Unbeknown to Wood, TW had recently met an aspiring young actor who would prove a more tenacious and important friend. In *Five O'Clock Angel* (1990), her memoir cum letters, Maria Britneva (later the Lady St. Just) recalls having befriended a "little man" who "looked unassuming and vulnerable" (St. Just, p. xviii) at a party given by John Gielgud. She and TW would soon exchange letters and begin to travel together.

This letter bears a reception date of June 16, 1948.]

108. *To Carson McCullers*

SH: Savoy Hotel London
July 5, 1948
[TLS w/ autograph marginalia
and postscript, 7 pp. Duke U]

Dearest Carson:

Found your letter waiting for me when I returned to the hotel just now from a rainy weekend at one of the great manor-houses of England where I was guest of an immensely wealthy old member of Parliament who married into the Guinness beer fortune, got rid of the lady but kept the fortune. The place is of Georgian period and somehow I felt suddenly as if I had walked into the setting of an Isak Dinesen tale, one of the Gothic ones, probably the one about the old lady that turned into a lively monkey and scrambled up the wall in the last scene: pure enchantment! The house was built so long and it seems to have absorbed the lives of many strange and wonderful and rather secretive people. For a while, after the owning family died out, it was turned into a nunnery. Then two young nuns were found drowned in the little swan-lake. This tragedy blighted the place: everyone said it was haunted. Ghosts were certainly walking the night I was there! I had an immense chamber with a regally canopied bed in a room that had once been the chapel of the house. I locked my door but about two A.M. while I was lying in bed reading Proces de Bourbons - a record of Marie Antoinette's trial - I heard stealthy footsteps. My blood ran icy! They stopped right outside my door. The doorknob turned very slowly: discovered the lock: then slowly turned back again and the footsteps, even lighter than before - withdrew! In the morning I discovered it was not a ghost but the host! - bringing me a hot drink and toast. A great joke was made about this, but I was too sleepy to really enjoy it.

I seem to have met practically everyone <u>but</u> Truman Capote. I have heard from several other sources that he has met <u>me</u>. Can I have been sleep-walking? For I have not consciously had that pleasure on this side of the Atlantic. It is mistyfying extremely. Aren't you allowing yourself to judge this little boy a bit too astringently? I know you must have reasons which I don't know of. I see him as an opportunist and a careerist and a derivative writer whose tiny feet have attempted to fit the ten-league boots of Carson McCullers and succeeded only in tripping him up absurdly. But surely not one of the <u>bad</u>-boys! His little face, as photographed by Cecil

Beaton against a vast panorama of white roses, has a look of pre-natal sorrow as if he were still in the womb and already suspected how cold the world is beyond the vaginal portals.

The writers I have seen here are Christopher Isherwood, E.M. Forster and, of course, Gore Vidal. Unfortunate things happened. Cristopher is going through a sort of unhappy climacteric. The sweetness has temporarily gone out of his nature and he felt called upon to tell Gore, very obliquely and through the mouth of his intimate companion, that he did not think Gore's work of paramount importance. Gore is not able to take this kind of criticism. A real <u>crise</u> developed. Gore spent three sleepless nights, and then left England.

Finally I met your bushy-faced friend, Bebe Berard, and I found him awfully nice. It was at one of the big London parties so we had only a short while to talk, but only of you. I told him that you adored him. He was deeply affected, for it seems that he has the same feeling for you. I saw a ballet that he had designed and it was the most beautiful decor I have seen.

France and Italy are full of your books, prominently displayed in every bookshop, but they are not yet distributed much in England. Why is that? Have you an agent here to look after your interests? Would you like me to investigate this?

I think I have, at long last, found the right hooks for a play but it will or may take me at least a year and a half or even two years to finish it for I know that it cannot be a repetition of what I have said before and yet it has to be a southern character portrait. I must believe in the possibility of such a thing being possible.

It is a small world with Pancho in it! There is a young man here who loaned him ninety dollars to pay a hotel bill in New York and he is still trying to recover it. It seems that Pancho became involved with two very wealthy women but they are now disillusioned and Pancho, at last report, was headed back South again. He reminds me rather pathetically of a bull in the arena with his black hide full of fancy darts from the picadors, charging madly this way and that, wherever the red silk flashes until finally sometime the sword behind the red silk will put a stop to him. A brave and wonderful black bull - but I am not a bull-fighter! My veronicas were not as quick as the horns.

I now look forward, actually, to returning to the States, provided this report is accurate of the southern withdrawal. By the time I arrive the play

will be in rehearsal which will keep me in New York most of the time. That is why I suggested you go to the sea now, someplace where I could join you for week-ends. But if you are comfortable and happy and at work in Nyack I understand you're wanting to stay there.

New Mown Hay and Mouchoir de Monsieur. I now have that fixed in my mind. I am tak[ing] ten days on the continent, at least passing through Paris, before the London opening and I will get the perfume for dear Cheryl as a bottled distillation of our mutual love for her.

Ever lovingly yours, Tennessee.

My week-end host was described by a catty friend as "a rose-baked sissy (city), half as old as time" which is a paraphrase of a line in some poem about Rome. funny?!!

[The manor house where TW was a guest reminded him of a "stately" old convent in Isak Dinesen's story "The Monkey" (1934).

Carson McCullers's early friendship with Truman Capote had been damaged by jealousy and a perception that *Other Voices, Other Rooms* was unduly imitative of her work, if not plagiarized. She warned TW that Capote "writes his friends (not me) that he is seeing you. What a opportunist that boy is - without any honor, or the minimum of dignity" (n.d., Private Collection).

Andrew Lyndon, a mutual friend, recalls that TW first saw Capote at a party in New York in 1947 and said admiringly, "'Baby, I think your little friend is charming! Just charming!'" (qtd. in Clarke, *Capote: A Biography*, 1988, p. 177). He and Capote would soon meet in Paris and return to the States on the *Queen Mary* amid laughter and high jinks (see *Memoirs*, pp. 150-151).

William Caskey, Christopher Isherwood's companion, thought Gore Vidal "typical American prep school." The three met in Paris in the preceding April when Vidal introduced himself and asked Isherwood "'how to manage'" (qtd. in *Diaries*, 1996) his career. E.M. Forster considered *Streetcar* a dull play to read but looked forward to "seeing it on the stage" (Forster to Isherwood, June 25, 1948, Huntington).

Christian Bébé Bérard designed sets and costumes for the London premiere of *Clock Symphony* (June 25, 1948), the ballet to which TW probably refers. His famous sets for *The Madwoman of Chaillot* (1945) were brought to New York for the 1948 production.

Pressure to diversify his theatre led TW to experiment with a biographical subject—Huey P. Long, the "Kingfish" of Louisiana politics—in "The Big Time Operators." His role as a corrupted idealist would be assumed by Chance Wayne in *Sweet Bird of Youth*. TW later noted that he did not envision the female lead as "the faded lily type of typical Williams heroine."

The perfume was intended as a gift for the producer Cheryl Crawford, a friend of McCullers who had recently advised her on staging *The Member of the Wedding*.

Penned in the upper margin of page 1 is the notation "Address me c/o H.M. Tennent Ltd., Globe Theatre, London."]

109. To Eric Bentley

> SH: Royal Crescent Hotel
> Brighton. [England]
> July 12, 1948
> [TLS, 3 pp. HRC]

Dear Mr. Bentley:

Yours is a kind of criticism that the theatre desperately needs and which is supplied by few others. However that is all the more reason why certain questionable attitudes of yours should be contested.

I think the most serious of these are two: first, a lack of respect for the extra-verbal or non-literary elements of the theatre, the various plastic elements, the purely visual things such as light and movement and color and design, which play, for example, such a tremendously important part in theatre such as Lorca's and which are as much a native part of drama as words and ideas are. I don't believe you are guilty of this, but I have read criticism in which the use of transparencies and music and subtle lighting effects, which are often as meaningful as pages of dialogue, were dismissed as "cheap tricks and devices". Actually all of these plastic things are as valid instruments of expression in the theatre as words, and needless to say, they add immeasurably to the general appeal: fortunately or unfortunately, I am not sure which, a general appeal is necessary and can and should be made for the sake of reaching more people without any vulgarization. On the other hand, it is easy for vulgarity to creep in, sometimes without the author's cognizance: there are many entrances for that sly actor!

Your other mistaken tendancy in my opinion is a curiously literal interpretation of things that have symbolic implication. I think that you were unfair to All My Sons in your Harper's Survey of the Theatre because you regarded the letter from the dead pilot son as purely and simply a letter instead of as a psychological revelation being objectified for dramatic purposes. I saw that play three times in New York and again here in London and was each time more profoundly moved by its superb structure,

its continual and building tension, the boldness with which idea and meaning was translated into action and object: the memorial broken in the storm: the horoscope prepared by the superstitious neighbor: the grape drink served in the arbor: - finally, by the time the letter and the suicide came along I was prepared fully to accept these superficially melodramatic occurences as symbols or concentrations of time and discovery and fate. Likewise it appeared that in my own play you were interpreting the black-suited figures in the final scene, which could have been death or any other form of fatal consequence, a bit too literally, as I had tried to make them abstract as possible. However the leniency we always have toward our own creation when under attack by others may enter into this argument.

I have seen in London the new play by your favorite Sartre. It is a great success, moving from the suburban Lyric Hammersmith to the West End very soon. You may be shocked by some of the purely theatrical dynamics in this play. I think it is Sartre's finest piece of theatre, and the intellectual freshness and purity is really quite wonderful. I have heard that Kermit Bloomgarten has bought it for New York and I should think Montgomery Clift would be perfect for the male lead. Here it is called <u>Crime</u> <u>Passionel</u> but in Paris it had a much better title: <u>Mains</u> <u>Sales</u>.

Best wishes, Tennessee Williams

[English-born and educated at Oxford and Yale, Eric Bentley (b. 1916) reviewed theatre for *Harper's Magazine* in the late 1940s and served as drama critic for the *New Republic* from 1952 to 1956. He has also published widely as an editor, translator, anthologist, and playwright.

All My Sons (1947) and *Streetcar* were among the plays cited by Bentley in *Harper's* annual theatre review for 1947-1948. Quite ironically, he thought, Arthur Miller had solved the problem of moral responsibility in *All My Sons* by the evasive technique of "a letter in which ALL is revealed." TW avoided such "cliches" in *Streetcar* and nearly crossed "the borderline of really good drama." The last scene answered Bentley's decisive question, "how deep does the play go? The episode of the black-coated couple from the madhouse compels the answer: not very" (March 1948). Bentley and TW would clash in the mid 1950s with a threat of legal action (see letter #300).]

110. To Helen Hayes

Hotel de l'Université
Rue de l'Université, Paris
30 July, 1948
[TLS, 2 pp. Private Collection]

Dear Helen:

It is hard for me to tell from the notices sent me this morning, which are very, very English, just how things went for the play but there can be no doubt that you had a resounding reception, and that is what I most wanted. Will you forgive me for not being there? I don't think Audrey or Mother will, but I am counting on your understanding, though I must, and most shamefully, admit that I do not altogether understand myself how I happened not to manage to make it. You may put this down to my "pixy behavior" and nobody knows better than I do that I have carried it much, much, much too far! I had looked forward to it intensely for such a long time: then the last few days I became enveloped in a cloud. Overwork. Nerves. A sort of paralysis. I had bought a ticket (plane) through a travel agency and was to pick it up the day before the flight. I work hard all that day. I suddenly remember I am to pick up the ticket. I rush out and suddenly I cannot remember the name or location of the travel-agency. Only Gore Vidal knows, for it was his agent. I cannot find Gore, he is out on the town. Finally, at seven P.M., I locate him by phone. He tells me where the agency is. I rush there. The agency is shut for the night. More rushing and stewing. Finally I find another agency which happens to be still open. I say I must get to London by seven P.M. tomorrow. Only one booking is available and that is on a plane at seven the next morning. Good, marvelous! I take it. All that night I sit up in my clothes, working and drinking black coffee so I will not miss the plane. About dawn I get queer sensations, palpitations: I think I am having a heart-attack. I rush to the bathroom and swallow a handfull of barbital tablets, almost a lethal dose, to quiet this nerve-crisis. I am hardly back from the bathroom when the black-out commences and I do not come out of it until several hours after the plane has left. From two until five in the afternoon I wait at the Gare des Invalides for a possible cancellation on some plane that might still get me into London in time for the play. No luck.

All this adds up to another terrific gaucherie on the part of Tennessee,

and I apologize for burdening you with an account of it. I only want you to know that I had, in Brighton, one of the truly deeply satisfying adventures of my life and to thank you for it from the bottom of a contrite heart.

Ever, Tennessee.

[A "terrific gaucherie" led TW to miss the opening of *The Glass Menagerie* on July 28. Perhaps he foresaw, as did Helen Hayes, that the Gielgud production would not repeat the success of the original. He also found London "dull" and the English "stuffy" and had discovered a more engaging situation in Paris. Gore Vidal was already in attendance and Truman Capote was expected from Italy. Sartre proved an elusive celebrity, but TW met Jean Cocteau and his companion, the actor Jean Marais.

The *Times* (London) reviewer was typical in his selective praise and invidious marking of national boundaries. Hayes had made "a great acting part out of conversational bromides," while *The Glass Menagerie* itself evolved "slow and sure in a very American way." Americans, the reviewer inferred, "must be the most patient of peoples" (July 29, 1948), if this Broadway hit were any indication. Binkie Beaumont assured TW that while the reviews were "not terribly impressive," the "general atmosphere" of the production was "one of great success" and business "excellent." The producer urged him not to "slip quietly back to America" (August 3, 1948, HRC) without making a return visit.]

111. To Walter Edwin Dakin

SH: Summer and Smoke Company
250 West 57th Street
New York 19, N.Y.
August 13, 1948.
[ALS, 4 pp. Columbia U]

Dear Grandfather -

It grieves me dreadfully to think of you spending a hot summer in Clarksdale when you could be so much more comfortable here or in some place like Monteagle.

Please take this check and remove yourself to cooler quarters. I am sure it will make you feel better and stronger. Heat can be debilitating even to a chicken, which you are not, exactly, though still the young member of the family.

The Menagerie seems to be a success in London, selling out every

night. Miss Hayes is not as good as Laurette Taylor but she is as good as any <u>living</u> actress. Lady Sibyl Colfax gave a dinner for Miss Hayes and me the opening night but as she did not invite the other members of the cast, I did not go. In fact, I remained in Paris and only came to London a couple of days before sailing for New York. I don't see how it is possible to mix Socialism and <u>snobbism</u> but the English manage to do it. I don't like them much.

Mother was in Paris when I left and was planning a short trip to Switzerland. I expect she'll be back here late this month. Dakin is also travelling and that is probably why you have not heard from him. Margo and Audrey send their love and we all wish you were here - and expect you soon. Wire me your plans when you make them. My address is 235 E. 58 and my phone number is El. 5-1570.

Much, much, much love - Tom.

[Persistent doubts led TW to propose that he take over direction of *Summer and Smoke* and that Margo Jones attend to production. She refused and banished the meddlesome author from rehearsals: "'I am the director and you better know that. You get off the stage, Tennessee'" (qtd. in Sheehy, *Margo*, 1989, p. 169). Tryouts in Buffalo, Detroit, and Cleveland were critically well received and indicated a successful premiere in New York (October 6).

Monteagle, in southeastern Tennessee, is near the University of the South, where Walter Dakin studied theology as a young man.

After watching Helen Hayes in tryouts of *The Glass Menagerie*, TW accurately predicted that she will "score a big hit in London. . . . If one still remembers Laurette a bit more vividly than he sees Helen that does not mean she is not wonderful" (to Kazan, July 19, 1948, WUCA).

Although aged, ill, and financially strapped, Lady Sibyl Colefax entertained visiting celebrities in London until her death in 1950.]

112. To Justin Brooks Atkinson

235 E. 58 Street [New York]
October 10, 1948
[TLS, 2 pp. BRTC]

Dear Brooks:

Margo says she has already thanked you for coming to our rescue but I want to add mine. I doubt that there is any gratitude much greater than

an author's for his one or two good notices in a storm of bad ones. Yours was not only good, it was beautiful, and not only beautiful but inspiring, for it made me feel that there was definitely some use in my continuing to try to bring poetic feeling into my work.

I do not at all agree with Maxwell Anderson's opinion that the critics have thrown a blanket over the poetic theatre but it is obvious that some of them are not doing it much intentional good and that is a pity for I think it is apparent that many theatre-goers are hungry for the difference that lyricism makes in plays. Summer has painful deficiencies: it often seems to me like a graceful cripple, but in a way I love it best of my plays. It is, in a way, the most affirmative: that is, spiritually affirmative, and although some reviews call it juvenile, it strikes me as the most grown-up in its thinking and feeling. The juvenile quality may be an awkwardness that ~~I am afraid always~~ goes with the handling of romantic material in such an unromantic age. And if it offered nothing else but a part for Margaret Phillips, I feel it would offer enough to make it welcome on Broadway. But with Phillips and Jo's set and Paul's music and Margo's tender direction, I do not quite see why six of the critics took such strong exception to it. Actually there was only one of the notices that made me mad. I guess you know which one I am talking about: I didn't read it but was told the contents. The others I felt were written in genuine disappointment which puzzles and troubles me but does not anger me at the writers. I wish it were possible to get some of them to go back again, for I have discovered while on the road with the show, that opinions would frequently improve at a second exposure, and if we could now get some friendlier follow-up articles I think the play might have a good chance of catching on here. Business so far has been very good, but of course they may be just rushing to see it in expectation of its imminent closing, and the audience response has been much warmer than opening night.

Rehearsals and the road-tour have made a jarring hiatus in my work, which I must now get back to. The new project is exciting but still in the woods and it will take more strength in each finger than I now have at this moment in my whole tired body!

My best regards to Orianne, as well as to you,

Ever, Tennessee.

[*Variety's* opening day headline—"Tenn. Williams' Take-Home Pay Now $7,500 WKLY" (October 6, 1948)—may have raised expectations of another smash hit, but only Atkinson found dramatic virtue in *Summer and Smoke*. The play was "charged with passion and anguish" and revealed once again TW's "almost unbearably lucid" (*New York Times*, October 7, 1948) knowledge of his characters. "Mawkish, murky, maudlin and monotonous" were the more typical descriptions of a play which seemed "juvenile" to many reviewers and compared unfavorably with *Streetcar*—still running strongly on Broadway. It was probably Robert Garland who angered TW by dubbing *Summer and Smoke* "'A Kiddy-Kar Called Conversation'" (*Journal American*, October 7, 1948). Critics praised the leads for having survived a "garrulous" script, while Margo Jones's "tender direction," as TW put it, received mixed notices.

Rehearsal of Summer and Smoke *(1948): Tennessee Williams, Margaret Phillips, Margo Jones, and Tod Andrews.*

Maxwell Anderson wrote in the aftermath of a savage attack on *Truckline Café* (1946), which closed after thirteen performances on Broadway. He protested the "enormous increase in the reviewers' power" and their virtual "censorship over the theatre" (*New York Times*, February 16, 1947).

The "exciting" new work is almost certainly "The Big Time Operators." A related script entitled "the puppets of the levantine" (n.d., HRC) was partially typed on letterhead of the "Summer and Smoke Company."]

113. To Margaret "Margo" Jones

235 East 58th Street
New York, N.Y.
October 27, 1948
[TLS, 1 p. HRC]

Dear Margo:

I drop in the play almost every night, and it seems to be holding up. Maggie says she is experimenting because she is not yet satisfied with her interpretation and feels she can do even better. Hank has taken her to task for this saying that the performance must not be allowed to vary from opening night. I think this a great mistake because the actors will remain interested if they feel some flexibility remains. They should be encouraged to work for new values as long as the established line is not altered. I have not observed any letdown whatsoever in their spirit of performance.

Now I want to take up what I suppose is a rather delicate matter. And since no delicacy is required between you and me, I will say plainly that I think you did a wrong thing in discharging and replacing Ellen James without my knowledge or consent, which, according to the Dramatists Guild contract, is one of the author's inalienable rights. You are about the only person in show business whose motives I never question. But your procedure is sometimes reminiscent of the Shuberts. How is that for plain speaking? Ha-ha. Ellen James is one of the plus qualities, and we don't have any plus qualities that we can safely throw out. I have seen the other girl and heard her read. She is a marvelous understudy for Maggie, and I heartily agree about hiring her in that capacity. The additional expense of retaining Ellen James in her present role is very slight. Liebling says she can be kept for $75.00 a week. I think we should do it. That is all I have to say about that.

I know that you are deep in the heart of Moliere. I shall soon be deep in the heart of North Africa or Italy. I have bought a new car, a Buick convertible, and I am trying to persuade grandfather to go abroad with me. Carson goes to court Friday. She is being sued for $50,000. She doesn't have $5.00. Quelle vie!

Love, Tenn.

TW/c

["Baffled and hurt," Margo Jones answered TW's rebuke by quoting a line from "The Purification" (1944): " 'If men keep honor, the rest can be arranged.'" She had "tried to live up to this and if I have failed - since honor is more than a word between us - there must surely be a way to understand each other again" (November 3, 1948, Private Collection). Jones might have added that Ellen James, the actor whose firing TW disapproved, had drawn no critical attention for her brief appearance in Scene Three. A wire from TW wishing Jones "mad success" (November 6, 1948, HRC) for an opening in Dallas may have eased the tension, but it did not discharge his resentment over the critical failure of *Summer and Smoke*.

TW wrote a flurry of letters on October 27, including one to his grandfather, who had returned to the Friends Home in Waynesville, Ohio: "Perhaps after Christmas . . . I shall go gypsying about Italy and North Africa. How would you like to join me? Is your gypsy instinct still that strong?" (October 27, 1948, Columbia U).

Carson McCullers and her former collaborator, Greer Johnson, agreed to submit their disputed contract to arbitration. A finding of November 8, 1948, held the contract to be in force for one year and empowered the Theatre Guild to produce *The Member of the Wedding* during that time using the joint script (see Carr, p. 311).]

114. To James "Jay" Laughlin

235 East 58th Street
New York, N.Y.
October 27, 1948
[TLS, 1 p. Houghton]

Dear Jay:

Please remember not to let ONE ARM be displayed for sale in bookstores. When I heard that Miss Steloff had ordered 200 copies, I became alarmed with visions of you and I pinned up like our one-armed hero. I hope that the book will be distributed as we planned, entirely by subscription. Let me know how you plan to distribute it. It is the most beautiful book you have yet made, and I am crazy about it.

Call me as soon as you can.

Sincerely, T. Williams

[Publication of *One Arm* was delayed by an incorrect copyright statement which Audrey Wood immediately noticed. The printing must be recalled, she wrote, lest the error "cause the stories to fall into the public domaine" (to Laughlin, October 27, 1948, HRC). Tipped into first edition copies of *One Arm* was "A SPECIAL

REQUEST" asking that the collection be sold "by personal solicitation and sub-scription rather than by general display. We are particularly anxious that the book should not be displayed in windows or on open tables."

In 1943 TW worked briefly for Frances Steloff, owner of the Gotham Book Mart, proving himself an inept clerk.]

115. To Walter Dakin Williams

235 East 58th Street
New York, N.Y.
October 27, 1948
[TLS, 1 p. HTC]

Dear Grandfather:

I am dictating just a short note to let you know I am well and satisfied with the outcome of the play production although it has left me feeling rather exhausted. Margo has gone back to Texas, but I am watching over the show. I was dreadfully disappointed that you were not here when I came back.

I want you to know that I have purchased a beautiful new car, a maroon-colored Buick convertible, at a bargain price, and we are going to take some kind of trip in it as soon as the situation here permits me to leave. Perhaps after Christmas I shall return to Europe and take the car with me and go gypsying about Italy and North Africa. How would you like to join me? Is your gypsy instinct still that strong? How would you like to come back to New York after you leave Waynesville? I am sure you remember Libby Holman, whom we visited in Connecticut. She has gone on tour and says she would love for us to stay at her house while she is gone. We would have a full staff of servants at our disposal, and, of course, my car. She and her mother send you their particular love and all of your many friends here speak of you continually and ask to be remembered to you.

Devotedly, Tom

[Edward Colton later advised against a trust for Rose Williams, citing technical problems which might leave her unprotected in future years (to TW, November 30, 1948, HTC). Precisely how the legal issues were resolved is unclear.

Investigation of private care for Rose led to correspondence with the director of Stamford Hall in Connecticut, who stated weekly costs "in the range $75 to $100" (Moore to Colton, November 4, 1948, HTC). Edwina warned TW not to

"do anything that will jeopardize your own financial security. I haven't laboured, and prayed, over it all these years just to see it dissipated" (November 28, 1948, Private Collection).]

116. To Jessica Tandy

[235 East 58th Street, New York]
November 2, 1948.
[TLSx, 1 p. Leavitt, p. 77]

Dear Jessica:

Many, many thanks for your letter on the Benton picture. You are so right that it really makes me ashamed of having lent my casual support to the idea. What you say about Blanche suddenly recalls to me all of my original conception of the character and what it was to me, from which you, in your delineation, have never once drifted away in spite of what I now realize must have been a continual pressure: that unwillingness of audiences to share a more intricate and special and sensitive response to things: their desire to participate more safely, familiarly, in the responses of an animal nature. I have almost forgotten (perhaps under this same pressure) that it was Blanche whom I loved and respected and whom I wished to portray, though I have never, please believe me, forgotten the exact and tender and marvelously understanding way that you brought her to life. -- I have such a divided nature! Irreconciliably divided. I look at Benton's picture and I see the strong things in it, its immediate appeal to the senses, raw, sensual, dynamic, and I forgot the play was really about those things which are opposed to that, the delicate half-approaches to something much finer. Yes, the painting is only one side of the play, and the Stanley side of it. Perhaps from the painter's point of view that was inevitable. A canvas cannot depict two worlds very easily: or the tragic division of the human spirit: at least not a painter of Benton's realistic type. Well, I am still an admirer of the painting, but, believe me, still more an admirer of yours for seeing and feeling about it more clearly than I did at first, and I should have felt the same way.

With love, Tennessee.

[The Thomas Hart Benton painting was both a Christmas present for Irene Selznick (from her estranged husband, David) and a publicity gimmick designed to launch *Streetcar* on the second year of its profitable run. *Look* magazine published the

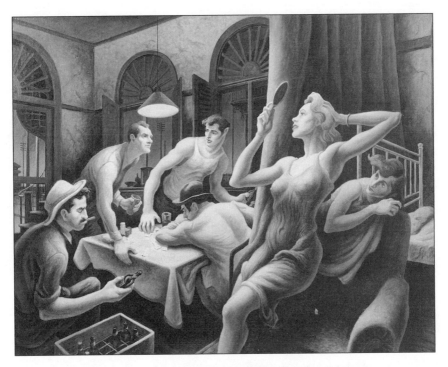

The Poker Night: *"Mr. Benton has naturally chosen to represent
the brutal aspects of 'Streetcar.'"*

painting on February 1, 1949, with remarks by TW which echoed a recent
controversy. Jessica Tandy (1909-1994) had declined to pose for a photographic
duplication of the painting on the grounds that it would confirm Benton's unbal-
anced view of *Streetcar* and "lead future audiences to think that they are going to
see sex in the raw." At issue was Tandy's claim that Benton's choice of the Poker
Night scene emphasized the "Stanley side" (to TW, n.d., Leavitt, p. 77) of the play
to the near exclusion of Blanche's more demanding role. TW's note in *Look* ends
diplomatically with praise for Benton's painting and tacit approval of Tandy's
objection: "Mr. Benton has naturally chosen to represent the brutal aspects of
'Streetcar' and he has done a colorful and dynamic job of it. It exists as a painting,
quite apart from its connection with the play, and that is as it should be" (p. 79).]

117. To Audrey Wood

[53 Arundel Place
Clayton, Missouri]
November 18, 1948
[TLS, 2 pp. HRC]

Dear Audrey:

I came home to find Grandfather practically as well as ever, and was vastly relieved on that account.

Since I got here I have been working on the average of six or eight hours a day. This evening even working on the graveyard shift! And have accomplished, I think, a good deal. It now looks as if "The Big Time Operators", which is the present title of play, might have a fairly complete first draft sometime this Spring, and I hope it won't take more than one re-writing. The story is not at all biographical but the material is drawn mostly from Huey Long, showing the main character in a mostly sympathetic light as a man very close to the people, fantastically uninhibited, essentially honest, but shackled with a corrupt machine and machine-boss. As a good half of the play deals with him as a young man (about 29, when first elected Governor) - though actually Long was a bit older than that - I am thinking now about Marlon Brando as in every respect but age the part fits him perfectly. D'you think he could put on age in a part to be acceptable at the end of the play as a man in his late thirties? - The age when Long died, I think. The combination of Kazan and Brando would be a stimulating assurance to work with. Would it be wise to approach Brando about his commitments or plans for next Fall, so he would keep this in mind as a pregnant possibility for him? Knowing that he would be free would be an encouragement. - The girl's part is very young: something like Anne Jackson but with a bit more pathos and delicacy, though she is not at all the faded lily type of typical Williams heroine. And I think there is a good part in it for Sidney Greenstreet as the corrupt but suave boss.

I would like for Tiz to try and get me the following reference works. Two biographies which I now have from the St. Louis library. "Huey Long: A Candid Biography" published by Dodge and written by Forrest Davis. "The Kingfish - Huey P. Long, Dictator" by Thomas O. Harris, published by the Pelican Publishing company, 339 Carondelet St. in New Orleans. Also two books written by Long himself which are called "Every Man a King" and the other "My First Days in the White House". I don't know

where these books are obtainable but I should think the information could be gotten from the library information desk or even Secty. of Louisiana, who might also be able to supply us with some "Memorial Volumes" which contain Long's speeches. I am going through Washington on my way back to New York and probably can pick up some material or books there. I have avoided, and will avoid reading, all <u>fiction</u> about Long as I don't want any unconscious coloration to creep into the play, and my character, Père Polk, will be pretty much my own creation with just as much of the Kingfish as I find theatrically enticing. For one thing he has plenty of sex-appeal, and that's what made me think of Brando for it.

This basement, or rathskeller, is a wonderful place to work! Right back of my table is Dakin's real "Seeburg" jukebox with colored lights and everything, which he bought out of a bar in one of his less judicious moments. I have played it constantly and got the mechanism all screwed up, but it still plays, however capriciously, sometimes stopping right in the middle of one record and starting another and sometimes not stopping at all. Since I threw a book at Dakin when he appeared on the stairs a few days ago I have been relatively unmolested. The jukebox, the typewriter, Grandfather and I are putting up a solid front - oh, yes, and a quart bottle of Old Taylor which I keep in reach but out of sight!

I plan to be back in New York about Thursday. Where is the <u>Streetcar</u> party now going to be, I wonder? - Tomorrow is my sister's birthday so we will probably drive out to the Snake Pit. The $650. a month places are out of the question. Are there no reasonable ones?

Love, Tenn.

The less said or known about my writing subject and plans the better, I think, at least till finished and copyrighted. - Want to see Sillcox soon as I return about the endowments.

[TW was free to visit Clayton now that Edwina and Cornelius were separated and the latter had departed for Knoxville.

Within a month TW's interest in "The Big Time Operators" had "dissolved," as he later informed Elia Kazan: "I couldn't convince myself that I cared enough about the character and ideas involved to put any fire into the writing" (see letter #140). Biographical subjects such as Huey Long had not proven congenial in the past, nor was TW likely to exceed the popular and critical success of *All the King's*

Men (1946), Robert Penn Warren's recent study of Long which received the Pulitzer Prize for Fiction.

Luise M. Sillcox was the executive secretary of the Authors' League and the affiliated Dramatists' Guild. TW planned to establish a fund so that grants could be made to such needy writers as Oliver Evans and Donald Windham.]

118. To Audrey Wood

[*Vulcania*]
Dec. 5, 1948.
[TLS w/ autograph postscript, 2 pp. HRC]

Dear Audrey:

I feel that I did the right thing when I got on this boat because I cannot live within phone-call of Broadway without feeling like a piece of a big machine, and a piece that doesn't fit properly. If I am to live and grow as an artist the direction of my life must be away from involvement in the frighteningly <u>unreal</u> realities of "The professional life". Lately I have felt drained and over-drawn. Being successful and famous makes such demands! I'm not equipped for it. I wanted it and still want it, with one part of me, but that isn't the part of me that is important or creative. I must dedicate myself, my life, to that part of me that is and make fewer, not more, concessions to the other.

You have been the greatest help to me in allowing me this necessary feeling of detachment from the business side of life, and I think that my brother can also be, as he has the legal and business sense that I lack. I hope that eventually you and he together can handle all that side of it between you so that I will not even have to think of it, as thinking of it weighs so heavily on my heart. I have asked him to come to New York, at my expense, and review my whole financial situation with you and Colton, decide about the foundation and the trust for my sister. Naturally you or he will let me know of what decisions are reached about it. Also I want him to study my tax-situation. He speaks Colton's language as he is now employed by a trust company and sits on various boards of corporations and is eminently equipped to judge in all such matters. I want him to get all my statements during my absence. I have never really been able to look at them, I just go blind when I take them out of the envelopes, and this does not make sense. All box-office and bank statements should go to him so I

won't have to worry about them at all. This he should do, as I am assuming the obligation of my sister's expensive care and he is also the heir to most of my estate (hypothetical as that may be). There may be certain disagreeable or even inconvenient aspects to this arrangement, but it does or will - I hope - give me a sense of security which I know you will see is the primary consideration. It is unfortunate that I have not been able to feel any security or understanding with Colton. He simply doesn't strike me that way. I know you want me to keep him and I shall but I must have this double check that my brother can give, for while one side of my nature is trustful as a child, the paranoiac side which is full of nervous apprehensions must also be considered if I am to live in peace among the clouds. If a human life-time contained one hundred more years than are ordinarily alloted, I am sure that I could reach a state of grace in which all these impurities would be rendered to ashes.

We have been in the Gulf stream these first three days of the voyage and it is as warm as Florida. I walk on the deck in my shirtsleeves. Work about four hours each morning, getting up at nine o'clock and going to bed at midnight. My tension is already going: the whites of my eyes have turned white again and I can sleep without seconal. Who knows what Africa will do, and the Arabs?

I left two trunks in the apartment which I want to have placed in storage, and various other things such as my Italian-bound copy of Hart Crane which I am afraid is outside the trunk, on the bookshelves in the front room. Joanna said she would be glad to see that these things are all packed away. She or Donnie can take care of my phonograph and my records. The big trunk should be locked and put in storage right away as it contains my journals. I was very loath to see Maria returning to the apartment as she is not a really good friend, I've found out. Bowles says she has been talking about me to Laughlin and others, saying that I am a lost soul that only she can redeem! - Just when I was beginning to think I might be wrong about Women!

There are probably many other things I can think of later, but I shall write as soon as I know which way the blackbird and the clown and I are going. (Blackbird is English for Merlo).

With love, 10.

P.S. Please let me know how "S & S" reacts to the termination of theatre parties. I pray it will not fold up like the tents of the Arabs.

[TW's attempt to allay fears of mismanagement and still remain detached from "the business side of life" is evident in following correspondence with his brother Dakin (see letters #119 and #120). At the same time TW was "very, very anxious" to avoid any rupture with Audrey Wood, whose services were indispensable and far in excess of mere literary representation.

The preceding months in New York were enlivened by Truman Capote, Gore Vidal, and especially Maria Britneva, who arrived in mid-September as TW's guest and reportedly remained to study at the Actors Studio with Elia Kazan. Her penchant for gossip amused TW, save when he was the subject. He later chided her "vocal part" for being "astonishingly active. You seem to say all the things that discreet people only think" (qtd. in St. Just, p. 13).

Earlier in the fall TW had "a quite sudden and accidental and marvelous re-encounter with Frank Philip Merlo" (*Memoirs*, p. 155). Of Sicilian descent, the twenty-six-year-old Merlo was born in Elizabeth, New Jersey, and served as a pharmacist mate in the Navy during World War II. With "the blackbird" and Paul Bowles, TW sailed on the *Vulcania* for Gibraltar and Tangier.

Summer and Smoke would not survive the "termination" of advance sales, which insured full houses on a short-term basis. Wood cabled TW at Fez, Morocco, on December 20 that the "weekly gross" was "sufficiently low" to endanger Rose's trust fund and advised a personal deposit of $3,000. On December 28 she reported a "business drop so great" that the play was "suddenly closing" (HRC) on January 1, 1949, after 102 performances—some $60,000 in debt.

The closing of *Summer and Smoke* without consultation shocked Wood, who informed Margo Jones that she could no longer represent her: "I fear you and I look at the so-called professional New York theatre from very different approaches" (January 5, 1949, HRC).]

119. To Walter Dakin Williams

"Vulcania"
Dec. 9, 1948
[TLS w/ enclosure, 1 p. Columbia U]

Dear Dakin:

Sorry I did not have a chance to get a letter off to you before I left New York. I am mailing this to you from Gibralter where we land this evening and at the same time mailing a letter to Audrey to let her know that I want you to make, at my expense, the trip to New York to confer with Colton about the trust fund for Rose (a half interest in Summer and Smoke) and also to get a clear picture of my financial situation particularly regarding taxes and the possible establishment of a foundation, a matter which

Audrey wanted me to discuss with an accountant before I left but which I did not have time to go into before sailing. Before any tax payments are made I want you to have a complete report on what these payments are to be. I, too, want to be informed of the amount of these payments before they are made, if necessary by cable, so that I will be morally and nervously prepared for my subsequent impoverishment, unlike last year when I only learned post facto. Please make every effort to exhaust all devices to save money on my taxes. I know this is asking a good deal of you, but since I am now to assume the financial responsibility for Rose I know you will see it is important, and fair, that everything be done to secure my finances so that I can continue this responsibility. I left a large envelope of various and miscellaneous business statements in the apartment with your name on it. This envelope contains all papers pertaining to my finances that I could find on the place, bank statements and box-office statements, and during my absence you will receive these statements which would otherwise be directed to me. I want you to hold them for me in Saint Louis till I get back to the States. If outside help appears necessary in tackling my tax-problem (an accountant or tax expert) I want you to call one in. Remember - or remind Colton - that all my living expenses in New York this last time should be deductible as I was there on business, the production of Summer and Smoke. Also much of my travelling expenses in Europe last year should be deductible, England for the Menagerie and France to collect royalties and arrange the future production of Streetcar. This is all I can think of at the moment. I will be very grateful to you, Dakin, for this help, and please give Audrey your cooperation and my thanks and love, also.

Tenn. / Tom

120. To Walter Dakin Williams

"Vulcania"
12/9/48
[TLS, 1 p. Columbia U]

Dear Dakin:

Writing this separately as I know you will not want to let Audrey see this part of the communication. I am very, very anxious to have you avoid betraying any sign of any distrust of her handling of my affairs as she is

morbidly sensitive where I am concerned. I have no reason to think there
has been any mishandling as I have not seen any evidence of it. You must
handle her with great tact and diplomacy: a breach in my relations with her
would be extremely dangerous and detrimental. I am asking you to watch
over my interests simply because I think it is wise to have a double-check -
especially when I am out of the country and may not even be accessible, at
times, to the postman, as I may be travelling around a good deal in the car.
So make every effort to give the trip and the conferences a friendly and
non-inquisitorial atmosphere, but do keep a sharp lookout at the same
time. If the statements do not seem right, if there are any important
discrepancies in them, please inform me first of what they are before you
take it up with Audrey and Colton. All this adds up to is one word: TACT!
Hope you will drop in to Summer and Smoke while you're in New York,
and give Audrey an expense account for your stay there, and enjoy
yourself. Love to mother and grandfather and you -

Love - Tom.

121. To Oliver Evans

[*Vulcania*]
[December 9, 1948]
[TLS, 1 p. HRC]

Dear Oliver:

From several hints that you dropped, with the delicacy of a thunder-clap,
I gathered that you might be in reduced circumstances and am hoping that the
enclosed "benefaction" will be of service. Otherwise I can see you going for
"Ottonte lire" in the Galleria or the Steps called Spanish, unless Maria is
active enough to hustle for you both.

They have just had the fire-drill which I did not participate in. The
Horse went up, so in case of fire I shall depend upon him to guide me to
the proper position. I doubt however that any of the life-boats would be
sufficiently Signorelli to suit me, so it is hardly worth bothering about, now,
is it?

I gave up on Ford Madox Ford, but in the ship's library I came across
The Aspern Papers by that original Auntie Fish, Henrietta James, and for
the first time I have been really thrilled by her writing. (I had never read her

before). I am now looking forward to practically everything the old girl has
written. Perhaps that is the "new world" that Irene saw me playing
Columbus to. Or am I a little bit late in discovering James? An odd
coincidence. I once wrote a play called "Lord Byron's Love Letter" - it is
in the collected one-acts - which has a startlingly similar story to it, but had
never even heard of this novella.

The passenger list is so appalling that it is not even printed! All you
have to do is look around to know why! Dorothy Gish we have only seen
from a distance. But there is a member of the crew, seen from an equal
distance, that I think you would somehow manage to establish contact
with if you were aboard. The food is excellent, excellent! I am eating nothing but proteins and am having a daily work-out and massage so that I will
not look quite so much like a Piggy-bank when I get to Manhattan.

We are due to arrive at Gibralter in an hour and I want to try to get
this letter off there. I promised Maria I'd write but can't think of anything
to say to her that I haven't said to you, especially since the Horse is getting
dressed and his image in the mirror directly above my typewriter is a little
distracting. I will try later.

With love, Tenn.

[The Spanish Steps in Rome and the Galleria in Naples were rendezvous of special
interest to TW and Oliver Evans.

The missed "fire-drill" may have inspired a one-act play by TW entitled
"Lifeboat Drill" (1979), a dark study of old age and marital unhappiness.

Henry James based *The Aspern Papers* (1888) upon the legend of Claire
Clairmont, half-sister of Shelley's second wife, Mary Godwin, and briefly the lover
of Lord Byron (and the mother of his daughter Allegra). As James recounts in his
preface, Claire had been approached in Florence by "an ardent Shelleyite" who cov-
eted literary papers which she presumably held. TW saw a coincidental relation
between the James story and his own one-act play "Lord Byron's Love Letter"
(1945). Walter Dakin's tale of an elderly woman who lived in Columbus,
Mississippi, and possessed a letter written by Byron has been identified as a source
for the sketch (see Leverich, p. 56).

Dorothy Gish last appeared on Broadway in *The Story of Mary Surratt* (1947).
In drafting "Daughter of Revolution," an early source for *The Glass Menagerie*,
TW inscribed the play "to Miss Lillian and Miss Dorothy Gish for either of whom
the part of Amanda Wingfield was hopefully intended by the author" (n.d., HRC).]

PART III
1949-1950

122. *To Audrey Wood*

[Hotel d'Inghilterra, Rome]
Jan. 11, 1949
[TLS w/ autograph postscript, 2 pp. HRC]

Dear Audrey:

I was very grateful for your long letter and the package of Xmas cards which I picked up today, the first real contact I have had with the States. I don't think there is any reason to take the Coen-Visconti-Downes row too seriously: it is impossible for an American to fix the blame or equity in this case. Obviously the person I want to make happy is Visconti as he is the one who is important to me here: he is practically the only legitimate manager in Italy. I have seen one of his productions, LIFE WITH FATHER, which is now running here and I thought it superior in quality to the New York show. The woman to play BLANCHE is a fine actress and perfect type for it, so I am annoyed with Fabio for making so much fuss. Actually I had met Visconti (in Sicily through Downes) a week or so before I established my first reluctant contact with Fabio, and had told Visconti I hoped he would do Streetcar so actually Fabio simply forced himself into the deal and then proceded to mess it up. It is true that Segre got credit and royalties for the translation of Menagerie, but Visconti says it had to be almost completely rewritten by Guerriri before the production. I cannot judge the right or wrong of all this, as I can only accept and compare the words of the opposite parties. Perhaps the best thing is to return the $300. to Coen and declare the agreement with him invalid: or else to pay Segre out of my royalties, as well as Guerriri. Of course I don't really care, as long as the show goes on and is well done.

The African Adventure was a mistake, as we arrived just at the start of the cold, rainy season. Our luggage was tied up in Gibralter so we could not leave Tangiers where we put up at a particularly dreadful place selected by Bowles for reasons of (his) economy. The meals cost about twenty-five cents but were scarcely worth it. There was no heat except for the fireplace in my room. Consequently the Bowles, Paul and Jane, were constant visitors which made it difficult to work. We delayed our departure for about ten days waiting for Bowles luggage to arrive - after ours finally had. His never showed up and we finally had to go on to Fez without it. Our first attempt to get across the Spanish Moroccan frontier was a fiasco. We arrived there at night in a torrential rain. Paul's twelve suitcases and our

four had to be taken through customs. While this was going on (interminably) the car got away, as we had left the brakes off, and started rolling downhill backwards. Frankie chased after it, as did many Arabs, and managed by a spectacular leap to get into it soon enough to avoid a serious crash. After all this we discovered that the car keys were lost. We dared not go on without them so we had to turn around and drive back to Tangiers. The keys were later found to have fallen down in the window socket of the car, only after we had notified the American consul that they had been stolen by the Spanish Moroccan customs officers and so caused a great disturbance. The next day we started out again, in another cloudburst. That day I found that I had developed a very peculiar affliction which is still with me. Whenever I lowered my head I felt a vibration all up and down my body like a ship with its propeller out of water. Also tingling sensations in my feet and fingers. This was naturally very disturbing and was one of the reasons I left Africa as I felt I should have some competent and intelligible medical advice. I saw an English-speaking doctor at Casablanca and have seen another one here in Rome and neither seem to take a very serious view of the affliction. I myself think it is probably a circulatory disorder due to strain and fatigue and other factors, such as no swimming. Paul had told me there was wonderful swimming in Morocco, but there was none. The weather was too cold and the pools were closed. I think it is the daily swimming that keeps me functioning passably well. My blood pressure is up, 145 over 100, which is not serious enough to explain the vibrations. I still have them, but now that I am swimming again, in the pool here in Rome, they're not quite so intense. If I get working well again, that will also help. Frankie is looking for an apartment for us. At present we have two rooms at a nice hotel, the Inghilterra, but there are too many tourists, desperate for conversation, hanging about the corridors and the bar, so that sometimes you don't really know that you have gotten out of New York or the Village. Through all of these tribulations Frankie has borne up wonderfully well, though he sometimes suffers from very bad headaches. My work was seriously interrupted, but the last few days I have been getting back at it again and have a room to myself for this purpose. It is true that I am working on a movie script: it is a screen version of one of the two plays I am working on. I alternate between the stage and screen script as they seem to be mutually helpful. I wish that I had a model movie-script containing the technical language of the film:

perhaps you know of a book containing material of this kind which you could send me. However I don't know how the item about Rossolini was conceived as I don't remember ever saying anything about such a notion. I would rather work with De Sica or Kazan if the film play becomes an actuality. De Sica has produced a magnificent new one (He did Shoe Shine) which is called Ladri di Bicyclette (Bicycle Thieves).

If Summer & Smoke is revived for the road I would be very happy, but I think it would be better to replace Andrews than Phillips, and most of all, a different director, as it was that end of the production that was most deficient in my opinion. I hope Jones has no more hold over the script, now that the play has closed. This does not mean we are enemies. Just wiser friends.

What about Rose?

With love, Tenn

Please mail Grandfather a box of good candy and a $100. check as a late Xmas present from me.

Dakin likes Colton and thinks I should keep him but also feels that he himself should have a retaining fee!

Tennessee Williams and Luchino Visconti: "Obviously the person I want to make happy is Visconti."

[The "African Adventure" ended after a dismal month with TW's arrival in Rome ca. January 6. He and Frank Merlo stayed at the Inghilterra, a fashionable hotel near the Spanish Steps, before returning to the apartment on via Aurora.

Luchino Visconti rejected the first translation of *Streetcar* (1947) commissioned by Fabio Coen, Audrey Wood's agent, on the grounds that it was derived from the New York production. Coen was also expected to pay for a second ordered by Visconti. TW typically complicated matters by approving each translation at a different time. The American reporter Donald Downes introduced TW to Visconti in 1948 and had apparently entered the "row."

Paul Bowles described TW as "violently perturbed by the Moslem scene" and surmised that his vibrations occurred "whenever things were not going smoothly" (*In Touch: The Letters of Paul Bowles*, ed. Miller, 1994, p. 200).

Manuscript sources (HRC) indicate that TW was at work on narrative, dramatic, and film versions of "The Roman Spring of Mrs. Stone" (1950), as the project was first entitled. The second play-in-progress is probably *The Rose Tattoo* (1951).

News that TW planned to write a screenplay with "an African background" for Roberto Rossellini surprised Audrey Wood. "True or false?" (January 8, 1949, HRC), she inquired.

Wood informed TW that the brief run of *Summer and Smoke* (1948) made an immediate tour impractical. The Theatre Guild, she added, was considering the play for a later subscription series and had asked that Margaret Phillips be replaced by a "star" (January 8, 1949, HRC). As producer, Margo Jones would oversee the eventual tour.]

123. *To Irene Mayer Selznick*

[Hotel d'Inghilterra, Rome]
1/16/49
[TLS w/ autograph marginalia, 1 p. Boston U]

Dear Irene:

I am now back in Rome, wondering why I ever left there and almost determined never to make that mistake again. Incidentally a big package, containing Nescafe, cocoa, chocolate bars, and condensed milk had been waiting for me in the post-office for several months and was finally delivered into my hands. It seemed like a gesture of yours: I cannot be sure for the outer package was nearly demolished and there was no record of the donor: if it is you, my thanks once again.

They are doing Streetcar in Rome, under the title Un Tram Che Se Chiamo Desiderio. There was a row and great litigation over a superfluity of translators, exactly twice as many as needed: I arrived on the scene like

the cowboy hero, just in time to halt an injunction and straighten things out to the complete happiness of all by the simple expedient of paying both translators out of my own royalties. After paying - just now according to the latest bulletin from home - $110,000. to the government, this little item was like the celebrated intercourse between the elephant and the mouse. You'll be happy to know that the Visconti production promises to be very exciting. There is no excess of restraint: in that respect it is more Italian than Dixie. Even the organist gets out of hand, at times: last night he and Blanche were closely competing in volume: she won out by a couple of pinwheel gestures but it was a photo-finish. I have a feeling it will suit the Italian public as their ordinary life is more theatrical than our theatre, for which God be praised.

We left Paul in Morocco. Everything was just exactly as he said it wasn't. It was cold, it was raining continually, there was no place to swim, the food was worse than in London - do you remember London? - and the natives might have been beautiful if they did not nearly all have scrofula or cataracts or ring-worm: anyway a visual appreciation of them was enough! I can't deny that Morocco is a mysterious and beautiful country, in spite of these things, and I am going back: not during the rainy season, however. (I still love Paul!)

I wish I could say that I am now quite well, but I'm not. I suffer from mysterious <u>Vibrations</u>: whenever I lower my head slightly I feel like an electric vibrator was running up and down my body! I guess it is high blood-pressure and I am going to see a doctor, recommended by the American consulate. A headline in a newspaper interview says: "Tennessee Williams Soffre Di 'Vibrazioni'!" Yes, there are reporters even in Rome. This condition interferes a bit with my work, however I don't think it is self-induced for that purpose.

Are there any picture deals at all imminent or likely for Streetcar? I hope too much money is not being demanded: if I could get, say, an assured income (after taxes) of three or four hundred a month out of it I would be very happy and I think some deal could be made on that basis. My brother, Dakin, is shocked that so far none of my earnings have been capital gain and that is why I am now broke again except for my government bonds ($60,000.). I remember we discussed this problem a bit when I had dinner in your apartment and you said some enlightening things about it: would that I could remember what they were! - Love, to you, Irene, and my warm greetings to all the passengers on the Streetcars.

Tennessee.

[*Un tram che si chiama desiderio* premiered at Rome's Theatro Eliseo on January 21, 1949, with Rina Morelli (Blanche), Vittorio Gassman (Stanley), and Marcello Mastroianni (Mitch) playing the leads. Rome was shocked by the candor of *Streetcar*, but critics deemed the production a triumph and lavished praise upon Visconti's politically inspired direction. Praise for TW was correspondingly diminished, but he admired the production nonetheless and observed that Gassman's Stanley wore "the tightest pair of dungarees" he had "ever seen on the male ass" (qtd. in Windham, pp. 229-230).

In later correspondence Audrey Wood reported a still "non-existent" market for film rights of *Streetcar*. Irene Selznick remained an alternate source of funding and seemed willing to co-produce if her father's studio—MGM—would only "open their mouth" (to TW, January 30, 1949, HRC). A fee of $750,000 and fear that Joseph Breen, Production Code administrator, would harshly censor *Streetcar* made buyers wary.

Penned in the upper margin is TW's mailing address, "c/o American Express, Rome."]

124. To Audrey Wood

[Hotel d'Inghilterra, Rome]
[January 1949]
[TLS w/ enclosure, 1 p. HRC]

Dear Audrey:

I have so far received no report on the grants which I had arranged through the Author's League. These are terribly important to the people concerned, and also to me. I cannot understand Miss Sillcox's apparent lack of courtesy in failing even to answer the applications. I know that she hasn't answered the one which I made for the Bowles for the address I gave her was care of me in Rome and it has been well over three weeks. What is the matter? Please check on it: find out whether or not she is intending to take any action. All the names that I gave her were people who deserved and needed this help very badly. I am enclosing a letter from Oliver Evans with a paragraph marked. At least a secretary might have acknowledged receipt of his application. Like all poets he is easily hurt or offended. The one thing I have accomplished this past year that I can look back on with gratification is making these grants and I want to be damned sure that they are followed through. The present treatment does not encourage me to make any further contribution through the League.

Incidentally I have also received no word about my sister, although I

understood that the money I gave Mother was to be used to transfer her to the private retreat near home.

Please tell Colton I want to know the exact maximum that I am allowed to give each year in the way of gifts, endowments, Etc., so that I can give that maximum (deductible). I feel that I could probably have given a great deal more than $5,000. if I had known what was allowable. Dakin says Colton wants his fee to be doubled ($2,000.) Is this true? So far I am not convinced that Colton has affected any substantial saving for me and don't see why I should increase his fee, especially if I must also pay Dakin which he seems to expect. I actually have very little money, not even enough to live on if the two companies of Streetcar should close: that is, without selling my bonds. Dakin feels, and I feel, too, that I must be sure, hereafter - assuming I have another play to sell - to make some deal by which I get to keep some of the procedes as "capital gain". We must keep that in mind. You see I am very depressed over the news of the tax-payment. . . .

With love, Tenn.

[Luise Sillcox, executive secretary of the Authors' League, was presumably slow to acknowledge applications to a fund established by TW. He had contributed $5,000 to the League and designated Oliver Evans, Paul and Jane Bowles, Carson McCullers, and Donald Windham as recipients.

TW feared that Edwina had been persuaded by Dr. Emmitt Hoctor, the superintendent, to leave Rose in the state asylum: "So far he has opposed (or neglected to do anything about) any suggestion that has been made for her improvement" (to Dakin Williams, n.d., Columbia U).

William Liebling assured TW that *Streetcar* was still profitable: "Last week, the New York company made over $26,000, and when the Chicago company leaves for the road, it will do capacity business for a long time. . . . So for Christ's sake stop worrying!" (January 25, 1949, HRC). The Broadway show would close on December 17, 1949, having earned a profit of $500,000. The national tour continued through the following spring.

This letter, which bears a reception date of January 24, 1949, was probably written in the week of January 16.]

125. *To Irene Mayer Selznick*

[45 Via Aurora, Rome]
[mid-February 1949]
[TLS, 1 p. Boston U]

Dear Irene:

I am still reading and studying letters #1-4: nobody has ever said so much about so much to so few! As Margo would say, Bless you darling! (But a little more sincerely than she always does). I had a hard time composing the cable about the English production. You are very, very persuasive about Mr. Olivier and Mme. his wife. You have evidently given the matter a great deal of consideration, and I am glad to see that you have included in your consideration that Mme. Olivier has not yet given us a ghost of an idea of her latent dramatic powers. But I believe, as you do, that Mr. Olivier is a smart cookie who would not want Vivien to lay anything bigger than ostrich egg on the London stage even in a play by an American author. In my cable I was being as explicit as possible, in so short a space. I still think an American company would be far better. However if the production is put off until 1950, the chances are that interest in the play would be considerably depleted and also that I might not be able to see it or want to if I could. I hope that isn't too mysterious-sounding! The prestige of an Olivier production would certainly be enormous and every bit as intriguing to me as to anyone else. If only we could be devastatingly frank with Sir Laurence, and say, Honey, we want <u>you</u> but could do without <u>her</u>! - After the Italian production I know it is possible to have a success even without the right Blanche, for the show has been a smash-hit here in Rome in spite of the fact that practically everyone agrees that the Blanche is wrong. They have moved it to a larger theatre and it is now in its fifth week and <u>I</u> am earning (though have not yet collected) 30,000 lire a night in spite of having to pay two translators out of my royalties.

Frank has gone to Sicily to visit his relatives there. I am lonely but have more energy for my work. I now have a script with a beginning a middle and an end, but there is still not much flesh on the bones and the animation is wanting. I'll finish this one, but maybe then I'll quit and develop my voice.

I'm as happy about Art's play as I could be about any play but my own. Please send me, or have Audrey send me, the New York notices, no matter how good they are! Don't send me anymore goodies, but if you feel in a

sending mood, as you often do, send something sweet to Grandpa. He is not too happy in Saint Louis. One letter says that Mother insists he is only pretending to be deaf and won't repeat anything to him so he has no idea what's going on in the house. In the next letter he says, she nags continually: "Oh, that tongue of hers!" A bit contradictory. Or maybe the electric ear is functioning better, now. One of my favorite anecdotes is of the Streetcar rehearsal when he produced the sound-effects tuning in on it.

To revert to London: I place it, like Pilate, in your hands, but please remember what a beating I took last summer in the London press and see that everything possible is done to protect us and the play, as distinct from Sir Laurence and his lady! And have it stated in the contract that no mention is to be made in the press of my figure being "short & squatty".

Love - 10.

[The Oliviers recently confirmed their availability for a London production of *Streetcar* (1949). Vivien Leigh was still primarily known for her role as Scarlett O'Hara in *Gone With the Wind* (1939)—a production of Irene Selznick's estranged husband, David—but her English stage credits were more extensive and varied than TW may have realized.

Rina Morelli's diminutive stature perhaps exaggerated her vulnerability and lessened the threat of Blanche's visitation. Nonetheless the press acclaimed both her casting and performance in *Streetcar*.

In Frank Merlo's absence TW summoned "Raffaello" and soon reported to Donald Windham—erroneously, it turned out—that he had "the clap" (qtd. in Windham, p. 231).

Death of a Salesman, by Arthur Miller, opened in New York on February 10, 1949.]

126. To Audrey Wood

[45 Via Aurora, Rome]
February 15, 1949.
[TLS w/ marginalia and
autograph postscript, 2 pp. HRC]

Dear Audrey:

I haven't meant to neglect you. In fact somewhere under all these papers is at least half a letter to you written weeks ago. But my little Secretary, or Interpreter, as the Italian press insist upon calling Frank, is visiting his

parent's cousins in Sicily and my affairs are much less well-organized than usual. A forlorn postcard today says he has caught the Flu and his Aunt won't let him out of the house but is planning a big dance to celebrate his recovery, when he recovers. Otherwise life here is well-ordered. The weather has been so fine that they've had to cut down on electricity because of a water-shortage and my evenings are spent in becoming candle-light. I have red, green and white candles in honor of the Italian flag, red for the blood of Italy, white for the snow of its mountains and green for its valleys. The late afternoons I take to the streets in my "lunghissima Buick Rosso" as it is described in the papers, and it is like navigating a battleship through narrow straits getting it in and out of the tiny avenues, it goes very slowly with great pomp and everybody shouts 'Que Bella Macchina!' and only Tyrone Power cuts a more important figure here. It is nick-named "Desiderio" in honor of the "Tram" which is still playing to very good houses in its fifth week. A beautiful set of photos is being sent you. The production was extraordinarily fine except for some over-acting (rather strenuous) on the part of the Morelli who plays Blanche. Could it be arranged for me to draw my Italian royalties while I am here, instead of having them all sent to New York? It would greatly facilitate my life here, as I would not have to frequent the money-changers. I was told this afternoon that only a statement from you, directed to the Authors Society in care of Fabio Coen, could release these royalties for my use here. I will also speak to Fabio about it. I have been exchanging some lively correspondance with Irene, including cables, about the London Streetcar. She says it is not practical to organize an American company before 1950. That seems too long to wait, and in that case I should like to know if you don't think it would be wise to accept an Olivier production? The prestige of his name, and his great gifts as a showman, must certainly be considered, although I have yet to see Vivian give a striking performance. But then neither did Morelli here - or rather, hers was much too striking - and the play was still a success "clamoroso". I will leave the matter in your hands (collective). . . .

I received today five complete sets of Arthur Miller notices, more than I ever received for any play of my own. Everybody seemed most anxious that I should know how thoroughly great was his triumph. I hope that I was pleased over it. If I was not it only goes to show what dogs we can be. At least it was a play that I liked by a man I look up to. Perhaps I am being over-cautious in saying I hope I was pleased because in the incorruptible

portion of my being (however small that may be) I felt an unmistakable beam of satisfaction. It is a deep, human play, warmly felt and written with a great simple dignity which comes out of Miller's own character, and the direction of it must have been a tremendous achievement for Gadge, because though I loved it, I thought the retrospective scenes would be hellishly difficult to stage. I am awfully anxious to see a picture of the set.

This is marvelous news about the imminent filming of "Menagerie". And tell Feldman that I will definitely come out as advisor anytime they want me. I can't commit myself to do any work on the script but still it might be possible for me to help with it, as it is so much to my interest (and the family's) for the picture to be done from a dignified script.

Please tell Eddie Colton for me that I am not really worried about "Capitol Gain" or anything else except my weight and my work and my occasional vibrations: those are my only real personal concerns right now. Once the tax-man has come and gone, like Santie Claus in reverse, I forget him until his next scheduled appearance. I do hope that I can manage, however, to accumulate enough money to bring me in a good monthly income, say, four or five hundred a month on which I could keep myself and a small Secretary and a big car.

Much love from your Italian client, 10.

Please kiss Luise for me, all have received their grants.

P.S. Please air mail copy of "Summer and Smoke" (the book) for Visconti.

[Tyrone Power lived in Rome while filming *Prince of Foxes* (1949). His recent marriage to Linda Christian drew hordes of unruly fans and reporters and received a papal blessing. Power's homosexual tendencies were perhaps known to TW.

Audrey Wood preferred to sell the film rights of *Streetcar* before mounting a London stage production and advised delaying the project until 1950, when an American cast and director could also be found (to TW, January 30, 1949, HRC). The critical "beating" of *The Glass Menagerie* (1945) in the preceding summer was not forgotten.

Notices for *Death of a Salesman* were uniformly positive and bore none of the reservations, moral or critical, which marked the reception of *Streetcar*. Elia Kazan, whose direction was also acclaimed, noted that Arthur Miller had learned from *Streetcar* how easily nonrealistic elements—"the retrospective scenes" to which TW refers—could be "blended with the realistic ones" (Kazan, p. 361).

Typed in the upper margin of page 1 is TW's name and mailing address, "American Express, Rome."]

127. To Irene Mayer Selznick

SH: Excelsior, Napoli
March 23, 1949.
[TLS w/ marginalia, 3 pp. Boston U]

Dear Irene:

I am travelling around with one suitcase, not large enough to contain your recent memoranda from the home-front so I am not sure that this will adequately cover the various problems brought up. But I take it, from the cable, that the most important question now pending, is who to put in Jessica's place for the summer. Of the two ladies, Deborah and Tallullah, I suspect the first is closer to the part: but isn't she also a little too much like Jessica, not enough contrast to spur a new interest, and does she have box-office draw? Tallullah certainly has the latter and certainly her interpretation would be an altogether new one and bound to stir interest. Frankly, I am ~~very~~ frightened of her, and I don't think she should be put in the play without very earnest assurance, from her, that she would play the play and not just Tallullah as she has been recently doing. In other words, we don't yet want the "Camp" streetcar! As I am so far away, I think I will delegate Audrey to represent my interest or voting power, in this matter. I'm perfectly sure that you and she together can weigh all the factors pro and con for each candidate, and Gadge, too, if he is still at all interested. Now as for the appeals from the London censor, I grudgingly acquiesce to his demands on every single point except the one relating to Allen Grey. Blanche's speech about her husband's homosexuality cannot be altered. There is nothing lurid or at all offensive in this speech, it is written with all requisite taste and delicacy and it is too important a thing to be deleted or changed, and if they will not accept the play with that speech, then it is clear to me that they just don't want the play produced in England and I would rather not have it done there if they don't want it. The other little textual changes demanded by the censors don't bother me much and can be done in rehearsal: I don't have either the book nor the script with me, nor even the list of the censor, so I can't refer to them now.

Grandfather is ecstatic over the candy, and over your kindness to him. He is quite in love with you, and I can think of no higher tribute that could be paid you than having won his heart so quickly and completely, for he has been a great cavalier, within the proper limits of his calling, and has known many ladies and admired only the best. A letter yesterday states that

he is "busily packing". Hitting the road again, to celebrate his 93rd birthday in Mississippi! The birthday is in April.

No important news of myself: except this: I have now rough drafts of three plays. That sounds ever so much better than it actually is. When I say rough I mean like a road through the jungle! All that I want out of God is time! I also need more energy, but if I get the time, I can manage, maybe not all three, but surely one.

Truman Capote is here. That stands in a little paragraph all by itself.

And one last paragraph to say thank you! Thank you for the letters and for everything, for being such a wonderful producer and such a good friend and such a great lady!

Love, Tenn.

[Jessica Tandy, Marlon Brando, and Kim Hunter left the cast of *Streetcar* on June 1 when their contracts expired. Tandy, the most difficult to replace, was succeeded by Uta Hagen, who had relieved her in the preceding summer and toured with the national company.

Tallulah Bankhead starred in a notorious revival of *Streetcar* in 1956. Her "roustabout reputation," as a critic put it, preceded the performance and confirmed TW's fears (see letters #321 and #323).

The Lord Chamberlain's Office cited blasphemous reference in *Streetcar* to "'Christ,'" as well as Stanley's crude linking of "'kidneys'" and "'soul.'" More serious was Blanche's disclosure of Allan Grey's homosexuality in Scene Six. "The Lord Chamberlain is of opinion," wrote his assistant, "that this passage should be altered making the young husband found with a negress instead of another man" (Gwatkin, July 12, 1948, HRC). Reports of the Olivier production indicate that Blanche's telling line—"the boy I had married and an older man who had been his friend for years"—was simply omitted. John Lehmann followed suit in publishing the first English edition of *Streetcar* (1949).

The "rough drafts" cited by TW are probably *The Roman Spring of Mrs. Stone*, *The Rose Tattoo*, and "The Big Time Operators" (n.d., HRC).]

128. *To Audrey Wood*

SH: Excelsior, Napoli
3/23/49
[TLS w/ autograph marginalia, 2 pp. HRC]

Dear Audrey:

I have just had a reunion with my typewriter which I had left at a hotel in Florence. It is now safely back, together with the manuscript notebook I had locked in the case, but I had several very anxious and frustrating days waiting for it.

Frank and I are on our way to the sea. We travelled this far, to Naples, with Capote and Jack Dunphy, one of your writers. I got to know Jack for the first time in Rome and I like him a lot. I'm not sure, however, that the four of us will continue to Ischia where Dunphy and Capote are going. I am not sure how much Capote I can take. He is completely disarming: and then all at once, out shoots the forked tongue! And the sting is all but mortal. But there are other islands, and we, Frank and myself, will probably spend a week on one of them.

I have a feeling that I am supposed to answer an accumulation of questions: right now I can't think of them. I have just written Irene saying that I delegated my voting power in the matter of Tandy replacements to you. That I would not alter the "Allen Grey" speech for London but would make all the other little changes or deletions.

Now as to the very grave question of future producers: I would rather not take that up seriously until I have a completed play script. As long as we are closely involved with Irene I think it would be extremely dangerous, certainly on my part, to make any commitment to another producer. I think she would be not merely bitter, but dangerously vindictive in such an event. I don't want to make any secret deal behind her back, not even with Cheryl Crawford who I think the world of. There is no reason to move on this till the play is ready, and nothing is lost by refusing to decide, even in our own minds, until the issue is imminent. I have three scripts, and if I finish one of them, the chances are that I will finish all three, but the if is still an if. I am depressed and anxious over my lack of health and energy mainly on account of my work which demands so much of my physical strength and nervous power. I must be well, or relatively well, to work well. And I still have these damned vibrations. Sounds like a neurotic symptom, but it isn't. Perhaps I should leave soon for Paris, as last year I felt stimulated as soon

as I went North. Now as ever I think only of how and where I can best function as a writer. Unfortunately the writer and the man are inseparable.

I would rather not sell the amateur rights to Summer & Smoke this year, which is another year in the high brackets. I would not be able to keep the money. Would much rather have it earn royalties for me over a long period as my own property. Speaking of "Summer" did you know that Margo (according to Anne Jackson according to Truman) made a speech to the cast saying that it was "the work of a dying man?" I would like to check on the authenticity of this report!   Much love -

10.

[Truman Capote and his new companion, Jack Dunphy, met TW and Frank Merlo in Rome and traveled with them to Naples. TW upset a table in Capote's lap after learning of Margo Jones's "speech" to the cast of *Summer and Smoke*. Anne Jackson, who played Nellie in the Broadway production, was apparently Capote's source. Capote denied repeating the story in malice but acknowledged the "mortal" nature of his "sting": "I didn't realize that I was touching the nerve nearest Tennessee's heart. He claimed he was dying every other day. It was his favorite gambit for getting sympathy. 'You don't know it, my dear,' he would say, 'but Ah'm a dyin' man!'" (qtd. in Clarke, *Capote: A Biography*, 1988, p. 196).

Audrey Wood lost patience with Irene Selznick who refused to underwrite the film version of *Streetcar*. She reminded TW that Selznick was "hopeful of getting" his next play and that this might be used as an "emotional weapon." Cheryl Crawford, Wood's choice to succeed Selznick, had been approached informally and was "very eager to do a Tennessee Williams play" (March 1, 1949, HRC).

TW rejected Wood's advice to sell "amateur rights" of *Summer and Smoke*. Wood later prevailed after informing him that payment would be spread over several years to lower the tax rate.

Penned in the upper margin of page 1 is TW's mailing address, "American Express, Rome."]

129. To Carson McCullers

SH: Excelsior, Napoli
3/23/49
[TLS, 2 pp. Duke U]

Dearest Carson:

I just discovered among my papers, when I was packing, a letter I had written you at least a month ago. That was just after I had heard that you

had moved into the city and had received a grant, and I was very happy over that news. But most of the letter, pertaining to myself, was a morbid chronicle, so it is just as well that I allowed it to remain among the discarded papers. I can't say I'm feeling a hell of a lot better now, but at least I don't feel obliged to raise such a lamentation. Rome has not done as much for me this year as it did last. For one thing, the winter seems to be everlasting. I've finally got tired of waiting for a warm sun and have set out in the Buick to find it. I may go on as far South as Sicily if I don't find any good swimming-places on the way. I am not alone, but in a way I am lonelier than if I were. Do you understand what I mean? Yes. I know you do. But that is the end of my lamentations; no more, no more! It is nobody's fault but my own. After a week or two in the sun, if I ever find it, I shall probably go up to Paris. I found it very stimulating last year, after the long stay in Rome, and I hope to God it works again this year. In a way the Buick is a burden: it is such an effort driving it around everywhere instead of just hopping on a plane.

I got copies of "Reflections" from both you and Laughlin. It seems absurd for me to write a preface to a great work by such a completely established writer and I should feel almost too embarassed to try, but I <u>will</u> try if you really want me to: that is, as soon as my present state of fatigue and depression has somewhat lifted, as soon as circumstances permit it to do so.

A certain young writer, I won't say his name, was in Rome for a brief while. It did not suit him and he has gone on to an island. The island is volcanic but the volcano is now extinct. In passing he managed to do a fair amount of mischief, but nothing really <u>tangible</u>. What is it?

I heard that you were travelling in the South. I may be back in the States, myself, sooner than I had originally planned. Let me hear from you!

Much, much love, Tenn.

[Carson McCullers wrote last to TW in the preceding January when she and Reeves, reconciled once again, shared an apartment in New York. She considered Rome "the right place" for TW and hoped that "no emotional ambivalence" involving "Frankie and Salvatore" (Raffaello) would arise to destroy his "peace." She also thanked him for the gift of a ring belonging to his sister, which she promised to treasure "always - or until the blessed time when Rose is well." The Authors' League grant, McCullers concluded, was "a rare bit of fortune": "How can I thank you?" (n.d., Duke U).

James Laughlin's plan to reprint McCullers's second novel, *Reflections in a Golden Eye* (1941), included a preface by TW.

The mischievous "young writer" to whom TW alludes is Truman Capote, as McCullers would have instantly guessed.]

130. To James "Jay" Laughlin

[45 Via Aurora, Rome]
4/10/49
[TLS w/ enclosure and autograph
marginalia, 1 p. Houghton]

Dear Jay:

I had quite a hard time writing this introduction since I didn't quite know what I was supposed to do with it, that is, what purpose it should serve, since Carson and her work are already so well-known and established. I may have taken altogether the wrong slant on it, particularly in the personal anecdotes and the stuff about her influence on a writer that will certainly be recognized as Capote. Please use your own judgement in trimming this down and editing it as much as you deem necessary or discreet and it might be a good idea to let Carson see it first, since it is her book. I honestly could not think of any other way of dealing with it. It was a good hard exercise but I don't want to try it again any time soon!

I have gotten the two reprints of Menagerie and Wagons and find them stunningly well done. After a disturbing period of apathy last winter, I am plowing ahead once more and have completed a first draft of a play and of a long story so if I come home next Fall it won't be empty-handed. We, Frankie and I, are going to London the end of this month for a conference with the Oliviers, and after that we will spend some time in Paris which I found very stimulating last year, but we are keeping the little apartment in Rome to return to when it is time to relax again. The days are one long blue and gold ribbon always unwinding and giving you an illusion of permanence of at least a physical kind, which is no small bargain. Vidal has not yet returned to Europe but Capote is now on Ischia with a new red-headed lover that he dotes on. They have radioactive springs on that volcanic island which are supposed to create enormous sexual vitality so perhaps Truman will have to leave Italy with a board nailed over his ass, which is the way a red-headed sailor once said a Mardi Gras visitor would

have to leave New Orleans! How is Carson? I haven't heard from her in a good while. Donnie's book is being rejected by all the big houses which is discouraging to him and mistifying to me. Maria is said to be on her way back to England in a few days and is arranging to be surprised by a big bon-voyage party and "shower".

Ever, Tenn.

<u>Lustig covers</u> a <u>dream</u>!

[James Laughlin flattered TW that his name was "very hot" and "would help to sell" the forthcoming edition of *Reflections in a Golden Eye*. He added, "Isn't it an awful commentary on our culture that a writer as great as Carson should have to have any help at all in getting her work to the public" (November 29, 1948, Houghton).

New Directions reprinted *The Glass Menagerie* and *27 Wagons Full of Cotton* (1945) in early 1949 without a copyright or a dust jacket fiasco. Laughlin also informed TW that he had earned the "tidy little sum" (April 14, 1949, Houghton) of $7,500 for sales in 1948.

TW refers to "completed" first drafts of *The Rose Tattoo* and *The Roman Spring of Mrs. Stone*.

Following the scene in Naples the parties traveled separately to the island of Ischia, where TW and Frank Merlo spent nearly two weeks. TW was reportedly jealous of Merlo's attraction to Capote, while Capote detected in Merlo "'a great crush'" (qtd. in Clarke, *Capote: A Biography*, p. 196) on Jack Dunphy.

TW described Ischia as "a dream" to Donald Windham and predicted that he would "like it best of anything in Italy" (qtd. in Windham, p. 237). He also urged Windham to "keep faith" while his novel *The Dog Star* (1950) was being circulated.

Penned in the upper margin is TW's mailing address, "American Express, Rome. (till April 20<u>th</u>)."]

131. To Audrey Wood

["the Neapolitan coast"]
[April 1949]
[TLS w/ autograph marginalia, 1 p. HRC]

Dear Audrey:

Frank and I are making a tour of sunny beaches along the Neapolitan coast before we face the rigors of a week in London with Irene. I have a feeling that condensed in that week will be all the harassments that you have experienced in two years of telephone conversations, and I say that still liking the woman and assuming that you still like her.

I have not known how to answer your wire about Ruth Ford Vs. Judith Evelyn. Truthfully when I saw Ruth, though I was disposed to like her, I felt that she made the whole character of Blanche seem totally phoney. I have always liked Evelyn and regarded her as an actress of remarkable power and thought she had that sort of looks that must depend on illusion that gave Blanche such physical pathos. So you see how difficult it is for me to wire an enthusiastic espousal of your side in this particular debate. When I think about the acting profession, I suspect it is about as heartbreaking as writing plays or representing playwrights!

Since I last wrote you I have been going through a relatively good period and working continually. I have finished a long story, about 35 pages, taken from one of the plays I was working on last year, The Roman Spring of Mrs. Stone, and which I now think would make a good movie script. I have discussed it slightly with De Sica, the best Italian director who made Shoe Shine and The Bicycle Thieves which has not yet been shown in the States and he is very anxious to do a film with me, is distinguished from most other big Italian directors by his simplicity and modesty and some understanding and use of English so I have a feeling that we could work together on a film if the proper arrangement could be worked out, that is, assurance of script-control for me so that I would have some creative satisfaction out of the work. It is a possible script for Garbo if she would be willing to play a woman of fifty still clinging to romance. I will have it typed in London and send you a copy.

The plays are right where they were when I last wrote but perhaps when I get North, and with the story off my hands, I will start forging ahead more rapidly on them.

While on Ischia I developed a suspicion of Truman almost equal to Carson's. How is Carson? I am worried for I haven't heard from her in quite a long while.

Love - 10.

P.S. DE SICA IS VERY ANXIOUS TO DIRECT MENAGERIE IN HOLLY-WOOD IF WARNERS ARE GOING TO DO IT. HE WILL BE FREE ABOUT SEPT. OR OCT. WHAT DO YOU THINK? Have been in touch with the Dieterlie-Magnani outfit. They have a fine story and I am thinking of going down to Stromboli when I get back from London, at least for the fun of it.

[Audrey Wood later reported that Uta Hagen had been signed to replace Jessica Tandy on Broadway and Judith Evelyn to replace Hagen on tour. Ruth Ford, a client of Liebling-Wood, was no longer in contention, having demanded a salary which Irene Selznick found excessive (to TW, April 19, 1949, HRC). Wood also noted in following correspondence that Irving Rapper had been hired to direct the film version of *The Glass Menagerie* (1950) and that Jane Wyman was set to play Laura. She closed by "doubly" begging TW "not to make any commitment" on *Streetcar* or any other play while "doing London town" (April 20, 1949, HRC) in May.

TW probably wrote this letter in the week of April 17, but it was not mailed until early-May, as a notation penned in the upper margin indicates: "Later - London - Everything went fine here. We leave for Paris tomorrow (5/9/49)."]

132. To Audrey Wood

[Paris]
5/13/49
[TLS, 1 p. HRC]

Dear Audrey:

We have just arrived in Paris from London and I have not yet seen Ninon or anyone else connected with the proposed Paris production so I can't make any comments on that. Things in London seemed to be in good shape when we left.

I have gotten the movie-script for the Menagerie. I think it would be disastrous to shoot this script as it now stands. There has been a general cheapening and bastardization which I think Hollywood cannot get away with any longer, against the tide of fine new pictures being made abroad as well as the advance evident in serious films made in America. The greatest damage has been done to the character of Amanda. As depicted in this film treatment she has lost all dignity and consequently all poetry and pathos. She is cheap and brassy. Not even the remnants of a lady but just a common and vulgar shrew. You can imagine how personally embarassing I find this to be. Also Laura's pathos has been turned to bathos through sentimentalization without any real heart or poetry left in it. I make these comments with full understanding of the necessary conversion to cinema appeal. And I make it because I think that all, including cinema, appeal has been sacrificed through lack of understanding and tasteful writing. There are still some good things in the script. The rearrangement

(of sequence) in the original material is not without some merits and advantages, particularly in the long scene of the gentleman caller, but I would say that practically all of the <u>new</u> material is so badly out of key and quality that it should be junked if the picture is to have any dignity, and I know I am right in feeling that this picture cannot succeed commercially or artistically unless that dignity is kept. Incidentally they should not put my name on the present script as author as it is obviously not my work, and a disgrace to any name that is signed to it, including ~~Arthur~~ Chas. Feldman's.

I wish that you and Eddie Colton would check on the following points: What are the percentage terms that we are given in the picture contract? In other words, the financial stake involved. Also, who is the director? I sincerely hope not Rappaport, as once mentioned, for he is known to be a just <u>competent</u> director and this film requires the finest, such as De Sica or Kazan or Wyler, especially since the script is now in such a mess of incomprehension. If I came out to work on it, how much artistic control would I be given? (Three questions) The last means that I would come if I were assured that I would be working with people, producer and director, that are tasteful and gifted enough to justify it. And that Mother and I have a good chance of making some money out of the picture.

As for Summer, certainly it shouldn't be revived without a fine director and a leading man better than Tod Andrews. I was shocked to hear that he had broadcast it, as he was the one person that I thought replacing might make a considerable difference, but that is characteristic of the Guild treatment, substitute for the good one and keep the lemon!

Will call Ninon this eve. -

Love - 10.

[Both Jean Anouilh and Jean Cocteau sought rights to a Paris production of *Streetcar* (1949). Audrey Wood's recommendation of Cocteau was tacitly approved when TW failed to answer correspondence. Ninon Tallon continued to represent Wood in France.

Charles Feldman reminded Wood that *The Glass Menagerie* script had not "changed fundamentally" (Wood to TW, May 18, 1949, HRC) since first read and approved by TW in July 1947. Feldman, though, had been forewarned of the present criticism. His assistant, Charles Abramson, read the script when it was first submitted and described the "conventional 'Boy Meets Girl' ending" as "too quick, too pat, and trite" (to Feldman, July 4, 1947, HRC). TW later accepted a screenwriting credit for *The Glass Menagerie*, as did the adapter, Peter Berneis.

On May 18 Wood detailed TW's "financial stake" in the film and regretted to say that the author has no legal rights over the choice of producer, director, actors, or script. She added that Irving Rapper—not H. Rappaport—was probably a more talented director than TW allowed (HRC).

In a second letter dated May 18, Wood predicted that John Shubert and the Theatre Guild, co-sponsors of the forthcoming tour of *Summer and Smoke*, would drop the play from consideration if TW demanded expensive changes in cast and direction (HRC).

The radio broadcast of *Summer and Smoke* (April 17, 1949) was co-sponsored by the United States Steel Corporation and The Theatre Guild on the Air. Robert Anderson wrote the adaptation and Dorothy McGuire and Tod Andrews spoke the leading parts.]

133. To Audrey Wood

[45 Via Aurora, Rome]
[late-May 1949]
[TLS, 2 pp. HRC]

Dear Audrey:

Today I received the best news that has come to me in a long time which is that my sister, Rose, is now out of the asylum for three days a week, in the custody of a lady in a neighboring town, that she has written home expressing her delight with the arrangement and was last seen "picking violets on her new friend's lawn". Now that I have this news, the realization of such long planning, I am very anxious to go ahead with the trust agreement giving her a half interest in "Summer & Smoke" and also to see that the play, if it goes on tour, will have every protection. I am considering coming home before the London production of Streetcar as I think my interests in America may be more pressing and important, as regards the Menagerie film and the Summer & Smoke tour. I want both of these things, so closely related to the welfare and satisfaction of my family, to be worked out as well as possible. I think the best protection (for all concerned) is to hold firm on certain points about which I have absolute conviction. I don't think a mere duplication of "S & S" will do any good. It must have the services of an imaginative director, possibly a new or young one, but one with more than stage manager's ability and license. I have always felt, very strongly, that the peculiarly dead effect created in many scenes of the play was due, unhappily, to the male lead having nothing but looks to contribute.

I like the idea of McGuire, but I am sure that someone better than Todd can be found in these post-war days when so many virile young actors with real ability can be had. See if you can't get an OK from the Shuberts to shop around both for a new male lead and a gifted young director who wouldnt demand, perhaps, any higher pay than a stage manager doing the job. I think the Oliviers would understand if I came home early to assist in the staging, as I wanted to do in the first place. Aside from Todd I would only insist on two other replacements, the Mexican Gonzales girl and the old doctor. I should prefer, of course, to replace Mrs. Winemiller and her husband as well, but I think we could get along with the same cast in all but the three parts I have mentioned, and with a new effort to inject life in the staging.

Now re: Menagerie a la Feldman. I am afraid I cannot retract anything I've said. I remember, and Feldman is perfectly right about this, that I expressed approval of the script in Hollywood but it was because I had been under the impression it would be something too awful to imagine. It wasn't that! And I certainly qualified my relief and approval. I said that I liked the way so much of the original script had been kept but I made it quite clear that I detested the new ending and that I thought all of the new material was a mere cheapening of the product, to no profitable end whatsoever. The cinema industry has shown great promise of new dignity in the last ten years or so, but this script is a most discouraging reversion to type. Mr. Feldman must remember that this play has toured the country and been very widely read. I doubt that he will find a single reviewer that will not jump down his throat for the grotesque distortion that is brought about by the phoney "Louis J. Singer ending". There are various ways of relieving the tragedy of the play if that seems necessary, but the one selected is almost the worst possible. Do you have a copy of my incomplete rewrite job on the script? I remember that it contained a suggestion for another ending, not to my entire satisfaction but certainly better than the awful Sunday-school-sentimental business that now brings the whole fabric of the play crashing down into ruins. Let us get the bull out of the china closet! If I thought the thing was hopeless I would dismiss it with a couple of sighs, but with the excellent cast that is lined up and Warners' back of it, there is still the possibility of making it into a great and successful picture. As for Rapper, I am relieved by some of his credits. The Corn Is Green was a pretty good picture, but he is still no one that I would have picked for the

job. Is there anyone beside Feldman that we can work on for a dignified script?

The long story developed into a novella. It is now about finished and I am looking for a typist who can read and write English.

What was this about being black words on white paper?! I never read your wonderful letters without seeing and hearing you just as if we were talking over a martini! But I doubt that I make such good sense.

With love, Tenn.

P.S. I am glad you read Feldmann my first letter, but think we must now handle him very politely and gently to get our concessions without insulting the man's idea of himself as a producer. I shall follow this, soon, with a detailed list of what is good and bad in the screen play, and some suggestions for new work on it. How late can they start shooting? Until they see the whites of my eyes?

[TW has apparently described his sister's first release from institutional care since 1937.

Irving Rapper's direction of *The Corn Is Green* (1945) led to Academy Award nominations for the best male and female supporting roles. Bette Davis starred as a crusading teacher who brings new ideas to a Welsh mining village.

On May 23, after a hiatus of several months, TW revived his journal, writing that he had just "about finished <u>Moon of Pause</u>," as *The Roman Spring* was provisionally entitled, but "prefer not to have any opinion of it yet."

Wood ended her second letter of May 18 by observing that she was "tired of coming out black words on white paper." Implied was frustration with TW's lassitude and inattention to business, which she soon made explicit by asking that he "rouse" himself "to some feeling of cooperation" (July 8, 1949, HRC).

This letter, which bears a reception date of May 31, 1949, was written in the week of May 22 in reply to Wood's recent correspondence.]

134. To Charles K. Feldman and Jerry Wald

[45 Via Aurora, Rome]
5/31/49
[TLx, 2 pp. U of Delaware]

Dear Mr. Feldman and Mr. Wald:

I am writing you jointly because I understand that you are jointly concerned as producers in the filming of my play, <u>The Glass Menagerie</u>,

and my subject is the present condition of the film-script which I have recently had the opportunity to read again.

I first saw an earlier version of this script in the summer of 1947, in Hollywood, and at that time I expressed to Mr. Feldman an agreeable surprise at the extent to which the material of the play had been kept in the screen version. I understood that this was an early, preliminary, draft of the screen-play and that it was still in a fluid state. My second reading of the screen-play, quite recently, was a good deal less agreeable for this is much closer to the date of actual shooting and I find that certain grave and important faults are still in the script and I think it is tremendously important, in every way, to everybody concerned, that these things should be eliminated before you shoot the picture and that some re-writing be done.

Let me say, before specific allusion to these defects, that I am only as concerned as I am because of my conviction, which I have always had very strongly, that this "property" has every chance of becoming a really great picture which would surpass its dimensions as a play. However the <u>basic</u> qualities of the play <u>must</u> be kept if it is going to come off successfully on the screen. The qualities that made it a successful play were primarily its true and fresh observation, its dignity, its poetry and pathos, for it had no great dramatic situations as a play nor has it any as a screen-play, and the story was slight and simple as it still is and must remain.

Now I feel that a great deal of the truth, dignity, poetry and pathos of this play has gone out the window, and this loss occurs through the insertion of certain little sequences and devices which can easily and quickly be cut out and replaced by something in keeping with the tone and quality of the play. I think you all know that I have no reputation of being "arty" or "highbrow", and that on the contrary I am known to be an exponent of sound and popular theatre which gets across to a large public, and nothing that I object to or suggest is going to hazard the popular acceptance of the screen-offering, but on the contrary, is especially intended to preserve and increase that appeal.

First of all, I specifically object to all the sequences involving "the other young man", the one who teaches art to the children and who provides "the happy ending". I object to him, first of all, because he is such a Sunday-school sissy of a character with no reality or interest, ~~a mouther of really indecently tired platitudes,~~ who brings to the story nothing but tedium and incredibility. He is a most palpable "device".

Now the whole play, in mood and quality, is keyed to the original type of ending and when something like this occurs, the poetry and the pathos so carefully built up in the preceding scenes are brought crashing to earth in splinters, and the final effect is one of bathos and sentimentality.

If the play had not been widely read, and seen in many parts of the country, where several companies have taken it on tour and presented it at little theatres, this distortion of its story and quality would not be so dangerous. But it is very well known, as a play, and all who liked or admired it as such will keenly resent the loss of its basic dignity on the screen, and reviewers will be likely to attack it.

The heartening message in the character of Laura is to those thousands of girls who do <u>not</u> find the dream-boy who sets everything magically right in the final sequence. This heartening message can be underscored and played up in the screen version without violating the essential meaning and truth of the play, and that is what I am appealing for in this letter. It is not a difficult (although very important) change to make, and although I am deep in other work and it is naturally pretty hard for me to revert to something I worked on five years ago, I will be happy to undertake these revisions provided that I have the assurance from you, the producers, that it is equally your will to make this a really true and dignified picture. I say that with hardly any doubt that it is so, for the work of Warner Brothers has hardly ever shown any lack of interest in these matters, but on the contrary has a high reputation for making honest pictures, and my acquaintance with Mr. Feldman, and the talks I had with him two years ago, indicated that he was also interested in making this a film of power and stature that would be creditable to us all.

Cordially,

[Charles Feldman (1904-1968) was an independent producer and Jerry Wald (1911-1962) a powerful supervisor at Warner Brothers with credits for such award-winning films as *Key Largo* (1948) and *Johnny Belinda* (1948).

The "sissy" who "teaches art to the children" was perhaps first encountered by Laura in an "artists' supply store" ("Italian Conference," June 27, 1949, HRC). Both scene and character—later identified as "Sterling"—were cut in revision of *The Glass Menagerie* script.]

135. To James "Jay" Laughlin

[45 Via Aurora, Rome]
<u>6/3/49</u>
[TLS, 2 pp. Houghton]

Dear Jay:

Many, many thanks for your letters. I am relieved that you are satisfied with the introduction to Carson's book. I had misgivings about it, and I still hope that you will let me have a look at the proofs before it goes into print. I was afraid, for one thing, that I might have written too much of a personal nature, and of course I was also a bit worried about the unavoidable comments on "imitators". I don't want to incur the wrath of Truman, which is probably worse than the wrath of God. I have not heard directly from Carson in a long time, not for about two months, but I have heard through Audrey that she has been in the South, is well, and that her play has been sold to the producers of Medea. I can't rejoice in that last bit of news for I am afraid that it may only bring her worry and grief, unless they pay her a good-sized advance to compensate for it.

Myself I have been terribly happy over some wonderful news about my sister. She is now out of the asylum for three days a week in the custody of an elderly couple in a pleasant country town in Missouri and Mother sent me five letters she had written expressing her great joy in the liberation. The letters were quite normal except that in one of them she sent her love to her offspring, of which of course she has none, but that seems a fairly harmless and comfortable delusion compared to the ones she used to suffer.

The story I mentioned has grown to the length of a novella, about 75 pages, and is still expanding, so I have neglected the play. This may turn out to be foolish of me but I don't seem to have any choice in the matter.

I cannot make up my mind about Book Find deal of selected writings. Sounds more like something to be done in the hypothetical future, but I would love very much to have a little volume of verse brought out that is all my own, with maybe a couple of stories for ballast. Is there any way we could print "Kingdom of Earth" or get it typed up? I am afraid the only copy may get lost. Do what you like about the Lawrence play. Perhaps it could be reserved to go with the eventual selection of poems and the stories: but dispose of it exactly as you think best.

Warners have sent a very stupid, commercial director over here to discuss the filming of "Menagerie" which they are now casting and will

start filming next Fall. The movie-script is a real abomination and I am raising hell about it, but perhaps quite helplessly as I have no legal control. The characters are all vulgarized, there is a ridiculous happy ending, the director has no taste or distinction, but they have rounded up a stunning array of actors, probably headed by Bette Davis and Jane Wyman, who recently won an Academy Award. Would you like to read a copy of the film-script just to see how awful they can be? Audrey could provide you with one. And do you think, since the play is really a dramatized memoir, I might sue them for libel if the characters are made too disgusting? The Mother, for instance, steals some money to bet on a race-horse! It is really worse than the proposed changes by Louis J. Singer. The director, Irving Rapper, is coming to see me for another conference at five o'clock, and the feathers will fly!

Paul and Jane Bowles are in Tangier. Lehmann in London is very happy over advance reactions to Paul's novel and I suspect it will make a real impression there. He now has the manuscript of Windham's novel which has been rejected by most of the big commercial publishers in the States.

Eyre de Lanux is a woman who was a great beauty, is now about 45 and I think she has recently had her face lifted while she was mysteriously away in Paris. She has a young Italian lover, a boy of 25, startlingly beautiful and the only real rascal that I have met in Italy. Her blind adoration of him is shocking! But quite understandable.

I have not yet located the painter (engraver?) you mentioned but I am sure I shall find him if he is still about Rome. The city is now at its loveliest, dangerously lovely for a person who should sit at home working all afternoon if he hopes to continue to get anywhere with his work.

Yours ever, 10.

Eyre's boy-friend, Paolo, recently brought her a two-year-old infant that he claims to be his bastard child and wants her to take care of it for him. It has no resemblance to him, it is obviously a trick of some kind. She has written a story about their "menage" as if it were being observed through the eyes of their cat. It is not yet good enough to send you, but perhaps the second draft will be.

[Carson McCullers later apologized for cutting a reference to a "bad-house" in TW's preface to *Reflections in a Golden Eye*. Her sister Rita Smith, fiction editor for *Mademoiselle*, had advised that it was "'too personal'" (n.d., Duke U), but McCullers invited TW to restore the passage if he wished.

Audrey Wood gave *The Member of the Wedding* (1950) to Robert Whitehead because of the producer's "taste" and "boldness" and anticipated sympathy for the author "on her first venture into playwriting" (Wood, *Represented by Audrey Wood*, 1981). Whitehead and Oliver Rea produced *Medea* in 1947.

TW would soon complete "an outline" of the "neglected" play, *The Rose Tattoo*, and seek the opinion of Wood and Elia Kazan.

James Laughlin's plan to join the Book Find Club—and its 30,000 members—in publishing an anthology of TW's writing did not materialize. Laughlin published special editions of "The Kingdom of Earth" (1954), a story which he considered "'clean dirt'" (to TW, December 18, 1948, Houghton), and "the Lawrence play" *I Rise in Flame, Cried the Phoenix* (1951).

John Lehmann issued Paul Bowles's first novel, *The Sheltering Sky* (1949), later in the fall. He was TW's English publisher and friend as well.

The painter and writer Elizabeth Eyre de Lanux was in her mid-fifties when she met TW in Rome. He later identified her as the model for Karen Stone in *The Roman Spring* and used details of her affair with the young writer Paolo Casagrande, as well as his given name. Laughlin's interest in de Lanux stems from a "charming little story" (to TW, May 25, 1949, Houghton) of hers which TW recommended for publication: "The Street of the Mouth-of-the Lion" (*New Directions Thirteen*, 1951).]

136. To Irene Mayer Selznick

[45 Via Aurora, Rome]
June 14, 1949.
[TLS, 1 p. Boston U]

Dear Irene:

I salute you with a fresh ribbon and I mean on the typewriter, not in my hair, although my curls are almost getting long enough to need one. But I believe you always liked me better when I needed a hair-cut.

We have been snowed under with American visitors. Most of them only pass through Rome and procede to Ischia where Capote and Auden are holding court, but we catch them both ways, going and coming, and are beginning to bend under the strain. Guess who is here right now? That's right! Little Maria. She arrived just as I was about to surrender the Roman field, so I am forced to remain a while longer to make some show of

hospitality. Of course I like seeing her, but at night I dream of the snowy solitude of the Dolomites, and I am sure it is not like the hills of Nebraska that the missionary in "Rain" dreamed about!

Irving Rapper was here to consult with me about the film-script for "Menagerie". I took quite a liking to him and perhaps we will be able to come to some fairly dignified compromise on the script. I read it again in Paris and was terribly shocked by the ending. I don't know why, but I didn't remember its being quite that bad, and in response to my howl of dismay, which reached Mr. Feldman by way of Audrey, they dispatched Rapper to pacify me. I rashly agreed to resume work on the film-script. Hate going back to it, but I couldn't let it be filmed that way without some effort to save it. I have been busy on that for the past couple of weeks. Unfortunately the only true ending was the one in the play, and the one I have now worked out, to satisfy their demand for "an up-beat", is the lesser of various evils - at best. They want me to come to Hollywood for further consultations in July, and Audrey wants me to come to New York the first of August to re-direct "Summer and Smoke" for the proposed road-tour sponsored by John Shubert. Both undertakings are important but the thought of returning to America before I have completed my work here is very alarming. It presents a dilemma. And then of course I feel that I may be wanted in England in August. "Yes is For a Very Young Man". I am too old to be saying yes so often when my anxious heart says no!

Maria is quite broken up over Poor Tom Heggen. I don't think she realized until his death that she cared for him so deeply, but now she is pensive and tearful a great deal of the time and one is obliged to treat her very gently. She appreciated your wire so much and speaks of you with great respect and fondness, which in my presence would be necessary anyhow.

Some very happy news from home. At long last my sister is having a change. She is under the special care of an elderly woman who takes her out of the sanitarium for three days of each week, and they have forwarded letters from Rose in which she expresses her great joy at this new arrangement. The letters are quite normal except that in one of them she sends "love to her off-spring" which is a bit of a surprise as we didn't know she had any. Perhaps the world of illusion isn't so bad. - How is Judith Evelyn, or is that too indiscreet a question? Frankie joins me in sending you love.

Love! - Tennessee.

[TW last saw Irene Selznick in London in early-May as plans for the English pro-duction of *Streetcar* were nearing completion. He and Vivien Leigh reportedly became "thick as thieves," while Laurence Olivier remained aloof and ominously "asked for freedom" to cut the play, which TW "gently refused" (Selznick, *A Private View*, 1983, pp. 322-323). A limited engagement of *Streetcar* was set to open in the following October.

"Little Maria" Britneva arrived in Rome on June 9 and found TW "very detached somehow, like something that is running down." She considered Frank Merlo "possessive and destructive of every relationship Ten has, which is bad, for an artist like Ten needs some impetus—happiness or unhappiness—not just the nervous reactions of a horse" (St. Just, pp. 19, 25). TW probably told Britneva of the "ugly, violent" (*Journal*, June 7, 1949) scenes with Merlo which preceded her arrival. Should they separate, TW foresaw that he "would go on living and enduring and I suppose turn him into a poem as I've done with others" (*Journal*, May/June 1949).

In Somerset Maugham's story "Rain" (1921), the missionary dreams of a prostitute whose breasts resemble the "hills of Nebraska." Maugham's once con-troversial story provided the tropical setting and the theme of religious hypocrisy for TW's first-known play, "Beauty is the Word" (1930/1984).

The recent death of Tom Heggen by drowning in a bathtub was ruled a probable suicide with the contributing cause an overdose of barbiturates. TW doubted the report, believing that Heggen, the young co-author of *Mister Roberts* (1948), "simply fell asleep" after careless use of drugs. TW attributed his death to the "shock of sudden fame" (*Journal*, May/June 1949), a lethal variety of his own "catastrophe of success." Britneva supplied the final ironic detail: Heggen "never took a bath!"

Selznick recently prevailed over Audrey Wood by hiring Judith Evelyn rather than Ruth Ford—Wood's client—to play Blanche in the national tour of *Streetcar*. TW appears to have enjoyed the battle of feminine wills, although Evelyn's difficult adjustment to the role supported Wood's position.]

137. To *Carson McCullers*

[45 Via Aurora, Rome]
6/18/49
[TLS, 1 p. Duke U]

Dearest Carson:

I am sorry there was such a long lapse in our correspondance. I have been away most of the time, London and Paris, as well as various places in Italy. And there has been an unbroken stream of arrivals from the States. I'm almost beginning to feel like the Mayor of Rome, except that I have no

golden key to offer, only an increasingly perfunctory sort of handshake and a hunted expression as I can seldom remember where I met them before, on Lexington avenue or Fire Island or Provincetown. Not that it makes much difference. One or two really good arrivals are expected, however: Oliver Evans is now crossing over and Donnie talks of coming later in the summer, and Maria Britneva is already here, a fugitive from London. Do you remember her? The little English girl who was much in evidence last Fall during the trial by "Summer". She is now here in Rome and I enjoy her company. She is full of a good kind of mischief. Most women hate her and few men know what to think of her. Last night she was arrested on suspicion of street-walking. She had strolled up into the park at two in the morning by herself. The cops fell in love with her, and bought her coffee in an all night cafe where the whores hang-out, and tried to make dates with her. Life here is full of little comedy denouements of that kind. I keep thinking how you would love it, and whenever I make a friend here I find myself wondering whether or not you would also like him or her, and I usually feel that you would. However I have a feeling that I will spend next year in the States. The Holy Year will make the town such a mess. They are already putting fig-leaves over the statues and forbidding white swimming-slips in the pools. I am thinking of Key West or San Francisco for next year, as New Orleans is still out of bounds due to the occupation by you-know-who. I have been working more lately, although the time is divided among poems and a novella and the play goes slowly. Really everything goes slowly in Rome, like old Father Tiber. Miss Buick has aged. Her rosey complexion has dimmed and her joints are creaking. She will have to be renovated, or open a tea-shop. Truman and Auden and Chester Coleman and various other of the spiteful sisterhood were all clustered on the little island of Ischia for several months but all at once there was some convulsion among them and they all came off at once. Truman and his paramour passed through town for a few days last week, Auden and Chester also at the same time. There was a great collision in the public rooms of the Inghilterra (hotel), all hissing and flapping like geese, and there are rumors that the island of Ischia has dropped back under the sea.

Frankie is sick. He has been running a high fever for several days with badly infected tonsils, has been on penicillin and sulfa and aspirin without much improvement, if any. I am worried about him, he is so quiet and pale and little-looking, all eyes and nose, like a baby sparrow, especially when

he has a chill, and I have no faith in the doctor. I have to go out now to find him a book, and pick up Maria before the cops get her again. Love to your mother and Rita and Reeves, and a whole lot to you. Be well and happy! I am delighted that you and Audrey have placed the play in good hands. And even happier about the new novel.

10

[Carson McCullers's preceding letter to TW ended with a plea, "Why why don't you write????" (n.d., Duke U).

"Holy Year," a time when special indulgences may be gained by the faithful, is observed every quarter-century by the Roman Catholic Church. Pilgrimage to Rome is a familiar part of the ancient ritual.

W.H. Auden and his companion Chester Kallman spent the summer of 1949 on the island of Ischia. Truman Capote has noted that Kallman "was extremely

Carson McCullers and director Harold Clurman examining the script of The Member of the Wedding *(1950): "I am delighted that you and Audrey have placed the play in good hands."*

rude to Tennessee and Frankie, and he made it a point not to invite them to their house. Tennessee was very hurt" (qtd. in Clarke, *Capote: A Biography*, p. 197).

TW's report of the "spiteful sisterhood" on Ischia amused McCullers, who also wondered how "Truman" had missed being "the flowergirl" (to TW, n.d., Duke U) at the recent wedding of Rita Hayworth and Prince Aly Kahn.

McCullers's "new novel" is *Clock Without Hands* (1961).]

138. To Justin Brooks Atkinson

[45 Via Aurora, Rome]
[mid-June 1949]
[TL, 1 p. HRC]

Dear Brooks:

Yesterday I got a letter from my friend Carson McCullers sending me a recent article of yours on Uta Hagen's performance in Streetcar, and I was deeply touched, as I have been often before, by your continuing interest in this old play of mine which must be tottering into a state of senesence although you write about it as if it were born yesterday.

I wrote you a long time, sometime last winter, but I didn't mail the letter, for I fell into a ridiculous state of gloom and apathy about that time, in which I felt almost as if it were presumptuous of me to maintain any contact with the outside world. Most of that feeling has worn off now, under the benign influence of the Roman sun, and the Romans, who are almost equally warm and golden. I have been through such cycles of depression before. As I grow older they seem to stay with me longer, but I am also better able to cope with them philosophically. I guess you can imagine, better than I can, what was the matter. The misfortune of "Summer" had some connection with it. I felt like a discredited old conjurer whose bag of tricks was exhausted. I had rough drafts of a couple of plays but lacked the confidence to go on with them as soon as I left the artificial exhileration of Manhattan. When my confidence began to return a little, I worked on poems and a novella, but have only just lately gotten seriously back to work on a play, and still can't say how soon it will be completed and still am not sure it is different enough from the others to be immune from the charge that my work is repetitive. The trouble is that you can't make any real philosophical progress in a couple of years. The scope of understanding enlarges quite slowly, if it enlarges at all, and the scope of

interest seems to wait upon understanding. In the meantime there is only continued observation, and variations on what you've already observed. I have noticed that painters and poets, and in fact all artists who work from the inside out, have all the same problem: they cannot make sudden, arbitrary changes of matter and treatment until the inner man is ripe for it. The blue period changes gradually to the rose, and of course there are some poets who never stop writing sonnets, and if their readers get weary of it, no one is to blame. The great challenge is keeping alive and growing as much as you can; and let the chips fall where they may!

[Brooks Atkinson declined to compare Jessica Tandy and Uta Hagen after Hagen assumed the role of Blanche on June 1. Her performance was "enlightened and exciting" and "thoroughly her own." Atkinson praised TW's "steel-like accuracy as a writer" once again and opined that *Streetcar* was still "one of the most glowing achievements of the Broadway theatre" (*New York Times*, June 12, 1949).

The unsigned typescript, unfolded and doubtless unmailed, was written in mid-June 1949 at the time of TW's preceding letter to Carson McCullers.]

139. To Audrey Wood

[45 Via Aurora, Rome]
6/21/49
[TLS w/ enclosure, 1 p. HRC]
Dear Audrey:

I am sending you herewith an outline of the long play on which I've been working off and on in Italy. I have kept a carbon of it which I may show to Gadge but would not have anybody else see it. So far I have not devoted myself to it at all consistently but I am leaving for a week or two in the northern lake country of Italy and am hoping that the change of climate will speed me up. Lack of physical energy has been a great detriment here, and if I push myself, I get hypertensive. That is one of the reasons I have been hesitant about committing myself to direct "Summer and Smoke" in New York. I seriously doubt that I would have the great physical endurance that sort of work calls for: that is, the long hours and strenuous final rehearsals. If I had a very good stage manager, of my own choice who could take over rehearsals when I was tired - then it would be feasible. Otherwise I doubt that the cost in energy would be worth while. Also I feel it would be foolish to put it on without a first rate cast. Someone better than Todd in the male part and

almost as good as Maggie for the girl. Would there be any, even the remotest, chance of interesting Marlon in the boy's part for a very limited engagement? And how about asking Mary Hunter to direct?

Arthur Miller and his wife are in town. We spent last evening with them and I am taking them out to dinner tonight. They are a lovely couple: he is so warm and honest a person one can hardly believe that he was ever on Broadway or in Hollywood. I mean he still seems quite innocent. Gadge is supposed to be here, or almost here, but so far no sign of it. I ran into John Garfield at a dancing place a couple of nights ago and he is all steamed up about the Streetcar picture deal. I have not yet studied it out completely but I have an idea that a Kazan picture would be a sure thing. There is no real need to worry about censorship as rape has been handled in "Johnny Belinda" and the slight alteration of a few lines ought to take care of the other angle. Oh, well. I will read Colton's letter again. Then try to make up my mind about it all. - Could you get Feldman-Rapper to engage Windham for the "Menagerie" movie script? He needs the money and I think he'd do a fine job.

Love, 10.

[The enclosed "outline" describes the basic argument of *The Rose Tattoo*: a middle-aged widow (Pepina) who idolizes her late husband (Rosario), the disclosure of his unfaithfulness by two spiteful female "clowns," and the appearance of a lover (Umberto) to break the spell of the past. The ardent love of Pepina's daughter (Rose) for a young sailor (Jack) forms a subplot which "develops into a mighty clash between mother and daughter" (Stornello, June 21, 1949, HRC). The play is set in a fishing village on the Gulf Coast and deals primarily with characters of Sicilian descent—TW's "Terra Trema" perhaps. The outline was also mailed to Elia Kazan, as following correspondence reveals.

John Shubert was now dealing directly with Margo Jones in planning the tour of *Summer and Smoke*. Audrey Wood advised TW of this "completely Shubertian" tactic and hoped that "Jones would {not} be fool enough" (July 8, 1949, HRC) to disregard their wish to revamp the cast.

Kazan offered to produce *Streetcar* in association with an independent film company linked to his friend John Garfield. The deal would require that Garfield "play the lead." At this time Kazan considered making the film without Production Code approval in order to retain the "integrity" (Colton to TW, May 6, 1949, HRC) of the play.

TW naively assumed that the rape scene in *Streetcar* and Allan Grey's homosexuality—the "other angle"—would meet little or no resistance from the censor. A

menacing score and severe lighting and shadow were used to suggest the impending rape in *Johnny Belinda*. Jane Wyman won an Academy Award for her role as a vulnerable young woman without speech or hearing who is raped and later exonerated for killing her attacker.

TW's recommendation of Donald Windham as screenwriter for *The Glass Menagerie* was belated, wishful thinking.]

140. To Molly and Elia "Gadge" Kazan

[45 Via Aurora, Rome]
7/12/49
[TLS w/ autograph marginalia, 2 pp. WUCA]

Dear Molly and Gadge:

I thank and love you both for the honesty of your letters and for the trouble you took to write them as you did when it would have been so much easier, I know, to have just been vague and nice about it. Fortunately I had already done some pretty brutal stock-taking of my self and accomplishments, or rather lack of them, on my trip through the lake country and by the time I got back to Rome, yesterday, the vapors of illusion were pretty thoroughly dispelled. So the letters were really only a confirmation, but one that was helpful. It is so good to be able to talk honestly with somebody about my dilemma as a writer! The simple truth is that I haven't known where to go since Streetcar. Everything that isn't an arbitrary, and consequently uninspired, experiment seems to be only an echo. This was true last year in Rome when I started and gave up at least four plays. When I went back to the States I seemed to be finding my way out of the predicament and I worked on a new play there, about a southern demagogue and with a social emphasis, which I thought I was seriously interested in and would push through to completion. But no sooner did I sail out of New York than my interest in it dissolved. I couldn't convince myself that I cared enough about the character and ideas involved to put any fire into the writing. Then I began to be badly frightened, and as always happens under that condition, I lost my objectivity. I wandered into work on "Stornello" simply because it seemed to demand so much less of me. It would have been more sensible to stop working, and just wait, with the hope that there would be a resurgence of energy that would allow me to continue the stronger themes that I had undertaken before I became so devitalized. But

to wait is hard, when there is much uncertainty, so I began to work again without really having the power. You will be glad to hear, though, that I hadn't gone very deep into this work, not even to a point where it would be difficult to give it up, and now that the whole problem has come to a head, and there is no more possibility of delusion and evasion, I feel strangely much calmer and less anxious about it. A good deal of that came to me through your letters, the very palpable sincerity of them, the lack of any crap of a comforting nature which really would have bothered me, and at the same time the feeling that you definitely cared. I doubt that anybody else, even Audrey, could have written me in quite that way about it. I don't need to tell you that the synopsis was not a real picture of the play that I had in mind. My efforts to make it sound lively made it sound cheap, but in the character of Pepina there was a lostness which I could feel and write about with reality, and would have, if I wrote it. The trouble was that I had already written so much about the same thing. In many ways writing is the most perilous and ephemeral of the talents, and you never know whether an impasse is only temporary or final, and the only real help lies in honesty with yourself and from others and keeping alive your interest in life itself.

To divert to the somewhat less serious topic of the picture. I have a long and confusing letter from Irene and a cable that apparently has some sort of connection with it. She is thinking in terms of Lillian Hellman and a script that will pass the Hays office, and while there is no direct reference to the terms of a sale, there are indications that she feels it would be foolishly Quixotic of her not to take advantage of a declining market. God knows I see her point about that, but it increases my longing to work out some kind of deal with you for the picture to be made honestly and at the same time to assure myself a few years of security in which to try to work out the various problems with which I am beset. A cable from Audrey makes no mention of Irene's project but demands my opinion of your offer which I had already given in the cable before I saw you in Rome. Is there any way you could acquire the rights by placing in - I believe "escrow" is the word - a down payment of forty or fifty thousand to be paid in ten thousand installments over a period of four or five years? And the rest of the payment to be a speculation upon the success of the picture, which I would be very happy to make if it were placed in your hands. You see why I couldn't get the whole payment at once and why, at the same time, I need the assurance that that much money would be definitely forthcoming. All

this is pure improvisation on my part, as I have not been in communication with Audrey or anyone else since the letter I showed you in Rome. I also sent Audrey a copy of the play synopsis, and perhaps that has stunned her into silence.

I have a feeling that Muni will come through with a fine performance for you, as I remember how strong he used to be in such early pictures as Scarface. You can bring him back to the surface.

With love, Tenn.

[TW's gloomy analysis of post-*Streetcar* writing includes "The Big Time Operators"—the "southern demagogue" play—as well as other works undertaken and presumably discarded.

Irene Selznick confidentially obtained a Production Code report which banned "sex perversion" in *Streetcar* and labeled the rape scene "unacceptable" because it "goes unpunished" (Breen to Paramount Pictures, June 27, 1949, Herrick). She swore TW to secrecy and explained that "in an effort to prevent a sale," the censor was often "much tougher before a property is sold" (July 1, 1949, Boston U).

Selznick also informed TW that she had hired Lillian Hellman to devise a strategy whereby *Streetcar* could "meet the Code and yet not lose substance" (July 1, 1949, Boston U). Hellman reported that omitting the "homosexual story" and the rape "need not fundamentally change" the play. The reason for Allan Grey's suicide might plausibly be obscured by Blanche's lack of knowledge or by her refusal to face the unpleasant truth. Blanche's capacity for self-deception could also be used to treat the rape as mere illusion (n.d., Irene Mayer Selznick Collection, Boston U).

Elia Kazan was apparently not involved in the production or funding of the *Streetcar* film.

Penned in the upper margin is TW's mailing address, "American Express, Rome."]

141. To Irving Rapper

[45 Via Aurora, Rome]
August 5, 1949.
[TLx, 1 p. HRC]

Dear Irving:

Here is the warehouse sequence. I am not enclosing picnic material because I hope that we may decide to eliminate it when we get together in California. It strikes me as a needless interruption of the continuity and it complicates the production without adding anything of material value to

the story, since we have already agreed that it is better to reserve the announcement of the coming caller for the fire-escape scene between mother and son, as it was done on the stage. The picnic and the rainstorm could have a certain picturesque pathos, but I am wondering, now, if we don't have enough background material without it, and also enough footage, and the inclusion of a picnic would, I should think, considerably add to the budget. Think and talk this over with Jerry Wald and wire me your reaction. I think you may now have sufficiently complete material to assess a budget and prepare a preliminary shooting-script. I don't imagine a final shooting-script is possible till after our California conferences.

I have introduced Jim in the warehouse, which was something we had agreed to consider. As I worked on the script it appeared more and more desirable to me to make this introduction here, to establish him as a character before he appears for the "big scene".

Irving, I don't know what to say about the ending. It really stumped me for quite a while and that is what held up my work on the script so much longer than I had expected. Your cable indicates a dissatisfaction with the ending that I submitted, but I wish that you could comment on it more specifically so that I could tell in what direction you feel it is wrong. Is it too much, or too little? It is certainly not a product of great inspiration! Even so, however, I feel it is a vast improvement on "The Sterling Character". My own difficulty is that in my heart the ending as it exists in the play was the artistically inevitable ending. While I assent to a new one, my heart belongs to the old one. Now I am not welching on our agreement to look for an up-beat, and I am not going to welch on it. I would be very grateful, though, for a repeated assurance from you and Jerry that there will be no pressure to reinstate "Sterling" or that kind of fairy-tale ending which we agreed would sacrifice the play's integrity. I think it is all right to suggest the possibility of "someone else coming". And that "someone else" remaining as insubstantial as an approaching shadow in the alley which appears in conjunction with the narrative line "The long delayed but always expected something that we live for" - it strikes me as constituting a sufficiently hopeful possibility for the future, symbolically and even literally, which is about as much as the essential character of the story will admit without violation. As you say we will undoubtedly find a solution in California, but it would add to my peace of mind if you could assure me now that there has been no reversion of opinion in favor of the old type of

ending. When the film comes to life I am sure we will all be surprised at how very little, how much less than we supposed, was needed to give the little anti-depressant we feel is called for.

Ever,

[Irving Rapper (1898-1999) directed Bette Davis in such notable Warner Brothers films as *Now, Voyager* (1942), *The Corn Is Green* (1945), and *Desperation* (1946). Friendship with Davis, a strong candidate to play Amanda at this time, may have influenced Rapper's appointment to direct *The Glass Menagerie*.

The "warehouse sequence" is one of several scenes written to add range and variety to the restricted setting of *The Glass Menagerie*. The "picnic material"—cut as TW advised—was also intended to diversify the film and to underscore the bleakness of the Wingfield apartment, to which the "sodden and dispirited" ("Italian Conference," June 27, 1949, HRC) family returns after the storm. The "announcement" of a gentleman caller was reserved for the "fire-escape scene" with Amanda and Tom which immediately follows.]

142. To James "Jay" Laughlin

[45 Via Aurora, Rome]
8/17/49.
[TLS w/ enclosures, 2 pp. Houghton]

Dear Jay:

Whatever decision you and Carson reach about the two prefaces is O.K. with me. My feeling was, when I read over the first version, that I appeared in that version to be talking too much about myself. If you revert to that original version I hope that you will preserve the cuts that I have made in it, particularly the long portion about "imitators". I believe that I scratched out (in the returned proofs) all but about two sentences of that material which was provoked mainly by a personal antagonism for Truman which I think should not be indulged in this place. I also wish you would compare the two versions very carefully, again, and perhaps something from the second, which I still believe had a great deal more dignity in keeping with the novel, could be appended or worked into the other.

I received yesterday a long letter from Carson, most depressing. "Health has failed steadily - can't walk more than half a block - neuritis has set in - damaged nerves constantly spastic - dreadful headache - nausea, prostration - a gland went wrong in the neck - prolonged suffering - a sort of

convulsion at dawn . . ." It sounds almost fantastic! Surely she has not been given any really intelligent diagnosis or therapy. I think she should be hospitalized for several months and exhaustively examined from every angle, physiological, emotional, Etc. Of course there needs to be a special branch of medicine for the understanding and treatment of such hypersensitive artists, but since they practically never have any money, they are simply condemned. I dread the play production that she is now facing as her emotional involvement is certain to be great. Clurman is a fine director for it, but when I last saw the script it was far from being in a state to produce.

I am sailing out of Naples on the twentieth, the crossing takes ten days, and must go directly to Hollywood when I land. My work on the movie script is practically complete but they are not yet satisfied with the ending and I think I shall have a fight with them about that. They say they don't want a fairy-tale ending but there is evidence of double-talk. At least I should learn something more about the technique of film-making which I can use creatively on some other assignment perhaps over here. I am on excellent terms with Rossollini and De Sica and Visconti and would enjoy working with any one of them. Last week had supper with Ingrid Bergman and Rossolini. Their "Fuck you" attitude toward the outraged women's clubs and sob-columnists is very beautiful and should have a salutary affect on discrediting those infantile moralists that make it so hard for anyone to do honest work and live honestly in the States. If Bergman has the moral courage she appears to have, it will be a triumph.

Several weeks ago I sent you two long poems, The Soft City and Counsel, which you haven't mentioned receiving. If you hate them, for God's sake Jay, don't hesitate to say so! I depend so much on your critical opinion as there are times when my own seems to fail me. I lose objectivity about my work, as everyone does at times, but you know that I am not morbidly sensitive to adverse opinion, but on the contrary, I am grateful for it. I showed Kazan and his wife a long synopsis of the play I had been working on. They both wrote me from London of their disappointment in it quite frankly and while I felt that the synopsis had not conveyed a true idea of the play as it existed in my conception, their criticism will be helpful when I go back to work on it, if I do. Whatever I do badly (even if it is everything!) I want to know, I want to be told! Honesty about failure is the only help for it.

I am enclosing two versions, first and second draft, of another poem. I

don't know which is the better or worse. Also the other ending to the Lawrence play. ~~I wonder if it would not be better to change Brett's name in the play to something like Brady, since the incident is fictitious and she might object. I don't believe Frieda would~~.

It is dreadful to leave here, but I have thrown a coin in the Fountain of Trevi.

Ever, 10

[TW recently drafted a second preface for *Reflections in a Golden Eye* and entrusted the final editing to James Laughlin. Neither personal elements nor a lengthy reference to "'imitators'" would appear in the published version, but TW probably annoyed Truman Capote by referring to "derivative talents" and Gore Vidal by ridiculing the "idea that a good novelist turns out a book once a year."

The affair of Ingrid Bergman and Roberto Rossellini during the filming of *Stromboli* (1949) caused an international scandal which forced Bergman to live and work in Europe until the mid 1950s. She divorced her Swedish husband to marry Rossellini and legitimize their unborn son.

"The Soft City" and "Counsel," poems by TW, first appeared in *New Directions Eleven* (1949).

The limited and the acting editions of *I Rise in Flame, Cried the Phoenix* (1951 and 1952, respectively) differ only in their staging of D.H. Lawrence's death—the later version briefer and less harrowing. In both editions the painter Dorothy Brett is renamed Bertha and cast as an officious disciple of Lawrence.]

143. To Frederic "Fritz" Prokosch

[Saturnia]
[late-August 1949]
[TLS, 1 p. Columbia U]

Dear Fritz:

Last year you gave me a copy of your book, <u>The Asiatics</u>, but I have only just now read it, while crossing back to the States, and I want you to know that I think it a great, an extraordinarily great, book, jewelled with wonderful images, with a wild and beautiful sort of freedom, almost anarchy, about it which I had certainly not expected, not even from your poetry, fine as that is but generally, maybe only because it is a shorter form, more subject to order. It has a feeling of freedom from usual form such as I remember finding only in Kafka or Joyce but it differs in richness of sensuosity, in pure luxury, from both of those writers. It is quite marvelous the way it surges along,

breaking, foaming, and then continuing like a wave washing right over its shores, a sense of flow, continual passage, richness, excitement unlike any other piece of writing I've known. I am still reading it, have not yet finished, but wanted to let you know immediately, though this letter may not reach you for quite a while, how very much it has moved me.

Ever, Tennessee.

[TW and Frank Merlo boarded the *Saturnia* in Naples and were due to arrive in New York on August 30.

Frederic Prokosch (1906-1989) has recalled talking "about love" with his "sad-eyed friend Tennessee Williams" (Prokosch, *Voices*, 1983, p. 253), whom he met in Rome in 1948. Prokosch held a doctorate in literature from Yale, but the popular and critical success of *The Asiatics* (1935) had released him from an unwanted academic career. The book's vivid setting, which reaches from Syria to China, was surprisingly based upon written sources rather than firsthand experience.

TW cabled Margo Jones from the *Saturnia* with a gibe about the forthcoming production of *Summer and Smoke*: "Suggest change title to August Madness" (August 25, 1949, Dallas Public Library).]

144. To Walter Edwin Dakin, Edwina Dakin and Walter Dakin Williams

SH: Hotel Bel-Air
701 Stone Canyon Road
Los Angeles 24 [California]
[early-September 1949]
[TLS, 2 pp. Columbia U]

Dear Grandfather, Mother & Dakin:

I am addressing you in order of seniority this time. Am living here in great luxury at the expense of Warner Bros. They have put me in a de luxe three-room suite. Swimming pool right outside the door, and have provided me with a Buick convertible since my own is stored in New York. Our relations have been very agreeable. We seem to be in complete agreement about the script. The vulgarities have been eliminated. I have re-written the whole thing according to my own ideas and I now think it has a chance to be a very successful picture. I have not yet made any definite plans but I intend to stay in America through the winter. They are planning to go to Saint

Louis to make some locations shots for the film. I will probably visit home at that time, which may be late this month or early October. It now seems definite that Gertrude Lawrence will play Amanda. I saw her test and it was amazingly good.

Don't know yet where I shall settle for winter. But I do plan to spend some time in Key West and I want Grandfather to join me there. I can pick him up in Saint Louis and we can drive down in my car. I sent Rose a box from New York. It contained a lovely compact and Roman scarf which I had bought in Italy, and a ten dollar bill. Let me know if she received it. This Saturday the producers are giving a formal party for me, and they say practically all of Hollywood will be there! Let me hear from you, care of Audrey. Oh - I signed the trust papers for Rose. As Summer and Smoke has re-opened in Chicago. I don't know, yet, how it is doing but the notices were better than it got in New York.   Love,

Tom.

[Finding an "'up-beat' for Laura at the end" (to Wood, July 29, 1949, HRC) of *The Glass Menagerie* proved TW's greatest difficulty in revising the screenplay. Before leaving Hollywood in late-September, TW completed a script which he naively thought final.

Bette Davis and Tallulah Bankhead tested for the role of Amanda, but it was the London-born Gertrude Lawrence, whose fame lay in stage musicals, who won the part. TW's endorsement of Lawrence—perhaps for benefit of family—belied his final verdict that her casting was "'a dismal error'" (qtd. in Morley, *Gertrude Lawrence*, 1981, p. 181).

The tour of *Summer and Smoke* opened in Chicago (September 5, 1949) to "better" reviews, although they were qualified and still mindful of *Streetcar*. Margo Jones's use of three actors rejected by TW led to a "big row" with Audrey Wood, who regretted that "legal technicalities" (to TW, August 22, 1949, HRC) forbade closing the show. Chicago reviewers admired the cast, including the disputed leads Tod Andrews and Katharine Balfour. TW later declared the production "a poor travesty of what it should have been" (qtd. in St. Just, p. 27).

Composition of this letter falls between TW's arrival in Los Angeles on September 5, 1949, and the "formal party" given in his honor on the 10th. The party, he observed, was "like a wet dream of Louella Parson's." He received his "first solid gold cigarette case" and saw his name "in blue letters in an illuminated block of ice!" (to Kazan, n.d., WUCA).]

145. *To Irene Mayer Selznick*

Western Union
New York
1949 Oct 12 PM 9 40
[Telegram, 1 p. Boston U]

PLEASE RELEASE YOUR BREATH DARLING DONT WANT YOU TO SUFFFO-
CATE BEFORE THE SHOW STARTS MUCH MUCH LOVE AND THANKS=

=TENNESSEE=

[Irene Selznick anxiously protected *Streetcar* as it was recast and reshaped by
Laurence Olivier for production in London. Olivier relieved the tension by writing
a detailed letter to TW in which he attributed many of the cuts to the special needs
of an English audience. "Deeply touched" by the gesture, TW cabled approval of
the revised script and regretted not having worked "more closely" (October 3,
1949, HRC) with the director.

   Streetcar opened at the Aldwych Theatre on October 12, 1949, drawing a
large, unruly crowd and causing intense public criticism of the play's "sooty"
subject matter and style. Vivien Leigh's Blanche won raves and played to full houses
for 326 performances.]

146. *To Paul Bowles*

1431 Duncan Street
Key West [Florida]
Nov. 19, 1949
[TLS w/ autograph marginalia, 1 p. HRC]

Dear Paul:

   We are very distressed to hear of your liver attacks and trust you are
now entirely recovered from them. Only you would declare the food in
England to be magnificent, just out of pure perversity I am sure, and
because you have been eating dried goat-meat in Morocco, which is
probably why you came down with a liver condition.

   I wish I had some good news to give you about the Menagerie music.
All I can definitely say is that we made a great effort. Played the records
for Jerry Wald and gave a set of them to Ann Warner who is Jack Warner's
exceedingly tiresome but good natured wife. What came of it all I have not
yet discovered. My communications since leaving Hollywood have been
more and more disturbing. Midnight telephones and wires, saying please

give us a little more up-beat at the end. Write scene between Laura and Tom after his departure to sea. Etc. No allusion to music and I have been either too sleepy or exasperated to think of it. There was nothing more to be done and yes is the most ambiguous word that you can get out of them. I shall have Audrey investigate again. You may be sure if they don't use your music it is simply because they are too stingy and the music too good. They only like music that goes Blah-blah-blah like a Brahms symphony by Irving Berlin, and always swelling to great inspirational crescendos.

There has been great excitement over your book in New York, especially the reviews, in which I am involved. Harvey Breit of the New York Times called me up and asked if I would review it. I said, Yes, indeedy, pie! He said 600 words. I said I could not be limited to that small a notice as I felt the book required a full page. We compromised on about 900, I believe. Gore was in my room when the call was received and took a great interest and I believe he is trying to get permission to review it for one of the other papers. Had no luck with the Trib and was going to try the Sat. Lit. when I pulled out of New York. I accused him, very unkindly and/or unjustly, of bitching up my notice. The day after I turned it in, and it was received very favorably by Breit, Gore had an interview with Breit in which the notice was discussed and read and the next day Breit called me back saying the publication of the notice was dubious and that a whole page had to be cut out which was the most pertinent part of it. First I blew up and said, Send it back, don't cut a word. Then I began to suspect a nigger in the wood-pile, meaning none other than G.V., so I called back and said I was willing to make a few deletions if necessary. It seems Gore had mentioned that the Trib wouldn't let him review the book because he was a friend of yours and Breit was now worried that there might be an objection about me, also, being your friend. Well, I accused Vidal to his face, of manipulation, and he was quite hurt and I now think that I was being unfair about it and owe him an apology. Today I got the proofs of the notice and it is almost as it was originally except they cut out a very lyrical last sentence about "time". It is a very favorable notice, of course, and I hope you will like it.

Tenn.

[TW, Frank Merlo, and Walter Dakin arrived in Key West ca. November 12. Dakin had flown from St. Louis to Jacksonville, where he was met and driven to the island which TW first visited in 1941.

"For purely personal reasons" (to TW, August 30, 1949, HRC)—an inveterate poverty—Paul Bowles asked that the "Menagerie music" which he composed for Broadway be used in the forthcoming film. Max Steiner eventually wrote a new score.

Reviewing the American edition of *The Sheltering Sky* (1949) allowed TW to belittle Gore Vidal and Truman Capote once again. He contrasted their "frisky antics" (*New York Times*, December 4, 1949, sec. 7, p. 7) in the preceding literary season with Bowles's masterly first novel, issued in the writer's thirty-eighth year. Vidal later denied any influence with the *New York Times* and attributed TW's "gratuitous swipe" to jealousy caused by his own history as "a late starter" (Vidal, *Palimpsest*, 1995, pp. 185-186).

Penned in the upper margin is the notation "We, Frank, Grandfather, and I, have taken this house in Key West for the winter & early spring. A new young writer, the rage of fashionable arty circles, named Speed Lamkin is also here. They call him the 'new Capote'. I thought the old one sufficient. Love - 10. (to Janie, too)."]

147. To Audrey Wood

[1431 Duncan Street
Key West, Florida]
11/?/49
[TLS, 1 p. HRC]

Dear Audrey:

I have not written you since getting here as I have been as preoccupied with the pleasures of living as the Madwoman of Chaillot. Every day has been like one of those sentimental ballads of Irving Berlin, blue skies, cottage small, sunshine and so forth. The little house is lovely, it is what they call a Bahama type house, white frame with a white picket fence and pink shutters. There are three bedrooms, a big combination living and dining room, two baths and a kitchen. Frank and I have moved to the upstairs room as the extremely loud conversations between Grandfather and the colored maid, Charleso Marie, make sleep impossible on the same floor level. Even earlier the roosters wake us up, but after the celebration of daybreak it is possible to get back to sleep. Next door is a magnificent black goat with big yellow eyes, surely one of God's most beautiful creatures, always straining at his rope as if he had an important errand to run if he could get loose. Only one block further is Speed Lamkin whom you may know or know of, sometimes referred to as the new Truman Capote. He doesn't write as well but is more agreeable. He is dissatisfied with Kay Brown because he wants to get a Hollywood job and she had not secured

one for him and wants to know if you could. Today he leaves for his home in Monroe, La., but Bigelow now occupying his New York apartment can give you all information.

President Truman and family arrived here today. Grandfather and Frank went down to see them pass along Duval street. Grandfather said that the President waved but he wasn't sure if it was at him or the crowd.

I share your concern about the King's Men. However I have not yet returned to work on the machine-boss play. Instead I rewrote the beginning of Stornello and about 40 pages of another novella. I think I will finish these items first, and in the meantime perhaps King's Men will come here or to Miami and I can see if there is too much resemblance. I am reducing Stornello to a minimal length so that it could be done on a double-bill with another longish short play like Camino Real, provided that Kazan can be coaxed into such a venture. This is not a very ambitious project but perhaps more reasonable, like placing your chips on odd or even rather than on one particular number. But the work goes much better here, so well that I have broken down the portable, now at the repair-shop, and have hired an upright machine. Did you get all the Camino revisions? There should be a new ending to Block 3, a new Block 5, and a new beginning to Block 8. Is there a chance, you think, of interesting Gene Kelly? There would also be a good part for him, as a sailor, in Stornello. Pepina and the Gypsy could be played by the same character actress. The Gypsy's daughter and Pepina's daughter could also be performed by one ingenue. Last week I also had to do a re-write on the opening narration for "Menagerie" as Jerry Wald wired me that they had changed their plans and wanted Tom on a ship. I hope they don't decide, now, to put Amanda on skates. I am very pleased over the sale to "Flair" and the amazing price received for it. You are very clever. But what has Bigelow done with poor Mrs. Stone?

Frank is going to New York, or more exactly, New Jersey, for Xmas but Grandfather and I have not yet steeled ourselves to the point of going home for the holidays. Perhaps we'll stay here. With love -

10.

[The "magnificent black goat" would soon appear in *The Rose Tattoo* as one of the play's comic effects.

A reviewer of Speed Lamkin's second novel, *The Easter Egg Hunt* (1954), mocked the "literary overtones of other writers, other books" (*New York Times*, March 7, 1954), and dispatched "the new Truman Capote."

The naval station in Key West served as a winter White House for the Truman administration. The arrival of the First Family on November 28, 1949, sets the date of this letter's composition.

The recent film premiere of *All the King's Men* (1949) raised or renewed "concern" about the originality of TW's "machine-boss" play, "The Big Time Operators."

Plans for a "double-bill" derive from TW's recent visit to the Actors Studio where Elia Kazan was rehearsing scenes from "Ten Blocks on the Camino Real" (1948): "'Oh, Kazan, we must do this. We must do this with one other play maybe, for Broadway'" (*Memoirs*, p. 165). The "Camino revisions" undertaken by TW were dated January 1950 and the project subsequently noted in the *New York Times* as set for a summer tryout. Kazan labeled the report "chatter and hopes" (to Wood, n.d., HRC) and delayed further work on the project "till spring" (to TW, n.d., HRC) when his latest film, *Panic in the Streets* (1950), would be complete.

The Glass Menagerie opens with a new prologue delivered by Arthur Kennedy—who plays Tom Wingfield—from the deck of a merchant ship.

"The Resemblance Between a Violin Case and a Coffin" (1950) appeared in the first number of *Flair* and brought the "amazing" sum of $750. So upset was Cornelius by TW's autobiographical story—in which he was termed "devilish"—that he issued a warning to Audrey Wood: "If he ever refers to my sisters or me in any of his writing I will make him regret it as long as he lives" (February 8, 1950, HRC).]

148. To Paul Bigelow

1431 Duncan
("The Annex")
[Key West, Florida]
12/4/49
[TLS w/ enclosure, autograph marginalia
and postscript, 1 p. Columbia U]

Dear Paul:

The Chief is in error. I swear by all that is holy, he give me the turquoise, he give me the goddam belt! Can I help it that Indians can't hold liquor? I took your advice about moving off the top floor. Told the Madam the tin roof made it too hot, so she put me downstairs in the basement. Much cooler. Trouble is the fucking janitor is absent-minded and locks the trap-door on me and the girls make so much noise they can't hear me holler. Tore my pink chiffon climbing out the coal-chute. But it is wonderful how the old styles are coming back, my Clara Bow hair-do, my kiss-me-quicks, and my low cut beaded gowns. And, honey, the Charleston has returned

and the Black Bottom is right around the corner. I always make an entrance when they play "Five Foot Two, Eyes of blue", and it's like you always said, Honey, vivacity goes a long way even when a girl is surrounded by jealous cats!

Speed has pulled out. He says his mother ordered him home but I wonder if that is why. He had got himself on the shit-list of the local queens by snatching off the one really butch sailor at a party they gave - about 10 minutes after he got there. He was doing a lot of work but in other respects I don't think the place quite suited him, as Speed, say what he will, gets a lot of bang out of smart society, God bless him. I don't blame him a bit, as who doesn't? I got to be very fond of him and will miss him a great deal. He has invited me to Monroe at Xmas. Grandfather and I may go to New Orleans about that time so I might drop up there for a day or so. I doubt, however, that I will be ready to go all the way to New York.

Working very hard here, and I think pretty well. Did 40 pages of a new novella and several scenes of an old play that I brought back from Italy are re-written. The new novella is my first attempt at an extended piece of humor in prose. It is a fantastic satire on a southern town that has become the seat of "A Project". (military, not theatrical, but otherwise not unlike the famous "Jones Project") However I must finish a play first.

Do let me see yours soon as you get a draft of it. I have such hopes for it. Must get out, now, to the beach. A girl makes her best contacts in the afternoon when she can see what she's doing. Frank is now happy here, Grandfather even more so. Hope you will find a chance to visit us after Xmas.

Love, 10

P.S. Am enclosing letter for Speed, urgent, don't have his address.

[TW appeared as a courtesan rather than a common whore in a similar campy spoof which Paul Bigelow received from Mexico City in 1945: "I made a brief appearance at the opera last night with 2 generals and 6 duennas but in spite of most discreet behavior on my part, there has been a wave of suicides and duels and every time I go out my carriage is drawn home by students" (postcard, June 8, 1945, Massee Collection). The whorehouse with a "tin roof" recalls a similar off-stage setting in *The Rose Tattoo* named the "Square Roof."

"The Knightly Quest" was finished in 1965 and published by New Directions the following year. The fictional "southern town" is based upon Macon, Georgia, where TW and Bigelow spent the summer of 1942. Fear of spies, heightened by the

Tennessee Williams and Grandfather Dakin, Key West:
"Must get out, now, to the beach."

presence of a nearby defense industry, led wary citizens to report them to the police as "'suspicious characters.'" After being detained and questioned, TW wrote presciently in the journal, "Macon swell background" (July 3, 1942). The "'Jones Project'" refers to a British scientific unit headed by the physicist R.V. Jones. He was decorated by President Truman for wartime research deemed critical in the use of radar.

Paul Bigelow's play, variously entitled "A Woman Who Came From a Boat" and "A Theme For Reason," has not been performed or published.

Penned in the lower margin is a reference to *The Rose Tattoo*, "finished first complete draft today!"]

149. To Carson McCullers

1431 Duncan
Key West [Florida]
12/6/49
[TLS w/ autograph marginalia, 1 p. Duke U]

Carson dear:

We are very, very happily situated here in a little white frame cottage, a sort of Tom Thumb house, with pink shutters and a white picket fence surrounding it. Directly across the street is a mangrove swamp extending to the sea which is about three blocks away. Last night the full moon, one of those great big yellow paper lantern moons, rose out of the mangrove swamp and over the palm tree and it was quite bewitching. But there are lots of mosquitos in the ointment and they seem peculiarly indifferent to citronella and spray-guns, evidently a strain that has developed immunity. They are only really bad when the wind blows off the swamp, and everything else is perfect.

The prodigy, Speed Lamkin, sometimes referred to as the "new Truman Capote" was here for a while, but he languished for the smart society of Manhattan and has now abandoned us. He was really a pretty nice kid and did not deserve the rather unfortunate title. Now for society we have only the White House Trumans and the sailors and our colored cook, Charleso Marie, who would make a good under-study for Bernice. Yesterday we saw a picture of Bernice, Frankie and John Henry in the Trib which somebody had on the beach. They do look perfect for the parts! Audrey is very elated over the casting, and it seems to me that the production is being handled with singular intelligence and good taste straight down the line. So far your best break was shaking off that malign combination of Guild, Collaborator and Crabtree. It seems to me that if the fates had not been in your corner you would never have managed such a favorable switch of management and director, not to mention the inspired casting. As for my coming to Philly, that is still in doubt, for I have Grandfather with me. He vehemently asserts that he will never again return to Saint Louis, you would think that he had escaped from a dungeon he is so happy to be here. We shall have to celebrate Xmas together, here in Key West it appears. But Frankie is going home for two weeks, and he will probably see you and the play while he is around New York and he will bring you good-luck as he has me. He has gone out, now, to pick up some

pictures we took with our new camera and if there are any good ones, I will enclose one for you. I hope you will observe that I have lost twelve pounds! I have cut down on my liquor to a limit of five drinks a day (Ah, Spartan soul that I am!) and eat only one meal, a big supper with heroic abstention from hot-biscuits and potatoes which are my two most favorite things in the world, almost! La Vida Es Pena! But perhaps next season you will see my picture in Welch's Grape-juice Ads.

I have at long last completed a first complete draft of a play but I don't think I shall do anything with it this season. The heat of Frankie's summer (your Frankie) should keep a cautious playwright under cover! - We send you our love, all three of us.

Tenn.

[TW refers to a publicity photo of Ethel Waters, Julie Harris, and Brandon de Wilde—principals in *The Member of the Wedding*—which had recently appeared in the *New York Herald Tribune*. The "malign combination" of the Theatre Guild, collaborator Greer Johnson, and director Paul Crabtree marked the early production history of the play. Contrary to reports, TW did not attend the Philadelphia opening and apologized to Carson McCullers in later correspondence.

TW's report of happiness, productivity, and abstemious habits was stated in part in an earlier letter to Audrey Wood, which ended with an urgent postscript: "Please have Dr. Frank E. Smith send me a supply of Seconal and phenobarbital tablets" (December 5, 1949, HRC).

Penned in the lefthand margin and keyed to the Truman reference in the second paragraph is the notation "I haven't seen them so far."]

150. To William Liebling

The Lighthouse
The New York Association for the Blind
111 East 59th Street, New York 22, N.Y.
December 20, 1949
[TLS w/ enclosure, 1 p. Todd Collection]

Dear Mr. Liebling:

There is so much useless spending of time and money and emotion on selfish ends that actually, finally, gets us no where that we really want to be, that all adds up eventually to zero. It seems to me that the few dispositions of these goods that do not add up eventually to zero, that are really creative

expenditures, are the ones that we make for non-selfish reasons such as the relief and the advancement and improvement of our afflicted fellow beings.

Of these none are more poignantly appealing, more deeply and touchingly needful than the ones that are blind. We all live in a good deal of darkness, but, they live in a darkness even greater than ours. Isn't it fortunate that sometimes the blind are really able to lead the blind?

Please forward your check payable to The Lighthouse in the enclosed envelope.

Sincerely yours, Tennessee Williams

[TW served as honorary chairman of the Theatrical Division of The Lighthouse, a charitable "association for the blind." In the preceding August the Lighthouse Players presented *Summer and Smoke* at the Mountain Playhouse in Jennerstown, Pennsylvania, with sightless actors in the cast. After some initial hesitation, Audrey Wood made a special release of the play to accommodate the group.]

151. To Margaret "Margo" Jones

1431 Duncan Street
Key West, Fla.
Jan. 2, 1950.
[TLS, 1 p. HRC]

Margo dear:

I am sorry to have let the holidays go by, or nearly by, without some word to you. At long last I have been completing a play, assembling a complete draft of it, which I shall take to New York for typing as soon as Frank returns from visiting his family in New Jersey for the holidays. It is a great relief but leaves me rather exhausted and I have done so little else since I got here in Key West. I have been disgracefully negligent. Most of my friends are mad at me. Particularly Donnie. He wrote me a month ago that he wanted me to make some comment for the dust-jacket of his book which Doubleday is bringing out in April, and it just slipped my mind until he wrote me a very cross letter indeed, implying that I was a faithless friend. You would think one writer would understand the preoccupations of another! As you are probably as busy and preoccupied as I am, you may understand better.

Jane and Tony Smith spent the holidays with us in Key West, and we

managed to create a semblance of Xmas spirit in spite of the summer warmth and the palm trees. They are really beautiful people, and since society here has been pretty limited, it was a great joy to have them. Grandfather is having the time of his life, all 92 years of it. He was looking distressingly frail when I picked him up in Jacksonville - he flew down from St. Louis to meet me there - but he's now gained a lot of weight and walks around briskly. He's crazy about Frankie who drives him around everywhere that he takes a notion to go, and he usually has a notion to go somewhere. Keeping up with his correspondance is a problem, too, as he can't see to write anymore. He swears that he will never return to St. Louis again. He and Mother don't get along so well anymore, she refuses to repeat things to him and he says he never knows what is going on in the house. Yet he also complains of her nagging him, which is a bit contradictory, and he has never forgiven Dakin for becoming a Roman Catholic.

We have a charming little house here, white frame with pink shutters. Frank and I have the upstairs which is an ideal place for working. There is an extra bedroom downstairs if you ever feel like paying us a visit. I shall be in New York for a week out of this month and the end of the month we go to Havana for a week (it is only a half hour by air from Key West), but we shall be here from now through April and whenever you want to take a little rest in the sun from your many labors, just let us know. You must be feeling like the title of your next New York production, after the strenuous routine that you have been following. Frank and I, and possibly Grandfather also (since he won't go back to St. Louis) are planning to return to Europe in the late Spring, after our lease on the house expires; I want to see the Paris production of Streetcar with Arletty and I also want to see if Magnani can talk English and would be interested in a job here. I can't think of any American actress of her type. I have taken off 13 pounds and feel somewhat rejuvenated and moderately at peace for the first time in perhaps three years. Some interesting people are beginning to arrive for the season. The nicest is Viola Veidt who is the daughter of the late Conrad Veidt. She is a bit of a lush and we have been drunk together the past 5 nights! Love & luck!

Tennessee.

[The dust jacket "comment" which TW belatedly wired—"Windhams first novel introduces finest young talent since Carson McCullers" (qtd. in Windham, p. 248)—eclipsed author and book and promised to offend Truman Capote and Gore Vidal as well.

An Old Beat-Up Woman, Margo Jones's "next New York production," would close in Boston on January 28, 1950. In the meanwhile Jones replied with typical gusto: "'Yes, honey, I sure do feel beat up and I love it!'" (qtd. in Windham, p. 251).

Jean Cocteau's production of *Un Tramway Nommé Désir* opened at the Théâtre Edouard VII in Paris on October 19, 1949, and ran for 233 performances. Arletty added a mysterious Blanche to the canon, while Cocteau's staging eroticized the visual effects of the play. Critics and audiences were again scandalized.

Shortly before his death in 1943, Conrad Veidt played the Nazi major in *Casablanca* (1942).]

152. To Jane Lawrence and Tony Smith

1431 Duncan Street
[Key West, Florida]
Jan. 5, 1950.
[TLS w/ autograph postscript,
2 pp. Smith Collection]

Dear Jane and Tony:

The house seemed awfully empty after you left till Frank got back last night. I don't know how we should have endured the holidays without you. Janie, I have only loved one book in my life as much as the Anabasis and that is my Crane which I don't have with me. I shall have a permanent library of two books, now, in all my travels. I have taken a quote from the Anabasis for my play, the one beginning O Slinger! Crack the nut of my eye - ram's skin painted red. (beginning and end of it is all I can reproduce at the moment). And the Rousseau snake-charmer is framed above my work-table in place of that innocuous little etching that came with the house. A cut-out of Valentino as Pan is also framed close beside it, replacing a sketch of a Scotch terrier which I always thought peculiarly uninteresting. Speaking of dogs, Tony's story of the Havana Exhibition has become the great cry in smart Key West society. Everybody is barking at everybody and saying "Dogs!" It has become the usual form of greeting and provokes great hilarity, as well it might. It is particularly fitting among the crowd that has adopted it. This week two great Scandinavians showed up, one of them 6'4" tall. Donnie and I met them at the Fifth avenue palace

of a exquisite East Indian prince named Dinisha. Don will remember. They told of attending a banquet given by Dinisha at which he ate only a single small nut, though there were endless courses and enormous hoopla. Grandfather was quite infatuated with the big Swede and insisted upon taking his arm and showing him the lime-tree and the two-story cactus plant. Then Frank arrived on the 9:30 bus and we had another little Christmas. He brought me several marvelous records, including Arensky's Waltz for Two Pianos which I have wanted a long time and a gold snake-ring with little diamond chips in it which is the nicest piece of jewelry I have owned and a huge bottle of Mitsouka, lest there be any doubt when I pass down Duval street. Frankie had lost weight at home and seemed glad to be back in our peaceful little world. A long wire from Audrey says they want me back on the West Coast to view the rough cut film of Menagerie but I am hoping, when I talk to Audrey long-distance after Carson's opening this evening, I can persuade them to send the film to New York so I won't have to go both places. The "stills" that Rapper sent me from Hollywood are really disgusting, the costumes and attitudes resembling Way Down East or Broken Blossoms, and I think it would be dreadful to go all the way out to the Coast just to be revolted! My collaborator, Oscar Saul, is furious with me, he says my lack of interest makes him feel insecure. All I can say is feeling insecure at $750. a week plus expenses should happen to me! <u>Girl</u>! as Fritzie would say. Or "<u>Bow</u> <u>Wow</u> - dogs . . . "

I guess this letter's all the writing I'll do today, as I couldn't start typing till Frank woke up which did not occur until 2 P.M. he was so exhausted, and I feel pretty stupid. But the weather at last is clear, it is a perfect beach-day. I wish I could show you my sister's latest letter: I believe it is her masterpiece. She used the word "implant" about six times, for sometime. Said she loved her new blouse and longed to implant it upon her clean, immaculate anatomy and wished that she had a brown skirt to implant with it. Finally said she was "implanting a stitch on a dish-towel, a brilliant, tragic one that she loved and hoped to bestow upon me". I guess it was the full moon. . . .

How is Buffie?

I am going to append to this letter, if possible in my stupefied condition, some additional "quotes" for Doubleday, but I hope you will use your own discretion about offering them to Donnie. The whole matter is apparently one of delicacy which I no longer know how to deal with, for Frank says

Don is still hurt over the quote, and I still don't understand how or why, except that there was the delay in getting it to him, and I have heard nothing from him since the cross letter. Is it the Flapper age that is coming back, or the age of the Prima Donna? I guess I would be equally at home in either, so have nothing to worry about! "High bosom or saucy butt, it is all the same to me! A turn, a twist, a flick of the wrist, for Mme. Tennessee!"

Much love, 10

P.S. Mailed "quotes" directly to ~~Doubleday~~ Don.

[Jane Lawrence (b. 1915) and Tony Smith (1912-1980) were married in California in 1943 with TW serving as their legal witness and informal honeymoon guest. Lawrence appeared in the original casts of *Oklahoma!* (1943) and *Where's Charley?* (1948) and later studied opera in Europe. An architect by training, Smith was associated with Frank Lloyd Wright before emerging in the 1960s as an artist who worked primarily in large-scale geometric forms. He appeared on the cover of *Time* magazine in October 1967 and was hailed as "the most dynamic, versatile and talented new sculptor" in America.

The "O Slinger!" epigraph from *Anabasis* (St.-John Perse, 1924) was used intermittently in drafts of *The Rose Tattoo*. The final line—"this world has more beauty than a ram's skin painted red!"—summarizes "the lyric as well as the Bacchantic impulse" (*Where I Live*, p. 55) which inspired the play.

"'Bow Wow - dogs'" refers to "'sex shows'" in Havana which TW was "crazy to see." A recent visitor, Smith reported that "they do every sexual act in the book and at the conclusion they get down on hands and knees, all barking like dogs, and one of the whores looks up and explains sweetly - 'Dogs!'" (TW to Kazan, January 27, 1950, WUCA).

Contrary to reports, TW did not attend the New York premiere of *The Member of the Wedding* (January 5, 1950). He planned instead to attend the opening of *Come Back, Little Sheba* on February 15 and to see *Member* at this time (to Wood, February 10, 1950, HRC).

The "disgusting" *Menagerie* "'stills'" reminded TW of D.W. Griffith's silent films *Broken Blossoms* (1919) and *Way Down East* (1920).

Charles Feldman bought film rights of *Streetcar* in the preceding October and hired Oscar Saul to write the adaptation. Saul's hope of working with TW for some four months led Frank Merlo to quip to Audrey Wood, "He does not know 'our boy' - does he?" (TW to Wood, addendum, n.d., HRC). TW's "only criticism" of Saul to date was that he "works a little too slowly" and "seems a little literal-minded in his approach, wants to explain and motivate things a little too carefully" (to Kazan, December 12, 1949, WUCA). Elia Kazan would soon agree to direct the

film, while Olivia De Havilland—acclaimed for her role as a mental patient in *The Snake Pit* (1948)—was the early choice to play Blanche DuBois.

TW quotes a letter from his sister Rose dated December 28, 1949: "I miss you. Am sorry that I couldn't bestow a present upon you that isn't my love. I am implanting a stitch on a dish towel that I can allot to you. It is a brilliant tragic one that I love, hope to bestow upon you" (Columbia U).]

153. *To Paul Bigelow*

[1431 Duncan Street
Key West, Florida]
1/13/50
[TLS w/ autograph postscript, 1 p. Columbia U]

Paul dear:

The holidays and attendant preoccupations made a great hiatus in my contacts with the world abroad. I'm not sure I have yet thanked you for the pyjamas which are the only ones for which I have ever had a positive attachment. Frank likes them equally and it is something of a contest which of us will wear them more though there is no question who wears them better.

I am immeasurably relieved (and even a little surprised) at the great success of Carson's play. I am sure this will do a great deal for her and once more it gives me a feeling of the existence of a Providence of some kind. I have not heard much about it yet. Only a few lines from Carson came yesterday enclosing an Ad with wonderful quotes for the play. When she recuperates from the strain I am sure that great psychological benefit will be apparent and I hope that she will then return to work on her novel. If I do not say that I hope she will immediately sit down to write another play, I trust you will understand my reasoning in the matter. You have been very remiss about social reportage? What is going on in the great world nowadays? A letter from Gore says he was to sail the 9th for Italy and eventually Ceylon. I wonder if Paul Bowles knows that he is coming? I have a copy of Gore's new book and I also have the much-celebrated first novel of Frederich Buechner whose dust-jacket photo out-shines any of the literary Apollos that have yet flowered among us. Is he at large in Manhattan, and what is the scuttlebut on this item? Where is Truman going to sail to? Or will he weather the storm in a fixed position? Fortunately Speed has yet to appear and I hope he has been to the right

photographer. I think this idea of cutting the photograph just at the line of the crotch (as in Buechner's) is the most provocative that has yet been devised. For Speed, however - not that I don't believe it would be equally becoming - I think a variation is indicated. The white roses, the reclining pose on the sofa, the amputated balls having already been exploited, what is there left for a girl to do on a dust-jacket this season but lick a peppermint-stick or bite her big toe?

Frankie and I (let's face it!) have fallen into virtual social oblivion here. A great old Queen Bee named Erna Shtoll or Shmole or something like that has arrived on the scene and become the center of gay society. Bedecked with yellow diamonds like 1000 watt bulbs on the marquee of a skating rink, she holds continual court on the beach and at the bars, the boys flock to her like gnats. But Erna and I took an instant aversion, one to the other. When I was introduced to her at the Bamboo Room (one evening during the holidays when I was quite drunk) she said loftily that she had met me twice before, both times in Tony's. The fact that I had no recollection even of being in Tony's more than once in my life did not improve matters any. She is a buxom widow of sixty and possibly regards me as a contender in the same weight class although I hope she acknowledges some disparity of years. I once had some modicum of social finesse in queen groups, and with queen Bees, but Frank has none whatsoever, he just looks blank and fiddles with his key-ring: so we are quite out of it. But there are still some compensating attractions. We hope that you will pay us a visit during the season. I was thinking of coming up to New York but only got as far as Miami and it seemed like far enough and came home the next day. - Is Audrey doing anything with Mrs. Stone? I think I have finished my play. I had it photostated in Miami and will send Audrey a copy today or tomorrow but am not yet ready for it to go out of her office except to the typist.

Much love - 10.

P.S. Gore has arrived in Key West for a week, and so has Mike James, son of Times editor, so the social situation has improved a bit.

[A Long Day's Dying (1950) was praised for craft and psychological insight and regarded as a promising first novel. The twenty-three-year-old author, Frederick Buechner, was not "at large in Manhattan" but teaching at the Lawrenceville School in New Jersey and later studying for the Presbyterian ministry, to which he

was ordained in 1958. To date his fiction and theological writing have produced a large and distinguished body of work.

"The white roses, the reclining pose on the sofa," refer to provocative photographs of Truman Capote by Cecil Beaton and Harold Halma, respectively.

TW mailed "Mrs. Stone" to Audrey Wood on November 11, 1949, for typing by Paul Bigelow and delivery to James Laughlin. Enclosed was a note in which TW discounted "the literary quality" (HRC) of the novella but expressed optimism for its potential as a film.]

154. To Alfred C. Kinsey

1431 Duncan
Key West, Florida
Jan. 18, 1950
[ALS, 2 pp. Kinsey Institute]

Dear Dr. Kinsey -

I am gratified by the attention you have given "Streetcar" since I feel that your work, your research and its revelations to the ignorant and/or biased public, is of enormous social value. I hope that you will continue it and even extend its scope, for not the least desirable thing in this world is understanding, and sexual problems are especially in need of it.

I am sailing for Europe around May 28 and will probably be in New York for a couple or three weeks prior to sailing (on the Ile de France). My agents are Liebling-Wood, Inc. if you want to get in touch with me at that time, or check on my whereabouts. Their address is 551 fifth ave.

I would welcome (and enjoy) the chance to discuss my plays with you whenever you find the occasion.

Cordially, Tennessee Williams

[Alfred Kinsey (1894-1956) informed TW that he and his staff at the Institute for Sex Research (University of Indiana) were "making an extensive study of the erotic element in the arts" and had examined *Streetcar* "in some detail." Many cast members had given their "histories" to the Institute, and so it seemed possible, Kinsey thought, "to correlate their acting with their sexual backgrounds" (January 14, 1950, Kinsey Institute). The premiere of *Streetcar* in December 1947 and the publication of *Sexual Behavior in the Human Male* (a collaboration of Kinsey and his staff) in the following month formed an intense focus of public sexual candor, and furor as well. TW declined to give his own sexual history when he Kinsey met later in November.]

155. To James "Jay" Laughlin

1431 Duncan St.
Key West, Fla.
<u>1/30/50</u>
[TLS, 1 p. Houghton]

Dear Jay:

I am delighted that you want to publish the novella separately in the Fall and that you think I've improved it. I am still making little revisions, from time to time; it might be helpful if you would go through it, sometime, very carefully and make a note of all those points at which the writing falls down. I may be doing this myself but of course I can't altogether rely on my own perception. Since it is such a short thing it should be possible to get it completely polished. Audrey and Bigelow were displeased with my original title, MOON OF PAUSE, but I like it much better than the one they prefer, THE ROMAN SPRING OF MRS. STONE, which I think is comparatively banal and much less pertinent but I have thought of another, DEBRIS OF GIANT PALMS, which derives from a passage of Perse's "Anabasis". I think I would prefer either that or the one I had first. Which do you like?

I have completed the long play THE ROSE TATTOO and had it typed up by Audrey. She has been rather cagey about it and my own feelings about it are tentative and mixed, I am afraid to read it over. Yesterday I wired her that I must have some comment, however brief and devastating that might be, and she wired back that was "very optimistic and thought it had the making of a great commercial vehicle". I am not sure that I feel very pleased about this reaction. So far I have never aimed at a commercial vehicle and I hope that I will never be willing to settle for that. I now have $113,000. in govt. bonds which is enough to live on in Sicily or Africa for the rest of my life without bothering about making money in the theatre. What I want, of course, is to continue to write honest works with poetic feeling but am haunted by the fear that I am repeating myself, now, have totally exploited my area of sensibility and ought to retire, at least publicly, from the field. The work on this play, begun last January in Rome, has exhausted me physically and nervously. I have suffocating spells in my sleep. Sometimes they wake me up but sometimes they are woven into my dreams, such as last night when I dreamed that I was trying desperately to crawl down a long corridor of a house in the vaccuum of a tornado.

Vidal arrived here about two weeks ago and since coming has written a really excellent short story, the best thing he has ever done in my opinion. I want you to see it, and so does he. Of course I also liked his story about "the street" (Some Desperate Adventure) which you didn't care for. I thought it was not well written but that it was the most honest expression of Vidal that he has yet offered. I am encouraging him to do it as a play. It could be terrifying as a study of the modern jungle. Vidal is not likable, at least not in any familiar way, but he and Bowles are the two most honest savages I have met. Of course Bowles is still the superior artist, but I wonder if any other living writer is going to keep at it as ferociously, unremittingly as Vidal! If only he will learn that people are not going to give a hoot for his manufactured pieces like "Search for a King", Etc.! He has a mania for bringing out one book a year! They are now stacked up like planes over an airport, waiting for the runway.

Audrey suggests that I come to New York but I am waiting for news that at least one swimming-pool has reopened. Since coming here I took off fifteen pounds by diet and swimming and I don't want to put it back on in one week of Manhattan high life.

Ever - 10.

[In titling "the novella," James Laughlin shared TW's current preference for "Debris of Giant Palms," while Audrey Wood and Paul Bigelow favored the eventual selection, "The Roman Spring of Mrs. Stone." "Moon of Pause," which refers to Karen Stone's menopausal experience, appeared earlier in *Summer and Smoke* in reference to Alma Winemiller's fading youth and the "cold dead peace" (August 1946, HRC) which lay ahead. The expression made Wood "acutely uncomfortable" (to TW, January 7, 1947, Columbia U) and was cut from the play.

"Tentative and mixed" feelings are evident in TW's present description of *The Rose Tattoo*: "I call this the 'kitchen sink draft' because I have thrown into it every dramatic implement I could think of. Perhaps all of them will work. Perhaps none of them will work. Probably a few of them will work" ("Note," January 1950, HRC).

From "outline" to first draft stage, there was development rather than fundamental change in the basic elements of *The Rose Tattoo*. Rosario's mistress, originally a voice heard "sobbing over the phone," was dramatically cast as Estelle Hohengarten, a thin blonde prostitute from Texas who appears in the opening and closing scenes. At the final curtain she and Pepina kneel to gather the ashes of Rosario—an addition to the outline as well—which Pepina has long venerated but impulsively scattered after learning of her husband's betrayal ("'Kitchen Sink' Draft," January 1950, HRC).

"Three Stratagems," the "excellent" story by Gore Vidal, appeared in *New Directions Twelve* (1950). The "manufactured" work, *A Search for the King* (1950), received mixed notices.]

156. To Elia "Gadg" Kazan

[1431 Duncan Street
Key West, Florida]
2/24/50
[TLS w/ autograph marginalia, 2 pp. WUCA]

Dear Gadg:

Your letter about the play makes it possible for me to go on with it. Audrey's reaction was ambiguous and stifling. Made me feel that the script might be something to pretend had not happened like public vomiting.

I think you see the play more clearly than I did. I have this creative will tearing and fighting to get out and sometimes the violence of it makes its own block. I don't stop to analyze much. I guess I don't dare to. I am afraid it would go up in smoke. So I just attack, attack, like the goat - but with less arrogance and power! Your phrase 'comic-grotesque mass to the male force' is particularly helpful as a definition. I shall try, now, doing it with only the one man, Alvaro, and a new scene in which Pepina is a widow proud and exalted in the memory of a great fulfilled love - almost absurdly puffed up in the invidious eye of the community: brought to her knees by the double shock of Rose's precocious flight into passion and the revelation of her dead husband's infidelity. Perhaps if she alone collects the ashes it will be enough, but I must confess I was enormously intrigued by the dramatic-pictorial value of the two women doing it - and I still don't see how that is in any way incongruous to the praise of the male force. Part of the story is Pepina's reconcilement to the eternal ambivalence (and frailties) of the human animal. She is converted from an ideal to a reality and finds that it is possible to forgive it and go on loving the broken idol. The male force is in those ashes which are all that is left of it and her gathering is her forgiveness and her reconcilement and being assisted by the other woman extended the forgiveness, in a way, to the whole race of man.

You have a passion for organization, for seeing things in sharp focus, which I don't have and which makes our combination a good one. Sometimes I can make a virtue of my disorganization by keeping closer to the

cloudy outlines of life which somehow gets lost when everything is too precisely stated. For instance you liked the play "Deep are the Roots" which I hated. I think you liked the orderly marshalling of forces on opposite sides, good and bad, and the message coming out in banner headlines, as it were, like the Los Angeles Examiner's announcement of Ingrid's baby. I much preferred "Death of a Salesman" where the good and bad, the pitiable and the heroic, were more cloudily intermingled in the single souls. The things that we do together will inevitably be somewhere between our two tastes in this matter. Thesis and antithesis must have a synthesis in a work of art but I don't think all of the synthesis must occur on the stage, perhaps about 40% of it can be left to occur in the minds of the audience. MYSTERY MUST BE KEPT! But I must not confuse it with sloppy writing which is probably what I have done in a good deal of Rose Tattoo.

I am terrified by the amount of work you still want to be done on "Streetcar". Why, honey, it looks like you want me to sit down and write the whole fucking thing over!!? This script is going to be the biggest patch-work quilt since the death of Aunt Dinah, and you might as well be reconciled to it. I am going to do my work on it in bits and pieces, taking little isolated segments of the Saul script and doing them over so that the replacements are made bit by bit and keeping as much of what's already done as possible, for as I explained to you the psychological block to the resumption of an old work before the satisfactory completion of a new work is a rugged thing to climb over. I think I have one exciting idea for the Stanley rape scene. No, don't have him go out to drink beer but have him suddenly smash the light-bulbs with the heel of a slipper. She cries out, 'What is that for?' - And he says, 'To see you better!' - Then dissolve as he approaches her - ("eyes blazing!")

I am going to do my version of the night-out with both the startling ideas that I had for it, the WONDER CLUB on Lake Pontchartrain with the boy singing in drag and the playing of the Varsouvianna but I will write it so that the first item can be easily eliminated from the script if you still dislike it. It appeals to me as a fresh and bold piece of screen material and a legitimate motive for Blanche's beginning to break: the dancing of the Varsouvianna - the music penetrating the powder-room where she has fled after the removal of the boy's wig - seems a marvelous springboard to the intensity of her monologue about Allan. Mitch: You mean he was like that boy in the female outfit? Blanche: No, no, no! He wasn't at all like

that, there was nothing the least bit - effeminate about him - but there was - Etc."

In the last scene I am going to return almost entirely to the play as you seem to feel, as I do, that is best. I thought of having a brief shot in the hospital of Stanley, Kiefaber and Shaw sitting on a bench outside Stella's room waiting to present their testimony - their names are spoken at the door and you dissolve to Blanche huddled in Eunice's apartment and the ants crawling into the icebox. Mr. Graves (highschool superintendant) might also be among the witnesses summoned by Stanley to secure the commitment.

While I was in New York I saw the THIRD MAN and was terrifically moved by it. Greatest camera shot I have ever seen was the huge ferris wheel, even better than any pictorial effect that I can remember in Eisenstein and it had the whole lyric image of Hart Crane's poem The Bridge in it, and, Christ, what music, what music! Can't we have something equally haunting back of Streetcar? And camera effects like that?! The story itself was rambling and told in too diffuse a fashion, not concentrated enough and not enough sustained tension. Dynamics too abstruse. But it is a magic piece. Of course I had my own degenerate ideas about the relationship between Orson and Joe Cotton which made the heroine of the film a little irrelevant: but there again, the audience was supplying 40% of the synthesis!

Yes, yes, yes, there are many things to be done between dark and daylight if God gives us six months more to pursue our illogical phantoms down celluloid and paper areaways! I hope that next year we will be in Rome shooting the posthumous life of Mrs. Stone. Possibly even with Garbo.

Love - 10.

[The "kitchen sink" draft of The Rose Tattoo was not "ready" for staging, Elia Kazan thought, but it had greater potential than the original outline. He advised TW to stress the "UNLOCKING" of Pepina and to reconsider the static, devotional ending which blocked her movement "towards freedom." Treating Rosario as a "memory" or "legend" and beginning the action much later, perhaps with the daughter's graduation, would help to realize the play as Kazan envisioned it: "A comic Mass between what man and woman are, and what they have made of themselves" (n.d., HRC).

Deep Are the Roots (1945) ran for 477 performances and helped to establish

Kazan's reputation as a successful Broadway director. The play conventionally studies the post-war "Negro problem" in the deep South.

The "night-out" scene at the "WONDER CLUB" (Scene Six) was retained in *Streetcar*, although a swing band rather than a "boy singing in drag" provided the entertainment. The Varsouviana was not played or danced, as TW preferred, but used as spectral accompaniment to Blanche's account of Allan Grey's death. No hospital "shot" or contingent of witnesses appears in the film.

The Third Man (1949), which was filmed in post-war Vienna, won the Academy Award for black and white cinematography (Robert Krasker). The "ferris wheel" in the bombed-out Prater was used to stage the famous meeting of Orson Welles and Joseph Cotten.

The Roman Spring of Mrs. Stone was filmed by José Quintero and released in 1961. Vivien Leigh, rather than Garbo, played the lead.

Penned in the lefthand margin of page 2 is the notation "dissolve from 3 men entering Stella's room to the deprecating ants crawling into icebox."

A briefer undated version of this letter is held by the HRC.]

157. To Gore Vidal

[1431 Duncan Street
Key West, Florida]
3/1/50
[TLS, 1 p. Houghton]

Fruit of Eden!

The first of your letters, the one mailed in packages, was forwarded to New York. I opened it and started to read it in the theatre when the lights went down. I never got past the first two sentences and unfortunately I left it in my program. I hope it has fallen into friendly hands and that it was not the sort of letter that would expose us to blackmail. The second I did get here. (We are back in Key West). The high point of my trip to New York was a week-end at Rhinebeck, arranged and conducted by Polly Bigelow. I became quite fond of Alice and also her husband who is not without charm. As you know, they have an indoor swimming pool and all the New York pools had been closed so it was a God send. I went to plays every night. The Cocktail Party was fascinating but nevertheless rather dull. The best was Inge's Come Back Little Sheba. Carson's was done so badly I found it difficult to appreciate, but there are standees at every performance. Lamkin was in evidence, but apparently about to leave for Hollywood. Audrey had got him a $250. week job with Charlie Feldman, like I had in

1943, but he seemed a bit wistful as though that were not quite what he had hoped to be in store for him. Truman I did not see at all: but he was purportedly present in New York. I had dinner with the Windham-Campbell menage. A very painful dinner, everyone on edge and very little to eat - the atmosphere full of a mysterious tension which I cannot understand or explain to myself and very saddening as I felt I had made every propitiatory gesture. I talked to Audrey about you. She had your letter and I assured her that she should certainly promote you with the studios if that was your wish. Hope you've heard from her. You should be able to get a better deal than Lamkin if you go after it. Polly is planning to visit us early in March but we are planning a trip to Havana first. He may occupy the house while we're away and spend a while with us after we get back. Professionally the trip was rather ambiguous. Audrey is sitting on the new script like an old hen, either because she doesn't really like it or because she doesn't want it to fall into the hands of a producer, I don't know which. I think she and Liebling hope to produce it themselves. I did show it to Kazan. He wrote a long letter about it, seemed sincerely interested and enthusiastic about most of it but wanted a different first act. So the work continues. I am tired to the point of collapse but perhaps the Havana trip will revive me. This literary life, my child, is no bed of thornless roses! Did you know that? But yesterday the social leaders of the town dropped in to see us. Grandfather was eating his rice krispies in the diningroom which, as you may remember, is continuous with the salon. I told him, Grandfather, The Newton Porters are here! He could not see the other end of the room and thought I was merely making some remark about them (it was quite early for a call) and he said, Goodness Gracious, what pests those people are! - An awkward moment ensued, as even at 92 there is a limit to what you can get away with.

Write me about Houston. I presume you're coming back to New Orleans? I may visit you there this Spring.

Love - 10.

[Paul Bigelow was a friend and companion of Alice Astor Bouverie, daughter of John Jacob Astor and mistress of Rhinebeck on the Hudson. She entertained a circle of artistic friends, including Gore Vidal, who first visited Rhinebeck in the preceding fall. The ubiquitous Speed Lamkin had introduced him to Bouverie.

T.S. Eliot's verse play *The Cocktail Party* premiered in New York on January

21, 1950, ran for a surprising 409 performances, and won the Drama Critics' Circle
Award as best foreign play of the season.

A romantic interest drew Vidal to Houston.]

158. To Audrey Wood

[Hotel Inglaterra, Havana]
[early-March 1950]
[TLS, 1 p. HRC]

Dear Audrey:

I have just this moment read your very touching and very beautiful
letter and it has done me a very great deal of good. Both yours and Kazan's
letters have helped me immensely in getting a clarification in my own mind
of what I want to do with the play, and I am going on with it. I now see
the woman, the little house, the little proprieties and black dummies and
parrot cage and all that as a sort of delicate, almost tissue-paper, fence built
lovingly around the instinct to protect and preserve and cherish which is
the meaning of WOMAN. And the goat bleating, the cries of children, the
wind banging the shutters, the roar of great trucks on the highway, the
fierce omni-present element of chance and destruction - as the careless
universe that besieges this little woman-built cosmos or womb. I hope that
all I do on the play, now, will bring this essential image and meaning out
more clearly so that it will illuminate the play and lift it above an ordinary
comedy or melodrama.

I am keeping the first part but with Rosario never seen, only heard
behind the drawn curtains between the two rooms, which are rose-colored
and bear the faint outlines of a rose. The second scene only a black
silhouette so that he is never visible to the audience. The other important
ideas I will discuss with you later. These only affect the PART ONE. I
thought it important to keep that part, as I don't want to lose Estelle
Hohengarten and the rose-colored silk shirt which are so important to the
working out of the (rounded) story.

We are now running out to the beach, and thank you again with all my
heart!

With my love, 10

[Elia Kazan's approach "sounds damned good," Audrey Wood wrote, but she fore-saw problems in revising *The Rose Tattoo* as Kazan had directed. Could Pepina's "passion" for Rosario be retained if he were a "minor" presence in the play? And lacking such "passion," might Pepina not seem bent on pleasure, a "last fling" with Alvaro, rather than mystical union with her husband?

Wood also foresaw the difficulty of casting Pepina if Anna Magnani, for whom the part was written, should prove unavailable. Still more formidable was the "task" of following *Streetcar*. In leaving the old "southern scene" and treating a new "class of people," TW had taken a "giant step forward," but she warned that this alone would not warrant production or satisfy the critics. "In other words - don't leap - but consider all these things and know that I love you dearly as a man and admire you as much as always as a writer" (March 5, 1950, HRC).

TW began to obscure Rosario's presence in a later draft of *The Rose Tattoo* (April 1950, HRC), but he was not yet willing to "lose" Estelle Hohengarten and the "rose-colored" shirt," as Kazan's approach would entail. Before Rosario's death, Estelle employed Pepina, a seamstress, to make a silk shirt for her lover, Rosario. Pepina later gave the garment to Alvaro in the hope, or delusion, that he was her husband incarnate.

This letter bears a reception date of March 8, 1950.]

159. To Jane Lawrence Smith

1431 Duncan
[Key West, Florida]
March 8, 1950
[TLS, 1 p. Smith Collection]

Dearest Janie:

What thrilling news that you will be in Italy with us! Audrey has always secured our passages through the Westover (I believe that's the name) travel agency which operates for a small fee. They get wonderful accomodations very quickly and are certainly worth the little extra expense. Frank and I are very dubious about the possibility of your getting steamship bookings in the second or tourist class this late on any ship sailing in May or even early summer. It is always much easier to get first class space. Why don't you fly over, either directly to Paris or Rome? It is almost completely safe, now, more so than land-plane travel and I should think bookings would be easier. I shall write Audrey, or her assistant who handles our transportation for us, that you're going over and would appreciate her assistance. Suggest you call Audrey and talk to her about

it. It would be so wonderful having you on the same boat with us and on the drive down to Rome, we would have such fun together!

The thing that we all dreaded but expected in Key West has finally happened. One of the New York queens was murdered in her bed last night by a sailor! The town is hot as a firecracker! Within half an hour after the news broke, the whole Erna gang had fled from the Keys in various and assorted convertibles. We were on our way to the movies when we heard. Queens could be seen scuttling in every direction like they had hornets up their asses! Five were picked up on the street and thrown into jail. You would think it was the queens that had killed the sailor, such was the panic amongst them. We made a round of the bars. Pat the drag-queen had gone into hiding. Michelle was white as a ghost. Lyle Weaver the organist at the Bamboo Room opened his program with "Nearer My God to Thee!" Shore police stood outside every bar and it was rumored that every queen in town would be locked up before daybreak. Only the night before our house-guest, Bigelow, had brought five sailors home with him - so we felt far from easy about the state of affairs and drove home by a back street. The murdered queen was an associate of the Erna gang. I am sure you remember Erna, the 60-year old nympho with all the yellow diamonds and coterie of swish. The sailor killed the guy with a copper ash-tray, splitting his head wide open. Police found them both still in bed. Details are not yet available as it happened after the paper was out. Frank is in town now, with Bigelow, getting more information. Mother arrives this evening on the 7:30 bus and we are just hoping that there will be no interviews with the police when we go into town to meet her! Thank God Frank and I had been leading a relatively quiet life. I expect it will be even quieter from now on! I am afraid it will cast a heavy shadow over Bigelow's visit.

There is really no other news at all comparable. I am still working on my play. Only Audrey and Gadge have seen it, both are very interested but felt it needed more work. I enjoy working on it as it continues to progress but wish I had the energy that I had in the old days! - the never-failing excitement.

Love to you and dear Tony - Tenn

[John Collins, 20, a sailor from the USS *Tringa*, and Atherton "Tony" Foster, 42, an artist from New York, drank heavily on the afternoon of March 7 and retired to Foster's apartment where the older man, Collins stated, made "unnatural

advances." Both were found disrobed on the bed, Foster having been struck fatally with a wooden ashtray stand. Collins was convicted of manslaughter—a grand jury had reduced the charge from first degree murder—and sentenced to seven years in prison. The jury recommended mercy.

TW informed Paul Bigelow that the "only unpleasantness" he experienced at the time was "in the Patio bar on the beach when a sailor came up to me and said, 'Didn't Oscar Wilde smoke a cigarette holder like that?' I made big eyes and said, 'Who is Oscar Wilde?' Social poise <u>always</u> comes in handy" (April 11, 1950, Columbia U).

Canceled in the letterhead is the imprint of the Hotel Inglaterra, Havana, where TW and Frank Merlo spent the past few days.]

160. To Audrey Wood

[1431 Duncan Street
Key West, Florida]
March 2?, 1950.
[TLS, 1 p. HRC]

Dear Audrey:

We have had a rather disturbing time of it lately. Mother took suddenly ill in Miami, two days after she left here and was removed to a hospital with a blood-count of 19,000. They thought she had an acute appendix and would have to be operated on. Frank and I flew to Miami but by the time we got there she had improved and the blood-count gone down to 11,000. Appendicitis was apparently ruled out as a diagnosis which makes it far more disturbing. The doctors feel she can fly to St. Louis Tuesday but must undergo a series of X-ray examinations as they now suspect "a diverticulum" of the intestinal tract. We have not told grandfather anything about this, but said a party was being given for mother by The Woman's Club of Miami and he accepted the story. When we left, yesterday, Mother seemed cheerful but naturally she is apprehensive. I know, from experience, how she must feel. She is flying back to St. Louis on Tuesday and I will phone the hospital daily to check on her condition.

Bigelow is still with us. The former under-Secretary of State, Sumner Welles, was here over the week-end. We had dinner with him one night, before the call to Miami. Bigelow has dined with him twice since on Maine lobster and vintage champagne at the Casa Marina but he left this morning (Welles) and now we have only each other.

I have your two letters about "Summer and Smoke" and the "Streetcar" picture deal. I think the entire script of "Summer" should be in the acting version, including the prologue but that a note should be included saying that the prologue may be omitted and that scene two was omitted in the Broadway production. I want the third act to correspond exactly to the version printed by New Directions. I don't think my work on the "Streetcar" scenario will occupy more than three weeks but I hope you'll get a good price for my services as it is going to be very difficult for me to return to that material now. I have already done considerable work on it and I am sure the final script will be a really good one. When I get closer to Saul's script I find a lot of valuable contributions that he has made, but the end must be much closer to the play. The rape can be suggested clearly without offense.

I read "The Rose Tattoo" aloud to Paul and Frank and was terribly shocked by the poor quality of the writing in it. Words that had rung true in my mind sounded quite wrong when I read them aloud: I suspect that it is even worse than the early versions of "Summer" "You Touched Me" or "Battle". This gives me great concern. I wonder if I have not reached the point of exhaustion that lies somewhere along every writer's trail. Yet I know that I can't stop writing for the simple reason that I can think of nothing else to do between the time I get up in the morning and the time I go swimming. I don't feel ~~gloomy or~~ desperate about this at all. Perhaps because I never expected to have any success as a writer and it never really became a part of my "modus vivendi". We have had extraordinary luck with what I had to offer and no complaints are in order.

When I talked to Dakin (about Mother) over long-distance, he said that Eddie Colton had been called on the carpet about my 1947 income tax deductions and there was danger of an assessment. How is that working out?

Love - 10.

[Sumner Welles resigned his position as FDR's under-Secretary of State following allegations (*New York Times*, August 4, 1943) that he had solicited porters on a Presidential train in 1940. In early 1950 he was convalescing in Palm Beach from a catalogue of ills.

Barrett Clark omitted the prologue because of the difficulty of casting children in amateur productions. Otherwise he followed TW's directions in publishing the "acting version" of *Summer and Smoke* (Dramatists Play Service, 1950).

Audrey Wood confirmed Elia Kazan's plan to begin filming *Streetcar* in August and asked TW to specify the time needed to do "a revised version" (March 17, 1950, HRC) of the screenplay. TW informed Kazan that she "demanded three weeks at six grand per from poor old Charlie" (March 23, 1950, WUCA). TW continued to underestimate the censor's objection to the rape scene in *Streetcar*.

This letter was probably written on March 20, 1950.]

161. To Audrey Wood

SH: Key West, Florida
March 27, 1950.
[TLS, 1 p. HRC]

Dear Audrey:

For some mysterious reason I've been able to work quite well lately and the play seems to be coming out of the bushes. If I decide that I want to have this play produced next season, and I now feel pretty sure that I will, I would like to have all the plans and arrangements for it (except, of course, casting) completed before I sail for Europe, so that I can enjoy my vacation. I do sincerely hope that everybody, you and Bill and Gadg, will be happy, or at least gracefully resigned, to whatever choice I make in the matter of a producer. I am sure you all must admit that it is more important that I should feel happy and at ease in this matter than anyone else, as my relations with the producer are probably the most important to the fate of the play - always the first consideration. And since I have worked so damned hard on this script (and in a way more alone-ly than any time before) it seems pretty obvious that the decision really ought to be mine, though I shall be as grateful as ever for the help and advice of everyone else that may be involved. I have just about given up the notion of producing myself. I feel that producing is a very separate and very consequential function, that it makes a tremendous difference: first, that the producer have intelligence, taste and power and experience, second: that the author should feel at ease or at home with the producer. I think it's a real vocation, and a full-time one, to which many are called but few chosen, and I myself don't feel the calling. This, of course, and everything else, can be discussed further when I get to New York. I now speak of production as a foregone conclusion not just because I am feeling much better satisfied with the script as I think it will finally be, but because I could not simply discard it

as a failure (without trial) without also discarding, by the same token and gesture, my career as a writer. As I said before, when the time comes, I can give that up, and certainly will give it up when it becomes unmistakably apparent I have nothing more to add to what I have had to say, but I doubt that what would be left of me would be much more edifying as experience or spectacle than the "posthumous life of Mrs. Stone". Another matter that I want treated with utmost confidence at the present. I am thinking of making Frankie a gift of part of The Rose Tattoo. I want him to feel some independance. His position with me now lacks the security and dignity that his character calls for. Perhaps I will give him ⅓ of it. I would like you to discuss this with Eddie and perhaps have the papers drawn up, quite secretly, so they will be ready for me to sign when I get to New York. Of course I don't want any reference made to this in our correspondance (except perhaps as "matter under discussion") until I have completely made up my mind about it in New York (before I sail) but I am interested in your opinion of it. Of course I am also hoping that a way will open for me to be of some help to Bigelow, of a more lasting nature for I am terribly fond of him and his position is such a precarious one which he has borne with touching gallantry for many years, but I want to do whatever I do without appearing to be giving alms - the alms-giver is "liked but not well-liked" and creates an uncomfortable feeling on both sides. - No other news deserving of comment except that we have acquired a white leghorn rooster and two Rhode Island red hens.

Love - Tenn.

[William Liebling once advised TW to form his own production company and to rely upon Liebling-Wood for backing. Rather than take the producer's standard fifty percent, the firm would be content with ten or fifteen and restore the remainder to the author. Such a plan, Liebling added, would help to shield TW from undue taxation (January 25, 1949, HRC). To the present letter Audrey Wood replied that "obviously all of us must resign ourselves to whatever choice you make re producer. Whatever producer is chosen however must present you with every possible financial advantage as author. Sure you will agree with me" (telegram, March 29, 1950).

"'Posthumous life'" refers to the psychological condition of "drifting" once Karen Stone's youth and beauty have faded and her stage career has ended. TW soon informed Wood that the title of the novella "is definitely 'The Roman Spring of Mrs. Stone'" (n.d., HRC).

Frank Merlo reportedly received ten percent of the profits from *The Rose Tattoo* (see Spoto, p. 173). The published version of the play was also dedicated "To Frank in return for Sicily."]

162. To Audrey Wood

SH: Western Union
Key West Flo
1950 Mar 28 PM 8 26
[Telegram, 1 p. HRC]

=BIRTHDAY ROSES IN ICE WATER AND ASPIRIN PERFECTLY GORGEOUS. I NEED SECCONAL TABLETS AND FRANKIE NEEDS HIS CHECK FOR THURSDAY LAST. THANKS AND LOVE=

TENNESSEE.

[TW's thirty-ninth birthday was the occasion of roses and Seconal.]

163. To Irene Mayer Selznick

1431 Duncan Street
Key West, Florida
April 5, 1950.
[TLS, 1 p. Boston U]

Dear Irene:

Your wire about Carson's award was the first to reach me. Nobody is to be congratulated but the author whose faith in the play was all but solitary. I blush to think how little faith I had in its success and that I actually thought it would be dangerous for Carson to have it produced. I am almost invariably wrong as a prophet of Broadway, for I thought that Inge's play would be the big hit, I saw no (commercial) hope for Eliot's and last year I was very dubious about the appeal of the "Salesman". Hereafter I will invest in any show that I think most likely to fail, and will probably wind up a strong rival of the Shuberts.

I have not forgotten your sailing-date. Isn't it April 15th? And I am still intending to have a script in your hands before then. Right now the second draft is at the typist's. She is a spinster with a heart condition who claims that any undue exertion might be fatal, so I cannot give her the hot-foot.

She has done 38 pages in about 3 days and it is a 130-page manuscript. She said she hoped to be through by Friday or Saturday which probably means Monday. Her typing is very beautiful - "frozen music" as a Mississippi lady once said in reference to St. Patrick's Cathedral - but a little, shall we say, - adagio? - Soon as completed I will shoot you a copy Air Mail Special in hopes it will catch your boat. For the sake of the author's nerves and vanity, and as a matter of general policy, we must not regard this as a submission for production. It's not yet time for that. I just want you to let me know what you think of it, as candidly, even brutally, as possible. I have told Audrey I am going to make up my own mind concerning everything in connection with this script which is the way it should be when one has worked on something so hard and against such odds, and she replied that she couldn't agree more completely. So I will probably decide for myself whether or not it ought to be produced and all the attendant circumstances, soon as I feel sufficiently objective about it. I do wish, while you're in Europe, you would check on Magnani for me, her command of English, her plans, Etc.? That is, if the play strikes you as being something that might appeal to her. - My feelings about the play go through continual and violent see-saws: fatuous contentment one day and despair the next. Perhaps Audrey is already consulting Bigelow and Inge about the sanitariums in Connecticutt. (for this client).

Liebling was here for one day, driving down from Coral Gables where he is recuperating from a virus infection. He looked very fit - the virus probably wishes that it had closed out of town.

There was a scandalous murder here last month, involving a middle-aged tourist and a sailor, and the town is what they call "hot". Many of our friends have been booked for vagrancy (of which there are 16 kinds in Florida law), sometimes for merely appearing on the street after dark. The overseas highway has been jammed with north-bound convertibles! - We plan to leave about the fifteenth, we hope voluntarily. Love -

10.

[*The Member of the Wedding* received seventeen of twenty-five votes in winning the Drama Critics' Circle Award for best play of the season. The Theatre Club and Donaldson prizes soon followed, while the Pulitzer went to *South Pacific* (1949).

TW described the same "violent see-saws" of emotion to Audrey Wood: "For a few days I will be in a state of euphoria, then I will suddenly hit bottom again.

No apparent reason except perhaps nervous exhaustion" (April 3, 1950, HRC). Wood replied that she felt "exactly the same way" and suggested they meet for "a nice drunken evening" (April 4, 1950, HRC).

Paul Bigelow, a production staff assistant of the Theatre Guild, kept William Inge sober and hidden from the press in a sanitarium near Greenwich, Connecticut, during rehearsals of *Come Back, Little Sheba*.]

164. To Oliver Evans

1431 Duncan Street
Key West [Florida]
7 April 1950
[TLS w/ autograph postscript, 1 p. HRC]

Dear Oliver:

The lament for your vanished youth is premature but well-fashioned. I have been lamenting mine, silently, for a long time now. What are your plans for the summer? We leave here a bit earlier than we expected. Last month a 43-year-old queen was clubbed to death by an ash-tray and a sailor, and as a reprisal for this terrible offense on the part of the queen, all the Bohemians in town are being picked up on the street and booked for vagrancy, given heavy fines and twelve hours to get off the Key. There are 16 different kinds of vagrancy in Florida law and I'm sure Frank and I, and perhaps even grandfather, would come under at least one of them! We will spend about a month in New York, then sail May 20th for Europe. I have finished my play, and the movie version of Streetcar which Kazan is going to shoot in August. I will probably come back for the shooting. Bigelow was here visiting us for a couple of weeks and I doubt that even you have ever received so many flattering attentions from the armed services. It reminded me of that bottle-capping machine they used to have in a window on Canal street! He got out just before they turned on the heat. Windham has already sailed for Europe, although his novel has not yet come off the press. Truman Capote is also reported to be considering another trip over. Paul Bowles is in India - he says Ceylon is the sexiest place he's ever been, and the natives are flirty as Mississippi maidens. Marian Vicarro was here and we renewed our friendship. She had Neal Thomas with her and Neal's lover who is a sad sack of a prissy sort of a queen. Poor Marian she doesn't seem to have found her bearings in the gay world although it is the only one she feels right in. She will have no fun playing the patsy to these

temperamental girls! - That was <u>not</u> Dame Selznick in the picture you sent us. The Dame is now quite handsome with her new boyish bob, and she looks well-fucked for a change. I don't know who the lucky man is. I hope she will like my new play - I have been working like a dog on it the whole time I've been here and am still quite uncertain about its merits.

Let me hear from you soon!

Love, 10.

I have lost 23 pounds!

[TW informed Maria Britneva that Oliver Evans had "resumed his duties at Nebraska, not omitting to drop by the bus-depot at odd moments, when classes are not in session." Evans would also improve Marion Vaccaro's gay company when he visited Miami in the following summer. TW observed that Vaccaro "is as big a queen as Oliver so they must be having a wonderful time together" (qtd. in St. Just, pp. 27 and 35). Their cruising would be recast in the story "Two on a Party" (1952).]

Tennessee Williams, Irene Selznick, and the "clown," Oliver Evans.

165. To Irene Mayer Selznick

[1431 Duncan Street
Key West, Florida]
4/10/50
[TLS w/ autograph postscript, 1 p. Boston U]

Dearest Irene:

If I had not promised to send you this script before sailing I would probably not have the courage to do so, for reading it over I am still desperately dissatisfied with it, I am not even sure that it is improved since the last draft. But a promise is a promise and an excuse is just an excuse, so I am letting you read it. Will you promise me one thing? Don't show it to anyone else! I am putting you on your honor, which I believe in!

You will understand why I am so hesitant and tentative about this script when you read it, and why I am so cagey about everything concerning. Since I cannot decide that I even want it produced, it is impossible at this point to submit it to anyone for a production. The item in Sunday's Times is totally incorrect and does not emanate from any source that I know of. Cheryl has shown great interest in my work, both in Rome and when she was here recently, but I have told her, as frankly as I am telling you, that I have too grave doubts about the script to allow it to be read or considered for production at this point. I am sure you know that I am being entirely honest with you on this point, as I would always be with you on any point concerning my work. There is never any double talk or double dealing in that department of my life. Gadg and Audrey, and now you, are the only ones that have read it. I read it aloud to Frank and Bigelow. I would appreciate it very much if you would mail this copy back to me from London, soon as you arrive there, care of Audrey. In your comments you may be as devastatingly candid as you please. There is no "icon" left to be "clastic"!

With love, 10.

(this is only copy with complete revisions to date, so will need for typing in N.Y.)

[TW hastened to assure Irene Selznick that Cheryl Crawford had not been offered *The Rose Tattoo*. Lewis Funke, source of the untimely rumor, based his "deduction" (*New York Times*, April 9, 1950) upon Crawford's recent visit to Key West and her earlier contact with TW in Rome.

Preceding the visit to Key West (April 3), Crawford defended her right to produce *The Rose Tattoo*: "I imagine Irene Selznick has been inquiring too. My feeling about this is that she was handed our best playwright on a golden platter, that she has not yet earned her right to such good fortune, and that some of us who have stuck with the theatre all of our working lives, taken great chances and done the first plays of many playwrights deserve the honor of producing Tennessee Williams" (to TW, March 9, 1950, U of Houston).]

166. *To Audrey Wood*

[1431 Duncan Street
Key West, Florida]
April 11, 1950.
[TLS, 2 pp. HRC]

Dear Audrey:

I am very, very grateful for your frank letter about producers. Of course the big question in my mind at the moment is not who I want to produce the new play but whether or not I really want it produced. That is what I said to Cheryl when she was here and what I wrote to Irene. I must admit that at the present time I feel much closer to Irene than Cheryl. The greatest personal loyalty I have is to you. The only loyalty that takes precedence over that is to my work, but it is hard for me to conceive of a situation in which those two loyalties might conflict seriously for long, they have always been so closely bound together. What I hope you will think about is the tremendous difference it makes to an author to feel "familiar and secure" with a producer he has to work with. Now if I were not a writer and you and Bill were not heads of a tremendously complex business organization I would say that the three of us would make the ideal team for production but to be realistic, we have, all three of us, great and pressing demands beyond the production of one (So far very shaky) little play. When I think about Irene I don't even ask myself if I like her or don't like her - although I am pretty sure that I do - I just know - without thinking about it - that the woman has demonstrated one of the most extraordinary powers of will, or drive, or vitality - or whatever you call it - that I've ever seen, and that's what I lack and what the rest of us don't have time for and what is, above everything else, most needed to give a delicate play the fortification and care it must have. Dear Cheryl, she's as delicate as the play itself, for all her tailored clothes and her square-set jaw, and her very clear

and honest blue eyes. I don't suppose, as a human being, I think any other producer quite measures up to her. After Irene, I suppose she's the one I'd want. But she just doesn't give the impression, somehow, of being vital or powerful enough to turn not only every stone but also some of the smaller mountains to achieve what she's after! But in conclusion I can only repeat what I said at the start. The question to decide first is whether or not the play should be produced. Then you and I can talk all this over and out about the producer. I have sent Irene a script, mailed it today, and in the letter I was very honest with her. I said it was not to be regarded as "submission for production", that I was not yet ready to talk or think in those terms - and - what is very true - I was most anxious simply to know what she thought of the script as it now stands - I am so far from being able to think or feel very clearly about it myself. I will get your copy off to you tomorrow, or Thursday - soon as I can get it assembled - I had to rush hers to catch her boat which sails Thursday midnight, and I told her to air mail the script back to you from London. As you see, I am being as prudent as ever!

Again, thanks for writing me how you felt, which always does the most good.

Love, Tenn

PS. Grandfather and I are coming up by train - we plan to leave next Tuesday - and Frank will drive the car up with an intellectual red-headed waitress as passenger. - We may never see him again! The reservations at the Sherry-N. will have to be moved forward. Frank will wire about this soon as the plans are quite final. Please alert Bigelow on swimming-pools! I have been working on film-script - hope to spend some time with Gadg preparing the ultimate draft.

P.S. (2) - Just got your wire. I have suspected right along that there was some gimmick involved in all the picture peoples' enthusiasm for "menagerie". I hope we can see it again as soon as I arrive in New York. - Reading your letter over about Irene, I must say that you are certainly not unique in your feeling about her personality problems. I was amazed, last Fall, to hear Brooks Atkinson, in Gadg's house, make something of the same observations about her. You may think it crazy of me to find these

traits in her somehow endearing - pathetic - "simpatico". My own hysteria is so like it, essentially, although mine is forcibly and cautiously controlled - but it gives me an understanding of hers. I wonder if you didn't really know her, and understand her, better when you first knew her, when we first talked about her in Charleston, S.C. So often the first perception is true and the later ones a distortion brought about by the strains that exist in all associations. - Obviously if we should all work together again on a production, there would have to be a frank discussion with Irene about the things that have made it difficult in the past, that there is to be no domination, no bullying, no unfair demands of time and energy - that you, especially, cannot be subjected to that sort of pressure - that there is no reason or need for it. I have a feeling that she is wise enough to recognize this without even being told - but should be told just the same! - in the creative world, everything good seems to be involved with a certain amount of excess - of "volonte de puissance" - an over-charged person that has to be controlled, if he or she submits to that control, is usually the best bet. The Whiteheads and Reas and Bloomgartens all leave me cold - I just "dummy up" in their presence. . . .

[Audrey Wood wrote that TW had not endured Irene Selznick "head-on, the physical body day after day for three years," during the production of *Streetcar*, and so he could more easily tolerate her intrusive manner and incessant demands. A strong personality herself, Wood admitted that she did not "function well" in the "vacuum of acquiescence" created by Selznick and urged TW "not to close the door to other possibilities." By recommending a group of "new managers," she anticipated her client's aversion to "the Whiteheads and Reas" and other conventional Broadway producers. Wood suggested once again that TW produce his own work and assured him that personal gain did not enter into her "thinking" (April 10, 1950, HRC).]

167. *To Carson McCullers*

[1431 Duncan Street
Key West, Florida]
April 1950
[TLS, 1 p. Duke U]

Dearest Carson:

All the news I have of you is indirectly, through Bigelow, Cheryl and Audrey, but that is my fault for I don't believe I have written since I last

saw you. I have been buried in work and am just now, finally, coming up to look around me a little. I have been working so hard for so long! I hope that for the next few months I will be willing and able to take it easy, relax, and get some enjoyment out of just living. I have felt <u>driven</u>, without even knowing why.

I gather from Bigelow that you are contemplating a trip to Ireland to visit Elizabeth Bowen. To me Ireland sounds so cold and wet somehow, I am much more drawn to Italy and France, but if you are charmed by Miss Bowen, of course that will be more important than the climate.

I do hope you are living in New York, now, instead of Nyack, for then we shall be able to see so much more of each other. Please let me know when you are sailing. That is, if it is within the next few days. We are leaving here this Sunday. Grandfather and I are going up by train and Frankie is driving up in the car with most of the luggage and with an intellectual red-headed waitress of great beauty. Perhaps we will never see him again! Our sailing date is May 20th on the Ile de France. I hope to spend some weeks in Paris. Perhaps Frank will precede me to Rome, or to Sicily, and I will follow him later by plane. My nerves must smooth out somewhere. Right now they are in a dozen frantic little knots! I shall devote the summer, not to work, but to a smoothing-out process, to making peace with myself and the world and the various phenomena of it.

The town has become pretty sad, Key West, I mean. About six weeks ago there was a murder, a middle-aged queen was beaten over the head with an ash-tray by a sailor. And as a reprisal for this ghastly offense on the part of the poor old queen, the town police have been prosecuting everyone around here who is a bit different-looking. A very ugly atmosphere has developed. Practically all the "Bohemians" have fled from the Keys. Frank and I are the sole survivors. I guess Grandfather's round collar made us appear more respectable but we have not been molested. But I stay home at night, I am actually afraid to go out on the downtown streets. A person can be arrested for sixteen different kinds of vagrancy and I'm sure I must come under at least one heading! One poor lad was picked up for having a "sissy walk"! Released on $250. bond and given a devastating lecture at court. Another poor belle known as "Tangerine" has altogether disappeared. We suspect she has committed suicide in the style of Key West. In the last ten years there have [been] 17 murders here and <u>no</u> convictions. When bodies are found they are nearly always called suicides, even when,

in at least one notorious instance, they are found with cement sacks for ballast and with hands and feet roped together at the bottom of a lagoon! - Suicide, mind you! - But I still love this part of the country, the water, the eternal turquoise and foam of the sea and the sky. If I ever buy property, I think it will be in the Caribbean.

It is so wonderful about the award. It will mean months more duration for the play, in New York and on the road and I should certainly think a movie-sale to boot. I feel so much better about you, knowing that now, at last, you must be free of anxiety about the material quantity of living. We will be at the Sherry-Netherland. I want grandfather to have a taste of real fine living while we are together. He refuses to go to Europe with us. Much love -

10. xxxxxxxxxx

[Carson McCullers and Reeves shared a fashionable apartment in New York at this time. TW thought her plan to visit Elizabeth Bowen in Ireland a "great mistake" and informed Paul Bigelow that he would not "consider" making such a trip with McCullers. "About Sister Woman," he added, "one must remember that psychic disturbance takes the place of orgasm and she may have all of that she longs for on the Irish moors, and out of it all may come another great novel" (April 11, 1950, Columbia U).

McCullers's health was still fragile but her financial prospects robust, as TW noted in further gossip with Bigelow: "The Smiths may finally have to abandon the pose of genteel destitution and face the fact that the family includes a money-maker of no small potential. I have been reading Tom Wolfe and it astonishes me how closely his family resembles theirs. Eliza and Bebe certainly should have met!" (April 11, 1950, Columbia U)—a reference to the penurious mothers of Thomas Wolfe and Lula Carson Smith.

TW planned to write to McCullers on April 11, 1950, the probable date of this letter's composition.]

168. To Irene Mayer Selznick

Sherry-Netherland Hotel [New York]
[April 1950]
[TLS, 3 pp. Boston U]

Dearest Irene:

It was indeed quite a letter, and yesterday afternoon, when I got it, was very black, the bottom of a long, descending arc that began with the play's

completion last month, broken only by the lift given by a brilliantly understanding (though highly critical) letter received from Gadg and a similar one from Molly and the enthusiasm of Bigelow when I read it aloud which had to be partly discounted as a friend's indulgence - a decline which continued by fairly gentle degrees until yesterday afternoon when your letter knocked the goddam bottom out of it and almost the top off me! For that afternoon, and the night that followed, I believed that you were right, that I had passed into madness and that power of communication was gone. Under the circumstances there [was] hardly any other conclusion to draw. Either you were "dead wrong" or I was crazy. Or that thing had happened which eventually happens to most lyric talents, the candle is burned or blown out and there's no more matches! - Then, of course, came the morning, consistent with its habit. I woke early, recognized Frank and Grandfather and even myself in the mirror - and had my coffee and sat down quietly and rationally to read over the script. Then the amazing thing came about. For the first time since this draft was completed, I liked what I had done and felt that I had done just exactly what I had meant to do in all but a few short passages, that in the play, as a whole, I had said precisely what I had wanted to say as well as it could be said, and the play existed.

Not a ballet, not a libretto, but a play with living characters and a theme of poetic truth, handled with more precision and stringency than ever before in my writing, and in a style, a medium (yes, highly plastic and visual but with those elements an integral, active and very articulate instrument of the play's total expression - not just "effects" for the sake of "effects" or symbols for the sake of being artily symbolic - but a way of saying more clearly, strongly and beautifully those things which could not have been said so well in language if they could have been said at all in language - a progress which I think very marked in the true use of theatre as distinguished from forms of verbal expression) - a medium worked out with tremendous difficulty in exact, or nearly exact, accord with the very clear and strong conception that it sprang from.

For the first time in my life I knew that I must take a solitary position of self-belief, as an artist, and that I could take it proudly because I had earned it. I had not skimped or scanted or hedged or cheated anytime, anywhere, during the year and four months in which I had struggled with the adversaries of doubt and disappointment and fatigue, the many mornings that were brick walls and the few that came open, the exhausting see-saw

of exhileration and despair, the continual, unsparing drain of all I had in me to give it. That was the history of it, and this was the culmination. I had to believe. I <u>believed</u>.

I hope you will forgive me now for indulging myself in argument with some of your points of objection. It will do me good. You say the emotion is "felt by the characters but not shared by the reader". I wonder if emotions in a play are usually, or even <u>ever</u>, shared by the reader? If they were, would there be any point in the production of a play, in translating it from the cold page to the warm and living instruments of the stage? Would there be any real need for great actors and brilliant directors and for designers and technicians? I don't think a play is so different from a sheet of music, and there are not many people who can read a sheet of music and hear the music in a way that would obviate an orchestra or singer. The parallel is particularly fitting to this particular play which consists, so much, as you have observed, of signals, notations, as though to various instruments whose playing together will create the expression. Then you say: "Were I to see rather than read the play, I fear I would be at a loss to understand the sources of sustained crisis under which Pepina labors". I venture to guess that with the collaboration of someone like Magnani and someone like Gadg you would find those "sources" far easier to understand, for then the play would come out of the notes and signals and would live before you. "Sustained crisis" is true. But throughout the play (which is about a "sustained crisis") that condition is fully documented and justified. It opens, for instance, with a highly emotional woman telling her passionately loved husband that she is to bear him a child. A crisis. The death of the husband is, of course, another crisis. But how is either of these difficult to understand? In the following acts of the play - the visual and violent "knife-scene" with the daughter, the devastating revelation of the husband's betrayal, first the struggle against it and finally, gradually, the acceptance of it - this, too, is sustained crisis, but I can't for the life of me see how it would seem <u>not</u> motivated, <u>not</u> comprehendible to any of us who have loved or suffered any great loss or disillusionment in our lives, I don't expect this sustained crisis, which is the play, to be felt in reading but I cannot doubt that in performance, with skill and power, an audience could be made to feel it deeply and to enjoy its katharsis. I was well-aware, while writing the play, that the high pitch of emotion in the characters, in keeping with their race, temperament and most of all with their situation, (the crises

in which they're involved) might make exhausting demands on everybody concerned. For this reason many of the scenes are deliberately low-keyed, particularly in the writing, the speeches, and the intensities are given quiet, almost submerged, forms of expression and the burden transferred as much as possible from the actor to the visual, plastic elements which you condemn as "effects". Scenes are cut-off and under-stated but always with at least some (muted) expression of the essential things, and the contrapuntal use of the children is like a modulated counter-theme or "cushion" to these intensities - (this will come out much more clearly in the final draft, for the separate play of the children developed very late in the play's composition). The great advance I have made in this play - technically, as a theatre-craftsman - is what you call its "penalizing minimum" of dialogue and the effects which you seem to think are extraneous ornamentation.

No, I feel no resentment about your letter and I do feel gratitude for your writing me what I hope was exactly what you felt, although I suspect you could have eliminated the pacifying reference to "ballet or libretto" and said, more bluntly, more kindly cruelly - I dislike it intensely! You're not the only one who does. I think Audrey and Bill are probably just as disappointed in it as you are. Who knows, at this point, who is right? But I would like to see it tried, produced, and I shall make an effort to see it.

Thanks and all the love as ever,

Tenn.

[Irene Selznick's letter of rejection made explicit what Elia Kazan and Audrey Wood had only implied: *The Rose Tattoo* was neither conceptually sound nor dramatically vital. The gravest problem lay with Pepina, whose motivation Selznick could neither "'know'" nor "feel." The myriad effects of the play—its "plastic medium"—were used "at the expense of the drama," she thought, or perhaps as compensation for the play's dramatic limitations. Selznick expressed no further interest in *The Rose Tattoo* and in closing forecast rather accurately TW's long-delayed success on Broadway: "If the 'doing' has been emotionally and artistically rewarding, I beg you to accept that return—it must lead to growth and to a more completely gratifying result in your next piece - or even the one after" (April 16, 1950, Boston U). Selznick went on to produce *Bell, Book and Candle*, a light comedy by John van Druten which opened the following November.

This letter was probably written in the week of April 16, 1950, after TW arrived in New York.]

*169. To Jack Warner, Jerry Wald, and
     Charles K. Feldman*

SH: The Sherry-Netherland
Fifth Avenue at 59th Street
New York 22, N.Y.
May 6, 1950.
[TLS, 5 pp. U of Delaware]

Dear Sirs:

I have now seen the picture three times, twice in a private screening room and finally with a regular audience in New Jersey and this letter is meant to convey as clearly as possible my own reaction to it, based on these three showings. I know and truly appreciate the tremendous enthusiasm that you have all felt and expressed for this picture, which you have made with great care. It was perhaps unfortunate that I had received nothing but highly laudatory comments on the film before I saw it, as I was not prepared to find any faults in it whatsoever. Consequently the first time I saw it, in the cold light of a private screening, my reactions were unavoidably more critical than those that you had expressed to me in your wires.

Let me begin by telling you the many things that I am grateful for and the things that I admire. First of all, the magnificent cast. I can't remember a picture in which four important actors give such uniformly fine performances and each so perfectly suited to the part. The performances of Jane Wyman and Arthur Kennedy are the best I have seen given by either of those two and have created the parts better than I have seen them in any of the stage productions of the play. Max Steiner has written a beautiful score, one that I think is really notable, which blends perfectly with the moods of the play. All of the comedy values in the picture have been brilliantly realized in Irving Rapper's direction and particularly by the playing of Lawrence and Kennedy. None of the "laughs" have been missed. I was particularly aware of this when I saw it before an audience in New Jersey. It was an audience that had come expecting to see "Cinderella", but I had the impression that the surprise on the program was generally agreeable to them. Even to my innately skeptical eye, the picture appears to have what you call "audience appeal", and being as much a showman as any of you, I think that is always a nice thing to have in any form of public entertainment.

Now I would not be willing to make any adverse comments at all if I didn't feel that certain things can still be done to protect and enhance the

property as it now exists. First of all, as a premise to these criticisms, I feel that the picture runs a bit longer than it should to have its maximum effect; perhaps as much as ten minutes can be eliminated with real improvement to the film. Since the changes that I have to suggest are nearly all in the form of editing, or clipping out, this is a happy circumstance. Unfortunately Irving was not able to supply me with a copy of the final shooting script so my notes cannot have exact page-and-line references.

The things that I object to most strenuously, and very strenuously indeed, are certain changes that were made in the script after I left Hollywood and which came to me as a complete and very distressing surprise when I first heard them from the screen. I understand why you decided to dramatize Amanda's recollection-scene, but it has the unfortunate effect of making her seem not just a romanticist, which she was to some degree, but an out-and-out liar. I am thinking particularly of her statement that she had "twenty-three proposals in a single evening". Of course the background for this fanciful reminiscence is much too elaborate and somehow it seems to lack any real nostalgia or poetry, it is more like a bit of an MGM musical suddenly thrown into the middle of the picture. I understand, also, why you may not be able to take this out of the film, but I am wondering if it could not be shortened a bit, or perhaps even done in softer, mistier focus and the "twenty-three serious proposals" drowned out by the music. However, I don't want to make a particular point of this.

What I do want to make a very particular point of is the script changes that have crept into Tom's "drunk-scene". Irving Rapper is coming back with specific notes on the lines that we thought could be removed from the scene. I can only assume that they were written in by the collaborator, Mr. Berneis. Irving knows exactly what these lines are and where they occur. It seems to me that they do untold damage to the dignity of the picture as a whole, the bathos and corny philosophizing are so incongruous to the spirit of the film as a whole. I must admit that at this point in the picture, I had to retire from the projection-room for a glass of water and that they cast a shadow over the entire remainder of the film. The second scene in the warehouse could be dropped out entirely without affecting the development of the story. I originally put it in to provide an occasion for Jim's invitation to dinner, but this scene has been entirely re-written by Mr. Berneis and the invitation no longer exists: consequently the scene is pointless except that it provides some additional footage for Kirk Douglas and a few

"yaks". The writing of the scene is amateurish and I believe that one of the jokes was borrowed from a well-known source. This scene, however, is not one of my really strong objections, I only feel that reducing it will result in a tighter picture.

A really strong objection concerns an insertion that has been made after Tom's final exit from the apartment. Laura follows him out into the alley and calls him back for the exchange of some more lines from the cornball department. It is the only scene in the entire picture where Miss Wyman's performance really weakens. Rapper has exact notes on this passage. The worst of these lines is "Send me your poems so I may travel with you". I would prefer the entire elimination of this little scene, which is anti-climactic and saccharine, but I particularly beseech you to eliminate the two or three utterances that Irving and I have noted upon the script. This, again, is a bit of editing that is entirely practicable and will help us immensely with the New York critics and all those who are familiar with "The Glass Menagerie" as a serious poetic play. Little touches like that, unimportant as they appear to be, can make a tremendous difference in critical attitude toward a film, to the impression of its dignity.

About the "new" gentleman-caller. In my script he was never visible on the screen. At the most, he was the sound of approaching footsteps and perhaps a shadow stretching before him as he came up the alley. This gives him a quality of poetic mystery and beauty which the picture badly needs in its final moments. Now we not only see him very plainly, his whole figure, but he is also provided with a full name, Richard Henderson. This little touch is going to stand out like a sore thumb and will gravely affect your critical reception, particularly in all those cities where the "Menagerie" has been known as a play. The light in Laura's eyes, and in her mother's, their glad "hellos" from the fire-escape were absolutely all the up-beat that the traffic could bear. As I remarked when I left my script with you, any more upbeat at this point is the straw that breaks the camel's back. I urge you most seriously to consider eliminating the shot of the actual figure coming up the alley and to remove the last name, both totally unnecessary to giving the picture its final "upbeat" and both extremely dangerous to a respect for the film's integrity among that relatively small, but terribly important, segment of the film public to which such things make a difference. (I don't think we should dismiss from our minds the possibility of an Academy Award, for instance.)

Tom's final narration is curiously lacking in real poetic feeling. We have all discussed this (Irving, Miss Wood and I) here in New York and we felt that this could be recorded again with a greater attention to the emotional quality of the lines and with the restoration of a couple of lines which Irving tells me - to my surprise and horror! - were cut out by the Breen office. The lines I think should be restored are the best, most lyric lines in the entire narration - "Then all at once my sister touches my shoulder. I turn around and look into her eyes. . . . Oh, Laura, Laura! I tried to leave you behind me. But I am more faithful than I intended to be. . . . "

Irving tells me that Breen made the disgustingly prurient charge that these lines (!!!!) contained a suggestion of <u>INCEST</u>! I cannot understand acquiescence to this sort of foul-minded and utterly stupid tyranny, especially in the case of a film as totally clean and pure, as remarkably devoid of anything sexual or even sensual, as the "Menagerie", both as a play and a picture. The charge is insulting to me, to my family, and an effrontery to the entire motion-picture industry! And I think you owe it to motion-pictures to defend yourselves against such prurience and tyranny by fighting it out with them. If I ever work in pictures, in America, I must know that my work is not at the mercy of the capricious whims that seem to operate in this office.

Well, boys, I have had my say! I am sure that you wanted me to have it, and I deeply appreciate your wanting me to have it and giving me the chance to have it. You have what is <u>almost</u> a fine picture. Don't let it remain anything less than what you are still able to make it, with only the exercise of a little scissors and paste.

Cordially and gratefully, Tennesee Williams

[Relatively few of the "changes" suggested by TW appear in the final print of *The Glass Menagerie*. Amanda's claim of "'twenty-three proposals'" was not "drowned out" by music, although the "recollection-scene" was apparently given a softer focus. The lengthy flashback was intended to create a youthful image for the fifty-one-year-old star, Gertrude Lawrence. "Otherwise," she once observed, Amanda "would have been only a character study of a middle-aged woman, and I don't want to get mother roles, and unglamorous ones at that" (qtd. in *New York Times*, October 16, 1949).

In the "'drunk-scene'" the only added, remaining, passage of "philosophizing" begins with Tom's wish that the magician's scarf cover the "whole ugly world," to which Laura replies that "the whole world is beautiful." The issuing of Jim's

invitation was removed from the warehouse sequence to enhance its announcement in the following fire-escape scene. The now "pointless" scene was not "dropped," although the "borrowed" joke was cut. So too was the line which TW most deplored—"'Send me your poems'"—in Tom's new departure scene. The inserted scene was designed, and retained, to strengthen the character of Laura, who confidently bids Tom "do what you've always wanted to do. Travel, write."

The shot of the "'new' gentleman-caller" was retained and is more "actual" than the allusive "sound" or "shadow" which TW preferred. The caller's last name was deleted, though, and the deep perspective of the alley maintained. Tom's final words are indeed flat: "And that is how I remember them, my mother and my sister. And so goodbye."

Joseph Breen, Production Code administrator, stated in his first report that Tom's memory of Laura should be "carefully scrutinized and possibly rewritten, to get away from the present suggestion of an incestuous attraction toward his sister" (to J.L. Warner, March 31, 1949, Herrick). He repeated the warning in later correspondence and apparently the offending lines were cut, although restored to the final print. TW seems not to have learned of Breen's objection until late in the production.]

170. To Paul Bigelow

Paris
6/7/50
[TLS w/ autograph postscript,
2 pp. Massee Collection]

Dear Paul:

So far we have not gone to London, not because Paris is too fascinating to leave but because I don't feel morally up to the rigors of London. I knew when I left New York the strain was going to hit me like a delayed-action bomb, and it did. I arrived here in a dreadful state of nervous fatigue and depression and am just beginning to pull out of it a little.

Sister Woman returned from Ireland promptly on schedule and apparently Elizabeth Bowen got herself out of a delicate situation with amazing grace and with no offense whatsoever. Of course Carson is talking of flying to London to join her there but it is only talk so far. She and Reeves came over to our little left-bank hotel the other day and spent the entire afternoon. Jane and Paul Bowles were also present. Poor Jane Bowles was so nervous that she drank half a bottle of vodka. Sister Woman and Reeves kept the chamber-maid hopping between our rooms and the wine-shop. Right in the

midst of this happy occasion the phone rang. It was long-distance, America calling Carson. It turned out to be the Martineaus. Florence was calling to inform them that Stanley had fallen "off the wagon" and pleading for advice and instructions. "Get Marty Mann!" cried Carson. Carson was then asked if Reeves had stayed, or gotten back, on the wagon. She said, Reeves is just drinking wine! And here was Reeves reeling about the room like a storm-wracked schooner. "Get Marty Mann! Tell her to get Marty Mann!" he shouted. Then both started babbling maudlinly into the phone at once, Oh, darling, oh, precious, oh, blessed, come right over here as soon as Stanley gets out of the hospital, we love you so much, we just adore you so much. Can Stanley talk? Oh, Stanley, love, how are you! Are you all right Stanley Precious? We love you so much, you know we just adore you. Honey, get Marty Mann and she'll pull you out of this thing! What, Stanley? Oh, Florence! What happened? Did he fall down? Oh, then call us back later, you precious sweet lovely thing, you! Etc. Etc. Etc. It must have been the longest and most intense transcontinental phone-call since the war ended, and the McCullers looked really happy and satisfied when they hung up and immediately sent out for another bottle of wine. Reeves called this morning, and I asked if they had had any further conversation with their producers and Reeves said, No. We just sent a cable confirming the talk on the phone!

So you see Paris is not really so far from New York, after all. I wonder if Rome will be any further? When I said we were getting an apartment in Rome (we hoped) Reeves immediately said, How many rooms? Oh, one and a half! I answered without a moment's reflection. There was a slight suggestion that Frank and I, being rather small people might be able to occupy the 'half' until I remembered that the 'half' room was really only a sort of a vestibule. Carson said, Oh, how lovely! I bet it's like Mrs. Spring's apartment in Rome, which I think was a slightly confused reference to my novel, the one that contained that extremely felicitous line about "amethyst dusk". . . .

The meeting between Reeves and Paul Bowles was not a happy one. Reeves said, Well, Son, how does it feel to be a published writer? Bowles looked like a Morrocan camel with a mouthful of the spiniest and most indigestible plant that grows on the desert. But the McCullers were so entranced over the good news about their producers that every response to their benign gestures struck them as expressing the most suitable gratitude

and delight. Carson told me three times, by careful reckoning, that I did not like her play. If she had told me once more I would have agreed with her, but luckily my final response was peculiarly inspired. When have I ever <u>not</u> liked anything you have ever done? For this I received a tender kiss on the lips. Paul Bowles was accorded the same tribute when their hosts came to take them away. Paul is terribly squeamish about any physical contact with anything not Arab and not under fifteen and he looked more like a Camel with something suddenly impossible to get down his throat than ever.

I am sorry to devote so much space to a really American topic but nothing has yet happened of a strictly European character that is worth noting. There is a vast and dreadful crowd of tourists here and we don't [know] where, how far South or East, it will be necessary to go to feel we have really left New York. But the Bowles are a pure delight as ever and, all in all, one might say the same of the McCullers, although quite naturally in a dissimilar fashion.

Much, much love, dearest Paul, Tenn.
(from Frank, too.)

Warmest regards to Alice! And to Jordan!

[TW and Frank Merlo landed at Plymouth on May 26. The "rigors of London" probably included bad food and bad trade as well as the truncated production of *Streetcar*, which closed on August 19, 1950, apparently unseen by TW.

Elizabeth Bowen's view of Carson McCullers as "a destroyer" may reflect the marital tension which she observed during the visit of Carson and Reeves in late-July. Bowen chose not "to be closely involved" (qtd. in Carr, p. 360) with McCullers, preferring the friendship of Eudora Welty, who had visited earlier in the spring.

Summarized were thirty years of counseling and advocacy in *Marty Mann Answers Your Questions about Drinking and Alcoholism* (1970). Reeves, who had been counseled by Miss Mann, recommended that Stanley Martineau, a co-producer of *The Member of the Wedding*, find similar help.

TW refers to "the amethyst light of prima sera" in Part Three of *The Roman Spring*.

The postscript refers to Alice Bouverie and Jordan Massee.]

171. To Cheryl Crawford

[Paris]
June 9, 1950
[TLS, 1 p. BRTC]

Dear Cheryl:

Your letter which I picked up this afternoon at American Express is the first ray of light that I have had from America. Gadg's letter, which was waiting for me when I arrived, attached to the censored "Streetcar" film-script, was most depressing. He said he was sorry that "he would not be able to do my play because of his film commitments". He mentioned Zapata, which I understand, but also mentioned the unfinished film-script by Arthur Miller. I don't see how or why an unfinished film-play would take precedence over my play, since surely its schedule is far more elastic at this time. I have written him twice, once from the boat, and again after receiving this very flat and cold announcement in Paris, and I told him how thoroughly bewildered I was by his sudden reversal of attitude. Do you know what to make of it? Perhaps you can get a clearer picture than I.

I felt so badly, after receiving his letter, that I gave up the idea of going to London and plunged into the anarchistic nightlife of Paris, which made me feel even worse. Now I have given that up, too, and we are leaving for Italy tomorrow or Monday.

I worked on the play all the while I was on the boat. I have a new ending which is free-er and wilder, involving the children instead of Estelle Hohengarten, and am re-writing the whole Rosario section. It is no use describing it but I will send you and Audrey the revised material as soon as it is completed. We have the name of a new Italian actress who speaks English, Lea Padovani. She is in the English film "Christ in Concrete" and is said to be similar in style to Magnani but younger. Of course I will make every effort to see and interest Magnani in Rome. If she can read English I don't [know] how she can fail to see herself as Pepina. Still another actress is Elena Zareschi but I don't know what she has appeared in. These names were given us by the Italian screen-writer of <u>Vive in Pace</u> whom we met here in Paris.

If Gadg is definitely out, I think we should consider Bobby Lewis as well as Danny Mann. In many ways the play would be especially suited to Bobby with his fine sense of style and poetry. Peter Brook is another name to bear in mind, but I am still hoping that Kazan is acting upon a temporary caprice.

I did not show the script to Olivier on the boat. I simply did not feel like exposing it again while I was still working on it and while I was still recuperating from the session with Molly.

You will hear from me soon after I settle in Italy or Sicily. More thanks than I can say for your belief!

Love from us both, Tenn.

[Successful productions of *Porgy and Bess* (1942), *One Touch of Venus* (1943), and *Brigadoon* (1947) established Cheryl Crawford (1902-1986) as an astute, tasteful manager and led to the staging of four plays by TW: *The Rose Tattoo*, as well as *Camino Real* (1953), *Sweet Bird of Youth* (1959), and *Period of Adjustment* (1960). Crawford's thrift as a producer was exceeded only by her intelligence and devotion to the theatre.

Lea Padovani's ability to look both "young" and "mature" (to TW, June 28, 1950, HRC) in *Christ in Concrete* (1949) was a valuable asset, Audrey Wood thought, in playing the role of Pepina. The arresting film title refers to an exploited bricklayer who drowns in concrete.

Robert Lewis's reputation as a sensitive director led to his recommendation by TW. *Come Back, Little Sheba* was Daniel Mann's first staging of a Broadway production.]

172. To Elia "Gadg" Kazan

Am. Ex. Co., Rome.
6/16/50
[TLS w/ autograph postscript, 3 pp. WUCA]

Dear Gadg:

When I finished your letter I had tears in my eyes, which was not very manly of me, but still in character, since I have never pretended to have much hair on my chest. The moisture came from relief, for your letter removed the doubt I had felt about your continued interest in my work and myself. I have too much reserve with people, as a rule, too much doubt and suspicion, but I had thrown all that overboard in my relations with you and had been totally honest and open with you, and something in the apparently cool tone with which you told me you would not be able to do "Rose Tattoo" hurt me a great deal more than the professional set-back. Now you have dispelled that feeling and we can forget it. In this letter I am going to be a great deal more unguarded than I have ever been in the past and I am

going to tell you a lot about myself and my life in the past few years because I think it may help you to understand my problems as a writer which I am now still able to hope will concern you. But that part of the letter I am going to save till the last. It is a sort of capsule-autobiography of the past five years and we should get through business matters first.

I did not see Vivien. I fell into a grim, nihilistic mood in Paris and could not go through with the planned trip to London but, plunged, instead, into the anarchistic nightlife that the city has to offer in spite of the Puritanical reforms that have lately gone on there.

I'm not worried about your not shooting the film on location as I know you will insist on getting a good studio set out of Warners. I am sorry you have changed your mind about the night-out scene which I truly liked and thought it was one place where the story was transposed into truly cinematic terms that gave it a value not in the stage version. To me Blanche's behavior in this sequence was clearly and sympathetically motivated, not hysterical but very normally human within the limits of her somewhat flighty nature. It could be toned down, if there were hysterical excesses, but basically I felt it was true and right and richly cinematic. Psychologically it couldn't be truer. She is not, at this point, madly in love with Mitch. How could she be? She is a woman desperate for understanding, affection, protection. But it isn't until the close of this scene that she comes to see that that is what he will give her, and at the point where she takes flight to the powder-room and calls up the old beau, she is hurt and clutching at straws. This could be made so very clear and poignant on the screen that I am surprised you have lost confidence in it. Don't listen to Leigh about script! The Oliviers are as bad as the Lunts in that Dept.

I don't mind the bits from scene four going back in, but I don't have a script with me, now, and can't visualize where they would go. However I am sure you must have a good place for them in mind. But do think earnestly about the night-out scene and consider whether you cannot play it down, in the heavy parts, so that the effect you fear, of a person already cracking up, can be avoided while still keeping the wonderful movement and vitality that it now has, and I am not just talking about the wind-blown flight down the stairs to the crumbling pier. In other words, I challenge your boldness.

Now let us talk about "Rose Tattoo". The fact that you have told Cheryl not to engage another director is a bit of encouragement and I am

clutching at it for all it is worth. Of course I now understand about Art's picture. You should have told me more about that originally. Under the circumstances I think it should take precedence over the play in your future plans. If the Zapata thing is out, does that leave a vacancy in your schedule, and where?

I'm not really very worried about the time-element myself, but I know that Cheryl has to know about it and that I don't want the play to open on Broadway later than March at the latest. If it has to open in the Spring, could it open in Chicago and stay out of town - with a lay-off during the summer - until the early Fall? My main concern, now, is to know that you want to do it and to continue my work on it. I feel that the Rosario part is coming richly to life, and perhaps Cheryl has told you that I have a new (alternative) ending which <u>may</u> be better than the two women. I know what youd dislike about the two women. It represents to you a retreat for Pepina. To me it was an advance on a realistic basis. But my objection to it is that it may be just a little bit cliché, a little expected or pat. Maybe that's only because of brooding too much about it. The other ending is really <u>wild</u> and it involves the children. - Of course Alvaro can't take the place of Rosario. Does anybody ever take the place of the first great love? What he accomplishes is her escape from the urn of ashes and her reconcilement with life! In the new ending I may go so far as to suggest, symbolically, that she will bear a child by him. I am sure that in playing the feeling will be one of affirmative statement, not decadent melancholy, because that is how I have conceived it. But the statement will have to have <u>pain</u> in it too. I think of this play as a dark, blood-red translucent stone that is twisted this way and that, to give off its sombre rich light, like the ring on the crooked finger of some wise and wicked old witch of beneficent character, or perhaps some old necromancer like Bigelow. In simpler terms, I think of it as having a curious light-dark quality, a stranger and richer mystery than my other plays have had. In that way, perhaps, less human, the way that the <u>interior</u> of the body is less familiarly human than the hands and face. It is more about perplexity than about pain. The mystery of one to another. The baffled look, the stammered speech, the incomplete gesture, the wild rush of beings past and among each other. All of that I am trying to get in one play, with a simple, commonplace story. During the past two years I have been, for the first time in my life, happy and at home with someone and I think of this play as a monument to that happiness, a house built of

images and words for that happiness to live in. But in that happiness there is the long, inescapable heritage of the painful and the perplexed like the dark corners of a big room. But the play is not at all personal, though it is dedicated to an intensely personal thing. At least I don't think it is personal, not as Menagerie or even as much as Streetcar, and the fact it is less personal (in a sense, more about a thing, a quality, than persons) may be what makes it seem inhuman to Molly. Now some of the above, especially the part about the blood-red stone, may not make much sense. I am not sure I would under-stand it myself, and I am talking about the play that exists in my conception and I don't know how near or far that is to the play on paper. Do you like Tchelitchew's painting "Cache-Cache" (Hide-and-Seek)? Stravinsky's Sacre du Printemps? Both of those works are masterpieces, and I have no right to compare this play to them, but they contain or suggest something of what I was trying to get and am still seeking in it which is what makes it so important to me. I hardly hope that I will be able to arrive at a full realization of this, but I think I will come close enough to make it felt as a disturbing and exciting experience in the theatre, even though it should happen to be a failure. With you, I don't think it would be. If you refuse to do it, I would still try to get it with someone like Lewis, Mann or Peter Brook, if any of them would attempt it. But of the directors I know, this is much closer to you. You have an emotional grasp of it. Not to have you would be a disaster, even before it opened. (I mean compared to what you could make it.) - One thing, very sad, I have got to face. I don't write with the effervesence that I used to. It comes harder. The peak of my virtuosity was in the one-act plays, some of which are like fire-crackers in a rope. Some of that came from sexual repression and loneliness which don't exist anymore for very good reasons, and some of it came from plain youth and freshness. As a compensation, I have a clearer, much clearer, sense of what I am doing. I have a deeper knowledge of life and people, and I think I have more sanity. As you can tell from this letter, my approach to my work is hysterical. It is infatuated and sometimes downright silly. I don't know what it is to take anything calmly although I know how to look like a fish on ice, as Maria Britneva describes me. I'll always be "a neurotic" but I don't think I am any longer in danger of becoming psychotic. But with that danger has also gone some of my uncontrolled vivacity as a writer.

Now I have written you everything but the autobiographical section, and thinking it over I know it is not necessary. For the past five years I have

been (intermittently but usually) haunted by a fear, which has made it necessary for me [to] work like somebody running out of a house on fire. Make out of that what you want to!

But right now concentrate, I hope, on making a great picture which only you can in America!

With love, Tenn.

I have gotten Alvaro into the first scene as a distant cousin who comes to request a loan for his three dependants: tentative and removable. I see the value in bringing him into the first part of the play: but was fearful of the changes it would call for in the later scenes. Perhaps they are not so formidable as I had thought. Pepina does not see Alvaro clearly in the first scene for she has turned the lights out to rest her eyes after sewing all day on "First Communion" dresses.

[TW answered Elia Kazan's rejection of *The Rose Tattoo* by writing that "an uncompleted film-script {"The Hook," by Arthur Miller} can be scheduled at any time in the future. . . . It makes it appear that the real reason is somewhere between the lines, which is evasive and not like you at all" (May 30, 1950, WUCA). Kazan's subsequent letter appears to have restored TW's confidence and explained the priority of Arthur Miller's script. Kazan may also have raised TW's hopes by mentioning that another film project of his, *Viva Zapata!* (1952), had encountered political difficulties in Mexico and might not be shot after *Streetcar* was finished. The same news had reached Audrey Wood in New York and led her to hope for Kazan's final "commitment" (to TW, June 16, 1950, HRC) to *The Rose Tattoo*.

Kazan apparently feared that TW's elaboration of the "night-out scene" in *Streetcar* would be incompatible with the measured closing, as Blanche and Mitch embrace: "Sometimes—there's God—so quickly!" No hysterical "flight" to the "powder-room" or to the "crumbling pier" was filmed.

TW met the surrealist painter Pavel Tchelitchew in the mid 1940s and spoofed his gloomy metaphysical themes with the sobriquet "Chilly Death." His experimentation with "interior landscapes" of the human body—*Hide and Seek* (1940-1942) a well-known example—intrigued TW. The title served provisionally during early draft stages of *Baby Doll* (1956).

The metaphorical "house on fire" and its haunting effect upon TW refer to his operation in May 1946.

Penned in the lower margin of page 1 is the notation "Let Art have <u>his</u> way! Commies go brah!" TW probably refers to Arthur Miller's defiant support of liberal causes, an activity which led the State Department to withhold his passport (see

letter #286) and the House Un-American Activities Committee to subpoena his testimony. The screenplay in question, "The Hook," was abandoned by Miller but proved the inspiration for Kazan's award-winning film *On the Waterfront* (1954).]

173. To Oliver Evans

[Hotel d'Inghilterra, Rome]
6/20/50
[TLS, 1 p. HRC]

Dear Oliver:

I was dreadfully shocked by the news of your accident. I do hope you've recovered from it. Isn't it strange that I always had the feeling, when you drove, that something terrible was going to happen? We are back in Rome but could not get back in our old apartment and are staying at the hotel Inhilterra while we look for a new Apt. We are seeing two this afternoon. Rome is not crowded by holy pilgrims as we had feared. In fact there seem to be fewer people than last summer. I have had two wonderful lays at the baths, one a fisherman from Capri and the other a Sicilian, blond, which are the best blonds in Europe. The last thing I did before I left America was to get Audrey hot on the problem of renewing your fellowship through the Authors' League. I don't know how much money there was left in it and unfortunately I can't make a new contribution to the fund until the money from my pictures starts coming in, sometime next winter. Right now I am just able to keep us going. I have finished a play and a novella. But the play's success is doubtful. It demands a really great actress like Magnani (the part is a Sicilian immigrant to America) and direction like Kazan's. Kazan is not entirely sold on the play and as yet I have no assurance that he will consent to do it. I am all at sixes-and-sevens, professionally. Wonder if should not quit writing. But there is only one other thing I like doing very much and you can't do that <u>all</u> the time. Or <u>can</u> you?

Our address is American Express, Rome. Let me know how things are working out. It is wonderful, wonderful news that you are transferring to City College, New York. That will make life so much easier for you, and we will see more of each other, if I am lucky next year (meaning if I am in New York for a production!)

Love, 10.

[To "the baths" of Rome TW added "the old Appian Way" as sexual rendezvous: "In the evenings, very late, after midnight, I like to drive out the old Appian Way and park the car at the side of the road and listen to the crickets among the old tombs. Sometimes a figure appears among them which is not a ghost but a Roman boy in the flesh!" (to Jane Lawrence Smith, June 29, 1950, Smith Collection).]

174. To Cheryl Crawford

[Hotel d'Inghilterra, Rome]
June 26, 1950
[TLS w/ marginalia and
autograph postscript, 2 pp. BRTC]

Dear Cheryl:

Your letters always buck me up when I am feeling down. I have not been able to rest since I left America. That is, I have not been able to quit working. I am too keyed up and things were too much "in the air" at the time of my sailing. I wanted to let everything go. Forget it. Have a good time when I arrived in Italy. But the Nemesis (feeling of incompletion, dissatisfaction, restlessness) stays with me, and every day I get up and go back to work as before, as if nothing were finished. Fortunately I seem to be working pretty well. The pity is that I am _not_ resting, which would probably be more important for me right now. But as Gorki said once: "The wisdom of life is deeper and wider than the wisdom of men". So perhaps it is life that is directing me to do this.

On the boat and in Paris I worked on the Rosario section but here in Italy I am working on the idea of beginning the play after Rosario's death, with the opening scene of Act Two. (Graduation morning). This eliminates both Rosario and Estelle Hohengarten, as well as one or two minor characters. It gives the play the classic unity of time and a great deal more compactness, generally. It sacrifices some values (the red silk shirt) but I think the added values are greater. When Natalia gets back from Capri in about ten days I am going to read her this version. She will help me with the Italian. I want nearly all the first dialogue in the knife scene to be in Italian. The action is explicit enough and the emotion would make Pepina revert to her native tongue.

Eleanora Mendellsohn was also suggested by Alice Bouverie when I read her the play in New York. Certainly should be looked into. All the reports on Magnani are discouraging, particularly from Natalia, who says that she

doesn't think she would consider any offer to go to America right now. I have not yet seen her but I shall continue to work on it. Today we are moving into a new apartment and I shall wait till we are settled and Natalia has returned from Capri to make a definite assault on Miss Anna. In the meantime I have gotten the names of a couple of others, Fulvia Mammi and one with a complete unspellable (from memory) second name, given me by Vittorio Gassman, who is, incidentally very interested and available for an American production. He played Stanley in the Roman Streetcar and is one of the world's (surely!) handsomest men as well as a fine actor. Perhaps is too romantic looking for the comedy values in Alvaro but he undresses like a dream, which I think is always good in a play that has some elements of sexuality in it. He speaks English, not well, but enough to master a part in that language. I will send you a picture of him presently, as we were photographed together at lunch by a Vogue photographer. Have you thought at all of Shirley Booth, or is she too "hot" right now to be approachable? There would be danger of too much similarity with her part in "Sheba". - Carson was drinking in Paris and so was Reeves, pretty heavily. Her trip to Ireland was apparently just pleasant. Not exciting. - Please keep after Gadg, and so will I, to the extent that it is possible through the mails. A cable and letter from Clurman wanting to direct. I didn't like his work in "Member", did you? It was curiously harsh and Broadwayese. I don't know what to say to him, since I like and admire him so much, intellectually and as a man.

I seem to be buying a house in Key West, according to cables from my lawyer. And Buffie has offered to rent me that apartment I loved so much in New York. It will be vacant the first of October and would be an ideal home during work on the play, whenever that may commence. I am glad you feel there is no need to rush things and that the casting of Pepina and the commitment of Kazan come first. I have a feeling that Kazan will like what I am doing in this last version of the play, as he originally said he thought Rosario was better as a memory and a legend and he felt the play broke into two parts with his death.

Frank sends his love, with mine, to both you and Ruth, and we hope you are finding rest and comfort in your Connecticutt dream-house.

Love, Tenn.

Friend saw Magnani at concert last night and said she expressed definite interest in seeing the play. An appt. is being arranged.

[TW quotes from an early story by Maxim Gorki entitled "My Fellow-Traveller" (1894).

Revision of *The Rose Tattoo* undertaken in Rome generally followed the approach suggested by Elia Kazan. Beginning the play on "Graduation morning" would cause a further obscuring of Rosario in preparation for Pepina's awakening. The elimination of Estelle Hohengarten would also require a new ending, as described in later correspondence (see letters #175 and #178). In the melodramatic "knife scene," Rose threatens suicide if Pepina will not relax her Sicilian discipline and accept the boy whom she loves, a sailor named Jack.

A native Roman, Natalia Danesi Murray married an American in the 1920s and lived thereafter in New York and Italy. She worked chiefly in broadcasting and publishing and in 1940 began an intimate relationship with the journalist Janet Flanner. She would prove a valuable liaison with Anna Magnani.

The Italian ancestry of Eleanora Mendelssohn explains her early consideration for the role of Pepina. Shirley Booth was "'hot'" after her award-winning performance in *Come Back, Little Sheba*. She played an aging romantic who lives in loneliness and reverie, as does Pepina.

Crawford and her companion Ruth Norman shared a "dream-house" named "Eastham."

Typed in the upper margin of page 1 is TW's mailing address, "American Express, Rome."]

175. To Audrey Wood

[Rome]
<u>July ?, 1950</u>
[TLS, 1 p. HRC]

Dear Audrey:

I really feel very deeply satisfied with the acquisition of a house, and I know that Grandfather will be equally pleased over it, for he was so happy there. It will also make a nice place for the others of the family to visit, especially my sister, when we are in New York. Incidentally Buffie Johnson has written to offer me her apartment at $400. a month. I wish I could take it for the few months I would be in New York for Tattoo as it would be an ideal refuge during that period of travail. You might contact her about it, possibly working out an exchange so that she could occupy my Key West house while I was in hers. She is now in Sag Harbor, New York with her new husband with whom she seems to be eminently satisfied. Hope he is likewise.

Tattoo is undergoing radical revisions. It now begins with the graduation morning as I finally decided that the Rosario section made it too long and unwieldy. I am building up the Pepina-Alvaro scenes as much as possible to give an effect of fullness. I think they are developing nicely. There is a new ending, without Hohengarten. I use the ancient woman ("La Fattuchiere") instead, and I have changed Pepina's name to Serafina which I think is prettier and more touching, since Serafina delle Rose means "Angel of the roses". In the end the old lady envelops her in her "grey shawl of pity" and beckons the curtain to fall. It makes a good curtain. I got the feeling that the other ending was a little pat or cliche, especially since the other woman does not, now, appear in the beginning of the play.

Magnani told a friend of mine she was eager to meet me and read the play but she does not answer her phone. She has a new villa in the country and is at present incommunicado with a new lover. Through Natalia Murray I will get in contact with other actresses such as Leah Padovani and Andreina Pagnani, a woman of 47, who is said to be the finest dramatic actress in Italy. How do you feel about Eleanora Mendolsohn? Cheryl wrote me about her. Can she play comedy well enough for the part? She is now touring in "Mad Woman" but I think she has a straight part.

What is this about the Bigelow "Sea Gull"! A marvelous idea. Is he going to produce it, or what? - My poor friend, Oliver Evans, was in a motor smash-up and is in the hospital. Is there any money for him at the Authors' League?

I don't know what to make of Gadg's behavior. I received a long letter from him, saying that the Miller picture was really very close to completion after much re-writing and that he was morally obligated to help with it. But he mentioned that the Zapata picture might fall through. I don't think we should allow him to escape us if any form of detention is availing!

Affectionate greetings to you and Bill, Tenn.

[Audrey Wood warmly approved TW's purchase of a house in Key West and assured him that he could afford the asking price of $22,500 without using his bonds (July 13, 1950, HRC). The Bahama-style cottage which TW formerly rented would see the gradual addition of a studio, guest house, pool, and the Jane Bowles Summer House, a gazebo built in memory of his friend.

Wood informed TW that he might be asked to adapt The Sea Gull (Chekhov, 1896) for a revival planned by Paul Bigelow. She had already listed for Bigelow "all the reasons" (to TW, July 7, 1950, HRC) why her client should avoid the project.

Further evidence of Elia Kazan's unpredictable "behavior" appeared in a *New York Times* report that Kazan had "no hesitancy" about directing *The Rose Tattoo* "if the script were held until he's available" (June 23, 1950). Wood did not "believe any of this" (HRC), as she informed TW on June 28.

The date of this letter falls between Wood's correspondence of July 7 and 13, 1950.]

176. *To John Lehmann*

[Rome]
10 July, 1950
[TLS, 1 p. Princeton U]

Dear John:

Rome is now the hottest it has been in 100 years, so Mrs. Stone and I are leaving Tuesday night for Vienna. If you know of any interesting public monuments we should see there, the address is American Express for about 10 days. Mrs. Stone says she wants to find "The Fourth Man" and I want to take a ride on that big ferris-wheel.

I am so glad you are going to do the novella separately. Jay has sent me a copy of his edition and the book looks fairly normal in <u>length</u> and the jacket design is superb, a fantastic bird-woman in very free style against a brilliant yellow and red.

If we sail from a northern port this time, I will make every effort, but no promise, to get over to London. I want to see you and your sisters and the Christopher Fry plays that I have heard so much about. Peter Ustinov is here doing Nero in the great MGM spectacle "Quo Vadis" which has already cost 8 million dollars and given employment to almost every street-walker in Rome: it will be a show-case of giovanni Romani if nothing else! They have a pack of lions, about 30 of them, a herd of fighting bulls, a brace of cheetas. The poveri raggazzi are quaking with terror of the scenes they have to act with this menagerie. Ustinov did not look too happy when the pair of cheetas walked on, supposedly pets of Octavia's, but perhaps he was only afraid they would steal the scene. A Vogue photographer wanted to take our picture together on Nero's throne and Ustinov said, "I don't share my throne with anybody!" - a queenly if not imperial remark!

A riverdici! Tenn.

[John Lehmann (1907-1989) lived in Vienna before the war and was coyly deemed familiar with the city's gay attractions. TW's prospective traveling companion Eyre de Lanux—"Mrs. Stone"—did not make the trip.

Lehmann originally planned to supplement the English edition of *The Roman Spring* (December 1950) with an additional story or two. Both he and James Laughlin, whose positions in British and American publishing were similar, preferred literature to commerce and encouraged adventurous new writing. By special arrangement with New Directions, Lehmann published the first English edition of TW's works before losing managerial control of his firm in 1952. Strict censorship laws apparently prohibited or discouraged an English edition of *One Arm* (1948).

Lehmann's sisters, Rosamond and Beatrix, author and actor, respectively, and the recent premiere of several verse plays by Christopher Fry were incentives for TW to visit London at this time.

Metro-Goldwyn-Mayer released *Quo Vadis?* in 1951.]

177. To Oliver Evans

[en route to Vienna]
7/13/50
[TLS, 1 p. HRC]

Dear Oliver:

I am as outraged as you by the notice in the Saturday Review. It is the most spiteful notice I've seen of a volume of poems since my own were reviewed by Randall Jarell. There is a close affinity between those two. They are both politician-poets, insanely jealous of anything genuinely lyrical. I shall write the editor of the Sat Lit but you must realize that my connection with the volume has probably done it a political disservice as I have always, for some reason, been particularly odious to the sort of professional litterateurs that write these notices. They loathe me because I have made some money out of writing and at the same time have dared to publish in avant-garde precincts. You must also remember that most of this spiteful sisterhood are thwarted queens. They usually lack the vitality or courage to have any good trade. They go to bed with each other, which puts them in a frightfully bad humor. There is something about your verse that smacks of sensual satisfaction and richness of experience and this they must deplore.

I am writing this on a train, on my way to Vienna. Rome was having the hottest summer in 100 years and I had to escape from it. I left Frank and the car and took off myself for a week or ten days. Eloi Bordelon and

William Richards, of New Orleans, were in Rome when I left. I think Eloi looks better than I have ever seen him, he has had some really miraculous skin-treatments or a marvelous new make-up for the pitted complexion was quite smooth. He told me that Frank Ford - do you remember him? - has brought out a book of poems. Frank was my best friend in New Orleans.

I have not had any response from Audrey or Sillcox about my repeated solicitations regarding the fund. It may be all gone. I bought a house in Key West, the one I occupied last winter, which I will make a permanent residence in America, and it will not be until my next play opens that I can make any fresh payments to the fund if it is now exhausted, but I am still waiting to hear. Audrey is interested in your work, for she sent me copies of both reviews, the Times and the Villa-nous one.

Suggest you read Aldington's new book on Lawrence, particularly the notices that brought about the suppression of "The Rainbow". Then you will not feel so badly or alone. Lawrence said: "I curse them all, body and soul, root, branch and leaf, to eternal damnation!" - I shall be exposed twice to the critics next year, with the short novel and the new play. I have a feeling that I shall have to buck a terrible tide of adverse criticism - the foreword to your volume is a straw in the wind. I am terribly sorry it worked against you like this, but you must rest assured that the beauty of the poems is ineluctable as this shining Alpine country that the train is now going through. I have rarely seen or heard people so moved by the reading of poems as I saw when Bigelow read yours aloud to a group in New York shortly before I left. Nobody takes Villa seriously, my dear! You will be in New York next year and there will be occasion to slit his throat, if you are after reprisal!

Love, Tenn.

[TW accused the editor of having loaded "the dice" by assigning such an "eclectic" (*Saturday Review*, August 19, 1950, p. 24) poet as José Garcia Villa to review the traditional lyrics of Oliver Evans (*Young Man With a Screwdriver*, 1950). Audrey Wood saw that Villa had "reviewed" TW's preface rather than Evans's poetry and instructed her client to think more "seriously" (July 7, 1950, HRC) about his own reputation. Villa "impressed" (to Villa, September 25, 1950, Private Collection) TW when he later offered to publish "The Kingdom of Earth" in a collection which he was editing. Villa reportedly worked for New Directions and knew of James Laughlin's reluctance to publish the story in America.

TW met Eloi Bordelon and William Richards in New Orleans in 1941. At the

time he and "the Bordelon" had a "bloody matrimonial break-up," leading TW to conclude that "Marriage is not for me!"

TW cites Richard Aldington's new biography, *D.H. Lawrence, Portrait of a Genius But . . .* (1950). Lawrence's courage and endurance inspired the earlier dedication of *Battle of Angels*: "Who was while he lived the brilliant adversary of so many dark angels and who never fell, except in the treacherous flesh, the rest being flame that fought and prevailed over darkness" (November 1939, HRC).]

178. To Cheryl Crawford

[Vienna]
July 14, 1950
[TLS w/ marginalia, 2 pp. BRTC]

Dear Cheryl:

I have gone to Vienna for a few days to escape the fierce heat of Rome, the hottest summer in 100 years. It is cooler, here, but the city has a feeling of profound desolation, for the first time making me feel the psychic, as well as material, ruin of western Europe. The city was far more destroyed than I had expected. They are tearing down the ruins and a great deal of re-building is going on so that the atmosphere is filled with an odor of dust, as if you were actually breathing that quality of ruin-beyond-repair which Vienna has. There is nothing hopeful or vigorous about the re-building. I watch the workmen from my hotel window, and they seem to be working in a kind of disgust, as if they knew it was useless. They work in a sort of stupor and sometimes they kick the wheel-barrow over and sit down on it with their face in their hands. Italy is like the wonderfully wise singing clown in King Lear, sad but making songs out of it, but here you see the different melancholy of the Germanic spirit, the lightless, graceless surrender to total defeat. Whoever created the myth of Viennese gaiety!? Sausages and beer and folk-songs still go on, but without any fresh impulse. Now and then you see a young man striding mightily along the street in lederhosen as if he were marching to band-music and you can guess the reason. He has been told that the West is dead but that a new life is coming out of the East! I am afraid that our dollars, our Marshall plan, have not given them the <u>spiritual</u> transfusion which they most need, the sign of a future which is not a continuation of the past which they breathe in the dusty air of their ruined city. And I suspect that the only way we can ultimately save

western Europe from what we are afraid of is by some ideological progress in ourselves beyond armaments and dollars, by transposing our democracy into a major key which is dynamic and fluid and truly representing the lightness and freedom that we know totalitarianism doesn't offer. Right now Europe is in a mood to take anything that seems altogether different from what they had in the past.

To descend to the personal level: I am still working hard on "Tattoo". As I think I told you, it now starts with the graduation morning and I have worked into the story a new element which changes the ending. It is now established in the story that Pepina received a supernatural sign when she conceived her two children, Rose and the son who died at birth the night of her husband's death. On the occasion of each conception she felt a burning pain on her left breast and saw, or imagined she saw, a stigmata, the rose tattoo of her husband appearing on it. Now in the end of the play, when she is kneeling to gather the ashes from the broken urn, the stigmata returns. She cries out. The ancient woman (La Fattuchiere) and others rush into the yard in response to her wild cries. She kneels with her breast exposed as the old woman enters the house, crying out: "The tattoo, the tattoo has come back! It means in my body another rose is growing!" The old woman, to comfort her, tells her, Yes, I see it, I see it clearly, Pepina! - and envelops her in the grey shawl of pity as the curtain comes down. - It should be felt by the audience that Pepina may be right, that she actually has received a sign that she has conceived by Alvaro. The danger is they might think she was crazy! We would have to obviate that danger by establishing the fact of the previous stigmatas - and Pepina's profound innate <u>mysticism</u>! - <u>not</u> madness! - I think that I have managed to establish these things in the revisions but of course I am very anxious to get the opinions of you and Audrey and also Gadg if he remains in the fold. So I am going to try to get a somewhat rough draft of this version of the play off to you before the end of the month. Myself, I feel very hopeful about it! - I am still hot on the elusive trail of Magnani. The day before I left Rome I was interviewed by an excellent young Italian writer and reporter for <u>L'Europa</u> and <u>Il Mondo</u>. I told him the story of the play and he was charmed by it and went immediately to the phone to call Magnani as he felt the part was very good for her. He was told that she was still out of town, at her hide-away in the country but he promised that he would be in touch with her by the time I returned from Vienna. Natalia is also going to

help but she has not yet heard the play. I may read it to her when this version is completed.

I was very happy over what you said about Mrs. Stone. My object in this novella was to show the ugly and awful mutations that may occur through the obsessive pursuit of a high position, the "power-drive" as we see it so much in our society, particularly in the theatre where it seems to be thrown in particularly sharp focus. And I wanted to make the reader feel more compassion than disgust for the rapacious bird-woman. I am terribly afraid of critical reactions to the book! I am sure they will find it "rotten", "decadent", Etc. and will revive the charge that I can only deal with neurotic people. My answer to that is that, of course, when you penetrate into almost anybody you either find madness or dullness: the only way not to find them is to stay on the surface. Madness I should put in quotes. I mean what is <u>considered</u> madness or neuroticism! - which is simply the inner distortions that any sensitive, mallable nature undergoes through experience in modern society.

Going out, now, to see more of Vienna.

With love, Tenn.

[Vienna was bombed by the Allies in 1943 and further damaged two years later when Russian troops liberated the city in house-to-house fighting. Russian sector guards alarmed TW: "They snatch the passport, grunt and throw it back at you, and you say 'Thank you' in a terrified whisper! . . . I hope we don't have to fight them!" (to Wood, July 13, 1950, HRC).

The announcement of Serafina's conception and stigmata was intended to unify the sensual and mystical elements of the play in the latest revised ending. The plan to begin *The Rose Tattoo* on "graduation morning" does not appear in subsequent draft stages and may be among those revisions which TW reported "throwing out" in mid-August.

Reviews of *The Roman Spring of Mrs. Stone* were sharply mixed and generally followed the line of "'decadent'" criticism feared by TW. The *Herald Tribune* critic wrote that Karen Stone "is tracked down . . . with the same inexorableness, and submitted to the same sexual crucifixion, that awaited Blanche DuBois or the heroine of 'Summer and Smoke.'" Why does TW "arrange his dramas like inquisitions, with torture preceding the confession, and death following?" (October 22, 1950).

Typed in the upper margin of page 1 is TW's mailing address, "American Express, Rome."]

179. *To Paul Bigelow*

[Rome]
August 3, 1950
[TLS, 2 pp. Duke U]

Dear Paul:

The news about the <u>Sea Gull</u> is by far the best to reach me from New York for a long, long time. As you know, I think it's the greatest of all modern plays, and probably the first really modern <u>poetic</u> play as well as the greatest. I think you are divinely appointed to produce it. I can't think of anyone else who would have a finer taste for its particular aura of period and atmosphere. I shudder to think what the Lunts must have done to it, and certainly the time is peculiarly ripe, after the fearful mutilation visited on Chekhov by the Logan-Hayes combination, to introduce to Broadway the <u>true</u> quality of his art, which I have never seen more than suggested, and then in London by an undistinguished company from the provinces. Ina Claire is a superb choice for Arcadina <u>provided</u>! - and I think she is enough of a really good actress to recognize that need - she does not try to convert it into a starring vehicle as the Lunts must have tried. If you could only get Margaret Phillips for the role of Nina! But what about direction? I think the question of director is far more critical than that of a new translation. I haven't read the Stark Young one but I should think it would have grace and style. After all, it is a Victorian piece, at least temporally. A certain elegance should be the keynote of its style in every department, not a chi-chi elegance but a poetic grace of speech as well as setting, costume and performance. The Chekhov translations which I <u>have</u> read - mostly those by Constance Garnett - are marred mostly by a certain stiffness, a stilted quality, which I am sure the original didn't have. I would be only too proud and happy to work with you on eliminating those touches, getting a more fluent and natural style of speech, and it would be a labor of love and refreshment for which I wouldn't want any other kind of remuneration than the pleasure and satisfaction of having a chance to do it. What I would most, if I were at all capable, love to do would be to collaborate on the <u>staging</u> of it, either with you or someone else more acquainted than either of us with the mechanics of stage direction. It would be a thrilling experience to help bring a play like that into its difficult, very delicate sort of reality. I know it can be done, and you are the right one to do it!

I am leaving in a few hours for the northern lake region as it has

become suffocatingly hot in Rome. I am stupefied. Cannot continue work here. I am hoping for some revival of energies in the north where there will be cool swimming. Frank is heading in the opposite direction, to Naples and Sicily. We'll both return here in a couple of weeks or possibly a bit less.

Oh, Paul, don't let anything deter or discourage you in this wonderful venture. I think it can be one of the few really memorable - quite unforgettable! - events in our American theatre! You can count on me for anything at all that I may be capable of doing in connection with it. I would love to see the Stark Young translation here in Europe if you or Audrey could get a copy of it to me.

                    Much love, Tenn.

P.S. Charlie wants me to come to Hollywood and has offered to pay our transportation and living expenses, so we will probably be returning to the States about the middle of the month, that is, starting back. They have sent me a final shooting script of "Streetcar", as assembled by Gadg, and he has done a really marvelous job on putting it together with great directness and economy of style. I think I have been unjust to Gadg about "Tattoo", that his reservations have been sincerely based on a lack of satisfaction with the script for reasons that were probably sound. It seems to me that trust in a person, if it is given after enough consideration, is practically never misplaced. Of all things it is the hardest for me to give, much harder than love, but I don't think I am ever wrong when I give it. I think about the play I will finally be guided by his decision. And Audrey's. If they still don't really and whole-heartedly like this final draft of it, I will abandon the idea of producing it, at least for this season. I have seen Magnani. She finally consented to meet me, and the meeting occured at a crowded sidewalk cafe, very carefully staged by Magnani who was in complete dominion. She looks marvelous, the sexiest looking woman on earth. She has taken off weight, and her body is quite beautiful. She has the warmth and vigor of a panther! She will not read the play till it is completely finished and she said she is far more interested in doing a film of it than on the stage in New York: that her film commitments will keep her occupied far into 1951. My guess is that she would quite definitely do the picture if it first had a success on the stage, but that it would be very difficult to ensnare her for Broadway, on exorbitant terms and with enormous power. Several people

here have suggested Mata or Marta Abba. I've never seen her. I don't think any other Italian actress would do. But I have heard of an American actress named Maureen Stapleton who is said to be a sort of American Magnani. Know anything about her?

Senta, per favore! Not a word to Sister Woman about my letter describing her phone conversation with the producers! She is already inclined to list me among her persecutors, I am afraid. Hope she arrived in good condition and that Li'l Pretty's condition has also undergone noticable improvement. Is it true that George Davis was fired from "Flair"? There are rumors that Windham has gone to Florence but nothing is reported on the remainder of the explosive colony at Taormina. I guess they are busy being photographed by Cecil Beaton among the old Greek ruins. I want so much to read the completed story you mention in your letter.

Tennessee Williams and the "legendary" Paul Bigelow.

[Plans to restage *The Sea Gull* led TW to "wonder if the present world atmosphere will not make the melancholy grace of Chekhov seem too old-fashioned?" (to Kazan, August 14, 1950, WUCA). Audrey Wood had questioned the expense of reviving the play (to TW, June 28, 1950, HRC) and in effect foretold the failure of Paul Bigelow's project.

Alfred Lunt and Lynn Fontanne starred—and Uta Hagen made her Broadway debut—in a Theatre Guild production of *The Sea Gull* in 1938. *The Wisteria Trees* (1950), loosely based upon *The Cherry Orchard* (1904), was written and produced by Joshua Logan and starred Helen Hayes. The lightly regarded adaptation of Chekhov had a modest run of 165 performances. The stage comedian Ina Claire was last seen on Broadway in *The Fatal Weakness* (1946).

In later correspondence TW restated his "dream" of directing *The Sea Gull*, with Marlon Brando and Stella Adler cast in leading roles. TW's adaptation entitled *The Notebook of Trigorin* had its world premiere at the Vancouver Playhouse in British Columbia in 1981. Allean Hale prepared the first edition (1997) for New Directions.

The summons to Hollywood led TW to reflect that "this Roman period has all the defects of the one before and very little of the occasional charm. I blame this on myself, my failure to lose myself in really satisfactory work, lack of accomplishment, disappointment in the play overshadowing the whole ambient of my present life" (*Journal*, July 26, 1950). Diminished too was "Frank's friendliness," which seemed "quite different" in Rome.

Carson McCullers and her husband "Li'l Pretty" separated once again after returning to the States in early-August.

TW began this letter in Rome shortly before he planned to leave for "the northern lake region." He went instead to Positano and then to "Naples," as indicated by a penned notation in the upper margin. The lengthy postscript may have been added in Naples and the letter mailed there.]

180. To Cheryl Crawford

[Rome]
8/11/50
[TLS, 1 p. BRTC]

Dear Cheryl:

You and Bigelow write the best letters I have ever received. I love the quotation from Whitman. What enviable serenity he had! With a spirit like that, and such assurance, it might almost be a pleasure to be a poet. I wonder if he ever had any doubts? It is odd, very odd, that not a single poem seems to express such a feeling. And yet it is not fatuous, nor is it conceited. You seem to feel that what he admires, and is confident of, in

himself is himself in life: that he does not separate himself from it. And the consoling things he says to himself seem really to be addressed to other people through himself. He understood the unanimity of mankind. That is the spirit from which an advanced democracy should have sprung, by-passing the Stalinist crowd.

The long-awaited meeting with Magnani has finally occured. She kept me waiting ¾ of an hour, and then sent a messenger to say that she was in front of Doney's the most crowded of the sidewalk cafes at the most crowded hour, and would receive me there. She was looking quite marvelous. She has taken off at least twenty pounds. Her figure is the very meaning of sex. Her eyes and her voice and style are indescribably compelling. She dominated the whole street. I was overwhelmed by her. But I have serious doubts about the advisability of putting her in a play, even if she consented. She was very direct. She said immediately that picture commitments tied her up until deep into 1951, that it would take her several months to prepare for a stage appearance. At first she pretended not to speak English but after a while she began to speak it, with a clear accent and surprising fluency. She demanded a script. I said she could see an early draft, that the final draft was not yet finished. This she refused to do. Said she would read only the final one. I am hesitant about showing her the final script. Plagiarism is so common in Italy, particularly of foreign writers. Her picture Volcano was very close to Bergman's Stromboli, and I would hate for an Italian film to come out using ideas from "Tattoo", possibly before it opened on the stage. I had the impression that it would be very easy to get her to do the picture. That she would do the play only under the most extravagant terms, with almost complete control over everything. I have the telephone number of Lea Padovani and will see her this week. Several people here have mentioned Marta Abba. Do you know anything about her? Audrey does. Would Maureen Stapelton be at all right? I have never seen her but have heard she is a somewhat Magnani type.

Eli Wallach as Kilroy in Gadg's scene from "Camino Real" is the closest thing that I have seen to Alvaro so far. Quinn does not seem to have quite the flexibility, the lightness and vivacity, that the part would require, especially as it is now written, although he does have the physical appearance and sexuality. Until we know about Gadg it is almost impossible to think much about casting, for he would be so essential to the use of fresh, inexperienced actors.

They want me to come back to the States sooner than I had planned, for further negotiations with the Breen office. I sent a wire yesterday saying I could fly from London Aug. 23 and am waiting to hear if that date is early enough. I want a chance to see some of the London theatre and a few more Italian actors, and also to rest a bit before the Hollywood-New York pressure is resumed, so soon after the long spell of work.

Love - 10.

[Anna Magnani, forty-two at the time of her meeting with TW, was scheduled to film *Bellissima* (1951) in mid 1951. *Vulcano* (1950), the title of her current film, was intended to echo the central symbol of the Rossellini-Bergman film *Stromboli* (1949). By linking the rival films, which were shot on nearby islands, the producer hoped to exploit the bitter ending of Magnani's affair with her former director.

Maureen Stapleton and Eli Wallach studied together at the Actors Studio and would play the leads in *The Rose Tattoo*. TW regarded the Studio, founded in 1947 by Elia Kazan, Robert Lewis, and Cheryl Crawford, as a source of fresh talent for the play.

"Negotiations with the Breen office" concern unresolved censorship problems in filming *Streetcar*.]

181. To Cheryl Crawford and Audrey Wood

[Rome]
8/15/50
[TLS w/ marginalia, 1 p. HRC]

Dear Cheryl and Audrey:

I am terribly alarmed over the startlingly early dates mentioned in your cable and Audrey's. The only date you had suggested before was a tentative booking for New Haven sometime in January which was far more reasonable in view of the fact that nobody has yet seen the final script - not even I! - and we haven't the ghost of an idea at this point who will direct or star in it. This summer in the dead heat of Rome I have felt like a tired horse at the last high hurdle. I have driven myself to keep working, by compulsion, not inspiration, and I am afraid that most of the progress I thought I was making was wishfull thinking. I am beginning to assemble the script. A lot of the revisions I am throwing out and reverting to earlier versions. Naturally some progress has been made, but not enough. If I could have rested completely, restored my nervous reserves - then made a

really fresh attack, the results would have been better. But somehow I couldn't rest and the advance can be measured in inches, instead of yards. I still believe that the flat stretches in the play will ultimately come to life, that I <u>will</u> eventually have a period of real stimulation again when I can do warm, spontaneous work that will suddenly illuminate the script where it is now like dusty glass. If Gadg were available it might be worth risking. He can do magic with fairly commonplace writing. Who else can? I feel as hurt as you must about his apparent dereliction - not resentful, but undeniably hurt! - but I still must acknowledge how badly this play needs him. - I think Mann did a good job on "Come Back, Little Sheba". But that was a far, far better play - just as a script - than Inge was given credit for writing. It almost directed itself. The texture of the writing was superb and it had a wonderful line of dramatic development, very clear and forceful, with only momentary lapses. As it now stands, this is not that good a play and not even <u>nearly</u> so easy a play to direct. This play remains what it was, the sketch for the best play that I have written, but still not <u>it</u>! - and a long way short of it. I think it would be sheer <u>folly to push it</u> into rehearsal in mid-October. I should have at least two months of rest in Key West and at least that much time should be devoted to seeking out the right people. The <u>absolutely</u> right people. Or at least, the absolutely right <u>Serafina</u>! - now that Magnani seems to be pretty definitely out. - So let's stall for time, at least keep all the dates fluid. If the play is <u>right</u>, it doesn't matter when it comes into town, really. If it <u>isn't</u> right, the time of the season is not going to help it enough to matter. - I have just about given up the idea of going to California. We will look over what I have done, all of us together, when I arrive in New York and have a completely, coldly objective round-robin discussion of it with no punches pulled. This may save us a lot of grief in the end! And I am able to take it. If it were done prematurely and failed, I am not sure that I <u>would</u> be able to take it. More later -

Much love, Tenn.

[Audrey Wood's cable ended any reasonable hope that Elia Kazan would stage *The Rose Tattoo*: "He is directing Zapata." Kazan recently informed Wood of this development and asked that she convey his regret to TW: "Tell Tennessee how badly I feel about it, which I do" (August 12, 1950, HRC). TW surveyed the damage in a separate letter to Wood and expressed a faint hope: "I don't feel badly about Gadg dropping out, I mean I don't feel <u>resentful</u> about it, although it is a

terrific set-back to the play. I don't think he was ever really sold on it. I would like to talk to him in the States before I think about Lewis or Mann as substitutes. If it is only the time element that eliminates him, perhaps it would be worth-while to wait for him" (August 15, 1950, HRC). Wood's cable also implored TW to return "immediately" (August 15, 1950, HRC) for rehearsals of *The Rose Tattoo* (October 16).

Typed in the upper margin is the notation "Having no carbon, I'm sending this to Audrey so she can read it first and pass it on to you, since it concerns you equally."]

182. *To Walter Edwin Dakin*

SH: Hotel Algonquin
59 West 44th Street
New York 18, N.Y.
9/13/50
[TLS, 1 p. HRC]

Dear Grandfather:

I have been so busy that I can scarcely believe that I have only been back in America for a week. Three things going at once, like Ringling Brothers circus - plans and casting for my new play, press-interviews for the opening of the "Glass Menagerie" in New York, and long-distance conferences with Charlie and Mr. Kazan about "Streetcar" which is now being filmed in California. I have not even had time to see Margo, who is in town directing a new play called "Southern Exposure". Now it seems that I will have to fly out to Hollywood this week-end, but will only need to stay a few days. Then fly back here to continue preparations for "The Rose Tattoo" which is the title of my new play. Frank is spending most of his free time at the dentist, which keeps him busy as me. I am still hoping we can get down to Key West in a short while. Maybe about the first of October. If the play goes into production so soon that we have to stay in New York, would you like to come up here and join us? We are looking for an apartment. That is, friends are looking for one for us and we will make sure it has a bedroom for you. The weather is beautiful in New York now, clear and pleasantly cool, and I know you would enjoy it.

Let me know your plans care of Audrey Wood, 551 Fifth Ave., and I will advise you of any new development in mine.

Much love, Tom

["On the sea, returning to what?" (*Journal*, September 1, 1950). TW sailed on the *Queen Elizabeth* and was due to arrive in New York on September 5. Frank Merlo's flight was delayed in Newfoundland: "I suppose the Horse went out and grazed a bit on the tundra" (qtd. in St. Just, pp. 36-37), TW later quipped to Maria Britneva.

A smash hit in Dallas, *Southern Exposure* (1950) flopped in New York and closed after twenty-three performances. "It shoulda stood in Texas," the critics advised the producer-director, Margo Jones.

Walter Dakin forwarded this letter to Edwina with a note that he was "very well and happy in the Gayoso," preferring, as he did, Memphis to St. Louis.]

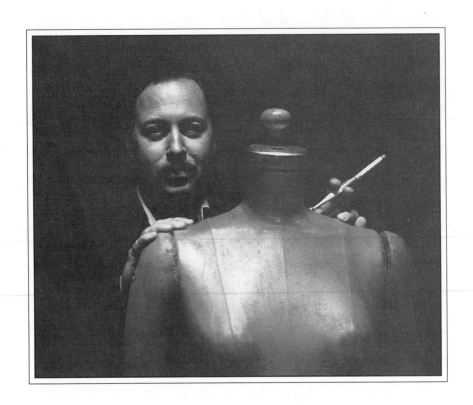

PART IV
1950 - 1952

Overleaf: "*Don't lean on my dummy. Sit down if you can't stand up.* *—What is the matter with you?*" (The Rose Tattoo, *1951*).

183. *To Irene Mayer Selznick*

SH: Hotel Bel-Air
701 Stone Canyon Road
Los Angeles 24
September 26, 1950
[TLS, 1 p. Boston U]

Dearest Irene:

Thank you so much for forwarding the sweet note from Peter, and all your other good offices. You are just an irrepresibly good producer! I cannot at this moment make any move about Peter, which I will explain more thoroughly when I see you in New York. We are flying back Wednesday night, day after tomorrow. A conference this week should make it fairly plain whether or not I can offer Peter the play.

Gadg is doing a brilliant job on Streetcar, and believe it or not, Madame Olivier is nothing less than terrific! I was almost startled out of my "sissy britches" - that is a term I picked up from Marion Davies to whom I was introduced a few nights ago by one Speed Lamkin, who has left very few stones unturned in this vicinity.

We are driving out, now, to see some more "rushes". They are up to the birthday party scenes.

Love from Tenn.

[Peter Brook's interest in directing *The Rose Tattoo* (1951) would not be realized, although Brook later staged the Paris production of *Cat on a Hot Tin Roof* (1956). Acclaimed productions of Cocteau, Sartre, and Christopher Fry, as well as a budding friendship with Irene Selznick, had brought the young British director to TW's attention.

TW was called to Hollywood to deal with censorship problems related to the filming of *Streetcar* (1947). Still unresolved was Blanche's discovery speech (Scene Six), which he was asked to revise "without hurting the content" or violating the censor's presumption that Allan Grey "was not homosexual" (Feldman to TW, September 12, 1950, HRC). Treatment of the rape scene, not yet filmed, would entail lengthy negotiation with the Production Code administrator, Joseph Breen.

Vivien Leigh, a major box-office star, replaced Jessica Tandy as Blanche and joined the remaining principals of the Broadway cast. By late-September Elia Kazan had reached Scene Eight of *Streetcar*.

Marion Davies starred in a series of films in the 1920s and '30s backed by her companion, William Randolph Hearst. Renowned for philanthropy and lavish parties, she battled alcoholism and the effects of polio in later life.

Elia Kazan directing Vivien Leigh and Kim Hunter in A Streetcar
Named Desire *(1951): "Madame Olivier is nothing less than terrific!"*

A composition date of September 25, 1950, is consistent with TW's plan to
return to New York on "Wednesday night" after nearly ten days on the West Coast.]

184. *To Walter Edwin Dakin*

SH: Gladstone
East 52nd Street at Park Avenue
New York 22
[September/October 1950]
[TLS w/ enclosure and
autograph postscript, 1 p. HRC]

Dear Grandfather:

We are now back in New York and plans for the production of my
new play THE ROSE TATTOO are getting under way very rapidly. It now
looks like I shall have to stay in New York for the next three months and

I am wondering if you would not like to come up here for a while. Frank and I are moving back into Buffie Johnson's apartment. Do you remember the place? It was on East Fifty-Eighth street and you said it looked like a Curiosity Shop. It is where you had the picture taken, containing the reference to your Civil War uniform. If you can come up we can find a place for you either very close to our apartment or in the Royalton Hotel or some other hotel that suits you, and you might enjoy staying here, at least till the cold weather commences which should not be for quite a while as it promises to be a pleasant Fall; the weather is now bright and warm. We would love to have you up here. I would almost rather go directly to Key West and occupy the new house there, but unfortunately my work demands that I stay close to Broadway till after the play opens. I expect that will be sometime in December. This week we are going to decide about a director. Mr. Kazan's picture-duties keep him on the West Coast so it has been necessary to find someone else.

The Glass Menagerie is doing well here, and Kazan and Miss Leigh are making a really great picture of Streetcar. Please let us know if you can come up. I know you don't mind flying. Frank will have plenty of time and your presence in the city would be a great joy and comfort as well as bringing good luck. I worry a great deal about your staying by yourself in Memphis or other places. Do you think Mother and Dakin would like to use the house in Key West till we go down there this winter? Apparently it suffered no damage in the hurricane, for we have no report of any. But it is pity to leave it unoccupied all this time.

Much love, Tom

Write us at 235 E. 58th Street. We tried to find an apartment with two bedrooms but all of them wanted us to sign leases for long terms or were frightfully expensive, or had some other serious disadvantage. As you know, the apartment on 58th Street suited me perfectly when I lived there.

Enclosing a little present.

[Factors of economy and availability led Cheryl Crawford to cast *The Rose Tattoo* from the ranks of the Actors Studio. Maureen Stapleton, a twenty-five-year-old with no major Broadway roles to her credit, won the part of Serafina, while Eli Wallach, an older and more experienced actor, joined the cast as Alvaro.

Association with the Actors Studio and successful staging of *Come Back, Little Sheba* (1950) occasioned Daniel Mann's selection as director. Boris Aronson was hired to design the set. Tryouts would begin in Chicago on December 29 and run for three or four weeks.

Bosley Crowther wrote that the "poignancy" (*New York Times*, September 29, 1950) of *The Glass Menagerie* (1945) had been diminished by indulging the comedic talents of Gertrude Lawrence. A few reviewers were more positive but only one considered the film version "excellent."

A preview of *The Glass Menagerie* in April led TW to play "a scene of anguish second only to Judith Anderson's proscenium-gnawing in 'Medea'" (*New York Journal-American*, July 31, 1950). Audrey Wood deplored the untimely report in Dorothy Kilgallen's column and assured the producer, Charles Feldman, that one of TW's "henchmen" (August 14, 1950, HRC) was responsible.

TW last rented the painter Buffie Johnson's apartment on East 58th Street in 1948.]

185. To Robert "Bobbie" Lewis

SH: Gladstone
East 52nd Street at Park Avenue
New York City - 22
October 10, 1950
[TLS, 1 p. Kent State U]

Dear Bobbie:

All I can do in this letter is to give you as earnestly as possible the reasons for the abrupt decision I made about direction of "Tattoo", none of which had anything to do with any lack of faith in your unique and wonderful powers as a director. As a matter of fact, that faith had grown during our few discussions. But I suddenly felt that I just couldn't wait all that time, that I had to get moving on it right away: otherwise the tension would build to a point that it would just tear me up. Being yourself a highly keyed man with a sense of what his work can mean to an artist, you must understand about that. The long dalliance with Gadg had a great deal to do with this explosive state of nerves and the absolute need to come to quick and final decisions. It was obvious that you were not in a position to speak in terms of early and definite dates. So I just did what I felt had to be done. As it is, we now have out of town bookings beginning December 7th and are going full steam ahead. The imminence, and the impetus, will help me shape the script for production and it will be as right by that time as it could ever be. The contact with you, and your astute

analysis of the play, meant a great deal to me. I am more grateful than I can easily say and I am sure that eventually we will work together on something if I am not kicked out of the theatre and if you will stay my friend.

Affectionately, 10.

[Robert Lewis (1909-1997), an original member of the Group Theatre (1931-1941), gave vital encouragement to TW when they met in New York in the early 1940s. His staging of *Brigadoon* (1947) was a critical and financial success which offset earlier "prestige failures" on Broadway. The timing of Lewis's current project was in conflict with plans to open *The Rose Tattoo* in late-December 1950.]

186. To Editor, *New York Herald Tribune Book Review*

235 E. 58th Street
New York, N.Y.
October 15, 1950
[TLS, 2 pp. HRC]

Dear Sir:

I am sending you a copy of the first paragraph of a letter that I have written my publisher, James Laughlin, of <u>New Directions</u>, as I feel that it partly concerns you.

Sincerely, Tennessee Williams

October 15, 1950

Dear Jay:

I deeply appreciate the long account you have given me of your promotion plans for "The Roman Spring". I know that this particular aspect of the publishing world is not what attracted you to it, anymore than it is the aspect of writing that is attractive to me. I must admit, though, that I am deeply concerned about the distribution of this book, and its reception, because it comes at a point in my life when I have a need for some confirmation or reassurance about my work's value. I certainly didn't get any from the notices the book has received in New York. I was startled and hurt not only by the harsh opinions but much more by the apparent lack of interest, as if the book (and my work in general) did not

seem even to merit a little attention. For instance, the fact that the
Herald-Tribune has ignored it completely, both in the daily and
Sunday book-review sections, is the worst sort of slap in the face,
not only to this one book, but also, I feel, to all the work I have
done, to my whole - position is not the word I want to use! But you
know what I mean. I feel that I have worked very hard and very
seriously over a considerable period, that I have not done anything
cheap or meretricious, that regardless of my known limitations as a
writer, I have shown taste and courage and do have honesty: and,
consequently, have a right to receive from journals that have literary
criticism, such as The Herald-Tribune, The New Yorker, Etc., the
minimal courtesy of some space within two or three weeks of the
publication date, a courtesy which I am sure they have extended
time and again to writers who make far less effort than I to explore
the world and experience of our time with some truth and significance. If other writers such as Edith Sitwell, Cristopher Isherwood,
Carson McCullers and Rosamund Lehmann have expressed an
admiration for the book which I know must be sincere, surely there
is something in it that merits a token of interest from the various
book-page editors, even though the book may not at all accord
with their personal tastes.

(FIRST PARAGRAPH OF A LETTER TO JAMES LAUGHLIN)

Tennessee Williams

[Harsh reviews of *The Roman Spring of Mrs. Stone* appeared in the *Times* and the
Saturday Review shortly after publication on September 27, 1950. Orville Prescott
dismissed the novella as "superficial, offensive and quite dull" (*New York Times*,
September 29, 1950). The *Herald Tribune* notice, printed on October 22, bore the
headline "Another Williams Victim" and went on to lament the author's morbidity
and the "sexual crucifixion" of his "heroines." TW's complaint did not appear in
the *Tribune*, although it may have hastened publication of the review.
    James Laughlin described a sluggish promotional campaign for *The Roman
Spring* with ads due to appear in the *New York Times* and the *Herald Tribune* on
October 29 (to TW, October 12, 1950, Houghton).]

187. To Joseph Ignatius Breen

235 E. 58th Street
New York, NY
October 29, 1950
[TLx, 2 pp. HRC]

Dear Mr. Breen:

Mr. Kazan has just informed me that objections have been raised about the "rape scene" in "Streetcar" and I think perhaps it might be helpful for me to clarify the meaning and importance of this scene. As everybody must have acknowledged by now since it has been pointed out in the press by members of the clergy of all denominations, and not merely in the press but in the pulpit - "Streetcar" is an extremely and peculiarly <u>moral</u> play, in the deepest and truest sense of the term. This fact is so well known that a <u>misunderstanding</u> of it now at this late date would arouse widespread attention and indignation.

The rape of Blanche by Stanley is a pivotal, integral truth in the play, without which the play loses its meaning, which is the ravishment of the tender, the sensitive, the delicate by the savage and brutal forces in modern society. It is a poetic plea for comprehension. I did not beg the issue by making Blanche a totally "good" person, nor Stanley a totally "bad" one. But to those who have made some rational effort to understand the play, it is apparent that Blanche is neither a "dipsomaniac" nor a "nymphomaniac" but a person of intense loneliness, fallibility and a longing which is mostly spiritual for warmth and protection. I did not, of course, disavow what I think is one of the primary things of beauty and depth in human existence, which is the warmth between two people, the so-called "sensuality" in the love-relationship. If nature and God chose this to be the mean of life's continuance on earth, I see no reason to disavow it in creative work. At the same time, I know what <u>taste</u> is and what <u>vulgarity</u> is. I have drawn a very sharp and clear line between the two in all of the plays that I have had presented. I have never made an appeal to anything "low" or "cheap" in my plays and I would rather die than do so. Elia Kazan has directed "Streetcar" both on the stage and the screen, with inspired understanding of its finest values and an absolute regard for taste and propriety. I was fortunately able to see, in "rushes", all but the last three scenes of the picture before I left California. Mr. Kazan has given me a detailed description of the scenes I didn't see as they now exist on the screen. I am really

amazed that any question should arise about censorship. Please remember that even in notoriously strict Boston, where the play tried out before Broadway, there was no attack on it by any responsible organ of public opinion, and on the screen the spiritual values of the play have been accentuated much more than they could be on the stage.

The poetically beautiful and touching performance of a great visiting artist, Vivien Leigh, has dominated the picture and given it a stature which surpasses that of the play. "A Streetcar Named Desire" is one of the truly great American films and one of the very few really moral films that have come out of Hollywood. To mutilate it, now, by forcing, or attempting to force, disastrous alterations in the essential truth of it would serve no good end that I can imagine.

Please remember, also, that we have already made great concessions which we felt were dangerous to attitudes which we thought were narrow. In the middle of preparations for a new play, on which I have been working for two years, I came out to Hollywood to re-write certain sequences to suit the demands of your office. No one involved in this screen production has failed in any respect to show you the cooperation, and even deference, that has been called for. But now we are fighting for what we think is the heart of the play, and when we have our backs against the wall - if we are forced into that position - none of us is going to throw in the towel! We will use every legitimate means that any of us has at his or her disposal to protect the things in this film which we think cannot be sacrificed, since we feel that it contains some very important truths about the world we live in.

Sincerely,

[Joseph Breen (1890-1965) vigorously administered the Production Code from 1934 until his retirement in the mid 1950s. The general principles of the Code—drafted in 1930 but weakly enforced by Breen's predecessor, Will Hays—forbade the production of any motion picture that would "lower the moral standard" of the audience, violate "correct standards of life," or ridicule "law, natural or human." Geoffrey Shurlock, Breen's assistant and successor, later observed that "Streetcar broke the barrier."

The troubling rape scene in Streetcar was "justified" by the "build-up speech" and then "left unpunished" insofar as "Stanley was concerned." Before filming began, the Production Code staff found TW and Elia Kazan uncooperative and "inclined to make speeches about the integrity of their art." A recommendation followed that the rape be "abolished" and Stanley made guilty of nothing more

serious than "violently" striking Blanche. Sensing evasion, the staff later warned against any "fence-straddling" (file memoranda, May 2, July 25, October 3, 1950, Herrick) device that would allow the scene to be variously interpreted as a rape or not. Kazan's solution to the impasse was accepted by Breen in early-November. The "build-up speech" was modified but a strong indication of rape remained in the final print. TW quickly supplied the lines with which Stanley was punished by Stella and the final concern of the censor relieved: "We're not going back in there . . ." (telegram, to Kazan, November 2, 1950, Herrick).]

188. To James "Jay" Laughlin

[235 East 58th Street, New York]
November 7, 1950
[TLS, 1 p. Houghton]

Dear Jay:

Many, many thanks for your letter about the play. Please do send your copy of it to Lustig. If he comes up quickly enough with a striking design I feel sure that Cheryl would be delighted to use it for playbills, advertisements, Etc. The values of the play being less literary than usual, I feel that it will be more impressive on the stage than it is in manuscript. At least, I hope so. The director, Danny Mann, is no fool, in fact he is a real New York intellectual but has humor and vitality to compensate for that defect. He says that "mood" is "doom" spelt backwards which probably means that I shall have to put up a fight for the plastic-poetic elements in the production. We shall see. If casting is completed by November 15th I can take a couple of weeks in Key West to train for the contest. The girl, Maureen Stapleton, is a God-send and the rest of the cast is being slowly and very carefully put together.

I am sorry you were mistaken about the novel moving up to ninth place on the best-seller list. In fact it moved quite strongly in the other direction. I doubt that there is any hope of resuscitating sales by further advertising. Do you think so? Perhaps it would be better to contribute the sum I was planning for the "Ad" to the Authors' League to be given to the Patchens. I have gotten another letter from Miriam saying that their situation has deteriorated still further. The letter is quite touching and while I have never liked Patchen's work very much I am sure that he deserves aid and perhaps I can make a tax-deductible contribution to them through the League. Would you check on that with Luise M. Sillcox. If she approves,

I can make out a check on my book-royalties, ear-marked for Patchen.

I am enclosing a short-story by Oliver Evans which I think has a great deal of charm. He wanted you to see it for possible inclusion in the annual.

Will call you this week, if I don't hear from you, about the contribution to League. Audrey can also advise you about it.

Ever, Tenn.

[James Laughlin described *The Rose Tattoo* as "a triumph of stage writing" and guessed that it "might be even more popular than Streetcar." Nonetheless he foresaw TW developing "along another line" (to TW, November 3, 1950, Houghton), as indicated by his earlier verse play "The Purification" (1944).

On November 5 *The Roman Spring of Mrs. Stone* fell from tenth to thirteenth place on the *New York Times* bestseller list and disappeared thereafter. It fared no better in the *Herald Tribune*.

In 1950 Kenneth Patchen had the first of three operations for chronic back pain and rheumatoid arthritis. TW did contribute to his care, as Patchen's wife, Miriam, had requested. New Directions published much of Patchen's experimental prose and verse.

Laughlin found the Oliver Evans story "derivative" (to TW, November 13, 1950, Houghton) and declined to publish it.]

189. To Cheryl Crawford

[1431 Duncan Street
Key West, Florida]
November ?, 1950
[TLS w/ autograph marginalia, 1 p. BRTC]

Dear Cheryl:

The cold wave affected even the Keys so I had to stay in and work instead of taking the rest in the sun that I had planned. Yesterday I mailed Audrey a bunch of final revisions which, together with the new material that I did just before leaving New York, should be incorporated in the script before we go into rehearsal. I think we should have a script conference a day or so before the start of rehearsals, to consider this new material and the script as it now stands. We are planning to leave December 3rd. If we fly back we could have the conference the next day. If we take the train, either that evening (of the next day) or the day following. I was greatly relieved by your wire about Boris' model. Long to see it. I hope it contains the embankment stairs that Milzener suggested, which I think is the best idea

that has been brought forward for the design in any of the discussions about it. Then I want to get together with David Diamond and Rose to see how their work is progressing. Perhaps they could all participate in this script-conference or general discussion as it would, then, be.

So far this season the critics have shown preposterous leniency, but it would be just my luck to have them exhaust their good-humor before we get in. If Florida were properly sunny, and I were getting enough swimming, this misanthropic state would not persist. But when one stays indoors continuing work on a script one has worked on and messed around with and fumed and fussed and fretted over for 23 almost solid months - and reads Westbrook Pegler and the tragic letters of Ezra Pound, starting off like a trumpet before the first World War and dying out to a penny-whistle in the mouth of an old man crumbling into lunacy - it is hard to keep a stout heart! Then I am depressed over grandfather. He is not as well as last year. He has a couple of skin-cancers on his face which have been treated by X-ray. The scabs are disfiguring and very distressing to him, since he has always taken such pride in his appearance. He is afraid they "look disgusting to people". I think they will clear up and Frank and I are trying hard to convince him of it.

The town has changed much for the worse, the campaign against "Bohemianism" still virulent, a spirit of suspicion making you feel uncomfortable when you go out in the evenings however innocently. Fortunately property values are thought to be increasing, and although I paid too much for this house, I may be able to get rid of it without much loss - if the present atmosphere continues, which I suppose it is bound to do, or even increase - in the event of a war. If Europe is cut off, I suppose I might try Mexico. I say "I" because I can't count on Frank remaining out of the service!

With love from "The Blue Boy" - Tenn.

[TW and Frank Merlo spent nearly two weeks in Key West, arriving ca. November 21 and returning to New York in early-December for rehearsals of *The Rose Tattoo*.

To date Boris Aronson had designed nearly forty Broadway shows, including the current hits *Season in the Sun* (1950) and *The Country Girl* (1950). In a recent interview he remarked that he was "'better known for the 'Lower Depths' than for the gayer sort of set'" (qtd. in *New York Times*, November 26, 1950). Early sketches for *The Rose Tattoo* show a path leading up the "embankment" which separates Serafina's cottage from the highway.

David Diamond, soon to begin a long residence in Italy, wrote incidental music for *The Rose Tattoo*, while Rose Bogdanoff designed the costumes.

Brooks Atkinson was one of the lenient critics who voted "raves" for *Bell, Book and Candle* (1950), the fanciful "trifle" (*New York Times*, November 15, 1950) produced by Irene Selznick and written and directed by John van Druten. The hit play had replaced *The Rose Tattoo* in Selznick's consideration and probably earned TW's disdain as a result. It was Selznick's "pretty pink and perfumed little dead pig of a baby" (TW to Kazan, November 18, 1950, WUCA).

The columnist Westbrook Pegler used a populist rhetoric to attack FDR, labor leaders, "furriners," and modern poets, whom he especially despised. TW was reading D.D. Paige's edition of *The Letters of Ezra Pound: 1907-1941* (1950).

"'Bohemianism'" was under attack in Washington as well as in Key West. A forthcoming Senate report demanded vigilance in keeping "perverts" off the "Government payroll" and strict enforcement of Civil Service rules in ousting those employed—some 3,700, it was thought, in "Washington alone" (*New York Times*, December 16, 1950).

The bungalow for which TW reportedly paid $22,500 in 1950 sold for $235,000 in 1991 and for more than a million dollars ten years later.

Penned in the upper margin is the notation "Enchanted by Boris design, just rec'd! Bigelow does not seem to know you have job for him (according to Audrey)." Paul Bigelow served as a production staff assistant to Cheryl Crawford.

Related correspondence suggests that TW wrote this letter on November 27, 1950.]

Boris Aronson, The Rose Tattoo *(1951): "Enchanted by Boris design."*

190. To Erwin Piscator

1431 Duncan
Key West, Fla.
December 1, 1950
[TLS, 1 p. Southern Illinois U]

Dear Dr. Piscator:

I am embarassed, and conscience-stricken, as I should be, by your gentle note of well-deserved reproach. I shall not say anything about my travels, or the awful concentration required by my work, but only that I am as interested as ever in what the Dramatic Workshop is doing and continually more and more impressed and admiring of its accomplishments and its endurance in the face of so much that is adverse in our present circumstances. I am not in New York or I would certainly have seen your adaptation of Kafka's great book. I hope to see it when I return in a few days. I have heard nothing but fine and exciting things about it. I feel it is one of the most significant works of our time.

Soon as the terrific strain and tension of this new play is over, I hope we can communicate more fully. I am proud to be a Board member and I hope that somehow or other I can manage to participate more than I have been able in the past.

My continual felicitations, my warm regards as ever,

Tennessee.

[Erwin Piscator (1893-1966), director of the Dramatic Workshop, scolded TW for having missed a production of *The Trial* (Kafka, April 1950) and solicited his contribution to an emergency fund-raising campaign. The need was caused by the separation of the Workshop—a liability in the conservative political climate—from its founding institution, the New School for Social Research. Neither TW's deference nor Piscator's "gentle" touch had marked earlier exchanges, when *Battle of Angels* (1940) was being considered for a Workshop production.

Membership on the Board of Trustees of the Workshop was later cited in TW's FBI file (obtained under the Freedom of Information Act) as evidence of questionable associations. An explanatory note stated that the Dramatic Workshop had been identified in 1948 "as a Communist front by the California Committee on Un-American Activities."]

191. To Edwina Dakin Williams and
Walter Edwin Dakin

[235 East 58th Street, New York]
12/16/50
[TLS, 1 p. Columbia U]

Dear Mother and Grandfather:

I was tremendously relieved to learn that Grandfather's wandering trunk had been tracked down and was eventually going to reach him. Now he can make public appearances in the style that suits him, and I'm sure he felt even more relieved than I did.

Frank and I are missing the warmth and tranquillity of Key West. But I am bearing up pretty well under the strain of rehearsals. Fortunately we had all the luck in casting the play. The girl playing the lead is almost as good an actress as Laurette Taylor. In fact, she is like a young Laurette, which pleases me especially because nobody else wanted to cast her in the part, since they felt her youth and lack of experience would be too great a handicap. But she has tremendous power and honesty in her acting and I think she is going to put the show over. She is an Irish girl, not pretty in any conventional way and considerably too plump, but she has more talent than any of the leading ladies of twice her age and half her size. The Director is not as gifted as Kazan but he works twice as hard, all day and half the night. It is his big chance. The Italian women in the cast are particularly touching and wonderful. Most of them were taken off relief when they got jobs in the play. They are natural born actors, although their experience was limited mostly to the Italian radio stations around New York. Then we have an old lady who must be in her eighties who was once a star in the London music-halls. She is playing "The Strega" - Italian for "witch". She is so deaf and blind that she has to be pushed on stage when her entrances come, but she is still a terrific performer, her name is Daisy Belmore. I hope that the fact that none of these people have been seen or known before on Broadway will give a special sense of reality to the production. There is great interest and speculation around about. Kazan and Irene are going to fly to Chicago and I hope we will put on such a good show that they will wish they had stayed at home! - since neither of them had courage enough to undertake it.

Irene's new play is a big success but also a big mess.

If you have any idea what Dakin and Rose would like for Christmas, please let me know. I shall try to do some shopping next week.

Marian Vacarro has come to New York. She put the car in a Miami storage garage where we can pick it up when we come back South. I am not sure I will have a chance to visit St. Louis, I seriously doubt it, as the last days of rehearsal, around Christmas, will need my close attention. The company leaves Christmas afternoon for Chicago where I will be staying at the Hotel Sherman.

Much love, Tom

[Cheryl Crawford and associates hesitated to give the "bravura" role to a near "unknown," as Maureen Stapleton has recalled: "Obviously they'd been impressed by my reading, but they seemed to want me to *promise* them I could succeed. First Crawford, then Mann, then Miss Wood asked for some sort of guarantee. What could I guarantee? . . . I finished talking and Tennessee jumped up from his chair, declaring, 'I don't care if she turns into a dead mule on opening night. I want her for the part!'" (qtd. in Stapleton, *A Hell of a Life*, 1995, p. 84).

Daisy Belmore's seventy-six years were filled with supporting roles on stage and screen, including a bit part in the classic *Dracula* (1931) film starring Bela Lugosi.]

192. To Margaret "Margo" Jones

235 E. 58th Street, New York.
December 1950
[TLS, 2 pp. Dallas Public Library]

Dearest Margo:

Your letters are always "a beaker full of the warm South". I am more and more keenly interested, all the time, in the progress of important theatres away from New York. There is something so awful about the finality of a Broadway production under the present scheme of things. One is so dreadfully at the mercy of a handful of men who display such an alarming lack of steady, definable standards. This season has been especially frightening with the great success of things like Bell, Book and Candle and all the fuss made over English importations that bore the be-Jesus even out of those who like poetry as much as I do. If one happens to run against the particular current of the moment, in this particular, very regional and provincial locality called Broadway, he is boxed down like a Punch or Judy and a play which may have come arduously but truly to life after a long struggle of two years or more is pitched off the professional

stage into the shadowy half-world of the non-professional little theatres here and there about the country and the limbo of the libraries. What is ANTA doing about it? It looks to me like ANTA is just another old Auntie! It is a convenient shop-window for stars to show themselves to exactly the same crowd under just about the same conditions. It is just another Broadway enterprise as far as it has demonstrated up till now. I do hope most passionately that you are serious about the national idea you were discussing when I last saw you. You are the person for it. I think you can give your personal excitement and fire to such a project and infect the whole country with it, and I think you should devote yourself to it, even though it may mean a temporary absence from Dallas or a division of your labors there. You should set up an office, probably here, get a full-time staff including the best publicity people and barn-storm about the country, presenting the idea and selling it to key people in all the cities where a theatre of this kind belongs. It would, I feel, have a profound effect on the whole cultural life of the nation which seems to be sinking into something almost worse than oblivion with the outlets of expression nearly all in the same old repressive hands. It would give the theatre a real new lease on life. Then any work of truth and vigor would have ten chances instead of one to reach the hearts of people that could respond to it.

I write this in a mood of personal anxiety about my own work but it is more than that. Do you realize that there is scarcely a newspaper, magazine, radio or TV station or cinema in the whole country that doesn't represent practically the same old tired, blind, bitter and dessicated attitude toward life? The Big Time Operators are all one guy and those are the qualities of him. So don't forget your youth and the crusading spirit of it! I would be very happy to take the stump with you when you are ready to start.

The "Tattoo" is going well, knock wood. We have all new people, new faces, mostly quite young, and a group of real Italian women who were taken off the relief rolls for this production. Most of them broke down and cried when they got their jobs! It's the most wonderful bunch of people I've ever seen collected in a show and it makes you feel a deep and frightening responsibility. If only it would make certain other people feel the same thing!

Let me hear from you again soon, and do, if you can, fly up sometime during our Chicago run. We open the 29th and may play there for four weeks at the Erlanger theatre.

With love, 10

Mother and Grandfather are occupying the house in Key West while we are away. We plan to return there in February.

[Verse plays by Christopher Fry—*The Lady's Not for Burning* and *Ring Round the Moon*—opened to acclaim in New York on November 8 and 23, 1950, respectively.

"ANTA" (American National Theatre and Academy) had recently launched a drama series in its new Playhouse on 52nd Street, formerly the Guild Theatre. The first offering—*The Tower Beyond Tragedy* (November 26, 1950), a verse play by Robinson Jeffers starring Judith Anderson as Clytemnestra—drew raves, especially from Brooks Atkinson, who deemed it "an inspired production" (*New York Times*, November 27, 1950).

TW "last saw" Margo Jones in the fall when she brought *Southern Exposure* (1950) to New York for an ill-advised production. Earlier in the summer she urged the Rockefeller Foundation to sponsor "a drive to create a national theatre" and Columbia University to "schedule a program of lectures" (Sheehy, *Margo*, 1989, p. 206) in support of the project.

This letter, which bears the imprint "Memphis, Tennessee," was probably written in mid-December 1950 in reply to Jones's latest correspondence (December 12, 1950, Dallas Public Library).]

193. To Christopher Isherwood

[235 East 58th Street, New York]
[December 1950]
[TLS, 1 p. Huntington]

Dear Chris:

I lost the long letter I wrote you on the train to Florida last month and it seems that I have also lost the advertising page from the Sunday Times book-section that Jay wanted me to enclose in this envelope, but you will doubtless see it. It contains your quote for Mrs. Stone, that poor lost lady, her epitaph in the world of letters, a very gracious and kind one for which I can't thank you enough, for she was much abused. Edith Sitwell and her brother, Osbert, also wrote me very nice things about the book but not knowing them as well as you, I didn't have the courage to ask them for permission to quote them.

"The Rose Tattoo" is in rehearsal. If for no other reason, the production will be notable for the return of Daisy Belmore, an octogenarian actress who successfully disguised the fact that was stone deaf and virtually blind when she read for the part. Fortunately she plays a Strega who has

little to do but chase a black goat off and on the stage and utter witless
cackles and imprecations from time to time. It may be necessary to tie a
string around her ankel to get her on and off on cue. You and Bill would
love her. And she would be an important addition to the ranks of "the
dreaded fog-queens". How is La. by the way, is the heat still on? Has
Speed recovered from his operation and returned to the Coast? Here it is
very, very dull. I was in the Blue Parrot last night, the gayest bar on the
bird-circuit. The queens were packed in so tight there wasn't even room
to grope in. They just stood there like a wierd assortment of animals that
had fled to the banks of a river from a forest fire. And blew smoke in each
other's faces and sang with the juke-box. "She's a nice girl, a proper girl,
but one of the roving kind!" There is a dreadful rumor that queens are
going to be drafted for the next one and that the draft age is being lifted to
35. This still excludes me but it takes in Frankie. I mean the admission of
queens, excludes me - not, of course, the extended age-limit! - I am still in
my te-eeens . . . Frankie has not yet been summoned but is very gloomy
with expectation. I am very gloomy without expectation.

    Is Caskey in or out of you-know-what?!!

                              Love, love! 10.

[TW met Christopher Isherwood (1904-1986) in Hollywood in 1943 while working as a screenwriter at MGM. He later claimed "great friendship" (*Memoirs*, p.
77) with Isherwood, who described their sexual history shortly after TW's death:
"We just found each other very sympathetic, and we went to bed together two or
three times, I imagine" (qtd. in Leverich, p. 502).

    Isherwood's "quote for Mrs. Stone" stated that TW "can bring tragic beauty
and humor to themes which lesser writers ought never to handle" (*New York
Times*, December 3, 1950).

    "'We are the dreaded fog queens!'" said TW, as he, Isherwood, and Bill
Caskey rode in a cab on a foggy night in London (June 1948). Isherwood recalls
that they began "to elaborate on the fantasy—how the respectable citizens shudder . . . and cross themselves as the dreaded fog queens ride by" (Isherwood, *Lost
Years*, 2000, p. 145).

    In December 1949 Isherwood was caught in the raid of a gay bar and held for
questioning by the Santa Monica police. He "denied being homosexual" but later
wished that he had made "a nationwide stink" (*Diaries*, December 6, 1949).
Presumably the "heat" continued.

    Baron de Charlus, Proust's aging homosexual, improbably refers to the "bird-
circuit" in *Camino Real* (1953): "They stand three-deep at the bar and look at

themselves in the mirror and what they see is depressing." The columnist Walter Winchell later reported that "liquor authorities" in New York, alerted by TW's reference, were "scrutinizing all hooch licenses" issued to such gaily named "joynts" (*New York Daily Mirror*, April 13, 1953) as the "Blue Parrot." Guy Mitchell's recording of "The Roving Kind" reached #4 on the charts in 1951.

The recent easing of "mental standards" for recruits helped to stabilize the draft age at nineteen through twenty-five. Frank Merlo, twenty-eight, was probably not in imminent danger of being drafted for service in the Korean War.

Caskey served three months (August-October 1950) for drunk driving in San Clemente, California. His long relationship with Isherwood was strained and would soon end.]

Christopher Isherwood: "We are the dreaded fog queens!"

194. To Edwina Dakin Williams and
Walter Edwin Dakin

SH: Hotel Sherman
Chicago 1, Ill.
1/6/51
[TLS, 1 p. Columbia U]

Dear Mother and Grandfather:

In the excitement of the past week we forgot to mail the household checks. Hope you have not been inconvenienced. I am including Marie's since I assume she has come back to work by now. We are anxious to keep her as we shall be back in Key West pretty soon now.

The opening was very exciting, a very warm response from a full house, the reviews were good except one who felt there was too much comedy for a serious play. He did not seem to realize that it <u>was</u> a serious play treated with humor. But he is coming back to see it again and will probably write a better piece. Business is improving. We have a fine theatre lined up in New York, the Martin Beck which is where you saw Cornell in Anthony and Cleopatra. I think I can get back to N.Y. the middle of this week. Chicago is so cold and unpleasant this time of year.

There was no time to do anything about Christmas but we will be able to send some little Advent remembrances later. Enjoyed Dakin's visit. He looked well and happy.

Much love, Tom.

[Sydney Harris wrote that the comedy of *The Rose Tattoo* violated the play's weighty thematics of spirit and flesh (*Chicago Daily News*, December 30, 1950). Claudia Cassidy, who had cheered for *The Glass Menagerie* during its perilous try-out in Chicago, was more positive but aware of serious lapses. *The Rose Tattoo* had not yet received "clairvoyant" direction, "mesmeric" acting, or "a luminous finale" (*Chicago Sunday Tribune*, December 31, 1950).

After the Chicago opening, Elia Kazan urged TW to examine "the last five minutes of the play" and to be sure that the ending was "fixed" (n.d., HRC). Eli Wallach has recalled the day when "Tennessee finally came in . . . and said, 'I want {Alvaro} to leave his shirt in the room when he runs up the hill. Then Serafina passes a bloodstained shirt up the hill'" (qtd. in Steen, *A Look at Tennessee Williams*, 1969, p. 292). This may be the "new ending" (to Laughlin, January 16, 1951, Houghton) to which TW referred in mid-January 1951 when the play was still in Chicago.

The season of Advent precedes Christmas in the liturgical calendar.]

195. To Justin Brooks Atkinson

[235 East 58th Street, New York]
Feb. 5, 1951
[TLS, 1 p. BRTC]

Dear Brooks:

Now that it is over, the waiting, I can tell you that I was scared out of my wits, as I knew that a sense of defeat at this point might have been altogether insurmountable. To know that you still like what I do is more reassuring than I can possibly tell you, for this play <u>was</u> a radical departure for me and there were many discouragements and uncertainties about it all the way along. After studying the notices, particularly yours, The News and The Trib, I feel invited to go on working for the theatre, and that is an invitation that I am only too eager to accept.

It was Orianne who let us know Saturday night that you were pleased with the play - in a telephone conversation sometime Saturday night, which made it possible to enjoy the after-opening party. So please give her my thanks, too.

Ever yours, Tennessee.

[Journal entries made before the preview and opening of *The Rose Tattoo* reveal a familiar pattern of renunciation and concern. "I mustn't ever again permit myself to care this much about any public success. It makes you little and altogether too vulnerable" (January 30, 1951). "Last night we had our first New York audience, invited - the show was down and I felt the response was not as good as Chicago" (February 1, 1951).

Atkinson found TW "in a good mood" in *The Rose Tattoo* and observed that he has written "the loveliest idyll for the stage in some time." Any fear that he might be "imprisoned within a formula" of despair was relieved by the joy and compassion of his new "comic play" (*New York Times*, February 5, 1951). Reviewers for the *Herald Tribune* and the *Daily News* were also charmed, but others faulted the play on moral or dramatic grounds, and one was "revolted" by "an unmentionable article" dropped on the stage—Alvaro's errant condom. Maureen Stapleton's Serafina was uniformly praised and *Variety* reported that *The Rose Tattoo* "Looks Hot" (February 7, 1951).]

196. To Irene Mayer Selznick

[1431 Duncan Street
Key West, Florida]
Feb. 27, 1951.
[TLS, 1 p. Boston U]

Dearest Irene:

Frank and I flew down here a week ago Friday and have had the whole family with us, Grandfather, Mother, and Dakin. I arrived with the Flu, Dakin took it and now Grandfather has it. He is a little better this morning. I think the knowledge that Mother is departing today for Saint Louis will hasten his recuperation, and I know it will be a relief to Frank and I to resume the Bohemian tenor of our ways. In the middle of April we plan to bring my sister down here with her nurse-companion for a few weeks. It will be her first long trip since she went in the sanitarium and the first time I have seen her in a long while. If it works out well, I hope it can be arranged to keep her down here most of the time. The place seems ideal for her as she adored Florida and ocean-bathing. I hope you will be here when Rose is here, for I know there would be a sympathy between you. (Frank says you were thinking of coming down. I hope so.) The production of "Tattoo" was a terrible drain on my energies. I was a wreck the last week in New York, but a satisfied wreck. If it had been a smash hit like "Streetcar" or a dismal failure like "Summer and Smoke", it would have been, either way, bad for me. As it is, I think it provides what is always most essential, a bridge to the future where I hope my best work still remains. Fortunately I had some work already under way, which it is easier to resume than it would be to start from scratch. Please thank John for the nice things he said in his Times Sunday magazine article. The wonderful and tremendously successful production of his play must be a source of great satisfaction to you, especially since he is such a fine person.

Love - Tenn.

[TW succeeded in transferring his sister Rose from Farmington State Hospital in Missouri to Stony Lodge, a private sanitarium near Ossining, New York. She lived in "her own cottage in the woods," as Dakin Williams has reported.

John van Druten called for "a new kind of playwriting" in which the "integrity of the author . . . takes precedence over all the older tricks and formulae of the

theatre." Van Druten looked to TW, Arthur Miller, and Carson McCullers, a trio of young writers who held "as much promise" as any he could "remember," to "freshen our own skill and talents and deep interest" in the theatre ("A Quarter Century of the Rialto," *New York Times*, February 25, 1951).]

197. To Oliver Evans

1431 Duncan St.
Key West, Fla.
3 March 1951
[TLS w/ enclosure, 1 p. HRC]

Dear Oliver:

I am somewhat disturbed by the beautiful but enigmatic first line of a poem, sent me in the form of a wire, which is the only communication received from you since I left New York. Frank suspected it was an obscure allusion to him, since he is the only person with whom I have "entered Rome", but neither slavery nor Christianity have been involved in our relations. We entered Rome as a pair of free pagans, and that is how we left it, and how we shall go back there, if we can return this summer. I am more inclined to think the allusion was to something unpleasant in my character or manner. I am not in a good position to defend myself except by saying that for some time I have been obsessed with the will to remain alive and continue my work and that most other things, except one or two relationships, have existed in a sort of penumbra outside that central mania. But you ought to know that you are one of those few things, and show an understanding and indulgence in times of strain, the sort of understanding I once hoped for from certain old friends who now look at me with pairs of animated ice-cubes and yet are said to have said that I said that they were going blind! If you think ill of me, now, it may please you to read the enclosed letter from a young Italian who claims that the gigolo in Mrs. Stone was based on his personality. It is a poison pen letter, that much I can make out, perhaps the worst that I have received since meeting those queens in the Automat on Sixth Avenue, and I am hoping you can translate it for me and see if it contains an actual threat. Frank was unable to make it out as he doesn't read Italian much, if any, better than I. I did gather that he considers me the Empire State Building of W.C.'s!

Grandfather has been in the hospital, seriously ill with Flu and

complications. He is now home but quite feeble and almost completely bed-ridden. If he is not in a critical condition, I will fly to New York next Thursday, this coming Thursday, to see the first East-coast pre-view of "Streetcar". And I will call you when I arrive in case you want to see it. Although I could not blame you for being tired of all my works, past, present or future. You have not shown me your new poems. I am jealous of them, for it has been at least five months since I have written a poem. (Some people say it's been longer!)

With love, Tenn.

[TW's failure to keep an appointment in New York offended Oliver Evans and probably led to his "enigmatic" verse: "It is with a Christian slave that one enters Rome" (TW to Healy, February 27, 1951, Columbia U). TW blamed the "'Flu'" in prior correspondence from Key West: "You know, honey boy, that I would never willingly miss an appointment with you!" (February 19, 1951, HRC).

In *The Roman Spring*, TW used the given name of Elizabeth Eyre de Lanux's young lover, Paolo Casagrande, as well as borrowed details of financial chicanery.]

198. *To Cheryl Crawford*

1431 Duncan
Key West, Fla.
March 3, 1951.
[TLS, 1 p. BRTC]

Dearest Cheryl:

There have been so many distractions that I really don't know whether I have written you or not since leaving New York! A seige of illness. I arrived here with the Flu. My brother, Dakin, took it, and then Grandfather. Dakin and Mother have left and poor Grandfather has just come back from the hospital in a dreadful condition, barely able to move, but thankful to be back at home with Frank and me. He will be 94 next month. I am terribly afraid that he won't last much longer. The doctor says that his lung congestion is symptomatic of a cardiac condition as much as the Flu. But he would not remain in the hospital which he said was 'a prison'. He is determined to survive! It is wonderful how even at his age the will to live can persist. We hustled Mother and Dakin back to Saint

Louis, for they depress him, and now there are just the three of us again. Frank is a wonderful nurse, and we have a negro maid who is devoted to Grandfather and gives him excellent diet and care. If he is sufficiently improved, I am flying to New York next Thursday to see the first East coast pre-view of "Streetcar". Feldmann wants to cut it, against Gadg's wishes, and I may be useful as a moral support to Gadg. I hope you can attend the pre-view with us. In spite of the Flu, and perhaps partly because of the fever, I have been unusually energetic and working hard every day. I think my happiness over "Tattoo" has been a moral support to me. I feel encouraged over the increase at the box-office. I don't suppose this is a season in which one can expect a continual sell-out. But I think if performance levels can be maintained, we should be set for a pretty good run. I hope Danny can keep in touch with the show. This has been my happiest

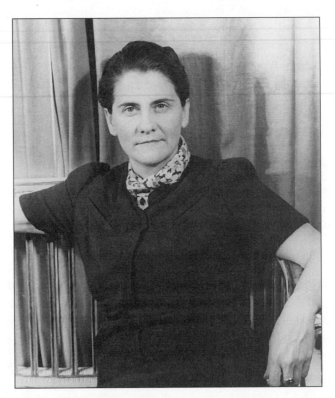

Cheryl Crawford, founding member of
The Group Theatre and The Actors Studio

experience in the theatre so far, since it came at a crucial point when a failure might have been final, but a success seems like the opening of another door.

Much love, Tenn.

[TW returned to New York in early-March to confer with Charles Feldman and Elia Kazan on the final editing of *Streetcar*. He later urged Feldman—under intense pressure from the Roman Catholic Legion of Decency—not to "exceed cuts we all agreed upon in New York" (see letter #210).

Cheryl Crawford reported advance sales of $75,000 as well as a healthy fourth-week gross of $27,600 for *The Rose Tattoo*. "I saw it Saturday afternoon," she added, "along with thirty-odd other standees. Maureen has grown in the part and all the performances were full and rich and fine" (to TW, n.d., HTC). A campaign launched by the publicist Wolfe Kaufman led to cast appearances on the RKO Pathe newsreel and the Ed Sullivan Show.]

199. To Audrey Wood

[1431 Duncan Street
Key West, Florida]
3/14/51
[TLS w/ enclosure and
autograph postscript, 1 p. HRC]

Dear Audrey:

Here is a suggested change for the last scene of "Tattoo" which I wish you would submit to Dannie. It may help alleviate some of the "moral" antipathy and doesn't constitute a serious concession.

On reflection, it seems to me that my feeling of depression at the two performances I saw was not attributable simply to the slackening of trade. I feel that the apathy of the audience, and perhaps to a considerable extent the slump of the box-office, is due to a loss of vigor in the general performance of the play. Some scenes it is true are stronger but the general effect, particularly in the last scene is weaker than it used to be. A softening of fibre, particularly in the crowd scenes. Unfortunately strength of attack is not Danny's strong point as a director. His staging never has the precision and force that Kazan could give to group movement on the stage, and so when the actors themselves get relaxed in the parts, the whole effect becomes flaccid. On interpretation, on physically quiet scenes, his work is

best and quite marvelous. I hope you will "look in" on the rehearsals of this new material, if it goes in, particularly the "telephone bit" and see that it has the necessary sharpness. I am a little vexed by Maureen's attitude toward continued work on the staging. She knows we have to put up a fight for this play and she ought to be more than willing to make a real effort. Confidentially, I think if the show goes on the road we ought to give serious consideration to the idea of getting Judith Anderson, not only for box-office draw but for professional attitude toward work. Talent is not enough, even in the young!

Love, Tenn

Grandfather much better!

[Brooks Atkinson later cited "the elimination of one lewd episode in the last act" (*New York Times*, June 3, 1951) of *The Rose Tattoo*—the still "unmentionable" condom.

    Variety reported on March 14 that "some straight plays skidded," including *The Rose Tattoo*, whose weekly gross fell to $24,200.

    The "'telephone bit'" used to reveal Rosario's infidelity was described as "bald" and "mechanical" in early reviews of *The Rose Tattoo*. TW's criticism of "the young" is underlined in red in the original typescript.

    TW planned to return to Key West on March 12, 1951, where in all probability he wrote this letter.]

200. To Audrey Wood

Western Union
Key West Flo
1951 Mar 19 AM 4 31
[Telegram, 1 p. HRC]

AUDREY WOOD=

PLEASE SEE IF YOU HAVE DUPLICATE OF ANY DRIVERS LICENSE FOR ME ARRESTED FOR TRAFFIC VIOLATION CANNOT LOCATE MY LICENSE APPEARING IN COURT TUESDAY MORNING LOVE=

TENNESSEE=

[TW's arrest was reportedly for drunken driving. Audrey Wood mentioned only an "accident" in later correspondence and implored TW to "please drive in such a fashion that you will live to be an old man, as old I hope as Rev. Dakin" (March 20, 1951, HRC).]

201. To Max Lerner

[1431 Duncan Street
Key West, Florida]
March 21, 1951
[TLx, 2 pp. HTC]

Dear Max Lerner:

Wolfe Kaufman sent me your article before you did and I had already planned to tell you that I think that you, for the first time to my knowledge, have placed your finger directly on the most demoralizing problem that the American playwright has to face. Although it does not loom very large against the present background of world affairs, the predicament of the playwright is a very peculiar one which holds considerable interest even to those outside the profession. But it is seldom that anyone outside the profession seems to give much thought to it. You are an exception which is extremely welcome.

In technical requirements alone, the writing of plays is probably the most complex of creative forms. I think it is also by far the most physically and nervously exhausting. It literally takes the strength of an ox, if you care deeply about it, to carry a play from conception all the way through to its opening night on Broadway. There are few playwrights, I think mainly because there aren't many willing or able to stand up under the grind.

As far as I know, you are the first to reflect in print on the exorbitant demands made by critics who don't stop to consider the playwright's need for a gradual ripening or development, time in which to complete it, a degree of tolerance and patience in his mentors during this period of transition. This does not mean that messy, bad, sloppy, work should be tolerated. No self-respecting playwright, still in possession of sanity, would condone it in himself, let alone expect it from hard-boiled critics. But this should be considered. It takes ten years of a man's life, usually, to grow into a new major attitude toward existence and the world he exists in. We all know that sometimes the growth is short-circuited, falls short of fulfillment. Our literary history is studded with F. Scott Fitzgeralds! - to mention an example no less pertinent for being outside the dramatic area. Many artists have smashed themselves trying to make this transition, and painfully often their critics have collaborated in the smash-up.

Painters have it better. They are allowed to evolve new methods, new styles, by a reasonably gradual process. They are not abused for turning out

creative variations on themes already stated. If a certain theme has importance, it may take a number of individual works to explore it fully. While he is evolving, growing as writer and person, the writer must go on working. Once he breaks the habit of work, his situation is most critical. He frequently becomes a lunatic or a lush or equal parts of both. The acuteness of sensibility that makes him an artist, if he is one, also makes him one of society's most vulnerable members. As for the playwright, people say: "Sure it's hard! But look at the money he makes?" -- Take it from me! No playwright who has come out since 1944 has a better than even chance of breaking even! He has a smash-hit once every five or ten years and he's in the same bracket of taxation that the industrialist is, who makes that much without fail every year!

It would help enormously if there were professional theatre centers outside of New York, so that the playwright would always be at the mercy of a single localized group. The reception of a play varies greatly wherever it goes on the road, especially if it is an experimental or controversial type of play. If only the WPA theatre had worked out! Some kind of state theatre seems to be the only eventual solution. But there are a thousand and one different messes in the world that have to be settled before people outside the theatre give a tinker's damn about the problem of the American playwright. We don't have it good right now. But does anybody? I think that most of us were born knowing that it was going to be bloody. But sometimes our critics ought to meet us half way - that is, if they want us to stand up under the unremitting strain of our profession. Some do, Brooks Atkinson, for instance, is consistently sympathetic to what he recognizes as something better than hack work. Others, such as the so-called Dean of American critics, Mr. Nathan, seems to want to blast us out of the ground at the first little sign of intransigeance, and the trouble is that they write so escruciatingly well! Do we have a chance? Whether we have one or not, the chance is that we will go on working, and usually for the love of it.

Sincerely,

[Max Lerner (1902-1992), prolific author, educator, and columnist, wrote that every successful playwright from Eugene O'Neill to TW has suffered "the critical American disease called The Recoils": "We spew up our welcoming hosannahs and ask the Genius to prove to us that he has not reverted to the bum he was before we discovered him." Consequently every play "must be a hit." TW "should be allowed

a chance to deepen his talent and give shape to his outlook without fear of being hounded for his lapses" (*New York Post*, March 6, 1951). A lightly edited version of TW's reply appeared in the *New York Post* on May 16, 1951, p. 44.

"The WPA theatre" (Works Progress Administration) sponsored some 64,000 performances and employed 10,000 theatre professionals during its brief tenure (1935-1939). Conservatives in Congress cut the welfare program in opposition to FDR's New Deal politics and the perceived radicalism of its offerings.

The HRC holds a briefer signed version of the letter dated Key West, March 19, 1951.]

202. To Oliver Evans

[1431 Duncan Street
Key West, Florida]
3/31/51
[TLS, 1 p. HRC]

Dear Oliver:

I was not unaware of your inebriate condition the last evening I saw you in New York, nor, I take it, was Dame Cabot or Miss Olivia De Havilland when you cried out, during her soliloquy on the apron of the stage: "Nothing can kill the beauty of the lines!" How those ladies may feel about it I am not in a position to say. One of the very few advantages of being my friend is that the point at which I become seriously offended, or even surprised, however moderately, is hard to reach. I had a pleasant little telephone conversation with Otis the morning after the night before. He warmly reiterated his welcome to Copenhagen and other capitals of Europe, so there is apparently no lasting rancor in that quarter. I should like very much to know the sequel to your conversations with Dame Cabot. I hope they didn't appear in the obituary column of the papers next day. I am sure it is the first time she has been exposed to such vigorous language. She must have spent the rest of the night in an oxygen tent.

I saw Marian in Miami. She had not yet left for New Orleans but was leaving that afternoon. Incidentally she loaned me fifty dollars as my purse had been snatched the night before during an encounter with a baby-faced thug in Biscayne Park. Fortunately I had very little money on me and succeeded in convincing him that my diamonds were worthless and he could not work the clasp on my watch. I told him that if he would just wait outside my hotel I would come out promptly with additional cash.

Needless to say I retired for the night, but the poor fool called me repeatedly on the phone, enquiring when I was coming down with the rest of his loot. Dirt is usually moronic, but this was a low-grade imbecile!

Grandfather is back on his feet, but the cook has gone on a binge and Frank has to assume her duties as well as the considerable demands already made upon him. My health? The new drugs remain intact. I tried one pill which seemed to cause a slight increase in my hypertension rather than otherwise. But the liquor supply is faithful. Now we are going out to the movies, as ever.

I love you, still and always, fratello mio!

Tenn.

[TW returned to New York in late-March to join Maureen Stapleton, Eli Wallach, and Boris Aronson in receiving "Tony" awards (March 25, 1951) for *The Rose Tattoo*. Sponsored by the American Theatre Wing, the "Tony" represented the first major prize of the season.

TW marked his fortieth birthday (March 26) by attending a lavish revival of *Romeo and Juliet*. Olivia De Havilland's Broadway debut as an aging Juliet (thirty-four) was not well received, as Oliver Evans, TW's companion, proclaimed from the audience. In *The Roman Spring*, Karen Stone was also miscast as Juliet in her final dramatic role.]

203. To James "Jay" Laughlin

[1431 Duncan Street
Key West, Florida]
4/1/51
[TLS, 1 p. Houghton]

Dear Jay:

Although I came here, ostensibly, for a rest I have been busier than usual working my way into another play. The initial stages are always the most strenuous, perhaps even worse than the final. I have been very nervous. Hypertensive. Bigelow took me to a fashionable doctor in New York who gave me some pills that are supposed to make my face flush and my ears buzz as they open the capillaries - distend the blood vessels, Etc. I took just one and felt far more hypertensive than usual so have put them on the shelf. I drink too much. About eight drinks a day at carefully spaced intervals. I am trying to work down to six. Perhaps I ought to stop working. But then I would explode from sheer ennui.

I hate to make any derogatory remarks about the Cummington boy's design. Strictly entre nous, it does look a bit like pigeon en casserole. But I sense that he feels very strongly about designing something for the book and it might be mean of us to frustrate him. The typography and paper are so beautiful. I do wish that Lustig was doing the front cover, however. I am charmed with the rose cover of the book of "Tattoo". The only other person I know who likes it is Donald Windham, but I like it very much indeed. I also love the ad, copy of which you sent me.

Thank you so much for the very detailed financial statements and I was agreeably surprised by the amount of funds. I hope sometime later in the Spring, when my own economic picture acquires more clarity, to make a new contribution to the Authors' League fund, earmarked for Oliver Evans. He is having an operation for his deafness and I would like to be able to help him with it. I may draw on my account with you for this purpose, perhaps about 1500. He is in desperate mental or nervous state, a great deal of which, I think, may be attributable to his affliction. Took eight sleeping pills one evening, fell down on the street and broke two ribs! Only quarts of black coffee saved him. On my birthday, while I was in New York, I took him to see "Romeo and Juliet" and when Miss De Havilland was delivering a soliloquy on the apron of the stage, Oliver, in the fourth row, suddenly cried out "Nothing can kill the beauty of the lines!" and tore out of the theatre. Later that night he called up an old lady who had formerly befriended him, a dowager from Boston who is the ranking member of the Cabot clan, and told her she was "just an old bitch and not even her heirs could stand her!" I think he deserves an endowment for life! Even if this intransigeant behavior persists.

Frank, Grandfather, and I are still in Key West. Until the end of April. We sail the middle of May for Europe, again.

                                        Ever, Tenn.

Love to Gertrude.

[The "play" in progress may be a revision of *Battle of Angels*, reportedly underway in March 1951, as indicated by correspondence with Maureen Stapleton, whom TW had asked to play the role of Myra or Vee (see Spoto, p. 174). Talks with Stapleton continued in New York, as well as the drafting of a poem whose title—"Orpheus Descending" (1952)—would replace *Battle of Angels*.

George Crandell, TW's bibliographer, reports that the first ten copies of *I Rise*

in Flame, Cried the Phoenix (1951) "were printed on Umbria paper and sold for $50.00 each." The original phoenix design gave way to a marbled pattern in shades of black and grey. TW admired the jacket of *The Rose Tattoo*—a luminous, burgeoning pink rose—and no doubt agreed with James Laughlin that "real innovators" such as the designer Alvin Lustig were "always ahead of the public taste" (to TW, April 20, 1951, Houghton).

Oliver Evans's recent call to the "dowager" Cabot punctuated an earlier outburst of candor, as reported by TW: "He told her that she had the manners of a fishwife," whereupon she forbade Evans "to enter her door" (qtd. in St. Just, p. 38).]

204. To Carson McCullers

[1431 Duncan Street]
Key West, Fla.
April 7, 1951
[TLS, 1 p. Duke U]

Dearest Carson:

It is a soft grey rustling muttering sort of a rainy afternoon with Frank gone from the house and the town and Grandfather dozing on the front room couch and me mixing a sad and lonely martini now and then and making a few ineffectual pecks at the typewriter. I decided this afternoon that I ought to stop writing and try to get close to life and people again. I feel that this obsession of work, work, work all the time has left me emotionally exhausted and only half a person. I wonder if I can quit? I wonder what I could find to take the place? Do you ever ask yourself that, and what do you think is the answer?

Last time I was in New York, about ten days ago I guess, I woke up in the night thinking about you, picked up the phone by my bed and sent you a wire. Did you get it? I was going to call you in the morning, but that morning I was very ill. Bigelow whisked me to a doctor. Then I left town with all kinds of anxieties and pills. I am a little better now, but not much.

This coming Wednesday my sister Rose arrives here with her nurse-companion to spend a week with us. It is the first long trip, or vacation, she has had since she went to the sanitarium about fifteen years ago. I sort of dread the meeting. It is bound to involve a lot of painful shocks, but we hope the change may help her, and if it does, that she will be allowed more freedom in the future.

Soon as Rose leaves I have to take Grandfather to Memphis and get him

settled there for the summer. Then we return to New York, and sail May 18th for Europe. Are you planning another trip abroad? This time we go without any definite plan and will probably stay over as long as the state of the world permits.

Grandfather was so pleased with your letter. He is fully recovered, yesterday took a dip in the ocean and is walking around as more or less nimbly as ever. Give Bebe my love, and Rita, and Reeves.

Much, much to you, Tenn.

I am reading Edith Sitwell's "A Poet's Notebook" with enormous pleasure. Is she still in the States, do you see her? Please tell her how much I am enjoying that book.

[Shortly before the opening of *The Rose Tattoo*, TW wrote that "the sunshine and the stars of Key West will be good regardless of how this crucial event turns out. The sea will comfort me, and perhaps it will even restore my power to work" (*Journal*, February 1, 1951).

TW was among the poets whose reception of Edith and brother Osbert Sitwell in 1948 produced a memorable scene—photographed and published by *Life* magazine (December 6, 1948)—at the Gotham Book Mart in New York. Edith Sitwell later met and befriended Carson McCullers at a party given in the poet's honor by TW and praised her as a "'transcendental writer'" (qtd. in Carr, p. 365).

A Poet's Notebook (1943) is Edith Sitwell's collection of aphorisms describing the nature and practice of poetry.]

205. To Audrey Wood

[Paris]
6/9/51
[TLSx, 1 p. HRC]

Dear Audrey:

We are in Paris for a few days after a long stay in London. Poor Maria Britneva is in trouble, pregnant by a married man, and having to have an abortion first of next week, which is dangerous as they think she is in the fourth month of it. She was in Paris with us for a couple of days but has now gone back to prepare for the operation. Don't mention this to anyone!

Mme. Tallant has not been in town so we will not get any more francs out of the Author's League this trip. There were a lot still left in the

strong-box at the Chase National Bank here, so we didn't really need them. I will get them out next time we come through Paris - the ones still held by the "League".

I am leaving tomorrow evening by train for Rome, Frank driving the new car down. We are pleased with it. We will have our original apartment in Rome, the one at 45 Via Aurora - not the one we had last summer which was so hot and uncomfortable. The telephone number there is 40779.

I do hope that "Tattoo" still survives. I expect momentarily to be informed of its demise!

Any chance of moving into the other theatre?

This week Oliver Evans will be having the operation for the recovery of his hearing - in Chicago. Could you check with Authors' League to see if he received the financial assistance I wanted them to give him? You can get his address through City College of New York, English department.

Saw a lot of Peter Brook and some of Irene in London. He seems to have replaced Binkie in her very flexible affections: hope she has better luck. The circumstances are more propitious, at least in one important respect.

With love to you and Bill, Tenn.

[TW and Frank Merlo sailed on the *Queen Mary*, due at Southampton on May 22. They spent approximately two weeks in London before leaving for Paris.

The name "Maria Britneva" has been razored from the first paragraph of the original typescript, but it remains in a signed photographic copy which serves as setting text.

After learning that royalties for *Streetcar* had been sent to the States, TW grumbled that "practically all of that will go to the government" (to Wood, September 9, 1951, HRC). Ninon Tallon continued to represent Audrey Wood in France.

The Rose Tattoo grossed $16,700 in the preceding week, down 40% from its earlier high.]

206. *To Justin Brooks Atkinson*

[45 Via Aurora, Rome]
June 12, 1951
[TLS, 2 pp. BRTC]

Dear Brooks:

I wrote you before on the stationary of the Queen Mary, because I gathered the impression from your new book that you had a special fondness for that ship. The letter got lost in the flurry of disembarkment at Southhamptom so I'm writing you, now, from Rome on stationary from a wonderful old hotel in London called the "Cavendish" which is the property of the only surviving mistress of Edward VII. I liked it even better than the Queen Mary.

The letter I lost was devoted mostly to praise of your book. I borrowed it from someone on the boat. It's the first time I've been almost literally unable to put down a piece of non-fiction. It's a book that comes close to the spirit of Thoreau, and I admired, and envied a little, the feeling of sensitive but tranquil adjustment to life in it, adjustment without conformity or surrender.

And I want to thank you for the recent article on my play. Cheryl just sent it to me. I am sure it has something to do with the cheering upturn of business that she mentioned. When I left New York there had been an alarming decline. About that 'unmentionable article' dropped on the floor. I would have removed it at once if it had not, somehow, failed to strike me as being at all vulgar, even though I knew it seemed that way to many people. Bohemianism seems to take such a strong hold on someone from a background so intensely Puritanical as mine was, once it is broken away from. Then I am always wanting to say and do things in a play that are not ordinarily done, to make it closer to common experience, to prove, at least to myself, that there is nothing in experience that cannot be admitted to writing. But I want to do this only <u>with taste</u>. The 'object', I thought, was a direct, bold and instant symbol of Serafina's conversion (in progress) from a non-realistic, romantic concept of the love-relation to one that was thoroughly, even somewhat grossly, down to earth! - From Rosario to a clown! And finding that life remains thrilling on either level.

I am back in Rome. I have not yet seen Mrs. Stone on the street but otherwise everything is much the same, which is good.

I wish you a pleasant summer, with birds and stars and ships, and I hope the Fall will bring an improved lot of plays.

Ever, Tenn.

[In *Once Around the Sun* (1951)—shipboard reading for TW—Atkinson recorded daily observations, including a reference to the liner upon which TW had recently sailed. The "noises" of Manhattan are "nervous, petty, sharp, impatient," he wrote, while "the voice of the *Queen Mary* is grand." Awareness of an earlier book by Atkinson, *Henry Thoreau, The Cosmic Yankee* (1927), may have prompted TW's reference to "the spirit of Thoreau."

Atkinson's "second view" of *The Rose Tattoo* was probably solicited by Cheryl Crawford to dispel the imminent box-office doldrums of summer. Atkinson still deplored TW's lapses in taste but he ended the article with quotable praise: "Behind the fury and uproar of the characters are the eyes, ears and mind of a lyric dramatist who has brought into the theatre a new freedom of style" (*New York Times*, June 3, 1951). Business did improve briefly but slumped badly in July and August.

"The streets are brilliant!" TW wrote to Oliver Evans after arriving in Rome: "The first night, a sailor from Trevisano. The next a Neapolitan at the baths. Tonight?" (June 13, 1951, HRC).]

207. To Audrey Wood

[45 Via Aurora, Rome]
June 1951
[TLS, 1 p. HRC]

Dear Audrey:

Such a great relief to learn you are mending rapidly. Frank sent the office a wire to send you three dozen red roses, the most roses I have ever sent anybody, and I do hope they got the wire and you got the roses! Isn't a sudden operation a frightening thing? To me it was sheer terror, which lasted a year afterwards, mainly because of the anesthesia, being <u>made</u> unconscious, but there is nobody else in this world quite as much a physical coward as I am, so I am sure it was not so difficult for you. Then, if I remember correctly, and I am sure that I do, I had <u>Pancho</u> with me and it was in a little hospital on a desert, filled with sinister-looking black nuns who seemed to be elderly usherettes in the lobby ~~portals~~ of the great beyond.

We are back in Rome. I am feeling well. I am writing three or four hours a day. I am nervous as a cat! - situation normal.

The new car is lovely. Frank put the first scratch on it, poor kid! But it isn't a serious scratch, and we think it's the most elegant car in Rome, all black and silver.

Rossellini wired me today that he had been calling me repeatedly but couldn't get through and gave me a number to call him, what about I don't know. Visconti wants me to re-write La Dame Aux Camellias for Anna Magnani to star in on the screen! - This - as Irene would say - I think I won't do! - I have not yet talked to Magnani, but I see her on the streets as often as I find myself there. A meeting is inevitable. Natalia Murray says that Visconti will do "Tattoo" in the Fall with an all-Sicilian cast except for the part of Serafina. I think it's a thrilling idea. Hope I can stay to see it. I have not yet talked directly to Visconti, but will this week. Right now he is directing Magnani in something for the screen, both being prima donnas there is bound to be an explosion that will make Stromboli look like a wet fire cracker.

Natalia Murray is going to America and wants to occupy our apartment, which is all right if we don't already have a tenant in it. I suppose the matter would have to be mentioned to Buffie. Natalia does not, apparently, expect to pay us anything, but that's all right. . . . . I think, however, she ought to pay for the phone and utilities while she is there, but if she doesn't offer to, perhaps we should be cavalier and say nothing about it.

We're back in our first apartment, 45 Via Aurora, phone number 460779.

Love - Tenn.

[The once energetic Audrey Wood felt "a great yearning to return to bed at all sorts of odd daylight hours" (to TW, July 2, 1951, HRC) following an appendectomy in early-June. Complications required a second procedure and a long recovery.

Luchino Visconti signed contracts in 1954 to stage The Rose Tattoo, but the project was vetoed by the Italian Censorship Bureau. He was currently directing Anna Magnani in Bellissima (1951) amid "continuous disagreements" with the star. The volcanic island on the northern coast of Sicily gave title and explosive climax to Roberto Rossellini's film Stromboli (1949).

The apartment on East 58th Street had been sublet and would not be available for Natalia Murray.

The numeral "25" has been penciled into the spaced, partially typed date, perhaps at Liebling-Wood.]

208. To Paul Bigelow

[45 Via Aurora, Rome]
July 3, 1951.
[TLS, 1 p. Massee Collection]

Dearest Paul:

I can't tell you how unhappy I am to hear that the jaw has been making you trouble, but I am also relieved that you are finally going to have the operation which I have always felt you should have had. This, my dear, is to be known hereafter as the "summer of operations", not merely the summer of 1951. Oliver has had his long delayed operation on his ear, and the first reports are most encouraging. The auditory nerve survived the operation, and the great danger was that it might be destroyed. Maria Britnieva, poor child, got into the immemorial trouble of warm-hearted ladies and is paying the price we never had to pay! Five days of "agonizing labor" she says and "two operations!" and the business is still going. Keep this under your Borsalino, pet! It is not supposed to be anything more exotic than ulcers. Then, Audrey! - Now, you! - Am I going to be next? - Ah, me . . . at this point you can imagine the deepest sigh of which I am capable.

I have had about 3 weeks of summer in Rome, and for the time being I think that's about enough. Lethargy has descended, work falls off, so I am planning a trip in the new Jaguar, probably to Spain, but stopping off at Perpignan to hear Pablo Cassales play his cello and to catch the end of the bull-fights at Pamplona, then on down to some good beach on the Costa Brava. I am not really, confidentially, well enough to make this trip by myself, but Frank and I have been together constantly too long and I think his present irritability means we ought to take separate trips. He may go to Vienna. As soon as Maria is able to travel, I think she will join me somewhere on the sea, for the benefit of both. I suppose it is safe to live with a lady who has just had such a severe demonstration of the consequences of uncontrolled passion. Of course I was never likely to forget them.

I will write you again when I get settled somewhere, and I hope by that time you will be all through with this distressing business.

Much, much love, 10.

[Jordan Massee described the operation on his former companion Paul Bigelow as "very serious, and not very successful."

Maria Britneva later attributed her own operation to "appendicitis" rather than "ulcers," adding that "although there were complications, their seriousness was gravely exaggerated by Tennessee" (St. Just, p. 41).]

209. *To Cheryl Crawford*

[45 Via Aurora, Rome]
[ca. July 9, 1951]
[TLS, 1 p. BRTC]

Dear Cheryl:

I am terribly disturbed over Paul's impending operation. I have had a long letter to him in my pocket for a number of days and I am going to get it off this afternoon when I post this one. I will be leaving here possibly tomorrow for a long auto trip, winding up on the Costa Brava, which is the Spanish Riviera north of Barcelona. The swimming is said to be marvelous there, I can see the bullfights, and I think the air will be more stimulating than it becomes here after a while.

Yesterday I met a young Porto Rican in a cafe. He had just come from New York and seen "Tattoo" and said that it was now being done completely without music. Naturally I was surprised and distressed to hear that. I don't think the composed music is essential to the play but I cannot imagine it without any music whatsoever. When we discussed it I thought it was planned to use the musicians who were sitting in the basement and have them play some simple folk tunes. Ideally, I would think a singer guitarist would be the thing! The play needs music more than any other I've had produced, partly because of the rather drastic transitions of mood that take place. Music helps the audience to follow emotionally. It softens the rough edges of which there are many, alas. I am sure the total absence of it would reduce the audience appeal far more than we can judge who have seen it so often, now, that our own reactions are mostly reminiscent. Please let me know . . .

I know, of course, the need for economy, but I would rather take lower royalties and have the music kept. For the tour, I do hope you can arrange to use a good Italian singer-guitarist. There is a man here that you heard at dinner one night in Rome - perhaps you remember him - if you don't, Natalia does! - His name is Alfredo del Pedo, he sings at the restaurant "Giorgio's" and has enormous charm at the age of sixty! I have an idea he would be delighted to go to America for the tour.

I am still working on the new "Summer". It has turned into a totally new play, even the conception of the characters is different, and it might very well be possible to present it again in the States, especially with a name like Peggy Ashcroft or Margaret Sullavan whom you mentioned. I don't think I will pick up my new scripts till Fall. I want to ruminate and gestate for a good while before I commit myself to another great trial. Note that I say 'great <u>trial</u>' <u>not</u> 'great play'! - Everybody here is very bitter over Mrs. Stone. They cross the street to tell me how much they hated it! They seem to think it was an attack on the city. - Actually I liked all the characters in that book, even the gigolo! - though I couldnt defend him. I think Mrs. Stone was superior to most of the people who tell me what a disgusting person she is.

love - 10.

[Audrey Wood later informed TW that she and Cheryl Crawford had agreed to suspend royalties when the weekly gross for *The Rose Tattoo* "hit" (August 7, 1951, HRC) a predetermined level.

TW recently asked the English producers of *Summer and Smoke* to "be patient" as he continued to revise the play: "About 80% of the brilliant progress" on the new script had "turned out to be pure illusion" (to Beaumont and Perry, June 12, 1951, HRC). Crawford soon received a more upbeat account: *Summer and Smoke* had "a straight, clean dramatic line for the first time, without the cloudy metaphysics and the melodrama that spoiled the original production" (June 14, 1951, BRTC). Alma and John were recast as near equals in sexual innocence, removing both the awkwardness of their shifting roles and the need for John's redemption. Mrs. Buchanan first appears in the "new" version as a socially ambitious mother who tries to block her son's relationship with Alma. (See "The Eccentricities of a Nightingale or The Sun That Warms the Dark," n.d., HRC.)]

210. To Charles K. Feldman

[July 1951]
[Telegram draft, 1 p. Columbia U]

Dear Charlie,

Gadg terribly disturbed over cuts made during his absence. Intends to remove his name from picture ~~unless these~~ I also feel grave mistake to

exceed cuts we all agreed upon in New York. A great picture can be botched by injudicious cutting. Don't let them spoil a great picture.

Love, Tennessee.

[The penciled note—probably a telegram draft—concerns unexpected censorship of *Streetcar* by the Roman Catholic Legion of Decency, which had rejected the Production Code seal of approval. Elia Kazan was not informed of last-minute cuts made by the producers to appease the Legion, which planned to give the film a "C" rating (Condemned). He described the cuts—some four minutes of footage—in an article designed to expose the sinister influence of the Catholic Church, the corresponding weakness of the producers, and the artistic violation of "the public, the author and myself" (*New York Times*, October 21, 1951). The Legion finally granted *Streetcar* a "B" rating to indicate a film that was "objectionable in part." The banned footage, including close-ups of Kim Hunter descending the stairs in the Poker Night sequence, has been restored in a "director's version."

Streetcar premiered on September 18, 1951, received excellent notices, and won the New York Film Critics award for best picture of the year.

The Legion criticism of *Streetcar* arose in early-July 1951, suggesting that TW may have drafted the telegram in Rome before leaving for Venice.]

211. To Audrey Wood

[Hotel Excelsior, Venice]
7/22/51.
[TLS, 1 p. HRC]

Dear Audrey:

I hope this finds you convalescing smoothly, but, alas, it leaves me in a depressed condition. The last few weeks have been fraught with misadventures. First of all, I smashed up the new car, the Jaguar. I was driving North, intending to spend some weeks on the Costa Brava of Spain as the Roman summer was taking my energy and I couldn't work. About one hundred miles out of Rome I became very nervous. I took a couple - or was it three? - stiff drinks from a thermos I had with me, and the first thing I knew there was a terrific crash! The car had gone into a tree at 70 miles an hour! - It had to be towed back to Rome. One side was virtually demolished. Repairs will take a month and one thousand dollars! But they say the car will look like new. - It was amazing that I was not seriously injured. My portable typewriter flew out of the backseat and landed on my head. Only a small

cut, no concussion, but the typewriter badly damaged! - Ever since, from the shock, I suppose, I have felt very tense. That is, more than usually so. I am now in Venice, on the Lido, but I don't like it here and will leave in a day or two for somewhere else. Frank did not come with me. He felt we needed a little vacation from each other. I didn't agree with him but felt it was wiser to pretend that I did. The work goes a little better out of Rome, but I am still feeling very disturbed. What a bad summer all of us are having! What have we done to deserve it?

How about Paul? Did he have his operation? One wonderful piece of news. Oliver writes me that his operation was a fabulous success, normal hearing completely restored in at least one ear. This will make a great difference for him and it gives me a sense of satisfaction to know that my money helped to accomplish it. Money does so little most of the time.

Maria also pulled through her operation, and is going back to her play. When it closes in August, she says she will join me somewhere on the sea, for a vacation.

I was shocked to learn - by chance, not by any word from Cheryl about it - that all of the music had been taken out of the play. I think this is a dreadful mistake. The play is built for music. It simply must not go out on tour without a singer-guitarist. I wish they would also be looking around for someone to replace the present Assunta, if it goes on tour, and that they will try to hold onto all the rest of the present cast.

Better news next time, I hope.

Love, Tenn.

P.S. Will you ask Bill what can be done about the insurance on the Jaguar? Was the Buick sold? If not perhaps I'd better hold onto it till I know the Jaguar can be successfully repaired.

[TW spent a week on the Lido in Venice bewildered and depressed by Frank Merlo's aloofness. "God knows how it is all going to work out. But I must try to be a little bit prudent, a little bit wise, and start drawing the sails of my heart back in, for the wind is against them" (*Journal*, ca. July 17, 1951).

Maria Britneva was an understudy in a London production of *The Three Sisters* (Chekhov, 1901). The present "Assunta" had a run-of-the-play contract and could not be replaced in *The Rose Tattoo*. Once the envy of Rome, TW's Buick was sold to the lyricist John Latouche, reportedly a former lover of Frank Merlo.]

212. To Theatre Musicians Union

[45 Via Aurora, Rome]
August 3, 1951.
[TLS, 2 pp. HRC]

Dear Sirs:

Let me state at the beginning, that I am second to no one that I know of in my enthusiastic endorsement of the organization or unionization of labor, which I think is essential, and I think it is also essential for artists to have protective unions. But anyone who likes unions, and what they do to protect workers and professional people and artists, is all the more deeply concerned when they appear to be operating to the detriment of the very ones they are supposed to protect through rigid and punitive rules which are not based on understanding or logic.

I am a professional worker and I belong to a union, the Dramatists' Guild.

Another union, which is yours, has committed a very damaging act against a work of mine, THE ROSE TATTOO. Incidentally, I devoted about three years to the composition of this play. It is not an opera or a musical, but it is a play in which the use of incidental music is extremely important. Music was composed for it, the sort of music suitable to its theme, setting and atmosphere, by one of our most gifted and famous American composers, David Diamond.

THE ROSE TATTOO was an artistic success but only a moderate commercial success, it has a large cast, a cast of twenty-some actors and its operating expenses are correspondingly high, not as high as they would be if "star names" were involved, but still high, and especially now, in the summer, when it has been running six months, it is necessary to practise some economies. All the while this play has been running we have had two sets of musicians, one actually playing, and one playing poker in the basement. Right on the face of it, this is a highly unreasonable situation. When business dropped off, we regretfully decided that in order to survive the summer months we would have to abandon the special musicians employed to play Mr. Diamond's music and use the ones who had been playing poker in the basement. Good Italian folk-tunes were substituted for the composed music, and the "special" musicians were released and we (at least I!) assumed that the unoccupied ones were going to take their place. No such thing! Some gimmick in your rules intervened. We still have the

musicians playing poker, or Canasta, in the basement, but we don't have any music whatsoever.

Now it may very well be that I have not received a clear picture of this remarkable situation. I spend most of my time working very intensely and as squarely and fairly as possible at my own profession, also unionized, and I may not have had the time or chance to acquaint myself as fully as I should with your point of view. I wish you would clarify it for me.

Why, specifically, is it impossible, now, for us to use the card-playing musicians in the basement? Why is the play stripped of music entirely, and we still have to pay for musicians?

Incensed is a mild word for how I feel about this, and I think this whole matter of musicians in the theatre must be brought out in the open as immediately and clearly as those concerned can bring it.

Sincerely, Tennessee Williams

P.S. I am not concerned about this matter merely as it affects THE ROSE TATTOO but as it affects a whole important segment of our modern theatre. Modern creative theatre is a synthesis of all the arts, literary, plastic, musical, Etc. THE ROSE TATTOO is a notable case in point since I think it has gone further than any recent legitimate American drama to demonstrate this fact, this synthesis of various creative elements, and when music is thrown out because of a highly illogical, a downright stupid misuse of protective rulings which are not protective but punitive, something has to be done, at least to clarify things.

[Cheryl Crawford fired the "'special musicians,'" but her plan to replace them with idle house musicians—currently on salary—was blocked by a union rule which forbade any change in orchestration after the opening of a play. TW argued in a covering letter to Cheryl Crawford and Audrey Wood that the absence of music "makes a radical, perhaps fatal, difference in the public response" (August 3, 1951, HRC) to *The Rose Tattoo*. Irene Selznick had fought, and won, a similar battle when the union classified *Streetcar* as a "drama with music," requiring added musicians and a higher pay scale.

Apparently either Wood or Crawford removed the impolitic references to "card-playing" and sent a revised version of the letter (August 3, 1951, HRC) to Local 802 of the American Federation of Musicians. The original signed typescript is used as setting text.]

213. To Gore Vidal

[Hôtel du Pont Royal, Paris]
8/13/51.
[TLS, 1 p. Houghton]

Dear Gore:

This has been what the Chinese would call "The summer of the long knives!" No one has been spared, not even the divine bird. Some of its brightest feathers are scattered upon the floor of the cage. Practically everyone has been operated on but you and Jo Healy. How are you feeling? Oliver has had his ear operation and has recovered normal hearing in at least one ear. Something has been done about Bigelow's jaw at Manhattan General. Maria Britnieva had a surgical experience in London. And of course Audrey.

My operation occured on the Via Aurelia between Rome and Genoa in my new Jaguar. I was driving it at 70 miles an hour, fortified by a couple or three stiff martinis, when a capricious truck came out of a side road and I decided to hit a large tree instead. One side of the car was demolished. My portable typewriter flew out of the backseat and crowned me just over the hairline. I have not had a bigger or more excited audience since the opening of "Menagerie". No one could believe that the divine bird was still able to flutter! But here, I am, in Paris! Waiting for the repairs on the car, which are taking six weeks and over a thousand dollars. The Little Horse remains in Rome. Yes, it's been the summer of the long knives.

I am staying at the Hotel du Pont Royal as the Hotel de L'Universite seems to be converted into the official headquarters of something or other quite different from what it was formerly the headquarters of. It is almost deserted, the town, except for "les mouches". I had to fight with them over my lunch, and I think they got away with most of the omelette.

Prokosch is back in Rome. We became quite chummy before I left there. He is finishing a new book called "Water Music" and seems to be in better spirits than I've ever known him to be. Incidentally he mentioned having coming across the opening chapter of Truman's new book in some periodical. Have you seen it, and if so, how are you feeling? - Buechner should be fucked, not published, and I am just the little guy who would like to do it, provided his photographs on dust-jackets are at least half as honest as yours. - Rome was disappointing this summer, especially the car was kaput so early in the season, and it was fearfully hot. I also took in

Munich (good cruising and 3 very good gay bars!) and a week at the Lido of Venice. Frank did Vienna and is going to do Sicily while I'm here. But I had my best time and most exciting lay in London, of all places. . . You know, we really should have done a real season there. If it were not for Grandfather, impatiently waiting for us in Memphis, I would not come back to the States at all this year. As it is, think I will stretch the visit through October.

I have been offered a house surrounded by a large wall in New Orleans, and may live there when I return, whether or not the Mexican remains. Write me in Rome, as I have to back there for the car and shall be travelling around for the next two or three weeks.

Love - 10.

[Before leaving Rome, TW read the "'new'" *Summer and Smoke* and was dealt "a staggering blow" by its "pitiful" quality, probably "the worst job" he had "ever done" (*Journal*, August 9, 1951). Relations with Frank Merlo, who displayed "all the warmth and charm of a porcupine," were still tense. The few days which TW spent alone in Paris produced an "itchy rash," a "gassy stomach," and insomnia, which was not relieved by "secconals" (*Journal*, August 15, 1951).

Gore Vidal was living in Duchess County, New York, finishing a new novel, and helping his father to run a small factory which made plastic bread trays. Frederic Prokosch planned to spend the coming year as a Fulbright Fellow at the University of Rome. He had spotted the "opening chapter" of Truman Capote's novella *The Grass Harp* (1951) in *Botteghe Oscure* (volume 7). Frederick Buechner's only published novel to date was his first, *A Long Day's Dying* (1950).]

214. To Audrey Wood

[Cavendish Hotel, London]
August 23, 1951
[TLS w/ autograph marginalia, 1 p. HRC]

Dear Audrey:

This has been a summer of wanderings. I am now in London, in response to a wire that reached me in Paris. Maria's first cousin who had lived with her since childhood is gravely ill, complications of diabetes and nephritis, and Maria wanted me to come over, so I did. I have been here about a week, am now waiting for my typewriter to be repaired the one that hit me on the head in the smash-up. It all started falling apart. I still

don't understand what my head can be made of! I have felt very odd this summer, but I'm not at all sure the typewriter can be blamed. They keep delaying the repair of the Jaguar. Now they say it won't be ready till September 8th and we are quite helpless, you can't make them do it any faster than they want to for love or money. Everything goes at a snail's pace during "the Solleone" (The lion sun) in Rome. Frank is still down there, unless he has gone to Sicily to visit his folks there. I have been travelling alone for the first time in three years, and in a way I guess it is good for me, it renews my self-reliance and possibly sharpens my wits a little, and it is a wonderful change for the Little Horse, a change which he had hinted rather broadly was about due.

I completed a first draft of the new "Summer and Smoke" (it has a different title and is almost a completely new play) but I have an idea Tennents will prefer to do the old one. This one is half an hour shorter and in its present condition it was not really ready to be read, extremely rough, but I let John Perry read it anyway, that is, I left it with him to be typed up and read if he wished to. If they do the old there is still a good deal of material in this one that can be used to improve it. I have not yet had an audience with Binkie Beaumont but I want you to know that I had lunch today with none other than Mr. T.S. Eliot the greatest living poet. He had Laughlin and I as guests to lunch at the Garrick Club, and he is the sweetest literary figure I've ever met, and fortunately I could speak with sincere admiration of his work, even of The Cocktail Party, and he seemed to be pleased. I had bought a first edition of The Cocktail Party and he inscribed it for me.

Carson is staying here in a house with a youngish and very seedy sort of mad poet, and I mean really mad, and it is really a menage. Fortunately there is one of those dedicated women there that look out for Carson, and I think she is in the bloom of a new infatuation for a middle-aged lady, the sister of John Lehmann, the one that is an actress. There is no further allusion to Edith Sitwell! I will see Carson tonight at John Lehmann's since we are both dining there. Tomorrow my repaired typewriter will return to me, and probably on Sunday I will fly back across the channel, to Paris, then on down to some "watering place" to "bathe".

I can't tell you how much I enjoyed and was relieved by your long, long letter, and the news that you are feeling like your self again.

Must leave, now, for dinner - Much love, Tenn.

[Maria Britneva's cousin lay "in a nightmarish state" during TW's present and later visit to London in October: "Shakes one's faith in the ultimate mercy even of nature" (*Journal*, October 6, 1951).

A Tennent staffer wrote that the "new" *Summer and Smoke* "amazed" everyone and "read like the first draft of a bad translation" (Kitty Black, *Upper Circle*, 1984, p. 188). In late-September Audrey Wood was still negotiating contracts with John Perry, the producer, and had "no idea which version" (to TW, September 20, 1951, HRC) of the play he would use. Perry soon clarified the situation: "Frankly, we could not have undertaken the production if Tennessee had insisted on the new version. It would be most unsuitable for this country, apart from the fact that it would have hardly played more than an hour and twenty minutes" (to Wood, September 25, 1951, HRC).

The McCullers saga took a strange turn in July when Reeves secretly left the hospital where he was being treated for alcoholism, boarded the *Queen Elizabeth* as a stowaway, and revealed himself to Carson midway through the voyage. He quickly returned to the States after the ship landed. In London McCullers lived with the "mad poet" David Gascoyne and apparently became infatuated with John Lehmann's younger sister, Beatrix (see Carr, pp. 375–381).

Penned in the upper margin is TW's mailing address, "Am. Ex. Rome."]

215. To Buffie Johnson Sykes

Cavendish Hotel, London
August 24, 1951.
[TL, 2 pp. HRC]

Dear Buffie:

I received in the mail yesterday a large and complete sheaf of correspondance between you and Audrey pertaining to the alleged damages and "theft" that occured in the apartment.

I doubt, Buffie, that you realize how preposterous your attitude and your charges are, it is charitable to have this doubt and I want to be as fair as I can under the circumstances, so I try to maintain this doubt. There is an element of (I hope) <u>unconscious</u> cruelty in your charges which is quite foreign to anything I have ever thought about you and which surprises and shocks me beyond expression. I know perfectly well that you must know, as you in fact admitted that distressing afternoon when you opened the cabinets and claimed that your jewels were stolen, that the last thing in the world that Frank and I would do or could be suspected of doing is stealing any of your belongings or even exposing them to any chance of theft. I have

never in my life touched anything that did not belong to me except one grape which I remember picking off a sidewalk stand as I walked past it with my father and mother when I was seven years old and I can still feel the slap that my father gave me and his roar of indignation. We do not steal things, not Frank, and not I, fortunately we neither have to nor want to. I cannot answer for the tenants you had in the apartment before we occupied it. It seemed to be Gerald's impression, I remember, that you were only imagining these depredations, at least that was the way it seemed to turn out the afternoon when you made the extremely offensive scene about the broken jewel-box. This I attributed only - as your husband did - to an attack of nerves, perhaps consequent on your recent illness and operation, but the present renewed charges of large and systematic thefts cannot be excused in that way, they are made cold-bloodedly and with an air of calculation which is simply unspeakable as coming from someone I had regarded once as a friend, and from an artist and a person that one would expect to have a sense of equity as well as good-breeding.

As for the neglect of the apartment, you know very well that we retained the maid that you had employed in the apartment and that we had her there every morning while we were occupying it and even sometimes during our absences to water and care for the precious plants in the patio, and that in addition to this, Frank's nephew came in every day when we were necessarily out of town on the road-tour of "The Rose Tattoo" to take care of the plants and the birds, none of which suffered while we were in the apartment except perhaps from the ordinary attritions of time, for you know that plants are not immortal. You took out the great rubber plant, in fact from time to time, having free access to the apartment in spite of our tenancy, you came and removed various things, whatever you wanted to take out, and we made no objection. You took out pictures, plants, furniture. In fact we came back from a short trip to find an almost new (and very inferior) set of furniture in the studio. You also know that "hand-carved" chair you speak of was broken before we came into the apartment, for we talked about it. You also know that you never - not repeatedly and not even once - suggested that the skylight be cleaned, and God knows I would loved to have had it cleaned if you did, for I was living there and its murky condition was far more distressing to me than it could have been to you at the distance of East Hampton. If you were seriously concerned about this skylight, why didn't you speak of it to me

or Frank? I have never, never, never in my life seen any of these articles you itemize as having been stolen from the apartment, and can you imagine anyone breaking into the place and sallying forth with a basket of Sevres vases, hand-painted Chinese screens, cupid-brackets and so forth? Can you seriously, for one moment, believe such a thing occured, and how or why would it!???

I do not intend to discuss this matter with you again outside of a court of law. And I assure you as earnestly as possible that I do not intend to be victimized by what it is most charitable to describe as your delusions. I don't think I have ever been quite so amazed by human behaviour in my life! Not of any individual that I have known.

Much more than incidentally, I think you should be rather ashamed of yourself for the relentless trial all this has been to Audrey during a summer when she was ill, had a severe operation and was supposed to rest. She was kind enough not to let me know about the affair till this week, as she knew how it would disturb me.

Sincerely,

[Buffie Johnson (b. 1912) complained to Audrey Wood that "serious and apparently systematic thefts" had taken place at her apartment on East 58th Street. She also charged that the property had so declined in "presentability and chic" during TW's occupancy that it would need "a complete new decoration" (July 17, 1951, Columbia U). In Memoirs TW described the apartment as "the loveliest" which he had occupied in New York and observed that Tony Smith had "designed" it for his—TW's—"old friend, Buffie Johnson" (pp. 151-152).

The printed version was revised by TW—a potentially libelous passage was canceled in a signed draft of the letter (August 24, 1951, HRC)—and sent to Liebling-Wood for retyping and delivery to Johnson.]

216. To Frank Merlo

SH: Cavendish Hotel
81 Jermyn Street
St. James's, S.W.1 [London]
August 29, 1951
[TLS, 2 pp. HRC]

Dear Little Horse:

We tried, Maria and I, to get you again on the telephone a couple of nights ago, from midnight until two, and the report was that you were not

in, so we gave it up at last and went to our separate beds. I am leaving here this evening by plane for Paris, and all in all, it has been a good visit. I am pretty done in, pretty tired, because I have been working hard and much better than I worked in Rome or Venice I do believe. The play script was completed here and is being typed at Tennents and John Perry seems to be serious about having it done at the Lyric Hammersmith, starting rehearsals about the middle of next month, September, and opening, I suppose, toward the end of October, and I really think we ought to stay over for it. By the way, Grandfather is back with mother, so I feel better about him. I think she will be nicer to him, since Dakin has been transferred to Sacramento and she will have no one but Grandfather in the house. Isn't it sad for her? I feel terribly sorry for the poor little old lady without her one last darling left in the nest! She wrote me a sweet letter, no reproaches, no sermon. Speaking of letters, Audrey sent me a sheaf of correspondance between herself and Buffie. Madame Sykes is planning to sue me for $975., theft and damages to her apartment. Says jewels were stolen, three Sevres vases, countless other valuables, precious heirlooms, that there had been systematic thefts over a long period during our occupancy. I sat right down and wrote her the most scorching letter that I've ever written, but I think this affair will terminate in a law-court. Fortunately I don't think she has any proof of any of these alleged stolen articles having been in the apartment, since she gave us no inventory when we moved in. Audrey has put the matter in Colton's hands. Isn't Buffie a regular shit and a bitch? I just can't hardly believe it!

Carson is here, and a fish couldn't drink so much without sinking. She is brooding and mooning over John Lehmann's sister, the middle-aged one on the stage who is said to be dikish. I called on Carson last night at her lodging-house, very pleasant, in Chelsea, and found her just sitting in a stupefied way on a sofa with a cigarette and a nearly empty bottle of sherry. She is coming over for lunch. Her physical condition has not changed but this all day and half the night drinking will lead to disaster. I am hoping she will go back to the States but she is planning to come to the continent. I don't think we could stand to have her in Rome in the state she is in. She needs psychiatric treatment worse than anyone I know, even myself, and it is heartbreaking.

Maria's cousin is a bit better but the ultimate outlook is hopeless. One doctor told us a few days ago she could only live three weeks, but she has

picked up since then and now is eating a little but hasn't had a bowel movement in about ten days, is too weak for an enema, and her kidneys rarely function.

Yesterday we went to see a polo match, Maria and I, with Hermione Baddeley, her 22 year old gay lover and a real Maharajah. Maria had a terrible fight with the young queen and it ended in tears. We had to get out of the car and walk a long ways before we found a taxi. The queen spit in Maria's face and called her the foulest names I've ever heard addressed to a woman by anyone but Pancho. Of course Maria provoked the quarrel by some untactful remark, called him "insufferably conceited" to his face.

I will only stay in Paris a couple of days, then I may go to St. Tropez for a little swimming, or I may even come straight on down to Rome, will let you know which the moment I've decided.

I'll be at the Pont Royal in Paris, till Thursday evening. <u>PLEASE</u> CHECK ON THE CAR AND MAKE SURE THEY REMEMBER THEY <u>PROMISED</u> TO HAVE IT COMPLETELY READY BY <u>SEPTEMBER EIGHTH</u>!

I've missed you an awful lot, both night and day, and Maria and I talk about you so much. But I think we needed this period away from each other.

Love, Tenn.

[*Summer and Smoke* would enter rehearsal in mid-October and have its London premiere on November 22. John Perry, an associate of Tennent Ltd., hired Peter Glenville as director.

Eddie Colton wrote that if Buffie Johnson "has any claim she had better litigate it," for "the burden of proof . . . will be upon her" (to Wood, August 22, 1951, HRC).

TW marked the death of Maria Britneva's cousin on October 11 with an elegy entitled "A Wreath for Alexandra Molostvova": "It is well to remember the chill of the vault made warm by the entrance of roses" (1956). TW wept at the Greek Orthodox service and "thought, of course, of Rose" (*Journal*, October 14, 1951).

Britneva later claimed that Hermione Baddeley's young lover, Laurence Harvey, provoked the "fight" by "extraordinarily abusive" (St. Just, p. 160) treatment of her. Baddeley hoped to play Serafina in the English production of *The Rose Tattoo* and had been introduced to TW by their mutual friend, the "Little Brit." Baddeley would not play Serafina, although she later starred as Mrs. Goforth in *The Milk Train Doesn't Stop Here Anymore* (1962/1963).

TW braced himself for the flight to Paris with "2 phenobarbs, 1 seconal, 1 martini." Their "magic," he knew, "isn't right, it isn't well, this cycle of sedation" (*Journal*, August 28, 1951).]

217. To Cheryl Crawford

SH: Hotel D'Angleterre, Copenhagen
Sept. 8, 1951.
[ALS, 4 pp. BRTC]

Dearest Cheryl -

This is a late town, but even here it is too late for me to pound a typewriter. I hope you can make out my nervous scrawl. I have been doing a tour of "Tattoo" openings in Scandinavia. There are to be eight, altogether; so far I have only seen one (very fine) in Copenhagen and another one, nearly as good, in Goteborg Sweden which has the finest stage (mechanically and in dimensions) I have ever seen.

The Danes are just as warm and lovable, in their own Northern way, as the wops. The Swedes are a little too serious and shy for a quick communication. All are fine actors, and I have never had such a warm-hearted welcome anywhere as I've had here. I needed it badly, for this has been a bad summer. I have been ill the whole time, I don't [know] whether in body or spirit or in both. I call it "The Summer of The Long Knives" - a paraphrase of a Chinese expression concerning a very difficult sort of night. I have travelled almost constantly, as if to run away from myself, and I have kept working, however badly.

Now I go back to Rome. Maybe this time the old spell will work. It didn't earlier. Then I go to London for their production of "Summer and Smoke" - I am not yet sure which version they plan to use, the new or old one. I prefer the new one, although it reflects the hysteria of my moods this summer. I want you to read it when I return to the States.

I think you have done a truly amazing job, holding the show together through the summer, keeping it going, and I make a deep bow, my forehead touching the floor, for it means a great deal to me, as you know. You are, when all is said and done, the very best of my various producers and I pray that God is willing to let me give you another play! -

Love, Tennessee.

[Frank Merlo joined TW for a "delightful" week in Copenhagen, as he cheerfully informed Walter Dakin. Tom's work, he added, was well known and admired by the Danes, including a "great gathering of university students" (September 26, 1951, HTC) which TW addressed. Lars Schmidt, Audrey Wood's agent in Scandinavia, confirmed the success of *The Rose Tattoo* and described TW as being

"in the very best humour" (to Wood, September 4, 1951, HRC). Privately TW wondered "why" he had come all the "way" to Copenhagen and resolved in the future to use a "two-letter word that says 'NO!'" (*Journal*, September 9 and 11, 1951).]

218. *To Audrey Wood*

[45 Via Aurora, Rome]
[September 28, 1951]
[TLS, 1 p. HRC]

Dear Audrey:

No, they didn't tell me about the goat. Did he die a natural death or was he killed by economy? Will not yield an inch on his replacement. Both the goat and music are essential to the play, and the elimination of both from the cast were not reported to me by the management. Of course I feel they did a good job keeping the show going through the summer, but on the road these economies won't do. I'd rather they closed the play than not have a goat or any music in it.

I've been working, working, working all summer but some of the time it's like a man trying to run with a sprained ankle. Most of the summer I spent on "Summer and Smoke" and I completed a script but both John Perry and the director, Peter Glenville, have decided in favor of the old one. Unfortunately the new version was only 57 pages and they didn't like it anyway. They are probably right, but if I had had more time, I would have preferred the new one.

I leave here tomorrow for Paris, then directly to London, will arrive there about October 1st and the address will be the Cavendish Hotel on Jermyn Street. Frank's driving the car up. The repairs were completed and it looks like new. We have receipts for the work which Frank will send for the insurance people.

I do hope the one-acts won't go into production till after the New Year. For one thing, it would be nice to have Wallach available. Then I will need some time on Camino Real if that's to be done. I have some re-writ on one scene of it, somewhere among my papers. Will shoot it off to you soon as it turns up. Perhaps Gadg and I can spend a week together in the country when I get back and work closely on the project. ~~He is such a slippery customer!~~ Do you really think he can be pinned down? He would do a

magnificent job and I think a success, with him, would be fairly certain. Can't think of anyone else who could handle those two plays.

I'm still happy over a long story I've been working on and I have a number of play scripts waiting for time and energy to be granted.

Please remember: "Goat and Guitar!" is the cry. This is the end of a long, hard day, and the end of a long, hard summer, and I suppose it is the beginning of a long, hard Fall, but what the hell, we are still with it!

MUCH LOVE, Tenn.

[*The Rose Tattoo* survived the summer and closed on October 27, 1951, after 306 performances. The tour began two days later in Montreal with Maureen Stapleton and Eli Wallach in the leads.

TW later claimed that the new script of *Summer and Smoke* had arrived "too late" to be used in the English production: "The original version of the play was already in rehearsal" (Author's Note, *The Eccentricities of a Nightingale*, 1964).

William Liebling revived an earlier project by proposing an evening of one-acts, including "Ten Blocks on the Camino Real" (1948) and "27 Wagons Full of Cotton" (1945). Elia Kazan, who was still intrigued by "Ten Blocks," had apparently agreed to direct the double bill, which Liebling would produce (Liebling to TW, September 14, 1951, HRC). TW warily observed, "Do I believe it? Well, hardly. Possible, just possible, in my cynical opinion. If {Kazan} did it would be as remarkable as if I really managed to write something good for a change" (*Journal*, September 16, 1951).

The "long story" in progress is "Three Players of a Summer Game" (1952). Drafted in Venice in July 1951, the promising story now seemed "Dull, dull!" and TW "hit the bottom!" (*Journal*, October 1, 1951).

This letter, misdated "8/28/51" by TW, has been assigned a date one month later as indicated by the sequence of events.]

219. To Audrey Wood

Cavendish [London]
October 27, 1951.
[TLS, 2 pp. HRC]

Dear Audrey:

I am very excited and a little dismayed and quite frightened over the rapid progress of plans for the short plays. I am frightened because I don't know what Gadg wants or expects of me. He talks of "work and work" (which sounds like an awful lot of it) but he doesn't say what it is to be,

and I have never worked as badly in my life as I have these past few months.

Of course I don't want to express these misgivings to Gadg at this point, for it might discourage his interest in the project but I think it is necessary to let you know. Yes, we had some talks about the play but I don't remember any specific, or even general, suggestions that he made, except that he seemed to feel it needed clarification. If he is coming to England and sailing back with Frank and me on the Elizabeth, of course there will be plenty of time to investigate his views. I do hope they don't include a desire to collaborate with me on the script! That is, to take part in the actual writing. On the other hand, Gadg has a very creative mind and he might stimulate me, provided his demands are not overwhelming and his ideas compatible with mine.

Of course what intrigues me most is the vision of "Audrey Wood Presents". It will inspire me to do all I can to make the presentation something worthy of all that our association has meant to me. A sentiment pompously expressed, but felt very truly. Gadg says he understands about that, and is happy.

Two questions: is it possible to get us a little apartment in New York with room for Grandfather? And!! Is there any truth in a wild report that Carson received from her mother that Cheryl and Bigelow were going to be married?!

Speaking of Carson! Confidentially, I have never seen her in quite such nervous disorder. When we arrived in London, she was staying at sort of a nursing-home in the country where she had apparently been placed by a female hypnotist on whom she had one of her immoderate "crushes". She suddenly came to London, early one morning, and wanted us to put her up in this little room that I use for work. It was obviously impossible to combine her life and ours in such small quarters, so through the assistance of an old acquaintance from New Orleans, one Valentina Sheriff, of Russian-Chinese background, we got her into the Ritz. Then all hell busted loose! Mme. Sheriff flew into a fury, not at poor Carson, but at us! Frank lost his Sicilian temper and called the Madame a few basic things in Carson's presence. I am afraid that our friendship with Carson is at least temporarily disrupted, for she was very cold to me at parting and declined my offer to see her off on the plane to New York, to which the female hypnotist had persuaded her to return.

It is a long, long and very involved story. I only hope that Carson doesn't turn it into one of her implacable vendettas. I love her and am very distressed about it.

Glenville and Margaret Johnson are doing great work on the play. But they have put the murder back into it. In fact, all my changes practically all of them, have been discarded and they have reverted almost entirely to the original script. Not very encouraging, is it.

About the apartment: of course we will only need it if it is true that the play goes into rehearsal in December. I have a horror of hotel-life in New York or I wouldn't bring up the problem. God knows enough already exist in our lives.

With love, Tenn

[Audrey Wood may have further "dismayed" and "frightened" TW by reminding him of Elia Kazan's unpredictable behavior. "What do you want to do? Whatever it is lets do it quickly. I'm getting nervous" (October 11, 1951, HRC), she added, in reference to a production of the "short plays."

Jordan Massee dismissed "the idea" of a Crawford-Bigelow marriage as "too absurd for words." Bigelow, he observed, was "100% gay" and Crawford "exclusively Lesbian."

Carson McCullers was treated unsuccessfully with hypnosis by Dr. Katherine Cohen, a psychiatrist.

Valentine Sherriff was a Russian-born divorcee who traveled widely and had introduced McCullers to a "motley assortment of Europeans and Americans" (Carr, p. 398) in Paris. Presumably TW met Sherriff in New Orleans, where she had married a wealthy husband and kept a walled house on Burgandy Street. Earlier in October she promised to supply TW with "100 seconals" (*Journal*, October 10, 1951).

Margaret Johnston played Alma Winemiller with "distinction" in the forthcoming London production of *Summer and Smoke*. After he and the director, Peter Glenville, had conferred on the script, TW resolved that the "murder" of the elder Buchanan "must go out - one way or another" (*Journal*, October 3, 1951).

TW sailed with Kazan on the Queen Elizabeth and did indeed take up "hotel-life in New York" after disembarking on November 12.]

220. To Peter Glenville

SH: Gladstone
East 52nd Street at Park Avenue
New York City - 22
[late-November 1951]
[TL, 1 p. HRC]

Dear Peter:

The report on "S.&S." is the most gratifying thing that's happened to me in a long time. I can't tell you how enormously I admire your work on the production, not only as the director but as a person, your understanding, your patience and sweetness. It was a completely happy experience working with you, and I shall always be indebted to you for restoring my faith in the play, and this just isn't the usual sentimental testimonial after a successful opening but what I would have felt regardless of how it had turned out. You are top man on the Totem pole!

Well, things are all screwed up over here. We are having a bloody time of it. Nobody seems right for the lead in "Camino Real" except Eli Wallach and he's on tour with "Rose Tattoo". We wanted Marlon but he is being maddeningly perverse, won't say yes or no, says he is going through an "emotional crisis" and is living in an almost empty apartment with a pet raccoon who scrambles into your lap and tries to unbutton your fly soon as you enter or assume a sitting position. Then Dame Selznick, with her inimitable gallantry, her superb sense of timing, bought and submitted a new play to Gadg almost as soon as we got off the boat in New York. It is a good play and for a while I wondered if she might not succeed in snatching Kazan away. But he is sticking with us, after all, and the Dame must cool her heels, at least until we open in February or the project blows up, which is still possible.

[Peter Glenville (1913-1996) trained in the Old Vic company and made his directorial debut on Broadway in 1949 with a program of one-acts by Terence Rattigan. His staging of *Summer and Smoke* at the Lyric-Hammersmith was deemed "admirable" by the reviewers. He later directed the film version of *Summer and Smoke* (1961) and the New York production of *Out Cry* (1973).

English reviewers of *Summer and Smoke* (November 22, 1951) praised the "beguiling pen" of the author and the "genuinely moving" treatment of Alma. Kenneth Tynan, TW's sharpest critic, found an "incompleteness" in the play which he considered the mark of "a minor talent." If TW's "characters, even at their best,

have a depleted look, it is probably because they start out with the disadvantage of being internally lame beyond all surgery" (*Spectator*, December 7, 1951).

Marlon Brando's "pet raccoon," Russell, reportedly slept with the star and was exercised on a leash.]

221. *To Irene Mayer Selznick*

SH: The Blackstone
Michigan Avenue at Balbo
Chicago 5, Illinois
December 1, 1951
[TLS, 2 pp. Boston U]

Dear Irene

Audrey says you were very disturbed over my only half serious remarks when we collided in that bar the night of Van Druten's opening. I didn't mean to disturb you, but I must say, in all honesty, that I am still wondering why you didn't mention, the night we were out together, what you were up to. Why didn't you say, Tennessee, I'm going to offer my new play to Gadge? Why did I only learn of it through Gadge, and Audrey didn't learn of it until after I had learned of it, and so forth! You can see why certain dark and ugly thoughts crept into my mind, and if you were disturbed, I can only assure you it was not half as much as I was disturbed. You know how vulnerable a writer is, sometimes even a producer! And how nervous one gets in the first stages of a production when it is still "touch and go", and you know what everything concerning my work means to me. I am glad that the only thing you were guilty of is thoughtlessness, for I don't believe, in my heart, that you would have had it in your heart to willfully injure me or my work.

Now let me congratulate you on having such a good play. I'm glad that Gadg will do it. I told him I thought he should.

Ever, Tenn.

[The casting of *Camino Real* drew TW to Chicago to scout Murray Hamilton—a potential Kilroy—in *The Moon Is Blue* (1951). The exquisitely named "Lincoln Baths" failed to enliven the trip, as TW informed Oliver Evans: They "were so dull tonight I put my clothes back on almost as soon as I took them off" (December 1, 1951, HRC).

TW apparently called Irene Selznick "'treacherous!'" (qtd. in St. Just, p. 51) for offering her "new play"—*Flight into Egypt* (1952), by George Tabori—to Elia

Kazan. She "shed a few feminine tears" and assured TW that she had "leaned over backwards" in consideration of his project, especially when Kazan said that it "was still in doubt" (December 4, 1951, Boston U). They met on November 28 at the premiere of John van Druten's latest play, *I Am a Camera* (1951).]

222. *To Paul Bigelow*

[Memphis, Tennessee]
PM: Memphis, December 4, 1951
[APCS, 1 p. Massee Collection]

Sol made big mistake booking me into "The Hide-Away". Mgr. says cannot use Petite Blonde type, wants dynamic red-head. I said I would take henna rinse but Mgr. very rude man. Need bus fare back to Sq. Roof. <u>Urgent</u>. Please advise!

Myrtle.

[The postcard extends a running joke with TW cast as "Myrtle," the Memphis prostitute in the story "The Kingdom of Earth" (1954). The impresario is probably "Sol" Hurok, while "Sq. Roof" refers to the sporting house in *The Rose Tattoo*. The razor-wielding figure in the background may allude satirically to Paul Bigelow's recent operation.]

223. *To Edwina Dakin Williams*

SH: Hotel Monteleone
New Orleans 12, U.S.A.
[late-December 1951]
[TLS w/ autograph postscript, 2 pp. HRC]

Dear Mother:

I feel very guilty about not visiting home for Christmas. I hope you understand how difficult it would have been. I've been operating under great pressure and had Grandfather with me. He can't take as much travel and excitement as he thinks he can. I flew to Memphis to pick him up. Kazan, his wife and I drove him down to Clarksdale, left him there while we drove about the Delta to collect background for a film that Kazan wants to make in the Delta based on my short plays. Then we picked up Grandfather again in Clarksdale and we all went back to New York, supposedly to start work on a stage production of "Camino Real". But meanwhile Liebling, who appointed himself the producer, decided it was too expensive a project to produce at this time. Nobody came forth with much money for it! So the stage production had to be postponed. I think it will be done in the early Fall, perhaps with somebody else at least as a co-producer. I am glad, now, that they came to that decision, although it was a disappointment at the time. Liebling could see nothing but the financial aspects of the plan, and was not even very efficient in handling those. I let him attempt it only because of Audrey, who is desperately anxious to give him something to do as he has become a terrible problem to her lately. So --- Grandfather and I are on our way to Key West, stopping off for a few days in New Orleans which he loves so much. He adores the restaurants here and always orders twice as much as he can eat, but he does enjoy it. We had our picture on the front page of the Times-Picayune and many old friends have been calling him.

It's lovely weather here, bright and warm. Frank will drive the car down to Key West to join us after New Year's. The car has just now arrived back in the country from England. Was shipped over at the expense of the manufacturer's, but it took a long time coming.

Grandfather says you will visit Clare in Florida so we will count on seeing you at that time. The Key West house is now vacant and waiting for us. I sent Rose a tweed coat (inter-lined) with hat and bag to match

from a shop on Fifth Avenue. Did it arrive, and did it fit her allright? I'm sending you a check.

With much love and all good wishes, Tom.

1431 Duncan, Key West (after Jan 1ˢᵗ).

[TW and his grandfather spent nearly two weeks in New Orleans before traveling to Miami and Key West.

Precisely when the film project coalesced is unclear. Plays of interest were "This Property is Condemned" (1941), "The Last of My Solid Gold Watches" (1943), "The Unsatisfactory Supper" (1946), and especially "27 Wagons Full of Cotton" (1945). The outcome, of course, was *Baby Doll* (1956).

William Liebling "appointed himself" producer of the one-acts in the preceding September. Elia Kazan later insisted that Cheryl Crawford join the production, whereupon Liebling intended to withdraw (Wood to TW, October 11, 1951, HRC). Plans for a double bill probably gave way in November or early-December to a single production of *Camino Real*, which was shelved thereafter because of casting and financial problems and a preliminary script.

A related story in *The Times-Picayune* quoted TW as still feeling "'defensive'" about the critical reception of *Summer and Smoke*. Although praised in England, the play had not been "'given a fair break on the American stage'" (December 27, 1951, p. 1).]

224. To Amado "Pancho" Rodriguez y Gonzalez

SH: The Robert Clay
Miami, Florida
January 10, 1952
[TLS, 1 p. HRC]

Dear Pancho:

I received and put on the little gold cross just before I caught the plane to Miami and it gave me a serene and happy flight, perhaps because it was blessed by the accompanying note with its assurances of your friendship and understanding. I enjoyed my visit to New Orleans, a great deal, but nothing pleased me more than to find you well and doing well and being contented and adjusted. Of all the old crowd that I saw again, you are the one who seems to have made the most progress toward maturity of heart and mind, and I am so glad that you have.

It was a very sweet thing for you to do!

<u>Thank you!</u>

Always fondly, Tennessee.

[TW later reflected upon his "last" meeting with Pancho Rodriguez: "One thing for which I don't pity myself is the two years we spent together when I was not a sick thing as I am now and you were you, wild, wonderful, a poem. . . . Walk tall, walk proud through this world. When I see you again, which I hope will not be in memory only, I want you to look as I last saw you, like a Spanish Grandee, with a touch of Montezuma, who could spit out the fires of the Inquisition, or trample them out with his bare feet, and laugh at Cortez" (n.d., Private Collection). The effusive remarks may have been written in April 1952, soon after the studio in Key West, to which TW refers, was completed.]

225. *To Oliver Evans*

1431 Duncan
K.W. Fla.
1/18/52
[TLS, 1 p. HRC]

Dear Oliver:

I meant to wire you soon as I heard of your award. I was thrilled over it as much as you must have been. I remember the poem very distinctly, it was one of the best you have written, and I hope the award will prove a spur to you in your writing as it should be.

I think you are being sly about the cuff-links. You know very well that you did not offer them to me until after I had exclaimed over their beauty one night at Lafitte's and I didn't accept them because I presumed you were offering them because I had admired them, the way Orientals are supposed to insist that you take anything you admire in their houses. As for your going to the airport, I didn't want to seem to impose the trip on you by seeming over eager to have you along, it was a long trip and I was not sure that Valentina would make the return agreeable to you, which apparently she didn't.

I had four days in Miami waiting for Frank. My old friend Gilbert Maxwell was with me constantly and drinking heavily all the time. He is making a living there by conducting private classes in creative writing.

Really, she is such a girl! She got so drunk at one of her classes, which I attended, that she could hardly stay in her chair in a reasonably vertical position. Was reading a short story aloud in a burlesk drunken fashion. There was a cat in the apartment that started leaping about. Miss Maxwell suddenly shrieked: "Silence! Please remember that this is a study-group!" The hostess timidly explained that the cat was making that noise, and Miss Maxwell cried out: "Well, the same thing goes for your fucking cat!" I had no trade there, but a slight, tender affair with a young queen who paints and is wasting away with some mysterious blood disease.

Bud Staples was already here when we arrived in Key West. He is with a gorgeous Bill Murphy type Adonis from Southern California. I took the boy home last night. Miss Merlo arrived in a taxi just as buttons were being undone on the front-room-sofa. There was a real Gotterdamerung to pay! Screams, protestations, fury and tears, winding up with Miss Merlo in her most becoming position on the living-room carpet and me wondering if Miss Southern California would be game for a second try under more discreet circumstances! - after being denounced as the whore of Babylon. I must say that Miss Merlo, when she is in a rage, pays very little attention to inequalities of size between her and the opponent.

Much love from Tenn.

[TW and his grandfather were joined in Miami by Frank Merlo and driven to Key West.]

226. To Paul Bigelow

SH: *The* Robert Clay
Miami, Florida
PM: January 18, 1952
[TL, 1 p. Columbia U]

SAYINGS OF MISS MAXWELL, JANUARY, 1952.

"I am in a very dangerous position for any creative person. Completely surrounded by people who worship and adore me!"

"Do you realize that I am almost 42?!!"

"I am at the age that women find most attractive!"

"She is in the book department at Burdine's, and simply adores me!"

"Look! She has my book on display!"

"I am compared to Thomas Wolfe as he would have written if he had controlled his style!"

"Darling, you are losing your hair!"
"My stomach is surprisingly flat. . . ."

"I am through with love!"

"I want you to meet somebody that you will be mad about. She works in the drag-show at Leon & Eddie's but don't let that fool you. Last Saturday a sailor pulled off her wig and she knocked him across two tables!"

"Tennessee? I am downstairs!"

MORE LATER.

[TW's visit to Miami restored a friendship with Gilbert Maxwell which began in New York in 1940. He and several other transplanted southerners, including

Donald Windham and Fred Melton, formed the first gay society which TW experienced as a young man. In a later biography, *Tennessee Williams and Friends* (1965), Maxwell wrote that similar "tastes" and "unhappy" family backgrounds had secured their friendship. The reunion inspired a list of "SAYINGS" in which TW gently mocked his friend's personal vanity and literary pretension. Vanity aside, Maxwell was a productive writer with three volumes of poetry and a recent novel to his credit.

The place of mailing is obscured in the postmark.]

227. To Elia "Gadg" Kazan

1431 Duncan,
Key West, Fla.
Jan. 21, 1952
[TL, 1 p. HTC]

Dear Gadg:

HELP! HELP! SEND ME A WRITER! This is an embarassing but realistic appeal. Pick him out very carefully. First a southerner, someone such as Hubert Creekmore or Eudora Welty or even Speed Lamkin who know the Delta country. Also, preferably, someone who has done enough film-writing, or some film-writing. I will pay the financial penalty out of my advance and I may even sacrifice the screen-writing credit provided that I am given full credit for the authorship of the one-act plays it's based on.

I really did mean it, Gadg, when I wired you that I would devote myself to this film, but, Baby, you know as well as I know, that, first of all, we've got to obey the first commands of our hearts. You know that or we wouldn't be so close to each other in spirit. So send me a writer, and believe that I want one for a respectable reason.

The reason is this: I've done the stuff in those plays, not a single thing in them is left unsaid and there they are, complete, not perfect by any manner or means, but really completed. Now I feel a lot of things left unsaid, crowding my fingers on the typewriter, but they don't seem to be an essential part of these short plays, and I can't kid myself and certainly don't want to kid you that they are. SO SEND ME A WRITER.

I will work with him. I'll work with him as closely as possible and still go on with the new work that's crowding my fingers.

I think that you and Audrey and Molly will understand about this, and won't, in your hearts, blame me for it.

Under separate cover - I'm exhausted right now - I'll give you a point-by-point reaction to your outline which was a really brilliant piece of work and one that makes a good, solid basis for the script-to-be. The first two parts of it I buy without reservation. The last part gets a little bit cloudy or arbitrary - both.

Nothing but good can come out of my working with someone else on this script, provided the someone else is wisely chosen. I want this film to be almost like a documentary in its background authenticity. Let's get a writer who really knows such things as the process of ginning cotton, or who will make a quick, concentrated study of it for us, on location, the sort [end of letter missing]

[On January 14, 1952, Elia Kazan gave preliminary testimony before the House Un-American Activities Committee regarding past Communist activities and associations. He admitted his brief membership (mid 1930s) in the Communist Party but declined for the moment to name other members, especially those associated with the Group Theatre. Two weeks later, an anxious, depressed Kazan began rehearsals of *Flight into Egypt*, which received mixed notices and closed after forty-six performances. TW and Frank Merlo were among the unlucky investors.

Audrey Wood advised TW to use Paul Bigelow as an assistant on the *Baby Doll* project and thus forego the personal expense and shared credit of a professional collaborator. He agreed but felt it "terribly unfair to require writer to assume all liabilities on a deal so full of speculation" (telegram, January 31, 1952, HRC). TW hoped to be put on salary by Charles Feldman, the likely producer, while film rights were being negotiated and a script prepared. The film's original working title, "The Twister," was replaced by a second, "Hide and Seek."

TW admired Kazan's "outline," especially the opening sequence of the "syndicate fire," which he thought "a beautiful, thrilling, dramatic and cinematic idea" (although later cut in revision). The ending described by Kazan may have seemed flat by contrast, as Archie Lee Meighan, his arson revealed, "turns defeated and slouches off" (to Kazan, January 23, 1952, WUCA).

TW cabled the Department of Agriculture for "technical information on cotton ginning" (February 4, 1952, HRC).]

228. *To Edwina Dakin Williams*

[1431 Duncan Street
Key West, Florida]
1/25/52.
[TLS w/ autograph marginalia, 1 p. HTC]

Dear Daughter and Mother:

We were delighted to get your letter but still are waiting to hear what disposition is being made of Dakin, and we are glad to know that you are planning to come South. Don't put it off long. The big downstairs room is waiting for you, ready whenever you can get here.

After two most delightful weeks in New York, excepting the snow and ice, Tom and I took the train to New Orleans, and had barely registered at the Monteleone when the owner of the hotel sent a great basket of fruit to us and when we went to pay the bill, discovered that we had been his guest the entire time we were there which was about two weeks. We were interviewed and photographed and got on the radio a couple of times. Soon as the paper was out, grandfather received a number of calls by phone from old friends from Tenn. and Miss. Chiefly among them, Mrs. Flournoy who later had us over on New Year's Day for Egg-nog and a drive about Audubon Park. Grandfather wishes to add that we had fruit-cake and nuts out of their own garden. Mrs. Flournoy's son is married to a lovely woman and they have a grown daughter, soon to be married. They have a charming home. She enquired a great deal about you.

On New Years morning Mr. and Mrs. Binnings whom I married in Clarksdale about 30 years ago took me to Early Communion. We flew down from New Orleans to Miami and stayed there about four days while Frank drove the Jaguar down from New York to pick us up. The car had been delayed by the big Atlantic storms but arrived in New York without damage. We are now settled here and everything is going smoothly. We have a middle-aged white woman working for us. She cleans well but cannot cook. Frank is cooking dinner for us, and doing it very well.

We are worried about your fingers. St. Louis is noted for its medical talent and should have cured the condition by this time. As soon as you hear about Dakin let us know.

The weather here has been lovely, warm as summer. We found the house in excellent condition but are still trying to get someone to cut our grass, as we have no gardening implements.

Edwina and Tennessee Williams, Key West.

Grandfather wishes me to add that our last few days in New Orleans we were the guests of Mrs. Sheriff who gave us her entire house while she stayed at a hotel. We would have remained longer in New Orleans but didn't want to accept too much. It was a wonderful visit and we plan to stop there again on the way North this Spring.

Grandfather says we have the prospects of a brilliant social season here. Ahem!

That's all, says Grandfather. I am working on a play and a film-script, the latter at the command of Audrey and Kazan and not according to my own wishes. Do come down soon as possible. Let us know when!

Much love, Tom & Grandfather

[TW was "too shy to be pleasant" and so his mother's forthcoming visit to Key West was "sad" (*Journal*, February 1952).

Penned in the upper margin is the notation "'Summer & Smoke' has transferred to Duchess Theatre in London - has been a hit in England and should make money for Rose's trust fund. 'Tattoo' still running in Copenhagen & Norway." Despite positive reviews, *Summer and Smoke* closed after forty-four performances at the Duchess.

This letter first appeared in Edwina Dakin Williams's memoir, *Remember Me to Tom*, 1963, pp. 226-227.]

229. To Cheryl Crawford

[1431 Duncan Street
Key West, Florida]
2/10/52.
[TLS, 1 p. BRTC]

Dear Cheryl:

It is a great encouragement to me to know that you are interested in "Camino". As I told you before I left New York, there was some indication that the Lieblings would consider an associate producer. I am increasingly dubious that Liebling will want to do the play in its final form. He felt that it could be financed for less than a hundred G's, but now that it is expanded into full length the cost will be greater and I seriously doubt that he will want to attempt it. It will have to be financially treated as a musical, and my problem, now, is to give it sufficient entertainment value to justify that expense. And I do think it should be produced by someone with experience in that field. I have gotten hold of the unabridged (12 volumes) Memoirs of Casanova and DuMas novel "Camille" and the material in the play is now based on the real histories of those characters. I think the play is essentially a plastic poem on the romantic attitude toward life. One thing I wanted to ask you about: is it possible to have scenery moved by dancers? I have a couple of interior set-pieces that I want moved on and off by masked dancers, sort of grotesque mummers with gargoyle masks, and I wondered if that would violate any union rule. It's important that the movement of these set-pieces should be part of the action so that there is no interruption. They move in and out of the street-facade on wagon-stages.

The film is going great. We did about 30 pages yesterday and at least that many today so that it is now almost finished as most of the material was already present in the plays. It is such a great part for Maureen. I almost wish "Tattoo" would close on the road before the film goes into production. I mean the Mrs. Meighan part. Paul is a great help. He types as fast as I can think, and his humor stimulates mine and we laugh our heads off while working. I think it is going to be a very original and strong picture. We're using "Wagons" "Solid Gold Watches" "Property Condemned" and "The Unsatis-factory Supper" and the transitions have worked very smoothly so that it all seems to be of one piece.

Glad you're not doing any more two week stands before you hit the coast. Didn't realize you were still on subscription in St. Louie. Much love -

Tenn.

[Cheryl Crawford's "experience" with musicals was extensive and successful, although her current production, *Paint Your Wagon* (1951), would lose money after a lengthy run. A budget drafted in the preceding December listed costs of $111,000 for mounting *Camino Real* ("Tentative Budget," December 4, 1951, HRC).

To expand and authenticate *Camino Real*, TW consulted *The Memoirs of Jacques Casanova*, reprinted in twelve volumes in 1928, and the Modern Library edition of *Camille*. From the Alexandre Dumas novel (1848) he drew details of Marguerite Gautier's life as a courtesan in Paris, including her improvident love for Armand Duval. Marguerite's friend, Prudence Duvernoy, states in early drafts of the play that "you've got to be realistic on the Camino Real!"

One of the "set-pieces" to which TW refers was probably intended for a retrospective scene at the Opéra Comique, where Marguerite and Armand first meet.

Carroll Baker rather than Maureen Stapleton played the role of Mrs. Meighan in *Baby Doll*.]

230. To Oliver Evans

[1431 Duncan Street
Key West, Florida]
20 February 1952
[TLS, 1 p. HRC]

Dear Oliver:

The best news I've had in a long time, baby, is that you're writing a novel. Much as I admire your poetry, and I have sincerely remarked countless times that you're the best of the current bards, I've always felt with equal earnestness that the latitude and depth of your experience and being would find its most complete and powerful expression in prose. Take that for what it may be worth as the opinion of a friend who wishes you better than well in whatever you undertake.

I have been just a little bit more than slightly bored with Key West this year, and I guess it's fortunate that I had a lot of work to do here. Frank has found a crowd he enjoys. They do the bars all night and he rolls in about daybreak. They're composed of the "after the lost generation" guys and dolls who live on liquor and "bennies" and the fringe of lunacy. Frank dances wildly with the dolls. Possibly lays the guys. I wouldn't know. I've had a dry run of it here as far as sex is concerned. Another queen hit the dust lately. She picked up dirt and was so severely chastised that she was not recognizable. Her eye-sockets, the bone, was knocked in

two inches from original position. She received 32 head-wounds anyone of which was sufficiently violent to kill her. Well, she daid! The sailor has confessed and is in the local calaboose. It struck terror to my heart, this little incident, and I do not venture far afield. Bigelow, however, cannot be discouraged and he averages about three or four tricks a night. He is the new "Florida Sweetheart." He is not staying in the house but in a place called Duke's Motel. Audrey sent him down here to apply the thumb-screws: to get me to work on the Kazan movie-script which I loathed doing but which is now done. I wonder if Bigelow's social activities will allow him time to type it up. He has given everyone around here the impression that he is my ghost-writer: somewhat annoying to me as I nearly killed myself batting the damned thing out and Miss Bigelow just sat there and put it on paper. She has just now been offered the position of chief play-reader for the Theatre Guild! About 12 grand a year.

We have a dainty little chameleon (lizard) in the house named Fairy May. She hides behind the oil paintings during the day but comes out in the evenings. Her tongue is twice as long as she is and she catches almost as many gnats and mosquitos as Bigelow does sailors.

Work hard, baby, and finish the book and get a big fat advance on it. We will do Europe this summer in the Jaguar! We will drive from Paris through Germany to Copenhagen in a blizzard of blonds. We will hit a tree at 90 miles an hour and our posthumous works will be on the Fall list.

I am impressed by Gore's new book. I cannot quarrel with your analysis of it, but I am deeply impressed by the cogency of the writing and the liquid smooth style. And I think your article proves that you can do a piece on him. Give him my love. Say that the bird gives her blessing.

Love, Tenn.

[Frank Merlo's "crowd" did not include TW: "It is 3 a.m. and Frank is still out - I've taken a sleeping tablet but I'll find it hard to sleep tonight. The same old dull tedious resentment and hurt - why do relationships have to be turned into duels. I don't want to fight - I want to trust and love and feel loved" (*Journal*, February/March 1952).

Reviews of Gore Vidal's "new" novel, *The Judgment of Paris* (1952), were mixed and the sales disappointing. John W. Aldridge wrote a condescending notice in the *New York Times*—as well as the literary study *After the Lost Generation* (1951), whose title TW applied to Merlo's "guys and dolls."]

231. To Cheryl Crawford

[1431 Duncan Street
Key West, Florida]
4/5/52
[TLS, 1 p. BRTC]

Dearest Cheryl:

I don't remember the date of your sailing but I have the impression it is soon, so Bon Voyage. Have a good time and a good rest and come back and not give a fuck, that's the only healthy attitude toward the present state of things here.

My trip to the Coast knocked me out, it was a dry run, there was really no point in going. Warners' stalled us with a lot of censorship objections and demands for revision without any signed contract. Audrey and Feldman think that Gadg's situation has a great deal to do with it. Gadg and Marlon and I were obviously screwed out of the Academy awards, and it was a hideous ordeal, sitting there with your bare face hanging out and pretending not to care. Gadg said he never saw anybody get so low in a chair, and I was afraid even to remove my flask from my pocket when Madame Clare Booth Luce got up on the platform and announced the writers awards. One part of me despises such prizes and the vulgar standards they represent, but another part of me wants to be "The Winner" of no matter what. When and how can we ever get over that, and have a dignified humility about us and a true sense of what matters?

I arrived on the Coast just too late for the L.A. stand of "Tattoo" but Audrey and Bill saw it and they said the performances were badly off, everybody was overacting and it wasn't the same show that it was in New York. Sorry to give you that report, but it was confirmed by practically everyone else, except Sheilah Graham who said it was "my best play". The San Francisco notices also seem to bear it out, one of them even complaining about Danny's staging. So "Tattoo" leaves me about where it found me, financially and morally, just as uncertain as before. That shows how demoralized I am. I should have some conviction about my own work.

If I were in good shape, "Camino" would be finished but I have only enough energy to work a couple of hours a day and the texture of the writing is very uneven, though formally it is very interesting, an extension of the free and plastic turn I undertook with "Tattoo". Nevertheless I will prepare a rough draft of the final version before I leave for Europe June 11th

and I do want you to see it, although it seems unlikely to me that it will strike you as a play that could be profitably and economically produced, it is such a screwy thing and would have to be given a very dressy production. Of course Gadg will get the first look at it.

Frankie is having himself a ball. I'm just a bit cross about it, but he is like a kid at play and somebody ought to be having a good time in this sand-lot even [if] it can't be me.

Your loving Tenn.

[Warner Brothers advised TW that the principal characters in "Hide and Seek" (February 19, 1952, U of Delaware) must be punished "for their transgressions." The censor added wryly that "any suggestions of sadism, etc., such as Vacarro's whip, should be de-emphasized - and Baby Doll's bruises will need a little salve" (March 24, 1952, HRC). An early draft submitted to Joseph Breen drew an expression of "concern" regarding "the low and sordid tone of the story as a whole" (to J.L. Warner, August 1, 1952, Herrick).

Continuing investigation of Elia Kazan by the House Un-American Activities Committee apparently made "Hide and Seek" more difficult to sell to Hollywood producers.

TW attended the Academy Awards ceremony (March 20, 1952) as a nominee in the writing division for *Streetcar*. Vivien Leigh, Karl Malden, and Kim Hunter won Oscars, while Marlon Brando, Elia Kazan, and TW were "screwed," as the unhappy author put it. *An American in Paris* (1951) won Best Picture award rather than the heavily favored *Streetcar*.]

232. To Audrey Wood

[1431 Duncan Street
Key West, Florida]
4/14/52
[TLS, 1 p. HRC]

Dear Audrey:

Here is part one of a long story or novella which I started last summer in Venice and have been working on now and then since. I think it could be published separately, and I don't know when I'll have time to get back to it, with Camino to prepare and more work to be done on the screenplay, so I wish you would have this part of it typed up, and, if you approve, submit it to some magazine such as Harper's Bazaar or Madamoiselle.

I think it has the situation and characters for a play or a film, eventually. I spoke of it to Jay while he was here and he thought it would make a good title story for a collection of stories that he wants to bring out along with the selected poems. The rest of it exists in rough draft.

The Jaguar has gone from bad to worse. I think it is questionable that it could safely complete our extensive trip through the South, without drastic rehabilitation. So I was wondering if it might not be better to place it in storage and buy a new Ford, that is, if I can afford to. I'll call you about that from New Orleans. Also I would like yours or Colton's opinion about the advisability of renting the house while we're away. Frank says Colton doesn't think I should rent it, and of course I'd rather not unless the economic situation requires it. The Studio turned out well, is now completed, but the contractor exceeded his estimate by about six hundred to our painful surprise. It does enhance the property a great deal, though, is really a complete separate living-unit.

Gadg's ad in the Times is a very sad comment on our Times. Will call you from New Orleans, probably next week-end.

With love, Tenn

["Three Players of a Summer Game" appeared in *The New Yorker* on November 1, 1952, and was reprinted by New Directions in *Hard Candy: A Book of Stories* (1954). Its "situation and characters" anticipate *Cat on a Hot Tin Roof* (1955).

Elia Kazan's second appearance before the House Un-American Activities Committee (April 10, 1952) led to the naming of seven former Communist members of the Group Theatre, including the playwright Clifford Odets. Kazan's "ad" in the *Times* described his own brief membership in the Party and rationalized the disclosure of former associates as necessary "to protect ourselves from a dangerous and alien conspiracy" ("A Statement," *New York Times*, April 12, 1952).]

233. To Justin Brooks Atkinson

SH: Hotel Monteleone
New Orleans 12, U.S.A.
[early-May 1952]
[TLS, 1 p. BRTC]

Dear Brooks:

My secretary just read me your new review of the village production of "Summer & Smoke" over the phone from New York and I am so happy over it I must tell you and thank you, and at the same time, though it doesn't personally concern me, I want to commend you on the solitary stand you took for Capote's play. I didn't see it and haven't read it but I know it must have been a work of sensitivity and charm as nobody can write more delicately than that odd little boy unless it is Carson McCullers.

These times must be difficult for a critic as they are for a writer.

I have been working like a beaver, I made a long play of "Camino Real", wrote a movie script, a long story and a couple of short plays this winter and Spring. I am tired, but I feel better inside. I was worried before. I couldn't get going on anything that seemed important to me.

Affectionate regards, Tennessee.

[TW planned to spend several weeks in New Orleans before visiting Columbus, Mississippi, with his grandfather.

The revival of *Summer and Smoke* (April 24, 1952) at the Circle in the Square was directed by José Quintero and starred Geraldine Page in a role which established her career. The arena production, Atkinson wrote, revealed "a poignantly intimate play that penetrates deep into the souls of two bewildered young people" (*New York Times*, May 4, 1952). While Quintero momentarily replaced Elia Kazan as TW's "biggest hope" (*Journal*, June 10, 1952), the production ran for a year and helped to launch the off-Broadway theatre movement.

Notices for Truman Capote's play *The Grass Harp* (1952) ranged from mildly sympathetic to cruel and succeeded in closing the production after thirty-six performances. Atkinson alone found dramatic strength and timely wisdom in Capote's delicate "idyll" (*New York Times*, March 28, 1952).]

234. *To Frank Merlo*

SH: The Gilmer Hotel
Columbus, Mississippi
May 9, 1952.
[TLS w/ autograph marginalia, 3 pp. HTC]

Dear Petit Cheval:

As you see from the enclosed photo, we have arrived in my point of origin on this unhappy planet. Doesn't my face look spiritual and my figure a shame? I haven't weighed since I left the Key but I'm sure I must have put on six or eight pounds, eating with Grandfather in New Orleans. Oliver gained even more and is downright plump, or was when we left him there. The last time I saw him he was cruising a nine-foot giant, following him into tea-rooms to see if he was built in proportion. I thought it wise to go home as both Oliver and the giant were quite drunk. We have seen all of Columbus and met most of the prominent people. The men are nearly all like elderly editions of Peter Lindamood, that is, elegant Auntie types. The Lindamood mansion is one of the show-places of town. But it is not real anti-bellum and it looks like the administration building of a girl's college. They don't think much of Peter here, as they say he writes his widowed mother about once a year and has run through his inheritance. I am told that he invested the last of it in this property on 58th street and if that doesn't pay off he'll be broke. Also met Blanchard's twin brother who was in a dreadful condition, staggering drunk, looked about twenty years older than Blanchard. Their house is a real decayed mansion, the windowshades are hanging in shreds. Met the lady who has Lord Byron's love-letter, she is mad as a hatter, was sitting crouched in a dark corner when we arrived. And this afternoon I am to meet another maddie, a cousin of mine named Miss Sadie Lanier. She has just returned from one of her many little visits to the State Asylum. And this evening I am going out with one of the elegant Aunties, a Mr. Patty, to a big lawn party on a plantation called Sugarlock. He said the company would not be appropriate for grandfather, so grandfather is dining elsewhere. I guess it is the "gay" plantation. This old girl used to sing in the church-choir with mother and said she went an octave higher than anyone else and seemed pleased when I told her that she had now lost her voice. The homes, the interiors, are just incredibly beautiful, almost everything in them is a price-less antique. But the people's ideas are older than their furniture. I am sorry you missed this trip and hope we can take it together some other time, it is

a strange part of the world and I feel as if I had always known it and I suppose I have.

The night spot, that is, the interesting one, is an old shack out on the highway called Bud & Dale's. Dale is a queen and Bud is a young lush and there are four B-girls, very pretty and all under twenty, and a great flock of boys from Mississippi State College which is 22 miles away. They all come in and hug Dale and fight over the four girls; inside liquor is forbidden, so they buy set-ups and drink outside. My Jaguar and quart of whiskey were a sensation but my popularity was excessive, there were so many around me that I couldn't get intimately acquainted with a single one, but I did get very drunk, stayed out till four A.M. and at seven grandfather was pounding my door with his cane. That was the morning this picture was taken, which may account for my expression.

If this sailor who's driving me from Memphis appears to be a good driver, I will only accompany him to the East coast, then let him drive the rest of the way alone and go ahead by train. I don't think I want to be with him long. He is one of a celebrated pair of love-birds in New Orleans, the two reigning beauties of the Quarter, and his conceit is second to none except his lover's. He shares the apartment of a poor little queen who is so unnerved by his charm that she shakes like a victim of cerebral palsy and she told me that one morning he slapped her because he woke up and found his shorts unfastened and thought she might have done him in his sleep. Both the two young lovers (not the martyred queen) are coming to New York expecting to set the town on its ears like nothing since the Rocky twins, and it will be a pleasure to see some of the bird-circuit bitches go to work on those girls and hone them down to life size.

We'll be in Memphis tomorrow night and hit the road for New York the next day or Tuesday, probably Tuesday. Anyway I'll call you before you get this letter.

Love - 10.

[The visit to Columbus, Mississippi, restored TW to his birthplace and Walter Dakin to friends and parishioners who fondly remembered his ministry at St. Paul's Episcopal Church (1905–1914). Although brief, the Columbus years formed the core of TW's southern childhood and his close relation with Rose.

Peter Lindamood was an aspiring writer who later returned to Columbus to care for his ailing mother. They were the last Lindamoods to live in the antebellum

Davis Patty, Walter Dakin, and Tennessee Williams, Columbus,
Mississippi, 1952: "Doesn't my face look spiritual and my figure a shame?"

home built by the prominent merchant family. Lindamood was friendly with the
poet Charles Henri Ford, who had lived in Columbus, and who is cited in present
correspondence by an arrow pointing to the Gilmer imprint and the penned notation, "hotel Ch. H. Ford was thrown out of for having dark trade!"

Sadie Lanier, the mad relative to whom TW refers, is not listed in official public records of Columbus or Lowndes County, Mississippi. Social Security files indicate that several women of the same name died in Alabama and Arkansas in the
1960s.

TW visited the Harrison-Evans plantation located some forty miles south of
Columbus near the former Indian village Shuqualak ("Sugarlock"). Davis Patty,
who did indeed sing in the choir of St. Paul's, was TW's guide for the evening.
Legend has it that the party at the so-called "'gay' plantation" supplied TW with
lines spoken by Big Daddy in *Cat on a Hot Tin Roof*: "Twenty-eight thousand acres
of the richest land this side of the valley Nile!" (Act Two).

A local historian has speculated that "Bud and Dale's" may be one of the so-called "home bars" which appeared during the Depression in converted houses or barns and which catered to different groups, including gay students from nearby Mississippi State University.]

235. To Walter Edwin Dakin

59 E. 54ᵗʰ Street [New York]
6/3/52.
[TLS, 2 pp. HRC]

Dear Grandfather:

I've been very busy since I got here. I had to do more work on the film script, then I had to prepare and give three public readings from my plays, stories and poems, then I had to get my play ready for typing, and all the social engagements, and seeing old friends, and so forth. This last week end I spent at Mrs. Bouverie's house in Rhinebeck. I'm sure you remember going there with me one time. I had a nice rest there. When I came back I had to give the third and final reading. I had packed houses for all three readings, and they say that they went off well. I was only nervous one time, the others I enjoyed doing it.

Frank's nephew Tony is being treated at the New Jersey state sanitarium. He has a mild form of dementia praecox. He and Frank are the same age and grew up as brothers so Frank is very disturbed over this and has to spend a great deal of time visiting him. The nephew is now taking insulin shock treatments.

I had to tell Liebling that he could not do my next play. So far there hasn't been any sign of resentment, but that may come out later. Kazan has left for Europe. He will meet us in Paris when we land. Then we'll have conferences on the production for next Fall, which will take place if he is pleased with the script. He hasn't seen it yet. Kazan was under great strain in New York. He had to testify before the committee and he gave the names of old friends who had been Communists when he was, fifteen years ago, and he feels quite guilty about it and left the country mainly on that account. It was a difficult thing to do, but he felt that it was a patriotic duty and so he did it.

I am feeling tired from all the activities and all the pressure since I returned to New York so the six days on the ocean will be a welcome rest.

We sail from here a week from Wednesday, June 11th is the date of the sailing. How I do wish that you were going with us this time! But I am sure you will be comfortable where you are. You must go to the mountains when it gets hot in Memphis. I imagine it's pretty warm there right now. We're not going to stay over long this time as we'll have to come back for the play if it's going to be produced in the early Fall. Frank and I will write you regularly from Europe. We'll have the old address, American Express in Rome.

I'm enclosing a check for June. Don't forget your solemn promise to me that you would spend and enjoy this money and not just put it away! You have a lot of money in your bank account and you must SPEND IT! - Audrey will mail check July & August.

Everybody enquires about you very fondly, Audrey, Bigelow, Irene, Cheryl Crawford, many others.

Do take care of yourself, and have a good time this summer.

Much, much love, Tom

[Anxious notations preceded TW's sailing on the *Liberté*: "I have been on edge for quite a while - very narrow margin indeed. Breathlessness at night, tension daily - diarrhea every A.M. F. has been pleasant enough but sort of separate. 'Camino' typed up - I havent dared read it yet" (*Journal*, June 10, 1952).

Canceled in the letterhead is the imprint of the Gladstone Hotel in New York.]

PART V
1952–1954

Overleaf: Elia Kazan examining the script of Camino Real *(1953).*
"You see <u>form</u> so clearly."

236. To Audrey Wood

[Hôtel du Pont Royal, Paris]
June 22, 1952
[TLS w/ autograph postscript, 3 pp. HRC]

Dear Audrey:

I must brief you very quickly on what has transpired in Paris between myself and the Turk. I was prepared for anything, but to my happy surprise he seemed to be very favorably impressed by the script and he says he wants to start rehearsals in late October. This suits me! I think it would be a mistake to put off this play till another season. Then it goes stale, I lose interest in it and so does everyone else. There isn't too much time to set up such a complicated production, but I think there's enough if we act with expedition. Gadg and I discussed everything but actors. We feel that Milzener ought to design unless a younger man appears who seems both original and safe. This should be investigated at once. Designs can be sent to me air mail special in Rome. Ballard should do the costumes. The composer: Alex North or Paul Bowles. Choreographer: Jerome Robbins or Anna Sokolov. Robbins is here in Paris and eager to see the script. All these people should start work early this summer, say, in early July. Gadg wants Cheryl to produce and I am inclined to agree with him, but I think she must forget economy in the initial expenditure and give the show a rich production, that must be thoroughly understood. Gadg says he will talk to her very frankly about it. I think her experience, her lack of other commitments or occupations, will mean a lot. The show will make great demands upon a producer, all of his or her time and capacity and experience, to organize it and keep things rolling smoothly among the various departments. This is not a show for anybody to make a debut in! I am sure, and have been sure for some while, that you and Bill would be most unwise to undertake it as your first venture into production. For one thing, I will need you to represent me versus producer. There are bound to be points of conflict where I will need protection strictly in my own corner, what with a tight producer and The Terrible Turk, although the latter has manifested, so far, only the lamb-like side of his nature. As for casting, I think Eli should have a script right away and be definitely committed. I would like for Stella Adler and perhaps Joseph Schildkraut to see the Marguerite-Jacques roles, but no commitments made yet. How about old Josephine Brown for the Gypsy? Or Old Prudence? I will return early, perhaps in August, so that

there will be plenty of time for casting before rehearsals start. The important thing is to keep Gadg occupied with it. Producer must be settled immediately, I would say as soon as he and you have talked to Cheryl and she has studied the script and assessed the budget. Not later than two weeks. For the other people, designer, composer, Etc., have to be tied up soon as possible. You said in your wire that preparations should take "many months". Ideally, yes, I agree, but there are too many uncertainties to make such a postponement advisable. For one thing, my health and my nerves. I want to be around and fully competent when this play is produced, I think I have earned the price of my admission to the show, and I do want to see it. Then it is certainly wise to use Gadg when he is ready. . . .

Do you think there would be the remotest possibility of interesting Olivier and Leigh in the Jacques-Marguerite roles?

Gadg made some fine suggestions. He didn't like Marguerite's scene with the gigolo in the last block, as he said there needed to be something to clarify her change, so I have written another scene to go there which I do think is better. I have also rewritten the first Marguerite-Jacques scene (block two) to introduce more strongly the longing to escape which builds to the big funicular scene. The opera-comique scene is too long, but cutting it is going to be a delicate operation. Obviously the show is going to run too long and Gadg thinks we ought to have _five_ weeks on the road. Remarkable coming from him. I should say at least four. He mentioned Chicago. I thought of Philly, Washington, and Boston. I think a total of 12 dancers, doubling in bits such as horses, dogs, streetcleaners, Etc., might be adequate but I have not yet studied the script from that angle. Costumes will be a large and important item, all the pictorial details have to be very well done, nothing skimped. That's why the production people have to get started pronto!

Maria arrives here tomorrow, with a broken heart, I suppose, and an empty purse. Rothschild surrendered 137,000 francs from his desk-drawer - for some reason we didn't go to the authors' league for the money! I wish you would get a statement directly from the Authors' League on what "Streetcar" made on its tour, which I thought was long and profitable. So far we have only gotten out of Rothschild-Tallant only about the equivalent of five or six hundred dollars, although from the Paris run, which we collected directly from the Society office, there were millions of francs, amounting to several thousands of dollars, I forget the exact figure, but

SELECTED LETTERS / 1952–1954

there is a curious discrepancy of size in the two amounts, even granted that the road tour may have been shorter and less profitable than the run in Paris. Incidentally, I found a letter in one of my pockets containing a check for $427. from the "readings" I gave in the village. You can deduct your percentage at that end. I had not noticed the letter till we unpacked on the boat.

Talked to Carson on phone. She has moved into her country house called the "Ancienne Presbyterre" about six miles from Paris, and she sounded rather faint and wistful on the phone. We'll see her before we leave. Reeves sounded drunk, definitely not like a man on anti-buse unless he was about to go into a coma. Please send grandfather a check for $200. the first of July and again the first of August. He is expecting it! And has promised that he will not leave it to the Episcopal church but spend it lavishly on high living in Dixie. Much love -

Tenn.

P.S. I have not had time to write the "essay" they want for the recordings. Tell Miss Roney that perhaps she could use something from my introduction to the published version of "Battle of Angels." States my philosophy of art. I also told Leonard Lyons I would write a "guest column" for him. Do you think he would use, instead, a humorous poem that I will send? Please enquire. I am doing a piece for the Sunday Times magazine.

P.S. Sending revisions air mail on Monday. Only copies so please have typed and inserted in the scripts.

[TW and Frank Merlo landed at Le Havre on June 17 and spent two weeks in Paris before leaving for Rome.

Following their meeting in Paris, Elia Kazan assured TW of his willingness to stage *Camino Real* (1953) "just as is," but he urged revision and went on to draft a nine-page letter of "suggestions" (n.d., Columbia U). In "late October" TW was still trying to please "The Terrible Turk," rehearsals and production a dim prospect.

William Liebling's withdrawal as producer of *Camino Real* bore no visible "sign of resentment." Audrey Wood made the formal announcement at this time, reminding TW in later correspondence that her husband had "laid out approximately $5,000.00" (July 4, 1952, HRC) in preparation. TW planned to reimburse the expense, as a following letter indicates.

The "opera-comique scene" was designed in part to recall the legend of

Marguerite Gautier (Camille), the sentimental whore who renounces her love for a handsome youth to preserve his good name and family prospects. TW finally eliminated the scene at Kazan's request, but in preparing *Camino Real* for publication, he restored two figures—Prudence Duvernoy and Olympe—associated with Marguerite's Parisian days and her meeting of Armand Duval at the opera.

Maria Britneva joined TW in Paris and remained to play an uncredited part in the John Huston film *Moulin Rouge* (1952). She soon cabled TW in Rome: "'AT IT LIKE KNIVES. HUSTON A STEAMING HOT CUP OF TEA'" (TW to Wood, July 8, 1952, HRC). TW had been delighted to learn in the spring that she and James Laughlin planned to marry, "when he was 'free of other obligations'" (St. Just, p. 55). Laughlin's marriage with Margaret Ellen Keyser, then in the process of dissolution, and his continuing affair with Gertrude Huston, a book designer at New Directions, were the main impediments.

Carson and Reeves McCullers sailed in the preceding January, spent several months in Rome, and settled near Paris in the village of Bachvillers. Before leaving the States, Carson learned of her election to the National Institute of Arts and Letters. Elected at the same time were Eudora Welty and TW.]

237. To Cheryl Crawford

[Hôtel du Pont Royal, Paris]
6/29/52
[TLS, 1 p. BRTC]

Dear Cheryl:

I wired Audrey a couple of nights ago that I had seen Magnani and her manager and that both had assured me she wants very much to do Tattoo. Then I had lunch with her and she assured me again. She is willing to do it in America with either De Sica or Visconti. She said she would actually prefer Visconti because he is "more sensual" but she was afraid that his old association with the "C.P." might keep him out of the States, in which case De Sica would be quite acceptable. She says she won't be free of other commitments until May. I think it is essential to move on this with the utmost expedition, for La Magnani is a capricious woman, the iron is now very hot, and if papers can be drawn up and money is ready, I think she is in the bag. I am leaving this evening for Rome. Suggest you get in touch with me there right away if you are still interested in making the film yourself and can sign her up. I am supposed to see her there when I arrive.

I have prepared a revised draft of "Camino" and am sending it right away. This is the one I want you to read. Gadg seemed pleased with the first and said he wanted to go into rehearsal with it in late October and would

see you as soon as he returned to the States for discussion. We both would like you to produce it, but are not sure that you will consider it a good financial risk, it will have to be budgetted very liberally to insure a full realization of its plastic values and of course it is a gamble. We both feel that you would understand it better than anyone else.

Do wish you were still in Europe, for this and the Magnani business!

Much love and also greetings to your fiance! Tenn

[Filming of The *Rose Tattoo* (1951) was delayed until late 1954 to accommodate "La Magnani," who finally agreed to play the role of Serafina. Ercole Graziadei informed Cheryl Crawford that his client's "last fee for a bilingual production" (August 1, 1952, HRC) was $90,000. Neither Vittorio de Sica nor Luchino Visconti would direct the film, nor did Crawford exercise her option to produce.

Audrey Wood warned Crawford, the eventual producer of *Camino Real*, that the play must "be done with artistic abandon and financial perfection." Crawford was enthusiastic, but she "spoke ruefully" to Wood of her "many succès d'estime" on Broadway, and of her need to have "both the esteem and the dough the next couple of times." *Camino Real* would require "further revision" (Wood to TW, July 4, 1952, HRC) to secure her interest.

TW closes with a playful allusion to Paul Bigelow, Crawford's unlikely "fiance!"]

238. To Elia "Gadg" Kazan

45 Via Aurora, Rome
7/14/52.
[TLS w/ autograph postscript, 2 pp. WUCA]

Dear Gadg:

First of all I want to say how lucky I think I am to have people like you and Audrey and Cheryl in my corner at this point. That this play should come off is of vital importance to me, and I am so happy and grateful that you are occupied with it! I received a letter from Audrey in the same mail as yours and I'm answering you both right now. I HAVE NOT YET GOTTEN YOUR NOTES! I presume they are waiting for me in Paris, at the American Express office. Perhaps it is just as well to let them rest there a few days, as I have just now, yesterday, sent my own revisions, about 22 pages of them, and perhaps you should digest those first before I take up yours. I am sure that yours will be good, as they always are, and stimulating to me, and you

know how sincerely I welcome them from you. Cheryl's suggestions and
criticisms will be very intelligent, and ably expressed, but I am not as sure
that they will be as useful as yours, as I know she has a bias in favor of a
certain element that is rarely present in my work. She expressed it best
when she says she loves a "hot light" at the end of her shows. This play
ends with a sort of "misty radiance" and I am not sure that will be, or can
be, hot enough to suit her; if you dissolve the shimmer of mystery over this
thing, you lose its fascination. It is up to me, now, to make the mystery of
it appealing enough, evocative and fascinating enough, to satisfy a large
and continuous audience. Of course it is also, perhaps even more at this
point, up to you and the other artists who will be engaged in it. You are all
correct about the problem lying in the Jacques-Marguerite story. I think I
have gone quite a ways toward solving it, but there may be still further to
go. What I am saying in their story is really a very clear and simple thing,
that after passion, after the carneval (which means 'farewell to flesh') there
is something else, and even something that can be more important, and
we've got to believe in it. Philosophically that is about as far as I can carry
their story without falsifying it, that is, without extending it beyond my
own convictions. I tried to explain the play to Huston and Ferrer at lunch
in Paris and I said it was a poetic search for a way to live romantically, with
'honor', in our times, royally under real conditions, and I think even as it
now stands the play fulfills this aim. I want to keep away from a Maxwell
Anderson sort of windiness and any sort of patness, make my points by
evocation and poetic allusion. Great clarity does not come out of life, only
people who die on the operating table die under a "hot light", and then it
is quickly extinguished, and one is not even sure of a "misty radiance"
except possibly in the recollections of one's more sentimental survivors! But
perhaps I am anticipating an objection which I won't be faced with. There
is very deeply and earnestly an affirmative sort of mysticism in this work,
and I want that to stand, and I want it also to be a very new and enthralling
piece of theatre which we can certainly make it, and that alone is a good deal.

Audrey is concerned about their losses as prospective producers which
she says amount to about $5,000., including her trip to Europe. I don't
want to impose this sum on the producer, whoever that may be, so I will
assure her in this letter that I am willing to make it up out of my own earnings, perhaps by scaling up her percentage to the point where the loss is
retrieved. I think she is right that Liebling shouldn't have to take this loss,

and since it is really my responsibility, I ought to make it up. Her letter was full of good sense, honest, clear, and thoughtful.

I am very relieved that you are seeing Jo. While the other departments can wait if <u>necessary</u>, I think design is so important and complex on this show that it ought to be under consideration right away. Also explore Whitehead as possibility.

You can't believe the heat here in Rome unless you are sitting right in the middle of it! I have made train reservations for Hamburg on 18<u>th</u>. It will be easier to think and work there. Tomorrow I'm having lunch with Magnani's lawyer. She is not only willing but eager to do "Tattoo" in America in May. Do you know anybody who would like to pick up that package?

Did you see Geraldine Paige's performance in "Summer and Smoke"? Perhaps we'll get together in Bavaria if you start this summer.

I ran the Jaguar into a low concrete post but at a moderate rate of speed, so only one fender was smashed this time. I think Maria is "Shacking up" with Huston in Paris: don't breathe a word of it, dear! She wires that he is a "Steaming hot cup of tea!"

That's all the gossip at this end of the line.

With lots of mountain violets, Tenn.

Later - Audrey wired revisions haven't come worried as I mailed them July 8<u>th</u> air.

[Elia Kazan's "notes" reveal sharp disappointment with Marguerite Gautier's role, especially in the opera scene, which Kazan could direct only for "moment to moment effects." Kilroy was "basically excellent," he thought, but his disappearance in the "middle section" of *Camino Real* created "a big hole" and left uncertainty regarding "his story" (n.d., Columbia U).

The "bias" which TW ascribed to Cheryl Crawford is also evident in Kazan's "notes," soon to be read by TW, and in his subsequent letters of criticism, which did little to absolve the playwright of "clarity."

Jo Mielziner's anticipated collaboration on *Camino Real* would be his fourth with TW.

In later correspondence TW identified the closing imagery of "mountain violets" with the affirmative values of *Camino Real*: "tenderness" and "humanity of feeling."

The HRC holds a briefer, undated draft of this letter.]

239. *To Gilbert Maxwell*

[45 Via Aurora, Rome]
7/15/52.
[TLS, 1 p. HRC]

Dear Gil:

You know me too well to require an apology for my failure to function properly in any sphere of human activity. It will not surprise you to learn that I have your manuscript with me, that I take it out from time to time and peruse it privately to my great solace and joy. I did not get to give it to Laughlin, for he did not return to New York until the very evening before my sailing, and we had a five-minute session in a restaurant before I dashed off to my lawyer's to make certain arrangements in case I should perish at sea. I have been meaning, and wanting to, tell you what a great success your poems were. I only wish my own had been half so well received. "Go Looking" always got a big hand and so did "Forfeits" and "Hand To Mouth". I limited myself to three or four of them at each reading, as I also had to read from my own works, stories and plays. As you know, I read badly, but nevertheless the poems came across through their own inextinguishable merits and made a deep impression on that (Always) minority which comes with anything like a potential sensibility to lyric things. I have, as I said, the manuscript right here with me in Rome, as I thought if I had a chance to, I would start working on a short preface. However I could mail it directly to Laughlin if you prefer. I am only going to be here a few more weeks, as I have to return some time in late August for a prospective stage production in Early Fall. It would probably be better for me to keep the verse with me, and take it personally to Laughlin and give him the pitch as soon as I get back. Don't you think so? Fortunately good poetry is something that keeps, but I do feel most ashamed of not having let you know about this sooner.

Grandfather is in Monteagle, which is in the mountains of Tennessee, and Tennessee is on the plains of Rome. But leaving tomorrow for a brief visit to Germany, which I hear is both cool and gay, while Rome is just gay. Look forward to seeing you in the early Fall. Be good. Take care of yourself. Don't worry about the novel. You know you can do it, and I know you will!

Love, Tenn.

[Gilbert Maxwell (1910-1979) asked for TW's help in placing a recent selection of his poetry with New Directions.]

240. To James "Jay" Laughlin

SH: Atlantic Hotel Hamburg
7/24/52
[TLS, 1 p. Houghton]

Dear Jay:

I've had you on my mind ever since I got to Europe but I just haven't had much chance to write a letter. We spent about a week in Paris with Maria, and I have never seen her looking so well, the stay on the sea had done her a world of good, her vitality was such that I simply could not keep up with her. I left her in good hands. She had lunch with John Huston, Jose Ferrer and myself the day before I left Paris and from then on, I take it, they took up where I had left off and I think she is not quite sure which of them she prefers and gives me to understand that both are mad for her, which I do not find in the least inconceivable, do you? The Russians are mad!

I had a lot of work to do and Rome was getting too hot for it so I left there after about two weeks and came up here to Hamburg which is very cool and invigorating. I thought I would be unknown up here. Quite the contrary! Had no sooner registered than reporters were calling and I had lots of pictures taken this afternoon. Alas, for the anonymous joys of the gay cabarets! - This hotel is so swanky that one cannot bring in friends at night, so don't be surprised if my next book of poems includes a lot of bucolics and eclogues and fauns and satyrs among the moonlit trees! Just so it doesn't also include the "polizie". Hamburg is really madder than the Russians.

Gadg is giving me many notes for revisions on "Camino" so I don't know just when I will get to work on the poems, but I will as soon as possible.

Affectionate greetings to Gertrude.

Yours ever, Tenn.

[In February 1952 TW delivered fifty-odd poems to James Laughlin which were graded "A" through "E" by the author. Nearly all appeared in TW's first book of verse, *In the Winter of Cities* (1956).]

241. *To Elia "Gadg" Kazan*

[45 Via Aurora, Rome]
[July 29, 1952]
[TL w/ autograph postscript, 2 pp. WUCA]

Dear Gadg:

First I want to apologize for the letter I gave Frank to mail you this morning and which he has probably already mailed. I want to apologize for the cutting things I said about Jo. Not true! Comforting, momentarily, to me, but not at all true. By denigrating Jo's work, who is honest and sober and gifted, who certainly has no axe to grind in attacking my work, who has indeed on the contrary contributed more than his share to giving my work the success it has had, I am playing a shoddy game which is despicable of me, and I want, now, to face the facts about myself, which are that I have been floundering around most of the time since Streetcar, flapping my arms in the air as if they were wings. Then striking at Jo because he had the honesty to say that's what I've been doing most of the time. If you people, you, Gadg, and Cheryl and Audrey and Jo and Molly, still take me seriously as a writer it is mainly because of what I did in the past. I can't say what is the matter, why I accomplish so little. I work, God knows! But I'm not as "charged" as I was, not as loaded. I have a sort of chronic fatigue to contend with. I used to have, say, two good days out of seven. Now I have about one good day out [of] fifteen or twenty. I have to "hypo" myself into thinking that stuff is good. Otherwise I'd have even more trouble in working. I feed on delusion, beg for encouragement. In this situation the sensible thing to do would be to quit for a time, as so many writers have done, such as Rilke, and wait and pray for a new start, for a new vision, a regeneration of the tired nerve cells. But you see I committed myself completely to the life of an artist. I froze out almost everything else. I don't know how to live as anything else. Day by day existence demands that I be working at something and that I believe that it is worth while! I have not made a success of life or of love. And if my work peters out, I am a bankrupt person. The only things I really have left are the affection of certain friends like you and Audrey and Cheryl, and the little comforts of liquor and food and sex and books, and the occasional feeling that I am still able to function as an artist on a worthwhile level of competence. You won't agree with this, since it would not be kind to, but let's skip that and go on to a realistic consideration of what's to be done about the present situation regarding this play.

This play is possible because it deals precisely with my own situation. Perhaps that's why I go on with it, even though it's basically an old work, not a new one. I think it is very likely my last one. I almost hope that it is. Except for some unexpected thing that will restore my old vigor, it would be better to put writing away, after this last job, and settle for whatever I could get out of just existing. Not existing has no appeal for me whatsoever. YOUR NOTES CAME THIS MORNING FROM PARIS. GADG, BELIEVE ME, THEY'RE BRILLIANT! Much better than the play. You see _form_ so clearly. I am going right back to work on the J-M scenes. The most provocative notes are on the return from the Opera, the excited speculations about the "Fugitivo", or whatever we call it, going directly into the Byron scene, and then the clash between Jacques and Marguerite about the heroic gesture of going through the arch. This morning I did some work on the opera scene and on a new ending. I usually work best when I have just come to a new place. I am going to Greece with Oliver when he arrives, and will be working continually on the script while we travel. Building to the "Fugitivo" is a straight, clear line, like a rocket that explodes at the height of its trajectory.

If we keep to that line, the story will have unity & a cumulative tension & a real climax. I am _terribly_ _stimulated_ by these notes, _fratello mio_!

[After ten days in Hamburg (ca. July 18-28), TW returned to Rome with the thought that he "must be more understanding" of Frank Merlo: "What else have I got, after all, but the 'Horse' and my memories? and my work" (_Journal_, ca. July 28, 1952).

Awaiting TW in Rome were Elia Kazan's long-delayed "notes," written after the June meetings in Paris, and a subsequent letter from Kazan reporting Jo Mielziner's "'v. negative' reaction" to _Camino Real_. TW lashed out at Mielziner, decrying his lack of "enthusiasm" for the play and denigrating his recent work on "cornball musicals" (to Kazan, July 29, 1952, WUCA).

TW's latest rewrites of _Camino Real_ had not, Kazan thought, solved "the problem" of Marguerite's vague motivation, nor had they "organically" integrated her "secondary" role with that of Kilroy, the presumed "emotional center" of _Camino Real_. Included with Kazan's "GENERAL POINTS" of discussion was a "SUGGESTED NEW OUTLINE" keyed to the play's "essential" story line: "How to die with dignity and honor and gallantry?" Kazan closed with a warning that Audrey Wood, Cheryl Crawford, and Jo Mielziner "all feel the confusion and lack of integration to a greater or less extent" (July 24, 1952, BRTC). TW "had hoped for too much," but he was "not crushed by this retrenchment" (_Journal_, July 29, 1952) of enthusiasm.]

242. *To Carson McCullers*

45 Via Aurora, Rome
8/?/52.
[TLS w/ enclosure, 1 p. Duke U]

Dearest Carson:

Your wire to Hamburg reached me just before I caught the train back to Rome. Hamburg was fascinating and I found that I liked the Germans surprisingly well in view of their reputation for bad conduct, but I got homesick after about a week, it was silly of me, but you know how one feels at times, and has to go running back where he came from even though it is actually no more home than any place else in the world.

Oliver Evans is some where in Europe but he is obviously annoyed with me and has not gotten in touch with me here. I think it is because I didn't wire him your address. He wanted to get the correct copy of that poem of yours that was badly mangled in "New Directions" as he wants to put it into the issue of Voices that he is editing and Laughlin has given permission but he doesn't have a true copy of the poem. Could you send one to "Voices" or to Oliver c/o me in Rome? I'm sure he'll turn up eventually and I can give it to him. What happened was that I didn't pick up my mail at American Express in Paris and it wasn't forwarded to me down here until just this week.

I'm enclosing still another fine notice of your book in England. Frank found this one in an English paper. It must have had a wonderful press there. Are you going to do anything about the dramatization of "Ballad"? After much initial enthusiasm, the interest in "Camino Real" seems to have subsided. Sober second thoughts, I suppose. It's awful how quickly a theatrical reputation declines on the market. A few years ago and I could have anything I wanted in the theatre, now I have to go begging. Two plays that didn't make money and, brother, you're on the skids! I wish we could spend a week or two working quietly together this summer, the way we did that wonderful summer in Nantucket, when you did "Member" and I did "Summer". The presence of someone else doing creative work is a comfort and a stimulation I think, for it is a lonely business. How is it on the estate? Is the dog having pups?

much love, 10.

[An earlier "notice" which TW sent to Carson McCullers described her as "such a mature writer that she makes most of her American contemporaries seem almost crude" (*The Observer*, July 20, 1952). Under review was an English anthology entitled *The Ballad of the Sad Café: The Novels and Stories of Carson McCullers* (1951).

In 1960 McCullers authorized Edward Albee to dramatize *The Ballad of the Sad Café* (1943). The final product disappointed her, as did the play's mixed reviews and brief run on Broadway (October 30, 1963-February 15, 1964). She later acknowledged that a lack of dialogue and action in the novella made it a poor subject for theatre.

Summer and Smoke (1948) and *The Rose Tattoo* (1951), the plays which had put TW "on the skids," lost $70,000 and $40,000, respectively, including the original Broadway show and tour.

Internal evidence suggests that TW wrote this letter on August 1 or 2, 1952, after returning to Rome.]

243. To Oliver Evans

45 Via Aurora, Rome.
8/5/52.
[TLS, 2 pp. HRC]

Dear Oliver:

What a relief to hear from you, I was afraid you might be in one of your Welsh rages because I had not responded to the cable and letter to Paris. I must explain about that. I did not call for mail at American Express in Paris, as I didn't expect any there. Consequently I missed the communications from you and also a long letter from Kazan, which led to serious misunderstandings. Finally all the Paris mail was forwarded to Rome, just last week, but you were already at sea so naturally I couldn't send you Carson's address or poem. Her address is "Ancienne Presbyterre", Bachivillers. Oise, France. She and Reeves came to Paris, both in a terrible shape. He was on liquor and sleeping tablets, she was on liquor. She said he had been threatening to kill himself and she must put him into a clinic. The next day she was threatening to kill herself and Maria was there and she didn't want me to leave the hotel with Maria because if we went out she was going to jump out of her window. It was all very upsetting. Then the next day she and Reeves went quietly back to the "Ancienne Presbyterre" but since then I have heard that they are going to sell that place and Reeves is in a clinic. I think if you can find a natural division between the two poems (they were simply run together in N.D.) that is all you need for Voices.

My dear, I was in Hamburg last week and guess who was staying in the same hotel! Miss Otis Taylor, the last of the Edwardian Aunties! We did the town together several nights, and I must say she is the most agreeable and charming company and I like her extremely much. There are three or four bars in Hamburg where the boys dance together and your sister did not miss a dance! She was the belle of the balls! Great strapping blonds whirled her about the floor to the Waltzes of Strauss, pursued her along the waterfront, kissed her among the ruins and seduced her incontinently between the cabarets. They would not allow her to rest. If they could not enter the hotel with her, which was, alas, often the case, owing to the manly roughness of their apparel, such was the heat of their passion that nothing would do but she must retire with them into the bushes. At one point she had to remain quite immobile, as if turned to marble, for about twenty minutes, in a peculiarly intimate pose with a Herculean blond who was resting his forehead on the trunk of a tree, while a policeman smoked a cigarette not ten yards away on the banks of the Alster. Eclogues and bucolics!

Why have you removed Athens from your itinerary? Miss Taylor says it is not to be believed, especially a certain park in the center of town. And aren't you coming to Rome? Please write me places and dates soon as you get this, so we can arrange to get together somewhere. I am about ready to take another trip. Rome is cool and lovely, now, and trade is abundant. You really must come here before you continue North, and Copenhagen is out of the question, completely, this summer, unless you already have your hotel reservations. The Olympic crowds. I walked and taxied all about Hamburg from midnight till five in the morning looking for a room where I could have a private conversation with one of my dancing partners. Not a room anywhere. At daybreak and after, we wound up in a whore house that rented us a bed for half an hour. You can't bring people into the good hotels after dark. And everything is booked up anyway. Better do southern Europe first, then make reservations for the northern places well in advance and don't go anywhere just expecting to find a room. Marian advised me by postcard from somewhere in Belgium that "she and Ed Birk and cousin Vac" are on the continent and going to Paris and then to Majorca. You'll probably run into them there. Let me know how that part of the continent is, I've never been there. The Jaguar is in good shape, we could take a trip.

Love, Tenn.

[Carson McCullers's threat of suicide did not detain or unduly alarm TW: "When I told her, Honey, sit tight, we'll see you later tonight, and whisked off to see Anna Magnani in preference to the big jump, I realized just what a hopelessly heartless old cynic I have become!" (qtd. in St. Just, p. 60).

Two poems by McCullers—"The Mortgaged Heart" and "When We Are Lost"—were accidentally "run together" when published in *New Directions Ten* (1948). Oliver Evans reprinted them separately in *Voices* (September-December, 1952), with a generous selection of poems by TW.]

244. To Liebling-Wood

SH: Western Union
Muenchen Via
1952 Aug 20
[Telegram, 1 p. HRC]

IN MUNICH WITH TERRIBLE TURK RETURNING ROME TOMORROW LOVE=

=TENNESSEE=

[Elia Kazan was in Munich to direct *Man on a Tightrope* (1953), a film whose timely subject matter was based upon the escape of a small, dilapidated circus from Communist Czechoslovakia. The "Terrible Turk" had invited TW to join him on location and draft "a rehearsal script" (July 24, 1952, BRTC) in accord with the new outline of *Camino Real*. TW thought it "a virtual return to the original script" and resented Kazan's intrusion: "I have fallen off remarkably in the esteem of my co-workers when they start dictating my work to me" (*Journal*, ca. August 17, 1952).]

245. To Ercole Graziadei

[45 Via Aurora, Rome]
September 6, 1952
[TL, 3 pp. Todd Collection]

Dear Dr. Graziedei:

Something happened yesterday evening which has caused me a good deal of perplexity and embarassment. A reporter from the Roman paper "Europeo" came to my apartment and asked me if I had any statement to make about the fact that my application for membership to the "Circolo de Golfo" had been turned down by the members. I was not sure that I

understood him correctly, as he didn't speak English, so I asked my Secretary, Frank, to come into the room, and the reporter then explained that "some Ambassador" had told him that I had "tried to get into the club" and that the nature of my writing, particularly of my novel "The Roman Spring of Mrs. Stone" was so objectionable that the "application" could not be accepted.

I am sure you must know what a humiliating sort of experience this was, and I do hope that you can give me a little more light on the subject. The reporter had sent a photographer to take my picture. Fortunately I was not at home at the time, and of course I declined to provide him with photographs or any statement at all in this connection.

I think it should be very well known, by this time, that I am probably the greatest Italophile, and especially "Romanophile", among all the writers who come here from America. I have very truly and deeply loved the Italian people. In all the interviews that I have given to the press, to radio, to television, in all the countries that I have visited, I have never failed, and with the most sincere feeling, to express my love and my gratitude to this city and to Italy where I have spent at least a total of two out of the last five years. This comes, for that reason - if it is true! - as a most disconcerting and deeply wounding sort of a shock.

Believe me, Dr. Graziedei, I have done nothing whatsoever to offend the officials or members of the club. As you know, I go there only to swim. I have a heart condition that makes swimming essential to my health. I usually go there late in the afternoon, swim twenty lengths, dry in the sun, and leave. I have met practically no one there except some Americans such as Mr. Cushing and the Van Renssaelers. I have brought a few guests to the club, such as Noel Coward, Janet Flanner, Natalia Danesi Murray, all of whom have behaved with the most complete propriety while they were there. My own social habits are always and everywhere considerate of those around me. I am very reserved, by nature. This is the first time, in my social experience, that I have been subjected anywhere to any kind of social ostracism, and I must say that it strikes me as curiously uncalled-for.

If it is true that members have objected to my short novel, which has not been published in Italy but which has come out in several other countries and which has been warmly appreciated by excellent critics - if this is true, I suspect that they have either not read the novel or else have completely failed to understand it. The book is a serious psychological study of an unhappy

American woman. It does <u>not</u> deal with Rome except as a poetic background to the tragedy of a woman, whose materialistic ambition and interests in her former life had left her with no spiritual resources when her youth was gone and who consequently found herself drifting into an emotional wilderness when the sterility of her old preoccupations became apparent to her. Probably the most eminent critic in England, Cyril Connolly, the editor of the late <u>Horizon</u>, England's best literary review, and American critics and writers such as Cristopher Isherwood and Carson McCullers, have attested to the serious quality of this work, and I am confident that it will be seen in its true light, a book with a significant moral import, highly relevant to our times, when it is reconsidered sooner or later. It is even better known that my latest play "The Rose Tattoo" was a warmly affectionate study of those lovable traits that I have found in your people. As a matter of fact, some people have felt that I am <u>too</u> sentimental about Rome and Italy. I don't think so.

Of course it is true that I am not a conventional member of the "haute bourgeoisie". I was well-born and I have been well-bred, but like most artists, in America and everywhere else in the world, I have no use for money or class snobbishness. I suppose my private life is unconventional, but it is discreetly unconventional, and I have always observed the proprieties of any group that I am thrown with. I live according to fairly strict moral principles, and the predominant tone of all my work is deeply and instinctively moral.

I am not writing this as a plea for reinstatement at the club. I am sailing October 2nd and I have no present plans for a return to Italy. If the action of the club has been truly reported to me, I cannot help but regard it as a totally gratuitous "slap in the face" from a quarter where I would least expect it. Because you were kind enough to offer me the use of the pool (I have never applied for permanent membership: I paid for a 3 months guest-membership solely in order to swim there), I thought I would let you know what happened, or what this journalist told me that he had been told had happened. I <u>would </u>very much like to know if the report is true.

Of course I also hope to talk to you again, before I leave here, about the Anna Magnani - Tattoo situation. I have been working so hard on my new play, which has involved trips to Germany for conference with Elia Kazan, and which has left me completely exhausted, now that it is finished, that I have been more or less "out of touch" with that project lately. But I did hear recently from Miss Crawford who says that at least two important

groups are very much interested in making the picture. My own interest is intense as ever, and now that the play is completed, I can give more attention to it than I have for the past month.

Please forgive me for troubling you with the other personal matter. But I'm sure you understand how something like that can hurt a person's feelings, especially when he knows it is not justified and when it casts a shadow over a place he has loved so sincerely.

Cordially

[TW was less than candid in appealing to Ercole Graziadei, who had introduced him to the private club and who was perhaps unaware of the event which now threatened disbarment: "The Mgr. called me from the pool to say 'guests had protested that Salvatore had gone in swimming without taking a shower'. Shouldn't have taken him out there. May result in loss of the pool which was my great and almost only comfort here this summer. Hate rich Italians!" (*Journal*, August 31, 1952). Salvatore Maresca, TW's former lover, reappeared during Frank Merlo's visit to Sicily (see letter # 256).

TW took revenge on the "'Circolo de Golfo'" by making it the retreat of a corrupt generalissimo in the latest draft of *Camino Real* (September 1952, HRC).]

246. To Audrey Wood

[45 Via Aurora, Rome]
9/12/52.
[TLS, 1 p. HRC]

Dear Audrey:

"To you from failing hands we throw the torch, Etc!"

Sorry about the delay but I have never felt quite so tired in my long and eventful life.

The Roman typist was terrible. It will have to be typed over, so I am sending you only one copy. Will edit and mail another copy to Gadg.

After much prompting and prodding, The Horse managed to get us bookings on the Queen Mary, sailing from South Hampton on October 2. I expect we'll be leaving here around the 20th so as to have a little time with Maria in London. She has a bit part in the Houston-Ferrer picture. We are going to store the car here, so we won't have to ship it back and forth.

Finally got a copy of Jack Dunphy's book. It is damned good. I really like his writing better than Truman's.

My own work has finally had social repercussions. I was informed that the members of the "Circolo de Golfo", a private club where I swim 20 lengths a day in a crystal-clear pool, would not accept me because of "The Roman Spring of Mrs. Stone". This news did not come directly from the club but from EUROPEO a picture-magazine. They arrived with photographers to get picture and statement from me. I gave them neither! Regret the pool but fortunately I was not kicked out till the end of the season.

With love, Tenn.

[Apropos of "failing hands," TW could find "no wings" in the revised draft of *Camino Real* which he mailed to Audrey Wood on September 15: "And such a long time on it! What a terribly tired old boy I've gotten to be" (*Journal*, September 6 or 7, 1952).

Jack Dunphy, a fiction client of Liebling-Wood, dedicated *Friends and Vague Lovers* (1952) to his companion, Truman Capote. The novel was fairly well received and reminded one critic of *The Roman Spring of Mrs. Stone* (1950) to which it bears a passing resemblance.]

247. To Jo Mielziner

[Hotel Excelsior, Naples]
[September 1952]
[TLS, 2 pp. BRTC]

Dear Jo:

Thanks for your letter and please forgive me for not replying sooner. I was in Germany when it arrived, conferring with Gadg in Munich, and after I returned there was a great deal of work to do. If the script is still not right, it isn't because of any lack of effort, I can assure you. I have virtually devoted a whole year to work on this one project. I'm not sure I should have. It never fails to excite me, but I think it is much the hardest thing I've ever tried to do. Now I've mailed a fairly definitive script to Audrey. I think this one is close enough to the final version that it should be submitted to producers, designers, Etc. as a basis for yes or no. I'm not saying it's good, I'm just saying it's just about the best that I can do with it, and I've said the same thing to Gadg. Gadg and I talked over the phone yesterday and we spoke of you and Gadg feels that you shouldn't commit yourself on the basis of "potentialities" (what the play <u>might</u> be) but how you feel about it

as it now stands. He thinks you ought to feel really satisfied with it - "enthusiastic" was his word - before you undertake to design it. I think we have to have an atmosphere of enthusiasm in order to contend with this very difficult project. That doesn't mean we have to say a lot of flattering things that we don't mean about it but simply that anyone engaged in it has to feel a genuine - what's the word? - emotional alliance with it. It can't be just another job for anybody. I know you don't take "jobs" but Gadg and I were both afraid you might out of loyalty, or something like that, want to undertake it without being really keen on it, and that wouldn't do.

I think the basic scenic problem is much what we talked about before. This is an intensely romantic script, and it needs a magic background. Real visual enchantment! - both in the set and the lighting. The set no longer has much technical difficulty. Fundamentally, it is just a plaza contained by three facades and three arches, one for the alley-way-out through the "Arch of Triumph", and two "Moorish-looking" arches downstage right and left. There is one interior the Gypsy's which could be dropped in or pushed in from the wings. The important thing is the visual atmosphere of a romantic mystery. I can't visualize your idea of a "bear-pit" and it doesn't strike a responsive chord. It doesn't sound beautiful, and I think the plaza should have the haunting loveliness of one of those lonely-looking plazas and colonnades in a Chirico - not like that but being emotionally evocative and disturbing to that degree.

Audrey will give you a copy of the new script, and that has more details in it about the design. But the important point is the one of "visual enchantment", and I do think there should be a single set (aside from the Gypsy's interior) which is changed only by lighting. That, of course - the lighting! - will be terribly important. I don't need to say so. - There won't be any spatial problem as there was with "Summer and Smoke" as you have a whole plaza, a few tables on a low terrace at one side, a small fountain in the middle, as the only things to occupy the exterior space aside from the actors and dancers.

I'm sailing Oct. 2nd on the "Mary". Gadg will be in New York a week later than I get there. I do hope you will have thought this out, whether you feel enough real interest or stimulation to work well on it and what you want to do with it if you do, when we get there, as it will be necessary to get organized very quickly if we have a production this season.

So far no producer is set, as scripts haven't gone out. I think Lucinda will probably be sent a script at the same time.

Ever, Tennessee

[Jo Mielziner (1901-1976) "felt like an ungrateful dog" for having criticized *Camino Real*: "I suppose it was my desire to have this be your greatest script of all." He suggested a "'labyrinth'" or "bear pit" to convey Kilroy's entrapment and hoped to use "projected images and patterns and colors" (to TW, August 26, 1952, HRC) to advance the various blocks. Mielziner's sets for *The Glass Menagerie* (1945), *Streetcar* (1947), and *Summer and Smoke* (1948) had deftly realized the psychological effects of restricted space, apparently the same challenge which he foresaw in *Camino Real*.

TW wrote this letter in Naples, probably in mid-September 1952, after completing the latest revision of *Camino Real*. As planned, he and Frank Merlo sailed from Southampton on October 2 and landed in New York on the 7th.]

248. To Gilbert Maxwell

"NIX ON NIXON CLUB"
59 E. 54th Street
New York, N.Y.
October 8, 1952
[TLS, 1 p. HRC]

Dear Gil:

I think some day you should write a book in the style of your letters, perhaps a book of letters about bringing culture to Miami in the fifties! (The decade, my dear, not your age!)

I have your poems, safe and sound, but Laughlin is knocking about the Orient for the Ford foundation which is getting out a journal of which he is editor, it is to be a compedium of world letters, and he is the hatchet man in the Far East at this moment. I read the poems to myself and aloud to guests. Go Looking, October Schoolroom, The Terrapin, are probably my favorites, but so many are lovely it's hard to choose. I can't guarantee that Laughlin, with his very modern bias, will be altogether sympathetic to the traditional lyric tone of most of these poems, but if he isn't, there are other houses. I've only been back two days, and Laughlin doesn't return till late November. Miss Bigelow is here. She has a rather ambiguous sort of a sinecure at the Theatre Guild. Nobody quite knows what her position is, but I did see her

literally spring up two flights of stairs to fetch Miss Helpburn a pack of Parliament cigarettes, for which gallantry she was rewarded by the sour comment that actors would smoke them up if they were left on the table. It seems that she had her name as co-producer on one of the playbills at Westport this summer. Perhaps she is really working into something there, but on the other hand she may be working out of it just as fast. She is very brisk and important, you'd hardly know Our Polly, and has put on a good deal of weight. You'd better send her the Mayo's diet. I took her to lunch. (She invited me) She had Hungarian goulash with noodles, a side order of French fries, a large salad and a butterscotch meringue pie. I had a lean lamb chop and lettuce with lemon juice, and that is the price we pay for our perennial figures! Are they worth it?!

I don't share your enthusiasm for Dick Orme. He is amusing and agreeable but can be a terrible bitch! Joel Harris I do like a great deal. Do you know Mary at Lafitte's, the former co-partner?

How long I stay here depends on whether or not the play just finished is to be produced this season, and that will not be quite definite till Kazan returns from Europe the end of this month. If it doesn't go on this season, I'll be seeing you about cranberry picking time and we can sell 'em together, with four arms. The old gentleman is enduring Saint Louis till we fetch him South again. I have been sending him an allowance of $200. a month to supplement his rather meagre pension from the Episcopal church. Yesterday Mother sent his last check back to me, saying he didn't need it since he was staying with her. I doubt very much that both of them are still alive in that house! - Love -

10.

[TW remarked earlier that Richard Nixon, the Vice-Presidential nominee, "looks like the gradeschool bully that used to wait for me behind a broken fence and twist my ear to make me say obscene things" (to Kazan, August 23, 1952, WUCA).

James Laughlin was the general editor of *Perspectives USA* (1952-1956), a publication financed by the Ford Foundation and primarily distributed abroad in foreign language editions to represent "the intellectual and artistic life of the United States" (qtd. in *New York Times*, April 7, 1952). Several stories by TW were reprinted in the quarterly, including "Three Players of a Summer Game" (1952).

Gilbert Maxwell's fourth collection, *Go Looking: Poems, 1933-1953*, was published by Bruce Humphries, Inc., in 1954. In a brief preface TW described the author as "a lyric talent of the first magnitude."

Paul Bigelow served primarily as co-director Terry Helburn's assistant at the Theatre Guild.

Richard Orme, Mary Collins, and Joel Harris were New Orleans figures associated with TW. Orme owned the property at 632 St. Peter Street which TW rented in 1946, while Collins was a co-owner of Café Lafitte in the French Quarter. Joel Harris was the grandson of Joel Chandler Harris, author of the Uncle Remus stories.]

249. To Elia "Gadg" Kazan

[59 East 54th Street, New York]
[October 1952]
[TL, 1 p. HRC]

Dear Gadg:

I do hope you are hurrying back here. Cheryl is eager to get started on the production which is quite natural since there is so much to be done, but she is making plans and decisions, I am afraid, that you ought to have a part in. I had a short letter from Jo. He says he is now "enthusiastic", but I know that Cheryl considers his fee too high and doesn't want to use him. She is also against Lucinda. She showed me a bunch of costumes sketched by some young man she's discovered. They look good to me. But all these matters should be considered by you. I don't feel that my position is at all strong without you. She says she has budgetted the show, tentatively, at $140,000. and it can break even at $19,000. These figures sound reasonable but my judgement in such matters is very incompetent, and this desire to get things at cut-rate, which is still manifest in the lady, is something that you can cope with much better than I. On the other hand, I think she is genuinely excited, now, over the project. How soon can we expect you on these shores?

This week-end I went to Philly to see the new Arthur Laurents play starring Shirley Booth. The play is thin, but pleasant and seems to appeal to the audience. Shirley magnificent in it. I was greatly impressed by Ben Edwards' set, it was practical, free, and imaginative, and he had lit it extremely well himself. I thought I'd mention this as I know you like his work, too. There's an Italian actor in it, DiLucca, who would make a fine Casanova.

Cheryl has a list of actors. Two I liked were Isa Miranda for Camille, March or Boyer for Casanova. I don't like the idea of using Merighi

(the fat woman in Rose Tattoo) for the Gypsy, do you? I think the Gypsy
and Old Prudence could be played by the same actress. I thought of
Josephine Brown.

Still working on script, taking it to St. Louis with me for a few days
visit with Mother and Grandfather.

Refrain: when do you get back?

Love,

[Added to Jo Mielziner's newfound "enthusiasm" for *Camino Real* was confidence
that its "difficult production problems" could be solved with "imagination" and
"ingenuity" (to TW, October 2, 1952, BRTC). Mielziner's withdrawal from the
project—a "bitter disappointment" to the designer—was presumably caused by a
"tight time schedule" (to TW, November 19, 1952, BRTC) rather than the
producer's inflexible thrift. Lucinda Ballard designed costumes for *Streetcar* but not
Camino Real.

The Time of the Cuckoo (1952) played in Philadelphia for two weeks
(September 29-October 11) and ran for a season on Broadway. The novice pro-
ducer Irene Selznick had closed the original version of the show—"Heartsong"—in
Philadelphia in 1947. No actor cited by TW was cast in *Camino Real*.

TW wrote to Maria Britneva on October 25 following a brief visit to Clayton:
"Dinky Dakin, sister Rose with attendant, Grandfather and Mother were all there,
one big happy family! I am still alive" (qtd. in St. Just, p. 61).

When Elia Kazan returned to the States in early-November, he was singularly
bent upon work and defying former friends and colleagues who had scorned his
cooperation with the House Un-American Activities Committee. "Only the discerning few could see what I was saying by my behavior: 'You can't hurt me; you
haven't penetrated my guard; I can beat you at any game you choose to play'"
(Kazan, p. 484).

TW wrote this letter after returning from Philadelphia, perhaps early in the
week of October 12, 1952.]

250. To Elia "Gadg" Kazan

[59 East 54th Street, New York]
[late-October 1952]
[TLS, 1 p. HRC]

Dear Gadg:

As Irene might phrase it: "This is to clarify my position" as stated in
the cable I sent you yesterday from Audrey's office after reading her copy

of your letter to Cheryl. Your letters are so portentous that they are being ~~distributed~~ passed among us like the one eye of the fatal sisters!

I am very, very disturbed by the fact that you say that you have not read the script but that it has been read by Freddie and Molly with a disfavor which I suspect you are under-stating.

I'm not going to give you any kind of a pitch for the play. Communication between you and me can be on a level where total honesty and simplicity prevail, for we are both about equally grown-up and knowing. I don't like being treated like a sensitive plant. I want to have it straight. I think I have already proved that I can take it.

I find it difficult to believe, anxiety and uncertainty notwithstanding, that there is still some irreconcilable difference in what you expect of the play and what I have given it. I haven't stopped working on the script a single day since the present draft was typed up and shall doubtless continue to work on it till it opens on Broadway, but of course the possibility must be faced that you have some basic objection which I, with all the willingness in the world, might still find myself unable to satisfy. And here I am sort of hung-up in New York, you in Europe, Grandfather in Memphis, the lease running out on the apartment and a new one to be signed or not signed almost immediately and some disposition to be made of the old gentleman and ourselves, Etc! Therefore it would be enormously valuable for you to refresh yourself, temporarily, in some way, just long enough to give the script one reading and let me know the extent of your dissatisfaction with it. I am sending you a set of the changes which I have made since the script was typed up - c/o Twenty-Foxes in Paris. They mostly affect the Marguerite material - blocks 12 & 13 - and Audrey and Cheryl feel they make a real improvement. I have greatly shortened the post-Gypsy scene between Jacques and Gutman and I am thinking of changing the position of Jacques' letter-scene in Block Five as it seems to impede the flow there. Perhaps it could be worked into the very first scene of the play in a condensed form. So you see I am not stopping work on play. I know there is work to be done. I only want to know if the work you want done and the work I want done can be brought close enough together to make it possible for us to put the show on this season. Can you give me "an estimate" real soon?

Love, Tenn.

[Fredric March, who starred in *Man on a Tightrope*, and Molly Kazan, Elia's wife, were the unwelcome critics of *Camino Real*. TW described Molly as "a pain" in her husband's "derriere" and as his own "bête-noir" (qtd. in St. Just, pp. 71 and 69).

"Communication" with TW was especially close after Kazan's damaging testimony in Washington: "We both felt vulnerable to the depredations of an unsympathetic world, distrustful of the success we'd had, suspicious of those in favor, anticipating put-downs, expecting insufficient appreciation and reward. The most loyal and understanding friend I had through those black months was Tennessee Williams" (Kazan, p. 495).

"Blocks 12 & 13" (Block Ten in the published text) of *Camino Real* bring the relationship of Marguerite Gautier and Jacques Casanova to a bittersweet finale, as she rejects his offer of love and departs for an encounter with a youthful hustler.]

251. To Edwina Dakin Williams

SH: *The* Robert Clay
Miami, Florida
Nov. 9, 1952
[TLS, 2 pp. HRC]

Dear Mother:

I am here at the Robert Clay hotel in Miami for a short rest as the state of indecision about the play production had gotten on my nerves. Kazan arrives in America this Tuesday and I won't know until a day or two later whether or not he is satisfied with the play script as it now stands. I thought it was better to let him and Cheryl thrash out their difficulties alone, with me at a restful distance till the decision is made. Of course if Gadg (Kazan) is now satisfied with the script and can reconcile his views with Cheryl's, I will return in about a week to start the production with them, but if an agreement isn't reached or if Gadg wants a good deal more work done on the script, I will procede to Key West and open the house there and Frank will come on down to join me. I think it is more likely, though, that I will be called back to New York. Before I left I wired Grandfather that I was coming down here, for at least a while, and have invited him to join me if he wishes to. I had to do this as I told him in St. Louis that we would be coming South in about two weeks. Now I would like to know if you feel able to stay with him in Key West (with Susie, of course) if I do have to go back to New York for the production. I feel that Key West would be better for grandfather than New York at a time when both Frank and I will be

pretty occupied with all the goings-on that are attendant on preparing a new play. If you can't make it, or Susie can't and you don't want to settle for Leona (our old maid, there) - I will take Grandfather back with me to New York. We have the bedroom for him even if we stay in the present apartment, and we've found another larger one which we will take if it's still available by the time a decision about the play has been reached, probably Wednesday or Thursday. I will be glad to pay Susie's salary ($35. a week) and transportation if you bring her down here with you and whatever other extra expenses are involved and my friend Gilbert Maxwell, who teaches here in Miami, can see about finding a place for Susie to stay here before you'd go on to Key West, or I could do that myself, since I could probably wait here till you arrive.

I sent Grandfather a special delivery letter last night explaining the situation. I hope he doesn't find it too confusing. I'm sure it will all work out, one way or another. My main consideration is making a comfortable arrangement for you and him. It would not be difficult, now, to have him in New York as I'm not likely to have much more work to do at home on the play, if the production starts now.

Incidentally our new dog has arrived, an English bull puppy only six weeks old, named "Mr. Moon". He is even cuter than Jiggs, is "paper-trained" and bursting with energy, a voracious eater, and addicted to cutting his teeth on shoes, trouser-cuffs and telephone wires. We have a little whip called a "persuader" to break him of these obnoxious habits. He gets up at daybreak and complains loudly till he is let out of the kitchen where he sleeps, but I don't suppose Grandfather would hear him and these anti-social practises will be corrected in time. Please write or wire soon as possible your plans. With love -

Tom.

[The "difficulties" faced by Elia Kazan and Cheryl Crawford were primarily financial, as TW noted in prior correspondence: "He demands an expensive production {of *Camino Real*}, she wants a modest one. I am sick of the whole thing and longing for Key West or Europe again" (qtd. in St. Just, p. 65). He warned Kazan that we may "find ourselves out of a producer unless some compromise can be effected between your prodigality and her caution" (October 21, 1952, WUCA). Crawford later reported that *Camino Real* was capitalized at $125,000, with the financial support of associates Ethel Reiner and Walter P. Chrysler, Jr.

While in Miami TW worked on a "double-volume" of poems and stories as

requested by James Laughlin. In correspondence with Robert MacGregor, Laughlin's editorial assistant, TW listed eight of the nine stories which eventually appeared in the collection *Hard Candy* (1954). "Kingdom of Earth" (1954) was tentatively penned in the margin and would require special treatment when published (November 9, 1952, Houghton).

"Jiggs" was the most petted of the Williams family dogs.]

252. To Paul Bowles

[1431 Duncan Street
Key West, Florida]
[January 1953]
[TLS, 1 p. HRC]

Dear Paul:

I'm writing you from my studio in Key West and the stains on the paper, the last remaining sheet on my work-table, are from an attempt at oil-painting. This is a heavenly place to work at anything creative. The studio is only one-room but is a complete living-unit as there is a bathroom built onto it and numerous electric outlets. A sky-light and jalousies on all sides and a ventilator fan for the hot days, lots of book-shelves and cabinets. When you're in America you and Janie must visit us here. Or you could occupy the house while we are away, either or both. The social life of the island is something appaling. I have given it up. I simply go to the movies and home to bed - after supper. The sky is constantly changing, the weather is soft and lovely and at least four days out of a week the water is perfect for swimming. I wish you would tell me more about your island in the Indian ocean. Why would I love it? Are the people beautiful and friendly? The next time we go abroad, which will be in the late Spring this year, we will plan to stay much longer, perhaps for a whole year or nine months, as I will not have another play next season and also because I don't want to do much writing. I want to rest from it a while as I haven't stopped for more than a week or two in the last fifteen years and I think the brain-cells are exhausted. That is if there are any such cells left in my personality complex! I think you are wise to come back to America for a while now, even if only to see what you are missing when you're away. Frank, Audrey, and I worked very hard on Gadg to get you for "Camino" and if the show had been put off till next season, as seemed likely at one

point owing to the determined resistance of Gadg's wife, we might eventually have won him over. He does like your music, but I think he and Molly Kazan have a real phobia about your writing. This comes from Molly, not Gadg. She is a dedicated person, the self-appointed scourge of Bohemia, and the year that "Sheltering Sky" came out, she sent us a carbon copy of a vitriolic review of it that she was trying unsuccessfully to market. It seemed to obsess her. I can't help thinking this attitude toward your writing has influenced Gadg against you as a composer. So far we have no composer and I doubt that there will be any original score. Probably we will just have a guitarist and selected tunes, although the play needs a score more than any other I've written. Gadg's tactical position is now very strong, and mine relatively very weak, as everything he has done has made money while my last two plays, Summer and Tattoo, have both lost money.

We saw a good deal of Janie in New York. She seems unusually well, is getting a little plump, and her play is going forward. She has a new third act. I haven't read it yet but she and Audrey both feel it is a distinct improvement. I finally got hold of "Two Serious Ladies" and it is one of my very favorite works of all time, it is altogether original and has a reality all its own, which is fearfully real. We have acquired an English-bull puppy named Mr. Moon who will be travelling with us from now on, poor creature, wherever we may go. Luckily he is blessed with an amiable nature.

Love - 10.

[TW spent the holidays with his mother and grandfather—and with Frank Merlo as well—in Key West and planned to return to New York in mid-January for rehearsals of Camino Real. Tryouts in New Haven (February 23-28) and Philadelphia (March 3-14) would precede the Broadway opening on March 19, 1953.

Paul Bowles composed music for The Glass Menagerie and Summer and Smoke, later for Sweet Bird of Youth (1959) and The Milk Train Doesn't Stop Here Anymore (1963). Bernardo Segall wrote the incidental score for Camino Real.

Correspondence between TW and the Kazans in the preceding December marked a crisis in plans for a spring production of Camino Real. Molly Kazan accused TW of having used his own "desperate" identification with the play as a "psychological weapon" against "friends and colleagues." She challenged him to "identify" instead with an audience and to write a first act with a climactic "carryover for Kilroy" (December 9, 1952, HRC).

Elia Kazan's "tactical" strength—occasioned by successful film work—was evident in the copious "suggestions" for revision of *Camino Real*, as repeated in recent correspondence. Kazan also urged TW to write a coherent first act—"You can forget the second act till rehearsal"—and accurately foresaw the consequences of failing to do so: "Thousand-odd people leaving their seats for the intermission not knowing what the hell we brought them to the theatre for in the first place" (December 10, 1952, HRC).

TW refers to Jane Bowles's play, *In the Summerhouse* (1953), and to her novel, *Two Serious Ladies* (1943).]

253. To Justin Brooks Atkinson

["on the train"]
March 24, 1953.
[TLS w/ marginalia, 1 p. BRTC]

Dear Brooks:

First of all, I want to thank you, as usual, for one of my most discerning and sympathetic notices, but then I want to ask you why, since you have seemingly understood so much, you have failed to understand a little bit more this time? I can't believe that you really think I have painted the world in blacker colors than it now wears, or that it is melancholia, psycopathic of me, to see it in those shades, and surely the final scenes of the play must have conveyed their true meaning which is far from negative, and which I truly believe: namely, that tenderness, humanity of feeling - "the violets in the mountains" - give the dying animal a sort of after-life, or triumph over his death. It seems to me that that point is almost too clear, too coarsely stated. I wanted no one to miss it. I think it makes this play the most affirmative one I have written. It may have been implicit in the others, I think it was, but here it is fairly shouted.

Pride tells me to keep a stoic silence about my hurt, but I don't think pride should prevail in my relations with you, the one who has most bravely, consistently stood by me in the past and for whom I have such grateful affection, in whom I feel such trust, and from whom I have no secrets as imperfect artist and person. Has this play alienated your old regard for my work? Do you feel as others that it is a "mish-mash" of muddy symbols and meaningless theatricalism, were you pulling your punches? No matter what you say, I think it would help me at this dark moment if you would level with me. All of us felt, reading your notice, that

you had things to say that you were refraining from saying, perhaps out of kindness, perhaps because you weren't sure.

I wanted to talk to you before I left town. Shyness prevented me from calling you myself but Margo said she tried to reach you but couldn't. - I'm writing this on the train, going back to Key West where I hope I'll be able to pick up some other work, now that nothing more can be done to help this one. It helps me to write you this and would help me still more if you feel inclined to answer.

Ever, Tennessee.

[Invective and ridicule dominated the opening-night reviews of *Camino Real*. It was, John Chapman wrote, "an enormous jumble of five-cent philosophy, $3.98 words, ballet, music, symbolism, allegory, pretentiousness, portentousness, lackwit humor, existentialism and overall bushwah" (*New York Daily News*, March 20, 1953). Atkinson was undaunted by the complexity of the play and judged the lyrical effect to be "as eloquent and rhythmic as a piece of music." He was shocked, however, by TW's "pessimism" and revolted by the "psychopathic bitterness" of *Camino Real*. His closing would not be quoted by any publicist: "Even the people who respect Mr. Williams' courage and recognize his talent are likely to be aghast at what he has to say" (*New York Times*, March 20, 1953).

Typed in the upper margin is TW's name and Key West address.]

254. To Walter Kerr

1431 Duncan Street
Key West, Fla.
March 31, 1953
[TLS, 2 pp. SHS of Wisconsin]

Dear Mr. Kerr:

I'm feeling a little punch-drunk from the feared but not quite fully anticipated attack at your hands and a quorum of your colleagues but I would like to attempt to get a few things off my chest in reply. Your original notice was too factually inaccurate, in a seemingly cynical way, to be answerable at all, but your Sunday notice, although equally adverse to the play, does seem to indicate some serious attention.

One night out of town Kazan and I were speculating about the probable critical reception in New York and I recall saying that I thought we would only get two good notices but that one of them would be Kerr's.

I was not at all sure of getting Atkinson's, because, although he's always been my main stand-by in the past, I felt that Brooks, although he's scrupulously fair toward anything he reviews, would be appalled by the episodes of decadance and brutality, - which he was, but which, as usual, he did not allow to prejudice his estimate of the work as a whole.

What I would like to know is, Don't you see that this play - as a concentrate, a distillation of the world and time we live in - surely you don't think it is better than a night-mare!? - is a clear and honest picture?

Two: don't you also recognize it as a very earnest plea for certain fundamental, simply Christian, attributes of the human heart, through which we might still survive?

Three: have you no appreciation of the tremendous technical demands of such a work, its complexities and difficulties, and at least the technical skill with which all of us involved in the production have managed to meet them? - As far as I remember at this moment, you made no mention more than perfunctory of music or choreography or the great plastic richness contributed by the designer, Lem Ayres, and you certainly did not go a step out of your way to give due tribute to such brilliant performances as Wallach's and Barbara Baxley's. Surely they had nothing to do with whatever alienated you from the play itself and I, who am hypercritical of all performers in a work of my own, can think of no performances but Laurette Taylor's that were so luminous and touching. And how about the work of Kazan? To undertake this play took a very notable courage, since no director ever tackled a play more difficult, and there were pieces of staging in it the like of which I know, and you know, that you'll wait many and many a season to see again.

To sum up:

Mr. Kerr, I believe in your honesty! I believe you said what you honestly think and feel about this play, but I don't think you fulfilled your entire obligation as a critic, since I think you didn't try very hard to encompass intentions and attitudes that are not and should not necessarily be coincident with your own. I hope I am talking sense to you. I am almost too tired and baffled to know what I'm saying, but that is only since March 20th. I did know what I was saying and doing in "Camino Real" and that it is one of my three best plays, that I worked on it two years for no financial profit but the two thousand dollar advance. Kazan and Ayres and I all waived royalties immediately after the N.Y. opening, and were all

Lemuel Ayers, full set design for Camino Real *(1953).*

taking the minimum. (This is a rather squalid parenthetical comment, but I want you to realize that this was not a big money-making scheme, if you had any such misapprehension about it! And Cheryl Crawford lost forty thousand on Rose Tattoo and stands to lose about three times that much on this one.)

If I had not been deluged, literally, with letters and wires expressing outrage over the play's critical reception, far more than for all my other plays put together, and if so many people had not come up to me after performances, when I waited in back of the house, with such unmistakably heart-felt enthusiasm, far more than I ever got, even, from any audience at "streetcar" - I wouldn't have the nerve to question your verdict. But silence is only golden when there is nothing to say and I still think I have a great deal to say no matter how badly I say it.

Cordially, Tennessee Williams

[Walter Kerr (1913-1996) restated much of his "Sunday notice" (*New York Herald Tribune*, March 29, 1953) in reply to TW's present correspondence. Evident in *The Rose Tattoo* and *Camino Real* was a movement "toward the cerebral" which

alarmed the reviewer and threatened the playwright. "Don't do it," he warned TW, for "what makes you an artist of the first rank is your intuitive gift for penetrating reality" without "junking {it} in the process" (April 13, 1953, HRC).

Kerr echoes pre-production correspondence in which Elia Kazan urged TW to integrate the "social" and "universal" aspects of *Camino Real*. Only then could he succeed in dramatizing "what is happening in the world of 1952" to those "irregulars" (November 17, 1952, HRC) with whom they both identified. The director and cast—especially Eli Wallach and Barbara Baxley, whose performances as Kilroy and Esmeralda were generally admired—survived the critical wreckage, but Kerr had little to say of their work because the production seemed "dead at the core."

Kazan later observed—and both author and producer agreed—that Lemuel Ayers had designed "a lugubrious realistic setting" (Kazan, p. 497) which lacked the "plastic richness" cited by TW. A former college friend of TW, Ayers had designed the sets for many Broadway shows, including *Oklahoma!* (1943).]

255. To Cheryl Crawford

[1431 Duncan Street
Key West, Florida]
3/31/53
[TLS, 1 p. BRTC]

Dear Cheryl:

Whenever I talk about you, I say: "Cheryl is a great fighter, she is always there when you need her." I can't possibly tell you what this experience has meant to me in the way of a reaffirmation of belief in people, and what can possibly stack up against that as a positive gain? Certainly nothing of a commercial nature!

Naturally it is not with a virginal freshness that I can continue work on the play now, but when I got back here I discovered among my old papers, left here last Spring, an introduction to play in which Quixote arrives, down an aisle of theatre, ranting and raving about the romantic quest above a loud singing wind, and it seems to me that would make a good way to begin. It involves slight changes in staging. I've also conceived a recapitulation of the Act One finale chase scene after Kilroy snatches his gold heart from the medical group. I think this gives a revival of pure physical activity which the play seemed to need after his death. The chase is now ghostly, almost all in his mind, no actual pursuers, but only sounds and voices, terminating in the box from which he leapt before. He leaps back into plaza at a point in Esmeralda's prayer. I'm working hard to get

this stuff in order and it should be mailed to you before the week-end. With all this discussion and controversy, and the precedent of Logan's work on "Wish You Were Here", I think we could interest people in post-production changes of this sort. I don't doubt that they will illuminate the play and add to the final effect, but they will increase the playing time somewhat. Cuts can be made to partially compensate for them, such as the Winchell bit which obviously didn't pay off in any support from him. I'm enclosing copy of letter I just wrote Kerr. I also wrote Brooks and Hawkins, though in much different vein. I think we ought to show fight in this situation.

Much love from 10.

["Do believe that I'll always be here fighting for you," Cheryl Crawford assured TW in the aftermath of *Camino Real*. She added that the *New York Times* planned to feature the "controversy" surrounding the play and "like a panther" (April 3, 1953, U of Houston) she had arranged for Edith Sitwell to write a letter of support. "May a visiting Englishwoman say how profoundly impressed and moved she was by 'Camino Real'" (*New York Times*, April 5, 1953), began Sitwell's defense.

Regarding "gain," Crawford lost no time in persuading Audrey Wood that *Camino Real* "might have a chance to run if we pay no royalties, at least until we see if we can get out of the woods" (March 25, 1953, HRC). The second-week gross fell far below house capacity, but Crawford felt that business was "tremendously encouraging" (April 3, 1953, U of Houston), as she informed TW.

The Don Quixote "introduction" cited by TW is probably the same "first scene" to which Elia Kazan refers in correspondence. He wrote that it was added to *Camino Real* after the Broadway opening because TW "thought it necessary" (to Leighton, July 30, 1957, HRC). Publication of the book in October 1953 saw Quixote's arrival transferred to a new prologue.

Joshua Logan attended the New Haven premiere of *Camino Real* and shared with TW and Elia Kazan both his general enthusiasm for the play and his specific advice for revision: "'Work through Kilroy'" (February 26, 1953, Library of Congress).

Logan's post-production doctoring of the musical *Wish You Were Here* (1952) had turned "a crying flop" into a "sold out {hit} with standing room for two years!" (Logan, *Josh* (1976).]

256. To Justin Brooks Atkinson

1431 Duncan Street
Key West, Fla.
April 3, 1953
[TLS, 4 pp. BRTC]

Dear Brooks:

You have no idea how much less lonely your letter made me feel, even though our points of view are as disparate as you say. It was not the mandatory failure of my play that so depressed me but the feeling that I was no longer able to communicate with the arbiters of that vocation to which I have completely committed myself and my life for the past fifteen years or more. Of course your letter is not the only one that has helped to relieve this feeling of being shut out and the door barred against me. Last night I got a special delivery letter from Edith Sitwell, posted just before sailing back to Europe, which was almost in itself enough to justify the trials that I've been through, and for many days, now, ever since the play began its pilgrimage in New Haven, an unprecedented, in my experience, flood of correspondance from people, many of whom objected as you did, to certain things in the play, some aspects of it, but who nearly all repeated that same thing, that it made them "feel less lonely". When so many people, more than were moving to write me about "Streetcar" and "Menagerie" put together - even, I believe, during the whole course of their long runs - tell me that it touched and moved them deeply, I can't keep on feeling that it was all in vain. No doubt some of these letters were prompted by compassion over the play's treatment by critics, but by far the majority of them had a tone which could only come from true feeling about the work itself. For myself I am comforted, but for the others involved in the production, particularly Gadg and Cheryl and some of the young actors, I can't help feeling outraged. My work will survive in print for later consideration and probably other productions, but all the passion and power which they spent on this single production is tied up with its fate and outlives it only in memory.

I do wish you had not misunderstood the removal of the gold heart. That heart was only his physical heart. I see, now, that making it gold may have been misleading. It was only a jest upon a cliché, "heart of gold". His living, physical heart was a heart of gold, often pawned in the past, so often, in fact, that even death couldn't break the habit, but his true

(spiritual) heart was not a removable or transactable thing, for he was, in spirit, the same Kilroy that he was before they cut his living heart out of him.

In writing fantasy it is terribly hard to know when you have violated the boundaries of audience acceptance. Some will allow you absolute license, others almost none, and I don't suppose there is any way of assuring a uniform disarmament, no matter how carefully or subtley you prepare them. A lot of the grotesque comedy in this work, and I think that is its dominant element, even though all of it had a serious import back of it, is tracable to the spirit of the American comic-strip and the animated cartoons, where the most outrageous absurdities give the greatest delight. I'm sure you've seen the movie cartoons where the characters are blown sky-high one moment and are skipping gaily about the next, where various members of their bodies are destroyed and restored in the flicker of the projector, and nobody seems to mind the implausibility of it. I thought that this art-form had softened up my American audiences for the manifest illogicalities of Camino! (More's the pity!) The Messrs. Chapman and Kerr - (I stopped reading the notices after those came out - except for Hawkins which a true friend read over the phone at 3 A.M. when a combination of nembutal and seconal still hadn't worked) - were obviously not willing to be budged one centimeter from the strictest of literal approaches, or at least moralistic attitudes, toward something that literally got down on its knees and begged for imaginative participation.

I know how different your world is from mine. I read the book which followed the course of a year in your life and which expressed a [philosophical] sweetness and serenity of spirit which I've [seen] expressed nowhere else in contemporary [writing] and so I know the difference in these worlds. [My] own world, Brooks, is not bitter nor brutal nor even reconciled to corruption, at least not inwardly, as it exists in me. But I must tell you that I have lived in "the lower depths", which are a large strata of society, have fought my way only partially up out of them, and my work is a record of what I have seen, heard, felt and known on the way. I have known intimately a world haunted by frustrate and dreadful longings. ("Keen for him, all maimed creatures, deformed and mutilated! His homeless ghost is your own!") I have even spent nights in southern jails - wrist handcuffed to ankle and made to crawl - and seen negro women kicked and bludgeoned up and downstairs because the circumstances of their lives had turned them to prostitution, I have lived intimately with the

outcast and derelect and the desperate and found in them the longing, passionate, and bravely enduring, and, most of all, the tender. I have tried to make a record of their lives because my own has fitted me to do so. And I feel that each artist is sort of bound by honor to be the voice of that part of the world that he knows. I came out of the world that you belong to, Brooks, and descended to those under levels, passing through various levels on the way, and I have tried to keep in touch with them all. It is only the upper levels that have rejected me. I was kicked out of a Roman country-club last summer (where I swam for relief from the heat and other therapeutic measures and conducted myself with the most fastidious propriety) - because of "The Roman Spring of Mrs. Stone" and the fact that a poor young Italian painter - not of the "noblesse" - but a clean and scrupulous character - was my guest one afternoon. Some of this feeling of outrage against hypocrasy and brutishness is expressed in my work, but I don't think protest alone would ever animate that work, it is mostly the animation that comes from the finding in people of those expressions of sensibilities and longings that were in Blanche and Alma and Serafina and Kilroy and Marguerite and Jacques, and that is what my work is really about, and when it stops being about those things it will be finished. (Me, too.)

In a memorable conversation with George Jean Nathan he remarked, "A wise man is a happy man." and I said, "Well, I am a fool." but I wondered then and have wondered since if he is really happier than I am or wiser. I don't think of myself as gloomy although I am technically what Joseph Wood Krutch once called me "a romantic pessimist". But I find life so terribly engaging that I think of death with the utmost abhorrence. I could go on and on about my "world" and attitude toward it, but I am sure you don't want or need that much elucidation of it. But before I sail in June I hope to see you and give you what I think is almost the most eloquent study yet made of what goes on in the world that I try to speak for, "The Collected Letters of Hart Crane" - and maybe also his biography by Philip Horton. A tragic world but not a negative one, and his greatest work was an American anthem - "The Bridge" - whose failure was mainly one of a too intense idealism for its material. You once gave me a book which I cherish, so it will be fair return. And I will also send you a published "Camino Real". I have probably exhausted your patience, now, but I hope I have not yet forfeited your friendship!?

Yours ever, Tenn.

["Two long hand-written letters" from Brooks Atkinson asking TW to explain how he "'got that way'" (TW to Kazan, April 16, 1953, WUCA) spurred the present correspondence.

In a secondary review Atkinson described *Camino Real* as "a sensitively composed fantasy," but he observed that only Byron and Quixote escape "the jail-yard of vice" envisioned by TW. Kilroy, "'heart of gold'" notwithstanding, succumbs to "the hopelessness and degeneracy" of the Camino Real. In closing Atkinson urged TW to "find a less malignant theme" (*New York Times*, March 29, 1953).

Atkinson's "serenity of spirit" was evident in *Once Around the Sun* (1951), shipboard reading for TW in 1951. With "Keen for him, all maimed creatures," La Madrecita mourns the death of Kilroy in *Camino Real* (Block Fifteen).

George Jean Nathan, long an antagonist of TW, ridiculed *Camino Real* as an "exhausting minstrel show," whose innumerable characters "make cracks none of the others can understand, and who are presided over by an interlocutor in the person of Williams whose too many pre-performance drinks have gone to his head" (*New York Journal American*, April 5, 1953).

TW cites the Brom Weber edition of *The Letters of Hart Crane, 1916-1932* (1952), and the Philip Horton biography, *Hart Crane: The Life of an American Poet* (1937).

The right-hand margin of the fourth paragraph is partially obscured in the original typescript. Editorial insertions appear in brackets.]

Margo Jones and Brooks Atkinson, Dallas.

257. To James "Jay" Laughlin

1431 Duncan St.
Key West, Fla.
April 5, 1953
[TLS, 2 pp. Houghton]

Dear Jay:

I want to thank you for the never-failing appreciation you have for anything good in my work. Your letter meant a great deal to me, since I went through a pretty black period after those notices came out. I had suspected that we would be blasted by a quorum of the critics, ever since New Haven Gadg and I had expected or feared it pretty certainly, but even so there was a degree of militant incomprehension that seemed like an order to get out and stay out of the current theatre.

I'm glad that you felt poetry in the play. I can't agree with you about Gadg. I don't think this play was nearly as easy for him as Streetcar or Salesman, it was a much harder and more complex job, and he was working with players at least half of which were dancers and had no previous speaking experience on the stage, an inadequate budget and far from adequate time in rehearsal and try-out on the road. Gadg is not as fond of verbal values as he should be, but of all Broadway directors he has the most natural love of poetry. Not a single critic seemed to have any sense of the abstract, formal beauty of the piece. They concentrated on what each thing might mean in a literal, logical sense, and I can't help thinking that there was a general feeling of ill-will among them at what seemed new and intransigent in the work. I have had a couple of letters from Atkinson, in London, expressing moral and chauvinistic indignation over the pessimism which he says "American audiences" will not accept, that they don't like it in Anouhil and Sartre and will not accept it from me. He repeated America and American several times as if the play was a violation of national respect. Nevertheless I think he, almost alone, did make an effort to divorce his personal repugnance from his professional appraisal, and was frank about the source of that repugnance. A couple or three nights ago I got a special delivery letter from Edith Sitwell, couched in the most extravagant heart-felt terms, for which I was rightly overcome with gratitude, and there has been a flood of letters from people known and unknown, more ever than I got during the whole course of Streetcar, saying their love of the play and anger at its reception. So although it is a great, almost overpowering,

professional setback for me, I don't feel altogether hopeless about it.

Your advice is good. I have nothing more to expect from Broadway and if I go on writing plays, it must be with an absolute uncompromising fidelity to myself alone, that is, quite purely from now on. They say, on good authority, that the life-expectancy of an American literary talent is about 15 years and I have already long-exceeded that mark, since I got my first pay-check for writing at sixteen and have written every day since that I was able to punch the type-writer keys and very few days when I wasn't can be remembered. But I think the pressure of things to say is as great as ever, if not greater, but a lot of the native energy is depleted and the time has come to let up a little, shift gears, work under less steam. It would be a good thing if I could stop altogether for a while, but I find my daily existence almost unbearably tedious without beginning it at the typewriter. Frank and I plan to go abroad, this year, for a really extended stay, in fact we are planning to go all the way around the world, beginning in Italy, then Spain, then North Africa, then Greece and Istanbul, then Helsinki for a festival production of some plays of mine, then on from the near East to the Orient, to Ceylon and India and Japan. Thence back to America, when it will be necessary to start trying to "make a living" again, as I will have nothing left but my bonds by that time. Early next month I'm going to try my hand at directing a play. The play is Donald Windham's family-portrait called "The Starless Air", structurally inept but very true and poetic, and there is a chance, if this Houston try-out goes well, I might return to the States to stage it for Broadway about Xmas time: it's about a family Christmas dinner in Georgia.

May I start sending you short-stories for the proposed collection? I have them with me and am getting them in shape. They will have to be typed at your end of the line, and I think they ought to be sold by subscription only, since I want to include some, such as "Two On A Party" that might precipitate an awful row in the present time of reaction.

Ever, Tenn.

[Reviews of the New Haven tryout accurately forecast trouble for *Camino Real*. *Variety* predicted that "the ultimate reception will be governed by the ratio of play-goers who look for stimulation rather than straight entertainment in their theatrical fare." The preliminary verdict was that *Camino Real* presented "a severe mental challenge to an audience" (February 25, 1953) and seemed an unlikely hit.

Following the New York opening of *Camino Real,* James Laughlin commiserated with TW and criticized Elia Kazan's direction for having obscured the play's "philosophical depth and tragic beauty" (March 26, 1953, Houghton). TW's defense of Kazan brought a harsh reply from Laughlin: "Nobody who really had a 'natural love of poetry' could have behaved the way he did over his former Communist friends. There are limits. Gadge loves money and fame. I hope they make him miserable" (April 11, 1953, Houghton).

Laughlin proposed that the "bulk" of the stories intended for *Hard Candy* be issued in "a public volume" and the more controversial ones—"Two on a Party" (1952), "Hard Candy" (1954), "The Kingdom of Earth" (1954)—held for "a separate limited edition" (to TW, April 11, 1953, Houghton).]

258. To Justin Brooks Atkinson

1431 Duncan
Key West [Florida]
[early-April 1953]
[TLS, 2 pp. HRC]

Dear Brooks:

My heart is very light this evening, your letters and a continual flood of others have very effectively stemmed the gravitation it felt when I packed my bags in Manhattan a couple of weeks ago, when I first poured out my woes to you. Although Camino has built steadily since it opened and Audrey Wood says it may do over 20 grand this week, none of us are receiving or expect to receive a penny royalty from it, but the work was done for exactly what it has gained, a communion with people. I wish, only, that it could continue longer, of course it can't very long. Preserving it on paper isn't enough, a published play is only the shadow of one and not even a clear shadow. The colors, the music, the grace, the levitation, the quick inter-play of live beings suspended like fitful lightning in a cloud, those things are the play, not words, certainly not words on paper and certainly not any thoughts or ideas of an author, those shabby things snatched off basement counters at Gimbel's. The clearest thing ever said about a living work, for theatre or any medium, was said in a speech of Shaw's in "The Doctor's Dilemma" but I don't remember a single line of it now, I only remember that when I heard it I thought, Yes, that's what it is, not words, not thoughts or ideas, but those abstract things such as form and light and color that living things are made of. But I do, as I say, feel

up-lifted and so does Kazan, who wrote me a long letter the other day when he returned from the country. Not the least of the spiritual benefits that both of us are so keenly aware of is something rare and fine that we found in the long work together, and even more in its failure than we could have found in its success: the fact that never once in the two years it took to plan and execute this job, and the tortuous aftermath of it, did either of us once disappoint or betray the other's faith. This may sound like not such a remarkable thing, but believe me, in theatre as I have known it, it is! It's almost incredible! At one point or another, when things begin to go badly, when the fighting gets thick, somebody almost always "chickens out" or covers up or turns "bitchy", but in this out-fit, not a single one did - so what's a failure? Gadg and I are going to work together, next on a film, of which I've already written the first draft, maybe even another play after that. Meanwhile I'm going to try my hand at directing, a play of Donald Windham's, in the Houston Playhouse, end of this month. I've never tried staging before and I hope I find that I am able to do it.

I'll be in New York about ten days before my sailing-date which is June 5th. Don't worry about being in the town or the country, I'll get in touch with you. I have a car and my Secretary, Frank Merlo, has a license to drive, if you happen to be in the country. We can drive out, and though I am even less able to express myself in talk than I am in writing, which is little enough, it will be a pleasure to try. It would not be inconvenient as I have four or five different friends in Connecticutt and up the Hudson, whose places we always make a tour of before sailing.

If Windham's play works out well (there still are problems) I will ask him to send you a copy. Both the Houston Playhouse and the Theatre Guild are considering it for Fall production on Broadway. It is a very true and simple play, potentially as lovely as "Member of the Wedding", and I hope that the try-out in the "round" in Houston will make Windham able to see and master the structural problems before a major production.

Ever, Tenn.

[*Camino Real* peaked at $19,600 in the fourth week of production. TW later amused Maria Britneva with a wry account of finances, noting that "Mother Crawford" took nearly everyone "off royalties" when the bad notices "came out" and that she hoped "to scrape along by such economies as lighting the stage by fire-flies and a smokey old kerosene lamp" (qtd. in St. Just, p. 75).

TW's reference to the "levitation" of performance reappears in the "Afterword" to the first and subsequent editions of *Camino Real*. Also reprinted there is the speech of the dying painter in *The Doctor's Dilemma* (Shaw, 1906): "I believe in Michelangelo, Velasquez and Rembrandt; in the might of design, the mystery of color, the redemption of all things by beauty everlasting and the message of art that has made these hands blessed. Amen" (Act IV).

TW completed a revised "first draft" of *Baby Doll* (1956)—"Hide and Seek," February 19, 1952, U of Delaware—at Key West in early 1952. His collaboration with Elia Kazan on the film project would be prolonged and at times contentious.

This letter, misdated "June 7 or 8, 1953" by TW, was written two months earlier in the week of April 5. The Houston Playhouse production of Donald Windham's play, *The Starless Air*, opened on May 13, 1953.]

259. To Walter Edwin Dakin

SH: Playhouse
Houston 2, Texas
5/3/53
[TLS w/ enclosure, 1 p. Columbia U]

Dear Grandfather

I'm here in Houston directing Don's play. It is a much harder job than I'd anticipated and I think I should have stuck to writing plays. But it's too late now to back out, I just have to struggle through with it as best I can. There is so much talk in the play and so little action. I have to wrack my brain inventing things for the actors to do while delivering their long speeches. Well, we open in about twelve days and I'll be leaving immediately afterwards, the quicker the better, as Houston is the dullest city I've ever been in. Joanna is wonderful to work with, patient, sympathetic and understanding. Don is pretty irritable, but I suppose any playwright would be under the circumstances. I'll be awfully tired when I get through this! A few quiet days in the mountains would be wonderful or even just at the Hotel Gayoso.

I'm glad you're comfortably situated. I should have mailed your raincoat and this check days ago, but it's been one continual "hassle" since I got here. Take care of yourself, but do have a good time with your old friends.

Give Alice and Nalle and Mrs. Rhodes my particular fond regards.

Much love, Tom.

My address is Hotel Shamrock or The Playhouse. Got your letter this morning so I guess you already knew it.

[TW spent approximately three weeks in Houston casting and rehearsing *The Starless Air*. The lead was played by Margaret Phillips, who starred in the original Broadway production of *Summer and Smoke*. Joanna Albus, formerly associated with Margo Jones in Dallas, founded the Playhouse in 1952.

Alice and Nalle and Mrs. Rhodes are friends of Walter Dakin.]

260. To James "Jay" Laughlin

SH: The Shamrock
Houston 5, Texas
[May 9, 1953]
[TLS w/ enclosure, 2 pp. Houghton]

Dear Jay:

I just got your letter and I thank you for your patience and understanding about this problem of getting the script ready for publication. Here is the introduction to the book. I had meant to devote this A.M., Saturday, to getting the book together, but last night a "crise" occured between myself and Windham. He accused me of "completely re-writing" his play while he was keeping "TV" and interview appointments, and having accordingly ruined it. It threw me into such a despondancy I couldn't sleep and this whole day I have been immobilized except for sitting and taking notes on an afternoon run-through. But tomorrow, Sunday, I really will buckle down to the script. I'm sorry to say the "Bigelow script" was hopeless. It was just a typed up copy of the prompt book and simply couldn't be published, as I say in this introduction. If I weren't involved in this directing job I could turn in a much smoother script for publication. However this one that I will mail to you on Monday will only need a little brushing up which I could do from proofs when I get back to New York about the end of next week. Affectly.

10.

[The enclosed "introduction" first appeared in the *New York Times* on March 15, 1953, shortly before the opening of *Camino Real*. The copy which TW revised for book publication is nearly the same as the original.

The "'crise'" occurred when Donald Windham, banned from rehearsals by the

director, found that TW "was writing and inserting speeches about mendacity that belonged in a play of his and not of mine. (They turn up, almost word for word, in *Cat on a Hot Tin Roof.*) Foreseeing the same fate for this play as for *You Touched Me* if I remained silent, I spoke out. A compromise was reached that allowed the script to be improved but kept it in my control" (Windham, p. 278).

In prior correspondence with Windham, TW cited the "*horrible mendacity*" of male characters in *The Starless Air* and described the "central theme" of the play as "revolt against lying!" (qtd. in Windham, pp. 275-276). His tactic for prompting authorial revision was vintage Kazan.]

Tennessee Williams and Donald Windham, Houston, 1953: "Last night a 'crise' occured between myself and Windham."

261. To Cheryl Crawford

SH: Hotel Gayoso
Memphis 1, Tenn.
May 17, 1953
[TLS, 1 p. BRTC]

Cheryl dear:

I'm spending a few days with Grandpa on my way back to New York. Bigelow and I flew here yesterday but he went on this morning in response to an urgent call from Terry.

Windham's play had a pretty good reception, though better for me than the play. We only had twelve days' rehearsal, so the work was intensive. I was amazed at how easily it went, the 8-hour sessions seemed to pass like an hour and there was a feeling of real creative activity and outlet in it for me. Of course I would prefer to stage the works of dead authors, or at least not the works of old friends, but if I can't write another play, and God knows whether I can or can't, I do believe I might be able to make a living as a director.

Phyllis Anderson and Audrey, as well as Bigelow and Langner, flew down for the occasion. What a very sweet person Phyllis is! I had never gotten to know her before. She is so gentle and reasonable and did a great deal to smooth over a very tense and disagreeable situation which had developed about the Playhouse which professional ethics forbid me to go further into.

I see by a movie fan-magazine that Brando would like to do a play for Cheryl Crawford. Is there anything specific in this?

See you soon!

Affectionately, Tenn.

[Donald Windham and his untried play were nearly eclipsed by the celebrity director, whose staging, one critic wrote, showed "exceptional insight into human nature." TW's prominence was further enhanced by a concurrent production of *The Rose Tattoo* at the Alley Theatre in Houston.

Reviewers found occasional brilliance in Windham's study of a declining southern family, but they doubted that *The Starless Air* had "enough power, sharpness and compulsion to interest an audience not especially susceptible to its Southern manners" (*Houston Post*, May 14, 1953).

Prominent visitors to Houston included Lawrence Langner, co-director of the Theatre Guild, who had taken an option on *The Starless Air* for a summer

production and a possible transfer of the play to Broadway—neither of which occurred.

Phyllis Anderson, wife of the playwright Robert Anderson, was Windham's agent at this time. She died in 1956, remembered by many on Broadway for having "led a whole new generation of playwrights into the theatre," as John Gassner wrote.]

262. *To Edith Sitwell*

SH: Hotel Gayoso
Memphis 1, Tenn.
May 17, 1953
[TLS, 2 pp. HRC]

Dear Dr. Sitwell:

I meant to write you much sooner but have been in the slough of despondancy which I only got out of by undertaking the staging of a friend's play in Houston, Texas, which was my first essay at direction. It turned out well and the forced activity was good for me and lifted the state of my spirit.

Immediately upon receiving your wire about "Camino" I wired you at the Hotel St. Regis in New York. I hope it reached you before you sailed. I'm sure that none of the messages of appreciation that I got about the play meant even half so much to me as yours, and without it the play's failure would have been far more crushing. I hope you understand this and how much I do thank you. Of course I knew already how warm and generous your attitude is toward works of others. I have read Denton Welch's journal which gives such touching testimony to this rare thing which distinguishes Edith Sitwell the woman as much as your work distinguishes you as a poet, or rather, which complements that work in the only suitable way.

"Camino" closed last Saturday. I don't think it needed to, for the last week's business was nearly double the week before and indicated that there was still a lot of interest in the play. But it was expensive to operate and the producer had not planned wisely. Like most brave people she had only made provisions against success. Not being brave, I always think in terms of possible failure, and yet when it comes it never fails to depress me. Nevertheless I am prepared for it and able to take suitable measures to cope with it.

I'm sailing June 5th but my boat lands at Havre and I shall make the quickest possible retreat to Rome. I shall be abroad until early November and it may turn out that I'll be in London sometime during that period, and if I do, I will surely get in touch with you.

Please believe that you have done a great deal to help me over a very difficult event in my life.

With "devoir", Tennessee.

[Edith Sitwell (1887-1964) wrote later in May to commiserate with TW over the closing of *Camino Real* and to declare the critics "fools!" for having rejected the play "out of sheer obstinacy." She consoled her friend with the thought that "when one can no longer raise" in the "stupid" an "absolute frenzy of hatred and anger - it means that one is dead" (May 24, 1953, Massee Collection).

Sitwell championed many young writers, including the novelist Denton Welch, who found it "so winey, so toxic, always to be hearing fine things about one's attempts from someone famous" (*The Journals of Denton Welch*, ed. De-la-Noy, 1984).

Camino Real closed on May 9, 1953, after sixty performances and a loss of $115,000. The final week's gross of $22,000 followed a sharp decline in business and was no doubt a reaction to the play's closing notice.]

263. To Edwina Dakin Williams

SH: Hotel Gayoso
Memphis 1, Tenn.
[ca. May 17, 1953]
[TLS, 2 pp. HRC]

Dear Mother:

I am spending a couple of days here with Grandfather enroute to New York, after a very strenuous three weeks in Houston, putting on Windham's play. It was my first attempt at direction and the results were gratifying, at least all the notices praised the direction but they were not so kind to the play. Actually the play was not quite ready to be produced, and what made it most unfortunate was that Windham, far from being grateful for my services, sat next to me while I was working with the actors, objecting to everything and giving them contrary directions. I finally had to ask him to stay out of the theatre till the initial staging was finished, which he took in very poor grace. Lawrence Langner of the Theatre Guild came

down for the opening, as did Bigelow and Audrey and some other Broadway figures. Langner wants me to stage the play in New York if it is done there, but I would be reluctant to involve myself again in a work of Windham's.

I am terribly, terribly concerned over the changes you are contemplating for Rose. Surely she won't be put back in the asylum! That, I am sure, would be the final blow, as she would almost certainly give up all hope if her limited freedom that she has with Mrs. Turner is taken away. I am convinced, from all evidence, that these state institutions are perfect nightmares - "Snake-pits". If Mrs. Turner won't keep her, someone else must. Please let me know about this before I sail for Europe June 5th.

Grandfather is about as well as when you last saw him and is having plenty of society here - too much for me! He is spending one more week here before he goes to Clarksdale where he intends to spend June. In July, about the first, he's planning to go to Tuckaway Inn. Are you going to join him there?

"Camino" closed last Saturday in spite of the fact that the final week did almost twice the business of the week before. Cheryl Crawford managed it very badly. She did not even put advertisements in The New Yorker or show-cards in the ticket-agency windows.

Of course this branded the play as a failure at the outset. I think it would be a mistake to trust her with another. Excitement and interest in the play was very high and if it had been properly exploited, it could have turned the tide. I am now busy preparing the manuscript for publication and Audrey has made contracts for its presentation here and there in Europe. "Rose Tattoo" has had a very successful opening in Paris and I will see it when I get there in June.

Grandfather says to give you his love and also the Widow Brown. I'm glad I stopped off to see him here as I was afraid he might not be comfortably settled. He is. If you could send Grandfather his "straw hat" he would be happy but says it is not necessary - a Knox panama, he says. He has the light grey one so it should not be essential.

Send Dakin my love. I do hope he gets the promotion, though it would be nice for you to have him back in Saint Louis, I suppose.

Much love, Tom.

[The precise date and circumstances of Rose Williams's departure from Stony Lodge in New York are unclear. An indication of her current status may be found in TW's correspondence with Elia Kazan: "I don't know who told you that my sister was worse. She is the same as ever but yours truly is just about ready to join her on that chicken-farm in Missouri. Her letters indicate that she thinks I am already there. She wrote me recently that the yard was full of 'tragic fowls' and she listed them by all our family names and said they were 'holding prayers' for me" (postmarked Le Havre, France, June 10, 1953, WUCA).]

264. *To Paul Bowles*

[11 Via Firenzie, Rome]
June 22, 1953.
[TLS, 2 pp. HRC]

Dear Paul:

We are back in Rome and have taken an apartment, a 4-floor walk-up which one cannot climb more than once a day and survive it, but it has two lovely terraces that catch the morning and afternoon sun and the portiere disappears after ten PM. So all in all it's a good deal.

Frank and the dog may remain here most of the summer but I am taking off for Spain and Tanger in a couple of weeks. I want to see some bull-fights and then I want to settle down near the beach in Tanger and get back in shape. I've been pretty seedy.

Today Luchino Visconti came to see us. He wanted me to do English dialogue for a film he is making with several American stars late this summer. I am simply not in condition, nervously, to undertake a job of this sort but I told him that you would be a perfect choice for it if you would be interested. He wanted me to write you at once and see if you'd like to. I dare say there would be a sizable increment. This he did not go into but there is American backing with stars such as Farley Granger involved. It might be worth your while if you are looking for "loot". He does not know your work as he cannot speak nor read English but I spoke of your books. He wants me to act in a "supervisory" capacity, which means that I would lend advice and assistance if needed. He wants to pay both of us but since I would not be doing any of the actual work I would - confidentially - turn over whatever I received to you. Visconti made the latest Anna Magnani film, "Bellissima", which is a great success now in America, and also a much greater film, "Terra Trema". He also has directed "Streetcar" and

"Menagerie" in the Italian theatre, and is by far the greatest stage director in Italy as well as a "grand Seigneur", the Viscontis being one of the three oldest families in the country - this is irrelevant but interesting, I think, since he is also very "leftish". I like him and I think his dealings would be completely equitable - this is relevant.

Has Ahmed come back? I hope so, for I sense your loneliness without him and it seemed a very good and workable relationship. I think what happened was a very temporary thing, a sort of "coup de feu" or derangement that came from the sudden collision of two very different cultures at a critical time. It is nothing that could not be understood by a man of your philosophical latitude. Of course I know very little about it all. Somehow I feel it is very sad for Libby . . . not for you.

I will let you know when I start for Spain, probably by air. I don't trust myself in a car, too many smash-ups, and the Jaguar is permanently off balance as a result. Besides there is more fluidity without one, and I have almost entirely gotten over my dread of the air. Is there a good hotel, <u>not</u> the <u>Rif</u>, near the beach in Tanger? Perhaps even the Rif would be tolerable in good weather. It was agreeable to hear of the bull-ring. I have a passion for corridas. I expect Frank and "Mr. Moon" would join me later. If you come to Rome we have an extra room for you here. We have this place for four months. You could work on one terrazza and me on the other. It is right over the opera house and we could hear them rehearsing as we worked! Tra la la! <u>LAAAAAAAAAA</u>! - very stimulating.

Love, Tenn.

[TW sailed on June 5 with little hope of serenity. "A neurosis," he wrote, "is worrying the ragged edges of my nerves and I was disturbed by a tearful scene put on by F's friend Ellen in front of others." The old "blue-devils" of fear and depression returned on the second day, TW still "running hard" (*Journal*, June 5 and 6, 1953) to elude them. He and Frank Merlo settled in Rome near the Teatro dell'Opera: "Tra la la! <u>LAAAAAAAAAA</u>!"

Senso (1954), the Luchino Visconti film to which TW refers, is set in Venice in the 1860s against the historical background of the Austrian occupation. Farley Granger played the role of Franz Mahler, an officer who is exposed as a traitor by his Venetian lover and executed by the Austrians for desertion.

Paul Bowles sailed unhappily for Tangier, while his companion Ahmed Yacoubi, a painter who had been adopted by smart society in New York, remained to enjoy a brief notoriety. He was currently "living in sin," Bowles remarked, at Libby Holman's estate in Connecticut. A famous torch singer,

Paul Bowles,
Tangier.

Holman lived under a shadow of suspicion after being charged in 1932 (although not prosecuted) with the murder of her husband, Smith Reynolds, a principal heir of the Reynolds tobacco fortune. Holman was a mutual friend of TW and Paul and Jane Bowles.]

265. *To Justin Brooks Atkinson*

11 Via Firenze, Rome
June 25, 1953
[TLS, 3 pp. BRTC]

Dear Brooks:

I had certainly meant to get in touch with you before I sailed this month but the long-delayed reckoning with my burned up nerves which I knew was coming but which I had skillfully evaded by keeping very busy, plunging into new work in Key West, and directing Windham's play in

Houston, did finally overtake me during that short period in New York. Practically every morning was like climbing out of a grave, and each one I asked myself, Can I call Brooks today? I did want very much to talk to you. But each day I obviously wasn't in a suitable state to see anybody but a few old friends who are accustomed to these recessive periods of mine. At such times, in company, I sit with a fixed, anxious smile and say nothing. I go to Rome each summer almost as a therapeutic measure. It is hard, even for me, to remain continually tense and anxious in this serene golden city, so now, as usual, I am coming out of it a little and by the time I return to the States I'll be ready to pick up and go on, perhaps with a new work of my own, if I work rapidly enough, perhaps to do Windham's play on Broadway for the Theatre Guild. I enjoyed directing. I was surprised to discover how satisfactory a creative outlet it was, and certainly it was good for me to change positions, to get a first-hand impression of what a director goes through with. I have a brand new appreciation of Gadg. I always loved and admired him, but when I consider how many times I "blew my top" at poor Windham and how often Gadg must have wanted to scream at me, but never did, I feel a real awe of his composure or control. Still I think that I can be a director at times when I have no work of my own to offer. The eight-hour periods seem to pass like a single hour and at the end of the day I would feel more refreshed than fatigued. And I felt the same satisfaction, when it went well, that I would have felt if it had been my own work. But direction is an art that has to be learned, like all arts, slowly, and while writing is a good preparation, it doesn't completely prepare you in place of experience. My dream is some day to direct "The Sea Gull" which is my favorite of all plays. I would like to have Brando as Constantine, Stella Adler as Mme. Arcadina, Geraldine Page as Nina, and maybe David Stewart could play Trigorin.

I have found an apartment here with two terraces, one that catches the morning sun and one for the afternoon, and yesterday I went to Magnani's. She wants to do two things, a film of <u>Rose Tattoo</u> which was written for her originally and she wants me to write her a modern de-sentimentalized version of "Camille". Censors have forbidden the showing of "Tattoo" on the Italian stage and also the release of the film of "Streetcar", but the best Italian stage director, Luchino Visconti, is keen to present "Camino" next season and I wonder if the church and/or government will permit it. Book-burning and banning and so forth is having a fearful ascendancy these

days, and that's why I think a single honest and courageously outspoken critic is more important to us right now than writers are, since the latter cannot function at all without the support of the first. What I value so highly in your criticism is that even when a work is personally distasteful to you, you are able to separate that subjective reaction to a remarkable degree from your objective evaluation of the thing itself. I hate works that are rooted in bitterness and hatred and disgust, such as Celline's and Malaparte's and Henry Miller's. These are black works and revolt me. But I catch flashes of a "tortured sensibility" in the best of Sartre. I don't mind a work being dark if it is rooted in compassion. In a notebook I once copied the following bit from Sartre's "Age of Reason": - "Various well-bred moralities had already discreetly offered him their services: disillusioned epicureanism, smiling tolerance, resignation, common sense, stoicism - all the aids whereby a man may savor, minute by minute, like a connoisseur, the failure of a life." - The sadness in this reflection is a genuine thing, truthful and therefore moving. Of course there must be more comfort in his existence than in his "existentialism" or he couldn't endure it, I agree with you about that. I'm sure he is comforted by the esteem of his followers, for instance, and by the excellent French wines and restaurants and the civilized freedom of thought that still prevails and is the great tradition in his country. Apparently he has no use for me. In the summer of 1948 I gave a cocktail party for theatrical friends in Paris and sent him a long wire, inviting him, to which he didn't respond, and during the party I heard he was in a bar nearby and dispatched a French writer to bring him over. He assured the writer he would come, but a short while later he strolled by my hotel without even looking up. Cocteau did not come, either, but he came early in the morning to explain why he couldn't come in the evening. As for Anouhil, all I know of his work is <u>Antigone</u> which seemed quite meaningless to me. If the sorrow and confusion and longing in a man's heart is eloquently expressed through art, I think it gives comfort and even exaltation to his audience, by making them feel less lonely. I had that experience lately at a play. It was Jane Bowles' <u>In A Summerhouse</u> which I saw in Ann Arbor shortly before I sailed. Although it was written before Carson's <u>Member of the Wedding</u> and bears no resemblance to it otherwise, it has a similar theme of spiritual isolation, it is one of the funniest and saddest and most original plays ever written. The feeling of loneliness in it was almost unbearably poignant but the effect was

heart-warming, it made me feel <u>not</u> alone. In fact, after seeing it three times, consecutively, I felt genuinely uplifted and peaceful for the first time in several months. The notices gave it no quarter but the audiences, although I'm not sure they knew what to make of it, were held fascinated and the producers are going to bring it into New York next Fall. Well, that's about all, right now - except for a funny remark that George Kaufmann made on the ship coming over about Eric Bentley's new book. He said the full title is "In Search Of A Theatre, and God Help It If I Find One!"

Yours ever, Tennessee.

[By late-June TW had "just about run through" the annual therapy of Rome. The work was "petering out" and things began to seem "a little too familiar": "I think I need the shock of something new to keep me from sinking into the old summer lethargy and stupefaction" (*Journal*, June 29, 1953). A trip to Spain followed in mid-July.

TW did not pursue Anna Magnani's request, or a similar bid by *Studio One*, a popular television showcase, to modernize the story of "Camille." A Visconti production of *Camino Real* also failed to materialize.

TW quotes the final lines of *The Age of Reason* (1945) by Jean-Paul Sartre.

A tryout cast featuring Miriam Hopkins and Mildred Dunnock could not save the new Jane Bowles play from harsh "notices" in Ann Arbor, Michigan. *In the Summerhouse* was panned by the critics as "pretentious, wordy nonsense" (*Detroit News*, May 20, 1953).

The Broadway producer-director George S. Kaufman mocked the title and pretention of Eric Bentley's collection of essays and reviews, *In Search of Theater* (1953).]

266. To Audrey Wood

11 Via Firenze
Rome
June 29, 1953
[TLS, 2 pp. HRC]

Dearest Audrey:

I always feel that there is a sort of telepathic communication between us across the Atlantic and I don't have to write you in order to let you know the general condition of things. So far things are okay. In Paris I saw the last two performances of "Rose Tattoo" before it shut down for the

summer. They say it will re-open in September. I am happy to report they did a fine job on it. Maria came over and it turned out that the Serafina, Leila Kedrova, was an old Russian friend of her mother's, and so they hit it off like a house afire, to the tune of thousands of francs at Russian night-clubs at my expense. But Kedrova is really superb, and I do wish they would use her in London. Her grunts alone are worth the admission price. She has great comedy and sexuality and her husband directed it well. It was really the first time I have seen the play truly performed, and this in spite of the stage being not much larger than a room at the "Y". Kedrova speaks some English and is eager to play in London and could pick up the language well enough to play it in a month or two. The truck-driver, also Russian, was equally good in his part. Do you suppose Binkie would be interested in having me direct the play, with Kedrova, for the Lyric-Hammersmith?

I have seen Magnani here in Rome. She invited me to her apartment and says she wants to make the film in Sicily with Brando, and that she thinks Mangiacavallo should be an American GI of Sicilian descent stationed there during the occupation. It sounds feasible enough, but is Brando interested and is an American film company prepared to produce it? She also wants me to write her a modern de-sentimentalized version of "Camille" to do on the stage in America, her idea is to do a reportory of three works, a musical revue, Rose Tattoo, and a "new Camille". A lady of limitless energy!

I had accumulated some francs from "Tattoo" but Ninon said she couldn't get them out on such short notice so the last day of my stay in Paris she came over with a check for $500. in francs, I believe it was 175,000 francs, which she said was an advance on "Summer and Smoke", which is now being translated by the lady who translated "Tattoo" and will be done at a still tinier theatre in the Fall. I signed <u>two</u> receipts (<u>not</u> carbons) for the francs, since she said one was to be sent to you and one for her to keep. Maria was highly skeptical about all this and I must say I think the handling of French royalties is something we had better keep an eye on, now that American earnings are at such an ebb.

We have taken an apartment at 11 Via Firenze. It has a terrace that catches the afternoon sun, and Frank and Mr. Moon are quite satisfied here, but since I can't use that wonderful swimming-pool at the country-club I was kicked out of, I feel restless in Rome and I think I'll fly

to Barcelona in a short time, and maybe wire Maria to join me in Madrid for a couple of weeks, as it is cheap there and I think I need the stimulation of a new background.

I talked to Carson on the phone in Paris and she was in great distress over Reeves. He has never stopped drinking and was then in the American hospital and she said she desperately wanted to talk to me about things and that I could drive out in their car which was at the hospital. I went to the hospital the next day with Maria but Reeves had checked out and the car was not there. I myself was feeling pretty seedy and did not attempt the trip to Bachivilliers by bus. The Carson-Reeves situation is apparently insoluble, I don't think there is anything anyone can do about it. Short of devoting your life to Carson, I don't see how you can help her, though she certainly needs help. Of course I feel guilty about it. I should have gone out there, somehow. But we left the next day for Rome. She had a French woman with her who answered the phone so at least her physical needs are being cared for.

How is Inge? Liquor seems to be the particular Nemesis of American writers. Says I, about to go inside for a Scotch on the rocks . . .

I've done some work on the film script and am also working on "Battle" and "Kingdom of Earth". Something should be finished by the time I get back to the States. Me or the cold war or something! Love to Liebling and to Bigelow, may God bless them, and Ida, may God bless her, and Grandfather and "Neesie" and Gadg - may God bless them and keep them in good health and spirits this summer as I hope he will try to keep me. May he do the same for Margo Jones and Joanna Albus and Alice Bouverie but may he be less concerned with the welfare of Geo. Jean Nathan than he is with that of the rat that bit off the nose of the little boy they call "Pig Face" in the slums of Chicago, because he has no nose, or even the rat that devoured the nine-months old baby, in the room that the Chicago News reporter mistook for an empty coal-bin. And God bless you and me, too!

Love, Tenn.

[Ninon Tallon sent an article in which TW had raved about Lila Kedrova, who played Serafina in the Paris production of *The Rose Tattoo* (1953). "Were you this happy," Audrey Wood asked her capricious client, for "I have known you to make speeches publicly and then confidentially tell me you were miserable!" (June 25, 1953, HRC).

"Binkie" Beaumont, managing director of Tennent Ltd., assumed that Peter Brook was TW's first choice to stage *The Rose Tattoo* in London. Beaumont's fear that censorship rulings would hinder the project had been confirmed in February when the Lord Chamberlain's office issued a list of mandatory "alterations." Before leaving Key West in April, TW approved the changes, including the removal of a vulgar reference to "the sex of a parrot" (February 17, 1953, HRC).

The prospect of Marlon Brando starring in *The Rose Tattoo* had unwelcome consequences, as Wood later informed TW (July 3, 1953, HRC). Hal Wallis, the producer with whom she was negotiating film rights, reasoned that signing Brando would make Anna Magnani expendable. He was unwilling to pay the $150,000 fee which she now asked.

William Inge's latest hit, *Picnic*, opened to strong notices on February 19, 1953, and won both the Pulitzer Prize and the Drama Critics' Circle Award—a feat last accomplished by Arthur Miller with *Death of a Salesman* (1949).

"Must soon decide whether to work on 'Battle of Angels' - 'Kingdom of Earth' or the film script," TW wrote concurrently in the journal. "Perhaps the wisest decision," he opined, "would be no work at all, but Spain would have to be awfully fascinating to make that tolerable" (June 29, 1953). Precisely when he began a dramatic adaptation of "The Kingdom of Earth" is unclear. The play was staged unsuccessfully in 1968 as *The Seven Descents of Myrtle*.]

267. To Carson McCullers

[Hotel Colón, Barcelona]
7/15/53
[TLS, 1 p. HRC]

Dearest Carson:

I've been having a rough time of it this summer. I was sick in Paris and haven't been well since. Right now I'm in Barcelona, resting on the beach, and Frank is in Rome. I have worried ever since I talked to you on the phone in Paris. I went out to the American hospital that Sunday to pick up your car and drive out to see you but Reeves had already checked out and we left that night for Rome. I do hope that both of you are better now, bad seasons are usually followed by relatively good ones. I've had a couple in a row but that's exceptional and I'm sure some relief is due. I don't know just how long I'll stay here. Relations with Frank had been strained and they reached the point where communication had ceased. After a couple of weeks of that I thought I'd better take off regardless of how little I felt like travelling. It's cool here and the beach is delightful. I have lunch on it every

day with a bottle of wine which is the world's most agreeable soporific and rest on the beach several hours. Paul Bowles is in Madrid and we'll probably get together in a few days. I got him a job writing dialogue in English for an Italian film. I didn't feel able to undertake the job myself and so persuaded Visconti to engage Paul. I guess we'll fly back to Rome together and perhaps the presence of another party we both like will relieve the tension with Frank which is probably the consequence of being together too constantly too long, and the fact he has never found a personal life for himself, that is any independant sort of activity. I understand it but I can't cope with it right now.

I understand that Miss Capote is in Europe, in Italy, but we have not collided. She is now reported to be at the fashionable resort of Portofino, which is much smarter than Capri. Did I tell you we have a dog? An English bull named Mr. Moon. I'm afraid the poor thing will perish on the streets of Rome as bulls don't stand heat well and Frank will not move without him, they are inseparable, Frank trots and he waddles after as rapidly as he can with that great jowly head of his barely clearing the sidewalk. Maria Britneva calls him "The Froggy Footman".

Our Roman address is 11 Via Firenze or American Express,

LOVE, 10.

[Carson and Reeves McCullers—still living at Bachvillers—entered the final dark months of their marriage in mid 1953 when Reeves attempted suicide. Carson quickly returned to the States once his plan for a double suicide became clear.

While Frank Merlo consorted with a "whore" named Alvaro, TW depended upon trade which was "brought in two or three times a week" (*Journal*, June 27 or 28, 1953). He soon grew "tired of begging for crumbs." The forthcoming trip to Spain was "the only answer," TW thought, to Merlo's behavior, "and maybe that only half one" (*Journal*, July 1 and 10, 1953).

"I spent 6 hours on the San Sebastian beach and had an affair in my cabana with someone procured by Franz" (*Journal*, July 11, 1953). *Suddenly Last Summer* (1958) would evolve from the Barcelona trip (July 10-20), as would the themes of sexual procurement and predation. TW also saw a band of "black-plucked-sparrow children shrilling about for bread and making percussive serenades with flattened out tin cans" (to Kazan, n.d., WUCA) who would reappear in the play as unwitting agents of retribution.

In Portofino "there was a gabble of voices, a cascade of laughter, a buzz of gossip" (Clarke, *Capote: A Biography*, 1988) to which TW and Merlo added their voices while visiting Truman Capote in August. Mr. Moon, however, was not

invited, since Capote had received as a gift a female bulldog. TW observed to Maria Britneva that "more than one bitch" (qtd. in St. Just, p. 77) now lived in Capote's house.]

268. To Audrey Wood

[Positano, Italy]
August 2?, 1953.
[TLS w/ autograph marginalia
and postscript, 2 pp. HRC]

Dear Audrey:

A supplement to the hasty letter we scribbled while checking out of the Excelsior in Naples, Maria and I. We are now in Positano, working on the Visconti film script. I know that I should have gotten in touch with you about this sooner but everything came up very rapidly. I got Bowles the job but his work on it, for a number of reasons, was disappointing, and so I felt obligated to do what I could to pull it together, since Visconti had taken him on my recommendation. Paul is not at all well, he has liver trouble and has fallen off to 112 pounds, and the Arab boy who travels with him has been driving him nearly insane. He was not in a condition to undertake this work but he desperately needed the money. I am doing all I can with the script but only accepting one week's salary, $500., the same as Paul was getting a week. Paul is still drawing salary and finishing his version of the script in Rome. Maria is helping me here and Visconti has employed her. Her position is somewhat vague but she gets $250 a month and is drawing $6. a day for expenses on this trip and afterwards when she is with the company in Verona and Venice where the film will be shot. Visconti is already shooting the battle scenes in Verona and Maria will join him soon as her work with me is finished. She will be employed about four months and she is terribly happy as it's the first decently paid job she's ever had. She's a great help to me in this week's work on the script. Fortunately I only have to re-write the three love scenes. The picture is "Urgano d'estate" and the stars are Alida Valli and Farley Granger. It is a big technicolor production with an English version as well as Italian. Maria thinks my work on it is good.

I haven't spoken of the "dossier" business. There didn't seem to be anything to say, it was almost too ridiculous to take seriously except that

its implications are so unspeakable. I really didn't know whether to laugh or cry! Of course the worst offense was the reference to you. I trust you have humor enough, now that the first shock is over, to see the funny side. I do. No use regarding it except as something out of Jonathan Swift. . . .

I found my letter of credit in the trunk of the car. Maria and I believe it was stolen from my luggage and put there after they found it couldn't be cashed without identifications.

As I said in last letter, I'm still working on my new version of "Battle". I think I can mail you the script before the end of August. The three principals are radically different. Myra is now the daughter of an Italian immigrant and the part might be fine for Isa Mirande. The part of Cassandra might be right for Julie Harris. The play itself is much less realistic and even wilder than before. I can't judge it, I only know it excites me to work on it, so I depend on you to read and decide about it, and I know you will tell me frankly what you think. Love -

Tennessee.

<u>Please</u> control those <u>spasms</u>!

[The long week that TW spent in Positano (August 25-September 2) was "productive and peaceful and, on the whole, quite pleasant" (*Journal*, August 31, 1953). He continued to revise *Battle of Angels* (1940) and began a promising new story entitled "Man Bring This Up Road" (1959). Mrs. Flora Goforth, the principal character, was "a composite of various vampires" (*Journal*, August 29, 1953) whom TW had known. She would be recast in *The Milk Train Doesn't Stop Here Anymore* (1962/1963).

Ahmed was traveling again with Paul Bowles but "not sleeping with him." Libby Holman, TW reported, said that "such relations were very evil and the opinions of a lady with thirty million dollars cannot be taken lightly by a young Arab whose family live in one room" (qtd. in Windham, p. 282).

Audrey Wood "frankly" evaluated the "new" *Battle of Angels* in late-September.

Penned in the upper margin of p. 1 is the notation "Write me c/o Am. Ex. Co., Rome."]

269. To Cheryl Crawford

SH: Harry's Bar, Venezia
PM: Venice, September 8, 1953
[APCS, 1 p. U of Houston]

Dearest Cheryl -

This is where good queens and bad go when they die in Europe. A few living ones also get here. Just saw the Aga Khan go staggering out followed by an impatient looking Begum. Maria is here. We are both working on a new film for Visconti which is to be a sort of wop "Gone With the Wind" in technicolor. Paul Bowles worked on it, too, and I think it may be beautiful if they don't f___ it up! Also writing on plays and film for Gadg. F. and Moon in Rome.

Good luck & Love - Tenn.

[The Visconti film in progress is *Senso*.]

Tennessee Williams and Maria Britneva on the Lido, 1953: "Maria calls me 'Forty Winks' because in the evenings I have a tendency to nod like the Dormouse in Alice."

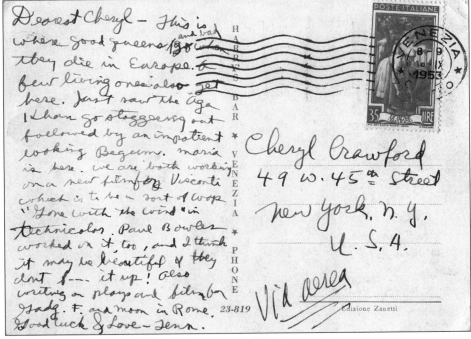

Dearest Cheryl — This is where good queens go and bad ones too they die in Europe. A few living ones also get here. Just saw the Aga Khan go staggering out followed by an impatient looking Begum. Maria is here. We are both working on a new film for Visconti which is to be a sort of Wop "Gone with the Wind" in Technicolor. Paul Bowles worked on it, too, and I think it may be beautiful if they dont f—— it up! Also writing on plays and film, by Sadie. F. and moon in Rome. Good luck & Love — Tenn.

Cheryl Crawford
49 W. 45th Street
New York, N. Y.
U. S. A.

Via Aérea

Edizione Zanetti

270. *To Edwina Dakin Williams and*
     Walter Edwin Dakin

[11 Via Firenze, Rome]
Sept. 19, 1953.
[TLS, 1 p. HRC]

Dear Mother & Grandfather:

I hope and presume that you are back together in Clayton. This has been the busiest summer that I've had in Europe. Working on two films and two plays and also doing a lot of travelling around.

The big news is that Anna Magnani, the Italian star, has finally come to terms with Paramount and the "Rose Tattoo" film deal is apparently all set. It will probably be filmed in America, on the Gulf coast, next summer. I called Anna and she is ecstatic about it and full of plans and suggestions and I will probably have to write the film-story, I hope for a good price. The exact terms of the movie-sale have not yet been told me by Audrey but I suspect she got a hundred thousand and a percentage of the distributor's gross.

Maria Britneva has been here most of the summer and I got her a job working on an Italian film, as well as Paul Bowles. He and I collaborated on the English dialogue, both getting $500. a week which is a good salary for Italy, though only one tenth of what I would get in America. But Visconti is the producer of my plays here and I felt obligated to him. Jane Lawrence and Tony Smith, Grandfather will remember them very well, just arrived in Rome and we will all get together for dinner tonight at a restaurant in the most beautiful plaza in Rome. The weather has turned cool but still bright.

I go to Helsinki for the Finnish premiere of "Tattoo" and to address the university there on the 28th October, and will sail for America immediately afterwards, arriving New York about November 8th.

Both of you take good care of yourselves. Much love,

Tom.

[Audrey Wood's threat "to push toward other producing bodies" (June 24, 1953, HRC) apparently convinced Hal Wallis to sign Anna Magnani for *The Rose Tattoo*.

The Finnish American Society informed TW of plans by the National Theatre to stage *The Rose Tattoo* in May and *The Glass Menagerie* in October. The productions would run concurrently during TW's forthcoming visit to Helsinki (March 2, 1953, HRC).]

271. *To Audrey Wood*

[11 Via Firenze, Rome]
September 19, 1953
[TLS w/ autograph postscript, 2 pp. HRC]

Dear Audrey:

I've worked harder this summer than any that I can remember but the quantity of work is much clearer than the quality. I know I ought to lay off it, to freshen up, but time seems short, and fewer and fewer things, as I grow older, seem to be interesting enough to fill a day with. This may be because I am tired. Maria calls me "Forty Winks" because in the evenings I have a tendancy to nod like the Dormouse in Alice.

I'm afraid I have been rather foolish about this picture and you may be cross about it, I mean the Visconti film work. When Bowles didn't do a satisfactory job, I felt obliged to take over since Visconti hired him at my recommendation, and this film is a crucial job for Visconti. He may never get another if it doesn't come off, and as you know, I have a very profound admiration for him and affection. Then also he gave Maria her first good job she's ever had in the theatre, at least from a money point of view, she's getting six dollars a day in living expenses and $250 a month salary. I have gotten only one thousand for two weeks work and of course I know I should have demanded more, especially since they are going to use my name, with Bowles, as English dialogue writer. But Visconti was "on the spot" and it seemed an occasion on which one ought to be self-forgetful. Do you agree?

Irene (Dame Selznick) is here and she says that you will be cross about it, so I am briefing you on all the circumstances.

Now I wish you would brief me on the "Tattoo" film deal. I don't know a thing about it. I called Magnani and she seemed ecstatic and was full of suggestions. We must go to Paris together to track down Brando - obviously she is mad for him! - the script must be half in English and half in Italian so that in the violent scenes she will not be reaching for words. And so forth and so forth. But she is genuinely delighted. What troubles me most is the suspicion that Dannie Mann will direct. I did so hope that it could be offered to Gadg for whom it was written along with Magnani, and who told me he would like to make a film of it, and I know he would if he could fit it into his schedule. Of course it might conflict with "27 Wagons", I don't know, but it seems to me the schedules could be juggled

around to arrange it. I can't see the intellectual Mr. Mann and the fiery Signora Magnani hitting it off together, nor can I see Dannie getting the poetry and wildness out of the script that it calls for. Please don't let Dannie know I have these reservations about him, I do think he is much superior to Irving Rapper, and I like him well enough personally despite the lack of any rapport between us. I would like to work on the script for Magnani with a director that would stimulate me as she does. With a fine director, "Tattoo" and Magnani would out-shine "Streetcar" and out-gross it, I do believe, but the director should be a plus value as well as the star.

I am still committed to appear in Helsinki October 28th so I'm afraid I'll have to make that trip, little as I like it. Then we couldn't sail till the first week in November. For a while I thought of calling it off and returning in early October but importunate wires and letters from the Finnish American society came in, and I succumbed.

Jane Lawrence and Tony Smith have just arrived,* seeing them tonight, and Paul Bowles and his Arabs have just got back from Istanbul where he went to do a travel piece for Holiday magazine.

I'm working on a play which I might possibly finish, in first draft, before I get back to the States and will now resume work on Gadg's film. How was "Tea & Sympathy" received? I hope well, although the theme struck me as rather improbable, not the circumstances but their solution.

With love, Tenn

*Jane is having a baby in January!

[TW and Paul Bowles shared the English dialogue credit for *Senso*. When finally shown in New York, the film was panned for being "closer to soap opera than Mr. Visconti imagined" (*New York Times*, July 9, 1968).

Audrey Wood last reported negotiating a "film deal" with Hal Wallis that would pay "$75,000 and 5% of the distributor's gross over $1,000,000" (to TW, July 3, 1953, HRC) for rights of *The Rose Tattoo*. Reservations aside, TW had approved Daniel Mann as director when he and Wood conferred in the preceding May.

Signs of the new play—*Cat on a Hot Tin Roof* (1955)—appear in the journal perhaps as early as February 1953. Donald Windham suggested as much in his complaint that lines written for *Cat* were appearing in his own play, *The Starless Air*, during rehearsals in May. TW further specified the origins of *Cat* with reference to "a short-long play based on the characters in 'Three Players'" which he drafted in Rome in summer 1953. He also ascribed his "terrible state of

depression" to the new play, which he could not seem to "grip" at this time (see letters #283 and #284).

Tea and Sympathy (1953), Robert Anderson's study of a naive schoolboy accused of homosexual tendencies, was directed by Elia Kazan and ran for 712 performances on Broadway. The play ended improbably, TW thought, with the restoration of the boy's masculinity by the wife of a teacher who was the main persecutor. Laura, speaking to Tom, delivers the closing line: "Years from now—when you talk about this—and you will—be kind."]

272. To Oliver Evans

[Granada, Spain]
10/7/53
[TLS 1 p. HRC]

Dear Oliver:

I am so sorry that you didn't come to Europe, as I kept hoping, for then you could be taking this trip with us and I'm sure you would enjoy it much more than I am. As you know, I'm the world's most fatiguable sight-seer, and here we are in Granada and I'm not even sure that I shall go to see the Alhambra, all I can think of is where they may be holding the bull-fights tomorrow and how quickly can we get to Tangier and have a little rest before sailing back to the States. We are travelling in two Jaguars, Paul's and mine. Paul with his Arab lover Ahmed and his chauffeur Mohammed in their Jaguar and Frank and I and Mr. Moon in ours. They have terrible rubber on their car, probably a result of so many trips through the Sahara and Spain, and we stop every few hours, sometimes less, to change the tires. Luckily I don't know how to do a thing so I just sit restlessly along the road and watch. The country, of course, is very beautiful, much like parts of Mexico, the mountains like the Sierra Madres. But the men are very disappointing to look at, after Italy, I have seen no one like Sebastian, even remotely, the food does not agree with me and I feel slightly ill all the time. However I dread going back to the States. I feel that the country is simply galloping into totalitarianism, now, what I see in the papers and magazines strikes terror in me. I wouldn't go back if it weren't for Grandfather waiting for me in St. Louis. I have been thinking we might go to New Orleans instead of Key West this time, it would be much more agreeable for the old man. Would you have an apartment for us to rent in your house? I've been happier those short times in New Orleans than anywhere else these last few years. Please forgive me for

the long delay in writing, it's been a terribly active summer for me, much moving around and Maria with us nearly the whole time. Now I've got her a job with Luchino Visconti who is making a big technicolor film that Bowles and I wrote the English dialogue for. They are shooting it near Vicenza, in Northern Italy, and later in Venice which will keep Maria busy till late December. She's loads of fun to be with and I do miss her. Will you please let me hear from you, where you are, what you're up to, c/o Paul Bowles, British Post Office, Tangier (Box #137). We'll probably be sailing in about three weeks. I haven't completed any new play and have no plans after we get back.

With love, Tenn.

[Evidence of "totalitarianism," as TW put it, was to be found in daily news reports of McCarthyism, loyalty boards, Smith Act trials (anti-sedition law), and other provisions against the Red scare. Earlier in June, Vincent Hartnett labeled Broadway "the last stronghold of show-business Marxists and their supporters" and placed TW in the second category by virtue of his "on-again, off-again flirtation with the Communist-front movement" ("New York's Great Red Way," *American Mercury*, June 1953). When challenged by TW's attorney, the editor of the *Mercury* defended Hartnett and threatened a full-scale exposé of the playwright's questionable associations. Hartnett was a primary contributor to *Red Channels* (1950), a pamphlet listing entertainment figures with alleged Communist ties or sympathies that was distributed to employers.]

273. To Audrey Wood

Hotel Rembrandt, Tangier
10/14/53
[TLS, 3 pp. HRC]

Dear Audrey:

We have arrived in Tangier with Paul Bowles after a ten day trip through Italy and Spain in the two Jaguars, Paul's and ours, and many vicissitudes and adventures along the way. Frank is now out investigating sailings out of Gibralter, the earliest likely prospect is the Andrea Doree on the 27th. Soon as we're booked onto something, we'll cable you, maybe before you get this letter. I want to get back soon as possible, now, as I'm worried about Grandfather.

Your long letter contained no mention of "Tattoo". Was the deal completed? A little good news about that would lift my spirit which was

somewhat downcast by your reaction to "the new Battle". I'm glad you wrote me so candidly about it. Your reaction to a script means much more to me than anyone else's, including the critics. Just before I sailed for Europe this time, Bill Inge said to me, Tenn, don't you feel that you are blocked as a writer? I told him that I had always been blocked as a writer but that my desire to write had always been so strong that it broke through the block. But this summer I'm afraid the block has been stronger than I am and the break-through hasn't occured. The situation is much plainer than the solution. There is a mysterious weakness and fatigue in my work now, the morning energy expires in about half an hour or an hour. I pick it up, artificially, with a stiff drink or two but this sort of "forced" energy is reflected in forced writing, which is often off-key and leaves me each day a little more depleted than the day before. I can't help thinking that there is something physiological at the root of this, some organic trouble that is sapping the physical vitality that I need for good work. I feel so "fagged out" in the evenings that I can hardly stay awake through a good movie and have lost all interest in any evening society but Frank's and Mr. Moon's.

Since the script simply doesn't "come off", I don't know if there is much point in telling you what I was aiming at but I will try to. What always bothered me in it was the juvenile poetics, the inflated style of the writing, so I tried to "bring it down to earth", to give the characters a tougher, more realistic treatment. Also I wanted to simplify the story-line, to make it cleaner and straighter, by eliminating such things as "The woman from Waco", Val's literary pretensions, the great load of background and atmospheric detail, and the hi-faluting style of Cassandra's speeches such as "Behold Cassandra, shouting doom at the gates!" and all that sort of crap which seemed so lovely to me in 1940. Unfortunately in 1940 I was a younger and stronger and - curiously! - more confident writer than I am in the Fall of 1953. Now I am a maturer and more knowledgeable craftsman of the theatre, my experience inside and outside the profession is vastly wider, but still the exchange appears to be to my loss. I don't need to tell you how hard I have worked to compensate for that loss, devotion to work is something we have in common.

However I still believe, although I don't have a copy of the script, that what I have done with it is defensible and that if, as a director, I had to choose among all the existing versions, this is the one I would want to put

on the stage. It's true that my conception of the characters is radically different, but I have re-written all of their speeches <u>since</u> this change of conception, and I think the disparity between the lyrical passages and the ordinary speech is justified by the heightened emotion at those times. It's only on rare occasions that our hearts are uncovered and their voices released and that's when poetry comes and the deepest emotion, and expression, of Val and Lady is no different from that of Val and Myra, both the new and the old conceptions of them would speak as they do at such moments. Lady is a woman coarsened, even brutalized, by her "marriage with death" as Val has been brutalized by the places and circumstances of his wanderings but at moments their true hearts and the true speech of their hearts break through and those are the lyrical passages of the play and I think they should have this contrast to the coarse common speech. The coarseness is deliberate and serves a creative purpose which is not sensational. Things like "perfect control of functions" are doubtless written too broadly and would have to be toned down in production but they are in character since Val has the sort of primitive innocense that would express such things freely without embarassment, he is outside of a world of conventional evasions and that is his meaning. I agree with you that the "Junior" bit might be offensive but that's of no importance. I think "sugar in the urine" is legitimate, it's just the sort of phrase that lower middle-class southern women use. As for the ending, I suspect that by the time you came to that, your interest had already been alienated because, unless there have been omissions in typing, what happens to Val is made completely clear, both in the speeches of the mob in the store and in the final bit when the conjure man gives his snakeskin jacket to Cassandra. When she is shot, Lady is covering Val. She falls and then she climbs up "his motionless body" - whence she staggers into the confectionery and dies out of sight, as she has always done in all the various versions. I think Cassandra's presence at that demise is "de trop" and should be removed. I also think it should be established that the doctor's office is right across the street from the store and that "there is a light in his window" so Lady's rushing out to confirm her pregnancy will seem more plausible.

Despite the coarse touches in the dialogue, I think the total effect of the play would be one of tragic purity, that is, when I have refined its texture a bit. Why did I make Lady the daughter of "a dago bootlegger"? I think it was just because the story of the burning of her father's wine garden

(I once called it "The Wine Garden of My Father") and her marriage to the man who burned it was poetically moving and significant, and because it fits the theme of the play, the destruction of the wild and lovely by "the dismembering Furies" that our civilized world produces.

Here the defense rests.

We have a room here with a great window that looks over two continents and the sea between them and all the ships that pass East and West, and it's a wonderful place in which to contemplate the end of the world and other grand and awful things that I wish I were able to get back into my writing.

Looking forward to that brass bed and red carpet which you say I have feathered my nest with in Manhattan.

Love, 10.

[Tangier held "no beauty" for TW, who left after a painful visit of two weeks. "It is just like Miami Beach thrown in the middle of some ghastly slums. The Arabs are inscrutable, you could never get to know them if you lived here a hundred years and they dislike and despise all Christians" (qtd. in St. Just, p. 80).

The "new" *Battle of Angels* was not merely "cleaner and straighter," as TW claimed, but it now lacked the "tragic love story" of Myra and Val which Audrey Wood associated with the original play. She also noted inconsistencies in characterization and dialogue and advised TW to "reconsider" who his "characters are in themselves and in relationship to each other" (September 28, 1953, HRC). In effect Wood confirmed TW's suspicion that his recent work had been "off-key, forced, hysterical," that the revised *Battle of Angels* was indeed "a fiasco" (*Journal*, August 13 and 23, 1953). The HRC holds a composite typescript of *Orpheus Descending* (September 1953) which is based upon the text mailed to Wood in September.

TW did not visit Helsinki as planned but returned directly to New York on the Andrea Doria, arriving November 2.]

274. *To Friend*

The Dylan Thomas Fund
November 10, 1953
[*Partisan Review*, January-February 1954, p. 128]

Dear Friend,

I am sure you have read in the press of the sudden and tragic death of the great poet Dylan Thomas. Thomas died of encephalopathy at St. Vincent's Hospital in New York on November 9th, after an illness of four days. He was only 39 years old. He was attended by one of the finest brain surgeons in New York and everything possible was done to save him.

Thomas' death is an incalculable loss to literature. His work was growing in stature with every year. But there is also a personal tragedy—he leaves a widow without means of support and three children—which gravely concerns his friends and admirers.

As spokesmen for a committee of his friends we are making this urgent appeal to you for a contribution to The Dylan Thomas Fund, which we have hastily organized, which will be used to meet his medical bills and funeral expenses and, if the response is as generous as we hope, to tide his family over the next difficult months.

Please send your check to The Dylan Thomas Fund, care of Philip Wittenberg, Treasurer, 70 West 40th Street, New York City. An accounting of disbursements from the Fund will be sent to the contributors at a later date.

For the DYLAN THOMAS FUND COMMITTEE

W.H. Auden
E.E. Cummings
Arthur Miller
Marianne Moore
Wallace Stevens
Thornton Wilder
Tennessee Williams

[Dylan Thomas arrived in New York in mid-October to direct the American premiere of his play *Under Milk Wood* (1953) and to collaborate with Igor Stravinsky on a new operatic work. His fatal illness was diagnosed as "a severe insult to the brain" caused by "alcoholic toxicity." James Laughlin, Thomas's American publisher, was instrumental in establishing the memorial fund.

TW chose lines from Thomas's poem "Do not go gentle into that good night" (1951) as epigraph for *Cat on a Hot Tin Roof.*]

275. To Oliver Evans

[323 East 58th Street, New York]
[late-November 1953]
[TLS, 1 p. HRC]

Dear Oliver -

I'm still lingering in New York, furnishing a two-room apartment on 58th Street, above Nicholson's cafe, which we will hold as a permanent pied-a-terre in New York, sub-leasing when we are abroad. I'm going through some of what you've been through. Just furnishing the two rooms has cost me $1600. But fortunately the rent is low, only $150. a month, and we can probably rent it for fifty more than we're paying. The rooms are charming, in a late Victorian style with a big glittering brass bed, a carpet sprinkled with garlands of roses, and much brass and colored glass in the decor. Frank will stay on here for at least a month after I go South. I will spend a few days in Saint Louis and bring Grandfather on down with me if I find him in condition to leave. I'm pretty sure he will be. Of course I would prefer to have a small furnished apartment for a month in New Orleans but will probably have to put up at the Monteleone or Saint Charles. However if you know of something that would be suitable for us (ground floor, with two bedrooms, or up a short flight of stairs), I wish you'd let me know. Do you think I could have the use of the Athletic Club pool? We have moved in Saint Louis, that is, Mother has bought a new house there, the address is 6360 Wydown Blvd. and I should be there about the end of this week or by early the next. I have someone, Mike Steen whom you may remember from New Orleans (a sailor at the time) to drive me down as he is going to Louisiana for the holidays. I'll come in the Ford convertible if Frank will ever bring it back from New Jersey where it was stored in his family garage. Have a lot to tell you but it will keep till we meet and I am momently expecting the arrival of someone Gore says I would love. I must get into a becoming peignoir and arrange the pillows on the chaise longue and see that the lights are subtle and the ice-cubes frozen. One bit of news: Carson McCullers' husband committed suicide last week in Paris. He had been planning it for more than a year and so terrorized her that she had fled from Europe to escape him. She is terribly disturbed because I don't think she had really expected him to do it. Love -

Tennessee.

[TW spent a pleasant month in New York visiting James Laughlin, Bob MacGregor, Gore Vidal, and Paul Bigelow. They "were all remarkably nice," including Frank Merlo, who was "on his rare best behavior" (*Journal*, December 4, 1953).

Mike Steen later interviewed friends and colleagues of TW and published their remarks in a collection entitled *A Look at Tennessee Williams* (1969).

Reeves McCullers died in Paris on November 19, 1953, from a probable overdose of barbiturates and alcohol. TW commented in 1972 that "'Reeves died, ultimately, out of great love for Carson. His was a desperate loneliness. Without her, he was an empty shell'" (qtd. in Carr, p. 403).

TW wrote this letter in the week of November 22, 1953, before visiting his family in Clayton.]

276. To Audrey Wood

SH: Hotel Monteleone
New Orleans 12, U.S.A.
12/23/53
[TLS, 3 pp. HRC]

Dear Audrey:

Just finished a good day's work on the film-script "Hide & Seek" or "Whipmaster". A couple of more equally good days should finish the job. I hated to quit work on the new "Battle" for this job but I sure can use the money if you can get it for me, and I hope you can! Now that I'm into it the work is interesting to me and I am pushing it fast and hard as I can, did 15 pages today and about 10 yesterday. As I told you, I'm only re-writing the beginning and end of the play and the sequences that formerly included the old salesman. I think the major problem is reconciling, artistically, the hilarious comedy which is the keynote of the film, and the very heavy "punishment for sins" ending of it demanded by the censors, but maybe that can be cheated a little the way we did the "moral ending" in Streetcar.

Are you getting any concrete concessions from Wallis? If he doesn't phrase the contract so that I am assured of script approval and choice of directors (if Danny should not do it) then I think the cash payments should be upped to at least one hundred thousand. I'm sure that was the figure he was prepared and able to pay if he had to pay it, and he has got to pay it unless he can give me an absolutely reliable check on the story and so forth.

I received a sweet letter from Danny Mann and will enclose an answer, as I don't know his address and perhaps you do.

A funny thing happened a couple of days ago, somebody called me and

identified himself as a nephew of Hal Wallis' wife, Louise Fazenda, and asked me how he could get in touch with Wallis, said he'd heard that he was going to do "Rose Tattoo" and that he had never been able to get in touch with him! I said it was much too early in the morning for me to solve such a weighty problem and to call me back later in the afternoon or evening, but he didn't.

Oliver Evans has completed his renovations on his French Quarter house, but his tenants moved out yesterday while he was giving a party for the officers on a French naval vessel which is paying a good-will visit to New Orleans. He wants Grandfather and I to occupy the vacated premises till the Key West house is ready. I don't know when that will be. I'm trying to get in touch with the realty company but they don't answer the phone this morning. Another possibility is Havana, but I think the sooner I get Grandfather settled down somewhere the better. He fell flat on his face in the Monteleone lobby night before last. He's very unsteady this year and I'm in constant dread that he'll break his hip-bone or something. Please make train or plane reservations for Frank right away! I can't manage alone in Key West. And Frank is likely to put if off unless the bookings are made for him. Please ask your travel agent to book him and Moon on something to Miami on or about Jan. 1st!

I'll manage to get there somehow in the car.

Now I must go downstairs and see if I can get the old man off his sofa in the lobby and into Gluck's restaurant next door for his creole gumbo and hot mince pie. Since that fall in the lobby, he has cut out the Manhattan cocktails.

We both send our love to you and Bill, Tenn.

[TW mailed the latest draft of "Hide & Seek" (n.d., HRC) to Audrey Wood with an admission that he had lost interest in the screenplay and hoped that "a southern writer" (January 15, 1954, HRC) could be found to complete it.

The "old salesman," Mister Charlie, derives from a one-act entitled "The Last of My Solid Gold Watches" (1943). Early drafts of *Baby Doll* begin with his arrival in the Mississippi Delta on the Yellow Dog train, but the role was cut in revision and the opening scene replaced by a more dramatic beginning.

Joseph Breen warned that Baby Doll's seduction in "Hide and Seek" represented a grave censorship problem, especially if treated as "a weapon of retribution against Meighan" (to J. L. Warner, August 1, 1952, Herrick). The warning, issued in 1952, had apparently stimulated thoughts about a "'moral ending'" for the film.

Hospitalization and the prospect of surgery for hemorrhoids would extend the New Orleans visit into the new year. Frank Merlo's arrival from New York led a distraught TW to proclaim that "my 'Horse' is my little world" (*Journal*, December 30, 1953). Oliver Evans added to his friend's abiding fear of cancer by repeating a doctor's warning that hemorrhoids "could become malignant" (*Journal*, January 1, 1954) without surgery.]

277. To Justin Brooks Atkinson

1431 Duncan St.
Key West, Fla.
Jan. 14, 1954
[TLS, 3 pp. BRTC]

Dear Brooks:

I'm so glad that Orianne was able to assemble that tricky little contraption for you and that you are pleased with it. A poet friend of mine, Oliver Evans, presented me with one in New Orleans and I was charmed by it and found out where he got it and thought that a critic who liked Miss Alma and Blanche would share my pleasure and theirs in this small and lyric adaptation of the great natural forces of heat and motion. I agree with you that it's a pity, to put it mildly, that these natural forces can't all be put to such innocent and charming uses or big ones that are equally benign. I went to a cocktail party in New Orleans that was completely still-born, dead and dull as ditch-water, until the lights were turned out and the angel chimes were set in motion, and then a mysterious softening and lightening of the atmosphere occured, and people started talking and being together in a warm and intimate way as if by magic, all through the influence of "The Angel Chimes", so I think they are more important than they look and worth the trouble of putting them together.

I read your Sunday piece on Jane Bowles' play and I blushed with that rather shameful satisfaction that you get from being favorably mentioned in print. I haven't had that satisfaction much lately and I am ashamed to admit that I was languishing for it. I hope you don't mind, or rather, I'm sure you don't, my taking exception to your assessment of the "Summerhouse". I wrote you about it early last summer and told you how much it had thrilled me at the try-out in Ann Arbor, which I saw just before I sailed for Europe. When I saw it again, just before I left for the South, this

Fall, it had undergone some alterations which were not for the good. Poor little Janie had succumbed, in the last act, to those well-meaning influences that surround the author of a play regarded as "special", and the efforts to motivate and clarify and justify the happenings in the play seemed to me to be at the expense of its purity and its "magic". Fortunately these efforts to make things clear were confined to the last act, and the two earlier acts were virtually the same as when I first saw them. But I don't think "The Queen of Tragedy" was a wise choice for the part of Mrs. Eastman-Cuevas. At least she wasn't at the Hartford opening which I attended. Miriam Hopkins, though not so powerful an actress, was much better in the part. She gave the greatest performance I've ever seen her give and was somehow exactly right for it. She had an off-beat humor and zany sort of extravagance that was both heartbreaking and hilarious, she was really Gertrude Eastman-Cuevas in the flesh. I think that this part is the subtlest part and the writing of the first two acts is the subtlest and most original theatre-writing of our times. I would have great, impossible, difficulty in writing a review of the play, so I thoroughly sympathize with your divided reactions. I mean I understand them. I wish, however, that critics could somehow devise a means of supporting plays which they can't approve or recommend as pieces of fine theatrical craftsmanship but which they recognize as having qualities much rarer than craftsmanship, a degree of sensibility and revelation which make them more important (don't they?) than all the hits of the season. Of course it would be wonderful, in fact, ideal, if a writer like Jane Bowles could also possess the professional know-how of a George Axelrod, but there is a jealous quarrel among the Muses which prevents this from being. I think, in other words, we need two separate and clearly defined standards of dramatic criticism, one for the George Axelrods and one for the Jane B's. They should not have to compete on the same terms in the same arena. In view of the fact that these two separate standards don't exist, or have never been openly defined in a way that's intelligible to the theatre public, the critics are probably being as fair as they can be, without favoring what they must feel are "special" interests.

As for myself, this is not a good time for me, I have been going through one of those long periods that have to be borne with patience because there is no other way to bear them. I have kept on working but my vitality is at a low ebb. I don't think this is discouragement, I think

it is simply fatigue, which I hope will be passing. There are certainly
lots of things I still want to do.

Yours ever, Tennessee.

P.S. I believe the biography I promised to give you was Phillip Horton's
biography of the American poet Hart Crane which I think is the most
illuminating picture yet drawn of a poet's difficulties in our modern world.
I'll send you my own copy, autographed by the author, but when I get back
to New York in the Spring I will give you another copy in exchange for that
one. If you find it interesting, you should also read Hart Crane's Collected
Letters which came out last Spring and which will fill out the picture and
relieve the gloom, as Crane himself was much brighter and livelier than his
life. The letters were published by "Hermitage" and edited by Brom Weber,
and I think they rank with the letters of D.H. Lawrence.

[TW "blushed" to be called "a consummate artist" whose lyricism had become "an
eloquent medium of theatrical expression." Such familiar praise by Atkinson
formed the core of his objection to *In the Summerhouse*, which premiered in New
York on December 29, 1953, and closed after fifty-five performances. "Scene by
scene," the Jane Bowles play was "original, exotic and adventuresome," but it left
the reviewer "in a muddle about the characters and with a feeling of flatness" (*New
York Times*, January 10, 1954) for the overall production. The clarifications reportedly imposed upon the script were not evident to Atkinson, nor did he share TW's
distaste for Judith Anderson, who replaced Miriam Hopkins as the imperious Mrs.
Eastman-Cuevas.

TW cites George Axelrod, author of the long-running comedy *The Seven Year
Itch* (1952), as a shrewd writer of popular Broadway fare. During the 1960s he
worked primarily in Hollywood, writing screenplays for *Breakfast at Tiffany's*
(1961) and *The Manchurian Candidate* (1962).]

278. To Cheryl Crawford

1431 Duncan St.,
Key West [Florida]
Jan. 22, 1954
[TLS, 2 pp. BRTC]

Dearest Cheryl:

Everybody who writes me from New York says, Isn't it wonderful,
Cheryl has a "big hit", and each one says it with true satisfaction as if it

was a personal success. I don't think anyone has ever had a hit that was enjoyed by so many people without a touch of the invidious in their reaction, and I can understand why. I feel the same way about it. I knew in Philadelphia that it would probably be a hit and it really did give me a wonderful feeling. Especially since the play is admirable. It is warm and witty and civilized and creditable to everybody in it, and I don't think I've ever seen better casting in the theatre. Of course you are justly famous for your casting. You have the greatest instinct for right actors in the theatre. I think this is the beginning of a new period for you. You needed just this little reassurance of luck to get you going again in full stride. Of course I have never seen you when you appeared disheartened. I don't think I ever will. It's hard to see how a person can be as strong as you are and still remain a presumably vulnerable thing of flesh and blood. We have forgotten about the Yankee spirit and you are a living reminder of what it was and apparently still can be.

I also like you for being honest and kind. . . .

So much for you!

I have the letters of Byron and I browse among them every night. It is impossible to get a book here which is a pity as there is no TV and the movies are old ones and bad ones and Frank and I are trying to stay away from the bars which are full of navy and navy intelligence, as they call it, and when we leave this island we don't want it to be on the famous "lavender bus" as they call it when you are told to get out. The weather is heavenly and all of us are feeling better. I was in the hospital for about a week in New Orleans. I had an attack of hemorrhoids, thrombosed, which is a complaint that is common among gentlemen of middle and late years and which is exquisitely painful. They were going to operate but at the last moment, observing my anxiety, they decided not to, and to see if the condition would not subside automatically, which it did and has now apparently disappeared. But they warned me that the hemmorrhoid veins should be removed if I want to avoid a possible recurrence. I may have this done in the Spring. I had to sleep under morphine several nights and I didn't enjoy it. I always felt like I was dying and didn't want to! Soon as I got out of the hospital, the same day, Grandfather and I took a plane for Miami. It took six hours, stopping at every cow-pasture! For several days afterwards I was so light-headed I couldn't walk a straight line but now I am feeling about as well as ever. I am working again, not easily, but with persistence and I hope I'll have something to show you in the Spring.

Devotedly, Tenn.

[Critics deemed *Oh, Men! Oh, Women!*, Cheryl Crawford's new production, "the funniest, wackiest, cockeyedest comedy to hit the Main Stem in a long time" (*New York Daily Mirror*, December 18, 1953). The story of a psychoanalyst who accidentally discovers his fiancée's sexual history premiered on December 17, 1953, and ran for 382 performances.

TW was probably reading a new selection of Byron letters edited by Jacques Barzun and published in 1953.

TW had good reason to shun "navy intelligence" in Key West. His FBI file indicates that the "Office of Naval Intelligence" has "secured statements from individuals who admitted participating in homosexual acts with Williams." Neither the date of the investigation nor the content of the "statements" is revealed in the file.]

279. To Gore Vidal

1431 Duncan Street
Key West, Fla.
January 27, 1954
[TLS, 2 pp. Houghton]

Dear Gore:

It seems that we just missed you here, which is regrettable as I had looked forward to the company of a bird in this place where the song bird is a very rare avis. There is a rumor that you may be coming back. Are you? The weather is divine here, the days blue and gold in continual succession, and those of our sisters who get around freely at night have reported sensational fortune. Little Arthur Williams is here, you may have crossed paths with him in Europe, he was on the Rome-Paris circuit for five or six years while we were on it. Frank can't stand him but I find him charming. He is very rich and utterly self-centered but he has a complete candor which is something that Latins cannot understand or tolerate, confusing it with bad taste, of which it is actually the opposite in my opinion. He is small and blond with a sort of gentle dry wit, small, perfect features, he looks rather like a much younger Lillian Gish or a gay little nephew of hers, he makes me think of that title of Elinor Wylies', "The Venetian Glass Nephew". But he has to have some dental work done and he is leaving today or tomorrow which is a pity as I shall then be a very solitary land bird among the gulls at South Beach. I do not go around at night. The bird was not well: plummetted to earth in New Orleans with a very dull thud and was confined to "Tuoro Infirmary" with an hideous affliction called

"thrombosed hemmorrhoids", which attacked the tail of the bird and brought it to earth like a good hunter's shot-gun. They were going to operate but decided, at zero hour, that the bird's anxiety made it a bad surgical risk and gave a reprieve on condition that the swelling, large as a hen's egg, subsided, which it gradually did, in the course of ten days. The bird's tail is now back to normal but they say that the hemmorrhoid veins should be cut in the Spring in order to prevent a recurrence. The pain was exquisite and the bird was pumped full of various drugs and morphine which had an upsetting affect on the circulatory system and the nerves. You know the repugnance with which the bird regards the prospect of its eventual demise. . . .

What I wanted to write you about today was your story in "New World Writing" which I finally read last night and which I must say is quite the best thing of yours I have seen to date. Unfortunately the first two pages are fairly routine, which threw me off it, when I first started to read it in New York, but it develops richly, in a new vein of yours that bodes very well for the future. The style is superbly smooth and polished and there are flashes of poetry in it that took me by surprise as I hadn't found them so much in your prose-writing before. It is written with impressive control and restraint, in fact it's one fault is an excessive diffidence about making its points. I thought the women in the library, "The Fatal Sisters" could have been pointed up just a bit more before he woke from his sun-nap to hear them plotting his destruction. And the scenes with the boy were cut just a tiny bit short of the point at which they would have been clearly comprehensible perhaps because you were afraid of evoking some echo of "Death in Venice", which I don't think should have bothered you, as all works of art that I can think of strike echos of others and the story is completely your own. This shade too much of diffidence is a fault on the side of the angel's, though it may prevent some people from getting as much from the story as there is there. I think it would make a fine play and I wish you had chosen it as the theme for the play you are working on. The people and background are very much at home with you and the fact that there is so much room for expansion in the story makes it a good play prospect.

Do write me some bulletins on New York if you're not coming back here soon. What happened to Paul and Janie? I talked to them over long-distance after the play opened but Janie was incoherent and Paul was very

cool and non-committal. He talked as if he thought the wires were tapped by the FBI. I only gathered that he was leaving this month for Tangier and that Ahmed would never be able to leave there, for Ceylon or anywhere else, because of trouble with passport. But Paul always takes the blackest possible view of a situation, a queer sort of defense against the jealous gods. I am trying to complete all manuscripts that are close enough to completion, so that I can leave for Ceylon or somewhere with a clean slate, that is, with nothing hanging over my head except the future which is quite enough to hang over any bird's head in these times.

Heard that Truman's mother died. Have you seen him? I saw Speed in Monroe but he was headed almost immediately for New York so must be there now. Oliver is living a very disordered life in New Orleans, cruising feverishly night and day and doing no work, but looks and seems to feel well.

Love, Tenn.

[Gore Vidal returned to New York at this time to develop a successful career in television writing.

The title of Elinor Wylie's novel *The Venetian Glass Nephew* (1925) refers to a creature made of glass who is brought to life by a necromancer's art.

"The Ladies in the Library" (1953), the Vidal story admired by TW, was dedicated to Alice Bouverie, whose estate on the Hudson may have provided setting and locale. The "Ladies," an incarnation of the mythological Fates, are overheard by a visiting writer as they plot his imminent death by a massive heart attack.

Truman Capote's mother Nina died on January 4, 1954, from an overdose of barbiturates and alcohol.]

280. To Jane Lawrence and Tony Smith

1431 Duncan
Key West [Florida]
Feb 8, 1954
[TLS, 1 p. Smith Collection]

Dear Jane & Tony:

I'm not able to write you a good letter right now, I'm not able to write anything good right now, but I don't want to let another day pass without telling you how happy I am over the birth of Clare Lanier. My middle name is also Lanier so I think of her as a relative.

In many ways you are the two most wonderful people that I have ever

known. I have always suspected that you actually are, it would not surprise me if I am right about that.

The child will be as wonderful as you both put together.

There's nothing I would like as well tonight as hearing Jane singing "My Bill" or Tosca or Carmen but all I hear is the palms scraping together and a distant radio.

Grandfather and Frank and I are back in Key West. The days are lovely but the nights are dull. But you remember how Key West is. We will be sailing back to Europe sometime in May by way of Gibralter and then up through Europe, with some stops in Spain and a long stay in Rome. Maybe after that we'll even take a boat to Ceylon with Paul Bowles and Ahmed, if Ahmed is permitted to leave Tangier by the French immigration authorities.

Grandfather says to give Clare Lanier his love and "apostolic blessing".

Mine to all three of you, Tennessee.

Town is dull this year, result of various acts of violence against queens in the past few seasons. One poor girl, a night auditor at the Casa Marina, was dispatched with <u>twenty-two</u> knife wounds by a party unknown. Blood was all over the apartment as if she had run till exhausted from room to room, probably defending herself as best she could with her manicure set and tweezers. Neighbors reported no out-cry. She probably had on her long-playing opera records, and didn't have time to turn them off as she flew!

281. To Lilla Van Saher

[1431 Duncan Street
Key West, Florida]
Feb 16, 1954
[TLS, 1 p. HRC]

Dear Lilla:

Sorry we just missed you in Key West, Regina St. Paul told us you'd been here. I trust we'll have better luck in the Spring. We plan to sail around the middle of May and will spend at least a month in New York before sailing. Our new address there is the floor above Cafe Nicholson on East Fifty-eighth street, phone is Murry Hill 8-6744. Gore will know when we get back or possibly when we're expected, and I do hope you'll be around.

The town is dead, no interesting society, almost no one to talk to. But the days are lovely. I get up at daybreak, work all morning and rest on the beach all afternoon, so the absence of any night-life is unimportant.

I'll fly over to Havana when some excitement becomes imperative.

Grandfather's still with us, and Frank and Mr. Moon.

It's kind of you to see my influence, favorably, in the current theatre season, but actually the only good play of the lot, "In The Summerhouse" was written long before any influence of mine existed. You'd love Jane Bowles: you might call her, she stays with Oliver Smith, the designer-producer, 28 W. 10th Street, A 1. 4-2085. She may be feeling depressed about the commercial failure of her play and you would be good for her, you have such a warm heart for other writers.

Ever yours, Tennessee.

[Lilla Van Saher (1912-1968), one of TW's "vampire" women, wrote *The Echo* (1947), a psychiatric novel, and *Macamba* (1949), a florid romance set in the Caribbean. TW described her as "a dominatrix" and dubbed her "the crepe de Chine Gypsy" (*Conversations*, p. 357).]

282. To Audrey Wood

SH: Hotel Nacional de Cuba, Havana
March 6, 1954
[TLS w/ autograph postscript, 2 pp. HRC]

Dear Audrey:

As you see I have removed to Cuba. Danny and I had three meetings and heart-to-heart talks before I left and everything was understood. I didn't think it wise to sign the contracts until we had gotten through to Hal Wallis, directly, about the matter of authorship. I don't know whether or not you read the "approach" that was submitted to us, but as Frankie remarked, it is actually a "retreat" and a very disastrous one. I suggest that you read it right away. You will agree with me about it. Remove the poetry from "Tattoo" and you have the cheapest kind of a grade B picture. There was no hint of poetry in this treatment. "Tattoo" is admirably suited to the screen. It will blossom out as a picture, even without Magnani, and with Magnani, it will have a stunning impact, IF-IF-IF! - it is not destroyed by

the writer. Consequently I feel that I am obligated, not only to the play and myself, but equally to Magnani, and all of us concerned, to make sure that the lyrical values, the plastic values, and so forth, are kept in it and given a chance to flower as <u>Magnani</u> will make them. ~~I don't believe that Wallis either appreciates Magnani or the play itself. Or he wouldn't even permit this~~.

I think that you can persuade Hal Wallis, not only of my good and honest and rational intentions, but of my taste and my capability to see that he has a script worthy of Anna Magnani, whether I have to do it alone, or with a ~~suitable~~ collaborator who will be willing to work <u>under my direction</u>, since I think it is reasonable to assume that I, who created the play and the characters in it, am best able to judge whether or not they are being re-created for the screen. Danny agrees with me about this a hundred percent and I know that you will. Perhaps Wallis does not want "Tattoo" but another film very loosely related to it. But he must remember that Magnani agreed to do "Tattoo" and that that is the play we are giving him. If he doesn't really like it, if he wants something else, then there is no point in continuing to deal with him. It would be another "Menagerie" or worse, for the episodes in "Tattoo" will be grotesque and Serafina a ridiculous slob <u>unless</u> it exists in the poetic atmosphere of the original ~~play~~.

I have already written the opening sequences of the film, up to the death of Rosario. I am <u>satisfied with the elimination of all censorable material</u>. But I am going to keep the boy kneeling before the shrine to promise that he will respect the daughter's innocence. This was disgustingly treated in the "approach", he promised that he would "honor his father and mother" and "punctured his finger with a needle" to make some sort of blood oath. This gives you an idea of the "approach". The kneeling to the shrine could never offend anybody, it never did, and on the screen it could be handled still more scrupulously, with absolute purity and touching devoutness.

I like the suggestion of Serafina actually going to the Square Roof to confront Estelle Hohengarten instead of calling her on the phone. <u>That's good</u>. (Maybe) I also like every opportunity of taking the picture outside the house. There is nothing I like better than freedom and movement, and Wallis should not be worried on that score.

Please try to sell him on three points: my taste, my professional capability and the humble objectivity that I think I now have developed in regard to my work.

I want to write you separately about Inge. I was terribly disturbed by the one-acts he gave me to read and which he demanded right back to show to Danny. I think he is going through what I went through after "Streetcar", post-success ~~trauma~~ "shock", but he is over-compensating in the wrong way. To exhibit this work is extremely damaging. I think you must deal with him as candidly as you do with me when I send you "crap". It's the only way to help a panicky writer. If I hadn't been leaving immediately for Cuba, I would have talked to him about this problem. Perhaps I will have a chance to before he returns to New York.

Love - 10.

How can I "make friends" with Wallis? I want to.

[TW expressed "fury over the 'Tattoo' script" developed by his collaborator, who "couldn't write 'I see the cat.'" He wished that he could "shut a door on all that dreary buy and sell side of writing and work purely again for myself alone. I am sick of being peddled. Perhaps if I could have escaped being peddled I might have become a major artist" (*Journal*, April 17, 1954). Joe Hazen, one of the film's co-producers, later informed TW that Hal Kanter was "off the script" (July 9, 1954, HRC). Daniel Mann was set to direct the film.

Censorship problems occasioned by *The Rose Tattoo* were last summarized in a Production Code report dated May 5, 1953. Joseph Breen advised that "romance rather than lust" guide the "big scene" between Alvaro and Serafina, and that Alvaro conveniently "pass out" from too much "wine" to avert any sexual intimacy. The advice, which was taken, would allow Serafina's daughter Rosa to "misconstrue" (to Wallis, May 5, 1953, Herrick) the suggestive events of the night. Restored to the film was the boy's promise to respect the "innocense" of Rosa, a distasteful reference which the censor preferred to delete. No Sicilian "blood oath" remained in the final print.]

283. To Audrey Wood

[1431 Duncan Street
Key West, Florida]
March 21, 1954
[TLS, 2 pp. HRC]

Dear Audrey:

Although I understand your letter about "Kingdom of Earth" and the practicality of your objections to the story's publication, I am distressed

over its omission from the book and have very little interest left in publishing these stories. I think "Kingdom" is by far my best and strongest piece of prose-writing. Without it the little book will be thin and pale as a leaf of under-nourished cabbage, and I would almost, perhaps quite, prefer not to have it brought out. It will not compare favorably to <u>One Arm</u>, people will say it's a "come down". With "Kingdom" they couldn't say that, even though that story might offend or disgust them. I wish that New Directions was willing to bring the book out much more privately and keep "Kingdom" in it, bring it out the way they did "I Rise in Flame", very de luxe and expensive and a small edition, not distributed by mail or through commercial book-stores but done strictly as an art venture and sold slowly without immediate profit. If it is a really exciting book, as it would be with Kingdom, it would have a much more permanent interest and eventually a bigger and more profitable sale. I don't mind at all if the <u>sales</u> are postponed till after these films are released if you really think it would hurt them. I don't think it would. On the contrary, I think the artistry of the story is defensible and that even if it is attacked by censors, it will not be damaging to my other projects.

MacGregor and I discussed, tentatively, a compromise arrangement, by which "Kingdom of Earth" would be "tipped into" a hundred or hundred and fifty "special" copies and held on reserve, for much more private distribution, at a higher price than the "trade edition". But I really don't think there should be a trade edition. It would suit me far better if there was only the special, private edition, distributed by hand directly by the publishers, to avoid legal trouble. I wouldn't suggest such a thing if I didn't think in the long run it would pay off at least as well. Actually the "queer" stories in the book will be more damaging than "Kingdom" which is merely sensual, if that is to be considered.

I hope I'll get a typed copy of "the new Battle" in a few days before we leave Key West. I'm eager to see how it reads. I think Act Two Scene one is particularly improved, but perhaps Carol should appear first at the store-entrance, perhaps during the altercation between Lady and Val, before she starts honking at the service-station, --- the store door could be locked and Val or Lady could shout, 'Not open!' --- I think it's much better not having Lady rush out to the doctor after the nurse charges her with pregnancy. Of course I know the play is pitched in an almost hysterical key, but if a non-realistic tone is established in staging right from the start, - also

in design, lighting, Etc. - it might be acceptable at least as "the work of a mad man". I'd like to show it to Gadg and Jose Quintero. Send me a couple of copies, one for notes.

I think I've done all the important scenes for "Tattoo" already. It is surprisingly easy, it takes to the screen by instinct.

I'm also pulling together a short-long play based on the characters in "Three Players" which I started last summer in Rome but don't expect that till you see it, as I might not like it when I read it aloud.

My feet still feel like I'm walking on two sponges! I am taking massive shots of Vitamin B12, in alternate cheeks, every other day, which is energizing but has no effect on the pedal extremities. I don't for one moment believe the doctor's opinion that it is "peripheral neuritis", it is something, all right, but not that! I want to have a medical check-up soon as I get back to New York to determine the true cause of the trouble: I think it is circulatory.

Jimmie Elliot wrote me a long, long letter about his plan to produce Raffaelo de Banfield's opera based on "Lord Byron's Love Letter". How do you feel about this? He said you approved. I think a production by Jimmie would need careful supervision as he has had nothing but flops and is still pretty young. I like the kid, though, and his enthusiasm is important. I guess there's not much to lose.

Bigelow's two-day visit has stretched and stretched, it's like the famous girdle called the Two-way stretch! But I love having him around, he livens things up considerably. It will be expensive, this pleasure, but I always feel that Bigelow is worth every cent he may cost you. IF - you can afford him . . .

Gertrude Houston was also here for a couple of days with a girl-friend. No allusions were made on either side to the Jay-Maria situation and she and her friend were rushing to meet a yacht in Miami and planning to join some oil-millionaire in Houston. Jay is definitely in India. I haven't heard a word from Maria! - the suspense is intolerable almost.

Love, Tenn

[Audrey Wood feared that publishing "The Kingdom of Earth" would cause publicity "detrimental" (to TW, March 18, 1954, HRC) to current and forthcoming film projects. The "sensual" story, drafted in 1942 and entitled "Spiritchel Gates" (HRC), is set in the Mississippi Delta and narrated by Chicken: "It's earth I'm after and now I am honest about it and don't pretend I'm nothing but what I am, a

lustful creature determined on satisfaction and likely as not to get my full share of it" (*Collected Stories*, p. 378). Chicken's determination leads indirectly to the death of Lot, his consumptive half-brother, and to the appropriation of Lot's prostitute-bride, Myrtle.

A "compromise" led New Directions to publish both a trade edition entitled *Hard Candy: A Book of Stories* (1954), and a limited edition entitled *The Kingdom of Earth with Hard Candy* (1954). TW demanded once again that his most controversial work not be openly sold or displayed in St. Louis.

The "short-long play" in preparation is *Cat on a Hot Tin Roof*.

Raffaello de Banfield wrote the music and TW the libretto for *Lord Byron's Love Letter: Opera in One Act*, which premiered in New Orleans on January 17, 1955. James Elliott produced the new opera on a bill which included the one-act "27 Wagons Full of Cotton."

TW informed Wood in early-February that the Laughlin-Britneva affair had been revived and that they planned to marry soon. TW, one of those chosen "'to hold the crown'" in the Russian Orthodox ceremony, quipped that "if this comes off, I'll be willing to <u>wear</u> the crown or even sit on it!" (February 1, 1954, HRC). Laughlin's untimely travel abroad only added to the mystery of his intentions. Gertrude Huston, formerly an intimate companion of the publisher, was visiting Key West with a friend.]

284. To Elia "Gadg" Kazan

[1431 Duncan Street
Key West, Florida]
March 31, 1954
[TLS, 2 pp. WUCA]

Dear Gadg:

You should never put off doing a play or a picture because when you do, somebody works on you, or you work on yourself, and the blood of art runs out through the mortal wound of excessive cogitation! Do you mind me telling you this? I am not afraid to say anything I want to say to you because I regard you as so close and true a friend that no dissimulation is necessary between us.

If you had hopped over here for a couple of days, we could have accomplished much more, batting ideas back and forth in talk than we can by exchanging letters about them in which each of us is determined to explain and defend his views and position.

The frog-gigging was your idea, I embraced it immediately as I do most

of your ideas which are so startling, so brilliantly apposite, so direct to the core of the story. A modern version of the medieval tournament with frog-sticks instead of lances and a panicky dyed blond as the lady fair and the mossy swamps of the deep South as the field of honor was a divinely apposite idea and one to which I made an immediate, humble obeisance. Now you have succumbed to the weakness of Hamlet. You have brooded and chewed over it for a year and a half, or more, and you have talked yourself out of it. Well, I still say it was a GREAT, GREAT IDEA! And you haven't talked me out of it. . . .

Sure, you could do a scene with a big party, but it wouldn't have anything like the dramatic poetry, the visual and symbolic richness of the men with the frog-sticks making human frogs of each other, rival phalluses - excuse me, phalli - I see what you mean when you say it comes out of a cocked hat, a magician's topper, but I don't agree with you, I don't think it does, I think it is an exactly parallel situation, and anyhow, it can easily be predicated or announced in one of the earlier scenes, Ruby can say they're going frog-sticking tonight and ball it up in the bayou! "What's fun about sticking frogs?" - "nothing, honey, if there was nothin' but frogs. . ." --- If we see the two men walking off side by side, after the very funny Gaston and Alfonso bit, one raging, grim, frustrate, the other, confident, smiling - the story is told. We know damned well that Vacarro isn't the frog! - that Meighan is already the stuck frog! - the story was completed, the whole thing actually resolved, when Vacarro put the horns on him, and after that all we want to do is hit hard and get out fast. The phone-bit is overdone. I don't think she should speak to God on the phone. After her conversation to the chief of police, she should drop the receiver exhaustedly into her lap and speak the words to God as if to herself in prayer, just holding the phone in her hand. I love the last line it gives us. "Scared in this big empty house". IT describes, or sums up, the whole individual human situation, alone and scared in a big empty house of a universe, so much too big for any single soul in it.

I had to pitch in and write the "Tattoo" script as the studio writer Wallis put on it did a shockingly bad job on it, worse than that other writer did on "Streetcar". Now Magnani and Lancaster are squabbling over top-billing, the gentleman wants to go in front of the lady and vice versa, and maybe she won't even do it, show-business is hell! - real frog-sticking!

Ask Audrey to let you read the re-write I did on "Battle of Angels".

I did it last summer in Rome and Spain. Audrey didn't like it and I did it over again here. Maybe she still doesn't like it, but I think it is an exciting and different piece of theatre and I would love to have your reaction to it. I also would like you to read a short-long play, originally a long one, called "A Cat on a Hot Tin Roof". It would require a curtain-raiser to make a full evening and the story is grim. I will show it to you before I sail for Europe May 15th. When are you leaving New York? I get there about the tenth of April, after delivering grandfather to the Gayoso lobby in Memphis.

Play it cool, baby!

Love, Tenn.

Skipper was here and should have had him a ball. For some reason this year the Island is over-run by beautiful nymphos, really attractive ones, who almost rape the men in public, let alone what they may do in private. They grope you at the bar and literally howl to be fucked. Won't take no for an answer if they can possibly get any other. I think Skipper was scared. He left mighty quick. But not as quick as Bigelow! - a cop named Buster walked into Logun's patio one night and took Bigelow by the seat of his pants and turkey-trotted him out to the paddy-wagon at the door. (I wasn't there but heard a vivid account) - It cost me five hundred bucks to get him off the keys the next morning. . . .

I thought this would give you a laugh, but please forget that I told you about it, please! You and I both love gossip. At heart I'm a back-fence biddy. . . .

[At first TW mildly resisted the "frog-sticking" conclusion of "Hide and Seek" because he had "never gigged frogs. Do you suppose the research dept. at Warners' could provide me with a graphic account of one?" (April 16, 1953, WUCA), he asked Elia Kazan. A draft of "Hide and Seek" dated March 25, 1954, includes a "Gaston and Alfonso bit" played by Archie Lee and Silva, who carry sharp gigs but tramp comically toward the bayou "side by side like a pair of sweethearts!" Violence is averted for the moment, as the scene dissolves to Baby Doll on the back porch of the Meighan residence calling the chief of police: "I'm all alone, I'm scared, in this - big - empty - house" (HTC). The present ending, Kazan may have felt, lacked a dramatic denouement and the necessary punishment of vice.]

285. To Audrey Wood

[1431 Duncan Street
Key West, Florida]
[ca. April 1, 1954]
[TLS w/ enclosure, 1 p. HRC]

Dear Audrey:

Here's a sort of rough draft of the play that threw me into such a terrible state of depression last summer in Europe, I couldn't seem to get a grip on it. I haven't done much with it since then, but I would like to have this draft typed up, so that I will at least be able to read it with less confusion. Although it is very wordy it is still too short and would need a curtain-raiser to make a full evening. But I do think it has a terrible sort of truthfulness about it, and the tightest structure of anything I have done. And a terrifyingly strong final curtain.

I am sending it to you a little prematurely since I am hitting the air-lanes with Grandfather this afternoon. Yesterday I sent you my work on "Rose Tattoo". I hope you will at least get the impression that I am still a hard-worker. . . .

A discouraging letter from Gadg. He wants a completely different ending to "Hide & Seek", although it was he who wanted me to end it with the frog-sticking party. I think that's an excellent ending and am not at all in sympathy with his new notions about it. I wrote him so. Is it true that he is going to do a play in the Fall by Robert Anderson? How can he do both? Is this the play you said you had for him? - I am getting jealous. . . .

With love, Tenn.

The news that Arthur Miller lost his passport is shocking and disgusting. It is also frightening to me, since I have not yet had any news of mine. Do you think they'll refuse it? I didn't send my old passport along with the application. Is that necessary? I am enclosing a letter of protest to the State Dept. but I will let you decide whether or not to send it. This is cowardly, but if I lost my passport, I would just curl up and die! - I have to get out of this country at least once a year, the way things are now. . . . Please make a copy of the letter and send the original to the State Dept, if you think this advisable. The other copy you might send to Arthur or to "The Times".

[The "rough draft" with a "strong final curtain" is *Cat on a Hot Tin Roof*. TW later reported some "messy" work on the play and worried that "the intrusion of the homosexual theme may be fucking it up again" (*Journal*, April 3, 1954).

Robert Anderson's new play *All Summer Long* opened on September 23, 1954, with direction by Alan Schneider rather than Elia Kazan. It closed after 60 performances on Broadway.

The enclosure regarding Arthur Miller's "lost" passport is printed as a separate letter.]

286. *The State Department*
Washington, D.C.

[1431 Duncan Street
Key West, Florida]
April 1, 1954
[TL, 1 p. HRC]

Dear Sirs:

I feel obliged to tell you how shocked I am by the news that Arthur Miller, a fellow playwright, has been refused a passport to attend the opening of a play of his in Brussels.

I know only the circumstances of the case that have been reported in the papers, but since I have been spending summers abroad since 1948, I am in a position to tell you that Mr. Miller and his work occupy the very highest critical and popular position in the esteem of Western Europe, and this action can only serve to implement the Communist propaganda, which holds that our country is persecuting its finest artists and renouncing the principles of freedom on which our ancestors founded it.

I would like to add that there is nothing in Arthur Miller's work, or my personal acquaintance with him, that suggests to me the possibility that he is helpful or sympathetic to the Communist or any other subversive cause. I have seen all his theatrical works. Not one of them contains anything but the most profound human sympathy and nobility of spirit that the American theatre has shown in our time and perhaps in any time before. He is one man that I could never suspect of telling a lie, and he has categorically stated that he has <u>not</u> supported Communism or been a Communist.

I don't think you have properly estimated the enormous injury that an action of this kind can do our country, even in the minds of those who are still prejudiced in our favor in Western Europe.

Yours respectfully,

[A spokesman for the State Department noted that Arthur Miller's application had been "rejected under regulations denying passports to persons believed to be supporting the Communist movement, whether or not they are members of the Communist party." Miller replied that he was not "'supporting any Communist movement,'" adding that "his plays would make more friends for American culture than the State Department" (*New York Times*, March 31, 1954). Miller planned to visit Brussels to attend the premiere of his play *The Crucible* (1953), a thinly veiled indictment of McCarthyism.

TW did not mail the letter of protest, fearing that his own passport would not be renewed for a sailing date of May 15 (see letter #294). Citation of a similar gesture of support for the "Hollywood Ten," screenwriters and directors investigated by the House Un-American Activities Committee in 1947, appears in TW's FBI file and was reported to the United States Information Agency in July 1954. At issue was TW's participation in a radio broadcast planned in 1950 which did not materialize.]

PART VI
1954–1957

Overleaf: Tennessee Williams and Anna Magnani.
"The sexiest looking woman on earth."

287. To Robert MacGregor

SH: Rembrandt Hotel, Tanger
5/29/54.
[TLS, 3 pp. Houghton]

Dear Bob:

Frank says he mailed the proofs to you yesterday. I'm sorry about the delay, I didn't realize you were in a hurry for them. I only came across one <u>serious</u> error, the omission of a phrase in "Hard Candy" which made a sentence meaningless, and I wrote the omitted phrase in the margin. Two or three stories are still here as I haven't yet read them. Mattress, 3 Players, Violin Case, The Vine and Widow Holly. As you have correct Mss. on these 4, it will be easy to check the proofs at your end. That is, if there is need for haste. I felt so fatigued, so run down, when I got on the boat that I knew I would loathe the stories if I read them. So I put it off till the last day of the voyage, when I was beginning to feel recovered. I liked most of them, especially "Two on a Party" which I almost wish were the title story of the book. Frank is disturbed over having both "Hard Candy" and "Mysteries of the Joy Rio" in the book. I think there should be a note stating that the latter is actually a first draft of the title story but that we felt there was enough difference to justify printing both. I think it might obviate some criticism, and criticism should certainly be obviated wherever possible, don't you think? I wonder if obviated is the right word. . . .

Now please do me this favor. Don't distribute the book anywhere that my mother would be likely to get her hands on it. That is, around Saint Louis. It must <u>not</u> be displayed in windows or on counters anywhere. Don't you agree? Or do you? My mother's reaction is the only one that concerns me. I think she would be shocked to death by "Two on a Party" - although it seems that she did get hold of "One Arm" somehow or other. It still makes me shudder to think of her reaction! She has aged greatly since. . .

Isn't it awful to have conventional blood ties? You just can't break them.

Soon as we landed in Tangier we found ourselves involved in the turbulent lives of the Bowles'. Jane is hopeless enamored of an Arab woman in the grain-market, a courtship which has continued without success for six years, and Paul's Arab, Ahmed, has moved out of his house, at least for "Rhamadan", a religious period of abstinence like our Lent, which is now going on here. A cannon which shakes the whole city is fired at 3 A.M.

announcing that eating, drinking, fucking must stop. It is fired again at 7 P.M. to signal the resumption of these practises, but Ahmed says that total abstinence is necessary in the third practise. Paul is languishing, liver trouble and paratyphoid came on him with Rhamadan.

It appears that we have inherited Maria for the summer. A letter was waiting for me at Gibralter in which she declared that she was brutally jilted and cannot stay in London, as everybody is sending her wedding presents and congratulatory messages. She is on a Mediterranean cruise to escape this humiliation. But she proposes to get off the boat at Corsica and come to Rome as she can't face London again under the circumstances. Funny as it does sound, I do feel sorry for her. Why did Jay propose to her if he wasn't prepared to go through with it? I wanted to have a quiet summer. . . . Of course when she arrives I will be happy to have her with us as she really does brighten a scene with her unquenchable spirits and love of fun. Jay says he was frightened of her vitality. Perhaps someone should have held his nose and made him swallow it for his own good, I can't see how, unless he is going to marry Gertrude after all, he will ever find anybody that will give him the lively companionship he seems to want and need.

Ever & truly, Tenn.

[Robert MacGregor (1911-1974) increasingly took over editorial tasks handled by James Laughlin at New Directions.

"Hard Candy" and "The Mysteries of the Joy Rio" are set in a "third-rate cinema" whose "galleries" have witnessed "every device and fashion of carnality" (*Collected Stories*, p. 103). So marked was their difference "in result" ("Editor's Note") that both stories would be published in *Hard Candy* (1954). TW preferred "Joy Rio," the early version, because of its greater compassion and unity (to MacGregor, March 1, 1954, Houghton).

MacGregor promised TW that relatively few copies of *Hard Candy* would be sent to St. Louis and that local book sellers had agreed to accommodate only preferred customers who "cannot be alienated" (August 24, 1954, Houghton).

TW was "shocked," if not surprised, by Laughlin's jilting of Maria Britneva. "Most of all," he wrote to her, "it seems so foolish, so pitiably foolish, of J. because you would have made him a perfect wife and would have given him a faith in himself, as a poet and as a person" (qtd. in St. Just, pp. 91-92). Audrey Wood reported a later conversation in which Laughlin expressed fear of Britneva's "'great will'" (to TW, July 19, 1954, HRC) and of her many social activities, both of which would interfere with his preferred manner of life.

Britneva's invitation to join TW in Rome came with an understanding that "we won't be wearing black chiffon or broken hearts on our sleeves, but enjoy the golden city in the golden summer" (qtd. in St. Just, p. 92).]

288. To Justin Brooks Atkinson

[Rome]
[early-June 1954]
[TLS, 2 pp. BRTC]

DEAR BROOKS:

Audrey Wood just stuck under my hotel door, here in Rome, your notice of "Purification" in Dallas and I can't even wait to get some decent paper on which to write you. Encouragement works in mysterious ways. I immediately sat down and conquered a scene in a play which had totally eluded and almost maddened and unmanned me for weeks past. Now my nerves are calm, my fingers don't shake, I look appreciatively out into the fine blue and gold morning that almost never fails to appear in Roman summer. Why are you so good to me? I certainly don't deserve it, although I do try to.

Did Margo really do a beautiful production? I think she sometimes can. She did a beautiful production of "You Touched Me" in Pasadena. Perhaps she failed to, with <u>Summer & Smoke</u> in New York because we were fighting. I am terribly attached to her, she has the quickest sympathies and warmest affections of any one I've ever known in my life, except my grandmother. And the deepest passion for the theatre. The tragedy is that her performance rarely lives up to her passion. Like a lover so anxious, so frightened of his desire, that he can't carry it through. . . . I have not been very good to her, have been cool and reserved since the clash over "Summer" but she has never seemed to resent it or hold it against me. She has true gallantry of spirit and ENORMOUS courage. I think what most annoyed me about "Summer" was not so much her refusal to let me work directly with the actors as the story, that came to me "round about", that she had made a speech to the actors saying that it was the work of "a dying playwright". I had been ~~terribly~~ ill at the time, but "dying" was the furthest thing from my intention, then or any time since, and anyway it struck me as an irrelevant or false and certainly not helpful sort of "appeal". Actors <u>always</u> do their best, and the real or imaginary sickness of an author

doesn't and shouldn't, couldn't, alter their contribution to the production.

Rome has never looked lovelier, than it does now, after the sick atmosphere of Tangier, which was only relieved by the beach and charm of Jane and Paul Bowles who make their home there, mostly because it's about the most economical place to live in the western half of the world.

Yours ever and truly and fondly, Tennessee.

[TW was "completely shattered by the 2 plane flights" from Tangier to Rome and reported "panic Panic!" in correspondence with Jane and Paul Bowles (6/?/54, HRC), whom he invited to visit the new ménage: "It is wonderful being all together in 1 place 'en famille' even when the horse sleeps with the chauffeur (??!)."

Margo Jones's staging of "The Purification" and "The Apollo of Bellac" (Jean Giraudoux, 1947) reassured Brooks Atkinson, who had come to regard the Dallas theatre project as "stock company merchandising." The plays, he wrote, "complement each other perfectly" and were "singularly beautiful" (*New York Times*, May 29, 1954) in their presentation. Jones had proven a sympathetic director of TW's early works, including "The Purification" in 1944.

In *Memoirs* TW recalled Jones's "speech" to the cast of *Summer and Smoke* (1948) and observed that "I did not like to be reminded that my apparent good health was so profoundly suspect" (p. 153).]

289. To Cheryl Crawford

[Rome]
[June 1954]
[TLS, 3 pp. BRTC]

Cheryl dear:

I hope you are not thinking badly of me because of my silence. I have been passing through, and still not out of, the worst nervous crisis of my nervous existence and I thought for a while I'd crack up. I've been approaching it for more than a year, evading with liquor and sedatives and distractions. But when it became imperative to stop work for a while, to take the rest I'd promised myself so long, I really fell apart at the seams. When I got up in the morning, there was nothing to do but draw deep, sighing breaths and exhale them and stare stupidly this way and that. What do people do with themselves when they don't work? Frank fusses over the dog for a couple of hours but I can't get interested in this new dog. I came to love Moon and he died and this new dog seems stupid and bad-tempered

to me, although he has the touching pathos of all small beings. (That is, except insects!) - I feel, now, that I should have remained in the States and possibly sought out some good psychiatrist or nerve-doctor this summer, regardless of my loathing of that sort of surrender or admission of helplessness. But the point has come when I can't rely on myself. The present "syndrome" is temporary at best. I go as far through the day as I can without a sleeping tablet. Then - sometimes before noon, rarely much after - I wash one down with a stiff drink. Five hours later the tension builds up again and I need another. So far I haven't exceeded three in the course of a day. But this is no good, it can't go on, you know, it is just temporizing. As Miss Alma said to the old doctor, "I don't see how I'm going to get through the summer." It has gotten so bad, Cheryl, that I don't dare to turn down a street unless I can sight a bar not more than a block and a half down it. Sometimes I have to stop and lean against a wall and ask somebody with me to run ahead and bring me a glass of cognac from the bar. . . . I don't understand what is back of these crises, panics. It could be simply a physical thing. Or it could be a physical expression of some deep mental crisis that's going on. I am telling you these embarassingly personal things because I think we have a relationship that permits confession and understanding. I could also tell Audrey, but unless she guesses, I am somehow too shy with her (always have been) to tell her things like that. - Now I do think that I can get through the summer but when I get back I want to tackle this dilemma in a radical way, even if it means submitting to analysis. Dr. Kinsey, after a four and a half hour talk in 1949 or 50, told me that I needed analysis and that he would recommend a good man for me. He seemed to realize that I was facing an eventual impasse, at which I am now arriving. I've put it off because of work and the need to travel. But now the sustained crisis has exhausted the working apparatus, so something has to be done to get at the root of it, even if it means facing something that I'm afraid to face. Lawrence said: "Face the facts and live beyond them". I've tried to live beyond them by not facing them and come to the logical pay-off that entails. I'll probably return earlier than usual this summer, perhaps in August, and if, in the meanwhile, you can get the name of some good man in the psychiatric field (perhaps through Kinsey), I think that I will be ready to give him a try. I don't want Inge's man, I don't like what he has done with Inge who seems to be living in a state of false complacense, peaceful on the surface, but with an apparent suspension of

his critical faculties at least regarding his own work, an "afflatus" that only makes him pompously self-satisfied and showing bad scripts around like fresh-plucked flowers. There is probably not more than one man who would be any good for me but I want to find him and find out, one way or the other, if I am susceptible to outside help. Without illusions. . . .

So much for the screaming "ME-mies"!

In spite of the state in which I worked on it, I still think "Orpheus" may have some, and possibly even enough, of the lyric beauty and intensity which I tried to put into it, to justify its production. Of course it was bound to suffer from its author's suffering to some extent. A line from Rabindranath Tagore: "With the shadow of my passion have I darkened your eyes." There is torment in this play, violence and horror - it is the under kingdom, all right! - that reflects what I was going through, or approaching, as I wrote it, but I think I may have managed, finally, at this point of stopping work on it, to keep the music over the thunder of disintegration. Perhaps if I had not been so tormented myself it would have been less authentic. Because I could not work with the old vitality, I had to find new ways and may have found some.

But I trust that our talks in New York made it clear that I want nothing but your usual absolute honesty from you, about this and anything between us, professionally or personally, something one can ask from very few people one knows in the course of a life-time. I certainly [don't] want the production of a play doomed to failure. So regard this work objectively as you can.

I'm enclosing the new third act and a new part of the second. I believe you got a script from Audrey, the one submitted just before I sailed, and you can insert these re-writes at the proper points. Then read it over, please, and let Gadg read it. I am keeping carbons of the new material for my own script.

I let Audrey read "Cat on a Tin Roof" while she was here and to my surprise she seemed to take a great liking to it, said the material excited her more than anything I've done since "Streetcar". But she doesn't find it complete in its present form and wants me to add another act to it. So far I don't agree with her. I think it tells a full story, though it is under conventional length, and that as soon, or if, I get back my creative breath, I can fill out these two acts (or 3 long scenes as they actually are) to a full evening without extending the story as I see it.

We have found an apartment, a pent-house with a terrace, looking over the Tiber and level with the evening flight of the "rondinelli", I have a club to swim at, Maria is expected, having been jilted by Laughlin, and so the external circumstances are not so bad. How are things in Glocamara? What of Bigelow? Surely he is back by now! If not, "attention must be paid to this man!"

With love, Tenn.

[Amid the "crisis" TW lamented his "heartbroken home. Mother. The sad distance come between us. My desperate old father. And the fate of Rose. And my soul, if I have one still, sighs and shudders and sickens" (*Journal*, June 6, 1954).

TW continued to revise *Orpheus Descending* (1957) in Tangier and Rome. A rewrite of Act III, scene 2, was "put in" the script on June 12 to further characterize Vee Talbott and intensify her blinding vision of Christ. The ending was also focused more sharply on Lady and Val with the removal of Carol Cutrere from the early part of the scene (n.d., HRC).

Audrey Wood recalls that she "stayed up until four in the morning" reading the untidy "'work script'" of *Cat on a Hot Tin Roof* (1955). She was "terribly excited" by the new play but demanded a "'third act,'" warning TW that "'it can't end with Big Daddy's speech, as it does. You've got to work on the story by sticking with Brick and Maggie'" (qtd. in Wood, *Represented by Audrey Wood*, 1981, pp. 165-166).

The "'rondinelli'" are the tiny birds of Rome which TW mentioned in *The Roman Spring of Mrs. Stone* (1950) and repeated in *Orpheus Descending*—as a symbol of escape from the corrupting influence of earth, citing the legend that they never touched earth until they died.

Linda vows that "attention must be paid" to her husband, Willy Loman, in light of his betrayal by a harsh economic order—in Act I of *Death of a Salesman* (Miller, 1949). TW would later use the same passage in poignant reference to Frank Merlo.

TW wrote this letter in June 1945, after moving on the 11th to the new apartment overlooking the Tiber.]

290. *To Audrey Wood*

Barcelona
8/5/54
[TLS w/ enclosure, 2 pp. HRC]

Dear Audrey:

Maria and I have been hopping around Europe like a pair of fleas, to escape the heat and lethargy of Rome. That little apartment turned out to be a regular oven. You don't need a stove, you just have to leave things out of the ice-box to cook them! Work was impossible. So Maria and I took off for Vienna, then to Venice where I saw Joe Mankiewicz, then back to Rome to see if it was cooler. It was hotter. So then we took off again to Barcelona. I am sorry that I will not meet Colton in Rome but maybe it's just as well to avoid any action on that "Summer and Smoke" deal till I am slightly more certain of how I am going to get along with Wallis. We talked about this in Rome and you agreed with me that it would be wise to delay. Of course I am greatly relieved by the news that Kanter is off the script but I feel that some additional assurances are necessary before making further commitments. I feel that the "Summer" deal should wait till I get back in the States, the end of September. (We're sailing with Magnani on the 22nd). Then you and I can discuss it in detail and make sure that we have the most protection obtainable. Films are more lasting than play productions and I'm afraid that my plays will be remembered mostly by the films made of them, and for that reason it is terribly important to me that I should get as much artistic control as possible in all film contracts. "Summer" could be done like a soap-opera, if it lacked this protection, and the reviews of "Mrs Leslie" make it clear that the critics, at least, are not buying that sort of thing anymore. Financially it looks like a good deal. But please let's wait till there's a final, really trustworthy, agreement on the "Tattoo" script, say, a week or two before they start shooting it, or at least till we can talk in New York the end of September. Do you agree? I sent the new ending from Rome. I am enclosing another version of Serafina's first scene, in the Ideal Grocery. It includes a meeting with Father de Leo which they seemed to desire. Magnani has received a script from Wallis and is having it translated into Italian. She is rightly very concerned over the script, as concerned as I am. I went through her script, scratching out the scenes which I am re-writing. (It was the yellow version they sent her.) If I am allowed to replace Kanter's stuff with my own, I think we will be in good shape. Neither Danny's nor

Hal's letters dealt at all specifically with our list of objections, the phrasing was disturbingly vague.

Their reaction to the new ending will be very significant.

I think it's very important that we maintain a completely friendly atmosphere, I don't want to seem unduly suspicious or "difficult" at this point, not till I am quite sure that a fight will be necessary. I am very hopeful that it can be avoided. In confidence: Mankiewicz described Wallis as "a cruel man". But I never accept other's opinions of people. Rarely agree with them. And the fact that Wallis wants to buy my plays is a great deal in his favor.

I enjoyed the meeting with Joe and we got along wonderfully in Venice. His ideas about "Orpheus" were interesting and showed a genuine concern, but I feel that his ideas are a bit too literal or realistic for a poetic play of this sort. He wants it too black and white. I'd prefer Gadg, if Gadg is at all interested. Meanwhile I am working steadily so that I'll have complete rough drafts of both "Cat" and "Kingdom of Earth" and my own final version of "Tattoo" when I return.

Oliver Evans is in Barcelona. He and Maria have gone off together to visit a young fisherman friend of Oliver's somewhere down the Coast but I expect them back this afternoon for the bull-fights. We'll probably fly to Madrid late this week but you'll get a wire if we do. I'll keep you informed of any moves that I make, never fear!

With love, Tenn

[Audrey Wood cabled producers Joe Hazen and Hal Wallis that Edward Colton had been sent to Rome to pacify TW on *The Rose Tattoo* script. To keep "peace on earth" (July 19, 1954, HRC), she advised that they not yet inform TW of their plan to retain "artistic control" of *Summer and Smoke*. Wallis produced the film in 1961.

About Mrs. Leslie (1954) was panned in the *New York Times* and *Variety* as a "saccharine saga" which is "only occasionally interesting." Daniel Mann directed and Shirley Booth played the lead in Wallis's current film.

The "Ideal Grocery" scene would expand the original setting of *The Rose Tattoo* and reveal Serafina's haughty pride in her unfaithful husband. The "new ending" to which TW refers, if the same as in the filmed version, involves a flagpole serenade by Alvaro, Serafina's return of the emblematic silk shirt, and the implied consummation of their "conversation."

On July 20 Wood asked Elia Kazan for his "very honest opinion" (July 20,

1954, HRC) of *Orpheus Descending*. Molly Kazan read the script first, deemed it "quite magical" though "not yet masterful," and warned that her husband was extremely "TIRED" (to Wood, July 30, 1954, HRC).

TW informed Wood of a recent exchange with "Poor little Maria": "I said she must forget Jay and go back to her old life. She said, What life? I have none. I said, Well, you've got to make one. Nobody can be that Russian this long!" (n.d., HRC).]

291. To Cheryl Crawford

"Amexco" Rome
August 23, 1954
[TLS, 1 p. HRC]

Dear Cheryl:

I am sorry about my last letter to you, I was a little bit drunk and feeling sorry for myself, I suppose. That's over now. I have been hopping all over Europe by plane with little Maria Britneva, like a pair of fleas, Vienna for a week, then ten days in Venice, Zurich, Rome again. Then off to Spain where we joined my poet friend Oliver Evans and took a trip by car along the Costa Brava, two weeks in Barcelona in which we saw seven bull-fights. "Mother's Ruin" is still a good friend of mine but I've cut down on it. Also rarely exceed one, and sometimes none of the "pinkies" in a day. And if I keep busy next Fall, and it looks like I'll have lots to do, I think I can keep off the analyst's couch a while longer, attractive tho it does seem in your current offering.

Cheryl, stop worrying about Orpheus, it is obviously not for you, that was apparent from our first phone talk about it last Spring. When I talk to you about it, it is only because I like to talk to you about my work, not because I am trying to sell it to you like a persistent huckster in the Medina. When you asked me, last Spring, why I didn't write a comedy - as if you didn't know that I only write for self-expression and that what I have to express is not, alas, a highly risible concept of the mysteries we live in - then I knew that on the conscious level you probably still want to do difficult, disturbing and challenging plays but that you now have a strong unconscious resistance to them, a circumstance that grew out of the terrible failure of Camino and the great success of "oh, Men, oh, Women!" and which is altogether understandable. But when you talk to Gadg about Orpheus -

Audrey wired me he likes it and may be able to do it in December - please don't low-rate it to him. Because I do honestly think you are wrong. Only one of the characters, Carol, is self-explanatory, and she is meant to be for she is a sort of sibyl or visionary, and I think the dynamics of the play are very powerful and that either Gadg or Mankiewicz, whichever does it, or even I, if neither of them will, could make it wildly exciting on the stage. That doesn't mean the critics would adore it, or it would be a big box-office hit, but I don't think either of those boys is afraid to reckon with chances, otherwise they wouldn't have done "Julius Caesar" and "Waterfront", even with Gielgud and Brando. "Out of this nettle, danger, Etc." - truest words the Bard ever lisped!

See you in Manhattan end of September. Fondly,

[TW returned to Rome after three weeks in Barcelona with "nothing" to show for his money but "boredom" and "irritation" (*Journal*, August 20, 1954). Maria Britneva's commanding behavior had removed any doubt of her possessive intentions. Oliver Evans would soon be offended by his portrait in *Hard Candy* and retaliate with a scurrilous postcard (see letter #312). In Rome the work went "not badly" but the "blue devils" returned after a brief respite. A claustrophobic attack in a cinema sent TW staggering "into the nearest bar. How disgusting! I must rise above it. I will" (*Journal*, August 23, 1954). Britneva recorded the episode and described "the terror of claustrophobia" which increasingly beset TW: "His heart pounds and pounds and he feels as though he were suffocating and panics, and so has to have a drink to relax" (St. Just, p. 97).

Cheryl Crawford's "offering" was probably Dr. Robert Laidlaw, a psychiatrist recommended to her by Alfred Kinsey, to whom she had relayed TW's earlier request.

TW recently learned of Crawford's opinion that production of "a fresh, new play" should ideally precede *Orpheus Descending*. Audrey Wood agreed and restated her wish that *Cat on a Hot Tin Roof* be developed into "a full evening" of theatre (Wood to TW, July 19, 1954, HRC).

Awaiting TW in Rome was a cable from Wood reporting Elia Kazan's preliminary interest in staging *Orpheus Descending*, "if you would do serious work" (August 16, 1954, HRC) on the script.

Julius Caesar (1953) and *On the Waterfront* (1954) were praised for imaginative direction by Joseph Mankiewicz and Elia Kazan, respectively. Marlon Brando played Mark Antony and the longshoreman Terry Malloy.

TW closes with a quotation from Shakespeare: "Out of this nettle, danger, we pluck this flower, safety" (*I Henry IV*, Act II.]

292. *To Edwina Dakin Williams and Walter Edwin Dakin*

[Rome]

[ca. August 23, 1954]

[TLS, 2 pp. HRC]

Dear Mother & Grandfather:

I've had to keep travelling about Europe this summer to escape the heat in Rome which was unusually bad this year and the attractive little apartment I described to you earlier turned out to be rather badly ventilated as it is divided into so many small rooms with windows opening mostly on a courtyard. Maria Britneva came to Rome and we flew to Zurich, then to Vienna, then to Venice, then back to Rome and then to Barcelona for two weeks where I met my friend Oliver Evans who was visiting there. We took an auto trip up the Mediterranean coast, called the Costa Brava, Oliver was searching for a place where he could live comfortably on the rent from his house in New Orleans, as he wants to spend a year in Spain and devote himself to writing instead of teaching in the States. Everywhere life was extremely cheap, you could live on fifty dollars a month, but we all agreed that the villages would be very tiresome after the first few days. So Oliver has now returned to the States, via Tangier, and will probably remain in New Orleans after all. We stayed in Spain about two weeks and when we got back here in Rome, the heat had broken. It is now delightfully cool and I'm enjoying the apartment again. We'll stay on here till September 22nd when we sail back to the States on the Andrea Doria with Anna Magnani.

I shall have to go out to Hollywood soon after I get back but can go through Saint Louis and spend some time with you. They want me to be on hand when they start shooting "Tattoo". They've finally decided to use a little town on the West Coast, close to the studio, instead of Mississippi or Florida. Which I think is sensible, as it is much less expensive and the less the picture costs the more I am likely to make out of it as my percentage comes after they recover the cost of the production. Kazan will be in Hollywood at the same time and Audrey cabled me that he is very interested in one of my new plays and might be able to do it on Broadway in December. Joe Mankiewicz is also interested in the same play and we have had talks about it in Venice and Rome. He's the man who made the recent film of Julius Caesar with Brando and Gielgud in the cast. Anyway it looks like I'll have a busy year ahead of me and I hope it will be profitable. Maybe Frank and Grandfather will have to open the house in Key West before I get there.

I bought Mother a lovely black lace mantilla, all sewn by hand, in Barcelona and will mail it from here. I thought it would look nice with her pearls and big tortoise shell comb for gala evenings. I think the Spanish ladies wear them to give them height as they are the tiniest women I've seen, few of them more than five feet.   Much love to you all,

Tom.

[Exteriors for *The Rose Tattoo* were filmed in Key West on a lot adjacent to TW's bungalow.

This letter is written on stationery of the Hotel Colón in Barcelona.]

293. To Audrey Wood

[Rome]
[early-September 1954]
[TLS, 2 pp. HRC]

Dear Audrey:

I agree in principle with what you say in your letter (August 25) but I feel there are circumstances to consider carefully in this instance. For one thing, I gathered that your enthusiasm for the "Cat" play is more or less contingent on my adding another act to it. To me the story is complete in its present form, it says all that I had to say about these characters and their situation, it was conceived as a short full-length play: there are three acts in it. First, Brick and his wife. Second, Brick and Big Daddy. Third, The family conference. They are short acts but complete, and I thought at least structurally the play was just right, I liked there being no time lapse between the acts, one flowing directly into the others, and it all taking place in the exact time that it occupies in the theatre. I would hate to lose that tightness, that simplicity, by somehow forcing it into a more extended form simply to satisfy a convention of theatre, would much rather risk the prejudice that might be incurred by bringing down a curtain at 10:30 or 10:45 and possibly raising it a little later to compensate. Or even using a good one act play as a curtain-raiser. It seems to me that all those one-act plays may have been just sitting there for this particular occasion to come along! Why not use one?

On the other hand, "Orpheus" is as ready as it will ever be. I will read it over when I get the manuscript but I doubt that there is much more I can

do to it, except maybe do a little more with the Carol bit in Act Three. I think it is nothing short of miraculous that two great directors want to do it, even with reservations. Now I think it is only fair that Gadg should let me know, at once, what he demands in the way of a re-write so that I can compare it with what Joe wants and decide which I can best satisfy, which is closer to my own point of view. The only way to deal with this situation is frankly and directly. Gadg wants to help me, I know. Why not tell him very frankly that I have this other offer, from Joe? In fact, I already wrote him about it a week or so ago, making it clear, however, that if he is willing to <u>commit</u> himself definitely to produce it, at a stated time this season, he should have it. Since Gadg has not written me, or approached me directly about this play or clearly stated what work he thinks it requires, and since Joe <u>has,</u> it appears likely to me that his interest is more nebulous or tentative of the two. I think he must be fair about this and put himself, imaginatively, in my uncomfortable but hopeful shoes. And make some definite move while there is still another "mighty director" somehow dangling on the same delicate line. Have I made myself clear? If not, I will send you a singing Western Union boy. On second thought, No, I might have to write the lyric.

Somehow I feel that you will work all this out with your usual unpar-allelled tact and perception, all I have to say, really, basically, is don't lose Joe unless you know you have Gadg, and when! Don't you think Mitchum is a great idea for Val? There's a wonderful piece on Mitchum in the August or September issue of Modern Screen which is almost Val's life story without Hollywood. Everyone here says Miranda is "N.G." Anyway Joe wouldn't use her and I doubt that Gadg would. I can't remember seeing Cortesi either, we'd better both have a look at her in something.

[Maria] is still here, and our domestic situation has deteriorated to a point where I am about to fly down to Sicily alone. I've been working only on "Kingdom of Earth" the last few weeks so that I'll have both of these new plays in complete first drafts when I get back to the States. Still sailing Sept. 22nd on the Doria with Magnani. Wallis leaves today. We got along well, I hope.

Love, Tenn.

["No one wants a Williams' play in New York this season more than I do," Audrey Wood assured her client, but she wished to observe the "order that is best for Tennessee Williams' career" rather than a "mighty" director. *Cat* seemed the more desirable property, assuming that TW could submit a full draft when he returned to New York

in late-September (to TW, August 25, 1954, HRC). Unacceptable to Wood was TW's earlier suggestion—restated in essence—that *Cat* be done with "Kingdom of Earth" on a double bill: "Although totally different in background, the plays are complementary in <u>theme</u> and would go well together" (TW to Wood, July 10, 1954, HRC).

Isa Miranda starred as Lady in the London production of *Orpheus Descending* (1959). Robert Mitchum did not appear in any work by TW.

The name "Maria" has been razored from the last paragraph in the original typescript. It is supplied in bracketed form.

This letter bears a reception date of September 7, 1954. The receiving office, however, was not Liebling-Wood but MCA (Music Corporation of America) to which the small firm founded in 1937 had recently been sold. Wood continued to represent her clients while her husband and business partner, William Liebling, partially retired.]

294. To Justin Brooks Atkinson

Sicily
Sept 4 1954
[TLS, 1 p. BRTC]

Dear Brooks:

Audrey Wood sent me a clipping from The Times bearing a letter from you to the editor about our recent decline of democratic freedom in the States. Her note said "I am deeply impressed by this". I am sure many people were. I certainly was. All the more deeply because I lacked the courage to write such a letter myself. When Art Miller lost his passport, I got as far as writing a letter to the State Department but only that far (didn't post it). I remembered that I had not yet received my own passport and I was afraid to antagonize the department and risk losing my own. That shows what an atmosphere of intimidation has come to exist among us. For a man in your position to speak up so boldly and clearly is not only brave but consequential. For courage is just as infectious as cowardice. I trust that now more and more of our writers and theatre people and so forth will dare to protest publicly against this creeping, sometimes galloping, decay of freedom. At least it has made us realize what a great and beautiful nation we belonged to, a few years back. Of course I don't believe our people will ever surrender as abjectly to these influences as, say, the Germans, Italians, and Russians, for we have never been serfs, peasants and slaves. Here in

Sicily, for instance, a sort of feudal serfdom still exists, also in much of Italy, and I'm afraid, to counter Communism, we should have shown more interest in propogating democracy among those countries that we were liberating from Fascism. We didn't make it sufficiently apparent to these people that democracy is something truly different from what they'd had before: so they got the idea that the only truly different thing would be communism. Same sort of blindness, inside and outside, when vision is most necessary. I wonder what pretty Mrs. Luce really thinks and says about things over here? I would love to hear her report to Mr. Dulles. De Gasperi's death was unfortunate for I believe he tried sincerely to check intemperate forces. He needed more inspiring fellowship on our side. I'll be leaving here soon. Each time more doubtful that I can get back again. And they are such beautiful people and there are so many cold eyes and hard faces elsewhere on earth! Yours ever,

10.

["Totalitarian attitudes and practices" cited by Atkinson include the refusal of passports and visas, domestic spying and the use of informers, the summoning of citizens before official committees "to answer for their personal ideas," the firing of civil servants "who do not parrot the party line," and various other restraints of traditional American freedom. The chief offender was Senator Joseph McCarthy, whom the "Government" had implicitly supported as "public prosecutor." "I wonder," Atkinson concluded, "if Americans really want it this way" (*New York Times*, August 16, 1954). Later he ruefully observed that Soviet induced "hysteria and fear" had made "most Americans McCarthyites in one degree or another" (to TW, September 23, 1954, BRTC).

Clare Boothe Luce, United States Ambassador to Italy, stirred controversy in early 1954 when off-the-record remarks critical of Italian politics—especially the Communist presence in labor and government—were reported in the press. John Foster Dulles, Secretary of State, was one of TW's favorite villains in international relations.

The death of former Italian Premier Alcide de Gasperi from a heart attack unnerved TW and revived his own "cardiac neurosis, in prodigious flower" (*Journal*, August 23, 1954).]

295. To Audrey Wood

[Rome]
Sept. [1954]
[TLSx, 2 pp. HRC]

Dearest Audrey:

All hell has broke loose here. Maria has denounced Frank as "common, ill-bred, Etc." and, at least for the past night, has removed herself from the premises. The trouble is that she wants to be treated constantly as a guest although, since she has been with us all summer, we can only treat her as a member of the family without giving up our agreeable pattern of life. Another trouble is that she is without any personal funds, to speak of, and is embarass-ingly dependant on us. She will not be realistic about this but wants us to entertain her titled friends at expensive restaurants, Etc., and when she leaves in the mornings, there is usually a message on the table giving us instructions of what to do. I tolerate this because I am very fond of her and am keenly aware of her emotional upset over being jilted by Jay, Etc. But Frank is nat-urally less inclined to put up with it and so it is "ending in tears". I do hope there can be some pacification before we separate next week.

Right now: Valentina Cortesi is here and reading script of new "Battle" with which she expresses great delight. I think she appears too young and beautiful for the part, she is really exquisite looking, but of course if she is a really fine actress that needn't rule her out. She had the idea, which doesn't seem bad to me, that her husband Richard Basehart might play opposite her as VAL. I just saw him do a great performance in an Italian film "La Strada" which got a prize at Venice, he seems a good type for it and is a fine actor. Please speak to Joe about this.

The news of Kazan is still ambiguous to me. I do wish he would write me about the script if he is truly interested in it. It would be a pity to lose Joe and then discover that Kazan wanted a sort of re-write that I could not attempt or agree with, which is always possible. Now that I've completed a very rough first draft, but a complete one, of "Kingdom of Earth" (or "The Seven Descents of Myrtle") I am working again on the new "Battle", doing over the Carol-Lady bit in the last act and I think that's the most critical point in the play and that I am making progress toward a solution of it.

"Big Nat" (Murray) is here. We're having dinner tonight with her and La Magnani, at 11 o'clock, if I don't die of hunger first. That's the hour when La Magnani is willing to take to the streets, not sooner. A wire today from

Wallis. "Ask Tennessee can he airmail rewrite Rosario scenes Plaza New York Mann meeting me there." The only thing wrong with that is that I really can't see any reason to re-write those scenes as they will play beautifully and they say exactly what they are meant to say. Mann said he thought Rosario should show more devotion to Magnani but it seems to me that the point is that <u>she</u> is the one that has the <u>devotion</u>, he has a mistress. Naturally he cares for her, maybe a lot, but in the stress of the situation it seems a little much to ask me to dramatize a great love on his part. I will attempt this, if it is really necessary, but can't we wait till I have talked with Mann in New York? It would not involve much re-writing but it is necessary to be quite clear, and agreed, about how to do this. Also there is the point that I am not on salary and have already far exceeded the three-weeks period of my employment as script-writer. How about that? And how about my expenses in California? I would be happy to settle for that, as a recompense for my continued services, but I don't think I should have to, or can afford, to go to California and stay there at my own expense, though I think my presence is essential, both for Magnani's security and the protection of the script. I am willing to live on a relatively modest level, of course. Can you work that out, you think? I am <u>worried</u> about money! - for the first time in ten years. . . .

Love, Tenn.

[Shortly before the blowup, Maria Britneva described Frank Merlo as "intelligent and good, but unfortunately very coarse." His "understanding," for which she was "grateful" (St. Just, p. 97), had apparently been exhausted.

Neither Valentina Cortese, twenty-nine at the time of her reading, nor her husband, Richard Basehart, appeared in *Orpheus Descending*.

Elia Kazan restated his wife's warning—"I'm quite exhausted. Out of gas. (petrol) No gissum left"—and offered to step aside if Joe Mankiewicz were "hot" to direct *Orpheus Descending*. Perhaps he should "wait for one of the new plays" (to TW, n.d., HRC), Kazan opined, signaling in effect his preference for *Cat on a Hot Tin Roof*.

Natalia Danesi Murray served as a personal assistant to Anna Magnani on the set of *The Rose Tattoo*. TW's reluctance to domesticate Rosario apparently prevailed. As filmed, he remains a shadowy character who ignores Serafina's announcement of "new life" in her body.

The names "Maria" and "Jay" have been razored from the first paragraph of the original typescript. They remain, however, in a photographic copy which serves as published text, and which bears a reception date of September 20, 1954.]

296. To Elia "Gadg" Kazan

[323 East 58th Street, New York]
[October 1954]
[TLS, 1 p. HTC]

Dear Gadg:

There is certainly no use in my trying to disguise or dissimulate the fact that I passionately long for you to do this play. But I can understand why you are afraid of its failure although I am not. I don't mean I think it couldn't fail. I think it not only could fail but has a fifty-fifty chance of failure, and know how much I have to lose from such a failure, but still I do passionately long for its production and for you to ~~produce~~ stage it because I think it does that thing which is the pure aim of art, the highest pure aim of art, which is to catch and illuminate truly and passionately the true, true quality of human existence. It so happens that the second act has the highest degree of dramatic tension. That has happened before in very fine plays and they have survived it. It has to be compensated, not by a trick or distortion but by charging the final scene with something <u>plus,</u> underlining and dramatizing as powerfully as possible the sheer <u>truth</u> of the material, it's very <u>lack</u> of shrewd showmanship, because I think critics and real theatre lovers will respect it all the more for not making some facile, easy, obvious concession to the things which a lot of people have complained about in us, both, a too professional, showy, sock-finish to theatre. Am I rationalizing again? Maybe, but on the other hand, I may be simply trying to articulate to you my side of the case.

You say that I didn't have faith in this play till you and Audrey liked it. Surely you understand <u>why</u>! I never had any confidence in my work, in fact I couldn't believe my ears when Audrey first told me that "Streetcar" was a good play because ever since 1946, the spring of it, I didn't see how I could do good things anymore. But God has been with me, and you and Audrey and a bunch of people who like truth stated with passion on the stage, no matter how cruel or black and often <u>bungling</u>, have noted and appreciated the fact that I continued to do it in spite of not thinking I could.

Even if "Cat" is not a good play, it's a goddam fiercely <u>true</u> play, and what other play this season is going to be <u>that</u>?

I resumed work this morning, at 8 A.M. after not much sleep, on Act Three, determined to get what you want without losing what I want.

(Assuming they are essentially the same thing, just conceived of in different fashions) I dare to believe that I can work this out, but it would help me immeasurably if you and some producer would give me a vote of confidence by committing yourselves to a date of production with the work still on the bench. I don't think that I would fail you. Of course I will be disappointed if you refuse, perhaps even angry at you - I was angry with you last night, too angry to sleep! - but I will not hate you for it, and we would still do something together again. I know that you are my friend.

                                         Ever, Tennessee.

P.S. Hope this doesn't sound like "a pitch"?

[With "great tensions and contentions," the decision to stage *Cat* was made after TW arrived in New York on September 30. He informed Maria Britneva in late-October that Elia Kazan was "genuinely enthusiastic about the script" and had "verbally" committed himself to direct the new play, with rehearsals set to begin on "February 1st" (qtd. in St. Just, pp. 101, 103).]

297. To Elia "Gadg" Kazan

[1431 Duncan Street
Key West, Florida]
Nov. 3, 1954
[TLS, 2 pp. WUCA]

Dear Gadg:

We arrived back here to find our whole property transformed into the Strega's house (next door to Serafina's), trees planted to hide our house and a dilapidated false front with tin roof built over my studio in the backyard. I hit the ceiling, that is, I would have hit it if there had been a ceiling to hit! I thought they had wrecked my studio and I charged out of the car like the strega's goat, shouting, "Who the blankety blank sonofabitches gave them permission to ruin my little house!" All the pent up emotion of the past week exploded, Grandfather's illness, my rage at mother and at life, all broke loose on the Paramount art department and production manager and assistants. I was not pacified till told that both houses would be completely repainted and that the hideous facade of my precious little studio could be removed without a scar on the original. But you should see the yard!

Practically all the junk and refuse in town has been heaped and scattered over it, and tomorrow comes the goat! Our next door nieghbor is getting twenty-five bucks a day for the use of his yard and porch but I guess all we're getting is free paint job when it's over. They start shooting daybreak tomorrow. I've never been this close to a movie production before and I must say that it's just too massive, too huge and implacable a machine, to be interesting. It no longer seems to have any relation to me or my own world, it's like some great Frankenstein that suddenly came clomping up to the door and took everything over. I am already bored with the whole thing, before it has started, and am interested only in plans for "Cat on a Tin Roof" and the return of sanity and quiet when the monster goes clomping back where it came from. I have just finished reading a ~~great~~ book "The Producer" by Richard Brooks which is an inside, almost documentary, account of how pictures are made. Incidentally, you are mentioned in it. Have you read it? Published by Cardinal reprints, originally by Simon & Schuster. Get it if you haven't. I think I'd rather read about making pictures than make them, it's too big, it involves too much money, it's a miracle when anything simple, true or creative manages to slip through, I suppose unnoticed by the boys on top, production heads, bankers and stockholders. That something like "Waterfront" or "Streetcar" can come out of it - man alive! <u>How</u>?! - Magnani, even Anna, looks shaken by the mass and weight of the mechanism. Wallis and Mann look like gleeful little boys who have just reached into their Xmas stockings! Are they kidding?

I suppose you have heard the sad news about Grandfather. He had a slight stroke just a couple of days before we arrived to pick him up for the winter. His left side is partially paralyzed and he is now in a nursing home in Saint Louis. We spent a week with him, he was improving a little when we left, but he says he is on his deathbed and since he would be 98 in April, it is not easy to argue him, or myself, out of it. It was so badly timed, however, as all this to-do in Key West would have been more thrilling to him than anyone else involved in it.

I am glad that in "Cat" we are getting off the chest some of the terrible things that we have to say about human fate. I want to keep the core of the play very hard, because I detest plays that are built around something mushy such as I feel under the surface of many sentimental successes in the theatre. I want the core of the play to be as hard and fierce as Big Daddy. I think he strikes the keynote of the play. A terrible black anger and ferocity, a rock-bottom honesty. Only against this background can his moments of tenderness, of longing,

move us deeply. This is a play about good bastards and good bitches. I mean it exposes the startling co-existence of good and evil, the shocking <u>duality</u> of the single heart. I am as happy as you are that our discussions have led to a way of high-lighting the good in Maggie, the indestructible spirit of Big Daddy, so that the final effect of the play is not negative, this is a forward step, a step toward a <u>larger</u> truth which will add immeasurably to the play's power of communication or scope of communication. More later. Anna, looking pale and scared, has just arrived at the door.

Next day: - whole town is on the street in front of the house and overflowing the whole premises except my studio which hides inviolate behind its false front. Three hours have been consumed in shooting about three minutes of the picture. Wallis made Marisa Pavan cry, which killed another half hour, by blowing his stack because she fluffed a line, the same one, in five takes. He is a hard customer!, that one. I wish he didn't want to buy my plays, or, rather, I wish somebody else <u>did</u> want to buy them, he is not hard in the right way, I am afraid. Danny is gentle. I am happy to say that he showed his annoyance to Wallis in the girl's defense. He and I will never have a true rapport but I respect and like him: he will never do anything great, I fear, without the collaboration of a Magnani, but he will always bring heart and - heart! - to his work, unless the Frankenstein takes it out of him.

Have just seen Magnani tear into the part! Forget that bit about her being nervous. That dame is nervous in a way that's terrific! She takes over like Grant did Richmond! And I must say that Danny has the good grace to be grateful for it, as he well should be, and even Hal Wallis began to grin a little. I was so shaken that on the way back from location, I had a "crise de nerfs" and had to stop a police car, yes, mind you, a police car! - to drive me home. I was shaking all over and the policeman was sympathetic . . . . An attack like the one I read you about from my journal. "Ten miles from no where and uphill all the way!"

(This letter is crazy because my nerves are shot right now.)

To get back to "Cat". I will not insult you by saying, "Don't ask me to sweeten it up." I know what you want. You don't want me to take the cliché route into tiresome old defeatism or romantic melancholy, you want me to make it hard, even savage, but with a respect for the quality of truth,

and the truth that there is: in the individual rising above himself, herself, at moments, under extreme pressure, to say or do something absolutely, uncompromisingly, true. And not self-loving only or self-pitying only.

This thing is going to come right, and I think soon enough for this season. I'm going to send off the new material sooner than I ought to, because we are late and have to work fast. Sometimes it's better that way. Work can die from delay and cogitation. Surprisingly, most of Maggie's stuff still fits our new conception of her. I was already unconsciously her friend when I wrote it. Please don't ask me to write over her part, I couldn't do it nearly as well, and all it really needs is bits of add and subtract. (Since we don't want to deny that she has the desperation and savagery of a cat on a tin roof).

Wired to ask if you could come down here when the film is finished here. I do hope you can, you'd like this place, and we could get the script right.

Love, 10.

[Hal Wallis has recalled the search for a shooting location in Key West: "We drove all over town looking for a wood frame house that would best fit the requirements as Serafina's home. Finally, I saw one . . . {that} looked perfect but there was a fence too close to it which enclosed a goat yard belonging to the house next door" (qtd. in Steen, *A Look at Tennessee Williams*, 1969). Wallis was surprised to learn that the owner was none other than the volatile author of *The Rose Tattoo*.

In *The Producer* (1951) Elia Kazan is mentioned as a socially conscious director. The author, Richard Brooks, later directed and wrote the screenplays for *Cat on a Hot Tin Roof* (1958) and *Sweet Bird of Youth* (1962).

The character of Maggie evolved from a sinister, domineering figure in "Three Players of a Summer Game" (1952). Her "more charming" development in *Cat*, as TW later put it, was consistent with the ending used for the Broadway production.]

298. To Audrey Wood

[1431 Duncan Street
Key West, Florida]
Nov 23, 1954
[TLS w/ enclosure, 1 p. HRC]

Dear Audrey:

I'm shooting this off to you before I've had a chance to consider it myself at all properly. I'm also sending, to save time, a copy to Gadg. I

agree with you that time must be considered now. I think Gadg must let us know right away if he is or isn't willing to make a definite commitment at a specific time, and soon enough for us to make other plans if he isn't. I am not at all sure that this new ending is what I want. Do you think it contains an echo of "Tea and Sympathy"? The other, harder, ending of it didn't. Here is another case of a woman giving a man back his manhood, while in the original conception it was about a vital, strong woman dominating a weak man and achieving her will. Also: does Big Daddy's reappearance really and truly add anything that's important to the story besides making it softer or sweeter or easier to take?

Christopher Isherwood strengthened my faith in the original play. I read him the first typed draft and he loved it, said he thought it in many ways my best play. He felt only that the story of Maggie-Brick-Skipper needed to be developed more fully to make it more clearly understood, what had actually happened, as that was the heart of the story. I've tried to do that in a re-write of the scene between Brick and Maggie about Skipper. I'm also now doing a re-write of the scene between Big Daddy and Brick about Skipper.

Should I go out to the Coast, to watch over the "Tattoo" shooting and at the same time confer with Kazan? Isherwood will be there and possibly the three of us could arrive at an agreement about the "Cat" script that would satisfy both Gadg and me. If Gadg wants "out", how about Jose Quintero? He is someone that I could work with and I think he would have sympathy and understanding of this script. Clurman is also a possibility but I think Jose is a better, fresher and more vital, director, and particularly one that I would find it easier to communicate with. Is Ben Gazzara still available? I am also interested in your suggestion of Dorothy McGuire. If I go to the coast, and Gadg remains interested, perhaps some casting could be done out there. . . .

Cast of "Tattoo" left last night, I am worn out and glad to resume the quiet life.

Don't you think it is important to get a producer lined up for "Cat" if it is really going to be produced this season? I don't want to produce it myself, I am not ready for that, I need the support of a top-flight management of experience and prestige to get it organized and provide the calm, workman-like atmosphere that such a delicate undertaking will need behind it.

My love, Tenn

[The enclosed revision of *Cat* led Elia Kazan to wire his approval and TW to write—as he flew nervously to Los Angeles—that "things look bright" (*Journal*, November 27, 1954).

The unwanted "echo of 'Tea and Sympathy'" (1953) refers to the ending of Robert Anderson's play, in which a schoolboy wrongly accused of homosexual tendencies is reassured by a sympathetic woman.

Reference to "the original conception" of *Cat* foreshadows TW's decision to publish both versions of the third act. At issue, as TW would state in a controversial "Note of Explanation," were Kazan's preference for the return of Big Daddy in Act Three, the development of Brick following his disclosure in Act Two, and the humanization of Maggie the Cat. These debated issues would guide the final stages of revision and give a theatrical shape to the so-called "Broadway Version" of Act Three.

Although both were reportedly "hot" for the play, neither Cheryl Crawford nor Irene Selznick would produce *Cat on a Hot Tin Roof*. With reference to experienced "management," TW doubtless intended to preempt consideration of William Liebling. Audrey Wood finally selected the Playwrights' Company.]

299. To Elia "Gadg" Kazan

[Beverly Hills Hotel
Beverly Hills, California]
November 31, 1954
[TLS w/ autograph postscript, 3 pp. WUCA]

Dear Gadg,

I've got to use a very light touch as I'm writing this at 4:30 AM in the Beverly Hills branch of Utter McKinley. This will also force me to be concise as opposed to abstruse in my statements.

I "buy" a lot of your letter but of course not all: possibly I "buy" more than half, and after a couple of nights studying it out, I think I understand it.

To be brief: the part I buy is that there has to be a reason for Brick's impasse (his drinking is only an expression of it) that will "hold water".

Why does a man drink: in quotes "drink". There's two reasons, separate or together. 1. He's scared shitless of something. 2. He can't face the truth about something. - Then of course there's the natural degenerates that just fall into any weak, indulgent habit that comes along but we are not dealing with that sad but unimportant category in Brick. - Here's the conclusion I've come to. Brick <u>did</u> love Skipper, "the one great good thing in his life which was true". He identified Skipper with sports, the romantic world of adolesence which he couldn't go past. Further: to reverse my original (somewhat tentative) premise,

I now believe that, in the deeper sense, not the literal sense, Brick is homosexual with a heterosexual adjustment: a thing I've suspected of several others, such as Brando, for instance. (He hasn't cracked up but I think he bears watching. He strikes me as being a compulsive eccentric). I think these people are often undersexed, prefer pet raccoons or sports or something to sex with either gender. They have deep attachments, idealistic, romantic: sublimated loves! They are terrible Puritans. (Marlon dislikes me. Why? I'm "corrupt") These people may have a glandular set-up which will keep them "banked", at low-pressure, enough to get by without the eventual crack-up. Take Brando again: he's smoldering with something and I don't think it's Josanne! Sorry to make him my guinea pig in this analysis (Please give this letter back to me!) but he's the nearest thing to Brick that we both know. Their innocense, their blindness, makes them very, very touching, very beautiful and sad. Often they make fine artists, having to sublimate so much of their love, and believe me, homosexual love is something that also requires more than a physical expression. But if a mask is ripped off, suddenly, roughly, that's quite enough to blast the whole Mechanism, the whole adjustment, knock the world out from under their feet, and leave them no alternative but - owning up to the truth or retreat into something like liquor. . . .

Maggie: What happened in here tonight between you and Big Daddy?

Brick: We - - - had a - - - talk. . . .

Maggie: About what? What about?

Brick: We - had a - talk! (Count 10: dead silence, Maggie the cat drawing a bead on him with her eyes, him at the proscenium, looking out into the house) - He says that I loved Skipper!

Maggie: Did you hit him with your crutch?

Brick: (Somewhat lifelessly) No, I didn't. - I mean - Yes, I did. . .

~~Maggie: (Abruptly) Thank you.~~

(X's quickly to liquor cabinet)

~~Brick: For what?~~

~~Maggie: (Count five in which she decides not to probe the topic above any further just now) It was gallant of you to save my face when I lied.~~

Then the "click" bit?

Also, in Act Two:

(Right after Brick has told "B.D." his Skipper story)

Brick: Now are you satisfied?

Big Daddy: - Are <u>you</u> satisfied?

Brick: What with?

Big Daddy: That half-ass story?

Brick: 'Half ass'?

Big: I'm not satisfied with it, you left something out, something is missing from it.

   (Phone rings in hall: the sound reminds Brick of something)

Brick: Yes. A telephone call in which Skipper made a, a, a! - "dictated confession" to me: and on which I hung up! - last time we spoke to each other. . .

Big Daddy: Who was it dictated by?

Brick: It was fed him by Maggie. - "The Cat".

Big Daddy: (After a pause) Anyhow now! - I think we've located the lie you're disgusted with. Your own to yourself! - You dug the grave of your friend and kicked him in it because you couldn't face the truth about something?

Brick: (Violent and sudden) <u>Who the hell can, can YOU</u>?! How about these birthday congratulations, these many happy returns when everybody but <u>you</u> knows there won't be any?

(You notice a transposition has occured: "Young and believing" is now before Skipper story)

- Don't you feel this does it? There's your plain and simple and believable reason: he had the problem I referred to above.

In a way, this is progress for Brick. He's faced the truth, I think, under Big Daddy's pressure, and maybe the block is broken. I just said maybe. I don't really think so. I think that Brick is doomed by the falsities and cruel prejudices of the world he comes out of, belongs to, the world of Big Daddy and Big Mama. Sucking a dick or two or fucking a reasonable facsimile of Skipper some day won't solve it for him, if he ever does such "dirty things"! He's the living sacrifice, the victim, of the play, and I don't want to part with that "Tragic elegance" about him. You know, paralysis in a character can be just as significant and just as dramatic as progress, and is also less shop-worn. How about Chekhov?

Now business. The above is just about as far as I can go with you. You've got to tell me, now, whether or not you will do this play this season. If not, I must go at once to New York and start setting up another production for it. I will not, I'm afraid, want to do it next season. You sort of said why in Anna's room Monday night. This play is too important to me, too much a synthesis of all my life, to leave it in hands that aren't mine, and I'm <u>longing to see it</u>!

Let's be brave. Now what do you have to lose?

My love, Tenn.

<u>Must have this letter back to copy the dialogue in it.</u>

[Elia Kazan's reassuring telegram (received November 27, 1954) was followed by "a 5 page letter" in which Kazan stated "his remaining objection" to *Cat*, apparently focused upon the character of Brick. "I do get his point," TW wrote, "but I am afraid he doesn't quite get mine. Things are not always explained. Situations are not always resolved. Characters don't always 'progress'. But I shall, of course, try to arrive at another compromise with him" (*Journal*, November 29, 1954).

Marlon Brando later wrote that he had been "afraid" for TW "because success sings a deadly lullaby to most people. Success is a real and subtle whore who would like nothing better that to catch you sleeping and bite your cock off. You have been as brave as any body I've known and its comforting to think about" (to TW, n.d., Columbia U).

The new Act Two dialogue was intended to offer "a reason" for Brick's "impasse" that would "'hold water,'" as Kazan had recently put it. Presumably the explanatory lines—published with little change in the first and later editions of *Cat*—do not violate the mystery of Brick's character, which TW further defended in a manuscript fragment held by the HRC: "The poetic mystery of BRICK is the poem of the play, not its story but the poem of the story, and must not be dispelled by any dishonestly oracular conclusions about him: I don't know him any better than I know my closest relative or dearest friend which isn't well at all: the only people we think we know well are those who mean little to us" (n.d.).

Rehearsals of *Cat* began on February 9, 1955, followed by a two-week tryout in Philadelphia (March 7-19).]

*Ben Gazzara and Burl Ives: "I can hop on one foot, and if I fall, I can crawl!" (*Cat on a Hot Tin Roof, 1955).

300. *To the Drama Editor*

[Beverly Hills Hotel
Beverly Hills, California]
[December 1954]
[TLS, 1 p. HRC]

To the Drama Editor:

I would like a little space to say simply that Mr. Eric Bentley has told an out-and-out lie, without the excuse of any possible misunderstanding, in his recently book-published claim that "A Streetcar Named Desire" (and "Death of a Salesman") were virtually co-authored by their director. Mr. Kazan who was the director of both my play and Mr. Miller's, was just as indignant as I am over this preposterous charge. At the time it first appeared, a strangely parenthetical supplement to Bentley's review of <u>Camino Real</u>, Mr. Kazan immediately wrote a note of protest about it, utterly disclaiming and denying any such thing. But it doesn't seem that Mr. Bentley's aim is to get at the truth. Consequently I feel obliged to point out, for whatever my word may be worth, that there isn't a line in "Streetcar" I didn't write, and that the interpretation of the play couldn't have been more exactly what the author had in mind when he wrote it. When I acknowledge the greatness of Kazan's direction (and Thank God for it) I think I do it more honestly than Bentley and I think Gadg appreciates it more from me. Into a play like "Streetcar" or "Salesman", the playwright has invested too much that is deeply personal, involving all his existence, to tolerate such a claim as Bentley has had the disgusting mischief and mendacity to publish.

Sincerely, Tennessee Williams

[Of grave concern to TW was Eric Bentley's claim that *Streetcar* (1947) had been "virtually" co-authored by Elia Kazan. TW's attorney threatened a suit if the publisher failed to "recall all outstanding copies" of *The Dramatic Event* (1954) and to "have the statement in question deleted" (Colton to Bentley and Horizon Press, December 2, 1954, HRC). Later printings retain the disputed passage, along with a prominently displayed note—formerly an addendum—in which Kazan is quoted as not having written "one line" of *Streetcar*. Bentley claimed nonetheless that his staging had profoundly altered the characterization, "without recourse to new dialogue." Bentley cited no correspondence from TW.

The printed letter represents a four-stage drafting process, as sources held by the HRC indicate. Related correspondence suggests that the letter—probably intended for publication in the *New York Times*—was written in the first two weeks of December 1954, before TW left California.]

301. To Walter Edwin Dakin

SH: Beverly Hills Hotel
Beverly Hills · California
[mid-December 1954]
[TLS, 1 p. HRC]

Dearest Grandfather:

I have fallen a little behind in my letters lately as I have been going through the busiest period in recent years, what with casting a play with Kazan and watching over the shooting of "Rose Tattoo". I don't even know precisely how long I've been out here, but I have to fly back tonight as Kazan is casting the new play in New York and I have to pass judgement tomorrow on Barbara Bel Geddes for the female lead. She is a fine actress who has appeared in a number of hits on Broadway but I am not sure she is right for this part so I have to return at once to take a look at her.

Anna Magnani and Burt Lancaster had their first fight on the set yesterday, as she was directing the scene and he didn't like it. So he walked off and there was a long and heated consultation before things could be resumed. Both are temperamental. I wish I could remain here as a referee is needed, but I shall just have to hope and pray that Danny Mann, the director, can keep peace between them long enough to finish the picture. So far the picture looks great. There's about two more weeks of work on it, at least.

Frank and the dog are flying to New York from Key West tomorrow so we'll all arrive there about the same time. I haven't gotten much rest or much sun this year, but so far I'm holding up pretty well under the pressure. The fact that I will have Kazan on the play is reassuring and takes a lot of anxiety off me. I just heard today that the Playwrights Company will be the producers, which is good, since they are much more generous with money than Cheryl Crawford who is a penny-pincher.

I talked to Dakin and Margo over long-distance a few days ago, he was visiting her in Dallas. He says he is "sweating out" his promotion which is a slang expression for waiting and hoping that he will get it. I hope so, too, and that if he does, he'll stay in the air-force till economic conditions in the country are more settled.

If I didn't have to put this play on now I would be in Saint Louis with you. I think about you every day. You must get out of bed as often as you can. I know it takes patience and effort, but we are depending on you to be

ready and able to return to Key West with us when we go back in the early
Spring. That's the nicest time of year there, you remember.

Much love from Tom

[TW rejoined Elia Kazan in New York in mid-December after spending two
"ghastly" (*Journal*, December 3, 1954) weeks in California bereft of friends and
sexual partners.

Kazan apparently told Barbara Bel Geddes, whom he directed in *Deep Are the
Roots* (1945), that she was the "joint choice" of author and director to play Maggie
the Cat. Audrey Wood's telegram (December 14, 1954, HRC) to that effect led TW
to examine her casting more closely after a hasty return to New York. Kazan later
admitted that Bel Geddes was his "kind of actress" (Kazan, p. 540), although not
TW's. Her work in *Cat* would lead to nomination for a Tony Award.

Filming of *The Rose Tattoo*—shifted to California for interior scenes—ended
in early-January 1955. Natalia Murray wrote at the time that the Production Code
office "gave praise to the film as well as to Anna's acting" (to Wood, January 9,
1955, HRC).

Walter Dakin, ninety-seven years of age, would not return to Key West following his recent stroke. He died on February 14, 1955. TW probably learned of
the sad event from Audrey Wood, who had been cabled by Edwina: "Please tell
Tom that Grandfather passed away at 630 this morning" (February 14, 1955,
HRC). According to Paul Bigelow, he "'left two small bequests, one hundred
dollars for Frankie Merlo, and one hundred dollars for me. It was all the old
gentleman had in the world'" (qtd. in Spoto, p. 200).

This letter was first printed in Edwina Dakin Williams's memoir, *Remember
Me to Tom*, 1963, pp. 229-230.]

302. To the Book Review Editor, Time

[323 East 58th Street, New York]
[January 1955]
[TL, 1 p. HRC]

Dear Sir or Miss or Madam:

I would like to suggest to you, without expressed rancor, that your
review of my six-year-old book of stories, ONE ARM, is a piece of critical
McCarthyism. I am a constant and constantly admiring reader and fan of
TIME, because it's the best news-coverage we have, and is especially
valuable to me in Europe in the summers when I can't get American papers,
and the quality of the reportorial writing is always good and often brilliant,

and because I was particularly impressed by your forthright and highly effective stand against the threat of McCarthy to our American principles. But now and again you shock me terribly by a corresponding (to McCarthy) type of intolerance, bordering on persecution, in your attitude toward the arts, theatre and literary. It is totally unworthy of everything else that you represent! "Human garbage" is a curiously un-Christian term to apply to those unfortunates that I (very admittedly!) have somehow been inclined to deal with more than with so-called "healthy and normal" individuals. If I went into the reasons for this, it would be unnecessarily apologetic. An artist must portray, as honestly as he can, what he knows. I have always done so. When you say I have raided "psycophathis sexualis for TV skits", are you being quite honest? What is there in any of these stories, either in content or style, that might conceivably be adaptable to TV as we now have it? These stories stretch all the way back, in time, to my adolescence, and God Knows, and I know, too, that they represent various degrees of writing skill, but you know as well as I know that they do not pander ever, in any way, to what is cheap or sensational anymore than my plays do.

[*One Arm and Other Stories* (1948)—reissued by New Directions in December 1954—"wears the scent of human garbage as if it were the latest Parisian perfume." The *Time* reviewer also surmised that TW had "raided" *Psychopathia Sexualis* (1886), Krafft-Ebing's study of sexual deviation, for his own case studies of "male and female prostitutes, harridans, and homosexuals." Only "Portrait of a Girl in Glass," which shone with "a luminous pity" (January 3, 1955, p. 76), escaped the harsh criticism. TW's letter did not appear in *Time* magazine.]

303. To Justin Brooks Atkinson

SH: Hollywood Roosevelt Hotel
Hollywood 28, California
1/25/55
[TLS w/ enclosure, 1 p. BRTC]

Dear Brooks:

We flew out here from New Orleans to see the rough-cut of "Rose Tattoo", which is still very rough but has promise of being a beautiful and moving film because of Magnani's great performance and Lancaster's surprisingly good one. Maureen and I, the night before I left New Orleans,

had someone read us your notice of the double-bill over the "blower", as
Maria calls phones, and I want to thank you for us both, Maureen and I,
for your kindness to the play and players. I agree with all you said, though
I feel sorry about de Banfield. I think he keyed his score to the remembered
romance rather than to the tawdry present existence of the old ladies, but
this pantomime in the background was too clumsily handled to justify the
soaring music. I think it ought to have another try somewhere, under
better conditions. There was a chance to bring Maureen into the Bijou on
a bill with "Trouble in Tahiti", the Leonard Bernstein musical, but all my
advisors in New York were dead set against it, so the project collapsed. I
hope it can be revived later, after my new long play has opened, perhaps in
the late Spring.

Anyway I thought the enclosed account of what happened between
play and opera on opening night might amuse you and Orianne. It is a very
mild account of what actually took place, since it doesn't include the
banshee cries and imprecations that paled even the most barbaric possible
interpretation that might have been given to those bloody wagons that had
passed before!

Thanks again, Brooks, as so often before, Tennessee.

[The New Orleans project was a "blunder," Atkinson wrote, despite "the good
will" of the local sponsors. His "kindness to the play and players," especially to
Maureen Stapleton who starred in "27 Wagons Full of Cotton" (1945), did not
include the direction, which Atkinson deemed "soft and maundering." The companion piece, "Lord Byron's Love Letter" (1945), was "demolished by a powerful
score and an orchestra of fifty instrumentalists" (New York Times, January 19,
1955). TW wrote the libretto and Raffaello de Banfield the excessive accompaniment. Publication of the book (Lord Byron's Love Letter: Opera in One Act,
Ricordi, 1955) coincided with the premiere on January 17, 1955. TW may have
enclosed an article published in the Times-Picayune on January 16 which reported
"madness" in the company as opening night approached.
    Atkinson would soon review Maria Britneva's performance as Blanche DuBois
in an off-Broadway production of Streetcar (March 3, 1955). She failed, he wrote,
"to express the inner tensions of that haunted gentlewoman" (New York Times,
March 4, 1955). A preliminary search of the Times has failed to locate the positive
review by Atkinson which Britneva quotes in Five O'Clock Angel (p. 112).]

304. To Elia "Gadg" Kazan

Tues, midnight at the St. James.
[March 1, 1955]
[Philadelphia, Pennsylvania]
[TLS w/ cover letter, 3 pp. WUCA]

Dear Gadg

Some notes and reflections on last run through in New York

The bare stage background in New York may have been partly responsible but it seemed to me that the last act of the play, the first part of Act III, suffers from an undue portentousness as if we were trying to cover up some lack of significant content by giving it a "tricky" or inflated style of performance.

In manuscript, in style of writing, this is almost the most realistic scene that I have ever written. I gave ~~enormous~~ care to restricting all the speeches to just precisely what I thought the person would say in precisely such a situation, I tried to give it the quality of an exact transcription of such a scene except for the removal of any worthless irrelevancies. I assumed, and still believe, that the emotional essence of the situation was strong enough to hold interest, and that the exact quality of experience, if captured truly, would give it theatrical distinction. Learning that someone deeply loved and long lived with is dying strikes me as being a material for strong drama, especially when played by Millie Dunnock, but to me, at least, I was continually distracted from the basically moving scene by details of staging and playing which seemed like a kind of legerdemain, as if it were necessary to conceal the actual scene rather than perform it. (Of course I am over-stating this, as usual, to make my point more vividly). There is a "poetry of the macabre" which I was creating in all the silly, trivial speeches that precede and surround the announcement to Big Mama, the fuss over what he ate at dinner, the observations about Keeley cure, anti-buse, vitamin B12, the southern gush and playfulness, these all contribute to a shocking comment upon the false, heartless, grotesquely undignified way that such events are treated in our society with its resolute concentration on the trivia of life. Practically all these values disappeared, for me at least, in a distractingly formalistic treatment of the situation. THE BASIC IDEA back of this formalism IS EXCELLENT! - Big Mama a victim in a pit or arena with her mockingly sympathetic, pitiless executioners gradually tightening a circle about her - this is a creative conception which

does not distort or violate in any way the original. But somehow the execution of the idea gets in the way of it. It would be much more effective if it were done more simply and naturally, almost precisely as it would be done in life, Big Mama seated with the others ranged at various positions about her, not in a pair of tight little groups whispering dummy-lines to each other. I don't think dummy-lines should ever be used in a play since they distract the actors from the truth of the scene they're playing: also faked whispers do the same thing. If the scene is really and truly too long, I will cut it, but first I would like to see it played more naturally and audibly, I would like to catch every line of the script in this scene except where there is a natural over-lapping. I think we ought to have a line-reading of this scene before you go back to work on it, which I hope you will do, so that we can re-evaluate the dialogue about which you and I have always had our greatest difference of opinion in the play.

I'm not happy over the interpretation of Doc Baugh whom I had conceived as a sort of gently ironical figure who had seen so much life and death and participated actively in so much of it that he had a sort of sad, sometimes slightly saturnine, detachment from the scene, a calm and kindly detachment, but he plays like a member of the family, in the same over-charged manner, like a fellow conspirator, especially at the moment when he starts abruptly forward as if about to deliver a speech and says the Keely cure bit at stage-center with such startling emphasis. It is off-beat, off-key little details like this which give the beginning of Act Three its curiously unreal look-for-the-rabbit-out-of-the-silk-hat air. . . I think this seriously impairs the effect of the more intense scene that follows and the play as a whole suffers from it. It can be very simply and easily corrected as the basic idea, as I said, is sound and good, it is simply a damaging over-elaboration and formalization. . . .

(Like a person apologizing profusely for something completely unnoticed by anyone but him.)

ATMOSPHERIC DETAILS, outbreak of storm and fireworks.

I think it is right to treat these unconventionally, non-realistically, as we do, but still they ought to be prepared for in a way that will make them <u>recognizable</u> as what they are. It is not natural or believable that there is

only the single burst of fire-works and that it occasions such a suddenly started and ended hullaballoo. Can't we have it preceded by some flashes of light in the sky as if from Roman candles, with some muted cries, before all hell breaks loose with the pyrotechnics that are so precisely cued, in a rather cornily symbolic way, by the Brick telling Big Daddy he is dying of cancer bit?

Same is true of the storm. I would like to hear every one of the very few lines in the script about the storm and I would like the storm to approach less abruptly. Otherwise it can only be a tornado or an atom-bomb going off as close as Clarksdale. . .

I love the noise of the storm fading into the lovely negro lullabye: that's a true and beautiful bit of non-realistic staging which comes at the right moment and isn't the least bit exaggerated, in fact I would like to hear the singing better.

You know, of course, that the first view of the setting gave me a horrible, almost death-dealing, blow this afternoon, so I won't go into that subject! I have never had a play that had to get by without visual atmosphere which fitted it, and I am terrified that this may be the first and last time! I have no one to blame but myself as I saw the sketches, but somehow I had always thought, well, Jo is a genius, and Gadg is a genius, and they know what they are doing and who am I to open my ass-hole about it. . .

Tomorrow I will try to think of some more things to squeal about. But now I am going downstairs for a drink and will leave this in your box without reading it over lest I get chicken and afraid to offend you.

I am being utterly sincere when I say that, on the whole, you have done one of your greatest jobs. I just want all of it to measure up to the truest and best of it, and to make it plain to everybody that this play is maybe not a great play, maybe not even a very good play, but a terribly, terribly, terribly true play about truth, human truth.

Devotedly, 10.

[TW warned in a brief cover letter that the depressing effect of the set, installed at the Forrest Theatre in Philadelphia, may have "influenced" his criticism of the final run through of *Cat* in New York.

Mildred Dunnock, an experienced, versatile actor, was last directed by Elia Kazan in *Death of a Salesman*. Her performance as Big Mama was admired in Philadelphia and New York.

Jo Mielziner's enthusiasm for *Cat* was unmistakable: "You have no idea, Tennessee, how exciting this is to work on. This makes up for months and months of slaving over trivia." He also acknowledged, and presumably shared, TW's "concern" that the setting "not turn into a coldly classical abstraction" (January 27, 1955, BRTC). Later correspondence (Wood to TW, April 12, 1955, HRC) confirmed TW's displeasure with Mielziner's set design and his wish not to represent it in the first edition of *Cat*. Kazan, by contrast, not only approved the setting but had also encouraged Mielziner to execute a design that would insure a non-realistic staging of the play (see Kazan, pp. 542-543).

The Philadelphia notices were glowing. *Cat* was a "powerful, free-swinging play" in which TW had "surpassed even the fire and quality" of *Streetcar*. Its "symphonic" construction, brilliantly orchestrated by Kazan, held the audience "in thrall." Act Three played well, especially the conclusion, in which Maggie entices Brick to "the marital bed" with a "hopeful hint for the future." *Variety* reported that the box office was "torrid" after the first week of performance.]

Jo Mielziner, full set design for Cat on a Hot Tin Roof *(1955).*

305. To Justin Brooks Atkinson

[323 East 58th Street, New York]
March 25, 1955
[TLS w/ autograph marginalia, 1 p. BRTC]

Dear Brooks:

Now that you've written your lovely notice I can tell you that I would have just died if you hadn't liked and praised "Cat", I would have literally just died! I can't explain to you or myself or anybody why the reception of this play meant so damnably much to me, why I was so disgustingly craven about it, why the wait for the morning notices to come out was the most unendurable interval of my life. Of course it's always been like that, every time since it started with that little theatre in Saint Louis in 1938, but it gets worse instead of better, and before I go through it again, I've got to sit down with myself long and privately and try to figure out what makes it and what I can do about it besides not writing more plays. It must stem from some really fearful lack of security, some abysmal self-doubt. Also it takes such ugly, odious tangential forms, such as my invidious resentment of Inge's great success despite my friendly attitude toward Bill and his toward me. I was consumed with envy of his play's success and could hardly discuss it with you when we met in the Village a week or so ago. Hideous competitiveness which I never had in me before! But after "Camino" I was plunged into such depths, I thought I would never rise from. I love writing too much, and to love anything too much is to feel a terror of loss: it's a kind of madness. Enough of this, since all I wanted to say was my heartfelt thanks. That's just a phrase when it appears on paper, but believe me I mean it!

Fondly, Tenn.

Some time I would like you to read the original (first) version of Cat before I re-wrote Act III for production purposes. Both versions will be published and, confidentially, I do mean confidentially, I still much prefer the original. It was harder and purer: a blacker play but one that cut closer to the bone of the truth I believe. I doubt that it would have had the chance of success that the present version has and since I had so desperate a need of success, and reassurance about my work, I think all in all Kazan was quite right in persuading me to shape Act III about the return of Big Daddy - in the original the family conference was interrupted not by a storm but by his off-stage cry when pain struck.

[So "limpid and effortless" was *Cat on a Hot Tin Roof* (March 24, 1955) that it seemed "not to have been written. It is the quintessence of life." While Atkinson ranked *Cat* as TW's "finest drama" (*New York Times*, March 25, 1955), his peers were less convinced of its unqualified merit. Walter Kerr cited a lack of candor; Robert Coleman found the characters "repulsive"; John Chapman slighted TW's "command," observing that the action seemed "pointless" at times. *Streetcar* did not, however, arise to judge *Cat* inferior, nor did the "unnatural relationship" of Brick and Skipper unduly concern the critics. Elia Kazan's direction and the work of the principal actors—Barbara Bel Geddes (Maggie), Burl Ives (Big Daddy), Ben Gazzara (Brick)—were uniformly admired. Presumed faults aside, *Cat* had immense theatrical power and would run for nearly 700 performances.

Only Richard Watts was troubled by the ending of *Cat* and perhaps intuitively shared TW's preference for the original version. The "apparent reconciliation" of Brick and Maggie seemed "almost a happy conclusion, yet the final impression is one of doom" (*New York Post*, March 25, 1955).

Atkinson hoped "to read the original version" of *Cat*, as he later informed TW. He was amazed, however, by TW's self-doubt: "I should think your popular success, if nothing else, would give you a feeling of command, for you, Arthur Miller and Bill Inge are the only contemporary playwrights who have been everywhere accepted as theatre artists of first rank" (March 30, 1955, HRC). Inge's latest success was *Bus Stop* (1955).

Penned in the upper margin is a note by Carson McCullers addressed to Atkinson: "I am so thankful you are in the theatre." The dating of the letter is also in her uncertain hand.]

306. To Walter Kerr

[323 East 58th Street, New York]
April 9, 1955
[TLS w/ enclosure, 1 p. SHS of Wisconsin]

Dear Mr. Kerr:

I liked your notices of "Cat" but I thought you brought up an arguable point about "evasions" so I have done the enclosed piece as a reply. Of course I would like to have it published. I feel it would interest everyone who is interested in the play and the various criticisms of it.

I'm now off to Key West or I would like very much to have a less formal discussion with you, but maybe we can have lunch or cocktails when I return in May.

Thank you for the keen intelligence and perception your notices of the play showed. I know that my ambiguities need examination of this kind.

Cordially, Tennessee.

["'Cat on a Hot Tin Roof' is a beautifully written, perfectly directed, stunningly acted play of evasion: evasion on the part of its principal character, evasion perhaps on the part of its playwright." At fault, Walter Kerr argued, was TW's "tantalizing reluctance" to dramatize Brick's "precise feelings" (*New York Herald Tribune*, March 25, 1955) for his friend Skipper. TW answered that ambiguity was a defense against "'pat' conclusions" and "facile definitions" and concluded that theatregoers should expect "views" rather than "certainties" (*New York Herald Tribune*, April 17, 1955; rpt. in *Where I Live*, pp. 70-74).]

307. To Players

SH: Western Union
Key West Flo
1955 May 2 PM 8 32
[Telegram, 1 p. HRC]

DEAR PLAYERS: I WANT YOU TO KNOW THAT I KNOW THAT YOU ALL GAVE ME THE PRIZES ALL MY LOVE=

=TENNESSEE=

[After *Cat* received the Pulitzer and the Drama Critics' Award, TW observed to Elia Kazan that prizes "do disturb one a little as they have so little, or so fantastically remote, a connection with the period and circumstances of work, the lonely, sometimes desperate, mornings of work and the doubts and so forth." Nonetheless "to have them gives you a deep down, slow-burning satisfaction. As if God had given a sign of being with you" (May 3, 1955, WUCA). Satisfying too was the financial performance of *Cat*, which played to standing room and was projected to return the original investment of $102,000 by late-May.]

308. To Cheryl Crawford

SH: Comodoro Hotel
Oceanfront at 72nd Street
Havana, Cuba
5/7/55
[TLS w/ autograph marginalia, 1 p. BRTC]

Dearest Cheryl:

Frank and I suddenly realized last night that your play had opened by this time and we hadn't heard, or said, a word about it. Excuses? A continual stream of guests, beginning with Carson and continuing through

Francoise Sagan and three other "froggies" and my publisher trying to unravel the devious threads of several scripts for publication of "Cat". And then just plain exhaustion, the most valid excuse of all. I don't need to tell you that we hope the "Honey" was a success. We'll be back in New York early next week, well, about the middle anyhow, so don't bother to write us a report down here. Hal Wallis got me on "the blower" as Maria calls phones, about an hour ago and is going to show us "Tattoo" in New York soon as we return. That will be an evening when we can all get together, us four, at least and have a quiet dinner together and then see what Vista-Vision has done to our play. And our Magnani. . .

I wish I could say something definite about Cheri but I've got too many things stacked up right now, a film to finish for Gadg, a couple of unfinished play scripts and a volume of verse to prepare for the printer. Besides it appears that Anna is keen on doing "Orpheus" right now and I don't want to distract her from that. I've been thinking, why not Jane Bowles for "Cheri"? We'll talk about it next week. Meanwhile, much love from your wandering brother Tom. . . .

T.

[Carson McCullers's visit to Key West consisted of "swilling" TW's liquor and "gobbling" his "pinkies" until the host "reeled with apprehension" (qtd. in St. Just, p. 113). Françoise Sagan was the nineteen-year-old author of *Bonjour Tristesse* (1954), a *succès de scandale* recently translated and published in the States. TW had interrupted her tour with an invitation to visit Key West, where she spent a "riotous two weeks" (Sagan, *With Fondest Regards*, 1985).

Cheryl Crawford's latest production, *The Honeys* (1955), was not "a success." Hume Cronyn and Jessica Tandy starred in the Roald Dahl comedy which closed after thirty-six performances. Crawford's interest in *Chéri* did not materialize. The Playwrights' Company unsuccessfully staged the Colette adaptation in 1959.

TW's complaint of "too many things" included making final revisions for a forthcoming book of poetry, planning a production of *Orpheus Descending*, in which Anna Magnani had recently shown interest, and finishing the "unfinished" script of *Baby Doll* (1956).

Penned in the upper margin with an arrow pointing to the Comodoro imprint is the notation "Don't forget this hotel, its a dream!"]

309. To Audrey Wood

SH: Hotel Excelsior, Roma
[early-June 1955]
[TLS, 1 p. HRC]

Dear Audrey:

I was thrilled to get a cable from Gadg last night which said "Brando Available". How authentic is this? Being available does not mean committed or signed, and I am from Missouri and my first name is Thomas! I got a letter from Brando, saying he was very seriously interested in <u>Orpheus</u>. . . . Anyhow it was most exciting, and if it is true that Brando is doing the film, it will be much easier for me to continue work on it. I am going through a bad time with work right now, it is difficult and slow. The events of the year have drained my nervous reserves, I guess. And I have to have a room to myself, and so far that has been impossible, travelling with Frank in a stateroom and a single hotel-room, and he is a late riser, you know. I will mail as much of the new material on the film as I think is fairly presentable on Saturday, as I wired you just now, with notes on further plans for it. The fact, or possibility, of having Brando should be a spur. I know how to write for that boy.

Had lunch with Gloria Swanson, just by chance, but have not yet seen Anna. I'm waiting till Frank catches up with me as conversation is much easier when he's about. He should arrive this evening. We have a huge bathroom, and I plan to work in there till we get an apartment. Tell Gadg to be patient, and I won't let him down.

The Olivetti just broke, the spacer came loose so I shall have to cut this short. I'll get it fixed bright and early tomorrow.

Lefkowitz cabled that the artistic control on "Summer" was all that could be "reasonably expected". How about the money? Was there any improvement in <u>that</u>? And what about the film sale of <u>Cat</u>? There is no reason to expect the bidding to get any hotter or the property to increase in value, so if I were you, dearie, I would dispose of it while that roof is still sizzling, and the cat jumping thereon, at whatever offer is highest. Otherwise - remember "Menagerie"?

Forgive my jaundiced eye.

Love, Tennessee.

[In correspondence Marlon Brando ranked *Orpheus Descending* as TW's "best play" and asked "exactly" when it would be staged. Magnani, he added, "doesn't frighten me. . . . She yearns to be subjigated in a way that is natural to all women but she can't find anybody with enough fire to "burn her down." Brando welcomed the chance to act with her, providing their roles were "equally volital." TW had apparently invited Brando to direct *Orpheus*, a prospect which both "thrilled" and "scared" the actor and led him to return the compliment: "You wrote your funky ass off in that play!" (n.d., Columbia U). Brando's reported interest in *Baby Doll* did not materialize.

TW recently hired Julius Lefkowitz as a business manager. The accountant's first letter (June 2, 1955, HRC) promised cogent advice with a dash and humor and literary taste.

Audrey Wood soon presented TW with a handsome offer for film rights of *Cat*. He wrote earlier to Elia Kazan that she "has 'folie de grandeur' about what she can get for the property" and asked that he talk "realistically" (n.d., WUCA) to her about the market.

TW wrote this letter in the week of June 5. The reception date of 5/13/55 is in error.]

310. To Audrey Wood

[Hotel Colón, Barcelona]
7/11/55
[TLS w/ autograph marginalia, 1 p. HRC]

Dear Audrey:

I'm afraid your patience, and Gadge's, will be sorely tried with me this summer, I am running away from something, but don't know what I am running away from. Each new place disappoints me, after a couple of days it seems like an awful mistake to have gone there. But when I return to Rome, that's no good either. Frank seems put out by my unexpectedly early return and the old routine is lifeless. Magnani is out-spokenly puzzled by my behavior, and I'm afraid we may lose her simply because I act like a Zombie whenever I am with her, despite my true affection for her and great desire to have her do the play. If only Brando would commit himself, this would set things going! Her romantic interest in him is luckily over but being a very sensible, as well as great, artist, she wants very much to work with him and is unwilling to make any definite commitment till he has made one, as she feels that his power and "draw" would give her the confidence to attempt an American play. Her English really has improved, though she hasn't been studying as much as she should.

Frank read me your long wire over the phone. The connection was so bad that I could only get bits of it, and I didn't know whether you were talking about "Orpheus" or "Cat" when you spoke of "ten year payments", Etc. "Rose Dakin Productions" is all right. I would prefer Williams-Wood, unless you feel it is necessary to disguise the identities of the producers. Also I think we ought to be in association with a name producer or one that has lots of the hard stuff. (The hard stuff I am talking about is money). - It's a phrase of Maria's.

I may go down to Tangier and talk to Bowles about doing background music for the play, I think we ought to use him since he wrote the music for the ballads to be used in the play, and I think this one does need music. Also I don't think we ought to delay about a director, Lewis or Clurman or Quintero, if Kazan is definitely unwilling, which I think is the case.

Unless my nervous problems work themselves out in the course of this "summer of the long knives", I am definitely going to start psychiatric treatment when I return in the Fall. Please send me right away to Rome the very first version of "Summer and Smoke", or maybe it was the second, anyway - the one that had film-sequences in it, so I can start immediately on the screen-play. I sent you this version from New Orleans in the winter of 1946, when I had the lunatic notion of using stage and screen in combo to tell the story. It has some good screen material that will be enormously useful to me now.

I am quite well, otherwise, except that I have a cold, from swimming in various unsanitary pools about Europe. Please try to get a payment to Rose's trust fund the earliest possible as Mother is waiting for this to make some better provisions for her comfort and care. If the payments must be delayed, then I think I should advance money to the fund if that can be worked out tax-wise by Lefkowitz. Have you heard that Louella Parsons had a stroke in Rome? One side of her face is twisted up very oddly, according to Jean Stein, who called on her there. I sent her roses and phoned several times, as I've always rather liked that old girl despite her silliness and prejudices.

With love, Tennessee.

[TW spent the better part of July in Barcelona. He thought Frank Merlo "put out" by his "unexpectedly early return" to Rome in June following a trip to Athens and Istanbul.

"Figures stagger imagination approve get the loot" (telegram, TW to Wood, July 2, 1955, HRC). MGM offered $500,000 for film rights of *Cat* with payments to be spread over ten years. Studio executives were also confident, Wood had noted, that they could "solve" (telegram, to TW, June 30, 1955, HRC) the censorship problems which filming *Cat* would entail.

Wood later thanked TW for suggesting that their production company be named "Williams-Wood" (August 3, 1955, HRC) rather than "RoseDakin," as she had proposed. *Orpheus Descending* was to be the first venture.

Julius Lefkowitz advised TW in prior correspondence to write the screenplay for *Summer and Smoke* as a way of protecting the "artistic integrity" (June 2, 1955, HRC) of the original work.

Penned in the upper margin is the notation "(will wire next address)".]

311. To Elia "Gadge" Kazan

[Hotel Colón, Barcelona]
[July 1955]
[TL, 3 pp. WUCA]

Gadge Baby:

My imagination, weary, jaded ole thing which it is this summer, was not exactly fired by your outline (which reached me yesterday, not till then, because of a bad-phone-connection between here and Rome so that Frank thought I meant to hold my mail there, until I called him again). On the contrary: it (my imagination) was somewhat chilled and dampened, and I will try to tell you why, without being unnecessarily expository. We get each other's points too readily, when there's one to be gotten, without a lot of wearisome palaver.

I feel that my own original conception of the film-story as a grotesque folk-comedy of the modern South, with some serious over-tones, carefully kept within the atmospheric frame of the story, is still the only right one. The course which you indicate for the ending is far too heavy, at least for a work that is to have any sort of artistic unity. You are talking about HEAVY DRAMA! - that winds up with a genteel woman's FULFILLMENT, Death for one man, prison for the other. I know that I have not been very fair with you because there was a point where I appeared to accept this sort of an ending, Meighan killing Silva, dragged off in chains, Etc. But that was before I became really "engaged" in this material, I had a couple of plays and play productions on my mind so I gave it all too little serious

consideration. If I had thought about it, I would have realized that to have tragedy on stage or screen you have to build up to it, everything has to be conceived and done in a way that establishes a premise for a tragic ending, mood and style of writing have got to prepare it. Otherwise, one thing defeats the other, the result is nowhere! So even before this summer, I discarded the idea of a heavy ending. I can't go back to it now, like a dog to his vomit, I would just puke it right back up again, because it is really indigestible, it will not sit on my critical stomach, nor would it sit on yours if you were sitting down here trying to lap it up yourself, because it is not only vomit, it is cold vomit, and vomit can only be lapped back up and successfully returned to the belly while it is hot. (I am trying to make you laugh but am probably just making you angry.) When Frank gets angry at me he sometimes shouts, 'What you want is a yes-man and I am nobody's yes-man!' I am saying, more quietly, the same thing to you, that is, if you persist in this folly . . . Baby Doll Meighan cannot be turned into a starring role for Grace Kelly or Deborah Kerr, it's a part for a sexy little comedienne, and as such, could be delightful and fresh and a great popular hit on the screen. Baby Doll is about as genteel as Paddy's Pig. Have you ever noticed her grammar, the cultural, intellectual and spiritual content of her speech and behavior? She is touchingly comic, a grotesquely witless creature, about as deep as kitty-cat's pee. Who the fuck gives a shit if she is, was, or ever will be "FULFILLED AS A WOMAN"? Besides, though I would be the last to denigrate the value of a good fuck, I don't think people are transformed, redeemed, fulfilled in this fashion, any more than you learn piano in ten easy lessons by mail. She gets laid, she gets laid good, maybe, and she will doubtless be having the most satisfactory summer of her life, but a person's fulfillment, if such a thing exists, can only occur through self-integration, a slow process, demanding, in the first place a degree of intelligence and maturity, at least enough to enable the person to see and know his own self. I am afraid this kind of fulfillment, the only kind that much matters, is not for the Baby Doll Meighans of this world. She can have a vaginal fulfillment and a fulfillment of the womb, but I can't see it going past that, and my knees ache with boredom at the thought of trying to take her, or make an audience take her, seriously as a "Fulfilled Woman"? You mention Pagnol. I am not sure I have seen a Pagnol film but the name suggests a lightness, a delicacy, a playfulness, in which case the film is now on the right track, though still a long way from its destination.

But I don't think a Pagnol atmosphere, if I am interpreting it rightly, can have an early Eugene O'Neill finish tacked onto it without the most serious disagreement between the two, each impaling the other upon a frog-gig!

And I said I was not going to be "Expository"!

Now here, in the crudest sort of a sketchy cornball fashion, is how I think the film might end. (Incidentally, I disagree with you entirely about the <u>end</u> of the play being the important or exciting part. I think the main dynamic lies in Silva's relentless, step-by-step sensual ravishment of this sexy little virgin-wife for revenge and for proof of the arson.) After the chop-sticks bit, SILVA goes to kitchen for ice-water. Back there he takes a stub pencil, hanging from a nail on kitchen wall, and scribbles the note of confession on the back of a receipt for milk or ice or something, folds it into his pocket and returns to parlor, finds whip which Baby Doll had childishly concealed in the piano-bench. Goes out, grinning, with ice-water to join her on porch. (I've sent Audrey a pretty good re-write on that bit). Step-by-step she is isolated with Vacarro, her panic-attraction-panic steadily building up, with or without the trip to Clarksdale, which I still like. (Why does it break the unity anymore than <u>your</u> idea of them going to the Brite Spot that night? We have created a geographic unity out of the whole community, I mean the early part of the film has already included the town in the frame or canvas.) - When the big chase scene culminates, serio-comically in the falling plaster in attic, Baby Doll's ankle caught between cracking lathes, he hands her the confession to sign before extricating her. This done, he gets her out. Then what does he do, to her astonishment, but go calmly downstairs and out of the house. She is amazed, disappointed. Defended virginity turns to frustrated libido. She calls down the stairs, and across the lawn, as he goes, 'Where you going?' - 'Home, for a nap, I didn't sleep good last night.' - 'Hey! - We got a bed left here.' - 'Where?' - 'The nursery!' - - - HE stops under the big pecan tree, leaps into it, suddenly, and springs down with a pecan in his mouth, cracks it between his teeth, and casually hands her the two nut-meats. This time she accepts without fastidious comment. He whistles reflectively for a moment: then says: "I'm sleepy, it's a long hot walk to my place . . . I'm five feet ten and one half. How long is the crib?' - 'The bars let down!' - 'Aw, you let down the bars, huh? Well - ' . . . . . He starts toward the house. We

dissolve to the nursery, seeing it for the first time, the pathos of a child's room in a house without children. Perhaps he winds up a musical top as she lowers the slats of the crib. He sighs and lies down. She remains standing over him. He looks up at her with one eye, winks slightly, and curls up with his back to her. SHE crouches beside the crib, which rocks, and rocks it very gently, beginning to sing 'Rock-A-Bye-Baby' - stopping at his first snore. The (phallic) whip slips from his fingers. She picks it up tenderly and replaces it in his loose, sleeping hand. So we fade out without proving, or disproving, that he laid her or not. The audience is free to think what it will. Anyhow something humanly touching has occured, or been stated, the child in man that meets and plays with and loves the child in woman.

Eli Wallach and Carroll Baker: "I'm five feet ten and one half. How long is the crib?" (Baby Doll, 1956).

As for the frog-gigging party: you can carry it on to the point where Meighan's nerve deserts him, he gives way before Silva, takes flight, slips and flounders in muddy water, falls sobbing to his knees among cypress-knees. . . .

Silva to Rock: 'Get him up. I'm goin' back for dry clothes.'

We close on Silva re-entering the old plantation house. It lights up!

- Meighan limping like a lame old dog back along the now deserted bayou.

- I still like the ending we have already, however.

- Do we go on with this thing, now, or deduct it from taxes as a human error? Write me in Rome. I'll be going back there in a few more days.

Love,

[Preserved in early drafts of *Baby Doll* is the "discarded" frog-gigging scene cited by TW: "We see a tall Negro bearing a man's body. . . . Baby Doll screams, the figures divide. Vacarro lies smiling mysteriously, eyes open, a gig through his bare belly. . . . Dissolve to Big Shot {Archie Lee Meighan} wading out of the water . . . the sheriff behind him" (n.d., HRC).

Elia Kazan's "outline" of *Baby Doll* was an older conception which had been delayed in delivery and superseded by a script that TW would eagerly approve (see letter #315). Kazan agreed nonetheless that the "HEAVY" ending which he had devised violated "the first nine-tenths of the picture." Wrong too, he thought, was the coy "Lady and the Tiger" ending which TW now proposed: it failed to satisfy "the interest in all three" characters. To soften the frog-gigging scene, Kazan suggested that Vacarro and Meighan be reconciled. Perhaps Meighan, bitten by a snake, could be tended by Vacarro "in some fantastic kind of brotherhood." It was, he admitted, a "weird idea," but it might restore the "grotesque style" (to TW, n.d., HRC) of the film.

Kazan apparently mentioned the French playwright and film director Marcel Pagnol. His Marseille trilogy had recently been adapted as a musical—*Fanny* (1954)—and staged successfully on Broadway.

As filmed, the "attic" and the "crib" scenes closely follow TW's direction. TW was no less variable than Kazan regarding the end of *Baby Doll*. In May he restated his preference for a final dissolve to a forlorn Baby Doll sitting on the back porch of the Meighan residence phoning the police—an ending which he boasted was almost "perfect!" and "practically censor-proof" (to Kazan, May 3, 1955, WUCA).

In June he described the present "crib" scene, with a final dissolve to Aunt Rose in the County Hospital, as a more suitable closing (to Kazan, n.d., WUCA).

A briefer signed version of this letter, dated July 23, 1955, is held by the HRC. The printed version bears a reception date of July 28, 1955.]

312. *To Frank Merlo*

[Hotel Colón, Barcelona]
[July 22, 1955]
[TLS, 2 pp. HTC]

Dearest Horse:

I am working on Red Cross to send you a "gift package" containing one dozen rolls finest Swan's down toilet tissue, one quart blood plasma, and a bottle of spirits of ammonia. (Ha ha, this is a joke!) More seriously, I am worried over the persistence of the complaint. I never had it that bad, even in Mexico when I first had it, and I hope you are being careful and seeing Anna's doctor. You really mustn't go to Sicily! You remember you had a bad attack of dysentery when you went there the first time, and also the summer heat there would be awfully hard on Buffo. If you want to take a trip, and I can understand why you might, I think you should try Capri or Positano or Amalfi. I could join you in Naples, when I leave here, sailing out of some Spanish port. I find the bathing, regularly, and the sun, does so much for me, physically. One does get run down in Rome. I've been remarkably well since I started spending my days on the beach. However Miss Egleston is back on the trail, now, she calls every day, almost, to announce she is waiting downstairs in the bar. I'm glad the fiesta Brava starts in Valencia this Sunday so I have a reason to cut out. Tynan is here with an English queen who has just done 18 months in Worms Scrubwood or Scrubwood Worms for the hideous offense of buggery! His victim was an RAF boy, his lover for three years. He tells me Tynan is a sadist, gets his kicks having girls put on little school-girl costumes and caning them about the legs till they dance and howl. Very pretty, I must say! Claude Marchand, the colored dancer, is also in Barcelona, with his English lover, and they are good company. Society snow-balls here. More and more, till you scarcely have a moment to yourself. It takes real strategy to contrive some precious hours of solitude. A wire from Audrey confirmed sale of Cat to Metro for half million, which means we don't have to worry about "the

hard stuff" for another ten years, I guess. We'll be old girls, by then, and can get our social security when it runs out, and by such little economies as saving old tea-bags and turning collars and cuffs, we can eke out a comfortable elderly existence in some quaint little cold-water walk-up in the west nineties, with an occasional splurge at the YMHA when a surviving Sitwell gives a reading there. I'm afraid my eyesight will be getting rather dim, by that time, but my hearing may hold up. I hope you will have stopped having diarrhea. Perhaps Miss Butterfly or Ladybird will have provided us with a warm-hearted, short-winded companion for our excursions to the corner delicatessen and to (as far as) Bloomingdale's on their 99¢ sales-days. Queens have settled for less in ten years' time. . .

Does this sound like Leslie Eggleston? No wonder. I've had him in my ears going in and coming out for the past six hours, without interval or respite. The poor thing has hepatitis, which is the only noticeable improvement, an improvement because he orders fewer drinks. One more bull-fight, tomorrow, and I am off for Valencia. Marian Vacarro sent me clippings about the death of poor Valentina Sheriff. ("How dare you talk to me like this in the Ritz!" - remember?) She was found dead in her negligee in a New Orleans hotel among various empty and half empty pill-bottles which are being analyzed by chemists to see which snuffed out her existence. Poor Valentina, as Marian said! - And then went blithely on about the gay crew on the banana boat to Venezuala that she was on lately. Letter from Paul Bowles said Oliver Evans had been there, very nervous, going to doctor daily for terrible head-aches. It is not a good year for us Bohemian type people, is it, ducks? Gadg sent me his outline for the film. Baby Doll must be a "Fulfilled woman", Silva dead, and Archie Lee in prison in the last reel. I had to write him a rather sharp reply. I told him that when you get mad at me you shout: 'What you want is a yes-man and I am nobody's yes-man' and I said that this was exactly how I felt about his fucking outline. . . .

If the paper was softer, I would send it to you, as a supplement to supplies in the bathroom.

I am being careful, as careful as I can be, and I hope that you are, too. Horazio could be worse, let him wash the car when you feel up to it again. He is a nice, honest boy, and you are safe with him, if you don't forget the "mother's aid" in the tube.

Audrey wired, also, that Brando is willing to play "Orpheus" in the Fall of '56, provided some changes were made in his part. I think he's

another one to be told to fuck off. Don't you? You'd better let Anna know about this. Also that Clurman is available in December. (This year.) I think we can do without the great ones in the male department if we can get her to learn English.

I bought Anna a very fine leather bag with her initials in gold-plate and I'm getting her a wide belt to go with it. I'm trying to find the right sort of comb and mantilla for <u>you</u>, something suitable for the bathroom at midnight.

Don't forget to wire me if you take a trip anywhere, Baby. You know how awful it would be for me to pop back to Rome, unexpectedly, and no Horse and no car! Just a few old blood-stains on the bathroom floor. . . .

I wouldn't know whether it was murder or mementos of chronic colitis! - No more cracks on that subject, I promise.

All my love to you, Tenn

[Frank Merlo was "so cross" that TW thought it wise "to stay on the hoof; besides, I am restless this summer" (qtd. in St. Just, p. 121).

TW reported an "icy" (qtd. in St. Just, p. 125) meeting with Oliver Evans in Barcelona. His friend had recognized himself as the vain, aging homosexual in "Two on a Party," reprinted in *Hard Candy* (1954). He answered at the time with a taunting postcard and a threatening note: "You are so ugly, how could you

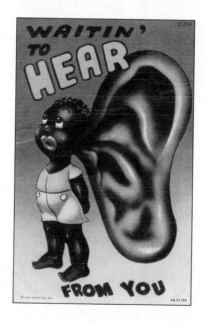

possibly interest anyone you didn't pay? Just read your new book & don't think you should return to New Orleans. A number of people join me in thinking it's very unhealthy for you - Love (not really) Oliver." (TW enclosed postcard and note in a letter to Elia Kazan dated September 16, 1954, WUCA.) The estrangement of friends ended in 1958, when Evans expressed new understanding of his portrait in *Hard Candy* and TW replied that his fondness for him had "never faltered" (November 15, 1958, HRC).]

313. *To Robert MacGregor*

SH: Hotel Colón, Barcelona
7/22/55
[TLS, 1 p. Houghton]

Dear Bob:

At last I got your letters, they were much delayed by a telephone misunderstand[ing], Frank thought I said to hold mail and I had told him to send it to me here, and this was not corrected till I called him again a week later, after waiting here all that time for the mail to come.

I do wish you could hold the book back, now, until I return to the States. It will doubtless be the only book of poems I will ever have published and I would like to be in closer touch with its preparation, there have already been misunderstandings. You haven't gotten all the poems on the list and you are not yet clear about the ones I want omitted. "The Angels of Fructification" should definitely go in, as it is one of the better ones. This is because I didn't have enough time to go over the collection with you before I sailed, but when I return, there'll be much more leisure and less pressure. I would like to confer with you about the cover design, and the type, for instance. Also I don't want any of the dates and places of composition at the ends of poems as they were in the "Five Poets" book. This is pretentiously silly so let's omit it, as an error of one's lyric youth corrected by prose reflection in middle years. Who gives a shit where and when I wrote these undistinguished verses? Only I. And I can remember. Also I still hope that somehow and sometime or other a better, more provocative, title will occur to me. I am enclosing a re-write of "Those Who Ignore the Appropriate Time Of Their Going". Does this strike you as a good title for the book, or is it too long and fancy? If you reflect upon it, it does describe or suggest a great deal about most of us. People expect me to provide good titles, and I

haven't this time, have I? - This re-write is only of the poem's last section. I would also like to change the beginning slightly, to:

> Those who ignore the appropriate time of their going
> are the most valiant explorers,
> going into a country that no one is meant to go into.

Could you send me the old version of the poem so I can fit it together with the revision?

I'm flying to Valencia tomorrow to attend a week of bull-fights with the English critic, Kenneth Tynan, who's doing a piece about me for Harper's Bazaar and is getting altogether too much confidential material here in Spain, though I am also getting a lot on him! Frank's in Rome. I will be returning there after the bull-fights, so you'd better address any mail to me there, #12 Via Corsini or c/o American Express.

Ever - Tennessee

[*In the Winter of Cities* was not published until June 1956, nor would it be TW's "only book of poems."

"Valentine to Tennessee Williams" appeared in *Mademoiselle* (February 1956) and was reprinted by the author, Kenneth Tynan, in *Curtains* (1961). In light of his harsh review of *Summer and Smoke*, Tynan wrote a surprisingly mild, conventional profile of TW. He cast him as a nomad, a hypochondriac, a solitary writer who "longs for intimacy, but shrinks from its responsibilities." Tynan's biographical summary followed the familiar outline of TW's painful departure from the South and prolonged exile in St. Louis. Unmentioned were personal and family matters including the illness of Rose. Tynan saved his aggression for Elia Kazan, who was accused of interfering with the composition of *Cat*. Tynan, drama critic for *The Observer* (London), drew from an autobiographical statement prepared by TW and dated July 26, 1955 (rpt. in Windham, pp. 301-307).]

314. *To Audrey Wood*

[Hotel Colón, Barcelona]
7/28/55
[TLS, 1 p. HRC]

Dear Audrey:

I still don't believe that you actually sold "Cat" for half a million. It's just fantastic. What a doll you are! I haven't adequately thanked you, and I'm afraid my importunities before the sale was consummated were inconsiderate of me. This is a down-beat summer, I just can't seem to get the work going, and that always throws me into a negative and unpleasant state of mind. Oh, well, you understand that, as you do most things. . .

I had to tell Gadg off, not rudely but firmly. He sent me a five-page outline for the film play which would have meant starting over from scratch even if I thought it was right, and it was corny as hell and old-fashioned melodrama that just wouldn't come off. I've stopped trying to work on it, at least until further word from him. If he's got any sense, he'll come to his senses, and leave me alone with the script to work it out my own way. I think he cheapened Cat, still think so, despite the prizes. That doesn't mean I doubt his good intentions, or don't like him, now, it's just that I don't want to work with him again on a basis in which [he] will tell me what to do and I will be so intimidated, and so anxious to please him, that I will be gutlessly willing to go against my own taste and convictions.

I'm still in Barcelona. The beach is wonderful, I swim a lot and it has picked up my physical condition, and there's the bull-fights. Frank's been sick all summer, first the hang-over from the hepatitis and then a fierce attack of colitis which went on for weeks. I don't think my company made him feel any better so it's just as well that I went away. Next year I'm going to insist that the boy go to a good analyst, he can afford it now and I can if he can't. I think these illnesses are a good part psychosomatic. He is haunted continually by the feeling of insufficiency, that he is dependant on me, and yet doesn't seem to be able to bring himself to the point of taking any positive action to change this state. We never joke and laugh together, which is bad, as jokes and laughter do so much to relieve the human dilemma, but he touches me deeply, and while I doubt that I have ever deeply loved him, according to my extremely romantic conception of what love should be - as distinguished from the pleasures of bed - still, he's given me an awful lot in a period when it was needed. So I want to

do all I can to help him find himself now, not just keep going over and over the same beaten track, following me, North, South, East and West, and making little abortive efforts, however violently shouted, to "say it isn't so". He's a true person, honest, intelligent, warm. "Attention must be paid to this man" before it's too late. His humility alone is great beauty.

I must, must get Brando's demands for his part soon, soon! If the demands are practicable, and Anna is willing to wait, then I wouldn't mind the delay till next the 1956 Fall. But if they are like most actors and directors demands, I'd rather forget him and try to find someone else. Anna suggested Jimmie Dean. I don't think that's a bad choice, except he's younger than Val ought to be. Clift is another possibility. Who else? I'm happy about Clurman, and I know that Anna would break through his tendancy to make a play a bit static or "fixed". Please tell him I am delighted that he may do it, and ask him to start thinking, planning for a mid-winter production. Anna is ready at that time. I think she would be so terrific, so true, in the role, that Brando is dispensable if difficult to please.

I will be back in Rome in about four days.

With love - 10.

PS. Please ask Bob MacGregor not to send poetry book to printers till he hears from me. I have further revisions and probably a different title. Would prefer holding it back till I return States late September. There is no hurry about it.

[Audrey Wood urged TW to spare himself and follow her own don't "ask" (August 3, 1955, HRC) policy regarding studio plans to censor *Cat on a Hot Tin Roof*. Such plans were already evident in an outline prepared by MGM and discussed with the Production Code staff before the sale of film rights. The proposed treatment would "stress the father-son relationship" and "omit any inference of homo-sexuality" between Skipper and Brick. Skipper would callously seduce Maggie, which Brick refuses to acknowledge until Big Daddy convinces him that his friend was "a rotter" (Production Code memorandum, June 23, 1955, Herrick).

Wood informed TW that Marlon Brando was still considering the lead in *Orpheus*, although he would not be available until fall 1956 and his commitment would entail difficult revision of the play. As written, the part of Val Xavier did not carry "enough weight," Brando thought, while the "blow torch ending" in which Val is emasculated was "tough to take" (August 4, 1955, HRC).

TW had not yet learned of Margo Jones's death on July 24, 1955, from exposure to a toxic cleaning agent. He later doubted the accidental nature of her death and surmised that Jones "may have had an abortion. That frequently results in uremic poisoning, if it goes wrong." It hurt TW "to think how often we laughed at dear Margo for her little silliness and paid too little attention to her great heart" (qtd. in St. Just, p. 124). His cable of condolence arrived after the funeral on July 26.]

315. To Elia "Gadg" Kazan

[12 Via Corsini, Rome]
[August 1955]
[TLx, 1 p. Private Collection]

Dear Gadg:

Frankie the Horse has just trotted in with the repaired Olivetti and I'm back on it, Baby. He also brought the script and your letter. I'm going to write you about it after only reading the first few pages and the last few pages. Later I'll write you a more dispassionate and qualified appraisal, but let me say right off, you're a better man than I am, Gunga Din! The end sounds great, it's great film-writing, perhaps it's even great writing. It doesn't sound like corn, it sounds like dynamite. (Remember! - I've only read about six pages, divided between the beginning and the end.) Of course you realize that if I use your stuff I will have to use your name as co-author, I couldn't honorably do otherwise. I would be happy to do this, and believe me I mean it. Owing people is shit. That is, owing a friend is shit. But nevertheless, the fact stays that I owe you what makes it possible for me to get through this summer, to live. A success when I had given up thought of anything but failure, and a sort of vague whimpering end to life. No, maybe not whimpering. Give the devil his due, I might not whimper. On the other hand, I might.

BELIEVE ME! - I've only read your letter and three pages at the beginning and about three at the end, but the shouting to the men on the bank with Archie Lee at the end of the gig, is great, great, great, great THEATRE! - What we live for, what we try to be in these silly makeshift existences of ours, and I pay you homage for it.

This is all for right now, Baby. But I hope that I will discover some way to persuade you to keep in "Chopsticks" and "Charm-bracelet" bits just as a sort of identification mark of my own that says, "Here lies Tennessee." -

You take the big guns, the heavy artillery, but let me have a little of my old little flute-playing here and there in the script to signify that I was your partner in it.

                                    True love,

[TW's refers to a shooting script of *Baby Doll* assembled by Elia Kazan which post-dates the rejected "five-page outline." In the new opening sequence Meighan leers at his sleeping virgin-bride through a peephole in the plaster. Staged in the conclusion is an epic battle between Vacarro and Meighan which ends with Meighan "shouting to the men on the bank" that he burned the syndicate gin: "I did it. I did it" (July 29, 1955, HTC). One of the silent witnesses, goaded by Vacarro to acknowledge the confession, kills the outsider with a rifle shot. This climactic scene was not filmed, nor would there be more than a trace of the original frog-gigging party—recast as a fishing expedition—in the final print. The present script ends with a close shot of Aunt Rose humming a lullaby to Baby Doll.

   Audrey Wood received a copy of this letter from Kazan and instructed TW not to offer him co-authorship of *Baby Doll*: "All of this should be handled by AW and not TW. You are a writer and not a business man. Stop making your own deals - I am much better as a dealer than you - Remember Metro Goldwyn Mayer!" (August 16, 1955, HRC).]

316. To the Editor, Theatre Arts

                                          [12 Via Corsini, Rome]
                                        [August/September 1955]
                                   [*Theatre Arts*, October 1955, p. 3]
Dear Sir:

   Due to my travels in Europe I was late in getting the July issue of your magazine containing the alleged interview with me ["Tennessee Williams: Ten Years Later"]. It is true that the interview took place; it took place very dimly, almost unconsciously, during the dreadful last week before the New York opening of my play *Cat*. But even considering the conditions under which I had this interview, I am not able to believe that I actually said the things that I am directly quoted as having said . . . I would certainly never be so unfaithful to the greatest lady of my life, Blanche Du Bois, to describe her as "weak," "pitiful," almost "a mental case." This, I know, I did *not!* In some respects Blanche, who went to the madhouse, was the most rational of all the characters I've created, and in almost all ways, she was the

strongest. She certainly fought on a much more desperate field than Maggie the Cat fights on, she fought with all odds against her and with unfailing valor, with gallantry that persisted and even reached its peak at the final curtain. It must be obvious to anyone that I prefer her to Maggie the Cat, though I have great admiration for both ladies. For very different reasons. It should also be obvious that I could never have denigrated *Camino Real* as something for which I can only ask for indulgence, granted after. I am not at all sure that it isn't the one I love most of my plays, though I know it commits the huge structural error of deviating from a straight narrative line. [Elia] Kazan and I both are very proud of this "failure" and talk of another production. My article in the [New York] *Herald Tribune* deals accurately with my attitude toward Brick's sexual nature, not the one given in quotes in this interview. I don't doubt that Arthur Waters was conscientious but I think it is necessary to be much more attentive to exact words and exact meanings when you use quotation marks in interviews, especially when you are interviewing someone who, under the circumstances, wants only to sit and wait as quietly as possible for the stroke of doom or deliverance. Finally, it is quite true that Kazan is my favorite director, but it was inaccurate and unkind, equally both, to suggest that I blamed *Rose Tattoo's* relative lack of success on its direction. Daniel Mann did a beautiful job on the stage version of *Tattoo* and a still more beautiful job on the film. Gadg would have demanded a stronger, tighter script from me: Danny was willing to take a chance on the script submitted.

Tennessee Williams
Rome, Italy

[Quotations attributed to TW—accurately or not—fail to convey his well-known preference for the ambiguity of character. Far too explicit were statements that "'Brick is definitely not a homosexual'" and that his drinking may be attributed to attacks on Skipper rather than his own "'personal involvement.'" Uncontested by TW were his reported opinions that the theatre was holding "its own" and that artistic standards for American films have "improved" (*Theatre Arts*, October 1955, p. 3; rpt. in *Conversations*, pp. 34-37).

The brackets and ellipsis were inserted by *Theatre Arts*.]

317. To Audrey Wood

[Rome/Paris]
[August/September 1955]
[TLS w/ enclosure, 2 pp. HRC]

Dearest Audrey:

The reaper is not only grim but active and rapid this season. It was Mel Ferrer that told me about Lem's death and it gave me a shock for Lem was my closest male friend at Iowa and I'd always been particularly fond of him. He was not only very gifted but also very kind and understanding. Mel said he died of leukemia after a three years' illness in which he carried on his work even when bed-ridden.

Wallis is here and we were at the Ferrers for dinner last night because Hal wants to sign Audrey Hepburn for Summer and Smoke. I think it's an excellent choice. Kurt Frings and his wife went along. Both of them struck me as having a merely surface geniality. Masking a lot of malice. I believe Hal is intending to get Ketti Frings to write the screen play for Summer and Smoke. I hope you will block this idea, she strikes me as having a basically vulgar mind. I'd rather work on it, if I find that I need a collaborator, with a male writer. I can handle the feminine side of the story but a good, sensitive male writer of quality could help me a lot with the action stuff, such as the fever epidemic and the melodramatic death of the old doctor. Also she would take the lion's share of the screenwriter's pay, no doubt, with Mr. Frings in her corner. I spoke of you and he said, 'I have never known such a domineering woman.' This did not please me at all as I feel you are quite the contrary.

Audrey Hepburn is fabulous! Truly! She was Miss Alma in the flesh! I can't think of better casting for this part. She has long thin arms, a long thin neck, long thin body and long thin legs - and eyes that break your heart with their youth and sweetness. No accent: exquisite grace. I almost found myself admiring Hal Wallis for thinking of her for it. Her price is $350,000 and he is willing to pay it! The deal is not yet completed but I had a distinct feeling that both she and Mel were very favorable to it. We discussed directors. Do you think the man who directed "Marty" would be right for it? Another one mentioned was William Wyler who directed her in "Roman Holiday".

I am flying to Stockholm on Wednesday where I will be the guest of the very rich Mrs. Lilla Van Saher Riwkin at the Castle Hotel. You can reach me there.

LATER - Found this unfinished letter among my papers when I got back here in Paris. This is my vague summer! - have been through everything but a flash flood at Inge's summer palace in Buck's County, PA. Seems to be good for me, never felt better in my life! - except that I don't write well. Now waiting here for Frank and Magnani to show. No word about when. But patience is a virtue in late summer or early Fall that one must respect. And practise. Saw Toby Roland (in London) about Tattoo. I like that man very much, and the director that he has in mind for Tattoo is the best in Europe, a young guy (23) named Peter Hall who put on "Waiting for Godot" now playing in London which I am not sure is not the greatest play of our time. Directed with absolute genius! - I'm trying to sell Roland on Stapleton as the lead. He has in mind a night-club performer that I never heard of. Lars Schmidt is coming here to confer with me about Tattoo for London and Cat for Paris. So things are jumping! I still have the new power-of-attorney. Haven't gotten around to notarizing it yet, but I will soon as I get back in the States where it can be done so much more easily. I'm sure there's no immediate crisis. Or is there? If there is, wire me. You're the only person that I trust in this world. You know that, don't you? But still I would prefer to go over the document with you prior to signing.

The matter of Orpheus is settled as far as I am concerned. We are going to produce it together. No playwrights! - in my heart it is hard for me to like any playwright who is still writing plays. Miller, yes! Inge, sometimes . . . . an ugly effect of the competitive system. They have to stun me with splendor that drives vanity out! Or I wish they'd quit writing as I have nearly this summer.

At this point, I'm afraid there is nothing to do about "Hide And Seek" but try very hard to like everything that Kazan suggests. I'm going out now (my first morning in Paris) to pick up his latest draft of it. Got a long-distance call from Jack Warner (from Cannes) praising the new script to the skies! Kazan probably writes better than it reads. However the script so far seems to be about 90% my stuff and I think he ought to be content with credit as the adaptor for screen. We'll talk about that in New York.

Is it possible that poor Rose is still in the State Asylum? If so, would you wire Mother that I want her to be transferred at once to Saint Vincent's in Saint Louis at my expense? I also have an old maid Aunt on my hands now. Dad has cut off her fifty-dollar-a-month allowance and I have to take it on. Please tell Lefkowitz. She can be deductible as a dependant. She is

Miss Ella Williams at 1633 West Clinch Ave., Knoxville, Tennessee. A wonderful old lady, very brave and proud, eighty years old. I have already sent her a check for $500. to tide her over the next few months but I think the monthly payments ought to be started to give her a feeling of security. I enclose her letter thanking me for the check so you can see her character.

With love, Tenn.

[The stage designer Lemuel Ayers died on August 14, 1955, at the age of forty.

Audrey Hepburn and her husband, Mel Ferrer, were evidently less "favorable" to *Summer and Smoke* than TW imagined. He later urged Hepburn not to consider the play a "downbeat" story: "It concerns victory of spirit over a circumstantial defeat which is only possible victory in life" (telegram, August 26, 1955, Herrick). Geraldine Page would play Alma in the 1961 film. The screenwriter Ketti Frings (*Come Back, Little Sheba*, 1952) had no hand in the production.

The trip to Scandinavia (ca. August 31-September 3) for the European premiere of *Cat* was "a mess!" as TW informed Maria Britneva. Lilla Van Saher apparently created a public relations fiasco in Stockholm by exploiting TW's presence. TW later implied that she had ruined his impending nomination for the Nobel Prize (see *Conversations*, p. 357). The play, if not the author, was "a huge success" (qtd. in St. Just, p. 127).

Casting, production, and censorship problems delayed the London premiere of *The Rose Tattoo* until 1959. Lea Padovani rather than Maureen Stapleton played the lead.

Audrey Wood recently criticized the Playwrights' Company for sloppy production of *Cat*. Presumably she hoped to moderate TW's high regard for the producing group and to strengthen the new corporation of Williams-Wood (Wood to TW, August 22, 1955, HRC).

No formal credit was given for the adaptation of *Baby Doll*. TW claimed the full screenwriting credit.

"Poor Rose" Williams was soon transferred to St. Vincent's Sanitarium in St. Louis County, where her custodial care began in 1937.

TW wrote the first part of this letter in Rome in the week of August 21, 1955. He added the "Later" part in Paris, probably in mid-September, after visiting Scandinavia, Hamburg, and London. The letter bears a reception date of September 19, 1955, three days before he and Frank Merlo sailed for the States.]

318. To Audrey Wood

[Comodoro Hotel, Havana]
Nov. 18 (or 20), '55
[TLS w/ autograph postscript
and enclosure, 2 pp. HRC]

Dear Audrey:

Frank told me over the phone yesterday that Otis Guernsey of the Trib wanted me to contribute a piece about Anna. Here it is. Will you please have it typed up and send copies to him and to me. I'm afraid it's a bit diffuse and over-length but I think the portrait is true and sympathetic. If the Trib doesn't take it, it might be submitted elsewhere.

Don't you think we are moving too slow on "Orpheus"? I think the dead-line for decisions from both Brando and Kazan should be the end of December, after Anna has arrived in the States. I also think it's imperative that she come over at that time, so we can sign her, and get the production under way. Until we know we have HER, it is hard to cast the others. I read the script over and I can't dispute Marlon's view that his part is weaker than hers. Nor can I see any way to expand it very appreciably without changing, adulterating, the truth of the play, and on this occasion, I am determined to express just me, not a director or actors. Almost everybody of taste that I have talked to about "Cat" are disturbed and thrown off somewhat by a sense of falsity, in the ending, and I don't want this to ever happen again, even if it means giving up the top-rank names as co-workers.

I have developed a sore gut and some fever, so I'm cutting my stay here short and flying back to Miami, this afternoon, unless I feel a lot better in the next few hours.

With love, Tenn.

P.S. Rose has been transferred to St. Louis hospital.

[TW spent the fall in New York and Key West before visiting Havana in mid-November. Staging *Orpheus* was uppermost in mind, but other projects vied for attention, especially the filming of *Baby Doll* and plans for European productions of *The Rose Tattoo* and *Cat*. A new play, *Sweet Bird of Youth* (1956/1959), was also underway at this time.

Publication of "Anna Magnani, Tigress of the Tiber," was timed to coincide with the release of *The Rose Tattoo* on December 12, 1955. TW wrote that the art

of Anna Magnani and Laurette Taylor was "closely related. Both owned that same uncanny sense of truth and measure and justice" (*New York Herald Tribune*, December 11, 1955, sec. 4, p. 3).

Casting *Orpheus* would be tedious and prolonged. Her son's hospitalization in Rome (the debilitating effects of polio) led Magnani to cancel plans for a late-December arrival in the States. Presumably she retained a strong interest in the play, although her financial terms—deemed "unconscionably exorbitant" by Audrey Wood—and demand for a brief engagement were inhibiting factors. Wood informed TW in the new year that signing Marlon Brando appeared "almost hopeless" (January 16, 1956, HRC), but as later correspondence reveals, his "final word" was still awaited in the following August.]

319. To Hodding and Betty Carter

[6360 Wydown Boulevard
Clayton, Missouri]
12/6/55
[TLS, 1 p. HRC]

Dear Hodding and Betty:

I had to cut my stay in Greenville a bit short in order to be back in New York for the premiere of Rose Tattoo and also get in a brief visit with what remains of the family here in Saint Louis. I am trying to write this letter on a machine that has probably not been used in the last twenty years, and is reluctant to return to active duty.

The boat trip

Interruption! Went downstairs to unpack my Olivetti. This is better. I was about to mention the boat-trip, the only, very delightful social event of my stay in Greenville. I would come back before the film's finished but I must admit that I had a feeling of being on the slopes of a very lively volcano. Saw and heard some things, nights out in the county, that made my hair stand on end. I think you're very, very brave! I pay you homage! (From my safe distance, physical courage not being one of my virtues.) I hear that Faulkner is going through the same thing as you. The script that I wrote for Kazan was not a "social comment" but if I know Kazan, I doubt that some rumbles of the tense and turbulent background will fail to make themselves heard in the completed work. I never believe in pointing the finger of shame or blame. I think Mississippi is handling this problem as well as Massachusetts

would handle the same problem if it existed up there. People are the same the world over. But ignoring the facts is totally unuseful. There are people like you in Mississippi, a lot of them I trust, and I think the present situation is a challenge to the innate nobility and sense of justice which I believe is part of the southern tradition.

Thanks to you, and good luck, with my fond regards,

Tennessee.

[Hodding Carter (1907-1972) won the Pulitzer Prize in 1946 for editorials opposing racial bigotry and segregation. He was the publisher-editor of the Greenville, Miss., *Delta Democrat-Times* for nearly four decades.

Elia Kazan cast TW as a wary visitor to the set of *Baby Doll* in Benoit, Mississippi. He attributed TW's abrupt departure to his feeling of banishment from the South for his sexual difference and his present fear of being "'insulted'" (qtd. in *Kazan on Kazan*, ed. Ciment, 1974, p. 74). TW was joined in Greenville by Lilla Van Saher.

Anna Magnani had "a triumphant field day," wrote Bosley Crowther in review of *The Rose Tattoo*. Although one might question the "validity" of Serafina's character and the "logic" of her "conversion to a natural life," the critic preferred not to quibble: Magnani "overwhelms all objectivity with the rush of her subjective force" (*New York Times*, December 13, 1955). She also overcame stiff competition from Susan Hayward, Katharine Hepburn, and Jennifer Jones to win the Oscar in her first American film.]

Elia Kazan (in sweater) and Tennessee Williams (on Kazan's left) on the Baby Doll *(1956) set in Benoit, Mississippi, 1955.*

320. To Elia "Gadg" Kazan

SH: *The* Robert Clay
Miami, Florida
[ca. early-January 1956]
[TLS, 2 pp. WUCA]

Dear Gadg:

I know you are always interested in my first reaction, which is always stronger and often better than my more considered reaction, so I wired you immediately after reading the "continuity" for the proposed ending, and this morning I am going to try to amplify or clarify that telegraphic out-cry of protest. No one knows better than I that in the heat of creation, which heat you are now enjoying in Greenville, cold as it is down there, you have an irresistible urge to expand, to blow up and burst the frame, of the work in progress. Maybe I have misinterpreted your continuity, despite prefatory comment that you always shoot more than you use, but! - You say that whenever I am in trouble I go poetic. I say whenever you are in trouble, you start building up a "SMASH!" finish. - As if you didn't really trust the story that goes before. It is only this final burst of excess that mars your film-masterpieces such as "East of Eden", and it is in these final fireworks that you descend (only then) to something expected or banal which all the preceding artistry and sense of measure and poetry - yes, you are a poet, too! no matter how much you hate it! - leads one not to expect. I simply can't believe that you have been shooting a film that demands a finish like this outline. I sense that you have been creating all of the values, and more, that we had in mind for a poignantly true, human, grotesquely humorous and touching, truly original piece of comedie humaine! It's all right, in fact it's wonderful, for Archie Lee to go berserk and shoot up the place, but when he kills a negro, somehow a false note is struck. Not false to the country. The hell with the Delta! But false to the key and mood of the story, because! - I don't think either you or I can accept a killing of a negro, whom we love, as just an ironical twist, just a final wry comment, as a tag to a tale which is endearingly close to universal human behavior till then. And killing a negro is not a part of universal human behavior, witness all the universal Archie Lees in this world who never killed a negro and never quite would! They would commit arson, yes, they would lie and cheat and jerk off back of a peep-hole, but they wouldn't be likely to kill a negro and slam the car door on his dying body and go on shooting and shouting, now,

would they?! Or if they do, and we are giving their portrait, everything in the picture has to be changed to meet this new comment, which is naturally more important than any preceding comment the picture has made. The wounding of a negro is more in scale. That might happen. Or maybe the shot goes wild and you add a very funny touch by Archie blasting the interior of the Pierce, opening the door and saying, 'Oh, you! Excuse me. . .' - And the colored boy gives a low whistle and looks up at God! - this is in the mood and the key, inside the frame, of the story. A killing is not so much a moral discrepancy as it is an artistic outrage of the film-play's natural limits. I think that ending I sent you, with the addition of the Baby Doll-Silva dialogue under the tree, comprises a very complete and satisfying finish to the story and stays inside the frame of it. Don't panic! And shoot wild as Archie Lee Meighan! I actually think you've got all the material from me that you need but I will supply more anyhow. But please have Jean Stein copy all the dialogue that belongs to the ending which I have so far sent you. When I unpacked my papers I found that I had left all of that stuff in New York. I am going to write out some speeches between Silva and the Marshall right now in case you decide to have an audible conference between them. I hope you don't. I think you have finished your story very, very powerfully and successfully before you come to the final bit and all you have to do is keep it in key, and in measure.

Love, Tenn.

[The *Baby Doll* company—including Eli Wallach (Silva Vacarro), Carroll Baker (Baby Doll), Karl Malden (Archie Lee Meighan), and Mildred Dunnock (Aunt Rose)—spent ten weeks on location in the Delta (November 1955-January 1956). Elia Kazan deplored the racial mores of the region and twice shielded Negroes from the police. Nonetheless he found the locals to be charmingly European in their rural culture and to have "great affection for each other" (qtd. in *Kazan on Kazan*, ed. Ciment, p. 75). With a single exception, they played all of the roles save the four principals.

As filmed, the finale of *Baby Doll* completes the "hide and seek" motif which originally entitled the script. Meighan, drunk and enraged by his wife's apparent seduction, goes "berserk" with a shotgun while Vacarro and Baby Doll crouch in a tree. The accidental killing of a Negro—the "false note" to which TW refers—does not occur in the film. Instead Meighan pulls open the door of an abandoned car only to find a Negro, to whom he politely says "excuse me."

Additional dialogue—typed on Hotel Greenville letterhead—stresses Vacarro's callous treatment of Baby Doll after Meighan's arrest has completed the theme of

revenge. "What about <u>ME</u>!?!" she cries, as Vacarro prepares to leave. "<u>Happy birthday to you</u>!" he replies. Baby Doll's unsureness regarding the future leads Aunt Rose to speak the closing line, "We'll find out tomorrow" (TW, "Sketch for possible new end of film," n.d., HRC).

TW's presence in Miami in early-January 1956 may support the speculative dating of this letter.]

321. *To Audrey Wood*

[1431 Duncan Street
Key West, Florida]
1/20/56.
[TLS, 1 p. HRC]

Dearest Audrey:

I have been too preoccupied with Tallulah and Streetcar to properly consider the problems of the next play. I agree that we should move at once to Paul Newman. Gore Vidal is here, and he says Paul is very eager to do the play. He has just come from Hollywood and saw Paul frequently there. It is possible that Newman will be better in the part than Brando, and will certainly cost less and play longer. The great problem, now, is to sell Magnani on him. Gore says she ought to see a print of his picture "The Rack". He thinks if she sees it, she will be convinced that he is an acceptable replacement for Brando. I think it may even be worth our while to fly together to Rome to show her this film and make an all-out effort to get her signed up.

This morning I did another re-write on the Val-Lady scene in Act Three. If it still seems right tomorrow, I will mail it to you.

Had a terrible fight with Tallulah. She screamed at me and I screamed back even louder, and she shut up! I flew to Key West and last night she called me and peace appears to be restored between us. Her first night was dreadful but her following performance, the next night, was legitimate and brilliant. She has it in her to play this part better than it has ever been played, the problem is to keep Tallulah inside the role of Blanche. Machiz understands, but is weak. After opening night, Jean Dalrymple and I discussed the possibility of replacing him with Jed Harris, and in which event I would forego my royalties. But the second night performance was so much better that I think this drastic (and cruel) step may not be

necessary. Even when she is bad, (Tallulah, not Blanche) the audience seems to adore her and we have played, so far, to packed houses, and Machiz phoned last night (collect!) to say that there were standees at both matinee and evening.

Maria is with us. Tallulah calls her 'That Cruikshank cartoon', 'that black-mailing bitch', and so forth. That was what precipitated the row. Also her sycophantic attendants had told her that I had deplored her opening performance in characteristically incontinent terms. . .

I think we must now make an all-out campaign to get Magnani signed up without Brando.

Love, 10

[In *The Rack* (1956) Paul Newman plays an Army captain accused of collaborating with the enemy while a prisoner in the Korean War. His performance was greatly admired, although Newman's looks would not please Anna Magnani.

The "fight" with Tallulah Bankhead began with TW's banishment from rehearsals of the *Streetcar* revival for making both star and director feel "self-conscious." The opening night performance, as reviewed by TW, was a disaster: "There were all these faggots in the house. Tallulah began to play to them. There was hardly anything else she could do. They insisted on it. And I got very drunk and at the conclusion of the evening I was sulking around and somebody said: 'Come over and speak to Tallulah.' And I said: 'I don't want to. She pissed on my play'" (qtd. in Brian, *Tallulah, Darling*, 1972, p. 204). *Streetcar* ran for three weeks (January 16-February 4, 1956) at the Coconut Grove Playhouse in Miami before transferring to City Center in New York.

Jean Dalrymple, executive director of the City Center Theatre Company, supervised the *Streetcar* revival. Herbert Machiz, thirty-three at the time, directed and brought the play to New York for a two-week engagement.

TW had apparently recommended that Maria Britneva play Stella in the forthcoming revival. Bankhead dismissed the idea after meeting her in New York: "How DARE you bring that Cruikshank cartoon to my apartment and tell me that she looks like my sister" (qtd. in Brian, *Tallulah, Darling*, p. 204). George Cruikshank was a Victorian illustrator with a talent for biting satire. Britneva was "rather impressed" that Bankhead knew of his work.]

322. *To Cheryl Crawford*

SH: Western Union
Key West Flo
1956 Feb 27 PM 1 55
[Telegram, 1 p. BRTC]

DEAREST CHERYL,

THANKS SO MUCH FOR YOUR WIRE. AM PLANNING TO TRY OUT BRAND NEW PLAY DISCRETELY AS POSSIBLE AT SMALL THEATER STUDIO M CORAL GABLES AM TRYING TO GET MAUREEN TO CONTRIBUTE HER SERVICES WITH PROMISE OF BROADWAY WHEN AND IF. WOULD LOVE FOR YOU TO SEE IT AND CONSIDER IT ALSO. YOU ARE STILL MY FAVORITE PRODUCER BY TEN COUNTRY MILES ESPECIALLY WHEN AUDREY WISHES. WILL CALL YOU SOON ABOUT DATES AND FURTHER DEVELOPMENTS MUCH LOVE

TENNESSEE=

[The "brand new play" evolved in part from "The Big Time Operators" (n.d., HRC), the Huey Long project which TW had shelved in late 1948. The premiere at Studio M Playhouse, Coral Gables, Florida, was set for April 16, 1956, with direction by George Keathley. Maureen Stapleton would not "contribute her services" to this or to any other production of *Sweet Bird of Youth*, as the work-in-progress was now entitled.]

323. *To the Drama Editor,* New York Times

"Drama Mailbag," *New York Times*
March 4, 1956, section 2, p. 3

To the Drama Editor:

To the considerable and lively controversy about Tallulah Bankhead as Blanche DuBois, in the recent City Center revival of my play, "A Streetcar Named Desire," I would like, "just for the record," as they say, to add my personal acknowledgment, praise and thanksgiving for what I think is probably the most heroic accomplishment in acting since Laurette Taylor returned, in the Chicago winter of 1944-45, to stand all her admirers and her doubters on their ears in "The Glass Menagerie."

I have loved all the Blanches I've seen, and I think the question of which was the best is irrelevant to the recent revival. Several weeks ago, on

the morning after the opening in Coconut Grove, Miami, Fla., the director
and I called on Miss Bankhead in her boudoir where this small, mighty
woman was crouched in bed, looking like the ghost of Tallulah and as quiet
as a mouse. I sat there gravely and talked to her with the most unsparing
honesty that I've ever used in my life, not cruelly, on purpose, but with an
utter candor. It seemed the only thing that could save the situation.

If you know and love Tallulah as I do, you will not find it reprehensible
that she asked me meekly if she had played Blanche better than anyone else
had played her. I hope you will forgive me for having answered, "No, your
performance was the worst I have seen." The remarkable thing is that she
looked at me and nodded in sad acquiescence to this opinion.

Contrary to rumor, I never stated publicly, to my sober recollection,
that she had ruined my play. What I said was phrased in barroom lingo. I
was talking to myself, not to all who would listen, though certainly into my
cups. But that morning, after the opening, Tallulah and I talked quietly and
gently together in a totally truthful vein.

She kept listening and nodding, which may have been an unprecedented
behavior in her career. The director and I gave her notes. I went back that
night, and every note she was given was taken and brilliantly followed in
performance. I left town, then, because I knew that I had hurt her deeply
(though for her good) and that she would feel more comfortable without
me watching her work.

I doubt that any actress has ever worked harder, for Miss Bankhead is
a great "pro," as true as they make them. I think she knew, all at once, that
her legend, the audience which her legend had drawn about her, presented
an obstacle which her deepest instinct as an artist demanded that she
conquer, and for those next three weeks she set about this conquest with a
dedication that was one of those things that make faith in the human
potential, the human spirit, seem far from sentimental: that give it justification. Think for a moment of the manifold disadvantages which I won't
name that beset her in this awful effort! She had only two weeks rehearsal.

When the play opened at the City Center, this small, mighty woman
had met and conquered the challenge. Of course, there were few people
there who had my peculiar advantage of knowing what she'd been
through, and only a few of her critics appeared to sense it. To me she
brought to mind the return of some great matador to the bull ring in
Madrid, for the first time after having been almost fatally gored, and facing

his most dangerous bull with his finest valor, a bullfighter such as Belmonte or Manolete, conquering himself and his spectators and his bull, all at once and together, with brilliant cape-work and no standing back from the "terrain of the bull." I'm not ashamed to say that I shed tears almost all the way through and that when the play was finished I rushed up to her and fell to my knees at her feet.

The human drama, the play of a woman's great valor and an artist's truth, her own, far superseded, and even eclipsed, to my eye, the performance of my own play. Such an experience in the life of a playwright demands some tribute from him, and this late, awkward confession is my effort to give it.

Tennessee Williams.

[Notices for the New York opening of *Streetcar* (February 15, 1956) were tempered by the inherent challenge of playing Blanche DuBois and by the unique complications which Tallulah Bankhead brought to the role. The "adoring saboteurs" who came to laugh on cue were disappointed by a performance which transcended the campy Bankhead legend. Brooks Atkinson was not alone, however, in thinking Bankhead miscast. Hers, he wrote, "is a personality that . . . is worldly and sophisticated, decisive and self-sufficient: it is fundamentally comic" (*New York Times*, February 16, 1956). TW later dismissed Bankhead's claim that he had written "every good role for her" but saluted the courage with which she had played "against the faggots" (1970; qtd. in *Conversations*, p. 154) in New York. Bankhead quipped in reply to the present tribute that "Mr. Williams' talents as a playwright are considerable, but in his manifesto he forever scuttled the ancient legend, *in vino veritas*'" (*New York Times*, March 11, 1956).

A draft version of this letter is held by the UCLA Research Library.]

324. To John Bernard Myers

[1431 Duncan Street
Key West, Florida]
3/15/56
[TLS, 2 pp. Columbia U]

Dear John

This is not a 'dear John' letter, believe me. . .

I did not talk to Jay Laughlin about Playbook preface but to Bob MacGregor. I talked to him one day before the opening at the Center and without having seen Herbert's work on the play since Miami. I talked to

both you and Herbert about my injured feelings and my feeling of betrayal in my personal relationship with Herbert during the play's preparation. That I felt he should have told me <u>not</u> to go away when Tallulah told me to <u>go</u>, that he should at least have called me to say that he was sorry I'd gone. Actually - being as wise as an old shit-house rat! - I could have done a great deal to benefit the production, both for Tallulah's sake and for Herbert's. But being much prouder than an old shit-house rat, I could not insist upon that privelege of remaining when I was dismissed by the star with the very clear acquiesence of the director.

That's all it amounts to, Baby, just that, and nothing more.

As for my regard for Herbert's work as a director, I think he came through a very severe test with colors that were not drooping. I have seen him do much better: I have seen "name directors" do worse!

My decision not to attempt a preface to the playbook was not because of any disappointment in Herbert professionally - in fact, the disappointment of a personal nature is now a thing of the past, among <u>un</u>-harbored resentments. I don't know all that went on in Herbert's mind during that period which prevented him from keeping in contact with me as he should have. That's all over! Done with! However you may think of me, I think of you as still being friends I am fond of. As for the preface, I couldn't possibly do it, now, simply because I have only two weeks in which to complete film script for "Summer and Smoke" and am, at the same time, producing the first draft of a new play at the Studio M in Coral Gables and am having to break my balls to steer it clear of disaster. Just an adventure, but the dynamics of a big play, which will some day emerge.

The saddest thing that could possibly come out of the Tallulah-Streetcar thing is that Herbert and I, through a complex of misunderstandings, should lose our love for each other, which was quite real, on my part, or otherwise I could never have felt such outrage when he seemed to dismiss me.

The whole thing had the elements of a poetic tragedy in modern terms, don't you think? I think everyone involved has grown through the experience. At least I am sure that I have. I was deeply grateful to Tallulah - having heard that she loathed my letter to the Times - for limiting her response to a couple of sentences merely saying that I was driven to drink. To which I was not unfamiliar beforehand. I have written to thank her. I want to write a play for her. She is quite possibly "the greatest demented artist of our time", as you called her. At any rate, she's an artist.

Love to you both, Tenn

Considering the personal elements which were involved, it is very likely that I am unable to properly assess Herbert's professional contribution, that it was much, much greater than I was able to judge. (I was not there.)

[John Myers (1919-1987), a contemporary art dealer, joined Herbert Machiz to present experimental plays at the Artists' Theatre in New York. Myers served as producer and artistic adviser while Machiz directed. At issue was a request that TW write a preface for *Playbook* (1956), a New Directions anthology to be dedicated to Myers and Machiz.

His Broadway debut with *Streetcar* drew little attention, but Machiz went on to direct three later plays by TW: *Garden District* (1958), *The Milk Train Doesn't Stop Here Anymore* (1962/1963), and *In the Bar of a Tokyo Hotel* (1969).

This letter is written on stationery of the Robert Clay in Miami.]

325. To Audrey Wood

<u>Key West</u> [Florida]
3/16/56
[TLS, 2 pp. HRC]

Dearest Audrey:

I am dividing my time about equally between the play and film-script which is unfortunate for the latter, but this is the first time in years that I have been able to work with unflagging interest on a play script for six and eight hours a day and though it will be a first draft that's exposed at Coral Gables, it has the dynamics of what I think may very well turn out to be the strongest play I have written. I've had to impose a terribly difficult task on the young director-producer George Keathley, since I have to keep shooting him revisions while he is in rehearsal with actors who are fairly inexperienced except for the one, Margaret Wyler, whom we brought down from New York. I've watched his work over a period of years, and, believe me, this is not another Herbert Machiz. He is crazy about the play. As fast as I send a new bit, he has it mimeographed in triplicates and shoots copies back to me. I am waiting till I feel I've done all I can, at this point, to send you a fairly definite acting version, to have copyrighted. A good deal of the writing is still rough and corny but it will have a great impact as theatre. We cast it very carefully, with the best talent that was available in the Miami area, and George is giving it every protection. On the marquee it says only: Play in Rehearsal, Watch for Opening date. There have been no

press-releases and won't be, if I can help it. I'm flying back to Miami this coming Monday to see how it's getting along.

Now about "Summer and Smoke": I have it all in my head! It's going to be amazingly easy to knock it out in full, soon as this immediate project, which surely deserves to take precedence, being a brand new creation and one that stirs me deeply, is squared away, in a few days now. Of course I feel regretful, if not guilty, about not giving film my full attention right now. But after all, you yourself admitted that it was a lousey deal and nothing much has been done to make it better. Honestly if they decided to drop it entirely, I would be happy. It would mean that I could have all of next summer to turn out the best film play I've done. And then make better terms for its sale later. The little that I have worked on the film play so far has convinced me that it can be as big as "Gone With The Wind" if I am permitted to work on it as a serious writer should work, not with a strict dead-line but with some sense of how a serious writer functions: not on a belt-conveyor, but with a reasonable adjustment to his best working-methods, involving contemplation and delicate revisions. "Rose Tattoo" was nominated for almost every reward <u>but</u> for script. I don't want that repeated. Craven submission to censorship, which films such as "Man With the Golden Arm" bucked with singular success, a deep-rooted fear of risking off-beat distinction, playing it dully safe, all conspired to turn a very hastily written but ~~highly~~ original and moving script into the closest possible approximation of a regular Hollywood property, raised above its level by one artist, Magnani, who simply couldn't be reduced to it. When people mention the picture, nobody praises the film itself, they just say: "God, that Magnani!" Well, for "Summer and Smoke" there won't be any Magnani. I ask that I be permitted to give them the only thing that they must know that they need, a really distinguished script on a play which is too peculiarly my own to be successfully handled by anyone else. I know and understand their problems, and I don't blame them for wanting to get this script as soon as they can. Reciprocally, they should know and understand <u>my</u> problems and speculate on the likelihood of my serving them best if I am not crowded now. If they <u>do</u> insist on a script on April Fool's day: I will give them one which will not be an April Fool's trick: but it will just be a pretty detailed sketch, along with those few scenes which depart most radically from the play done on Broadway, such as the doctor's killing, (the casino scene in which the old doctor smashes up the gaming

tables with his cane and is shot by Gonzales), the fever epidemic and the reformation of young Dr. John. All the rest fits so naturally into a film scenario that all I have to do is transcribe it with those cuts and plastic and mobile freedoms that the screen gives. A work that only requires about two or three weeks of undistracted attention. (At least for a 1st reading draft)

But you know that my salvation, truly, depends on my being able to go on turning out new works, and even though faith may falter in my power to do so, we should cling to it still.

Tell Bill I'll be in Miami Monday evening and can see Cloris Leachman any time thereafter. Frank says she's a fine actress. I don't know her work. If necessary, I can fly up to New York to participate in solving these replacement problems for "Cat". Hope you liked Sidney Blackmer.

Love, Tenn.

PS. I have decided to remove the suggestion of a <u>castration</u> from <u>Orpheus</u>. I don't think it is necessary and since the new play ends in a similar act of violence which is much more necessary and organic, to theme and development of story, am willing to sacrifice it in <u>Orpheus</u>. What do you think? I think it was one of things that disturbed Marlon, and that such an incident should only be used in a play when it is organically essential to the play's meaning, Etc.

[*Sweet Bird of Youth* claimed TW's "full attention" in advance of the premiere. Work on the *Summer and Smoke* film script was delayed accordingly.

The Rose Tattoo was nominated for eight Academy Awards, including Best Actress (won) and Best Picture. Nominations for art direction, cinematography, costume, editing, and music accentuate the lack of any recognition for screenwriting.

Otto Preminger "bucked" the Production Code by treating the forbidden subject of drug addiction in *The Man with the Golden Arm* (1955). The film was released without Code approval.]

326. To Edwina Dakin Williams

[1431 Duncan Street
Key West, Florida]
PM: Key West, March 18, 1956
[ALS, 3 pp. HTC]

Dear Mother -

I'm so sick of the typewriter I'm using a pen, have been working 6 or 8 hours a day and that studio is beginning to get pretty hot. It's warm as mid-summer, now, in Key West, and only one room is air-conditioned, but there's a breeze at night. Our faithful old "retainer" Leoncie is back with us, she comes and goes on my bicycle in a snow white, severely starched linen dress, yelling and waving to all the neighbors as she approaches or makes her departure. Our house has become a regular stop for the sight-seeing buses and cars in Key West. They all want to see where "Rose Tattoo" was shot. So Leoncie and Mr. Anderson (old Charlie) are having a lot of public attention. Frank does practically all the cooking, has bought an out-door charcoal grill for chicken, steak, Etc. We eat "mighty good".

I am trying out the first draft of a new play very secretly at a tiny theatre in Coral Gables just to size it up for myself. Most of my present work is on this. I'm afraid Paramount will have to wait a while longer for the "Summer & Smoke" film script. I wish they would just let it go, as I am not at all pleased with the terms of the contract, and think I could have gotten much more for it, elsewhere. But Harold Clurman has been signed to direct it, and he is a brilliant director.

I had to cancel flight to St. Thomas due to work here.

I hope to go North by way of New Orleans and St. Louis next month.

Nice letter today from Dakin. He seems to expect to return to St. Louis before next Xmas.

Much love - Tom.

[Edwina noted that her son's "Key West ménage is made up of Frank, Leoncie, a Bahama maid, two bulldogs and a parrot." She was seventy-one at this time and would soon be hospitalized in St. Louis with an emotional disorder.

This letter first appeared in Edwina Dakin Williams's memoir, *Remember Me to Tom*, 1963, p. 219.]

327. To Joseph H. Hazen and Hal B. Wallis

1431 Duncan St.
Key West [Florida]
March 28, 1956
[TLS, 1 p. Herrick]

Dear Joe: and Hal:

When an actress in Hollywood gets pregnant I believe you call it an act of God and make allowances for it and the schedule is adjusted to this unavoidable circumstance. A parallel thing has happened to me, quite unexpectedly: I was knocked up with an idea for a play. Plays are what I live for! You know that. I had to push everything else aside till 'the delivery'. I did some work on the screen play but it is not nearly finished. Only a few scenes are done. It was not a matter of choice. I do have a sense of responsibility, but I feel that my first responsibility is always to new work. Enough defense of this thing which I know you will understand.

The play is now finished. It's already in rehearsal and will open (sort of a sneak try-out) at Studio M, Coral Gables, about the middle of April. Obviously this means that I am not going to give you a finished film-script on the first. Also, obviously, you will be justified, from a contractual point of view, in cancelling the deal or in consigning the film-script to another writer. For your sake, as well as my own, if the delay is inexcusable, I would rather have you call the whole deal off than have someone else do a script which only I could transpose to the screen successfully. It is so completely my own material and my own style, and of all my plays, this is the one that already existed most clearly in my mind as a screen-play. It can be completed faster than I did "Rose Tattoo", all the material for it is in my head and in the various versions of it that I have on my work table. However the fact remains that we had agreed on a dead-line which I can't meet. I will be back in New York by the end of April and after the play opens, or sooner, I can give my undivided attention to the film. I would guess, sincerely, that I could complete a good script for you before I sail for Europe late in May. The question is, are you willing to give me that much extension? I am not worried about the money for the film-script. If you feel that you can't wait, and want to put someone else on it right away, you certainly have that privelege. I doubt that it would turn out satisfactorily, but if it doesn't, you can always engage me for revision with shared credit at whatever weekly pay Audrey thinks right for it. I will accept 'shared

credit' provided that I don't finally have to write it all myself. I was very, very happy about the choice of Harold Clurman to direct the script, and I know that Harold and I can work together to give you a picture that will win more awards than "Tattoo": that is, if you feel that you can grant this temporal allowance. Time is of the essence, I know, but the right screen-play is more so.

I know I thanked you verbally for the tape-recorder but I'm afraid I haven't yet written you what a valuable acquisition it is. I still work mostly on the typewriter, but in revisions it is very helpful to read the stuff to the recorder and hear the lines spoken back to me on it.

I wish you would forward this letter to Hal: it is written to you both, naturally. This bad start is my fault and I do want a chance to compensate for it.

Ever yours, Tenn.

[Hal Wallis (1899-1986) and Joe Hazen (1898-1994) purchased film rights of *Summer and Smoke* in the preceding July. The contract specified that TW deliver a first draft of the script by April 1, 1956. Peter Glenville rather than Harold Clurman eventually directed the film.]

328. To Joyce Croft Williams

1431 Duncan St.
Key West, Fla.
4/20/56.
[TLS, 1 p. HRC]

Dear Joyce:

Dake must have told you what a bad letter-writer I am. I wanted to write you at once how much I appreciated your letter about "Tattoo" but I was immersed in a try-out production of a new play here in Miami (Coral Gables, to be specific) and it's taken all my time and energy lately. It was well-received here and will probably go on Broadway sometime next season.

I'm so glad Dakin is returning from the Far East, I think he's had enough military life. I wish he would get started in law-practise and work into politics which is in the Williams (Tennessee) tradition. I think our father was the first Williams who never held a political office since colonial days.

If you'll forgive the impropriety of the suggestion, I hope you'll make me an uncle. I'd love a nephew or niece as much as a child of my own. Right now I'm going out to look for a new puppy. The bull-dog, Buffo, died suddenly a few weeks ago and left an awful void. A friend is driving me over to "The Beach" to look at a little Boxer.

I'm going to join Mother in New Orleans late this month, spend a week with her there. She hasn't been at all well this year and I don't want to leave the States, for my summer trip abroad, without a visit with her. We'll call you from there in case you might be able to drive over for a week-end with us.

Love, Tom

[Dakin Williams and Joyce Croft (b. 1921) married in October 1955 before Dakin was dispatched to Taiwan as a legal affairs officer. Prior assignments in California and Texas followed his recall to active duty in 1951 as a captain in the Air Force. Dakin later served as an Assistant United States Attorney in Eastern Illinois and ran unsuccessfully for several statewide offices. He and Joyce did indeed make an "uncle" of TW by adopting two daughters.

This letter is written on stationery of the Towers in Miami.]

329. To Cheryl Crawford

SH: *The* Towers
Miami, Florida
5/?/56.
[TLS, 1 p. BRTC]

Dearest Cheryl:

I'm late writing you because of a flood of visitors, Mother, Maria, and Bigelow all at once, and Kazan and yesterday Audrey again, and also continual re-writing on the play. A big new piece went in last night, replacing the church and hospital bits which are now handled as exposition at Boss Finley's house. Yesterday was the first performance of this new material and it was not as much improvement as I had hoped, due partly, perhaps, to its newness, but also I'm afraid to an over load of exposition. It leaned heavily on the ingenue who is the weakest member of the cast. Audrey kept a tight mouth about it. I could not gather at all clearly from her manner or anything she said whether or not she felt an

important advance had been made. I guess I have to work this thing out alone. And stop seeking confirmation from others in the profession. Kazan saw it before the changes and promised to come back to catch it again after the changes went in, but he is still in Sarasota with Budd Schulberg, working on their film, and has not set a definite date for his return if he makes one. I'll wait a few more days to see if he does. Meanwhile we continue to turn away patrons every night and put up folding chairs for special ones.

Keathley is coming to New York right after we close here, May 20th, because of Margrit Wyler's return to Europe. I do hope we can devise something for him. I think he is gifted, and that contact with the New York theatre would provide him with the technical skill which is his one serious deficiency. I do admire and like him, and I know that you do.

Your letter meant much more to me than any other reaction I've had. It's too early to discuss a New York production more than tentatively. Everything rests on me, now, and on my ability to solve the play's problems this summer. I shall devote myself [to] it, even if it means turning over my film-committment, Summer and Smoke, to another writer. I really would have no choice, unless this thing works out very quickly. I want to talk to you soon as I get back to New York, and show you the changes.

Much love, Tenn.

P.S. I have been drinking too much because of tensions. Do you think I ought to stay in New York and try to lick that problem, or let it ride for the summer, with whatever control I can manage on my own hook, till I have finished a satisfactory draft of this work? I don't think I could do both at the same time.

[TW invited Elia Kazan and Jo Mielziner to "look at" the Studio M production of *Sweet Bird of Youth*. Both were sufficiently impressed, it appears, to collaborate on the later Broadway version (March 10, 1959).

Boss Finley appears in "The Big Time Operators" as a shady political figure who blocks the affair of his daughter Rose and Phil Beam (Heavenly and Chance Wayne on Broadway). Their plot line was complicated in later drafts by the redefined and expanded role of the Princess—originally conceived as Artemis Pazmezoglu, a male exile from Vienna. Dropped in the evolution of *Sweet Bird* was Pere, the Huey Long figure who defies Boss Finley after being raised to the governorship by his machine.

The "church and hospital bits" refer to Rose Finley's exalted experience on

Easter morning that the "power to bear <u>life</u>" has been restored following her abortion and hysterectomy. After the church service, she demands that x-rays be taken at the hospital to confirm the restoration. The so-called "'<u>miracle</u> pictures'" show only the effect of "a well-performed operation" (*Sweet Bird of Youth*, May 1956, HRC), as the surgeon, Dr. Scudder, concludes. Reviews of *Sweet Bird* in the Miami press were positive, if brief and amateurish.

George Keathley considered the Playhouse a steppingstone to New York, but he feared that "the 'means' might strangle the possible 'end'" (to Wood, April 27, 1956, HRC). He directed at least two additional plays by TW: a Broadway revival of *The Glass Menagerie* (1965) and the Chicago production of *Out Cry* (1971).

Cheryl Crawford reminded Audrey Wood that producing *The Rose Tattoo* (1951) and especially *Camino Real* (1953) had entailed creative risk without "financial advantage" to herself. She also attributed her unlucky refusal of *Cat* to such losses but hoped "desperately to be involved" (April 24, 1956, HRC) with the production of *Sweet Bird of Youth*.

Crawford cited problems of scenic arrangement and continuity in *Sweet Bird* but assured TW that she was moved by its power. "I hope, hope, hope" (April 25, 1956, U of Houston) was her closing plea for consideration.]

330. To Christopher Isherwood and Don Bachardy

[*The* Towers, Miami]
May 12/ '56
[TLS, 1 p. Huntington]

Dearest Cris and Don:

Those sweet people the Masslinks gave me your address which I had carefully stashed away in my Key West studio. I am totally benumbed by throwing on a play, like a fit, in Coral Gables. Reached the point of exhaustion from which there is no return, or so it appears to me now, living on Milltowns, seconals and double shots of vodka with a splash of orange juice. Frankie couldn't take it and has gone to New York: a purely geographic separation. We are supposed to sail May 31st for Europe on a Greek boat I'd never heard of, the Queen Frederica, because Jane Bowles will be on it and it puts in at Gibralter where we can see Paul. However I just might, at the last moment, switch plans and go West instead. That is, East by way of West. I feel that I've had Europe and would like to see places like Japan and Ceylon and China. Also I have had Key West for reasons too multiple and complex to go into, though maybe they could be described as simple boredom. Do you think we would be happy on the West Coast? I

thought maybe we could buy a little ranch and collect animals and have a swimming pool on it. I'm going to New York in a few days. Let me hear from you, will you? The address is 323 E. 58th Street.

With my love, Tenn.

[Don Bachardy (b. 1934), a well-known portraitist, was Christopher Isherwood's new companion.

George Keathley visited Key West in the preceding March and found tensions between TW and Frank Merlo to be raw. He witnessed a blowup which led Merlo to pack and leave with a familiar parting shot, "'I'm not your goddamned yes-man!'" Keathley surmised that he had missed the "'prelude'" to this quarrel but not the aftermath in which "'they separated more and more'" (qtd. in Spoto, p. 205).

TW and Merlo sailed on the *Queen Frederica* (May 31, 1956) with Jane Bowles and Lilla Van Saher. They were scheduled to arrive at Gibraltar on June 7.]

Lilla Van Saher, Jane Bowles, and Tennessee Williams aboard the Queen Frederica, *1956.*

331. To Audrey Wood

[51 Via Del Babuino, Rome]
June 29, 1956
[TLS, 2 pp. HRC]

Dear Audrey:

I am very relieved by the news that Jimmie McGhee has the job. It would have been quite impossible for me to tackle it this summer, alone. Jimmie has taste, as well as theatre sense and a certain amount of experience behind him, and what is most important in this instance, we have, I believe, a similar kind of "sensibility". I know how little that term implies to big Hollywood studios, but nevertheless it is the important element in dealing with this film. A typical Hollywood writer would not succeed in turning it into a commercial picture, as the studio would conceive it, but oddly enough I think that Jimmie and I, working together with mutual understanding, can do just that, as well as keeping its artistic worth. Jimmie will do most of the actual new writing, and of course should have equal screen credit. I will give him all of my old material on the play to work with and will keep a constant eye on his progress without being a Simon Legree.

Of course I would love to have done this all by myself, but I can't tell you how tired, how totally exhausted, I feel this summer! I knew this feeling was coming, and it has come, and I hope that, like most things that come it will also go! All that I am fit for, at the moment, is bits and pieces of patchwork on "Orpheus" and "Bird", if "Bird" ever flies here. About next year's production, I think the situation ought to be kept "fluid".

Anna unmistakably is very anxious to do "Orpheus", but she feels that even four months is too long a run in a play! She hopes to whittle it down. Maybe to two months! I find it difficult to believe that Paramount would be willing to absorb such a big loss as a two months run of a hundred thousand dollar production would call for. What's your opinion? I think they would hedge on the production and it would be second rate if not third or fourth. I don't think, even with Anna, as complex and challenging a play as "Orpheus" could make a good impression without all the best talents that the theatre can offer involved in its production, do you?

Harold Clurman is here, and he thinks that Stella Adler would be great in the part, and that with her, Brando might be available. Again: what do you think? Stella is not necessarily too old for the part, but she has become

such a special sort of figure, such an overwhelmingly glamorous <u>great lady</u> that I wonder if she could give the part the necessary sort of earthiness and pathos. I think of her more as Mrs. Stone in a Roman Spring, or summer . . . What do you think, again?

Anna was not pleased with the pictures of Newman. She said his face was coarse, unpoetic. She wants to see pictures of Franciosa. - It occurs to me that she may be bluffing about the two-months run and that if she really liked a certain player opposite her, she might be willing to play <u>four</u>. After all, time passes quickly, and I feel that Frank and I could keep her amused in Manhattan if we stayed in constant attendance on her and there was Mr. X to take over "after hours", not necessarily her co-star. Here she has a new lover: he is 23 years old. I don't take it seriously, even if she does, she orders the boy around [like] a flunkey and I don't [think] she notices <u>all</u> of his facial expressions as he receives these orders! - How about Ben Gazzara? He was too fat when I last saw him but if he could shed a few pounds, he might look right, and I think his quality is intense and poetic. Also he is not married, now, is he?

Anna has lost a lot of weight but I am not sure that her English has improved much if any. Her ego surpasses mine but is more excusable.

We have moved into a charming apartment at #51 Via Della, Babuino but Frank smashed up the MG on the road to Rome. We are using a rented car. When the MG is repaired, I think I will drive down to Sicily so I can have the daily swims that are so important to my well-being, relative as that is under all circumstances.

Happy to hear that Marjorie opened well. What are the other replacements going to be like?

With love, Tenn.

[James Poe and Meade Roberts shared the screenwriting credit for *Summer and Smoke* when the film was released in 1961.

Resumed at this time, the journal records "an almost unbroken decline in health and spirits" as well as "unprecedented weakness" (ca. July 28, 1956) in TW's writing. He later observed that "some people think I like pain, suffering. That's bull! There is nothing more painful than pain and I long to escape it but my nature and the circumstances of my life imposed it on me, and I could find no escape." Adding to the desolation of TW's ninth summer in Rome was "another big row with F, who's now quit the house" (August 6, 1956).

Stella Adler, fifty-five and married to Harold Clurman, eventual director of *Orpheus*, would not play Lady in the stage production. She was revered by Marlon Brando as a teacher and mentor.

TW surmised that Gabriel, Anna Magnani's new lover, "blows the horn satisfactorily." He added in wry correspondence with Maria Britneva that "Anna still has the disconcerting habit of pounding her abdomen, so I guess you would call it a two-piece band!" (qtd. in St. Just, p. 135).]

332. *To William Liebling*

SH: Hotel Colón, Barcelona
July 21, 1956
[TLS, 1 p. HRC]

Dear Bill:

I loved and appreciated your letter but I think you are being unduly concerned over an unimportant matter. I mean you know how I am inclined to speak out tactlessly but honestly about things, especially when I am under great nervous tension. Isn't there a little bit of justice on both sides? There usually is in all matters of disagreement. Surely if you were not representing the actor you would have felt, as strongly as the management felt and as I did, that maybe his demanded increase in salary was a little bit bigger than ought to be demanded so late in the run of a show that was falling off at the box-office? You see, Bill, you can't avoid being in a "divided position" when you are representing the actors in the show and also representing the show. I value all that you said in your letter, especially your devoted watch over the production and the excellent choices you have suggested in the re-casting such as that marvelous actress now playing Big Mama and I know you would never sell the play down the river for the sake of larger commissions, but, Bill, at the same time, you are simply OBLIGED to try to get as large a price for an actor as he wants, and usually actors ask for more than a play, late in its run, with falling box-office, can afford to pay them without cutting down on their stay. That's all I meant. I only meant that you were in a difficult position. I am astonished and full of admiration that you are able to handle it so well, with such fairness, but I wish that you were not placed in such a position for it creates this kind of tension between us.

Honest speech is bound to hurt feelings. In Florida, for instance, you suggested that I give up "Orpheus Descending" as a play and liquidate it

as a financial asset by selling outright to the movies. This is a play that will be destroyed by the movies at least as an honest and passionate work of art. I will have no interest in it as a film unless Magnani plays it and even then I will probably only be interested and satisfied by her performance as I was in the case of "Rose Tattoo". I worked, God, what a long, long time on that script as a play. As a <u>PLAY</u>! It stung me terribly to have it proposed that I send it to the glue-factory.

You see? You didn't mean to hurt me and I didn't mean to hurt you. We are BOTH kind people and we are both sincerely fond of each other, but sometimes there is a divergent point of view, and when those times occur, frank speech is preferable to hypocritical silence. Do you agree with me about this?

Love, 10.

[At issue, TW thought, was Bill Liebling's "'divided position'" in supervising *Cat on a Hot Tin Roof* and representing Alex Nicol, who replaced Ben Gazzara as Brick. Liebling denied TW's "intimation" of conniving and self-interest, claiming that Nicol's recent salary demand, while high, had been met to protect the "welfare" of the play. *Cat's* profit to date of $425,000, he added, bore out the wisdom of hiring topflight actors. Liebling later apologized for having offended TW with the advice to film *Orpheus Descending* and dispense with a Broadway production. He had hoped to relax a burdened writer by shedding a play which always seemed "out in the cold" (to TW, July 6 and August 6, 1956, HRC).]

333. To Jim Adams

SH: Hotel Colón, Barcelona
July 21, 1956.
[TLS, 1 p. Rendell]

Dear Jim:

I have also been going through a sort of nervous crisis, which has kept me from answering your letter earlier. I knew it was coming, as I was terribly worn out when I left New York, I nearly always go to pieces for a while in the summer as a way of recovering from the strains of the other seasons. After you've been through a few of these periods you know that they come and go and you just "sweat it out". Of course you have to do certain things, mostly things of a physical nature to improve your general

condition, such as spending as much time as possible in the sun and also, preferably, by the sea. I tried Rome for a few weeks but got feeling worse all the time, I flew to Barcelona where there is a good beach only five minutes from this hotel and after a week of sun-bathing and swimming I feel much better and I think I can get thru the summer without much further disturbance. Of course New York is more difficult, but there are some good pools and you can even get to the sea now and then if you don't mind a long subway ride. I enjoyed my first few years in New York. I think you may too when you have found your bearings. Do you see or hear from Bigelow? I think he's a genuinely warm and good person, at least he has always been in his relations with me which have lasted for 16 years now. What are you doing about studying for theatre, or have you really given that up? I thought, sincerely, that your reading showed talent, but unless you yourself are convinced that you want to be an actor, and are willing to buck the long, or fairly long, period of preparation, of waiting for a "break", well, it may not be worth the struggle. Or anguish! But, finally, we always do what we want or <u>need</u> to do, there isn't much conscious choice.

We are flying back to New York about the middle of September, yes, flying this time, for the first time, that is, across the ocean. I have seen three bull-fights this week and now I am going to another which is a double-header with twelve bulls and six matadors, twice the usual number of each. It is a great theatre, and pageantry. Let me hear from you soon, Jim.

Fondly, Tom.

Write me at 51 Via Babuino, Rome, or c/o American Express there, Rome.

[Jim Adams and TW, distant cousins, were probably related through the Otte branch of the family which settled in Tennessee in the 1880s. Adams wrote first to TW, who replied in March 1956 that his relative seemed to be "struggling" with himself and searching for "a 'different' life" following his graduation from college. TW enclosed a small check: "Lets say it's from Aunt Rose" (March 5, 1956, Rendell). To Maria Britneva he recommended Adams as "a very nice, naive kid" (qtd. in St. Just, p. 134).]

334. To Audrey Wood

SH: Hotel Colón, Barcelona
[ca. July 21, 1956]
[TLS, 4 pp. HRC]

Dear Audrey:

I think it is a highly Quixotic gesture for a major Hollywood studio to offer a half million dollars for a play that hasn't yet been completed, which is still in first draft, but that is too large a sum for me to regard with frivolity so if they really want to negotiate on the basis of a brief synopsis, I will try to provide one.

I would say that "Sweet Bird of Youth" has the biggest and clearest theme of any work I have done to this point. It is almost a synthesis of the ideas in the other plays, come to a needle-point of clarity, and directness.

It is about: the betrayal of people's hearts by the subtle progress of a corruption which is both personal and social, the two influences, the native power-drive of the individual and the false values with their accent on being "top-dog", on fierce competition for a superior position, that defeat the possible true and pure and compassionately loving relations between people.

The two principal protagonists are a boy who almost "made the grade" but was always blocked by something just short of what he longed for, and a middle-aged woman who was a great star in films, who had a career like Garbo's, and quit when she felt that her youth and beauty were failing: retired to places abroad and to various easy distractions and bought pleasures and finally to the illusory, brief comfort of drugs.

She was importuned by old friends and business associates to attempt a "come-back picture". She made it. She returned to America to attend the premiere. When she saw her face on the screen, bearing the history of her long and erratic departure from the vocation which she had lived for, she fled in panic from the theatre, fled from the city without any communication with anybody she knew, and landed in a Florida hotel where she registered under the name she acquired by her fourth marriage as Princess Pazmezoglu, in a rather naive and inefficient attempt at obscurity, and there plunged deeper, continually, in the drugged state of semi-oblivion which is what an artist has left when he abandons his art, because, for some mysterious reason related to the passage of time and the accent on false values and youth's loss, its moral and physical process of degeneration, -

well, there seemed to be nothing else left for her to do. She acquired a hard and cynical kind of wisdom in this world to which she had retreated. But in the Florida hotel, she met a boy, Phil Beam, who was employed there as a beach-boy. He, too, had arrived at a breaking point in his life. He had started out with enormous promise and every apparent gift. He was exceptionally goodlooking and had exceptional charm. He seemed the boy most likely to succeed. He almost did, countless times, but something always held him just short of what he aimed at. He recognized "The Princess" as the retired star, Ariadne Del Lago, and, being used by this time, he is now thirty, to prostituting what is left of his youth, looks, and charm for the "chance to make good" he still hopes for, he makes himself valuable to her as a sort of "caretaker-lover" from whom she has no secrets, including her use of drugs, but "holds out for something", keeps the relation between them a little bit short of satisfaction to "hold her interest".

The Princess is asked to leave the Florida hotel when the odor of the smoked drugs (hashish) drifts into the corridor, and the boy drives her off, along the old Spanish trail of the conquistadors, toward a Texas town where she has oil-wells that she wants to sell at a huge profit (She is already very rich) and then on to the West Coast, where she will launch the boy on his passionately longed-for career in films, she being a major stock-holder in a sort of third rate Hollywood studio. A contract exists between them. But the boy has stopped at the town of Saint Cloud on the Gulf Coast.

He has stopped there because it is where he started. He was born in this town and he has kept coming back to it because his life-long sweetheart lives there, the daughter of a local political boss whose power and influence are much greater than local and who is now about to enter "the national arena".

The boy cannot resist the chance to be seen driving about Saint Cloud in the magnificent Mercedez-Benz of the Princess, and blowing the long silver trumpets at the street-crossings and being seen by the townspeople who had come to regard him as a failure, in such apparent splendor. But the main objective of his return is to re-claim the girl: the two of them used to be the handsomest and most glamorous young pair in Saint Cloud.

He has hit upon a shrewd and vicious device to enslave his travelling-companion, the Princess Pazmezoglu. In the first act of the play, when they wake up together in the Hotel Belvedere of Saint Cloud, she has suffered

an eclipse of memory, an attack of amnesia, perhaps mostly voluntary, and he has concealed under the bed a tape-recorder, and he leads her to make admissions, while they take the drug together, that would disgrace her. Her memory clears up. She recalls the come-back picture and the shock of anticipated fiasco that she had fled from. She turns to the boy, passionately, for the necessary distraction, love-making: then he discloses the trick. However the Princess trumps his ace. She laughs at his threat of blackmail and easily secures the upper hand again and forces him to serve her as a "kept lover": then signs some traveller's checks for him as a "token of some satisfaction". He goes. He leaves her alone in the hotel room, with her drugs, her oxygen mask for her attacks of panicky "air-shortage" and her recollection of a blasted dream of coming back as an artist.

The play, then, shifts to the sweetheart of Phil Beam and to her father, Boss Finley, and brother, Boss Finley, Junior. This scene establishes the fact that the girl, Valerie has become an object of scandal that threatens the Boss's political career. She had an illegal operation done on her after Phil's last visit to Saint Cloud. We have already heard about this in the first scene of the play, when the doctor, George Scudder, who had performed the operation on her, calls on Phil in the hotel room, before the Princess has wakened from her drugged sleep, and warns him to get out of town and without disclosing all that had happened to Valerie, implies that Phil will "be cut, too" if he doesn't leave town at once.

Boss Finley demands that his daughter appear on the platform with him, that night, at a meeting of "The Youth for Tom Finley Club" - to "scotch the rumors" about her, dressed all in white like a virgin with lilies of the valley pinned on her. The Boss is running for office on the issue of white supremacy. He is a comical but foully hypocritical character, who has had a mistress of twenty years, Miss Lucy, whom he keeps in great luxury at the Hotel Belvedere.

When Valerie defies her father and refuses to appear on the platform with him, he discloses that Phil Beam has returned to Saint Cloud and says that if she doesn't comply with his demand, that Phil Beam will suffer an operation, performed by Dr. Scudder, under force, that will correspond to the one that she has suffered, which has deprived her of her life-bearing organs.

That is the basic situation of the play.

The following scenes include a scene in the cocktail lounge of the hotel, where Miss Lucy finally makes it clear to Phil Beam what has happened to

Valerie, as a result of his last stay in Saint Cloud, a scene between Phil and Valerie's maiden Aunt in which he begs to see her but is turned away from the house and almost caught by the police car that arrives to take Valerie to the "rally". A scene between Phil and the Princess in which he tries to force her to call a famous columnist who has been her faithful friend, all the years, to launch a publicity campaign about the "two young stars of tomorrow", himself and Valerie. The Princess makes the call and is informed by the columnist that the defeat she fled from was not, after all, a defeat but that, on the contrary, the picture has scored an enormous success and that the industry is gasping for her. The "rally" of the "Youth for Tom Finley Club" at which Valerie Finley stands on one side of her father and Tom Junior on the other while the Boss sounds the tocsin for the white supremacy battle. A heckler in the crowd shouts a question about the "mysterious operation" performed on Boss Finley's daughter at the Thomas J. Finley hospital and this incites a riot, the heckler being dragged into the palm garden and pistol-whipped there.

After the Princess has learned of her unsuspected triumph in her "come-back" she turns on Phil with righteous outrage and laughs at his attempt to use her to advance himself and the wild dream of co-starring with Valerie and the Princess in a picture. She exposes him as a "pitiful monster". She admits: "I am a monster, too" but points out that she has created "out of the passion and torment of her life" something that won her an inextinguishable light of acclaim, while all that he has is "a crown of laurel, put on his head too early, and already withered". That he has gone past something he couldn't afford to go past, the meridian of his youth.

Phil rushes once more to the girl's house. She has returned there from the disastrous rally which she had attended to protect him. She is alone in the house. The police car has rushed back to the riot, after returning her home. He speaks to her, pleads with her, through a latched screen door to forget everything that's happened and to come away with him in the car of the Princess. She refuses to see, refuses to come to the door, they talk without facing each other, she in the parlor, he on the porch, by the locked screen door under the relentlessly turning light from Point Lookout. Finally, his exhortation failing, he attempts to force entrance. She runs to the phone and calls a panicky warning. Phil still refuses to leave. She warns him of her father's threat to castrate him as she was "cut" after he had last

come back to Saint Cloud. Still he stays on the porch. He waits for the telephone warning to bring the doctor, The Boss, and Tom Junior to the house. He speaks the tragic import of the play as a soliloquy. Then the three men arrive and he is removed without protest.

Valerie remains. She comes out on the porch. A car is heard driving up. The Princess in a taxicab has spotted her car and approaches the porch, calling for Phil Beam. Valerie stares at her mutely. There is a far away cry. Valerie turns away in horror. The Princess is frightened, we hear the lament in the air, a sound-effect which has occured off-and-on in the play. The Princess, panicky, tells the cab driver to remove her luggage to her own car and directs him to drive her out of the town, leave his cab there - she'll pay whatever he asks for. . . .

Valerie turns back to the audience and calls out: "Oh, Lady, wrap me in your starry blue robe, make my heart your perpetual novena!" - So the play ends.

This is a terribly bad, ragged, dislocated synopsis of it, but I don't think I can ever give a synopsis of my plays, this one especially not.

If you can get half a million for it, I will eat my Olivetti!

Love, 10

P.S. Dearest Audrey: It was awfully hard, for some reason, for me to write this synopsis. I suggest that you have it done over by Bigelow, using this as a base, and tell him I will give him five grand if it results in a half million dollar film sale! I have left out such important plot points as the scene between Scudder and Phil in the first act and Phil's effort to discover what exactly has happened to the girl. Bigelow knows the play well enough to rectify these omissions and give a more complete and organized synopsis. In the next few days I will send you some important re-writes on "Orpheus".   Much love, Tenn.

[Audrey Wood cabled TW on July 2 that she had "just ended extremely encouraging meeting with Metro re financing and preproduction deal Sweet Bird Hope to have definite proposition before end this week" (July 2, 1956, HRC). Albert S. Rogell (Roxbury Productions) and Metro-Goldwyn-Mayer were the eventual producers of Sweet Bird of Youth.

This letter, received on July 23, 1956, was probably written at the time of TW's preceding correspondence with William Liebling.]

335. *To Audrey Wood*

[51 Via Del Babuino, Rome]
8/1/56
[TLS w/ autograph marginalia, 1 p. HRC]

Dearest Audrey:

I hope you're back from a refreshing vacation. I wish that I was. This is the worst summer I have spent in Europe. For some reason which I can't account for I haven't been able to sleep, on an average, more than 2½ or 3 hours a night and have been depressed most of the time. We are in a very unfortunate apartment. Everybody comes out and screams in the court-yard at about Seven A.M. and goes on screaming till long after dark. I go to the window and shout: 'Sta Zit, sta zit!' like Serafina in her most violent moments but the Wops just ignore me. The dog barks sympathetically in protest but Frank goes on snoring, sleeping the sleep of the just, being Italian, immune to loud voices, as a disturbance.

Anna plans to sail for the States about September 26 on the sister ship of the ill-fated Andrea Doria and wants us to go with her, in fact insists on it. I wanted to fly over this time. At least I wanted to get back earlier since there is so much to be arranged for the "Orpheus Production". To answer your questions, relayed through Lefkowitz by wire this morning, I think we ought to start rehearsals soon after arrival in States. Maybe two weeks after. And plan on a month out of town and book a New York theatre for some date in December. Jean Dalrymple has offered the City Center and I think it might be a good place for a two-months run to occur. I stood at the back of the house when Streetcar played there and it didn't seem to be distractingly big, and the weekly gross at capacity would almost pay off the production. Of course I assume we would do capacity business with a fine production even if we got mixed notices on the play. The notices on Anna will inevitably be raves.

I'm having my final re-writes on the play typed up and will mail copies this week-end. They only affect third act, the difficult section with Carol.

"Sweet Bird" was so appallingly mixed up, despite my directions to typist, that I have not been able to read it this summer, let alone work on it. I shall try to tackle it again when I return to Stateside.

Not a single word from Mother since I left, and no report on whether or not Rose has been transferred to the Institute for Living, as her Saint Louis doctor suggested and to which I consented.

What's to become of Bigelow without Bouverie? Did you know Maria is married? She married Peter Saint Juste, an old beau of hers in London, and I believe the title of 'Lady' goes with it. She's on her honeymoon, on the continent, and will probably descend to Rome before long. Is she still on my pay-roll? I think we might drop her, now, and the funds can be diverted to my old maid Aunt in Knoxville if that venerable spinster survives, she has been living on fifty a month, and is at least 80, and not at all well.

You haven't written me this summer. Am I in the dog-house, for any number of imaginable reasons?

                                             Love, Tenn.

Essential get SCENE DESIGNER!

[TW inferred that the previous lodger left the noisy premises "to escape from his eighty-five-year-old termagant and shrew of a mother who has a *connecting* apartment. . . . When she falls silent for more than twenty minutes we can only suspect that {the servants} have brained her" (qtd. in St. Just, p. 135).

Carol Cutrere's entrance in Act Three of *Orpheus* is probably the "difficult section" to which TW refers. In a draft fragment she alludes to the myth of Orpheus and charges Lady with Val's earthly corruption (n.d., HRC). The passage was replaced with an impersonal reference to the modern wasteland, "sick with neon."

Alice Astor Bouverie died on July 19, 1956. Her friend and frequent companion Paul Bigelow was not a legatee of the will.

Maria Britneva acquired a title and a classic Palladian house in Wiltshire when she married Peter St. Just on July 25, 1956.

Penned in the upper margin is TW's mailing address, "Amexco, Rome."]

336. To Audrey Wood

                                    [51 Via Del Babuino] Rome.
                                                     8/25/56
                                              [TLS, 1 p. HRC]

Dear Audrey:

I've been out of touch with the world these past ten days which I spent at Ravello and Positano on the sea. I came back to find Magnani in a stew. I gather from Frank that she wants me to give her a cut of the picture-sale money. It seems that she doesn't feel she is being adequately recompensed

for her stage-appearance, that her expenses in New York will run higher than her pay. Frank says this is my fault because I let her know that you had worked out a very good contract for me with Wallis which gave me a hundred thousand more in tax-savings. Perhaps Frank understands Magnani better than I do, since they have the same sort of blood in their veins, but I cling romantically to the feeling that she just wants another demonstration of devotion to her, as right now, being in love with an Italian boy young enough to play her son on the screen, she must be a lonely woman. Of course I don't think I <u>should</u> have to pay Magnani, but I am willing to make some gesture of that sort if getting her on the stage depends on it. Sometimes I wonder if it would not have been better to use an American actress in the stage production and let Anna do just the film. Then again I think how thrilling she will be in some of the scenes, and feel, again, that all the hassle will justify itself in the end.

<u>LATER</u>.

- - - I've talked to you on phone since above paragraph and also had another meeting with Anna. I am still willing to give her a share of my profits on the screen-play, if that will make her satisfied. What I am much more concerned about is her willingness to adapt herself to our theatre system. She has to accept our casting and our director, and the script that she's given, and I think she should perform at least one matinee a week. Her chief concern about the director is whether or not he will give her "freedom to create in her own way". I have assured her that Clurman would do that, within all reasonable limits, that he is profoundly sympathetic to creativity in the people he works with. The main difficulty, here, is that in Italy the theatre is not regarded seriously. And it is the one thing that I <u>do</u> regard very seriously in my work. I think Jurow and Graziedei must make it very plain to her that she will have her creative freedom but that she must not trespass upon ours, author's, director's and producer's, which is for her protection as well as ours, as she would be working in a theatre system that she doesn't know. I am also concerned over her English. She has not been studying the language. She apparently expects to master it in the one or two months in New York before she goes into rehearsal. Especially if we are playing in a large house, like The Palace, it's essential that she deliver her lines with clarity and assurance.

I think I understand and I know that I love Anna, but I don't want to make this play, on which I have worked long and hard, just a show-piece

for Magnani. Since the final revisions I have made this summer (some of which you've received) I am confident that it can stand on its own legs and though another actress would be a compromise, I feel that with very careful casting and a fine production, it could get the sort of notices and popular support that would insure a long run. To sacrifice the long run is an important concession which I have already made to her, much more important than giving up any sum of money to her. These things have to be made clear to Anna, by Jurow, through Graziedei since she is frighteningly inclined to concentrate on her own interests, result of working so long in the Italian film-industry where it's every man for himself, with a vengeance!

I think you might have a preliminary talk with Jurow about these matters and set up a conference with him for the evening of the day I get to New York or as soon thereafter as possible. With love

Tenn.

[A play script of *Orpheus* submitted to the Production Code staff by Hal Wallis drew criticism for "excessive emphasis upon sex" and the absence of a "'voice for morality'" (Shurlock to Wallis, July 30, 1956, Herrick). Audrey Wood was negotiating film rights with Wallis, although they would eventually be purchased by Martin Jurow and Richard Shepherd.]

337. To Anna Magnani

[51 Via Del Babuino, Rome]
August 26, 1956.
[TLS, 1 p. HTC]

Dearest Anna:

I will be going to see Ercole in about an hour but I would like to point out to you, directly and beforehand, my own side of the situation. I am not sure that you realize that I am also making a large financial sacrifice. I am limiting the Broadway run of what I truly believe is my most important play, on which I have written very long and very hard, over a period of many years, to a two-months run, as if I thought that its only value rested in the fact that it would be played by Anna Magnani. My established royalties are ten percent of the weekly box-office gross plus about ten percent of the profits of the play or even fifteen. This means that I am going to lose about two hundred and fifty thousand dollars if the play has

the success that I believe it would have. Then I am also losing another hundred and fifty thousand on the picture sale, since a long-run success, such as "Cat on a Hot Tin Roof", has a picture sale of half a million dollars and a percentage, while I am taking for "Orpheus" only $350,000. plus percentage.

The idea of sharing my picture-profits with you is not very distressing or disturbing to me, as I am not so much interested in money right now. My great concern is whether or not you really and truly <u>want</u> to do the stage-play. Perhaps you would rather not. Perhaps you would rather confine yourself to the film, in which case the stage part could be taken by an American actress who would doubtless be inferior to you in the part but would play it for the usual run of a successful play and make it possible for us to have a profitable stage production, seen by a great many people, playing to large audiences for a long time, in New York and on the road.

I am mentioning this alternative possibility so that you will not feel that you are trapped or compelled to do something that you would rather avoid, because you may feel that the language barrier presents you with too great a risk on the stage. I cannot honestly attempt to minimize the fact that this particular risk does exist. At the present time, your English is certainly not adequate for a New York stage appearance and there is the question of whether or not you can make it ready in time for the start of the production this coming winter.

Needless to say, since you know how deeply I feel about this dream of ours, it would be a grave disappointment to see another actress create the part of Lady on the stage. My primary motive in writing this professional letter to you is so that you will not feel <u>obliged</u> to do something which you may regard as a great risk and sacrifice and feel reluctant to do it.

Meanwhile, my love as always, Tennessee.

[TW assumed that a two-month run of *Orpheus Descending* would be compatible with the proposed sale of film rights to Hal Wallis. He was later advised of the contractual terms which made such a brief engagement impossible, as he informed Anna Magnani (1908-1973). Ercole Graziadei, Magnani's agent, would attempt to maintain high salary terms for his client, which TW emphatically dismissed as a cause for his reluctance to cast Magnani on Broadway.]

338. To Edwina Dakin Williams

[323 East 58th Street, New York]
Sept. 24, 1956
[TLS, 1 p. Columbia U]

Dearest Mother:

It was a great shock to me to find a telegram saying you were in the hospital when I got back from visiting Rose in Hartford. However my phone conversations with Dr. Alexander and Dr. Gildea have been reassuring, as they say that you are only suffering from a nervous upset caused by worry and tension, and they feel that a short hospital rest is all that you need. I asked them if I should come to Saint Louis and they did not advise me to. However if you want me to come, I'll be glad to. I have had a very tiring summer myself and there has been a great deal of tension and strain connected with the preparations for a new play production this winter. I was planning, and had made arrangements, to fly down to the Virgin Islands and spend a couple of weeks resting completely on the beach, which is my kind of hospital. Of course I would give this up if you feel you need me in Saint Louis right now, but neither of the doctors thought that you had any serious or organic trouble and that you would be all right by the time I came back. I will arrange to come back through Saint Louis and by that time I'm sure you will be quite recovered: at least, so I gathered from the doctors' reports. Also I will be in a much better condition. I have been as nervous as a "cat on a hot tin roof" myself, lately. A writer's life is no bed of roses! And it [is] a bed of thorns when he is writing for the stage. As Amanda said in "Menagerie": "It calls for Spartan endurance".

I think that I straightened out things at Rose's hospital in Hartford. I was very unhappy over her appearance. She had on a shabby house-dress and a cheap cotton sweater that clashed with it in color and her hair looked greasy and was cut too short. I told them she must be encouraged to keep herself dressed nicely and must go to the beauty parlor twice a week, as I feel that pride in appearance is an excellent therapy, especially for women. The second time I saw her, (I went on Friday and again on Saturday) - she was dressed better and in better spirits. She does not complain about the staff at the Institute, she just says she would like to be back in Saint Louis and practise on the grand piano at home. I brought her a pretty little inexpensive wrist-watch, but they put it away for her. She <u>does</u> need one of her coats. All she seems to have now, is a short woolen jacket, and of

course it is going to be quite chilly in Connecticutt in a short time now. She asked for her "Spring coat", but did not seem to want the fur one right now. She gave me a list of other things she wanted which I passed on to her doctor who said he would check on whether or not she actually needed them or just imagined she did. When I get back here I will pay her another visit, and will see her every two or three weeks while I am in the North this winter. If I am not satisfied with things there, I think we should try something else, but we ought to give the place a fair chance first.

Do take a good rest in the hospital. You can write me c/o Audrey and it will be forwarded to me at once. Her address is 598 Madison Ave., c/o MCA.

Much love, Tom.

[TW returned to New York in early-September and reportedly sublet an apartment on East 36th Street, where he worked apart from Frank Merlo.

TW informed Maria Britneva that his mother "had been put in a psychiatric ward, suffering from paranoia. She thought her colored maid was trying to poison her and the colored chauffeur to murder her, result of her disturbance over the anti-segregation violence in the South, and had not eaten for days and was in a state of hallucination" (qtd. in St. Just, p. 139).

For several months Rose Williams was an unhappy patient at the renowned Institute of Living in Hartford, Connecticut, apparently her fifth residence in as many years. She soon returned to Stony Lodge in Ossining, New York. A visit by Frank Merlo produced an "encouraging report," which TW conveyed to Edwina: Rose "looked lovely" and "talked completely normally" (n.d., HRC).]

339. To Kermit Bloomgarden

SH: The New Flamboyant Hotel
St. Thomas, Virgin Islands
September 28, 1956
[TLS, 1 p. SHS of Wisconsin]

Dear Kermit:

I am deeply touched by your wire, believe me. If I had known earlier that you wanted to produce a play for me perhaps we would have worked it out but now it's too late. It wasn't till the day before I left New York that I finally gave up the idea of producing with Audrey. Then I began to see that the emphasis was being put on things that were not my true concern,

and we broke up the corporation. I asked Audrey and Clurman to offer the play to some good, experienced producer who could guarantee a house for us. As it was already so late, I think that the matter of booking a house took priority in their choice. Also my demand for immediate action. The Stevens-Whitehead group were immediately accessible and seemed to offer us the assurance of a house. I've had Roger Stevens as a producer before and the relationship was excellent. However I do sincerely hope that some time you and I can get together as I respect so highly your values in the theatre, your dedication to plays that have something to say of value in our time.

Again, many thanks, and all my best wishes,

Sincerely, Tennessee.

[Apparently the break-up of the Williams-Wood corporation left no public trace of hard feelings, nor is there any indication of the "things" which alarmed TW. Kermit Bloomgarden (1904-1976) advised TW that his name "will get a theatre faster than Bloomgarden, or Stevens or Whitehead. Don't let it interfere with your choice again" (October 15, 1956, SHS of Wisconsin). Robert Whitehead and Roger L. Stevens, associates of the Producers Theatre, formally agreed in early-October to stage *Orpheus Descending*.]

340. To the Editors of Time

[The New Flamboyant Hotel
St. Thomas, Virgin Islands]
September 28, 1956
[TLS, 1 p. *Time* Inc. Archives]

Dear Sirs:

Much as I am flattered by your reference to me, in the book section, as "the high priest" of something, even something called "Merde", I must put in my two cents worth of protest. I feel that scatology is notably absent from my work. However if I did make references of that nature, I would not exercise the subterfuge of a foreign word for it.

The gentleman quoted, Dean Fitch, may have gone to "Cat On A Hot Tin Roof" but he went to it with a pair of tin ears and came out of it with a tin horn to blow. "Cat" is the most highly, intensely moral work that I have produced, and that is what gives it power. It is an out-cry of fury, from start to finish, against those falsities in life that provide a good

fertilizer for corruption. What it says, in essence, through the character of Big Daddy, is this: when your time comes to die, do you want to die in a hot-bed of lies or on a cold stone of truth?

Mr. Fitch takes dangerous exception to "honesty". Is that, now, to be put down as a dirty word like the word "intellectual"? If so, then all American artists must beware. We are in for a revival of cultural Fascism. Of course there are such things as false "intellectuals" and false "honesty", but the damage to us all that may derive from attaching odium to these words by slick sophistries about them, such as purveyed by Dean Fitch, talking about "stars over the dump heap" in feeble paraphrase of Oscar Wilde, is much more important than the virtue of pointing out their occasional misappropriations.

I propose that writers concerned with honesty are more likely to be honest than those who are <u>not</u> concerned with it, and I would like to see a list of those works that Dean Fitch approves along with those he condemns, it would be more fully instructive.

Sincerely, Tennessee Williams

[Robert Elliot Fitch, dean of the Pacific School of Religion (Berkeley, California), claimed that a "'cult'" of talented contemporary writers was intent upon deifying "'dirt.'" Hemingway, O'Neill, Norman Mailer, and James Jones were "merde mystics," whose "special ethic of honesty" was designed to replace Christian values with a debased secular morality. TW, current "high priest of the cult," epitomized the "*mystique* of obscenity," especially in *Cat*, whose "final merit" was "'to describe the town dump so that we smell the garbage'" ("Mystique de la Merde," *Time*, October 1, 1956).

Printed in *Time* (October 22, 1956, pp. 11-12) was a heavily edited version of TW's original letter, the last two paragraphs cut entirely.]

341. To Cheryl Crawford

SH: The New Flamboyant Hotel
St. Thomas, Virgin Islands
[early-October 1956]
[TLS, 2 pp. BRTC]

Dear Cheryl:

You shouldn't have listened to anything I said, at least not with such a critical ear, after that nightmare trip to Hartford. I was outraged by the

world and the human situation and myself, myself mostly, and anybody that was mentioned, Terry or Jesus Christ or anybody, would have seemed monstrous to me. I have no real hard feelings against Terry. It makes me smile now to remember calling her "A BEAST OF THE APOCALYPSE!" As a matter of fact, Terry has always seemed oddly likable to me despite the fact that she's even more selfish than I am and even less able to be helpfully engaged in other's concerns. But of course I know her very little. I don't know why I should [have] harked back to an incident of sixteen years ago and something she blurted out to cover up her embarassment and the sense of shame that she couldn't admit herself without feeling obliged to do something for someone in whom she was disappointed and whose catastrophe she wasn't able or willing to cope with.

I was also very angry at you because you said such a cruel thing about my ravaged sister, that she was "just a body". It doesn't jive, that remark, with the sentimental side of your nature. She isn't any more just a body than you and I are, and if you looked at her, at her tortured face and observed her desperate effort to meet the terrible moment of facing the person she loved most as a girl, and to whom she was closest, and knew that she was a lunatic being visited by him in a bug-house, a plush-lined snake-pit, I don't see how you could call her just a body. Madness doesn't mean the cease of personality, it simply means that the personality has lost touch with what we call reality, and I think, myself, that their mental and emotional world is much more vivid than ours is.

I regret that instant of anger which simply struck out, conveniently, at your friend Terry. We're all inclined to project our own guilt into others, and strike at them in order to spare ourselves.

It's lovely here, lonely, but very therapeutic. I'm stretching out the stay as long as I can.

About Orpheus: Don't you remember telling me that it would only impress you as the work of an unproduced young playwright, a work of promise but not a play for production? I showed it to you first.

I think the best thing Bigelow's friends can do for him is to draw him back into the theatre where he seemed to be at home and to function with real creative interest. He's had too much dependance on people for someone with his basic strength of character and originality of mind. And they've all let him down. Alice's failure to put him in her will is a shocking thing, but it jives with my observations of the very rich ones. Bigelow has

had that jaw condition since 1941, he has learned to live with it, and since he's had it and lived with it that long, I don't think there's any imminent gravity about it, and that the minor operation will probably relieve or remove the pain, and he must pick up his life as it was before the rupture with Jordan and the affair with Alice. I hope that Boris will need him, as he did in "Tattoo", to assist in the setting, if that will be a temporary assistance to Paul, and I always feel that his connection with a production is enormously valuable.

I'm working again on "Sweet Bird of Youth" and the work's going better with the improvement in physical condition.

See you sometime this month. My love to Ruth, and to you.

Tenn.

[The "incident" to which TW refers followed the disastrous premiere of *Battle of Angels* in 1940. Terry Helburn, co-director of the Theatre Guild, consoled the crest-fallen playwright with an unforgettable line: "'Well, at least you're not out of pocket'" (qtd. in Leverich, p. 395).

Boris Aronson—rather than Jo Mielziner, who was strongly drawn to the project—designed the set for *Orpheus Descending*. There is no indication that Paul Bigelow served as a production assistant.]

Boris Aronson, full set design for Orpheus Descending *(1957)*

342. To Anna Magnani

[*The* Towers, Miami]
[ca. early-October 1956]
[TLS, 2 pp. HTC]

Dearest Anna:

Here is what has happened. When I arrived in New York I received the first complete and clear picture of the proposed deal with Wallis. It contained a clause of which I had no knowledge before, namely, that the $125,000. production would be paid out of my money for the film and would be about half of it. This total amount could be lost if, for some reason, the play either closed out of town, before coming into New York, or if it received bad notices and failed in New York. If we were coming into New York for a reasonable run, say a run of six months, it might be worth the gamble, but coming in for only two months it is the sort of wild speculation which I am not in a position to make. You know that I am taxed 87 or 90 percent of my earnings each year so that I have not been able to accumulate much money for a very uncertain future which also involves the care of my sister ($800. a month), a spinster Aunt, partial support of my mother, Frank, and the maintenance, off and on, of the present Lady St. Just who has been deserted by her new husband with a five pound note.

All of my advisors, here, think that the idea of doing "Orpheus" for two months on Broadway is fantastic. They think it would be a great injustice to the play, in which they all believe strongly, and feel that it would [be] a slap in the face of the American theatre which has conferred on me its highest awards. They also feel that it creates a bad impression for you. Also it would be necessary to put the play in a theatre much too large for it, a huge barn of a theatre, the Palace on Broadway or the Globe. The whole production would have the atmosphere of a stunt, it would antagonize the press and create hostility throughout the American theatre.

Now I know that you would make every effort to bring the play into New York, once you'd started upon it, but many unforeseen things might come up. For instance, I am not sure that you know what it is like to try out a new play on the road. Almost every evening changes are made in the script, new speeches are put in, old speeches are cut out. I must tell you, with all love and honesty in my heart, that I am not of the opinion that your command of the English language is adequate to this sort of thing. It would drive you crazy, it might make you collapse. Because I could not

possibly sacrifice my play by failing to make those adjustments which are always necessary in the preparation of a new play for a Broadway opening.

Of course the terms demanded for you are extremely high, but please believe me when I say to you that it is not my unwillingness to meet your salary terms that have brought me to the conclusion that either we must persuade you to play for six months on Broadway, or release you from this "act of homage" to me which would certainly be an almost unbearable strain upon your nerves, emotions, and physical power. I doubt that you will feel yourself able to play for six months. That being the case, wouldn't it be better, dear Anna, for you to just come to make the picture? The picture will not be given to any other actress you can count on that. Then after you've made the picture and become very familiar with the part and mastered the English language, then you could have a short, triumphant run in the play on Broadway, perhaps at the City Center. I think this could be worked out.

You know my plays usually run, if successful for a year and a half or two years. I receive over a thousand dollars a week, on the average, over this period. Eighty-seven or ninety percent of this goes to the government but I have deductible expenses and am able to live well and travel and meet my sentimental and moral obligations to others while a successful play is running. Therefore I would be suffering an enormous loss by putting on a play for such a short period that it would be unlikely even to recover the initial cost of the production, not to mention the loss of my share of its profits and the loss of half its film-sale value through the necessity of having to finance it by borrowing from a film studio with a pre-production deal which is unfavorable to me.

Audrey will write you about this matter more knowingly than I can, and I'm sure you will also hear from Jurow. But please do let me hear from you as soon as possible, whether or not you feel able to play on Broadway long enough to do the play justice and to spare me a financial loss which I am not able to bear.

All my love as ever, Tennessee

Still haven't mailed this letter because I wasn't sure, yet, that I had said to you precisely what was most important to say. I think you will believe me when I say that money doesn't come first but that what I am committed to, first, is the service of the theatre. I could give the theatre an exciting starring vehicle with you in the role of Lady but the play itself would be

bound to suffer through something as simple as your difficulty with the English language. I will have to make continual changes in the script of this play all through its month of try-outs before coming into New York. You know, as well as I know, that it would be impossible for you to change speeches nightly. Probably no one could play this part better than you, even with perfect command of English, but the play itself would have to be denied the fluid, quick-changing, condition which is necessary to bring it into New York successfully. You would make a desperate effort to cope with this necessity. It would exhaust you. It would almost kill you. I don't think it is the right time to ask you to go through such an ordeal which might, after all, turn out to be a failure, damaging to your prestige.

[A partial draft, typed on stationery of the Towers in Miami, refers to the "long letter" (n.d., HTC) printed above. It was probably written in Miami in early-October 1956 after TW returned from a lonely trip to St. Thomas. Precisely when Anna Magnani and Marlon Brando withdrew from the *Orpheus* production is unclear, but the roles were assumed on Broadway by Maureen Stapleton and Cliff Robertson. Magnani and Brando appeared in the film version *The Fugitive Kind* (1959).]

343. *To Harold Clurman and Robert Whitehead*

[323 East 58th Street, New York]
[ca. late-October 1956]
[TLS, 1 p. HTC]

Dear Harold & Bob:

Before we get into this thing too deep, I think we ought to face and cope with, or decide not to cope with, certain conditions of this play production. To begin with, I have lived with this play and these characters for sixteen years, with great concentration and love, and you have made a recent acquaintance with them. By the time this production has opened, if it does open, you may know them as well or better than I do, but at the present moment my familiarity with them and understanding of them is much, much greater than yours. You will find me absolutely adamant in casting the parts. I will demand to have precisely the actor that I think most suitable for each part because I respect the work, despite all its fault, I respect it as much as any play I have written and I am determined, for your sake as well as mine, to give it the protection of my so much longer and

deeper understanding of it than yours. Yesterday, I felt sort of isolated, as if I stood in one corner, and you two in another. This sort of situation predicates the possibility of a play-production full of contention and dissention and so forth, with the author an embattled minority faced by a pair who see eye to eye but not as clearly as he naturally sees it. However I can't stand the strain of such a situation. You noticed that I drank more than usual yesterday and it was because I suddenly felt that I was being backed into a corner as a minority of one. I respect the function of a producer but I feel that before he undertakes to produce a play he must accept the author's conception of the important characters and meaning of the play as a whole and not seek to adjust them to his own personal point-of-view, which is too recent to be penetrating. That doesn't mean that he shouldn't express his point-of-view or that it might not prove valuable. What it means, primarily, is that he SHOULD express it. Emphatically and clearly as possible to director and author so that the disparities among the different points-of-view can be aired and settled in the very beginning, before a destructive opposition develops. But it must be understood that <u>my</u> conception prevails. Not that it is fixed and frozen, but that it must necessarily be adhered to ----- I think it's imperative that the three of us, and Audrey, have a conference before we go any further in which there must be a totally candid comparison of our possibly variant points-of-view about the play's characters and meaning, and I think this should occur before we continue the readings on Monday. I am sending this special delivery to the office. I don't have any carbon paper on hand so I am mailing this one copy to Bob. We can begin by reading it - this letter - aloud and go on from there. Among the things I want to discuss is my very strong feeling that $75,000. is much too modest a capital investment in a play of this kind, which simply must be supported by the highest production values. No compromises! I don't approve of any unnecessary expenditures but I think that stinting on this production indicates a lack of faith in it, and we can't start on that premise with any safety. I don't myself see how it could be capitalized at less than a hundred grand with a twenty percent over-call. I notice in <u>Variety</u> that "Light A Penny Candle" is capitalized at $85,000. with the same over-call of twenty percent and I cannot accept the idea that this play can get by with less. We have a large cast and I want a truly shining production. . . . or <u>none</u>!

Sincerely, Tennessee.

[Harold Clurman (1901-1980), principal founder of the Group Theatre (1931-1941), and Robert Whitehead (1916-2002), former director of ANTA, brought exceptional taste and experience to the production of *Orpheus Descending*. TW's defensiveness was doubtless inspired by the bittersweet experience of *Cat*.

Earlier in the fall TW opposed the casting of Cliff Robertson as Val Xavier. Audrey Wood instructed her client to listen to her "with both ears" (telegram, October 3, 1956, HRC) and rethink his position. Robertson replaced Robert Loggia during the Philadelphia tryout and opened on Broadway.

TW drafted an "Imaginary Interview" in which he stated the "theme" of *Orpheus Descending*: "More tolerance and respect for the wild and lyric impulses that the human heart feels and so often is forced to repress, in order to avoid social censure and worse" (n.d., HTC). Precisely how the director and producer had violated this conception is unclear. Maureen Stapleton, who played Lady, has stated that rehearsals were tense and that use of the prologue (finally removed) caused sharp disagreement (see Spoto, p. 212).

TW briefly visited St. Louis and returned to New York in mid-October with Edwina. The closing reference to an article in *Variety*, dated October 24, 1956, suggests that he wrote to Clurman and Whitehead toward the end of the month.]

344. To Cheryl Crawford

[1431 Duncan Street
Key West, Florida]
December '56
[TLS, 2 pp. U of Houston]

Dearest Cheryl:

A note in Winchell's column a few days ago said that "Girls of Summer" had risen from 16 grand to 28 grand in one week, and I do hope this is an accurate report, for it pained me to find such a depressed note in a letter from someone who, to me at least, if not to us all, is synonymous with "semper invictus" as it applies to the spirit.

I find it dismaying as you do that you have this run of bad luck. But that's how it goes, rough as a cob sometimes, and sometimes smooth as silk. I have had a remarkably good time lately, feeling well and relaxed (for me!), and with a renewal of energy which made it possible for me to complete rough sketches of two plays in a few weeks time, but now I'm exhausted again, the spurt of energy has subsided. Tonight my stomach is swollen up like a basketball and hot as fire. I can't even take a drink. I am not at all sure it is not the presence of mother. Mom is here. She could not stay in Saint Louis. She said 'That outfit would put her back in the

bug-house', so she descended to Florida. I don't know why she affects me like this, but I feel that everything she says and everything she looks is an implied criticism. Guilt, I suppose. I love her and feel sorry for her, but she drives me somewhat crazy.

Poor Miss Brinda is in heat. We took her to the Vet this afternoon and the vet said he had never seen a worse specimen of any breed of a dog than she is and he would not recommend the perpetuation of her line by breeding her. Funny, but I think she's the most charming animal I've ever known. Maybe because both of us are equally wall-eyed, and would be equally bad bets for perpetuation of our lines.

Ivan Oblolensky (no less!) called me long-distance from New York a few days ago about Paul. They want to go ahead with the operation right away and Ivan wanted me to go fifty-fifty on the cost of it which is $1500. I asked him: "Didn't your mother leave Paul any money?" Answer: "Unfortunately not." - Me: — "What a pity. . ." - Then I assured him that I would guarantee a fifty percent of the cost but that with two members of my family very expensively not well, I did hope he could raise the money through other channels, but that if he didn't, I would certainly under-write the project. Paul says a wonderful thing about rich people, the very rich ones: "They have a phenomenal faith in the efficacy of small sums!"

Anyway, it is good to do something for such a rare person as Paul even if you can't, at the moment, afford to.

For your own sake, honey, I am glad you are not doing "Orpheus". I think it is a beautiful and true play that says something very clearly but I don't think many people are going to like what it says. I was frightened by Brooks write-up of "Menagerie". He indicated that he thought I had become harsh and cruel, since then, and this may mean that I will lose my only consistently good critic, the next time around. You must not do anything risky, the next time, and "Orpheus" is a big risk.

We will have to break camp soon, but we will be coming back in the Spring. It would be nice if you and Ruth could visit us then and of course you could use the house anytime we are away. It's a sweet little place and the air and the sky and the water are the best I have found in the States with the possible exception of Taos, but that doesn't have the water.

Will be seeing you soon.

Love, 10.

[Cheryl Crawford's run of "bad luck" included *The Honeys* (1955), *Mister Johnson* (1956), and *Girls of Summer* (1956), none of which reached sixty performances on Broadway.

Miss Brinda was the ungainly successor of Signor Buffo, who died from heat exhaustion.

The publisher-financier Ivan Obolensky is the son of Alice Astor and her first husband, Prince Serge Obolensky. Her large estate was whittled down by debt, taxes, and legal fees, leaving fewer than two million dollars for the legatees.

A City Center revival of *The Glass Menagerie* (November 21, 1956)—starring Helen Hayes, formerly a reluctant Amanda—led Brooks Atkinson to contrast this "delicate and moving" early work with TW's later plays: "There is a streak of savagery in his work now. The humor is bitter. The ugliness is shocking" (*New York Times*, November 22, 1956).

TW broke "camp" in Key West to attend the New York premiere of *Baby Doll* on December 18, 1956. The film was condemned by the Roman Catholic Legion of Decency and denounced from the pulpit by Francis Cardinal Spellman, who forbade the faithful to see it under pain of sin. *Time* magazine declared *Baby Doll* "just possibly the dirtiest American-made motion picture that has ever been legally exhibited" (December 27, 1956).

Spending Christmas with Rose—"quite pretty again"—reassured TW that her "sweetness, patience, and poise" had survived the "snake-pits." She remains, he wrote to Maria St. Just, "an unmistakable lady" (qtd. in St. Just, p. 141).]

345. To Edwina and Walter Dakin Williams

[323 East 58th Street, New York]
[February 1957]
[TLS, 2 pp. HTC]

Dear Mother and Dakin:

The Chicago production of "Orpheus" has been called off due to "an act of God". The tent collapses in a cloud-burst, slightly injuring 43 people. I'm sorry about the casualties but somewhat relieved that we don't have to open the play in a tent in Chicago, and so are the actors. Since I won't be going to Chicago, Mother perhaps you would like to visit New York. We could drive out to see Rose. I visited her last Sunday and was distressed by the fact that she has lost so much weight, eighteen pounds, and was refusing to wear her new teeth. She claims they upset her stomach. Also she had been picking at her face again and made a sore on her forehead. The head doctor, Dr. Bernard, feels it may be necessary to give

her a few mild shock treatments to bring her out of this present phase of disturbance. At the advice of my analyst, I got in touch with a specialist in Lobotomy cases who will go out and take a look at her before a decision is reached about the shock treatments. She was doing quite well at Stony Lodge till lately. I guess we have to expect these recurrent lapses, and I feel she is in the best possible hands. However she is still longing for St. Louis and after she gets through this present disturbed condition, we might discuss the question of transferring her to the place Dakin mentioned near his air-base so that he could keep an eye on her and she could have an occasional visit at home. Aside from the lost weight, she seemed physically well and did not complain of anything. We took her in town and she bought twelve bars of soap, although I had seen about twice that many in her room at the Lodge. SHE had laid them out on the window sill, each on its own little nest of tissue paper like a bunch of holy candles. She also wanted a box of candy. She consulted the "Doctor in her ears" about which box to select and he advised her to pick out the biggest. It seems that milk and candy are the only things she wants to eat right now, but they are giving her vitamin injections to keep up her strength.

I will let you know what the specialist decides in the next few days.

Anna Magnani is here in New York and Audrey is negotiating with Hal Wallis who wants to buy "Orpheus" for her. Sam Spiegel, producer of "Waterfront" is also bidding for it as a vehicle for Ingrid Bergmann, so with interest from two competitive quarters, we may realize a good movie sale after all.

Love, Tom

[Reviews of *Orpheus Descending* in Washington (February 21-March 2) and Philadelphia (March 5-16) were mixed and business only fair. The *Variety* reviewer considered *Orpheus* a potential hit but stressed both the "reminiscent" nature of the play—"a murky tale of inbred, hard-eyed people in a Mississippi village"—and its structural limitations. A more negative critic in Washington described TW as his "own prisoner" and concluded that *Orpheus* is "murky, ineffective and sometimes tasteless" (*Washington Post and Times Herald*, February 22, 1957). The Philadelphia notices were stronger on the whole, but the play was viewed unfavorably in relation to TW's earlier hits and the box office remained fairly soft.]

346. To Justin Brooks Atkinson

[323 East 58th Street, New York]
3/24/57
[TLS, 1 p. BRTC]

Dear Brooks:

I believe I've always written you a letter of thanks for an appreciative review after openings of my plays and I see no reason to discontinue the practise on this occasion even though the appreciation, on this occasion, was more qualified than usual. It seems to me that several of the critics failed to regard the play in its true light, as a dramatic poem. I remember when I went to Copenhagen when "Rose Tattoo" opened there, the leading drama critic remarked to me, 'This isn't a play, it's a poem.' I think the same remark holds true of 'Orpheus Descending' but it was apparently regarded as a melodrama, and naturally I don't know for sure if I am right or the critics are right. But I do know that critics are more objective about a playwright's work, as a rule, than he is. Anyway I would love to see you again, after all this time, and have a frank talk with you. I've always felt a silly embarassment about having social contact with theatre critics because I feared it might seem like an attempt to disarm them in their attitude toward my work. But I've reached a certain stop, or point of departure, in my professional life, now, and I think it would help to discuss things with you, if you are not disinclined. I want to present my side of the argument that seems to have come up between us. And I want, even more, to hear yours expressed with a more private frankness, and I think I can take it. After the past few weeks, I think I can take anything at all. And since I know that you do care seriously about my work, I think you might also welcome the occasion to take the kid gloves off and put the verbal boxing gloves on with me. I think it would help me. So will you call me, anytime early this week? I'm at my typewriter for about three hours every day, from about ten to one P.M. with a phone by me, so unless you feel that I am past all redemption, please do call me.

Ever affectionately yours, Tenn.

Phone number: Plaza 5-9741

[Praise for *Orpheus Descending* was tepid at best and forecast an unsuccessful run on Broadway (March 21-May 18, 1957). Occasional "streaks" of poetry failed to compensate for a dramatic structure that was "loosely woven," unsure in its "progressions," and "not soundly motivated," as Atkinson observed. He did not find "savagery" in the work, as TW feared, but oddly thought *Orpheus* one of TW's "pleasantest plays" (*New York Times*, March 22, 1957). Walter Kerr found "essential artifice" rather than unsureness at the core of the work and concluded that its "passions" were mere "excuses for handsome big scenes" (*New York Herald Tribune*, March 22, 1957). Maureen Stapleton and Cliff Robertson gave strong performances, but attendance steadily declined and the show closed after sixty-eight performances, some $65,000 in the red.]

347. To Elia "Gadg" Kazan:

SH: *The* Towers
Miami, Florida
April 3, 1957.
[TLS, 2 pp. WUCA]

Dear Gadg:

Frank read me your letter over the phone and I am truly grateful for your frankness about the play. I have had to absorb a great deal of very frank criticism of my work on this time around, and I can't see that it has done me any harm. I feel a little bit better than usual, as a matter of fact. Of course it could be the "anesthesia of shock". But I have been living for years with an always partially and sometimes completely "blocked" talent, which was only quite free in "Streetcar" and for the very special reason that I thought I was dying, and that thought eclipsed the anxiety which had always blocked my talent. Of course I was ten years younger, then, too. We know what youth is, don't we? However I came back with "Cat" and it could happen again. I still hope that it will. I know that of all the people I've known and worked with, you are probably the one that most shares that hope with me. When Budd Schulberg said to me, opening night of "Orpheus", at intermission in a bar, that you were hurt because I hadn't invited you to the opening, I said, That's impossible. He knows me too well. He knows me better than anyone in the world. - I meant that. I think you do. I think we know each other, despite the huge differences in our natures, so well that we can't hurt each other. Maybe the correspondances in our natures are bigger than the differences, after all. We are both

obsessed by the same thing. Work. Saying. Speaking out our hearts, and though we both bear in our different ways a great burden of guilt, I believe we have atoned for most of it in our devotion to honest creative work.

Am I wrong in thinking that if you had directed "Orpheus" it would have been one of our great successes? I don't think so. I think your appreciation of its basic truth would have inspired me to lift it above its theatricalism, such as the boy entering on the dead cue of the Choctaw cry, and you could have made the "prologue speech" work so that the story could have risen out of an eloquent premise. You could have staged the ending so it would play and score. You would have found the "key" in which the play is written, not just intellectually but with an artist's and poet's vision, and gotten a stunning performance from Maureen all the way through.

Here is my program: have a complete change this summer, go to Japan and Hong Kong and so forth. In the Fall, take up residence again in New Orleans, and start analysis there if I still feel I need it and there is a good analyst there. Try to kick the liquor habit or cut down on it. I'm not an alcoholic, I almost never get drunk, but I do drink too much and my working hours in the morning are affected by resulting hang-overs and depression. Cultivate a cooler, more objective attitude toward my work, and recapture some of my earlier warmth and openness in relation to people, which began to go when I began to be famous.

Love, Tenn.

INDEX OF RECIPIENTS

Letters are cited by reference number in the Index of Recipients.

GENERAL INDEX

WORKS INDEX

pany effort goes into training the graduate rather than his boss. Yet it is the boss who really has the power to create the climate which will lead to rebellion, conformity, or creative individualism. If the companies care whether their new hires use one or the other of these adaptation strategies, they had better start looking at the behavior of the first boss and training him for what the company wants and hopes for. Too many bosses concentrate on teaching too many peripheral values and thus undermine the possibilities for creative individualism and organization improvement.

Conclusion

The essence of management is to understand the forces acting in a situation and to gain control over them. It is high time that some of our managerial knowledge and skill be focused on those forces in the organizational environment which derive from the fact that organizations are social systems who do socialize their new members. If we do not learn to analyze and control the forces of organizational socialization, we are abdicating one of our primary managerial responsibilities. Let us not shrink away from a little bit of social engineering and management in this most important area of the human side of the enterprise.

References

Blau, P. M. & Scott, R. W. *Formal Organizations.* San Francisco: Chandler, 1962.

Goffman, E. *Asylums.* Garden City, N.Y.: Doubleday Anchor, 1961.

Schein, E. H., Schneier, Inge, and Barker, C. H. *Coercive Persuasion.* New York: W. W. Norton, 1961.

Schein, E. H. "Management Development as a Process of Influence," *Industrial Management Review* (M.I.T.), 1961, 2, 59–77.

Schein, E. H. "Forces Which Undermine Management Development," *California Management Review, V,* Summer, 1963.

Schein, E. H. "How to Break in the College Graduate," *Harvard Business Review,* 42, 1964.

Schein, E. H. "Training in Industry: Education or Indoctrination," *Industrial Medicine and Surgery,* 1964, 33.

Schein, E. H. *Organizational Psychology.* Englewood Cliffs, N.J.: Prentice-Hall, 1965.

Schein, E. H. "The Problem of Moral Education for the Business Manager," *Industrial Management Review* (M.I.T.), 1966, 8, 3–14.

Schein, E. H. "Attitude Change During Management Education," *Administrative Science Quarterly,* 1967, 11, 601–628.

Schein, E. H. "The Wall of Misunderstanding on the First Job," *Journal of College Placement,* February/March, 1967.

SURPRISE AND SENSE MAKING: WHAT NEWCOMERS EXPERIENCE AND HOW THEY COPE IN ENTERING UNFAMILIAR ORGANIZATIONAL SETTINGS

MERYL REIS LOUIS

There is growing concern that current organizational entry practices do not adequately ease the transition of new members into work organizations. Voluntary turnover during the first 18 months on the job is increasing among college graduates in first career jobs, and reports of mounting disillusionment among new recruits are accumulating in college placement offices and in corporate personnel departments. That these trends are found despite growing attention by companies to new member orientation highlights both the difficulty of bringing newcomers on board and the need for improved organizational entry practices.

The purpose of this article is to present a perspective to fill some gaps in current approaches to organizational entry. This perspective proposes that an appreciation of what newcomers typically experience during the transition period and how they cope with their experiences is fundamental to designing entry practices that facilitate newcomers' adaptation in the new setting.

A Model of the Newcomer Experience

In order to understand the processes by which newcomers cope with entry and socialization experiences, we must first understand that experience. In the following pages we identify some key features of the newcomer experience and outline a model for understanding the processes of newcomers' coping, or sense making. It is proposed that change, contrast, and surprise constitute major features of the entry experience. Although all refer to differences associated with entering new settings, they focus on separate types of differences.

Entry Experiences

Change. "Change" is defined here as an objective difference in a major feature between the new and old settings. It is the newness of the "changed to"

This paper was prepared specifically for this volume. An expanded version first appeared in *Administrative Science Quarterly,* June 1980, Vol. 25, 226–251.

situation that requires adjustment by the individual. The more elements that are different in the new situation as compared with the previous situation, the more the newcomer potentially has to cope with. This is true even though differences represent improvements over the previous situation. Defined more elaborately, change is publicly noted and knowable; that is, there is recordable evidence of a difference. Evidence includes new location, addresses, telephone numbers, title, salary, job description, organizational affiliation, perquisites, etc. Such evidence exists in advance of the transition. In fact, changes themselves are knowable in advance.

With the start of a new job, the individual experiences a change in role and often professional identity, from student to financial analyst, for instance. Such role changes are often accompanied by changes in status. Similarly, there are often major differences in basic working conditions. Discretion in scheduling time, opportunities for feedback, and peer interaction may be very different at work versus in school, in field sales versus marketing research or management.

Schein (1971) has stated that an individual entering an organization crosses three boundaries: functional, hierarchical, and inclusionary. Together, the boundaries represent three more dimensions of change for newcomers. The newcomer takes on a set of tasks within a functional area (e.g., marketing, finance) and must learn how they are to be accomplished. The newcomer also acquires a position in the hierarchy, implying supervisory authority over subordinates and reporting responsibility to a superior.

A more informal but no less crucial boundary is the inclusionary one, which refers to one's position in the informal information and influence networks. Influence and information access from the previous situation can seldom be transferred into the new situation. As a result, newcomers usually hold peripheral rather than central positions in the inclusionary network. Over time they may develop access and influence bases, but initially they are usually "on the outside." Based on this view of change, we can generally expect a transition from school to a first full-time, career-related job to be accompanied by more changes and, therefore, more to cope with than a transition from one work organization to another, especially when the new job is similar to the previous one.

Contrast. The second feature of the entry experience is a contrast, which is personally rather than publicly noticed and is not, for the most part, knowable in advance. Contrast, an effect described by gestalt psychologists (Koffka, 1935; Kohler, 1947), involves the emergence within a perceptual field of "figure," or noticed features, against ground, or general background. Particular features emerge when individuals experience new settings. Which features emerge as figure is, in part, determined by features of previously experienced settings. Both differences between settings and characteristics within (new) settings contribute to the selection of features experienced as figure. For example, how people dress in the new setting may or may not be noticed or experienced as a contrast by the newcomer, depending in part on whether dress differs between new and old settings. The presence of a difference in dress is a necessary but not sufficient precondition for the noticing of a contrast. Similarly, the absence of windows may or may not emerge through the contrast effect as a distinguishing feature of the new setting, depending on the individual and the full set of potential contrasts in the situation. Contrast is, therefore, person-specific rather than indigenous to the organizational transition. That is, for two people undergoing the same change (e.g., leaving Stanford and entering Merrill Lynch), different contrasts will emerge.

A special case of contrast is associated with the process of letting go of old roles, which often seems to continue well into the socialization process. The prolonged letting go in organizational entry seems to differ markedly from the situation in tribal rites of passage and total institution inductions. In typical entry situations, no newcomer transition ritual erases all trace of the old role before the new role is taken on. Instead, newcomers voluntarily undertake the role change, change only one of the many roles they simultaneously hold, and carry into the new role memories of experiences in old roles. The first time the newcomer is involved in almost any activity in the new role (e.g., a professor uses the computer or library or has a manuscript typed at the new university), the memory of the corresponding activity in one or more old roles may be brought to mind. The process is similar, though on a less emotionally charged scale, to the event-anniversary phenomenon that occurs in adjusting to the death of a loved one. As experiences from prior roles are recalled, contrasts are generated, and a variety of subprocesses may be triggered. For instance, the newcomer may evaluate aspects of the new role using old-role experiences as anchors on internal comparison scales. Or the newcomer may try to incorporate aspects of the old into the new role or resist the new role in favor of the old role.

Based on the natural limits of human capabilities for perceptual processing (Miller, 1956), we surmise that there may be some maximum number of contrasts to which individuals can attend simultaneously. In addition, it appears that for individuals in new situations, some minimum number of the contrasts emerge. The contrasts represent subjective differences between new and old settings by which newcomers characterize and otherwise define the new situation.

Surprise. The third feature of the entry experience is surprise, which represents a difference between an individual's anticipations and subsequent experiences in the new setting. Surprise also encompasses one's affective reactions to any differences, including contrasts and changes. Surprise may be positive (e.g., delight at finding that your office window overlooks a garden) and/or negative (e.g., disappointment at finding that your office window cannot be opened). The subject of anticipation and, therefore, surprise may be the job, the organization, or self. Anticipations may be conscious, tacit, or emergent; either overmet or undermet anticipations can produce surprise. Figure 1 summarizes several forms of surprise in relation to three dimensions for understanding organizational entry phenomena. It is presented to illustrate some typical sources and forms of surprise and is not intended to be inclusive.

Several forms of surprise often arise during the transition and require adaptation on the part of the newcomer. Only the first three can be traced directly to Figure 1. The first form of surprise occurs when conscious expectations about the job are not fulfilled in the newcomer's early job experiences. Unmet expectations, as typically used, refers to undermet conscious job expectations, shown as the shaded area in Figure 1.

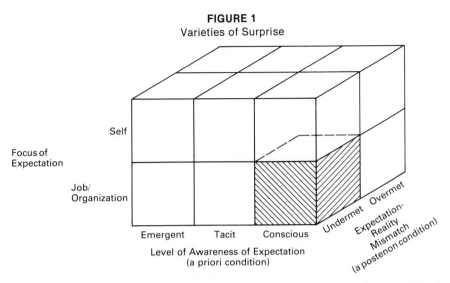

FIGURE 1
Varieties of Surprise

Focus of Expectation
- Self
- Job/Organization

Level of Awareness of Expectation
(a priori condition)
- Emergent
- Tacit
- Conscious

Undermet — Overmet
Expectation-Reality Mismatch
(a posterion condition)

A second form of surprise that may occur during transitions arises when expectations (both conscious and unconscious) about oneself are unmet. Choice of the new organization is often based on assumptions about one's own skills, values, needs, etc.

During transitions, errors in assumptions sometimes emerge, and the newcomer must cope with the recognition that he or she is different from his or her previous perceptions of self. For example, "I chose this job because it offered a great deal of freedom; now I realize I really don't want so much freedom."

A third form of surprise arises when unconscious job expectations are unmet or when features of the job are unanticipated. Job aspects not previously considered important stand out as important because their presence or absence is experienced as undesirable. As one newcomer said, "I had no idea how important windows were to me until I'd spent a week in a staff room without any." This is an example of both an inadequacy in anticipations that produces surprise and a contrast that indicates a typical overlap between the two features.

A fourth form of surprise arises from difficulties in accurately forecasting internal reactions to a particular new experience. "What will happen" (the external events) may be accurately anticipated, whereas "how it will feel" (the internal experience of external events) may not be accurately assessed by the individual. How new experiences will feel, as opposed to how the individual expected them to feel, is difficult to anticipate and often surprising. The difference is analogous to the distinction that can be drawn between "knowing about" in a cognitive sense and "being acquainted with" in an experiential sense. "I knew I'd have to put in a lot of overtime, but I had no idea how bad I'd feel after a month of 65-hour weeks, how tired I'd be all the time." In this example, the facts were available to the individual and were accepted; what was inaccurately anticipated and, therefore, surprising was how it would "actually feel," the subjective experience. The individual in this example might interpret his experience as, "I don't have as much energy as I thought," a form of unmet expectation about self.

A fifth form of surprise comes from the cultural assumptions that new-comers make. Surprise results when the newcomer relies on cultural assumptions brought from previous settings as operating guides in the new setting, and they fail. Van Maanen (1977: 20) describes the situation as follows:

> a newcomer assumes that he knows what the organization is about, assumes others in the setting have the same idea, and practically never bothers to check out these two assumptions. What occurs upon experience is that the neophyte receives a surprise of sorts . . . in which he discovers that significant others . . . do not share his assumptions. The newcomer must then reorient himself relative to others . . . through a cognitive revision of his previously taken-for-granted assumptions.

Since cultures differ between organizations, a cognitive framework for expressing and interpreting meanings in a particular culture must be developed in and for the specific culture in which it will be used.

A final point about surprise is necessary. Both pleasant and unpleasant surprises require adaptation. However, traditional formulations of unmet expectations implicitly treat only undermet expectations or unpleasant surprises. In the future, it will be important to include both overmet and undermet expectations in considering surprises that contribute to newcomers' entry experiences.

The picture of the newcomer experience developed here suggests that the strategy of enhancing the realism only of conscious preentry job expectations is not adequate. Similarly, strategies to ensure that conscious preentry job expectations are not underfulfilled (unmet) in early job experiences are also not sufficient. Ultimately, both views seek to aid newcomers by reducing the extent of their unmet expectations. Both implicitly deny the near inevitability of the myriad unanticipated and even impossible to anticipate changes, contrasts, and surprises attendant on entering substantially different organizational settings. Unmet conscious job expectations constitute merely one subset of surprise.

It is proposed that appreciation of changes, contrasts, and surprises characteristic of newcomers' entry experiences is essential in designing organizational structures that facilitate newcomer transitions. In essence, they constitute a part of the experiential landscape of individuals during transitions into unfamiliar organizational settings.

Sense Making

How Individuals Cope with Surprise. Individuals detect and interpret surprises through what can be called a *sense-making process.* Sense making can be viewed as a recurring cycle comprised of a sequence of events occurring over time. The cycle begins as individuals form unconscious and conscious anticipations and assumptions, which serve as predictions about future events. Subsequently, individuals experience events that may be discrepant from predictions. Discrepant events, or surprises, trigger a need for explanation, or postdiction, and, correspondingly, for a process through which interpretations of discrepancies are developed. Interpretation, or meaning, is attributed to surprises. Based on the attributed meanings, any necessary behavioral responses to the immediate situation are selected. Also based on attributed meanings, understandings of actors, actions, and settings are updated and predictions about future experiences in the setting are revised. The updated anticipations are analogous to alterations in cognitive scripts.

The cycle as described focuses on the more rational elements in sense making. It is meant to represent general stages in understanding one's experience, rather than the literal process by which all individuals respond to each experience. It is crucial to note that meaning is assigned to surprise as an output of the sense-making process, rather than arising concurrently with the perception or detection of differences.

In making sense, or attributing meaning to surprise, individuals rely on a number of inputs. Their past experiences with similar situations and surprises help them in coping with current situations. Individuals are also guided by their more general personal characteristics, including predispositions to attribute causality to self, others, fate, etc. [e.g., the locus of control (Rotter, 1966) and anomie (McClosky and Schaar, 1963)], as well as their orienting purposes in the situation and in general. Another input that shapes how sense is made of surprise is the individual's set of cultural assumptions or interpretive schemes, that is, internalizations of context-specific dictionaries of meaning, which "structure routine interpretations and conduct within an institutional area" (Berger and Luckmann, 1966: 138). In addition, information and interpretations from others in the situation contribute to the sense-making process. Figure 2 summarizes the model and presents it in relation to the features of entry experiences described earlier in the section.

What Newcomers Need. In order to assess the special needs of newcomers during sense making, we compare their situation in general with that of insiders. The experiences of newcomers differ in three important ways from

FIGURE 2
Sense Making in Organizational Entry

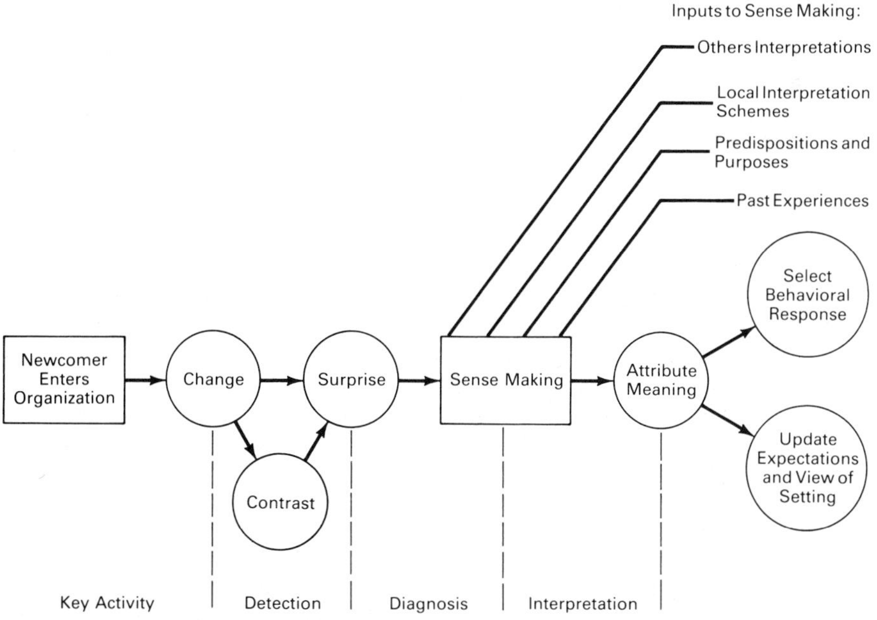

those of insiders. First, insiders normally know what to expect in and of the situation. For the most part, little is surprising or needs to be made sense of. Second, when surprises do arise (e.g., not getting an expected raise), the insider usually has sufficient history in the setting to interpret them more accurately or to make sense based on relevant knowledge of the immediate situation. An insider probably knows, for instance, whether the denied raise is due to company-wide budget cuts or is related to job performance and whether it is an indication of how the future may unfold or a temporary situation. Third, when surprises arise and sense making is necessary, the insider usually has other insiders with whom to compare perceptions and interpretations.

The comparison of newcomers' and insiders' experiences suggests that two types of input to sense making shown in Figure 2 may be problematic for newcomers: local interpretation schemes and others' interpretations. Concerning local interpretation schemes, newcomers probably do not have adequate history in the setting to appreciate as fully as insiders might why and how surprises have arisen. With time and experience in the new setting, they may come to understand how to interpret the actions of superiors and others and what meanings to attach to events and outcomes in the work setting. According to Berger and Luckmann (1966), during the early stages in a new setting, newcomers internalize context-specific dictionaries of meaning used by members of the setting. At the outset, however, newcomers typically are unfamiliar with these interpretation schemes of the new setting. And, as we saw earlier, they are usually unaware of *both* their need to understand context-specific meaning dictionaries, or interpretation schemes, and the fact that they are unfamiliar with them (Van Maanen, 1977).

As a result, newcomers often attach meanings to action, events, and surprises in the new setting using interpretation schemes developed through their experiences in other settings. Based on these, inappropriate and dysfunctional interpretations may be produced. For example, what it means to "take initiative" or "put in a hard day's work" in a school situation may be quite different from its meaning in a work setting. In essence, this constitutes a variation on the kind of surprise that arises when tacit job-related expectations are unmet. Newcomers may also attribute permanence or stability to temporary situations, or vice versa (Weiner, 1974). Or newcomers may see themselves as the source or cause of events when external factors are responsible for outcomes (Weiner, 1974). Similarly, one's understanding of why a superior responds in a particularly harsh manner may be inadequate. Overpersonalized attributions may result in the absence of knowledge about how that superior typically behaves toward other subordinates or without relevant background information, for instance, about the superior's recent divorce, lack of promotion, or reduction in scope of authority and responsibility.

The dysfunctional effects of such interpretational errors can be seen by tracing how the responses chosen are influenced by the meanings attributed in situations. In a series of studies by Weiner (1974), subjects attributing events to stable causes changed behavior more often than did subjects attributing events to unstable or temporary causes (e.g., the boss is always like this, or the boss is going through a rough, but temporary, period). In laboratory experiments, shifts in subjects' affect were more likely to result from personal, or internal, attributions than from external attributions (e.g., the boss doesn't like me, or the boss treats everyone harshly). Although further work is needed to assess the extent to which Weiner's findings hold in organizational settings, it seems obvious that individuals select responses to events at least in part on the basis of the meaning they attach to them. Decisions to stay in or leave organizations and feelings of commitment or alienation would appear to follow from sense made by newcomers of early job experiences.

The second type of input that makes sense making problematic for newcomers is information and interpretations from others in the situation. In comparison to the situation of insiders, newcomers probably have not developed relationships with others in the setting with whom they could test their perceptions and interpretations. Since reality testing is seen as an important input to sense making, it seems particularly important for newcomers to have insiders who might serve as sounding boards and guide them to important background information for assigning meaning to events and surprises. Insiders are seen as a potentially rich source of assistance to newcomers in diagnosing and interpreting the myriad surprises that may arise during their transitions into new settings. Insiders are already "on board;" presumably, they are equipped with richer historical and current interpretive perspectives than the newcomer alone possesses. Information may also come through insider/newcomer relationships, averting and/or precipitating surprises. These relationships might also facilitate the newcomer's acquisition of the context-specific meaning dictionary or interpretation scheme.

The framework presented here suggests that sense made of surprises by newcomers may be inadequate in the absence of relevant information about organizational, interpersonal, and personal histories. Inputs to sense making from sources in the organization balance the inputs provided by the newcomer (i.e., past experiences, personal predispositons, and interpretive schemes from old settings), which are likely to be inadequate in the new setting. Until newcomers develop accurate internal maps of the new setting, until they appreciate local meanings, it is important that they have information available for amending internal cognitive maps and for attaching meaning to such surprises as may arise during early job experiences.

Implications for Research and Practice

Summary

Previous work on organizational entry has lacked a theoretical framework for understanding what newcomers experience and how they cope with their experiences in entering unfamiliar organizational settings. We proposed a new perspective to fill that gap. The new perspective first provided a picture of what the newcomer is likely to experience. Conceptual categories were created to distinguish among features of the entry experience. *Change* was said to represent the external, objective differences in moving from one organization to another (e.g., a change in physical location, title, salary). *Contrast* was used to refer to those differences that emerge in the newcomer's perceptual field as personally significant, as subjectively experienced characteristics of the new situation. *Surprise* was used to refer to differences between newcomers' anticipations of and actual experiences in the organization. Anticipations may be formed before or after entering the organization; anticipations and other action-guiding assumptions (e.g., cultural assumptions) may be conscious, tacit, and/or emergent, and anticipations can be focused on oneself, as well as the job, the organization, and its culture.

How newcomers cope with their entry experiences was the subject of the second component of the new perspective. We developed a model of newcomers' processes of coping based on the earlier picture of the newcomers' experience. The sense-making model we proposed focused on the cognitive processes that individuals employ in organizational settings to cope with surprise and novelty. We identified newcomers' special sense-making needs. In particular, they need help in interpreting events in the new setting, including surprises, and help in appreciating situation-specific interpretation schemes or cultural assumptions. We saw that insiders are a potentially rich source of such help.

Research Implications

The perspective provides a theoretical framework for understanding which aspects or dimensions of socialization into new work settings are critical and why. It suggests that socialization practices that facilitate sense making and, in the process, encourage appreciation of the local culture and acquisition of a setting-specific interpretation scheme ultimately facilitate adaptation to the new setting and progress through the stages of socialization. Practices that facilitate sense making provide the newcomer with relevant and reliable information. Specific information is made available in response to newcomers' needs, rather than in advance, according to what is considered to be organizationally efficient. The information comes from someone who knows and is willing and able to share with the newcomer a particular part of "how things operate around here." Other newcomers do not have this information, and written orientation material usually does not give it. The perspective leads us to expect that *in-response* socialization practices facilitate sense making and adaptation far more effectively than *in-advance* practices. And, similarly, practices in which insiders, rather than other newcomers, are the newcomers' primary associates and informal socializing agents should facilitate adaptation.

Although several socialization dimensions developed in previous studies touch on aspects of socialization suggested by the perspective, none does so exclusively. For instance, although formal (versus informal) socialization usually implies in-advance socialization, it conveys a set of other characteristics as well. Formal orientations typically process several newcomers at one time; they tend to present a great deal of general information representing official policy, rather than actual practice. In individual (versus collective) socialization, the newcomer probably has greater access to insiders as associates (rather than other newcomers), who are willing to speak "off the record" and share local norms with the newcomer. But individual socialization is also more likely to be informal than formal, confounding the picture further. Finally, in serial (versus disjunctive) socialization, insiders who previously held the role that the newcomer is assuming are present in the organization. Although suggesting that insiders may be among the newcomer's associates, serial socialization does not rule out the possibility that other newcomers are the primary associate group for the newcomer. Therefore, we suggest that future research specifically examine the separate effects of dimensions of socialization derived from the theoretical framework described here.

The surprise and sense-making perspective bears on recruit turnover research in a number of ways. The turnover approach to organizational entry has focused on newcomers' conscious preentry expectations about the job. Yet the perspective proposed here suggests that surprise may arise from tacit and even emergent anticipations and assumptions, as well as from conscious expectations. It also suggests that expectations are not formed once and for all before entering the new setting, but evolve and are periodically revised as a result of sense made of surprises. Furthermore, it indicates that assumptions about oneself (e.g., what I can and want to do) may lead to surprises that have at least as much impact as expectations about the job. On the basis of the variety of sources and types of surprise typically experienced in entering organizations, we suggest that the narrow view of unmet expectations adopted in earlier research should be broadened in future research. In addition, the separate effects of initial and disconfirmed expectations and overmet as well as undermet expectations should be assessed. Future research is also needed to explore the underlying psychological processes by which expectations, and surprise in general, affect individuals. Toward that end, the sense-making model presented here provides a theoretical outline of some basic processes by which surprise precipitates sense making and through which individuals select responses to surprise.

Other implications for future research include the need to understand the processes by which cultural knowledge is acquired. Although we saw that surprise may result when cultural assumptions from old settings are not supported in new settings, we have not yet traced how newcomers learn the ropes and come to appreciate the local culture of the new setting. One way to pursue the question is to examine how culture is manifested in organizational settings and from there to trace how cultural manifestations are transmitted.

Another area in which future research is needed is the transition from the old role itself, the leave-taking aspect of changing roles. How do newcomers in modern organizations let go of old roles as they take on new ones? Two alternative explanations of the letting-go process have been suggested here. In a *tabula rasa* process, initiates are stripped of old roles before taking on new roles. In an *event anniversary* process, letting go occurs gradually as experiences in the new role trigger recall of complementary experiences in old roles. The relative merit of each as an explanation of letting go during organizational entry is a question for future research.

Finally, further work is needed on surprise and sense making. Specific subprocesses within the sense-making cycle have not been adequately articulated. Perceptual and cognitive processes overlap from the detection to the interpretation of surprise. How do the processes interface? In terms of surprise, what personal and situational factors influence the newcomer's "novelty" threshold? Why do some people seem to thrive on novelty, whereas others seem burdened and surprised by almost any novel experience?

Practical Implications

Previous research has favored strategies for managing newcomers' entry into work organizations that provide individuals with more accurate (realistic) initial expectations, through a Realistic Job Preview. In contrast, strategies developed from the perspective developed here take as given the near inevitability that newcomers will experience some unmet expectations and, more generally, surprise in entering unfamiliar organizational settings. Strategies based on the present framework would aim to intervene in the newcomer's cycle as sense is made of surprise, rather than merely attempting to prevent one form of surprise, the unmet conscious preentry job expectation.

What this means at the practical level is that, at a minimum, certain secrecy norms, the sink-or-swim, learn-on-your-own philosophy, and sanctions against sharing information among office members are dysfunctional for newcomers and for their employing organizations as well. Each of these restricts possible sources of relevant information available to newcomers. On the other hand, fostering links between newcomers and their insider peers or non-supervisor superiors would be beneficial. Superiors can support informal associations between newcomer and co-worker insiders or more formal programs, such as buddy systems, in which insiders receive skills training and serve as guides for newcomers. Informal sponsor and mentor links between junior and senior members offer other models of relationships through which information, perceptions, and interpretations of events in the organization can be exchanged.

Another potential aid for newcomers is the appraisal process. Timely formal and informal feedback from superiors to newcomers about their performance may reduce the stress-producing uncertainty of "not knowing how you're doing," and replace possibly inaccurate self-appraisals with data from superiors, which guide the newcomer's subsequent assessments of equity in the situation. An early appraisal could provide newcomers with an understanding of the process and criteria of performance evaluation. With such firsthand knowledge, the newcomer can be expected to make more reality-based self-assessments; in addition, he or she is better equipped to interpret other events related to evaluation, a crucial area in the newcomer's early organizational life. An early appraisal could be treated as a collaborative sense-making session, in which the superior helps the newcomer try on a portion of an important insider's interpretive scheme.

Finally, there are implications for newcomers themselves and for those who help prepare them to select and enter organizations. It would be beneficial for newcomers to enter organizations with an understanding of the nature of entry experiences: why it is likely that they may experience surprises during the socialization period; why they, as newcomers, are relatively ill equipped to make accurate sense of surprises arising during early job experiences; and how they might proactively seek information from insiders at work to supplement their own inadequate internal interpretive schemes. Toward that end, college curricula and placement activities could, as a matter or course, provide students with a preview of typical entry experiences and ways to manage them.

The implications for research and practice are based on the assumption that newcomers are ill equipped to make sense of the myriad surprises that potentially accompany entry into an unfamiliar organization. It has been proposed that entry practices that enhance newcomers' understandings of their experiences in and of new organizational settings will facilitate newcomers' adaptation. Socialization practices should be developed that help provide newcomers with insiders' situation-specific interpretive schemes. The insiders' view can supplement and balance natural inadequacies in newcomers' sense-making tendencies and can hasten the development of more adequate long-term self-sufficient functioning. Furthermore, it is likely that supplementing newcomers' sense making will facilitate accuracy in newcomers' interpretations of their immediate experiences, on the basis of which individuals choose affective behavioral responses to early experiences on the job and in the organization.

References

Berger, Peter and Thomas Luckmann. *The Social Construction of Reality: A Treatise in the Sociology of Knowledge.* New York: Doubleday, 1966.

Koffka, Kurt. *Principles of Gestalt Psychology.* New York: Harcourt Brace Jovanovich, 1935.

Kohler, Wolfgang. *Gestalt Psychology.* New York: Mentor, 1947.

McClosky, Herbert and John H. Schaar. "Psychological Dimensions of Anomy." *American Sociological Review,* 30: 14–40, 1963.

Miller, George A. "The Magical Number Seven, Plus or Minus Two: Some Limits on Our Capacity for Processing Information." *Psychological Review,* 63: 81–96, 1956.

Rotter, Julian B. "Generalized Expectations for Internal versus External Control of Reinforcement." *Psychological Monographs: General and Applied,* 80, No. 1, 1966.

Schein, Edgar H. "The Individual, the Organization, and the Career: A Conceptual Scheme." *Journal of Applied Behavioral Science,* 7: 401–26, 1971.

Van Maanen, John. "Experiencing Organization: Notes on the Meaning of Careers and Socialization." In John Van Maanen (ed.), *Organizational Careers: Some New Perspectives,* 15–45. New York: Wiley, 1977.

Weiner, Bernard. *Achievement Motivation and Attribution Theory.* Morristown, N.J.: Silver Burdett, 1974.

2 learning and problem solving

R&D ORGANIZATIONS AS LEARNING SYSTEMS

BARBARA CARLSSON
PETER KEANE
J. BRUCE MARTIN

In comparison with the relatively systematic, logical, and planned processes of some organizations, R&D processes often appear to be disorderly and unpredictable— difficult, if not impossible, to manage. However, the hypothesis that the primary output of R&D is *knowledge* (incorporated in formulas and specifications) suggests that its major process is *learning*. We have confirmed that, when R&D activities are viewed as part of a learning process, much of what appears disorderly is seen to have an underlying order. Furthermore, we have determined that this perspective is useful for describing, understanding, and improving the R&D process.

Linear models of technical innovation may be useful in describing key steps in the R&D process and in documenting projects after the fact but are not particularly helpful in understanding the process in real time. Linear models can describe what happened but not *how* it happened, and tend to reinforce the belief in a kind of orderliness which does not exist (see Figure 1).[1]

The model we *have* found to be descriptive of the way learning occurs in R&D organizations is based on D. A. Kolb's work on individual experiential learning.[2] Kolb postulates a four-step repetitive cycle, which provides the

Reprinted by permission of the authors and publisher from *Sloan Management Review*, Spring, 1976.

The authors are indebted to David A. Kolb, whose work has provided the foundation for this paper, and to Richard Beckhard, who introduced us to Kolb and encouraged our work.

[1]This paper is no exception. The relatively orderly description of our research bears little resemblance to the actual cycling and recycling, false starts, definition and redefinition of hypotheses and objectives which occurred. However, Harvard Business School Professor Charles J. Christenson has described God as "using an inelegant method to design the world but cleaning up His approach in the published version." At least we are in good company.

[2]See Kolb [6].

FIGURE 1

Linear Models of Technical Innovation

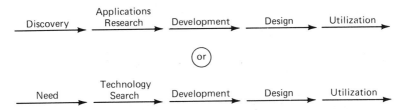

framework for the model shown in Figure 2. This cycle is summarized as follows:

> Immediate concrete experience is the basis for observation and reflection. These observations are assimilated into a "theory" from which new implications for action can be deduced. These implications, or hypotheses, then serve as guides in acting to create new experiences.[3]

We have generalized Kolb's work, which focuses on the individual learning process, to the organizational learning process.

Kolb's learning process requires orientations that are polar opposites: active and reflective; concrete and abstract. The shifting orientation results in four kinds of activity, each of which is required at some stage of the learning process.

1. *Divergence (concrete* and *reflective).* This kind of activity is required to seek background information and sense opportunities, investigate new patterns, recognize discrepancies and problems, and generate alternatives. Literature browsing and Brainstorming are techniques which may be used to aid this kind of activity.

2. *Assimilation (abstract* and *reflective).* This kind of activity is required to develop theory, compare alternatives, establish criteria, formulate plans and hypotheses, and define problems. Grounded Theory techniques are designed to aid this kind of activity.[4]

3. *Convergence (abstract* and *active).* This kind of activity is required to select among alternatives, focus efforts, evaluate plans and programs, test hypotheses, and make decisions. Venture Analysis techniques are designed to aid this kind of activity.

4. *Execution[5] (concrete* and *active).* This kind of activity is required to advocate positions or ideas, set objectives, commit to schedules, commit resources, and implement decisions. PERT and Critical Path Scheduling are techniques frequently used to aid this kind of activity.

Organizations differ in their capabilities for performing the tasks associated with each of the stages. There are predictable strengths associated with an appropriate skill level in each stage and there are predictable weaknesses associated with either an excess or a deficiency in any stage. Figure 3 outlines some of these strengths and weaknesses.

[3]See Kolb [6], p. 2.
[4]See Glaser and Strauss [3].
[5]We have chosen the term "Execution" rather than "Accommodation," the more precise term used by Kolb, as the label for this stage of the Learning Model. We found that the term "Accommodation" is frequently misunderstood because of its connotations of passivity and compromise.

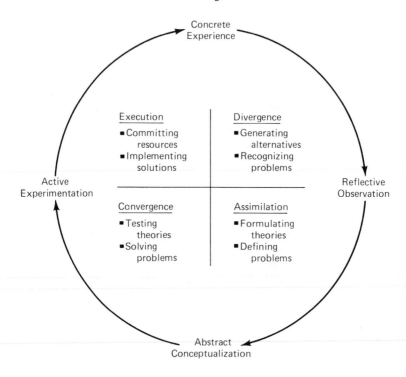

FIGURE 2
The Learning Model

Experimental Validation

In a series of experiments, we have demonstrated that the Learning Method provides a useful description of the R&D process in a way which permits strengths and weaknesses to be assessed, identifies bottlenecks, and provides cues to remedial action. We asked R&D managers what factors inhibited innovation in their individual areas. We found that most of their responses fit into the patterns of strengths or weaknesses predicted in Figure 3. The following are a few examples.

Comment	Corresponding Strength or Weakness
"We're not idea poor, but we do need people to push ideas."	Strength in divergence Lack of execution
"Timetables are sometimes too tight to let people explore."	Excessive execution Too little divergence
"We execute well; we need to develop needs."	Sufficient execution Too little divergence
"We allow ourselves to be diffuse; we need more focus."	Lack of convergence
"We lack conceptualization—fitting all the elements into a full concept."	Lack of assimilation
"We lack good ideas."	Lack of divergence

FIGURE 3
Strengths and Weaknesses

Concrete
Experience

Execution		Divergence	
Strength:	Accomplishment Goal-oriented action	Strength:	Generation of alternatives Creativity
Excess:	Trivial improvements Tremendous accomp- lishment of the wrong thing	Excess:	Paralyzed by alternatives
Deficiency:	Work not completed on time Not directed to goals	Deficiency:	Inability to recognize problems/opportunities Idea poor

Active   Reflective

Experimentation   Observation

Convergence		Assimilation	
Strength:	Design Decision making	Strength:	Planning Formulating theory
Excess:	Premature closure Solving the wrong problem	Excess:	Castles in the air No practical application
Deficiency:	No focus to work Theories not tested Poor experimental design	Deficiency:	No theoretical basis for work Unable to learn from mistakes

Abstract
Conceptualization

These data not only suggest that major elements of the R&D process can be expressed in terms of the Learning Model, but also confirm that organizations can develop "flat spots" which may be described in terms of the Learning Model.

In another experiment, we devised a scheme for scoring biweekly progress reports which are written by professional members of our organizations.[6] For each report, this scoring scheme provided a measure of the effort in each stage of the learning process. We applied this scoring scheme to several series of reports written by individual staff members. Our findings, which are summarized below, supported our hypothesis that the Learning Model is descriptive of the dynamics of R&D projects.

1. Most of the subjects appeared to be following a clockwise sequence through the stages of the Learning Model; that is, a report scoring relatively high in Assimilation was likely to be followed by a report relatively high in Convergence, which was likely to be followed by a report high in Execution, etc.

2. A researcher who had no familiarity with the content of the reports or

[6]The scoring system was quite complex and specific to the particular reports which were being evaluated. The system consisted essentially of assigning each sentence to a stage of the Learning Model, and totaling the number of sentences in each stage. We are grateful to Sherry Ewald and Paula Miller for their efforts in the sometimes arduous task of scoring the documents.

with the authors could from the scores alone predict with accuracy the strengths and weaknesses of the projects. For example, from a series of scores indicating consistently high levels of Assimilation and Execution, and consistently low levels of Divergence and Convergence, one of the researchers correctly predicted that the project would be suffering from a lack of creativity (Divergence) and lack of focusing and testing of hypotheses (Convergence) prior to execution of new activities, and that these deficiencies could result in executions that failed without adding to understanding.

3. The effect of management interventions could be observed in the scores. For example, late in the project cited above there was a sharp but temporary shift into the Convergence stage. Although we observed the shift, we did not know its cause. Subsequent discussions with the manager revealed that the shift was the result of his probing questions about their research design, and confirmed his fear that the effect of his action had been only temporary.

In a third experiment we collected historical data on the progress of a project and extended the data into real time by periodic interviews with members of the project team. We found that key steps in the progress of the project could be interpreted as representing a clockwise sequence through the Learning Model as shown in Figure 4. A list of the activities involved with the project (corresponding to the numbers on the diagram) and a list of the information inputs which occurred during the project (corresponding to the letters on the diagram) follow Figure 4. Critical examination of this analysis by other project managers and their higher-level R&D managers confirmed that the model represented the realities of the project. The higher-level managers were particularly reassured by the sense of order given to a set of events that had not seemed nearly so orderly at the time.

We have subsequently analyzed other projects in the same manner and found less orderly progression around the model. We found instances of stages being skipped, of project teams "stuck" in a stage, and even instances of reverse (i.e., counterclockwise) movement through the stages. The managers involved generally agreed that the pictures were accurate and that the deviations indicated problems deserving of management attention.

Use of the Model

We can testify to the usefulness of the Learning Model from our own experience. Our individual strengths are in different stages of the model and our efforts to work together often involved more conflict than the task seemed to warrant. As we learned more about the Learning Model, we each developed an appreciation of the contributions of the other members of our group. Our working relationships are greatly improved; now if we find ourselves pulling in different directions, we refer to the Model for resolution.

In the course of our experiments, we have exposed the Learning Model to a large number of R&D managers and project team members, and have received responses suggesting that the Model also has been useful to them. Sharing the Learning Model with others in our organization has been most productive when we have communicated the *concept,* and allowed others to discover applications for themselves. Kolb has developed a Learning Style Inventory which we have found very useful in these discussions.[7] The Learning Style Inventory is a brief pencil-and-paper test which gives the subject an indication of his preference for activity in each of the stages of the Learning Model. Members of work teams who shared their individual results have invariably found important differences among themselves, and usually came quickly to understand how these differences in "Learning Style" have influenced their process of working together. Individuals who prefer Execution are likely to be impatient with Assimilation, and Divergers are likely to find Convergers stodgy and stifling of creativity. An understanding of individual differences has generally led to an interest in understanding the Learning Model, which has in turn led to the kinds of learning and applications reported below.

One project team had been having difficulty in understanding why the character of their interactions with each other shifted sharply from meeting to meeting. In some meetings they found themselves open to new ideas, free to raise questions, and valuing the inputs of other members. In other meetings they found themselves rejecting new ideas, making few significant comments on each other's work, and generally rejecting those ideas which were offered. After being exposed to the Learning Model, they realized that the first condition prevailed when the project was in a Divergence stage, and the latter occurred when the project required Convergence or Execution.

FIGURE 4
Project History in Terms of the Learning Model

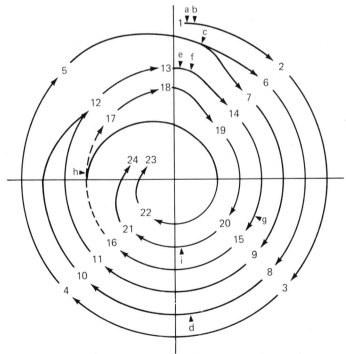

[7]Kolb [5] describes the development of the Learning Style Inventory, which has been published in Kolb, Rubin, and McIntyre [7].

List of the Activities for Figure 4

1. Planning activity initiated by a management question: "What businesses should this division be in?"
2. Generation of nine alternatives.
3. Establishment of criteria for selection made jointly with marketing.
4. Evaluation of the nine alternatives against the criteria resulting in the selection of three projects to pursue.
5. Assignment of staff to activate three projects, one of which is the subject of this study.
6. Identifying the options for positioning the product in the market.
7. Identifying the potential process routes to making the product.
8. Establishing the criteria for deciding the competitive targets.
9. Examining standing criteria in the division for choice of processes, and weighting flexibility higher than normal for this project.
10. Deciding on the specific objective for this product.
11. Choosing the process route to be developed.
12. Making the product and placing a consumer test.
13. Obtaining consumer test results that confirmed that the product targets had been met.
14. Generation of alternatives for obtaining a more favorable economic position in the marketplace.
15. Analyzing the alternatives from the standpoint of the user.
16. Selection of the specific target and the attribute to be optimized.
17. Making the product and placing a consumer test. (The path from 16 to 17 is shown as a broken line because the work was incomplete, i.e., the consumer test was placed without having the optimum product.)
18. Obtaining and analyzing consumer test results which were worse than predicted.
19. Generation of alternatives for the project in view of the outcome of the consumer test.
20. Reexamination of criteria.
21. Optimizing product/process variables.
22. Specifying the process details for the test market production and trimming costs to fit within the appropriation. (The path from "h" to 22 is shown as a solid line, because the intervening steps were obviously taken even though they were not specified as activities, e.g., each item of cost was questioned and trimmed if not justified.)
23. Meeting specific requirements for the test market plant.
24. Making product and placing next consumer test.

List of the Information Inputs for Figure 4

a. Management input—desire to capitalize on a new technology and desire to be of service to society.
b. Consumer input—a generally recognized, unmet consumer need.
c. Technical input—temporary transfer in of a scientist familiar with the new technology.
d. Marketing input—desired product target.
e. Economic input—cost estimate for test market plant much higher than expected.

f. Management input—in view of the projected costs, the business opportunity is seen as unattractive.

g. Marketing input—proposal for new product targets.

h. Management input—appropriation for test market (much lower than original estimate).

i. Management input—top management confirmation of overall market strategy and requirements.

Discussions with the manager of the same project team provided the basis for a new concept of the role of the project manager. Traditionally the manager's role has been viewed primarily as one of planning, organizing, directing and controlling. When organizations are viewed as learning systems, the manager's role can be viewed as one of providing leadership in the learning process. The following observations developed out of our conversations with the manager of this team.

1. When the development of a product is going smoothly, the manager's role will involve thinking and planning about the next stage, and will be 90° to 135° ahead of that of the team members. For example, if the team is engaged in Execution, the manager will be thinking about the possible alternatives for the project when the results of Execution are known; if the team is engaged in idea generation, the manager's role will involve thinking about the criteria for solution. By concentrating on what is to come, the manager exerts a useful pull on the project.

2. In time of crisis, when the team is finding it difficult to move through the learning cycle, the role requires the manager to move into the same stage as the project team. For example, the manager may work with the team to develop theories to explain an unexpected result or to help in the pilot plant when there is a critical deadline.

3. The manager must take care that he does not move too far ahead of the project team, thus not only losing sensitivity to their current problems but also confusing them with regard to the path they should take. The manager should avoid pulling the team *across* the Model instead of *around* it.

This same manager used his knowledge of the work team process and his understanding of his role of leadership in the learning process to devise a special plan for supporting the work of one of the team members. The team member had come forward with a proposal to investigate some leads which might result in options which would be alternative or supplemental to those which the team was soon to execute. The manager recognized the merits of the proposal but also recognized that the team member was proposing to involve himself deeply in the Divergence stage of the Model, while the rest of the team was involved in the Convergence and Execution stages. The manager described his strategy to prevent unproductive conflict between the Divergence of the team member and the Convergence of the rest of the team: "I built a fence around the Divergence quadrant and told him to stay in it and the others to stay out." He thus encouraged and supported the team members's independent pursuit of the learning process until it came into phase with the learning process of the rest of the team.

In still another instance, a group of technical information specialists found the model useful in suggesting ways they could increase their effectiveness in providing technical information to project teams. They realized that the information needs of project teams vary according to the stage of the learning process as shown below.[8]

Stage	Activity	Information Need
Divergence	Generation of alternatives Creativity	Specific alternatives Stimulation to the process of generating alternatives (e.g., information about Brainstorming)
	Problem/opportunity sensing	State of the art State of the world
Assimilation	Planning Formulating theory	Policy Planning methodology Strategy models
	Establishing criteria	Evaluation criteria
Convergence	Interpretation of data Narrowing down alternatives	Screening/selection techniques
	Design of experiments Decision making Evaluation of outcome	Experimental design Political science knowledge
Execution	Execution of plan Implementation of decision	Feedback on results (Monitoring techniques)
	Goal setting	Information on need

Implications for Management of R&D

The Learning Model provides a basis for several kinds of action which can be taken by management to improve the R&D process.

Staffing decisions can be made in light of the Learning Model. The assignment of individuals with requisite skills in each of the stages of the learning process should result in improving that process. The balance of skills required is likely to shift over the course of a project. In the earliest cycles through the learning process (e.g., during concept and prototype development), skills in the Divergence and Assimilation stages are likely to be most critical. Later (e.g., when the design is fixed and engineering specifications are being prepared) skills in Convergence and Execution become most critical. Shifts in assignment of individuals during the project life may, in *some* instances, not only improve the progress of the project, but also permit individuals to have assignments which match their preferences and abilities.[9]

Organization policies and reward systems can be used to support an appropriate balance of learning activities. It is our observation (which is supported by research reported by Kolb[10]) that organizations and professional

[8]Thomas J. Allen (private communications) has suggested that the information needs of R&D projects vary with the kind of project (e.g., research, service, engineering) and with the maturity of the project.

[9]We caution against the assumption that the learning preferences of individuals are fixed. It has been our observation that for many individuals learning style preference is highly situational.

[10]See Kolb [6].

FIGURE 5

FIGURE 5

Intervention Strategies

Concrete
Experience

Execution	Divergence
Critical path scheduling	Brainstorming
Goal-setting	Synectics
	Creative problem solving
	Browsing
	Literature
	Visiting
	General consultants

Active   Reflective
Experimentation   Observation

Convergence	Assimilation
Decision trees	Thinking
Design of experiments	Manipulating data
Calculations	Extracting grounded theory
Methods consultants	Game theory
Experimenting	Management information
	"Expert" consultants

Abstract
Conceptualization

disciplines often develop values which favor activity in one learning stage over the others. When these values are out of balance with the needs of the organization the kinds of problems outlined in Figure 3 can result. Managers can help restore appropriate balance.

Specific problems can be identified and strategies for remedial action suggested by reference to the Learning Model. The most common specific problems, we expect, will arise when an individual or team is either stuck in or deficient in a learning stage. Some of the techniques which can be used in these situations are shown in Figure 5.

Implications beyond R&D Organizations

We believe the experience of the technical information specialists can be generalized to many other support organizations. For example, management science groups are sometimes seen as only helpful in decision making (Convergence), and even then only when risks can be quantified and defined.[11] Another view suggests that management science can provide benefits much more broadly.[12] We believe that the ability of management scientists to provide these benefits is dependent upon their sensitivity to the stage of the learning cycle of the organization (or individual) they are supporting. The table

[11]For example, see Arcand [1].
[12]For example, see Hammond [4].

below relates Hammond's categories of benefits to the corresponding stages of the Learning Model.

Potential Benefits of Management Science*	Corresponding Stage of the Learning Model
1. Provides a structure to a situation which is initially relatively unstructured to the manager.	Assimilation
2. Extends the decision maker's information processing ability.	Divergence
3. Facilitates concept formation.	Assimilation
4. Provides cues to the decision maker.	Assimilation/Convergence
5. Stimulates the collection, organization and utilization of data which might not otherwise be collected.	Divergence
6. Frees from mental set.	Divergence/Assimilation

*The list of benefits is taken directly from Hammond [4], pp. 9–11.

While our research and applications have been almost entirely within R&D systems, we believe the Learning Model has parallel applications in other kinds of systems. The importance of the Model to an organization will be proportionate to the importance of production of new knowledge as an organizational goal. To the extent that technical, social and political turbulence is forcing even the most stable organizations and institutions to adopt a learning orientation if they are to survive, we expect the Learning Model to be increasingly useful.[13]

References

1. Arcand, C. G., "Bureaucratic Innovation: The Failure of Rationality." *Chemtech,* 1975, pp. 710–714.

2. Bennis, W. G., and Slater, P. E. *The Temporary Society,* New York: Harper & Row, 1968.

3. Glaser, B. G., and Strauss, A. L. *The Discovery of Grounded Theory: Strategies for Qualitative Research.* Chicago: Aldine Publishing Company, 1967.

4. Hammond, J. S. "The Roles of the Manager and Management Scientist in Successful Implementation." *Sloan Management Review,* Winter 1974, pp. 1–24.

5. Kolb, D. A. *The Learning Style Inventory: Technical Manual,* Boston. Mass.: McBev and Co., 1976.

6. Kolb, D. A. "On Management and the Learning Process." *California Management Review,* Spring 1976.

7. Kolb, D. A.; Rubin, I. M.; and McIntyre, J. M. *Organization Psychology: An Experiential Approach,* 2nd ed. Englewood Cliffs, N.J.: Prentice-Hall, 1974, pp. 23, 25.

8. Schein, E. H. *Organizational Psychology,* Englewood Cliffs, N.J.: Prentice-Hall, 1965.

9. Schon, D. A. *Beyond the Stable State,* New York: Random House, 1971.

[13]For example, see Bennis and Slater [2], Schon [9], and the discussion of the "adaptive-coping cycle" appearing in Schein [8].

DOUBLE LOOP LEARNING IN ORGANIZATIONS

CHRIS ARGYRIS

Several years ago the top management of a multibillion dollar corporation decided that Product X was a failure and should be dropped. The losses involved exceeded $100 million. At least five people knew that Product X was in serious trouble six years before the company decided to stop producing it. Three were plant managers who lived daily with the production problems. The two others were marketing officials, who perceived that the manufacturing problems could not be solved without expenditures that would raise the price of the product to the point where it would no longer be competitive in the market.

There are several reasons why this information did not get to the top sooner. At first, those lower down believed that with exceptionally hard work they might turn the errors into success. But the more they struggled the more they realized the massiveness of the original mistake. The next task was to communicate the bad news so that it would be heard above. They knew that, in their company, bad news would not be well received at the upper levels if it was not accompanied by suggestions for positive action. They also knew that top management was enthusiastically describing Product X as a new leader in its field. Therefore, they spent much time in composing memos that communicated the realities yet would not be too shocking to top managers.

Middle managers read the memos and found them too open and forthright. Because they had done the production and marketing studies that resulted in the decision to produce Product X, the memos from lower level management had the effect of questioning the validity of their analysis. They wanted time to "really check" these gloomy predictions and, if they were true, to design alternative, corrective strategies. If the pessimistic information was to be sent upward, they wanted it accompanied by optimistic action alternatives. Hence further delay.

Once the middle managers were convinced that the predictions were valid, they began to release some of the bad news, but they did so in measured doses. They managed the releases carefully to make certain they were "covered" if management became upset. The tactic they used was to cut the memos drastically and summarize the findings. They argued that the cuts were necessary because top management was always complaining about receiving long memos. The result was that the top received fragmented information underplaying the severity of the problem (not the problem itself) and overplaying the degree to which line middle management and the technical people were in control of the problem.

Top management, therefore, continued to speak glowingly about the product, partially to ensure that it would get the financial backing it needed from within the company. Lower level managers became confused and eventually depressed because they could not understand the continued top management support nor the reason for the studies that were ordered to evaluate the production and marketing difficulties they had already identified.

Their reaction was to reduce the frequency of their memos and the intensity of the alarm they expressed while simultaneously turning the responsibility for dealing with the problem over to middle management people. When local plant managers, in turn, were asked by their foremen and employees what was happening, the only response they gave was that the company was studying the situation and continuing its support. This bewildered the foremen, but led them to reduce their concern.

How Organizations Learn

I should like to use this case to explain a view of organizational learning. First, however, a few definitions and concepts are in order. Organizational learning is a process of detecting and correcting error. Error is for our purposes any feature of knowledge or knowing that inhibits learning. When the process enables the organization to carry on its present policies or achieve its objectives, the process may be called single loop learning. Single loop learning can be compared with a thermostat that learns when it is too hot or too cold and then turns the heat on or off. The thermostat is able to perform this task because it can receive information (the temperature of the room) and therefore take corrective action.

If the thermostat could question itself about whether it should be set at 68 degrees, it would be capable not only of detecting error but of questioning the underlying policies and goals as well as its own program. That is a second and more comprehensive inquiry; hence it might be called double loop learning. When the plant managers and marketing people were detecting and attempting to correct error in order to manufacture Product X, that was single loop learning. When they began to confront the question whether Product X should be manufactured, that was double loop learning, because they were now questioning underlying organization policies and objectives.

In this organization, as in many others, norms had developed that admonished people: "Do not confront company policies and objectives, especially those top management is excited about." Thus to communicate the truth upward about the serious problems of Product X would, in addition to confronting a company policy, violate an organizational norm. But in order for this norm to be followed it must have been protected by another norm that states, "You cannot openly confront norms that tell you not to confront policies and objectives." In other words, in order to maintain the first norm a lot of information about error hiding would have to be camouflaged. So we have norms embedded within norms that inhibit double loop learning.

The Double Bind

To complicate matters, when employees adhere to a norm that says "hide errors," they know they are violating another norm that says "reveal errors." Whichever norm they choose, they risk getting into trouble. If they hide the error, they can be punished by the top if the error is discovered. If they reveal the error, they run the risk of exposing a whole network of camouflage and deception. The employees are thus in a double bind, because whatever they do is necessary yet counterproductive to the organization, and their actions may even be personally abhorrent.

One common way to reduce the tension that results from conflicting aims is to begin to conceive of the error hiding, deception, and games as part of normal organizational life. The moment individuals reach this state, they may also lose their ability to see the errors. This is one reason some employees are genuinely surprised and hurt when they are accused of behaving disloyally and immorally by those (usually outsiders) who discover the longstanding practices of error hiding.

Note what has happened. The camouflaging of technical errors is done by individuals using acceptable human games and organizational norms. The hiding of every important instrumental error, therefore, implies the existence of human games, and these in turn imply the existence of games to hide the games.

It is rare, therefore, that an organization is able to use double loop learning for its instrumental and policy issues if it cannot do so for the games and norms. The reason is that the games and norms act to prevent people from saving what they know about the technical or policy issues. The subordinates who knew about the problems of Product X did not say so directly because it would have violated organizational norms and games that everyone respected and played in order to survive.

Long-Term Problems

Under these conditions, if double loop learning occurs, it would be because of: (1) a crisis precipitated by some event in the environment (for example, a recession or a competitor producing a better product); (2) a revolution from within (a new management) or from without (political interference or takeover); (3) a crisis created by existing management in order to shake up the organization.

These choices entail several long-range problems. First, the change usually comes long after its necessity has been realized by alert individuals or groups within the organization. The delay teaches these persons that their alertness and loyalty are not valued. Second, those who are not alert or not as involved are reinforced in their behavior. They learn that if they wait long enough and keep their reputations clean, someone else will someday take action. Third, change under crisis and revolution is exhausting to the organization. Fourth, such changes usually reinforce the factors that inhibit double loop learning in the first place. Hence, from the standpoint of organizational learning processes, there would be no change.

How Organizations Survive

What keeps organizations effective if all this is true? First, organizations are quite good at single loop learning. Second, since most private and public organizations are unable to learn by the double loop method, the costs can be built into the price or tax structures. But there may be a limit to price and tax increases, and this way out may be the road toward economic and political instability. Third, many people are struggling to counteract these processes of organizational rigidity and deterioration, especially at upper levels. The result is that in our society executives work overtime and employees work the regular hours. Fourth, the processes I am concerned about have only recently become so potent in advanced industrial societies that they cannot be ignored.

Thus an ongoing national survey of peoples' belief in the ability of organizations to get things done shows that public confidence reached a peak in the late 1960s, and since then it has been deteriorating. At the same time, information science technology and managerial know-how have continued to increase in sophistication.

Why is it that organizations appear to be less effective as the technology to manage them becomes more sophisticated? The answer is, I believe, that the management theory underlying the new sophisticated technology is the same as the one that created the problem in the first place. Take New York City as an illustration. All types of new managerial committees and new leaders have been introduced to deal with the troubled fiscal situation. They are correcting many single loop errors, but, if we can judge from the newspaper accounts, they are having much more difficulty in confronting the double loop question. The newspapers have, for example, cited several instances where cuts in municipal service budgets had not been made nearly a year after they were promised. Or, if unions are now willing to forgo raises for their members in order to prevent layoffs, have they been helped to examine the errors in their thinking that led to the problems in the first place?

During the Lindsay administration, I talked with several of the top city financial people. Although finance is not my field, it was not difficult to see the games being played with budgets and to identify some of the possible dangers. When I raised some questions, they responded that I did not understand big city administration and politics. They insisted that no one would let a big city go bankrupt. Double loop learning will occur only when these officials examine and alter their willingness to play financial games, which they know are counterproductive, as well as their assumptions that they will remain in control.

Actually, this type of thinking is going on in all parts of our society. Doctors and lawyers know that medical and legal services are inadequate (especially for the poor), and that pressure is building to remedy the situation; yet they have resisted setting up machinery to evaluate how their own actions affect the distribution of their services.

Someday even our newspapers may suffer a reduction in their autonomy. I predict this because of what I found in the study of a leading newspaper. The top executives felt helpless in creating within their own organization the conditions they insisted should exist in the White House and in state and city governments.[1] And just as the existing climates in those governmental bodies might lead to corruption and distortion, I found the same to be true in the newspapers. Why should our nation protect the managers of a newspaper when they are unable to create the milieu they themselves argue is necessary if truth is to be served?

The final result ironically will also be counterproductive. Society will create agencies to monitor the organizations and the professions. But it is difficult if not impossible for outside agencies to monitor the quality of the learning processes without becoming enmeshed in the organization. If people from *within* an organization can hide these processes from their own superiors, how will an outside agency discover them?

Why is double loop learning so rare? Asking this question is like asking why illness is so prevalent. A thorough answer would generate a network of interconnected factors so complex that it would seem unmanageable. I do not think, however, we have reached the point where the problem is unsolvable.

Inhibiting Factors

Donald Schon and I have been conducting research that we believe has identified a few of the more critical factors that inhibit double loop learning in organizations.[2] In order to explain these findings, I must first introduce some concepts.

Model I Assumptions

People have theories that they use to plan and carry out their actions. "If you want to motivate people to perform, pay them well and inspect their production closely" is an example of a proposition contained in many executives' theories for action.

Yet we found that few people are aware that they do not *use* the theories they explicitly espouse, and few are aware of those they do use. If people are unaware of the propositions they use, then it appears that they design for themselves private assumptions that are not genuinely self-corrective. Thus they are prisoners of their own theories.

If this finding sounds questionable, let me assure you that I was doubtful myself about our early results. But, as we began to develop a model of the assumptions we saw people using, which we call Model I (*see Exhibit 1*), the pieces began to fall into place.

The validity of the theories that most people use to design and carry out their actions is tested by their effectiveness in achieving the values people hold. Schon and I have identified four basic values that people who operate by Model I assumptions always seem to strive to satisfy and that govern their behavior. They are (1) to define in their own terms the purpose of the situation

[1]Chris Argyris, *Behind the Front Page* (San Francisco: Jossey-Bass, 1974).
[2]Chris Argyris and Donald Schon, *Organizational Learning* (Reading, Mass.: Addison-Wesley, to be published).

EXHIBIT 1
Theories of Action

Governing Variables for Action	Action Strategies for Actor	Consequences on Actor and His Associates	Consequences on Learning	Effectiveness
I	*II*	*III*	*IV*	*V*
Model I				
1 Achieve the purposes as I perceive them.	1 Design and manage environment so that actor is in control over factors relevant to me.	1 Actor seen as defensive.	1 Self-sealing.	
2 Maximize winning and minimize losing.	2 Own and control task.	2 Defensive interpersonal and group relationships.	2 Single loop learning.	Decreased.
3 Minimize eliciting negative feelings.	3 Unilaterally protect self.	3 Defensive norms.	3 Little testing of theories publicly.	
4 Be rational and minimize emotionality	4 Unilaterally protect others from being hurt.	4 Low freedom of choice, internal commitment, and risk taking.		
Model II				
1 Valid information.	1 Design situations or encounters where participants can be origins and experience high personal causation.	1 Actor seen as minimally defensive.	1 Testable processes.	
2 Free and informed choice.	2 Task is controlled jointly.	2 Minimally defensive interpersonal relations and group dynamics.	2 Double loop learning.	Increased.
3 Internal commitment to the choice and constant monitoring of the implementation.	3 Protection of self is a joint enterprise and oriented toward growth.	3 Learning-oriented norms.	3 Frequent testing of theories publicly.	
	4 Bilateral protection of others.	4 High freedom of choice, internal commitment, and risk taking.		

Source: Exhibit 1 taken from Chris Argyris and Donald Schon, *Theory in Practice* (San Francisco: Jossey-Bass, 1974).

in which they find themselves, (2) to win, (3) to suppress their own and others' feelings, and (4) to emphasize the intellectual and deemphasize the emotional aspects of problems.

To satisfy these governing variables, people tend to use unilateral behavioral strategies such as advocating a position and simultaneously controlling others in order to win that position, controlling the tasks to be done, and secretly deciding how much to tell people and how much is to be distorted, usually to save somebody's face.

The reader can now begin to see why Model I theories of action might be difficult to correct. First, the actors do not invite confrontation of the inconsistencies within their theories or the incongruities between what they espouse and what they actually use. To do so would allow for the possibility that someone else could get control or that someone else could win, and negative feelings might be aroused—all violations of the governing variables.

The people observing the actor usually see and react to his or her inconsistencies and incongruities. However, they often hold the same theories of action, and so they say nothing, lest they upset the actor and be seen as insensitive and undiplomatic.

A Practical Example

These governing variables and behavioral strategies are deeply rooted. I was leading a seminar with 15 line officers of a large holding company (mostly presidents of divisions) and 8 financial officers of these divisions plus the headquarters financial officer and the head of the entire company. During the discussion, I began to realize that the line officers were seriously concerned that the financial types with their financial information systems seemed to be getting increasing power with the chief executive officers. The finance people, who sensed this concern and interpreted it as natural defensiveness, wished they could do something about it.

Because both groups wanted to correct the problem, I asked the line and financial officers each to write a short case. On the right-hand side of the page they were to write, in scenario form, how they would go about discussing the issue with their financial or line counterparts. On the left-hand side they were to write anything that they thought or felt about the situation but probably would not communicate. I then summarized the findings on both sides and presented these to both groups.

Some interesting patterns emerged from an analysis of the cases. In all 23 cases, the scenarios dealt primarily with skin-surface aspects of the problem. For example, the line officers focused on the frustrations connected with filling out so many forms, the inability to get financial results quickly enough, and yet being loaded—indeed overloaded—with information that they did not need. The financial officers, on the other hand, said the forms were complex because the banks demanded the information, or, if the reports were not coming out fast enough, they would try to speed them up.

In both groups the information in the column of thoughts and feelings *not* discussed was central to the problem. For example, "Here comes the runaround again," and "Why don't they say that they want to control this place?" or "He [the financial man] demands reports to impress his boss."

Moreover, the members of each group knew they were withholding information and covering up feelings. They also guessed that the others were doing the same. However, information that each side considered incomplete or distorted was not up for discussion. If people could not discuss these issues, they still had to solve them, so they would have to make inferences about others' views. They could test inferences only indirectly and were unable to discuss how they tested an idea.

Primary Inhibiting Loops

The example just mentioned illustrates one of the conditions people create when they attempt to solve double loop problems. All parties withheld information that was potentially threatening to themselves or to others, and the act of coverup itself was closed to discussion.

Thus it was highly probable that the people in each group would view much of the information they received from others as being inconsistent, vague, and ambiguous. The detection and correction of error under these conditions is highly unlikely. To compound the problem, the qualities of inconsistency, vagueness, and ambiguity themselves are not discussable. Thus feedback loops are created that play a primary role in inhibiting double loop learning.

Schon and I have collected nearly 3,000 such cases from executives, government leaders, trade union officials, lawyers, architects, health professionals, ministers, and educators at all levels of education. Thus what I am talking about is not a characteristic solely of business managers. Nor, by the way, are these findings limited to capitalist nations. The data available indicate that people in socialist countries also use Model I.

I am not asserting simply that people do not behave according to what they consider to be their theories for action. That would not be a particularly new finding. I am saying that people espouse theories that they use to design and manage their actions, of which they are unaware. If people simply did not behave consistently with their own theories, then it might follow that the corrective action is to alter behavior. In a study of six corporate presidents, I found that trying to change behavior is not sufficient and indeed could lead to behavior that is transitory and superficial.[3]

For example, an overcontrolling president may learn to be less controlling without altering the Model I values that govern his behavior such as unilaterally controlling a situation and maximizing his chance of winning. Under these conditions the president may become undercontrolling by letting his subordinates alone, by "giving them their head." But, if difficulties arise, he will again behave in accordance with his private assumptions and will strive to regain unilateral control.

His subordinates will then conclude that the original reduction of control was probably only a tactic. In other words, under stress the president's old leadership style resurfaces because the assumptions underneath it have not been altered.

Changing private assumptions involves helping people to become aware of these internal maps; helping them to see how their present assumptions are counterproductive for the very kind of learning they need to be effective (for example, how to combine articulate advocacy of their views with questioning by others of these views); providing them with new assumptions that reduce

---

[3]See my book, *Increasing Leadership Effectiveness* (New York: Wiley-Interscience, 1976).

greatly the counterproductive consequences; showing them how to move from old to new assumptions; and teaching them the skills necessary to implement the new behavior in work settings.

This may appear to be an overly rational approach to changing human behavior. My experience in actual seminars is quite the contrary. The emotional and intellectual aspects of the whole human being become involved. I will return to this point after I say more about the kind of world people create who use Model I assumptions to design their actions.

Secondary Inhibiting Loops

As we have seen, people create loops to protect the primary inhibiting loops, and so we have loops nested within loops that inhibit learning. Model I blinds people to their weaknesses. For instance, the six corporate presidents were unable to realize how incapable they were of questioning their assumptions and breaking through to fresh understanding. They were under the illusion that they could learn, when in reality they just kept running around the same track.

President A told the group that Vice President Z, whom he had viewed as a prime candidate to be the next president, was too submissive and did not show enough initiative. The presidents questioned A carefully, and they soon produced evidence that A might be the cause of Z's behavior. A was surprised and irked about his own lack of awareness, but he was pleased with the help he got. He invented a solution based on the new diagnosis, which was, in effect, "to lay off the vice president and give him more breathing space."

His colleagues were able to help A to see that the solution was simplistic. As one said, "If I were Z and you suddenly changed by letting me alone, I would wonder if you had given up on me." A, again surprised and irked, nevertheless learned. Next, he tried out the solution that he and the others finally designed, with his peers acting as Z. In all cases, what he produced was not what he and they had invented.

The point to this story is that A honestly thought that he was doing the right things. What he learned was that he did not have the skills to discover, to invent, to produce double loop solutions, *and* that he was unaware of this fact.

What happens is that people provide incomplete and distorted feedback to each other; each knows that this is the case; each knows that the other knows; and each knows that this game is not usually discussable. The second set of factors, therefore, that helps to create secondary inhibitions are the games people play in order not to upset each other. These games can become complex and spread quickly throughout an organization.

For example, the R&D people, not being able to meet a promised deadline, assure the top management that they have at least enhanced the state of the art. Then there are the budget games, such as "throwing the dead cat into the other department's yard." There is also the game of starting a crisis in order to get attention and to obtain more of the scarce financial resources.

These factors tend to reinforce each other. Eventually they form a tight system that inhibits individual and organizational learning. I call this a Model 0-1 (*see Exhibit 2*) learning system, and I have found such a system in most of the organizations I have studied, both private and public, product- or service-oriented.

The result is that people are taught to have a limited set of maps for how

EXHIBIT 2

Model O-1: Learning Systems That Inhibit Error Detection and Correction

1 Information that is inaccessible, vague, inconsistent, incongruent	
▲	
2 Interacts with	
▼	
3 Model theories-in-use (advocacy coupled with unilateral coercion;	
▼	
4 Primary inhibiting loops	Feedback loop to 2, 3
▼	
5 Unawareness of inability of discover--invent--produce double loop solutions. Counterproductive group dynamics (win-lose dynamics; nonadditivity; conformity; group-think). Counterproductive intergroup dynamics (polarization of issues; destructive warfare). Counterproductive organizational norms and activities (games of deception; systems are expected to be brittle and unchangeable).	
6 Secondary inhibiting loops	Feedback loop to 2, 3, 4, 5
▼	
7 Correctable errors (errors of which people are aware and whose discovery and correction pose minimal threat to individuals and to systems; whose discovery is a threat but whose camouflage is more threatening). Uncorrectable errors (errors whose discovery is a threat to individuals and to system of hiding error)	Feedback loop to 2, 3, 4, 5, 6
▼	
8 Camouflage error Camouflage primary and secondary loops Camouflage the camouflage Protective activities	Feedback loop to 2, 3, 4, 5, 6, 7
▼	
9 Decreased double loop learning increased double binds	Feedback loop to 2, 3, 4, 5, 6, 7, 8

they must act, and they erect elaborate, defensive smoke screens that prevent both themselves and anyone else from challenging either their actions or the assumptions on which they are based.

Changing the Learning System

There appear to be at least two different ways to alter Model 0-1 learning systems. The first is the use of workshops and seminars. The strategy is to get a group of people (usually away from the office) to sit down and level with each other. The sessions are managed by an expert in group dynamics and problem solving. The president gives his or her blessing and assures people that no one will be hurt if he or she speaks the truth. In well-designed sessions and where subordinates believe the president, the results are encouraging. Problems do come to the surface and get discussed. Moreover, solutions are devised, and schedules for implementation are defined.

But I do not know of any of these workshops (including those I have helped to design) where the unfreezing and the increased problem-solving effectiveness continued or extended to other problems. After a month or so back at home, the spirit seems to wane. Also, if someone tries to say something risky, it usually is accompanied by the comment, "In the spirit of our meeting. . . ." The idea is to invoke the conditions of openness that had been created temporarily during the workshop.

The reason these workshops have little long-lasting impact is that they do not deal directly with the organizational learning systems that created or permitted the problems to arise in the first place. The first requirement for changing these learning systems is that people must develop internal assumptions that are different from Model I. Model II shows such a result (see *Exhibit 1* on page 50).

The underlying aims of Model II are to help people to produce valid information, make informed choices, and develop an internal commitment to those choices. Embedded in these values is the assumption that power (for double loop learning) comes from having reliable information, from being competent, from taking on personal responsibilities, and from monitoring continually the effectiveness of one's decisions.

Model II is not the opposite of Model I. For example, its governing values are not to accomplish the purpose as others see it or to give control to everyone, or to deemphasize the intellectual and emphasize the emotional aspects, at the expense of problem solving.

Significant misunderstandings have arisen in our society because this distinction was not taken seriously. Since Model I overemphasizes ideas and rationality, many in management education go to the other extreme and emphasize the expression of feelings even to the point of suppressing ideas. Not only is this polarization ineffective; it misses the point that feelings have meanings and meanings are intellectual phenomena. Without focusing on meanings it is not possible to ascertain whether feelings are valid or productive.

Another example of a misplaced emphasis is the recent push toward participation by employees in organizations, by citizens in communities, and by students in schools. The idea was to give these groups more power in the decision-making process. It was assumed that students or employees could enhance the effectiveness of the decision-making process. This policy overlooked the fact that such participation would probably increase the number of people with Model I assumptions, who, in turn, would create even more complicated learning systems.

If students and workers had genuinely different views, neither they nor the managers would deal with them effectively. We are now coming to realize that participation should be related to competence to solve problems effectively; and such competence in turn is related to internal assumptions, not to whether people are superiors or subordinates, male or female, young or old, or members of a minority or the majority.

A key result of using Model II is ability to combine the skills of advocacy with those of encouraging inquiry and confrontation of whatever is being advocated. For example, the presidents with whom I worked had little difficulty in being articulate or inviting inquiry, but initially they found it almost impossible to combine the two. Moreover, they predicted that their subordinates would not believe them if they did combine the two, and that they would focus on advocacy and ignore the inquiry. The predictions turned out to be correct.

The Dilemmas of Power

The predisposition to polarize in order to ignore or to suppress dilemmas and paradoxes is a crucial problem for leaders trying to deal with double loop issues. Until recently, the inability to deal with the dilemmas was not critical because management had so many other problems to solve. The point is that the older and more successful a system is, the more likely it is that its participants will find themselves dealing with dilemmas and paradoxes that have been shunted aside during the early development of the system.

The "dilemmas of power" represent important issues for all future leaders. The six presidents identified several crucial ones for them: (1) how to be strong, yet admit the existence of dilemmas; (2) how to behave openly, yet not be controlling; (3) how to advocate and still encourage confrontation of their views; (4) how to respond effectively to subordinates' anxieties in spite of their own; (5) how to manage fear, yet ask people to overcome their fears and become more open; (6) how to explore the fear of understanding fear; and (7) how to gain credibility for attempts to change their leadership style when they are not comfortable with such a style.

Finally, Model II emphasizes the building of trust and risk taking, plus stating of positions in such a way that they are publicly testable so that self-sealing processes can be reduced.

It is not easy for people to move from Model I toward Model II because, as mentioned before, they tend to be unaware that they cannot perform according to Model II. Becoming aware of this fact tends to be frustrating to them, especially since they have always been taught that the basis for change is to understand and to believe in the necessity for it. But, as the presidents found out, understanding and believing in Model II did not ensure that they would be able to produce Model II behavior.

The other frustrating aspect was demonstrated in the presidents' seminar. The participants soon found that, while they were trying to help themselves and each other move toward Model II, they created a learning system that made it highly unlikely that they would ever succeed. So, in order to move toward Model II, the presidents had to examine the learning system that they had just created and begin to change it.

Moving Ahead

In the new learning system people would advocate their views in ways that would invite confrontation, positions would be stated so that they could be challenged, and testing would be done publicly. Group and intergroup defenses would be dealt with as they arose. Games such as camouflaging information would be discussed when they were relevant.

The emphasis would be on double loop learning, which means that underlying assumptions, norms, and objectives would be open to confrontation. Also any incongruities between what an organization openly espoused as its objectives and policies and what its policies and practices actually were could also be challenged.

But underlying assumptions and governing variables cannot be effectively questioned without another set against which to measure them. In other words, double loop learning always requires an opposition of ideas for comparison.

As these new learning systems take hold, they tend to decrease the primary and secondary loops plus the organizational games that inhibit learning. This, in turn, should increase the amount of successful experience with double loop learning. People would then raise their aspirations about the quality and magnitude of change their organization can take.

Effects of the System

The reader may ask what difference this makes to the bottom line. I will show that it can make a difference, but first I should like to join those business executives and scholars who argue that the bottom line is not a tough enough criterion to use to evaluate the importance of double loop learning. It is not enough to ask, for example, what the profit of the company is. A tougher question is whether the company can continue to make a profit. Moreover, as we have seen with the rise of consumerism and corporate responsibility, if top management does not take a broader view of profit, legislation will be passed that will permit outsiders to require corporations to do so.

The second comment I would make is that research on double loop learning is in its infancy. To my knowledge, the experiment with the six presidents is the first of its kind anywhere. Also, apparently there is no organization of any kind that has a full-fledged model that goes beyond Model II. We have to implant these new learning systems to see how we can ensure their taking hold and growing. The best and toughest evaluation period for double loop learning in an organization is three to five years.

I believe that to argue that management does not have the time for such trials is wrong for two reasons. First, I do not believe that there is any real choice. If organizations do not become double loop learners (without revolutions and crises), they will be taken over. That will lead to disaster because, regardless of the organization that takes over, it, too, will not be a double loop learner. The second reason is that the transition does not require that an organization stop what it is doing. The capacity for double loop learning does not inhibit single loop learning; indeed, it usually helps it. So an organization does not threaten its present level of effectiveness by striving to become more effective in its learning.

I have followed the six presidents described for four years as they have attempted to introduce the new ideas in their organizations. Their task has been difficult, and they have made many errors. But, instead of hiding the errors, they are learning from them. This, in turn, provides a realistic model for the vice presidents, who have just begun to become aware of the new concepts.

In one of the companies, the vice presidents were able to tell the president that for years they thought that a certain division should be closed down but, because they felt the division was the president's pet interest, they presented the financial results to him so as to hide their belief. Once this situation surfaced, action was taken to close down the division.

During the recent recession the same group of officers were able to cut their expense budgets by 20% in record time and without hiding from each other what they were doing. The games of politicking and throwing the dead cat in the other group's yard were reduced. Moreover, since they were all significantly more committed to monitoring the new budget, the implementation was much more effective.

In another company, the chief executive officer decided to turn over the company he had started to a new president who was more managerially oriented than he. The vice presidents agreed that it would be a good idea, provided the founder would permit the new president to truly manage the company. To convince them that he meant business, the chairman withdrew almost completely.

After one year, it became apparent that the new president was a failure. Eventually, at the insistence of the executives and the banks, the chairman had to reenter the company and replace the president. The banks and several of the members of the board recommended strongly that the changeover be abrupt and without the advance knowledge of the vice presidents.

The chairman decided instead to deal with the problem in conjunction with the people involved. He asked the president if he wanted to join in the process of transition. The president wanted to have only one session with the vice presidents, after which he left. The chairman held several sessions with the vice presidents, and they planned the transition in order to have a minimally disruptive effect upon the organization. The result was that the production and marketing errors were quickly corrected, and the company returned to a healthy financial status much sooner than expected. Equally important, to the chairman, was that the entire incident provided an opportunity to develop a much more cohesive top management team.

Finally, the presidents have shown important changes as human beings and as leaders. They all reported that they were less "tied up" inside and that they were more able to advocate what they believed while still inviting inquiry. They were all beginning to deal more effectively with the dilemmas of power.

It is not easy to create organizations capable of double loop learning, but it can be done. Even with minimal awareness the results are encouraging. The chief executive officer and his immediate subordinates are the key to success, because the best way to generate double loop learning is for the top to do it.

3 individual motivation and organizational behavior

THE TWO FACES OF POWER

DAVID C. MCCLELLAND

For over twenty years now I have been studying a particular human motive—the need to Achieve, the need to do something better than it has been done before. As the investigation advanced, it became clear that the need to Achieve (technically n Achievement) was one of the keys to economic growth because men who are concerned about doing things better have become active entrepreneurs and created the growing business firms which are the foundation stones of a developing economy (see McClelland, 1961). Some of these heroic entrepreneurs could be regarded as leaders in the sense that they seldom were leaders of men. The reason is simple: n Achievement is a one man game which need not involve other people at all. Boys who are high in n Achievement like to build things or make things with their hands, presumably because they can tell easily whether they have done a good job of work. A boy who is trying to build as tall a tower as possible out of blocks can measure very precisely and easily how well he had done. He is in no way dependent on someone else to tell him how good it is. So in the pure case the man with high n Achievement is not dependent on the approval of others; he is concerned with improving his own performance, and as an ideal type, he is most easily conceived as a salesman or an owner-manager of a small business, where he is in a position to watch carefully whether his performance is improving.

But in studying such men and their role in economic development, I ran head on into problems of leadership, power and social influence which n Ach clearly did not prepare a man to cope with. For as a one-man firm grows larger, it obviously requires some division of function, some organizational structure. Organizational structure involves relationships among people, and sooner or later someone in the organization has to pay attention to getting

This paper has been prepared as a commentary on the lack of leadership in contemporary America as noted by John Gardner in his paper, "The anti-leadership vaccine."

people to work together, or dividing up the tasks to be performed, or to supervising the work of others, and so on. Yet it is fairly clear that a high need to Achieve does not equip a man to deal effectively with managing human relationships. For instance, a salesman with high n Achievement does not necessarily make a good sales manager. For as a manager, his task is not to sell, but to inspire others to sell which involves a different set of personal goals and different strategies for reaching them. I shall never forget the moment when I learned that the president of one of the most successful achievement-oriented firms we had been studying scored exactly zero in n Achievement! Up to this point I had fallen into the easy assumption that a man with a high need to Achieve does a better job, gets promoted faster, and ultimately ends up as president of a company. How then was it possible for a man to be head of an obviously achieving company and yet score so low in n Achievement? At the time I was tempted to dismiss the finding as measurement error, but now I see it as a dramatic way of calling attention to the fact that stimulating achievement motivation in others requires a different motive and a different set of skills than wanting achievement satisfaction for oneself. For some time now our research on achievement motivation has shifted its focus from the individual with high n Achievement to the climate which encourages him and rewards him for doing well (see Litwin and Stringer, 1968). For no matter how high a person's need to Achieve may be, he cannot succeed if he has no opportunities, if the organization keeps him from taking initiative or does not reward him if he does. As a simple illustration of this point, we have found in our recent research in India that it did no good to raise achievement motivation through training if the man was not in charge of his business. That is to say, even though he might now be "all fired up" and prepared to be more active and entrepreneurial, he could not in fact do much so long as he was working for someone else who had the final say as to whether any of the things he wanted to do would in fact be done. In short, the man with high n Achievement seldom can act alone, even though he might like to. He is caught up in an organizational context in which he is being managed, controlled or directed by others. Thus to understand better what happens to him, we must shift our attention to those who are managing him, to those who are concerned about organizational relationships, to the leaders of men.

Since managers are primarily concerned with influencing others, it seems obvious that they should be characterized by a high need for Power and that by studying the power motive we could learn something about the way effective managerial leaders work. That is to say, if A gets B to do something, A is at one and the same time a leader (i.e., he is leading B), and exercising some kind of influence or power over B. Thus leadership and power are two closely related concepts and if we want to understand effective leadership better, we may begin by studying the power motive in thought and action. What arouses thoughts of being powerful? What kinds of strategies does the man employ who thinks constantly about gaining power? Are some strategies more effective than others in influencing people? In pursuing such a line of inquiry, we are adopting an approach which worked well in another area. Studying the achievement motive led to a better understanding of business entrepreneurship. Analogously, studying the power motive complex may help us understand managerial leadership better.

But there is one striking difference between the two motive systems which is apparent from the outset. In general, individuals are proud of having a high need to Achieve, but dislike being told they have a high need for Power. What is it about the concern for power which distinguishes it from most other motives which are socially approved? It is a fine thing to be concerned about doing things well (*n* Achievement) or making friends (*n* Affiliation), but why is it reprehensible to be concerned about having influence over others (*n* Power)? The vocabulary behavioral scientists use to describe power relations is strongly negative in tone. Consider one of the major works that deals with people concerned with power, *The Authoritarian Personality.* In it they are pictured as harsh, sadistic, fascist, Machiavellian, prejudiced, and neurotic. Ultimately, concern for power leads to Nazi-type dictatorships, to the slaughter of innocent Jews, to political terror, police states, brainwashing and exploitation of helpless masses who have lost their freedom. Even less political terms for power have a distinctively negative flavor: dominance-submission, competition, zero sum game (if I win, you lose). It is small wonder that people don't particularly like being told they have a high need for Power.

The negative reactions to the exercise of power became vividly apparent to me in the course of our recent research efforts to develop achievement motivation (McClelland and Winter, 1969). Out of our extensive research on the achievement motive, we conceived of ways in which it might be increased through short intensive courses. At first people were interested and curious. It seemed like an excellent idea to develop a fine motive like *n* Achievement, particularly among under-achievers in school or relatively inactive businessmen in underdeveloped countries. But most people were also skeptical. Could we really do it? It turned out that many remained interested only so long as they were really skeptical about our ability to change motivation. As soon as it became apparent that we could indeed change people, and in a relatively short period of time, then many observers started to worry. Was it really ethical to change people's personalities? Weren't we brainwashing them? What magical power were we employing to change an underlying personality disposition which had presumably been laid down in childhood and laboriously stabilized over the years? We then became aware of the fundamental dilemma confronting anyone who gets involved in the "influence game." He may think that he is exercising leadership, i.e., influencing people for their own good, but if he succeeds, he is likely to be accused of manipulating people. We thought our influence attempts were benign. In fact we were a little proud of ourselves. After all, weren't we giving people a chance to be more successful at business and in school? Yet we soon found ourselves attacked as potentially dangerous "brainwashers." To some extent ordinary psychotherapy avoids these accusations because the power the therapist has seems to be relatively weak. Therapy doesn't work very well or very quickly, and when it does the therapist can say that the patient did most of the work himself.

But consider the following anecdote. Johnny was a bright but lazy sixth grade student in math. His parents were quite concerned that he was not motivated to work harder and were delighted when the psychologists explained that they had some new techniques for development motivation that they would like to expose Johnny to. After all, he spent practically all of his evenings watching TV and the parents felt that he could surely be employing his time better. Soon after the motivation training regime started in school, they noticed a dramatic change in his behavior. Now he spent all his time studying math. He never watched television but stayed up late working long hours and soon got way ahead of his class in advanced mathematics. Then the parents began to worry. What in the world had the psychologists done to their Johnny to produce such a dramatic change in his behavior? They wanted him changed, but not *that* much. They reacted very negatively to the power that the psychologists seemed to have had over him.

An experience like this was enough to make us yearn for the detached scientist, consulting expert role so vividly described by John Gardner (1965) as the preferred role for more and more young people today. For the scientist ordinarily does not intervene (i.e., exercise power) directly in human or social affairs. He observes the interventions of others, reports, analyzes, and advises, but never takes responsibility himself. In this case our research had led us to intervene actively and even that small, relatively benign exercise of influence led to some pretty negative responses from the public. My own view is that young people avoid leadership roles not so much because their professors brainwash them into believing it is better to be a professional, but because in our society in our time and perhaps in all societies at all times, the exercise of power is often viewed very negatively. People are suspicious of a man who wants power. He is suspicious of himself. He doesn't want to be in a position where he might be thought to be seeking power and influence in order to exploit others.

Yet clearly this negative face of power is only part of the story. Power must have a positive face too. For after all, people cannot help influencing each other. Organizations cannot function without some kind of authority relationships. Surely it is necessary and desirable for some people to concern themselves with management, with working out influence relationships that make it possible to achieve the goals of the group. A man who is consciously concerned about working out the proper channels of influence is surely better able to contribute to group goals than a man who neglects or represses power problems and lets working relationships grow up higgledy-piggledy. So our problem is to try to understand these two faces of power. When is it bad and when is it good? Why is it often perceived as dangerous? What aspects are viewed favorably? When is it proper and when improper, to exercise influence? Are there different kinds of power?

It will not be possible to answer all of these questions definitively, but recent research on the power motive as it functions in human beings with the curious fact that turned up in the course of what are technically "arousal" studies. When an experimenter gets interested in a new motive, he ordinarily begins to study it by trying to arouse it in a variety of ways to see how it influences what a person thinks about. Then these alterations in thought content are worked into a code or a scoring system which will capture the extent to which he is concerned about achievement or power or whatever motive state has been aroused. Thus, Veroff (1957), when he began the study of the power motive, asked student candidates for office to write imaginative stories while they were waiting for the election returns to be counted. He contrasted these stories with those written by other students who were not candidates for office. That is, he assumed that the students waiting to hear if they had been elected were in a state of aroused power motivation and that their stories would reflect this fact as contrasted with stories of students not in such a state. From the differences in story content he derived a coding system for *n* Power (need for Power) which centered on the greater concern for having influence over others present in the stories of student candidates for election. Later arousal studies by Uleman (1965) and Winter (1967) further defined the essence of *n* Power as a concern for having a *strong impact on others.* That is, when power motivation was aroused in a variety of ways, students thought more often about people having strong impact on others. This is true not only for student candidates for office awaiting election returns, but also for student experimenters who are about to demonstrate their power over subjects by employing a winning strategy in a competitive game that they had been taught beforehand (Uleman, 1965).

What surprised us greatly was to discover that drinking alcohol also increased such power thoughts in men. This discovery was one of those happy accidents that sometimes occurs in scientific laboratories when two studies thought to be unrelated are proceeding side by side. Certainly when we began studying the effects of social drinking on fantasy, we had no idea that alcohol would increase power fantasies. Yet we early found that it increased sex and aggression fantasies and one day it occurred to us that certain types of exploitative sex and certainly aggression were instances of "having impact" on others and therefore could be considered part of an *n* Power scoring definition. We later found that drinking in small amounts increases the frequency of power thoughts even outside the field of sex and aggression altogether. This finding by itself did not at first mean very much to us, but it served to focus attention on two further questions. What was the relationship between *n* Power and drinking! And is it worthwhile to distinguish between a more primitive sex and aggression power imagery, as aroused by heavy drinking, and a more socialized type of interpersonal influence aroused in other ways? Winter (1967) conducted an extensive study of power fantasies and related activities among college students that shed some light on both of these questions. He found that some students with high *n* Power scores did in fact tend to drink more heavily, and that some of them held more offices in student organizations. The interesting fact was that these were not the same people. That is, a student with high *n* Power either drank more heavily or he was a club officer, though he was usually not both, possibly because heavy drinking would prevent him from being elected to a responsible office. In other words, Winter identified alternative manifestations of the power drive—either heavy drinking or holding office. Clearly these activities appear to lie along some dimension of inhibition of socialization, with drinking representing a less socialized, more primitive expression of power whereas holding public office represents a more socialized form of having impact.

Other studies have added to this picture, and while it is still not altogether clear, its main outlines can be readily sketched. There are two faces of power. One might be described as a kind of unsocialized concern for personal dominance. It is aroused in men by drinking alcohol and probably by other techniques like threat of physical violence that have not yet been tested experimentally. At the fantasy level, it expresses itself in terms of thoughts of exploitative sex and physical aggression. At the level of action, it leads to heavier drinking, more trouble from drinking, more casual sexual contacts (in which the goal seems to be sexual exploitation rather than love), and a tendency to watch TV shows dealing with crime and violence.

The other face of the power motive is more socialized. It is aroused by the possibility of winning an election, or the expectancy that one will be able to win over another in a competitive game. At the fantasy level it expresses itself in terms of more conventional thoughts of persuasion and interpersonal influence. So far as activities are concerned, people concerned with the more socialized aspect of power participate more often in competitive sports, even as adults, and end up more often as officers in the organizations which they join. It is useful to think of the two aspects of the power motive as having developed at different points in the life of a child. The more direct and less socialized form of expressing power, as in direct physical aggression, appears to occur earlier as the child tries to get what he wants simply by pushing another child out of the way. Later on he must learn more acceptable and more inhibited means of influencing other people.

Certain characteristics of the power syndrome cannot readily be classified as belonging to either aspect of it exclusively. Consider for example the control of resources. If someone wants to have impact on others, he should accumulate resources like physical strength, wealth or information which can be used to impress other people or control what they do. If he is stronger, he can threaten to beat up someone if he doesn't do what he says. If he is richer, he can reward the other person for compliance or punish him by withdrawal of funds for noncompliance. Or if he knows something that the other person does not know, he can use this information to influence what happens to the other person. In his study of university students Winter employed a measure of what he called *prestige possessions* which included such things as a refrigerator, a well-equipped bar, certain types of collegiate "artifacts" (like pins, beer mugs, etc.), owning a motorcycle, and so on. He found that ownership of prestige supplies was significantly correlated with the n Power score, but more significantly it belonged to the cluster of activities which we have described as expressing unsocialized personal power desires. At least at the college level, control of these resources goes with exploitative sex and heavy drinking. Yet a moment's reflection will show that prestige symbols may be an important part of more socialized influence attempts. Thus then we were trying to convince Indian businessmen that they should come to our motivation training courses because their achievement motivation could be developed, we relied heavily on the prestige of scientific findings and our association with a major American university. A political leader must employ the prestige of his office and his distinguished record of public service as means of persuading people to accept his leadership in public affairs. In such cases it seems safer to conclude that the characteristic does not belong exclusively to either the negative or positive aspect of the power syndrome. Rather it can be employed either in the service of a primitive or a more socialized power attempt.

We have made some progress in distinguishing two aspects of the power motive, but what exactly is the difference between the way the two are exercised? Again a clue came from a very unexpected source. It is traditional in the literature of social psychology and political science to describe a leader as someone who can evoke feelings of obedience or loyal submission in his followers. A leader is sometimes said to have charisma if, when he makes a speech, for example, the members of his audience are swept off their feet and feel they must submit to his overwhelming authority and power. In the extreme case they are like iron filings that have been polarized by a powerful magnet. He is recognized as supernatural or superhuman; they feel submissive, loyal, devoted, obedient to his will. Certainly this is one common description of what was happening in mass meetings addressed by Hitler or Lenin. As great demagogues they established their power over the masses which followed loyally, obediently.

Winter wished to find out just exactly what kinds of thoughts the members of an audience had when exposed to a charismatic leader. In other words he wanted to find out if this common picture of what was going on in the minds of the audience was in fact accurate. So he exposed a group of business school students to a film of John F Kennedy's Inaugural Address as President of the United States sometime after he had been assassinated. There was no doubt that this film was a highly moving and effective presentation of a charismatic leader for such an audience at this time. After the film was over he asked them to write imaginative stories as usual and contrasted the themes of their stories with those written by a comparable group of students after they had seen a film explaining some aspects of modern architecture. Contrary to expectation, he did not find that the students exposed to the Kennedy film thought more afterward about submission, following, obedience, or loyalty. Instead the frequency of power themes in their stories increased. It is certainly not too far fetched to interpret this as meaning that they felt strengthened and uplifted by the experience. They felt more powerful, rather than less powerful and submissive. This is an extremely interesting finding because it suggests that the traditional way of explaining the influence a leader has on his followers has not always been entirely correct. He does not force them to submit and follow him by the sheer overwhelming magic of his personality and persuasive powers. This in fact is to interpret leadership in terms of the kind of primitive aspect of the power syndrome we described above, and leadership has been discredited in this country because social scientists have often used this primitive power image to explain how the leader gets his effects. Rather he is influential in quite a different way by strengthening and inspiriting his audience. Max Weber, who is the source of much of the sociological treatment of charisma, recognized that such leaders obtained their effects through "begeisterung," a word which means "inspiration" rather more than its usual translation, "enthusiasm."[1] The leader arouses confidence in his followers. They feel better able to accomplish whatever goals he and they share. Much has been made of whether his ideas as to what will inspire his followers came from God, from himself, or from some intuitive sense of what the people need and want. But whatever the source he cannot inspire them unless he expresses vivid goals and aims which in some sense they want. And of course the more he is meeting their needs, the less "persuasive" he has to be. But in no case does it make much sense to speak as if his role is to force submission. Rather it is to strengthen and uplift, to make people feel like origins, not pawns (deCharms, 1968). His message is not so much: "Do as I say because I am strong and know best. You are children with no wills of your own and must follow me because I know better," but "Here are the goals which are true and right and which we share. Here is how we can reach them. You are strong and capable. You can accomplish these goals." His role is to clarify what goals the group should achieve and then create confidence in its members that they can achieve them. John Gardner has described these two aspects of the leadership role very well

[1]For a fuller discussion of what Weber and other social scientists have meant by charisma, see Eisenstadt, 1968, and Tucker, 1968.

when he said that leaders "can conceive and articulate goals that lift people out of their petty preoccupations, carry them above the conflicts that tear a society apart, and unite them in the pursuit of objectives worthy of their best efforts" (1965).

So the more socialized type of power motivation cannot and does not express itself in a leadership pattern which is characterized by more primitive methods of trying to have personal impact. Social scientists have been too much impressed by the dominance hierarchies established by brute force among lower animals in their thinking about the power motive. Such methods may be effective in very small groups, but if a human leader wants to be effective in influencing large groups, he must come to rely on much more subtle, and socialized forms of influence. He necessarily gets more interested in formulating the goals toward which groups of people can move. And if he is to move the group toward achieving them, he must define the goals clearly and persuasively and then he must be able to strengthen the will of the individual members of the group to work for those goals. To be sure, if he is a gang leader, he may display power characteristics, like exploitative sex and physical aggression which we have been characterizing as typical of less socialized forms of power, but even here to the extent that he is a leader of a large group he is effective because he knows how to encourage them to pursue such goals, perhaps in this case by the technique of his own example in dislaying more primitive, less socialized forms of power.

Some further light on the two faces of power was shed by our experience in trying to exert social leadership by offering achievement motivation development courses for business leaders in small cities in India. As noted above, when we began to succeed in these efforts, some observers began to wonder whether we were coarsely interfering in people's lives, perhaps spreading some new brand of American imperialism by foisting achievement values on a people that had gotten along very well without them. Their reaction is not unlike the one just described in which an outsider seeing a leader sway an audience concludes that he must have some mysterious magical power over the audience. Did we have a similar kind of "power over" the Indian businessmen who came for motivation training? Were we a new type of psychological Machiavelli?

Certainly we never thought we were. Nor, we are certain, did the businessmen perceive us as very powerful agents. How then did we manage to influence them? What happened was very much like the process of social leadership as described by John Gardner. First, we set before the participants certain goals which we felt would be desired by them—namely, to be better businessmen, to improve economic welfare in their community, to make a contribution in this way to the development of their country as a whole, to provide a pilot project that the rest of the underdeveloped might copy, and to advance the cause of science. These goals ranged all the way from the specific and personal—improving one's business—to improving the community, the nation and the world. In our experience neither a personal selfish appeal nor an altruistic social appeal is as effective by itself as the combination of the two. At any rate, these certainly were objectives that interested the businessmen we contacted. Second, we provided them with the means of achieving these goals, namely, the courses in achievement motivation development which we explained were designed to make them personally better able to move quickly and efficiently toward these objectives. What we had to offer were some new types of training in goal setting, planning, and risk taking which research had shown would help a man become a more effective entrepreneur. All of this was explained as a simple matter of fact which it was. No one was pressured to undergo this training or pursue these goals. If there was any pressure perceived, it is clearly in the eyes of the outside observer noting the effects of our intervention; it was not in the minds of the participants at the time. Third, the major goal of all of our educational exercises was to make the participants feel strong, like origins rather than pawns. Thus we insisted that the initial decision to come must be their own. They should not come out of a sense of obligation or desire to conform. In fact we pictured the training as so difficult that a high degree of personal involvement would be necessary to complete it. During the training we never set goals for them. They set their own goals for what they would try to do either in the course or for the next few months after the course. We never made psychological analyses of their test behavior which we either kept for our private diagnosis or presented to them as evidence of our superior psychological knowledge. Rather we taught them to analyze their own test records and to make their own decisions as to what a test score meant. After the course they set up their own association to work together for common community goals. We did not provide them with technical information about various types of new business they might enter. If they wanted such information, they had to go search for it themselves. We did not have a fixed order of presenting course materials, but constantly asked the participants to criticize the material as it was presented and to direct the staff as to what new types of presentation were desirable. Thus it turned out that we had behaved all along like effective leaders in our ceaseless efforts to make the participants feel strong, competent and effective on their own. We expressed in many ways our faith in their ability to act as origins and solve their own problems. In the end many of them justified our faith. They became more active, as we expected them to, and once again validated the ubiquitous psychological finding that what you expect other people to do they will in fact tend to do (see Rosenthal, 1968). Furthermore we have good evidence that we succeeded only with those businessmen whose sense of personal efficacy was increased. This expresses the ultimate paradox of social leadership and social power: to be an effective leader, you have to turn all your so-called followers into leaders. No wonder the situation is a little confusing not only to the would-be leader, but also to the social scientist observing the process!

Now let us put together the various bits and pieces of evidence about the nature of power and see what kind of a picture they make. The negative face of power is characterized by the dominance-submission mode. If I win, you lose. It is more primitive in the sense that the strategies employed are adopted earlier in life before the child is sufficiently socialized to learn more subtle techniques of influence. In fantasy it expresses itself in thoughts of exploitative sex and direct physical aggression. In real life it leads to fairly simple direct means of feeling powerful—like drinking heavily, chasing women, acquiring some kinds of "prestige supplies," or watching "the fights" on television. It does not lead to effective social leadership for the simple reason that a person whose power drive is fixated at this level tends to treat other people as pawns rather than as origins. And people who feel they are pawns tend to be passive and useless to the leader who is getting his childish satisfaction from dominating them. As

Galbraith points out, slaves are the poorest, most inefficient form of labor ever devised by man. If a leader wants to have real far reaching influence, he must make his followers feel powerful and able to accomplish things on their own.

The positive face of power is characterized by a concern for group goals, for finding what goals will move them, for helping the group to formulate them, for taking some initiative in providing members of the group with the means of achieving such goals, and for giving group members the feeling of strength and competence they need to work hard for such goals. In fantasy it leads to a concern with persuading, forming new organizations, expressing the viewpoint of a given organization and so on. In real life, it leads to an interest in sports, politics, and holding office. It treats members of a group more as origins than as pawns. Even the most dictatorial leaders have not succeeded without instilling in at least some of their followers a sense of power and strength to pursue the goals he has set. This is often hard for outside observers to believe, but that is because they do not experience the situation as it is experienced by inside group members. One of the characteristics of being an outsider who notices only the success of an influence attempt is that he tends to convert what is a positive face of power into its negative version. He believes the leader must have "dominated" because he was so effective whereas in fact direct domination could never have produced so large an effect.

Why? Why is a successful influence attempt so often perceived as an instance of personal domination by a leader? One answer lies in the simplifying nature of social perception. The observer notices that a big change in the behavior of a group of people has occurred. He also can single out one or two people as having been leaders in some way involved in the change. He does not know how the leaders operated to bring about the change since he was not that intimately involved in the process. So he tends to perceive it as an instance of application of primitive power, or simple dominance and submission. The more effective a leader is, the more personal power tends to be attributed to him, no matter how he goes about getting his effects.

There is also a realistic basis for the frequent misperception of the nature of leadership. In real life the actual leader is balancing on a knife edge between expressing personal dominance and the more socialized type of leadership. He may present first one face of power, then the other. The reason lies in the simple fact that even if he is a socialized leader, he must take initiative in helping the group form its goals. How much initiative? How persuasive should he attempt to be? At what point does his clear enthusiasm for certain goals verge over into personal, authoritarian insistence that those goals are the right ones whatever the members of the group may think? If he takes no initiative, he is no leader. If he takes too much, he becomes a dictator, particularly if he tries to shut off the process by which members of the group can participate in shaping the group goals. Furthermore, there is a particular danger for the man who has demonstrated his competence in shaping group goals and in inspiriting group members to pursue them, for in time both he and they may assume that he knows best and he may almost imperceptibly shift from being a democratic to an authoritarian leader. There are safeguards against slipping from the more socialized to the less socialized expressions of power. One is psychological: the leader must thoroughly learn the lesson that his role is not to dominate and treat people like pawns, but to give strength to others and make them feel like origins. If they are to be truly strong, he must continually consult them and be aware of their wishes and desires. A firm faith in people as origins prevents the development of the kind of cynicism that so often characterizes authoritarian leaders. The other safeguard is social: democracy provides a system whereby the group can throw out the leader if they feel he is no longer properly representing them or formulating goals with them that the group wants to achieve.

Despite these safeguards, Americans remain unusually suspicious of the leadership role for fear that it will become the vehicle of personal abuse of power. Students do not aspire to leadership roles becuase they are sensitive to the negative face of power and suspicious of their own motives. Furthermore, they know if they are in a position of leadership, they will be under constant surveillance by all sorts of groups which are ready to accuse them of personal abuse of power. Americans have probably less respect for authority than almost any people in the world. The reasons are not hard to find. Many Americans immigrated here in the first place to avoid tyranny in other countries. We have come to hate and fear authority in many of its forms because of its excesses elsewhere. As a nation, we are strongly committed to an ideology of personal freedom and noninterference by government. We cherish our free press as a guardian of our freedom because it can ferret out tendencies toward the misuse or abuse of personal power before they become dangerous to the public. In government and also in many other types of organizations, we have developed elaborate systems of checks and balances or divisions of power which make it hard for any one person or group to abuse power. In government power is divided three ways—among the executive, the legislative and the judicial branches. In business it is divided among management, labor, and the owners. In the universities the trustees, the administration and students share power. In many of these organizations there is also a system for rotating leadership to make sure that no one gains enough power over time to misuse it. A Martian observer might conclude that as a nation we are excessively, almost obsessively, worried about the abuse of power.

But the wonder of it is that any leadership can be exercised under such conditions. For look at the situation from the point of view of a would-be leader. He knows that if he takes too much initiative, or even if he doesn't, he is very likely to be severely attacked by some sub-group as a malicious, power hungry status seeker. If he is in any way a public figure, he may be viciously attacked by the press for any mis-step or chancy episode in his past life. Even though the majority of the people are happy with his leadership, a small vociferous minority can make his life unpleasant. Furthermore, he knows that he will not be the only leader trying to formulate group goals. If he is a Congressman, he has to work not only with his fellow Congressmen, but with representatives of independent sources of power in the Presidency and the bureaucracy. If he is a college president, he has to cope with the relatively independent sources of power in his trustees, the faculty and the student body. If he is a business manager, he must share power with labor leaders. Furthermore, he knows that his tenure of office is very likely to be temporary. It is chancy whether he will get in a position to exert leadership. So there is no use preparing for it. If he does get in he won't stay long. So he should spend his time now preparing for what he will do before and after his short tenure in office. Under these conditions why would any promising young man aspire to be a leader? He begins by doubting his motives and ends by concluding that even if he believes his motives to be altruistic, the game is scarcely worth the candle. In other words, the antileadership vaccine, which John Gardner speaks of, is partly supplied by the negative face that power wears in our society and the extraordinary lengths we have gone to protect ourselves against it.

It is much safer to pursue a career as a professional advisor where one is assured some continuity of service, freedom from public attack (because after all one is not responsible for decisions), certainty that one's motives are good, and the peace of mind that comes from knowing that power conflicts have to be settled by someone else.

Is there any remedy for the situation? How can immunity against the antileadership vaccine be strengthened? For some immunity surely needs to be built up if our society is not to go floundering about for lack of leadership. I would personally concoct a remedy which is one part changes in the system, one part rehabilitation of the positive face of power, and one part adult education. Let me explain each ingredient in turn. I feel least confident in speaking about the first one because I am neither a political scientist, a management expert, nor a revolutionary, yet as a psychologist I do feel that America's concern about the possible misuse of power verges at times on a neurotic obsession. To control the abuses of power, is it really necessary to divide authority so extensively and to give such free license to anyone to attack a leader in any way he likes? Doesn't this make the leadership role unnecessarily difficult? John Gardner, I am sure, is aware of how difficult it is to get qualified people to want to be college presidents in present-day America. But who in his right mind would want the job under most operating conditions today? A president has great responsibility—for raising money, for setting goals for the institution that faculty, students and trustees can share, for student discipline, for appointment of a distinguished faculty and so forth—yet he often has only a very shaky authority with which to carry out these responsibilities. What authority he has, he must share with the faculty (many of whom he cannot remove no matter how violently they disagree with the goals set for the university), with the trustees and with the students who speak with one voice one year and quite a different one two years later. I am not now trying to defend ineffective college presidents no matter what they do. I am simply trying to point out that our social system makes his role an extraordinarily difficult one. Furthermore, other democratic nations, like Britain, have not found it necessary to go to such extremes to protect their liberty against possible encroachment by power hungry leaders. Some structural reform definitely seems called for. It is beyond the scope of this paper to say what it might be. The possibilities range all the way from a less structured system in which all organizations are conceived as temporary with task force leaders (see Bennis and Slater, 1968) to a system in which leaders are given more authority or offered greater protection from irresponsible attack. But surely the problem deserves serious attention. If we want better leaders, we will have to find ways of making the conditions under which they work less frustrating.

The second ingredient in my remedy for the antileadership vaccine is rehabilitation of the positive face of power. This paper is an effort in that direction. Its major thesis is that many people, including both social scientists and potential leaders, have consistently misunderstood or misperceived the way in which effective social leadership takes place. They have confused it regularly, as we have pointed out, with the more primitive exercise of personal power. The error is perpetuated by people who speak of leaders as "making decisions." Such a statement only serves to obscure the process by which the decision is arrived at. It suggests that the leader is making a decision arbitrarily without consulting anyone, exercising his power or authority for his own ends. It is really more proper to think of an effective leader as an educator. In fact the word "educate" comes from the Latin *educare* meaning "to lead out." The relationship between leading and educating is much more obvious in Latin than it is in English, although the Latin word *dux* (leader) does appear in several English words like conductor, as in the sense of a leader of an orchestra. Effective leaders are educators: they lead people out by helping set goals for a group, communicating them widely throughout the group, taking initiative in formulating means of achieving the goals, and finally, inspiriting the members of the group to feel strong enough to work hard for those goals. Such an image of the exercise of power and influence in a leadership role should not frighten anybody and should convince more people that power exercised this way is not only not dangerous but of the greatest possible use to society.

Our experience in developing businessmen in India has led me to propose the third ingredient in my formula for producing better leaders—namely, psychological education for adults. What impressed me greatly about the results we obtained in India was the apparent ease with which adults can be changed, by the methods we used. The dominant view in American psychology today is still that basic personality structure is laid down very early in life and is very hard to change later on. Whether the psychologist is a Freudian or a learning theorist, he believes that early experiences are critical and shape everything a person can learn, feel and want throughout his entire life span. As a consequence many educators have come to be rather pessimistic about what can be done for the poor, the black or the dispossessed who have had damaging experiences early in life. Such traumatized individuals have developed nonadaptive personality structures that are difficult, if not impossible, to change later in life, or so the reasoning goes. Yet our experience with the effectiveness of short-term training courses in achievement motivation for adult businessmen in India and elsewhere does not support this view. I have seen men change, many of them quite dramatically, after only a 10-day exposure to our specialized techniques of psychological instruction. They have changed the way they thought, the way they talked, and what they spent their time doing; their businesses improved. The message is clear: adults can be changed, often with a relatively short exposure to specialized techniques of psychological education. The implication for the present discussion is obvious: if it is true, as John Gardner argues, that many young men have learned from their professors in the colleges and universities that the professional role is preferable to the leadership role, then psychological education offers society a method of changing their views and self conceptions when they are faced with leadership opportunities. The type of psychological education needed will of course differ somewhat from the simple emphasis on achievement motivation in the courses offered for entrepreneurs. More emphasis would have to be given to managing motivation in others. More explanations would have to be given of the positive face of leadership as an educational enterprise to give participants a better idea of how to be effective leaders. But such alterations in the nature of the courses are quite feasible. In fact they have been tried out and repeatedly we have discovered that leaders are not so much born as made. And we have been working in places where most people would feel there was not much leadership potential—namely, among the poor and dispossessed. Yet we have found over and over again that even among people who have never thought of themselves as leaders or attempted to have influence in any way in poverty areas, real leadership performance can be elicited by our specialized techniques of psychological education. We need not be so pessimistic about possibilities for change in adults. Real leaders have been developed in such disadvantaged locations as the Delmarva Peninsula in the United States, the black business community in Washington, D.C., or the relatively stagnant small cities of India. So I can end on an optimistic note. Even if the leadership role today is becoming more and more difficult and people tend to avoid it for a variety of reasons, science has again come at least partly to the rescue by providing society with new techniques for developing the leaders that are needed for the world of tomorrow.

References

Bennis, W. G. and P. E. Slater. *The Temporary Society.* New York: Harper & Row, 1968.

Eisenstadt, S. N. *Charisma, Institution Building, and Social Transformation: Max Weber and Modern Sociology.* Chicago, Illinois: The University of Chicago Press, 1968.

Litwin, G. H. and R. A. Stringer. *Motivation and Organizational Climate.* Harvard University, Graduate School of Business Administration, Division of Research, 1966.

McClelland, D. C. *The Achieving Society.* Princeton, N.J.: Van Nostrand, 1961.

McClelland, D. C. *et al., Alcohol and Human Motivation.* New York: The Free Press (in press).

McClelland, D. C. and D. G. Winter, *Motivating Economic Achievement.* New York: The Free Press, 1969.

Tucker, R. C. "The Theory of Charismatic Leadership." *Daedalus,* 1968, *97*, 731–756.

Uleman, J. "A New TAT Measure of the Need for Power." Unpublished doctoral dissertation, Harvard University, 1965.

Veroff, J. "Development and Validation of a Projective Measure of Power Motivation." *Journal of Abnormal and Social Psychology,* 1957, *54*, 1–8.

Weber, M. *Theory of Social and Economic Organization.* New York: The Free Press, 1957.

Winter, D. G. "The Need for Power in College Men: Action Correlates and Relationship to Drinking." Chapter 5 in D. C. McClelland *et al., Alcohol Power and Inhibition.* Princeton, N.J.: Van Nostrand (in press).

Winter, D. G. "Power Motivation in Thought and Action." Unpublished doctoral dissertation, Harvard University, 1967.

THAT URGE TO ACHIEVE

DAVID C. MCCLELLAND

Most people in this world, psychologically, can be divided into two broad groups. There is that minority which is challenged by opportunity and willing to work hard to achieve something, and the majority which really does not care all that much.

For nearly twenty years now, psychologists have tried to penetrate the mystery of this curious dichotomy. Is the need to achieve (or the absence of it) an accident, is it hereditary, or is it the result of environment? Is it a single, isolatable human motive, or a combination of motives—the desire to accumulate wealth, power, fame? Most important of all, is there some technique that could give this will to achieve to people, even whole societies, who do not now have it?

While we do not yet have complete answers for any of these questions, years of work have given us partial answers to most of them and insights into all of them. There is a distinct human motive, distinguishable from others. It can be found, in fact tested for, in any group.

Let me give you one example. Several years ago, a careful study was made of 450 workers who had been thrown out of work by a plant shutdown in Erie, Pennsylvania. Most of the unemployed workers stayed home for a while and then checked back with the United States Employment Service to see if their old jobs or similar ones were available. But a small minority among them behaved differently: the day they were laid off, they started job-hunting.

They checked both the United States and the Pennsylvania Employment Office; they studied the "Help Wanted" sections of the papers; they checked through their union, their church, and various fraternal organizations; they looked into training courses to learn a new skill; they even left town to look for work, while the majority when questioned said they would not under any circumstances move away from Erie to obtain a job. Obviously the members of that active minority were differently motivated. All the men were more or less in the same situation objectively: they needed work, money, food, shelter, job security. Yet only a minority showed initiative and enterprise in finding what they needed. Why? Psychologists, after years of research, now believe they can answer that question. They have demonstrated that these men possessed in greater degree a specific type of human motivation. For the moment let us

---

refer to this personality characteristic as "Motive A" and review some of the other characteristics of the persons who have more of the motive than other persons.

Suppose they are confronted by a work situation in which they can set their own goals as to how difficult a task they will undertake. In the psychological laboratory, such a situation is very simply created by asking them to throw rings over a peg from any distance they may choose. Most persons throw more or less randomly, standing now close, now far away, but those with Motive A seem to calculate carefully where they are most likely to get a sense of mastery. They stand nearly always at moderate distances, not so close as to make the task ridiculously easy, nor so far away as to make it impossible. They set moderately difficult, but potentially achievable goals for themselves, where they objectively have only about a 1-in-3 chance of succeeding. In other words, they are always setting challenges for themselves, tasks to make them stretch themselves a little.

But they behave like this only if *they* can influence the outcome by performing the work themselves. They prefer not to gamble at all. Say they are given a choice between rolling dice with one in three chances of winning and working on a problem with a one-in-three chance of solving in the time alloted, they choose to work on the problem even though rolling the dice is obviously less work and the odds of winning are the same. They prefer to work at a problem rather than leave the outcome to chance or to others.

Obviously they are concerned with personal achievement rather than with the rewards of success *per se,* since they stand just as much chance of getting those rewards by throwing the dice. This leads to another characteristic the Motive A persons show—namely, a strong preference for work situations in which they get concrete feedback on how well they are doing, as one does, say in playing golf, or in being a salesman, but as one does not in teaching, or in personnel counseling. A golfer always knows his score and can compare how well he is doing with par or with his own performance yesterday or last week. A teacher has no such concrete feedback on how well he is doing in "getting across" to his students.

The *n* Ach Person

But why do certain persons behave like this? At one level the reply is simple: because they habitually spend their time thinking about doing things better. In fact, psychologists typically measure the strength of Motive A by taking samples of a person's spontaneous thoughts (such as making up a story about a picture they have been shown) and counting the frequency with which he mentions doing things better. The count is objective and can even be made these days with the help of a computer program for content analysis. It yields what is referred to technically as an individual's *n* Ach score (for "need for Achievement"). It is not difficult to understand why people who think constantly about "doing better' are more apt to do better at job-hunting, to set moderate, achievable goals for themselves, to dislike gambling (because they get no achievement satisfaction from success), and to prefer work situations where they can tell easily whether they are improving or not. But why some people and not others come to think this way is another question. The evidence suggests it is not because they are born that way, but because of special training they get in the home from parents who set moderately high achievement goals but who are warm, encouraging and nonauthoritarian in helping their children reach these goals.

Such detailed knowledge about one motive helps correct a lot of common sense ideas about human motivation. For example, much public policy (and much business policy) is based on the simpleminded notion that people will work harder "if they have to." As a first approximation, the idea isn't totally wrong, but it is only a half-truth. The majority of unemployed workers in Erie "had to" find work as much as those with higher *n* Ach, but they certainly didn't work as hard at it. Or again, it is frequently assumed that *any* strong motive will lead to doing things better. Wouldn't it be fair to say that most of the Erie workers were just "unmotivated"? But our detailed knowledge of various human motives shows that each one leads a person to behave in *different ways*. The contrast is not between being "motivated" or "unmotivated" but between being motivated toward A or toward B or C, etc.

A simple experiment makes the point nicely: subjects were told that they could choose as a working partner either a close friend or a stranger who was known to be an expert on the problem to be solved. Those with higher *n* Ach (more "need to achieve") chose the experts over their friends, whereas those with more *n* Aff (the "need to affiliate with others") chose friends over experts. The latter were not "unmotivated"; their desire to be with someone they liked was simply a stronger motive than their desire to excel at the task. Other such needs have been studied by psychologists. For instance, the need for Power is often confused with the need for Achievement because both may lead to "outstanding" activities. There is a distinct difference. People with a strong need for Power want to command attention, get recognition, and control others. They are more active in political life and tend to busy themselves primarily with controlling the channels of communication both up to the top and down to the people so that they are more "in charge." Those with high *n* Power are not as concerned with improving their work performance daily as those with high *n* Ach.

It follows, from what we have been able to learn, that not all "great achievers" score high in *n* Ach. Many generals, outstanding politicians, great research scientists do not, for instance, because their work requires other personality characteristics, other motives. A general or a politician must be more concerned with power relationships, a research scientist must be able to go for long periods without the immediate feedback the person with high *n* Ach requires, etc. On the other hand, business executives, particularly if they are in positions of real responsibility or if they are salesmen, tend to score high in *n* Ach. This is true even in a Communist country like Poland: apparently there, as well as in a private enterprise economy, a manager suceeds if he is concerned about improving all the time, setting moderate goals, keeping track of his or the company's performance, etc.

Motivation and Half-Truths

Since careful study has shown that common sense notions about motivation are at best half-truths, it also follows that you cannot trust what people tell you about their motives. After all, they often get their ideas about their own motives from common sense. Thus a general may say he is interested in achievement (because he has obviously achieved), or a businessman that he is interested only in making money (because he has made money), or one of the majority of unemployed in Erie that he desperately wants a job (because he knows he needs one); but a careful check of what each one thinks about and how he spends his time may show that each is concerned about quite different things. It requires special measurement techniques to identify the presence of n Ach and other such motives. Thus what people say and believe is not very closely related to these "hidden" motives which seem to affect a person's "style of life" more than his political, religious or social attitudes. Thus n Ach produces enterprising men among labor leaders or managers, Republicans or Democrats, Catholics or Protestants, capitalists or Communists.

Wherever people begin to think often in n Ach terms, things begin to move. Men with higher n Ach get more raises and are promoted more rapidly, because they keep actively seeking ways to do a better job. Companies with many such men grow faster. In one comparison of two firms in Mexico, it was discovered that all but one of the top executives of a fast growing firm had higher n Ach scores than the highest scoring executive in an equally large but slow-growing firm. Countries with many such rapidly growing firms tend to show above-average rates of economic growth. This appears to be the reason why correlations have regularly been found between the n Ach content in popular literature (such as popular songs or stories in children's textbooks) and subsequent rates of national economic growth. A nation which is thinking about doing better all the time (as shown in its popular literature) actually does do better economically speaking. Careful quantitative studies have shown this to be true in Ancient Greece, in Spain in the Middle Ages, in England from 1400–1800, as well as among contemporary nations, whether capitalist or Communist, developed or underdeveloped.

Contrast these two stories for example. Which one contains more n Ach? Which one reflects a state of mind which ought to lead to harder striving to improve the way things are?

Excerpt from story A (4th grade reader): "Don't Ever Owe a Man—The world is an illusion. Wife, children, horses and cows are all just ties of fate. They are ephemeral. Each after fulfilling his part in life disappears. So we should not clamour after riches which are not permanent. As long as we live it is wise not to have any attachments and just think of God. We have to spend our lives without trouble, for is it not time that there is an end to grievances? So it is better to live knowing the real state of affairs. Don't get entangled in the meshes of family life."

Excerpt from story B (4th grade reader): "How I Do Like to Learn—I was sent to an accelerated technical high school. I was so happy I cried. Learning is not very easy. In the beginning I couldn't understand what the teacher taught us. I always got a red cross mark on my papers. The boy sitting next to me was very enthusiastic and also an outstanding student. When he found I could not do the problems he offered to show me how he had done them. I could not copy his work. I must learn through my own reasoning. I gave his paper back and explained I had to do it myself. Sometimes I worked on a problem until midnight. If I couldn't finish, I started early in the morning. The red cross marks on my work were getting less common. I conquered my difficulties. My marks rose. I graduated and went on to college.''

Most readers would agree, without any special knowledge of the *n* Ach coding system, that the second story shows more concern with improvement than the first, which comes from a contemporary reader used in Indian public schools. In fact the latter has a certain Horatio Alger quality that is reminiscent of our own McGuffey readers of several generations ago. It appears today in the textbooks of Communist China. It should not, therefore, come as a surprise if a nation like Communist China, obsessed as it is with improvement, tended in the long run to outproduce a nation like India, which appears to be more fatalistic.

The *n* Ach level is obviously important for statesmen to watch and in many instances to try to do something about, particularly if a nation's economy is lagging. Take Britain, for example. A generation ago (around 1925) it ranked fifth among 25 countries where children's readers were scored for *n* Ach—and its economy was doing well. By 1950 the *n* Ach lvel had dropped to 27th out of 39 countries—well below the world average—and today, its leaders are feeling the severe economic effects of this loss in the spirit of enterprise.

Economics and *n* Ach

If psychologists can detect *n* Ach levels in individuals or nations, particularly before their effects are widespread, can't the knowledge somehow be put to use to foster economic development? Obviously detection or diagnosis is not enough. What good is it to tell Britain (or India for that matter) that it needs more *n* Ach, a greater spirit of enterprise? In most such cases, informed observers of the local scene know very well that such a need exists, though they may be slower to discover it than the psychologist hovering over *n* Ach scores. What is needed is some method of developing *n* Ach in individuals or nations.

Since about 1960, psychologists in my research group at Harvard have been experimenting with techniques designed to accomplish this goal, chiefly among business executives whose work requires the action characteristics of people with high *n* Ach. Initially, we had real doubts as to whether we could succeed, partly because like most American psychologists we have been strongly influenced by the psychoanalytic view that basic motives are laid down in childhood and cannot really be changed later, and partly because many studies of intensive psychotherapy and counseling have shown minor if any long-term personality effects. On the other hand we were encouraged by the nonprofessionals: those enthusiasts like Dale Carnegie, the Communist ideologue or the Church missionary, who felt they could change adults and in fact seemed to be doing so. At any rate we ran some brief (7 to 10 days) "total push" training courses for businessmen, designed to increase their *n* Ach.

Four Main Goals

In broad outline the courses had four main goals: (1) They were designed to teach the participants how to think, talk and act like a person with high *n* Ach, based on our knowledge of such people gained through 17 years of research.

For instance, individuals learned how to make up stories that would code high in *n* Ach (i.e., how to think in *n* Ach terms), how to set moderate goals for themselves in the ring toss game (and in life). (2) The courses stimulated the participants to set higher but carefully planned and realistic work goals for themselves over the next two years. Then we checked back with them every six months to see how well they were doing in terms of their own objectives. (3) The courses also utilized techniques for giving the participants knowledge about themselves. For instance, in playing the ring toss game, they could observe that they behaved differently from others—perhaps in refusing to adjust a goal downward after failure. This would then become a matter for group discussion and the man would have to explain what he had in mind in setting such unrealistic goals. Discussion could then lead on to what a person's ultimate goals in life were, how much he cared about actually improving performance v. making a good impression or having many friends. In this way the participants would be freer to realize their achievement goals without being blocked by old habits and attitudes. (4) The courses also usually created a group *esprit de corps* from learning about each other's hopes and fears, successes and failures, and from going through an emotional experience together, away from everyday life, in a retreat setting. This membership in a new group helps a person achieve his goals, partly because he knows he has their sympathy and support and partly because he knows they will be watching to see how well he does. The same effect has been noted in other therapy groups like Alcoholics Anonymous. We are not sure which of these course "inputs" is really absolutely essential—that remains a research question—but we were taking no chances at the outset in view of the general pessimism about such efforts, and we wanted to include any and all techniques that were thought to change people.

The courses have been given: to executives in a large American firm, and in several Mexican firms; to underachieving high school boys; and to businessmen in India from Bombay and from a small city—Kakinada in the state of Andhra Pradesh. In every instance save one (the Mexican case), it was possible to demonstrate statistically, some two years later, that the men who took the course had done better (made more money, got promoted faster, expanded their businesses faster) than comparable individuals who did not take the course or who took some other management course.

Consider the Kakinada results, for example. In the two years preceding the course 9 men, 18 percent of the 52 participants, had shown "unusual" enterprise in their businesses. In the 18 months following the course 25 of the individuals, in other words nearly 50 percent, were unusually active. And this was not due to a general upturn of business in India. Data from a control city, some forty-five miles away, show the same base rate of "unusually active" men as in Kakinada before the course—namely, about 20 percent. Something clearly happened in Kakinada: the owner of a small radio shop started a chemical plant; a banker was so successful in making commercial loans in an enterprising way that he was promoted to a much larger branch of his bank in Calcutta; the local political leader accomplished his goal (it was set in the course) to get the federal government to deepen the harbor and make it into an all-weather port; plans are far along for establishing a steel rolling mill, etc. All this took place without any substantial capital input from the outside. In fact, the only costs were for four 10-day courses plus some brief follow-up visits every six months. The men are raising their own capital and using their own resources for getting business and industry moving in a city that had been considered stagnant and unenterprising.

The promise of such a method of developing achievement motivation seems very great. It has obvious applications in helping underdeveloped countries, or "pockets of poverty" in the United States, to move faster economically. It has great potential for businesses that need to "turn around" and take a more enterprising approach toward their growth and development. It may even be helpful in developing more *n* Ach among low-income groups. For instance, data show that lower-class Black Americans have a very low level of *n* Ach. This is not surprising. Society has systematically discouraged and blocked their achievement striving. But as the barriers to upward mobility are broken down, it will be necessary to help stimulate the motivation that will lead them to take advantage of new opportunities opening up.

Extreme Reactions

But a word of caution: Whenever I speak of this research and its great potential, audience reaction tends to go to opposite extremes. Either people remain skeptical and argue that motives can't really be changed, that all we are doing is dressing Dale Carnegie up in fancy "psychologese," or they become converts and want instant course descriptions by return mail to solve their local motivational problems. Either response is unjustified. What I have described here in a few pages has taken 20 years of patient research effort, and hundreds of thousands of dollars in basic research costs. What remains to be done will involve even larger sums and more time for development to turn a promising idea into something of wide practical utility.

Encouragement Needed

To take only one example, we have not yet learned how to develop *n* Ach really well among low-income groups. In our first effort—a summer course for bright underachieving 14-year-olds—we found that boys from the middle class improved steadily in grades in school over a two-year period, but boys from the lower class showed an improvement after the first year followed by a drop back to their beginning low grade average (see the accompanying chart). Why? We speculated that it was because they moved back into an environment in which neither parents nor friends encouraged achievement or upward mobility. In other words, it isn't enough to change a man's motivation if the environment in which he lives doesn't support at least to some degree his new efforts. Negroes striving to rise out of the ghetto frequently confront this problem: they are often faced by skepticism at home and suspicion on the job, so that even if their *n* Ach is raised, it can be lowered again by the heavy odds against their success. We must learn not only to raise *n* Ach but also to find methods

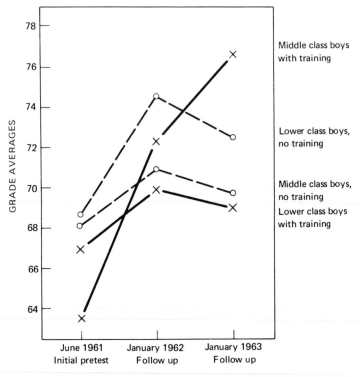

GRADE AVERAGES

Middle class boys
with training

Lower class boys,
no training

Middle class boys,
no training

Lower class boys
with training

June 1961   January 1962   January 1963
Initial pretest   Follow up   Follow up

In a Harvard study, a group of underachieving 14-year-olds was given a six-week course designed to help them do better in school.

Some of the boys were also given training in achievement motivation, or *n* Ach (solid lines). As graph reveals, the only boys who continued to improve after a two-year period were the middle-class boys with the special *n* Ach training.

Psychologists suspect the lower-class boys dropped back, even with *n* Ach training, because they returned to an environment in which neither parents nor friends encouraged achievement.

of instructing people in how to manage it, to create a favorable environment in when it can flourish.

Many of these training techniques are now only in the pilot testing stage. It will take time and money to perfect them, but society should be willing to invest heavily in them in view of their tremendous potential for contribution to human betterment.

THE NEED FOR CLOSE RELATIONSHIPS
AND THE MANAGER'S JOB

RICHARD E. BOYATZIS

The results of research on the affiliative motive are somewhat contradictory although they tend to relate high levels of this motive with poor performance as a manager. Boyatzis (1972) proposed a new theory of affiliation motivation in which he claimed there are two forms of the motive: one is called *affiliative assurance* and the other *affiliative interest*. With these types of affiliation motivation in mind, prior findings are reconciled into clear patterns of behavior: one would lead to effective performance of a manager's job, and the other would not.

The Manager and His Subordinate

Past research on the affiliation motive has shown that a person with a high level of that motive would act in some ways which are necessary to a manager's job, such as communicating with others and understanding their feelings. Such a person may also exhibit behavior which inhibits the manager in effectively performing his job, such as seeking the approval of subordinates.

A corporate unit or "spin-off" (research and development organizations, in particular) headed by a manager with a high need for affiliation does not do as well as do other similar organizations (Harris, 1969; Wainer and Rubin, 1969). Such a manager prefers to work in collaboratively structured groups and in a relaxed atmosphere (deCharms, 1957; French, 1955). Both of these situational factors are often difficult to establish because of economic pressures and requirements of the marketplace.

A manager with a high need for affiliation would strive for approval from his subordinates and superiors (Byrne, 1961), he would be sensitive to others' facial expressions and their feelings (Atkinson and Walker, 1956), and if the manager and his subordinate were to disagree, the manager would change his attitude to one which was more acceptable to the subordinate's, especially if the manager likes the subordinate (Burdick and Burnes, 1958; Byrne, 1961).

If this manager with a high need for affiliation were given a choice as to which of his subordinates he would like to work with on a task, he would choose the subordinate with whom he has a close, friendly relationship—even if this person were less competent to perform the task than another subor-

Prepared specifically for this volume.

dinate (French 1956). He would also choose a subordinate less likely to reject his offer, rather than choose a more qualified subordinate (Rosenfeld, 1964).

The manager with a high need for affiliation is so concerned about his relationships that performance objectives of his job become confused. The goal of building and maintaining friendly relations supersedes a concern over the effectiveness of his organizational unit's performance toward corporate objectives. But, he sincerely believes that friendly relations are *necessary* to healthy corporate performance.

In contrast to these findings, several studies have shown that a person with affiliation motivation demonstrates behavior which contributes to the effectiveness of corporate performance. Lawrence and Lorsch (1967) report that effective "integrators" (managers whose function is to integrate the work of various people or units) rank higher in the need for affiliation than their less effective peers.

Kolb and Boyatzis (1970) showed that people who were effective at helping others change their behavior were higher in the need for affiliation than their less effective counterparts. This is relevant because one of the manager's functions is to "help" his subordinates develop their behavioral skills to more effectively perform their present job, as well as to aid the subordinate in planning his career development.

After several days with this effective affiliation motivated manager, you would notice that he spent more time communicating with subordinates (Noujaim, 1968) and writing, calling, and visiting friends (Lansing and Heyns, 1959) than would other managers you know. The disposition to communicate with others is a critical aspect of the manager's job. Without that communication, it is very difficult to integrate people's efforts in a manner which builds their commitment to their work.

The evidence is somewhat contradictory. On the one hand, managers with high affiliation motivation exhibit behavior which interferes with their job and the poor performance of their organizational units show it. On the other hand, aspects of a manager's job require some of the behavior demonstrated by a person with affiliation motivation. Is it a matter of degree—i.e., do managers who show ineffective behavior stemming from affiliative concerns have levels of affiliation motivation which are too high? Or is it a function of the way in which they experience and express their affiliation motive?

Grasping or Concern?

A manager may have a low, moderate, or high concern about close relationships relative to his other concerns, such as concerns about having impact on others, prestige or reputation, attempting to do better against a standard of excellence, or doing something unique, to mention a few.

Affiliative concerns which are moderate or high with respect to other concerns may lead a manager to increase the performance of his unit and develop commitment in his subordinates, or it may cause him to act in a way which interferes with his job. The difference in the effects of a person's affiliative motive is determined by the *type* of affiliation motive.

As a result of methodological and conceptual difficulties, I contend that the research on the need for affiliation taps primarily the *affiliative assurance* form of the motive. The early experiments performed in an attempt to develop

a method of measuring the need for affiliation based their research on a definition of affiliation motive as a striving for close relationships in the sense of
security needs (Shipley and Veroff, 1952; Atkinson, Heyns, and Veroff, 1954).
The arousal of the motive in these studies consisted of having individual
members of fraternities stand, while others in his group described them on an
adjective checklist (used in two studies), or using people adversely affected by
being rejected from a fraternity during a rush period (used in one study). Both
techniques bias the measuring system in a way which causes the measure of affiliation motivation to tap the person's concerns about being evaluated, being
accepted or rejected more than his unanxious concerns about being a part of
close relations. The component of anxiety about being rejected or negatively
evaluated by friends was probably present in people who participated in the
studies.

A preliminary attempt to separate the affiliative assurance motive from the
affiliative interest motive demonstrated support for the theory, but lacked
enough substantial results to consider it a definitive theoretical and
methodological solution to the problem of measuring affiliation motives
(Boyatzis, 1972). The support found did confirm the basic notion that the two
forms exist, and they do determine different forms of interpersonal behavior.

A manager with a high affiliative assurance motive will basically be concerned about obtaining assurance as to the security and strength of his close
relations. He will be anxious about not being rejected. This concern leads him
to look for "proof" of others' commitments to him and to avoid issues or conflict which may threaten the stability of the relationship. He would tend to be
jealous or possessive of his subordinates (and possibly of his superior), search
for communications which support the closeness of the relationship, and look
for signs of approval from the others around him. He would avoid conflict
situations by smoothing things over, or abdicating his role in intervening to
resolve the conflict. *It is this assurance form of affiliation motivation which
would interfere with a person's work as a manager.* It would be his "grasping"
onto close relationships which would drain his energy and absorb his time. He
would spend time seeking approval and security, rather than doing his job.

The manager with an assurance motive would be concerned about the subordinate's feelings toward him and the job. He would be looking for acceptance
and approval from the subordinate. This manager would equate the subordinate's happiness in the job with acceptance of the manager as a person, and
would not feel comfortable confronting the subordinate with negative feedback on job performance. He might even ignore this type of information to
avoid the interpersonal situation of telling the subordinate. The rules of
behavior in his relationship to his subordinates would include much concern
but little openness—for example, the subordinate would not be allowed to
disagree with the manager or give him negative feedback because it would
threaten the relationship.

The manager would not look forward to a transfer or promotion of him or
his subordinates, but, instead would like to keep them all in the family. The
objectives of this manager's organizational unit would be ambiguous to his
subordinates. Although corporate objectives would be evident, the manager
would actually be spending time working on the relationships, and at times, at
the expense of performance objectives.

The manager with predominantly an affiliative interest motive would want the subordinate to feel a part of a human organization. The rules of behavior in his relationships would include interpersonal concern and openness, and because the relationship was in the context of the whole organization, there would be a sense of closeness evolved from working together toward performance objectives. This would not threaten, or diminish, the manager's feelings of closeness to his subordinates.

This type of manager could evaluate a subordinate's piece of work, give him negative or positive feedback, and not communicate a positive or negative overall evaluation of the subordinate as a person. As a result of the openness and concern over the subordinate's welfare, a climate of trust would be established which would encourage the subordinate to make his motives or concerns clear to the manager. This would enable the manager to direct the subordinate's work more effectively, designing his subordinate's job in a manner which responded to his motives or concerns.

Such a manager would be enthusiastic about the transfer or promotion of one of his subordinates, not feeling the separation as a loss and would look forward to establishing a close relationship with a new subordinate.

It is the affiliative interest form of the motive which would lead to increased managerial effectiveness. Such a person's show of "concern" would not occur at the expense of goal-oriented behavior.

Most organizational theorists emphasize the importance of personnel feeling as a part of an organization. The manager with an affiliative interest motive can stimulate those feelings on a human level by making it clear that the subordinate's thoughts and feelings are important to him. The manager with an assurance motive has a tendency to confuse his subordinates. They are not sure whether the quality of interpersonal relationships is the most important factor on the job, or if it is performance toward organizational objectives. The objectives of this manager's performance are often toward building and maintaining a set of close relationships.

In his relationship to his superior, the manager with an assurance motive would be looking for approval and acceptance. He would exaggerate in his mind the relevance of positive feedback and would tend to ignore negative feedback. With some negative feedback, he might assume that the superior did not like him as a person and he would not utilize the information to improve performance, but begin to withdraw from the job.

He would do things which would please the superior and make him notice. Constantly seeking more personal contact, such a manager would not take moderate risks in job assignments and would prefer to stay away from challenging tasks which might result in failure. He might also do the opposite, which is to accept task assignments which are high-risk (challenging, but hardly attainable) in the hope that if he succeeds, his superior would appreciate him greatly.

The manager with an affiliative interest motive would be able to separate interpersonal relationships and job performance issues. Feedback to him, or from him to his superior, could be related to a task and not have implications for the future quality of their relationship. Informal meetings with the interest-type manager and his superior would be more relaxed than such encounters with an assurance-type manager.

The reader should remember that the afflilation motive is but one of many motives of the individual. The character of the person's affiliative motive will interact with his other motives in a variety of ways. Providing a person who has either type of affiliative motive with a warm, interpersonal environment in which to work will stimulate him. In particular, a person with an assurance motive will not be able to devote energy to objectives other than maintaining relationships if he does not feel like an accepted part of the organizational unit. A manager with such a motive may find it difficult to stimulate goal-oriented thinking and behavior in his subordinates because of his needs.

Toward a Genuine Concern

Managers with relatively low concerns about close relationships compared to other concerns will find the performance of their organizational unit increasing and turnover decreasing if they develop the ability to demonstrate genuine concern toward others around them.

Managers with high affiliative assurance motives would find the performance of their units increasing if they could realize that people around them do not necessarily want to reject them. Their relationships are a part of a work organization whose main objectives are performance toward corporate objectives. The concerns for assurance are this manager's needs, not his subordinates' or superior's needs.

A healthy and productive organization is a humane effort toward corporate performance objectives. By increasing the behavior which would appear to emanate from an affiliative interest motive, a manager will create a climate of interpersonal concern and trust which builds the capability of the organization to reach its objectives and grow.

References

J. W. Atkinson, R. W. Heyns, and J. Veroff, "The Effect of Experimental Arousal of the Affiliation Motive on Thematic Apperception," *Journal of Abnormal and Social Psychology,* 1954, *49,* 405–410.

J. W. Atkinson and Walker, "The Affiliation Motive and Percpetual Sensitivity to Faces," *Journal of Abnormal and Social Psychology,* 1956, *53,* 38–41.

R. E. Boyatzis, "A Two-Factor Theory of Affiliation Motivation" (unpublished doctoral dissertation, Harvard University, 1972).

H. A Burdick and A. J. Burnes, "A Test of 'Strain Toward Symmetry' Theories," *Journal of Abnormal and Social Psychology,* 1958, *57,* 367–370.

D. Byrne, "Anxiety and the Experimental Arousal of the Affiliation Need," *Journal of Abnormal and Social Psychology,* 1961, *63,* 660–662.

D. Byrne, "Interpersonal Attraction as a Function of Affiliation Need and Attitude Similarity," *Human Relations,* 1961, *14,* 283–289.

R. deCharms, "Affiliation Motivation and Productivity in Small Groups," *Journal of Abnormal and Social Psychology,* 1957, *55,* 222–226.

E. G. French, "Some Characteristics of Achievement Motivation," *Journal of Experimental Psychology,* 1955, *50,* 232–236.

E. G. French, "Motivation as a Variable in Work Partner Selection," *Journal of Abnormal and Social Psychology,* 1956, *53,* 96–99.

H. Harris, "An Experimental Model of the Effectiveness of Project Management Offices" (unpublished Master's dissertation. Massachusetts Institute of Technology, 1969).

D. A. Kolb and R. E. Boyatzis, "On the Dynamics of the Helping Relationship," *Journal of Applied Behavioral Sciences,* 1970.

J. B. Lansing and R. W. Heyns, "Need for Affiliation and Four Types of Communication," *Journal of Abnormal and Social Psychology,* 1959, *58,* 365–372.

P. R. Lawrence and J. W. Lorsch, "New Management Job: The Integrator," *Harvard Business Review,* 1967, *45,* 142–151.

K. Noujaim, "Some Motivational Determinants of Effort Allocation and Performance" (unpublished doctoral dissertation. Massachusetts Institute of Technology, 1968).

H. Rosenfeld, "Social Choice Conceived as a Level of Aspiration," *Journal of Abnormal and Social Psychology,* 1964, *3,* 491–499.

T. E. Shipley and J. Veroff, "A Projective Measure of Need for Affiliation," *Journal of Experimental Psychology,* 1952, *43,* 349–356.

H. A. Wainer and I. M. Rubin, "Motivation of Research and Development Entrepreneurs," *Journal of Applied Psychology,* 1969, *53,* 178–184.

4 personal growth and career development

THE INDIVIDUAL, THE ORGANIZATION, AND THE CAREER: A CONCEPTUAL SCHEME

EDGAR H. SCHEIN

Introduction

The purpose of this paper is to present a conceptual scheme and a set of variables which make possible the description and analysis of an individual's movement through an organization. We usually think of this set of events in terms of the word "career," but we do not have readily available concepts for describing the multitude of separate experiences and adventures which the individual encounters during the life of his organizational career. We also need concepts which can articulate the relationship between (1) the career seen as a set of attributes and experiences of the *individual* who joins, moves through, and finally leaves an organization, and (2) the career as defined by the *organization*—a set of expectations held by individuals inside the organization which guide their decisions about whom to move, when, how, and at what "speed." It is in the different perspectives which are held toward careers by those who act them out and those who make decisions about them, that one may find some of the richest data for understanding the relationship between individuals and organizations.

The ensuing discussion will focus first on structural variables, those features of the organization, the individual, and the career which are the more or less stable elements. Then we will consider a number of "process" variables which will attempt to describe the dynamic interplay between parts of the organization and parts of the individual in the context of his ongoing career. Basically there are two kinds of processes to consider: 1) the influence of the organization on the individual, which can be thought of as a type of *acculturation* or

The ideas in this paper derive from research conducted from 1958–1964 with funds from the Office of Naval Research, Contract NONR 1841 (83) and subsequently with funds from the Sloan Research Fund, M.I.T. Reprinted from Sloan School of Management, M.I.T., Working Paper No. 326-68, with permission of Edgar H. Schein.

adult socialization; and 2) the influence of the individual on the organization, which can be thought of as a process of *innovation* (Schein, 1968).

Both socialization and innovation involve the relationship between the individual and the organization. They differ in that the former is initiated by the organization and reflects the relatively greater power of the social system to induce change in the individual, whereas the latter is initiated by the individual and reflects his power to change the social system. Ordinarily these two processes are discussed as if they were mutually exclusive of each other and as if they reflected *properties* of the organization or the individual. Thus certain organizations are alleged to produce conformity in virtually all of their members, while certain individuals are alleged to have personal strengths which make them innovators wherever they may find themselves. By using the concept of career as a process over time which embodies many different kinds of relationships between an organization and its members, I hope it can be shown that typically the same person is both influenced (socialized) and in turn influences (innovates), and that both processes coexist (though at different points in the life of a career) within any given organization.

I. The Structure of the Organization

Organizations such as industrial concerns, government agencies, schools, fraternities, hospitals, and military establishments which have a continuity beyond the individual careers of their members can be characterized structurally in many different ways. The particular conceptual model one chooses will depend on the purposes which the model is to fulfill. The structural model which I would like to propose for the analysis of careers is not intended to be a general organizational model; rather, it is designed to elucidate that side of the organization which involves the movement of people through it.

My basic proposition is that the organization should be conceived of as a three-dimensional space like a cone or cylinder in which the external vertical surface is essentially round and in which a core or inner center can be identified. What we traditionally draw as a pyramidal organization on organization charts should really be drawn as a cone in which the various boxes of the traditional chart would represent adjacent sectors of the cone but where movement would be possible within each sector toward or away from the center axis of the cone. Figure 1 shows a redrawing of a typical organization chart according to the present formulation.

Movement within the organization can then occur along three conceptually distinguishable dimensions:

1. *Vertically*—corresponding roughly to the notation of increasing or decreasing one's *rank* or *level* in the organization;
2. *Radially*—corresponding roughly to the notion of increasing or decreasing one's *centrality* in the organization, one's degree of being more or less "on the inside";
3. *Circumferentially*—corresponding roughly to the notion of changing one's function or one's division of the organization.

Whether movement along one of these dimensions is ever independent of movement along another one is basically an empirical matter. For present purposes it is enough to establish that it would be, in principle, possible for an in-

FIGURE 1
A Three Dimensional Model of an Organization

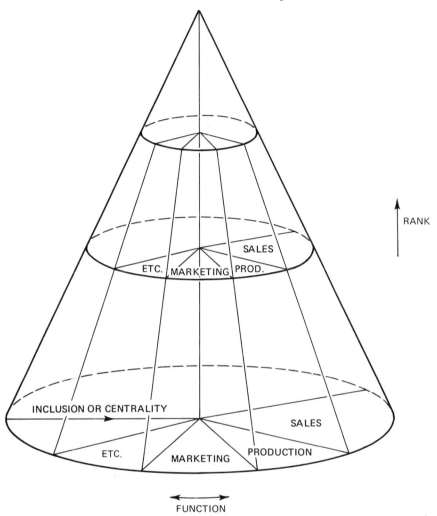

dividual to move along any one of the dimensions without changing his position on either of the other ones.

Corresponding to the three types of movement one can identify three types of *boundaries* which characterize the internal structure of the organization:

1. *Hierarchical boundaries*—which separate the hierarchical levels from each other;

2. *Inclusion boundaries*—which separate individuals or groups who differ in the degree of the centrality;[1]

3. *Functional or departmental boundaries*—which separate departments, divisions, or different functional groupings from each other.

[1]The organization as a multi-layered system corresponds to Lewin's concept of the personality as a multi-layered system like an onion (Lewin, 1948).

Boundaries can vary in (1) *number,* (2) *degree of permeability,* and (3) type of *filtering properties* they possess. For example, in the military there are a great many functional boundaries separating the different line and staff activities, but the overall policy of rotation and keeping all officers highly flexible makes these boundaries highly permeable in the sense that people move a great deal from function to function. On the other hand, a university would also have many functional boundaries corresponding to the different academic departments, but these would be highly impermeable in the sense that no one would seriously consider the movement of an English professor to a Chemistry department, or vice versa. A small family-run business, to take a third example, is an organization with very few functional boundaries in that any manager performs all of the various functions.

Similarly, with respect to hierarchical or inclusion boundaries one can find examples of organizations in which there are many or few levels, many or few degrees of "being in," with the boundaries separating the levels or inner regions being more or less permeable. The external inclusion boundary is, of course, of particular significance, in that its permeability defined the ease or difficulty of initial entry into the organization. Those companies or schools which take in virtually anyone but keep only a small percentage of high performers can be described as having a highly permeable external inclusion boundary, but a relatively impermeable inclusion boundary fairly close to the exterior. On the other hand, the company or school which uses elaborate selection procedures to take in only very few candidates, expects those taken in to succeed, and supports them accordingly, can be described as having a relatively impermeable external inclusion boundary but no other impermeable boundaries close to the exterior.

Further refinement can be achieved in this model if one considers the particular types of filters which characterize different boundaries, i.e., which specify the process or set of rules by which one passes through the boundary. Thus hierarchical boundaries filter individuals in terms of attributes such as seniority, merit, personal characteristics, types of attitudes held, who is sponsoring them, and so on. Functional boundaries filter much more in terms of the specific competencies of the individual, or his "needs" for broader experience in some scheme of training and development (the latter would certainly not be considered in reference to a hierarchical boundary). Inclusion boundaries are probably the most difficult to characterize in terms of their filtering system in that the system may change as one gets closer to the inner core of the organization. Competence may be critical in permeating the external boundary, but factors such as personality, seniority, and willingness to play a certain kind of political game may be critical in becoming a member of the "inner circle."[2] Filter properties may be formally stated requirements for admission or may be highly informal norms shared by the group to be entered.

With reference to individual careers, organizations can be analyzed and described on the basis of (1) number of boundaries of each type, (2) the boundary permeability of the different boundaries, and (3) the filtering system which characterizes them. For example, most universities have two hierarchical boundaries (between the ranks of assistant, associate, and full professor), two inclusion boundaries (for initial entry and tenure), and as many functional

[2]One of the best descriptions of such filters in an organization can be found in Dalton's (1959) discussion of career advancement in the companies to be studied.

90

boundaries as there are departments and schools. Filters for promotion and tenure may or may not be the same depending on the university, but will generally involve some combination of scholarly or research publication, teaching ability, and "service" to the institution. Organizations like industrial ones which do not have a tenure system will be harder to diagnose as far as inclusion filters go, but the inclusion boundaries are just as much a part of their system. The variables identified thus far are basically intended as a set of categories in terms of which to describe and compare different types of organizations in respect to the career paths they generate.

A final variable which needs to be considered is the *shape* of the three-dimensional space which characterizes the organization. The traditional pyramidal organization would presumably become in this scheme a cone. An organization with very many levels could be thought of as a very steep cone, while one with few levels could be thought of as a flat cone. The drawing of the organization as a cone implies, however, that the highest level person is also the most central which is, of course, not necessarily the case. If the top of the organization is a management team, one might think of a truncated cone; if there is a powerful board of directors who represent a higher level but a wider range of centrality one might think of an inverted cone, the point of which touches the apex of the main cone and which sits on top of the main one. In universities where the number of full professors is as large as the number of assistant professors, one might think of the organization more as a cylinder with a small cone on top of it representing the administration.

I am not stating any requirements that the shape of the organization be symmetrical. If a certain department is very large but very peripheral, it might best be thought of as a large bulge on an otherwise round shape. If one considers internal inclusion boundaries one may have some departments which are in their entirety very central and thus reach the vertical axis (core), while other departments do not contain anyone who is very central in the organization and thus do not reach the core at all. The shape of the inner core is also highly variable. It may be an inverted cone which would imply that the number of central people *increases* with rank. Or it might be a cylinder which would imply that there are equal numbers of central people at all ranks. Or it might be some highly asymmetrical shape reflecting the reality that the number of central people varies with length of service, department, political connections with higher ranks, access to critical company informations, etc.[3]

Some Problems of Measuring Organizational Structure

The problem of measurement varies greatly as a function of the degree to which boundaries and their filtering characteristics are explicitly acknowledged by a given organization and by wider society. Thus, hierarchical boundaries which separate levels are a widely accepted fact of organizational life and the rules for permeating them tend to be fairly explicit. To the extent that implicit informal factors do operate it becomes more difficult to measure the filtering properties of the hierarchical boundaries in any given organization.

Functional boundaries are generally the easiest to identify because our typical analysis of organizations emphasizes different functions and depart-

[3]Dalton (1959) has identified what he calls "vertical cliques" which cover different ranks as well as departments of an industrial organization.

ments. Similarly, the rules of entry to a function or department tend to be fairly explicit.

The inclusion boundaries are the hardest to identify and measure because to a considerable extent their very existence usually remains implicit. While it may be clear to everyone in a company that there is an inner circle (which may cut across many rank levels), this fact may be denied when an outsider probes for the data. The filtering mechanism may be even more difficult to identify because even the willing informant, including members of the inner circle, may be unclear about the actual mechanisms by which people move toward the center. Even the *concept* of centrality is unclear in that it does not discriminate between (1) an individual person's *feeling* of being central or peripheral, and (2) some *objective criterion* of his actual position in the organization's social structure.

In the discussion thus far I have meant by the term "centrality" the person's objective position as measured by the degree to which company secrets are entrusted to him, by ratings of others of his position, and by his power. His subjective rating of himself might correlate highly with these other measures and thus might prove to be a simpler measuring device, but it does not basically define centrality because a person may misperceive his own position.

It may be argued that I have over-stated the assumption that the organization is an integrated unified entity. It may after all be only a group of individual people or sub-groups coordinating their activities to some degree but operating from quite different premises. Therefore there are no "organizational" boundaries, only individual approaches to the movement and promotion of their subordinates.

There is ample evidence for the assertion that people who associate with each other around a common task for any length of time *do* develop group boundaries of various sorts and a set of norms which define their probability and filtering properties (e.g., Homans, 1950). But it is quite possible that several such groups co-exist within a larger social system and develop different norms. In applying the concepts which I am outlining in this paper it is therefore necessary to identify as the "organization" a group which has interacted for a sufficient length of time to have developed some common norms. Later, in analyzing the progress of a career, it will of course be necessary to consider the difficulties which are created for the individual as he moves from a group with one set of norms about boundaries to another group with a different set of norms about boundaries, even though both groups are part of the same larger organization.

II. The Structure of the Individual

Any given individual can be thought of as a more or less integrated set of social selves organized around a basic image or concept of self. His basic temperament, intellectual equipment, learned patterns of feeling expression, and psychological defenses underlie and partially determine this self-image and the kinds of social selves which the individual constructs for himself to deal with his environment. But our focus is on the constructed selves which make it possible for the individual to fulfill various role expectations in his environment, not on the more enduring underlying qualities.

I am using the concept of a constructed social self in the sense of Mead (1934) and more recently Becker (1961) and Goffman (1955, 1957, 1959), as a set of assumptions about, perceptions of, and claims on a given social situation in which role expectations may be more or less well defined. The basic rules of conduct and interaction in terms of which the person orients himself to any social situation are largely culturally determined, but these basic rules still leave each individual a wide latitude in how he will choose to present himself in any given situation (the "line" he will take), and how much social value or status he will claim for himself (his "face").

This conception of the individual places primary emphasis on those aspects of his total being which are the most immediate product of socialization, which most immediately engage other persons in daily life, and which are most dependent on the reinforcement or confirmation of others. For example, at a *basic* level, a person may be temperamentally easily frustrated, may have developed a character structure around the repression of strong aggressive impulses, and may rely heavily on denial and reaction-formation as defense mechanisms. These characteristics describe his basic underlying personality structure but they tell us practically nothing of how he presents himself to others, what his self-image is, how he takes characteristic occupational or social roles, how much value he places on himself, and what kind of interaction patterns he engages in with others.

Focusing on his constructed selves, on the other hand, might show us that this person presents himself to others as very even tempered and mild mannered, that in group situations he takes a role of harmonizing any incipient fights which develop between others, that he tries to appear as the logical voice of reason in discussions and is made uneasy by emotions, that he prefers to analyze problems and advise others rather than getting into action situations (i.e., he prefers some kind of "staff" position), and that he does not get too close to people or depend too heavily upon them. None of the latter characteristics are inconsistent with the basic structure, but they could not have been specifically predicted from the basic structure. Persons with the same kind of underlying character structure might enter similar interactive situations quite differently. In other words, I am asserting that it is not sufficient to describe a person in terms of basic personality structure, if we are to understand his relationship to organizations. Furthermore, it is possible to analyze the person's functioning at the social self level and this level of analysis is most likely to be productive for the understanding of career patterns and the reciprocal influence process between individual and organization.

Each of us learns to construct somewhat different selves for the different kinds of situations in which we are called on to perform, and for the different kinds of roles we are expected to take. Thus, I am a somewhat different person at work than at home; I present myself somewhat differently to my superior than to my subordinate, to my wife than to my children, to my doctor than to a salesman, when I am at a party than when I am at work, and so on. The long and complex process of socialization teaches us the various norms, rules of conduct, values and attitudes, and desirable role behaviors through which one's obligations in situations and roles can be fulfilled. All of these patterns become part of us so that to a large extent we are not conscious of the almost instantaneous choices we make among possible patterns as we "compose ourselves" for entry into a new social situation. Yet these patterns can be immediately brought to consciousness if the presented self chosen is one which does not fit the situation, that is, fails to get confirmation from others.

Failure to get confirmation of a self which involves a certain claimed value is felt by the actor as a threat to his face; he finds himself in a situation in which he is about to lose face if he and the others do not take action to reequilibrate the situation (Goffman, 1955). A simple example of this process can be seen if a person presents himself to others as a humorous fellow who can tell a good joke, tries telling a joke which turns out not to be seen as funny, and "recoups" or avoids the loss of face which is threatened by the silence of others by humorously derogating his own joke telling ability, thereby signaling to the others that he is now claiming a different and somewhat less "valuable" (i.e., more humble) self. The others may signal their acceptance of the latter self by various reassurances, but all parties know very well the unmistakable meaning of the silence following the first joke.

The various selves which we bring to situations and from which we choose as we present ourselves to others, overlap in varying degrees in that many of the attributes possessed by the person are relevant to several of his selves. Thus, emotional sensitivity may be just as relevant when a person is dealing with a customer in a sales relationship as it is with his wife and children in a family relationship. The person's attributes and underlying character structure thus provide some of the common threads which run through the various social selves he constructs, and provide one basis for seeking order and consistency among them.

Another basis for such order and consistency is to be found in the role demands the person faces. That is, with respect to each role which the person takes or to which he aspires, one can distinguish certain central expectations, certain essential attributes which the person must have or certain behaviors he must be willing to engage in, in order to fulfill the role minimally (pivotal attributes or norms). Other attributes and behaviors are desirable and relevant though not necessary (*relevant* attributes or norms), while still another set can be identified as irrelevant with respect to the role under analysis, though this other set may define various "latent" role capacities the person may have (*peripheral* attributes or norms).[4] The pivotal, relevant, and peripheral attributes of a role will define to some degree the filters which operate at the boundary guarding access to that role.

These changes which occur in a person during the course of his career, as a result of adult socialization or acculturation, are changes in the nature and integration of his social selves. It is highly unlikely that he will change substantially in his basic character structure and his pattern of psychological defenses, but he may change drastically in his social selves in the sense of developing new attitudes and values, new competencies, new images of himself, and new ways of entering and conducting himself in social situations. As he faces new roles which bring new demands, it is from his repertory of attributes and skills that he constructs or reconstructs himself to meet these demands.

A final point concerns the problem of locating what we ordinarily term as the person's beliefs, attitudes, and values at an appropriate level of his total

---

[4]This analysis is based on the distinction made by Nadel (1957) and utilized in a study of outpatient nurses by Bennis *et al.* (1959).

personality. It has been adequately demonstrated (e.g., Adorno *et al.,* 1950; Smith, Bruner, and White, 1956; Katz, 1960) that beliefs, attitudes, and values are intimately related to basic character structure and psychological defenses. But this relationship differs in different people according to the functions which beliefs, attitudes, and values serve for them. Smith *et al.* distinguish three such functions: (1) *reality testing*—where beliefs and attitudes are used by the person to discover and test the basic reality around him; (2) *social adjustment*—where beliefs and attitudes are used by the person to enable him to relate comfortably to others, express his membership in groups, and his social selves; and (3) *externalization*—where beliefs and attitudes are used to express personal conflicts, conscious and unconscious motives, and feelings.

The kind of function which beliefs and attitudes serve for the individual and the kind of flexibility he has in adapting available social selves to varying role demands will define for each individual some of his strengths and weaknesses with respect to organizational demands and the particular pattern of socialization and innovation which one might expect in his career.

For example, a given individual might well have a number of highly labile social selves in which his beliefs and attitudes serve only a social adjustment function. At the same time, he might have one or more other highly stable selves in which he shows great rigidity of belief and attitude. The process of socialization might then involve extensive adaptation and change on the part of the person in his "labile" social selves without touching other more stable parts of him. He might show evidence of having been strongly influenced by the organization, but only in certain areas.[5] Whether this same person would be capable of innovating during his career would depend on whether his job would at any time call on his more stable social selves. The activation of such stable selves might occur only with promotion, the acquisition of increasing responsibility, or acceptance into a more central region of the organization.

When we think of organizations infringing on the private lives of their members we think of a more extensive socialization process which involves changes in more stable beliefs and attitudes which are integrated into more stable social selves. Clearly it is possible for such "deeper" influence to occur, but in assessing depth of influence in any given individual–organizational relationship we must be careful not to overlook adaptational patterns which look like deep influence but are only the activation of and changes in relatively more labile social selves.

Some Problems of Measuring Individual Structure

I do not know of any well worked out techniques for studying a person's repertory of social selves, their availability, lability, and associated beliefs and attitudes. Something like rating behavior during role-playing or socio-drama would be a possible method but it is difficult to produce in full force the situational and role demands which elicit from us the social selves with which we play for keeps. Assessment techniques which involve observing the person in actual ongoing situations are more promising but more expensive. It is possible that a well motivated person would find it possible to provide accurate data

---

[5]For a relevant analysis of areas which the organization is perceived to be entitled to influence, see Schein and Ott (1962) and Schein and Lippitt (1965).

through self-description, i.e., tell accurately how he behaves in situations that he typically faces.

If observation and interview both are impractical, it may be possible to obtain written self-descriptions or adjective check-list data (where the adjectives are specifically descriptive of interactional or social behavior) in response to hypothetical problem situations which are posed for the individual. The major difficulty with this technique would be that it is highly likely that much of the taking of a social self is an unconscious process which even a well motivated subject could not reconstruct accurately. Hence his data would be limited to his conscious self-perceptions. Such conscious self-perceptions could, of course, be supplemented by similar descriptions of the subject made by others.

III. The Structure of the Career

The career can be looked at from a number of points of view. The individual moving through an organization builds certain perspectives having to do with advancement, personal success, nature of the work, and so on (Becker *et al.*, 1961). Those individuals in the organization who take the "organizational" point of view, build perspectives in terms of the development of human resources, allocation of the right people to the right slots, optimum rates of movement through departments and levels, and so on. A third possible perspective which one can take toward the career is that of the outside observer of the whole process, in which case one is struck by certain basic similarities between organizational careers and other transitional processes which occur in society such as socialization, education, and acculturation of immigrants, initiation into groups, etc. If one takes this observer perspective one can describe the structure and process of the career in terms of a set of basic *stages* which create transitional and terminal *statuses* or *positions,* and involve certain psychological and organizational processes (see Table 1).

In the first column of the Table 1, I have placed the basic stages as well as the key transitional events which characterize movement from one stage to another. The terminology chosen deliberately reflects events in organizations such as schools, religious orders, or fraternities where the stages are well articulated. These same stages and events are assumed to exist and operate in industrial, governmental, and other kinds of organizations even though they are not as clearly defined or labelled. Where a stage does not exist for a given organization, we can ask what the functional equivalent of that stage is. For example, the granting of tenure and the stage of permanent membership is not clearly identified in American business or industrial concerns, yet there are powerful norms operating in most such organizations to retain employees who have reached a certain level and/or have had a certain number of years of service. These norms lead to personnel policies which on the average guarantee the employee a job and thus function as equivalents to a more formal tenure system.

It should be noted that the kind of stages and terminology chosen also reflects the assumption that career movement is basically a process of learning or socialization (during which organizational influence is at a maximum), followed by a process of performance (during which individual influence on the organization is at a maximum), followed by a process of either becoming obsolete or learning new skills which lead to further movement. These are

TABLE 1
Basic Stages, Positions, and Processes Involved in a Career

Basic Stages and Transitions	Statuses or Positions	Psychological and Organizational Processes: Transactions between Individual and Organization
1. Pre-entry	Aspirant, applicant, rushee	Preparation, education, anticipatory socialization
Entry (trans.)	Entrant, postulant, recruit	Recruitment, rushing, testing, screening, selection, acceptance ("hiring"); passage through external inclusion boundary; rites of entry; induction and orientation
2. Basic training, novitiate	Trainee, novice, pledge	Training, indoctrination, socialization, testing of the man by the organization, tentative acceptance into group
Initiation, first vows (trans.)	Initiate, graduate	Passage through first inner inclusion boundary, acceptance as member and conferring of organizational status, rite of passage and acceptance
3. First regular assignment	New member	First testing by the person of his or her own capacity to function; granting of real responsibility (playing for keeps); passage through functional boundary with assignment to specific job or department
Sub-stages 3a. Learning the job 3b. Maximum performance 3c. Becoming obsolete 3d. Learning new skills, etc.		Indoctrination and testing of person by immediate work group leading to acceptance or rejection; if accepted further education and socialization (learning the ropes); preparation for higher status through coaching, seeking visibility, finding sponsors, etc.
Promotion or leveling off (trans.)		Preparation, testing, passage through hierarchical boundary, rite of passage; may involve passage through functional boundary as well (rotation)
4. Second assignment Sub-stages	Legitimate member (fully accepted)	Processes under no. 3 repeat
5. Granting of tenure Termination and exit (trans.)	Permanent member Old timer, senior citizen	Passage through another inner conclusion boundary Preparation for exit, cooling the mark out, rites of exit (testimonial dinners, etc.)
6. Post-exit	Alumnus emeritus, retired	Granting of peripheral status

relatively broad categories which are not fully refined in the table. For example, in the case of becoming obsolete a further set of alternative stages may be provided by the organizational structure—(1) retraining for new career; (2) lateral transfer and permanent leveling off with respect to rank, but not necessarily with respect to inclusion; (3) early forced exit (early "retirement"); (4) retention in the given stage in spite of marginal performance (retaining "dead wood" in the organization).

In the second column of the table are found the kinds of terms which we use to characterize the statuses or positions which reflect the different stages of the career. In the third column I have tried to list the kinds of interactional processes which occur between the individual and the organization. These processes can be thought of as reflecting preparation of the incumbent for boundary transition, preparation of the group for his arrival, actual transition processes such as tests, rites of passage, status conferring ceremonies, and post transition processes prior to preparation for new transitions.[6]

Basically the dynamics of the career can be thought of as a *sequence of boundary passages*. The person can move up, around, and in, and every career is some sequence of moves along these three paths. Thus, it is possible to move primarily inward without moving upward or around as in the case of the janitor who has remained a janitor all of his career but, because of association with others who have risen in the hierarchy, enjoys their confidences and a certain amount of power through his opportunities to coach newcomers.

It is also possible to move primarily upward without moving inward or around, as in the case of the scarce highly trained technical specialist who must be elevated in order to be held by the organization but who is given little administrative power or confidential information outside of his immediate area. Such careers are frequently found in universities where certain scholars can become full professors without ever taking the slightest interest in the university as an organization and where they are not seen as being very central to its functioning.

The problem of the professional scientist or engineer in industry hinges precisely on this issue, in that the scientist often feels excluded in spite of "parallel ladders," high salaries, frequent promotions, and fancy titles. Moving in or toward the center of an organization implies increase in power and access to information which enables the person to influence his own destiny. The "parallel ladder" provides rank but often deprives the professional in industry of the kind of power and sense of influence which is associated with centrality.

Finally, movement around without movement in or up is perhaps most clearly exemplified in the perpetual student, or the person who tries some new skill or work area as soon as he has reasonably mastered what he had been doing. Such circumferential or lateral movement is also a way in which organizations handle those whom they are unwilling to promote or get rid of. Thus, they get transferred from one job to another, often with the polite fiction that the transfers constitute promotions of a sort.

In most cases, the career will be some combination of movement in all three dimensions—the person will have been moved up, will have had experience in several departments, and will have moved into a more central position in the organization. Whether any given final position results from smooth or even movement or represents a zig-zagging course is another aspect to consider. Because sub-cultures always tend to exist within a large organization, one may assume that any promotion or transfer results in some *temporary* loss of centrality, in that the person will not immediately be accepted by the new group into which he has been moved. In fact, one of the critical skills of getting ahead may be the person's capacity to regain a central position in any new group into which he is placed.[7] In the military service, whether a person is ultimately accepted as a good leader or not may depend upon his capacity to take a known difficult assignment in which he temporarily loses acceptance

[6]See Strauss (1959) for an excellent description of some of these processes.

[7]In a fascinating experiment with children, Merei, 1941, showed that a strong group could resist the impact of a strong leader child and force the leader child to conform to group norms, but that the skillful leader child first accepted the norms, gained acceptance and centrality, and then began to influence the group toward his own goals.

and centrality and to succeed in spite of this in gaining high productivity and allegiance from the men.

The attempt to describe the career in terms of sequential steps or stages introduces some possible distortions. For example, various of the stages may be collapsed in certain situations into a single major event. A young man may report for work and be given as his first assignment a highly responsible job, may be expected to learn as he actually performs, and is indoctrinated by his experiences at the same time that he is using them as a test of his self. The whole assignment may serve the function of an elaborate initiation rite during which the organization tests the man as well. The stages outlined in the chart all occur in one way or another, but they may occur simultaneously and thus be difficult to differentiate.

Another distortion is the implication in the chart that boundaries are crossed in certain set sequences. In reality it may be the case that the person enters a given department on a provisional basis before he has achieved any basic acceptance by the organization so that the functional boundary passage precedes inclusion boundary passage. On the other hand, it may be more appropriate to think of the person as being located in a kind of organizational limbo during his basic training, an image which certainly fits well those training programs which rotate the trainee through all of the departments of the organization without allowing him to do any real work in any of them.

A further complexity arises from the fact that each department, echelon, and power clique is a sub-organization with a sub-culture which superimposes on the major career pattern a set of, in effect, sub-careers within each of the sub-organizations. The socialization which occurs in sub-units creates difficulties or opportunities for the person to the degree that the sub-culture is well integrated with the larger organizational culture. If conflicts exist, the person must make a complex analysis of the major organizational boundaries to attempt to discover whether subsequent passage through a hierarchical boundary (promotion) for example, is more closely tied to acceptance or rejection of subcultural norms (i.e., does the filter operate more in terms of the person's capacity to show loyalty even in the face of frustration or in terms of disloyalty for the sake of larger organizational goals even though this entails larger personal risks?).

IV. Implications and Hypotheses

Thus far I have tried to develop a set of concepts and a kind of model of the organization, the individual, and the career. The kinds of concepts chosen were intended to be useful in identifying the interactions between the individual and the organization as he pursues his career within the organization. We need concepts of this sort to make it possible to compare organizations with respect to the kinds of career paths they generate, and to make it possible to describe the vicissitudes of the career itself. Perhaps the most important function of the concepts, however, is to provide an analytical frame of reference which will make it possible to generate some hypotheses about the crucial process of organizational influences on the individual (socialization) and individual influences on the organization (innovation). Using the concepts defined above, I would now like to try to state some hypotheses as a first step toward building a genuinely socio-psychological theory of career development.

Hypothesis 1. Organizational *socialization* will occur primarily in connection with the passage through hierarchical and inclusion boundaries; efforts at *education* and *training* will occur primarily in connection with the passage through functional boundaries. In both instances, the amount of effort at socialization and/or training will be at a maximum just prior to boundary passage, but will continue for some time after boundary passage.

The underlying assumption behind this hypothesis is that 1) the organization is most concerned about correct values and attitudes at the point where it is granting a member more authority and/or centrality, and 2) the individual is most vulnerable to socialization pressures just before and after boundary passage. He is vulnerable before because of the likelihood that he is anxious to move up or in and is therefore motivated to learn organizational norms and values; he is vulnerable after boundary passage because of the new role demands and his needs to reciprocate with correct attitudes and values for having been passed. It is a commonly observed organizational fact that a griping employee often becomes a devoted, loyal follower once he has been promoted and has acquired responsibility for the socialization of other employees.[8]

Hypothesis 2. Innovation, or the individual's influence on the organization, will occur *in the middle* of a given stage of the career, at a maximum distance from boundary passage.

The person must be far enough from the earlier boundary passage to have learned the requirements of the new position and to have earned centrality in the new sub-culture, yet must be far enough from his next boundary passage to be fully involved in the present job without being concerned about preparing himself for the future. Also, his power to induce change is lower if he is perceived as about to leave (the lame duck phenomenon). Attempts to innovate closer to boundary passage either will meet resistance or will produce only temporary change.

Hypothesis 3. In general, the process of socialization will be more prevalent in the early stages of a career and the process of innovation late in the career, *but both processes occur at all stages.*

Figure 2 attempts to diagram the relationships discussed above. The boundaries that are most relevant to these influence processes are the hierarchical ones in that the power of the organization to socialize is most intimately tied to the status rewards it can offer. One cannot ignore, however, the crucial role which inclusion boundaries and centrality may play in affecting the amount of socialization or innovation. If it is a correct assumption that genuinely creative innovative behavior can occur only when the person is reasonably secure in his position, this is tantamount to saying that he has to have a certain amount of acceptance and centrality to innovate. On the other hand, if the acceptance and centrality involves a sub-culture which is itself hostile to certain organizational goals, it becomes more difficult for the person to innovate (except in reference to sub-cultural norms). This is the case of the men in the production shop with fancy rigs and working routines which permit them to get the job done faster and more comfortably (thus innovating in the service of sub-group norms), yet which are guarded from management eyes and used only to make

[8]See also Lieberman (1956) for an excellent research study demonstrating attitude change after promotion.

FIGURE 2
Socialization and Innovation During the Stages of the Career

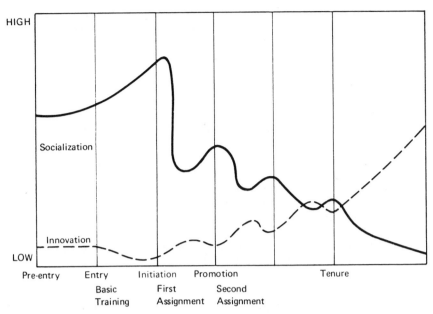

life easier for the men themselves. One thing which keeps these processes from being shared is the sub-group pressure on the individual and his knowledge that his acceptance by the sub-group hinges on his adherence to its norms. Innovation by individuals will always occur to some degree, but it does not necessarily lead to any new ideas or processes which are functional for the total organization.

Whether or not organizational innovation occurs, then becomes more a function of the degree to which sub-group norms are integrated with the norms and goals of the total organization. In complex organizations there are many forces acting which tend to make groups defensive and competitive, thus increasing the likelihood of their developing conflicting norms (Schein, 1965). Where this happens the process of innovation can still be stimulated through something akin to the "heroic cycle" by which societies revitalize themselves. Campbell shows how the myth of the hero in many cultures is essentially similar (Campbell, 1956). Some respected member of the total organization or society is sent away (freed from the sub-group norms) to find a magic gift which he must bring back to revitalize the organization. By temporarily stepping outside the organization the person can bring back new ideas and methods without directly violating sub-group norms and thus protect his own position as well as the face of the other group members.

Hypothesis 4. Socialization or influence will involve primarily the more labile social selves of the individual, while innovation will involve primarily the more stable social selves of the individual, provided the individual is not held captive in the organization.

I am assuming that if socialization forces encounter a stable part of the person which he is unable or unwilling to change, he will leave the organization if he can. On the other hand, if a given way of operating which flows from a stable portion of the individual is incompatible with other organizational procedures or norms, i.e., if innovation is impossible, the individual will also leave. The only condition under which neither of these statements would hold is the condition in which the individual is physically or psychologically unable to leave.

Hypothesis 5. A change in the more stable social selves as a result of socialization will occur only under conditions of coercive persuasion, i.e., where the individual cannot or does not psychologically feel free to leave the organization.

Conditions under which coercive persuasion would operate can be produced by a variety of factors: a tight labor market in which movement to other organizations is constrained; an employment contract which involves a legal or moral obligation to remain with the organization; a reward system which subtly but firmly entraps the individual through stock options, pension plans, deferred compensation plans and the like.

If conditions such as those mentioned above do operate to entrap the individual and, if he in turn begins to conform to organizational norms even in terms of the more stable parts of his self, he will indeed become unable to innovate. It is this pattern which has been identified by Merton as operating in bureaucratic frameworks and which writers like W. H. Whyte have decried with the label of "organizational man." It should be noted, however, that this pattern occurs only under certain conditions; it should not be confused with normal processes of socialization, those involving the more labile parts of the person's self and the more pivotal role requirements or norms of the organization.

An important corollary of this hypothesis is that if organizations wish to insure a high rate of innovation, they must also insure highly permeable external boundaries, i.e., must insure that employees feel free to leave the organization. The less permeable the exit boundary, the greater the pressures for total conformity.

Summary

In this paper I have tried to present a set of concepts about the nature of the organization, the nature of the individual, and the nature of the career—the set of events which tie the individual and the organization together. My purpose has been to provide a frame of reference and a set of concepts which would make it possible to think in more empirical terms about a variable like "career," yet which would relate this variable both to organizational and psychological variables. Using concepts such as "organizational boundaries," labile and stable "social selves," career stages and transitional processes, I have tried to identify some hypotheses about organizational influences on the individual (socialization) and individual influences on the organization (innovation).

References

Adorno, T. W. *The authoritarian personality.* New York: Harper, 1950.

Becker, H. S. *et al., Boys in white.* Chicago: University of Chicago Press, 1961.

Bennis, W. G. *et al.,* The role of the nurse in the OPD. Boston University Research Rept. No. 39, 1959.

Campbell, J. *The hero with a thousand faces.* New York: Meridian, 1956.

Dalton, M. *Men who manage.* New York: Wiley, 1959.

Goffman, E. On face work, *Psychiatry,* 1955, 18, 213–231.

Goffman, E. Alienation from interaction *Human Relations,* 1957, 10, 47–60.

Goffman, E. *The presentation of self in everyday life.* Garden City, N.Y.: Doubleday Anchor, 1959.

Homans, G. C. *The human group.* New York: Harcourt Brace, 1950.

Katz, D. (ed.) Attitude change, *Public Opinion Quarterly,* 1960, 24, 163–365.

Lewin, K. *Resolving social conflicts.* New York: Harper, 1948.

Lieberman, S. The effects of changes in roles on the attitudes of role occupants. *Human Relations,* 1956, 9, 385–402.

Mead, G. H. *Mind, self, and society.* Chicago: University of Chicago Press, 1934.

Merei, F. Group leadership and institutionalization. *Human Relations,* 1941, 2, 23–39.

Nadel, F. *The theory of social structure.* Glencoe, Ill.: Free Press, 1957.

Schein, E. H. & Ott, J. S. The legitimacy of organizational influence. *American Journal of Sociology,* 1962, 6, 682–689.

Schein, E. H. *Organizational psychology.* Englewood Cliffs, N.J.: Prentice-Hall, 1965.

Schein, E. H. & Lippitt, G. L. Supervisory attitudes toward the legitimacy of influencing subordinates. *Journal of Applied Behavioral Science,* 1966, 2, 199–209.

Schein, E. H. Organizational socialization. Industrial Management Review (M.I.T.), 1968.

Smith, M. B., Bruner, J. S., and White, R. W. *Opinions and personality,* New York: Wiley, 1956.

Strauss, A. *Mirrors and masks.* Glencoe, Ill.: Free Press, 1959.

GOAL-SETTING AND
SELF-DIRECTED BEHAVIOR CHANGE

DAVID A. KOLB

RICHARD E. BOYATZIS

Two recent developments, one theoretical and one practical, have led behavior change researchers to pay more attention to self-directed techniques of behavior change. In practice, there is a growing demand for behavioral science solutions to human problems. More and more individuals are seeing that the various forms of psychotherapy can provide viable solutions to their personal problems. In addition, social welfare agencies are seeking to change their role from that of policeman and distributor of government funds to that of an agent for individual and community development. This growing demand for the practical application of behavioral science knowledge has made practitioners painfully aware of the fact that, using the existing techniques of behavior change which are so dependent on the change agent for their success, there can never be enough professionally trained personnel to meet this demand. So in desperation the practitioner is asking, "How crucial am I in the change process? Is it possible to develop change techniques that people can use themselves?"

Until recently the theoretical answer has been no. Therapeutic models of change, both the analytic and learning theory based, have conceived of the patient as passive and reactive. In the tradition of their medical origins it is the doctor who was the active and curative agent in the therapeutic process. In an analysis of psychological journals, Allport (1960) found that psychologists exclusively used a reactive model of a man to interpret their results. In the psychologist's mind man was an animal who reacted to stimuli and who was controlled by his environment. The concept of will—man's ability to control and change his own behavior—was nowhere to be found in respectable psychological theories. The idea of self-directed change appeared only in common sense psychologies like those of Norman Vincent Peale and Dale Carnegie.

This research was supported in part by the Industrial Relations Section, Sloan School of Management, M.I.T. Computation was done at the M.I.T. Computation Center. We wish to express our appreciation to William McKelvey, Sara Winter, James Curtis and Robert Zuckerman for assistance in research design and administration, to George Farris for assistance in data interpretation, and to Robert Euritt, George Farris, Michael Fulenwider, William McKelvey, Irwin Rubin, Suresh Srivastva and Sara Winter who served as T-Group trainers, and to the students who through their efforts made this research possible.

Currently, however, there are a great number of theorists who challenge the reactive conception of man. Hartmann, Kris and Loewenstein (1947) and other ego psychologists began to reinterpret psychoanalytic theory laying increasing emphasis on the power of ego processes in the rational direction and control of one's behavior. More recently White (1957) has detailed the research evidence for pro-active, competence motivation in human beings— motives urging men and animals to ignore safety and security, and to take on new, difficult, and challenging tasks. Of this group of men it is perhaps Carl Rogers who has been most influential in applying the new growth-oriented theory of man to the practice of behavior change. He created an entirely new theory and method of psychotherapy—client-centered therapy (1951). As the name implies, in client-centered therapy the client is the active and curative agent in the therapeutic relationship. The therapist's job is to create in a nondirective way the therapeutic conditions which will facilitate self-inquiry and personal growth in the client. By emphasizing man's creative and problem-solving abilities and his growth potential the pro-active theorists imply that self-directed change is not only theoretically possible but that it occurs as a natural life process.

These two conflicting models of man pose something of a dilemma, for we cannot accept one and discard the other without doing an injustice to the data. Research evidence and common sense observations can be marshalled to support both theories—man is passive and controlled by his environment as well as creative and self-directing. The noted ethologist Konrad Lorenz (1963) suggests, however, that this dilemma is an illusion. There is no contradiction, he maintains, between the fact that man's behavior is governed by causal stimulus-response type laws and the fact that man strives toward goals and can modify his behavior by an act of will. "The appreciation of the fact that life processes are directed at aims or goals, and the realization of the other fact that they are, at the same time, determined by causality, not only do not preclude each other but they only make sense in combination. If man did not strive toward goals, his questions as to causes would have no sense; if he has no insight into cause and effect, he is powerless to guide effects toward determined goals, however rightly he may have understood the meaning of these goals . . . (p. 231). Increasing knowledge of the natural causes of his own behavior can certainly increase a man's faculties and enable him to put his free will into action . . . (p. 232)."

Thus in his integration of the two models of man Lorenz suggests a methodology for self-directed change. If we can increase an individual's understanding of the psychological laws which govern his behavior, we can increase his capacity for self-direction. To explore the characteristics of the process of self-directed change we have developed a simple method for self-directed behavior change.

The major emphasis of the method is on self-research. Each subject is encouraged to reflect on his own behavior, and to select a limited and well-defined goal which he would like to achieve. The next step is to undertake a continuing and accurate assessment of his behavior in the area related to his change goal. He keeps an objective record of his behavior in this area, generally in the form of a graph which measures progress toward the goal from day to day. The subject decides for himself how long the project should continue and when his goal is attained.

When business-school students used this method to change themselves as part of their participation in self-analytic groups (Kolb, Winter, and Berlew, 1968), two factors were found that predicted the students' success in changing. Change was found to be related to the individual's commitment to his change goal and the amount of feedback he received from other group members during the last half of the group. Improving the change method to increase goal commitment and feedback increased the percentage of students successfully attaining their goals from 5% to 61%.

The research reported in this paper is a more detailed exploration of the dynamics of the goal-setting process in self-directed behavior change. More specifically, we seek answers to the following questions:

1. Does conscious goal-setting facilitate goal achievement?
2. What characteristics of the goal-setting process are related to subsequent success or failure in goal-achievement?

Goal-Setting and Goal-Achievement

There has been a great deal of attention given to the relationship between goal-setting and goal-achievement in the psychological literature. Most of these studies, however, have been conducted in the level of aspiration experimental paradigm and have been concerned mainly with the question— How does successful or unsuccessful goal-achievement affect goal-setting? (Lewin, *et al.* 1944; Festinger, 1942; Frank, 1941). The major result of these studies has been that success increases aspirations and failure, to a lesser extent, decreases aspirations. Comparatively little attention has been given to the reverse question which is central to understanding the role of goal-setting in self-directed behavior change—How does goal-setting affect success in goal-achievement?

McClelland's theory of motivation gives a partial answer to this question (McClelland, 1965). Motives in his theory are affectively toned associative networks arranged in a heirarchy of importance within the individual. In other words a motive is an emotionally toned pattern of thinking. The influence which a motive holds over an individual's behavior is determined by the extent to which this pattern of thinking dominates an individual's consciousness. Hundreds of studies have been conducted within this theoretical framework showing the relationship between achievement motivation and behavior as well as other motives such as power, affiliation, aggression and sex (McClelland, 1961; Atkinson, 1958). In addition a number of behavior change programs have reported success in changing achievement motivated behavior by changing (among other things) the position of the achievement motive in a person's motive hierarchy by helping him develop and clearly conceptualize the associative network defining the motive (Kolb, 1965; McClelland, 1965; Litwin and Aronoff, 1971). These studies all lend support to the notion that dominance of a goal (i.e., achievement desires) in consciousness will lead to behavior toward that goal (i.e., achievement related behavior).

Organizational psychology provides another source of evidence for the importance of conscious goal-setting for goal achievement. The field has long recognized the importance of goal-setting and programs of management by objectives have made this process quite explicit in industrial management

(Drucker, 1954). Studies of organizations have shown productivity and satisfaction are greater when the worker sets his own goals (Likert, 1967; McGregor, 1960). One excellent field study of performance appraisal interviews by Kay, French, and Myer (1962) gives empirical support to the hypothesis that conscious goal-setting leads to goal achievement. The authors found that when managers' improvement needs were translated into specific goals during performance appraisal interviews, 65.2% of these goals were subsequently achieved. When improvement needs were not translated into specific goals only 27.3% were subsequently accomplished. Kay and French conclude that, "Appreciable improvements in performance were realized only when specific goals were established with time deadlines set and results measures agreed upon. Regardless of how much emphasis the manager gave to an improvement need in the appraisal discussion, if this did not get translated into a specific goal, very little performance improvement was achieved" (p. 1).

Two studies in the level of aspiration literature have attempted to show the effect that stating a level of aspiration has a subsequent peformance. Kausler (1959) gave a simple arithmetic test to three groups of students, two of which were asked to state levels of aspiration. He found that when mathematical ability was held constant those who were asked to state their level of aspiration performed significantly better than those who were not. Rao (1956) conducted an experiment in which he examined the effects of level of aspiration and feedback on peformance. His conclusion was that task performance was decreased when either a level of aspiration was not stated or feedback was withheld.

Finally, our previous research on self-directed behavior change (Kolb, Winter, and Berlew, 1968) suggested that when the self-directed change method was modified to emphasize conscious goal-setting the percent of successful goal achievement increased from 44% to 61%.

There is, then, some empirical support for the hypothesis that conscious goal-setting facilitates goal achievement. The purpose of the study reported here is to ascertain whether conscious goal-setting will facilitate the achievement of personal improvement goals by individuals using the self-directed behavior change method.

> *Hypothesis I.* Individuals will change more on those dimensions of their self-concept which they define as relevant to their consciously set change goal than they will on dimensions of their self-concept which they define as not relevant. This difference will be independent of the difficulty of the change goal.

This hypothesis differs from those of previously reported research in that it does not involve an experimental manipulation of the independent variable, goal-setting. This difference overcomes one problem with previous research designs but creates another. The problem with the previous experimental designs is that it is impossible to determine whether the improvements in performance were a result of conscious goal-setting or a result of the influence attempts of the experimenter which are inherent in asking an individual to set goals. By asking a person to say how many arithmetic problems he is going to do or by defining with him what specifically he is going to do to improve his job performance the experimenter or manager is in effect telling the person to achieve the goal. Research on the social psychology of experimental situations suggests that this influence, even if unconscious, can be very great (Milgram,

1968; Orne, 1962; Rosenthal, 1963). In the current experiment, subjects are free to choose whatever goal they wish thus eliminating the effect of experimenter persuasion. The problem with the current design, however, is that it is difficult to conclude that it is conscious goal-setting that causes greater goal achievement. Individuals may simply choose goals that are easier to achieve. In an attempt to overcome this problem we will test whether goal-setting facilitates change in difficult as well as easy goals.

Characteristics of the Goal-Setting Process

In addition to assessing the effect of conscious goal-setting on goal achievement, this research seeks to determine those characteristics of the goal-setting process which facilitate goal achievement. From a content analysis of individuals' initial goal statements five hypotheses will be tested. These include an exploration of the individual's awareness of his goal, his expectation of success, and his level of psychological safety. The remaining two hypotheses are concerned with the individual's evaluation of his progress—the extent to which he proposes to measure his progress and the degree to which he controls his own reinforcement and evaluates himself.

Awareness. Most forms of psychotherapy attempt to increase the patient's awareness of the forces affecting his behavior with the implicit assumption that this insight will change the patient's behavior. Two recent psychotherapy research programs have been able to define the role of awareness in personality change more specifically. Gendlin, *et al.* (1968) has devised a process measure of what he calls the client's focusing ability. He describes the role of focusing ability in therapy as follows:

> The therapist calls the client's attention to an as yet unclear partly cognitive and situational complex which is concretely felt by the client. The client must then be willing and able to focus his attention directly on this felt complex so that he can concretely feel and struggle with it (p. 218).

Gendlin finds that clients who display this kind of focusing ability in therapy interviews improve after therapy while those who do not show focusing ability do not improve. Truax and Carkhuff (1964) have developed a process measure which they call intrapersonal exploration that is similar to focusing ability in that it emphasizes awareness of feelings associated with one's problems. They also find that presence of intrapersonal exploration in psychotherapy interviews is indicative of successful change.

In a study of the personality characteristics of individuals who are successful in self-directed behavior change projects Winter, Griffith, and Kolb (1968) found results that suggest that successful change is a function of one's ability to maintain awareness of the dissonance between one's ideal self and one's current self.

> *Hypothesis II.* Individuals who are successful in achieving their change goal will initially show a greater awareness of forces related to that change goal than will individuals who are unsuccessful in achieving their change goal.

Expectation of Success. A number of studies in psychotherapy have shown that an individual's expectations of success or failure can in fact determine his success or failure in therapy (Goldstein, 1962; Frank, 1963). We would predict that this would be even more likely in a self-directed change project since the individual plays a more central role in his own change effort.

> *Hypothesis III.* Individuals who are successful in achieving their change goals will show in their initial goal choice papers more indications that they expect success than will individuals who are not successful in achieving their goal.

Psychological Safety. The concept of psychological safety is one which many students of the behavior change process have felt to be essential for successful change (Maslow, 1954; Rogers, 1951; McClelland, 1965; Schein, 1968). Rogers gives some insights into how lack of psychological safety (threat) or its presence can effect the goal-setting process:

> Any experience which is inconsistent with the organization of the self (or structure) may be perceived as a threat, and the more of these perceptions there are, the more rigidly the self-structure is organized to maintain itself.

> Under certain conditions, involving primarily complete absence of any threat to the self-structure, experiences which are inconsistent with it may be perceived, and examined, and the structure of self revised to assimilate and include such experiences (Rogers, 1951, p. 508).

Thus if a person experiences low psychological safety he is likely to defensively distort his weaknesses and be unable to commit himself to new ideals which are different from his present self.

> *Hypothesis IV.* Individuals who are successful in achieving their change goals will indicate greater psychological safety during the goal-setting process than will individuals who are not successful.

Measurability of the Change Goal. In addition to goal-setting, previous research on self-directed change has shown that information feedback related to one's change goal is essential for achievement of that goal (Kolb, Winter, and Berlew, 1968). It seems important, therefore, that a person's change goal be conceived in such a way that feedback from others and the environment could modify it, i.e., the goal should be measurable. We have already mentioned the Kay, French, and Myer study which found improvements in performance only "when specific goals were established with time deadlines set and results measures agreed upon." If an individual has defined his goal in such a way that he can measure whether or not he is achieving it, then he should be more capable of identifying and using feedback.

> *Hypothesis V.* Individuals who are successful in achieving their change goals will be more likely to give consideration to measuring progress toward their goal than those who are not successful.

Self-Controlled Evaluation. The final hypothesis is related to one of the initial assumptions underlying the self-directed change method—that changes in behavior are most likely to be successful if the process of changing is seen by the individual to be under his own control. The previously cited Kay, French, and Myers study found that if a subordinate viewed his efforts in the goal-setting process of equal importance and efficacy as his superior's, his achievement of these goals was significantly higher than those who viewed their influence in the process as minimal or less than they deserved. We have already mentioned organizational studies which show the importance of self control in the goal-setting process.

This need for self control of the change process extends beyond initial goal-setting to a need for self control of the process of evaluating progress toward the goal. The studies by Rotter and his associates of internal versus external control of reinforcement (Lefcourt, 1966) have found distinct differences between people who see positive and negative events as being a consequence of their own actions and, therefore, under their personal control (Internality) and people who see positive and negative events as caused by external forces and beyond personal control (Externality). Rotter finds that:

> The individual who has a strong belief that he can control his own destiny is likely to:
>
> 1. be more alert to those aspects of the environment which provide useful information for his future behavior
> 2. takes steps to improve his environmental condition
> 3. place greater value on skill or achievement reinforcements and be generally more concerned
> 4. be resistive to subtle attempts to influence him (Rotter, 1966, p. 25).

Thus from Rotter's research we would predict that individuals who see the evaluation of their progress as being self-controlled and self-reinforced will be more successful than those who see evaluation as being controlled by others.

Rogers, in his attempts to identify the characteristics of effective helping relationships, also stresses the importance of self-evaluation:

> I have come to feel that the more I can keep a relationship free of judgment and evaluation, the more this will permit the other person to reach the point where he recognizes that the locus of evaluation, the center of responsibility, lies within himself. The meaning and value of his experience is in the last analysis something which is up to him and no amount of external judgment can alter this. (Rogers, 1961, p. 55).
>
> *Hypothesis VIA.* Individuals who are successful in achieving their change goals will be more likely to feel that the control of reinforcement that they receive during the change process rests with themselves than those who are not successful.
>
> *Hypothesis VIB.* Individuals who are successful in achieving their change goals will be less likely to feel that control of reinforcement that they receive during the change process rests with others than those who are not successful.

Experimental Procedure

The experimental procedure used in this study is a modification of earlier applications of the self-directed change method to self-analytic groups (Kolb, Winter and Berlew, 1968; Winter, Griffith and Kolb, 1968). The setting for the experiment was a semester-long course in psychology and human organization, required of master's candidates in management at the M. I. T. Sloan

School. Offered as an optional part of the course, 111 students participated in 30 hours of T-Group training usually divided into two 2-hour sessions each week. There were 8 groups of approximately 15 students each. These groups were structured slightly differently from the traditional T-Group method (see Schein and Bennis, 1965, chapter 3) in that they were focused around a task—helping one another achieve personal change goals via the self-directed change method. Students chose, at the beginning of the T-Group, individual change goals which they wanted to achieve. They picked goals like having more empathy, being a more effective leader, and talking more; and customarily they shared these goals with other group members asking them for feedback on their progress. This procedure served to define clearly the groups' task as one of helping others achieve their personal change goals.

The students were about 1/2 undergraduates and 1/2 master's candidates in management. There were two females. About 10% of the students were foreign nationals with varying degrees of fluency in the English language. Subjects varied in age from 19 to 35 with most in their early twenties.

Before the T-Groups began students were asked to write a short paper describing how they saw themselves behaving in a group situation and how they would ideally like to behave in the same situation. They were asked to fill out a 60-pair semantic differential describing their real and ideal selves. It was made clear to the students that these papers would not affect their course grade.

The students then heard a lecture on self-directed change, including a discussion of factors influencing behavior change and several case studies. After the lecture, during the first week of the T-Groups, students chose change goals relevant to their behavior in groups. Each person was asked to write a short paper describing his goal and answer certain questions regarding the goal and his commitment to it. This goal-choice paper was designed to provide data about the characteristics of the person's initial goal. Students were given the following outline to assist them in writing their papers.

The Process of Goal Choice:

    I. Self-evaluation
      1. What are your major strengths and weaknesses in a group as you see them?
      2. Are there any areas in which you really want to change?
      3. Why do you feel these changes would be desirable?
    II. Focusing on one measurable goal
      1. Describe as accurately and concretely as possible the goal you have chosen to work toward.
      2. What considerations influenced your choice of this particular goal?
      3. How do you plan to measure your progress toward this goal? How will you know when you have attained it? What change will be observable to others?
    III. Anticipating the change process
      1. Given your choice of the above goal, what are the factors in yourself, in other people, and in the environment which will help or hinder your progress?

Included with the goal choice paper assignment was a list of the 60 adjective pairs from the real-self, ideal-self semantic differential. Students were asked to circle those adjective pairs which "best represented the dimensions along which you plan to change." This data was used to determine those aspects of an individual's self-concept which were related to his change goal for testing Hypothesis I.

At the end of each T-Group session each member was asked to fill out a feedback form on which they recorded the feedback they received from others that day. The forms also asked for a daily rating of progress. The purpose of these feedback forms was to stimulate students' awareness of the feedback they were receiving.

The project concluded with a written report by each student on their self-directed change project. In the report they were asked to describe their change process and their success in achieving their goal. They were also asked to indicate their success in changing on a five point scale ranging from (1) "I have made no progress in achieving my goal," to (5) "I have completely achieved my goal."

In conjunction with their final report, students completed again the real-self, ideal-self semantic differential.

Identification of High Change and Low Change Subjects. Three measures of change were used in this study. The first is based on the discrepancy between real-self descriptions and ideal-self descriptions on the semantic differential. A before discrepancy score was obtained by subtracting the ideal score from the real score of each pair of adjectives on the forms filled out at the beginning of the experiment. An after discrepancy was obtained the same way using the forms filled out at the conclusion of the experiment. To obtain the change score for each adjective pair the magnitude of the after discrepancy was subtracted from the magnitude of the before discrepancy. Thus a positive score would indicate that a person was closer to his ideal-self after his change project than he was before.

An average *goal-related* change score was then computed for each subject by totaling the change scores for each of the adjective pairs he checked as describing his change goal and dividing by the number of adjective pairs checked. An average non-goal-related change score was computed for each subject by following the same procedure for those adjectives which he did not check. These two scores were used to test Hypothesis I.

The second change measure is based on the subjects' self evaluation of their success in achieving their change goal (the five point rating scale included in their final report). It is used in order to make results gathered here comparable with the results of previous research (Kolb, Winter, and Berlew, 1968; Winter, Griffith, and Kolb, 1968) which used an experimenter rating of success in goal achievement based on a reading of subjects' final reports. The subjects' rating was used because it was felt that the subject's own rating of his success might more accurately represent aspects of his own experience than the experimenter's rating. A comparison of the former experimenter ratings of the final report with the subjects' ratings show an 85% agreement between the scores.

The third measure of change is based on the group leaders' ratings of change. The group leader of each T-Group was asked to indicate each individual's change toward his goal on a five-point scale. The Kendall Tau correlation between these leader ratings and the subject's own ratings was .35 ($p < .01$). In addition a significant correlation (.39, $p < .01$) was found between the subject's rating of his success and his average goal-related change score on the semantic differential.

To form a group of clearly successful and a group of clearly unsuccessful subjects, the 51 individuals (in the self-rated change analysis) and the 35 individuals (in the case of the trainer rated change analysis) who were reported to have made moderate progress in achieving their goals were eliminated from data analysis. This left a group of low change subjects who reported "no progress" or "very slight progress" ($N = 32$ for self-rated change and $N = 34$ for trainer rated change) and a group of high change subjects who reported "almost completely achieving my goal" or "completely achieving my goal" ($N = 28$ for self-rated change and $N = 42$ for trainer rated change).

The hypotheses concerning the characteristics of the goal-setting process associated with success or failure in goal achievement were tested using both the self rated and trainer rated measures of change.

Results

Hypothesis I was concerned with the effect of goal-setting on goal achievement. The data describing the test of this hypothesis are shown in Table 1. Individuals showed an average change of .35 on adjective dimensions related to their goal while showing an average change of .16 on non-goal related dimensions. This difference is highly significant ($p < .005$, 1-tail). An inspection of the adjective pairs that individuals indicated as relevant to their change goal showed that the median number of pairs indicated by an individual was 12 of the 60 adjectives. The number of adjectives indicated ranged from 1 to 46. The median number of times that any single adjective pair was checked was 22 with a range of 4 to 88. From this it can be concluded that individuals tended to use several adjective dimensions to describe their change goal and that all of the 60 adjective dimensions on the semantic differential were used.

TABLE 1

Self Concept Change in Goal-related and Non-goal-related Dimensions

	Average Change per Adjective Dimension		
	Goal-related Dimensions	Non-goal-related Dimensions	Significance of Differences[1]
All adjective dimensions	.35 $n = 111$	.16 $n = 111$	$< .005$
Easy change dimensions	.52 $n = 110$	.31 $n = 110$	$< .03$
Moderate dimensions	.19 $n = 96$	.17 $n = 96$	$< .30$
Difficult change dimensions	.17 $n = 105$	.02 $n = 105$	$< .035$

[1]Wilcoxon matched pairs signed rank test, 1-tail.

To determine whether these differences were simply a result of the fact that subjects tended to choose easy dimensions to change on, a measure of difficulty of change was computed for each adjective dimension. This was accomplished by computing the average change score for each of the 60 adjective dimensions when this dimension was not circled as relevant to the individual's change goal. This change score became an operational definition of difficulty of change without the benefit of goal-setting. The adjectives were rank ordered according to this change score and then divided into three groups of twenty—a group of easy change adjective dimensions, a moderate group and a group of difficult change dimensions. For each group the mean change per dimension when these adjectives were not goal related was then compared to the mean change when the adjectives were described as goal related. (The reader will note that the sample size is depleted in these comparisons since in some cases, for example, an individual might not describe any easy adjectives as related to his change goal.) The result of these comparisons show significantly more change on goal related dimensions in the easy and difficult dimensions and a similar but small and insignificant difference in the moderate dimensions. Although the small facilitating effect of goal-setting on moderately difficult adjective dimensions is difficult to explain, the facilitating effect shown on both easy and difficult dimensions suggests that the results for all adjective dimensions were not simply a result of choosing easy adjectives.

To further test this relationship, goal-related change and non-goal-related change were correlated with the subject's own estimation of the difficulty of his goal which he indicated on a five-point scale at the time of his goal choice. In both cases there was no significant relationship ($r = -.04$ in both instances). An inspection of scatter plots for both correlations showed no indication of a curvilinear relationship. Thus we conclude that the effect of goal-setting or goal achievement is not due to the adjective difficulty or to self-perceived difficulty of goal achievement.

Hypothesis II. Awareness and Goal Achievement. The goal choice papers of high change and low change subjects were scored for the number of forces which they mentioned as affecting their change goal. The coding scheme developed by Thomas, Bennis, and Fulenwider (1966) was used to score the papers for (1) the total number of forces mentioned, (2) the number of forces which facilitated progress toward the goal, (3) the number of forces which inhibited progress toward the goal, (4) the number of self-related forces, and (5) the number of other-related and environmental forces. The papers were scored on these and all other categories to be described by a scorer who was unaware of the subjects' change score. A sample of 15 papers scored by two independent coders showed a 98% agreement in scoring.

The following are examples of the different types of forces scored in the goal-choice papers. The word in parenthesis after the statement describes whether the force was self or other related.

> 1. Inhibiting Forces:
>
> "I'm afraid of letting my feelings be known, I'm afraid of making mistakes in front of the group." (self)
>
> "If the group is prepared to sit back and just listen obviously I am going to receive little stimulus to improve communication as they do not seem able to reach my level." (others)
>
> 2. Increasing Forces:
>
> "I can accept criticism from others, so that others will accept criticism from me." (self)

"The factors that might help my progress are my innate appreciation for competition and recognition (self), as well as encouragement from the group to initiate ideas." (others)

The average total number of forces and the average number of the sub-types of forces are shown for High and Low change groups in Table 2. The data confirm the hypothesis that high change subjects show a greater initial awareness of forces relating to their change goal. Although no specific hypotheses were made about the sub-types of forces, the data is interesting but unclear. Successful changers according to the self-rated change scale see significantly more

TABLE 2

High and Low Change Subjects' Awareness of Forces Related to Their Change Goal

	Self-Rated Change			Trainer-Rated Change		
	High Change Subjects $N = 28$	Low Change Subjects $N = 32$	Level of Significance[1]	High Change Subjects $N = 42$	Low Change Subjects $N = 34$	Level of Significance[1]
Mean number of forces mentioned	3.69	2.44	< .02	3.16	2.23	< .04
Mean number of facilitating forces	1.76	.75	< .001	1.42	1.29	NS
Mean number of inhibiting forces	1.93	1.69	NS	1.88	.94	< .006
Mean number of self-related forces	2.07	2.03	NS	2.09	1.64	< .05
Mean number of other related forces	1.62	.41	< .0001	1.02	.58	NS

[1]Mann–Whitney U-Test, 1-tail for total number of forces, 2-tail for sub-groupings.

facilitating forces and other related forces while successful changers according to the trainer-rating scale see significantly more inhibiting and self-related forces.

Hypothesis III. Expectations of Success and Goal Achievement. All of the goal choice papers were scored for statements which indicated that the writer expected to be successful in achieving his goal. Statements like the following were scored—"I expect to achieve my goal by the end of the course." Only explicit statements of expectations of success were scored. Statements of desire for success ("I want to achieve my goal") or a conditional expectation ("If I can keep active, I expect to arrive at my goal") were not scored. Two independent scorers showed an 82% agreement on scoring expectations of success. In the self-rated change analysis, 43% of the subjects in the high change group stated in their goal choice papers that they expected success; only 9% of the low change subjects stated success expectations. This difference is highly significant ($p < .001$). In the trainer-rated change analysis, 26% of the subjects in the high change group stated an expectation of success and 9% of the subjects in the low change group stated an expectation of success. This difference is also statistically significant ($p < .03$).

Hypothesis IV. Psychological Safety and Goal Achievement. The goal choice papers of high and low change subjects were scored for psychological safety according to the following category definition:

Negative Statements of Psychological Safety
One point is given for each statement by a person of feeling threatened. This is determined by statements of feelings like shy, withdrawn, ineffective, worthless (feeling unworthy), uneasy in front of people, afraid of others, others' reactions, of himself, and feeling self-conscious. General statements of a "lack of self-confidence" were not coded. Evidence of feelings must be present.

Examples of negative statements are:
"I am afraid of not being accepted or included by them."

"This, coupled with my inner feelings of uneasiness in front of a group . . ."

Positive Statements of Psychological Safety
One point is given for each statement by a person of feeling safe in the environment. This is coded by statements like: feeling successful, having good ideas, and being a good leader.

Examples of positive statements are:
"I find I have the ability to stimulate thought by bringing up cogent questions and comments."

"I see myself as perceptive of group members and motives." The total psychological safety score equals total negative statements minus total positive statements.

Two independent coders showed a high reliability ($r = .89$) on psychological safety scores.

In the case of self-rated change, subjects who were successful in achieving their goal had a mean psychological safety score of .28 while unsuccessful subjects had a mean psychological safety score of 1.31 (low scores indicate high psychological safety). The difference between the two groups is significant at the .05 level (1-tail) using the Mann–Whitney U-Test. In the case of trainer-rated change, high changers showed a mean psychological safety score of .29 while low changers showed a mean score of 1.23 (again, a low score indicates high psychological safety). Although the difference is not significant using a Mann–Whitney U-Test ($p = .10$, 1-tail), the trend is in the same direction as that found using the self-rated measure of change tending to substantiate the hypothesis. We can thus conclude that subjects who were successful in changing were more psychologically safe during the initial goal-setting process than subjects who were not successful.

Hypothesis V. Measurement and Goal Achievement. Although students were instructed to give consideration in their goal choice papers to how progress toward their goal might be measured, some did so and others did not. The following is an example of a subject who stated a method for measuring his progress:

> I intend to measure my success by two methods: (1) by an intuitive feeling of how much I have contributed to the group activity during a session, and (2) by actually measuring the number of times that I verbally participate during a group meeting.

The number of high change subjects and low change subjects who mentioned a measurement method were compared. While only 34% of the low change subjects mentioned a method for measuring progress, 79% of the high change subjects mentioned a measurement method in the self-rated change analysis. This difference is highly significant ($p < .001$). In the case of trainer-rated change, 61% of the high change subjects mentioned a method of measuring progress toward their goal, while 41% of the low change subjects mentioned a method of measurement. This difference is also significant ($p < .04$).

Hypothesis VIA and VIB. Self Evaluation, Other Evaluation and Goal Achievement. The goal choice papers of high and low change subjects were coded for indications of self evaluation of progress toward their goal and for indications of group evaluation of progress. Examples of self evaluation methods are, "I will record the number of times I speak up in the group on a graph and evaluate my progress after each session," "I will observe how uneasy I feel each time I speak and will know I am progressing toward my goal when I start to feel comfortable." Examples of group evaluation methods are, "The group will tell me how at ease I look each time I speak, and whether or not I appear to be improving," "The others in the group will tell me whether or not my statements are coherent and relevant to the subject being discussed."

Two independent scorers showed a 90% agreement on both group and self-evaluation categories. To test hypothesis VIA the percent of subjects in the high and low change groups who showed self-evaluation methods were compared. In the self-rated change analysis, 64% of the high change subjects indicated a self-evaluation method while only 32% of the low change subjects indicated a self-evaluation method ($p < .006$, 1-tail). In the trainer-rated analysis, 57% of the high changers indicated a self-evaluation method while 35% of the low changers indicated a self-evaluation method ($p < .02$, 1-tail). Hypothesis VIB was tested by comparing the percent of subjects in the high and low change groups who indicated group-evaluation methods. In the case of self-rated change, 28% of the low change subjects indicated a group evaluation method while 32% of the high change subjects indicated a group evaluation method. In the case of trainer-rated change, 20% of the low changers indicated a group evaluation while 21% of the high changers indicated a group evaluation. Neither of these differences were in the direction predicted or were statistically significant. Thus it appears that self-controlled evaluation facilitates goal achievement while group-controlled evaluation is unrelated to goal achievement.

Conclusions and Implications

The experiment presents convincing evidence that conscious goal-setting plays an important role in the process of self-directed behavior change. Individuals tend to change more in those areas of their self-concept which are related to their consciously set change goals. These changes are independent of the difficulty of the change goal and thus do not appear to be a result of an initial choice of easy to achieve goals. The results would suggest a modification of those Freudian and learning theory based approaches to behavior change that treat consciousness as an epiphenomenon by placing heavy emphasis on unconscious forces and behavioral conditioning. While this experiment, since it does not involve an experimental manipulation of goal setting, does not con-clusively prove that conscious goal-setting caused the subsequent changes in self-concept, taken with other experimental studies cited in this paper it does strongly suggest that conscious goal setting facilitates goal achievement.

The analysis of the initial goal descriptions of subjects who were subse-quently successful and unsuccessful in achieving their goals provides evidence for those specific characteristics of the goal setting process which are crucial for goal achievement. Awareness of forces related to the change goal, high ex-pectations of success, high psychological safety, a concern for measuring pro-gress, and an emphasis on self-controlled evaluation all appear to be precur-sors of successful goal achievement.

While the data in this experiment are not sufficiently quantified to allow tests of the interrelationships among the variables identified as important characteristics of the goal-setting process, the results suggest some tentative outlines for a cybernetic model of behavior change. Nearly every student of personality and behavior change has recognized that human personality is a dynamic feedback system with self-sustaining and self-reinforcing qualities. Sullivan, for example, sees this aspect of personality (which he calls the self system) to be the major stumbling block to constructive personality change. Hall and Lindsey (1957) describe his concept of the self system this way:

> The self system as the guardian of one's security tends to become isolated from the rest of the personality; it excludes information that is incongruous with its present organization and fails thereby to profit from experience. Since the self guards the person from anxiety, it is held in high esteem and protected from criticism. As the self system grows in complexity and independence it prevents the person from making objective judgments of his own behavior and it glosses over obvious contradictions between what the person really is and what his self system says he is (p. 139).

Since individuals tend to act in accord with their self system, threats to the self system will cause a person's activities to become more and more inappropri-ate and rigid leading to further failure and insecurity which in turn leads to further distortions in the self system and so on. The characteristics of the goal-setting process which we have found to be associated with successful self-directed change give some clues about the nature of the intervening variables in this process. Figure 1 shows how the goal-setting characteristics fit into a cybernetic model of the change process. Interrelationships among the variables are simplified to illustrate the dominant feedback loop. For purpose of illus-tration, let us describe the interaction of these characteristics in an unsuc-cessful change process beginning with low psychological safety. Low psycho-logical safety can lead to decreased awareness. This decrease in awareness would in turn lead to a decreased sense of self-control which would lead to fewer expectations of success. Low expectations of success would produce few attempts to achieve the goal which would in turn produce fewer opportunities for feedback from the environment. All this would tend to produce failure in achieving the goal. The failure feelings thus aroused would tend to further decrease psychological safety producing an amplification of this positive feed-back loop.

FIGURE 1

A Simple Cybernetic Model of Behavior Change and Helping Interventions

Implications for Helping Interventions

This cybernetic model of the behavior change process suggests several intervention strategies that may serve to create more effective helping relationships with individuals who are seeking change. Since feedback loops are composed of elements which need not have a prior or an hierarchical causal order, helping interventions can be directed to the point or points in the feedback loop where they will be most effective in producing change. As Phillips and Wiener put it:

> Within the cybernetic framework, although not unique to it, variables are selected and regulated in the feedback chain which are most amenable to manipulation and control. In structured therapy, elusive causes are not sought that might operate to produce a disordered system: the therapist goes directly to the element (information) in the feedback loop that has a meaningful coefficient of efficiency in maintaining the loop, and he proceeds immediately to try to insert the change (1966, p. 96).

Thus, cybernetic models of the change process hold forth the promise of an eclectic approach to the choice of helping strategies based on research which identifies those elements in the feedback loop which have the highest "coefficient of efficiency."

The simplified model of change shown in Figure 1 suggests seven types of intervention which may prove effective in breaking into the self-defeating cycle of failure.

1. *Supportiveness.* Rogerian theory has been based primarily on the supportive strategy of increasing the clients' security and self-confidence through the therapists' unconditional positive regard, accurate empathy, and genuineness (Rogers, 1961). Truax and his associates (Truax and Carkhuff, 1964) have shown that these three therapist characteristics are related to constructive personality change in both Rogerian and other forms of therapy. In addition they find that the presence of these variables in the therapist are positively related to intrapersonal exploration on the part of the patient. These results suggest that supportive interventions aimed at increasing psychological safety have a relatively higher coefficient of efficiency in that they produce positive change and gains in another element in the feedback loop—awareness (intrapersonal exploration).

2. *Collaborative goal-setting.* Attempts to increase awareness of personal improvement goals through an explicit process of collaborative goal setting have not often been a part of behavior change programs. However, the use of this strategy in achievement motivation training programs and in organizational settings as well as in research on self-directed behavior change suggests that goal-setting procedures may indeed by a highly effective intervention method. In fact, a careful examination of behavior therapy method of change suggests that in addition to applying, for example, the principles of reciprocal inhibition (Wolpe, 1958) the therapist is also leading the patient through a process of explicit goal setting. By asking the patient to define and rank order the fear evoking situations in his life and then telling him to try to relax while visualizing the weakest fear situation until he masters it and then proceeding to the next weakest and so on, the therapist is in effect helping the patient to set realistic goals and work to achieve them in a way that is quite similar to the self-directed change method. At this point no research evidence exists which can tell us whether it is the process of reciprocal inhibition or collaborative goal-setting which is the change producing intervention. Similar questions can be raised about other behavior therapy methods.

3. *Emphasis on self-direction.* While few therapeutic systems place a heavy emphasis on self control of the change process in their methodology, it is a common assumption that true psychotherapeutic change does not occur until the patient works through his dependence upon the therapist and achieves self-direction. The literature on cognitive dissonance gives experimental evidence for the importance of self-direction in attitude change. These experiments show that attitude change is greatest and most enduring when the person feels that he has freely chosen to alter his point of view (Secord and Backman, 1964). Recognizing the importance of self-direction in personality change, self-help societies like Alcoholics Anonymous and Synanon (for narcotics addicts) have made the principles of personal responsibility and voluntary commitment to change a central part of their ideology. DeCharms (1968) has formulated a concept of self-direction which he calls the origin-pawn variable. In a recent

program of research he has been successful in increasing academic performance by training ghetto children to be origins rather than pawns.

4. *Manipulation of expectations.* Research evidence on the impact of an individual's expectations on his own chances for successful change has already been presented. As yet few direct attempts have been made to directly increase individuals' expectations of success. A significant exception is the previously cited work on achievement motivation training. That manipulation of expectations can produce behavior change is shown by a well-executed study by Rosenthal and Jacobson (1968). They found that intellectual gains could be produced in children by nothing more than giving names of children who had been selected at random to their new teachers at the beginning of the school year and describing them to these teachers as children who could be expected to show unusual gains in inteligence during the year. This research suggests that helping interventions that increase expectations of success may be a very effective method of breaking the cycle of failure.

5. *Behavior monitoring and control.* Behavior therapy attempts to elicit behaviors consistent with constructive personality change goals are of two types—stimulus control and modeling (Schwitzgebel and Kolb, 1974). In stimulus controls methods environmental conditions which serve as either discriminating or eliciting stimuli for desired behavioral responses are used to increase the probability of a desired response, or decrease a response to be avoided. A simple example would be the case of the student who moves his study area away from his bed in order to keep from falling asleep. Modeling can be defined as "the systematic provision of opportunities for observing the behavior of others, wherein the cues to behavior came from the behavior of others. In short, this is vicarious learning" (Brayfield, 1968, p. 480). A number of studies, most notably by Bandura and Walters (1963), have shown that the observation of a given behavior in a model increases the occurence of that behavior.

In self-directed behavior change projects another method has been successfully used to elicit goal directed behavior—behavior monitoring. By keeping continuous records of progress toward their goal, subjects are constantly reminded of the goal they are trying to achieve, thus producing more attempts to achieve the goal (Zach, 1965; Goldiamond, 1965; Schwitzgebel, 1964). The fact that high change subjects in the research presented in this paper gave more attention than low change subjects to how their progress could be measured provides additional evidence for the efficiency of behavior-monitoring procedures.

6. *Selective reinforcement.* Perhaps the best documented strategy for producing change is the manipulation of environmental feedback through the use of selective reinforcement. The methods of operant shaping and intermittent positive reinforcement have been used to alter such insignificant behaviors as use of pronouns and such major behavioral patterns as delinquent behavior and schizophrenic symptoms (Schwitzgebel and Kolb, 1973). Research on self-directed change suggests that in certain circumstances the total amount of information feedback may also be related to change (Kolb, Winter, and Berlew, 1968).

7. *Manipulation of results.* A final intervention method which deserves consideration is the manipulation of results of change. While this method has not

been used systematically as a therapeutic intervention, it is a common device in experimental research. For example, the literature on level of aspiration is replete with examples of artificial manipulation of performance results, which show measurable changes in future goal-setting and performance. While there are obvious problems of credibility for the change agent with such artificial distortions of reality this method might prove to be a promising helping strategy.

It can be seen from the above discussion that the elements of the goal-setting process that are crucial for successful goal achievement as well as feedback from the environment and the final change score itself may all be changed by helping interventions. The task for future research is to determine how effective these interventions, taken singly or in combination, can be in changing the cycle of insecurity and failure to one of psychological safety and success. The most effective intervention strategy may well prove to be the information feedback procedures of behavior therapy approaches in combination with the goal-setting procedures of self-directed change.

References

Allport, G. W. *Personality and social encounter.* Boston: Beacon Press, 1960.

Aronoff, J., Litwin, G. Achievement motivation training and executive advancement, *Journal of Applied Behavioral Science,* 1971, Vol. 7, 215–229.

Atkinson, J. W. (Ed.) *Motives in fantasy, action and society.* Princeton, N.J.: Van Nostrand, 1958.

Bandura, A. and Walters, R. H. *Social learning and personality development.* New York: Holt, Rinehart and Winston, 1963.

Brayfield, A. Human resources development, *American Psychologist,* 1968, Vol. 23, 479–482.

DeCharms, R. *Personal causation.* New York: Academic Press, 1968.

Drucker, P. F. *The practice of management.* New York: Harper Brothers, 1954.

Festinger, L. A theoretical interpretation of shifts in level of aspiration, *Psychological Review,* 1942, Vol. 49, 235–250.

Frank, J. D. Recent studies of the level of aspiration, *Psychological Bulletin,* 1941, Vol. 38, 218–226.

Frank, J. D. *Persuasion and healing.* New York: Schocken Books, 1963.

Gendlin, E., Beebe, J. III, Cassens, J., Klein, M., and Gaerlander, M. Focusing ability in psychotherapy, personality and creativity, in, *Research in psychotherapy: Vol. III,* American Psychological Association, 1968.

Goldiamond, I. Self-control procedures in personal behavior problems, *Psychological Reports,* 1965, Vol. 17, 851–868.

Goldstein, A. *Therapist-patient expectancies in psychotherapy.* New York: Pergamon Press, 1962.

Hartman, H. E. and Loewenstein, R. M. Comments on the formation of psychic structure, in, *The psychoanalytic study of the child.* New York: International University Press, Vol. 2, 1947.

Hall, C. S., Lindzey, G. *Theories of personality.* New York: Wiley & Sons, 1957.

Kausler, D. H. Aspiration level as a determinant of performance, *Journal of Personality,* 1959, Vol. 27, 346–351.

Kay, E., French, W., and Meyer, H. *A study of the performance appraisal interview,*

Management Development and Employee Relations Services, General Electric, New York, 1962.

Kolb, D. A. Achievement motivation training for under-achieving high school boys, *Journal of Personality and Social Psychology,* 1965, Vol. 2, 783–792.

Kolb, D. A., Winter, S., and Berlew, D. Self-directed change: Two studies, *Journal of Applied Behavioral Science,* 1968, Vol. 4, 453–473.

Lefcourt, H. M. Internal versus external control of reinforcement, *Psychological Bulletin,* 1966, Vol. 65, 206–220.

Lewis, K., Dembo, T., Festinger, L., Sears, P. S. Level of aspiration, in, *Personality and behavior disorders.* New York: Ronald Press, 1944.

Likert, R. *The human organization.* New York: McGraw-Hill, 1967.

Lorenz, K. *On aggression.* New York: Harcourt, Brace and World, 1963.

Maslow, A. *Motivation and personality.* New York: Harper Brothers, 1954.

McClelland, D. C. *The achieving society.* New York: Van Nostrand, 1961.

McClelland, D. C. Toward a theory of motive acquisition, *American Psychologist,* 1965, Vol. 20, 321–333.

McGregor, D. *The human side of enterprise.* New York: McGraw-Hill, 1960.

Milgram, S. Behavioral study of obedience, in, *Interpersonal dynamics.* Homewood, Ill.: Dorsey Press, 1968.

Orne, M. On the social psychology of the psychological experiment: With particular reference to demand characteristics and their implications, *American Psychologist,* 1962, Vol. 17, 776–783.

Phillips, E. L. and Wiener, D. *Short-term psychotherapy and structured behavior change.* New York: McGraw-Hill, 1966.

Rao, K. U. The effect of interference with certain aspects of goal-setting on level of aspiration behavior, *Psychological Studies,* 1959, Vol. 1, 1–10.

Rogers, C. R. *Client centered therapy.* Boston: Houghton Mifflin, 1951.

Rogers, C. R. *On becoming a person.* Boston: Houghton Mifflin, 1961.

Rosenthal, R. On the social psychology of the psychological experiment: The experimenter's hypothesis as unintended determinant of experimental results, *American Scientist,* 1963, Vol. 51, 268–283.

Rosenthal, R. and Jacobson, L. Teacher expectations for the disadvantaged, *Scientific American,* 1968, Vol. 218, 19–23.

Rotter, J. B. Generalized expectancies for internal versus external control of reinforcement, *Psychological Monographs,* 1966, Vol. 80.

Schein, E. H. Personal change through interpersonal relationships, *Interpersonal dynamics.* Homewood, Ill.: Dorsey Press, 1968.

Schein, E. H. and Bennis, W. G. *Personal and organizational change through group methods.* New York: Wiley & Sons, 1965.

Schwitzgebel, R. A simple behavioral system for recording and implementing change in natural settings. Unpublished doctoral dissertation, Harvard School of Education, 1964.

Schwitzgebel, R. and Kolb, D. A. *Changing human behavior: Principles of planned intervention,* New York: McGraw-Hill, 1974.

Secord, P. F. and Backman, C. W. *Social psychology.* New York: McGraw-Hill, 1964.

Thomas, J., Bennis, W., and Fulenwider, M. Problem analysis diagram. Unpublished manuscript, Sloan School of Management, M.I.T., 1966.

Truax, C. and Carkhoff, R. For better or for worse: The process of psychotherapeutic personality change, in, *Recent advances in the study of behavior change.* Montreal: McGill University Press, 1964.

White, R. W. Motivation reconsidered: The concept of competence, *Psychological Review,* 1959, Vol. 66, 297–333.

Wolpe, J. *Psychotherapy by reciprocal inhibition.* Stanford: Stanford University Press, 1958.

Zachs, J. Collaborative therapy for smokers. Unpublished manuscript, Harvard University, 1965.

CAREER DEVELOPMENT, PERSONAL GROWTH, AND EXPERIENTIAL LEARNING

Donald M. Wolfe

David A. Kolb

Career development involves one's whole life, not just occupation. As such, it concerns the whole person—needs and wants, capacities and potentials, excitements and anxieties, insights and blindspots, warts and all. More than that, it concerns him/her in the ever-changing contexts of his/her life. The environmental pressures and constraints, the bonds that tie him/her to significant others, responsibilities to children and aging parents, the total structure of one's circumstances are also factors that must be understood and reckoned with. In these terms, career development and personal development converge. Self and circumstance—evolving, changing, unfolding in mutual interaction—constitute the focus and the drama of career development.

I. Current Perspectives on Learning and Adult Development

The overwhelming bulk of the theory and research on personality development has focused on childhood stages and processes. Since the time of Freud's early work on psychosexual development, the emphasis even among researchers with quite different theoretical orientations (e.g., Piaget) has been on the impact of early experiences and maturational factors on the structure of adult personality, which is presumably quite stable, past adolescence. This is in keeping with our general cultural orientation, which treats the first 20 plus years as formative, after which one is, or should be, "mature." The predominant structures of both family life and our educational system are geared to these assumptions.

Primary and secondary education and much of college are aimed toward the acquisition of broad areas of knowledge and skills which can be applied to many fields of work; specialized training through trade or professional schools or apprenticeships for a specific career is, in educational terms, the last formative step toward becoming a full adult. The implicit assumption is that one can learn by the mid-twenties those things one needs to know to pursue a successful life career, in spite of our common knowledge that job changes are frequent and often necessary later in life.

In recent years there has been a growing interest in more differentiated views of career development, recognizing that "success" often leads to promotions which require new knowledge and competencies and that "failures" may require a new start in a different field. In any event, the earlier assumptions are oversimplified and distressingly off-target—people can and do learn and develop throughout their life spans, and there are many significant turns in the road which require new learning for many, if not all, career paths. Maturity in life and career is more appropriately viewed as a continuing process of unfolding than as a status achieved once and for all.

The scientific study of personality development, in spite of its major emphasis on the childhood years, has in recent years begun to address the processes of growth throughout the life cycle. In 1950 Erikson published the first of several seminal works on his epigenetic eight-stage model of psychosocial development throughout the life cycle, building on Freud's theory of psychosexual development. This work, in particular, has stimulated the current generation of work on the adult stages of development [cf. Levinson et al. (1974, 1977), Gould (1972), Neugarten (1968), and Havighurst (1972)—popularized by Sheehy (1976)]. In Erikson's model (and in others as well) the stages are precipitated by the convergence of internal and environmental forces which require a new kind of adaptation and from which one undertakes the development of new capacities and strengths. In childhood, the internal forces emerge primarily from biological maturation (e.g., the sexual awakening at puberty), and even in later life, biological changes (acute illness, physical deterioration) may impose new adaptive responses. But for the most part, the inner forces for change in adults derive from psychological needs.

Environmental forces are similarly more predictable in the early years—mothers no longer tolerate giving constant attention to the post-infancy child, with increasing mobility of the two- to three-year-old, parents must put the brakes on at least the more destructive and intrusive behavior; and so on. In the adult stages the environmental forces vary more widely from one career path to another (career defined quite broadly to incorporate both occupational roles and other major walks of life, e.g., childbearing). Nonetheless, for the adult as for the child, significant external events (e.g., the birth of a first child, taking on new major work assignments, becoming responsible for aging parents, being blocked from long-dreamed-of achievements), whether planned or haphazard, produce changes in the environmental press to which one must adapt. In any case, the emerging centrality of new developmental tasks, marking entry to a new stage, is always a joint function of personal and situational factors. Research on adult development must also have this dual focus.

The Phases and Developmental Tasks of Adult Life

While there are minor disagreements among the authors mentioned above, a general model is emerging from their collective research efforts. The essential features of this model are:

1. Personality deveopment throughout the life cycle occurs through a succession of relatively predictable phases.
2. Within each phase there is a cycle of intensity and quiescence—a disruption to the quasi-stationary equilibrium (in Lewin's terms) of one's former pattern of adaptation, leading to intense coping efforts and heightened activity (often involving significant changes in orientation and situational arrangements), followed by establishment of a new equilibrium.

3. The disequilibrium is generated, in each phase, by the emergence of a new focal conflict or dilemma created by new internal forces, environmental pressures and demands, or both.
4. One can cope with the focal conflict in defensive, or developmental ways (i.e., the consequences may be positive or negative, growthful or regressive).
5. Growth involves the active engagement in a set of "developmental tasks" appropriate to resolving the focal conflicts and satisfying personal needs and social responsibilities.

Havighurst (1977) defines a developmental task as one that "arises at or about a certain period in the life of the individual, successful achievement of which leads to his happiness and to success with later tasks, while failure leads to unhappiness in the individual, disapproval by the society, and difficulty with later tasks." He sees the young adult (20 to 35) as faced with two basic tasks: "He wants to explore possibilities, before making some permanent choices, expecially about his occupational career. At the same time he wants to get himself established in a life structure which offers continuity and growth." The specific developmental tasks of this period are (1) selecting a mate, (2) starting a family, (3) rearing children, (4) managing a home, (5) getting started in an occupation, and (6) taking on civil responsibility. The major striving during this period (according to Neugarten, 1963) is toward establishing mastery over the outer world. Hence, one's orientation is largely other-directed, in keeping with his concerns about where and how he "fits" in society. Major preoccupations are achievement and recognition.

Toward the end of this period, many people begin to reexamine their purposes, drives, and life-style. They take stock of their accomplishments and resources and begin to question what they should do with the rest of their lives. That is to say, they enter the (often disconcerting) *midlife transition.*

In middle adulthood the frenetic turning inward of the midlife transition mellows to a more quiet preoccupation with the inner life, associated with an acceptance of the limited time left in life and with increased confidence in oneself and what one can do. The developmental tasks of middle adulthood, according to Havighurst, are (1) achieving mature social and civil responsibility, (2) assisting teenaged children to become responsible and happy adults, (3) reaching and maintaining satisfactory performance in one's occupational career, (4) developing adult leisure-time activities, (5) accepting and adjusting to the physiological changes of middle age, and (6) adapting to aging parents.

The life cycle thus can be conceived as spanning these broad phases: the formative years up to age 18 to 20, early adulthood to age 35 to 40, and middle–late adulthood. Each of these can be further subdivided for special purposes; in fact, many people experience a much larger number of phases as the conditions of their lives change. We distinguish these three because they typically involve quite different stances toward life, each with its special developmental dissection. In childhood and adolescence, the focus is on *acquisition* of those interests, values, propensities, and competencies that make one a unique person ready to live in the adult world.

The next 15 to 20 years or so constitute a period of differentiation and specialization during which the person finds his place in that world and learns how to function more or less effectively within it. Generally, during this period one's focus is outward, attending to environmental possibilities and constraints and what one needs to do to adapt to and master living in one's life structure (the pattern of roles, groups, and organizations which we have included under the umbrella term circumstances).

Sometime in midlife there tends to be a (not always deliberate or articulated) questioning and reexamination of one's life and turning inward of focus aimed toward a more effective and comfortable *integration* of the whole self and life circumstances. There is, of course, nothing magical about age per se; the shift from one phase to another, while fairly predictable, varies considerably from person to person, depending both on her/his psychological condition and on how s/he is viewed and treated by others.

We think it is also important to differentiate life phases from developmental stage or level. The phases Sheehy identifies, for example, reflect age-related conditions and challenges of life. Developmental tasks are set before one. These may or may not be faced and worked through in developmental ways. Consequently, personal growth or increased maturity may or may not accrue from them. Growth in terms of enhancement of self-insight, wisdom, competence, ego strength, adaptability, or personal integrity (while perhaps correlated with the movement through life phases) clearly reflects a different conceptual dimension. Changing circumstances and adjustments to them do not automatically imply personality development, although they often provide the conditions and stimulus for growth to occur.

Changing Life Structures

The transition from one life phase to another is often marked by some significant circumstantial change (e.g., marriage, divorce, moving to a new community, taking a new job) or internal changes in meanings, attitude, or purpose, calling for a rearrangement of one's relationship to the structures in his/her environment. Levinson refers to such changes as "marker events."

Much about one's circumstances is influenced by forces outside oneself. Some changes (e.g., death of a loved one) are imposed upon the person—s/he is a victim of her/his circumstances. S/he has no choice. Nevertheless, people generally have a great deal of choice in life structure. Even in situations totally defined and structured by others, it is the person, more often than not, who chooses whether to involve himself/herself in that situation.

To a considerable extent, once in a situation, much can be done to alter one's environment—to restructure conditions and relationships in ways that make them more fitting and fulfilling for the person. For example, a manager may not have full choice in what responsibilities fall within his/her purview or which subordinates will be assigned to his/her area, but s/he often has considerable latitude in determining how tasks will be approached and in style of management (e.g., participative, or group-centered vs. unilateral or one-on-one supervision). Similarly, family members can often renegotiate responsibilities for various household tasks.

In these terms, adaptation is a two-way street; one can alter the situation to fit himself/herself as well as adjusting herself/himself to fit the situation. One is active agent as well as sometimes pawn in the flux of changing life structures. Choice in entering, altering, and leaving various environmental structures is ultimately what gives one at least some mastery over circumstances. A consequence of this is that, just as people can create or find living arrangements that give some modicum of comfort, security, and gratification, they can seek out and build new life structures that provide conditions and experiences for further personal development.

Learning as the Core Process of Development

Movement through life's phases may occur with dramatic or only minor changes in circumstantial structure. Similarly, it may coincide with substantial or with little or no personal growth and development. One may adapt to new circumstances or new life demands in old ways and, in spite of modification in behavior, remain essentially unchanged by the experience. Yet the changing pressures, conditions, and opportunities are often the ground for new spurts in personal growth.

The difference between mere readjustment and development is a function of the learning that occurs through the experience. Personal development involved increasing self-insight and recognition and acceptance of one's complex, ever-changing dynamics. It also involves increased understanding of one's world and how it works. It involves increased capacity for taking responsibility for oneself, coupled with increased competence in pursuing one's ends in personally fulfilling and socially beneficial ways. All of these increases come about through a variety of learning processes—processes that can occur in any setting and continue throughout one's life.

II. The Theory of Experiential Learning

Experiential learning theory provides a model of learning and adaptation processes consistent with the structure of human cognition and the stages of human growth and development. It conceptualizes the learning process in such a way that differences in individual learning styles and corresponding learning environments can be identified. The core of the model, shown in Figure 1, is a simple description of the learning cycle; of how experience is translated into concepts which, in turn, are used as guides in the choice of new experiences.

FIGURE 1
The Experiential Learning Model

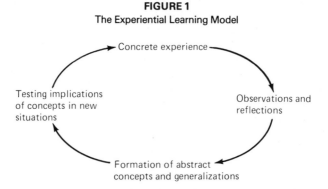

Learning is conceived of as a four-stage cycle. Immediate concrete experience is the basis for observation and reflection. These observations are assimilated into a "theory" from which new implications for action can be deduced. These implications or hypotheses then serve as guides in acting to create new experiences. The learner, if s/he is to be effective, needs four different kinds of generic adaptive abilities: *concrete experience* abilities (CE), *reflective observation* (RO) abilities, *abstract conceptualization* (AC) abilities, and *active experimentation* (AE) abilities. That is s/he must be able to involve herself/himself fully, openly, and without bias in new experiences (CE); s/he must be able to observe and reflect on these experiences from many perspectives (RO); s/he must be able to create concepts that integrate her/his observations into logically sound theories (AC); and s/he must be able to use these theories to make decisions and solve problems (AE). Yet this ideal is difficult to achieve. Can anyone become highly skilled in all these abilities, or are they necessarily in conflict? How can one be concrete and immediate and still be theoretical?

A closer examination of the four-stage learning model would suggest that learning requires abilities that are polar opposites and that the learner, as a result, must continually choose which set of learning abilities s/he will bring to bear in a specific learning situation. More specifically, there are two primary dimensions to the learning process. The first dimension represents the concrete experiencing of events at one end and abstract conceptualization at the other. The other dimension has active experimentation at one extreme and reflective observation at the other. Thus, in the process of learning, one moves in varying degrees from actor to observer, from specific involvement to general analytic detachment.

These two dimensions represent the major direction of cognitive development identified by Piaget. In his view, the course of individual cognitive development from birth to adolescence moves from a phenomenolistic (concrete) view of the world to a constructivist (abstract) view and from an egocentric (active) view to a reflective internalized mode of knowing. Piaget also maintains that these have also been the major directions of development in scientific knowledge (Piaget, 1970).

Many other cognitive psychologists (e.g., Bruner, 1960, 1966; Harvey, Hunt, and Shroeder, 1961) have identified the concrete/abstract dimension as a primary dimension on which cognitive growth and learning occurs. Goldstein and Scheerer suggest that greater abstractness results in the development of the following abilities:

1. To detach one's ego from the outer world or from inner experience.
2. To assume a mental set.
3. To account for acts to oneself; to verbalize the account.
4. To shift reflectively from one aspect of the situation to another.
5. To hold in mind simultaneously various aspects.
6. To grasp the essential of a given whole: to break up a given into parts to isolate and to synthesize them.
7. To abstract common properties reflectively; to form hierarchic concepts.
8. To plan ahead ideationally, to assume an attitude toward the more possible, and to think or perform symbolically (1941, p. 4).

Concreteness, on the other hand, represents, according to these theorists, the absence of these abilities, the immersion in and domination by one's immediate experiences. Yet the circular, dialectic model of the learning process would imply that abstractness is not exclusively good and concreteness exclusively bad. Witkin's (1962, 1973) extensive research on the related cognitive styles of global vs. analytic functioning has shown that both extremes of functioning have their costs and benefits; the analytic style includes competence in analytical functioning combined with an impersonal orientation, while the global style reflects less competence in analytic functioning combined with greater social orientation and social skill. Similarly, when we consider the highest form of learning—creativity—we see a requirement that one be able to experience anew, freed somewhat from the constraints of previous abstract concepts. In psychoanalytic theory this need for a concrete childlike perspective in the creative process is referred to as regression in service of the ego (Kris, 1952). Bruner (1966), in his essay on the conditions for creativity, emphasizes the dialectic tension between abstract and concrete involvement. For him the creative act is a project of detachment and commitment, of passion and decorum, and of a freedom to be dominated by the object of one's injury.

The active/reflective dimension is the other major dimension of cognitive growth and learning. As growth occurs, thought becomes more reflective and internalized, based more on the manipulation of symbols and images than overt actions. The modes of active experimentation and reflection, like abstractness/concreteness, stand in opposition to one another. Kagan's (Kagan and Kogan, 1970) research on the cognitive-style dimension of reflection–impulsivity suggests that extremes of functioning on this continuum represent opposing definitions of competence and strategies for achieving. The impulsive strategy is based on seeking reward for active accomplishment, while the reflective strategy is based on seeking reward through the avoidance of error. Reflection tends to inhibit action, and vice versa. For example, Singer (1968) has found that children who have active internal fantasy lives are more capable of inhibiting action for long periods of time than are children with little internal fantasy life. Kagan et al. (1964) have found, on the other hand, that very active orientations toward learning situations inhibit reflection and thereby preclude the development of analytic concepts. Herein lies the second major dialectic in the learning process—the tension between actively testing the implications of one's hypotheses and reflectively interpreting data already collected.

Individual Learning Styles

Over time, accentuation forces operate on individuals in such a way that the dialectic tensions between these dimensions are consistently resolved in a characteristic fashion. As a result of our hereditary equipment, our particular past life experience, and the demands of our present environment, most people develop learning styles that emphasize some learning abilities over others. Through socialization experiences in family, school, and work, we come to resolve the conflicts between being active and reflective and between being immediate and analytical in characteristic ways. Some people develop minds that excel at assimilating disparate facts into coherent theories, yet these same people are incapable of, or uninterested in, deducing hypotheses from the theory. Others are logical geniuses but find it impossible to involve and surrender themselves to an experience. And so on. A mathematician may come to place great emphasis on abstract concepts, while a poet may value concrete experience more highly. A manager may be primarily concerned with the active application of ideas, while a naturalist may develop his/her observational skills highly. Each of us in a unique way develops a learning style that has some weak and strong points.

We have developed a brief self-descriptive inventory called the Learning Style Inventory (LSI) to measure differences in learning styles along the two basic dimensions of abstract/concrete and action/reflection (Kolb, 1976). While the individuals tested on the LSI show many different patterns of scores, we have identified four statistically prevalent types of learning styles. We have called these four styles the converger, the diverger, the assimilator, and the accommodator. The following is a summary of the characteristics of these types based both on our research and on clinical observation of these patterns of LSI scores.

The *converger's* dominant learning abilities are abstract conceptualization (AC) and active experimentation (AE). His/her greatest strength lies in the practical application of ideas. We have called this learning style the "converger" because a person with this style seems to do best in those situations, such as conventional intelligence tests, where there is a single correct answer or solution to a question or problem (Torrealba, 1972). His/her knowledge is organized in such a way that, through hypothetical–deductive reasoning, s/he can focus it on specific problems. Liam Hudson's (1966) research in this style of learning (using different measures than the LSI) shows that convergers are relatively unemotional, preferring to deal with things rather than people. They tend to have narrow interests, and often choose to specialize in the physical sciences. Our research shows that this learning style is characteristic of many engineers (Kolb, 1976).

The *diverger* has the opposite learning strengths of the converger. S/he is best at concrete experience (CE) and reflective observation (RO). His/her greatest strength lies in his/her imaginative ability. S/he excels in the ability to view concrete situations from many perspectives and to organize many relationships into a meaningful "gestalt." We have labeled this style "diverger" because a person of this type performs better in situations that call for the generation of ideas, such as in a "brainstorming" idea session. Divergers are interested in people and tend to be imaginative and emotional. They have broad cultural interests and tend to specialize in the arts. Our research shows that this style is characteristic of persons with humanities and liberal arts backgrounds. Counselors, organization development consultants, and personnel managers often have this learning style.

The *assimilator's* dominant learning abilities are abstract conceptualization (AC) and reflective observation (RO). His/her greatest strength lies in his/her ability to create theoretical models. S/he excels in inductive reasoning; in assimilating disparate observations into an integrated explanation (Grochow, 1973). S/he, like the converger, is less interested in people and more concerned about abstract concepts, but s/he is less concerned with the practical use of theories. For him/her it is more important that the theory be logically sound and precise. As a result, this learning style is more characteristic of the basic sciences and mathematics rather than the applied sciences. In organizations, this learning style is found most often in the research and planning departments (Kolb, 1976; Strasmore, 1973).

The *accommodator* has the opposite strengths of the assimilator. S/he is best at concrete experience (CE) and active experimentation (AE). His/her greatest strength lies in doing things; in carrying out plans and experiments and involving himself/herself in new experiences. S/he tends to be more of a risk taker than people with the other three learning styles. We have labeled this style "accommodator" because S/he tends to excel in those situations where s/he must adapt himself/herself to specific immediate circumstances. In situations where the theory or plans do not fit the facts, s/he will most likely discard the plan or theory. (The opposite type, the assimilator, would be more likely to disregard or reexamine the facts.) S/he tends to solve problems in an intuitive, trial-and-error manner (Grochow, 1973), relying heavily on other people for information rather than her/his own analytic ability (Stabell, 1973). The accommodator is at ease with people but is sometimes seen as impatient and "pushy." His/her educational background is often in technical or practical fields such as business. In organizations, people with this learning style are found in "action-oriented" jobs, often in marketing or sales.

Developmental Stages: An Experiential Learning Perspective

In addition to providing a framework for conceptualizing individual differences in style of adaptation to the world, the experiential learning model suggests more normative directions for human growth and development. As we have seen in the previous section, individual learning styles affect how people learn, not only in the limited educational sense, but also in the broader aspects of adaptation to life, such as decision making, problem solving, and life-style in general. Experiential learning is not a molecular educational concept, but a molar concept describing the central process of human adaptation to the social and physical environment. It, like Jungian theory (Jung, 1923), is a holistic concept that seeks to describe the emergence of basic life orientations as a function of dialectic tensions between basic modes of relating to the world. As such, it encompasses other more limited adaptive concepts, such as creativity, problem solving, decision making, and attitude change, that focus heavily on one or another of the basic aspects of adaptation. Thus, creativity research has tended to focus on the divergent (concrete and reflective) factors in adaptation, such as tolerance for ambiguity, metaphorical thinking and flexibility, while research on decision making has emphasized more convergent (abstract and active) adaptive factors, such as the rational evaluation of solution alternatives.

From this broader perspective, learning becomes a central life task, and how one learns becomes a major determinant of the course of his/her personal development. The experiential learning model provides a means of mapping these different developmental paths and a normative adaptive ideal—a learning process wherein the individual has highly developed abilities to experience, observe, conceptualize, and experiment.

The human growth process is divided into three broad developmental stages. The first stage, *acquisition*, extends from birth to adolescence and marks the acquisition of basic learning abilities and cognitive structures. The second stage, *specialization*, extends through formal education and/or career training and the early experiences of adulthood in work and personal life. In this stage, development primarily follows paths that accentuate a particular learning style. Individuals shaped by social, educational, and organizational socialization forces develop increased competence in a specialized mode of adaptation that enables them to master the particular life tasks they encounter in their chosen career (in the broadest sense of that word). This stage, in our thinking, terminates at midcareer, although the specific chronology of the transition to stage 3 will vary widely from person to person and from one career path to another. The third stage, *integration*, is marked by the reassertion and expression of the nondominant adaptive modes or learning styles. Means of adapting to the world that have been suppressed in favor of the development of the more highly rewarded dominant learning style now find expression in the form of new career interests, changes in life-styles, and/or innovation and creativity in one's chosen career.

Through these three stages, development is marked by increasing complexity and relativism in dealing with the world and one's experiences, and by higher-level integrations of the dialectic conflicts between the four primary genotypic adaptive modes—concrete experience, reflective observation, abstract conceptualization, and active experimentation. With each of these four modes, a major dimension of personal growth is associated. Development in the concrete experience adaptive mode is characterized by increases in *affective complexity*. Development in the reflective observation mode is characterized by increases in *perceptual complexity*. Development in the abstract conceptualization and active experimentation modes are characterized by increases in *symbolic complexity* and *behavioral complexity*, respectively.

In the early stages of development, progress along one of these four dimensions can occur with relative independence from the others. The child and young adult, for example, can develop highly sophisticated symbolic proficiencies and remain naive emotionally. At the highest stages of development, however, the adaptive commitment to learning and creativity produces a strong need for integration of the four adaptive modes. Development in one mode precipitates development in the others. Increases in symbolic complexity, for example, redefine and sharpen both perceptual and behavioral possibilities. Thus, complexity and the integration of dialectic conflicts among the adaptive modes are the hallmarks of true creativity and growth.

Figure 2 graphically illustrates the experiential learning model of growth and development as it has been outlined thus far. The four dimensions of growth are depicted in the shape of a cone, the base of which represents the lower stages of development and the apex of which represents the peak of development—representing the fact that the four dimensions become more highly integrated at higher stages of development. Any individual learning style would be represented on this cone by four data points on the four vertical dimensions of development. Thus, a converger in developmental stage 2 (specialization) would be characterized by high complexity in the symbolic and behavioral modes and lower complexity in the affective and perceptual modes. As s/he moved into stage 3 of development, her/his complexity scores in the affective and perceptual modes would increase.

While we have depicted the stages of the growth process in the form of a simple three-layer cone, the actual process of growth in any single individual life history probably proceeds through successive oscillations from one stage to another. Thus, a person may move from stage 2 to 3 in several separate subphases of integrative advances followed by consolidation or regression into specialization. (For a more detailed description of this development model, see Kolb and Fry, 1975.)

III. Learning Press of Disciplines and Careers

Situations differ in the adaptational demands they place on the person in two major ways. First, they differ in degree of complexity: some situations are

FIGURE 2
The Experiential Learning Theory of Growth and Development

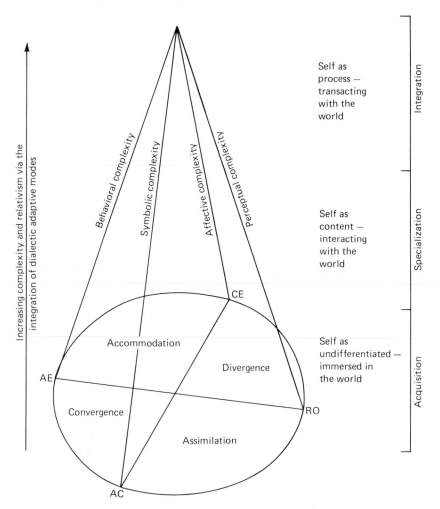

simple, familiar, predictable, and consequently easy to understand and deal with, while others are complex, turbulent, and highly taxing of one's coping resources.

Second, they differ in the kinds of adaptive response that tends to be effective. For example, many interpersonal situations call for a heightened sensitivity to emotional dynamics and nuances. Active listening and tuning in to others through skills in concrete experiencing is more effective than, for example, withdrawing into reflection or categorizing others in abstract terms. Other problems are more readily dealt with through creation and application of abstract analytic schemes. Consequently, it is important in examining career possibilities, to differentiate the kind as well as the degree of complexity within which one must function.

The concept of environmental learning press is based on differential complexity inherent in the situation—on the kind of learning process that facilitates adaptation. But learning press implies more than that. It also reflects the fact that practice in dealing with a particular kind of complexity stretches the person's capacity for dealing with it more readily. A situation that demands experimenting with behavioral alternatives enhances and reinforces active experimentation, to the extent that the person engages in this process. One expands his/her learning and adaptive processes through exercising them. Hence, a particular environment may be a fertile field for enriching one or another generic adaptive competence. Thus, given an appropriate methodology, environments can be assessed for the extent to which they require and thereby stimulate development on each of the four basic learning modalities.

We do not mean to imply that a press toward a particular style of learning necessarily results in that kind of learning. Just as one acquires through childhood and adolescence some capacity to engage in learning modes, one also acquires a variety of ways of coping with overwhelming or intolerable complexity. Complex situations can be defended against as well as engaged in. Among the ways one can deal defensively with complex situations are selective inattention, polarizing (black–white thinking), stereotyping, intellectualizing, withdrawing, impulsive action, and routinization.

A mismatch of style and press is more apt to lead to a defensive response and to an artificial simplification of situational complexity. Divergers are apt to turn aside the challenge and tedium of abstract analysis in favor of pursuing new excitements, or to resist and delay making the decisions required for taking action when that is called for. Convergers, on the other hand, are apt to ignore or stereotype others in favor of applying abstract principles to problem solving. The former often defends against symbolic and behavioral complexity, while the latter defends against the affective and perceptual. Accommodators and assimilators likewise have their ways of reducing and defending against kinds of complexity with which they are ill-equipped to deal.

Differential Learning Press across Academic Disciplines

Let us turn now to the question of whether different fields involve characteristic kinds of complexity and therefore press toward particular adaptive competencies. More particularly, we are concerned with whether the two-dimensional learning style grid might accurately portray the similarities, differences, and interrelations among fields. To explore this question, we examined data collected in the 1969 Carnegie Commission on Higher Education study of representative American colleges and university. These data consisted of 32,963 questionnaires from graduate students in 158 institutions and 60,028 questionnaires from faculty in 303 institutions. Using tabulations of these data reported in Feldman (1974), *ad hoc* indices were created of the abstract/concrete and active/reflective dimensions for the 45 academic fields identified in the study. The abstract/concrete index was based on graduate-student responses to two questions asking how important an undergraduate background in mathematics and humanities were for their fields. The mathematics and humanities questions were highly negatively correlated (-.78). The index was computed using the percentage of graduate-student respondents who strongly agreed that either humanities or mathematics were very important:

$$\frac{\text{\% math important} + (100 - \text{\% humanities important})}{2}$$

Thus, high index scores indicated a field where a mathematics background was important and humanities was not important.

The active/reflective index used faculty data on the percent of faculty in a given field who were engaged in paid consultation to business, government, and so on. This seemed to be the best indicator on the questionnaire of the active, applied orientation of the field. As Feldman observed, "Consulting may be looked upon not only as a source of added income but also as an indirect measure of the 'power' of a discipline, that is, as a chance to exert the influence and knowledge of a discipline outside the academic setting" (1974, p. 52). The groupings of academic fields based on these indices are shown in Figure 3.

The indices produce a pattern of relationships among academic fields that is highly consistent with other studies (see Biglan, 1973) and with the learning style data (reported in a later section). The results support the widely shared view that cultural variation in academic fields divide the academic community into two camps, the scientific and the artistic (e.g., Snow, 1963; Hudson, 1966). They also suggest that this is usefully enriched by the addition of a second dimension of action/reflection or applied/basic. When academic fields are mapped on this two-dimensional space, a fourfold typology of disciplines emerges. The *natural sciences and mathematics*, calling for assimilative adaptive skills, are appropriately clustered in the abstract/reflective quadrant, while the abstract/active quadrant incorporates the *science-based professions*, most notably the engineering fields, reflecting their requirements for skills in convergence around applied problems. The *social professions* (such as education, social work, and law) press for accommodative competencies and are found in the concrete/active quadrant. The concrete/reflective quadrant encompasses the *arts, humanities, and social sciences*, all of which tend to be enriched by divergent mentalities.

Some fields seem to include within their boundaries considerable variation on these two dimensions of learning style. Several of the professions (particularly management, medicine, and architecture) are themselves multidisciplinary, including specialities that emphasize different learning styles. Medicine requires both a concern for human service and scientific knowledge. Architecture has requirements for artistic and engineering excellence. Management involves skill at both quantitative and qualitative analysis: dealing with things and dealing with people. Several of the social sciences, particularly psychology, sociology, and economics, can vary greatly in their basic inquiry paradigm. Clinical psychology emphasizes divergent learning skills, while experimental psychology emphasizes convergent skills; industrial and educational psychology emphasize practical accommodative skills. Sociology can be highly abstract and theoretical (as in Parsonian structural functionalism) or concrete and active (as in phenomenology or ethnomethodology). Some economics departments may be very convergent, emphasizing the use of econometric models in public policy, while others are divergent, emphasizing economic history and philosophy.

Indeed, every field will show variation on these dimensions within a given department, between departments, from undergraduate to graduate levels,

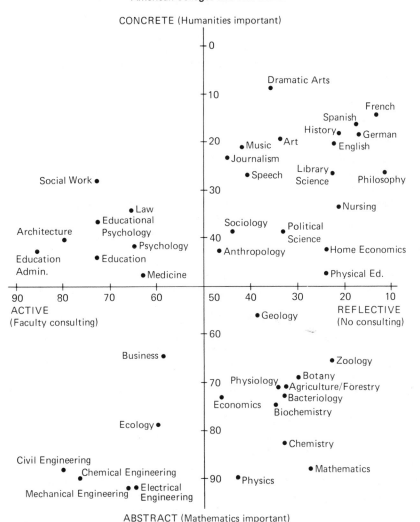

FIGURE 3

Concrete/Abstract and Active/Reflective Orientations of
Academic Fields Derived from the Carnegie Commission Study of
American Colleges and Universities

and so on. The purpose of this analysis is not to "pigeonhole" fields but to identify useful dimensions for describing variations in the learning/inquiry process that characterize different career paths.

The Structure of Knowledge. When one examines fields in the four major groupings we have identified—the social professions, the science-based professions, humanities/social science, and natural science/mathematics—it becomes apparent that what constitutes valid knowledge in these four groupings differs widely. This is easily observed in differences in how knowledge is reported (e.g., numerical or logical symbols, words, or images), in inquiry methods (e.g., case studies, experiments, logical analysis), or in criteria for evaluation (e.g., practical vs. statistical significance). In this typology the professions are predominately discrete in their inquiry strategy, seeking to understand particular events or phenomena, while the basic disciplines are integrated in their inquiry strategies, seeking structures or processes that apply universally. The scientific professions and basic disciplines are predominately analytic, seeking to understand wholes by identifying their component parts, while the social/humanistic fields tend to be synthetic, believing that the whole can never be explained solely by its component parts.

Learning Press in Professional Education

The data presented above deal with learning press as a generalized direction of a field—the dominant "style" of the field, analogous to the learning style of a person. But if we are to understand how learning press reinforces and enhances development of adaptive competencies, we must take a more microscopic look. What are the specific conditions, events, and social psychological processes through which the environmental press impacts the person?

In educational settings, a major focal point for learning press is the immediate learning environment, determined primarily by teachers and the course designs. For example, we have found correlations between the learning styles of students and the learning styles of teachers they found influential, as well as correlations between student learning styles and preference for educational methods, such as lectures, small-group discussions, and so on (Kolb, 1976). Fry (1977) has developed a reliable assessment procedure for determining the extent to which a given learning environment stimulates development on the four basic learning style modes: affective complexity, perceptual complexity, symbolic complexity, and behavioral complexity. His technique examines five areas of a learning environment: (1) objectives, (2) principal focus and source of information, (3) nature of feedback and rewards, (4) the learner's role, and (5) the teacher's role.

Table I identifies characteristics of the four "pure" types of learning environments. In each case, practice in and reinforcement of the associated leaning mode is required and supported. Formal lectures, textbook reading, and test taking exemplify symbolically complex situations intended to expand one's capacity for abstract conceptionalization. Most graduate seminars and paper writing assignments are both perceptually and symbolically complex, reinforcing reflective as well as conceptualizing skills. On the other hand, field placements in social work or clinical fields involve both concrete experiencing and active experimenting, stretching one's competence in dealing with affective and behavioral complexity.

From Fry's analysis it becomes clear that enhancement of those generic adaptive competencies most relevant to a particular career field is a function not just of *what* is learned, but also of *how* it is learned and under what immediate conditions in the educational context. Pedagogical strategies and teaching styles can be congruent or incongruent not only with the subject matter, but also with the adaptive competencies required for success in the field. Initial socialization into a career field occurs perhaps most forcefully through these processes.

TABLE 1
Characteristics of Educational Environment Which Press toward
and Reinforce Basic Learning Modes

1. Affectively complex environments are characterized by:
   a. Focus on here-and-now experiences.
   b. Legitimization of expression of feelings and emotions.
   c. Situations structured to allow ambiguity.
   d. High degree of personalization.

2. Perceptually complex environments are characterized by:
   a. Opportunities to view subject matter from different perspectives.
   b. Time to reflect and roles (e.g., listener, observer) that allow reflection.
   c. Complexity and multiplicity of observational frameworks.

3. Symbolically complex environments are characterized by:
   a. Emphasis on recall of concepts.
   b. Thinking or acting governed by rules of logic and inference.
   c. Situations structured to maximize certainty.
   d. Authorities respected as caretakers of knowledge.

4. Behaviorally complex environments are characterized by:
   a. Responsibility for setting own learning goals.
   b. Opportunities for real risk taking.
   c. Environmental responses contingent upon self-initiated action.

The Learning Press of Work Roles and Environments

Adaptation and learning are called for in every context throughout life. In most work settings, one is interdependent with a variety of others who have a stake in how the assigned role is performed. These others (colleagues, clients, supervisors, subordinates, and others with whom s/he interacts) each hold expectations about what s/he should and should not do, how problems should be handled, and how relationships should be maintained. In some fields the issues are restricted to task behaviors, but in many the expectations go beyond this to what one should believe and how one should think and feel.

When these role expectations are communicated, through word or action, they become *role pressures*. They are most apt to be expressed, of course, when one's behavior violates expectations or when other conditions call for a change in behavior. It is through these sometimes distinct, but often subtle and indirect pressures that one learns, day by day, how to be in his/her career.

Four functions are involved in virtually every endeavor: perceiving, thinking, acting, and feeling, and any of these may be the target of role expectations. Consequently, we think of expectations being in the perceptual domain if they deal with what the person becomes aware of, recognizes, and attends to. At the group or organizational level, this has to do with a shared sense of reality. In highly stable situations where simple, routine tasks are to be performed, a common sense of reality is readily maintained with little active communication of role expectations. Turbulent situations or those which require simultaneous attention to many facets and issues are more apt to involve role pressures having to do with the person's awareness or observational capacities. Thus, we can assess roles (and career lines) in terms of their relative perceptual complexity.

Roles that involve complex analysis, synthesis, and problem solving tend to be rich in symbolic complexity. People in such roles (e.g., researchers, educators) tend to be evaluated in terms of the depth and quality of their thought processes and their ability to integrate complex issues through abstract reasoning. Role pressures on this dimension tend to deal with logic, comprehensiveness, keeping abreast of knowledge development, potential applications, and the like.

In other fields the emphasis is on action—on decision making and generating useful results. Managers, engineers, physicians, nurses, and many trades deal with high degrees of behavioral complexity. Role pressures tend to focus on the quality of decisions taken and solutions achieved. How one deals with the facts in the situation to produce valued outcomes is the major concern of role senders.

Affective complexity is central to certain roles (e.g., psychiatrist, personnel manager, social worker, minister, actor) and is generally highly valued in the humanities and arts. Role pressures in the affective domain are apt to focus on having an appropriate value system and using it with empathy and understanding.

At any given time, whatever one's career, one may be subjected to role pressures in any of these domains—perceptual, symbolic, behavioral, or affective—but clearly those roles which center on one or another tend to reinforce specialization in a corresponding learning style. Early in one's career the press is often specialized, only to be broadened in later phases. For example, engineers generally experience the strongest role press in the symbolic and behavioral domains, but with advancement to management positions, there is increasing pressure to attend also to the affective and perceptual. Thus, changing roles may generate conflict for the person, but may also be the stimulus for increased integration.

Role Constellations and Life-Styles

Most of us occupy several roles during any given phase of life. That is, one is not only a butcher but also a parent/spouse, a neighbor, a member of the committee on social problems at church, a volunteer fireman, and an umpire for the Little League. Each of these roles involve relationships and expectations. Each holds its potential for learning, fulfillment, and stress. They may all contribute to specialization in learning and adaptive style or toward complementarity of different styles.

Role constellations vary along several dimensions that may have important consequences for adult development. They range from simple to complex, depending on the number of separate roles and contexts one engages in. They vary in the extent to which one role dominates the others (e.g., for many housewives, being a mother is central at all times and colors engagement in every other role). They vary in unity vs. disjointedness: some people manage to keep their various roles and role relationships quite isolated from one another —working in the city with one set of colleagues but never taking work or colleagues to their homes in the suburbs.

The pattern of one's role constellation may yield a unified sense of self; that is, one carries the same identity, interests, and adaptive style into all roles. It is equally possible, depending on the constellation, for one to be a "different person" in each role (e.g., to be strong and domineering at work, passive and dependent at home, aloof in community relations, and a "tiger" with a hidden lover). One's life-style, in this sense, may promote learning and stretching one's capacities in some areas while retarding development in others. It may contribute to specialization as well as balancing toward integration.

The transition from adolescence to early adulthood involves a great many changes in one's life structure. The provisional selection of a career and one's first job as an adult are marker events in the resolution of adolescent identity confusion. Entering the adult world begins the elaboration and confirmation of one's newly formed identity. This involves the actualization of one's personal dreams of adult accomplishment, entering a career that holds promise of implementing those dreams, and arranging a new life structure that supports adult–adult relationships, personal fulfillment, and opportunity for the future. Interpersonal issues take on new significance as the person works through the departure from family of origin toward independent life and reaches toward intimacy in selecting a mate and starting a family.

During this early adult transition, one is torn between the need to make career and marital choices which will establish structure, direction, and stability and the desire to keep open the options and possibilities for further development. For some, college offers an extended opportunity to explore various fields, try out relationships with potential partners, and get to know themselves better before making the critical and seemingly irreversible life decisions. In any event, one strives to make choices that yield a good match between personal aspirations and dispositions, on the one hand, and environmental demands, opportunities and resources, on the other. One seeks not just any nitch in the adult world, but one that fits oneself and one's adaptive style.

In the experiential learning theory of career development, stability and change in career paths is seen as resulting from the interaction between internal personality dynamics and external social forces in a manner much like that described by Super and co-workers (1963). The most powerful development dynamic that emerges from this interaction is the tendency for there to be a closer and closer match between self characteristics and environmental demands. This match comes about in two ways: (1) environments tend to change personal characteristics to fit them (i.e., socialization), and (2) individuals tend to select themselves into environments that are consistent with their personal characteristics. Thus, career development in general tends to follow a path toward accentuation of personal characteristics and skills (Feldman and Newcombe, 1969; Kolb, 1973b), in that development is a product of the interaction between choices and socialization experiences that match these dispositions, and the resulting experiences further reinforce the same choice disposition for later experience. Many adult life paths follow a cycle of job, education, and life-style choices that build upon the experiences resulting from similar previous choices. Indeed, the common stereotype of the successful career is a graded ladder of similar experiences on which one climbs to success and fulfillment.

Learning Styles and Career Choice

To illustrate this process, let us first examine the relationship between individuals' learning styles and their career choice. If we examine the undergraduate major of the individuals in a sample of 800 practicing managers and graduate students in management, a correspondence can be seen between their Learning Style Inventory (LSI) scores and their initial career interests (Kolb, 1976). This is done by plotting the average LSI scores for managers in the sample who reported their undergraduate college major (see Figure 4); only those majors with more than 10 people responding are included.

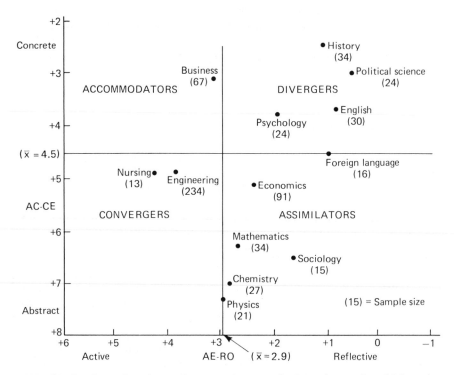

FIGURE 4

Average LSI Scores on Active/Reflective (AE–RO)
and Abstract/Concrete (AC–CE) by Undergraduate College Major

The distribution of undergraduate majors on the learning style grid is quite consistent with theory. Undergraduate business majors tend to have accommodative learning styles, while engineers on the average fall in the convergent quadrant. History, English, political science, and psychology majors all have divergent learning styles. Mathematics and chemistry majors have assimilative learning styles along with economics and sociology. Physics majors are very abstract, falling between convergent and assimilative quadrant. Subsequent studies have consistently replicated this basic pattern of relationship between undergraduate majors and learning styles (Kolb, 1976), a pattern that directly corresponds to the typology of career fields presented earlier (see Figure 3). What these studies show is that undergraduate education is a major factor in the development of learning style. Whether this is because individuals are shaped by the fields they enter or because of selection/evaluation processes that put people into and out of disciplines is an open question at this point. Most probably both factors are operating—people choose fields that are consistent with their learning styles and are further shaped to fit the learning norms of their field once they are in it. When there is a mismatch between the field's learning norms and the individual's learning style, people will either change or leave the field.

Although the data above are suggestive of some general correspondence between learning styles and careers, they do not offer evidence for the accentuation process. In a first attempt to examine the details of this process, Plovnick (1971) studied a major university department using the concepts of convergence and divergence defined by Hudson (1966). He concluded that the major emphasis in physics education was on convergent learning. He predicted that physics students who had divergent learning styles would be more uncertain of physics as a career and would take more courses outside the physics department than their convergent colleagues. His predictions were confirmed. Those students who were not fitted for the convergent learning style required in physics tended to turn away from physics as a profession, while those physics students having a convergent style continued to specialize in physics, both in their course choice and their career choices.

In another study of MIT seniors (Kolb, 1973b), we further examined the consequences of matches and mismatches between student learning style and discipline demands. Several criteria were used to choose four departments whose learning style demands matched the four dominant learning styles. To study the career choices of the students in the four departments, each student's LSI scores were used to position him/her in the LSI grid with a notation of the career field s/he had chosen to pursue after graduation. If the student was planning to attend graduate school, his/her career field was circled. If the accentuation process were operating in the career choices of the students, we should find that those students who fall in the same quadrant as the norm of their academic major should be more likely to pursue graduate training and careers related to that major, while students with learning styles that differ from their discipline norms should be more inclined to pursue other careers and not attend graduate school in their discipline. We can illustrate this pattern by examining students in the mathematics department (Figure 5). Ten of the 13 mathematics students (77 percent) whose learning styles are congruent with departmental norms choose careers and graduate training in mathematics. Only two of the 13 students (15 percent) whose learning styles are not congruent plan both careers and graduate training in mathematics (these differences are significant using the Fisher exact test $p < .01$). Similar patterns occurred in the other three departments.

To further test the accentuation process in the four departments, we examined whether the student's choice/experience career development cycle indeed operated as an accentuating positive feedback loop. If this were so, those students whose learning style dispositions matched and were reinforced by their discipline demands should show a greater commitment to their choice of future career field than those whose learning styles were not reinforced by their experiences in their discipline. As part of a questionnaire, students were asked to rate how important it was for them to pursue their chosen career field. In all four departments, the average importance rating was higher for the students with a match between learning style and discipline norms (the differences being statistically significant in the mechanical engineering and economics departments). Thus, it seems that learning experiences that reinforce learning style dispositions tend to produce greater commitment in career choices than those learning experiences that do not reinforce learning style dispositions.

To examine if this correspondence between learning styles and career field continued in the jobs individuals held in midcareer, we studied about 20 man-

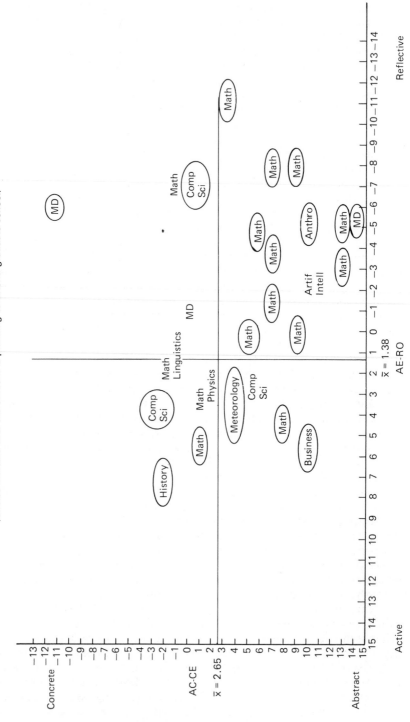

FIGURE 5

Career Field and Graduate School Plans for Mathematics Majors as a Function of Their Learning Styles
(Circles indicate that the student is planning to attend graduate school)

agers from each of five functional groups in a midwestern division of a large American industrial corporation. The five functional groups are described below, followed by our hypothesis about the learning style that should characterize each group given the nature of their work.

1. Marketing ($n = 20$). This group is made up primarily of former salespersons. They have a nonquantitative "intuitive" approach to their work. Because of their practical sales orientation in meeting customer demand, they should have accommodative learning styles (i.e., concrete and active).

2. Research ($n = 22$). The work of this group is split about 50/50 between pioneer research and applied research projects. The emphasis is on basic research. Researchers should be the most assimilative group (i.e., abstract and reflective), a style fitted to the world of knowledge and ideas.

3. Personnel/Labor relations ($n = 20$). In this company, people from this department serve two primary functions, interpreting personnel policy and promoting interaction among groups to reduce conflict and disagreement. Because of their "people orientation," these workers should be predominantly divergers, concrete and reflective.

4. Engineering ($n = 18$). This group is made up primarily of design engineers who are quite production-oriented. They should be the most convergent subgroup (i.e., abstract and active), although they should be less abstract than the research group. They represent a bridge between thought and action.

5. Finance ($n = 20$). This group has a strong computer, information-system bias. Financial workers, given their orientation toward the mathematical task of information system design, should be highly abstract. Their crucial role in organizational survival should produce an active orientation. Thus, finance group members should have convergent learning styles.

Figure 6 shows the average scores on the active/reflective (AE–RO) and abstract/concrete (AC–CE) learning dimensions for the five functional groups. These results are consistent with the predictions above, with the exception of the finance group, whose score is less active than predicted (it fell between the assimilative and the convergent quadrants). The LSI clearly differentiates the learning styles that characterize managers following different career paths within a single company.

We draw two main conclusions from this research. First, the experiential learning typology seems to provide a useful grid for mapping individual differences in learning style and for mapping corresponding differences in the environmental demands of different career paths. As such, it is a potentially powerful tool for describing the differentiated paths of career development. Second, the research data present enticing, if not definitive, evidence that early career choices tend to follow a path toward accentuation of one's learning style. Learning experiences congruent with learning styles tend to positively influence the choice of future learning and work experiences that reinforce that particular learning style. On the other hand, those who find a learning or work environment incongruent with their learning style tend to move away from that kind of environment in future learning and work choices. The research to date suggests that accentuation is a powerful force in early career development. Correspondingly, the major cause of change or deviation from accentuation in the early career results from individual choice errors in choosing a career environment that matches the individual style. The primary reason for the strength of the accentuation forces in early career seems to stem from identity pressures to choose a specialized job and career. Integrative fulfillment needs seem to have second priority at this time.

FIGURE 6

Average LSI Scores on Active/Reflective (AE-RO) and
Abstract/Concrete (AC-CE) by Organizational Functions

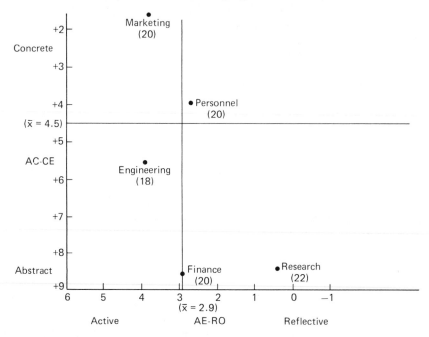

V. Midcareer Transition and the Move Toward Integration

The developmental model of experiential learning theory holds that specialization of learning style typifies early adulthood and that the role demands of career and family are likely to reinforce specialization. We expect, however, that this pattern changes in midcareer. Specifically, we expect that as individuals mature, accentuation forces play a smaller role. On the contrary, the approach of the middle years brings with it a questioning of one's purposes and aspirations, a reassessment of life structure and direction. For many, choices made earlier have led down pathways no longer rewarding, and some kind of change is needed. At this point many finally face up to the fact that they will never realize their youthful dreams and that new, more realistic goals must be found if life is to have purpose. Others, even if successful in their earlier pursuits, discover that they have purchased success in career at the expense of other responsibilities (e.g., to spouse and children) or other kinds of human fulfillment.

Erikson identifies this as the crisis of generativity vs. stagnation. Continued accentuation of an overspecialized version of oneself eventually becomes stultifying—one begins to feel stuck, static, in a rut. The vitality of earlier challenges too easily is replaced by routinized application of well-established solutions. In the absence of new and fresh challenges, creativity gives way to merely coping and going through the motions. Many careers plateau at this time and one faces the prospect of drying up and stretching out the remaining years in tedium. Finding new directions for generativity is essential.

There is considerable agreement among adult development scholars that growth occurs through processes of differentiation and hierarchic integration and that the highest stages of development are characterized by personal integration. From the perspective of experiential learning theory this goal is attained through a dialectic process of adaptation to the world. Fulfillment, or individuation as Jung calls it, is accomplished by expression of nondominant modes of dealing with the world and their higher-level integration with specialized functions. For many, the needs of modern society are seen to be in direct conflict with these individual needs for fulfillment. Jung puts this case as follows:

> The favoritism of the superior function is just as serviceable to society as it is prejudicial to the individuality. This prejudicial effect has reached such a pitch that the great organizations of our present day civilization actually strive for the complete disintegration of the individual, since their very existence depends upon a mechanical application of the preferred individual functions of men. It is not man that counts but his one differentiated function. Man no longer appears as man in collective civilization; he is merely represented by a function—nay, further, he is even exclusively identified with this function and denied any responsible membership to the other inferior functions. Thus, the modern individual sinks to the level of a mere function because it is this that represents a collective value and alone affords a possibility of livelihood. But as Schiller clearly discerns, differentiation of function could have come about in no other way: "There was not other means to develop man's manifold capacities than to set them one against the other. This antagonism of human qualities is the great instrument of culture; it is only the instrument, however, for so long as it endures, man is only upon the way to culture" (Jung, 1923).

Yet the implication of Schiller's observation is that while human beings are the instrument of culture in their specialized adaption, they are creators of culture through integrative fulfillment. This can be illustrated by comparing the development of scientific knowledge and the personal career paths of scientists. As Piaget (1970) and others (e.g., Kuhn, 1962) have documented, the historical development of scientific knowledge has been increasingly specialized moving from egocentrism to reflection and from phenomenalism to constructivism—in experiential learning terms from active to reflective and concrete to abstract. Yet the careers of highly successful scientists follow a different path. These individuals make their specialized abstract/reflective contributions often quite early in their careers. With recognition of their achievements, comes a new set of tasks with active and concrete demands. The Nobel prize winner must help to shape social policy and to articulate the ethical and value implications of his/her discoveries. The researcher becomes department chairperson and must manage the nurturance of the younger generation. So in this career, and most others as well, the higher levels of responsibility require an integrative perspective that can help shape cultural responses to emergent issues. In fact, there are integrative developmental challenges at all occupational levels. Many first line supervisors for example, have created personal job definitions that transcend the specialized boundaries of their trade to include the development of younger workers and the building of meaningful community and family relationships.

There is little argument that integrative development is important for both personal fulfillment and cultural development. Yet little research has been done on the integrative phase of adult development. The only study to date on learning styles in later phases of adult development was conducted by Clark et al. (1977). Their study compared cross-sectional samples of accountant and marketing students and professionals at various career stages. The learning styles of marketing and accounting MBA's were similar, being fairly balanced on the four learning modes. Lower-level accountants had convergent learning styles, and this convergent emphasis was even more pronounced in middle-level accountants, reflecting a highly technical emphasis in the early and middle stages of accounting careers. The senior-level accountants, however, were accommodative in their learning style, reflecting a greater concern with client relations and administration than with technical functions. Marketing professionals at the lower level also were convergent in learning style but became highly concrete at middle-level responsibilities, reflecting a shift from technical to creative concerns. The senior marketing personnel had accommodative learning styles similar to those of senior accountants, probably reflecting the same client and management concerns.

These results indicate that progression to new challenges, even within a given career path, calls for giving up excessive reliance on a specialized style in favor of integrating nondominant (and thus underdeveloped) functions. Thus, many forces—both internal and environmental—generate this period of reexamination and transition to middle adulthood.

The Experience of Crisis in Midlife Transition

Within each of life's major stages, the person maintains a relative balance of personal and situational factors. That is not to say, *static*, for one can be quite active in the pursuit of relevant developmental tasks, not to mention in the management of the vagaries of day-to-day life. The equilibrium is reflected, rather, in the patterning of living arrangements (e.g., role relationships in family, school, work tend to persist), and there is general continuity of meaning and purpose. The transitions from one stage to the next, although not always dramatic, tend to be experienced as discontinuities, as disruptions in the flow of life, involving some break with past orientations and arrangements to make room for new developmental tasks.

At times, as often happens in the transition from juvenile to adolescent, the transition is a major upheaval, frought with a loss of orientation and purpose. Conditions and events lose their old meanings and are not yet understandable in new terms. Old perspectives no longer quite handle the significant realities and possibilities one senses only dimly. One enters a period of confusion, restlessness, and uncertainty.

Some degree of reorientation is in order for everyone at this stage, requiring a giving up or breaking from some of the old patterns and frameworks. However, many hold doggedly to those things that have provided security, comfort, acceptance from others, or satisfactions. In the face of uncertainty about what comes in their place, the breaking of old patterns is disorienting and anxiety-producing. Consequently, some respond to the middle years with stubborn resistance to change.

When the change is abrupt and pervasive, as in divorce or being fired from a job held over many years, the tension and disorientation reach crisis proportions. Confusion, acute anxiety, depression, anger, resentment, and a sense of help-lessness, hopelessness, or worthlessness are not uncommon emotional reactions at such times. The transition, even if growthful in the long run, may be very painful and debilitating for a time.

For a great many people, the transition is difficult and prolonged—the term "midlife crisis" is most apt. As we currently conceive it, a midlife crisis is distinguished from a more evolutionary developmental transition by a number of interrelated characteristics:

1. It is unanticipated or at least unplanned.
2. There is a loss of self-direction and control; the person feels as though events are happening to him/her.
3. Changes are not bounded but expand to encompass the person's whole life space (e.g., a divorce leads to abandoning friends, changing job, moving away, and so on).
4. It creates acute stress and anxiety, influencing the person's day-to-day coping behavior (e.g., inability to concentrate, labile emotions, accident-proneness).
5. Attempts to cope with the crisis are rigid and stereotyped, dominated by black-white thinking. They create more problems than they resolve, producing a vicious downward spiral.

The plaguing dilemma, if the transition involves crisis of any real intensity, is that usual modes of coping interfere with both learning and environmental manipulation. Anxiety, rigidification, and loss of focus undermine those very learning processes that would resolve the crisis and facilitate new growth. Similarly, typical responses to environmental stress—withdrawal, avoidance, attack are seldom effective in setting to right those conditions which create the stress. In the short run, those natural, human reactions to crisis are of service to immediate self-maintenance, but they also tend to prolong the crisis without the understanding and help of others or the good fortune of being able to lay low without the rest of one's world going to hell.

Learning and Change in the Transition Process

Whatever the content of the issues and concerns one faces in midlife, there are two process agendas to be addressed if the transition is to be productive in terms of growth and development: changing environmental conditions and investments in personal learning.

To the extent that the transition is precipitated by significant environmental events (e.g., loss of job, divorce) or by internal changes that make one's circumstances untenable or dissatisfying, the transition is likely to call for some kinds of environmental change. For some, this means a rather massive pulling up of roots and moving to a new job in a new location. Others may find that relatively small scale modifications in certain key work or family roles are sufficient.

Role expectations and demands tend to dominate one's life space in early adulthood. One lives by the oughts and shoulds associated with many roles. At some level, one is driven by both career and family role requirements, whether those demands are expressed by others or by the power of the situation (e.g., the needs of a newborn child). One *is* what one's role calls for, in the extreme, especially if the rewards for specialization are ample.

For many individuals, however, withdrawal of reward for accentuation may be a precondition for the emergence of fulfillment concerns. Our notion here is that rewards for accentuation are often so powerful and overwhelming that the individual develops what we call a role-encapsulated ego. That is, rewards for specialized role performance tend to prevent the emergence of nondominant fulfillment needs. Thus, in many cases, withdrawal of these rewards may have to precede the awareness of fulfillment needs.

People as they approach midlife are seldom content to have their lives totally defined from the outside. The other-directedness of early adulthood must give way to a greater sense of being one's own person. This shift alone usually requires some renegotiation of roles, even when the content of one's role-related activities remains the same. Relationships with colleagues, boss, spouse, and children undergo subtle, if not dramatic change. Especially during the transition itself, the role-boundedness of many people's lives must be relieved to make room for the exploration of new possibilities.

The transition from early to middle adulthood involves a breaking from the authority of role expectations toward a centering in oneself as the source of purpose, meaning, and action. Instead of being driven, the mature person becomes the driver. This is not to say that with the transition, one no longer performs his/her roles or cares about the expectations of others. Rather, it means that one begins to recognize the role (and the social structure within which it is embedded) as a platform from which s/he can accomplish purposes s/he owns. The role belongs to her/him, not s/he to the role.

As one become autonomous from the excessive demands of role expectations, s/he becomes her/his own person—a nonrole person. Among other things, this is essential preparation for the time when, through retirement, increasing independence of one's children and the like, one begins a full disengagement from roles altogether, to live out his life with integrity. Increasing personal autonomy and centeredness is part and parcel of the integration of adaptive styles.

A growthful transition inevitably involves the person in new learning ventures, directed both inward and outward. It is a time for giving up some of the illusions and pretenses associated with early adult adaptation. A successful resolution requires more accurate and comprehensive self-knowledge—hence, the turn to introspection and the questioning of one's ambition, drives, wants, and capacities. Thus, learning, especially during critical transitions, is highly personal.

If there is any significant change of scene, one also moves into an active phase of learning about new environmental realities and how they can be understood in terms relevant to one's new purposes. Moreover, a change of career or even taking on new responsibilities in the community is apt to require the development of new competencies or the refinement of underutilized ones. Gaining new knowledge and skills often makes the difference between stagnation and development.

The developmental challenge of the midlife transition is to face up to and move toward those personal and situational changes that show promise of growth and authenticity without causing undue pain or disruption to oneself or others.

Not everyone, of course, faces up to that challenge. Many do not find or recognize the need; life seems to be tolerable in its current plan. Others, fearing the stress and turmoil, retreat not only from change but even from very deep questioning. Still others find it genuinely fulfilling and recommit to present structures and directions.

Generally, we see the midlife transition as a constructive move toward human fulfillment, toward becoming a whole person and rounding out a life worth living. As in other developmental transitions, the internal psychological work and resultant behavioral and situational changes are the mechanisms through which one corrects the excesses and deficiencies of one's former adaptations. Under favorable conditions, the midlife transition involves minor recalibration on many issues and reorientation toward investing time and energy in those things one cares most about. The move is toward living more authentically, creatively, and harmoniously.

References

Biglan, A., "The Characteristics of Subject Matter in Different Academic Areas," *Journal of Applied Psychology*, 57, (1973), 195-203.

Bruner, Jerome S., *On Knowing: Essays for the Left Hand*. (New York: Atheneum, 1966).

Bruner, Jerome S., *The Process of Education*. (Cambridge, Mass.: Harvard University Press, 1960).

Clark, Diana, et. al., "A Study of the Adequacy of the Learning Environment for Business Students in Hawaii in the Fields of Accounting and Marketing," a Working Paper, (University of Hawaii School of Management, 1977).

Feldman, Kenneth, and Theodore Newcombe, *The Impact of College on Students*, Vols. I and II, (San Francisco: Jossey-Bass, Inc., 1969).

Feldman, Saul D. (ed.), *Escape from the Doll's House*. (New York: McGraw-Hill, 1974).

Fry, R., "Diagnosing Professional Learning Environments: An Observational Framework for Matching Learner Styles with Types of Situational Complexity," Ph.D. Dissertation, (Cambridge, Mass.: Massachusetts Institute of Technology, Sloan School of Management, 1977).

Goldstein, K., and M. Scheerer, "Abstract and Concrete Behavior: An Experimental Study with Special Tests," *Psychological Monographs*, 53, (1941).

Gould, Robert, "The Phases of Adult Life: A Study in Developmental Psychology," *American Journal of Psychiatry*, 129, (1972), 521-531.

Grochow, Jerrold, "Cognitive Style as a Factor in the Design of Interactive Decision-Support Systems," an unpublished Doctoral Dissertation, (Cambridge, Mass.: Massachusetts Institute of Technology, Sloan School of Management, 1973).

Harvey, O. J., D. Hunt, and H. Schroeder, *Conceptual Systems and Personality Organization*. (New York: John Wiley & Sons, Inc., 1961).

Havighurst, Robert, "The Life Cycle," *The Future American College*. Edited by A. Chickering. (San Francisco: Jossey-Bass, Inc. In press. 1979).

Hudson, Liam, *Contrary Imaginations*. (Middlesex, England: Penguin Books, 1966).

Jung, C. G., *Psychological Types*. (London: Pantheon Books, Inc., 1923).

Kagan, J. and N. Kogan, "Individual Variations in Cognitive Processes," *Carmichael's Manual of Child Psychology*, (3rd ed.), Vol. 1. Edited by P. H. Mussen, (New York: John Wiley & Sons, 1970).

Kagan, Jerome, Bernice L. Rosman, Deborah Day, Joseph Albert, and William Phillips, "Information Processing in the Child: Significance of Analytic and Reflective Attitudes," *Psychological Monographs*, 78(1), (1964).

Kolb, David, *The Learning Style Inventory: Technical Manual*. (Boston, Mass.: McBer and Co., 1976).

Kolb, David, "Toward a Typology of Learning Styles and Learning Environments: An Investigation of the Impact of Learning Styles and Discipline Demands on the Academic Performance, Social Adaption and Career Choices of M.I.T. Seniors," a Working Paper, No. 688-73, (Cambridge, Mass.: Massachusetts Institute of Technology, Sloan School of Management, 1973).

Kolb, David, and Ronald Fry, "Toward an Applied Theory of Experiental Learning," *Theories of Group Processes*. Edited by Cary L. Cooper. (New York: John Wiley & Sons, Inc., 1975).

Kris, Ernst, *Psychoanalytic Explorations in Art*. (New York: International Universities Press, 1962).

Kuhn, Thomas, *The Structure of Scientific Revolutions* (2nd ed.). (Chicago: University of Chicago Press, 1970).

Levinson, Daniel, "The Mid-Life Transition: A Period in Adult Psycho-Social Development," *Psychiatry*, (May 1977).

Neugarten, Bernice L. (editor), *Middle Age and Aging*. (Chicago: University of Chicago Press, 1968).

Piaget, Jean, *The Place of the Sciences of Man in the System of Sciences*. (New York: Harper & Row, Inc., 1974).

Plovnick, Mark S., "Primary Care Career Choices and Medical Student Learning Styles," *Journal of Medical Education*, 50, (1975), 849-855.

Sheehy, Gail, *Passages*. (New York: E. P. Dutton & Co., Inc., 1976).

Singer, Jerome, "The Importance of Daydreaming," *Psychology Today*, 1(11), (1968), 18-26.

Snow, Charles P., *The Two Cultures: And a Second Look*. (New York: Cambridge University Press, 1970).

Sofer, Cyril, *Men in Mid-Career*. (New York: Cambridge University Press, 1970).

Stabell, C., "The Impact of a Conversational Computer System on Human Development Perspective," Master's Thesis, (Cambridge, Mass.: Massachusetts Institute of Technology, Sloan School of Management, 1973).

Strasmore, M., "The Strategic Function Reevaluated from the Organization Development Perspective," Master's Thesis, (Cambridge, Mass.: Massachusetts Institute of Technology, Sloan School of Management, 1973).

Super, D., et. al., *Career Development Self Concept Theory*. (Princeton, N.J.: Princeton College Entrance Exam Board, 1963).

Torrealba, D., "Convergent and Divergent Learning Styles," Master's Thesis, (Cambridge, Mass.: Massachusetts Institute of Technology, Sloan School of Management, 1972).

Witkin, H. A., "The Role of Cognitive Style on Academic Performance and in Teacher/Student Relationships," *Research Bulletin*, 73(11). (Princeton, N.J.: Educational Testing Service, 1973).

Witkin, H. A., et. al. *Psychological Differentiation*. (New York: The Halsted Press Division of John Wiley & Sons, Inc., 1974).

5 group dynamics

THE NATURE OF
HIGHLY EFFECTIVE GROUPS

RENSIS LIKERT

We concluded in Chapter 8 that the form of organization which will make the greatest use of human capacity consists of highly effective work groups linked together in an overlapping pattern by other similarly effective groups. The highly effective work group is, consequently, an important component of the newer theory of management. It will be important to understand both its nature and its performance characteristics. We shall examine these in this chapter, but first a few words about groups in general.

Although we have stressed the great potential power of the group for building effective organizations, it is important to emphasize that this does *not* say that all groups and all committees are highly effective or are committed to desirable goals. Groups as groups can vary from poor to excellent. They can have desirable values and goals, or their objectives can be most destructive. They can accomplish much that is good, or they can do great harm. There is nothing *implicitly* good or bad, weak or strong, about a group.

The nature of the group determines the character of its impact upon the development of its members. The values of the group, the stability of these values, the group atmosphere, and the nature of the conformity demanded by the group determine whether a group is likely to have a positive or negative impact upon the growth and behavior of its members. If the values of the group are seen by the society as having merit, if the group is warm, supportive, and full of understanding, the group's influence on the development of its members will be positive. A hostile atmosphere and socially undesirable or unstable values produce a negative impact upon the members' growth and behavior.

Loyalty to a group produces pressures toward conformity. A group may demand conformity to the idea of supporting, encouraging, and giving recognition for individual creativity, or it may value rigidity of behavior, with seriously narrowing and dwarfing consequences. This latter kind of pressure for conformity keeps the members from growing and robs the group of original ideas. Many writers have pointed to these deleterious effects of conformity. They often overlook the capacity of groups to stimulate individual creativeness by placing a high value on imaginative and original contributions by their members. As Pelz's findings, reported in Chapter 2, demonstrate, groups can contribute significantly to creativity by providing the stimulation of diverse points of view within a supportive atmosphere which encourages each individual member to pursue new and unorthodox concepts.

Some business executives are highly critical of groups—or committees—and the inability of committees to accomplish a great deal. Their criticisms are often well warranted. In many instances, committees are wasteful of time and unable to reach decisions. Sometimes the decisions, when reached, are mediocre. Moreover, some members of management at various hierarchical levels use committees as escape mechanisms—as a way to avoid the responsibility for a decision.

The surprising thing about committees is not that many or most are ineffective, but that they accomplish as much as they do when, relatively speaking, we know so little about how to use them. There has been a lack of systematic study of ways to make committees effective. Far more is known about time-and-motion study, cost accounting and similar aspects of management than is known about groups and group processes. Moreover, in spite of the demonstrated potentiality of groups, far less research is being devoted to learning the role of groups and group processes and how to make the most effective use of them in an organization than to most management practices. We know appreciably less about how to make groups and committees effective than we know about most matters of managing.

We do know that groups can be powerful. The newer theory takes this into account and tries to make constructive use of the group's potential strength for developing and mobilizing human resources.

In this and other chapters the use of the term "group" may give the impression that groups have the capacity to behave in ways other than through the behavior of their members. Thus, such expressions appear as the "group's goals," "the group decides," or the "group motivates." In many instances, these expressions are used to avoid endless repetition of the words, "the members of the group." In other instances, something more is meant. Thus, in speaking of "group values," the intent is to refer to those values which have been established by the group through a group-decision process involving consensus. Once a decision has been reached by consensus, there are strong motivational forces, developed within each individual as a result of his membership in the group and his relationship to the other members, to be guided by that decision. In this sense, the group has goals and values and makes decisions. It has properties which may not be present, as such, in any one individual. A group may be divided in opinion, for example, although this may not be true of any one member. Dorwin Cartwright puts it this way: "The relation between the individual members and the group is analogous to the distinction made in mathematics between the properties of a set of elements and the properties of the elements within a set. Every set is composed of elements, but sets have properties which are not identical with the properties of the elements of the set.''

The Highly Effective Work Group

Much of the discussion of groups in this chapter will be in terms of an ideal organizational model which the work groups in an organization can approach as they develop skill in group processes. This model group, of course, is always part of a large organization. The description of its nature and performance characteristics is based on evidence from a variety of sources. Particularly important are the observational and experimental studies of small groups such as those conductd by the Research Center for Group Dynamics (Cartwright & Zander, 1960; Hare et al., 1955; Institute for Social Research, 1956; Institute for Social Research, 1960; Thibaut & Kelly, 1959). Extensive use is made of data from studies of large-scale organizations (see Chapters 2 to 4). Another important source is the material from the National Training Laboratories (Foundation for Research on Human Behavior, 1960d; National Training Laboratories, 1953; National Training Laboratories, 1960; Stock & Thelen, 1958). The NTL has focused on training in sensitivity to the reactions of others and in skills to perform the leadership and membership roles in groups.

In addition to drawing upon the above sources, the description of the ideal model is derived from theory. Some of the statements about the model for which there is little or limited experimental or observational data have been derived directly from the basic drive to achieve and maintain a sense of importance and personal worth. At several points in this chapter and Chapter 12 the author has gone appreciably beyond available specific research findings. The author feels, however, that the generalizations which are emerging based on research in organizations and on small groups, youth, and family life, personality development, consumer behavior, human motivation, and related fields lend strong support to the general theory and the derivations contained in this book.

It has been necessary to go beyond the data in order to spell out at this time in some detail the general pattern of the more complex but more effective form of organization being created by the higher-producing managers. The author hopes that the theory and model proposed will stimulate a substantial increase in basic and developmental research and that they will be tested and sharpened by that research.

The body of knowledge about small groups, while sufficiently large to make possible this description of the ideal model, is still relatively limited. Without question, as the importance of the work group as the basic building block of organizations becomes recognized, there will be a great increase in the research on groups and our knowledge about them. The over-all pattern of the model described here will be improved and clarified by such research. Our understanding of how to develop and use groups effectively will also be greatly advanced.

The following description of the ideal model defines what we mean by *a highly effective group*. The definition involves reference to several different variables. Each of them can be thought of as a continuum, i.e., as a characteristic which can vary from low to high, from unfavorable to favorable. For example, a group can vary from one in which there is hostility among the members to one in which the attitudes are warm and friendly. The ideal model is at the favorable end of each variable.

The Nature of Highly Effective Work Groups

The highly effective group, as we shall define it, is always conceived as being a part of a larger organization. A substantial proportion of persons in a company are members of more than one work group, especially when both line and staff are considered. As a consequence, in such groups there are always linking functions to be performed and relationships to other groups to be maintained. Our highly effective group is not an isolated entity.

All the persons in a company also belong to groups and organizations outside of the company. For most persons, membership in several groups both within and outside the company is the rule rather than the exception. This means, of course, that no single group, even the highly effective work group, dominates the life of any member. Each member of the organization feels pressures from membership in several different groups and is not influenced solely by loyalty to any one group.

Since the different groups to which a person belongs are apt to have somewhat different and often inconsistent goals and values, corresponding conflicts and pressures are created within him. To minimize these conflicts and tensions, the individual seeks to influence the values and goals of each of the different groups to which he belongs and which are important to him so as to minimize the inconsistencies and conflicts in values and goals. In striving for this reconciliation, he is likely to press for the acceptance of those values most important to him.

The properties and performance characteristics of the ideal highly effective group are as follows:

1. The members are skilled in all the various leadership and membership roles and functions required for interaction between leaders and members and between members and other members.

2. The group has been in existence sufficiently long to have developed a well-established, relaxed working relationship among all its members.

3. The members of the group are attracted to it and are loyal to its members, including the leader.

4. The members and leaders have a high degree of confidence and trust in each other.

5. The values and goals of the group are a satisfactory integration and expression of the relevant values and needs of its members. They have helped shape these values and goals and are satisfied with them.

6. In so far as members of the group are performing linking functions, they endeavor to have the values and goals of the groups which they link in harmony, one with the other.

7. The more important a value seems to the group, the greater the likelihood that the individual member will accept it.

8. The members of the group are highly motivated to abide by the major values and to achieve the important goals of the group. Each member will do all that he reasonably can—and at times all in his power—to help the group achieve its central objectives. He expects every other member to do the same. This high motivation springs, in part, from the basic motive to achieve and maintain a sense of personal worth and importance. Being valued by a group

whose values he shares, and deriving a sense of significance and importance from this relationship, leads each member to do his best. He is eager not to let the other members down. He strives hard to do what he believes is expected of him.

9. All the interaction, problem-solving, decision-making activities of the group occur in a supportive atmosphere. Suggestions, comments, ideas, information, criticisms are all offered with a helpful orientation. Similarly, these contributions are received in the same spirit. Respect is shown for the point of view of others both in the way contributions are made and in the way they are received.

There are real and important differences of opinion, but the focus is on arriving at sound solutions and not on exacerbating and aggravating the conflict. Ego forces deriving from the desire to achieve and maintain a sense of personal worth and importance are channeled into constructive efforts. Care is taken not to let these ego forces disrupt important group tasks, such as problem-solving. Thus, for example, a statement of the problem, a condition which any solution must meet, a suggested solution, or an item of relevant fact are all treated as from the group as a whole. Care is taken so that one statement of the problem is not John's and another Bill's. A suggested solution is not referred to as Tom's and another as Dick's. All the material contributed is treated as *ours*: "One of our proposed solutions is *A,* another is *B.*" In all situations involving actual or potential differences or conflict among the members of the group, procedures are used to separate the ego of each member from his contribution. In this way, ego forces do not stimulate conflict between members. Instead, they are channeled into supporting the activities and efforts of the group.

The group atmosphere is sufficiently supportive for the members to be able to accept readily any criticism which is offered and to make the most constructive use of it. The criticisms may deal with any relevant topic such as operational problems, decisions, supervisory problems, interpersonal relationships, or group processes, but whatever their content, the member feels sufficiently secure in the supportive atmosphere of the group to be able to accept, test, examine, and benefit from the criticism offered. Also, he is able to be frank and candid, irrespective of the content of the discussion: technical, managerial, factual, cognitive, or emotional. The supportive atmosphere of the group, with the feeling of security it provides, contributes to a cooperative relationship between the members. And this cooperation itself contributes to and reinforces the supportive atmosphere.

10. The superior of each work group exerts a major influence in establishing the tone and atmosphere of that work group by his leadership principles and practices. In the highly effective group, consequently, the leader adheres to those principles of leadership which create a supportive atmosphere in the group and a cooperative rather than a competitive relationship among the members. For example, he shares information fully with the group and creates an atmosphere where the members are stimulated to behave similarly.

11. The group is eager to help each member develop to his full potential. It sees, for example, that relevant technical knowledge and training in interpersonal and group skills are made available to each member.

12. Each member accepts willingly and without resentment the goals and expectations that he and his group establish for themselves. The anxieties, fears, and emotional stresses produced by direct pressure for high perform-

ance from a boss in a hierarchical situation are not present. Groups seem capable of setting high performance goals for the group as a whole and for each member. These goals are high enough to stimulate each member to do his best, but not so high as to create anxieties or fear of failure. In an effective group, each person can exert sufficient influence on the decisions of the group to prevent the group from setting unattainable goals for any member while setting high goals for all. The goals are adapted to the member's capability to perform.

13. The leader and the members believe that each group member can accomplish "the impossible." These expectations stretch each member to the maximum and accelerate his growth. When necessary, the group tempers the expectation level so that the member is not broken by a feeling of failure or rejection.

14. When necessary or advisable, other members of the group will give a member the help he needs to accomplish successfully the goals set for him. Mutual help is a characteristic of highly effective groups.

15. The supportive atmosphere of the highly effective group stimulates creativity. The group does not demand narrow conformity as do the work groups under authoritarian leaders. No one has to "yes the boss," nor is he rewarded for such an attempt. The group attaches high value to new, creative approaches and solutions to its problems and to the problems of the organization of which it is a part. The motivation to be creative is high when one's work group prizes creativity.

16. The group knows the value of "constructive" conformity and knows when to use it and for what purposes. Although it does not permit conformity to affect adversely the creative efforts of its members, it does expect conformity on mechanical and administrative matters to save the time of members and to facilitate the group's activities. The group agrees, for example, on administrative forms and procedures, and once they have been established, it expects its members to abide by them until there is good reason to change them.

17. There is strong motivation on the part of each member to communicate fully and frankly to the group all the information which is relevant and of value to the group's activity. This stems directly from the member's desire to be valued by the group and to get the job done. The more important to the group a member feels an item of information to be, the greater is his motivation to communicate it.

18. There is high motivation in the group to use the communication process so that it best serves the interests and goals of the group. Every item which a member feels is important, but which for some reason is being ignored, will be repeated until it receives the attention that it deserves. Members strive also to avoid communicating unimportant information so as not to waste the group's time.

19. Just as there is high motivation to communicate, there is correspondingly strong motivation to receive communications. Each member is genuinely interested in any information on any relevant matter that any member of the group can provide. This information is welcomed and trusted as being honestly and sincerely given. Members do not look "behind" the information item and attempt to interpret it in ways opposite to its purported intent. This interest of group members in information items and treatment of such items as valid reinforces the motivation to communicate.

20. In the highly effective group, there are strong motivations to try to influence other members as well as to be receptive to influence by them. This applies to all the group's activities: technical matters, methods, organizational problems, interpersonal relationships, and group processes.

21. The group processes of the highly effective group enable the members to exert more influence on the leader and to communicate far more information to him, including suggestions as to what needs to be done and how he could do his job better, than is possible in a man-to-man relationship. By "tossing the ball" back and forth among its members, a group can communicate information to the leader which no single person on a man-to-man basis dare do. As a consequence, the boss receives all the information that the group possesses to help him perform his job effectively.

22. The ability of the members of a group to influence each other contributes to the flexibility and adaptability of the group. Ideas, goals, and attitudes do not become frozen if members are able to influence each other continuously.

Although the group is eager to examine any new ideas and methods which will help it do its job better and is willing to be influenced by its members, it is not easily shifted or swayed. Any change is undertaken only after rigorous examination of the evidence. This stability in the group's activities is due to the steadying influence of the common goals and values held by the group members.

23. In the highly effective group, individual members feel secure in making decisions which seem appropriate to them because the goals and philosophy of operation are clearly understood by each member and provide him with a solid base for his decisions. This unleashes initiative and pushes decisions down while still maintaining a coordinated and directed effort.

24. The leader of a highly effective group is selected carefully. His leadership ability is so evident that he would probably emerge as a leader in any unstructured situation. To increase the likelihood that persons of high leadership competence are selected, the organization is likely to use peer nominations and related methods in selecting group leaders.

An important aspect of the highly effective group is its extensive use of the principle of supportive relationships. An examination of the above material reveals that virtually every statement involves an application of this principle.

Leadership Functions

Several different characteristics of highly effective groups have been briefly examined. The role of the leader in these groups is, as we have suggested, particularly important. Certain leadership functions can be shared with group members; others can be performed only by the designated leader. In an organization, for example, the leader of a unit is the person who has primary responsibility for linking his work group to the rest of the organization. Other members of the group may help perform the linking function by serving as linking pins in overlapping groups other than that provided by the line organization, but the major linking is necessarily through the line organization. The leader has full responsibility for the group's performance and for seeing that his group meets the demands and expectations placed upon it by the rest of the organization of which it is a part. Other members of the group may share this responsibility at times, but the leader can never avoid full responsibility for the adequate performance of his group.

Although the leader has full responsibility, he does not try to make all the decisions. He develops his group into a unit which, with his participation, makes better decisions than he can make alone. He helps the group develop efficient communication and influence processes which provide it with better information, more technical knowledge, more facts, and more experience for decision-making purposes than the leader alone can marshal.

Through group decision-making each member feels fully identified with each decision and highly motivated to execute it fully. The over-all performance of the group, as a consequence, is even better than the excellent quality of the decisions.

The leader knows that at times decisions must be made rapidly and cannot wait for group processes. He anticipates these emergencies and establishes procedures with his group for handling them so that action can be taken rapidly with group support.

The leader feels primarily responsible for establishing and maintaining at all times a thoroughly supportive atmosphere in the group. He encourages other members to share this responsibility, but never loses sight of the fact that as the leader of a work group which is part of a larger organization his behavior is likely to set the tone.

Although the leader accepts the responsibility associated with his role of leader of a group which is part of a larger organization, he seeks to minimize the influence of his hierarchical position. He is aware that trying to get results by "pulling rank" affects adversely the effectiveness of his group and his relationship to it. Thus, he endeavors to deemphasize status. He does this in a variety of ways that fit his personality and methods of leading, as for example by:

1. Listening well and patiently.
2. Not being impatient with the progress being made by the group, particularly on difficult problems.
3. Accepting more blame than may be warranted for any failure or mistake.
4. Giving the group members ample opportunity to express their thoughts without being constrained by the leader pressing his own views.
5. Being careful never to impose a decision upon the group.
6. Putting his contributions often in the form of questions or stating them speculatively.
7. Arranging for others to help perform leadership functions which enhance their status.

The leader strengthens the group and group processes by seeing that all problems *which involve the group* are dealt with by the group. He never handles such problems outside of the group nor with individual members of the group. While the leader is careful to see that all matters which involve and affect the whole group are handled by the whole group, he is equally alert not to undertake in a group-meeting agenda items or tasks which do not concern the group. Matters concerning one individual member and only that member are, of course, handled individually. Matters involving only a subgroup are handled by that subgroup. The total group is kept informed, however, of any subgroup action.

The leader fully reflects and effectively represents the views, goals, values, and decisions of his group in those other groups where he is performing the function of linking his group to the rest of the organization. He brings to the group of which he is the leader the views, goals, and decisions of those other groups. In this way, he provides a linkage whereby communication and the exercise of influence can be performed in both directions.

The leader has adequate competence to handle the technical problems faced by his group, or he sees that access to this technical knowledge is fully provided. This may involve bringing in, as needed, technical or resource persons. Or he may arrange to have technical training given to one or more members of his group so that the group can have available the necessary technical know-how when the group discusses a problem and arrives at a decision.

The leader is what might be called "group-centered," in a sense comparable with the "employee-centered" supervisor described in Chapter 2. He endeavors to build and maintain in his group a keen sense of responsibility for achieving its own goals and meeting its obligations to the larger organization.

The leader helps to provide the group with the stimulation arising from a restless dissatisfaction. He discourages complacency and passive acceptance of the present. He helps the members to become aware of new possibilities, more important values, and more significant goals.

The leader is an important source of enthusiasm for the significance of the mission and goals of the group. He sees that the tasks of the group are important and significant and difficult enough to be challenging.

As an over-all guide to his leadership behavior, the leader understands and uses with sensitivity and skill the principle of supportive relationships.

Many of these leadership functions, such as the linking function, can be performed only by the designated leader. This makes clear the great importance of selecting competent persons for leadership positions.

Roles of Membership and Leadership

In the highly effective group, many functions are performed either by the leader or by the members, depending upon the situation or the requirements of the moment. The leader and members, as part of their roles in the group, establish and maintain an atmosphere and relationships which enable the communication, influence, decision-making, and similar processes of the group to be performed effectively. This means not only creating positive conditions, such as a supportive atmosphere, but also eliminating any negative or blocking factors. Thus, for example, groups sometimes have to deal with members who are insensitive, who are hostile, who talk too much, or who otherwise behave in ways adversely affecting the capacity of the group to function. In handling such a problem, the group makes the member aware of his deficiency, but does this in a sensitive and considerate manner and in a way to assist the member to function more effectively in the group. The members of most ordinary groups stop listening to a member who expresses himself in a fuzzy or confused manner. In a highly effective group, the members feed back their reaction to the person involved with suggestions and assistance on how to make his contributions clear, important, and of the kind to which all will want to listen. Friendly assistance and coaching can help a member overcome excessive talking or help him to learn to think and express himself more clearly.

Benne and Sheats (1948) have prepared a description of the different roles played in well-functioning groups. These roles may at times be performed by one or more group members, at other times by the leader. The list, while prepared on the basis of roles in discussion and problem-solving groups, is useful in considering the functions to be performed in any work group which is part of a larger organization.

The following material is taken from the Benne and Sheats article (pp. 42–45) with slight modifications. Group roles are classified into two broad categories:

> 1. *Group task roles.* These roles are related to the task which the group is deciding to undertake or has undertaken. They are directly concerned with the group effort in the selection and definition of a common problem and in the solution of that problem.

> 2. *Group building and maintenance roles.* These roles concern the functioning of the group as a group. They deal with the group's efforts to strengthen, regulate, and perpetuate the group as a group.

Group Task Roles

> The following analysis assumes that the task of the group is to select, define, and solve common problems. The roles are identified in relation to functions of facilitation and coordination of group problem-solving activities. Each member may, of course, enact more than one role in any given unit of participation and a wide range of roles in successive participations. Any or all of these roles may be performed, at times, by the group "leader" as well as by various members.

> 1. *Initiating-contributing:* suggesting or proposing to the group new ideas or a changed way of regarding the group problem or goal. The novelty proposed may take the form of suggestions of a new group goal or a new definition of the problem. It may take the form of a suggested solution or some way of handling a difficulty that the group has encountered. Or it may take the form of a proposed new procedure for the group, a new way of organizing the group for the task ahead.

> 2. *Information seeking:* asking for clarification of suggestions made in terms of their factual adequacy, for authoritative information and facts pertinent to the problems being discussed.

> 3. *Opinion seeking:* seeking information not primarily on the facts of the case, but for a clarification of the values pertinent to what the group is undertaking or of values involved in a suggestion made or in alternative suggestions.

> 4. *Information giving:* offering facts or generalizations which are "authoritative" or involve presenting an experience pertinent to the group problem.

> 5. *Opinion giving:* stating beliefs or opinions pertinent to a suggestion made or to alternative suggestions. The emphasis is on the proposal of what should become the group's view of pertinent values, not primarily upon relevant facts or information.

6. *Elaborating:* spelling out suggestions in terms of examples or developed meanings, offering a rationale for suggestions previously made, and trying to deduce how an idea or suggestion would work out if adopted by the group.

7. *Coordinating:* showing or clarifying the relationships among various ideas and suggestions, trying to pull ideas and suggestions together or trying to coordinate the activities of various members or sub-groups.

8. *Orienting:* defining the position of the group with respect to its goals by summarizing what has occurred, departures from agreed upon directions or goals are pointed to, or questions are raised about the direction the group discussion is taking.

9. *Evaluating:* subjecting the accomplishment of the group to some standard or set of standards of group functioning in the context of the group task. Thus, it may involve evaluationg or questioning the "practicality," the "logic," or the "procedure" of a suggestion or of some unit of group discussion.

10. *Energizing:* prodding the group to action or decision, attempting to stimulate or arouse the group to "greater" activity or to activity of a "higher quality."

11. *Assisting on procedure:* expediting group movement by doing things for the group—performing routine tasks, e.g., distributing materials, or manipulating objects for the group, e.g., rearranging the seating or running the recording machine, etc.

12. *Recording:* writing down suggestions, making a record of group decisions, or writing down the product of discussion. The recorder role is the "group memory."

Group Building and Maintenance Roles

Here the analysis of member-functions is oriented to those activities which build group loyalty and increase the motivation and capacity of the group for candid and effective interaction and problem-solving. One or more members or the leader may perform each of these roles.

1. *Encouraging:* praising, showing interest in, agreeing with, and accepting the contributions of others; indicating warmth and solidarity in one's attitudes toward other group members, listening attentively and seriously to the contributions of group members, giving these contributions full and adequate consideration even though one may not fully agree with them; conveying to the others a feeling that—"that which you are about to say is of importance to me."

2. *Harmonizing:* mediating the differences between other members, attempting to reconcile disagreements, relieving tension in conflict situations through jesting, or pouring oil on troubled waters, etc.

3. *Compromising:* operating from within a conflict in which one's ideas or position is involved. In this role one may offer a compromise by yielding status, admitting error, by disciplining oneself to maintain group harmony, or by "coming half-way" in moving along with the group.

4. *Gate-keeping and expediting:* attempting to keep communication channels open by encouraging or facilitating the participation of others or by proposing regulation of the flow of communication.

5. *Setting standards or ideals:* expressing standards for the group or applying standards in evaluating the quality of group processes.

6. *Observing:* keeping records of various aspects of group process and feeding such data with proposed interpretations into the group's evaluation of its own procedures. The contribution of the person performing this role is usually best received or most fittingly received by the group when this particular role has been performed by this person at the request of the group and when the report to the group avoids expressing value judgments, approval, or disapproval.

7. *Following:* going along with the group, more or less passively accepting the ideas of others, serving as an audience in group discussion and decision.

The *group task roles* all deal with the intellectual aspects of the group's work. These roles are performed by members of the group during the problem-solving process, which usually involves such steps as:

1. Defining the problem.
2. Listing the conditions or criteria which any satisfactory solution to the problem should meet.
3. Listing possible alternative solutions.
4. Obtaining the facts which bear on each possible solution.
5. Evaluating the suggested solutions in terms of the conditions which a satisfactory solution should meet.
6. Eliminating undesirable solutions and selecting the most desirable solution.

The *group building and maintenance roles* are, as the label suggests, concerned with the emotional life of the group. These roles deal with the group's attractiveness to its members, its warmth and supportiveness, its motivation and capacity to handle intellectual problems without bias and emotion, and its capacity to function as a "mature" group.

The membership roles proposed by Benne and Sheats, while they are not definitive or complete, nevertheless point to the many complex functions performed in groups and dealt with by leader and members. The members of a highly effective group handle these roles with sensitivity and skill, and they see that the emotional life of the group contributes to the performance of the group's tasks rather than interfering with them.[1]

The highly effective group does not hesitate, for example, to look at and deal with friction between its members. By openly putting such problems on the table and sincerely examining them, they can be dealt with constructively. An effective group does not have values which frown upon criticism or which prevent bringing friction between members into the open. As a consequence, it does not put the lid on these emotional pressures, causing them to simmer below the surface and be a constant source of disruption to the performance of group tasks. The intellectual functions of any group can be performed without bias and disruption only when the internal emotional tensions and conflicts

[1]Although the Benne and Sheats list does not define each category unambiguously, it is useful in helping a group analyze and improve its processes. Another list has been prepared by Bales (1950) which has relatively precise definitions. The Bales list will be of interest to those who wish to do research on group processes or who wish to observe and analyze them systematically.

have been removed from the life of the group. Differences in ideas are stimulating and contribute to creativity, but emotional conflict immobilizes a group.

Group building and maintenance functions and group task functions are interdependent processes. In order to tackle difficult problems, to solve them creatively, and to achieve high performance, a group must be at a high level of group maintenance. Success in task processes, fortunately, also contributes to the maintenance of the group and to its emotional life, including its attraction to members and its supportive atmosphere.

In the midst of struggling with a very difficult task, a group occasionally may be faced with group maintenance problems. At such times, it may be necessary for the group to stop its intellectual activity and in one way or another to look at and deal with the disruptive emotional stresses. After this has been done, the group can then go forward with greater unity and will be more likely to solve its group task constructively.

The leader and the members in the highly effective group know that the building and maintenance of the group as well as the carrying out of tasks need to be done well. They are highly skilled in performing each of the different membership and leadership roles required. Each member feels responsible for assuming whatever role is necessary to keep the group operating in an efficient manner. In performing these required roles, the member may carry them out by himself or in cooperation with other group members. Each exercises initiative as called for by the situation. The group has a high capacity to mobilize fully all the skills and abilities of its members and focus these resources efficiently on the jobs to be done.

The larger the work group, the greater the difficulty in building it into a highly effective group. Seashore (1954) found that group cohesiveness, i.e., attraction of the members to the group, decreased steadily as work groups increased in size. This finding is supported also by other data (Indik, 1961; Revans, 1957).

To facilitate building work groups to high levels of effectiveness it will be desirable, consequently, to keep the groups as small as possible. This requirement, however, must be balanced against other demands on the organization, such as keeping the number of organizational levels to a minimum. This suggests the desirability of running tests and computing the relative efficiencies and costs of different-sized work groups. It is probable also that the optimum size for a group will vary with the kind of work the group is doing.

The highly effective group as described in this chapter, it will be recalled, is an "ideal model." It may sound completely unattainable. This does not appear to be the case. There is impressive evidence supporting the view that this ideal can be approximated, if not fully reached, in actual operations in any organization. This evidence is provided by the highest-producing managers and supervisors in American industry and government. If the measurements of their work groups and the reports of their work-group members are at all accurate, some of these managers have built and are operating work groups strikingly similar to our ideal model.

This chapter started by observing that groups can have constructive or destructive goals and can achieve these goals fully or partially, that there is nothing inherently good or bad about groups. If we reflect on the nature and functional characteristics of the highly effective group, however, some qualification of our initial comments may be warranted. In the highly effective group, the members can and do exercise substantial amounts of influence on the group's values and goals. As a consequence, these goals reflect the long-range as well as the short-range needs, desires, and values of its members. If we assume that the long-range desires and values will reflect, on the average, some of the more important long-range values and goals of the total society, we can draw some inferences about the highly effective group. These groups will, in terms of probability, reflect the constructive values and goals of their society. They are likely to be strong groups seeking "good" goals.

GROUPTHINK

IRVING L. JANIS

"How could we have been so stupid?" President John F. Kennedy asked after he and a close group of advisers had blundered into the Bay of Pigs invasion. For the last two years I have been studying that question, as it applies not only to the Bay of Pigs decision-makers but also to those who led the United States into such other major fiascos as the failure to be prepared for the attack on Pearl Harbor, the Korean War stalemate and the escalation of the Vietnam War.

Stupidity certainly is not the explanation. The men who participated in making the Bay of Pigs decision, for instance, comprised one of the greatest arrays of intellectual talent in the history of American Government—Dean Rusk, Robert McNamara, Douglas Dillon, Robert Kennedy, McGeorge Bundy, Arthur Schlesinger Jr., Allen Dulles and others.

It also seemed to me that explanations were incomplete if they concentrated only on disturbances in the behavior of each individual within a decision-making body: temporary emotional states of elation, fear, or anger that reduce a man's mental efficiency, for example, or chronic blind spots arising from a man's social prejudices or idiosyncratic biases.

I preferred to broaden the picture by looking at the fiascos from the standpoint of group dynamics as it has been explored over the past three decades, first by the great social psychologist Kurt Lewin and later in many experimental situations by myself and other behavioral scientists. My conclusion after pouring over hundreds of relevant documents—historical reports about formal group meetings and informal conversations among the members—is that the groups that committed the fiascos were victims of what I call "group think."

Psychology Today, November 1971. Copyright © 1971 Ziff-Davis Publishing Company. Reprinted by permission of *Psychology Today* magazine and the author.

"Groupy"

In each case study, I was surprised to discover the extent to which each group displayed the typical phenomena of social conformity that are regularly encountered in studies of group dynamics among ordinary citizens. For example, some of the phenomena appear to be completely in line with findings from social-psychological experiments showing that powerful social pressures are brought to bear by the members of a cohesive group whenever a dissident begins to voice his objections to a group consensus. Other phenomena are reminiscent of the shared illusions observed in encounter groups and friendship cliques when the members simultaneously reach a peak of "groupy" feelings.

Above all, there are numerous indications pointing to the development of group norms that bolster morale at the expense of critical thinking. One of the most common norms appears to be that of remaining loyal to the group by sticking with the policies to which the group has already committed itself, even when those policies are obviously working out badly and have unintended consequences that disturb the conscience of each member. This is one of the key characteristics of groupthink.

1984

I use the term groupthink as a quick and easy way to refer to the mode of thinking that persons engage in when *concurrence-seeking* becomes so dominant in a cohesive ingroup that it tends to override realistic appraisal of alternative courses of action. Groupthink is a term of the same order as the words in the newspeak vocabulary George Orwell used in his dismaying world of *1984*. In that context, groupthink takes on an invidious connotation. Exactly such a connotation is intended, since the term refers to a deterioration in mental efficiency, reality testing and moral judgments as a result of group pressures.

The symptoms of groupthink arise when the members of decision-making groups become motivated to avoid being too harsh in their judgments of the leaders' or their colleagues' ideas. They adopt a soft line of criticism, even in their own thinking. At their meetings, all the members are amiable and seek complete concurrence on every important issue, with no bickering or conflict to spoil the cozy, "we-feeling" atmosphere.

Kill

Paradoxically, soft-headed groups are often hard-hearted when it comes to dealing with outgroups or enemies. They find it relatively easy to resort to dehumanizing solutions—they will readily authorize bombing attacks that kill large numbers of civilians in the name of the noble cause of persuading an unfriendly government to negotiate at the peace table. They are unlikely to pursue the more difficult and controversial issues that arise when alternatives to a harsh military solution come up for discussion. Nor are they inclined to raise ethical issues that carry the implication that *this fine group of ours, with its humanitarianism and its high-minded principles, might be capable of adopting a course of action that is inhumane and immoral.*

Norms

There is evidence from a number of social-psychological studies that as the members of a group feel more accepted by the others, which is a central feature of increased group cohesiveness, they display less overt conformity to group norms. Thus we would expect that the more cohesive a group becomes, the less the members will feel constrained to censor what they say out of fear of being socially punished for antagonizing the leader or any of their fellow members.

In contrast, the groupthink type of conformity tends to increase as group cohesiveness increases. Groupthink involves nondeliberate suppression of critical thoughts as a result of internalization of the group's norms, which is quite different from deliberate suppression on the basis of external threats of social punishment. The more cohesive the group, the greater the inner compulsion on the part of each member to avoid creating disunity, which inclines him to believe in the soundness of whatever proposals are promoted by the leader or by a majority of the group's members.

In a cohesive group, the danger is not so much that each individual will fail to reveal his objections to what the others propose but that he will think the proposal is a good one, without attempting to carry out a careful, critical scrutiny of the pros and cons of the alternatives. When groupthink becomes dominant, there also is considerable suppression of deviant thoughts, but it takes the form of each person's deciding that his misgivings are not relevant and should be set aside, that the benefit of the doubt regarding any lingering uncertainties should be given to the group concensus.

Stress

I do not mean to imply that all cohesive groups necessarily suffer from groupthink. All ingroups may have a mild tendency toward groupthink, displaying one or another of the symptoms from time to time, but it need not be so dominant as to influence the quality of the group's final decision. Neither do I mean to imply that there is anything necessarily inefficient or harmful about group decisions in general. On the contrary, a group whose members have properly defined roles, with traditions concerning the procedures to follow in pursuing a critical inquiry, probably is capable of making better decisions than any individual group member working alone.

The problem is that the advantages of having decisions made by groups are often lost because of powerful psychological pressures that arise when the members work closely together, share the same set of values and, above all, face a crisis situation that puts everyone under intense stress.

The main principle of groupthink, which I offer in the spirit of Parkinson's Law, is this:

> *The more amiability and esprit de corps there is among the members of a policy-making ingroup, the greater the danger that independent critical*

thinking will be replaced by groupthink, which is likely to result in irrational and dehumanizing actions directed against outgroups.

Symptoms

In my studies of high-level governmental decision-makers, both civilian and military, I have found eight main symptoms of groupthink.

1 Invulnerability

Most or all of the members of the ingroup share an *illusion* of invulnerability that provides for them some degree of reassurance about obvious dangers and leads them to become overoptimistic and willing to take extraordinary risks. It also causes them to fail to respond to clear warnings of danger.

The Kennedy ingroup, which uncritically accepted the Central Intelligence Agency's disastrous Bay of Pigs plan, operated on the false assumption that they could keep secret the fact that the United States was responsible for the invasion of Cuba. Even after news of the plan began to leak out, their belief remained unshaken. They failed even to consider the danger that awaited them: a world-wide revulsion against the U.S.

A similar attitude appeared among the members of President Lyndon B. Johnson's ingroup, the "Tuesday Cabinet," which kept escalating the Vietnam War despite repeated setbacks and failures. "There was a belief," Bill Moyers commented after he resigned, "that if we indicated a willingness to use our power, they [the North Vietnamese] would get the message and back away from an all-out confrontation. . . . There was a confidence—it was never bragged about, it was just there—that when the chips were really down, the other people would fold."

A most poignant example of an illusion of invulnerability involves the ingroup around Admiral H. E. Kimmel, which failed to prepare for the possibility of a Japanese attack on Pearl Harbor despite repeated warnings. Informed by his intelligence chief that radio contact with Japanese aircraft carriers had been lost, Kimmel joked about it: "What, you don't know where the carriers are? Do you mean to say that they could be rounding Diamond Head (at Honolulu) and you wouldn't know it?" The carriers were in fact moving full-steam toward Kimmel's command post at the time. Laughing together about a danger signal, which labels it as a purely laughing matter, is a characteristic manifestation of groupthink.

2 Rationale

As we see, victims of groupthink ignore warnings: they also collectively construct rationalizations in order to discount warnings and other forms of negative feedback that, taken seriously, might lead the group members to reconsider their assumptions each time they recommit themselves to past decisions. Why did the Johnson ingroup avoid reconsidering its escalation policy when time and again the expectations on which they based their decisions turned out to be wrong? James C. Thompson Jr., a Harvard historian who spent five years as an observing participant in both the State Department and the White House, tells us that the policymakers avoided critical discussion of their prior decisions and continually invented new rationalizations so that they could sincerely recommit themselves to defeating the North Vietnamese.

In the fall of 1964, before the bombing of North Vietnam began, some of the policymakers predicted that six weeks of air strikes would induce the North Vietnamese to seek peace talks. When someone asked, "What if they don't?" the answer was that another four weeks certainly would do the trick.

Later, after each setback, the ingroup agreed that by investing just a bit more effort (by stepping up the bomb tonnage a bit, for instance), their course of action would prove to be right. *The Pentagon Papers* bear out these observations.

In *The Limits of Intervention,* Townsend Hoopes, who was acting Secretary of the Air Force under Johnson, says that Walt W. Rostow in particular showed a remarkable capacity for what has been called "instant rationalization." According to Hoopes, Rostow buttressed the group's optimism about being on the road to victory by culling selected scraps of evidence from news reports or, if necessary, by inventing "plausible" forecasts that had no basis in evidence at all.

Admiral Kimmel's group rationalized away their warnings, too. Right up to December 7, 1941, they convinced themselves that the Japanese would never dare attempt a full-scale surprise assault against Hawaii because Japan's leaders would realize that it would precipitate an all-out war which the United States would surely win. They made no attempt to look at the situation through the eyes of the Japanese leaders—another manifestation of groupthink.

3 Morality

Victims of groupthink believe unquestioningly in the inherent morality of their ingroup; this belief inclines the members to ignore the ethical or moral consequences of their decisions.

Evidence that this symptom is at work usually is of a negative kind—the things that are left unsaid in group meetings. At least two influential persons had doubts about the morality of the Bay of Pigs adventure. One of them, Arthur Schlesinger Jr., presented his strong objections in a memorandum to President Kennedy and Secretary of State Rusk but surpressed them when he attended meetings of the Kennedy team. The other, Senator J. William Fulbright, was not a member of the group, but the President invited him to express his misgivings in a speech to the policymakers. However, when Fulbright finished speaking the President moved on to other agenda items without asking for reactions of the group.

David Kraslow and Staurt H. Loory, in *The Secret Search for Peace in Vietnam,* report that during 1966 President Johnson's ingroup was concerned primarily with selecting bomb targets in North Vietnam. They based their selections on four factors—the military advantage, the risk to American aircraft and pilots, the danger of forcing other countries into the fighting, and the danger of heavy civilian casualties. At their regular Tuesday luncheons, they weighed these factors the way school teachers grade examination papers, averaging them out. Though evidence on this point is scant, I suspect that the group's ritualistic adherence to a standardized procedure induced the members to feel morally justified in their destructive way of dealing with the Vietnamese people—after all, the danger of heavy civilian casualties from U.S. air strikes was taken into account on their checklists.

Victims of groupthink hold stereotyped views of the leaders of enemy groups: they are so evil that genuine attempts at negotiating differences with them are unwarranted, or they are too weak or too stupid to deal effectively with whatever attempts the ingroup makes to defeat their purposes, no matter how risky the attempts are.

Kennedy's groupthinkers believed that Premier Fidel Castro's air force was so ineffectual that obsolete B-26s could knock it out completely in a surprise attack before the invasion began. They also believed that Castro's army was so weak that a small Cuban-exile brigade could establish a well-protected beachhead at the Bay of Pigs. In addition, they believed that Castro was not smart enough to put down any possible internal uprisings in support of the exiles. They were wrong on all three assumptions. Though much of the blame was attributable to faulty intelligence, the point is that none of Kennedy's advisers even questioned the CIA planners about these assumptions.

The Johnson advisers' sloganistic thinking about "the Communist apparatus" that was "working all around the world" (as Dean Rusk put it) led them to overlook the powerful nationalistic strivings of the North Vietnamese government and its efforts to ward off Chinese domination. The crudest of all stereotypes used by Johnson's inner circle to justify their policies was the domino theory ("If we don't stop the Reds in South Vietnam, tomorrow they will be in Hawaii and next week they will be in San Francisco," Johnson once said). The group so firmly accepted this stereotype that it became almost impossible for any adviser to introduce a more sophisticated viewpoint.

In the documents on Pearl Harbor, it is clear to see that the Navy commanders stationed in Hawaii had a naive image of Japan as a midget that would not dare to strike a blow against a powerful giant.

5 Pressure

Victims of groupthink apply direct pressure to any individual who momentarily expresses doubts about any of the group's shared illusions or who questions the validity of the arguments supporting a policy alternative favored by the majority. This gambit reinforces the concurrence-seeking norm that loyal members are expected to maintain.

President Kennedy probably was more active than anyone else in raising skeptical questions during the Bay of Pigs meetings, and yet he seems to have encouraged the group's docile, uncritical acceptance of defective arguments in favor of the CIA's plan. At every meeting, he allowed the CIA representatives to dominate the discussion. He permitted them to give their immediate refutations in response to each tentative doubt that one of the others expressed, instead of asking whether anyone shared the doubt or wanted to pursue the implications of the new worrisome issue that had just been raised. And at the most crucial meeting, when he was calling on each member to give his vote for or against the plan he did not call on Arthur Schlesinger, the one man there who was known by the President to have serious misgivings.

Historian Thompson informs us that whenever a member of Johnson's ingroup began to express doubts, the group used subtle social pressures to "domesticate" him. To start with, the dissenter was made to feel at home, provided that he lived up to two restrictions: 1) that he did not voice his doubts to outsiders, which would play into the hands of the opposition: and 2) that he kept his criticisms within the bounds of acceptable deviation, which meant not challenging any of the fundamental assumptions that went into the group's prior commitments. One such "domesticated dissenter" was Bill Moyers. When Moyers arrived at a meeting, Thompson tells us, the President greeted him with, "Well, here comes Mr. Stop-the-Bombing."

6 Self-Censorship

Victims of groupthink avoid deviating from what appears to be group consensus; they keep silent about their misgivings and even minimize to themselves the importance of their doubts.

As we have seen, Schlesinger was not at all hesitant about presenting his strong objections to the Bay of Pigs plan in a memorandum to the President and the Secretary of State. But he became keenly aware of his tendency to suppress objections at the White House meetings. "In the months after the Bay of Pigs I bitterly reproached myself for having kept so silent during those crucial discussions in the cabinet room," Schlesinger writes in *A Thousand Days*. "I can only explain my failure to do more than raise a few timid questions by reporting that one's impulse to blow the whistle on this nonsense was simply undone by the circumstances of the discussion."

7 Unanimity

Victims of groupthink share an *illusion* of unanimity within the group concerning almost all judgments expressed by members who speak in favor of the majority view. This symptom results partly from the preceding one, whose effects are augmented by the false assumption that any individual who remains silent during any part of the discussion is in full accord with what the others are saying.

When a group of persons who respect each other's opinions arrives at a unanimous view, each member is likely to feel that the belief must be true. This reliance on consensual validation within the group tends to replace individual critical thinking and reality testing, unless there are clear-cut disagreements among the members. In contemplating a course of action such as the invasion of Cuba, it is painful for the members to confront disagreements within their group, particularly if it becomes apparent that there are widely divergent views about whether the preferred course of action is too risky to undertake at all. Such disagreements are likely to arouse anxieties about making a serious error. Once the sense of unanimity is shattered, the members no longer can feel complacently confident about the decision they are inclined to make. Each man must then face the annoying realization that there are troublesome uncertainties and he must diligently seek out the best information he can get in order to decide for himself exactly how serious the risks might be. This is one of the unpleasant consequences of being in a group of hardheaded, critical thinkers.

To avoid such an unpleasant state, the members often become inclined, without quite realizing it, to prevent latent disagreements from surfacing when they are about to initiate a risky course of action. The group leader and the members support each other in playing up the areas of convergence in their thinking, at the expense of fully exploring divergencies that might reveal unsettled issues.

"Our meetings took place in a curious atmosphere of assumed consensus," Schlesinger writes. His additional comments clearly show that, curiously, the consensus was an illusion—an illusion that could be maintained only because the major participants did not reveal their own reasoning or discuss their idiosyncratic assumptions and vague reservations. Evidence from several sources makes it clear that even the three principals—President Kennedy, Rusk and McNamara—had widely differing assumptions about the invasion plan.

8 Mindguards

Victims of groupthink sometimes appoint themselves as mindguards to protect the leader and fellow members from adverse information that might break the complacency they shared about the effectiveness and morality of past decisions. At a large birthday party for his wife, Attorney General Robert F. Kennedy, who had been constantly informed about the Cuban invasion plan, took Schlesinger aside and asked him why he was opposed. Kennedy listened coldly and said, "You may be right or you may be wrong, but the President has made his mind up. Don't push it any further. Now is the time for everyone to help him all they can."

Rusk also functioned as a highly effective mindguard by failing to transmit to the group the strong objections of three "outsiders" who had learned of the invasion plan—Undersecretary of State Chester Bowles, USIA Director Edward R. Murrow, and Rusk's intelligence chief, Roger Hilsman. Had Rusk done so, their warnings might have reinforced Schlesinger's memorandum and jolted some of Kennedy's ingroup, if not the President himself, into reconsidering the decision.

Products

When a group of executives frequently displays most or all of these interrelated symptoms, a detailed study of their deliberations is likely to reveal a number of immediate consequences. These consequences are, in effect, products of poor decision-making practices because they lead to inadequate solutions to the problems being dealt with.

First, the group limits its discussions to a few alternative courses of action (often only two) without an initial survey of all the alternatives that might be worthy of consideration.

Second, the group fails to reexamine the course of action initially preferred by the majority after they learn of risks and drawbacks they had not considered originally.

Third, the members spend little or no time discussing whether there are nonobvious gains they may have overlooked or ways of reducing the seemingly prohibitive costs that made rejected alternatives appear undesirable to them.

Fourth, members make little or no attempt to obtain information from experts within their own organizations who might be able to supply more precise estimates of potential losses and gains.

Fifth, members show positive interest in facts and opinions that support their preferred policy; they tend to ignore facts and opinions that do not.

Sixth, members spend little time deliberating about how the chosen policy might be hindered by bureaucratic inertia, sabotaged by political opponents, or temporarily derailed by common accidents. Consequently, they fail to work out contingency plans to cope with foreseeable setbacks that could endanger the overall success of their chosen course.

Support

The search for an explanation of why groupthink ocurs has led me through a quagmire of complicated theoretical issues in the murky area of human motivation. My belief, based on recent social psychological research, is that we can best understand the various symptoms of groupthink as a mutual effort among the group members to maintain self-esteem and emotional equanimity by providing social support to each other, especially at times when they share responsibility for making vital decisions.

Even when no important decision is pending, the typical administrator will begin to doubt the wisdom and morality of his past decisions each time he receives information about setbacks, particularly if the information is accompanied by negative feedback from prominent men who originally had been his supporters. It should not be surprising, therefore, to find that individual members strive to develop unanimity and esprit de corps that will help bolster each other's morale, to create an optimistic outlook about the success of pending decisions, and to reaffirm the positive value of past policies to which all of them are committed.

Pride

Shared illusions of invulnerability, for example, can reduce anxiety about taking risks. Rationalizations help members believe that the risks are really not so bad after all. The assumption of inherent morality helps the members to avoid feelings of shame or guilt. Negative stereotypes function as stress-reducing devices to enhance a sense of moral righteousness as well as pride in a lofty mission.

The mutual enhancement of self-esteem and morale may have functional value in enabling the members to maintain their capacity to take action, but it has maladaptive consequences insofar as concurrence-seeking tendencies interfere with critical, rational capacities and lead to serious errors of judgment.

While I have limited my study to decision-making bodies in Government, groupthink symptoms appear in business, industry and any other field where small, cohesive groups make the decisions. It is vital, then, for all sorts of people—and especially group leaders—to know what steps they can take to prevent groupthink.

Remedies

To counterpoint my case studies of the major fiascos, I have also investigated two highly successful group enterprises, the formulation of the Marshall Plan in the Truman Administration and the handling of the Cuban missile crisis by President Kennedy and his advisers. I have found it instructive to examine the steps Kennedy took to change his group's decision-making processes. These changes ensured that the mistakes made by his Bay of Pigs ingroup were not repeated by the missile-crisis ingroup, even though the membership of both groups was essentially the same.

The following recommendations for preventing groupthink incorporate many of the good practices I discovered to be characteristic of the Marshall Plan and missile-crisis groups:

1. The leader of a policy-forming group should assign the role of critical evaluator to each member, encouraging the group to give high priority to open airing of objections and doubts. This practice needs to be reinforced by the leader's acceptance of criticism of his own judgments in order to discourage members from soft-pedaling their disagreements and from allowing their striving for concurrence to inhibit criticism.

2. When the key members of a hierarchy assign a policy-planning mission to any group within their organization, they should adopt an impartial stance instead of stating preferences and expectations at the beginning. This will encourage open inquiry and impartial probing of a wide range of policy alternatives.

3. The organization routinely should set up several outside policy-planning and evaluation groups to work on the same policy question, each deliberating under a different leader. This can prevent the insulation of an ingroup.

4. At intervals before the group reaches a final consensus, the leader should require each member to discuss the group's deliberations with associates in his own unit of the organization—assuming that those associates can be trusted to adhere to the same security regulations that govern the policy-makers—and then to report back their reactions to the group.

5. The group should invite one or more outside experts to each meeting on a staggered basis and encourage the experts to challenge the views of the core members.

6. At every general meeting of the group, whenever the agenda calls for an evaluation of policy alternatives, at least one member should play devil's advocate, functioning as a good lawyer in challenging the testimony of those who advocate the majority position.

7. Whenever the policy issue involves relations with a rival nation or organization, the group should devote a sizable block of time, perhaps an entire session, to a survey of all warning signals from the rivals and should write alternative scenarios on the rivals' intentions.

8. When the group is surveying policy alternatives for feasibility and effectiveness, it should from time to time divide into two or more subgroups to meet separately, under different chairmen, and then come back together to hammer out differences.

9. After reaching a preliminary consensus about what seems to be the best policy, the group should hold a "second-chance" meeting at which every member expresses as vividly as he can all his residual doubts, and rethinks the entire issue before making a definitive choice.

How

These recommendations have their disdavantages. To encourage the open airing of objections, for instance, might lead to prolonged and costly debates when a rapidly growing crisis requires immediate solution. It also could cause rejection, depression and anger. A leader's failure to set a norm might create cleavage between leader and members that could develop into a disruptive power struggle if the leader looks on the emerging consensus as anathema. Setting up outside evaluation groups might increase the risk of security leakage. Still, inventive executives who know their way around the organizational maze probably can figure out how to apply one or another of the prescriptions successfully, without harmful side effects.

They also could benefit from the advice of outside experts in the administrative and behavioral sciences. Though these experts have much to offer, they have had few chances to work on policy-making machinery within large organizations. As matters now stand, executives innovate only when they need new procedures to avoid repeating serious errors that have deflated their self-images.

In this era of atomic warheads, urban disorganization and ecocatastrophes, it seems to me that policymakers should collaborate with behavioral scientists and give top priority to preventing groupthink and its attendant fiascos.

6 problem solving in groups

LEADERSHIP PRINCIPLES
FOR PROBLEM SOLVING CONFERENCES

Norman R. F. Maier

It is possible for a discussion leader to increase the ability of a group of people to solve problems by means of the application of certain principles. No claim is made that the nine principles described below constitute a complete list, and it is also possible that the number eventually may be reduced to fewer and more fundamental principles. The reader may find that some of the principles overlap in certain respects. Nevertheless, the principles stated below are adequate in their present form to serve as a guide to the discussion leader.

Principle 1

Success in problem solving requires that effort be directed toward overcoming SURMOUNTABLE *obstacles.* If we think of a problem situation as one in which obstacles block us from reaching a goal, it follows that some of these obstacles will be more readily overcome than others. As a matter of fact, a problem will be insoluble if attempts are made to reach a goal over an insurmountable obstacle. This means that persistent attempts to overcome some obstacles might be doomed to failure. Success in problem solving, therefore, depends on locating obstacles that can more readily be overcome.[1]

It is the common tendency to persist in following an initial approach to a problem. In other words, a particular obstacle is selected and pursued despite the fact that it cannot be overcome. Usually this obstacle is the most obvious

---

Reprinted with permission of the publisher from Norman Maier, *Problem Solving and Creativity,* (Monterey, Calif.: Brooks/Cole Publishing Company, 1970). 1970).

[1]N. R. F. Maier, "An Aspect of Human Reasoning," *Brit. J. Psychol.,* 1933, 24, 144–155.

or is one that previous experience has suggested. For example, medical research reveals that the innoculation of a serum to create immunity has been a successful approach for dealing with some diseases so it tends to be followed for others. In business it is not uncommon to approach new problems with approaches previously found successful. Yet difficult problems require new and unusual approaches; if they did not, they would not be difficult problems.

A common tendency that frequently leads to a failure is associated with the attempt to solve a problem by locating a person or group that is at fault. For example, a solution to international problems that require another nation to behave differently may meet with failure because the problem solvers cannot control the action they recommend. Lacking such control, when it is essential to the solution, represents an insurmountable obstacle. A solution that cannot be effectuated falls short of solving the problem and hence leads us only to the insurmountable obstacles. Successful solutions must be workable.

Principle 2

Available facts should be used even when they are inadequate. A solution that was effective in one situation becomes favored and is used in new situations even when the similarity between the old and new situation is superficial. The assumption that the situations are the same tends to detract from a careful examination of the facts that are available.

When a good deal of information is available, problem solvers are more prone to work with the evidence. There is then enough information given to permit them to reject some solutions. However, in the absence of adequate information, it becomes more difficult to be selective and as a consequence imagination and biases dominate the problem solving.[2]

Principle 3

The starting point of a problem is richest in solution possibilities. The solution of a problem may be envisaged as a route from the starting point to the goal. The process of thinking about a solution is like proceeding along a particular route. Once one starts in a particular direction one moves away from certain alternatives and thus reduces the number of possible alternative directions that may be pursued.

Each route may confront one with obstacles. As discussion of a problem proceeds, successive obstacles present themselves. A group may have successfully by-passed two obstacles along the way and then find difficulty with others that face them at their advanced stage of progress. Because of this partial success in moving forward, it is difficult for them to revert and start all over again, yet a new start is the only way to increase the variety of solution possibilities. For example, a great deal of progress was made with propeller-driven planes; however, they had limitations. They were not able to fly above a certain height because of the lack of atmosphere. Increasing their power and design could raise the flying ceiling somewhat; nevertheless, the need for

[2]N. R. F. Maier, "Screening Solutions To Upgrade Quality: A New Approach to Problem Solving Under Conditions of Uncertainty," *J. Psychol.*, 1960, 49, 217–231.

atmosphere limited the ceiling for propeller-driven craft. A plane with an entirely different power plant—the jet engine—represented a fresh start in aviation.

In the usual problem-situation a person develops certain ideas about solutions. This means he moves from the starting point in a particular direction toward the goal. Thus the supervisor who wishes to improve phone-answering services in his office by eliminating or reducing personal calls finds it difficult to think of approaches that do not limit personal calls. Rather he thinks of different approaches for *limiting* personal calls and loses sight of the original goal of improving phone-answering service. The solution reached now becomes confused with the problem. This is why statements of problems frequently contain suggestions of solutions. Obviously such statements of problems are so near the goal that they limit other solution possibilities. Such suggested solutions may be unacceptable and unimaginative.

In order to get a better appreciation of the starting point of a problem, a discussion leader should ask himself why he wishes or favors a certain solution. What purpose does my solution serve? Such a question may suggest the nature of the starting point of the problem. Spending time with the group to explain the prime objective, therefore, represents a procedure for finding the starting point.

All solutions represent methods for reaching a goal, but frequently sight is lost of the starting point. Rather the goal becomes an ideal toward which to strive. Practical consideration, however, requires that we reach a goal from the point at which we find ourselves. It may be unrealistic to get to an ideal goal from certain points. If one could start over again, more problems could be solved, or more ideal goals could be reached, but this is not realistic problem solving. A solution always is a path *from* the starting point *to* a goal, and sight of this starting point should not be lost.

Principle 4

Problem-mindedness should be increased while solution-mindedness is delayed. By nature people progress too rapidly toward a solution. This is what is meant by solution-mindedness. This tendency is similar to the phenomenon known as the Zeigarnik[3] effect. Once a task is begun psychological forces are set up to push the task to completion. The reader will understand how he himself resists being interrupted while engaged in a task and how he worries over unfinished activities. It is only natural, therefore, that since the goal of a problem is to find a solution, energy and activity toward accomplishing this end are set in motion.

This means that in almost any discussion the responses of various persons tend to interrupt the thinking process of one another, and this is often disturbing. It is only natural for a dominant person to push through his ideas, and when he happens to be the leader, the value of group participation is lost.

Experimental evidence supporting the value of delaying the reaching of a

[3]B. Zeigarnik, "Ueber das Behalten von erledigten und unerledigten Handleungen." *Psychol. Forsch.,* 1927, 9, 1–85. M. Ovsiankina, "Die Wiederaufnahme unterbrochener Handlungen." *Psychol. Forsch.* 1928, 11, 302–379.

solution and spending more time focusing on the problem is available.[4] Common experience also may be cited.

It is not uncommon to find that people who disagree about solutions later find that they have not even agreed on the problem. The first prerequisite to reaching agreement on a solution would seem to be one of reaching agreement on the problem. The reader also will recall that when he asks his friends for help on a problem, they offer suggestions before he has finished his statement of the problem.

It is apparent that a discussion leader can cause a group to be more problem-minded. Usually he is a strong force in encouraging solution-mindedness. He must not only inhibit this tendency, but encourage problem-mindedness in his group in the process of improving his discussion leadership.

Principle 5

Disagreement can lead either to hard feelings or to innovation, depending on the discussion leadership. Two strong forces make for conformity: fear of the leader's unfavorable judgment and fear of unfavorable responses from the group to which one belongs. These factors unfortunately operate only too frequently in group discussion so that the leader must be prepared to deal with both of them. Experimental evidence in support of this conclusion is to be found in several of our recent studies.[5]

Almost everyone has learned that he can get into more trouble by disagreeing with his boss than by agreeing with him. This is the kind of learning that develops "yes-men." In most organizations, conferees need a great deal of encouragement to feel free to disagree with the boss. This does not mean that disagreeing is a virtue. Rather the subordinate must feel free to disagree if he is to contribute the best of his thinking. The leader takes the first steps in reducing conformity by withholding judgment, entertaining criticism, and trying to understand strange ideas.

The dangers of disagreeing with the majority members of one's own group or with society in general is less readily learned. The dissenter and the innovator sometimes find themselves popular and sometimes unpopular. For this reason, any hard feelings created by disagreement are not too apparent. However, an additional factor also operates. This is the security gained in "going along with the crowd." When people are unsure of themselves they are particularly prone to follow group opinion rather than risk a deviant opinion.[6] Conformity to group standards becomes unfortunate when it inhibits free expression or when the group rejects the person who innovates without examining or understanding his contributions. A majority does not have to prove or justify itself because it does not have to change minds, but a minority can be laughed down and hence is denied the opportunity to prove itself. Original ideas are new so the original person frequently finds himself in the minority.

[4]N. R. F. Maier and A. R. Solem, "Improving Solutions by Turning Choice Situations into Problems." *Pers. Psychol.* 1962, 15, 151–157.

[5]N. R. F Maier and J. J. Hayes, *Creative Management,* New York, John Wiley & Sons, Inc., 1962.

[6]E. L. Walker and R. W. Heyns, *An Anatomy for Conformity,* Englewood Cliffs, N.J., Prentice-Hall, 1962.

This means that he may not only be a lonely person, but will have to justify many of his views.

When one person disagrees with another, the latter is inclined to feel that he has been attacked. As a consequence he feels hurt, defends himself, or becomes angry and counter-attacks. Such emotional reactions lead to interpersonal conflict and this type of interaction tends to worsen. As a result, some people avoid hurting others. "Good" group members, therefore, tend to be sensitive to group opinion and become careful in expressing their views. As a matter of fact, they may find that the easiest way to be careful is to avoid disagreeing. People who get along with other participants by conforming may be good group members, but they also become poor problem solvers.[7] Members cannot learn from one another by agreeing. They can avoid generating hard feelings but eventually they may become bored. Satisfaction in group problem solving should come from task accomplishment, otherwise the group activity is primarily social.

We therefore are confronted with the fact that because disagreeing with others frequently leads to injured pride and interpersonal conflict, it is considered to be poor manners. In attempts to avoid trouble, people learn to refrain from disagreeing and hence move toward conformity. However, that alternative also is undesirable. The resolution of this dilemma is not only to prevent the suppression of disagreement but to encourage a respect for disagreement and thereby turn it into a stimulant for new ideas. How is this to be done?

First of all, each individual can learn to be less defensive himself, even if he cannot expect this tolerance from others. This is not much of a gain but it can be a personal one. A group leader, however, can accomplish a good deal in this respect. The leader of a group discussion can create a climate where disagreement is encouraged, he can use his position in the group to protect minority individuals, and he can turn disagreements among group members into situational problems. This is a second of the important skill areas for reducing the undesirable aspects of conformity, and in addition this skill in group leadership makes for innovation by using disagreement constructively.

Group thinking has a potential advantage over individual thinking in that the resources making for disagreement are greater in a group. Group thinking also has a potential disadvantage in that the dominant thinking may be that of the majority. The leader's responsibility is to capitalize on the advantages and avoid the disadvantages of group processes.

While organizations search for creative talent and attempt to develop it, the creative talent already present in the organization is being depressed at all levels. In a recent study[8] the solutions of four person groups taken from four populations differing in organizational orientation were compared. The problem used involved an industrial situation in which the need for a change in work procedure was raised.

The results showed that the least creative solutions came from management

[7]L. R. Hoffman, "Homogeneity of Member Personality and Its Effect on Group Problem-Solving," *J. Abn. Soc. Psychol.,* 1959, 58, 27–32. L. R. Hoffman and N. R. F. Maier, "Quality and Acceptance of Problem Solutions by Members of Homogeneous and Heterogeneous Groups," *J. Abn. Soc. Psychol.,* 1961, 62, 401–407.

[8]N. R. F. Maier, "Organization and Creative Problem Solving," *J. Appl. Psychol.* 1961, 45, 277–280.

groups, better solutions came from students in the school of business administration, still better ones from students in a college course on industrial psychology, while the greatest number of innovative solutions came from students in Liberal Arts courses. It appears that the farther the problem solvers were removed from organizational experience, the more innovative were their solutions. Unless something is done to prevent it, awareness of organization structure suppresses innovation. The key factor seems to be the perception of the role of the boss in introducing and gaining acceptance of change.

Principle 6

The "idea-getting" process should be separated from the "idea-evaluation" process because the latter inhibits the former. "Idea-evaluation" involves the testing and the comparison of solutions in the light of what is known, their probability for succeeding, and other practical considerations. It is the practical side of problem solving and is the phase of problem solving when judgment is passed on solutions. "Idea-getting" requires a willingness to break away from past experience. It is this process that requires an escape from the bonds of learning and demands that we search for unusual approaches and entertain new and untried ideas.

Robert Ingersoll once said "Colleges polish the pebbles and dim the diamonds." This may be an overstatement, but it points up the dual aspect of learning. It is the creative potentials that are inhibited by knowledge. Insofar as education teaches us what is known, it develops us and permits us to meet situations that have been previously met. In this way our problem solving is enhanced—our knowledge can generalize—and this is polish. However, in order to escape from the search into the past, new combinations of elements must be generated. The process of learning is to build associative bonds between elements of experience that are found and observed in conjunction with one another. Thus we learn names of things, we relate causes with effects, and we compare and see likenesses and differences. Creativity, however, requires the combination of elements and events that have never been experienced together—the generation of a new route from the starting point to the goal, made up of parts of old routes.

In other words, creativity requires the ability to fragment past experience to permit the formation of new spontaneous combinations. In contrast, learning requires the ability to combine or connect elements that have been contiguous to each other in our experience. Since these two abilities are basically different, they do not necessarily go together. One person may possess an unusual learning ability and be uncreative, another may be unusually creative but not be outstanding in learning ability. Both the abilities to learn and to fragment experience are necessary for good problem solving. However, the second of these has been largely overlooked because of our emphasis on the study of learning.[9]

In order to illustrate the difference between learning and fragmenting, let us

[9]N. R. F. Maier. "Selector-Integrator Mechanisms in Behavior." In: *Perspectives in Psychological Theory* (Ed. by B. Kaplan and S. Wapner). New York: International Universities Press, 1960.

turn to the string problem which we have used widely in our research. This problem requires that the ends of two strings hanging from the ceiling be tied together. They are spaced so that a person cannot reach one while holding the other. With the aid of strings or sticks one could readily solve this problem. However, the only tool available is a pair of pliers, so the obvious solutions are excluded. Past experience has associated this tool with certain functional uses and as a consequence it becomes less likely to be seen as a weight than would an ordinary piece of metal. The creative solution requires that a pendulum be constructed by using the pair of pliers as a pendulum weight. Thus the distant string can be made to swing within reach. To find this solution the old associate bonds must be broken in order to permit the pliers to become a pendulum bob. When this new connection is made (pliers fastened to the string) and the pendulum is discovered, there is a sharp change in functional meanings. It is this change in meaning that causes the experience of insight. Sudden insights are associated with creative discoveries because the new meaning is not gradually built up through experience, but comes suddenly as a result of a spontaneous new combination.[10]

The acquisition of knowledge, such as college training, actually may give an individual a mental set that reduces his creativity in certain respects, even though such knowledge is valuable in other ways. This is because the educated person may attempt to solve a problem by applying what he knows, and although this would be a successful approach on some occasions, it would not be a creative solution. This set prevents him from making up unique solutions and thereby developing a combination of parts that cannot be found in his past. Thus a potentially creative person (a diamond) might be dimmed (in Ingersoll's sense) by a knowledge of standard or known approaches to a problem.

Past learning, practical considerations, and evaluation all tend to depress flights of imagination—the forward leap that is based on a hunch (insufficient evidence). Creative thinking is a radical rather than a conservative look at a problem situation and requires encouragement if it is to be nurtured. To demand proof of new ideas at a time of their inception is to discourage the creative process.

However, creative ideas and insane ideas sometimes are difficult to distinguish. Both represent a departure from the common and traditional ways of thinking; both are new and unique to the person. But there is also a difference. The creative idea has a basis in objective reality, even though the evidence to convince others is inadequate; in contrast, the product of the insane mind is made up of elements derived largely from internal stimulation, such as hallucinations and imagined events.

The discussion leader can delay a group's criticism of an idea by asking for alternative contributions and he can encourage variety in thinking by encouraging the search for something different—something new. Turning ideas upside down, backwards, trying out different combinations of old ideas all represent ways to encourage the expression and generation of new ideas.

[10]N. R. F. Maier, "Reasoning in Humans, II. The Solution of a Problem and its Appearance in Consciousness," *J. Comp. Psychol.*, 1931, 12, 181–194.

Principle 7

Choice-situations should be turned into problem-situations. The characteristic of a choice-situation is one of being confronted with two or more alternatives. As a consequence, behavior is blocked until one of the alternatives is selected. The characteristic of a problem-situation, on the other hand, is one of being confronted with an obstacle that prevents the reaching of a goal. Behavior is blocked until the obstacle can be removed or surmounted. Creative alternatives tend to be overlooked in choice-situations because a choice is made between the obvious alternatives. The fact that such alternatives exist directs the energy toward making a choice and thus detracts from the search for additional alternatives.

Creative or unusual alternatives, not being among the obvious ones, are unlikely to characterize behavior in choice-situations because activity is directed toward a choice between existing alternatives. Something must be done to delay this choice until the possibility of additional alternatives is explored. This is something the discussion leader can do. Since the unusual alternatives are not readily apparent it is necessary to encourage considerable searching.[11]

The discovery or creation of solutions is inherent in the nature of problem solving. This means that the discussion leader should approach each choice-situation as one in which the possibility of additional alternatives exists. When he encourages this searching behavior in group discussion, he is turning a choice-situation into a problem-situation. Only after other alternatives are found or invented should the process of making a choice be undertaken.

Principle 8

Problem-situations should be turned into choice-situations. Because problem-situations block behavior, the natural reaction for people is to act on the first solution that is obtained. The objective in problem-situations is to remove or get around an obstacle. As a consequence, the discovery of the first successful possibility tends to terminate the search. The fact that one solution is found does not preclude the possibility that there may be others, yet people frequently behave as though this were the case.

If the leader accepts the first solution as a possibility, he may then ask the group to see if they can find another solution. If a second and even more solutions are obtained, the problem-situation will have been turned into a choice-situation. The opportunity to make a choice must necessarily improve the final decision because a choice between alternatives is permitted and the better one can win.

A recent study from our laboratory reveals that a second solution to a problem actually tends to be superior in quality to the first. This is not surprising when one realizes that a second solution requires further searching. Continued searching tends to lead to less obvious discoveries and these are likely to be the more innovative possibilities. Other factors may also favor the superior quality of the second solution. A dominant leader or certain vocal members may have

[11]N. R. F. Maier, *The Appraisal Interview,* New York: John Wiley & Sons, Inc., 1958.

pushed their ideas because of their ability to dominate, thereby discouraging the development of disagreement in the groups. Hoffman[12] in reviewing a number of studies, believes that balanced conflict, in which opposing members are equally strong, favors creative solutions. Such conflict requires an innovative solution, he believes, because one point of view cannot dominate over another. Both alternatives are likely to be obvious alternatives for conflicting parties and hence each might be overlooking something.

Turning problem situations into choice situations thus has two advantages. It leads to more unusual solutions, which would tend to be the more creative; and it permits the opportunity to select the best of the alternatives.

Decision-making requires both choice behavior and problem-solving behavior. To identify decision-making either with choice behavior or with problem solving is to restrict its function. Both activities go on in decision making, and since the two processes differ, it is desirable to make capital of the difference and thereby upgrade each.

Principle 9

Solutions suggested by the leader are improperly evaluated and tend either to be accepted or rejected. When the discussion leader conducts a discussion with his subordinates he is in a position of power so that his ideas receive a different reception than those coming from participants. This point is basic to the group decision process. In this connection an experiment by Solem[13] nicely illustrates the principle. He found that discussion leaders acting as superiors had more successful conferences when they did not have a chance to study a problem beforehand. When they studied a problem and reached a decision before the discussion, they tended to express their ideas. As a result, the discussion was diverted into a reaction to their ideas so that alternatives were not generated. The tendency of members was either to show acceptance or rejection reactions to the leader's ideas. Thus the leader's previous study of a problem caused the group to reach less acceptable and poorer decisions.

Even when the discussion leader has no formal authority over the group his position is seen as one of power. Actually such a leader exerts considerable power by merely approving or disapproving of ideas that are expressed. Thus a leader's suggestions are either blindly followed or resented rather than weighed.

The best way to avoid these two undesirable reactions is for the leader to refrain from introducing his views or passing judgment on the ideas expressed by participants. His job is to conduct the discussion and show his proficiency in this regard. In applying these principles his position becomes analagous to that of a symphony orchestra conductor. He plays no instrument but makes use of the instruments of the participants. Similarly the discussion leader uses the minds of conferees and is interested in the best end results. At this point the analogy breaks down because the orchestra conductor has a particular outcome in mind, while the discussion leader strives for acceptable and high quality solutions, not his particular one.

[12]L. R. Hoffman, "Conditions for Creative Problem Solving," *J. Psychol.,* 1961, 52, 429-444.

[13]A. R. Solem, "An Evaluation of Two Attitudinal Approaches to Delegation." *J. Appl. Psychol.,* 1958, 22, 36-39.

Quality and *acceptance* are essential dimensions in decision-making.[14] The quality dimension refers to the objective features of a decision—in other words, how does it square with the objective facts? The acceptance dimension refers to the degree to which the group that must execute the decision accepts it—in other words, how does the group feel about the decision? High quality and high acceptance are both needed for effective decisions. This means that group discussion must effectively deal with both facts and feelings.

A major problem is raised because the methods for dealing with facts are quite different from those for dealing with feelings. The skilled conference leader must recognize when he is dealing with facts and ideas and when he is confronted with feelings and biases. The difference is not always too apparent because feelings are often couched behind made-up reasons or rationalizations. Diagnostic skill therefore is one of his leadership requirements.

Once he is able to make diagnostic judgments his next step is to deal effectively with each. The skills for removing conference obstacles in the form of feelings and in the form of ideas are quite different, and each set of skills has its place.

The problem-solving principles discussed in this paper are primarily relevant to handling the intellectual aspects of discussion. In dealing with emotional aspects the leader performs a more permissive function and serves more in the role of a group counselor.

The skill requirements in conference leadership are not difficult to learn. The problem lies more with the interference caused by old habits. Once one can break away from these and get a fresh start, the battle is half won. The first step is to recognize the existence of qualitative distinctions. No one skill is best for all purposes. If the basic distinctions are made, progress in each area becomes relatively easy.

[14]N. R. F. Maier and J. J. Hayes, *Creative Management, op. cit.*

PLANNING ON THE LEFT SIDE
AND MANAGING ON THE RIGHT

Henry Mintzberg

In the folklore of the Middle East, the story is told about a man named Nasrudin, who was searching for something on the ground. A friend came by and asked: "What have you lost, Nasrudin?"

"My key," said Nasrudin.

So, the friend went down on his knees, too, and they both looked for it.

After a time, the friend asked: "Where exactly did you drop it?"

"In my house," answered Nasrudin.

"Then why are you looking here, Nasrudin?"

"There is more light here than inside my own house."

This "light" little story is old and worn, yet it has some timeless, mysterious appeal, one which has much to do with the article that follows. But let me leave the story momentarily while I pose some questions—also simple yet mysterious—that have always puzzled me.

First: Why are some people so smart and so dull at the same time, so capable of mastering certain mental activities and so incapable of mastering others? Why is it that some of the most creative thinkers cannot comprehend a balance sheet, and that some accountants have no sense of product design? Why do some brilliant management scientists have no ability to handle organizational politics, while some of the most politically adept individuals cannot seem to understand the simplest elements of management science?

Second: Why do people sometimes express such surprise when they read or learn the obvious, something they already must have known? Why is a manager so delighted, for example, when he reads a new article on decision making, every part of which must be patently obvious to him even though he has never before seen it in print?

Third: Why is there such a discrepancy in organizations, at least at the policy level, between the science and planning of management on the one hand, and managing on the other? Why have none of the techniques of planning and analysis really had much effect on how top managers function?

What I plan to do in this article is weave together some tentative answers to these three questions with the story of Nasrudin around a central theme, namely, that of the specialization of the hemispheres of the human brain and what that specialization means for management.

The Two Hemispheres of the Human Brain

Let us first try to answer the three questions by looking at what is known about the hemispheres of the brain.

Question One

Scientists—in particular, neurologists, neurosurgeons, and psychologists—have known for a long time that the brain has two distinct hemispheres. They have known, further, that the left hemisphere controls movements on the body's right side and that the right hemisphere controls movements on the left. What they have discovered more recently, however, is that these two hemispheres are specialized in more fundamental ways.

In the left hemisphere of most people's brains (left-handers largely excepted) the logical thinking processes are found. It seems that the mode of operation of the brain's left hemisphere is linear; it processes information sequentially, one bit after another, in an ordered way. Perhaps the most obvious linear faculty is language. In sharp contrast, the right hemisphere is specialized for simultaneous processing; that is, it operates in a more holistic, relational way. Perhaps its most obvious faculty is comprehension of visual images.

Although relatively few specific mental activities have yet been associated with one hemisphere or the other, research is proceeding very quickly. For example, a recent article in *The New York Times* cites research which suggests that emotion may be a right-hemispheric function.[1] This notion is based on the finding that victims of right-hemispheric strokes are often comparatively untroubled about their incapacity, while those with strokes of the left hemisphere often suffer profound mental anguish.

What does this specialization of the brain mean for the way people function? Speech, being linear, is a left-hemispheric activity, but other forms of human communication, such as gesturing, are relational rather than sequential and tend to be associated with the right hemisphere. Imagine what would happen if the two sides of a human brain were detached so that, for example, in reacting to a stimulus, a person's words would be separate from his gestures. In other words, the person would have two separate brains—one specialized for verbal communication, and the other for gestures—that would react to the same stimulus.

This "imagining," in fact, describes how the main breakthrough in the recent research on the human brain took place. In trying to treat certain cases of epilepsy, neurosurgeons found that by severing the corpus callosum, which joins the two hemispheres of the brain, they could "split the brain," isolating the epilepsy. A number of experiments run on these "split-brain" patients produced some fascinating results.

In one experiment doctors showed a woman epileptic's right hemisphere a

[1] Richard Restak, "The Hemispheres of the Brain Have Minds of Their Own." *New York Times,* 25 January 1976.

photograph of a nude woman. (This is done by showing it to the left half of each eye.) The patient said she saw nothing, but almost simultaneously blushed and seemed confused and uncomfortable. Her "conscious" left hemisphere, including her verbal apparatus, was aware only that something had happened to her body, but not of what had caused the emotional turmoil. Only her "unconscious" right hemisphere knew. Here neurosurgeons observed a clear split between the two independent consciousnesses that are normally in communication and collaboration.[2]

Now, scientists have further found that some common human tasks activate one side of the brain while leaving the other largely at rest. For example, a person's learning a mathematical proof might evoke activity in the left hemisphere of his brain, while his conceiving a piece of sculpture or assessing a political opponent might evoke activity in his right.

So now we seem to have the answer to the first question. An individual can be smart and dull at the same time simply because one side of his or her brain is more developed than the other. Some people—probably most lawyers, accountants, and planners—have better developed left-hemispheric thinking processes, while others—artists, sculptors, and perhaps politicians—have better developed right-hemispheric processes. Thus an artist may be incapable of expressing his feelings in words, while a lawyer may have no facility for painting. Or a politician may not be able to learn mathematics, while a management scientist may constantly be manipulated in political situations.

Eye movement is apparently a convenient indicator of hemispheric development. When asked to count the letters in a complex word such as *Mississippi* in their heads, most people will gaze off to the side opposite their most developed hemisphere. (Be careful of lefties, however.) But if the question is a specialized one—for example, if it is emotionally laden, spatial, or purely mathematical—the number of people gazing one way or another will change substantially.

Question Two

A number of word opposites have been proposed to distinguish the two hemispheric modes of "consciousness," for example: explicit versus implicit; verbal versus intuitive; and analytic versus gestalt.

I should interject at this point that these words, as well as much of the evidence for these conclusions, can be found in the remarkable book entitled *The Psychology of Consciousness* by Robert Ornstein, a research psychologist in California. Ornstein uses the story of Nasrudin to further the points he is making. Specifically, he refers to the linear left hemisphere as synonymous with lightness, with thought processes that we know in an explicit sense. We can *articulate* them. He associates the right hemisphere with darkness, with thought processes that are mysterious to us, at least "us" in the Western world.

Ornstein also points out how the "esoteric psychologies" of the East (Zen, Yoga, Sufism, and so on) have focused on right-hemispheric consciousness (for example, altering pulse rate through meditation). In sharp contrast, Western psychology has been concerned almost exclusively with left-hemispheric consciousness, with logical thought. Ornstein suggests that we

[2]Robert Ornstein, *The Psychology of Consciousness* (San Francisco: W. H. Freeman, 1975), p. 60.

might find an important key to human consciousness in the right hemisphere, in what to us in the West is the darkness. To quote him:

> Since these experiences [transcendence of time, control of the nervous system, paranormal communication, and so on] are, by their very mode of operation, not readily accessible to causal explanation or even to linguistic exploration, many have been tempted to ignore them or even to deny their existence. These traditional psychologies have been relegated to the "esoteric" or the "occult," the realm of the mysterious—the word most often employed is "mysticism." It is a taboo area of inquiry, which has been symbolized by the Dark, the Left side [the right hemisphere] of ourselves, the Night.[3]

Now, reflect on this for a moment. (Should I say meditate?) There is a set of thought processes—linear, sequential, analytical—that scientists as well as the rest of us know a lot about. And there is another set—simultaneous, relational, holistic—that we know little about. More importantly, here we do not "know" what we "know" or, more exactly, our left hemispheres cannot articulate explicitly what our right hemispheres know implicitly.

So here is, seemingly, the answer to the second question as well. The feeling of revelation about learning the obvious can be explained with the suggestion that the "obvious" knowledge was implicit, apparently restricted to the right hemisphere. The left hemisphere never "knew." Thus it seems to be a relevation to the left hemisphere when it learns explicitly what the right hemisphere knew all along implicitly.

Now only the third question—the discrepancy between planning and managing—remains.

Question Three

By now, it should be obvious where my discussion is leading (obvious, at least, to the reader's right hemisphere and, now that I write it, to the reader's left hemisphere as well). It may be that management researchers have been looking for the key to management in the lightness of logical analysis whereas perhaps it has always been lost in the darkness of intuition.

Specifically, I propose that there may be a fundamental difference between formal planning and informal managing, a difference akin to that between the two hemispheres of the human brain. The techniques of planning and management science are sequential and systematic; above all, articulated. Planners and management scientists are expected to proceed in their work through a series of logical, ordered steps, each one involving explicit analysis. (The argument that the successful application of these techniques requires considerable intuition does not really change my point. The occurrence of intuition simply means that the analyst is departing from his science, as it is articulated, and is behaving more like a manager.)

Formal planning, then, seems to use processes akin to those identified with the brain's left hemisphere. Furthermore, planners and management scientists seem to revel in a systematic, well-ordered world, and many show little appreciation for the more relational, holistic processes.

What about managing? More exactly, what about the processes used by top managers? (Let me emphasize here that I am focusing this discussion at the

[3]Ibid., p. 97.

policy level of organizations, where I believe the dichotomy between planning and managing is most sharp.) Managers plan in some ways, too, (that is, they think ahead) and they engage in their share of logical analysis. But I believe there is more than that to the effective managing of an organization. I hypothesize, therefore, that *the important policy processes of managing an organization rely to a considerable extent on the faculties identified with the brain's right hemisphere.* Effective managers seem to revel in ambiguity; in complex, mysterious systems with relatively little order.

If true, this hypothesis would answer the third question about the discrepancy between planning and managing. It would help to explain why each of the new analytic techniques of planning and analysis has, one after the other, had so little success at the policy level. PPBS, strategic planning, "management" (or "total") information systems, and models of the company—all have been greeted with great enthusiasm; then, in many instances, a few years later have been quietly ushered out the corporate back door. Apparently none served the needs of decision making at the policy level in organizations; at that level other processes may function better.

Managing from the Right Hemisphere

Because research has so far told us little about the right hemisphere, I cannot support with evidence my claim that a key to managing lies there. I can only present to the reader a "feel" for the situation, not a reading of concrete data. A number of findings from my own research on policy-level processes do, however, suggest that they possess characteristics of right-hemisphere thinking.[4]

One fact recurs repeatedly in all of this research: the key managerial processes are enormously complex and mysterious (to me as a researcher, as well as to the managers who carry them out), drawing on the vaguest of information and using the least articulated of mental processes. These processes seem to be more relational and holistic than ordered and sequential, and more intuitive than intellectual; they seem to be most characteristic of right-hemispheric activity.

Here are ten general findings:

1. The five chief executives I observed strongly favored the verbal media of communication, especially meetings, over the written forms, namely reading and writing. (The same result has been found in virtually every study of managers, no matter what their level in the organization or the function they supervised.) Of course verbal communication is linear, too, but it is more than that. Managers seem to favor it for two fundamental reasons that suggest a relational mode of operation.

[4]These findings are based on (a) my observational study of the work of five chief executives reported in *The Nature of Managerial Work* (New York: Harper and Row, 1973) and in "The Manager's Job: Folklore and Fact" (HBR July–August 1975, p. 49); (b) a study of twenty-five strategic decision processes reported in "The Structure of 'Unstructured' Decision Processes," coauthored with Duru Raisinghani and Andre Theoret, to appear in a forthcoming issue of *Administrative Science Quarterly;* and (c) a series of studies carried out under my supervision at McGill University on the formation of organizational strategies over periods of decades, reported in "Patterns in Strategy Formation," Working Paper I.A.E., Aix-en-Provence, France, submitted for publication.

First, verbal communication enables the manager to "read" facial expressions, tones of voice, and gestures. As I mentioned earlier, these stimuli seem to be processed in the right hemisphere of the brain. Second, and perhaps more important, verbal communication enables the manager to engage in the "real-time" exchange of information. Managers' concentration on the verbal media, therefore, suggests that they desire relational, simultaneous methods of acquiring information, rather than the ordered and sequential ones.

2. In addition to noting the media managers use, it is interesting to look at the content of managers' information, and at what they do with it. The evidence here is that a great deal of the manager's inputs are soft and speculative—impressions and feelings about other people, hearsay, gossip, and so on. Furthermore, the very analytical inputs—reports, documents, and hard data in general—seem to be of relatively little importance to many managers. (After a steady diet of soft information, one chief executive came across the first piece of hard data he had seen all week—an accounting report—and put it aside with the comment, "I never look at this.")

What can managers do with this soft, speculative information? They "synthesize" rather than "analyze" it, I should think. (How do you analyze the mood of a friend or the grimace someone makes in response to a suggestion?) A great deal of this information helps the manager understand implicitly his organization and its environment, to "see the big picture." This very expression, so common in management, implies a relational, holistic use of information. In effect, managers (like everyone else) use their information to build mental "models" of their world, which are implicit synthesized apprehensions of how their organizations and environments function. Then, whenever an action is contemplated, the manager can simulate the outcome using his implicit models.

There can be little doubt that this kind of activity goes on all the time in the world of management. A number of words managers commonly use suggest this kind of mental process. For example, the word "hunch" seems to refer to the thought that results from such an implicit simulation. "I don't know why, but I have a hunch that if we do *x,* then they will respond with *y.*" Managers also use the word *judgment* to refer to thought processes that work but are unknown to them. *Judgment* seems to be the word that the verbal intellect has given to the thought processes that it cannot articulate. Maybe "he has good judgment" simply means "he has good right-hemispheric models."

3. Another consequence of the verbal nature of the manager's information is of interest here. The manager tends to be the best informed member of his organization, but he has difficulty disseminating his information to his employees. Therefore, when a manager overloaded with work finds a new task that needs doing, he faces a dilemma: he must either delegate the task without the background information or simply do the task himself, neither of which is satisfactory.

When I first encountered this dilemma of delegation, I described it in terms of time and of the nature of the manager's information; because so much of a manager's information is verbal (and stored in his head), the dissemation of it consumes much of his time. But now the split-brain research suggests that a second, perhaps more significant, reason for the dilemma of delegation exists. The manager may simply be incapable of disseminating some relevant information because it is removed from his verbal consciousness. (This suggests that we might need a kind of managerial psychoanalyst to coax it out of him!)

4. Earlier in this article I wrote that managers revel in ambiguity, in complex, mysterious systems without much order. Let us look at evidence of this. What I have discussed so far about the manager's use of information suggests that their work is geared to action, not reflection. We see further evidence for this in the pace of their work ("Breaks are rare. It's one damn thing after another"); the brevity of their activities (half of the chief executives' activities I observed were completed in less than 9 minutes); the variety of their activities (the chief executives had no evident patterns in their workdays); the fact that they actively exhibit a preference for interruption in their work (stopping meetings, leaving their doors open); and the lack of routine in their work (only 7% of 368 verbal contacts I observed were regularly scheduled, only 1% dealt with a general issue that was in any way related to general planning).

Clearly, the manager does not operate in a systematic, orderly, and intellectual way, puffing his pipe up in a mountain retreat, as he analyzes his problems. Rather, he deals with issues in the context of daily activities—the cigarette in his mouth, one hand on the telephone, and the other shaking hands with a departing guest. The manager is involved, plugged in; his mode of operating is relational, simultaneous, experiential, that is, encompassing all the characteristics of the right hemisphere.

5. If the most important managerial roles of the ten described in the research were to be isolated, *leader, liaison,* and *disturbance handler* would certainly be among them. (The other seven are *figurehead, monitor, disseminator, spokesman, negotiator, entrepreneur,* and *resource allocator,* and the last two are also among the most important roles.) Yet these three are the roles least "known" about. *Leader* describes how the manager deals with his own employees. It is ironic that despite an immense amount of research, managers and researchers still know virtually nothing about the essence of leadership, about why some people follow and others lead. Leadership remains a mysterious chemistry; catchall words such as *charisma* proclaim our ignorance.

In the *liaison* role, the manager builds up a network of outside contacts, which serve as his or her personal information system. Again, the activities of this role remain almost completely outside the realm of articulated knowledge. And as a *disturbance handler* the manager handles problems and crises in his organization. Here again, despite an extensive literature on analytical decision making, virtually nothing is written about decision making under pressure. These activities remain outside the realm of management science, inside the realm of intuition and experience.

6. Let us turn now to strategic decision-making processes. There are 7 "routines" that seem to describe the steps involved in such decision making. These are *recognition, diagnosis, search, design, screening, evaluation/choice,* and *authorization.* Two of these routines stand out above the rest—the *diagnosis* of decision situations and the design of custom-made solutions—in that almost nothing is known of them. Yet these two stand out for another reason as well: they are probably the most important of the seven. In particular, diagnosis seems to be *the* crucial step in strategic decision making, for it is in that routine that the whole course of decision making is set.

It is a surprising fact, therefore, that diagnosis goes virtually without mention in the literature of planning or management science. (Almost all of the later literature deals with the formal evaluation of given alternatives, yet this is often a kind of trimming on the process, insignificant in terms of determining actual outcomes.) In the study of the decision processes themselves, the managers making the decisions mentioned taking an explicit diagnostic step in only 14 of the 25 decision processes. But all the managers must have made some diagnosis; it is difficult to imagine a decision-making process with no diagnosis at all, no assessment of the situation. The question is, therefore, *where* did diagnosis take place?

7. Another point that emerges from studying strategic decision-making processes is the existence and profound influence of what can be called the *dynamic factors*. Strategic decision-making processes are stopped by interruptions, delayed and speeded up by timing factors, and forced repeatedly to branch and cycle. These processes are, therefore, dynamic ones of importance. Yet it is the dynamic factors that the ordered, sequential techniques of analysis are least able to handle. Thus, despite their importance, the dynamic factors go virtually without mention in the literature of management science.

Let's look at timing, for example. It is evident that timing is crucial in virtually everything the manager does. No manager takes action without considering the effect of moving more or less quickly, of seizing the initiative, or of delaying to avoid complications. Yet in one review of the literature of management, the authors found fewer than 10 books in 183 that refer directly to the subject of timing.[5] Essentially, managers are left on their own to deal with the dynamic factors, which involve simultaneous, relational modes of thinking.

8. When managers do have to make serious choices from among options, how do they in fact make them? Three fundamental modes of selection can be distinguished—analysis, judgment, and bargaining. The first involves the systematic evaluation of options in terms of their consequences on stated organizational goals; the second is a process in the mind of a single decision maker; and the third involves negotiations between different decision makers.

One of the most surprising facts about how managers made the 25 strategic decisions studied is that so few reported using explicit analysis; only in 18 out of 83 choices made did managers mention using it. There was considerable bargaining, but in general the selection mode most commonly used was judgment. Typically, the options and all kinds of data associated with them were pumped into the mind of a manager, and somehow a choice later came out. *How* was never explained. *How* is never explained in any of the literature either. Yehezkel Dror, a leading figure in the study of public policy making, is one of the few thinkers to face the issue squarely. He writes:

> Experienced policy makers, who usually explain their own decisions largely in terms of subconscious processes such as "intuition" and "judgment," unanimously agree, and even emphasize, that extrarational processes play a positive and essential role in policymaking. Observations of policymaking behavior in both small and large systems, indeed, all available description

[5]Clyde T. Hardwick, and Bernard R. Landuyt, *Administrative Strategy and Decision Making,* 2nd ed. (Cincinnati: South-Western, 1966).

of decisional behavior, especially that of leaders such as Bismarck, Churchill, DeGaulle, and Kennedy, seem to confirm that policy makers' opinion.[6]

9. Finally, in the area of strategy formulation, I can offer only a "feel" for the results since my research is still in progress. However, some ideas have emerged. Strategy formulation does not turn out to be the regular, continuous, systematic process depicted in so much of the planning literature. It is most often an irregular, discontinuous process, proceeding in fits and starts. There are periods of stability in strategy development, but also there are periods of flux, of groping, of piecemeal change, and of global change. To my mind, a "strategy" represents the mediating force between a dynamic environment and a stable operating system. Strategy is the organization's "conception" of how to deal with its environment for a while.

Now, the environment does not change in any set pattern. For example, the environment does not run on planners' five-year schedules; it may be stable for thirteen years, and then suddenly blow all to hell in the fourteenth. And even if change were steady, the human brain does not generally perceive it that way. People tend to underreact to mild stimuli and overreact to strong ones. It stands to reason, therefore, that strategies that mediate between environments and organizational operations do not change in regular patterns, but rather, as I observed earlier, in fits and starts.

How does strategic planning account for fits and starts? The fact is that it does not (as planners were made so painfully aware of during the energy crisis). So again, the burden to cope falls on the manager, specifically on his mental processes—intuitional and experiential—that can deal with the irregular inputs from the environment.

10. Let me probe more deeply into the concept of strategy. Consider the organization that has no strategy, no way to deal consistently with its environment; it simply reacts to each new pressure as it comes along. This is typical behavior for an organization in a very difficult situation, where the old strategy has broken down beyond repair, but where no new strategy has yet emerged. Now, if the organization wishes to formulate a new strategy, how does it do so (assuming that the environment has stabilized sufficiently to allow a new strategy to be formulated)?

Let me suggest two ways (based on still tentative results). If the organization goes the route of systematic planning, I suggest that it will probably come up with what can be called a "main-line" strategy. In effect, it will do what is generally expected of organizations in its situation; where possible, for example, it will copy the established strategies of other organizations. If it is in the automobile business, for instance, it might use the basic General Motors strategy, as Chrysler and Ford have so repeatedly done.

Alternatively, if the organization wishes to have a creative, integrated strategy which can be called a "gestalt strategy," such as Volkswagen's one in the 1950s, then I suggest the organization will rely largely on one individual to conceptualize its strategy, to synthesize a "vision" of how the organization will respond to its environment. In other words, scratch an interesting strategy, and you will probably find a single strategy formulator beneath it.

[6]Yehezkel Dror, *Public Policymaking Re-Examined* (Scranton: Chandler, 1968), p. 149.

Creative, integrated strategies seem to be the products of single areas, perhaps of single right hemispheres.

A strategy can be made explicit, can be announced as what the organization intends to do in the future, only when the vision is fully worked out, if it ever is. Often, of course, it is never felt to be fully worked out hence the strategy is never made explicit and remains the private vision of the chief executive. (Of course, in some situations the formulator need not be the manager. There is no reason why a manager cannot have a creative right-hand man—really a left-hand man—who works out his gestalt strategy for him, and then articulates it to him.) No management process is more demanding of holistic, relational, gestalt thinking than the formulation of a creative, integrated strategy to deal with a complex, intertwined environment.

How can sequential analysis (under the label *strategic planning*) possibly lead to a gestalt strategy?

Another "famous old story" has relevance here. It is the one about the blind men trying to identify an elephant by touch. One grabs the trunk and says the elephant is long and soft; another holds the leg and says it is massive and cylindrical; a third touches the skin and says it is rough and scaly. What the story points out is that—

> Each person standing at one part of the elephant can make his own limited, analytic assessment of the situation, but we do not obtain an elephant by adding "scaly," "long and soft," "massive and cylindrical" together in any conceivable proportion. Without the development of an overall perspective, we remain lost in our individual investigations. Such a perspective is a province of another mode of knowledge, and cannot be achieved in the same way that individual parts are explored. It does not arise out of a linear sum of independent observations.[7]

What can we conclude from these ten findings? I must first reemphasize that everything I write about the two hemispheres of the brain falls into the realm of speculation. Researchers have yet to formally relate any management process to the functioning of the human brain. Nevertheless, the ten points do seem to support the hypothesis stated earlier: *the important policy-level processes required to manage an organization rely to a considerable extent on the faculties identified with the brain's right hemisphere.*

This conclusion does not imply that the left hemisphere is unimportant for policy makers. I have overstated my case here to emphasize the importance of the right. The faculties identified with the left hemisphere are obviously important as well for effective management. Every manager engages in considerable explicit calculation when he or she acts, and all intuitive thinking must be translated into the linear order of the left if it is to be articulated and eventually put to use. The great powers that appear to be associated with the right hemisphere are obviously useless without the faculties of the left. The artist can create without verbalizing; the manager cannot.

Truly outstanding managers are no doubt the ones who can couple effective right-hemispheric processes (hunch, judgment, synthesis, and so on) with effective processes of the left (articulateness, logic, analysis, and so on). But there will be little headway in the field of management if managers and re-

[7]Ornstein, p. 10.

searchers continue to search for the key to managing in the lightness of ordered analysis. Too much will stay unexplained in the darkness of intuition.

Before I go on to discuss the implications for management science and planning, I want to stress again that throughout this article I have been focusing on processes that managers employ at the policy level of the organization. It seems that the faculties identified with the right-hemispheric activities are most important in the higher levels of an organization, at least in those with "top-down" policy-making systems.

In a sense, the coupling of the holistic and the sequential reflects how bureaucratic organizations themselves work. The policy maker conceives the strategy in holistic terms, and the rest of the hierarchy—the functional departments, branches, and shops—implement it in sequence. Whereas the right-hemispheric faculties may be more important at the top of an organization, the left-hemispheric ones may dominate lower down.

Implications for the Left Hemisphere

Let us return to practical reality for a final word. What does all I've discussed mean for those associated with management?

For Planners and Management Scientists

No, I do not suggest that planners and management scientists pack up their bags of techniques and leave the field of management, or that they take up basket-weaving or meditation in their spare time. (I haven't—at least not yet!) It seems to me that the left hemisphere is alive and well; the analytic community is firmly established, and indispensable, at the operating and middle levels of most organizations. Its real problems occur at the policy level. Here analysis must co-exist with—perhaps even take its lead from—intuition, a fact that many analysts and planners have been slow to accept. To my mind, organizational effectiveness does not lie in that narrow-minded concept called "rationality"; it lies in a blend of clear-headed logic *and* powerful intuition. Let me illustrate this with two points.

1. *First, only under special circumstances should planners try to plan.* When an organization is in a stable environment and has no use for a very creative strategy—the telephone industry may be the best example—then the development of formal, systematic strategic plans (and main-line strategies) may be in order. But when the environment is unstable or the organization needs a creative strategy, then strategic planning may not be the best approach to strategy formulation, and planners have no business pushing the organization to use it.

2. *Second, effective decision making at the policy level requires good analytical input; it is the job of the planner and management scientist to ensure that top management gets it.* Managers are very effective at securing soft information; but they tend to underemphasize analytical input that is often important as well. The planners and management scientists can serve their organizations effectively by carrying out ad hoc analyses and feeding the results to top management (need I say verbally?), ensuring that the very best of analysis is brought to bear on policy making. But at the same time, planners need to

recognize that these inputs cannot be the only ones used in policy making, that soft information is crucial as well.

For the Teacher of Managers

If the suggestions in this article turn out to be valid, then educators had better revise drastically some of their notions about management education, because the revolution in that sphere over the last fifteen years—while it has brought so much of use—has virtually consecrated the modern management school to the worship of the left hemisphere.

Should educators be surprised that so many of their graduates end up in staff positions, with no intention of ever managing anything? Some of the best-known management schools have become virtual closed systems in which professors with little interest in the reality of organizational life teach inexperienced students the theories of mathematics, economics, and psychology as ends in themselves. In these management schools, management is accorded little place.

I am not preaching a return to the management school of the 1950s. That age of fuzzy thinking has passed, thankfully. Rather, I am calling for a new balance in our schools, the balance that the best of human brains can achieve, between the analytic and the intuitive. In particular, greater use should be made of the powerful new skill-development techniques which are experiential and creative in nature, such as role playing, the use of video-tape, behavior laboratories, and so on. Educators need to put students into situations, whether in the field or in the simulated experience of the laboratory, where they can practice managerial skills, not only interpersonal but also informational and decisional. Then specialists would follow up with feedback on the students' behavior and performance.

For Managers

The first conclusion for managers should be a call for caution. The findings of the cognitive psychologists should not be taken as license to shroud activities in darkness. The mystification of conscious behavior is a favorite ploy of those seeking to protect a power base (or to hide their intentions of creating one), this behavior helps no organization, and neither does forcing to the realm of intuition activities that can be handled effectively by analysis.

A major thrust of development in our organizations, ever since Frederick Taylor began experimenting in factories late in the last century, has been to shift activities out of the realm of intuition, toward conscious analysis. That trend will continue. But managers, and those who work with them, need to be careful to distinguish that which is best handled analytically from that which must remain in the realm of intuition, where, in the meantime, we should be looking for the lost keys to management.

⌐ managing
work teams

FACTORS INFLUENCING THE EFFECTIVENESS
OF HEALTH TEAMS

IRWIN RUBIN
RICHARD BECKHARD

Introduction

In the first part of the article, several key variables known to be of importance in any group situation are discussed. These variables are drawn from behavioral science knowledge and their dynamics. The particular relevance of these general variables to a specific situation is discussed next. The situation chosen is an interdisciplinary health team[1] working to deliver comprehensive family-centered care[2] to the residents of a low-income urban area. The success or failure of such a highly interdependent diverse group is, in large measure, a function of how well they work together—their group process.[3] Finally, in the last section, we discuss one alternative response to the question: What can you do about it? A model is described for intervening directly into the life of a team to help them improve the way they work together. An actual case study of the application of this model is then discussed.

Abridged and reprinted from I. M. Rubin and R. Beckhard, "Factors Influencing the Effectiveness of Health Teams." *Milbank Quarterly,* July, 1972, pp. 317–335.

[1]The "average" team in this center consisted of a full-time internist, a full-time pediatrician, two full-time nurses, and four to six full-time family health workers drawn from the community. Available on a part-time basis were a dentist, a psychiatrist, in addition to the back-up support of X-rays, labs, and the like. A team was responsible for 1,500 families in a particular geographical area.

[2]We pay little attention to this paper to the very important question of the organization of which the health team is a part. For an intensive discussion of the organizational issues involved in the delivery of health care see R. Beckhard, "The Organizational Issues in Team Delivery of Health Care," *Milbank Quarterly,* 1971.

[3]For an excellent and readable description of group process, see E. H. Schein, *Process Consultation.* Reading, Mass.: Addison-Wesley Publishing Co., 1969.

While many readers will not themselves be members of an interdisciplinary health team, the concepts discussed and issues raised should nonetheless be easily generalizable. By combining both theory and practice, this article will enable the reader to more easily see the "real world" relevance of group process.

The Dynamics of Groups

In this section, we will present and briefly define seven selected characteristics or variables known to be of importance in any group situation. Each characteristic can be viewed as a scale or yardstick against which one can ask the question: Is this particular group (made up of certain kinds of people, trying to do a given task in this situation) located where it needs to be on each of these scales to function most effectively?

Goals or Mission

A team or group has a *purpose*. There exists a reason (or reasons) for the formation of the group in the first place. In any group, therefore, there will be issues like:

1. How clearly defined are the goals? Who sets the goals?
2. How much agreement is there among members concerning the goals? How much commitment?
3. How clearly measurable is goal achievement?
4. How do group goals relate to broader organizational goals? To personal goals?

Since a group's very existence is to achieve some goal or mission, these issues are of central importance.

Role Expectations—Internal

In working to achieve their goals, group members will play a variety of *roles*. There exists among the members of a group a set of multiple expectations concerning role behavior. Each person, in effect, has a set of expectations of how each of the other members[4] *should* behave as the group works to achieve its goals. In any group, therefore, there exist questions about:

1. the extent to which such expectations are clearly defined and communicated (role ambiguity);
2. the extent to which such expectations are compatible or in conflict (role conflict); and
3. the extent to which any individual is capable of meeting these multiple expectations (role overload).

These role expectations are messages "sent" between the members of a

[4]For an excellent study of this concept of role sets see R. N. Kahn, *et al., Organizational Stress: Studies in Role Conflict and Ambiguity* (New York: Wiley, 1964).

group. Generally, the more uncertain and complex the task, the more salient are issues of role expectations.

Role Expectations — External

Any individual is a member of several groups. Each group of which he is a member has expectations which can influence his behavior. The Director of Pediatrics in a hospital, for example, is "simultaneously" the manager of his group, a subordinate, a member in a group of peers (directors of the functional areas), a member of a hospital staff, a father, husband, etc.

Each of these "reference" groups, as they are called, holds expectations of a person's behavior. Together they can be ambiguous, in conflict, or create overload. These multiple *reference group* loyalties can create significant problems for an individual in terms of his behavior as a *member* of a particular group. While the source of the conflicts involved in the question of reference group loyalties is external to a particular group, they can have significant *internal* effects.

Decision-Making

A group is a problem-solving, decision-making mechanism. This is not to imply that an entire group must always make all decisions as a group. The issue is one of relevance and appropriateness; *who* has the relevant information and *who* will have to implement the decision. A group can choose from a range of decision-making mechanisms including decision by default (lack of group response), unilateral decision (authority rule), majority vote, consensus, or unanimity.

Each form is appropriate under certain conditions. Each will have different consequences both in terms of the amount of information available for use in making the decision, and the subsequent commitment of members to implement the decision.

Similarly, when a group faces a conflict it can choose to (a) ignore it, (b) smooth over it, (c) allow one person to force a decision, (d) create a compromise, or (e) confront all the realities of the conflict (facts and feelings), and attempt to develop an innovative solution. The choices it makes in both of these areas will significantly influence group functioning.

Communication Patterns

If, indeed, a group is a problem-solving, decision-making mechanism, then the effective flow of information is central to its functioning. Anything which acts to inhibit the flow of information will detract from the group effectiveness.

There are a range of factors which affect information flow. At a very simple level there are architectural and geographical issues. Meeting space can be designed to facilitate or hinder the flow of communication. Geographically separated facilities may be a barrier to rapid information exchange. There are also numerous more subtle factors. Participation—frequency, order, and content—may follow formal lines of authority or status. High-status members may speak first, most, and most convincingly on all issues. The best sources of information needed to solve a problem will, however, vary with the problem.

Patterns of communication based exclusively on formal lines of status will not meet many of the group's information needs. People's feelings of freedom to participate, to challenge, to express opinions also significantly affect information flow.

Leadership

Very much related to the processes of decision-making and communication is the area of leadership. To function effectively, a group needs many *acts of leadership*—not necessarily one "leader" but many leaders. People often misinterpret such a statement as saying "good groups are leaderless." This is not the intent. Depending on the situation and the problem to be solved, different people *can* and *should* assume leadership. The formal leader of a group may be in the best position to reflect the "organization's" position on a particular problem. Someone else may be a resource in helping the formal leader and another member clarify a point of disagreement. All are examples of *necessary acts of leadership.* It is highly unlikely that in any group there will be one person capable of meeting all of a group's leadership needs.

Norms

Norms are unwritten (often untested explicitly) rules governing the behavior of people in groups. They define what behavior is "good or bad," "acceptable or unacceptable" if one is to be a functioning member of this group. As such, they become very powerful *determinants* of group behavior and take on the quality of laws—"It's the way we do things around here!" Their existence is most clear when they are violated—quiet uneasiness, shifting in one's seat, joking reminders, are observable. Repeated violation of norms often leads to expulsion—psychological or physical.

Norms take on particular potency because they influence all of the other areas previously discussed. Groups develop norms governing leadership, influence, communication patterns, decision-making, conflict resolution, and the like. Inherently, norms are not good or bad. The issue is one of appropriateness—does a particular norm help or hinder a group's ability to work.

These seven factors, then, are characteristics of any group situation. Where a particular group needs to be on each of these "yardsticks" is a function of the situation. We turn now to look at these factors within the setting of health teams.

The Dynamics of a Health Team

Our intention in this section is to look at these factors affecting group functioning and to relate them to a group⁵ setting (community-based, total health

---

'By group practice we mean situations wherein people are together over long periods of time working on a common task. More temporary groups like the group formed to do a particular operation in a hospital are not included in our discussion. Even in many temporary groups, such as short duration task forces or committees, many of the process factors discussed can be observed to be in operation.

care). The center in which we have worked[6] is the particular situation from which we will draw examples and observations. However, the issues raised are, in our view, very broadly relevant.

Goals or Mission

A health team striving to provide "comprehensive family-centered health care" faces uncertainties substantially different from those one might find in a hospital setting. The goals[7] in a hospital are relatively clear: remove the gall stone, deliver the baby. Success is measurable and clear. Seldom are social factors of prime importance. The thrust is curative and the emphasis is medical.

The community-oriented health teams we have studied experience considerable uncertainty over their mission. "Comprehensive" means the team cannot ignore *social* problems and emphasize the "relative security and certainty" of medical problems. There is considerable anxiety generated because the team does not really know when and if it is succeeding. The questions of *priorities* and time allocations become complicated; how does one decide between competing activities in the absence of clearly defined goals? A team member wonders if she should spend half a day trying to arrange for a school transfer for a child or should she see the other patients scheduled for visits.

No one member of the team has been trained to be knowledgeable in all the areas required. Yet, the complexity of the task demands that doctors become involved in social problems; nurses become the supervisors of paraprofessional family health workers who are an integral part of the team; and these community-based family health workers become knowledgeable in diagnosing and treating psychiatric problems. This is not to say everyone should become an expert at solving all problems. The requirements are for considerable information collection, sharing, and group planning so that the *team* has all the available information to deploy its total resources to the task.

The anxieties and frustrations created by the complexity of the task are *inevitable*—an inherent part of providing "comprehensive" care.[8] A major team dilemma is one of managing short- versus long-run considerations—to give itself short-run security and direction while not losing sight of its long-run global goal.

[6]For a more detailed preliminary report of our activities in this setting see: Fry, R. E. and Lech, B. A., "An Organizational Development Approach to Improving the Effectiveness of Neighborhood Health Care Teams: A Pilot Program." Unpublished Master's thesis, Sloan School of Management. Massachusetts Institute of Technology, June, 1971. (Copies available from Dr. Martin Luther King, Jr. Health Center, 3674 Third Avenue, Bronx, New York 10456.)

[7]If one takes a *total* hospital as a group, many similar issues appear. Revens, for example, argues that the central task in a hospital is the management of anxiety. This is very analogous to the position we take *vis-a-vis* a health team. The only difference is that the problems are more visible in the smaller social system of an ongoing group. See R. W. Revens, *Standards for Morale: Cause and Effect in Hospitals.* (London: OXford University Press, 1964).

[8]A very useful tool for diagnosing the forces impinging upon a team is called life space or force field analysis. For more detail, see Fry and Lech, *op. cit.,* and an article by Kurt Lewin, in W. Bennis, K. Benne. and R. Chin, *The Planning of Change,* 2nd ed. (New York: Holt, Rinehart, and Winston, 1969).

The nature of the task—comprehensive family-centered health care—demands a highly diverse set of skills, knowledge, backgrounds. In creating a team, many "cultures" are of *necessity* being mixed and asked to work together.

As a result of educational background and training, the doctors are accustomed to being primary (if not sole) authority and most expert in medical issues. The specialist role for which they have been so well trained and which is so appropriate in a hospital setting comes under pressure in a health team. As a team member, in addition to his specialist skills, the doctor is asked to become more of a generalist. He needs to teach other health workers some of his medical knowledge. He also needs to *learn* from them more about the social problems facing the community and the character, mores, and values of the particular patient population.

Doctors tend to maintain strong psychological ties with their professional specialty groups. The stronger these ties for a physician, the more difficult it will be for him to develop needed team loyalty. His sense of professionalism stems from these external reference groups. The careful hospital-type workup he has been so well trained to do may not be feasible or appropriate in the face of the hectic schedule generated by large numbers of patients. The conflict may become one around "professional standards." Comprehensive group practice may require a redefinition of these standards and perhaps even the redefinition of a professional.

Both the nurses and family health workers tend to bring a history of submissiveness. The nurses have been trained to be submissive to doctors. In this setting, nurses find themselves as *coordinators* of the work of a team *including doctors*—a complete role reversal.

Family health workers in this case are local community residents who, after six months of clinical training, suddenly find themselves defined as "colleagues" with middle-class physicians. They bring a deep concern for social problems coupled with the best understanding of what will or will not work with patients (their friends and relatives!). The team needs their knowledge of the cultural norms of the community and their commitment to social issues. Their background and passive posture is often a barrier to the realization of these expectations.

Whereas the nurses and doctors have a professional reference group, the family health workers as yet have none. The resulting feelings of "homelessness" are heightened by their liaison role at the interface between the team and the community.[9] Their membership and acceptance in the community is crucial to the team's ability to be of service. They alone can serve to bridge the cultural gaps which exist.[10]

This set of conditions differs markedly from the hospital setting where strong reference group loyalties and clearly defined role expectations are common. Behaviors learned during one's individual preparation are appropriately applicable in the vast majority of situations. Although professionals and

[9]Such people have been called marginal men. A foreman in a factory is another example since he is caught between the management culture and the worker culture.

[10]The very notion of a team approach to the delivery of health care may, for example, force a redefinition of the norm of privacy between doctor and patient. The norm may need to be adapted to encompass team and patient.

paraprofessionals work in the same organization, seldom, if ever, are they asked to work in highly interdependent on going stable groups.

A part of being a member of a highly interdependent team is the need to develop new loyalties and learn how to do some new things—not anticipated or covered during individual training. In fact, it is very unlikely that, in the face of the mission of providing "comprehensive family-centered health care," clearly defined, complete job descriptions will ever be feasible.[11] This reality puts great stress on a team's ability to learn and adapt by itself. In response to a particular problem, the question cannot be "Whose job is it?" but may instead have to be "Who on the team is capable?" or "Who needs to learn how to handle this situation?"

Decision-Making

The inherent uncertainties in its mission and the diverse mix of skills represented on a health team suggest that decisions can seldom be appropriately made in a routine, programmable, or unilateral manner. This is in sharp contrast to the majority of cases in the hospital setting where there is the relative clarity and certainty of the goals and clearly defined roles and lines of authority.

One difficulty in any on going team is the need to differentiate a variety of decision-making situations. In an attempt to be "democratic and participative" a team might try to make all decisions by consensus as a team. This represents a failure to distinguish, for example, (a) who has the information necessary to make a decision, (b) who needs to be *consulted before* certain decisions get made, and (c) who needs to be informed of a decision, after it has been made. Under certain circumstances, the team may need to strive for unanimity or consensus; in other cases, majority vote may be appropriate.

Perhaps the greatest barrier to effective decision-making in highly interdependent health teams stems again from the "cultural" backgrounds of team members. Doctors are used to making decisions by themselves or in collaboration with peers of equal status—other doctors or highly educated professionals. At the other extreme, the community residents who work on the team are used to being passive dependent recipients of others' decisions. Yet many times, on a health team, the doctor and the community workers *are and must behave as peers*—neither one possessing all the information needed to solve a particular problem or make a particular decision. Furthermore, there are many times when the doctor is the one who needs information held by another health worker. When a conflict develops, the required discussion which will lead to consensus is difficult to achieve; forcing, compromise, or decision by default may result. Commitment to decisions is low with the result being that many decisions have to be remade several times—"I thought we decided that last week!" or "Didn't we decide that you would do such and such?"

The team approach to delivery of health care puts great stress on the need for numerous and various inputs to many decisions. When the decision-

---

[11]Many organizations are realizing the needs for such fluid role relationships. A job is now viewed as "a man in action in a particular situation at a particular moment." Such "job descriptions" must be constantly renegotiated and updated to account for *both* changes in the man and the situation.

making process is inappropriate, less information is shared, commitment is lowered, and anxiety and frustration are increased.

Communication Patterns/Leadership

Issues of communication patterns and leadership can be handled together for, as was true in the case of decision making as well, the central theme is one of "influence." The leadership or influence structure—to which we have all become so accustomed via our family, educational, and organizational experiences and which is appropriate for a hospital operating room, for example—will be incapable of responding to the diversity of issues with which a health team must deal. In this setting, *each member* is a resource. He must have open channels to all the other members. Because of the complexities in this type of group, a number of communication norms are required: openness (leveling) and a *person-to-person* relationship which has enough mutual trust to enable each person to "tell it like it is."

Team practice cannot work if *roles* talk to *roles*—a much more personal mutual dependency is required. Influence, communication frequency, and leadership should be determined by the nature of the problem to be solved not by hierarchical position, by seating position, educational background, or social status.

With respect to leadership in particular, the teams we have studied relied on the model they knew best—in this case, *"follow the doctor."* Continued reliance on that model will result in an overemphasis on medical versus social issues, a lack of shared commitment to decisions (which doctors sometimes interpret as "lack of professional attitude"), and less than complete sharing of information, all of which affect the task performance directly.

Norms

Much of what we have described is reflected in a group's *norms*. The teams we have studied have exhibited several powerful norms:

1. "In making a decision, silence means consent."
2. "Doctors are more important than other team members"; "We don't disagree with them"; "We wait for them to lead."
3. Conflict is dangerous, *both* task conflicts and interpersonal disagreements—"It's best to leave sleeping dogs lie."
4. Positive feelings, praise, support are not to be shared—"We're all 'professionals' here to do a job."
5. The precision and exactness demanded by our task negate the opportunity to be *flexible* with respect to our own internal group processes. (This may be a carryover from the hospital operating room environment where the last thing you need is an innovative idea as to how to do things better!)

The effects of these norms, and others like them, is to guarantee that a team gets caught in a negative spiral.[12] While the norms are those of rigidity, the complexity of the environment and the task to be done demand flexibility. The

[12]It is in this regard that our thinking is very similar to Revens'. The ineffective management of inherent anxiety results in more anxiety creating a negative feedback loop and a self-reinforcing downward spiral. See Fry and Lech, *op. cit.*

frustrating, anxiety-provoking quality of the task places great demands for some place to recharge one's emotional battery. The team is potentially such a place.

In addition to these specific norms of flexibility, support, and openness of communication, there is a set of higher order norms which are essential. Task uncertainty and environmental changes require that a team develop a capacity to become self-renewing—to become a *learning* organism. Learning requires a climate which legitimizes controlled experimentation, risk taking, failure, and evaluation of outcomes. In the absence of norms which support and reinforce these kinds of behaviors, a team will end up fighting two enemies—*its task and itself.*

There exists, in other words, a unique connection between what a team does (its *task*) and how it goes about doing it (its *internal group processes*). At a very simple level, the health care analogy would be: If a team is to treat a family as an integrated unit (its task), the team itself must, in many ways, operate as a highly integrated "family unit" (its internal group processes). Without this ability to maintain itself a health team will, like many other "pieces of equipment," eventually burn itself out. In the interim, work continues to get done but more and more energy is demanded to "move the machine forward."

To summarize, the "internal process" issues we have discussed will occur in any group. They cannot be wished away or ignored for long without some cost. Nor are they the result—as is frequently assumed—of basic personality problems. More often team members have difficulty functioning together because of ambiguous goal orientations, unclear role expectations, dysfunctional decision-making procedures, and other such process issues.

If a health team is first to survive and second to grow, it must, as we have said, develop an attitude and a capability for building and renewing itself as a team. It can do this first by becoming aware of how its internal group processes influence its ability to function and second by learning how to manage these process or maintenance needs in a more productive manner.

We turn now to a brief case illustration of an effort aimed at helping health teams move closer to this ideal of becoming self-renewing or learning organisms.

A Case Study of a Health Team Improvement Effort[13]

Our efforts at helping teams improve their functioning relied heavily upon a very simple but powerful model—the action research approach.[14] The basic flow of activities can be depicted in the following manner:

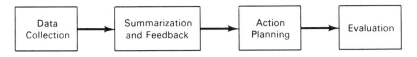

[13]Our initial efforts at intervention into two health teams are reported in detail in Fry and Lech, *op. cit.* We have to date completed initial interventions with six health teams. Similar activities are planned for other teams in the future as well as follow-up activities to reinforce our initial efforts. Four of our students—Ron Fry, Bern Lech, Marc Gerstein, and Mark Plovnick—have worked closely with us in these efforts.

[14]For an excellent description of this model and its applicability in a wide variety of situations see R. Beckhard, *Organization Development: Strategies and Models.* Reading, Mass.: Addison-Wesley Publishing Co., 1969.

In this setting, the initial activity with a health team involved interviewing each member individually—using both openended questions and checklist ratings. Questions asked related directly to the seven process factors discussed earlier such as team goals, level of participation, decision-making styles, etc. These data were then summarized and fed back *anonymously* to the entire team.

Team members' reactions to the data presented during this feedback session were varied. For some, the result was one of surprise—"I didn't realize people felt that way about this team!" Others were surprised to find many of their own concerns widely shared. Before the feedback session, many people believed they were the only ones experiencing certain difficulties. The most frequent reaction could be characterized as follows: "These problems have been around—*under the surface*—for a long time. Now they have been collected, summarized, and are out on the table for all of us to see."

The teams, in other words, were provided with an *image* or *picture* of their present state based on information (feelings as well as facts) collected from the most valid sources available—the team members themselves. As a result of the interview feedback process, teams *owned* the information (verbatim quotes were used to exemplify a particular issue) and *shared* the image of their present state—"It's out on the table for all of us to see." These two elements of *shared ownership* helped to create a heightened desire and commitment on the part of team members to solve their problems.

In order to cope with the large number of complex problems reflected in the information and to move most effectively into action planning, the health teams had to:

1. prioritize the multiple issues reflected in their data;
2. decide upon the most appropriate format to use (total group, homogeneous versus heterogeneous subgroups, etc.) to generate solution alternatives;
3. develop a clear and shared set of *change objectives* or goals—an image of what a more ideal or improved state would be;
4. allocate individual and subgroup responsibilities to implement chosen actions; and
5. specify mechanisms and procedures for checking progress (follow-up).

The problem-solving skills, attitudes, norms, etc., needed to accomplish the above "process work" were *very similar* to behaviors needed to successfully accomplish "task work." This unique connection between task and process can be clarified with the following example.

A salient problem in each health team concerned their regularly scheduled 1½ hour weekly team conference meetings. These meetings represented the one time each week when the entire team met together. The intent was to discuss patient family cases, learn from each other's experiences, work on common problems and the like. The pervasive feeling with regard to these meetings was one of frustration and dissatisfaction. They were dull, a waste of time, and a time for some people to "lecture" about their pet topics.

The way the team managed itself (its process) during these meetings in fact made the situation more difficult. The negative spiral to which we referred earlier was operating to drain energy and commitment required to solve patient problems.

The specific action plans developed and subsequent team improvement interventions were, in each case, a product of the particular issues reflected in the data collected initially from a team. Regardless of the problem, the same action research model, with minor variations was applied. For example, action plans aimed at improving the team conference meeting included:

1. the formation of agenda planning committees:
2. systems of rotating chairmen to help all team members enhance their skills at running a meeting;
3. designation of observers, on a rotating basis, to help the team evaluate —*at the end of each meeting*—the impact of its own group dynamics.[15]

While many consultant interventions were aimed at helping a team to solve problems it *presently* felt, longer run considerations also guided consultant behavior. Whenever feasible, a team was helped to see the connection between *what* they were doing (their task) and *how* they were going about it (their internal group process). This expanded awareness helped to develop an attitude (norm) toward change which legitimized *managed experimentation and learning*. In other words, if a team is to become self-renewing, it must be willing to experiment in a *controlled way*—to try new ways of working, evaluate and learn from the consequences of these efforts, and use this new learning in the planning and implementation of future efforts. On the assumption that the action research approach we used represented a generalizable problem-solving model, we continuously worked to help the teams to internalize this model so that they could apply it when confronted with future problems.

DYNAMICS OF GROUPS THAT EXECUTE OR MANAGE POLICY

RONALD FRY
IRWIN RUBIN
MARK PLOVNICK

Introduction

Dilemmas faced by the middle manager are well known. For example, Aram (1976) has observed that this person must motivate, but also alter, individual needs of others in order to achieve collective actions; must exercise authority with humaneness; must apply rules and policies with equity, yet allow for special needs and considerations of individuals in order for them to develop; and as a leader must both adhere to and change group norms in order to maintain effectiveness over time. Occupants of such roles are caught betwixt and between. The executive washroom lies some distance above: a con-

From R. Payne and C. Cooper, eds. *Groups at Work*. John Wiley & Sons, Inc., New York, 1981.

stant source of aspiration and motivation. The keys are few, however, so the competition will be stiff. Some distance below lies the old gang: a group perhaps recently left. The middle manager is no longer one of the troops and is not yet one of the generals. S/he lives in a state of limbo . . . a kind of no-man's land. Zander (1979) has argued further that the better the occupants of these positions practice "good management techniques" the more vulnerable they become to coercive derisive tactics of others. In the face of such hostility or unfair treatment, they must remain cool, calm, and dignified. The better the manager, the more s/he tends to be "on stage" all the time.

Our intent in this chapter is to examine a class of groups in organizations whose life space and dynamics parallel, in many ways, those of the manager caught in the middle. These are groups that execute or manage policy. For the sake of convenience we will refer to these groups as *middle groups.*

Since no group—top, middle, or bottom—exists totally in isolation, we will begin by looking at the organization as a whole. . . as a series of interlocking groups. This will provide a picture of the unique environment in which middle groups function. In so doing, we shall focus heavily on a concept which we label the *mirror image.* This is a phenomenon whereby a middle group experiences the effects of a problem reflected upon it by a group above it in the organizational hierarchy, usually an executive level, policy *setting* group. After a focus on the ways in which the functioning of a middle group is influenced by its environment (primarily top groups), we will then look within the middle group itself. The focus will be upon factors that influence a middle group's ability to execute or manage policy. Key examples will be illustrated in actual case vignettes. The final section will deal with a description of the individual and group level skills needed to cope with the particular problems faced by middle groups.

A Framework for Analysis

Beckhard's (1972) general model of task-group functioning provides the basis for our analysis of middle group functioning. Basically, this model says that task groups meet in order to manage issues related to their goals, roles (allocation of work), procedures (ways work gets done), and relationships. To this notion we would add two key propositions. The first is that a task group also meets to manage issues resulting from its surrounding *system* or environment. As we shall see for middle groups in particular, it is impossible to conceive of a group existing in a vacuum. Thus, in addition to goal, role, procedure, and interpersonal issues these groups experience and manage internally, they will also experience, and thus need to manage, issues resulting from organizational structure, reward and promotion systems, training policies, interfaces with other groups at their own and other organizational level, and sometimes interfaces with the environment outside the organization. Rubin and Beckhard's (1972) field studies of interdisciplinary health care teams supports the resulting model of factors influencing work-group functioning shown (Figure 1).

The vertical arrows speak to the second addition to Beckhard's basic model. In essence, these five factors are thought to be casually linked in the sense that interpersonal conflicts are more often than not *symptoms* of real conflicts in

FIGURE 1

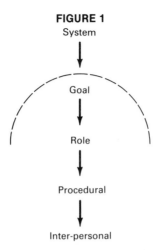

system, goal, role, or procedural areas (Plovnick et al., 1975). Similarly, disagreement over how to make a decision, a procedural issue, is often the result of unclear or conflicted expectations over who does what, i.e., a role issue. Even goal conflicts are sometimes symptoms of conflicting mandates given the group by others in the overall organization, i.e., a systems issue. For the sake of convenience we shall refer to this hierarchical model as the SGRPI model (S for system, G for goal, etc.). Using this model, let us move to the particular kinds of dilemmas faced by middle groups: those groups that lie somewhere beneath the chief executive and corporate planners, and who must execute and manage policies set by the executives for the majority of the employees in the total system.

System Issues Faced by Middle Groups

The major "systems" issue, or environmental factor, that influences a middle group is the top group (or groups) from which it receives the policies it must manage or execute. Many lower level groups have tasks which are highly constrained or, at least defined, by the technology they use (e.g., an assembly group or programming group). Furthermore, they can make their own decisions about roles (who operates what), procedures (scheduled maintenance, speed of operation), and interpersonal issues. On the other hand, a middle group derives its primary work from others above it and often does not have *any* impact on this task (i.e., policy to implement). Indeed, whether or not the middle group can or will influence its basic mandate is a crucial goal issue to be addressed, as we will discuss in the next section. Beyond setting the basic task for the middle group, the top group also greatly influences the role, procedural, and interpersonal factors a middle group experiences in its daily life. The structure of the organization and/or executive fiat often dictates *who* is on the middle group and thus can create desirable role complementarity or undesirable role confusion or conflict. Structurally, a middle group often is not alone, particularly in larger systems. There are several middle groups executing or managing various policies set down by upper groups. Hence, any one middle group may find itself competing with another in order to succeed in its policies,* often at the expense of another middle group's policies. This is often seen in situations where a marketing group, trying their best to execute given policies, runs into resistance from a production or research and development group who are also trying to operate in their own best interests. Procedurally, the top group often influences the middle group's ways of doing things via the middle group's leader or manager who is typically a member of that top group: what Likert (1961) has labeled the "linking pin." As such s/he is accustomed to "a way of doing things" which may be best for determining policy, but may also be less desirable for managing policy. Thus, in middle groups, styles of decision making, ways of running meetings, how conflicts are dealt with, etc., can often *mirror* the way things are done in the top group(s) from which the middle group's leader comes. Similarly, interpersonal conflicts in middle groups are typically handled as they are in top groups because members at the middle level are attuned to the norms, or what it takes to get ahead, of the "executive suite." This is not as true for lower groups who exist in areas more distant from the executive suites and have norms and standards that reflect more their function or physical technological environment.

In essence, what is being suggested is that the main systems issue that middle groups face is the danger(s) inherent in *mirroring* the key environmental force acting on them, namely the top group. Using the SGRPI model, this is akin to saying that one group's management (or lack of it) of goals, role, procedural, and interpersonal issues creates a set of influences that become a systems force for groups below them. This systems force can have a facilitative or dysfunctional impact on the lower group's GRP or I issues as it goes about its work.

For the middle group, this mirroring dynamic creates a sort of Catch 22: they are trying to do a completely different task (manage or execute policy) from the top group (who set the policy), but feel pressure to function in a manner akin to the top group with respect to problem definition, role allocations, decision-making procedures, conflict management, etc. They are also trying to do this in a collaborative environment while coping with the competitive pressures created by so many in the middle striving for so few positions at the top. For the middle group to manage its goals, roles, procedures, and relationships in fundamentally different ways from how things are done above it may get the job done better, but may also cause its members to look like deviants and become less desirable for promotion.

Mintzberg (1979) illustrates this Catch 22 well in his analysis of divisional structures. In the headquarter's attempts to monitor divisional behavior on a personal basis, the group executive visits the middle group (Division Management) often to "keep in touch" or to "avoid any surprises." Tensions can often develop around doing things "his way," thus tending to more centralization or doing things differently in ways better suited to the specific tasks at hand. If the executive "wins," the middle group emulates the top and may not get its task (executing and managing) accomplished most effectively. If the middle group "wins," headquarters distances themselves and evaluates only on output, and usually only the economic measure of it. So even if a good job is done, the personal relationship and understanding between middle and top

---

*One need only look at the way budgets get handled in most organizations. A middle group which underruns its budget may well get chastized for poor planning and take a cut in next year's budget. Neither of these responses can be construed as a reward for good performance.

group members that may be the key to any promotion for members of the middle group is lost.

Given this mirroring tendency, or dilemma, of middle groups, we now turn to a more specific analysis of issues these groups will face in trying to manage their own work.

Internal Characteristics of Middle Groups

Middle groups experience a series of dynamics that are unique from other groups in the organization. In terms of the SGRPI model, the goals, roles, procedures, and interpersonal factors can be used to understand some of these peculiarities facing middle groups.

Goals

Goal issues are perhaps the most difficult problems faced by middle groups. Furthermore, because of the subsequent impact of goal ambiguity and conflict on role, procedural, and interpersonal issues, goal problems are also the most critical for these groups to resolve. In the middle group the primary source of difficulty in determining goals stems from the group's hierarchical location—being in the middle.

Middle groups tend to experience great difficulty in establishing an identity or philosophy. Top-level groups, by comparison, are generally recognized as needing to deal with the highly ambiguous task of setting overall organizational mission, policy, and strategy (e.g., to increase sales and profits). Their rewards are predicated upon overall organization success. They recognize that theirs is an ambiguous task and the power and control they enjoy in being at the top takes some of the anxiety out of the fuzziness of their goals.

Lower level groups likewise experience relatively low goal ambiguity. Their task is generally clearly and operationally defined. The parameters of effective performance are also usually fairly explicit (e.g., increase widget production by 15 percent).* The first-line supervisor does experience some problems in having to relate both to management and labor simultaneously, but these issues are generally felt in the role, procedural, and interpersonal areas rather than goal areas.

The middle group, however, is often fundamentally unclear as to whether their goals are, or should be, fuzzy and abstract, or concrete and operational. Partly this results from unclear or inconsistent expectations communicated by top management. Even with clear mandates, however, most middle groups are still faced with the challenge, ultimately, of interpreting higher level expectations and molding them into an acceptable statement of their group's core mission, goals, and priorities for others to use.

The very description of these groups—"groups that execute or manage policy"—suggests inherent goal conflicts. To *execute* policy is to carry out well-defined operational objectives—yourself. To *manage* policy is to infer objectives and to see to it that others own them, and carry them out. Essentially a

---

*This is often true, even in the face of unclear policy from the middle group, because of the constraints or demands of the technology. That is, certain objectives related to output, rate, or quality are tied to the type of process, degree of automation, type of task interdependency, etc., all dictated by the particular kind of technology in use.

middle group must decide if it is more of a doer group or more of a support group. At one extreme, a middle group's primary mission might revolve around "helping employees to understand/internalize/prioritize organizational policies." † At another extreme, the mission might revolve around "announcing and insuring strict compliance to policies set from above." The role and procedural implications both within a middle group and between a middle group and lower groups are dramatically different depending on which of these two mission orientations most represents the reality.

As implied in our model, if a middle group is experiencing what appears to be a mission or goal-related conflict, one natural place to look for the cause would be the environment or system which surrounds it—the group(s) above it. What expectation has the policy-setting group sent (through its linking-pin representative—the formal boss) to the middle group? Is it clear, unambiguous, and free of internal incompatibilities and inconsistencies? If not, then the middle group is bound to experience difficulty in working through its own GRPI issues and its functioning will suffer accordingly. Since the cause lies in its environment, in this case the policy-setting group above, so too does the ultimate solution. And hence, another mission dilemma for a middle group: to influence or consult the policy *setters* above (an often risky venture for people in no-man's land), or to dutifully serve as interpreters and administrators of what is given to them (also risky vis-à-vis the subordinate workforce).

Suppose that the policy-setting group has clear, unambiguous, unconflicted expectations of the middle group enabling the middle group to define its mission clearly. This represents the essential start but it is not, in and of itself, sufficient. There remains the issue of the consistency or congruence between the middle group's goals and several related procedural issues under the control of the top group. Consider the effects of an incongruity between a mandated mission from the top and another system issue—the reward system in the organization. A mandated mission to a middle group such as "develop new products" may require very high levels of interdependence both within any one middle group and between various middle groups. Yet, in most organizations the typical formal reward system—which reflects a *policy* decision of a procedural type from the top group to the entire organization—strangles collaboration and nurtures competition. To behave collaboratively in most organizations, over any length of time, is thus highly irrational. This "rationality" of successful managers is reflected in Schein's (1978) study of MIT alumni. In categorizing his sample by type of career anchor (a pattern of self-perceived talents, motives, and values that serve to guide, constrain, stabilize, and integrate a person's career) only 18 percent were identified as having "managerial" career anchors. In this category, "interpersonal competence" to work with others to achieve organization goals was only one of three foci: the other two being analytical competence and emotional competence to address crises. The remaining 82 percent of the sample were seen to have even less collaboratively oriented career anchors labeled as technical/functional, autonomy, creativity (i.e., entrepreneurial), and security. The real pay-offs, typically, come from individual success and achievement. Thus, corporate procedures may further complicate middle group goal setting and achievement.

†Further to this, as one staff under a general manager put it, "We're here to protect the people in the plant from his (the GM's) personal style."

As the SGRPI model indicates, problems with goals often lead to problems with roles. The middle group's dilemma, regarding their mission, executor, or manager of policy, translates into ambiguity and conflict regarding functional responsibilities of middle group members. For example, a product manager must decide whether his/her role is personally to make and oversee the implementation of all decisions regarding the product, or to organize and coordinate those responsible for the product (i.e., marketing, manufacturing, engineering, research and development, etc.) into a team that can make and implement product-related decisions. In the latter case the product manager is a coordinator and many day-to-day decisions can be made without her or his personal presence. However, the product managers within an organization (a middle group) may be unclear as to how they are to function in this regard—doers or coordinators.

With increased supervisory responsibility and high personal aspirations to succeed in high status jobs added to the above demands for innovative problem solving and decision making, role conflict would seem inevitable. This is supported in Kahn et al.'s (1964) study of role stress where they found middle managers reporting the largest amount of role conflict (90 percent of sample above median score on conflict index). This was much higher than either the group above (54 percent of top management cases over median score) or the group below (60 percent of second-level supervisors over median score). It appears that such large role conflict scores reflect a goals/roles paradox for middle groups: by attending to their aspirations to do well in the eyes of top managers, the middle group may tend toward the "executor" role to fulfill the goal they perceive the top wants to achieve and in a way the top might do it. In so doing, however, they subject themselves to increased demands to change their supervisory, decision-making, etc., behavior from peers and subordinates who may prefer the more "managerial" or coordinative role.

Often the skills and experiences of middle group managers also limit their flexibility in these role areas. As "graduates" of lower level management they may rely heavily on the skills that made them successful in previous positions. Frequently these earlier jobs were highly technical (versus managerial) in nature and lead the middle group to behave more like implementors than managers. More often than not what is learned from past experience in lower level groups is the message: "if you want it done right, do it yourself!" This is particularly true in professional groups like physicians, engineers, or teachers. Engineering managers may prefer to work at the bench rather than at the meeting table. An M.D. in an administrative position, director of emergency services for example, may find it difficult to delegate decision making to the staff since all of a physician's professional training emphasizes that the doctor is the only qualified authority for most decisions.

Because the managers comprising middle groups come from a variety of backgrounds and orientations their perceptions of appropriate roles often conflict. Middle groups may, for example, find it difficult to manage areas of overlapping responsibility between group members, each accustomed to clear operational responsibilities, or whose prior work required them to be individual contributors and, when successful, individual recipients of praise or reward.

Procedures

Many of the procedural problems a middle group faces regarding decision making, communicating, conflict resolution, etc., are symptomatic of unresolved goal or role issues. Suppose, however, the goal and role issues were well in hand. Procedural decision—the how we should work together issues—are meant to flow from and be consistent with the nature of the task (goal) and role allocations.

The particular danger in a middle group is the pressure which can be left to mirror the procedure of the group above it—when the tasks of the two groups are different. In subtle but powerful ways the linking-pin boss brings in norms of behavior learned while s/he is a member of the top group. It is the dilemma of those in the middle.

The sense of limited opportunities which is more evident in middle managers than elsewhere adds to the competitive pressure to look good to the top. Lower level groups perceive a large number of middle level jobs available and see the quality of aspirants as "mixed." In the top management groups there is a sense of having "made it" and the competition for the one job available, Chief Executive Officer, is fairly "up-front" and manageable. Middle group managers may not feel as though they have made it yet and perceive limited promotional opportunities with much talented competition for those few opportunities.

Interpersonal Issues

Again, the existence of interpersonal issues, or personality conflicts, is often a consequence of unresolved system, goal, role, or procedural issues. In the summary of research on conflict in organizations, Katz and Kahn (1978) find that personality and other predisposing factors have been shown to have weak and irregular effects on organization conflict in comparison to the influence of situational/organizational factors related to the administration of rules and procedures.

The ambiguity and conflict in middle group goals and roles can lead to relatively high levels of stress and anxiety in these groups which can exacerbate any real or potential interpersonal conflicts. Yet middle groups can still have some very real interpersonal issues stemming from their position in the organization. The juxtaposition in middle groups of managers from differing backgrounds and with differing orientations creates potential stylistic incompatibilities. Finally, the struggle to the top of the organization can set the stage for some fierce clashes over conflicting personal goals and ambitions. While some of these same conditions can be found in other groups, middle groups seem to provide unusually fertile turf for interpersonal conflict.

The preceding discussion describes some of the types of problems middle groups experience internally in their goals, roles, procedures, and interpersonal relationships. It is usually the case that the conditions creating a problem in any one category tend to lend to difficulties in the other categories as well. The following two case studies illustrate this dynamic.

This case deals with the Construction Division (C.D.) of a large, high technology electronics company. The Construction Division was responsible for the building and maintenance of the organization's physical plant. There were six major facility sites within the company. The C.D. had a Site Manager at each of these locations who reported directly to the C.D. Manager. Three functional specialists from staff groups and staff assistant to the C.D. Manager rounded out the C.D. team as shown in Figure 2.

As part of a systematic team development effort, based on the SGRPI model (Rubin et al., 1978), the team very early on had to address the question of the C.D. team Core Mission. In preparation for this, each individual member (eleven in total) wrote out their own response to the question:

"As *I* see it, our Core Mission as a team is...."

During a team development session the team would share and discuss their individual perceptions. They would then work toward one synthesized statement which reflected an agreed upon view of the team's Core Mission. The output, in other words, would be an agreed upon response to the following:

"As *we* see it, our Core Mission as a team is...."

Exhibit 1 contains each individual's actual response to the pre-meeting homework assignment: "As *I* see it, our Core Mission as a team is...."

While at first glance this may look like a surprising conglomeration of unrelated perspectives, it is not at all atypical. Several very predictable patterns can be seen in these individual "answers" to the same question.

Diagnostic Confusion

One thing which becomes immediately clear is the tendency all groups have to mix and lump SGRP and I issues. The diagnostic question was intended to focus on Core Mission—"What business are we in, as a team?"—a goal-level question. What comes out are goal-type responses *and* role-type responses *and* procedural-type responses *and* interpersonal-type responses. This type of confusion is particularly prevalent in middle groups and speaks to the general difficulty they experience in setting goals.

Conflicting Internal Orientations

The C.D. team became involved in a team development effort in the first place in part because there seemed to be a host of persistent interpersonal conflicts—particularly between the C.D. Manager and the Site Managers, and the staff representatives. As mentioned previously, there are a variety of issues

FIGURE 2

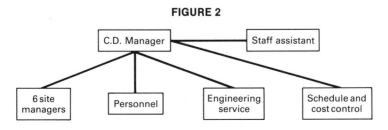

EXHIBIT 1
C.D. Team
Individual Core Mission Input

C.D. Manager
To construct all site and building facilities and chemical installation from information supplied by the engineering departments and/or customers.

This construction to be performed within quality, cost, and time schedules as specified and agreed upon. The actual physical work to be performed in the field by either our own shops or outside contracting firms.

Personnel Representative
To construct facilities in the most efficient manner possible, utilizing the talents of the organization.

Engineering Service Representative
Manage all space and facilities construction as defined by engineering services to insure least cost, highest quality, and minimum interruption of corporate functions.

Schedule and Cost Control Liaison
To efficiently provide a construction service to the Corporation by the management of and/or participation in all construction projects. Completely controlling costs, quality, manpower, and schedules.

Quality Control Representative
Provide with efficient means to obtain quality construction services at a reasonable cost.

Site Manager 1
A solid construction team is our desired goal.
1. Our mission, as I see it, is to bring various groups within our team closer together.
2. It is my goal to understand the Construction Engineering Management job better.
3. A better working relationship between trades groups and engineers will guarantee a better overall work output.
4. Stop feeling that my job is the only important one and let's move out of isolation within groups.
5. More job-related discussions between Line Managers and Construction Engineering Managers.

Site Manager 2
To work together to get our jobs done.

To share our knowledge and specialties even though we have different areas of work and we are often on our own.

Site Manager 3
To coordinate the administration of the Construction Department Personnel and of construction efforts both inside and outside at the various sites.

Site Manager 4
Management of the facilities type construction needs of the Corporation.

This includes both the urgent or secret, small confidential or nonpublic needs to be performed by the in-house group as well as the public and large type of construction to be performed by contracting with outside contracting firms.

We are the construction expertise of . . . (the Corporation).

Employ minority contractors wherever possible.

Site Manager 5
Complete responsibility for the management of all new construction work connected with the Company's space needs and/or chemical requirements. Additionally, the Department makes its resources available as requested by the Machinery Construction Department.

Site Manager 6
To have a better and closer working relationship with the members in this room, to get their task done effectively. To make sure that each one of us understands his role and what the impact could have if we do not work with each other—understanding the real world that we have to work with is the key to our improvement.

that increase the likelihood of interpersonal conflict in middle groups. Many of the interpersonal issues identified in this case were symptomatic of more fundamental goal, role, and procedural conflicts that can be inferred from these Core Mission inputs.

The C.D. Manager, a civil engineer from the "old school," saw the team's Core Mission being "to *construct all* site...." Several of the Site Managers with more formal management training (notably Site Managers 4 and 5) saw the team's Core Mission being "Complete responsibility for the *management* of all new...." These differences are not all unlike the difference between managing policy or executing policy discussed earlier. In the past, given this team's conflict avoidance tendency, this difference was passed off as one of semantics. It is anything but a semantic difference. Rather, it reflects a very basic boundary definition issue. The role and procedural implications of "to construct..." versus "to manage the construction..." are dramatically different. The inability to resolve this basic mission-related issue in the past resulted in the C.D. team having to continuously deal with problems that pop up in procedural areas (Should/should not staff people attend our meeting?), role areas (Who decides whether or not to have a subcontractor?), and in interpersonal areas (What is taking you guys so long to get started?). The ultimate decision, in this case to be responsible for the *management* of all construction, served to clarify and unblock a host of previously persistent energy drains.

Conflicting External Expectations

As discussed earlier, a middle group's functioning is influenced by its surrounding system or environment, particularly the goal, role, and procedural-type inputs it gets from the groups above it. We can see a small but nonetheless notable example of this in the case of the C.D. team.

The corporate mandate to the C.D. team included elements of quality and cost and, as Site Manager 4 pointed out, the employment of minority (primarily black) contractors. The C.D. team, in other words, had a piece of the larger organization's social responsibility mission. Hiring minority contractors could easily conflict with highest quality, lowest cost expectations.

The source of this conflict lies outside the C.D. team itself. A policy-setting group above it has sent what is potentially an incompatible set of expectations. The C.D. Manager, through his linking-pin function, must try to clarify this conflict within the top-level group of which he is a member. Then, as the formal leader of the C.D. team, he can input a clearer mandate from the group above. Ultimately, however, the C.D. team must interpret its mandate in its own way, and integrate top management's expectations into the C.D. core mission.

Line/Staff Conflicts

Because the C.D. consisted of managers with diverse backgrounds (engineering, finance, personnel) there was considerable confusion regarding the contributions various team members could and should make. The site managers went so far as to question the relevance of the staff representatives at team meetings. The staff people in turn complained about underutilization, being left out of important decisions and communications, etc. What was necessary was to examine the potential contribution of each team member, and negotiate a level of involvement. Ultimately the team did this as part of their team-building program. In general the site managers were pleasantly surprised by the contributions the staff people were capable of making.

The C.D. case demonstrates some of the SGR issues middle groups experience and must manage, particularly in the areas of identity and goal setting. The following case describes important problems in the areas of roles and procedures.

The B.P. Case

This case centers around the management team of a body parts (B.P.) division of an automobile manufacturer. In this particular case, this middle group has a clear and agreed to goal of *managing* policies set down by corporate executives and interpreted by the general manager of the B.P. Division (and leader of this group). These policies concern the number, type, and quality of body parts to be designed, engineered, manufactured, and shipped to the automotive assembly division of the corporation. During a formal, "task-oriented" team development program (Rubin et al., 1978), this group determined their mission to be one of "managing" policy, and in discussing role and procedural issues they faced, they essentially developed a communication and problem-solving structure as shown (Figure 3).

With this team structure, divisional policies would be discussed collectively so that engineering, quality control, finance, personnel, and manufacturing heads could all engage with one another in an *interdependent* atmosphere to best *manage* the policies mandated to them. It was also mutually decided by this team that because their "core mission" was to manage policy, their efforts should be focused on selling, guiding, and helping subordinates to do work, not doing the work themselves (something they were each good at, or they would not have been in this group in the first place).

This philosophy and agreements about goal, role, and procedural issues helped this middle group to lead its division to one of their most profitable years and increased status and recognition in the large corporation. It was also felt by the group's members to have contributed to reduced turnover in the group and better interpersonal feelings, as our SGRPI model would predict.

This rather bright picture began to change as the sale of automobiles diminished due to rising energy costs, cyclical decrease in demand, and a general economic slowdown occurred. Gradually, this group's environment (the top group) began to operate in a "crisis mode." If inventories were not being turned as frequently, if production schedules slowed, if quality standards fell, if deliveries to assembly plants were late, executives (who set the policies) would call down to various members of this team to get an answer to

FIGURE 3

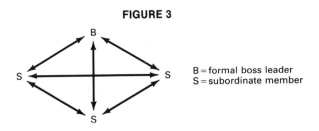

B = formal boss leader
S = subordinate member

220

the problem. Consequently, as the mirroring phenomenon discussed earlier would predict, each member would act on his/her own to either solve the problem (thereby doing the work versus managing it) or by calling someone else below to gather information without consulting any other members of the team. Thus, their internal dynamics changed as a result of system forces on them. Now they behaved as in Figure 4.

As a consequence, role expectations that had been clear before now became conflicted as any member might call someone into another's area to get an answer for someone higher up, thereby going into another member's "turf" without consent or consultation. Collaborative procedures gave way to one-on-one conferences or publicly reporting one's "findings" about some problem in the group before the problem had ever been discussed by the group. Lastly, and probably most importantly, the mutual trust and cohesiveness of this group began to break down as the causal effects of system/goals/roles/procedural issues finally resulted in increased anger and frustration with each other. Members began to resent others for finding answers for the top group first, for calling their people without their knowledge, and for not doing things that had been agreed to or scheduled previously because they were reacting to the unilateral and crisis-oriented requests of the top group.

Thus, several forementioned aspects of the SGRPI model came into play in the B.P. group. First, by working through their own GRPI issues (and not automatically mirroring their top group) they achieved a good, productive atmosphere with minimal symptomatic interpersonal issues. As the system around them changed, however, so did their ability to manage their GRPI issues. And as they mirrored an autocratic, crisis-oriented, do versus manage climate around them, their work as a group began to falter. Agreed to tasks were not done on time while members were busy reacting in a one-on-one fashion to top group requests.* Role ambiguity led to more private and competitive procedures which finally resulted in interpersonal mistrust and anger.

With both the C.D. and B.P. cases in mind, let us now turn finally to a discussion of what group and individual skills can help to anticipate and manage these dilemmas that can and do occur in middle groups.

FIGURE 4

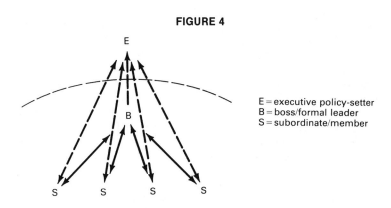

E = executive policy-setter
B = boss/formal leader
S = subordinate/member

*Both the formal (salary increases, etc.) and informal (norms about pleasing one's boss) reward system in most organizations guarantees and reinforces this dysfunctional pattern.

Implications and Summary

The hierarchical SGRPI model and the mirror dynamic discussed above have important implications for middle groups and their formal leaders. The power of the hierarchical SGRPI model lies first in its usefulness as a diagnostic tool to help group leaders and groups, themselves, to understand factors that may be getting in the way of doing their work effectively. The typically chaotic and ambiguous world of the middle group described in this chapter can thus be made more predictable, if not more manageable.

In addition to providing diagnostic clarity, the model provides a built-in intervention sequence: goal issues to be dealt with before role issues, the latter prior to procedural issues, and so on. The author's experiences with their task-oriented team development program (Rubin et al., 1978), developed from the SGRPI model, have shown this sequence of interventions to be particularly useful to middle groups and their managers where, as we have argued, the definition of task (e.g., manage versus execute) and allocation of role responsibilities are typically ambiguous. The tendency of most persons in these groups to attribute their inability to address this ambiguity to interpersonal conflicts has, in our experience, immobilized any potential energy to overcome the negative effects of such confusion and ambiguity. In Argyris and Schön's (1974) terms, their "espoused theories" are to do what is best to accomplish tasks, meet objectives, etc., but their "theories in use" are rather to scapegoat someone as being the block to team effectiveness, or to wait for the system to transfer, recruit, or otherwise readjust the team's personnel to achieve a better mix of personalities. By providing these managers and groups with a conceptual model and skills that help them focus on goal, role, and procedural issues *before* trying to deal with true interpersonal conflicts (which are seldom resolved—only managed), this task-oriented approach to team development has helped these managers to develop more congruent espoused and in-use theories.* They can get to a position where, if they espouse goal, task, and other organizational criteria to be the most important, they can behave in conjunction with these beliefs by applying the SGRPI model.

The sequential nature of the SGRPI model also helps the formal leader to see his/her choice points about what to work on, and when. In the role of linking-pin or boundary spanner, she/he has the opportunity and responsibility to work on the system(s)-level forces impacting on his/her group's functioning. To do this the formal leaders of middle groups will find that they must interface with others who sit below, alongside, and above them in the organizational hierarchy. The personal influence and negotiation skills required to operate effectively in the midst of such potentially conflicting crosscurrents must be learned and practiced. These influence skills are particularly critical when, as we have seen, a middle group may need to consciously resist the pressure to function like a top group. The manager of a middle group must first be able to diagnose the influence behavior demanded by the situation and second be able to behave flexibility to respond. †

---

*It should be noted that this task-oriented approach to team development differs in focus from other interpersonal and group-process oriented technologies currently in use. Comparisons of these basic approaches to team building, focusing on goal, role, procedural, or interpersonal issues are offered by Beer (1976). For a comprehensive view of alternative team building techniques focusing more on P and I issues, see Dyer (1977).

†For a further description of training efforts designed to develop these personal influence and negotiation skills, see Berlew and Harrison (1977).

The formal manager is also the key to avoiding dysfunctional mirroring of the top group. First, the dynamic of mirroring must be understood and its symptoms noticed or diagnosed. The task-oriented approach to team building helps in this regard for it forces an explicit focus on appropriate ways to organize the undertaking of a task and thereby minimizes inappropriate attention to issues of politics, style preferences of top managers, and the like.

Acting on the kinds of awareness noted above is easier said than done, however. To do any of what has been suggested as necessary to improve middle groups requires that the goup leader often go against some fairly deeply entrenched attitudes or assumptions. One such assumption we have continuously observed regarding groups is that "over time things will work themselves out." In our view, groups left to their own devices will not likely reach anywhere near their full potential. Some form of systematic, planned development intervention is essential. It is time to treat groups/teams as the complex pieces of human machinery they are and to train them to work well.

If the wishful thinking mode is to become passé, so too must the tendency to focus on persons versus situations. The typical strategy for a poorly functioning middle group is a transfusion of new blood—the "Red Cross" approach—or individual training—a "Statue of Liberty" approach—where in the "poor, weak, tired" individual members are sent to a training program of some sort. While individual training is important and mismatches do occur necessitating these "transfusions," the SGRPI model points to the critical importance of addressing specific situational or environmental issues—S, G, R, P—before assuming inter- or intrapersonal issues are causal to the problems at hand.

This environmental focus again puts great pressures on the formal leader of a middle group. Because managers of middle groups are almost to the top, they are often rather resistant to raise S, G, R type issues within the group of which they are a member. To do so in most organizations is to run the risk of being seen as disloyal and/or questioning the wisdom of one's superiors. Yet it is exactly the raising of these issues which is essential to the management of the interface between top and middle groups and the effective functioning of the middle groups themselves.

We are reminded, in closing, of a brief Sufi parable which captures the essence of what life must be like for middle groups and their managers. A snake says to a frog: "If you carry this message to my friend at the top of the mountain, you can eat all the flies which are buzzing around me." The frog reflected for a moment and responded very thoughtfully: "The job seems fine but I'm not sure I can handle the compensation."

References

Aram, J. (1976) *Dilemmas of Administrative Behavior.* Englewood Cliffs, N.J.: Prentice-Hall.

Argyris, C., and Schön, D. (1974) *Theory in Practice: Increasing Professional Effectiveness.* San Francisco: Jossey-Bass.

Beckhard, R. (1972) "Optimizing Team-building Efforts," *Journal of Contemporary Business,* **1**, 3, 23-32.

Beer, M. (1976) "The Technology of Organization Development", in M. Dunnette, ed., *Handbook of Industrial and Organizational Psychology.* Chicago: Rand McNally, pp. 955-61.

Berlew, D., and R. Harrison (1977) *Positive Power and Influence Workshop.* Boston: Situation Management Systems, Inc.

Dyer, W. G. (1977) *Team Building: Issues and Alternatives.* Reading, Mass.: Addison-Wesley.

Kahn, R. L., D. Wolfe, R. Quinn, and J. Snoek (1964) *Organization Stress: Studies in Role Conflict and Ambiguity.* New York: Wiley.

Katz, D., and R. L. Kahn (1978) *The Social Psychology of Organizations,* 2nd ed, New York: Wiley.

Likert, R. (1961) *New Patterns of Management.* New York: McGraw-Hill.

Mintzberg, H. (1979) *The Structuring of Organizations.* Englewood Cliffs, N.J.: Prentice-Hall.

Plovnick, M., R. Fry, and I. Rubin (1975) "New Developments in O.D. Technology," *Training and Development Journal, 29,* 4, 19–28.

Rubin, I., and R. Beckhard (1972) "Factors Influencing the Effectiveness of Health Care Teams," *Milbank Memorial Fund Quarterly,* **July,** 317–35.

Rubin, I., M. Plovnick, and R. Fry (1978) *Task Oriented Team Development.* New York: McGraw-Hill.

Schein, E. (1978) *Career Dynamics: Matching Individual and Organizational Needs.* Reading, Mass.: Addison-Wesley.

Zander, A. (1979) *Groups at Work.* San Francisco: Jossey-Bass.

8 managing conflict among groups

MANAGING CONFLICT AMONG GROUPS

L. DAVE BROWN

Conflict among groups is extremely common in organizations, although it often goes unrecognized. Managing conflict among groups is a crucial skill for those who would lead modern organizations. To illustrate:

> Maintenance workers brought in to repair a production facility criticize production workers for overworking the machinery and neglecting routine maintenance tasks. The production workers countercharge that the last maintenance work was improperly done and caused the present breakdown. The argument results in little cooperation between the two groups to repair the breakdown, and the resulting delays and misunderstandings ultimately inflate organization-wide production costs.

> A large manufacturing concern has unsuccessful negotiations with a small independent union, culminating in a bitter strike characterized by fights, bombings, and sabotage. The angry workers, aware that the independent union has too few resources to back a protracted battle with management, vote in a powerful international union for the next round of negotiations. Management prepares for an even worse strike, but comparatively peaceful and productive negotiations ensue.

> Top management of a large bank in a racially mixed urban area commits the organization to system-wide integration. Recruiters find several superbly qualified young black managers, after a long and highly competitive search, to join the bank's prestigious but all-white trust division and yet, subsequently, several leave the organization. Since virtually all the managers in the trust division are explicitly willing to integrate, top management is mystified by the total failure of the integration effort.

These cases are all examples of conflict or potential conflict among organizational groups that influence the performance and goal attainment of

---

Prepared specifically for this volume.

the organization as a whole. The cases differ in two important ways.

First, the extent to which the potential conflict among groups is *overt* varies across cases: conflict is all too obvious in the labor–management situation; it is subtle but still evident in the production–maintenance relations; it is never explicit in the attempt to integrate the bank's trust division. It is clear that *too much* conflict can be destructive, and much attention has been paid to strategies and tactics for reducing escalated conflict. Much less attention has been paid to situations in which organizational performance suffers because of *too little* conflict, or strategies and tactics for making potential conflicts more overt.

Second, the cases also differ in the *defining characteristics* of the parties: the production and maintenance groups are functionally defined; the distribution of power is critical to the labor and management conflict; the society's history of race relations is important to the black–white relations in the bank. Although there has been much examination of organizational conflict among groups defined by function, there has been comparatively little attention to organizational conflicts among groups defined by *power differences* (e.g., headquarters–branch relations, some labor–management relations) or by *societal history* (e.g., religious group relations, black–white relations, male–female relations).

It is increasingly clear that effective management of modern organizations calls for dealing with various forms of intergroup conflict: too little as well as too much conflict, and history-based and power-based as well as function-based conflicts. This paper offers a framework for understanding conflict among groups in the next section, and suggests strategies and tactics for diagnosing and managing different conflict situations.

Conflict and Intergroup Relations

Conflict: Too Much or Too Little?

Conflict is a form of interaction among parties that differ in interests, perceptions, and preferences. Overt conflict involves adversarial interaction that ranges from mild disagreements through various degrees of fighting. But it is also possible for parties with substantial differences to act as if those differences did not exist, and so keep potential conflict from becoming overt.

It is only too clear that it is possible to have *too much* conflict between or among groups. Too much conflict produces strong negative feelings, blindness to interdependencies, and uncontrolled escalation of aggressive action and counteraction. The obvious costs of uncontrolled conflict have sparked a good deal of interest in strategies for conflict reduction and resolution.

It is less obvious (but increasingly clear) that it is possible to have *too little* conflict. Complex and novel decisions, for example, may require pulling together perspectives and information from many different groups. If group representatives are unwilling to present and argue for their perspectives, the resulting decision may not take into account all the available information. The Bay of Pigs disaster during the Kennedy Administration may have been a consequence of too little conflict in the National Security Council, where critical information possessed by representatives of different agencies was suppressed to preserve harmonious relations among them (Janis, 1972).

In short, moderate levels of conflict—in which differences are recognized and extensively argued—are often associated with high levels of energy and involvement, high degrees of information exchange, and better decisions (Robbins, 1974). Managers should be concerned, in this view, with achieving levels of conflict that are *appropriate* to the task before them, rather than concerned about preventing or resolving immediately all intergroup disagreements.

Conflict among Groups

Conflict in organizations takes many forms. A disagreement between two individuals, for example, may be related to their personal differences, their job definitions, their group memberships, or all three. One of the most common ways that managers misunderstand organizational conflict, for example, is to attribute difficulties to "personality" factors, when it is, in fact, rooted in group memberships and organizational structure. Attributing conflict between production and maintenance workers to their personalities, for example, implies that the conflict can be reduced by replacing the individuals. But if the conflict is, in fact, related to the differing goals of the two groups, *any* individual will be under pressure to fight with members of the other group, regardless of their personal preferences. Replacing individuals in such situations without taking account of intergroup differences will *not* improve relations.

Groups are defined in organizations for a variety of reasons. Most organizations are differentiated horizontally, for example, into functional departments or product divisions for task purposes. Most organizations also are differentiated vertically into levels or into headquarters and plant groups. Many organizations also incorporate in some degree group definitions significant in the larger society, such as racial and religious distinctions.

A good deal of attention has been paid to the relations among groups of relatively equal power, such as functional departments in organizations. Much less is known about effective management of relations between groups of unequal power or those having different societal histories. But many of the most perplexing intergroup conflicts in organizations include all three elements—functional differences, power differences, and historical differences. Effective management of the differences between a white executive from marketing and a black hourly worker from production is difficult indeed, because so many issues are likely to contribute to the problem.

Intergroup relations, left to themselves, tend to have a regenerative, self-fulfilling quality that makes them extremely susceptible to rapid escalation. The dynamics of escalating conflict, for example, have impacts within and between the groups involved. *Within* a group (i.e., within the small circles in Figure 1), conflict with another group tends to increase cohesion and conformity to group norms (Sherif, 1966; Coser, 1956) and to encourage a world view that favors "us" over "them" (Janis, 1972; Deutsch, 1973). Simultaneously, *between*-groups (i.e., the relations between the circles in Figure 1) conflict promotes negative stereotyping and distrust (Sherif, 1966), increased emphasis on differences (Deutsch, 1973), decreased communications (Sherif, 1966), and increased distortion of communications that do take place (Blake and Mouton, 1961). The *combination* of negative stereotypes, distrust, internal militance, and aggressive action creates a vicious cycle: "defensive" aggression by one group validates suspicion and "defensive" counteraggression by the other, and the conflict escalates (Deutsch, 1973) unless it is counteracted

FIGURE 1
Varieties of Intergroup Conflict

A. Functional
   Differences:
   Maintanance and
   Production

   M = Maintenance
   P = Production
   ◄━► = Overt Conflict

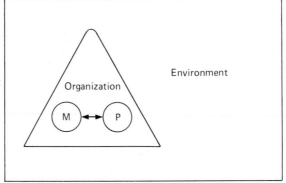

B. Power
   Differences:
   Management and
   Labor

   Mt = Management
   L = Labor
   ◄━► = Escalated
         Conflict

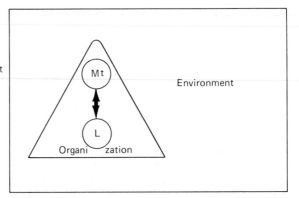

C. Societal
   Differences:
   Black and
   White Managers

   W = Whites
   B = Blacks
   ◄--► = Covert
          Conflict

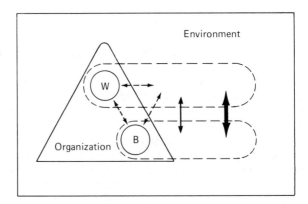

by external factors. A less well understood pattern, in which positive stereotypes, trust, and cooperative action generates a benevolent cycle of increasing cooperation may also exist (Deutsch, 1973).

To return to one of the initial examples, both the maintenance concern with keeping the machines clean and the production concern with maximizing output were organizationally desirable. But those concerns promoted a negative maintenance stereotype of production ("too lazy to clean the machines") and a production stereotype of maintenance ("want us to polish the machine, not use it") that encouraged them to fight. Part A of Figure 1 illustrated the overt but not escalated conflict between the parties.

Introducing power differences into intergroup relations further suppresses communications among the groups. The low-power group is vulnerable, and so must censor communication—such as dissatisfaction—that might elicit retaliation from the high-power group. In consequence, the high-power group remains ignorant of information considered sensitive by the low-power group. The long-term consequences of this mutually reinforcing fear and ignorance can be either escalating oppression—a peculiarly destructive form of too little conflict—or sporadic eruptions of intense and unexpected fighting (Brown, 1978).

The fight between the small independent union and the large corporation described at the outset illustrates the potential for outbursts of violent conflict when the parties are separated by large differences in power. The small union felt unable to influence the corporation at the bargaining table, and so used violence and guerilla tactics to express its frustration and to influence management without exposing the union to retaliation. Part B of Figure 1 illustrates the positions of the parties and the quality of their conflict.

Conflicts among groups that involve societal differences may be even more complicated. Differences rooted in societal history are likely to be expressed in a network of mutually reinforcing social mechanisms—political, economic, geographic, educational—that serve to *institutionalize* the differences. Societal differences do not necessarily imply power differences between the groups, but very frequently the effect of institutionalization is to enshrine the dominance of one party over another. Relations among such groups within organizations are strongly influenced by the larger society. Organizational tensions may be the result of environmental developments that the organization cannot control. In addition, differences associated with histories of discrimination or oppression may involve strong feelings and entrenched stereotypes that can lead to explosive conflict. Societal differences in organizations call for careful management that permits enough overt conflict so the differences are understood, but not so much that they are exacerbated.

The failure to integrate the trust division illustrates the problem of managing institutionalized racism. The black recruits had all the technical skills for success, but they could not join the all-white clubs or buy a house in the all-white suburbs where their colleagues lived, played, and learned the social ropes of the trust business. Nor could they challenge top-level decisions to keep them away from the oldest (and richest) clients ("who might be racist and so take their business elsewhere"). But the failure to face the potential conflicts—among members of the organization and between the organization and its clients—in essence made it impossible for the black managers to become full members. This situation is diagrammed in Part C of Figure 1.

Diagnosing the Conflict

Diagnosis is a crucially important and often-neglected phase of conflict management. Since conflict problems are often not recognized until after they have become acute, the need for immediate relief may be intense. But intervention in a poorly understood situation is not likely to produce instant successes. On the contrary, it may make the situation worse.

The manager of conflict should at the outset answer three questions about the situation:

1. At what level or levels is the conflict rooted (e.g., personal, interpersonal, intergroup, etc.)?
2. What role does s/he play in the relations among the parties?
3. What is a desirable state of relations among the parties?

A conflict may be the result of an individual, an interpersonal relationship, an intergroup relationship, or a combination of the three. If the manager understands the contributions of diffferent levels, s/he can respond appropriately. It is generally worthwhile to examine the conflict from *each* of these perspectives early in the diagnosis.

The position of the manager vis-a-vis the parties is also important. Managers who are themselves parties to the dispute are likely to be biased, and almost certainly will be perceived by their opponents as biased. Actual bias requires that the manager be suspicious of his/her own perceptions and strive to empathize with the other party; perceived bias may limit the manager's ability to intervene credibly with the other party until the perception is dealt with. Conflict managers who are organizationally superior to the parties may not be biased in favor of either, but they are likely to have poor access to information about the conflict. For such persons special effort to understand the parties' positions may be necessary. Third parties that are respected and seen as neutral by both sides are in perhaps the best position to intervene, but they are a rare luxury for most situations. In any case, awareness of one's position vis-a-vis the parties can help the manager avoid pitfalls.

Finally, a conflict manager needs to develop a sense of what is too much and what is too little conflict among the parties—when is intervention merited, and should it increase or decrease the level of conflict? Relations among groups may be diagnosed in terms of attitudes, behavior, and structure, and each of those categories have characteristic patterns associated with too much and too little conflict.

Attitudes include the orientations of groups and group members to their own and other groups—the extent to which they are aware of group interdependencies, the sophistication of group representatives about intergroup relations, and the quality of feelings and stereotypes within groups. Too much conflict is characterized by blindness to interdependencies, naiveté about the dynamics and costs of conflict, and strong negative feelings and stereotypes. Too little conflict, in contrast, is marked by blindness to conflicts of interests, naiveté about the dynamics and costs of collusion, and little awareness of group differences.

Behaviors include the ways in which groups and their members act—the levels of cohesion and conformity within groups, the action strategies of group representatives, the extent to which interaction between the groups is marked by escalating conflict or cooperation. Too much conflict often involves monolithically conforming groups, rigidly competitive action strategies, and escalating aggression among the groups. Too little conflict is associated with undefined or fragmented groups, unswervingly cooperative action strategies, and collusive harmony and agreement in place of examination of differences.

Structures are underlying factors that influence interaction in the long term—the larger systems in which parties are embedded, structural mechanisms that connect the parties, group boundaries and long-term interests, and regulatory contexts that influence interaction. Too much conflict is promoted by undefined or differentiated larger systems, lack of integrative mechanisms that link the groups, clearly defined and conflicting group interests and identities, and few rules or regulations to limit conflict. Too little conflict is encouraged by a shared larger system that suppresses conflict, no mechanisms to promote examination of differences, vague definitions of conflicting group interests and identities, and regulations that discourage overt conflict.

These diagnostic categories and the earmarks of too much and too little conflict are summarized in Table 1. Attitudinal, behavioral, and structural aspects

TABLE 1
Diagnosing Conflict among Groups

Area of Concern	General Issue	Symptoms of Too Much Conflict	Symptoms of Too Little Conflict
Attitudes	Awareness of similarities and differences	Blind to interdependence	Blind to conflicts of interest
	Sophistication about intergroup relations	Unaware of dynamics and costs of conflict	Unaware of dynamics and costs of collusion
	Feelings and perceptions of own and other group	Elaborated stereotypes favorable to own and unfavorable to other group	Lack of consciousness of own group and differences from other group
Behavior	Behavior within groups	High cohesion and conformity; high mobilization	Fragmentization; mobilization
	Conflict management style of groups	Overcompetitive style	Overcooperative style
	Behavior between groups	Aggressive, exploitative behavior; preemptive attack	Avoidance of conflict; appeasement
Structure	Nature of larger system	Separate or underdefined common larger system	Shared larger system that discourages conflict
	Regulatory context for interaction	Few rules to limit escalation	Many rules that stifle differences
	Relevant structural mechanisms	No inhibiting third parties available	No third parties to press differences
	Definition of groups and their goals	Impermeably bounded groups obsessed with own interests	Unbounded groups aware of own interests

of intergroup relations tend to interact with and support one another. The result is a tendency to escalate either the conflict or the collusion until some external force exerts a moderating effect. Thus, intergroup relations are volatile and capable of rapid escalatory cycles, but they also offer a variety of leverage points at which their self-fulfilling cycles may be interrupted by perceptive managers.

Intervention to promote constructive conflict may involve *reducing* conflict in relations with too much or *inducing* conflict in relations with too little. In both cases, intervention involves efforts to disrupt a cyclical process produced by the interaction of attitudes, behavior, and structure. Interventions may start with any aspect of the groups' interaction, although long-term change will probably involve effects in all of them. More work has been done on the problem of reducing conflict than on inducing it—but conflict-reduction strategies often have the seeds of conflict induction within them.

Changing *attitudes* involves influencing the ways in which the parties construe events. Thus *altering group perceptions of their differences or similarities* may influence their interaction. Sherif (1966), for example, reports reduction in intergroup conflicts as a consequence of introducing superordinate goals that both groups desired but whose achievement required cooperation; emphasizing interdependencies may reduce escalated conflict. On the other hand, inducing conflict may require deemphasizing interdependencies and emphasizing conflicts of interest. Attitudes may also be changed by *changing the parties' understanding of their relations.* Increased understanding of the dynamics of intergroup conflict and its costs, for example, may help participants reduce their unintentional contributions to escalation (e.g., Burton, 1969). By the same token, increased understanding may help parties control the development of collusion (Janis, 1972). *Feelings and stereotypes may also be changed* by appropriate interventions. Sharing discrepant perceptions of each other has helped depolarize negative stereotypes and reduce conflict in a number of intergroup conflicts (e.g., Blake, Shepard, and Mouton, 1964), and consciousness raising to clarify self and other perceptions may help to increase conflict in situations where there is too little. Attitude-change interventions, in short, operate on the ways in which the parties understand and interpret the relations among the groups.

Changing *behaviors* requires modifying ways in which group members act. *Altering within-group behavior,* for example, may have a substantial impact on the ways in which the groups deal with each other. When members of a highly cohesive group confront explicitly differences that exist *within* the group, their enthusiasm for fighting with outside groups may be reduced. Similarly, an internally fragmented group that becomes more cohesive may develop an increased appetite for conflict with other groups (Brown, 1977). A second behavior-changing strategy is to *train group representatives to manage conflict more effectively.* Where too much conflict exists, representatives can be trained in conflict-reduction strategies, such as cooperation induction (Deutsch, 1973) or problem solving (Filley, 1975). Where the problem is too little conflict, the parties might benefit from training in assertiveness or bargaining skills. A third alternative is to *monitor between-group behavior,* and so influence escalations. Third parties trusted by both sides can control escalative tendencies or lend credibility to reduction initiatives by the parties that might otherwise be distrusted (Walton, 1969). Similarly, conflict induction may be an outcome of third-party "process consultation" that raises questions about collusion (Schein, 1969). Behavior-change strategies, in summary, focus on present activities as an influence on levels of conflict, and seek to move those actions into more constructive patterns.

Changing structures involves altering the underlying factors that influence long-term relations among groups. A common alternative is to *invoke larger system interventions.* Conflict between groups in the same larger system is often reduced through referring the question at issue to a higher hierarchical level (Galbraith, 1971). A similar press for conflict induction may be created when too little conflict results in lowered performance that catches the attention of higher levels. A related strategy for managing conflict is to *develop regulatory contexts* that specify appropriate behaviors. Such regulatory structures can limit conflict by imposing rules on potential fights, as collective bargaining legislation does on labor–management relations. Changes in regulatory structures can also loosen rules that stifle desirable conflict. A third strategy is the *development of new interface mechanisms* that mediate intergroup relations. Integrative roles and departments may help to reduce conflict among organizational departments (Galbraith, 1971), while the creation of ombudsmen or "devil's advocates" can help surface conflict that might otherwise not become explicit (Janis, 1972). Another possibility is *redefinition of group boundaries and goals,* so the nature of the parties themselves is reorganized. Redesigning organizations into a matrix structure, for example, in effect locates the conflicted interface within an individual to ensure that effective management efforts are made (Galbraith, 1971). Alternatively, too little conflict may call for clarifying group boundaries and goals so the differences among them become more apparent and more likely to produce conflict. Structural interventions typically demand heavier initial investments of time and energy, and they may take longer to bear fruit than attitudinal and behavioral interventions. But they are also more likely to produce long-term changes.

These strategies for intervention are summarized in Table 2. This sample of strategies is not exhaustive, but it is intended to be representative of interventions that have worked with groups that are relatively equal in power and whose differences are primarily related to the organization's task. The introduction of power differences and societal differences raises other issues.

Power Differences

Relations between high-power and low-power groups are worth special examination because of their potential for extremely negative outcomes. The poor communications that result from fear on the part of the low-power group and ignorance on the part of the high-power group can result in either extreme oppression (too little conflict) or unexpected explosions of violence (too much).

It is understandable that high-power groups prefer too little conflict to too much, and that low-power groups are anxious about the risks of provoking conflict with a more powerful adversary. But organizations that in the short run have too little conflict often have too much in the long term. Inattention to the problems of low-power groups requires that they adopt highly intrusive influence strategies in order to be heard (e.g., Swingle, 1976). So the comfort of avoiding conflict between high- and low-power groups may have high costs in the long run.

TABLE 2
Intervening in Conflict among Groups

Area of Concern	General Issue	Strategies for Too Much Conflict	Strategies for Too Little Conflict
Attitudes	Clarify differences and similarities	Emphasize interdependencies	Emphasize conflict of interest
	Increased sophistication about intergroup relations	Clarify dynamics and costs of escalation	Clarify costs and dynamics of collusion
	Change feelings and perceptions	Share perceptions to depolarize stereotypes	Consciousness raising about group and others
Behavior	Modify within-group behavior	Increase expression of within-group differences	Increase within-group cohesion and consensus
	Train group representatives to be more effective	Expand skills to include cooperative strategies	Expand skills to include assertive, confrontive strategies
	Monitor between-group behavior	Third-party peacemaking	Third-party process consultation
Structure	Invoke larger system interventions	Refer to common hierarchy	Hierarchical pressure for better performance
	Develop regulatory contexts	Impose rules on interaction that limit conflict	Deemphasize rules that stifle conflict
	Create new interface mechanisms	Develop integrating roles of groups	Create "devil's advocates" or ombudsmen
	Redefine group boundaries and goals	Redesign organization to emphasize task	Clarify group boundaries and goals to increase differentiation

Managing conflict between high- and low-power groups requires dealing in some fashion with their power differences, since those differences drastically affect the flow of information and influence among the parties. A prerequisite to conflict management interventions may well be *evening the psychological odds,* so that both groups feel able to discuss the situation without too much risk. Evening the odds does not necessarily mean power equalization, but it does require trustworthy protection (to reduce the fear of low-power groups) and effective education (to reduce the ignorance of high-power groups). Given psychological equality, interventions related to attitudes, behavior, and structure that have already been discussed may be employed to promote constructive levels of conflict (e.g., Brown, 1977). It should be noted that for differently powerful groups the boundary between too much and too little conflict is easily crossed. Managers may find themselves oscillating rapidly between interventions to induce and interventions to reduce conflict between such groups.

To return once again to an initial example, the history of fighting and violence between the small union and the corporation led the latter's managers to expect even worse conflict when faced by the international union. But voting in the international in effect evened the odds between labor and management. Violent tactics considered necessary by the small union were not necessary for the international, and the regulatory structure of collective bargaining proved adequate to manage the conflict subsequently.

Organizations are increasingly forced to grapple with societal differences. These differences are typically not entirely task-related; rather, they are a result of systemic discrimination in the larger society. Group members enter the organization with sets toward each other with which the organization must cope to achieve its goals. Societal differences are most problematic when they involve histories of exploitation (e.g., blacks by whites, women by men), and successful conflict management of such differences requires more than good intentions.

Managing societal differences in organizations may call for evening the odds, as in managing power differences, since societal differences so often include an element of power asymmetry. But coping with societal differences may also require more, since the effect of institutionalization is to ensure that the differences are preserved. *Invoking pressures from the environment* may be required even to get members of some groups into the organization at all. External forces such as federal pressure for "equal opportunity" and expanding educational opportunities for minorities can be used to press for more attention to societally based conflicts within organizations. Organizations may also develop *internal counterinstitutions* that act as checks and balances to systemic discrimination. A carefully designed and protected "communications group," which includes members from many groups and levels, can operate as an early warning system and as a respected third party for managing societal intergroup tensions in an organization (Alderfer, 1977).

The bank's failure to integrate the trust department turned largely on institutionalized racism. The decision to hire black managers was made partly in response to environmental pressure, and so overcame the initial barrier to letting blacks into the division at all. But once into the division, no mechanisms existed to press for overt discussion of differences. Without that discussion, no ways could be developed for the black managers to scale the insurmountable barriers facing them. The bank colluded with its supposedly racist clients by protecting them from contact with the new recruits. Although the first step—recruiting the black managers—was promising, trust division managers were unable to make the differences discussable or to develop the mechanisms required for effective management of the black–white differences in the division.

Conclusion

It may be helpful to the reader to summarize the major points of this argument and their implications. It has been argued that relations among groups in organizations can be characterized by too much or too little conflict, depending on their task, the nature of their differences, and the degree to which they are interdependent. This proposition suggests that *conflict managers should strive to maintain some appropriate level of conflict,* rather than automatically trying to reduce or resolve all disagreements. Effective management of intergroup conflict requires both understanding and appropriate action. Understanding intergroup conflict involves diagnosis of attitudes, behaviors, structures, and their interaction. *Effective intervention to increase or decrease conflict requires action to influence attitudes, behaviors, and structures grounded in accurate diagnosis.*

Power differences between groups promote fear and ignorance that result in reduced exchange of information between groups and the potential for either explosive outbursts of escalated conflict or escalating oppression. Evening the odds, at least in psychological terms, may be a prerequisite to effective intervention in such situations. *Managers must cope with fear, ignorance, and their consequences to effectively manage conflicts between unequally powerful groups.*

Societal differences institutionalized in the larger society may further complicate relations among groups in organizations by introducing environmental events and long histories of tension. Managing such differences may require invocation of environmental pressures and the development of counterinstitutions that help the organization deal with the effects of systemic discrimination in the larger society. *Environmental developments produce the seeds for organizational conflicts, but they also offer clues to their management.*

The importance of effective conflict management in organizations is increasing, and that development is symptomatic of global changes. We live in a rapidly shrinking, enormously heterogeneous, increasingly interdependent world. The number of interfaces at which conflict may occur is increasing astronomically, and so are the stakes of too much or too little conflict at those points. If we are to survive—let alone prosper—in our onrushing future, we desperately need skilled managers of conflict among groups.

References

Alderfer, C. P. Improving Organizational Communication Through Long-Term Intergroup Intervention. *Journal of Applied Behavioral Science, 13,* 1977, 193–210.

Blake, R. R., and Mouton, J. S. Reactions to Intergroup Competition Under Win–Lose Conditions. *Management Science, 4,* 1961.

Blake, R. R., Shepard, H. A., and Mouton, J. S. *Managing Intergroup Conflict in Industry,* Ann Arbor, Mich.: Foundation for Research on Human Behavior, 1964.

Brown, L. D. Can Haves and Have-Nots Cooperate? Two Efforts to Bridge a Social Gap. *Journal of Applied Behavioral Science, 13,* 1977, 211–224.

Brown, L. D. Toward a Theory of Power and Intergroup Relations, in *Advances in Experiential Social Process,* edited by C. A. Cooper and C. P. Alderfer. London: Wiley, 1978.

Burton, J. W. *Conflict and Communication: The Use of Controlled Communication in International Relations,* London: Macmillan, 1969.

Coser, L. A. *The Functions of Social Conflict.* New York: Free Press, 1973.

Deutsch, M. *The Resolution of Conflict.* New Haven, Conn.: Yale University Press, 1973.

Filley, A. C. *Interpersonal Conflict Resolution.* Glenview, Ill.: Scott, Foresman, 1975.

Galbraith, J. R. *Designing Complex Organizations.* Reading, Mass.: Addison-Wesley, 1971.

Janis, I. *Victims of Groupthink.* Boston: Houghton-Mifflin, 1972.

Lawrence, P. R., and Lorsch, J. W. *Organization and Environment.* Boston: Harvard Business School, 1967.

Robbins, S. P. *Managing Organizational Conflict.* Englewood Cliffs, N.J.: Prentice-Hall, 1974.

Schein, E. H. *Process Consultation.* Reading, Mass.: Addison-Wesley, 1969.

Sherif, M. *In Common Predicament.* Boston: Houghton-Mifflin, 1966.

Swingle, P. G. *The Management of Power.* Hillsdale, N.J.: Erlbaum Associates, 1976.

Walton R. *Interpersonal Peacemaking.* Reading, Mass.: Addison-Wesley, 1969.

TACTICS OF LATERAL RELATIONSHIP: THE PURCHASING AGENT

GEORGE STRAUSS

This is a study of the tactics used by one functional group in an organization—purchasing—to influence the behavior of other functional departments of relatively equal status. It deals in part with "office politics" and "bureaucratic gamesmanship."

Most studies of human relations in management have dealt with *vertical* relations between superiors and subordinates or between line and staff.[1] Yet the purchasing agent's[2] internal relationships (as opposed to his external relationships with salesmen) are almost entirely *lateral;* they are with other functional departments of about the same rank in the organizational hierarchy— departments such as production scheduling, quality control, engineering, and the like. Most agents receive relatively little attention from their superiors; they must act on their own, with support being given by higher management only in exceptional cases. They are given broad freedom to define their own roles and are "controlled" chiefly by the client departments with which they deal.

Although purchasing is technically a staff department, its relations with other departments can best be analyzed in terms of work flow rather than according to the typical staff-line concept. At the beginning of the typical work flow the sales department receives an order; on the basis of this the engineering department prepares a blueprint; next the production scheduling department initiates a work order for manufacturing and a requisition for purchasing; with this requisition the purchasing department buys the needed parts.

But this process does not always work smoothly. Each department has its

---

Reprinted from *Administrative Science Quarterly,* 7, No. 2 (1962), 161–186. Used by permission of Administrative Science Quarterly and George Strauss.

[1]There have been many studies of lateral relations within or among primary work groups, but such studies have been concerned primarily with rank-and-file workers, not management. Three notable studies of horizontal relations within management are Melville Dalton, *Men Who Manage* (New York, 1959); Elliot R. Chapple and Leonard Sayles, *The Measure of Management* (New York, 1961); and Henry A. Landsberger, "The Horizontal Dimension in a Bureaucracy," *Administrative Science Quarterly,* 6, (1961), 298–332.

[2]Henceforth, I shall refer to the purchasing agent as the "agent."

specialized point of view which it seeks to impose on others, and each department is struggling for greater authority and status. The purpose of this exploratory study is to illustrate the range of tactics available in the interdepartmental conflict which almost always results.

Research Method

The research methodology included a considerable number of informal contacts with agents, observation of them at work for periods of up to one week, twenty-five formal interviews, a written questionnaire, a review of purchasing journals, and an analysis of how agents, both individually and in groups, handled specially prepared case problems.[3] In the selection of firms to be studied there was a strong bias in favor of those with large engineering staffs, since agents in these firms face the most complex problems.

The discussion which follows will be largely impressionistic and will deal with broad aspects of tactics used by purchasing agents, since their problems vary greatly and various means are used to solve them. It should also be noted that the examples illustrate extreme cases, which, being extreme, illustrate some of the basic dilemmas which most agents face, though often in an attenuated form. This study is primarily concerned with the agent himself, the man who heads the purchasing office. It does not directly concern the buyers and expediters under him or the added complications that occur when division or plant agents have a staff relationship with a corporation-wide purchasing office.

Causes of Friction

The agent originally had two primary functions: (1) to negotiate and place orders at the best possible terms—but only in accordance with specifications set by others—and (2) to expedite orders, that is, to check with suppliers to make sure that deliveries are made on time. This arrangement gave the agent broad power in dealing with salesmen but made him little more than an order clerk in terms of power or status within the company.

The ambitious agent feels that placing orders and expediting deliveries are but the bare bones of his responsibilities. He looks upon his most important function as that of keeping management posted about market developments: new materials, new sources of supply, price trends, and so forth. And to make this information more useful, he seeks to be consulted before the requisition is drawn up, while the product is still in the planning stage. He feels that his technical knowledge of the market should be accorded recognition equal to the technical knowledge of the engineer and accountant.

Specifically, the ambitious agent would like to suggest (1) alternative

[3] I am indebted for assistance to the Buffalo and Northern California Association of Purchasing Agents and to the chairmen of their respective Committees for Professional Development, Messrs. Roger Josslyn and M. J. McMahon. Helpful criticism was provided by Profs. Delbert Duncan, E. T. Malm, and Lyman Porter at the University of California, Berkeley; Prof. John Gullahorn of Michigan State College; Prof. Leonard Sayles at Columbia University; and Dean Arthur Butler and Prof. Perry Bliss at the University of Buffalo. Part of the research was done while the author was a research associate at the Institute of Industrial Relations, University of California, Berkeley.

materials or parts to use, (2) changes in specifications or redesign of components which will save money or result in higher quality or quicker delivery, and (3) more economical lot sizes, and to influence (4) "make or buy" decisions. The agent calls these functions "value analysis."

One way of looking at the agent's desire to expand his influence is in terms of interaction. Normally orders flow in one direction only, from engineering through scheduling to purchasing. But the agent is dissatisfied with being at the end of the line and seeks to reverse the flow. Value analysis permits him to initiate for others. Such behavior may, however, result in ill feeling on the part of other departments, particularly engineering and production scheduling.

Conflicts with Engineering

Engineers write up the *specifications* for the products which the agents buy. If the specifications are too tight or, what is worse, if they call for one brand only, agents have little or no freedom to choose among suppliers, thus reducing their social status internally and their economic bargaining power externally. Yet engineers find it much easier to write down a well-known brand name than to draw up a lengthy functional specification which lists all the characteristics of the desired item. Disagreements also arise because, by training and job function, engineers look first for quality and reliability and thus, agents charge, are indifferent to low cost and quick delivery, qualities of primary interest to purchasing.

All these problems are aggravated by the "completion barrier." Usually the agent seeks to change specifications only after the engineer has already committed his plans to blueprints and feels he has completed his work—in fact, he may be starting another project; the agent's interference inevitably threatens the engineer's feeling of accomplishment and completion. In any case engineers are jealous of their professional status and often resent the efforts of the agent to suggest new techniques or materials. These are areas in which the engineer feels that he is uniquely competent. Finally, agents are particularly anxious to prevent "backdoor selling" which occurs when a salesman bypasses them and seeks to influence someone else in the organization (usually an engineer) to requisition the salesman's product by name or—more subtly—to list specifications which only this product can meet. Backdoor selling threatens the agent's status in two ways: (1) it encourages specification by brand and (2) it makes both salesmen and engineers less dependent on him.

Conflicts with Production Scheduling

The size of the order and the date on which it is to be delivered are typically determined by production scheduling. The agent's chief complaint against scheduling is that delivery is often requested on excessively short notice—that schedulers engage in sloppy planning or "cry wolf" by claiming they need orders earlier than they really do—and thus force the agent to choose from a limited number of suppliers, to pay premium prices, and to ask favors of salesmen (thus creating obligations which the agent must later repay). Schedulers, on the other hand, claim that "short lead times" are not their fault, but the fault of the departments farther up the line, such as engineering (which delays its blueprints) or sales (which accepts rush orders). In addition agents claim that schedulers order in uneconomic lot sizes and fail to consider inventory costs of the savings from quantity discounts. In some instances, as we shall see, the purchasing agent seeks to solve these problems through combining production scheduling, inventory control, and purchasing into one "materials handling" department, which he hopes he will head.

Techniques for Dealing with Other Departments

Normally the agent attempts to fill requisitions as instructed. The majority of interdepartmental contacts are handled routinely and without friction in accordance with standard operating procedures. Yet many difficult problems cannot be easily programmed. Other departments are constantly placing pressures on the agent, who must take countermeasures, if only to preserve the *status quo*. And if the purchasing agent wishes to expand his power aggressively, as many do, he will inevitably run into conflict.

Understandably, then, successful agents have developed a variety of techniques for dealing with other departments, particularly when they wish to influence the terms of the requisitions received. These techniques will first be summarized briefly under five general headings and then be discussed in greater detail.

1. *Rule-oriented tactics*
    a. Appeal to some common authority to direct that the requisition be revised or withdrawn.
    b. Refer to some rule (assuming one exists) which provides for longer lead times.
    c. Require the scheduling department to state in writing why quick delivery is required.
    d. Require the requisitioning department to consent to having its budget charged with the extra cost (such as air freight) required to get quick delivery.
2. *Rule-evading tactics*
    a. Go through the motions of complying with the request, but with no expectation of getting delivery on time.
    b. Exceed formal authority and ignore the requisitions altogether.
3. *Personal-political tactics*
    a. Rely on friendships to induce the scheduling department to modify the requisition.
    b. Rely on favors, past and future, to accomplish the same result.
    c. Work through political allies in other departments.
4. *Educational tactics*
    a. Use direct persuasion, that is, try to persuade scheduling that its requisition is unreasonable.
    b. Use what might be called indirect persuasion to help scheduling see the problem from the purchasing department's point of view (in this case it might ask the scheduler to sit in and observe the agent's difficulty in trying to get the vendor to agree to quick delivery).
5. *Organizational-interactional tactics*
    a. Seek to change the interaction pattern, for example, have the scheduling department check with the purchasing department as to the possibility of getting quick delivery *before* it makes a requisition.
    b. Seek to take over other departments, for example, to subordinate scheduling to purchasing in an integrated materials department.

Note that neither the over-all categories nor the tactics listed under them are all-exclusive and that there is a great deal of over-lapping. They are proposed not as comprehensive tools of analysis, but merely as fairly common examples of bureaucratic gamesmanship.

Each agent interviewed in the study was evaluated in terms of his reported success (in terms of specific accomplishments) in getting other departments to accept a wider role for purchasing. Although this measure was crude and subjective,[4] there seemed to be quite clear differences between the tactics used by those who looked upon their job description as a defensive bastion and those who sought to expand their power beyond it. (Note that success is measured here in terms of expansion of power, rather than money saved for the company.)

Rule-Oriented Tactics

The tactics listed below are rule-oriented in the sense that the agent's approach is perfectly legitimate under the formal rules of the organization. Agents who emphasize these tactics seem to fit into Melville Dalton's category of "systematizers."

Appealing to the Boss

According to traditional organizational theory, whenever two executives on about the same level cannot agree, they should take the problem to their common superior for solution. Yet, most agents looked upon this as a drastic step, to be taken only when other means failed.

Only five of the agents interviewed mentioned appealing to their superior as a reasonably common means of dealing with interdepartmental problems. In three cases low status seemed to be largely responsible for their inability to handle problems on their own.

Two of these agents were new to the job. For example, one was a man in his early twenties, who had only a few months' experience and who commented that his chief problems were his age and his inability to understand what engineers were talking about. This man met daily to review his problems with his boss and commented that his boss ran interference for him, at least in big problems.

The purchasing agent of a large scientific laboratory was very successful in extending his authority. In dealing with research departments, however, he used the laboratory manager "as a buffer between me and the department heads." But in regard to equipment-maintenance departments, whose heads had much lower status than did the scientists, he commented that "if there were differences, I would discuss them with them. If we didn't agree, the laboratory manager would have to arbitrate. But this has never happened here." Significantly, this agent did not have a college degree, while many of the scientists were Ph.D's.

[4]*Reported* success obviously involves a fair amount of wishful thinking—aspiration rather than accomplishment—but for the general character of this study this limitation was not too serious. It should be emphasized, however, that whether an agent was a successful expansionist depended not only on his own personality and his choice of techniques but also on the institutional characteristics of the organization in which he worked.

The other two agents who frequently worked through their superiors came from branch plants of nation-wide firms, which placed strong emphasis on individual responsibility to live within rigid rules.

The more expansionist agents rarely relied on their superiors to help them in interdepartmental disputes (in part because they had little success in doing this). They often explained that they would take problems to a man's superior if necessary but that they rarely found it necessary. Many repeated versions of the following:

> We have a policy against engineers having lunch with salesmen. Since the engineer is on my level I couldn't *tell* him to stop it. But in a nice way I could talk to him. If this didn't work, I'd see the plant manager.
>
> *Q:* Have you ever done this [appealed to the boss]?
> *A:* No.

The general feeling, particularly among stronger agents, was that too frequent reference to the superior would weaken their relations both with the superior and with their fellow employees. ("After all, you've got to live with them.") To bring in top management too often would, in effect, be an admission that the agent could not handle his own problems. Moreover there is a myth in many corporations of being "one great big happy family," and, as a consequence, it is difficult to bring conflicts out in the open. Furthermore, since the agent is usually the aggressor, in the sense that he is seeking to expand his power beyond its formal limits, he is unlikely to go to the boss unless his case is unusually good.

On the other hand, the threat of going to the boss loses its effectiveness as a weapon if the threat is *never* carried out. The following quotation summarizes a common position:

> It depends on how much fuss you want to make. If it is really important, you can tell him you will discuss it with his boss. But, I don't want you to get the wrong impression. If you have to resort to this, you are probably falling down on the job. By and large, we have a good relationship with our engineers. However, there are times when you have to take a tough position. You aren't doing your job if you always go along with them in a wishy-washy fashion."

One agent explained how he "educated" engineers to accept substitute products instead of insisting on one brand.

We prepared our evidence and we were all set to take it to the top—and then, at the last minute, we backed down and told them it was too late in the game. But we indicated that in the future we would take similar issues to the top and they knew we would. So there has been much more understanding. . . . You have to risk making a few enemies once in a while.

Use of Rules

A second traditional bureaucratic means of dealing with other departments is to cite applicable rules or to rely on a formal statement of authority (such as a job description). For instance, an agent may circumvent pressure to place an order with a given company by referring to company rules requiring competitive bidding on all purchases in excess of $10,000. Most agents agreed, in theory, that rules of this sort are useful weapons, but they varied greatly in the extent to which they relied upon them in practice.

Some agents went very much "by the book," day in and day out. In general, these were men without college training, and they worked for larger, rule-oriented companies that were not changing rapidly. In answer to questions, these men often said, "This matter is governed by corporate policy" or made references to manuals and procedures. They also had a tendency to draw the lines of responsibility quite tightly, so that there were few areas of joint decision making; for example, "Engineering has the final word as far as specs are concerned. But we decide from whom to buy, provided they meet the specs." On the other hand, many agents operated very effectively without any formal written statement of their authority; their authority was understood by everybody in the organization and there was no need to put it in writing.

The evidence suggests that the most successful expansionists preferred to operate informally until there was an open conflict with another department. When this happened, they were very glad to refer to rules to bolster their position. Thus, paradoxically, we found strong agents who worked hard to introduce purchasing manuals and then paid relatively no attention to them in daily practice. In effect these agents take the position of "speak softly and carry a big stick." Indeed, the use of rules involves an implicit threat to appeal to higher management if the rules are not obeyed. ("When everyone in the organization knows what your responsibility is—and that you are backed up—then there is no need to mention it constantly.")

If flexibly used, procedure manuals provide the agent with an added bargaining weapon in dealing with other departments. Even though he may permit rules in the manual to be ignored most of the time, he can always do this as a favor in return for which he may ask favors. And the rules put a legal stamp on his efforts whenever he decides to ensnarl another department in a mass of red tape. But the expansionist agent must be careful not to become too rule-oriented. After all, his goal is to expand his influence beyond the areas over which rules give him definite authority—not to retreat behind them.

Requiring Written Acceptance of Responsibility

Another bureaucratic technique used by many agents is to require others to justify their decisions in writing. For example, if a production scheduler orders a part for delivery with very short lead time, the agent can ask him to explain in writing why there is such a rush. He hopes the scheduler will be embarrassed unless he has a good excuse—and in any case, the effort will make him reluctant to make such last-minute requests in the future. Certainly this helps expose the scheduler who constantly cries "wolf."

Agents may ask for written explanations to clear themselves. Just as often, however, this is done to make others hesitate or to have evidence against them later. In insisting that such reports be written, the purchasing agent can refer to company rules or to possible audits. Thus in asking for such a statement, agents often say, "I need it to document my records."

Again, it is the weaker, noncollege agent who makes the most persistent use of such tactics. Many seem to feel that an approach of this sort is cowardly and defeatist. As one put it, "If you are trying to get a man to say 'yes,' I don't see any value in forcing him to put his 'no' in writing. Then he will never move."

And another said, "I suppose you do punish an engineer by forcing him to give you a long written explanation, but that's hardly the way to win friends or advance your point of view." Furthermore, "You can always ask an engineer to give you a formal test result, but if he wishes he can always make the test fail."

Financial Charges

Cost-accounting procedures may also be used as a lever. A number of agents made comments like this:

> Whenever I get a request for a rush delivery, I ask the department which wants it whether they are willing to authorize overtime[5] or air freight. Since this gets charged against their budget, they usually hesitate a bit. If they go along I know they really need it. And if they have too many extra charges the auditor starts asking questions.

This tactic resembles the one previously discussed, particularly when the agent enters a statement into his records that the product would have been cheaper had the requisition been received on time. (Some companies charge in-bound freight to the budget of the purchasing or traffic department; in such cases purchasing's leverage is somewhat less effective.)

Some companies have what is often called an efficiency (or profit) improvement plan. According to such a plan each department (and sometimes each executive) receives credit[6] for the cost savings which can be attributed to the department's activities. Agents in two companies reported that engineers showed little enthusiasm for value analysis because the purchasing department got all the credit, even though part of the work was done by the engineering department. The situation greatly improved in one of these companies when "primary" credit was transferred to engineering, with purchasing retaining "participating" credit.

Rule-Evading Tactics

Literal Compliance

In dealing with pressures from other departments the agent can always adopt a policy of passive resistance—that is, he can go through the motions in hopes of satisfying the demands. This tactic of feigned acceptance[7] is often used with production scheduling. For instance, after completing a lengthy phone call in which he half-heartedly tried to persuade a vendor to make a very quick delivery, an agent commented, "My buyer tried already and I knew that they just weren't going to be able to deliver that soon. Still production scheduling was screaming and they threatened to go to the plant manager. So I tried to handle it in such a way as not to hurt my relations with the vendor. They knew why I had to call."

[5]That is, the vendor is authorized to make an extra charge for having his men work overtime.
[6]Though there is no direct pay-off, performance under the plan is often taken into account in determining bonuses or promotions.
[7]Dalton, *op. cit.,* p. 232.

This game of passive resistance can be skillfully played in such a way as to set a trap for the other department.

Example. One agent told how he dealt with an engineer who had placed a requisition for one company's products after having been lavishly entertained by its salesman. The agent wrote a long memo explaining why he felt this to be a poor choice and presented it to the engineer in a fashion which he knew the engineer would reject. The agent then placed the order. As he had predicted, the products arrived late and were totally inappropriate. The subsequent investigation led both to this engineer's transfer and demotion and to other engineers having greater respect for the agent's advice.[8]

It should be noted, however, that these tactics were reported by only a minority of agents. In almost every case the agent was "weak" (in terms of expansionism) or worked in large companies where there was considerable emphasis on following formal rule books. Instead of passively seeming to accept unreasonable requests, the stronger agents actively oppose them.

Exceeding Authority

Occasionally agents may revise the terms of requisitions on their own initiative, even though they have no formal authority to do so. For instance, an agent may extend a lead time if he knows the production scheduler has set the delivery date much earlier than is really required. Where a requisition calls for a given brand, he may purchase a substitute which he feels sure is an equivalent. Or, he may buy a larger quantity than requested in order to take advantage of quantity discounts.

When an agent revises requisitions in this manner, he may or may not tell the requisitioning department what he is doing. In either case he is exceeding his formal authority. In effect, he is daring the requisitioning department to make an issue of it. This requires considerable courage. No sensible agent will expose himself in this way unless (1) his over-all political position is secure and (2) he feels the terms of the original requisition were clearly so unreasonable that the requisitioning department will hesitate to raise the issue and expose its mistake.

Most agents were reluctant to use this tactic. Even if they could safely change orders in a given case, continual flouting of the requisitioning department's desires would create too much antagonism in the long run.

Personal-Political Tactics

Friendships and exchange of favors are used in almost every organization to get things done and to oil the wheels of formal bureaucracy. The agent is no exception to this rule; yet the author found to his surprise that informal relations played a less important role than he had expected. Agents, on the whole, seemed oriented to doing things "through channels."

None of the tactics which follow are contemplated by the company's formal

---

[8]A tactic like this can always backfire. The agent himself may be blamed for the failure.

scheme; all involve the use of personal relations. It would seem that Dalton's "adapters" would make greatest use of these tactics.

Friendships

Most agents prefer to deal with friends. Friendships help reduce the kinds of tensions to which agents are commonly subject. Even where friendship is not involved, it is easier to deal with people when you know their idiosyncrasies and special interests. Not surprisingly, comments like this were common: "[In handling problems] friendships count a lot. Many of the people here started when I did twenty-five years ago. We are all at about the same level and most of them are pretty good friends of mine. A lot is a matter of trust and confidence."

Agents seem to rely on friendship contacts as a means of communication and of getting quick acceptances of proposals that could be justified on their merits in any case. Rarely do agents rely on friendship alone. As one put it, "You can accomplish some things on the basis of friendship, but you can't do too much or you will strain your friendship."

Exchange of Favors

To some extent agents operate on the principle of "reward your friends, punish your enemies," and are involved in a network of exchange of favors—and sometimes even reprisals. Favors of various sorts may be given. Most agents are under pressure to make personal purchases, for example, to help someone in management buy a set of tires at wholesale rates. Since there are usually no formal rules as to such extracurricular purchasing, the agent has a strong incentive to help those who help him most. Similarly an agent is in a position to suggest to a salesman that it might be strategic to take a "co-operative" engineer to lunch. And there are always people in management who would like him to do a favor for a friend or relative who is a salesman or who owns a small business.

Other favors are more work-related. An agent may expedite delivery for a production scheduler who normally gives plenty of lead time for his orders but who now has a real emergency on his hands. Or he may rush parts for an engineer who is building a prototype model. "If a man is reasonable with me," one agent commented, "I'll kill myself to get him what he wants." The agent is less likely to exert himself for the man who has been uncooperative in the past. Yet, in general, agents seem to play down the exchange of favors, perhaps because they have relatively few favors to offer, other than trivial ones such as personal purchases or lunches for salesmen.[9]

The use of reprisals can be seen most clearly in dealing with salesmen. As one agent put it, "I play ball with those who play ball with me. If a salesman operates behind my back, he's going to have a hell of a time getting me to give him an order." Reprisals are more risky in dealing with management.

Example. One assistant agent, for example, told how he "delayed" getting catalogues for "uncooperative" engineers and gave "slow service" to

9Reciprocity in the broader sense, as suggested by Gouldner and others, is, of course, inherent in the entire framework of relations discussed here. Cf. Alvin W. Gouldner, "The Norm of Reciprocity: A Preliminary Statement," *American Sociological Review,* 25 (1960), 161–177.

engineers who habitually cried wolf. However, both this man's supervisor and his personnel director expressed concern over his poor human relations and his tendency to antagonize others.

The typical agent, however, seemed to feel that if he used such techniques he ran the risk of permanently impairing his relations with others. Furthermore, these techniques might always backfire; for example, if production were delayed because components were delivered late, he would be blamed.

Interdepartmental Politics

In addition to their personal relations with people, agents inevitably get involved in interdepartmental power struggles. Indeed, as the following quotation suggests, the agent is often a man in the middle, subject to conflicting pressures from all sides:

Production scheduling wants quick delivery, engineering wants quality, manufacturing wants something easy-to-make, accounting wants to save money, quality control has their own interests. And then you've got to deal with the supplier—and present the supplier's position back to your own organization (sometimes you think you are wearing two hats, you represent both the supplier and the company). Everybody has his own point of view and only the agent sees the over-all picture.

Much of the agent's time is spent seeking informal resolution of such problems[10]—and in these meetings he often acts as a mediator. The following is a common situation:

Example. Production scheduling has been pushing hard to get early delivery of a particular component (perhaps because the sales department has been pressing for increased production). In response to this pressure the vendor puts new, inexperienced men on the job. But when the components are delivered, quality control declares the work is sloppy, rejects it *in toto,* and wants to disqualify the vendor from doing further work for the company. Production scheduling and vendor are naturally upset; the vendor insists that the defects are trivial and can be easily remedied; and purchasing is placed in the difficult position of trying to mediate the issue.

If the agent is not careful in situations like this, he may become a scapegoat; everyone may turn on him and blame him for the unhappy turn of events. On the other hand, the successful agent is able to play one pressure off against another and free himself—or he may enlist the support of a powerful department to back him. If he is shrewd, he can get both sides to appeal to him to make the final decision and thus gain prestige as well as bestow favors which he may later ask returned.

Like it or not, agents of necessity engage in power politics. In doing this, they necessarily develop allies and opponents. Each department presents a special problem.

1. *Engineering.* Unless the relationship with engineering is handled with great tact, engineering tends to become an opponent, since value analysis invades an area which engineers feel is exclusively their own. Purchasing is at a disadvantage here. Engineers have the prestige of being college-trained ex-

---

[10]Dalton (*op. cit.,* pp. 227–228) points out the function of meetings in short-circuiting formal means of handling problems.

perts, and engineering is much more strongly represented than purchasing in the ranks of higher management.

2. *Manufacturing.* There is often a tug of war between purchasing and manufacturing over who should have the greatest influence with production scheduling. These struggles are particularly sharp where purchasing is trying to absorb either inventory control or all of production scheduling.

3. *Comptroller.* The comptroller is rarely involved in the day-to-day struggles over specifications or delivery dates. But when purchasing seeks to introduce an organizational change which will increase its power—for example, absorbing inventory control—then the comptroller can be a most effective ally. But the agent must present evidence that the proposed innovation will save money.

4. *Sales.* Sales normally has great political power, and purchasing is anxious to maintain good relations with it. Sales is interested above all in being able to make fast delivery and shows less concern with cost, quality, or manufacturing ease. In general, it supports or opposes purchasing in accordance with these criteria. But sales is also interested in reciprocity—in persuading purchasing "to buy from those firms which buy from us."

5. *Production scheduling.* Relations with production scheduling are often complex. Purchasing normally has closer relations with production scheduling than any other department, and conflicts are quite common. Yet these departments are jointly responsible for having parts available when needed and, in several companies at least, they presented a common front to the outside world. Unfortunately, however, production scheduling has little political influence, particularly when it reports relatively low down in the administrative hierarchy.

The shrewd agent knows how to use departmental interests for his own ends. Two quotations illustrate this:

> Engineering says we can't use these parts. But I've asked manufacturing to test a sample under actual operating conditions—they are easy to use. Even if engineering won't accept manufacturing's data, I can go to the boss with manufacturing backing me. On something like this, manufacturing is tremendously powerful.

> [To get acceptance of new products] I may use methods and standards. Or I might go to engineering first and then to methods and standards if engineering shows no interest. If I go to methods and standards I got to emphasize the cost-saving aspect [as contrasted to engineering's interest in quality].

Educational Tactics

Next we come to a set of tactics designed to persuade others to think in purchasing terms.

Direct Persuasion

Direct persuasion—the frank attempt to sell a point of view—is, of course, the agent's typical means of influencing others. Successful persuasion means "knowing your products backwards and forwards. . . building your case so that it can't be answered. . . knowing what you are talking about."

Most agents feel it essential that they have complete command of the facts, particularly if they are to bridge the status gap and meet engineers on equal terms. As one of them said, "The engineer thinks he is the expert; the only way you can impress him is to know more than he does." Thus many agents go to considerable lengths to acquire expertise; they spend a great deal of time learning production processes or reading technical journals.

Yet some of the stronger agents pointed out that too much expertise can be dangerous in that it threatens the other man's status. "Never put a man in a corner. Never prove that he is wrong. This is a fundamental in value analysis. It doesn't pay to be a know-it-all." Thus some agents look upon themselves primarily as catalysts who try to educate others to think in purchasing terms:

> Actually it is an asset not to be an engineer. Not having the [engineering] ability myself, I've had to work backwards. I can't tell them what to do but I can ask questions. They know that I'm not trying to design their instrument. . . . You have to give the engineer recognition. The less formal you are in dealing with them the better. It doesn't get their dander up.

Indirect Persuasion

Recognizing the danger of the frontal approach, agents often try forms of indirection—manipulation, if you like—which are designed to induce the other departments to arrive at conclusions similar to those of the agent but seemingly on their own. For example:

> We were paying $45.50 a unit, but I found a vendor who was producing a unit for $30 which I felt would meet our needs just as well. There was a lot of reluctance in engineering to accept it, but I knew the engineer in charge of the test was susceptible to flattery. So I wrote a letter for general distribution telling what a good job of investigating he was doing and how much money we'd save if his investigation was successful. . . . That gave him the motivation to figure out how it *could* work rather than how it *could not* work.

Indirect persuasion often involves presenting the facts and then letting the other person draw his own conclusions. The agent may ask the engineer to run a test on a product or even simply attach a sample of the product to an inter-office buck slip, asking, "Can we use this?" Similarly, choosing which salesmen may see engineers, he can indirectly influence the specification process. (In fact, once an agent decides that a product should be introduced, he and the salesman will often co-ordinate their strategies closely in order to get it accepted by others in management.)

Most agents feel engineers should have no part in negotiating prices; they feel this would be encroaching on purchasing's jurisdiction. But one successful agent encourages engineers to help out in the bargaining because "that's the best way I know to make these engineers cost conscious." Another arranges to have foremen and production schedulers sit in while he negotiates delivery dates with salesmen. "In that way they will know what I'm up against when they give me lead times which are too short for normal delivery."

Organizational factors play an important part in determining (1) whether the agent's relations with other departments will be formal or informal (for example, whether most contacts will be face-to-face, by phone, or in writing), (2) whether it will be easy or hard for other departments to initiate for purchasing, and (3) whether purchasing can make its point of view felt while decisions are being considered—or can intervene only after other departments have already taken a position. All these involve interaction patterns. We shall consider here only two types of organizational changes: informal measures which make it easier for other departments to initiate change in the usual flow of orders and formal changes involving grants of additional authority.

Inducing Others to Initiate Action

In most of the examples discussed here, the agent seeks to initiate change in the behavior of other departments. He is the one who is trying to change the engineer's specifications, the production scheduler's delivery schedules, and so forth. The other departments are always at the receiving (or resisting) end of these initiations. As might be expected, hard feelings are likely to develop if the initiations move only one way.[11]

Recognizing this, many of the stronger agents seem to be trying to rearrange their relations with other departments so that others might initiate changes in the usual work flow more often for them. Specifically they hope to induce the other departments to turn instinctively to purchasing for help whenever they have a problem—and at the earliest possible stage. Thus one agent explained that his chief reason for attending production planning meetings, where new products were laid out, was to make it easier for others to ask him questions. He hoped to encourage engineers, for example, to inquire about available components before they drew up their blueprints. Another agent commented, "I try to get production scheduling to ask us what the lead times for the various products are. That's a lot easier than our telling them that their lead times are unreasonable after they have made commitments based on these."

Some purchasing departments send out what are, in effect, ambassadors to other departments. They may appoint purchase engineers, men with engineering background (perhaps from the company's own engineering group) who report administratively to purchasing but spend most of their time in the engineering department. Their job is to be instantly available to provide information to engineers whenever they need help in choosing components. They assist in writing specifications (thus making them more realistic and readable) and help expedite delivery of laboratory supplies and material for prototype models. Through making themselves useful, purchase engineers acquire influence and are able to introduce the purchasing point of view before the "completion barrier" makes this difficult. Similar approaches may be used for quality control.

Work assignments with purchasing are normally arranged so that each buyer can become an expert on one group of commodities bought. Under this

---

[11]Actually, of course, initiations do occur in both directions. The production schedulers initiate for the agent when they file requisitions and the engineers initiate when they determine specifications. This normal form of programmed, routine initiation is felt to be quite different from the agent's abnormal attempts to introduce innovation. This distinction is quite important.

arrangement the buyer deals with a relatively small number of salesmen, but with a relatively large number of "client" departments within the organization. A few agents have experimented with assigning men on the basis of the departments with which they work rather than on the basis of the products they buy. In one case work assignments in both purchasing and scheduling were so rearranged that each production scheduler had an exact counterpart in purchasing and dealt only with him. In this way closer personal relations developed than would have occurred if the scheduler had no specific individual in purchasing to contact.

Even the physical location of the agent's office makes a difference. It is much easier for the agent to have informal daily contacts with other departments if his office is conveniently located. Some companies place their agents away from the main office, to make it easier for salesmen to see them. Although this facilitates the agents' external communications, it makes their internal communications more difficult. Of course, those companies that have centralized purchasing offices and a widespread network of plants experience this problem in an exaggerated form. Centralized purchasing offers many economic advantages, but the agent must tour the plants if he is not to lose all contact with his client departments.

Value analysis techniques sharply highlight the agent's organizational philosophy. Some agents feel that value analysis should be handled as part of the buyer's everyday activities. If he comes across a new product which might be profitably substituted for one currently used, he should initiate engineering feasibility studies and promote the idea ("nag it" in one agent's words) until it is accepted. Presumably purchasing then gets the credit for the savings, but resistance from other departments may be high. Other agents, particularly those with college training, reject this approach as unnecessarily divisive; they prefer to operate through committees, usually consisting of engineers, purchasing men, and production men. Though committees are time consuming, communications are facilitated, more people are involved, more ideas are forthcoming—and, in addition, the purchasing department no longer has the sole responsibility for value analysis.

To the extent that he allows others to take the initiative the agent himself must take a passive role. Not all agents are emotionally prepared to do this.[12] Some feel that it smacks too much of the "order clerk." A number commented, in effect, "I don't want to be everyone's door mat." Many asked questions like, "How far do you go in cost estimating, in getting quotes for hypothetical orders? . . . What do you do if a man throws a label at you and says get me some of this? After all, our time is limited."

Formal Organizational Change

The final approach is for the agent to seek to expand the formal grant of authority given his department (which might mean a larger budget too), as, for example, to place other functions such as traffic, stores, or even inventory control and production scheduling in one combined materials department. Agents who exert their energies in this direction generally reject the "human relations" or "participative" approach to management. They like to resolve

---

[12]After all, a certain type of active, initiating sort of personality is required if the agent is to bargain successfully with suppliers; it is hard for the same individual to adopt a passive role within the organization.

problems through memoranda ("it helps keep emotions down") and are not particularly optimistic about the possibilities of converting other departments to think in purchasing terms ("after all every department has its own point of view—that's natural"). They spend considerable time developing statistical means of measuring their own efficiency and that of their subordinates, and they are more likely to be in companies that have similar philosophies. For example, one agent explained why value analysis in his organization was concentrated in the purchasing department, "[Our company] doesn't believe in joint assignments or committees. If a man isn't competent to do the job himself, then we find another man. We don't want weak sisters." And another argued, "The responsibility must be concentrated in one department or another. It can't fall between two stools."[13]

Choice of Techniques

The foregoing list of tactics is presented not as a formal typology but merely to illustrate the *range* of techniques available to the agent. Most agents use all of these techniques at one time or another, depending on the problem. A different technique might well be used in introducing a major policy change than in handling routine orders. In trying to promote changes, one agent observed:

> You have to choose your weapons. I vary them on purpose. . . . I ask myself, who has the final decision? How does the Chief Engineer operate? What does he delegate? What does he keep for himself? It all involves psychological warfare. Who are the people to be sold? Who will have the final say?

And even in dealing with one problem, a mixture of tactics will generally be used. Nevertheless, the over-all strategies used by various agents seem to vary greatly in terms of which tactics receive the greatest emphasis.

1. Some agents seek formal grants of power (for example, to get inventory placed under purchasing); others merely seek influence (for example, to persuade inventory control to order in more economic lot sizes).

2. Some agents want to influence decisions *before* they are made (for example, through encouraging engineers to turn instinctively to purchasing for help whenever they are even considering the use of a new component); others *after* (for example, through having their decisions upheld often enough for engineering to hesitate to make an issue of a request whenever purchasing questions a specification).

3. Some agents think in terms of their long-run position and thus seek to improve procedures; whereas others are interested chiefly in exerting their influence in each conflict as it comes along.

We have already noted a difference between successful expansionists and those content with their roles as they are. On the whole, expansionists seemed to be more likely to choose informal tactics such as indirect persuasion, inducing others to make changes in the work flow, and interdepartmental politics. They had long-run strategies and sought to influence decisions before they were made. Those who were successful in achieving more formal power were

---

[13]Yet it could be argued that the committee system does not itself divide responsibility; it merely recognizes the fact that responsibility for value analysis is of necessity divided among departments.

also well aware of the value of informal influence; those who merely *talked* about formal power seemed to be relatively unsuccessful even in informal influence. In fact, one of the most noticeable characteristics of successful expansionists was their flexibility. Most were equally adept at using both formal and informal tactics and were not averse to turning the formal organization against itself.

Differences in success in expansionism seem to be due to a number of factors:

1. *Technology.* Obviously the agent cannot expand very much in a service industry or one where only raw materials are bought. He has his greatest chance for power in companies which make goods to order and in which there is a great deal of subcontracting.

2. *Management philosophy.* Where lines of authority are sharply drawn, the agent has little chance to extend his influence—except through direct seizure of another department's power, which is not easy. Note the comments of one agent in a highly rule-oriented company:

> We are a service department. . . We must see that parts are here at the proper time. . . . I usually let engineering pretty much make its own decisions. I may try to persuade an engineer to accept a new product. But if he says "no" all I can do is wait till he gets transferred and try to persuade his succesor.

Of the agents interviewed, the most successful was one in a company which had just introduced a new management and in which all relationships were in flux.

3. *Education.* Purchasing agents who were college graduates seemed to be more expansionist than those who were not. This may be due to their higher level of aspiration. Moreover, any company that appoints a college graduate may well expect to grant him greater influence. The college-trained man may feel more as an equal of the engineer and therefore more willing to come into conflict with him.

Furthermore, the more educated men (and particularly those with a business school background) seemed more prone to rely on techniques that were informal and not rule-oriented. Specifically, they were less likely to rely on formal statements of authority, to require others to take formal responsibilities for decisions, or to insist that an agent should "yell loudly whenever his rights are violated"; and they were more willing to work through committees.[14]

Conclusion

Traditional organization theory emphasizes authority and responsibility; it deals largely with two types of relationships: (1) those between superiors and subordinates, which it conceives as being primarily authoritarian (though

[14]These conclusions are consistent with the findings of the questionnaire sample ($N = 142$). The results are in the direction indicated for both degree of education and business school background (each taken separately) although only three out of eight relationships are significant at the .05 level. The questionnaire data are somewhat suspect, however, since the values which agents report are not always consistent with their observed behavior: in answering questionnaires many agents seem to place greater emphasis on formal techniques than they do in practice.

perhaps modifiable by participation, general supervision, and the like) and (2) those of staff and line, which are nonauthoritarian. Though the purchasing department is traditionally classified as a staff department, my own feeling is that the staff-line dichotomy in this case (as perhaps for most other purposes) tends to obscure more problems than it illuminates. As we have seen, the purchasing department's relations with other departments cannot be explained by any one simple phrase, such as "areas of responsibility," "exchange of favors," "advice," "control," or the like. Instead the skillful agent blends all these approaches and makes use of authoritarian and persuasive tactics as the situation requires. His effectiveness is largely dependent on the political power he is able to develop.

Recent authors have suggested that the study of organization should begin first with "the work to be done and resources and techniques available to do it."[15] The emphasis is on the technology of the job ("technology" being defined broadly to include marketing problems and the like as well as external environment) and the relationships between people which this technology demands. "Organizations should be constructed from the *bottom up,* rather than from the *top down.* In establishing work-group boundaries and supervisory units, management should start with the actual work to be performed, an awareness of who must co-ordinate his job with whom, when, and where."[16]

Some of us who are interested in this area are groping toward a concept of *work flow,* meaning the communications or interactions required by the job and including the flow of raw materials and products on the assembly line, the flow of paper work when a requisition moves through engineering, scheduling, and purchasing, as well as the flow of instruction, which may move down the chain of command from president to janitor.

This has been an exploratory study of the interrelationship between power struggles and lateral work flow. Of particular interest in this study, are: (1) the agent's strong desire for increased status, which upsets the stability of his relationship with other departments, (2) his attempts to raise his status through influencing the terms of the requisitions he receives and thus make interactions flow both ways, (3) the relatively limited interference on the part of higher management, which makes the lateral relationship especially important for the agent, (4) the "completion barrier," which requires the agent to contact an engineer before a blueprint is finished if the agent is to be successful in influencing the terms of the requisition, and (5) the differing vested interests or terms of reference of the various departments, which make agreement more difficult.

Finer mapping and more intensive research into interdepartmental relations is required; interactions should be precisely counted[17] and work should be done with specialties other than purchasing.

[15]Wilfred Brown, *Explorations in Management* (London, 1960), p. 18. See Chapple and Sayles, *op. cit.;* William F. Whyte, *Men at Work* (Homewood, Ill., 1961).

[16]George Strauss and Leonard R. Sayles, *Personnel: The Human Problems of Management* (Englewood Cliffs, N.J., 1960), p. 392. The sentence is Sayles's.

[17]Albert H. Rubenstein of Northwestern University has completed an unpublished quantitative study of communications within a purchasing department.

⑨ interpersonal communication

ACTIVE LISTENING

CARL R. ROGERS
RICHARD E. FARSON

The Meaning of Active Listening

One basic responsibility of the supervisor or manager is the development, adjustment, and integration of individual employees. He tries to develop employee potential, delegate responsibility, and achieve cooperation. To do so, he must have, among other abilities, the ability to listen intelligently and carefully to those with whom he works.

There are, however, many kinds of listening skills. The lawyer, for example, when questioning a witness, listens for contradictions, irrelevancies, errors, and weaknesses. But this is not the kind of listening skill we are concerned with. The lawyer usually is not listening in order to help the witness adjust, cooperate, or produce. Our emphasis will be on listening skills of the supervisor or manager that will help employees gain a clearer understanding of their situations, take responsibility, and cooperate with each other.

Two Examples

The kind of listening we have in mind is called "active listening." It is called "active" because the listener has a very definite responsibility. He does not passively absorb words which are spoken to him. He actively tries to grasp the facts and the feelings in what he hears, and he tries, by his listening, to help the speaker work out his own problems.

To get a clearer picture of what active listening means, let us consider two different approaches to the same work problem. The example is set in the printing industry, but the behavior of the men could surface in any organization.

Reprinted by special permission of the Industrial Relations Center of the University of Chicago and the authors.

Example No. 1:

Foreman: Hey, Al, I don't get this rush order. We can't handle any 50,000 run today. What do they think we are?

Supervisor: But that's the order. So get it out as soon as you can. We're under terrific pressure this week.

F: Don't they know we're behind schedule already because of that press breakdown?

S: Look, Kelly, I don't decide what goes on upstairs. I just have to see that the work gets out and that's what I'm gonna do.

F: The guys aren't gonna like this.

S: That's something you'll have to work out with them, not me.

Example No. 2:

F: Hey, Ross. I don't get this rush order. We can't handle any run of 50,000 today. What do they think we are?

S: They're pushing you pretty hard aren't they Kelly?

F: They sure are and I'm getting sore. We were just about back to schedule after the press breakdown. Now this comes along.

S: As if you didn't have enough work to do, huh?

F: Yeah. I don't know how I'm going to tell the pressman about this.

S: Hate to face him with a rush order now, is that it?

F: I really do. Joe is under a real strain today. Seems like everything we do around here is rush, rush, rush!

S: I guess you feel it's unfair to load anything more on him today.

F: Well, yeah. I know there must be plenty of pressure on everybody to get the work out, but—well, Joe doesn't deserve all the rush orders. But, if that's the way it is—I guess I'd better get the word to him and see how I can rearrange the work flow.

There are obviously many differences between these two examples. The main one, however, is that Ross, the supervisor in the second example is using the active-listening approach. He is listening and responding in a way that makes it clear that he appreciates both the meaning and the feeling behind what Kelly is saying.

Active listening does not necessarily mean long sessions spent listening to grievances, personal or otherwise. It is simply a way of approaching those problems which arise out of the usual day-to-day events of any job.

To be effective, active listening must be firmly grounded in the basic attitudes of the user. We cannot employ it as a technique if our fundamental attitudes are in conflict with its basic concepts. If we try, our behavior will be empty and sterile, and our associates will be quick to recognize such behavior. Until we can demonstrate a spirit which genuinely respects the potential worth of the individual, which considers his rights and trusts his capacity for self-direction, we cannot begin to be effective listeners.

What We Achieve by Listening

Active listening is an important way to bring about changes in people. Despite the popular notion that listening is a passive approach, clinical and research evidence clearly shows that sensitive listening is a most effective agent for individual personality change and group development. Listening brings about changes in people's attitudes toward themselves and others, and also brings about changes in their basic values and personal philosophy. People who have been listened to in this new and special way become more emotionally mature, more open to their experiences, less defensive, more democratic, and less authoritarian.

When people are listened to sensitively, they tend to listen to themselves with more care and make clear exactly what they are feeling and thinking. Group members tend to listen more to each other, become less argumentative, more ready to incorporate other points of view. Because listening reduces the threat of having one's ideas criticized, the person is better able to see them for what they are and is more likely to feel that his contributions are worthwhile.

Not the least important result of listening is the change that takes place within the listener himself. Besides the fact that listening provides more information about people than any other activity, it builds deep, positive relationships and tends to alter constructively the attitudes of the listener. Listening is a growth experience.

How to Listen

The goal of active listening is to bring about changes in people. To achieve this end, it relies upon definite techniques—things to do and things to avoid doing. Before discussing these techniques, however, we should first understand why they are effective. To do so, we must understand how the individual personality develops.

The Growth of the Individual

Through all of our lives, from early childhood on, we have learned to think of ourselves in certain, very definite ways. We have built up pictures of ourselves. Sometimes these self-pictures are pretty realistic but at other times they are not. For example, an average, overweight lady may fancy herself a youthful, ravishing siren, or an awkward teenager regard himself as a star athlete.

All of us have experiences which fit the way we need to think about ourselves. These we accept. But it is much harder to accept experiences which don't fit. And sometimes, if it is very important for us to hang on to this self-picture, we don't accept or admit these experiences at all.

These self-pictures are not necessarily attractive. A man, for example, may regard himself as incompetent and worthless. He may feel that he is doing his job poorly in spite of favorable appraisals by the organization. As long as he has these feelings about himself he must deny any experiences which would seem not to fit this self-picture, in this case any that might indicate to him that he is competent. It is so necessary for him to maintain this self-picture that he is threatened by anything which would tend to change it. Thus, when the organization raises his salary, it may seem to him only additional proof that he is a fraud. He must hold onto this self-picture, because, bad or good, it's the only thing he has by which he can identify himself.

This is why direct attempts to change this individual or change his self-picture are particularly threatening. He is forced to defend himself or to completely deny the experience. This denial of experience and defense of the self-picture tend to bring on rigidity of behavior and create difficulties in personal adjustment.

The active-listening approach, on the other hand, does not present a threat to the individual's self-picture. He does not have to defend it. He is able to explore it, see it for what it is, and make his own decision as to how realistic it is. He is then in a position to change.

If I want to help a man or woman reduce defensiveness and become more adaptive, I must try to remove the threat of myself as a potential changer. As long as the atmosphere is threatening, there can be no effective communication. So I must create a climate which is neither critical, evaluative, nor moralizing. The climate must foster equality and freedom, trust and understanding, acceptance and warmth. In this climate and in this climate only does the individual feel safe enough to incorporate new experiences and new values into his concept of himself. Active listening helps to create this climate.

What to Avoid

When we encounter a person with a problem, our usual response is to try to change his way of looking at things—to get him to see his situation the way we see it, or would like him to see it. We plead, reason, scold, encourage, insult, prod—anything to bring about a change in the desired direction, that is, in the direction we want him to travel. What we seldom realize, however, is that under these circumstances we are usually responding to *our own* needs to see the world in certain ways. It is always difficult for us to tolerate and understand actions which are different from the ways in which *we* believe *we* should act. If, however, we can free ourselves from the need to influence and direct others in our own paths, we enable ourselves to listen with understanding, and thereby employ the most potent available agent of change.

One problem the listener faces is that of responding to demands for decisions, judgments, and evaluations. He is constantly called upon to agree or disagree with someone or something. Yet, as he well knows, the question or challenge frequently is a masked expression of feelings or needs which the speaker is far more anxious to communicate than he is to have the surface questions answered. Because he cannot speak these feelings openly, the speaker must disguise them to himself and to others in an acceptable form. To illustrate, let us examine some typical questions and the type of answers that might best elicit the feeling beneath it.

Employee's Question	Listener's Answer
Just who is responsible for getting this job done?	Do you feel that you don't have enough authority?
Don't you think talent should count more than seniority in promotions?	What do you think are the reasons for your opinion?
What does the boss expect us to do about those broken-down machines?	You're tired of working with worn-out equipment, aren't you?
Don't you think my performance has improved since the last review?	Sounds as if you feel your work has picked up over these last few few months?

These responses recognize the questions but leave the way open for the employee to say what is really bothering him. They allow the listener to participate in the problem or situation without shouldering all responsibility for decision-making or actions. This is a process of thinking *with* people instead of *for* or *about* them.

Passing judgment, whether critical or favorable, makes free expression difficult. Similarly, advice and information are almost always seen as efforts to change a person and thus serve as barriers to his self-expression and the development of a creative relationship. Moreover, advice is seldom taken and information hardly ever utilized. The eager young trainee probably will not become patient just because he is advised that, "The road to success is a long, difficult one, and you must be patient." And it is no more helpful for him to learn that "only one out of a hundred trainees reach top management positions."

Interestingly, it is a difficult lesson to learn that *positive evaluations* are sometimes as blocking as negative ones. It is almost as destructive to the freedom of a relationship to tell a person that he is good or capable or right, as to tell him otherwise. To evaluate him positively may make it more difficult for him to tell of the faults that distress him or the ways in which he believes he is not competent.

Encouragement also may be seen as an attempt to motivate the speaker in certain directions or hold him off rather than as support. "I'm sure everything will work out O.K." is not a helpful response to the person who is deeply discouraged about a problem.

In other words, most of the techniques and devices common to human relationships are found to be of little use in establishing the type of relationship we are seeking here.

What to Do

Just what does active listening entail, then? Basically, it requires that we get inside the speaker, that we grasp, *from his point of view*, just what it is he is communicating to us. More than that, we must convey to the speaker that we are seeing things from his point of view. To listen actively, then, means that there are several things we must do.

Listen for Total Meaning. Any message a person tries to get across usually has two components: the *content* of the message and the *feeling* or attitude underlying this content. Both are important, both give the message *meaning*. It is this total meaning of the message that we must try to understand. For example, a secretary comes to her boss and says: "I've finished that report." This message has obvious factual content and perhaps calls upon the boss for another work assignment. Suppose, on the other hand, that the secretary says: "Well! I'm finally finished with your damned report!" The factual content is the same, but the total meaning of the message has changed—and changed in an important way for both supervisor and worker. Here sensitive listening can facilitate the work relationship in this office. If the boss were to respond by simply giving his secretary some letters to type, would the secretary feel that she had gotten her total message across? Would she feel free to talk to her boss about the difficulty of her work? Would she feel better about the job, more anxious to do good work on her next assignment?

Now, on the other hand, suppose the supervisor were to respond, "Glad to get that over with, huh?" or "That was a rough one, wasn't it?" or "Guess you don't want another one like that again," or anything that tells the worker that he heard and understands. It doesn't necessarily mean that her next work assignment need be changed or that he must spend an hour listening to the worker complain about the problems she encountered. He may do a number of things differently in the light of the new information he has from the worker—but not necessarily. It's just that extra sensitivity on the part of the supervisor that can transform an average working climate into a good one.

Respond to Feelings. In some instances the content is far less important than the feeling which underlies it. To catch the full flavor or meaning of the message one must respond particularly to the feeling component. If, for instance, our secretary had said, "I'd like to pile up all those carbons and make a bonfire out of them!" responding to content would be obviously absurd. But to respond to her disgust or anger in trying to work with the report recognizes the meaning of this message. There are various shadings of these components in the meaning of any message. Each time the listener must try to remain sensitive to the total meaning the message has to the speaker. What is she trying to tell me? What does this mean to her? How does she see this situation?

Note All Cues. Not all communication is verbal. The speaker's words alone don't tell us everything he is communicating. And hence, truly sensitive listening requires that we become aware of several kinds of communication besides verbal. The way in which a speaker hesitates in his speech can tell us much about his feelings. So too can the inflection of his voice. He may stress certain points loudly and clearly, and he may mumble others. We should also note such things as the person's facial expressions, body posture, hand movements, eye movements, and breathing. All of these help to convey his total message.

What We Communicate by Listening

The first reaction of most people when they consider listening as a possible method for dealing with human beings is that listening cannot be sufficient in itself. Because it is passive, they feel, listening does not communicate anything to the speaker. Actually, nothing could be farther from the truth.

By consistently listening to a speaker you are conveying the idea that: "I'm interested in you as a person, and I think that what you feel is important. I respect your thoughts, and even if I don't agree with them, I know that they are valid for you. I feel sure that you have a contribution to make. I'm not trying to change you or evaluate you. I just want to understand you. I think you're worth listening to, and I want you to know that I'm the kind of person you can talk to."

The subtle but most important aspect of this is that it is the *demonstration* of the message that works. Although it is most difficult to convince someone that you respect him by *telling* him so, you are much more likely to get this message across by really *behaving* that way—by actually *having* and *demonstrating* respect for this person. Listening does this most effectively.

Like other behavior, listening behavior is contagious. This has implications for all communications problems, whether between two people, or within a large organization. To insure good communication between associates up and down the line, one must first take the responsibility for setting a pattern of listening. Just as one learns that anger is usually met with anger, argument with argument, and deception with deception, one can learn that listening can be met with listening. Every person who feels responsibility in a situation can set the tone of the interaction, and the important lesson in this is that any behavior exhibited by one person will eventually be responded to with similar behavior in the other person.

It is far more difficult to stimulate constructive behavior in another person but far more valuable. Lisening is one of these constructive behaviors, but if one's attitude is to "wait out" the speaker rather than really listen to him, it will fail. The one who consistently listens with understanding, however, is the one who eventually is most likely to be listened to. If you really want to be heard and understood by another, you can develop him as a potential listener, ready for new ideas, provided you can first develop yourself in these ways and sincerely listen with understanding and respect.

Testing for Understanding

Because understanding another person is actually far more difficult than it at first seems, it is important to test constantly your ability to see the world in the way the speaker sees it. You can do this by reflecting in your own words what the speaker seems to mean by his words and actions. His response to this will tell you whether or not he feels understood. A good rule of thumb is to assume that one never really understands until he can communicate this understanding to the other's satisfaction.

Here is an experiment to test your skill in listening. The next time you become involved in a lively or controversial discussion with another person, stop for a moment and suggest that you adopt this ground rule for continued discussion. Before either participant in the discussion can make a point or express an opinion of his own, he must first restate aloud the previous point or position of the other person. This restatement must be in his own words (merely parroting the words of another does not prove that one has understood, but only that he has heard the words). The restatement must be accurate enough to satisfy the speaker before the listener can be allowed to speak for himself.

You might find this procedure useful in a meeting where feelings run high and people express themselves on topics of emotional concern to the group. Before another member of the group expresses his own feelings and thought, he must rephrase the *meaning* expressed by the previous speaker to that person's satisfaction. All the members in the group should be alert to the changes in the emotional climate and the quality of the discussion when this approach is used.

Problems in Active Listening

Active listening is not an easy skill to acquire. it demands practice. Perhaps more important, it may require changes in our own basic attitudes. These changes come slowly and sometimes with considerable difficulty. Let us look at some of the major problems in active listening and what can be done to overcome them.

To be effective in active listening, one must have a sincere interest in the speaker. We all live in glass houses as far as our attitudes are concerned. They always show through. And if we are only making a pretense of interest in the speaker, he will quickly pick this up, either consciously or subconsciously. And once he does, he will no longer express himself freely.

Active listening carries a strong element of personal risk. If we manage to accomplish what we are describing here—to sense the feelings of another person, to understand the meaning his experiences have for him, to see the world as he sees it we risk being changed ourselves. For example, if we permit ourselves to listen our way into the life of a person we do not know or approve of—to get the meaning that life has for him we risk coming to see the world as he sees it. We are threatened when we give up, even momentarily, what we believe and start thinking in someone else's terms. It takes a great deal of inner security and courage to be able to risk one's self in understanding another.

For the manager, the courage to take another's point of view generally means that he must see *himself* through another's eyes—he must be able to see himself as others see him. To do this may sometimes be unpleasant, but it is far more *difficult* than unpleasant. We are so accustomed to viewing ourselves in certain ways—to seeing and hearing only what we want to see and hear—that it is extremely difficult for a person to free himself from the need to see things his way.

Developing an attitude of sincere interest in the speaker is thus no easy task. It can be developed only be being willing to risk seeing the world from the speaker's point of view. If we have a number of such experiences, however, they will shape an attitude which will allow us to be truly genuine in our interest in the speaker.

Hostile Expressions

The listener will often hear negative, hostile expressions directed at himself. Such expressions are always hard to listen to. No one likes to hear hostile words or experience hostility which is directed against them. And it is not easy to get to the point where one is strong enough to permit these attacks without finding it necessary to defend himself or retaliate.

Because we all fear that people will crumble under the attack of genuine negative feelings, we tend to perpetuate an attitude of pseudo-peace. It is as if we cannot tolerate conflict at all for fear of the damage it could do to us, to the situation, to the others involved. But of course the real damage is done by the denial and suppression of negative feelings.

Out-of-Place Expressions

Expressions dealing with behavior that is not usually acceptable in our society also pose problems for the listener. These out-of-place expressions can take the extreme forms that psychotherapists hear—such as homicidal fantasies or expressions of sexual perversity. The listener often blocks out such expressions because of their obvious threatening quality. At less extreme levels, we all find unnatural or inappropriate behavior difficult to handle. Behavior that brings on a problem situation may be anything from telling an "off-color" story in mixed company to seeing a man cry.

In any face-to-face situation, we will find instances of this type which will momentarily, if not permanently, block any communication. In any organization, expressions of weakness or incompetency will generally be regarded as unacceptable and therefore will block good two-way communication. For example, it is difficult to listen to a manager tell of his feelings of failure in being able to "take charge" of a situation in his department because *all* administrators are supposed to be able to "take charge."

Accepting Positive Feelings

It is both interesting and perplexing to note that negative or hostile feelings or expressions are much easier to deal with in any face-to-face relationship than are positive feelings. This is especially true for the manager because the culture expects him to be independent, bold, clever, and aggressive and manifest no feelings of warmth, gentleness, and intimacy. He therefore comes to regard these feelings as soft and inappropriate. But no matter how they are regarded, they remain a human need. The denial of these feelings in himself and his associates does not get the manager out of the problem of dealing with them. The feelings simply become veiled and confused. If recognized they would work for the total effort; unrecognized, they work against it.

Emotional Danger Signals

The listener's own emotions are sometimes a barrier to active listening. When emotions are at their height, when listening is most necessary, it is most difficult to set aside one's own concerns and be understanding. Our emotions are often our own worst enemies when we try to become listeners. The more involved and invested we are in a particular situation or problem, the less we are likely to be willing or able to listen to the feelings and attitudes of others. That is, the more we find it necessary to respond to our own needs, the less we are able to respond to the needs of another. Let us look at some of the main danger signals that warn us that our emotions may be interfering with our listening.

Defensiveness. The points about which one is most vocal and dogmatic, the points which one is most anxious to impose on others—these are always the points one is trying to talk oneself into believing. So one danger signal becomes apparent when you find yourself stressing a point or trying to convince another. It is at these times that you are likely to be less secure and consequently less able to listen.

Resentment of Opposition. It is always easier to listen to an idea which is similar to one of your own than to an opposing view. Sometimes, in order to clear the air, it is helpful to pause for a moment when you feel your ideas and position being challenged, reflect on the situation, and express your concern to the speaker.

Clash of Personalities. Here again, our experience has consistently shown us that the genuine expression of feelings on the part of the listener will be more helpful in developing a sound relationship than the suppression of them. This is so whether the feelings be resentment, hostility, threat, or admiration. A basically honest relationship, whatever the nature of it, is the most productive of all. The other party becomes secure when he learns that the listener can express his feelings honestly and openly to him. We should keep this in mind when we begin to fear a clash of personalities in the listening relationship. Otherwise, fear of our own emotions will choke off full expression of feelings.

Listening to Ourselves

To listen to oneself is a prerequisite to listening to others. And it is often an effective means of dealing with the problems we have outlined above. When we are most aroused, excited, and demanding, we are least able to understand our own feelings and attitudes. Yet, in dealing with the problems of others, it becomes most important to be sure of one's own position, values, and needs.

The ability to recognize and understand the meaning which a particular episode has for you, with all the feelings which it stimulates in you, and the ability to express this meaning when you find it getting in the way of active listening, will clear the air and enable you once again to be free to listen. That is, if some person or situation touches off feelings within you which tend to block your attempts to listen with understanding, begin listening to yourself. It is much more helpful in developing effective relationships to avoid suppressing these feelings. Speak them out as clearly as you can, and try to enlist the other person as a listener to your feelings. A person's listening ability is limited by his ability to listen to himself.

Active Listening and Organization Goals

"How can listening improve productivity?"

"We're in business, and it is a rugged, fast, competitive affair. How are we going to find time to counsel our employees?"

"We have to concern ourselves with organizational problems first."

"We can't afford to spend all day listening when there is work to do."

"What's morale got to do with service to the public?"

"Sometimes we have to sacrifice an individual for the good of the rest of the people in the organization."

Those of us who are trying to advance the listening approach in organizations hear these comments frequently. And because they are so honest and legitimate, they pose a real problem. Unfortunately, the answers are not so clear-cut as the questions.

Individual Importance

One answer is based on an assumption that is central to the listening approach. That assumption is: the kind of behavior which helps the individual will eventually be the best thing that could be done for the work group. Or saying it another way: the things that are best for the individual are best for the organization. This is a conviction of ours, based on our experience in psychology and education. The research evidence from organizations is still coming in. We find that putting the group first, at the expense of the individual, besides being an uncomfortable individual experience, does *not* unify the group. In fact, it tends to make the group less a group. The members become anxious and suspicious.

We are not at all sure in just what ways the group does benefit from a concern demonstrated for an individual, but we have several strong leads. One is that the group feels more secure when an individual member is being listened to and provided for with concern and sensitivity. And we assume that a secure group will ultimately be a better group. When each individual feels that he need not fear exposing himself to the group, he is likely to contribute more freely and spontaneously. When the leader of a group responds to the individual, puts the individual first, the other members of the group will follow suit, and the group comes to act as a unit in recognizing and responding to the needs of a particular member. This positive, constructive action seems to be a much more satisfying experience for a group than the experience of dispensing with a member.

Listening and Productivity

As to whether or not listening or any other activity designed to better human relations in an organization actually makes the organization more productive—whether morale has a definite relationship to performance is not known for sure. There are some who frankly hold that there is no relationship to be expected between morale and productivity—that productivity often depends upon the social misfit, the eccentric, or the isolate. And there are some who simply choose to work in a climate of cooperation and harmony, in a high-morale group, quite aside from the question of achievement or productivity.

A report from the survey Research Center at the University of Michigan on research conducted at the Prudential Life Insurance Company lists seven findings related to production and morale. First-line supervisors in high-production work groups were found to differ from those in low-production groups in that they:

1. Are under less close supervision from their own supervisors.
2. Place less direct emphasis upon production as the goal.
3. Encourage employee participation in the making of decisions.
4. Are more employee-centered.
5. Spend more of their time in supervision and less in straight production work.
6. Have a greater feeling of confidence in their supervisory roles.
7. Feel that they know where they stand with the company.

After mentioning that other dimensions of morale, such as identification with the company, intrinsic job satisfaction, and satisfaction with job status, were not found significantly related to productivity, the report goes on to suggest the following psychological interpretation:

> People are more effectively motivated when they are given some degree of freedom in the way in which they do their work when every action is prescribed in advance. They do better when some degree of decision-making about their jobs is possible than when all decisions are made for

them. They respond more adequately when they are treated as personalities than as cogs in a machine. In short if the ego motivations of self-determination, of self-expression, of a sense of personal worth can be tapped, the individual can be more effectively energized. The use of external sanctions, or pressuring for production may work to some degree, but not to the extent that the more internalized motives do. When the individual comes to identify himself with his job and with the work of his group, human resources are much more fully utilized in the production process.

The Survey Research Center has also conducted studies among workers in other industries. In discussing the results of these studies, Robert L. Kahn writes:

In the studies of clerical workers, railroad workers, and workers in heavy industry, the supervisors with the better production records gave a larger proportion of their time to supervisory functions, especially to the interpersonal aspects of their jobs. The supervisors of the lower-producing sections were more likely to spend their time in tasks which the men themselves were performing, or in the paper-work aspects of their jobs.

Maximum Creativeness

There may never be enough research evidence to satisfy everyone on this question. But speaking from an organizational point of view, in terms of the problem of developing resources for productivity, the maximum creativeness and productive effort of the human beings in the organization are the richest untapped source of power available. The difference between the maximum productive capacity of people and that output which the organization is now realizing is immense. We simply suggest that this maximum capacity might be closer to realization if we sought to release the motivation that already exists within people rather than try to stimulate them externally.

This releasing of the individual is made possible first of all by listening, with respect and understanding. Listening is a beginning toward making the individual feel himself worthy of making contributions, and this could result in a very dynamic and productive organization. Profit making organizations are never too rugged or too busy to take time to procure the most efficient technological advances or to develop rich sources of raw materials. But technology and materials are but paltry resources in comparison with the resources that are already within the people in the organization.

G. L. Clements, of Jewel Tea Co., Inc., in talking about the collaborative approach to management says:

We feel that this type of approach recognizes that there is a secret ballot going on at all times among the people in any business. They vote for or against their supervisors. A favorable vote for the supervisor shows up in the cooperation, teamwork, understanding, and production of the group. To win this secret ballot, each supervisor must share the problems of his group and work for them.

The decision to spend time listening to employees is a decision each supervisor or manager has to make for himself. Managers increasingly must deal with people and their relationships rather than turning out goods and services. The minute we take a man from work and make him a supervisor he is removed from the basic production of goods or services and now must begin relating to men and women instead of nuts and bolts. People are different from things, and our supervisor is called upon for a different line of skills completely. These new tasks call for a special kind of person. The development of the supervisor as a listener is a first step in becoming this special person.

COMMUNICATION: THE USE OF TIME, SPACE, AND THINGS[1]

ANTHONY G. ATHOS

It was amazing to me to discover how many ways we have of talking about time. We have time, keep time, buy time, and save time; we mark it, spend it, sell it, and waste it; we kill time, pass time, give time, take time, and make time. With so many ways of dealing with time in the English language, we must be as sensitive to it as Eskimos are to snow, for which they have many words and no small respect.

Our American[2] concepts of time are that it is continuous, irreversible, and one-dimensional. Recent movies that shuffle the sequence of events so that they do not proceed in the same order as they "do" in "real" time, including flashaheads as well as the old standard flashbacks, are effective in disturbing us into powerful experiencing precisely because they deny our long-standing assumptions about time. We often seem to experience tomorrow as spatially in front of us and yesterday as almost literally behind us. With some effort we might be able to think of today as the space we were just in and the space we will very soon be in as we walk in a straight line. "Now" is even harder for many Americans, and it seems we experience it as the space filled by our bodies.

Perhaps that is why such interesting variations exist in different parts of the United States in orientations toward time. My personal experience in New England leads me to see people here as more oriented toward the past and the future than toward the present. Southern Californians seem more present-and future-oriented, with some important emphasis upon now (and thus greater familiarity with their bodies). The Latin Americans I know seem more past-and present-oriented. My point here is that we differ in our experiencing of time (as contrasted with our ways of thinking about it), focusing upon dif-

---

Reprinted by permission of the author and publisher from A. G. Athos and J. Gabarro, *Interpersonal Behavior* (Englewood Cliffs, N.J.: Prentice-Hall, Inc., 1978).

[1]Some of the ideas in this chapter were developed in a lecture given by Anthony G. Athos which was first published in *Behavior in Organizations: A Multidimensional View*, by A. G. Athos and R. E. Coffey, Prentice-Hall, Englewood Cliffs, N.J., 1968. The author is greatly indebted to the stimulation of Edward T. Hall's *The Silent Language* (Premier paperback, 1961) and *The Hidden Dimension* (Doubleday, 1966). Hall's work is much recommended to those who find that this brief discursive introduction stimulates further interest in a different and more systematic approach.

[2]"United States" and "America" refer here to the whole country, ignoring the considerable differences in the "cultures" of Hawaii, Alaska, Texas, and other parts of the whole.

ferent aspects of it. Yet there is a tendency for us to assume that it is linear "in" space: i.e., as a "straight line" from the past through the present into the future.

Of course, those who live more in touch with nature, say, farmers or resort operators, might also see time as cyclical. The earth makes its daily round of the sun; the seasons, like circles, "each mark to the instant their ordained end" and cycle again. And many of us, on an island vacation, for example, "unwind" like a corkscrew from what we left behind, slowly lose our concerns for tomorrow, and relax into letting days happen so that each merges with the one before and into the one after as an experienced, continuous present. The loosening delight of such vacations is in contrast with our more usual patterns, wherein our concerns about time can easily become compulsive.

Accuracy

I can recall being in Athens, Greece, and asking my Greek cousin "How long does it take to walk from here to the library?" I was staying with her family and I wanted to spend the afternoon at the library and leave there in time to get back home for a 6 P.M. appointment with an American friend. She said, "Not long." I replied with some irritation "No. I need to know, so I can stay there as long as possible. How long does it take?" She shrugged and said "It's a short walk." I said with a frown "Come on. I want to know exactly. How long?" With great exasperation she finally dismissed me with "A cigarette!" Well, I felt a bit defeated, if a little amused, for to her a 10- or even 20-minute error in estimate would have been simply irrelevant. Any greater precision would confine her. Yet we want to know *exactly*. Our concern for accuracy is enormous. Where else but in the Western industrialized world would watches get advertised as not being off more than a few seconds a month? Where else would people literally have timepieces strapped to their bodies so they can be sure they "keep on time"? Because of our concern for accuracy, the way we use time in our culture "talks" to other people.

Many men can remember the first time they ever drove to pick up someone for a date. It's not surprising that many of us got there a bit early and drove around the block a while so as not to communicate our anxiety or eagerness too openly. To arrive at 7:00 for a 7:30 date is to "tell" the other about these feelings and may result in "seeming" naive, unless the boy can explain it away. To arrive at 8:00 for a 7:30 date "says" you feel somewhat indifferent, and a decent explanation is required if the evening is to make any sense at all. Similarly, it is not uncommon for professors to assume that a student who is frequently late for class "doesn't care." Most get angry as a result. Students tend to assume that professors who are late to class also don't care very much. Time thus often "tells" caring, whether accurately or not.

We also use time to tell how we feel and see others in terms of relative status and power. If the President of the United States called you to Washington to talk with him next Tuesday at 3 P.M., it is unlikely that you would arrange your flight to arrive at National Airport at 2 P.M. You would most likely want very much to be sure you were at the White House no later than 3 P.M., and might very well get to Washington on Monday to be certain nothing would go wrong. Because of the great difference between the status of the President and the rest of us, we would likely feel that any inconvenience in waiting ought to be ours.

The same can be true in companies. If the president of a large organization calls a young salesman to his office for a 3 P.M. meeting, the chances are awfully good that the salesman will arrive before 3 P.M., even if he walks around the block for an hour, so as not to arrive "too early."

Imagine two men who are executives in the same large company, whose respective status is virtually the same but who are very competitive in many ways. One calls the other on the phone, and asks him to come to his office for a meeting at 1 P.M. that afternoon. (Notice that one is initiating, which generally indicates higher status; that he is specifying the place and the time, which diminishes the other's influence on those decisions; and that the "invitation" comes only a few hours before the intended meeting, which may imply that the other has nothing more important to do.) The chances are good that the second man will not arrive before or even at 1 P.M. for the meeting, unless his compulsiveness about time in general is so great that it overcomes his feelings about being "put down" (in which case he has lost a round in their competition and may be searching for a "victory" during the meeting). He might well arrive late, perhaps 5 minutes, which is enough to irritate but not openly insult, and then offer either no apology or only a very casual one. The way he handles time in this setting will communicate to the first executive, and so he may plan his response as carefully as a choreographer plans a ballet. Yet little of the process may be fully conscious for him. As Hall says in the title of his book, these are often truly silent languages for many of us.

The longer people are kept waiting, the worse they feel. If the young salesman who was invited to his company president's office for a 3 P.M. meeting arrives at a "respectful" 2:50 and is told by the secretary to have a seat, he remains relatively comfortable until 3 P.M. If the secretary waits until 3:10 to phone the president and remind him the salesman is there, she may communicate (i.e., the salesman may "hear") that she thinks a 10-minute wait is about all she can handle without feeling that the salesman will be feeling the first pangs of being unwanted. If she hangs up the phone and says "He'll be right with you" and the clock continues to tick until 3:25, she might feel impelled to say something about how busy the president is today (i.e., "Don't feel bad. It's nothing personal."). By 3:45 the salesman is likely to be somewhat angry, since he is likely to assume that the president doesn't really care about seeing him. If the president comes out of his office (note this use of space) to get the salesman and apologizes for being late and explains why (especially if the explanation includes information about "the top" that the salesman is not usually aware of), the salesman may "forgive" his boss ("That's all right. I don't mind at all. Your time is more important than mine.") and all can go well. If the president buzzes his secretary and tells her to send the salesman in, and then proceeds directly to the business at hand, the salesman is likely to be torn between the anger he feels and the fear of expressing it, which may affect their meeting without either knowing why. In short, then, the longer a person is kept waiting, the more "social stroking" is required to smooth ruffled feathers. Awareness of the process can reduce its power to discomfort when you are on the receiving end, and can increase your skill at helping others to realize when you were not deliberately, with intent, trying to "put them down." Being "thoughtless" and thus "hurting other's feelings" is all too often just what we call it: thoughtless. Thinking about our uses of time can, after an awkward self-consciousness, lead to an increase in intuitive, out-of-awareness skill in dealing with self and others.

Using time to manipulate or control others is common, even if we who do so are unaware of it. I once hired a gardener on a monthly contract to care for my yard. When we were discussing the arrangements, I felt somewhat uncertain that he would do all I wanted done or do it to my satisfaction. My feelings of mistrust were expressed by focusing upon time. I wanted to know precisely what day of the week he would come and how many hours he would stay. He seemed to understand and said "Thursday. Four hours."

Well, he actually did come on Thursday once in a while, but he also came on every other day of the week except Sunday and Monday. He never to my knowledge stayed four hours even when I happened to be home. I was sure I was being "taken" until it occurred to me the yard had never looked so good and everything really needing to be done was done.

The gardener apparently thought in terms of planting and cutting and fertilizing cycles. He felt his duty was to the yard, not to me. He sent me bills about every three or four months and then he often had to ask me what I owed him. He trusted me completely to pay him what he deserved. He worked in terms of seasons of the year, and I was trying to pin him down to an hourly basis. My attempt to replace my mistrust with the brittle satisfaction of controlling another person, in time, would eventually have led him to quit or me to fire him. I was lucky to see what was happening, and I left him alone. We got along fine.

Time is viewed as both precious and personal, and when we allow someone to structure our time, it is usually in deference to his or her greater status or power. This is especially true when we would rather be doing something else, as is the case with some employees in many organizations who "put in their time" from nine to five. Many people today are looking for an opportunity to "do their own thing" (when they can figure out what that is) and their reluctance to be controlled vis-à-vis a dimension as personal as time is reflected in such questions as "How much of your time is yours?", "Did you take time to smell the flowers?", and "Do you own your life?" "Private time" (such as weekends) is often "intruded upon" by work, with the notable exception of the Pacific Northwest, where it is generally regarded more strongly as "non-work" time.

The use of time to define relationships can also be seen in most marriages. How many Americans do you know who work through the dinner hour or into the night without calling their spouses? By contrast, people in other cultures often handle the time of their arrival home differently. In Greece I found that dinner was served at my uncle's house whenever he came home—and that might be anywhere from 6 to 9 P.M. This variation in the use of time, as well as my dealings with the gardener, introduces still another major notion about time.

Scarcity

We seem to see time as a limited resource for each person, so we think that what they choose to do with what time they have is a signal about how they feel about us. You are already experienced with the application of this notion. We all have feelings about how frequently we "ought" to see certain persons in order to express a "suitable" amount of affection. Take visits home to see your parents. Some students go home every weekend, some only on vacations, some only on holidays, some every few years, and some never. But almost all parents are pleased, assuming they like their children, to find their offspring choose to visit them rather than do something else. There is a mutual exclusivity operating here. If you go home to see your parents, they know you did so at the expense of some other option. If your other options were attractive, they hear you care enough about your relationship with them to forego some other pleasure. Simply choosing to "spend your time" with them is thus a gift of sorts and a signal about your sentiments. The same is true with other people, of course, especially subordinates in an organization.

Even when the choice of how or with whom we spend our time is not really our own, others may "hear" a communication about our feelings. If you and two other persons begin to meet after class once a week for a beer and then you take a part-time job that forces you to go directly from class to work, your absence in the pub will be "understood" as out of your control (given the choice you made to work). But the loss of interaction must be made up elsewhere or your friends will probably feel that you "withdrew."

Some people are really tough on this one. You may have three final exams to study for and a broken leg, and like most professors some friends will insist you come to the appointed meeting and bring your leg with you. And yet there need be no unreasonable demands involved for misunderstandings to occur. Perfectly reasonable people can think we don't care for them because we do something else rather than see them. They can misjudge the importance to us of the something else and be ignorant of the conditions that made it important. A supervisor who spends more time per day with one subordinate because the tasks being done temporarily require closer supervision may communicate to other subordinates, especially if time with them is temporarily reduced, that the supervisor "cares" more about what the one subordinate is doing, and perhaps will come to care more about that person than them. There may be more than a little truth in this. Sociologists have noted that it is not uncommon for positive sentiment to increase as the frequency of interaction increases, albeit with several important exceptions (including the problem of formal authority).

We sometimes experience with new friends an increase in frequency of interaction that accelerates beyond a point of equilibrium, given the importance the relationship comes to have for one or both persons. Then, if one person begins to withdraw a bit in order to adjust the frequency of contact to the kind and amount of sentiment, the other person—especially if s/he is desirous of more frequent interaction—tends to feel hurt. This hurt can lead them to react by further reducing or demanding increases in the frequency of contact, and until someone says openly what they are feeling, the cycle can proceed to the destruction of the relationship.

The scarcity of time for a person at a given moment is also his/her "cost" of time. When two people "spend" time together in any activity, communication will be strained and difficult unless the time being spent has approximately the same value for each participant. This is obvious when we by chance meet a friend in the street or hallway; if one begins to chat and the other is in a hurry, the encounter is bound to be a little awkward even if the person "short of time" explains why.

Our notion that time is scarce fits most Americans' feelings that things should be ordered, and that earlier is better than later. First born, first position, number two man, fourteenth in a class of 655, top 10 percent all assume meaning because of their position.

Early promotions in business or an advanced degree in two years instead of three are seen as praiseworthy, even if some run right by what they are trying to catch. These notions of time sequence are not inborn; they are culturally conditioned. Edward Hall reports that it takes the average child a little more than twleve years to master time and the concepts of order. I am constantly reminded of this by my young daughter, who recently asked: "But how long away is Friday?"

The point of this is, again, that time is seen as scarce, and thus whom you choose to "give your time to" is a way of measuring your sentiments. Just being more aware of this can help you recognize the usefulness of simply saying, out loud, what the meaning of your choice is for you. And, of course, such awareness also helps prevent you from assuming (without awareness of the assumption) the meanings of other persons without checking their intent.

Repetition

Finally, time has meaning for us in terms of repetition of activities. Some of our personal rhythms are so intimate and familiar to us that we are unaware of them. Most of us eat three meals a day, for example, not two, not five. The culture assumes that lunch is at noon for the most part, and this was probably defined originally in response to what people experienced in terms of hunger. But the convention also becomes a structure to which we adapt and with which we become familiar. When we experience an interruption of our pattern, we often become irritated. I can recall, for example, that I found it difficult to adjust to a change in schedule on my first teaching job. For several years as a doctoral candidate, I had had coffee at 10 o'clock with a group of congenial colleagues. The coffee hour became one of the central social functions of my day, in addition to a means of getting some caffeine into my reluctantly awakening body. When I began teaching I had a 9 o'clock and a 10 o'clock class three days a week, and I was troubled by the 10 o'clock class and adjusted by bringing a cup of coffee into class with me. The pattern was so well developed and so valued within me that I was willing to "break a norm" (and, in fact, a rule) against food in the classrooms in order to have my 10 o'clock coffee. It sounds like a small matter, and in one sense it is, but it makes my point even if it is a trivial example. There are daily cycles we are used to, and while there are many we share, there are others relatively unique to each of us. The closer to the body any repetitions of activity come, the more important they are to us.

Take seasons of the year, for example. In areas that have weather rather than climate, say, New England rather than southern California, the use of time varies from season to season as activities change. People in Boston not only put away their silver and use their stainless steel in August, but they give different kinds of parties with different time rules than they do in winter. In general, the rules are relaxed, more variety is "allowed," and time is less carefully measured for meaning.

Our rhythms are also influenced by our feasts and holidays and rituals. Christmas, Easter, Rosh Hashonah, Chanukah, Father's Day, Thanksgiving, Memorial Day, and the like, all have their "time" in the year. It has been hypothesized that Christ was really born in August, and the December celebration of his birth came about because the people of northern Europe had long had a pagan winter festival which they were used to. In any event, we are accustomed to certain activities and feelings in connection with each "special day."

Take Christmas, for example. Most businesspeople know there will be less work done just prior to and after Christmas than is usual. People experience a need for closeness, for family, for ritual, for the nostalgia of past Christmases, for gift giving and midnight services. They eat more and drink more and even get fond of their old Aunt Minny. It is a time set aside for warmth, affection, children, family, friends, and ritual.

The Greeks, however, celebrate their Easter much as we do our Christmas, and mark their Christmas almost as casually as we do our Easter. If you were to spend Christmas in Athens, you would likely sense something as missing. If you were there on Easter, you would get a "bonus." If you were in the United States working on a job that peaked in volume between December 20 and January 3, say in a post office, and you had to work long hours, the chances are you would feel quite resentful. The rhythms of our days, our weeks, our months, our years are all deeply familiar to us even if we are unaware of them. Any serious disruption of any of them is felt as deprivation. Just being aware of this can help you in many ways—planning changes, for example. Can you see why major changes in work design or location or personnel are particularly resented during the Christmas holidays?

Then, for students (and nowadays nearly everyone in the country spends at least twelve years as one, and more are spending sixteen or even eighteen), certain rhythms that matter are established. Where else in our culture do people get promoted every year for anything better than dreadful work? Where else can people choose their bosses (professors) so as to avoid certain ones, and where else can they drop one of them with no penalty after several weeks work? If you look at the assumptions students naturally take with them to work from school, you can see why the yearly immigration of graduates into business is such a trauma for both students and companies. Subculture shock is what it is.

A subsummary may help here. Basically, all I am saying is that time is important to us in many ways, that *when* you do what you do says things to others about what you feel, and that the "rules" about time vary from setting to setting. If you will just watch for one day what is going on in your life vis-à-vis time, I think you will see some interesting things. How you and others use time to communicate would make a terrific din if "talking" with time made noise.

Space

Space is a language just as expressive as time. Indeed, as hinted above, it is hard to separate it from the language of time, but it is useful to try.

More Is Better Than Less

The chances are good that you have seen various business organizations. The chances are even better that you found the size of offices related to the status of people there. It is rare indeed to find a company president occupying a smaller office than his subordinates, and it is not uncommon to find the top person ensconced in a suite of rooms. One of the ways we "tell" about the importance of people is by the amount of space we assign to them. Space, like time, is a scarce and limited resource.

I recall a distinguished senior professor returning to school after a long and nearly fatal illness. He was being moved from his old office to a new one in an air-conditioned new building, largely because the dean of his school believed the air conditioning would be of help to him. The professor may have thought he "heard" something else, for as I passed his office one day I found him on his hands and knees measuring his new office with a 12-inch ruler. It was a good deal smaller than his prior office, and from how he behaved later I think he was "learning" that his illness had diminished his importance to the school, so that he was reduced to a small office. It would be amusing if it were not so painful.

Another time I was being toured through a new and beautiful office building of a large corporation. The president's office was handsome indeed, but when I was taken next door to the executive vice president's office, I realized that the VP had a larger and recognizably more stunning space in which to work. I later asked my guide, an officer of the company, if the president and executive vice president had been vying for power. He looked surprised and defensively asked "Why do you ask?" I told him what I saw in the use of space. He laughed and said "Another theory bites the dust! The VP's office is better because he has charge of sales in this district and his office is our best example of what we can do for customers."

A year later the VP and president came into open conflict in seeking the support of the board of directors, and the VP left the organization. Of course, the offices were not "the" cause. But they were a signal that something was off. There are few organizations that can accept incongruence in the use of space when it communicates so clearly to hundreds of employees. In the company mentioned, I heard later, a frequent question in the executive ranks prior to the VP's departure was: "Who is running this place?"

Of course, we observe this in everyday life. We want larger houses on more land. We want lots with a view. (Although I notice few people with a picture window looking out at the view. What we want, I suspect, is mostly the illusion of an enlargement of our space.) Yet other people are more comfortable in smaller spaces. Latin people love to be awed by cathedrals and vistas in parks, but they seem to enjoy being "hugged" by smaller rooms at home and at work. The smaller space apparently is associated with warmth and touch and intimacy, while larger spaces are associated with status and power and importance. Perhaps this is why entering a huge office intimidates many of us. We almost physically inflate the person who occupies it. In any event there is a strong tendency in organizational subcultures to relate the amount of space assigned to individuals to their formal status or organizational height. Check this out around school or in any business. When the pattern does not hold, something interesting may be going on.

Private Is Better Than Public

As a doctoral candidate I was first given a desk in a large room with many other desks, then was "upgraded" to a cubicle with 6-foot walls and an open top, then to a private office. It was minuscule, but I could close it and be alone or private within it. When I began working as a professor, I shared an office with two others, then I shared it with one other, and now once again I have my own private office, roughly twice as big as my last one. Sequence and size are what matter here. It is "better" to have your own space than to share it, and it is "better" if it can be closed off for privacy than if it is open to the sight or hearing of others. And each "advantage" was distributed by rank, and by seniority within rank.

We use much the same thinking about country clubs or pools or university clubs. By excluding some others, on whatever criteria, we make it feel more private to us. And we apparently like that. The very process of exclusion marks the boundaries of our space both physically and socially, and, of course, psychologically. When we say that a person is "closed," we mean that we are excluded from him/her and vice versa. Thus, the process of defining the extent to which our various spaces are private is complex. As we set our boundaries we also exclude. And we need our own space, as we also at times need to be "open." Yet in organizations, it is clearly the rule that private offices are better than public ones. To go from a large but public office to a smaller but private one is a mixed blessing, but often the balance is favorable. For we are not like Miss Garbo who wants to be alone, but we do want to be able to be alone or private when we wish.

A powerful illustration of the value we place on privacy took place in the 1920s. A coal company in West Virginia owned the houses in which its miners lived. When the miners struck, the company took the doors off the houses. It is not hard to imagine the wrath of the miners. Another example is the automobile company that took the doors off the men's room stalls in the 1950s to discourage workers from long toilet breaks. The response in this instance was also very strong, and understandably so. When a space is designed for activity that is close to our body, we value its privacy all the more. Our free-flowing modern houses almost always have doors on at least two rooms, the bedroom and the bathroom. Perhaps that infamous "key to the executive men's room" is of more utility than arbitrary status.

Given the importance we attach to privacy, the way we use the space we have "talks" to others. If we have a private office and shut its door to speak with someone, we announce a message to that person and to those outside. We are saying "This conversation is important and not to be overheard or casually interrupted." Neither the person nor those outside know whether the news is good or bad, but they do know that you care about it and they may make unwarranted assumptions. For we close off our space for more private or personal behavior. Whether it is angry or loving, we intend to focus importantly.

Higher Is Better Than Lower

A few years ago I watched my three-year-old daughter playing "I'm the king of the castle" with friends. They laughingly fought each other for position at the top of a small steep hill. Each wanted to be on top, to be higher up than the others—in this instance, quite literally, in space. When they grow up, I fell to musing, they'll jockey for height with less laughter and more discomfort.

Perhaps our desire to be higher rather than lower is inherited from our primitive ancestors or perhaps it comes from such childlike games, or rather from the important business of being little for so long, and thus less powerful than we might wish. In any event, houses higher on the hill, from Hong Kong to Corning, are "better" (and usually more expensive) than those below. The view is often cited as the reason, but I doubt it. It's more likely a residue of our childhood that probably reaches back in evolution far beyond the Greeks, who built the Acropolis on a sharp-rising rock for protection as much as grandeur. Much as dogs still circle about before they lie to sleep (a still visible link to their wild forebears, who circled to crush tall grass into a kind of nest), we seek height for reasons in large part lost to us.

We move up in organizations, or "climb the ladder." We go up to the head office and down to the shop. We call the wealthiest people the upper classes and the poorest the lower classes. Much of our imagery for what we value is in terms of up and down. People from Boston go "down" to Maine, although it is north of Boston. Allegedly this is because early travelers were referring to tides, but it also fits the notion of some Bostonians that Boston is the apex from which one can only go down.

On a more concrete level, the ground-floor walk-in legal aid centers that have opened their doors in deprived neighborhoods are less frightening to prospective clients partly because of their ground-level location. Here again space speaks. To be higher than you is to be better than you.

Near Is Better Than Far

Really, this one can be just the reverse of what it says. It depends upon whether sentiments are positive or negative. Near is better if the sentiments are positive. Far is better if the sentiments are negative.

In a business organization, it is not uncommon for the offices near the boss to be more highly valued than those farther away. If the chief executive officer is on the third floor, the others on that floor are also assumed to be privileged. They are closer to the top person and thus have more opportunities for informal interaction, as well as the formal designation of spatial assignment near the boss's space.

The same principle holds at formal dinner parties, where nearness to the host is valued. The farther down the table one is placed, the lower one's status at the dinner. In branch organizations that cover large territories a common problem is that each branch develops internal loyalties greater than the loyalty to the head office. The distance from the center of the organization impedes communication.

Thus when the sentiments are positive, being near is better than being far away. As I mentioned, the reverse can also be true. People prefer to increase distance when their sentiments are negative.

In Is Better Than Out

We seem to assume that people who work inside are better than those who work outside, perhaps because of the respective associations with mental and manual work. Baseball teams prefer to be in their own field, their most familiar space. Often when we are uneasy or anxious we move to our own space. In it we feel more secure.

The basic difference between in-out and near-far is that the former works from a specific point while the latter is a matter of degree. But they are closely related. For example, a few years ago a wedding was to take place in the side chapel off the main seating area of a church. The number of guests exceeded the number of seats in the chapel. So decisions needed to be made about who sat in the chapel and who sat outside it. There were thus created two "classes" of guests: those sitting inside and those sitting outside, yet within each class there was a sliding scale at work. How close to the front of your class were you seated? I can tell you those who sat at the back of the second class felt like relative "outsiders." Certainly, they were not among the "in" group.

Naturally these five dimensions of space are related. An office that is smaller but private and near an important executive may be highly desirable in spite of its size. When you consider the impact of space, you must look at the possible influence of each of the five dimensions and how they can balance each other in specific settings, as well as how they influence the use of time as a language.

Interpersonal Space

On a more personal level we have another silent language related to space. We have the general notion that we own the space around us, much like an invisible bubble. Others are to stay outside the bubble except when powerful feelings—of intimacy or anger—are being expressed. Touch is especially to be avoided in our culture, with the same exceptions. How many times have you sat next to a stranger in a movie theater and jockeyed for the single armrest? Since touching is out, it often ends up under the arm of the bolder person, who risks touch.

I recall an amusing yet painful incident at a recent cocktail party. A woman, newly arrived from Israel, was talking with an American male of Swedish descent. Her conception of the proper distance from her face to his was about half the distance he apparently felt comfortable with. She would step in, he would step back. She virtually chased him across the room before they both gave up. She dismissed him as "cold." He saw her as "pushy." Each had a different notion of the appropriateness of distance given their relationship, and neither could feel comfortable with the other's behavior.

When someone with a different notion of the use of interpersonal space steps into our bubble we feel either uncomfortable and crowded, aggressed upon and threatened, or expectant of affection. Getting that close in the United States is for many a hit-or-kiss affair.

In addition, in our mouthwashed, deodorant-using culture the idea of smelling another's body or breath is often thought to be repugnant. The experience is avoided except in lovemaking, and even there many perfume away all traces of personal odor. Yet some people enjoy being close enough to others in public settings to feel their body warmth and smell their natural odors, and they touch others more often than we do. When we meet such people we have a terrible time because they "say" things, in the way they use space, that we do not appreciate or understand. They, in turn find us as difficult as we find them.

Yet within this huge country there are many subgroups with variations in their use of interpersonal space. Men walking down the street in the Italian district of Boston often do so arm-in-arm, something one would seldom, if ever, see around most universities in the Boston area. And in any large business organization, you can see the effects of variations in the use of space complicating relationships. A warm, expressive executive who feels comfortable touching the arm or shoulder of a subordinate may make him exceedingly uncomfortable if he is the nontouch, keep-your-distance type. You can watch your own behavior here to see how you use your own space and how you react to others who behave differently. Just being aware of it helps a great deal.

Since the American experience of smell, body warmth, and touch is so poorly developed, most of what we say to each other using these media does not take place in our awareness. But it does take place. Communication by smell, largely a chemical process, is far more extensive than we think. Edward Hall reports that in discussing olfactory messages with a psychoanalyst, a skillful therapist with an unusual record of success, he learned that the therapist could clearly distinguish the smell of anger in patients at a distance of 6 feet or more. Schizophrenic patients are reputed to have a characteristic odor and Dr. Kathleen Smith of St. Louis has demonstrated that rats readily distinguish between the smell of a schizophrenic and a nonschizophrenic. If chemical messages are this powerful, one wonders how many of what we consider to be well-hidden feelings are being "telegraphed" by the smells we are unable to disguise.

If smell as a communicator is out of awareness, how much more so is the skin as a major sense organ. Yet the skin has remarkable thermal characteristics and apparently has an extraordinary capacity both to emit and detect infrared heat. Under stress or strong emotion, we can send out thermal messages which can be "read" by perceptive individuals (usually spouses, lovers, or children) who can get within 2 feet. Getting "red in the face" in anger or embarrassment or sexual arousal is so common we hardly think about it. Yet the coloration of skin talks, too.

In summary, remember that people use space to say things they are often unaware of, but highly responsive to. To the extent that you can become more aware of your own behavior and that of others, you can be more skillful at "saying" what you mean to others and "hearing" what they mean. It is a fascinating exploration.

Things

This aspect of communication is so easily grasped that I will just briefly present 10 rather obvious generalizations. Each points to what I see as a major assumption operating in our culture. Each naturally has exceptions, and each interacts with the others much as the various dimensions of space modify outcomes, and relate to time.

1. *Bigger is better than smaller.* Until recently, the automobile has been a good example in the United States. Except for small sports cars, bigger cars (which, see below, are often more expensive) were generally regarded as better than smaller.
2. *More is better than fewer.* Two cars, houses, etc., are better than one.
3. *Clean is better than dirty.* The American fetish under attack.
4. *Neat and orderly is better than messy and disorderly.* A clean desk may communicate efficiency, while a messy one may "say" you are disorganized in many settings.
5. *Expensive is better than cheap.* Original works of art are "better" than reproductions.
6. *Unique is better than common.* Ditto.
7. *Beautiful is better than ugly.* Ditto.

8. *Accurate is better than inaccurate.* Back to Acutron.

9. *Very old or very new is better than recent.* Victorian furnishings are now becoming "old" enough to be of increasing value after 60 years of being "recent."

10. *Personal is better than public.* One's own object, say, chair or desk, is valued as a possession. In offices, as in homes, the boss or host often has "his" chair and others usually stay out of it. The news photo of a student sitting in the chair of the president of Columbia University during the 1969 uprising was used so often because it showed someone breaking this "rule."

Summary

Just as the various aspects of space are interrelated (remember the small but private office near the boss?) and influence the uses of time as language, so, too, do both overlap with our use of things. If that same office near the boss has an expensive, one-of-a-kind Persian rug and antique furniture, it can become even more valued, even though it is small.

The way we and others use time and space and things talks. If you are deaf to the messages, you miss much of the richness of what is being said by you and others. If you start "listening" consciously, you can begin to appreciate more of the subtle languages that are in use and thus gradually increase your personal intuitive skill in being with other persons in and out of organizations.

References

Hall, Edward J. *The Silent Dimension.* New York: Premier Paperback, 1961.

Hall, Edward J. *The Hidden Dimension.* New York: Doubleday, 1966.

Sommer, Robert. *Personal Space: The Behavioral Basis of Design.* Englewood Cliffs, N.J.: Prentice-Hall, 1966.

Steele, Fred I. *Physical Settings and Organization Development.* Reading, Mass.: Addison-Wesley, 1973.

DEFENSIVE COMMUNICATION

JACK R. GIBB

One way to understand communication is to view it as a people process rather than as a language process. If one is to make fundamental improvement in communication, he must make changes in interpersonal relationships. One possible type of alteration—and the one with which this paper is concerned—is that of reducing the degree of defensiveness.

Reprinted from the *Journal of Communication*, XI, No. 3 (September 1961), 141–48, by permission of the author and the publisher.

"Defensive behavior" is behavior which occurs when an individual perceives threat or anticipates threat in the group. The person who behaves defensively, even though he also gives some attention to the common task, devotes an appreciable portion of his energy to defending himself. Besides talking about the topic, he thinks about how he appears to others, how he may be seen more favorably, how he may win, dominate, impress or escape punishment, and/or how he may avoid or mitigate a perceived or an anticipated attack.

Such inner feelings and outward acts tend to create similarly defensive postures in others; and, if unchecked, the ensuing circular response becomes increasingly destructive. Defensive behavior, in short, engenders defensive listening, and this in turn produces postural, facial, and verbal cues which raise the defense level of the original communicator.

Defensive arousal prevents the listener from concentrating upon the message. Not only do defensive communicators send off multiple value, motive, and affect cues, but also defensive recipients distort what they receive. As a person becomes more and more defensive, he becomes less and less able to perceive accurately the motives, the values, and the emotions of the sender. The writer's analyses of tape recorded discussions revealed that increases in defensive behavior were correlated positively with losses in efficiency in communication.[1] Specifically, distortions became greater when defensive states existed in the groups.

The converse also is true. The more "supportive" or defense reductive the climate the less the receiver reads into the communication distorted loadings which arise from projections of his own anxieties, motives, and concerns. As defenses are reduced, the receivers become better able to concentrate upon the structure, the content, and the cognitive meanings of the message.

Categories of Defensive and Supportive Communication

In working over an eight-year period with recordings of discussions occurring in varied settings, the writer developed the six pairs of defensive and supportive categories presented in Table 1. Behavior which a listener perceives as possessing any of the characteristics listed in the left-hand column arouses defensiveness, whereas that which he interprets as having any of the qualities designated as supportive reduces defensive feelings. The degree to which these reactions occur depend upon the personal level of defensiveness and upon the general climate in the group at the time.[2]

Evaluation and Description

Speech or other behavior which appears evaluative increases defensiveness. If by expression, manner of speech, tone of voice, or verbal content the sender

---

[1] J. R. Gibb, "Defense Level and Influence in Small Groups," in *Leadership and Interpersonal Behavior*, ed. L. Petrullo and B. M. Bass (New York: Holt, Rinehart & Winston, 1961), pp. 66–81.

[2] J. R. Gibb, "Sociopsychological Processes of Group Instruction," in *The Dynamics of Instructional Groups*, ed. N. B. Henry (Fifty-ninth Yearbook of the National Society for the Study of Education, Part II, 1960), pp. 115–35.

TABLE 1

Categories of Behavior Characteristic of Supportive
and Defensive Climates in Small Groups

Defensive Climates	Supportive Climates
1. Evaluation	1. Description
2. Control	2. Problem orientation
3. Strategy	3. Spontaneity
4. Neutrality	4. Empathy
5. Superiority	5. Equality
6. Certainty	6. Provisionalism

seems to be evaluating or judging the listener, then the receiver goes on guard. Of course, other factors may inhibit the reaction. If the listener thinks that the speaker regards him as an equal and is being open and spontaneous, for example, the evaluativeness in a message will be neutralized and perhaps not even perceived. This same principle applies equally to the other five categories of potentially defense-producing climates. The six sets are interactive.

Because our attitudes toward other persons are frequently, and often necessarily, evaluative, expressions which the defensive person will regard as nonjudgmental are hard to frame. Even the simplest question usually conveys the answer that the sender wishes or implies the response that would fit into his value system. A mother, for example, immediately following an earth tremor that shook the house, sought for her small son with the question: "Bobby, where are you?" The timid and plaintive "Mommy, I didn't do it" indicated how Bobby's chronic mild defensiveness predisposed him to react with a projection of his own guilt and in the context of his chronic assumption that questions are full of accusation.

Anyone who has attempted to train professionals to use information-seeking speech with neutral affect appreciates how difficult it is to teach a person to say even the simple "Who did that?" without being seen as accusing. Speech is so frequently judgmental that there is a reality base for the defensive interpretations which are so common.

When insecure, group members are particularly likely to place blame, to see others as fitting into categories of good or bad, to make moral judgments of their colleagues, and to question the value, motive, and affect loadings of the speech which they hear. Since value loadings imply a judgment of others, a belief that the standards of the speaker differ from his own causes the listener to become defensive.

Descriptive speech, in contrast to that which is evaluative, tends to arouse a minimum of uneasiness. Speech acts which the listener perceives as genuine requests for information or as material with neutral loadings is descriptive. Specifically, presentations of feelings, events, perceptions, or processes which do not ask or imply that the receiver change behavior or attitude are minimally defense-producing. The difficulty in avoiding overtone is illustrated by the problems of news reporters in writing stories about unions, Communists, Negroes, and religious activities without tipping off the "party" line of the newspaper. One can often tell from the opening words in a news article which side the newspaper's editorial policy favors.

Speech which is used to control the listener evokes resistance. In most of our social intercourse someone is trying to do something to someone else—to change an attitude, to influence behavior, or to restrict the field of activity. The degree to which attempts to control produce defensiveness depends upon the openness of the effort, for a suspicion that hidden motives exist heightens resistance. For this reason attempts of non-directive therapists and progressive educators to refrain from imposing a set of values, a point of view, or a problem solution upon the receivers meet with many barriers. Since the norm is control, non-controllers must earn the perceptions that their efforts have no hidden motives. A bombardment of persuasive "messages" in the fields of politics, education, special causes, advertising, religion, medicine, industrial relations, and guidance has bred cynical and paranoidal responses in listeners.

Implicit in all attempts to alter another person is the assumption by the change agent that the person to be altered is inadequate. That the speaker secretly views the listener as ignorant, unable to make his own decisions, uninformed, immature, unwise, or possessed of wrong or inadequate attitudes is a subconscious perception which gives the latter a valid base for defensive reactions.

Methods of control are many and varied. Legalistic insistence on detail, restrictive regulations and policies, conformity norms, and all laws are among the methods. Gestures, facial expressions, other forms of non-verbal communication, and even such simple acts as holding a door open in a particular manner are means of imposing one's will upon another and hence are potential sources of resistance.

Problem orientation, on the other hand, is the antithesis of persuasion. When the sender communicates a desire to collaborate in defining a mutual problem and in seeking its solution, he tends to create the same problem orientation in the listener; and, of greater importance, he implies that he has no predetermined solution, attitude, or method to impose. Such behavior is permissive in that it allows the receiver to set his own goals, make his own decisions, and evaluate his own progress—or to share with the sender in doing so. The exact methods of attaining permissiveness are not known, but they must involve a constellation of cues, and they certainly go beyond mere verbal assurances that the communicator has no hidden desires to exercise control.

Strategy and Spontaneity

When the sender is perceived as engaged in a stratagem involving ambiguous and multiple motivations, the receiver becomes defensive. No one wishes to be a guinea pig, a role player, or an impressed actor, and no one likes to be the victim of some hidden motivation. That which is concealed, also, may appear larger than it really is, with the degree of defensiveness of the listener determining the perceived size of the suppressed element. The intense reaction of the reading audience to the material in the *Hidden Persuaders* indicates the prevalence of defensive reactions to multiple motivations behind strategy. Group members who are seen as "taking a role," as feigning emotion, as toying with their colleagues, as withholding information, or as having special sources of data are especially resented. One participant once complained that another was "using a listening technique" on him!

A large part of the adverse reaction to much of the so-called human relations training is a feeling against what are perceived as gimmicks and tricks to fool or to "involve" people, to make a person think he is making his own decision, or to make the listener feel that the sender is genuinely interested in him as a person. Particularly violent reactions occur when it appears that someone is trying to make a stratagem appear spontaneous. One person has reported a boss who incurred resentment by habitually using the gimmick of "spontaneously" looking at his watch and saying, "My gosh, look at the time—I must run to an appointment." The belief was that the boss would create less irritation by honestly asking to be excused.

Similarly, the deliberate assumption of guilelessness and natural simplicity is especially resented. Monitoring the tapes of feedback and evaluation sessions in training groups indicates the surprising extent to which members perceive the strategies of their colleagues. This perceptual clarity may be quite shocking to the strategist, who usually feels that he has cleverly hidden the motivational aura around the "gimmick."

This aversion to deceit may account for one's resistance to politicians who are suspected of behind-the-scenes planning to get his vote; to psychologists whose listening apparently is motivated by more than the manifest or content-level interest in his behavior, or to the sophisticated, smooth, or clever person whose "oneupmanship" is marked with guile. In training groups the role-flexible person frequently is resented because his changes in behavior are perceived as strategic maneuvers.

Conversely, behavior which appears to be spontaneous and free of deception is defense reductive. If the communicator is seen as having a clean id, as having uncomplicated motivations, as being straightforward and honest, and as behaving spontaneously in response to the situation, he is likely to arouse minimal defense.

Neutrality and Empathy

When neutrality in speech appears to the listener to indicate a lack of concern for his welfare, he becomes defensive. Group members usually desire to be perceived as valued persons, as individuals of special worth, and as objects of concern and affection. The clinical, detached, person-is-an-object-of-study attitude on the part of many psychologist-trainers is resented by group members. Speech with low affect that communicates little warmth or caring is in such contrast with the affect-laden speech in social situations that it sometimes communicates rejection.

Communication that conveys empathy for the feelings and respect for the worth of the listener, however, is particularly supportive and defense reductive. Reassurance results when a message indicates that the speaker identifies himself with the listener's problems, shares his feelings, and accepts his emotional reactions at face value. Abortive efforts to deny the legitimacy of the receiver's emotions by assuring the receiver that he need not feel bad, that he should not feel rejected, or that he is overly anxious, though often intended as support giving, may impress the listener as lack of acceptance. The combination of understanding and empathizing with the other person's emotions with no accompanying effort to change him apparently is supportive at a high level.

The importance of gestural behavioral cues in communicating empathy should be mentioned. Apparently spontaneous facial and bodily evidences of concern are often interpreted as especially valid evidence of deep-level acceptance.

Superiority and Equality

When a person communicates to another that he feels superior in position, power, wealth, intellectual ability, physical characteristics, or other ways, he arouses defensiveness. Here, as with the other sources of disturbance, whatever arouses feelings of inadequacy causes the listener to center upon the affect loading of the statement rather than upon the cognitive elements. The receiver then reacts by not hearing the message, by forgetting it, by competing with the sender, or by becoming jealous of him.

The person who is perceived as feeling superior communicates that he is not willing to enter into a shared problem-solving relationship, that he probably does not desire feedback, that he does not require help, and/or that he will be likely to try to reduce the power, the status, or the worth of the receiver.

Many ways exist for creating the atmosphere that the sender feels himself equal to the listener. Defenses are reduced when one perceives the sender as being willing to enter into participative planning with mutual trust and respect. Differences in talent, ability, worth, appearance, status, and power often exist, but the low defense communicator seems to attach little importance to these distinctions.

Certainty and Provisionalism

The effects of dogmatism in producing defensiveness are well known. Those who seem to know the answers, to require no additional data, and to regard themselves as teachers rather than as co-workers tend to put others on guard. Moreover, in the writer's experiment, listeners often perceived manifest expressions of certainty as connoting inward feelings of inferiority. They saw the dogmatic individual as needing to be right, as wanting to win an argument rather than solve a problem, and as seeing his ideas as truths to be defended. This kind of behavior often was associated with acts which others regarded as attempts to exercise control. People who were right seemed to have low tolerance for members who were "wrong"—i.e., who did not agree with the sender.

One reduces the defensiveness of the listener when he communicates that he is willing to experiment with his own behavior, attitudes, and ideas. The person who appears to be taking provisional attitudes, to be investigating issues rather than taking sides on them, to be problem solving rather than debating, and to be willing to experiment and explore tends to communicate that the listener may have some control over the shared quest or the investigation of the ideas. If a person is genuinely searching for information and data, he does not resent help or company along the way.

Conclusion

The implications of the above material for the parent, the teacher, the manager, the administrator, or the therapist are fairly obvious. Arousing defensiveness interferes with communication and thus makes it difficult—and sometimes impossible—for anyone to convey ideas clearly and to move effectively toward the solution of therapeutic, educational, or managerial problems.

10 interpersonal perception

EMPATHY REVISTED:[1] THE PROCESS OF UNDERSTANDING PEOPLE

FRED MASSARIK

IRVING R. WECHSLER

Mike Corey walked into his office, fifteen minutes behind schedule. Through the glass partition Mike caught a glimpse of his boss. Arthur Blick looked up briefly as Mike slid into his chair. A number of signs obscured the full view: "Tomorrow We Finally Have to Get Organized," "THINK," "Wait Till Next Time—You Have Done Enough Damage for Now." Mike tried to look inconspicuous, though his mind was working rapidly. He was late for the third straight day. Oh, there were good reasons all right . . . one day his wife needed to be driven downtown and *she* wasn't ready—one day he had a terrible headache . . . and then . . . today. . . . His thoughts shifted abruptly—it really didn't matter as long as Blick was in a good mood. . . . Mike had some very definite ideas about what kind of guy his boss was. Usually he wasn't a bad sort; businesslike, but human too. If you had a big problem, he probably would listen. Still he was so darn changeable, and you had to hit him "just right" if you wanted to get along. This morning Blick seemed preoccupied . . . he looked up as if he hardly saw you, yet the way he spun back to his desk telegraphed "bad news."

This was Jean Krugmeier's first day on her job. She liked being an employ-

---

[1]The area covered by this article has been subject to systematic study only in very recent years. It is still much in flux, and few findings of certainty are as yet available. As we seek to lay out some of the problems, methods, and results with which this research is concerned, we are much aware of the tentative nature of our comments. The technically-inclined reader is urged to examine R. Tagiuri and L. Petrullo, *Person Perception and Interpersonal Behavior* (Stanford, Conn.: Stanford University Press,1958); F. Heider, *Psychology of Interpersonal Relations* (New York: John Wiley and Sons, 1958); and U. Bronfenbrenner, J. Harding, and M. Gallwey, "The Measurement of Skill in Social Perception" in D. C. McClelland, *et al., Talent and Society* (Princeton, N.J.: Van Nostrand Co., 1958).

ment interviewer. People were interesting, and it would be a novel experience to sit behind a desk all day. The initial two interviews proceeded uneventfully. The third applicant wanted to be foreman of the shipping gang. He was a young, burly 250 pounder who said that he used to work in the steel mills near Gary. He spoke loudly, with much self-assurance. "Some sort of a bully—a leering Casanova of the hot-rod set," Jean thought. Jean always did dislike guys like this, especially this sort of massive redhead. Just like her kid brother used to be—"a real pest!" The more he bragged about his qualifications, the more Jean became annoyed. It wouldn't do to let her feelings show; interviewers are supposed to be friendly and objective. She smiled sweetly, even if she did have a mild suspicion that her antagonism might be coming through. "I am sorry, we cannot use you just now," she said. "You don't seem to have the kind of experience we are looking for. But we'll be sure to keep your application in the active file and call you as soon as something comes up. Thank you for thinking of applying with us."

Looking at Social Perception

These anecdotes serve to illustrate the all-pervasive role that *social perception* plays in our lives. Forming impressions of people is a part of our daily experience, yet we rarely single out the process for explicit consideration.

Mike Corey was very much concerned with making the correct perceptual assessment of Arthur Blick's mood for the morning. Of course, he reacted without specifically worrying about his *empathy*.[2] He did what came naturally. The physical obstructions in the glass partition between the two offices were not the only barriers between these men. Mike's own views, attitudes, and feelings contributed to the difficulties, and so in turn did Blick's behavior, which provided Mike with only a limited amount of information (or *cues*). The fact that the entire relationship was set in the context of a given office situation both aided and impeded the extent to which Mike Corey could accurately perceive the relevant aspects of his boss's personality.

Jean Krugmeier probably does not think of herself as a prejudiced person. She may associae the term "prejudice" primarily with racial intolerance. She argues vociferously that people must have an "open mind." Still, like all of us, she too has "blind spots" and uses "shortcut thinking" which gives her a distorted picture of reality. Her feelings about burly redheaded men are very much like any other prejudice. They are supported by a *stereotype* that, in essence, says: "All of them are alike!" Thus, Jean's feelings may be irrational, her mind may be closed, and her social perception less than accurate because she subconsciously prevents relevant information about people "of this sort" from reaching her.

The Illusion of Objectivity

Most of us pride ourselves on our ability to look at people in a dispassionate, objective manner. Yet the psychological realities are that every time we have a personal contact we *do* form favorable or unfavorable impressions

[2]In this context, we shall treat as synonymous the concepts *empathy, understanding of people, social sensitivity,* and *accuracy in social perception.*

that influence our social behavior. We all have some positive or negative feelings in our interpersonal experiences. We *do* like or dislike in varying degrees, even if we are not always willing or able to recognize our true feelings.

Social perception is the means by which people form impressions of and, hopefully, understand one another. *Empathy*, or *social sensitivity*, is the extent to which they succeed in developing *accurate impressions*, or actual understanding, of others.[3] Social perception is not always rational or conscious; thus it follows that empathy is not necessarily the result of conscious, rational effort. For some, it may just seem to "happen," while others may develop it only after much training and living experience.

Three basic aspects of social perception must be considered: (1) *the perceiver*, the person who is "looking" and attempting to understand; (2) *the perceived*, the person who is being "looked at" or understood; and (3) *the situation*, the total setting of social and nonsocial forces within which the act of social perception is lodged.[4] We have already encountered "perceivers" Mike Corey and Jean Krugmeier, and their respective "perceived" counterparts, Arthur Blick and the burly job applicant.

The Perceivers and the Perceived

Perceivers and perceived need not be single individuals. Entire *social groupings* may do the "looking" or may be "looked at." We can, for example, conceive of the social perceptions existing between two rival departments of a corporation, with each department viewing the other with possible hostility or competitive jealousy. Similarly, we may distinguish social perceptions among small work groups, among large companies, and even among nations. Indeed any group of people, as well as any given person, can be a principal participant in the process of social perception.

The perceiver and perceived are not billiard balls on a flat table top. Their interactions do not usually produce obvious one-to-one cause-and-effect relations, for the perceived and the perceiver both possess personalities of great complexity. Social perception developes in the give-and-take among these *personalities-in-action*.

What is termed "personality" for the individual may be viewed as a unique pattern of "group characteristics" for the social grouping, be it work group, department, company, or nation. This pattern does not result from a simple addition of the personalities of individual members, although these individual personalities do have an impact. Rather, the social grouping's "personality" results from its formal and informal traditions, and from its accepted ways of "doing things." For example, some groups operate rigidly "according to the book"; others are more flexible and freewheeling. Some groups are highly integrated, with close and supportive relationships existing among their mem-

---

[3]Many complexities are involved in the actual measurement of social sensitivity. The definition given here is a kind of practical shortcut, useful for most everyday applications. For a consideration of the conceptual issues, see, for example, N. L. Gage and L. J. Cronbach, "Conceptual and Methodological Problems in Interpersonal Perception," *Psychological Review*, LXII (1955), 411–422; and L. J. Cronbach, "Processes Affecting Scores on 'Understanding of Others' and 'Assumed Similarity,' " *Psychological Bulletin*, LII (1955), 177–193.

[4]This approach is in harmony with Robert Tannenbaum and Fred Massarik, "Leadership: A Frame of Reference," *Management Science*, IV, 1 (October, 1957), 1–19.

bers; others are torn by antagonistic cliques and by intense rivalries. Some groups set high and constant standards for the admission of new members; others are more open and lax in their membership requirements.[5]

Patterns of Perceiving

The process of social perception can be graphically portrayed in a variety of ways. If I stands for "individual," and G for any grouping of individuals (and if the arrow stands for the act of perceiving), we may consider such relations as the following:

Perceiver to Perceived
Type-A I $\rightarrow$ I (Individual to Individual)
Type-B I $\rightarrow$ G (Individual to Grouping)
Type-C G $\rightarrow$ I (Grouping to Individual)
Type-D G $\rightarrow$ G (Grouping to Grouping)

Our anecdotes were of the Type-A variety—one individual perceiving another individual. Jean Krugmeier's perception of the job applicant, however, was influenced by a Type-B perception, her view of all burly, red-headed men—a view that she as an individual held for a broader (though tenuous) grouping of persons. Under conditions beyond those already described, Mike Corey may be perceived in a Type-C relationship by his fellow employees, a grouping that may view him with envy and anger because of his ability to get away with lateness without apparent untoward consequences.

Type-D perceptions become important particularly in attempts to analyze the nature of complex organizations, such as large sections or departments, entire firms, or other entities composed of various subgroups. For instance, a management consultant may wish to assess the way in which the Sales Department views the Credit Department—how the Research Section sees the Development Branch—or how Employee Relations relates to Wage and Salary Administration—and vice versa.

The four types of perceptual processes noted so far are relatively straightforward: Type-A, interindividual perception; type-B, an individual's perception of a grouping; Type-C, a grouping's perception of an individual; and Type-D, intergroup perception. Yet in each type countless obvious as well as hidden distortions can and do occur which prevent the perceiver from obtaining a faithful image. These breakdowns in communications, which we shall need to explore further at a later point, magnify their effects when we consider what might be termed *higher-order perception*.

As Mike Corey, for instance, forms his perceptions of Arthur Blick, he also considers the way in which Blick reciprocates. In other words, Corey is very much concerned to know how Blick feels about him. Corey makes assumptions about Blick's view of him which may or may not be correct. He may "think" that Blick hardly saw him, when—if he were to probe Blick's true

[5]Among the better-known approaches to the analysis of a group's personality is that of J. K. Hemphill and C. M. Westie, "The Measurement of Group Dimensions," *Journal of Psychology*, XXIX (1950), 325–342. Many sociologists have also made important contributions in this area; see, for example, Robert Dubin, *The World of Work* (Englewood Cliffs, N.J.: Prentice-Hall, 1958); and Melville Dalton, *Men Who Manage* (New York: John Wiley Sons, in press).

reaction—he might learn that Blick saw Corey very well indeed and was actively annoyed with his repeated tardiness. The extent to which one accurately recognizes someone else's reactions to oneself defines a special kind of social sensitivity—the ability to assess correctly what another person "thinks" about you.

Above, we are dealing with a "perception of a perception." We may conceive of a theoretically infinite series of social perceptions that begin as follows:

1. First-order perceptions: how the perceiver views the perceived (as illustrated by Types A, B, C, and D).
2. Second-order perceptions: how the perceiver "thinks" the perceived views the perceiver.
3. Third-order perceptions: how the perceiver "thinks" the perceived views "the perceiver's perception of the perceived," *etc.*

By the time we reach third-order perceptions, the pattern has become immensely problematical. Any further higher order adds to the complexity. Fortunately, most of our actual perceptions governing interactions with others probably do not get more involved than those defined by the first or second order.

One Empathy—Or Many?

There may be several different "empathies." Some perceivers seem more skillful in seeing beneath the surface and in ferreting out correct perceptions from vast networks of superficial psychological defenses. Others are more capable in hurdling the abyss that separates their actual observations of cues from the more remote recesses of behavior that they are seeking to understand. Some excel in painstakingly accumulating fragments of perceptual evidence and piecing them together. Others have a unique capacity for the elegant sweep that pulls together quickly and accurately a broad complexity of social phenomena.

Understanding social groupings rather than individuals involves unique problems and may require different skills of perception from those needed in understanding individuals. The talent for sizing up group opinion is probably different from the "diagnostic skills" needed for understanding a specific employee. An executive of a large corporation, for instance, may excel in accurately assessing opinions and attitudes of union and work force, but he may need to sharpen his skills in empathizing with his fellow corporate officers.

The probable existence of several "empathies" is not surprising if we consider the diversity of the factors at work. We have available a tremendous variety of cues that we may draw on in order to understand how another person thinks or feels, and these make differential demands upon our skills to draw inferences that will yield accurate perceptions.

Cues: Raw Material of Perceiving

Cues are often direct: through words, gestures, facial expressions, and specific behavioral acts, they are transmitted to the perceiver (interpreter) directly by the perceived (communicator), sometimes consciously, sometimes subconsciously. At other times, the perceiver gets his insights second hand—as by gossip, through reference letters, or by comments overheard during a coffee-break.

Some cues are more obvious in their apparent meaning. A broad smile and a friendly hello usually reflect a clear expression of personal warmth, while a vague wave of the hand is considerably more ambiguous and thus more difficult to interpret.

Some cues are more clear-cut than others. A girl's approximate age—the beautician's art notwithstanding—is likely to be more easily assessable than the meaning of a Mona Lisa-like smile; and despite best intentions, it may be virtually impossible to base an analysis of a person's basic psychological motivations on a casual martini-clouded social contact.

The psychological leap to be made from the cues available to what we seek to understand presents another consideration. As Mike Corey viewed his boss Blick, he had knowledge of Blick's customary office behavior. He had observed Blick before and under roughly similar conditions. Past cues provided a good base of present generalizations. On the other hand, Mike Corey might want to join Blick's country-club set. There he would need some insights into the latter's social behavior. Corey would search for some implicit theory, derived from Blick's on-the-job reactions, the only reactions with which he is actually familiar. He would try to extrapolate from Blick's available pattern of cues into a relatively distant and different situation, and risk empathic failure in the process.

The Perceiver's Background

The perceiver brings to the task of understanding others two sets of interrelated characteristics: (1) his general background, *demographic characteristics;* and (2) his unique self, *personality characteristics.*

Demographic characteristics are those broad sociological aspects of the individual which, for the most part, are easily definable, specific, and outside the more subtle ebb-and-flow of personality as such. Age, sex, nationality, religion, number of siblings, occupation, and economic level are illustrative.

When the psychologist Ronald Taft[6] reviewed studies on the relation of certain demographic attributes to social perceptual skill (especially empathy for individuals rather than for social groupings), he formed conclusions such as the following: (a) ability to judge emotional expression in others increases with age in children, but does not seem to increase further with age in adulthood; (b) sex differences in empathy are negligible, but there may be a very slight edge in favor of women.

Thus it seems that when dealing with adults, such as those encountered in business, age alone provides no free ticket to social perceptual wisdom. Although—hopefully—age may bring increases in some areas of technical knowledge, the process of getting older in and of itself does not lead to heightened empathy. Further, there does not seem to be much substance to the widely held assumption that women are "better judges" of people than men; the controversy on this point is not fully resolved.

More significant relationships emerge from an analysis of dynamic *personality characteristics.* Taft's attempt to find common threads in the web of available research leads him to postulate rather substantial association be-

6See R. Taft, "The Ability to Judge People," *Psychological Bulletin*, LII (1955), 1-23.

tween emotional adjustment and empathy. A person's emotional adjustment hinges primarily on how he sees himself and how he feels about himself—it is closely linked to his *self-concept*.

One's self-concept provides a kind of psychological "base of operations" that inevitably affects relations with family, friends, business associates, and strangers. Some aspects of the self-concept are at the surface of personality; these are the *publicly held attitudes*—the things we don't mind telling other people about ourselves and our views of the world. And there are some feelings about the self of which we are aware, but which we do not want to share with others—these are the *privately held attitudes* to the self. And buried still deeper are the *subconscious and unconscious aspects*—feelings about "who" we are and "what" we are that somehow we cannot face up to, even to ourselves. The theories of psychoanalysis and depth psychology deal at length with these "disassociated" parts of the self, which as subtly disturbing, often powerful sources of internal turmoil may affect and hinder a person's effective functioning.

Barriers and Aids to Empathy

The individual who has resolved most of his internal conflicts appears in a better position to direct his energies to the understanding of others. He is likely not to meet "booby traps" of his own unconscious devising that prevent accurate perception. The *healthy personality* is based upon a fundamental self-acceptance at all levels—public to unconscious. It relies on an openness to experience, a willingness to respond realistically to relevant cues; it exhibits a lack of dogmatism and a capacity for responding to the world flexibly and dynamically. When we are under pressure, or in a state of anxiety, we are less likely to perceive accurately the motives and actions of those about us. It is only when we have reached a fair give-and-take balance between ourselves and the world that we are in a secure position to venture important human relations judgments.

In light of this, is it likely that in a Nirvana of perfect psychological equilibrium all social perceptions would be accurate? On the basis of what we know, the answer is no. In order to understand others, there must be some driving force, some motivation, some problem. Such cause or problem implies the existence of some tensions within the perceiver. In a fully tensionless state—in a hypothetical state of perfect adjustment—there could be no reason to care about understanding anything or anybody. As a result there would be little meaningful social perception or social interaction. As too many cooks are said to spoil the broth, too many tranquilizers seem to spoil the well-springs of human understanding. While excess tension reduces empathy, its complete absence induces a state of apathy.

The Special Case of Self-Insight

Empathy and self-insight tend to go hand in hand, although the evidence is by no means all in.[7] Fortunate, they say, is the individual who knows how

[7]See, for example, J. S. Bruner and R. Tagiuri, "The Perception of People" in G. Lindzey (editor), *Handbook of Social Psychology*, II (Cambridge, Mass.: Addison-Wesley Publishing Co., 1954), 645–646.

much or how little he truly knows about himself—who is aware of his own capacities, limitations, motivations, and attitudes.

The sole tool that we bring to the task of understanding others is our own personality. The cues we receive from the outside must be processed through the perceptual equipment that is "us"—through lenses of our own background and expectations. If we are to be successful in assessing the meaning of cues that impinge on us, we must become aware of the distortions that may be introduced by our "built-in" perceptual equipment.

A realistic view of our perceptual limitations, and of the kinds of aberrations we tend to introduce in what we see and hear, should help us to make allowances in interpreting the world around us. If, for instance, we are aware that people who seem to be weak and submissive make us irrationally angry, we may be able to develop safeguards against our own unreasonable anger and ultimately gain a more realistic understanding of the motivations of the other person.

Self-insight does not come easy. Many factors militate against it. Central among these is our system of *psychological defenses*—the ways in which we systematically and unconsciously protect ourselves from facing what might be real or imagined threats to our personal security.

These protective distortions—which frequently concern our perceptions of others—help us make reality more palatable. There is no human being alive who is without some pattern of psychological defenses. Unfortunately, the cost of excessive utilization of defenses is the progressive removal from reality. Without some controlled and mild forms of self-delusion, adjustment of the ordinary everyday sort may be difficult. Yet the defenses that we bring into play as we seek to understand ourselves and others seduce us into various states of unreality; they make us see that which is *not* there, and hide that which might be apparent.

In our illustrations of Mike Corey and Jean Krugmeier, not much may have been at stake. However, similar processes, affected by the distortions of psychological defenses, influence decisions of major importance: for example, the selection and promotion of top management personnel, the establishment of budgetary commitments, the theme of advertising campaigns, or the assessment of company performance.

The Force of Attitude

One particularly pervasive pattern of personal defenses found in industry, which interferes with the process of understanding others, is characterized by a high degree of *authoritarianism*, with concurrent *rigidity in perception* and *intolerance for ambiguity*. The authoritarian person seems to need to view the world in clearly defined segments, some strictly black, others strictly white. He does not make much room for gradations—things are clearly good or abominably bad, people friendly or hostile, nations with us or against us. Thus, the authoritarian unconsciously fails to recognize subtle but significant interpersonal phenomena, because he is unable to evaluate shades of gray for what they are.[8] Extreme nonauthoritarian personalities—"nothing is definite—all is a matter of shading"—also encounter difficulties in understanding others

[8]See T. W. Adorno, E. Frenkel-Brunswik, D. J. Levinson, and R. N. Sanford, *The Authoritarian Personality* (New York: Harper & Bros., 1950).

since they too have a singularly single-minded view of what the world and its inhabitants are like.

The attitudes with which we approach the task of understanding others, then, do a great deal to determine just what we will be able to see. Attitudes basically serve as organizing forces that order in some preliminary manner the potential chaos and complexity confronting us. They give meaning to what we are prepared to see and hear. As such, they serve a necessary and useful function.

"Playing the Odds"

The question of whether the holding of stereotypes is necessarily detrimental to accurate social perception deserves consideration. If we define a "stereotype" as an *inaccurate* perception of a given grouping, it follows logically that stereotypes are hindrances. But, more generally, we *do* need to be able to type people by means of broad and flexible generalizations. In that sense, a realistic view of a group of individuals (a kind of "accurate stereotype") may increase the odds for accuracy in our perception of others. Thus we may make assumptions about the characteristics of a specific company's board of directors, about the honor graduates of a college, or about women secretaries. We frame enlightened guesses concerning the manner in which a directive will be interpreted by first-line supervision, the way in which a sales campaign on bottled beer will be received by the housewives in Suburbia, or how the new profit-sharing plan suggested by the union's bargaining committee will strike the company attorney. This kind of "typing," while based upon prior perceptions of individuals and groups, necessarily is a kind of oversimplification; still its use in a consciously wary manner is a constant necessity if we are to relate to people.

Since understanding people involves relative probabilities of being right, caution is always in order. We must ever attempt to remain open to a constant flow of new information which may help us alter our perceptions in the light of changing circumstances. It is the danger of fossilization—the pitfall of "hardening" perceptions irrationally—that needs to be avoided.

Link between Perceiver and Perceived

The personality of the perceived also determines the success of social perception. Ultimately it is the relationship that emerges between perceiver and perceived which becomes crucial. *Communication* linking the two—the sending and receiving of messages (involving feelings as well as content)—becomes raw material underlying the process of understanding others. Cues are messages from the perceived to the perceiver. In each instance, the perceiver "samples" certain small units of behavior that come from the perceived. While these samples in a statistical sense are neither random nor necessarily representative, they form the basis for generalizations that constitute predictions about the behavior of others. As communications develop, a person becomes both perceiver and perceived—sending and receiving cues of great variety and with high speed.

In the relationship between perceiver and perceived it becomes important for the perceiver to elicit cues from the perceived which will do the most to reveal, on a sample basis, the relevant aspects of the perceived's feelings, thoughts, and potential behavior. This ability to break through a person's outer veneer, to penetrate false fronts, has two facets: (1) the perceiver's *skill in facilitating the "sending" of cues* by the perceived, and (2) the perceiver's *skill in picking up and interpreting properly* the cues that have been sent.

Jean Krugmeier, for example, by eliciting fully the attitudes and aspirations of her job applicant might have succeeded in bringing to the surface relevant cues that might have made possible a more sensible evaluation of his potential. She might have reduced the applicant's defensiveness by proving herself receptive to his comments and accepting of him as a person, by listening for his feelings as well as meaning, and by communicating to him her understanding of his point of view.

As we engage in the process of understanding people, our hope for ever increasing accuracy rests partially with our ability to get *feedback* on how others view the accuracy of our perceptions. We must remain in tune with the reactions of others—not in order to become blind automata, but rather to doublecheck and review the validity of our own perceptions.

The Danger of "Expertise"

Usually we receive feedback from members of our own *reference groups*—our families, friends, and business associates. These are the people whose opinions about us usually matter to us. Especially parents and close relatives who haved provided us with experiences which make us what we are often continue to give us, as Robert Burns so aptly put it, "the giftie . . . to see oorsels as ithers see us."

At times, the validity of our insights and understanding of people is assessed by experts, by psychiatrists or psychologists who have been trained in personality diagnosis and behavior prediction. Unfortunately, research has shown that some of these experts, in spite of their intellectual grasp of interpersonal relations, are rather inept judges of people. This startling paradox has some rather persuasive explanations to account for it. First, intellect alone—though a slight help—does not guarantee empathy. More importantly, for some people too much knowledge is a dangerous thing! For them, there exists the danger of *overreaching*. They are confronted with the ever present temptation to read into cues complex "deeper" meanings which in reality may not be there at all. This is the pitfall of imagining psychological ghosts behind each casual remark, simply because of some intellectual predisposition to make interpretations at more esoteric levels.

For experienced clinicians, the process of feedback here again proves to be a partial safeguard. If all too often our views of others, though psychologically "sophisticated," find no confirmation, either by the subject of our perception or through the perceptions of other observers, we may suspect that we are overreaching in our search for perceptual accuracy.

The Situation: Arena for Feelings

Regardless of the specific situation in which social perception takes place, some positive feelings of varying intensity will be exchanged between perceiver and perceived. These feelings condition the process of social perception. They set up *halos* which reduce the accuracy of empathic judgments. If we believe that some persons "can do no wrong," if we are enamored of their righteousness and virtue, if we blindly approve of everything they do—we will be unable accurately to assess their less desirable characteristics or behaviors. The inverse is equally true; pervasive hostility and prejudice also obliterate any chance for a realistic appraisal of people's positive characteristics.

A more subtle manifestation of the impact of feelings on perceptual accuracy can be found in the process of *naive projection* (assuming similarity), the attributing by the perceiver of his own characteristics to the perceived. If few cues are available to the perceiver, if he is unable to utilize those that are available, or if his feelings toward the other person are in fact similar to those he has about himself, projection may become his significant *modus operandi*. The vacuum that might be filled by meaningful cues is taken up by assumptions implying that the perceived resembles the perceiver.

Assuming similarity to another person is neither intrinsically a barrier nor a block to accurate social perception. If the perceived really *is* much like the perceiver with respect to the characteristics involved in the judgment, assuming similarity is clearly warranted. Although some unique psychological perceptual skill may or may not have been at work, accurate social perception will result.

One can visualize an extreme situation in which the major prerequisite for social perceptual accuracy is the knack for picking out associates who resemble us with regard to relevant personality dimensions. If we succeed in this selection, be our choice conscious or unconscious, all we may need in order to understand them is to assume that they are, more or less, replicas of ourselves. Obviously, reality rarely permits this uncritical, though convenient, approach. More likely we may find that we assume similarity where none exists, thus hindering social sensitivity by the unwarranted assumption.

A blind assumption, on the other hand, that we do *not* resemble others (or a particular "other") can also lead to misperception. In most cases, the perceiver and the perceived do share in common some attitudes, feelings, and similar personality characteristics. The challenge confronting us is to recognize those elements that we have in common with other individuals, while at the same time noting the differences that make us unique. Likewise, when dealing with many people, we need to learn to discriminate the relevant differences among them, while remaining aware of the similarities which they, as a group, share. Thus, as a particular boss considers a group of subordinates, he must ask—and answer—these four questions:

1. In what respects is each of these persons like me?
2. In what respects does each of these persons differ from me?
3. In what ways do all these people resemble one another?
4. In what ways is each of these people unique from every other?

Clearly, this is a large order.

The *relative stress* with which people relate to one another also influences their ultimate empathy toward each other. As superiors, for instance, we may find it relatively easy to size up properly the feelings and attitudes of our subordinates; as subordinates our anxieties may becloud our perceptions of our superiors' intent and attitudes. The well-known phenomenon of "seeing red" when angered and the notion that "love is blind" represent classic illustrations of the befogging effect of strong emotions on social perception.

Most accurate social perception, it seems, occurs under conditions which do not involve extremely charged feelings.

Because each individual approaches the task of social perception in his own particular situation, his personal receptivity will be influenced by the nature of this situation. An executive who operates in an environment of "yes-men" may come to be attuned to hearing "yes," even if the real sound is more like "maybe." An amusing cartoon series of medical specialists on vacation shows a plastic surgeon fascinated by the Sphinx in Egypt, a urologist intrigued by the shapes of swimming pools, and a gynecologist marveling at the fertile life in the farm's pigsty.

The *broader culture*, too, provides certain expectations and highlights specific types of cues. The "Man in the Gray Flannel Suit," the "Rate Buster," the "Organization Man," the "Huckster," the "Tycoon"—all of these are cultural types which are readily found on the American business scene, and whose existence is typically recognized by those of us who share a common cultural heritage.

Pay-Off for Empathy

Whatever its correlates and roots, empathy provides a "road map" defining properly the social world confronting the perceiver. There is no guarantee, however, that even the most understanding perceiver will be able to behave appropriately, even if his road map is clear and accurate. He further requires an adequate repertoire of behaviors—*behavioral flexibility*—to provoke the kinds of action that will most effectively attain the goals he seeks.

Social sensitivity and social effectiveness do not necessarily go hand in hand. In *The Outsider,* Colin Wilson[9] draws the portrait of the cultural hero who sees too much, whose perceptions penetrate all too well, but who tragically lacks the customary social skills for functioning within the reality that he perceives.

"Seeing too much," if not buttressed by an appropriate range of available behaviors, can indeed prove a threat to self and others and thereby reduce ultimate social effectiveness. In terms of actual pay-off, having too much empathy may well be as detrimental as having too little. Seeing the surrounding social world in proper perspective is useful only if knowledge can be successfully implemented by action.

As an executive faces the myriad decisions he needs to make, it becomes quite clear that he must master two tasks: he must learn to see accurately the human, as well as the inanimate, factors of the total scene; and he must acquire the skills of action which, while based upon accurate perception, tap well-springs of behavior that ultimately lead to the successful attainment of personal and organizational goals.

Social effectiveness can be developed. For some people, dealing with feelings is as easy as recognizing and manipulating facts. For others, the world of emotions is mysterious indeed. The improvement of social skills is a many-sided challenge. Neither intellectual learning nor emotional experience alone suffice. Nor is the heightening of social sensitivity the sole sacrosanct cure-all. Experiences are needed that reach the full personality. Increased social effectiveness depends on a "tool-kit" of appropriate behaviors, in addition to enhanced understanding of social situations. Special clinically-oriented train-

[9]Colin Wilson, *The Outsider* (Boston: Houghton Mifflin Co., 1956).

ing experiences[10] hold promise to bring about integrated intellectual, emotional and behavioral learnings that can make for greater effectiveness in dealing with others.

PERCEPTION: IMPLICATIONS FOR ADMINISTRATION

SHELDON S. ZALKIND
TIMOTHY W. COSTELLO

Management practice is being increasingly influenced by behavioral science research in the areas of group dynamics, problem solving and decision making, and motivation. One aspect of behavior which has not been fully or consistently emphasized is the process of perception, particulary the recent work on person perception.

In this paper we shall summarize some of the findings on perception as developed through both laboratory and organizational research and point out some of the administrative and managerial implications. We discuss first some basic factors in the nature of the perceptual process including need and set; second, some research on forming impressions; third, the characteristics of the perceiver and the perceived; fourth, situational and organizational influences on perception; and finally, perceptual influences on interpersonal adjustment.

Nature of the Perceptual Process

What are some of the factors influencing perception? In answering the question it is well to begin by putting aside the attitude of naive realism, which suggests that our perceptions simply register accurately what is "out there." It is necessary rather to consider what influences distort one's perceptions and judgments of the outside world. Some of the considerations identified in the literature up to the time of Johnson's 1944 review of the research on object

Reprinted from *Administrative Science Quarterly*, VII (September 1962), 218–35, by permission of the authors and the publisher. Portions of this article were originally presented at the Eighth Annual International Meeting of The Institute of Management Sciences in Brussels, August 1961.

[10]Sensitivity Training is one approach designed to improve a person's behavioral flexibility. For a description see, for example, Irving R. Weschler, Robert Tannenbaum, and John H. Zenger, *Yardsticks for Human Relations Training*, Adult Education Association Monograph No. 2 (Chicago: Adult Education Association, 1957). Similar programs sponsored by the National Training Laboratories in Group Development are described in numerous publications, especially those authored by Leland P. Bradford.

perception (where distortion may be even less extreme than in person perception) led him to suggest the following about the perceiver[1]:

1. He may be influenced by considerations that he may not be able to identify, responding to cues that are below the threshold of his awareness. For example, a judgment as to the size of an object may be influenced by its color even though the perceiver may not be attending to color.

2. When required to form difficult perceptual judgments, he may respond to irrelevant cues to arrive at a judgment. For example, in trying to assess honesty, it has been shown that the other person's smiling or not smiling is used as a cue to judge his honesty.

3. In making abstract or intellectual judgments, he may be influenced by emotional factors—what is liked is perceived as correct.

4. He will weigh perceptual evidence coming from respected (or favored) sources more heavily than that coming from other sources.

5. He may not be able to identify all the factors on which his judgments are based. Even if he is aware of these factors he is not likely to realize how much weight he gives to them.

These considerations do not imply that we respond only to the subtle or irrelevant cues or to emotional factors. We often perceive on the basis of the obvious, but we are quite likely to be responding as well to the less obvious or less objective.

In 1958, Bruner, citing a series of researches, described what he called the "New Look" in perception as one in which personal determinants of the perceptual process were being stressed.[2] Bruner summarized earlier work and showed the importance of such subjective influences as needs, values, cultural background, and interests on the perceptual process. In his concept of "perceptual readiness" he described the importance of the framework or category system that the perceiver himself brings to the perceiving process.

Tapping a different vein of research, Cantril described perceiving as a "transaction" between the perceiver and the perceived, a process of negotiation in which the perceptual end product is a result both of influences within the perceiver and of characteristics of the perceived.[3]

One of the most important of the subjective factors that influence the way we perceive identified by Bruner and others, is *set*. A study by Kelley illustrated the point.[4] He found that those who were previously led to expect to meet a "warm" person, not only made different judgments about him, but also behaved differently toward him, than those who were expecting a "cold" one. The fact was that they simultaneously were observing the same person in the same situation. Similarly, Strickland indicated the influence of set in determining how closely supervisors feel they must supervise their subordinates.[5] Because of prior expectation one person was trusted more than another and

[1]D, M. Johnson, "A Systematic Treatment of Judgment," *Psychological Bulletin*, XLII (1945), 193–224.

[2]J. S. Bruner, "Social Psychology and Perception," in *Readings in Social Psychology,* ed. E. Maccoby, T. Newcomb, and E. Hartley (3d ed.; New York, 1958), pp. 85–94.

[3]H. Cantril, "Perception and Interpersonal Relations," *American Journal of Psychiatry*, CXIV (1957), 119–26.

[4]H. H. Kelley, "The Warm–Cold Variable in First Impressions of Persons," *Journal of Personality*, XVIII (1950), 431–39.

[5]L. H. Strickland, "Surveillance and Trust," *Journal of Personality*, XXVI (1958), 200–215.

was thought to require less supervision than another, even though performance records were identical.

Forming Impressions of Others

The data on forming impressions is of particular importance in administration. An administrator is confronted many times with the task of forming an impression of another person—a new employee at his desk, a visiting member from the home office, a staff member he has not personally met before. His own values, needs, and expectations will play a part in the impression he forms. Are there other factors that typically operate in this area of administrative life? One of the more obvious influences is the physical appearance of the person being perceived. In a study of this point Mason was able to demonstrate that people agree on what a leader should look like and that there is no relationship between the facial characteristics agreed upon and those possessed by actual leaders.[6] In effect, we have ideas about what leaders look like and we can give examples, but we ignore the many exceptions that statistically cancel out the examples.

In the sometimes casual, always transitory situations in which one must form impressions of others it is a most natural tendency to jump to conclusions and form impressions without adequate evidence. Unfortunately, as Dailey showed, unless such impressions are based on important and relevant data, they are not likely to be accurate.[7] Too often in forming impressions the perceiver does not know what is relevant, important, or predictive of later behavior. Dailey's research furthermore supports the cliche that, accurate or not, first impressions are lasting.

Generalizing from other research in the field, Soskin described four limitations on the ability to form accurate impressions of others.[8] First, the impression is likely to be disproportionately affected by the type of situation or surroundings in which the impression is made and influenced too little by the person perceived. Thus the plush luncheon club in which one first meets a man will dominate the impression of the man himself. Second, although impressions are frequently based on a limited sample of the perceived person's behavior, the generalization that the perceiver makes will be sweeping. A third limitation is that the situation may not provide an opportunity for the person perceived to show behavior relevant to the traits about which impressions are formed. Casual conversation or questions, for example, provide few opportunities to demonstrate intelligence or work characteristics, yet the perceiver often draws conclusions about these from an interview. Finally, Soskin agrees with Bruner and Cantril that the impression of the person perceived may be distorted by some highly individualized reaction of the perceiver.

But the pitfalls are not yet all spelled out; it is possible to identify some other distorting influences on the process of forming impressions. Research has brought into sharp focus some typical errors, the more important being stereotyping, halo effect, projection, and perceptual defense.

[6]D. J. Mason, "Judgments of Leadership Based upon Physiognomic Cues," *Journal of Abnormal and Social Psychology*, LIV (1957), 273–74.

[7]C. A. Dailey, "The Effects of Premature Conclusion upon the Acquisition of Understanding of a Person," *Journal of Psychology*, XXIII (1952), 133–52.

[8]W. E. Soskin, "Influence of Information on Bias in Social Perception," *Journal of Personality*, XXII (1953), 118–27.

The word "stereotyping" was first used by Walter Lippmann in 1922 to describe bias in perceiving peoples. He wrote of "pictures in people's heads," called stereotypes, which guided (distorted) their perception of others. The term has long been used to describe judgments made about people on the basis of their ethnic group membership. For example, some say, "Herman Schmidt [being German] is industrious." Stereotyping also predisposes judgments in many other areas of interpersonal relations. Stereotypes have developed about many types of groups, and they help to prejudice many of our perceptions about their members. Examples of stereotypes of groups other than those based on ethnic identification are bankers, supervisors, union members, poor people, rich people, and administrators. Many unverified qualities are assigned to people principally because of such group memberships.

In a research demonstration of stereotyping, Haire found that labeling a photograph as that of a management representative caused an impression to be formed of the person, different from that formed when it was labeled as that of a union leader.[9] Management and labor formed different impressions, each seeing his opposite as less dependable than his own group. In addition, each side saw his own group as being better able than the opposite group to understand a point of view different from its own. For example, managers felt that other managers were better able to appreciate labor's point of view than labor was able to appreciate management's point of view. Each had similar stereotypes of his opposite and considered the thinking, emotional characteristics, and interpersonal relations of his opposite as inferior to his own. As Stagner pointed out, "It is plain that unionists perceiving company officials in a stereotyped way are less efficient than would be desirable. Similarly, company executives who see all labor unions as identical are not showing good judgment or discrimination."[10]

One of the troublesome aspects of stereotypes is that they are so widespread. Finding the same stereotypes to be widely held should not tempt one to accept their accuracy. It may only mean that many people are making the same mistake. Allport has demonstrated that there need not be a "kernel of truth" in a widely held stereotype.[11] He has shown that while a prevalent stereotype of Armenians labeled them as dishonest, a credit reporting association gave them credit ratings as good as those given other ethnic groups.

Bruner and Perlmutter found that there is an international stereotype for "businessmen" and "teachers."[12] They indicated that the more widespread one's experience with diverse members of a group, the less their group membership will affect the impression formed.

An additional illustration of stereotyping is provided by Luft.[13] His research suggests that perception of personality adjustment may be influenced by stereotypes, associating adjustment with high income and maladjustment with low income.

[9]M. Haire, "Role Perceptions in Labor-Management Relations: An Experimental Approach," *Industrial Labor Relations Review,* VIII (1955), 204-16.

[10]R. Stagner, *Psychology of Industrial Conflict* (New York, 1956), p. 35.

[11]G. Allport, *Nature of Prejudice* (Cambridge, Mass., 1954).

[12]J. S. Bruner and H. V. Perlmutter, "Compatriot and Foreigner: A Study of Impression Formation in Three Countries," *Journal of Abnormal and Social Psychology,* LV (1957), 253-60.

[13]J. Luft, "Monetary Value and the Perception of Persons," *Journal of Social Psychology,* XLVI (1957), 245-51.

The term "halo effect" was first used in 1920 to describe a process in which a general impression which is favorable or unfavorable is used by judges to evaluate several specific traits. The "halo" in such case serves as a screen keeping the perceiver from actually seeing the trait he is judging. It has received the most attention because of its effect on rating employee performance. In the rating situation, a supervisor may single out one trait, either good or bad, and use this as the basis for his judgment of all other traits. For example, an excellent attendance record causes judgments of productivity, high quality of work, and so forth. One study in the U.S. Army showed that officers who were liked were judged more intelligent than those who were disliked, even though they had the same scores on intelligence tests.

We examine halo effect here because of its general effect on forming impressions. Bruner and Taguiri suggest that it is likely to be most extreme when we are forming impressions of traits that provide minimal cues in the individual's behavior, when the traits have moral overtones, or when the perceiver must judge traits with which he has had little experience.[14] A rather disturbing conclusion is suggested by Symonds that halo effect is more marked the more we know the acquaintance.[15]

A somewhat different aspect of the halo effect is suggested by the research of Grove and Kerr.[16] They found that knowledge that the company was in receivership caused employees to devalue the higher pay and otherwise superior working conditions of their company as compared to those in a financially secure firm.

Psychologists have noted a tendency in perceivers to link certain traits. They assume, for example, that when a person is aggressive he will also have high energy or that when a person is "warm" he will also be generous and have a good sense of humor. This logical error, as it has been called, is a special form of the halo effect and is best illustrated in the research of Asch.[17] In his study the addition of one trait to a list of traits produced a major change in the impression formed. Knowing that a person was intelligent, skillful, industrious, determined, practical, cautious, and warm led a group to judge him to be also wise, humorous, popular, and imaginative. When warm was replaced by cold, a radically different impression (beyond the difference between warm and cold) was formed. Kelley's research illustrated the same type of error.[18] This tendency is not indiscriminate; with the pair "polite–blunt," less change was found than with the more central traits of "warm–cold."

In evaluating the effect of halo on perceptual distortion, we may take comfort from the work of Wishner, which showed that those traits that correlate more highly with each other are more likely to lead to a halo effect than those that are unrelated.[19]

[14]J. S. Bruner and A. Taguiri, "The Perception of People," in *Handbook of Social Psychology*, ed. G. Lindzey (Cambridge, Mass., 1954), chap. xvii.

[15]P. M. Symonds, "Notes on Rating," *Journal of Applied Psychology*, VII (1925), 188–95.

[16]A. Grove and W. A. Kerr, "Specific Evidence on Origin of Halo Effect in Measurement of Morale," *Journal of Social Psychology*, XXXIV (1951), 165–70.

[17]S. Asch, "Forming Impressions of Persons," *Journal of Abnormal and Social Psychology*, LX (1946), 258–90.

[18]Kelley, *op. cit.*

[19]J. Wishner, "Reanalysis of 'Impressions of Personality,'" *Psychological Review*, LXVII (1060), 96–112.

A defense mechanism available to everyone is projection, in which one relieves one's feelings of guilt or failure by projecting blame onto someone else. Over the years the projection mechanism has been assigned various meanings. The original use of the term was concerned with the mechanism to defend oneself from unacceptable feelings. There has since been a tendency for the term to be used more broadly, meaning to ascribe or attribute any of one's own characteristics to other people. The projection mechanism concerns us here because it influences the perceptual process. An early study by Murray illustrates its effect.[20] After playing a dramatic game, "Murder," his subjects attributed much more maliciousness to people whose photographs were judged than did a control group which had not played the game. The current emotional state of the perceiver tended to influence his perceptions of others; i.e., frightened perceivers judged people to be frightening. More recently, Feshback and Singer revealed further dynamics of the process.[21] In their study, subjects who had been made fearful judged a stimulus person (presented in a moving picture) as both more fearful and more aggressive than did non-fearful perceivers. The authors were able to demonstrate further that the projection mechanism at work here was reduced when their subjects were encouraged to admit and talk about their fears.

Sears provides an illustration of a somewhat different type of projection and its effects on perception.[22] In his study projection is seeing our own undesirable personality characteristics in other people. He demonstrated that people high in such traits as stinginess, obstinacy, and disorderliness, tended to rate others much higher on these traits than did those who were low in these undesirable characteristics. The tendency to project was particularly marked among subjects who had the least insight into their own personalities.

Research thus suggests that our perceptions may characteristically be distorted by emotions we are experiencing or traits that we possess. Placed in the administrative settings, the research would suggest, for example, that a manager frightened by rumored organizational changes might not only judge others to be more frightened than they were, but also assess various policy decisions as more frightening than they were. Or a general foreman lacking insight into his own incapacity to delegate might be oversensitive to this trait in his superiors.

Perceptual Defense

Another distorting influence, which has been called perceptual defense, has also been demonstrated by Haire and Grunes to be a source of error.[23] In their research they ask, in effect, "Do we put blinders on to defend ourselves from seeing those events which might disturb us?" The concept of perceptual defense offers an excellent description of perceptual distortion at work and

[20]H. A. Murray, "The Effect of Fear upon Estimates of the Maliciousness of Other Personalities," *Journal of Social Psychology*, IV (1933), 310–29.

[21]S. Feshback and S. D. Singer, "The Effects of Fear Arousal upon Social Perception," *Journal of Abnormal and Social Psychology*, LV (1957), 283–88.

[22]R. R. Sears, "Experimental Studies of Perception. I. Attribution of Traits," *Journal of Social Psychology*, VII (1936), 151–63.

[23]M. Haire and W. F. Grunes, "Perceptual Defenses: Processes Protecting an Original Perception of Another Personality," *Human Relations*, III (1958), 403–12.

demonstrates that when confronted with a fact inconsistent with a stereotype already held by a person, the perceiver is able to distort the data in such a way as to eliminate the inconsistency. Thus, by perceiving inaccurately, he defends himself from having to change his stereotypes.

Characteristics of Perceiver and Perceived

We have thus far been talking largely about influences on the perceptual process without specific regard to the perceiver and his characteristics. Much recent research has tried to identify some characteristics of the perceiver and their influence on the perception of other people.

The Perceiver

A thread that would seem to tie together many current findings is the tendency to use oneself as the norm or standard by which one perceives or judges others. If we examine current research, certain conclusions are suggested:

1. *Knowing oneself makes it easier to see others accurately.* Norman showed that when one is aware of what his own personal characteristics are, he makes fewer errors in perceiving others.[24] Weingarten has shown that people with insight are less likely to view the world in black-and-white terms and to give extreme judgments about others.[25]

2. *One's own characteristics affect the characteristics he is likely to see in others.* Secure people (compared to insecure) tend to see others as warm rather than cold, as was shown by Bossom and Maslow.[26] The extent of one's own sociability influences the degree of importance one gives to the sociability of other people when one forms impressions of them.[27] The person with "authoritarian" tendencies is more likely to view others in terms of power and is less sensitive to the psychological or personality characteristics of other people than is a non-authoritarian.[28] The relatively few categories one uses in describing other people tend to be those one uses in describing oneself.[29] Thus traits which are important to the perceiver will be used more when he forms impressions of others. He has certain constant tendencies, both with regard to using certain categories in judging others and to the amount of weight given to these categories.[30]

[24]R. D. Norman, "The Interrelationships among Acceptance–Rejection, Self–Other, Insight into Self, and Realistic Perception of Others," *Journal of Social Psychology*, XXXVII (1953), 205–35.

[25]E. Weingarten, "A Study of Selective Perception in Clinical Judgment," *Journal of Personality*, XVII (1949), 369–400.

[26]J. Bossom and A. H. Maslow, "Security of Judges as a Factor in Impressions of Warmth in Others," *Journal of Abnormal and Social Psychology*, LV (1957), 147–48.

[27]D. T. Benedetti and J. G. Hill, "A Determiner of the Centrality of a Trait in Impression Formation," *Journal of Abnormal and Social Psychology*, LX (1960), 278–79.

[28]E. E. Jones, "Authoritarianism as a Determinant of First-Impressions Formation," *Journal of Personality*, XXIII (1954), 107–27.

[29]A. H. Hastorf, S. A. Richardson, and S. M. Dombusch, "The Problem of Relevance in the Study of Person Perception," in *Person Perception and Interpersonal Behavior*, ed. R. Taguiri and L. Petrullo (Stanford, Calif., 1958).

[30]L. J. Cronbach, "Processes Affecting Scores on 'Understanding of Others' and 'Assumed Similarity,' " *Psychology Bulletin*, LII (1955), 173–93.

3. *The person who accepts himself is more likely to be able to see favorable aspects of other people.*[31] This relates in part to the accuracy of his perceptions. If the perceiver accepts himself as he is, he widens his range of vision in seeing others; he can look at them and be less likely to be very negative or critical. In those areas in which he is more insecure, he sees more problems in other people.[32] We are more likely to like others who have traits we accept in ourselves and reject those who have the traits which we do not like in ourselves.[33]

4. *Accuracy in perceiving others is not a single skill.* While there have been some variations in the findings, as Gage has shown, some consistent results do occur.[34] The perceiver tends to interpret the feelings others have about him in terms of his feeling toward them.[35] One's ability to perceive others accurately may depend on how sensitive one is to differences between people and also to the norms (outside of oneself) for judging them.[36] Thus, as Taft has shown, the ability to judge others does not seem to be a single skill.[37]

Possibly the results in these four aspects of person perception can be viewed most constructively in connection with earlier points on the process of perception. The administrator (or any other individual) who wishes to perceive someone else accurately must look at the other person, not at himself. The things that he looks at in someone else are influenced by his own traits. But if he knows his own traits, he can be aware that they provide a frame of reference for him. His own traits help to furnish the categories that he will use in perceiving others. His characteristics, needs, and values can partly limit his vision and his awareness of the differences between others. The question one could ask when viewing another is: "Am I looking at him, and forming my impression of his behavior in the situation, or am I just comparing him with myself?"

There is the added problem of being set to observe the personality traits in another which the perceiver does not accept in himself, e.g., being somewhat autocratic. At the same time he may make undue allowances in others for those of his own deficiencies which do not disturb him but might concern some people, e.g., not following prescribed procedures.

The Perceived

Lest we leave the impression that it is only the characteristics of the perceiver that stand between him and others in his efforts to know them, we turn now to some characteristics of the person being perceived which raise problems in perception. It is possible to demonstrate, for example, that the status of the person perceived is a variable influencing judgments about his behavior. Thibaut and Riecken have shown that even though two people behave in iden-

[31]K. T. Omwake, "The Relation between Acceptance of Self and Acceptance of Others Shown by Three Personality Inventories," *Journal of Consulting Psychology*, XVIII (1954), 443–46.

[32]Weingarten, *op. cit.*

[33]R. M. Lundy *et al.,* "Self Acceptability and Descriptions of Sociometric Choices," *Journal of Abnormal and Social Psychology*, LI (1955), 260–62.

[34]N. L. Gage, "Accuracy of Social Perception and Effectiveness in Interpersonal Relationships," *Journal of Personality,* XXII (1953), 128–41.

[35]R. Taguiri, J. S. Bruner, and R. Blake, "On the Relation between Feelings and Perceptions of Feelings among Members of Small Groups," in *Readings in Social Psychology*.

[36]U. Bronfenbrenner, J. Harding, and M. Gallway, "The Measurement of Skill in Social Perception," in *Talent and Society*, ed. McClelland *et al.* (Princeton, N.J., 1958), pp. 29–111.

[37]R. Taft, "The Ability to Judge People," *Psychological Bulletin,* LII (1955), 1–21.

tical fashion, status differences between them cause a perceiver to assign different motivations for the behavior.[38] Concerning co-operativeness, they found that high status persons are judged as wanting to co-operate and low status persons as having to co-operate. In turn, more liking is shown for the person of high status than for the person of low status. Presumably, more credit is given when the boss says, "Good morning," to us than when a subordinate says the same thing.

Bruner indicated that we use categories to simplify our perceptual activities. In the administrative situation, status is one type of category, and the role provides another. Thus the remarks of Mr. Jones in the sales department are perceived differently from those of Smith in the purchasing department, although both may say the same thing. Also, one who knows Jones's role in the organization will perceive his behavior differently from one who does not know Jones's role. The process of categorizing on the basis of roles is similar to, if not identical with, the stereotyping process described earlier.

Visibility of the traits judged is also an important variable influencing the accuracy of perception.[39] Visibility will depend, for example, on how free the other person feels to express the trait. It has been demonstrated that we are more accurate in judging people who like us than people who dislike us. The explanation suggested is that most people in our society feel constraint in showing their dislike, and therefore the cues are less visible.

Some traits are not visible simply because they provide few external cues for their presence. Loyalty, for example, as opposed to level of energy, provides few early signs for observation. Even honesty cannot be seen in the situations in which most impressions are formed. As obvious as these comments might be, in forming impressions many of us nevertheless continue to judge the presence of traits which are not really visible. Frequently the practical situation demands judgments, but we should recognize the frail reeds upon which we are leaning and be prepared to observe further and revise our judgments with time and closer acquaintance.

Situational Influences on Perception

Some recent research clearly points to the conclusion that the whole process of interpersonal perception is, at least in part, a function of the *group* (or interpersonal) context in which the perception occurs. Much of the research has important theoretical implications for a psychology of interpersonal relations. In addition, there are some suggestions of value for administrators. It is possible to identify several characteristics of the interpersonal climate which have direct effect on perceptual accuracy. As will be noted, these are characteristics which can be known, and in some cases controlled, in administrative settings.

Bieri provides data for the suggestion that when people are given an opportunity to interact in a friendly situation, they tend to see others as similar to themselves.[40] Applying his suggestion to the administrative situation, we can

[38]J. W. Thibaut and H. W. Riecken, "Some Determinants and Consequences of the Perception of Social Causality," *Journal of Personality*, XXIV (1955), 113-33.

[39]Bruner and Taguiri, *op. cit.*

[40]J. Bieri, "Change in Interpersonal Perception Following Interaction," *Journal of Abnormal and Social Psychology*, XLVIII (1953), 61-66.

rationalize as follows: Some difficulties of administrative practice grow out of beliefs that different interest groups in the organization are made up of different types of people. Obviously once we believe that people in other groups are different, we will be predisposed to see the differences. We can thus find, from Bieri's and from Rosenbaum's work, an administratrive approach for attacking the problem.[41] If we can produce an interacting situation which is cooperative rather than competitive, the likelihood of seeing other people as similar to ourselves is increased.

Exline's study adds some other characteristics of the social context which may influence perception.[42] Paraphrasing his conclusions to adapt them to the administrative scene, we can suggest that when a committee group is made up of congenial members who are willing to continue work in the same group, their perceptions of the goal-directed behavior of fellow committee members will be more accurate, although observations of purely personal behavior (as distinguished from goal-directed behavior) may be less accurate.[43] The implications for setting up committees and presumably other interacting work groups seem clear: Do not place together those with a past history of major personal clashes. If they must be on the same committee, each must be helped to see that the other is working toward the same goal.

An interesting variation in this area of research is the suggestion from Ex's work that perceptions will be more influenced or swayed by relatively unfamiliar people in the group than by those who are intimates.[44] The concept needs further research, but it provides the interesting suggestion that we may give more credit to strangers for having knowledge, since we do not really know, than we do to our intimates, whose backgrounds and limitations we feel we do know.

The *organization*, and one's place in it, may also be viewed as the context in which perceptions take place. A study by Dearborn and Simon illustrates this point.[45] Their data support the hypothesis that the administrator's perceptions will often be limited to those aspects of a situation which relate specifically to his own department, despite an attempt to influence him away from such selectivity.

Perception of self among populations at different levels in the hierarchy also offers an opportunity to judge the influence of organizational context on perceptual activity. Porter's study of the self-descriptions of managers and line workers indicated that both groups saw themselves in different terms, which corresponded to their positions in the organization's hierarchy.[46] He stated that managers used leadership-type traits (e.g., inventive) to describe themselves, while line workers used follower-type terms (e.g., coopera-

[41]M. E. Rosenbaum, "Social Perception and the Motivational Structure of Interpersonal Relations," *Journal of Abnormal and Social Psychology*, LIX (1959), 130–33.

[42]R. V. Exline, "Interrelations among Two Dimensions of Socjometric Status, Group Congeniality and Accuracy of Social Perception," *Sociometry*, XXIII (1960), 85–101.

[43]R. V. Exline, "Group Climate as a Factor in the Relevance and Accuracy of Social Perception," *Journal of Abnormal and Social Psychology*, LV (1957), 382–88.

[44]J. Ex, "The Nature of the Relation between Two Persons and the Degree of Their Influence on Each Other," *Acta Psychologica*, XVII (1960), 39–54.

[45]D. C. Dearborn and H. A. Simon, "Selective Perception: A Note on the Departmental Identifications of Executives," *Sociometry*, XXI (1958), 140–44.

[46]L. W. Porter, "Differential Self-Perceptions of Management Personnel and Line Workers," *Journal of Applied Psychology*, XLII (1958), 105–9.

tive). The question of which comes first must be asked: Does the manager see himself this way because of his current position in the organization? Or is this self-picture an expression of a more enduring personal characteristic that helped bring the manager to his present position? This study does not answer that question, but it does suggest to an administrator the need to be aware of the possibly critical relationship between one's hierarchical role and self-perception.

Perceptual Influences on Interpersonal Adjustment

Throughout this paper, we have examined a variety of influences on the perceptual process. There has been at least the inference that the operations of such influences on perception would in turn affect behavior that would follow. Common-sense judgment suggests that being able to judge other people accurately facilitates smooth and effective interpersonal adjustments. Nevertheless, the relationship between perception and consequent behavior is itself in need of direct analysis. Two aspects may be identified: (1) the effect of accuracy of perception on subsequent behavior and (2) the effect of the duration of the relationship and the opportunity for experiencing additional cues.

First then, from the applied point of view, we can ask a crucial question: Is there a relationship between accuracy of social perception and adjustment to others? While the question might suggest a quick affirmative answer, research findings are inconsistent. Steiner attempted to resolve some of these inconsistencies by stating that accuracy may have an effect on interaction under the following conditions: when the interacting persons are co-operatively motivated, when the behavior which is accurately perceived is relevant to the activities of these persons, and when members are free to alter their behavior on the basis of their perceptions.[47]

Where the relationship provides opportunity only to form an impression, a large number of subjective factors, i.e., set, stereotypes, projections, etc., operate to create an early impression, which is frequently erroneous. In more enduring relationships a more balanced appraisal may result, since increased interaction provides additional cues for judgment. In his study of the acquaintance process, Newcomb showed that while early perception of favorable traits caused attraction to the perceived person, over a four-month period the early cues for judging favorable traits became less influential.[48] With time, a much broader basis was used which included comparisons with others with whom one had established relationships. Such findings suggest that the warning about perceptual inaccuracies implicit in the earlier sections of this paper apply with more force to the short-term process of impression forming than to relatively extended acquaintance-building relationships. One would thus hope that rating an employee after a year of service would be a more objective performance than appraising him in a selection interview—a hope that would be fulfilled only when the rater had provided himself with opportunities for broadening the cues he used in forming his first impressions.

[47]I. Steiner, "Interpersonal Behavior As Influenced by Accuracy of Social Perception," *Psychological Review*, LXII (1955), 268–75.
[48]T. M. Newcomb, "The Perception of Interpersonal Attraction," *American Psychologist*, XI (1956), 575–86.

Summary

Two principal suggestions which increase the probability of more effective administrative action emerge from the research data. One suggestion is that the administrator be continuously aware of the intricacies of the perceptual process and thus be warned to avoid arbitrary and categorical judgments and to seek reliable evidence before judgments are made. A second suggestion grows out of the first: increased accuracy in one's self-perception can make possible the flexibility to seek evidence and to shift position as time provides additional evidence.

Nevertheless, not every effort designed to improve perceptual accuracy will bring about such accuracy. The dangers of too complete reliance on formal training for perceptual accuracy are suggested in a study by Crow.[49] He found that a group of senior medical students were somewhat less accurate in their perceptions of others after a period of training in physician-patient relationships than were an untrained control group. The danger is that a little learning encourages the perceiver to respond with increased sensitivity to individual differences without making it possible for him to gauge the real meaning of the differences he has seen.

Without vigilance to perceive accurately and to minimize as far as possible the subjective approach in perceiving others, effective administration is handicapped. On the other hand research would not support the conclusion that perceptual distortions will not occur simply because the administrator says he will try to be objective. The administrator or manager will have to work hard to avoid seeing only what he wants to see and to guard against fitting everything into what he is set to see.

We are not yet sure of the ways in which training for perceptual accuracy can best be accomplished, but such training cannot be ignored. In fact, one can say that one of the important tasks of administrative science is to design research to test various training procedures for increasing perceptual accuracy.

[49]W. J. Crow, "Effect of Training on Interpersonal Perception," *Journal of Abnormal and Social Psychology,* LV (1957), 355-59.

11 managing differences in the multicultural organization

MOTIVATION, LEADERSHIP, AND ORGANIZATION: DO AMERICAN THEORIES APPLY ABROAD?

GEERT HOFSTEDE

A well-known experiment used in organizational behavior courses involves showing the class an ambiguous picture—one that can be interpreted in two different ways. One such picture represents either an attractive young girl or an ugly old woman, depending on the way you look at it. Some of my colleagues and I use the experiment, which demonstrates how different people in the same situation may perceive quite different things. We start by asking half of the class to close their eyes while we show the other half a slightly altered version of the picture—one in which only the young girl can be seen—for only five seconds. Then we ask those who just saw the young girl's picture to close their eyes while we give the other half of the class a five-second look at a version in which only the old woman can be seen. After this preparation we show the ambiguous picture to everyone at the same time.

The results are amazing—most of those "conditioned" by seeing the young girl first see only the young girl in the ambiguous picture, and those "conditioned" by seeing the old woman tend to see only the old woman. We then ask one of those who perceive the old woman to explain to one of those who perceive the young girl what he or she sees, and vice versa, until everyone finally sees both images in the picture. Each group usually finds it very difficult to get its views across to the other one and sometimes there's considerable irritation at how "stupid" the other group is.

Cultural Conditioning

I use this experiment to introduce a discussion on cultural conditioning. Basically, it shows that in five seconds I can condition half a class to see something different from what the other half sees. If this is so in the simple

---

classroom situation, how much stronger should differences in perception of the same reality be between people who have been conditioned by different education and life experience—not for five seconds, but for twenty, thirty, or forty years?

I define culture as the collective mental programming of the people in an environment. Culture is not a characteristic of individuals; it encompasses a number of people who were conditioned by the same education and life experience. When we speak of the culture of a group, a tribe, a geographical region, a national minority, or a nation, culture refers to the collective mental programming that these people have in common; the programming that is different from that of other groups, tribes, regions, minorities or majorities, or nations.

Culture, in this sense of collective mental programming, is often difficult to change; if it changes at all, it does so slowly. This is so not only because it exists in the minds of the people but, if it is shared by a number of people, because it has become crystallized in the institutions these people have built together: their family structures, educational structures, religious organizations, associations, forms of government, work organizations, law, literature, settlement patterns, buildings and even, as I hope to show, scientific theories. All of these reflect common beliefs that derive from the common culture.

Although we are all conditioned by cultural influences at many different levels—family, social, group, geographical region, professional environment—this article deals specifically with the influence of our national environment: that is, our country. Most countries' inhabitants share a national character that's more clearly apparent to foreigners than to the nationals themselves; it represents the cultural mental programming that the nationals tend to have in common.

National Culture in Four Dimensions

The concept of national culture or national character has suffered from vagueness. There has been little consensus on what represents the national culture of, for example, Americans, Mexicans, French, or Japanese. We seem to lack even the terminology to describe it. Over a period of six years, I have been involved in a large research project on national cultures. For a set of 40 independent nations, I have tried to determine empirically the main criteria by which their national cultures differed. I found four such criteria, which I label dimensions; these are Power Distance, Uncertainty Avoidance, Individualism-Collectivism, and Masculinity-Femininity. To understand the dimensions of national culture, we can compare it with the dimensions of personality we use when we describe individuals' behavior. In recruiting, an organization often tries to get an impression of a candidate's dimensions of personality, such as intelligence (high-low); energy level (active-passive); and emotional stability (stable-unstable). These distinctions can be refined through the use of certain tests, but it's essential to have a set of criteria whereby the characteristics of individuals can be meaningfully described. The dimensions of national culture I use represent a corresponding set of criteria for describing national cultures.

Characterizing a national culture does not, of course, mean that every person in the nation has all the characteristics assigned to that culture. Therefore, in describing national cultures we refer to the common elements

The Research Data

The four dimensions of national culture were found through a combination of theoretical reasoning and massive statistical analysis, in what is most likely the largest survey material ever obtained with a single questionnaire. This survey material was collected between 1967 and 1973 among employees of subsidiaries of one large U.S.-based multinational corporation (MNC) in 40 countries around the globe. The total data bank contains more than 116,000 questionnaires collected from virtually everyone in the corporation, from unskilled workers to research Ph.D.s and top managers. Moreover, data were collected twice—first during a period from 1967 to 1969 and a repeat survey during 1971 to 1973. Out of a total of about 150 different survey questions (of the precoded answer type), about 60 deal with the respondents' beliefs and values; these were analyzed for the present study. The questionnaire was administered in the language of each country; a total of 20 language versions had to be made. On the basis of these data, each of the 40 countries could be given an index score for each of the four dimensions.

I was wondering at first whether differences found among employees of one single corporation could be used to detect truly national culture differences. I also wondered what effect the translation of the questionnaire could have had. With this in mind, I administered a number of the same questions from 1971 to 1973 to an international group of about 400 managers from different public and private organizations following management development courses in Lausanne, Switzerland. This time, all received the questionnaire in English. In spite of the different mix of respondents and the different language used, I found largely the same differences between countries in the manager group that I found among the multinational personnel. Then I started looking for other studies, comparing aspects of national character across a number of countries on the basis of surveys using other questions and other respondents (such as students) or on representative public opinion polls. I found 13 such studies; these compared between 5 and 19 countries at a time. The results of these studies showed a statistically significant similarity (correlation) with one or more of the four dimensions. Finally, I also looked for national indicators (such as per capita national income, inequality of income distribution, and government spending on development aid) that could logically be supposed to be related to one or more of the dimensions. I found 31 such indicators—of which the values were available for between 5 and 40 countries—that were correlated in a statistically significant way with at least one of the dimensions. All these additional studies (for which the data were collected by other people, not by me) helped make the picture of the four dimensions more complete. Interestingly, very few of these studies had even been related to each other before, but the four dimensions provide a framework that shows how they can be fit together like pieces of a huge puzzle. The fact that data obtained within a single MNC have the power to uncover the secrets of entire national cultures can be understood when it's known that the respondents form well-matched samples from their nations: They are employed by the same firm (or its subsidiary); their jobs are similar (I consistently compared the same occupations across the different countries); and their age categories and sex composition were similar—only their nationalities differed. Therefore, if we look at the differences in survey answers between multinational employees in countries A, B, C, and so on, the general factor that can account for the differences in the answers is national culture.

within each nation—the national norm—but we are not describing individuals. This should be kept in mind when interpreting the four dimensions explained in the following paragraphs.

Power Distance

The first dimension of national culture is called *Power Distance*. It indicates the extent to which a society accepts the fact that power in institutions and organizations is distributed unequally. It's reflected in the values of the less powerful members of society as well as in those of the more powerful ones. A fuller picture of the difference between small Power Distance and large Power

FIGURE 1

The Power Distance Dimension

Small Power Distance	Large Power Distance
Inequality in society should be minimized.	There should be an order of inequality in this world in which everybody has a rightful place: high and low are protected by this order.
All people should be interdependent.	A few people should be independent: most should be dependent.
Hierarchy means an inequality of roles, established for convenience.	Hierarchy means existential inequality.
Superiors consider subordinates to be "people like me."	Superiors consider subordinates to be a different kind of people.
Subordinates consider superiors to be "people like me."	Subordinates consider superiors as a different kind of people.
Superiors are accessible.	Superiors are inaccessible.
The use of power should be legitimate and is subject to the judgment as to whether it is good or evil.	Power is a basic fact of society that antedates good or evil. Its legitimacy is irrelevant.
All should have equal rights.	Power-holders are entitled to privileges.
Those in power should try to look less powerful than they are.	Those in power should try to look as powerful as possible.
The system is to blame.	The underdog is to blame.
The way to change a social system is to redistribute power.	The way to change a social system is to dethrone those in power.
People at various power levels feel less threatened and more prepared to trust people.	Other people are a potential threat to one's power and can rarely be trusted.
Latent harmony exists between the powerful and the powerless.	Latent conflict exists between the powerful and the powerless.
Cooperation among the powerless can be based on solidarity.	Cooperation among the powerless is difficult to attain because of their low-faith-in-people norm.

Distance societies is shown in Figure 1. Of course, this shows only the extremes; most countries fall somewhere in between.

Uncertainty Avoidance

The second dimension, *Uncertainty Avoidance,* indicates the extent to which a society feels threatened by uncertain and ambiguous situations and tries to avoid these situations by providing greater career stability, establishing more formal rules, not tolerating deviant ideas and behaviors, and believing in absolute truths and the attainment of expertise. Nevertheless, societies in which uncertainty avoidance is strong are also characterized by a higher level of anxiety and aggressiveness that creates, among other things, a strong inner urge in people to work hard. (See Figure 2.)

Individualism-Collectivism

The third dimension encompasses *Individualism* and its opposite, *Collectivism.* Individualism implies a loosely knit social framework in which people are supposed to take care of themselves and of their immediate families only, while collectivism is characterized by a tight social framework in which people distinguish between in-groups and out-groups; they expect their in-group (relatives, clan, organizations) to look after them, and in exchange for

FIGURE 2

The Uncertainty Avoidance Dimension

Weak Uncertainty Avoidance	Strong Uncertainty Avoidance
The uncertainty inherent in life is more easily accepted and each day is taken as it comes.	The uncertainty inherent in life is felt as a continuous threat that must be fought.
Ease and lower stress are experienced.	Higher anxiety and stress are experienced.
Time is free.	Time is money.
Hard work, as such, is not a virtue.	There is an inner urge to work hard.
Aggressive behavior is frowned upon.	Aggressive behavior of self and others is accepted.
Less showing of emotions is preferred.	More showing of emotions is preferred.
Conflict and competition can be contained on the level of fair play and used constructively.	Conflict and competition can unleash aggression and should therefore be avoided.
More acceptance of dissent is entailed.	A strong need for consensus is involved.
Deviation is not considered threatening; greater tolerance is shown.	Deviant persons and ideas are dangerous; intolerance holds sway.
The ambiance is one of less nationalism.	Nationalism is pervasive.
More positive feelings toward younger people are seen.	Younger people are suspect.
There is more willingness to take risks in life.	There is great concern with security in life.
The accent is on relativism, empiricism.	The search is for ultimate, absolute truths and values.
There should be as few rules as possible.	There is a need for written rules and regulations.
If rules cannot be kept, we should change them.	If rules cannot be kept, we are sinners and should repent.
Belief is placed in generalists and common sense.	Belief is placed in experts and their knowledge.
The authorities are there to serve the citizens.	Ordinary citizens are incompetent compared with the authorities.

FIGURE 3

The Individualism Dimension

Collectivist	Individualist
In society, people are born into extended families or clans who protect them in exchange for loyalty.	In society, everybody is supposed to take care of himself/herself and his/her immediate family.
"We" consciousness holds sway.	"I" consciousness holds sway.
Identity is based in the social system.	Identity is based in the individual.
There is emotional dependence of individual on organizations and institutions.	There is emotional independence of individual from organizations or institutions.
The involvement with organizations is moral.	The involvement with organizations is calculative.
The emphasis is on belonging to organizations; membership is the ideal.	The emphasis is on individual initiative and achievement; leadership is the ideal.
Private life is invaded by organizations and clans to which one belongs; opinions are predetermined.	Everybody has a right to a private life and opinion.
Expertise, order, duty, and security are provided by organization or clan.	Autonomy, variety, pleasure, and individual financial security are sought in the system.
Friendships are predetermined by stable social relationships, but there is need for prestige within these relationships.	The need is for specific friendships.
Belief is placed in group decisions.	Belief is placed in individual decisions.
Value standards differ for in-groups and out-groups (particularism).	Value standards should apply to all (universalism).

that they feel they owe absolute loyalty to it. A fuller picture of this dimension is presented in Figure 3.

Masculinity

The fourth dimension is called *Masculinity* even though, in concept, it encompasses its opposite pole, *Femininity.* Measurements in terms of this dimension express the extent to which the dominant values in society are "masculine"—that is, assertiveness, the acquisition of money and things, and *not* caring for others, the quality of life, or people. These values were labeled "masculine" because, *within* nearly all societies, men scored higher in terms of the values' positive sense than of their negative sense (in terms of assertiveness, for example, rather than its lack)—even though the society as a whole might veer toward the "feminine" pole. Interestingly, the more an entire society scores to the masculine side, the wider the gap between its "men's" and "women's" values (see Figure 4).

A Set of Cultural Maps of the World

Research data were obtained by comparing the beliefs and values of employees within the subsidiaries of one large multinational corporation in 40 countries around the world. These countries represent the wealthy countries of the West and the larger, more prosperous of the Third World countries. The Socialist block countries are missing, but data are available for Yugoslavia

FIGURE 4

The Masculinity Dimension

Feminine	Masculine
Men needn't be assertive, but can also assume nurturing roles.	Men should be assertive. Women should be nurturing.
Sex roles in society are more fluid.	Sex roles in society are clearly differentiated.
There should be equality between the sexes.	Men should dominate in society.
Quality of life is important.	Performance is what counts.
You work in order to live.	You live in order to work.
People and environment are important.	Money and things are important.
Interdependence is the ideal.	Independence is the ideal.
Service provides the motivation.	Ambition provides the drive.
One sympathizes with the unfortunate.	One admires the successful achiever.
Small and slow are beautiful.	Big and fast are beautiful.
Unisex and androgyny are ideal.	Ostentatious manliness ("machismo") is appreciated.

(where the corporation is represented by a local, self-managed company under Yugoslavian law). It was possible, on the basis of mean answers of employees on a number of key questions, to assign an index value to each country on each dimension. As described in the box on page 311, these index values appear to be related in a statistically significant way to a vast amount of other data about these countries, including both research results from other samples and national indicator figures.

Because of the difficulty of representing four dimensions in a single diagram, the position of the countries on the dimensions is shown in Figures 5, 6, and 7 for two dimensions at a time. The vertical and horizontal axes and the circles around clusters of countries have been drawn subjectively, in order to show the degree of proximity of geographically or historically related countries. The three diagrams thus represent a composite set of cultural maps of the world.

Of the three "maps," those in Figure 5 (Power Distance × Uncertainty Avoidance) and Figure 7 (Masculinity × Uncertainty Avoidance) show a scattering of countries in all corners—that is, all combinations of index values occur. Figure 6 (Power Distance × Individualism), however, shows one empty corner: The combination of Small Power Distance and Collectivism does not occur. In fact, there is a tendency for Large Power Distance to be associated with Collectivism and for Small Power Distance with Individualism. However, there is a third factor that should be taken into account here: national wealth. Both Small Power Distance and Individualism go together with greater national wealth (per capita gross national product). The relationship between Individualism and Wealth is quite strong, as Figure 6 shows. In the upper part (Collectivist) we find only the poorer countries, with Japan as a borderline exception. In the lower part (Individualism), we find only the wealthier countries. If we look at the poorer and the wealthier countries separately, there is no longer any relationship between Power Distance and Individualism.

The 40 Countries: Abbreviations Used in Figures 5, 6, and 7

ARG	Argentina	FRA	France	JAP	Japan	SIN	Singapore
AUL	Australia	GBR	Great Britain	MEX	Mexico	SPA	Spain
AUT	Austria	GER	Germany (West)	NET	Netherlands	SWE	Sweden
BEL	Belgium	GRE	Greece	NOR	Norway	SWI	Switzerland
BRA	Brazil	HOK	Hong Kong	NZL	New Zealand	TAI	Taiwan
CAN	Canada	IND	India	PAK	Pakistan	THA	Thailand
CHL	Chile	IRA	Iran	PER	Peru	TUR	Turkey
COL	Colombia	IRE	Ireland	PHI	Philippines	USA	United States
DEN	Denmark	ISR	Israel	POR	Portugal	VEN	Venezuela
FIN	Finland	ITA	Italy	SAF	South Africa	YUG	Yugoslavia

FIGURE 5

The Position of the 40 Countries
on the Power Distance and Uncertainty Avoidance Scales

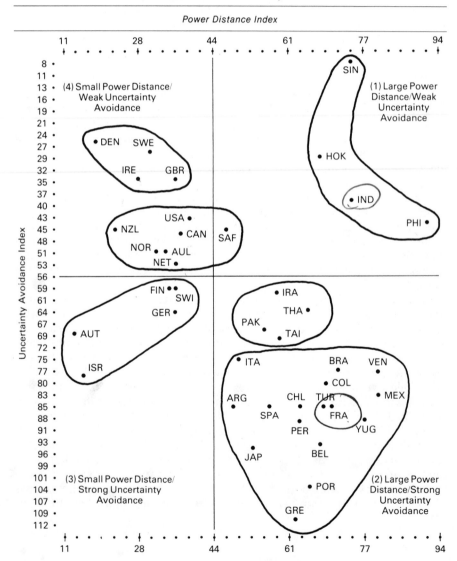

FIGURE 6

The Position of the 40 Countries
on the Power Distance and Individualism Scales

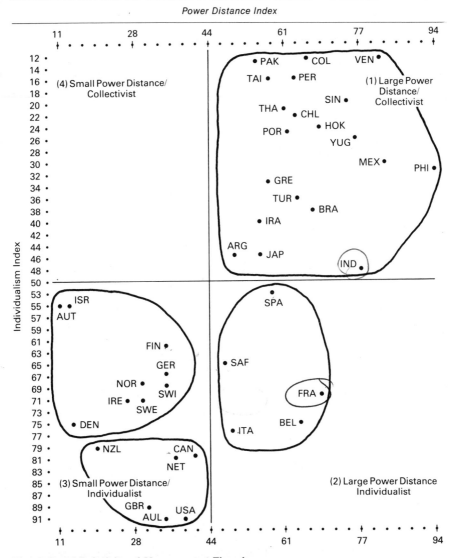

The Cultural Relativity of Management Theories

Of particular interest in the context of this discussion is the relative position of the United States on the four dimensions. Here is how the United States rates:

- On *Power Distance* at rank 15 out of the 40 countries (measured from below), it is below average but it is not as low as a number of other wealthy countries.

- On *Uncertainty Avoidance* at rank 9 out of 40, it is well below average.

317

FIGURE 7

The Position of the 40 Countries
on the Uncertainty Avoidance and Masculinity Scales

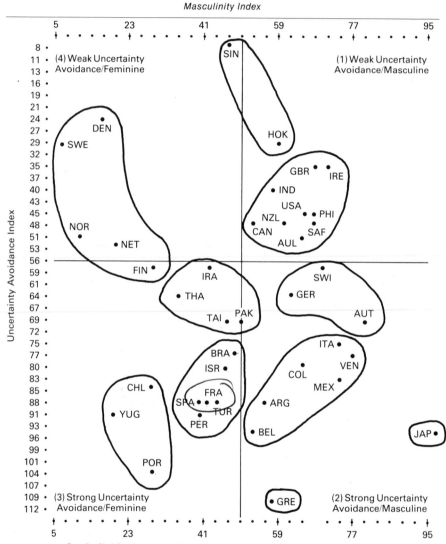

- On *Individualism* at rank 40 out of 40, the United States is the single most individualist country of the entire set (followed closely by Australia and Great Britain).

- On *Masculinity* at rank 28 out of 40, it is well above average.

For about 60 years, the United States has been the world's largest producer and exporter of management theories covering such key areas as motivation, leadership, and organization. Before that, the centers of theorizing about what we now call "management" lay in the Old World. We can trace the history of management thought as far back as we want—at least to parts of the Old

Testament of the Bible, and to ancient Greece (Plato's *The Laws* and *The Republic*, 350 B.C.). Sixteenth-century European "management" theorists include Niccolo Machiavelli (Italy) and Thomas More (Great Britain); early twentieth-century theorists include Max Weber (Germany) and Henri Fayol (France).

Today we are all culturally conditioned. We see the world in the way we have learned to see it. Only to a limited extent can we, in our thinking, step out of the boundaries imposed by our cultural conditioning. This applies to the author of a theory as much as it does to the ordinary citizen: Theories reflect the cultural environment in which they were written. If this is true, Italian, British, German, and French theories reflect the culture of Italy, Britain, Germany, and France of their day, and American theories reflect the culture of the United States of its day. Since most present-day theorists are middle-class intellectuals, their theories reflect a national intellectual middle-class culture background.

Now we ask the question: To what extent do theories developed in one country and reflecting the cultural boundaries of that country apply to other countries? Do American management theories apply in Japan? In India? No management theorist, to my knowledge, has ever explicitly addressed himself or herself to this issue. Most probably assume that their theories are universally valid. The availability of a conceptual framework built on four dimensions of national culture, in conjunction with the cultural maps of the world, makes it possible to see more clearly where and to what extent theories developed in one country are likely to apply elsewhere. In the remaining sections of this article I shall look from this viewpoint at most popular American theories of management in the areas of motivation, leadership, and organization.

Motivation

Why do people behave as they do? There is a great variety of theories of human motivation. According to Sigmund Freud, we are impelled to act by unconscious forces within us, which he called our id. Our conscious conception of ourselves—our ego—tries to control these forces, and an equally unconscious internal pilot—our superego—criticizes the thoughts and acts of our ego and causes feelings of guilt and anxiety when the ego seems to be giving in to the id. The superego is the product of early socialization, mainly learned from our parents when we were young children.

Freud's work has been extremely influential in psychology, but he is rarely quoted in the context of management theories. The latter almost exclusively refer to motivation theories developed later in the United States, particularly those of David McClelland, Abraham Maslow, Frederick Herzberg, and Victor Vroom. According to McClelland, we perform because we have a need to achieve (the achievement motive). More recently, McClelland has also paid a lot of attention to the power motive. Maslow has postulated a hierarchy of human needs, from more "basic" to "higher": most basic are physiological needs, followed by security, social needs, esteem needs, and, finally, a need for "self-actualization." The latter incorporates McClelland's theory of achievement, but is defined in broader terms. Maslow's theory of the hierarchy of needs postulates that a higher need will become active only if the lower needs are sufficiently satisfied. Our acting is basically a rational activity by which we expect to fulfill successive levels of needs. Herzberg's two-factor theory of motivation distinguishes between hygienic factors (largely corresponding to Maslow's lower needs—physiological, security, social) and motivators (Maslow's higher needs—esteem, self-actualization); the hygienic factors have only the potential to motivate negatively (demotivate—they are necessary but not sufficient conditions), while only the motivators have the potential to motivate positively. Vroom has formalized the role of "expectancy" in motivation; he opposes "expectancy" theories and "drive" theories. The former see people as being *pulled* by the expectancy of some kind of result from their acts, mostly consciously. The latter (in accordance with Freud's theories) see people as *pushed* by inside forces—often unconscious ones.

Let us now look at these theories through culture-conscious glasses. Why has Freudian thinking never become popular in U.S. management theory, as has the thinking of McClelland, Maslow, Herzberg, and Vroom? To what extent do these theories reflect different cultural patterns? Freud was part of an Austrian middle-class culture at the turn of the century. If we compare present-day Austria and the United States on our cultural maps, we find the following:

- Austria scores considerably lower on Power Distance.
- Austria scores considerably higher on Uncertainty Avoidance.
- Austria scores considerably lower on Individualism.
- Austria scores considerably higher on Masculinity.

We do not know to what extent Austrian culture has changed since Freud's time, but evidence suggests that cultural patterns change very slowly. It is, therefore, not likely to have been much different from today's culture. The most striking thing about present-day Austrian culture is that it combines a fairly high Uncertainty Avoidance with a very low Power Distance (see Figure 5). Somehow the combination of high Uncertainty Avoidance with high Power Distance is more comfortable (we find this in Japan and in all Latin and Mediterranean countries—see Figure 5). Having a powerful superior whom we can both praise and blame is one way of satisfying a strong need for avoiding uncertainty. The Austrian culture, however (together with the German, Swiss, Israeli, and Finnish cultures), cannot rely on an external boss to absorb its uncertainty. Thus Freud's superego acts naturally as an inner uncertainty-absorbing device, an internalized boss. For strong Uncertainty Avoidance countries like Austria, working hard is caused by an inner urge—it is a way of relieving stress. (See Figure 2.) The Austrian superego is reinforced by the country's relatively low level of Individualism (see Figure 6). The inner feeling of obligation to society plays a much stronger role in Austria than in the United States. The ultrahigh Individualism of the United States leads to a need to explain every act in terms of self-interest, and expectancy theories of motivation do provide this explanation—we always do something *because* we expect to obtain the satisfaction of some need.

The comparison between Austrian and U.S. culture has so far justified the popularity of expectancy theories of motivation in the United States. The combination in the United States of weak Uncertainty Avoidance and relatively high Masculinity can tell us more about why the achievement motive has become so popular in that country. David McClelland, in his book *The Achieving Society,* sets up scores reflecting how strong achievement need is in many countries by analyzing the content of children's stories used in those countries to teach the young to read. It now appears that there is a strong relationship between McClelland's need for achievement country scores and the combination of weak Uncertainty Avoidance and strong Masculinity charted in Figure 7. (McClelland's data were collected for two historic years—1925 and 1950—but only his 1925 data relate to the cultural map in Figure 7. It is likely that the 1925 stories were more traditional, reflecting deep underlying cultural currents; the choice of stories in 1950 in most countries may have been affected by modernization currents in education, often imported from abroad.)

Countries in the upper righthand corner of Figure 7 received mostly high scores on achievement need in McClelland's book; countries in the lower lefthand corner of Figure 7 received low scores. This leads us to the conclusion that the concept of the achievement motive presupposes two cultural choices—a willingness to accept risk (equivalent to weak Uncertainty Avoidance; see Figure 2) and a concern with performance (equivalent to strong Masculinity; see Figure 4). This combination is found exclusively in countries in the Anglo-American group and in some of their former colonies (Figure 7). One striking thing about the concept of achievement is that the word itself is hardly translatable into any language other than English; for this reason, the word could not be used in the questionnaire of the multinational corporation used in my research. The English-speaking countries all appear in the upper righthand corner of Figure 7.

If this is so, there is reason to reconsider Maslow's hierarchy of human needs in the light of the map shown in Figure 7. Quadrant 1 (upper righthand corner) in Figure 7 stands for *achievement motivation,* as we have seen (performance plus risk). Quadrant 2 distinguishes itself from quadrant 1 by strong Uncertainty Avoidance, which means *security motivation* (performance plus security). The countries on the feminine side of Figure 7 distinguish themselves by a focusing on quality of life rather than on performance and on relationships between people rather than on money and things (see Figure 4). This means *social motivation:* quality of life plus security in quadrant 3, and quality of life plus risk in quadrant 4. Now, Maslow's hierarchy puts self-actualization (achievement) plus esteem above social needs above security needs. This, however, is not the description of a universal human motivation process—it is the description of a value system, the value system of the U.S. middle class to which the author belonged. I suggest that if we want to continue thinking in terms of a hierarchy for countries in the lower righthand corner of Figure 7 (quadrant 2), security needs should rank at the top; for countries in the upper lefthand corner (quadrant 4), social needs should rank at the top, and for countries in the lower lefthand corner (quadrant 3) *both* security and social needs should rank at the top.

One practical outcome of presenting motivation theories is the movement toward humanization of work—an attempt to make work more intrinsically interesting to the workers. There are two main currents in humanization of work—one, developed in the United States and called *job enrichment,* aims at restructuring individual jobs. A chief proponent of job enrichment is Frederick Herzberg. The other current, developed in Europe and applied mainly in Sweden and Norway, aims at restructuring work into group work—forming, for example, such semiautonomous teams as those seen in the experiments at Volvo. Why the difference in approaches? What is seen as a "human" job depends on a society's prevailing model of humankind. In a more masculine society like the United States, humanization takes the form of masculinization, allowing individual performance. In the more feminine societies of Sweden and Norway, humanization takes the form of femininization—it is a means toward more wholesome interpersonal relationships in its deemphasis of interindividual competition.

Leadership

One of the oldest theorists of leadership in world literature is Machiavelli (1468–1527). He described certain effective techniques for manipulation and remaining in power (including deceit, bribery, and murder) that gave him a bad reputation in later centuries. Machiavelli wrote in the context of the Italy of his day, and what he described is clearly a large Power Distance situation. We still find Italy on the larger Power Distance side of Figure 5 (with all other Latin and Mediterranean countries), and we can assume from historical evidence that Power Distances in Italy during the sixteenth century were considerably larger than they are now. When we compare Machiavelli's work with that of his contemporary, Sir Thomas More (1478–1535), we find cultural differences between ways of thinking in different countries even in the sixteenth century. The British More described in *Utopia* a state based on consensus as a "model" to criticize the political situation of his day. But practice did not always follow theory, of course: More, deemed too critical, was beheaded by order of King Henry VIII, while Machiavelli the realist managed to die peacefully in his bed. The difference in theories is nonetheless remarkable.

In the United States a current of leadership theories has developed. Some of the best known were put forth by the late Douglas McGregor (Theory X versus Theory Y), Rensis Likert (System 4 management), and Robert R. Blake with Jane S. Mouton (the Managerial Grid®). What these theories have in common is that they all advocate participation in the manager's decisions by his/her subordinates (participative management); however, the initiative toward participation is supposed to be taken by the manager. In a worldwide perspective (Figure 5), we can understand these theories from the middle position of the United States on the Power Distance side (rank 15 out of 40 countries). Had the culture been one of larger Power Distance, we could have expected more "Machiavellian" theories of leadership. In fact, in the management literature of another country with a larger Power Distance index score, France, there is little concern with participative management American style, but great concern with who has the power. However, in countries with smaller Power Distances than the United States (Sweden, Norway, Germany, Israel), there is considerable sympathy for models of management in which even the initiatives are taken by the subordinates (forms of industrial democracy) and with which there's little sympathy in the United States. In the approaches toward "industrial democracy" taken in these countries, we notice their differences on the second dimension, Uncertainty Avoidance. In weak Uncertainty Avoidance countries like Sweden, industrial democracy was started in the form of local experiments and only later was given a legislative framework. In strong Uncertainty Avoidance countries like Germany, industrial democracy was brought about by legislation first and then had to be brought alive in the organizations ("Mitbestimmung").

The crucial fact about leadership in any culture is that it is a complement to subordinateship. The Power Distance Index scores in Figure 5 are, in fact, based on the values of people as *subordinates*, not on the values of superiors. Whatever a naive literature on leadership may give us to understand, leaders cannot choose their styles at will; what is feasible depends to a large extent on the cultural conditioning of a leader's subordinates. Along these lines, Figure 8 describes the type of subordinateship that, other things being equal, a leader can expect to meet in societies at three different levels of Power Distance—subordinateship to which a leader must respond. The middle level represents what is most likely found in the United States.

Neither McGregor, nor Likert, nor Blake and Mouton allow for this type of cultural proviso—all three tend to be prescriptive with regard to a leadership style that, at best, will work with U.S. subordinates and with those in cultures—such as Canada or Australia—that have not too different Power Distance levels (Figure 5). In fact, my research shows that subordinates in larger Power Distance countries tend to agree more frequently with Theory Y.

A U.S. theory of leadership that allows for a certain amount of cultural relativity, although indirectly, is Fred Fiedler's contingency theory of leadership. Fiedler states that different leader personalities are needed for "difficult" and "easy" situations, and that a cultural gap between superior and subordinates is one of the factors that makes a situation "difficult." However, this theory does not address the kind of cultural gap in question.

In practice, the adaptation of managers to higher Power Distance environments does not seem to present too many problems. Although this is an unpopular message—one seldom professed in management development

FIGURE 8

Subordinateship for Three Levels of Power Distance

Small Power Distance	Medium Power Distance (United States)	Large Power Distance
Subordinates have weak dependence needs.	Subordinates have medium dependence needs.	Subordinates have strong dependence needs.
Superiors have weak dependence needs toward their superiors.	Superiors have medium dependence needs toward their superiors.	Superiors have strong dependence needs toward their superiors.
Subordinates expect superiors to consult them and may rebel or strike if superiors are not seen as staying within their legitimate role.	Subordinates expect superiors to consult them but will accept autocratic behavior as well.	Subordinates expect superiors to act autocratically.
Ideal superior to most is a loyal democrat.	Ideal superior to most is a resourceful democrat.	Ideal superior to most is a benevolent autocrat or paternalist.
Laws and rules apply to all and privileges for superiors are not considered acceptable.	Laws and rules apply to all, but a certain level of privileges for superiors is considered normal.	Everybody expects superiors to enjoy privileges; laws and rules differ for superiors and subordinates.
Status symbols are frowned upon and will easily come under attack from subordinates.	Status symbols for superiors contribute moderately to their authority and will be accepted by subordinates.	Status symbols are very important and contribute strongly to the superior's authority with the subordinates.

courses—managers moving to a larger Power Distance culture soon learn that they have to behave more autocratically in order to be effective, and tend to do so; this is borne out by the colonial history of most Western countries. But it is interesting that the Western ex-colonial power with the highest Power Distance norm—France—seems to be most appreciated by its former colonies and seems to maintain the best postcolonial relationships with most of them. This suggests that subordinates in a large Power Distance culture feel even more comfortable with superiors who are real autocrats than with those whose assumed autocratic stance is out of national character.

The operation of a manager in an environment with a Power Distance norm lower than his or her own is more problematic. U.S. managers tend to find it difficult to collaborate wholeheartedly in the "industrial democracy" processes of such countries as Sweden, Germany, and even the Netherlands. U.S. citizens tend to consider their country as the example of democracy, and find it difficult to accept that other countries might wish to develop forms of democracy for which they feel no need and that make major inroads upon managers' (or leaders') prerogatives. However, the very idea of management prerogatives is not accepted in very low Power Distance countries. This is, perhaps, best illustrated by a remark a Scandinavian social scientist is supposed to have made to Herzberg in a seminar: "You are against participation for the very reason we are in favor of it—one doesn't know where it will stop. We think that is good."

One way in which the U.S. approach to leadership has been packaged and formalized is management by objectives (MBO), first advocated by Peter Drucker in 1955 in *The Practice of Management*. In the United States, MBO has been used to spread a pragmatic results orientation throughout the organization. It has been considerably more successful where results are objectively measurable than where they can only be interpreted subjectively, and, even in the United States, it has been criticized heavily. Still, it has been perhaps the single most popular management technique "made in U.S.A." Therefore, it can be accepted as fitting U.S. culture. MBO presupposes:

- That subordinates are sufficiently independent to negotiate meaningfully with the boss (not-too-large Power Distance).
- That both are willing to take risks (weak Uncertainty Avoidance).
- That performance is seen as important by both (high Masculinity).

Let us now take the case of Germany, a below-average Power Distance country. Here, the dialogue element in MBO should present no problem. However, since Germany scores considerably higher on Uncertainty Avoidance, the tendency toward accepting risk and ambiguity will not exist to the same extent. The idea of replacing the arbitrary authority of the boss with the impersonal authority of mutually agreed upon objectives, however, fits the small Power Distance/strong Uncertainty Avoidance cultural cluster very well. The objectives become the subordinates' "superego." In a book of case studies about MBO in Germany, Ian R. G. Ferguson states that "MBO has acquired a different flavor in the German-speaking area, not least because in these countries the societal and political pressure toward increasing the value of man in the organization on the right to co-determination has become quite clear. Thence, MBO has been transliterated into Management by Joint Goal Setting (Führung durch Zielvereinbarung)." Ferguson's view of MBO fits the ideological needs of the German-speaking countries of the moment. The case studies in his book show elaborate formal systems with extensive ideological justification; the stress on *team* objectives is quite strong, which is in line with the lower individualism in these countries.

The other area in which specific information on MBO is available is France. MBO was first introduced in France in the early 1960s, but it became extremely popular for a time after the 1968 student revolt. People expected that this new technique would lead to the long-overdue democratization of organizations. Instead of DPO (Direction par Objectifs), the French name for MBO became DPPO (Direction *Participative* par Objectifs). So in France, too, societal developments affected the MBO system. However, DPPO remained, in general, as much a vain slogan as did Liberté, Egalité, Fraternité (Freedom, Equality, Brotherhood) after the 1789 revolt. G. Franck wrote in 1973, "I think that the career of DPPO is terminated, or rather that it has never started, and it won't ever start as long as we continue in France our tendency to confound ideology and reality. . . ." In a postscript to Franck's article, the editors of *Le Management* write: "French blue- and white-collar workers, lower-level and higher-level managers, and 'patrons' all belong to the same cultural system which maintains dependency relations from level to level. Only the deviants really dislike this system. The hierarchical structure protects against anxiety; DPO, however, generates anxiety. . . ." The reason for the anxiety in the French cultural context is that MBO presupposes a depersonalized authority in the form of internalized objectives; but French people, from their early childhood onward, are accustomed to large Power Distances, to an authority that is highly personalized. And in spite of all attempts to introduce Anglo-Saxon management methods, French superiors do not easily decentralize and do not stop short-circuiting intermediate hierarchical levels, nor do French subordinates expect them to. The developments of the 1970s have severely discredited DPPO, which probably does injustice to the cases in which individual French organizations or units, starting from less exaggerated expectations, have benefited from it.

In the examples used thus far in this section, the cultural context of leadership may look rather obvious to the reader. But it also works in more subtle, less obvious ways. Here's an example from the area of management decision making: A prestigious U.S. consulting firm was asked to analyze the decision-making processes in a large Scandinavian "XYZ" corporation. Their report criticized the corporation's decision-making style, which they characterized as being, among other things, "intuitive" and "consensus based." They compared "observations of traditional XYZ practices" with "selected examples of practices in other companies." These "selected examples," offered as a model, were evidently taken from their U.S. clients and reflect the U.S. textbook norm—"fact based" rather than intuitive management, and "fast decisions based on clear responsibilities" rather than the use of informal, personal contacts, and the concern for consensus.

Is this consulting firm doing its Scandinavian clients a service? It follows from Figure 7 that where the United States and the Scandinavian culture are wide apart is on the Masculinity dimension. The use of intuition and the concern for consensus in Scandinavia are "feminine" characteristics of the culture, well embedded in the total texture of these societies. Stressing "facts" and "clear responsibilities" fits the "masculine" U.S. culture. From a neutral viewpoint, the reasons for criticizing the U.S. decision-making style are as good as those for criticizing the Scandinavian style. In complex decision-making situations, "facts" no longer exist independently from the people who define them, so "fact-based management" becomes a misleading slogan. Intuition may not be a bad method of deciding in such cases at all. And if the implementation of decisions requires the commitment of many people, even a consensus process that takes more time is an asset rather than a liability. But the essential element overlooked by the consultant is that decisions have to be made in a way that corresponds to the values of the environment in which they have to be effective. People in this consulting firm lacked insight into their own cultural biases. This does not mean that the Scandinavian corporation's management need not improve its decision making and could not learn from the consultant's experience. But this can be done only through a mutual recognition of cultural differences, not by ignoring them.

Organization

The Power Distance × Uncertainty Avoidance map (Figure 5) is of vital importance for structuring organizations that will work best in different countries. For example, one U.S.-based multinational corporation has a worldwide policy that salary-increase proposals should be initiated by the employee's direct superior. However, the French management of its French subsidiary interpreted this policy in such a way that the superior's superior's superior—three levels above—was the one to initiate salary proposals. This way of working was regarded as quite natural by both superiors and subordinates in France. Other factors being equal, people in large Power Distance cultures prefer that decisions be centralized because even superiors have strong dependency needs in relation to their superiors; this tends to move decisions up as far as they can go (see Figure 8). People in small Power Distance cultures want decisions to be decentralized.

While Power Distance relates to centralization, Uncertainty Avoidance relates to formalization—the need for formal rules and specialization, the assignment of tasks to experts. My former colleague O.J. Stevens at INSEAD has done an interesting research project (as yet unpublished) with M.B.A. students from Germany, Great Britain, and France. He asked them to write their own diagnosis and solution for a small case study of an organizational problem—a conflict in one company between the sales and product development departments. The majority of the French referred the problem to the next higher authority (the president of the company); the Germans attributed it to the lack of a written policy, and proposed establishing one; the British attributed it to a lack of interpersonal communication, to be cured by some kind of group training.

Stevens concludes that the "implicit model" of the organization for most French was a pyramid (both centralized and formal); for most Germans, a well-oiled machine (formalized but not centralized); and for most British, a village market (neither formalized nor centralized). This covers three quadrants (2, 3, and 4) in Figure 5. What is missing is an "implicit model" for quadrant 1, which contains four Asian countries, including India. A discussion with an Indian colleague leads me to place the family (centralized, but not formalized) in this quadrant as the "implicit model" of the organization. In fact, Indian organizations tend to be formalized as far as relationships between people go (this is related to Power Distance), but not as far as workflow goes (this is Uncertainty Avoidance).

The "well-oiled machine" model for Germany reminds us of the fact that Max Weber, author of the first theory of bureaucracy, was a German. Weber pictures bureaucracy as a highly formalized system (strong Uncertainty Avoidance), in which, however, the rules protect the lower-ranking members against abuse of power by their superiors. The superiors have no power by themselves, only the power that their bureaucratic roles have given them as incumbents of the roles—the power is in the role, not in the person (small Power Distance).

The United States is found fairly close to the center of the map in Figure 5, taking an intermediate position between the "pyramid," "machine," and "market" implicit models—a position that may help explain the success of U.S. business operations in very different cultures. However, according to the common U.S. conception of organization, we might say that *hierarchy is not a goal by itself* (as it is in France) and that *rules are not a goal by themselves.* Both are means toward obtaining results, to be changed if needed. A breaking away from hierarchic and bureaucratic traditions is found in the development toward matrix organizations and similar temporary or flexible organization systems.

Another INSEAD colleague, André Laurent, has shown that French managers strongly disbelieve in the feasibility of matrix organizations, because they see them as violating the "holy" principle of unit of command. However, in the French subsidiary of a multinational corporation that has a long history of successful matrix management, the French managers were quite positive toward it; obviously, then, cultural barriers to organizational innovation can be overcome. German managers are not too favorably disposed toward matrix organizations either, feeling that they tend to frustrate their need for organizational clarity. This means that matrix organizations will be accepted *if* the roles of individuals within the organization can be defined without ambiguity.

The extreme position of the United States on the Individualism scale leads to other potential conflicts between the U.S. way of thinking about organizations and the values dominant in other parts of the world. In the U.S. Individualist conception, the relationship between the individual and the organization is essentially calculative, being based on enlightened self-interest. In fact, there is a strong historical and cultural link between Individualism and Capitalism. The capitalist system—based on self-interest and the market mechanism—was "invented" in Great Britain, which is still among the top three most Individualist countries in the world. In more Collectivist societies, however, the link between individuals and their traditional organizations is not calculative, but moral: It is based not on self-interest, but on the individual's loyalty toward the clan, organization, or society—which is supposedly the best guarantee of that individual's ultimate interest. "Collectivism" is a bad word in the United States, but "individualism" is as much a bad word in the writings of Mao Tse-tung, who writes from a strongly Collectivist cultural tradition (see Figure 6 for the Collectivist scores of the Chinese majority countries Taiwan, Hong Kong, and Singapore). This means that U.S. organizations may get themselves into considerable trouble in more Collectivist environments if they do not recognize their local employees' needs for ties of mutual loyalty between company and employee. "Hire and fire" is very ill perceived in these countries, if firing isn't prohibited by law altogether. Given the value position of people in more Collectivist cultures, it should not be seen as surprising if they prefer other types of economic order to capitalism—if capitalism cannot get rid of its Individualist image.

Consequences for Policy

So far we have seriously questioned the universal validity of management theories developed in one country—in most instances here, the United States.

On a practical level, this has the least consequence for organizations operating entirely within the country in which the theories were born. As long as the theories apply within the United States, U.S. organizations can base their policies for motivating employees, leadership, and organization development on these policies. Still, some caution is due. If differences in environmental culture can be shown to exit between countries, and if these constrain the validity of management theories, what about the subcultures and counter-cultures within the country? To what extent do the familiar theories apply when the organization employs people for whom the theories were not, in the first instance, conceived—such as members of minority groups with a different educational level, or belonging to a different generation? If culture matters, an organization's policies can lose their effectiveness when its cultural environment changes.

No doubt, however, the consequences of the cultural relativity of management theories are more serious for the multinational organization. The cultural maps in Figures 5, 6, and 7 can help predict the kind of culture difference between subsidiaries and mother company that will need to be met. An important implication is that identical personnel policies may have very different effects in different countries—and within countries for different subgroups of employees. This is not only a matter of different employee values; there are also, of course, differences in government policies and legislation (which usually reflect quite clearly the country's different cultural position). And there are differences in labor market situations and labor union power positions. These differences—tangible as well as intangible—may have consequences for performance, attention to quality, cost, labor turnover, and absenteeism. Typical universal policies that may work out quite differently in different countries are those dealing with financial incentives, promotion paths, and grievance channels.

The dilemma for the organization operating abroad is whether to adapt to the local culture or try to change it. There are examples of companies that have successfully changed local habits, such as in the earlier mention of the introduction of matrix organization in France. Many Third World countries want to transfer new technologies from more economically advanced countries. If they are to work at all, these technologies must presuppose values that may run counter to local traditions, such as a certain discretion of subordinates toward superiors (lower Power Distance) or of individuals toward ingroups (more Individualism). In such a case, the local culture has to be changed; this is a difficult task that should not be taken lightly. Since it calls for a conscious strategy based on insight into the local culture, it's logical to involve acculturated locals in strategy formulations. Often, the original policy will have to be adapted to fit local culture and lead to the desired effect. We saw earlier how, in the case of MBO, this has succeeded in Germany, but generally failed in France.

A final area in which the cultural boundaries of home-country management theories are important is the training of managers for assignments abroad. For managers who have to operate in an unfamiliar culture, training based on home-country theories is of very limited use and may even do more harm than good. Of more importance is a thorough familiarization with the other culture, for which the organization can use the services of specialized crosscultural training institutes—or it can develop its own program by using host-country personnel as teachers.

Acknowledgments

This article is based on research carried out in the period 1973–78 at the European Institute for Advanced Studies in Management, Brussels. The article itself was sponsored by executive search consultants Berndtson International S.A., Brussels. The author acknowledges the helpful comments of Mark Cantley, André Laurent, Ernest C. Miller, and Jennifer Robinson on an earlier version of it.

Selected Bibliography

The first U.S. book about the cultural relativity of U.S. management theories is still to be written, I believe—which lack in itself indicates how difficult it is to recognize one's own cultural biases. One of the few U.S. books describing the process of cultural conditioning for a management readership is Edward T. Hall's *The Silent Language* (Fawcett, 1959, but reprinted since). Good reading also is Hall's article "The Silent Language in Overseas Business" (*Harvard Business Review,* May–June 1960). Hall is an anthropologist and therefore a specialist in the study of culture. Very readable on the same subject are two books by the British anthropologist Mary Douglas, *Natural Symbols: Exploration in Cosmology* (Vintage, 1973) and the reader *Rules and Meanings: The Anthropology of Everyday Knowledge* (Penguin, 1973). Another excellent reader is Theodore D. Weinshall's *Culture and Management* (Penguin, 1977).

On the concept of national character, some well-written professional literature is Margaret Mead's "National Character," in the reader by Sol Tax, *Anthropology Today* (University of Chicago Press, 1962), and Alex Inkeles and D.J. Levinson's, "National Character," in Lindzey and Aronson's *Handbook of Social Psychology,* second edition, volume 4 (Addison-Wesley, 1969). Critique on the implicit claims of universal validity of management theories comes from some foreign authors: An important article is Michel Brossard and Marc Maurice's "Is There a Universal Model of Organization Structure?" (*International Studies of Management and Organization,* Fall 1976). This journal is a journal of translations from non-American literature, based in New York, that often contains important articles on management issues by non-U.S. authors that take issue with the dominant theories. Another article is Gunnar Hjelholt's "Europe Is Different," in Geert Hofstede and M. Sami Kassem's reader, *European Contributions to Organization Theory* (Assen, Netherlands: Von Gorcum, 1976).

Some other references of interest: Ian R. G. Ferguson's *Management by Objectives in Deutschland* (Herder und Herder, 1973) (in German); G. Franck's "Epitaphe pour la DPO," in *Le Management,* November 1973 (in French); and D. Jenkins's *Blue- and White-Collar Democracy* (Doubleday, 1973).

Note: Details of Geert Hofstede's study of national cultures have been published in his book, *Culture's Consequences: International Differences in Work-Related Values* (Beverly Hills: Sage Publications, 1980).

FALSE GRIT

WARREN BENNIS

There's a mythology of competence going around that says the way for a woman to succeed is to act like a man. One proponent of this new "man-scam" is Marcille Gray Williams, author of *The New Executive Woman: A Guide to Business Success,* who advises women to "learn to control your tears. Mary Tyler Moore may be able to get away with it, but you can't. Whatever you do, don't cry." Women in increasing numbers are enrolling in a variety of training and retraining programs which tell them that if they dress properly (dark gray and dark blue) and talk tough enough (to paraphrase John Wayne, "A woman's got to do what a woman's got to do"), they'll take another step up the ladder of success. Which explains why training programs for women (and men too) have become a booming growth industry.

What we see today are all kinds of workshops and seminars where women undergo a metaphorical sex change, where they acquire a tough-talking, no-nonsense, sink-or-swim macho philosophy. They're told to take on traits just the opposite of those Harvard psychoanalyst Dr. Helen H. Tartakoff assigns to women: "endowments which include the capacity for mutuality as well as for maternity . . . for creativity as well as receptivity. In short," she sums up, "women's feminine heritage, as caretaker and peacemaker, contains the potential for improving the human condition."

Ironically, men are simultaneously encouraged to shed the same masculine character traits that women are trying to imitate through their own form of nonassertiveness and in sensitivity training programs. So it's O.K., even better than O.K., for old Charlie to cry in his office. How marvelous. How liberating. Women impersonate the macho male stereotype and men impersonate the countermacho stereotype of the women.

It's time to move beyond "sex differences" and "sex roles," beyond the myths of female and male impersonations, to a more sophisticated understanding of women in organizations. Instead of retraining women *as individuals* to acquire appropriate dress or assertiveness, we have to face up to the organization as a culture—as a system which governs behavior. For, according to research findings, the impact of the organization on success or failure is

---

Reprinted from *Savvy Magazine,* June 1980, with permission of the author.

much greater than that of personality characteristics—or, for that matter, sex differences.

This realization avoids the "blame the victim" approach which explains executive success in terms of individual dispositions (whether created by temperament or socialization). The villains of the piece turn out to be complex organizations, whose power structures and avenues for opportunity routinely disadvantage those people not particularly sophisticated about how such organizations work. More often than not, those people are women, since they tend to have had less experience in learning the ropes of organizational life. This perspective suggests a different kind of strategy for the elimination of sex discrimination than the "sex roles" school of thought. Instead of retaining women (or men, for that matter) and trapping all concerned in a false dream, it's necessary to take a look at the very nature of complex organizations. It is these systems and the roles within them that women must understand. And it is, at bottom, these complex organizations which should bear the burden of change, not the women subjected to weekend bashes where male-chauvinist Pygmalion games are played to the tune of "Why Can't a Woman Be More Like a Man?"

Alfred North Whitehead cautioned us wisely: "Seek simplicity and then distrust it." To put it kindly, the trouble with too many sex-difference, sex-role training programs is that they seek simplicity but forget to distrust it. And no wonder. Simplicity is easier. It's easier to transform individuals than to transform creaky, complex systems with their bureaucratic sludge and impenetrable webs of self-interest. It's a lot easier to change an Eliza Doolittle than Victorian England's class structure. The trouble is: When Eliza returns to her old habitat in Covent Garden, the old familiar behaviors return almost immediately, and everything she learned from Professor Higgins is extinguished in days. This "fade out" effect has occurred wherever individuals are trained or re-educated outside the organizational context. What's easier can be dangerously off target.

When I discussed this with Boris Yavitz, Dean of Columbia University's Graduate School of Business, he told me, "What I fear is that women will try to take on the attributes of men in a wrong-headed attempt to disprove the old stereotypes." The women he sees in his program have all the intellectual equipment necessary for success in business; they're motivated, directed, purposeful. "We never set out eight years ago to bring in women by making it easy," says Yavitz; "and yet in the last eight years our female enrollment has increased from 5 percent to 40 percent of the school. We are holding exactly the same standards we have always held, and the women are doing superbly." As they are, by the way, in all top graduate schools of management. M.I.T. accepts from 25 percent to 40 percent as do Harvard, Stanford, Chicago, and Wharton, the bastions of management-education excellence in this country. Women's competence is well documented. From all reports, they are capable on the job—and, Yavitz adds, "They prove their competence without the need for sporting hair on their chests."

Organizations, thankfully, are too complicated for the popular delusion of simplicity and certainty, the false-grit tunnel vision of a John Wayne. The fact is that there is no one set of rules, of programmed behavior, dress or skills that can apply to women or men in their attempts to succeed. Perhaps the most convincing documentation of this point is a study of 1,800 successful managers recently completed by the American Management Associations (A.M.A.). From this study, a profile emerges: Effective managers are social initiators; they anticipate problems and possible solutions. They build alliances, bring people together, develop networks. Their competencies cluster in several areas: *social-emotional maturity* (composed of such traits as self-control, spontaneity, perceptual objectivity, accurate self-assessment, stamina, adaptability); *entrepreneurial abilities* (efficiency, productivity); *intellectual abilities* (logical thought, conceptual ability, the diagnostic use of ideas and memory); and *interpersonal abilities* (self-presentation, interest in the development of others, concern with impact, oral communication skills, the use of socialized power, and concern with relationships).

The A.M.A. study is, without question, some of the most complete, systematic research ever undertaken on the attributes of the good manager. I see nothing in its findings that would give men or women (with whatever "natural endowments" one attributes to sex roles) an edge. I would also wager that most astute observers of the managerial landscape would agree with the study. Yavitz, for one, describes the effective manager as possessing "the ability for true communication—I don't mean the glib view, that you're communicating when you make a great pitch." He insists that two-way communication is imperative: "A manager must be perceptive, must understand what she's hearing, and then be able to convey the ideas clearly to others . . . must be flexible enough to acknowledge that there are competing constituencies and must be sensitive enough to listen to the emotion and spirit behind the words as well as to the content . . . and she must be able to synthesize what she's heard, to put together something as close to the optimal solution as possible, something that makes sense.

"The manager must be able to persuade, explain, convince others why this solution is more sensible and beneficial for the whole cluster of constituencies than another solution. I surmise," he concludes, "that a high sense of responsibility and commitment, ability to cope with ambiguity, and a continuing sense of curiosity and willingness to learn are critical attributes for the successful manager."

Does either sex have a monopoly on the constellation of traits identified by the A.M.A. research or by Dean Yavitz?

A better explanation of success, it seems to me, is that those who are favorably placed in organizational structures are more likely to be successful, independent of gender, than those less favorably placed. By "favorably placed" I mean: (1) having the support of one's subordinates, (2) having clear goals and a similarly clear path to them, and (3) being empowered by the organization with appropriate means to reward and punish one's subordinates. When these conditions are present, we have what scholars refer to as "situational favorableness."

Complex organizations vary enormously. Specifically, they vary with respect to their "cultures." Some organizations are formalistic in nature, rigid, hierarchical; others are collegial, relying on agreement and consensus; while still others tend to be personalistic, concerned with the self-actualization of their employees. Within organizations, too, there can be great cultural differences. Just compare Bell Telephone's Murray Hill Labs with its international headquarters at Basking Ridge, New Jersey. It's hard to find a man without a beard or with a tie at the Bell Labs at Murray Hill, and equally hard

Three Types of Organizational Cultures

	Formalistic	Collegial	Personalistic
Basis for decision	Direction from authority	Discussion, agreement	Directions from within
Form of control	Rules, laws, rewards, punishments	Interpersonal, group commitments	Actions aligned with self-concept
Source of power	Superior	What "we" think and feel	What *I* think and feel
Desired end	Compliance	Consensus	Self-actualization
To be avoided	Deviation from authoritative direction; taking risks	Failure to reach consensus	Not being "true to oneself"
Time perspective	Future	Near future	Now
Position relative to others	Hierarchical	Peer	Individual
Human relationships	Structured	Group oriented	Individually oriented
Basis for growth	Following the established order	Peer group membership	Acting on awareness of self

to find a man without a tie and with a beard at Basking Ridge. The accompanying table contrasts the values and behavior of three types of organizational systems.

Success depends greatly on being able to diagnose the particular organizational culture within which one is embedded and to develop the flexibility to respond and initiate within that structure. There's nothing sex-related about it. All that's required are the knowledge and the personal skills that that most famous of all salesmen, Professor Harold Hill of "The Music Man," expounded: "Gotta know the territory."

From Hobbes to Freud, the special character of Western (most especially American) development has been an awareness of the heterogeneity of human experience and an accentuated consciousness of the power of the individual to overcome or shape his circumstances. As Isaiah Berlin shows in his *Russian Thinkers,* the Russian tendency has always been for the system—always the senior partner to self-affirmation—to move toward hegemony. In the United States, that partnership has been reversed, with self-affirmation in the ascendance. There is, as Mounier, the French political writer, has warned us, a "madness in both those who treat the world as a dream and . . . a madness in those who treat the inner life as a phantom." To apply this to systems, there are those who view organizations as mirages, with no reality except that which we give them. This is one kind of madness. The other madness is that of those, like the Russians and some *echt* Marxist thinkers, who will not deal with, or even recognize, aspects of their personality, dispositions, if you will, that stem from our inner souls, or private lives. For the sake of our collective sanity, we must recognize the validity and reality of each—by organization and personality—for without that total embrace, our perspective will be dangerously skewed.

In any case, it would be a grave error to fall into the trap of underestimating the power of organizations and conceiving of executive success as dependent on toughness or softness, assertiveness or sensitivity, masculinity or femininity. That popular delusion has already caused too much damage, both to individuals who are impersonating males and females, and to the institutions for which they work.

AN EVALUATION OF ORGANIZATIONAL DUE PROCESS IN THE RESOLUTION OF EMPLOYEE/EMPLOYER CONFLICT

JOHN D. ARAM

PAUL F. SALIPANTE, JR.

In the last decade, employee/employer relationships in the United States have been strongly influenced by federal legislation expanding the rights and protection of employees. Issues involving equal employment opportunity, pension management, job safety, and protection against recrimination for cooperation with a variety of regulatory agencies cut across white- and blue-collar lines and apply to unionized and nonunionized personnel. The current approach to resolving conflict by executive or judicial units of government is in sharp contrast to the previous national labor policy, which held that disputes are best settled through direct bilateral negotiation or through mediation and arbitration by neutrals. Employee/employer conflict in the newer area of "employee rights" is identified by (1) issues that apply more widely than to union settings alone, and (2) governmental, rather than private sector, establishment of the grounds and procedures for pursuing grievances. A key question is whether an effective private system of industrial jurisprudence is available to organizations and employees that will provide a workable alternative to further governmental action by offering the benefits of direct, private settlement rather than the costs, delay, and acrimony often accompanying litigation (Coulson, 1978).

Although the labor relations literature has discussed union grievance systems since the 1930s, it is only since Evan's (1961) article on "Organization Man and Due Process of Law" that due process systems have been explicitly considered in the literature of organization and administration. A number of subsequent articles have addressed the theory, incidence, and application of organizational due process (Evan, 1962a, 1962b, 1965, 1975; Ewing, 1977a, 1977b, 1977c; Scott, 1965, 1966, 1969; Selznick, 1969).

Our purpose in this paper is to review the literature on the development and performance of grievance resolution or due process systems in private employment settings. We first address the meaning and justification of due process in the workplace. Then, types of due process are identified and criteria for evaluating their effectiveness are derived and applied. Employee/employer conflict and grievance procedures are discussed with respect to issues involving the statutory rights of individuals, organizational norms and rules, and societal norms. We identify a set of conditions for the effective development

Reprinted from the *Academy of Management Review,* Vol. 6, No. 2, 1981, 197–204.

of organizational systems of conflict resolution, and suggest future directions for inquiry in this area.

The Meaning and Justification of Due Process in the Workplace

Substantive and Procedural Due Process

Any discussion of due process must begin with the difference between substantive and procedural due process, a long-standing distinction of jurisprudence. *Substantive due process* treats of the rationale or purpose of laws, ensuring that a person's life, liberty, or property is not arbitrarily taken away. *Procedural due process* concerns the fairness of procedures in applying the law, rather than the fairness of the substance of the law itself. Procedural standards are not fixed, but are often relatively well defined. For example, in criminal cases the procedural elements of a timely notice of charges, the right to counsel, rules governing introduction of evidence, rights of cross-examination and of appeal, and so forth are well established (Harron, 1977).

Procedural due process is pertinent to any institutional judgment. In a context of appraising the role of due process in American institutions, Forkosch (1958) argued that due process is a general concept rather than a set of fixed procedures. Reflecting on the Supreme Court's manner of defining due process, he concluded that "there has always been a majority of the High Court which has rejected the formulation of discrete, tangible, substantive, or procedural check-points, preferring, instead, to set up a mosaic of an historical, economic, political, sociological, and legal process against which the particular situation can be cast and evaluated." Forkosch also argues that the terms "adequate" and "fair" are more appropriate for analysis than specific actions such as "notice" and "hearing."

This perspective has merit in the application of the concept to employment settings. It emphasizes the purpose, objectives, and values to be served by an organizational due process system and confronts the organization at a policy level concerning its objectives and standards for internal justice. At the same time, it permits flexibility in specific procedures. The absence of fixed definitions and procedures for due process puts a premium on distinct formulations of intent and procedures by organizational policy makers.

Justifications for Due Process Systems

Various justifications have been offered for applying the concept of due process to work organizations. One argument takes a pragmatic view of the present statutory rights of employees and the widening application of constitutional rights to employment settings (Ewing, 1977a). In this view, organizational due process is a fair and less costly means of resolving disputes than litigation.

A second justification for bringing due process to the workplace has been presented by Phillip Selznick (1969), who finds the concept of due process at the heart of the law of governance. He questions whether this particular principle of public governance can and should be applied to private organizations, then argues that it should, because (1) there are already areas of blurred distinction between public and private law, (2) laws of governance apply to all rule-making authority, and (3) institutions must develop fair means for participants to attain and transfer statuses and roles that have value to them. Selznick provides a rationale for relating due process as a principle to new employee/employer realities and the underlying public attitudes that have served as wellsprings of legislative support.

A final justification for due process is consistent with A.O. Hirschman's (1970) concept of "voice" (verbal or written dissent or advice) as a type of feedback from employees and thus as a mechanism of recuperation and adaptation. Due process systems can include procedures for planning and altering personnel policies as well as for settling specific disputes.

These three justifications for organizational due process are based, respectively, on practical necessity, on a normative view of the sociology of the law, and on a theory of organizational recuperation. Although no one justification may be persuasive, the convergence of the three encourages further evaluation of the concept.

The Nature and Effectiveness of Procedures of Due Process

Whatever the function an organization's decision makers intend for a due process system, questions of feasibility must be raised before specific procedures are adopted. How to define procedures is not obvious; procedures that are practical for one organization may not be so for another, and procedures seen as feasible by an organization's decision makers may prove to be unworkable in the view of employees. Some insight can be gained on these issues by reviewing the range and incidence of procedures used by organizations, and by applying criteria of effectiveness to them.

Design Issues Indicated by Previous Research

Research by Scott (1965) and by Ewing (1977b) has established that a significant percentage of business organizations have some type of due process. Scott's survey of 793 firms in 6 industries found that 35 percent of the firms had some form of appeal system and 11 percent had formal appeal systems. In Ewing's more recent questionnaire study of due process in organizations among *Harvard Business Review* subscribers, the frequency of specific procedures was found to vary greatly. For example, only about 10 percent of the sample reported the presence of a corporate ombudsman, but other procedures, such as an executive "open door policy," were reported by over 60 percent of the respondents. Though marred by obvious methodological weaknesses, Ewing's comparison of subscriber responses in 1971 and 1977 is provocative because it indicates that an increasing number of firms are adopting procedures that reflect a serious concern with due process. For example, the incidence of management grievance committees increased from 9 to 14 percent over this period.

An initial conclusion, then, is that a reasonable number of firms have procedures to implement due process—certainly enough to indicate that it is practical for many firms. Regarding general feasibility, Scott found that the incidence of formal appeal systems was greater in larger firms and in industries marked by relatively lower job mobility. These findings suggest that due process is either more necessary or more feasible in such firms and industries.

Beyond these basic issues of incidence and feasibility lie the more difficult questions of choice of procedures and their effectiveness. Both Scott and Ewing made distinctions between procedures they saw as "advanced" or "tough" and those they labeled "early" or "soft." Scott implied that firms go through an evolutionary development from informal policy, to formal policy without specified procedures, to formal policy and specified procedures. Scott's and Ewing's typologies of procedures appear compatible with each other and they suggest two dimensions underlying their categorizations. One is the *degree of formality of appeal procedures.* High formality connotes explicit statements concerning (1) appealable issues, (2) steps to be followed in presenting a complaint, and (3) roles and responsibilities of parties in the resolution of the conflict. A second dimension is the *degree of independence from management of the final decision maker.* The separation of the judicial function from managerial positions in favor of staff offices, grievance committees, review boards, and outside arbitrators is evident in the tougher procedures cited by Scott and Ewing.

Though the analysis of effectiveness is not explicit in their work, the typologies of procedures used by Scott and Ewing imply that more "advanced" procedures are more effective. Is there, in fact, a correlation between effectiveness and procedural formality and independence of the final decision maker? Empirical research has not addressed this question sufficiently, although recommendations assuming such a correlation have been made, based on institutional studies and general experience with union grievance systems (International Labor Office, 1965). Given the lack of research, our approach is to develop criteria by which to evaluate alternative procedures of due process. These criteria will then be applied to the questions of decision-maker independence and procedural formality.

Criteria for Evaluating Procedures of Due Process

The framework for specifying criteria is Hirschman's (1970) analysis of "exit" and "voice" as recuperative mechanisms for organizations that are, for whatever reason, threatened with loss of support by major constituencies. Hirschman's analysis primarily concerns customers' decisions to change their purchases to a substitute product (exit) or to seek corrective changes in the firm's product or service (voice), but he also identifies the choice for dissatisfied employees as leaving the organization or seeking change in it. Of particular interest are the conditions in which voice will be elected over exit by a discontented employee.

Hirschman argues that employees are generally more predisposed than consumers to voice as an expression of dissatisfaction. Because employees usually have fewer options than do consumers, the benefits of voice as well as the cost of exit are usually greater for employees than for consumers. Thus, the problem is to create specific organizational mechanisms that capitalize on employees' natural predispositions toward voice.

While Hirschman does not explicitly consider criteria for evaluating means of voicing complaints, he does stress that for voice to function as a recuperative force, it must be more attractive than exit. His thinking can be extended on two points in the present context. First, one might say that voice, through an internal appeal system, must be more attractive to the individual than either exit or external voice (litigation). Second, the attractiveness of internal appeal depends on (1) a perception that a situation can be corrected because the organization has both the capability and willingness to change, and (2) the presence of advantages to the individual of an internal rather than an external resolution.

These two factors imply four criteria for evaluating appeal systems. To increase the first factor—employees' perceptions that the situation has a reasonable chance to be corrected through internal appeal—the appeal system must be seen as offering a fair settlement. If employees do *not* feel that a complaint will receive a fair hearing—i.e., that change or redress is not achievable from a just complaint—the appeal system will not be attractive. Of course, fairness also implies that reasons for a lack of change are understood and are found acceptable.

To increase the second factor—the advantage of internal appeal—the system must have several positive characteristics in comparison with the external alternatives: (a) timely resolution, to reduce the period of uncertainty and the loss of benefits stemming from continuance of the decision being appealed; (b) ease of utilization, to minimize the time and effort required to file and follow through on an appeal; and (c) protection from recrimination, so that future benefits such as raises and promotions are not threatened by the filing of an appeal. Because the more valuable employees are often those for whom exit opportunities are most readily available, the advantages of internal appeal must be perceived as significant to avoid loss of these employees.

The determinants of attractiveness of internal appeal have led to four evaluation criteria: fairness of settlement, timeliness of settlement, ease of utilizing the system, and protection from loss of future benefits. If any one of these criteria is not met, an internal appeal system will not be used.

These criteria do not address the effect of due process on line management, another obvious concern to the organization's decision makers. Some advantages (Salipante and Aram, 1978; Yenny, 1977) and some disadvantages (Epstein, 1975) to management have been touched on, but the question needs more extensive examination.

Decision-maker independence. If these four criteria are applied to the design issues identified earlier, the criterion of most relevance to the question of decision-maker independence is the perceived fairness of settlement. If an appeal system is to be used in preference to external litigation, it must be at least roughly comparable in the prospect of a fair decision. One would suspect that the more independent the final decision maker from the party charged in a grievance, as would be a federal judge or arbitrator, the greater the perceived fairness of settlement.

The ultimate step of a grievance hearing before an outside arbitrator has become a key and proven part of American labor relations (Slichter, Healy, and Livernash, 1969). Refusals by the courts to review most arbitrated decisions based on labor contracts have strengthened the role of arbitrators, and the faith of labor and management in them. Appeal systems providing arbitration as the final step thereby promise high general acceptance on the criterion of fairness of settlement.

It is important to note that arbitration is being discussed here as the final available step of an appeal system, and not as the expected resolution step for the vast majority of appeals. Studies have shown only a small percentage of complaints passing to arbitration for resolution (Gandz, 1978; Martin, n.d.).

Formality of procedures. The second design issue of due process systems is the degree to which appeal procedures are formally specified. There appears to be no simple relationship between formality and effectiveness. The presence of highly formalized grievance procedures in most labor agreements suggests that unions and managements find value in formalization. Kuhn (1961), however, found that dispute resolution also depended on informal political processes within the union and between union and management. Others (McKersie and Shropshire, 1962; Slichter et al., 1969) have argued that an effective union/management system settles most grievances at an early informal stage. In general, one may conclude that formalized procedures are often functional, but may also be incomplete.

The criteria for attractiveness of appeal systems suggest that formal procedures, if properly designed, do offer potential advantages. With regard to the perceived-fairness-of-settlement criterion, formal systems can increase a grievant's perception of receiving a fair hearing if they provide an advocate or supporter for the grievant. This supporter could be another employee of the grievant's choice, a staff assistant, or legal counsel.

Consider next the criterion of timeliness of resolution. Formal systems with few steps and a short time limit on each step should offer faster resolution than an informal system, since the latter has no requirement that a decision ever be reached. However, a formal system that establishes a progression of many steps may inhibit timely resolution. Some union systems have been criticized on these grounds (deVyver, 1976), leading to calls for expeditious grievance procedures. In fact, labor courts in several European countries offer faster resolution than is typically available in an American union system (Aaron, 1971).

Formal systems can also offer advantages according to the criterion of effort required to utilize the system. A clearly defined system with relatively few steps and with a staff designated to assist grievants can be used with little effort. In contrast, informal systems may require much effort simply to determine what the alternatives for appeal are, to whom to appeal, and in what manner. Complex formal systems having many steps and requiring extensive documentation of appeals can also require great effort.

Protection from recrimination is the final criterion to be considered. The phenomenon of recrimination against whistle-blowers is well known and has been frequently documented in the press (e.g., Stevens, 1978). Well-designed formal systems can provide some measure of protection; one method for reducing recrimination is to impose a strong penalty for its use. This would be easier in a formal system, since specific penalties could be spelled out and means of enforcement provided.

The preceding discussion suggests that appropriately designed formal systems promise advantages in terms of employee use. However, formality may make the appeal system less effective than trusted informality if the system is inaccessible, requires many steps and delays before a final decision, or has no protection from recrimination.

A final consideration is whether a single, uniform due process system is appropriate for resolving all employee/employer conflicts or whether differentiation of the resolution process according to type of conflict is warranted. This question concerns the utility of a general-purpose due process system versus several selective procedures addressed to particular types of conflict.

There appears to be no available classification of organizational conflict that elucidates the role of due process as a procedure of corrective justice (Thomson, 1976). For example, Tannenbaum (1965) discusses economic, power, and psychological sources of conflict in the union/management context, but these global categories shed little light on specific types of employee grievances and their resolution. More recently, Gandz's (1978) analysis of grievance arbitration adapted Thomas's (1977) categories of conflict: pseudo-conflict, common problem conflict, and conflict of interest. Only the latter category addresses issues pertinent to due process systems.

Closer to the topic of appeal systems, Evan (1965) conducted a comparative study of superior/subordinate conflict and perceptions of appeal procedures in private and public research laboratories. In this study, conflict was classified as *technical,* meaning disagreements over the means or ends pertaining to the work; *administrative,* referring to disagreements concerning procedures, policies, and allocation of resources; or *interpersonal,* including personality clashes and barriers to interpersonal communication. Although more specific to the workplace, these categories are still general and do not distinguish between a variety of specific disputes—for example, whether the grievance is for personal redress or correction of a general organization practice, or whether the grounds for complaint are established in law, involve an internal norm or expectation, or are anchored in an external social value.

Our own classification of conflict is based on known precedents and principles for settling disputes. We offer this typology as a point of departure for differentiating specific applications of due process systems.

Conflicts Involving Statutory Rights

The type of conflict having the best-defined and clearest basis for resolution concerns issues defined by public statutes. The original laws, a substantial body of regulatory guidelines and compliance procedures, and judicial norms are available to clarify and ensure the rights of employees. Even though various aspects of these laws and regulations may be the subject of intense controversy (e.g., When does affirmative action become reverse discrimination?), employee rights and required employer actions are generally clear.

The major issue for due process systems in confronting conflict arising within an area covered by law is what relation to expect and seek between internal appeal mechanisms and external courts. An organization's policy makers, seeing the possibility of simultaneously addressing the same complaint in two different forums, may question the value of internal appeal.

What, then, might be the relation between internal resolution and external litigation? The direction of an answer can be found in the Supreme Court ruling in *Alexander* vs. *Gardner-Denver Co.* (415 U.S. 36, 7 FEP Cases 81, 1974), in which a central question was whether an arbitration decision concerning a discrimination charge is subject to judicial review. The Court found that arbitration in employment discrimination claims cannot be binding, but it also outlined the conditions by which an arbitrator's decision could be given weight in any subsequent judicial proceedings: the presence of nondiscrimination provisions in the collective bargaining agreement, the degree of procedural fairness in the arbitration proceedings, the adequacy of the arbitration record, and the expertise of the arbitrator.

Expanding on the role of arbitration in employment discrimination claims, Edwards (1976) proposed a set of rules for the arbitration process, among which was employee agreement not to simultaneously pursue the claim in another forum during arbitration. In principle, at least, this rule might be incorporated into a variety of internal appeal systems.

The Supreme Court's decision appears to affirm the role of private mechanisms of resolving disputes where statutory or constitutional rights are involved, while not asking more from the private system than can realistically be expected. The benefit of a private mechanism, especially evident with a provision for arbitration, should be to reduce the burden of time and expense for both employee and employer.

Conflicts Involving Organizational Norms

A second type of conflict concerns grievances about actions in which an individual perceives negative personal consequence or penalty, but has little external legal recourse. This is the area of such diverse issues as discipline, discharge, salary and promotion, and arbitrary or otherwise unfair treatment. This area of conflict is guided by the collective bargaining agreement in the case of a unionized workforce and simply by organizational policy and the power of individual workers or work groups (Roy, 1952; Dalton, 1959) in the case of a nonunionized workforce and for exempt personnel in general.

Designing a due process system for resolving conflicts of this type seems to require a painstaking effort to determine the criteria and norms of fairness for the specific organization. One of the problems in developing these policies may be significant differences between occupational groups in the concept of fairness itself. Selznick (1969), in an attitude survey of a large group of employees, found substantial differences in definitions of fairness between occupational groups. Fairness, to unskilled workers, meant primarily "equal treatment for all." This definition became successively less important within more skilled, administrative, and professional occupational groups, for whom "recognition of individual abilities" was the predominant meaning. Also, large differences in attitudes were found across occupational groups with respect to conditions for discharge and the importance of recognition of highly skilled employees.

We have argued that a major issue for due process systems dealing with conflicts covered by statutory rights is the relationship between internal and external forums. We now argue that, for individual conflicts *without* recourse to external forums, a major issue is incorporating the different values and concepts of various hierarchical levels, educational levels, and occupational groups into policies—statements of appealable issues and norms of fairness—governing due process systems. The potential role of arbitration in this class of disputes is also guided by these same considerations. Individuals who have expertise and experience in the arbitration of issues concerning the relevant employee level or occupational group should be designated as arbitrators.

Conflicts Involving Societal Norms

Appropriateness of organizational actions with respect to societal expectations appears to be even less well defined than statutory issues or problems of internal organizational norms. This third type of conflict occurs when an organizational member questions or challenges an organizational policy or action on the basis of its moral or social effect. Members may be in conflict with the organization with respect to the safety of consumer product design, the ethics of conducting business in a particular country, or the ethical and professional conduct of officials. Such conflicts, loosely referred to as "whistle blowing," covers a wide range of potential disclosures and complaints of members. This appears to be the least well-understood area of conflict, the one of least accumulated practical experience. The key issue here is understanding and specifying social norms that could guide organizational policy. Whereas conflicts of organizational norms call for developing an organizational consensus (although perhaps one differentiated by segments of the organization), this third type of conflict presents the more difficult task of determining societal consensus.

A variation of this type of conflict involves a challenge to the legality of an organization's actions, such as price-fixing, unfair trade practices, insider trading, or fraud. In these cases, the alleged action is legally prohibited, but the process for challenging the action within the corporation is rarely defined. The potential for this type of conflict is greatest for corporate lawyers, accountants, and top managers.

The board of directors is, institutionally, the body responsible for integrating the organization with society and it may be able to assume explicit responsibility for resolving conflicts that have external ethical, social, or legal ramifications. Outside directors might be considered to have a responsibility for defining social norms and expectations for organizational practices, for hearing grievances of this type, and for ensuring compliance with the law. Boards having audit, public affairs, or public responsibility committees could include due process in this area of conflict with their other functions. Such means appear to be appropriate and practical for resolving conflicts related to societal implications of organizational actions.

This preliminary classification of types of conflict depends on the focus of definition of norms. The major types of conflict involve statutory rights, organizational norms, and social norms, including compliance with the law. It would be reasonable to draw at least two conclusions from this typology. First, any or all of these types of conflict can be seen as recuperative mechanisms for the organization: each has the potential for correcting errors of organizational action. Second, the effectiveness of a due process system can be enhanced by a specific matching of forums of dispute settlement with the types of conflict.

Concluding Remarks

Our discussion has focused on due process from the perspectives of organizations and of individual employees. The larger societal question is whether private systems of conflict resolution can be effective in the absence of institutionalized support for employees. In other words, can procedures for settling disputes be effective in areas in which employees are not supported by a union or by government regulation? Can they also play a constructive role where such institutional support presently exists?

Exploring these questions has led to consideration of the functions that organizational due process might serve, to evaluation of procedural formality and decision-maker independence as criteria for system effectiveness, and to development of a typology of employee/employer conflict and conflict resolution. The argument running through this review offers conditional positive support for the possibility of private systems of conflict resolution. If employers consciously formulate objectives and standards of justice, and if procedures are designed with a high degree of decision-maker independence and balanced formality, internal due process systems can serve an institutional role in resolving employee/employer conflicts. The analysis also suggests that the effectiveness of due process systems can be augmented by differentiating types of conflict and providing selective mechanisms of resolution.

The topic of due process in work organizations calls for much greater conceptual development, practical experimentation, and systematic research. The broad issue is the role that internal appeal systems can play in employee/employer conflict. More specific questions are: What are possible types of procedures for internal due process? What are their differential consequences? To what circumstances and types of conflict are they applicable? How can they relate to external forums of conflict resolution? How can they be developed? What organizational policies are necessary to support them?

The subject of employee rights presents a significant challenge to the management of organizations. Those who take up the challenge will enjoy an unusual opportunity to integrate scholarly and practical interests and to serve both individuals and institutions.

References

Aaron, B. "Contemporary Issues in the Grievance and Arbitration Process. In *Collective Bargaining Today: Proceedings of the Collective Bargaining Forum* (New York, 1970). Washington, D.C.: Bureau of National Affairs, 1971.

Coulson, R. "New Fringe Benefit: Voluntary Arbitration of Job-Rights Claims." *New York Law Journal*, 1978, *179*(1), 4.

Dalton, M. *Men Who Manage*. New York: Wiley, 1959.

DeVyver, F. "Grievance Systems in American Industry." *Australian Quarterly*, June 1976, pp. 34–43.

Edwards, H. "Arbitration of Employment Discrimination Cases: A Proposal for Employer and Union Representatives." *Labor Law Journal*, 1976, *27*, 265–277.

Epstein, R. "The Grievance Procedure in the Non-union Setting: Caveat Employer." *Employee Relations Law Journal*, 1975, *1*, 120–127.

Evan, W. "Organization Man and Due Process of Law." *American Sociological Review*, 1961, *26*, 540–547.

——. "Due Process of Law in Military and Industrial Organizations." *Administrative Science Quarterly*, 1962, *7*, 187–207. (a)

——. "Public and Private Legal Systems." In Evan, W. (ed.), *Law and Society*. New York: Free Press, 1962, pp. 165–184. (b)

———. "Superior-subordinate Conflict in Research Organizations." *Administrative Science Quarterly,* 1965, *10,* 52–64.

———. "Power, Conflict, and Constitutionalism in Organizations." *Social Science Information,* 1975, *14,* 53–80.

Ewing, D. *Freedom Inside the Organization: Bringing Civil Liberties to the Workplace.* New York: McGraw-Hill, 1977. (a)

———. "What Business Thinks About Employee Rights." *Harvard Business Review,* 1977, *55,* 81–94. (b)

———. "Winning Freedom on the Job: From Assembly Line to Executive Suite." *Civil Liberties Review,* July/August 1977, pp. 8–22. (c)

Forkosch, M. "American Democracy and Procedural Due Process." *Brooklyn Law Review,* 1958, *24,* 143–253.

Gandz, J. *Grievance Arbitration.* Working Paper Series No. 206, School of Business Administration, University of Western Ontario, 1978.

Harron, T. *Law for Business Managers: The Regulatory Environment.* Boston: Holbrook Press, 1977.

Hirschman, A. *Exit, Voice, and Loyalty: Responses to Decline in Firms, Organizations, and States.* Cambridge, Mass.: Harvard University Press, 1970.

International Labor Office. *Examination of Grievances and Communications within the Undertaking.* Geneva, 1965.

Kuhn, J. *Bargaining in Grievance Settlement.* New York: Columbia University Press, 1961.

Martin, J. *Equal Employment Opportunity Complaint Procedures and Federal Union/Management Relations: A Field Study.* Unpublished manuscript, Wayne State University, Detroit, Mich., no date.

McKersie, R. and W. Shropshire. "Avoiding Written Grievances: A Successful Program." *Journal of Business,* 1962, *35,* 135–152.

Roy, D. "Quota Restriction and Goldbricking in a Machine Shop." *American Journal of Sociology,* 1952, *67,* 427–442.

Salipante, P. and J. Aram. "The Role of Special Grievance Systems in Furthering Equal Employment Opportunities." In *Proceedings of the Industrial Relations Research Association,* August 1978.

Scott, W. *The Management of Conflict.* Homewood, Ill.: Irwin, 1965.

———. "An Issue in Administrative Justice: Managerial Appeal Systems." *Management International,* 1966, *6,* 37–53.

———. "Organization Government: The Prospects for a Truly Participative System." *Public Administration Review,* 1969, *29,* 43–53.

Selznick, P. *Law, Society, and Industrial Justice.* New York: Russell Sage Foundation, 1969.

Slichter, H., J. Healy and E. Livernash. *The Impact of Collective Bargaining on Management.* Washington, D.C.: Brookings Institution, 1969.

Stevens, C. "The Whistle Blower Chooses Hard Path." *Wall Street Journal,* Nov. 11, 1978, p. 36.

Tannenbaum, A. "Unions." In J. G. March (ed.), *Handbook of Organizations.* Chicago: Rand-McNally, 1965, pp. 710–763.

Thomas, K. "Conflict and Conflict Management." In M. D. Dunnette (ed.), *Handbook of Industrial and Organizational Psychology.* Chicago: Rand-McNally, 1977, pp. 889–935.

Thomson, A. *The Grievance Procedure.* Lexington, Mass.: Lexington Books, 1976.

Yenny, S. "In Defense of the Grievance Procedure in a Non-union Setting." *Employee Relations Law Journal,* 1977, *2,* 434–443.

⎡⎾⎾⎿ leadership and decision making

DECISION MAKING AS A SOCIAL PROCESS: NORMATIVE AND DESCRIPTIVE MODELS OF LEADER BEHAVIOR

VICTOR H. VROOM
ARTHUR G. JAGO

Introduction

Several scholarly disciplines share an interest in the decision-making process. On one hand, there are the related fields of operations research and management science, both concerned with how to improve the decisions which are made. Their models of decision making, aimed at providing a rational basis for selecting among alternative courses of action, are termed normative or prescriptive models. On the other hand, there have been attempts by psychologists, sociologists, and political scientists to understand the decisions and choices that people do make. March and Simon [6] were among the first to suggest that an understanding of the decision-making process could be central to an understanding of the behavior of organizations—a point of view that was later amplified by Cyert and March [1] in their behavioral theory of the firm. In this tradition, the goal is understanding rather than improvement, and the models are descriptive rather than normative.

Whether the models are normative or descriptive, the common ingredient is a conception of decision making as an information-processing activity, frequently one which takes place within a single manager. Both sets of models focus on the set of alternative decisions or problem solutions from which the choice is, or should be, made. The normative models are based on the conse-

Reprinted by permission of the authors and publisher from *Decision Sciences,* Vol. 5, 1974.

The research contained in this article was sponsored by the Organizational Effectiveness Research Program, Office of Naval Research (Code 452) under Contract to the senior author (No. N00014-67-A-0097-0027; NR 177-935). Reproduction in whole or in part is permitted for any purpose of the United States Government.

quences of choices among these alternatives, the descriptive models on the determinants of these choices.

In this article, the authors take a somewhat different, although complementary, view of managerial decision making. They view decision making as a social process with the elements of the process presented in terms of events between people rather than events that occur within a person. When a problem or occasion for decision making occurs within an organization, there are typically several alternative social mechanisms available for determining what solution is chosen or decision reached. These alternatives vary in the person or persons participating in the problem-solving and decision-making process, and in the relative amounts of influence that each has on the final solution or decision reached.

There are both descriptive and normative questions to be answered about the social processes used for decision making in organizations. The normative questions hinge on knowledge concerning the consequences of alternatives for the effective performance of the system. The dimensions on which social processes can vary constitute the independent variables, and criteria of the effectiveness of the decisions constitute dependent variables. Ultimately, such knowledge could provide the foundation for a specification of the social and interpersonal aspects of how decisions *should be* made within organizations.

Similarly, the descriptive questions concern the circumstances under which alternative social processes for decision making *are* used in organizations. The dimensions on which social processes vary become the dependent variables, and characteristics of the manager who controls the process and the nature of the decision itself provide the basis for the specification of independent variables.

Vroom and Yetton [10] provided a start to an examination of both normative and descriptive questions through an examination of one dimension of decision making—the extent to which a leader encourages the participation of his subordinates in decision making. Participation in decision making was a logical place to start since there is substantial evidence of its importance and of the circumstances surrounding different consequences of it [3] [9] [11].

The purpose of this article is twofold: (1) to provide a brief summary of the objectives, methods, and results of the research pertaining to both normative and descriptive models of decision processes used in organizations (described in detail in Vroom and Yetton [10]); (2) to describe some recent extensions of the previous work, including an empirical investigation designed to explore facets of decision making not previously studied.

Vroom and Yetton concern themselves primarily with problems or decisions to be made by managers with a formally defined set of subordinates reporting to them. In each problem or decision, the manager must have some area of freedom or discretion in determining the solution adopted, and the solution must affect at least one of the manager's subordinates. Following Maier, Solem, and Maier [4], they further make a distinction between group problems and individual problems. If the solution adopted has potential effects on all immediate subordinates or some readily identifiable subset of them, it is classified as a group problem. If the solution affects only one of the manager's subordinates, it is called an individual problem. This distinction is an important one because it determines the range of decision-making processes available to the manager. Table 1 shows a taxonomy of decision processes for both types of problems. Each process is represented by a symbol (e.g., AI, CI,

GII, DI) which provides a convenient method of referring to each process. The letters in the code signify the basic properties of the process (A stands for autocratic; C for consultative; G for group; and D for delegated). The roman numerals that follow the letters constitute variants on that process. Thus AI represents the first variant on the autocratic process, AII the second variant, and so on.

The processes shown in Table 1 are arranged in columns corresponding to their presumed applicability to either group or individual problems and are arranged within columns in order of increasing opportunity for the subordinate to influence the solution to the problem.

The discrete alternative processes shown in Table 1 can be used both normatively and descriptively. In the former use, they constitute discrete alternatives available to the manager or decision maker who presumably is motivated to choose that alternative which has the greatest likelihood of producing effective results for his organization. In the latter use, the processes constitute forms of behavior on the part of individuals which require explana-

TABLE 1

Decision-making Processes

For Individual Problems	*For Group Problems*
AI You solve the problem or make the decision yourself, using information available to you at that time.	AI You solve the problem or make the decision yourself, using information available to you at that time.
AII You obtain any necessary information from the subordinate, then decide on the solution to the problem yourself. You may or may not tell the subordinate what the problem is, in getting the information from him. The role played by your subordinate in making the decision is clearly one of providing specific information which you request, rather than generating or evaluating alternative solutions.	AII You obtain any necessary information from subordinates, then decide on the solution to the problem yourself. You may or may not tell subordinates what the problem is, in getting the information from them. The role played by your subordinates in making the decision is clearly one of providing specific information which you request, rather than generating or evaluating solutions.
CI You share the problem with the relevant subordinate, getting his ideas and suggestions. Then *you* make the decision. This decision may or may not reflect your subordinate's influence.	CI You share the problem with the relevant subordinates individually, getting their ideas and suggestions without bringing them together as a group. Then *you* make the decision. This decision may or may not reflect your subordinates' influence.
GI You share the problem with one of your subordinates and together you analyze the problem and arrive at a mutually satisfactory solution in an atmosphere of free and open exchange of information and ideas. You both contribute to the resolution of the problem with the relative contribution of each being dependent on knowledge rather than formal authority.	CII You share the problem with your subordinates in a group meeting. In this meeting you obtain their ideas and suggestions. Then, *you* make the decision which may or may not reflect your subordinates' influence.
DI You delegate the problem to one of your subordinates, providing him with any relevant information that you possess, but giving him responsibility for solving the problem by himself. Any solution which the person reaches will receive your support.	GII You share the problem with your subordinates as a group. Together you generate and evaluate alternatives and attempt to reach agreement (consensus) on a solution. Your role is much like that of chairman, coordinating the discussion, keeping it focused on the problem, and making sure that the critical issues are discussed. You do not try to influence the group to adopt "your" solution and are willing to accept and implement any solution which has the support of the entire group.

tion. In the balance of this paper we will attempt to keep in mind these two uses of the taxonomy and will discuss them separately.

A Normative Model of Decision Processes

What would be a rational way of deciding on the form and amount of participation in decision making to be used in different situations? Neither debates over the relative merits of Theory X and Theory Y [7], nor the apparent truism that leadership depends on the situation are of much help here. The aim in this portion of the research is to develop a framework for matching a leader's behavior, as expressed in the alternatives presented in Table 1, to the demands of his situation. Any framework developed must be consistent with empirical evidence concerning the consequences of participation and be operational so that a trained leader could use it to determine how he should act in a given situation.

The normative model should provide a basis for effective problem solving and decision making by matching the desired decision process with relevant properties of particular problems or decisions to be made. Following Maier [5], the effectiveness of a decision is thought to be a function of three classes of outcomes, each of which may be expected to be affected by the decision process used. These are:

1. The quality or rationality of the decision.
2. The acceptance or commitment on the part of subordinates to execute the decision effectively.
3. The amount of time required to make the decision.

Space prevents an exposition of the empirical evidence concerning the consequences of participation, but the reader interested in these questions is referred to Vroom [9], and Vroom and Yetton [10, pp. 20–31] for a presentation of that evidence. Since the research program began, a number of normative models for choosing among alternative decision processes have been developed. Each revision is slightly more complex than its predecessor but, in the minds of both developers and users, also more accurate in forecasting the consequences of alternatives. Most of these models have been concerned solely with group problems (the right hand column in Table 1). In Vroom and Yetton [10] virtually all of the discussion of normative models is oriented toward group problems; although, in their discussion of further revisions and extensions of the model, they discuss the possibility of a model for both individual and group problems and present a tentative model which governs choice of decision processes for both types.

Figure 1 shows the latest version of a model intended to deal with both types of problems. Like previous models, it is expressed in the form of a decision tree. Arranged in the form of simple Yes–No questions that a leader could ask himself about the decision-making situation he is presently confronting.[1] To use the model, one starts at the left-hand side of the tree and works toward the right-hand side, asking oneself the questions pertaining to any box that is encountered. When a terminal node is reached, a number will be found

[1]For a detailed definition of these attributes and of criteria to be used in making Yes–No judgments, see Vroom and Yetton [10, pp. 21–31].

FIGURE 1

Decision-Process Flow Chart for Both Individual and Group Problems

A. Is there a quality requirement such that one solution is likely to be more rational than another?
B. Do I have sufficient info to make a high quality decision?
C. Is the problem structured?
D. Is acceptance of decision by subordinates critical to effective implementation?
E. If I were to make the decision by myself, is it reasonably certain that it would be accepted by my subordinates?
F. Do subordinates share the organizational goals to be attained in solving this problem?
G. Is conflict among subordinates likely in preferred solutions? (This question is irrelevant to individual problems.)
H. Do subordinates have sufficient info to make a high quality decision?

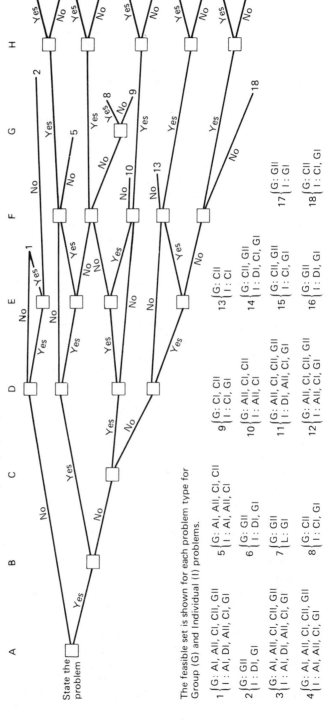

The feasible set is shown for each problem type for Group (G) and Individual (I) problems.

1 { G: AI, AII, CI, CII, GII
    I : AI, DI, AII, CI, GI

2 { G: GII
    I : DI, GI

3 { G: AI, AII, DI, AII, CI, GII
    I : AI, DI, AII, CI, GI

4 { G: AI, AII, CI, CII, GII
    I : AI, AII, CI, GI

5 { G: AI, AII, CI, CII
    I : AI, AII, CI

6 { G: GII
    I : DI, GI

7 { G: GII
    L: GI

8 { G: CII
    I : CI, GI

9 { G: CI, CII
    I : CI, GI

10 { G: AII, CI, CII
     I : AII, CI

11 { G: AII, CI, CII, GII
     I : DI, AII, CI, GI

12 { G: AII, CI, CII, GII
     I : AII, CI, GI

13 { G: CII
     I : CI

14 { G: CII, GII
     I : DI, CI, GI

15 { G: CII, GII
     I : CI, GI

16 { G: GII
     I : DI, GI

17 { G: GII
     I : GI

18 { G: CII
     I : CI, GI

designating the problem type and one or more decision-making processes considered appropriate for that problem. Within each problem type there are both individual and group problems, and the feasible set of methods is different for each.

The decision processes specified for each problem type are not arbitrary. The specification of the feasible set of decision processes for each problem type is governed by a set of ten rules that serve to protect the quality and acceptance of the decision by eliminating alternatives that risk one or the other of these decision outcomes. These rules, consistent with existing empirical evidence concerning the consequences of participation, are shown in Table 2 in both verbal and set-theoretic form. It should be noted that the rules are of three distinct types. Rules 1 through 4 are designed to protect the quality or rationality of the decision; Rules 5 through 8 are designed to protect the acceptance of or commitment to the decision; and Rules 9 through 10 eliminate the use of group methods for individual problems and vice versa. The decision tree is merely a convenient structure for applying these rules, and, once the problem type has been determined, the rules have all been applied. It can be seen that there are some problem types for which only one method remains in the feasible set, and others for which two, three, four, or even five methods remain in the feasible set.

When more than one method remains in the feasible set, there are a number of ways in which one might choose among them. One method, called Model A and discussed at length by Vroom and Yetton, uses the number of manhours required by the process of decision making. They argue that if the alternatives within the feasible set are equal in the probability of generating a rational decision which subordinates will accept, a choice among them based on the time requirement of each will be of maximum short-run benefit to the organization.

The basis for estimating the relative requirements in manhours for the alternatives given for group problems is simple. Vroom and Yetton argue that more participative processes require more time. Therefore, the ordering of the methods shown for group problems in terms of manhours is perfectly correlated with the degree of participation they permit (AI $<$ AII $<$ CI $<$ CII $<$ GII). However, the extension of the model to cover individual problems complicates this picture, since the decision process which provides greatest opportunity for subordinate influence, DI, is certainly less time consuming than GI, which requires reaching a solution which has the agreement of both superior and subordinate. While the differences in time requirements of the alternatives for individual problems is not nearly so great as the differences in the alternatives for group problems, we have assumed an ordering such that AI $<$ DI $<$ AII $<$ CI $<$ GI. The reader will note that the ordering of alternatives from left to right within the feasible sets for each problem type in Figure 1 reflects this assumption. Thus, for both group and individual problems, the minimum-manhours solution is assumed to be the alternative furthest to the left within the feasible set.

There are, however, other bases for choice within the feasible set. A manager may wish to choose the most participative alternative that can be used while still producing rational and acceptable solutions to organizational problems. Such a position could be grounded in humanistic considerations, emphasizing the intrinsic value of participation, or on pragmatic considerations, such as the utility of participation in developing informed and responsi-

TABLE 2

Rules Underlying the Normative Model

1. *The Leader Information Rule*

If the quality of the decision is important and the leader does not possess enough information or expertise to solve the problem by himself, then AI is eliminated from the feasible set.

2. *The Subordinate Information Rule:*

(applicable to individual problems only)

If the quality of the decision is important and the subordinate does not possess enough information or expertise to solve the problem himself, then DI is eliminated from the feasible set.

3a. *The Goal Congruence Rule*

If the quality of the decision is important and the subordinates are not likely to pursue organizational goals in their efforts to solve this problem, then GII and DI are eliminated from the feasible set.

3b. *The Augmented Goal Congruence Rule*

(applicable to individual problems only)

Under the conditions specified in the previous rule (i.e., quality of decision is important, and the subordinate does not share the organizational goals to be attained in solving the problem) GI may also constitute risk to the quality of the decision taken in response to an individual problem. Such a risk is a reasonable one to take only if the nature of the problem is such that the acceptance of the subordinate is critical to the effective implementation and prior probability of acceptance of an autocratic solution is low.

4a. *The Unstructured Problem Rule (Group)*

In decisions in which the quality of the decision is important, if the leader lacks the necessary information or expertise to solve the problem by himself and if the problem is unstructured, the method of solving the problem should provide for interaction among subordinates. Accordingly, AI, AII, and CI are eliminated from the feasible set.

4b. *The Unstructured Problem Rule (Individual)*

In decisions in which the quality of the decision is important, if the leader lacks the necessary information to solve the problem by himself and if the problem is unstructured, the method of solving the problem should permit the subordinate to generate solutions to the problem. Accordingly, AI and AII are eliminated from the feasible set.

5. *The Acceptance Rule*

If the acceptance of the decision by subordinates is critical to effective implementation and if it is not certain that an autocratic decision will be accepted, AI and AII are eliminated from the feasible set.

6. *The Conflict Rule*

(applicable to group problems only)

If the acceptance of the decision is critical, an autocratic decision is not certain to be accepted and disagreement among subordinates in methods of attaining the organizational goal is likely, the methods used in solving the problem should enable those in disagreement to resolve their differences with full knowledge of the problem. Accordingly, AI, AII and CI, which permit no interaction among subordinates, are eliminated from the feasible set.

7. *The Fairness Rule*

If the quality of the decision is unimportant, but acceptance of the decision is critical and not certain to result from autocratic decision, the decision process used should permit the subordinates to interact with one another and negotiate over the method of resolving any differences with full responsibility on them for determining what is equitable. Accordingly, AI, AII, CI, and CII are eliminated from the feasible set.

8. *The Acceptance Priority Rule*

If acceptance is critical, not certain to result from an autocratic decision and if (the) subordinate(s) is (are) motivated to pursue the organizational goals represented in the problem, then methods which provide equal partnership in the decision-making process can provide greater acceptance without risking decision quality. Accordingly, AI, AII, CI, and CII are eliminated from the feasible set.

9. *The Group Problem Rule (Group)*

If a problem has approximately equal effects on each of a number of subordinates (i.e., is a group problem) the decision process used should provide them with equal opportunities to influence that decision. Use of a decision process such as GI or DI, which provides opportunities for only one of the affected subordinates to influence that decision, may in the short run produce feelings of inequity reflected in lessened commitment to the decision on the part of those "left out" of the decision process and in the long run be a source of conflict and divisiveness.

10. *The Individual Problem Rule (Individual)*

If a problem affects only one subordinate, decision processes which unilaterally introduce other (unaffected) subordinates as equal partners constitute an unnecessary use of time of the unaffected subordinates and can reduce the amount of commitment of the affected subordinate to the decision by reducing the amount of his oportunity to influence the decision. Thus CII and GII are eliminated from the feasible set.

ble behavior [10]. A model based on these considerations is termed Model B.

The reader should note that both Models A and B are consistent with the rules which generate the feasible set. They merely represent different bases for choice within it. Model A chooses the method within the feasible set which is the most economical method in terms of manhours. Its choice is always the method furthest to the left in the set shown in Figure 1. Model B chooses the most participative method available within the feasible set, which is that method closest to the bottom of Table 1. Model A seeks to minimize manhours, subject to quality and acceptance constraints, while Model B seeks to maximize participation, subject to quality and acceptance constraints. Of course, when only one process exists within the feasible set, the choices of Model A and B are identical. Perhaps the best way of illustrating the model is to show how it works in sample situations. Following are a set of actual leadership problems,[2] each based on a retrospective account by a manager who experienced the problem. The reader may wish, after reading each case, to analyze it himself using the model and then to compare his analysis with that of the authors.

> *Case I.* You are president of a small but growing Midwestern bank, with its head office in the state's capital and branches in several nearby market towns. The location and type of business are factors which contribute to the emphasis on traditional and conservative banking practices at all levels.
>
> When you bought the bank five years ago, it was in poor financial shape. Under your leadership, much progress has been made. This progress has been achieved while the economy has moved into a mild recession, and, as a result, your prestige among your bank managers is very high. Your success, which you are inclined to attribute principally to good luck and to a few timely decisions on your part, has, in your judgment, one unfortunate by-product. It has caused your subordinates to look to you for leadership and guidance in decision making beyond what you consider necessary. You have no doubts about the fundamental capabilities of these men but wish that they were not quite so willing to accede to your judgment.
>
> You have recently acquired funds to permit opening a new branch. Your problem is to decide on a suitable location. You believe that there is no "magic formula" by which it is possible to select an optimal site. The choice will be made by a combination of some simple common sense criteria and "what feels right." You have asked your managers to keep their eyes open for commercial real estate sites that might be suitable. Their knowledge about the communities in which they operate should be extremely useful in making a wise choice.
>
> Their support is important because the success of the new branch will be highly dependent on your managers' willingness to supply staff and technical assistance during its early days. Your bank is small enough for everyone to feel like part of a team, and you feel that this has and will be critical to the bank's prosperity.
>
> The success of this project will benefit everybody. Directly, they will benefit from the increased base of operations, and, indirectly, they will reap the personal and business advantages of being part of a successful and expanding business.

[2]For additional problems and their analysis, see Vroom and Yetton [10, pp. 40-44].

	Analysis	Synthesis	
A	(Quality?) = Yes	Problem Type	14-Group
B	(Leader's Information?) = No	Feasible Set	CII, GII
C	(Structured?) = No	Model A Behavior	CII
D	(Acceptance?) = Yes	Model B Behavior	GII
E	(Prior Probability of Acceptance?) = Yes		
F	(Goal Congruence?) = Yes		
G¹	(Conflict?) = No		
H¹	(Subordinate Information?) = Yes		

¹The question pertaining to this attribute is asked in the decision tree but is irrelevant to the prescribed behavior.

Case II. You are regional manager of an international management consulting company. You have a staff of six consultants reporting to you, each of whom enjoys a considerable amount of autonomy with clients in the field.

Yesterday you received a complaint from one of your major clients to the effect that the consultant whom you assigned to work on the contract with them was not doing his job effectively. They were not very explicit as to the nature of the problem, but it was clear that they were dissatisfied and that something would have to be done if you were to restore the client's faith in your company.

The consultant assigned to work on that contract has been with the company for six years. He is a systems analyst and is one of the best in that profession. For the first four or five years his performance was superb, and he was a model for the other more junior consultants. However, recently he has seemed to have a "chip on his shoulder," and his previous identification with the company and its objectives has been replaced with indifference. His negative attitude has been noticed by other consultants, as well as by clients. This is not the first such complaint that you have had from a client this year about his performance. A previous client even reported to you that the consultant reported to work several times obviously suffering from a hangover and that he had been seen around town in the company of "fast" women.

It is important to get to the root of this problem quickly if that client is to be retained. The consultant obviously has the skill necessary to work with the clients effectively. If only he were willing to use it!

	Analysis	Synthesis	
A	(Quality?) = Yes	Problem Type	18-Individual
B	(Leader's Information?) = No	Feasible Set	CI, GI
C	(Structured?) = No	Model A Behavior	CI
D	(Acceptance?) = Yes	Model B Behavior	GI
E	(Prior Probability of Acceptance?) = No		
F	(Goal Congruence?) = No		
H¹	(Subordinate Information?) = Yes		

¹The question pertaining to this attribute is asked in the decision tree but is irrelevant to the prescribed behavior.

Case III. You have recently been appointed manager of a new plant which is presently under construction. Your team of five department heads has been selected, and they are now working with you in selecting their own staffs, purchasing equipment, and generally anticipating the problems that are likely to arise when you move into the plant in three months.

Yesterday, you received from the architect a final set of plans for the building, and, for the first time, you examined the parking facilities that are available. There is a large lot across the road from the plant intended primarily for hourly workers and lower level supervisory personnel. In addition, there are seven spaces immediately adjacent to the administrative offices, intended for visitor and reserved parking. Company policy requires that a minimum of three spaces be made available for visitor parking, leaving you only four spaces to allocate among yourself and your five department heads. There is no way of increasing the total number of such spaces without changing the structure of the building.

Up to now, there have been no obvious status differences among your team, who have worked together very well in the planning phase of the operation. To be sure, there are salary differences, with your Administrative, Manufacturing, and Engineering Managers receiving slightly more than the Quality Control and Industrial Relations Managers. Each has recently been promoted to his new position, and expects reserved parking privileges as a consequence of his new status. From past experience, you know that people feel strongly about things which would be indicative of their status. So you and your subordinates have been working together as a team, and you are reluctant to do anything which might jeopardize the team relationship.

Analysis		Synthesis	
A (Quality?) = No		Problem Type	2-Group
D (Acceptance?) = Yes		Feasible Set	GII
E (Prior Probability of			
Acceptance?) = No		Model A Behavior	GII
G¹ (Conflict?) = Yes		Model B Behavior	GII

¹The question pertaining to this attribute is asked in the decision tree but is irrelevant to the prescribed behavior.

Case IV. You are executive vice president for a small pharmaceutical manufacturer. You have the opportunity to bid on a contract for the Defense Department pertaining to biological warfare. The contract is outside the mainstream of your business; however, it could make economic sense since you do have unused capacity in one of your plants, and the manufacturing processes are not dissimilar.

You have written the document to accompany the bid and now have the problem of determining the dollar value of the quotation which you think will win the job for your company. If the bid is too high, you will undoubtedly lose to one of your competitors; if it is too low, you would stand to lose money on the program.

There are many factors to be considered in making this decision, including the cost of the new raw materials and the additional administrative burden of relationships with a new client, not to speak of factors which are likely to influence the bids of your competitors, such as how much they *need* this particular contract. You have been busy assembling the necessary data to make this decision but there remain several "unknowns," one of which involves the manager of the plant in which the new products will be manufactured. Of all your subordinates, only he is in the position to estimate the costs of adapting the present equipment to their new purpose, and his cooperation and support will be necessary in ensuring that the specifications of the contract will be met. However, in an initial discussion with him when you first learned of the possibility of the contract, he seemed adamantly opposed to the idea. His previous experience has not particularly equipped him with the ability to evaluate projects like this one, so that you were not overly influenced by his opinions. From the nature of his arguments, you inferred that his opposition was ideological rather than economic. You recall that he was actively involved in a local "peace organization" and, within the company, was one of the most vocal opponents to the war in Vietnam.

	Analysis	Synthesis	
A	(Quality?) = Yes	Problem Type	8 or 9 Individual
B	(Leader's Information?) = No	Feasible Set	CI, GI
C	(Structured?) = Yes	Model A Behavior	CI
D	(Acceptance?) = Yes	Model B Behavior	GI
E	(Prior Probability of Acceptance?) = No		
F	(Goal Congruence?) = No		
H[1]	(Subordinate Information?) = No		

[1]The question pertaining to this attribute is asked in the decision tree but is irrelevant to the prescribed behavior.

Toward a Descriptive Model

So far, we have been concerned only with normative or prescriptive questions. But, how do managers really behave? What decision rules underlie their willingness to share their decision-making power with their subordinates? In what respects are these decision rules similar to or different from those employed in the normative model?

The manner in which these questions are posed is at variance with much of the conventional treatment of such issues. Frequently, leaders are typed as autocratic or participative or as varying on a continuum between these extremes. In effect, autocratic or participative behavior is assumed to be controlled by a personality trait, the amount of which varies from one person to another. The trait concept is a useful one for summarizing differences among people, but allows no room for the analysis of intra-individual differences in behavior. Following Lewin's [2] classic formulation $B = f(P,E)$, we assumed that a leader's behavior in a given situation reflects characteristics of that leader, properties of the situation, and the interaction of the two.

Two somewhat different research methods have been used in studying the situational determinants of participative behavior. The first method [10, chapter 4] utilized what we have come to refer to as "recalled problems." Over 500 managers, all of whom were participants in management development programs, provided written descriptions of a group problem which they encountered recently. These descriptions ranged in length from one paragraph to several pages and covered virtually every facet of managerial decision making. Each manager was then asked to indicate which of the methods shown on the right hand side of Table 1 (AI, AII, CI, CII, GII) he had used in solving the problem. Finally, each manager was asked a set of questions concerning the problem he had selected. These questions corresponded to attributes in the normative model.

Preliminary investigation revealed that managers perceived the five alternatives as varying (in the order shown in Table 1) on a scale of participation but that the four intervals separating adjacent processes were not seen as equal. On the basis of the application of several scaling methods [10, pp. 65-71], the following values on a scale of participation were assigned to each process: AI = 0; AII = .625; CI = 5.0; CII = 8.125; GII = 10.

Using the managers' judgments of the status of the problems they described on the problem attributes as independent variables and the scale values of their behavior on the problem as a dependent variable, it is possible to use the method of multiple regression to determine the properties of situations; i.e., problems, which are associated with autocratic or participative behavior. It is also possible to insert the managers' judgments concerning their problems into the normative model and to determine the degree of correspondence between managerial and model behavior.

Several investigations have been conducted using this method—all of which have been restricted to group problems and the decision processes corresponding to them. The results are consistent with the view that there are important differences in the processes used for different kinds of problems. Specifically, managers were more likely to exhibit autocratic behavior on structured problems in which they believed that they had enough information, their subordinates lacked information, their subordinates' goals were incongruent with the organizational goals, their subordinates' acceptance of the decision was not critical to its effective implementation, and the prior probability that an autocratic decision would be accepted was high. Thus, many (but not all) of the attributes contained in the normative model had an effect on the decision processes which managers employed, and the directions of these effects are similar to those found in the model. However, it would be a mistake to conclude that the managers' behavior was always identical to that of the model. In approximately two thirds of the problems, nevertheless, the behavior which the manager reported was within the feasible set of methods prescribed for that problem, and in about 40% of the cases it corresponded exactly to the minimum manhours (Model A) solution.

Several observations help to account for differences between the model and the typical manager in the sample. First, as is apparent from an inspection of Figure 1, the normative model incorporates a substantial number of interactions among attributes, whereas no such interactions appeared in the results of the regression analysis. Second, the magnitude of the effects of two attributes pertaining to the acceptance or commitment of subordinates to decisions was considerably weaker in the descriptive than in the normative model, suggesting that these considerations play less of a role in determining how people behave. This inference was further supported by the fact that rules designed to protect the acceptance of the decision in the normative model were violated far more frequently than rules designed to protect decision quality.

The results of this research were supportive of the concept of intra-personal variance in leadership style and helped to identify some of the situational factors influencing leaders' choices of decision processes. There were, however, some key methodological weaknesses to this research. Limited variance in and intercorrelations among problem attributes restricted the extent to which situational effects could be determined with precision. Furthermore, the fact that subjects selected and scored their own problems may have led to confounding of individual differences and situational effects. Finally, since only one problem was obtained from each manager, it was impossible to identify interactions between person and situational variables, i.e., idiosyncratic rules for deciding when and to what extent to encourage participation by subordinates.

The methodological problems inherent in the use of "recalled problems" dictated a search for another method with which to explore the same phenomenon. The technique selected involved the development of a standardized set of administrative problems or cases, each of which depicted a leader faced with some organizational requirement for action or decision making. Managers were asked to assume the role of leader in each situation and to indicate which decision process they would employ.

Several standardized sets of cases were developed using rewritten accounts of actual managerial problems obtained from the previous method. These sets of cases, or problem sets, were developed in accordance with a multi-factorial experimental design, within which the problem attributes were varied orthogonally. Each case corresponded to a particular combination of problem characteristics, and the entire set of cases permitted the simultaneous variation of each problem attribute. To ensure conformity of a given case or problem with the specifications of a cell in the experimental design, an elaborate procedure for testing cases was developed [10, pp. 97–101], involving coding of problems by expert judges and practicing managers.

This method showed promise of permitting the replication of the results using recalled problems with a method that avoided spurious effects stemming from the influence of uncontrolled variables on problem selection. Since the use of a "repeated measures design" permitted a complete experiment to be performed on each subject, the main effects of each of the problem attributes on the decision processes used by the subject could be identified. By comparing the results for different subjects, the similarities and differences in these main effects, and the relative importance of individual differences and of situational variables could be ascertained.

Vroom and Yetton worked exclusively with group problems and with an experimental design which called for thirty cases. The results, obtained from investigations of eight distinct populations comprising over 500 managers, strongly support the major findings from the use of recalled problems, both in terms of the amount of correspondence with the normative model and the specific attributes of situations which tended to induce autocratic and participative decision processes. Moreover, the nature of the methods used made it possible also to obtain precise estimates of the amount of variance attributable to situational factors and individual differences. Only 10% of the total variance could be accounted for in terms of general tendencies to be autocratic or participative (as expressed in differences among individuals in mean behavior on all thirty problems), while about 30% was attributable to situational effects (as expressed in differences in mean behavior among situations).

What about the remaining 60% of the variance? Undoubtedly, some of it can be attributed to errors of measurement, but Vroom and Yetton were able to show that a significant portion of that variance can be explained in terms of another form of individual differences, i.e., differences among managers in ways of "tailoring" their approach to the situation. Theoretically, these can be thought of as differences in decision rules that they employ concerning when to encourage participation.

A Follow-Up Investigation

The descriptive results reported thus far are but a cursory account of the previous work of Vroom and Yetton [10]. The territory which they explored, however, represents only one-half of the domain originally mapped out in the introductory section of this article. As we have pointed out repeatedly, all of their empirical investigations dealt exclusively with group problems. The extended model (Figure 1), including both individual and group problems, was the focus of the follow-up investigation reported below; questions to be answered concerned differences between descriptive models of behavior on group versus individual problems, and the extent of manager agreement with the yet-untested extension of the normative model.

Since the use of standardized cases in testing the group model provided consistent and richer data than use of recalled problems, only standardized cases were employed in this investigation. Like previous problem sets, a new set of cases was constructed, drawing from those group problems included in previous sets and individual problems rewritten from a large sample of actual decision-making situations.

If each of the eight dichotomous attributes (Figure 1) were varied independently for both group and individual problems, 2^9 or 512 unique combinations of attribute characteristics could be generated. To reduce the size to a workable number of combinations to be included in the revised problem set, a number of "nesting" procedures dictated by obvious interrelationships among the attributes were used. Five principles, the first three of which were employed by Vroom and Yetton [10] in previous sets, convey these procedures:

> *Principle 1:* Leader's information *(B)*, problem structure *(C)*, and subordinates' goal congruence *(F)* are varied only when there is a quality requirement *(A)* to the problem.
>
> *Principle 2:* Problem structure *(C)* is varied only when the leader does not have sufficient information *(B)* to make a high-quality decision.
>
> *Principle 3:* The prior probability of acceptance of an autocratic solution *(E)* is varied only when acceptance of the decision by subordinates is critical for effective implementation *(D)*.
>
> *Principle 4:* Subordinate information *(H)* is varied only in individual problems having a quality requirement *(A)*.
>
> *Principle 5:* Conflict among subordinates *(G)* is varied only in group problems.

The rationale for the first three of these procedures is discussed by Vroom and Yetton [10, pp. 95–97]. Principle 4 reflects the irrelevance of subordinate information to the effectiveness of decisions lacking a quality requirement, and the irrelevance of subordinate information to the behavior of the normative model for group problems. Similarly, Principle 5 is based on the fact that potential conflict or disagreement among a set of subordinates is both difficult to manipulate in problems affecting only a single subordinate and irrelevant to the behavior of the model on individual problems.

The applications of these five nesting principles reduced the number of problem cases required from 512 to 81. These 81 cells in the experimental design represented 72 cases in which there was a quality requirement (36 group, 36 individual) and 9 cases without a quality requirement. This number was further reduced by 50 percent sampling of the cells having a high-quality requirement, the cells chosen being balanced with respect to the remaining variables. In addition to the sampling, three individual problems with low-quality requirements were included to decrease the high-low ratio for this attribute. Although confounding some higher-order interactions, this process reduced the number of standardized problems required while retaining the desirable property that certain main effects are orthogonal.

Cases thought to meet the specifications of the above design were coded on each attribute by expert judges and managers in a manner similar to that of problems used in previous problem sets. Those with ambiguous status on any attribute were revised until criteria for their inclusion in a given cell in the experimental design were met. When all 48 problems or cases had been selected, they were assigned numbers in accordance with a random process and administered to subjects, all of whom were practicing managers.

The managers studied were all participants in a management development program in which the senior author played an instructional role. The program was similar to that described in Vroom and Yetton [10, chapter 8]. In working on the problem set, each manager was asked to assume the role of leader in each of the 48 situations and to indicate the decision process (from the two columns in Table 1) that he would use in each situation. Each knew that he would receive an individualized computer printout representing an analysis of his leadership style, but was naive with regard to the model, problem attributes, or the basis for construction of the problem set.

Managers in three distinct management development programs were studied using this method. The three populations varied most obviously in the heterogeneity of the managerial jobs performed by the participants. A brief description of each population follows:

Population 1 (P1)—High Heterogeneity, $N = 30$

. . . highly diverse group, one-half of whom were managers from business firms. The industries they represented included oil, steel, pulp and paper, aircraft, and banking; and their locations included Greece, Iran, Switzerland, Egypt, and the United States. The other half were military officers from the Air Force, Army, Marines, and Navy; and their functions ranged from publications to research and development.

Population 2 (P2)—Moderate Heterogeneity, $N = 40$

. . . group of middle managers from a large industrial corporation producing a wide variety of electrical products. The managers came from many operations of the company including space products, environmental systems, steam turbines, and consumer products. Their functions within these operations included manufacturing, engineering, finance, marketing, and employee relations.

Population 3 (P3)—Low Heterogeneity, $N = 28$

... group of department heads from the research center of a large public utility specializing in tele-communications.

Discrimination between Group and Individual Problems

Of foremost importance was whether the managers' behavior would reflect the distinction between group and individual decision-making situations. Since CII and GII are decision-making processes applicable only to group problems, their use on individual problems would indicate that managers do not discriminate between these types of situations. Use of GI and DI on group problems would indicate a similar confusion. The mean frequency of decision process choices on the 24 group and 24 individual cases (Table 3), suggests that managers do discriminate between the two types of problems. The average manager chose, for group problems, processes that are designed for exclusive use in individual problems only 0.25 times in 24. He chose group decision-making processes for individual problems less than 0.80 times in 24. These data provide strong support for the fact that managers implicitly distinguish group from individual problems, a distinction that is basic to the broader structure of the normative model.

TABLE 3

Mean Frequency of Process Choice
on Group and Individual Problems ($N = 98$)

Process	Group Problems	Individual Problems	Difference[1]
AI	3.24	4.62	$p < .001$
AII	2.48	2.11	ns
CI	4.05	5.99	$p < .001$
CII	7.50	0.47	p .001
GI	0.09	6.30	$p < .001$
GII	6.48	0.31	$p < .001$
DI	0.16	4.20	$p < .001$

[1]Repeated measures T-test (two-tailed).

The data in Table 3 also suggest that managers behave more autocratically in situations affecting only one subordinate than in situations affecting a group. Use of AI and CI, comparatively autocratic processes common to both the group and individual models, is significantly greater on individual than on group problems. Consequently, use of the more participative processes relevant to group situations (CII and GII) is greater than the use of the more participative processes (GI and DI) relevant to interaction with single subordinates.

Individual and Situational Main Effects

Using standardized cases, Vroom and Yetton [10] were able to attribute 30% of the variance in participation on group problems to situational determinants. The use here of standardized individual problems also lends itself to such analysis. Before fitting a linear model to the data, however, the newly included decision processes, GI and DI, required assignment of values on a scale of participation. Using the same scaling technique employed for group processes, GI was assigned a value of 8.125 and DI a value of 10.

These values can now be used in an effort to calculate the amount of variance in decision processes attributable to the problem and to the individual manager. The analysis, which treats problem and individual as nominal variables, was identical to that used by Vroom and Yetton [10]. It was carried out separately for group and individual problems and for each of the three populations. Table 4 reports the results.

TABLE 4
Percent Total Variance Attributable
to Problem and Individual Differences

	Group Problems				Individual Problems			
	P1	P2	P3	ALL	P1	P2	P3	ALL
Due to problem	31.0%	39.6%	45.8%	34.7%	39.7%	49.2%	50.6%	44.0%
Due to individual	11.4%	7.3%	7.4%	11.7%	7.7%	8.8%	5.3%	8.7%

The data on group problems clearly replicate the earlier finding of Vroom and Yetton. Situational differences account for about 35% of the variance in managers' behavior, while individual differences account for a much lower 12%. Thus, the amount of influence of situational factors in determining choice of a leadership method on group problems is roughly three times the influence of individual differences. This ratio is even higher when one looks at individual problems, where the influence of situational factors appears to be roughly five times the influence of individual differences.

The amount of variance attributable to individual differences and to shared situational effects might be expected to vary with the homogeneity of the roles carried out with the populations studied. If the nature of the work performed has anything to do with the development of a leadership style, as reflected in behavior on the standardized cases, then one would expect to find that managers performing more homogeneous roles would be less different from one another. A comparison of the proportion of explained variance attributable to individuals and to situations for the three populations strongly supports this prediction. In fact, the ratio of shared situational effects to individual effects for P3, the most homogeneous population studied, is 9.6 to 1 for individual problems, compared with 5.6 and 5.2 for P2 and P1, respectively. For group problems, the ratio for P3 is 6.2, compared with 5.4 and 2.7 for P2 and P1, respectively.

Problem Attributes as Determinants of Behavior

The results shown in Table 4 corroborate Vroom and Yetton's earlier findings with respect to the relative importance of situational factors and traits of authoritarianism-participation in determining decision processes used on group problems. It also extends those conclusions to individual problems with an indication that situational variables play an even stronger role relative to traits.

However, the results presented so far do not indicate what situational variables are important in influencing behavior on standardized cases. The experimental design underlying the problem set makes it possible to assess the direction and magnitude of the effect of the eight problem attributes in determining the decision process used by the 98 managers studied.

Two methods were used in the analyses of the data:

1. *The main effects* of each problem attribute were computed by subtracting the mean scale value of the decision processes used on all problems selected to represent a low value of the attribute from the mean scale value of the decision processes on all problems selected to represent a high value of that attribute. Since the method of scaling the decision processes accords larger scores to more participative processes, a positive value for the main effect of a given attribute indicates a tendency for that attribute to result in use of more participative methods by a typical manager.

Calculations of main effects of attributes were made separately for group and individual problems. The number of problems representing high and low values of each attribute is given by the experimental design. It should be noted that calculations of main effects of some attributes were based on less than the entire set of problems, due to the use of the nesting principles mentioned above.

2. *Multiple regressions* were performed separately for behavior on group and individual problems. Level of participation was the dependent variable, and problem attributes were the independent variables. A value of 1 was given to the problem attribute if the attribute was present, and -1 if the attribute was absent from the problem. When one variable was nested within another, assumptions had to be made to permit a complete specification of all attributes for all problems. (This requirement of multiple regression distinguishes it from the previous method in which main effects could be based on only a subset of the cases.) The assumptions used follow directly from the nesting principles discussed earlier.[3]

The principle advantage of the second method is its usefulness in determining the proportion of situational variance attributable to the influence of each problem attribute.[4] The results from both methods are shown in Table 5.

All but one of the mean main effects have the same sign for both group and individual problems. Furthermore, the signs are consistent with the direction of effect on attributes of the behavior of Model A in all but two of the fourteen effects studied. Subjects tended to show more participation on problems in which the leader lacked relevant information, particularly if the problem was also unstructured. They showed more participation on problems that required subordinate acceptance than on problems that did not, especially when they lacked the expert, legitimate, or referent power to gain that acceptance from an autocratic decision. Finally, managers were found to show more

---

[3]The assumptions used for this purpose are as follows: (1) $A = -1 \rightarrow B = 1, C = 1, F = 1$; (2) $B = 1 \rightarrow C = 1$; (3) $D = -1 \rightarrow E = 1$ and (4) $A = -1 \rightarrow H = 1$.

[4]The regression method (Overall and Spiegel [8, pp. 315–317]) derives main effect estimates from an additive (no interaction) model and includes interaction parameters only to evaluate deviation from the additive model. Overall and Speigel claim this method is appropriate when the problem is conceived as a multiclassification factorial design, but computational difficulties, or unequal cell frequencies, prevent employment of conventional analysis of variance techniques. No findings relevant to interactions among problem attributes are presented here, although data concerning such interactions for group problems are presented in Vroom and Yetton [10].

participation when subordinates shared organizational goals than when they did not.

The one problem attribute which appears to have a differential effect on the two types of problems is attribute A—the existence of a quality requirement. The same set of managers tended to encourage a greater degree of participation by their subordinates on group problems with a quality requirement and on individual problems without a quality requirement. Additional examina-

TABLE 5

Main Effects of Problem Attributes and Their
Contribution to Situational Variance

Problem Attributes	Group Problems			Individual Problems		
	Mean Main Effect [1]		% Situational Variance	Mean Main Effect [1]		% Situational Variance
Quality requirement	1.72	$(1.46)^2$	5.6%	−0.45	$(1.01)^2$	1.2%
Leader's information	−0.44	(−3.44)	0.4	−1.67	(−3.23)	3.2
Structure	−1.69	(−5.00)	7.5	−0.83	(−1.88)	1.4
Importance of acceptance	0.65	(3.36)	1.1	1.90	(2.27)	5.7
Prior probability	−2.44	(−6.72)	20.6	−0.94	(−5.63)	2.4
Goal congruence	0.46	0.97	0.4	3.51	(2.85	40.8
Conflict	−1.30	(0.42)	8.4	—	—	—
Subordinate information	—	—	—	0.87	(1.46)	5.0

[1]Main effects are significantly different from zero at the .001 level or beyond (two-tailed T-test).
[2]Figures in parentheses show main effects calculated for Model A's behavior on same problems.

tion of the frequency of use of each decision process on problems with high and low quality requirements indicates that the effects of this problem attribute are not linear across the participation scale, particularly for individual problems. The existence of a quality requirement militates against the use of AI for group problems and against the use of both AI and DI for individual problems. CI is the model style for the individual problems with a quality requirement while CII is the model process for group problems.

Two other attributes were varied only within one set of 24 problems and provided no basis for comparison of group and individual problems. As found previously by Vroom and Yetton, managers responded to potential conflict and disagreement among subordinates by becoming more autocratic on group problems. In this respect, they differed from Model A, which showed a small but positive effect. They also responded to a high level of subordinate information and expertise by becoming more participative on individual problems. The latter is a new finding but not an unexpected one.

While the direction of the main effects of the comparable problem attributes are similar, their magnitudes are not. The contribution of each attribute, considered alone, to the explanation of situational variance is also shown in Table 5.[5]

[5]The experimental design and the method of coding attributes for the regressions result in some multicollinearity among independent variables. It appears, however, that any confounding is negligible, since only variables with very low main effects are affected. Since the experimental design and coding method were consistent for group and individual problems, multicollinearity does not contribute to the observed differences between the two types of problems.

Prior probability of acceptance of an autocratic decision (attribute E) is the most important determinant of participation on group problems, explaining 20.6% of the situational variance. However, it explains only 2.4% of that variance for individual problems. Apparently, the degree to which a leader possesses enough power to gain acceptance of his own decision is more relevant to his handling of matters affecting the entire system under his direction than to matters affecting only a single subordinate. It is possible that the greater time required for the more participative approaches to group problems, relative to those for individual problems, limits their use to situations in which the leader cannot gain acceptance of his own ideas. "If you can sell your own solution, then sell it—you save time that way" is more consistent with managers' behavior on group problems than on individual problems. It also is interesting to note that this difference is consistent in direction with the main effects for Model A, also shown in the table.

A second problem attribute to possess markedly different explanatory power for group and individual problems is goal congruence (attribute G). It accounts for an overwhelming 40.8% of the problem variance in decision processes for individual problems but less than one-half of 1% of the variance for group problems. The set of managers studied were extremely reluctant to delegate problems to subordinates who did not share the goals to be achieved. (DI was used in only 0.3% of such instances.) However, they did not exhibit the same reluctance to use the GII process in situations of low mutual interest. Conceivably, the fact that an entire set of subordinates does not share the goals to be achieved in a problem which affects them all constitutes a signal to many managers for the use of participative methods in order to effect a greater rapprochement with system objectives. On the other hand, alienation of a single subordinate constitutes a less serious problem. He can typically be replaced or "brought into line" at a later time. The results shown as main effects for Model A are similar in direction, but the difference is not nearly as large.

Agreement with the Normative Model

Effects of the problem attributes on the behavior of 98 managers reported in Table 5 bear reasonable similarity to the role of the attributes in the normative model. A comparison of Model A main effects of each problem attribute with the observed values reveals that similarity. Indeed, the directions of main effects calculated for Model A are identical to those shown for the behavior of the managers for 12 of 14 comparisons. Even the two main effects with a different sign are instructive.

A more accurate indication of similarity between the behavior of the model and that of the managers studied may be seen by examining the frequency with which their choices of decision processes were in agreement with the feasible set, Model A, and Model B choices. These data, along with certain other aggregate indices of behavior, are shown in Table 6.

It can be seen that agreement with all three indices shows significantly higher agreement between the normative model and managers' behavior on individual problems than on group problems. For example, the number of instances of

TABLE 6
Managers' Agreement with the Normative Model

	Short-Term Model (A)		Developmental Model (B)		Manager's Behavior			
	Group	Ind.	Group	Ind.	Group	Ind.	^{r}Grp.,Ind.	$^{Diff\,1}$Grp.,Ind.
Agreement with feasible set	24	24	24	24	16.34	19.81	0.25**	$p < .001$
Agreement with Model A	24	24	9	9²	7.78	10.59	0.17	$p < .001$
Agreement with Model B	9	9²	24	24	7.29	9.34	0.27**	$p < .001$
MLP³	4.43	4.09	9.30	8.13	6.25	5.47	0.71**	$p < .001$
Mean within-person variance	18.84	15.92	0.82	3.91	12.19	12.53	0.51**	ns

**Correlations significant at .01 level or beyond.
[1]Repeated measures 7-test (two-tailed).
[2]These values reflect the fact that there are 9 group and 9 individual problems that have feasible sets which contain one alternative that satisfies both the Model A and the Model B requirement.
[3]Mean level of participation (MLP) is the mean scale value of selected decision processes.

agreement with the feasible set is 16.34 (68%)[6] for group problems but 19.81 (82.5%) for individual problems.

This difference cannot be attributed to the number of feasible responses for group and individual problems. Indeed, a random assignment of decision processes in each subset of problems would yield the same expected agreement with the feasible set—9.57, or about 40%, for both individual and group problems. However, an inspection of the structure of the model shown in Figure 1 reveals another possible basis for the difference in agreement rates for individual and group problems. It will be noted that GII—the most participative process for group problems—stands alone within the feasible set for 5 of the 18 types of group problems. However, there are none of the 18 types of individual problems for which DI—the most participative method for individual problems —stands alone. If a given manager found the loss of control inherent in either delegation or group decision making threatening, and never employed either process in the 48 cases, he would automatically violate the feasible set on five group problems but would not necessarily exhibit any rule violations on individual problems.

For both kinds of problems, agreement with Model A exceeds agreement with Model B, although the difference for group problems does not reach conventional levels of statistical significance. Larger differences were found by Vroom and Yetton for their population of over 500 managers. It is likely that the substantially higher level of participation on group problems for the populations reported here prevents the replication of these results.

The fourth row in the table shows mean level of participation (MLP) for Model A, Model B, and for the 98 managers studied. It is worth noting that managerial behavior tends to be more participative than Model A but more autocratic than Model B. Of perhaps greater interest is the fact that the

[6]This figure is comparable to the 69.7% agreement reported by Vroom and Yetton for 551 managers on 30 group problems.

behavior of managers and that of both models is more autocratic on individual than on group problems.

The final row in the table shows the average within-person variance in behavior across problems for the managers studied and the variance for the two models. Managerial behavior exhibits less variance across situations than Model A but substantially more variance than the highly participative Model B.

The second column from the right shows correlations between various indices of behavior on group and individual problems. Managers who use participative methods on group problems also tend to be more participative on individual problems. In fact, the correlation of 0.71 between MLP on group and individual problems, each based on 24 problems, approaches Vroom and Yetton's estimate of 0.81 for the reliability of a 30-problem test using solely group problems. This finding clearly refutes a speculation which launched the inquiry into the relationship between behavior on group and individual problems. In an earlier phase of the research, several managers who received feedback based on group problems depicting their behavior as autocratic relative to their peers insisted that, while they were opposed to group meetings for the purpose of making decisions, they really believed in delegation. Such an assertion is inconsistent with the correlation and mean difference of power sharing on the two types of problems.

The correlation between variance in behavior on group and individual problems is likewise supportive of consistency in style in dealing with these two kinds of problems. Those who exhibit variety in their approaches to dealing with group problems also exhibit variety in their approach to individual problems, to a degree which comes close to the reliability of this property within group problems alone.

There is also a tendency for managers whose behavior is consistent with the model for group problems to behave consistently with the model for individual problems. However, the correlation reported for the three indices of agreement with the normative model are both smaller in magnitude and smaller in relation to estimated reliabilities than the previous two coefficients.

When a manager's behavior is outside the feasible set of alternatives for a given problem, his choice of decision process violates at least one of the ten rules described earlier. Identification of the relative frequency of violations of each of those rules provides a clearer understanding of the bases of agreement or disagreement with the normative model.

Table 7 shows (1) the rules; (2) the number of applicable group and individual problems to each rule, i.e., the maximum number of times each rule could be violated in the 48-case problem set; (3) the mean observed probability of violation[7] of each rule; and (4) an expected probability of rule violations,[8] assuming a random assignment of choices consistent with the total frequency distribution of

[7]Probabilities of violation of a given rule are calculated by dividing the frequency of violation by the frequency of applicability of the rule within the 48-case problem set. This transformation permits comparisons to be made across rules [10, pp. 146–147].

[8]Expected probabilities of rule violations were based on random assignment of process choices constrained only by the mean distribution of decision processes in each subset of 24 problems. These probabilities reflect the rule violations expected of a person who maintained the mean frequency of use of each process but who did not discriminate among problems in his allocation of processes.

choices. The difference between expected and observed (Expected-Observed) can be taken as evidence of discrimination between problems to which the rule is applicable and problems to which the rule is not applicable. A positive difference is indicative of discrimination consistent in direction with the model and a negative difference indicative of discrimination opposite in direction to the model.

TABLE 7
Comparison of Observed and Expected
Probability of Rule Violation (N = 98)

Rule	Applicable Cases (Grp., Ind.)	Group Problems			Individual Problems		
		Obs.	Exp.	Diff.[1]	Obs.	Exp.	Diff.[1]
1 $A \cap \bar{B} \to \bar{A}I$	(12,12)	.037	.135	$p < .001$	.025	.193	$p < .001$
2 $A \cap \bar{H} \to \bar{D}I$	(0,9)	—	—	—	.026	.175	$p < .001$
3A $A \cap \bar{F} \to \bar{G}II,\bar{D}I$	(9,9)	.260	.270	ns	.003	.175	$p < .001$
3B $A \cap (\bar{D} \cup E) \cap \bar{F} \to \bar{G}I$	(0,6)	—	—	—	.092	.262	$p < .001$
4A $A \cap B \cap \bar{C} \to \bar{A}I,\bar{A}II,\bar{C}I$	(6,0)	.284	.407	$p < .001$	—	—	—
4B $A \cap B \cap \bar{C} \to \bar{A}I,\bar{A}II$	(0,6)	—	—	—	.128	.281	$p < .001$
5 $D \cap \bar{E} \to \bar{A}I,\bar{A}II$	(8,8)	.079	.238	$p < .001$	.131	.281	$p < .001$
6 $D \cap \bar{E} \cap G \to \bar{A}I,\bar{A}II,\bar{C}I$	(4,0)	.263	.407	$p < .001$	—	—	—
7 $\bar{A} \cap D \cap \bar{E} \to \bar{A}I,\bar{A}II,\bar{C}I,\bar{C}II$	(2,2)	.765	.730	ns	.087	.530	$p < .001$
8 $D \cap \bar{E} \cap F \to \bar{A}I,\bar{A}II,\bar{C}I,\bar{C}II$	(3,3)	.466	.730	$p < .001$	.320	.530	$p < .001$
9 Group $\to \bar{G}I,\bar{D}I$	(24,0)	.011	.224	$p < .001$	—	—	—
10 Ind. $\to \bar{C}II,\bar{G}II$	(0,24)	—	—	—	.032	.307	$p < .001$
Weighted Average	(68,79)	.138	.280	$p < .001$	.061	.266	$p < .001$

[1] T-test (one-tailed).

The weighted average of rule violations for group and individual problems shows that rules tend to be violated less than half as frequently on individual as on group problems. This finding is consistent with the previous observation of substantially greater agreement with the feasible set on individual problems. Nonetheless, a comparison of weighted averages with expected probabilities shows greater-than-expected conformity with the rules of the model for *both* kinds of problems. This global indicator of consistency with the model is perhaps less revealing than a detailed examination of the results for each rule. Vroom and Yetton [10, pp. 147-149] had previously found that acceptance rules (5-8) had generally higher observed probabilities of rule violations than quality rules (1-4). With few exceptions, the same results were obtained here, but the inclusion of expected rates of violation for each rule as a standard of comparison reveals that acceptance rules (due to a greater inclusiveness in processes eliminated) are expected to have higher violation rates.

A more appropriate basis for determining consistency between a rule and managerial behavior is the degree of difference in behavior between those problems to which the rule is applicable and behavior on the entire set of problems. A comparison of expected and observed rates of violation of rules relevant to individual problems shows substantial evidence that these managers are tending to make the kinds of discriminations made in the rules. Observed values are always significantly less than expected values. When comparing across rules, it is evident that rule 8 is the only rule relevant to individual problems which is violated with some notable frequency. This rule prohibits use of processes other than GI and DI when the acceptance by an individual subordinate of a decision is critical, when the prior probability of his acceptance of an autocratic decision is low, and when the subordinate shares the goals to be obtained.

A similar comparison for group problems tells a quite different story. For two of the eight rules, the difference between observed and expected values is not significant. Rule 7, the Fairness Rule, is, in fact, violated slightly more frequently than expected, based on random choices, and Rule 3a is violated almost as frequently as expected. A recomputation of the weighted average of observed probability of rule violations for group problems eliminating Rules 3a and 7 yields a value of 0.096. While still greater than the observed probability for individual problems (0.061), this calculation shows that, in large measure, the disparity between agreement with the feasible set on group versus individual problems can be attributed to managers' inappropriate use of the GII process, i.e., their reluctance to use the GII process on problems which are essentially matters of fairness and equity (Rule 7), and their willingness to use GII on problems where their subordinates do not share the goals of the organization (Rule 3a).

Discussion and Summary

In this paper a normative model of social processes for decision making was presented. This model represented a slightly elaborated and refined version of a model presented in Vroom and Yetton [10]. We share the previous authors' view that such models are far from perfect but can serve a useful function in stimulating research which, in time, will be reflected in better models.

The latter half of this paper was devoted to questions related to how managers do select decision processes—to the factors which influence the degree to which they share their decision-making power with their subordinates. In pursuing these questions, we also relied heavily on the previous work of Vroom and Yetton by using a set of standardized cases selected in accordance with an experimental design. Each case depicted a leader faced with a problem to solve, and subjects were asked to assume his role and to select from a specified list of decision processes the one they would employ. The major difference from Vroom and Yetton was in the nature of the experimental design used in the construction of the "problem set." Whereas Vroom and Yetton's design utilized 30 "group problems" and five decision processes, the design used here provided for seven decision processes and 24 group and 24 individual problems. This design permitted the additional exploration of relationships between behavior on each kind of problem, and of the consistency of the behavior on the latter with the normative model.

The results are supportive of previous conclusions drawn by Vroom and Yetton but augment them in several significant ways. The managers studied do make the discrimination between group and individual problems required by the normative model and select from the appropriate class of decision methods for each problem. Furthermore, the role that the problem attributes play in affecting managers' behavior on the two kinds of problems are distinct in several respects. Therefore, a descriptive model to account for the circumstances under which managers share their decision-making power with subordinates must incorporate a distinction between group and individual problems and the differences in the effects of problem attributes on each kind of problem.

Agreement between the normative model and managers' behavior is substantially higher for individual problems than for group problems, although both exceed chance. The principal bases for deviations from the model on group problems lie in the circumstances surrounding the use of group decision making (GII). Managers are exceedingly reluctant to employ GII on problems without a quality requirement but involving substantial components of fairness and equity and, consequently, exhibit higher-than-expected violations of Rule 7. On the other hand, they make greater use of GII in problems with a quality requirement when the interests of subordinates do not coincide with organizational goals—a use that is prohibited by Rule 3a in the model. The disagreement with the normative model for individual problems is, in large measure, due to a reluctance to employ participative methods (DI and GI) as a means of obtaining needed commitment to a course of action from a subordinate.

The results presented here provide further evidence against the explanatory power of a trait of authoritarianism-participation in accounting for the decision processes used by managers. While managers who tend to employ power-equalization methods on group problems also tend to use such methods on individual problems ($r = .71$), there is wide variance in the processes used in different situations. The variance in behavior that can be attributed to situational characteristics is many times larger than the variance that is attributable to individual differences. From these results, it makes substantially more sense to talk about autocratic and participative situations rather than autocratic and participative managers. The results presented reinforce the earlier conclusion of Vroom and Yetton from their investigation of group problems and suggest that a similar but stronger conclusion can be drawn with respect to individual problems.

Finally, the results presented indicate that the relative explanatory power of situational and individual difference variables is probably not independent of the similarity in roles performed by the managers in the population. The greater the homogeneity within the population, the smaller the proportion of variance attributable to mean differences among managers, and the greater the tendency to respond in a similar fashion to situational demands. The obvious implication is that the nature of the role occupied by the manager shapes his leadership style, but the manner in which this occurs is a subject for further investigation.

References

1. Cyert, R. M., and J. G. March, *A Behavioral Theory of the Firm,* Englewood Cliffs, N.J.: Prentice-Hall, 1963.
2. Lewin, K., "Frontiers in Group Dynamics," *Field Theory in Social Science,* edited by D. Cartwright (New York: Harper, 1951), pp. 188–237.
3. Lowin, A., "Participative Decision Making: A Model, Literature Critique, and Prescriptions for Research," *Organizational Behavior and Human Performance,* 3, 1968, pp. 68–106.
4. Maier, N. R. F., A. R. Solem, and A. A. Maier, *Supervisory and Executive Development: A Manual for Role Playing,* New York: Wiley, 1957.
5. Maier, N. R. F., "Problem-solving Discussions and Conferences," *Leadership Methods and Skills,* New York: McGraw-Hill, 1963.

6. March, J. G., and H. A. Simon, *Organizations*, New York: Wiley, 1958.

7. McGregor, D., *The Human Side of Enterprise*, New York: McGraw-Hill, 1960.

8. Overall, J. E., and D. K. Spiegel, "Concerning Least Squares Analysis of Experimental Data," *Psychological Bulletin*, 72, 1969, pp. 311–322.

9. Vroom, V. H., "Industrial Social Psychology," *Handbook of Social Psychology*, edited by G. Lindzey and E. Aronson (Reading, Mass.: Addison-Wesley, 1970), 5, pp. 196–268.

10. Vroom, V. H., and P. W. Yetton, *Leadership and Decision-Making*, Pittsburgh: University of Pittsburgh Press, 1973.

11. Wood, M. T., "Power Relationships and Group Decision Making in Organizations," *Psychological Bulletin*, 79, 1973, pp. 280–293.

MANAGERIAL BEHAVIOR
AND CAREER PERFORMANCE

J. PETER GRAVES

Most writers and researchers of career issues mention in passing the importance of the manager to subordinate growth and development. However, little direct attention is focused on this individual as a source of tremendous benefit or harm to subordinate's careers. Most organizations, for their part, include development of subordinates as a criterion for managerial performance appraisal. But when deadline push comes to economic shove, it is subordinate development that ends up on the back burner.

The point must not be overlooked that employee development is a long-term consideration competing for the attention of a manager beset with short-term pressures. It takes time, hence costs money, to involve subordinates in goal setting, information sharing, delegation, and so on. It is easy to say in nearly any situation, "If we don't solve the short-run aspects of this problem, there might not be a long run to worry about." In situations of rapid change and economic constraint, the pressures to deal with problems with a short-run perspective are enormous.

Organizations seldom view the issue of career development to be a concern of management at all. Rather, the personnel department, employee development division, or other staff groups are charged with providing career planning and development. Some of these programs are excellent; most are at best harmless. But a watchword of advice common to all of them is "take charge of your own career."

While a significant degree of responsibility for career growth certainly rests with the individual, the impact of managerial decision making and organizational policy is often either ignored or treated as a benign force, readily amenable to any individual's career plan. The effect of line management is so pervasive, however, that it may be considered a well-established and ongoing

From C. B. Derr (ed.) *Work, Family, and the Career.* NY Praegar, 1980.

system for the development of careers. Every time a person is promoted, assigned a new job, given additional responsibilities, and so on, a career development decision has been made. It is likely to be a decision with greater impact than individuals acting on their own initiative could effect.

The Manager and Careers

A careful analysis of a long-prevalent pattern of career development has recently been reported by Thompson and Dalton (1976) and Graves (1977). The result of their research, based on 1,500 scientists and engineers in five research and development organizations, permits a meaningful discussion of the ways managers can positively affect the career growth of those they supervise.

Career Stages

The pattern observed by these researchers described career development in terms of stages. Each stage differs from the others in activities, relationships, and psychological adjustments. Moreover, successful performance at each stage is a prerequisite for success in the next. Individuals who continue to move through these stages retain their high performance ratings; those who do not move tend to be less valued by their organization.

Stage 1. Four stages are identified, with stage 1 noted as the apprenticeship period. Here an individual works under relatively close supervision and direction. In addition, most highly successful professionals have an informal mentor at this time. Surprisingly, some people stay in this stage most of their careers and are never able to assume independent responsibility for their own work. However, that group represents a small minority. The majority, whether having had a mentor or not, make the transition into the next stage.

Stage 2. The second stage is one of independence and specialization. A majority of professionals look forward to having their own project or area of responsibility. Earning this opportunity and taking advantage of it moves a person into stage 2. Most of the solid professional work in the organization is done by individuals in this category. About 40 percent of the professionals in the organizations surveyed are in stage 2. From an individual point of view, it is risky to remain in this stage because managers have rising expectations as a person's age and salary level increase. As a result, those who remain in this stage after 40 tend to receive lower performance ratings. Professionals who move into stages 3 and 4 are quite successful in avoiding that fate.

Stage 3. The role of the professional in stage 3 changes from one of being concerned with one's own development and progress to one in which a substantial effort is expended on behalf of others. Not all individuals do this in the same way nor in identical roles. Some may become mentors to other younger professionals. Others, by the strength of their technical contributions, become valued consultants to groups in and out of the organization. Still others move into the administrative structure of the organization and away from the technical aspects of the work.

Stage 4. The professionals who move into this stage do so because they begin to exercise a significant influence over the future direction of the organization; they are engaged in wide and varied interactions both in and out of the organization; and they are involved in the sponsoring and development of promising people within the organization. Stage 4 people are heavily involved in external relationships. This outside contact is critical because it not only brings information into the organization, but it also gives the organization the visibility it needs to market its goods and services.

It has been suggested that the stages are just another way of looking at the same old levels of organizational hierarchy, giving the pyramid but another name. It is true that there are many managers in stages 3 and 4, but the researchers found many nonmanagers there also. In stage 3, for example, 65 percent of the professionals were not in supervisory positions; in stage 4, 26 percent were not. Thus, in the organizations surveyed, a significant proportion of the professionals were able to remain contributors in their technical specialties and still be highly valued by the organization.

The Need for a Flexible Approach

To arrive at the point of valued contribution as either a manager or non-manager takes more than just an awareness of the direction of necessary growth. While individuals can and should have a significant impact on the development of their careers, managerial actions sometimes exert strong, if not the dominant, influence on subordinates' careers.

The model of career stages carries with it clear implications for the kinds of managerial actions and attitudes that help the development of subordinates' careers. Since it is not likely that all subordinates will be at the same point in their careers, it is necessary for the managerial behavior to be appropriate to the career stage of the subordinate. As individuals may be viewed to be developing through stages, so also must the nature of supervision adapt to the career growth of those supervised.

For example, it is important that the person in stage 1 have a meaningful relationship with a mentor. Whether this mentor is the manager or another senior professional, the supervisor can greatly assist the establishment of the relationship. The supervisor must tolerate the individual's need for greater detail and clarity in the assignments received. The need for frequent and realistic feedback on performance is greater in this stage. Professionals at this stage in their careers should be encouraged to complete all training or education in the basic knowledge of their occupation, perhaps earning an advanced degree. The manager's encouragement, approval, and in some cases tolerance of the special conditions in this stage are essential for the subordinate's success.

In contrast to stage 1, the professional in stage 2 requires an entirely different set of circumstances. The individual should begin to devote significant time and effort to a specific project area or specialty. This work should be more challenging and of longer duration than stage 1 assignments. The individual should begin to make important project or job decisions and should receive and accept greater responsibility in determining what to do and how to do it. Continuing education activities should be directed toward sharpening technical skills in a specialty. It is very important to develop a specialty in this stage, but the manager should carefully monitor the status and future of the project or specialty this individual is working on. Stage 2 professionals are highly vulnerable to shifts in priority and funding of their work area.

In the same manner, the nature of supervision that is required for continued growth through stage 3 and 4 must be appropriate to the work history, talents, and aspirations of the individual. This places a tremendous burden on the manager to be aware of and sensitive to the needs of each subordinate.

Even without the model of career stages, a manager who is honest with subordinates and keeps them informed on job-related matters, involves them in meaningful goal setting, and delegates challenging work will have a positive effect on their careers. Such values are common to most programs of management education and development. A common vehicle for the communication of these values in many organizations is the assessment center. It is one such assessment center sponsored by Syntex Corporation and called the Career Development Center (CDC), which provided the basis for the study reported here.

The Present Investigation

Subjects and Data Gathering

The subjects for this study were 90 managers from 20 large organizations in technology-based industries and utilities. All subjects had been participants in the CDC. The time since participation ranged from 12 to 48 months, averaging about 30 months. The subjects occupied first-level and middle-management positions in their organizations, with an average salary of $23,410 in late 1976. Their average age in 1976 was 36.39 years. Most had a bachelor's degree, a third had completed master's degrees, and a few the doctorate degree.

The study was an attempt to understand better the relationship between managerial behavior and job performance. A variety of measures of behavior and attitudes were obtained and then compared with indexes of job performance.

Predictors of performance. Some of the measures of behavior and attitude were obtained at the assessment center. These data included test scores on instruments such as FIRO-B, Gordon Personal Inventory and Profile, verbal and abstract reasoning, and reading skills. Measures of managerial behavior commonly stressed by assessment centers were also obtained. All of these data, for the purposes of this study, were considered predictors of managerial performance and were to be compared with current indexes of performance for their predictive validity.

Present behaviors. Data concerning another set of behaviors were gathered at the same time as current performance data by means of the Objective Judgment Quotient (OJQ), the highly reliable assessment instrument developed by Wyvern Research Associates. This instrument was completed by the subject, the subject's superior, and two colleagues (subordinates or peers). The results provided a measure of each of 14 behaviors for every subject.

Job performance. Two measures of job performance were obtained. One measure used was a reflection of salary growth rate over the recent past. The specific index used was percent salary increase per month since CDC participation. The second measure of job performance was obtained at the same time as the OJQ instrument was completed. The subject, the subject's superior, and two colleagues rated the subject on a six-point scale according to the degree of perceived similarity to "the most effective manager you have ever known." Subjects were rated high if they were seen as very similar in behavior to effective managers, low if seen as not comparable at all. The persons rating were cautioned not to compare the subject to the highest paid or most upwardly mobile, but the most effective. It thus was hoped to obtain two performance indexes that reflected organizational recognition of on-the-job performance and similarity to effective managers.

Results

The examination of primary interest was to determine if assessment center measures of behavior and attitudes are good predictors of managerial performance. The results were surprising for two reasons.

The first surprise was that very few of the measurements from the assessment center were good predictors of future managerial performance. Of 11 skill areas observed and assessed at the CDC, only two—conflict resolution and delegation—were significantly related to future performance.

Even more surprising was that while the two performance measures related to each other, they did not bear uniform relationships to all of the other variables. Some behaviors were positively related to one performance measure, but negatively related to the other. Only three variables were positively related to both performance indexes, while for 15 others, their correlations with the two performance scores were significantly different from each other. It thus became apparent that it was more meaningful to distinguish between salary growth rate and managerial effectiveness when discussing the relationship between behavior and performance.

Success and effectiveness. Success is the term applied to the performance measure of salary growth rate. It is likely to be a fairly sensitive indicator of organizational recognition. *Effectiveness* is the term applied to the evaluation provided by superiors and colleagues regarding the subject's actual job performance.

It should not be surprising that success and effectiveness were found to be related positively to each other, but the relationship is more complicated than a single correlation coefficient would indicate. The two indexes are not simply different ways of measuring the same phenomenon. This is seen by the manner in which behavioral, biographical, and test data relate to both success and effectiveness.

Figure 1 attempts to visually represent the direction and strength of each variable of interest on the two dimensions of success and effectiveness. The dashed lines indicate levels of statistical confidence beyond which the correlation coefficients for a variable are significantly different. The variables beyond the dashed lines do not relate in the same way to success as they do to effectiveness.

The variables in Figure 1 can generally be classified into three categories: those behaviors that are positively related to both success and effectiveness, those that are negative on effectiveness and positive on success, and those that are positive on effectiveness and negative on success. Of primary interest to the present discussion are the last two categories. It appears as though a number of qualities or skills important to climbing the job ladder are negatively related to

FIGURE 3.1.

Eighteen Variables of Importance and Their Relationship to Success and Effectiveness
(Each dot represents a pair of correlation coefficients for that variable)

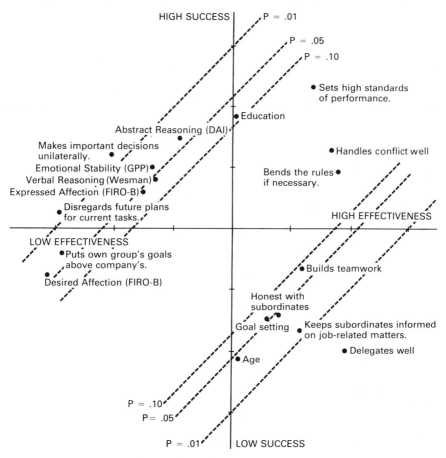

effective performance in the managerial role. The obverse of this appears also to be the case, namely, that some behaviors strongly related to effectiveness are negatively related to organizational ascendancy.

Successful and Effective Management

For purposes of further discussion, successful management will be defined by those variables to the upper left of the dashed lines in Figure 1. This managerial approach stresses individual, unilateral action by managers toward short-term goals of their own work unit. Verbal and reasoning abilities are important as well as a controlled public image, that is, one who is not given to much emotion or excitability.

Effective management embodies the behaviors to the lower right in Figure 1. Delegation, team building, goal setting, honesty with subordinates, and keeping them informed on job-related matters are the central behaviors in this approach.

We Get What We Reward

It is well known that behaviors that are rewarded will tend to continue, while behaviors that are unrewarded will not persist. It probably would be an oversimplification to conclude that rewarding successful management is a clear example of hypocrisy. It is likely that most of the organizations represented by the subjects of this study would say that they desire and support effective management. They may even claim a systematic process for evaluating and rewarding the proper managerial behavior. But therein lies part of the problem. When appraising the performance of managers, one tries to set up straightforward, objective criteria against which performance can be measured and ultimately rewarded. Such efforts might be successful in situations of high structure and predictability, but will not work when applied elsewhere. To focus on the visible aspects of the manager's job is usually to consider only the public behaviors and the short-term results of recent decisions. Even the much-touted management by objectives (MBO) is seldom a solution to this dilemma. Under most MBO systems, goals in areas where quantification is difficult often go unspecified. Behaviors such as team building and delegation often go unrewarded simply because they are hard to observe.

Effective Management and Subordinate Growth

The model of career stages provides a helpful perspective from which to view one's own career and the careers of others. But even without an explicit model, effective management will positively aid the development of subordinate careers. Keeping subordinates informed on job-related matters, meaningful goal setting, and the delegation of challenging work are behaviors that create a climate favorable to growth and development.

On the other hand successful management, by focusing on short-range objectives and unilateral decision making, creates a climate generally unfavorable to subordinate growth. Important job-related decisions about subordinates are typically made with little input from those affected. Long-range concerns, of which employee development is an example, are sacrificed for short-term objectives.

Successful management is not a new phenomenon. Rather, it is a new name for a managerial approach that has been around for a long time. Its effect on subordinate careers has attracted little attention in the past because of the pattern of organizational growth through the 1950s and 1960s. In growing organizations the development of subordinates is achieved largely through promotions and reassignments. As organizational growth slows or levels off, there are fewer positions to stimulate employees to learn and acquire new skills. Career development then becomes more dependent on managerial actions that provide challenge and stimulation within the context of the present job.

Reactions and Remedies

Subordinate Reactions

There are predictable reactions to successful management by subordinates who perceive little opportunity for meaningful growth. It must be pointed out that many will do nothing either because they are unaware of career issues, or the costs of individual action are too great.

The career change. Successful management gives the career-minded subordinate the feeling of being boxed in. Faced with this frustration, many believe they must leave the organization or even the occupation to escape. This may solve the personal dilemma, but do nothing to change the factors that caused it. Subordinates may even contribute to the recurrence of such practices in the organization they leave. When those who cannot tolerate a certain state of affairs leave the organization, the only ones left will be those who can. A similar situation occurs in the various processes of government when honest and upright citizens refuse to participate because of the dishonesty of the incumbents. The incidence of dishonest practices is thereby likely to increase, not decrease.

Retaliation. While not a realistic alternative, a commonly observed behavior pattern by individuals frustrated and helpless to improve their situation is retaliation. Regardless of its precise form—simple resistance to direction or even larceny and sabotage—such behavior illustrates the vast creative potential that can be turned against the organization. (There may be some uncomfortable with the choice of the term *creative potential,* preferring to reserve it for appropriate contributions to organizational goals. But anyone familiar with such resistance must agree that there are many ingenious forms of antiorganizational behavior.) These activities contribute little, if anything, to the improvement of the organization and nothing to career development.

Unionization. Professionals in greater numbers are considering various forms of unions, associations, and collective bargaining as means of self-protection and to effect organizational change. It is a peculiarity of professionals, as a category of personnel, that neither of these objectives is meaningfully achievable through unionization. It has been observed that the individual who turns to a union for protection from management is merely switching from being subject to the whims of one group to being subject to the whims of another. That the situation is so simple is doubtful, but the success of the union is, in large measure, dependent on its ability to organize its members into a uniform, homogeneous power block. This has precisely the same effect upon career development as when management treats subordinates as a homogeneous, monolithic block, desirous of the same things, motivated by similar opportunities, and possessing common aspirations. In either instance, the individual's career goals must fit the strictures deemed appropriate by the leaders, be they union or company. On the other hand, the kind of supervision implied by the model of career stages is highly individualized, treating each subordinate in terms of that person's unique characteristics and aspirations. Furthermore, the polarization between management and nonmanagement that tends to occur with unionization would seriously impair, if not destroy altogether, the mentor/apprentice relationship as well as the relationships between management and nonmanagement in stages 3 and 4.

Organizational Remedies

In contrast to the steps available to individuals to deal with the effects of successful management, which have little substantive impact on the situation, there are practical steps that the organization can take to improve the prospects for meaningful career development.

New inputs to the decision process. It is important that attention be drawn to the impact of decisions affecting job assignments, promotions, and the like. When such decisions are made without involving others, and with an eye to short-run as opposed to long-range concerns, there is great risk of negative effects on careers. It is not necessary to make such decisions in public; rather, the decision simply should involve more persons than the manager acting alone. Other managers, the individuals affected by the issue, and interested third parties may be considered for input to such decisions.

Career monitoring. A form of ombudsman has been suggested as a means of providing organizational support for the airing of problems associated with careers. Presumably, this would be an individual with some influence and respect in the organization, such as a manager, former manager, or even a number of such individuals who each take a rotating turn in this role. It would be this person's responsibility to mediate the complaints that arise from personnel decisions and act as an interested third party on important considerations.

A chief engineer in a research and development organization has set up a system to monitor the changing of job assignments. He has determined that each person should have a major new assignment at least every four years. Consequently, he has directed that the name of any engineers not reassigned in four years be submitted to him monthly. If any name remains on the list for more than two or three months, the chief engineer begins to ask some pressing questions of the manager of that engineer.

Optimal organizational design. The matrix organizational design has been suggested as a means of focusing attention on careers. One characteristic of such a structure is that each person has two bosses: a product or project manager and a functional manager. Under this arrangement, one manager worries about getting the task completed, and the other worries about staffing, job assignments, compensation, and so on. The functional manager has responsibility for the career development of the professionals in the group. If a person has been working in a narrow specialty too long, the functional manager has the power to approach the project manager to try to get the individual into a new area to develop greater breadth. This type of organization is not simple, nor is it a panacea, but it increases the visibility and legitimacy of career issues.

Reward the right behaviors. Ultimately, for these suggestions to have positive effect, they must be backed by genuine organizational improvement toward effective management and away from successful management. Managers will persist in a behavior or pattern of behaviors as long as there is incentive to do so. In the simplest terms, this means the organization must reward effective management. A knowledge of effective management alone is insufficient incentive to change; individuals must believe that it is to their personal as well as the organization's benefit to be concerned with career development.

To reward effective management, organizations must do a better job of measuring managerial performance. As mentioned earlier, most appraisal systems contribute to such problems rather than assist in their resolution. Fortunately, new methods such as the scaled comparison are becoming available to permit more bias-free measurement of managerial performance across a range of important behaviors.

As an organization moves in the direction of effective management, the climate becomes more supportive of long-range concerns such as career development. But one need not be a great fan of career development to value such a shift. Effective management is, after all, exactly that—effective. When this kind of supervision is also rewarded, the distinction between effectiveness and success will become meaningless.

References

Graves, J. P. 1977. "Now Even Obsolescence May Be Obsolete: A New Look at Careers and Their Development" (Paper presented at the National CIEC Conference of the American Society of Engineering Education, San Antonio, Tex., January 21).

Thompson, P. H. and G. W. Dalton. 1976. "Are R&D Organizations Obsolete?" *Harvard Business Review,* Nov.–Dec., pp. 105-16.

STRATEGIES, STRUCTURES, AND PROCESSES OF ORGANIZATIONAL DECISION

JAMES D. THOMPSON

ARTHUR TUDEN

Despite the apparent importance of decision-making for theories of administration and the considerable attention recently devoted to the topic, present models and knowledge of decision-making have generated few hypotheses about administration, and they have not been adequately linked with organizational models.

A major deficiency of most decision models has been that they are economically logical models seeking to describe maximization processes. These *econo-logical* models have utility as criteria against which to reflect behavior, but they have contributed little toward the explanation or prediction of behavior.

Simon has achieved a major break-through with his "satisficing" model.[1] This is much more than the mere substitution of one word or one concept for another, for Simon's model is a *psycho-logical* model designed to describe and predict behavior. Its full significance seems not yet to be widely recognized.

This psychological model of decision-making is essentially one dealing with individual human beings. It applies equally to purposive choices of a personal or an organizational nature. Its generalizability is, however, both a source of power and of limitation, for it does not deal explicitly with the particular phenomena which surround the making of decisions in organizational contexts.

As a companion to the psychological model, therefore, we wish to develop *sociological* models. We believe they will point to important decision-making behavior which has been observed in organizations but which is neither described nor predicted by econological or psychological models.

We will attempt to show (1) that there are several types of decisions to be made in and on behalf of collective enterprises, (2) that each type of decision calls for a different strategy or approach, (3) that there are several varieties of organizational structures which facilitate these several strategies, and (4) that the resulting behavior defines variations in decision processes. It has been our purpose to construct models which are neither culture-bound nor discipline-bound, containing no evaluative or normative elements.

Reprinted from James D. Thompson and Arthur Tuden, *Comparative Studies in Administration* (Pittsburgh: University of Pittsburgh Press, 1959) by permission from the author and publisher.

[1]Herbert A. Simon, "A Behavioral Model of Rational Choice," *Quarterly Journal of Economics,* February, 1955; reprinted in Simon, *Models of Man,* New York: John Wiley & Sons, 1957.

"Choice" from among alternatives seems to be the end-point of decision-making, but the term "decision" will not be confined simply to ultimate choice. Rather, "decision" will refer to those activities which contribute to choice, including recognizing or delimiting and evaluating alternatives as well as the final selection. Thus an individual may have responsibility for making a final choice on behalf of an organization, but if others help him delimit or evaluate alternatives we will not describe that individual as *the* decider.[2]

The term "decision" in this paper should also be understood to refer to organizational decisions. Personal decisions, i.e., choices presumed by an individual to have consequences only for himself, are excluded.[3] Likewise, unconscious choices or habits are not within the scope of this paper.

The term "decision unit" will be used to refer to that individual or group within an organization which has power, responsibility, or authority to choose, on a particular issue, for the organization. To illustrate, in American jurisprudence, "the court" may be the appropriate organization, but the power to decide certain issues is assigned to a single presiding judge as the decision unit; other issues are assigned to a jury as the decision unit; still others are assigned to a panel of justices as the decision unit.

Types of Decision Issues

The notion of differing types of issues calling for decisions is not new. More than a decade ago Simon distinguished ethical from factual decisions[4] but no one seems to have extended his analysis. More recently there has been considerable discussion of decision-making under the differential conditions of certainty, risk, and uncertainty.[5] Dorwin Cartwright has suggested distinguishing among judgment, preference-ranking, and "actual decision-making" (which he defines as commitment to action).[6] There have, however, been few attempts to build typologies of issues or decisions.

A typology of issues will enable the sorting out of (a) those aspects of decision situations which *confront* decision units from (b) those actions which decision units may take in such situations.

The main elements of decision—found both in the econological and psychological models available—seem to be three: (1) alternative courses of ac-

[2]For the notion of "composite decisions" see Herbert A. Simon, *Administrative Behavior,* New York: Macmillan, 1957. See also R. Tannenbaum and F. Massarik, "Participation by Subordinates in the Managerial Decision Making Process," *Canadian Journal of Economics and Political Science,* August, 1950.

[3]This distinction is made by Chester I. Barnard, *Functions of the Executive,* Cambridge, Mass.: Harvard University Press, 1936.

[4]Simon, *Administrative Behavior* (first edition), 1945.

[5]For examples, see the collection of papers edited by M. J. Bowman, *Expectations, Uncertainty and Business Behavior,* New York: Social Science Research Council, 1958; and R. D. Luce and H. Raiffa, *Games and Decisions,* New York: John Wiley & Sons, 1957.

[6]In Bowman, *op. cit.*

tion, (2) differential consequences of the several alternatives (means), and (3) evaluation of the potential outcomes on some scale of desirability (ends).[7]

We will work with two of those three variables, dropping "alternative courses of action," since by definition a unit called upon to decide is aware of at least one pair of alternatives. Before working with the remaining two variables, however, we wish to redefine them slightly in order to achieve greater generalizability.

The notion of "consequences of alternative courses of action" assumes only a concern with present and future, not with past actions. Yet it seems reasonable, for example, to conceive of the trial jury as a decision unit which works backward from one present fact, e.g., a corpus delecti, to choose one of several possible past actions which may account for the present fact. This sequence may also characterize certain decisions in scientific research and in audits or inspections. The notion of *causation,* as applied to several alternatives, seems to us to subsume both questions of present and future states and questions of past actions which may explain present states.

We would also like to avoid some of the possible implications of such terms as desirability scale, which is inanimate, and to substitute for them some term with more explicit behavioral overtones. For this purpose we will speak of *preferences about outcomes.* In conceiving of our major variables as *causation* and *preferences,* we have gained a certain flexibility without losing the value of previous work on economic models. The means-ends approach falls within our scheme, but we have the added advantage of being able to include other approaches too.

Since we are dealing with organizations—social systems—it cannot be taken for granted that causation will be "known" as soon as a decision issue appears, nor can it be assumed that the organization is certain of its preferences regarding the several alternatives apparent. Often the organization's decision unit cannot simply choose, but must act to determine what its knowledge or beliefs are regarding cause-and-effect relationships, and what its preferences are about the postulated effects.

Now, if the two variables *causation* and *preferences* are reflected against the additional question of whether there is *agreement or consensus within the decision unit* about those two matters, it is possible to construct a four-fold typology of decision issues.

| | | Preferences about Possible Outcomes | |
		Agreement	Disagreement
Beliefs about Causation	Agreement	Computation	Compromise
	Disagreement	Judgment	Inspiration

[7]We believe this is not inconsistent with the statements of such diverse writers as Simon, *Models of Man (op. cit.)*; Irwin D. J. Bross, *Design for Decision,* New York: The Macmillan Co., 1953; Richard C. Snyder in Roland Young (ed.) *Approaches to the Study of Politics,* Evanston: Northwestern University Press, 1958; Jacob Marschak in Paul Lazarsfeld (ed.) *Mathematical Thinking in the Social Sciences,* Glencoe, Illinois: The Free Press, 1954; and Bernard Berelson in Berelson, Paul Lazarsfeld and William McPhee, *Voting,* Chicago: University of Chicago Press, 1954.

The labels in the four cells—computation, judgment, compromise, and inspiration—are descriptive of four *strategies* which we believe are appropriate for the four types of decision issues. In the following section we will elaborate on those strategies, and connect them with certain types of social structures. For the time being we will deal only with "pure" cases.

Pure Strategies and Structures

Decision by Computation

Where there is agreement regarding both causation and preference, i.e., where a preference hierarchy is understood and where knowledge is available or believed to be available, decision-making is a technical or mechanical matter. In its extreme form, this situation requires no genuine choice, since the problem-solution appears as common sense.[8]

But in many instances, the appropriate techniques for equating cause–effect knowledge with known preferences are quite complicated. The data may be so voluminous for example, that only an electronic calculator can make sense of them. Likewise, the particular sequences of action involved in the techniques may be hard to master and difficult to carry out, so that only the highly trained specialist can arrive at an appropriate choice. In either event, the strategy for decision is straight-forward analysis, and we term this decision by computation.

A structure for computation. Assuming for the moment complete freedom to build an organization which will face *only* computation issues, and that our guiding norms are economy of effort and efficiency of performance, what kind of organization shall we build?

This will be an organization of specialists, one for each kind of computation problem we can anticipate, and we want to introduce four constraints or rules to: (1) prohibit our specialists from making decisions in issues lying outside their spheres of expert competence, (2) bind each specialist to the organization's preference scale, (3) route all pertinent information to each specialist, and (4) route every issue to the appropriate specialist.

The organization which we have just built contains the heart of what Max Weber described as the "pure type" of bureaucracy. This bureaucratic model is clearly expressed in the "formal" or "official" structure of the great majority of business firms, governmental agencies, and military units. For each of these, presumably, preferences can be stated with some clarity. Members are appointed to positions only so long as they embrace those preferences. Moreover, bureaucracy is formulated on the assumption that rules or procedures can be established for classes of cases or problems, and that the events which will call for organizational decisions are repetitive or

---

[8]Simon notes that what he terms "programmed" choice situations sometimes elicit behavior which suggests that the choice has been made in advance. In these cases, he says, there is a well-established procedure that leads through a series of steps to a determinate decision. He also stresses that programmed decisions may involve a very great amount of computation before choice is actually made. See his paper in Bowman, *op. cit.*

serial events for which expert competence can be developed.[9] Candidates for these positions are expected to hold licenses or degrees indicating successful completion of training for the specialized positions, or to pass tests.

It is in these organizations that the concept and practice of "delegation" seems most widespread, and that decision units officially are comprised of single individuals. Expert specialization means that the organization can enjoy the economy of assigning problems to individuals or their electronic counterparts.

Decision by Majority Judgment

Where causation is uncertain or disputed, although preferences are clearly known and shared, decision-making takes on new difficulties. Lacking in acceptable "proof" of the merits of alternatives, the organization must rely on judgment.[10] Triangulation illustrates this simply and clearly. Each member of the three-man team is presumed competent by virtue of his training and his equipment to make a judgment, but because none has indisputable and complete evidence, none is permitted to make the decision alone, and no member may outvote or override the judgment made by other members. But triangulation is a special case of the more general problem—special because each judge focuses on the same empirical phenomenon from his own special vantage point. More frequent, perhaps is the case where there is not only differential perception but also differential interpretation, and this is most clearly illustrated by the voting situation in which the collective judgment determines the decision. We will refer to this strategy of organizational decision as one of majority judgment.

A structure for majority judgment. What kind of organization shall we build as an ideal one to handle only judgmental problems? This is to be an organization of wise and knowing men, operating according to constraints or rules which: (1) require fidelity to the group's preference hierarchy, (2) require all members to participate in each decision, (3) route pertinent information about causation to each member, (4) give each member equal influence over the final choice, and (5) designate as ultimate choice that alternative favored by the largest group of judges—the majority.

What we have just described may be labelled, for lack of a better term, a *collegium.* This concept has been used in ecclesiastical literature to refer to a self-

---

[9]Bowman, in *Expectations, Uncertainty, and Business Behavior, op. cit.,* commenting on the papers read at the conferences, notes that only two authors focus on cases involving nonseriability. She comments that "Neglect of the higher degrees of uncertainty (or nonseriability) was undoubtedly deliberate in some instances, reflecting the hypothesis that businessmen ignore parameters about which they cannot at least make reasonably informed guesses, and that they commonly avoid taking actions the outcomes of which are characterized by extreme uncertainty. . . . However, problems involving the more extreme degrees of uncertainty were probably bypassed for another reason, the obvious difficulty of dealing with them systematically." p. 5.

[10]See Leon Festinger's important distinction between "social reality" and "external reality" as bases for the validation of opinions of group members. Festinger, "Informal Social Communication," *Psychological Review,* 1950, pp. 271–292.

governing voluntary group, with authority vested in the members.[11] Whatever this type of organization is labelled, the social science literature does not seem to contain formal models of it, as it does for bureaucracy.

Nevertheless, this type of organization is described in case studies of "voluntary associations" and in the constitutions and by-laws of many organizations, including many American universities and trade unions. All of these not only take steps to "get out the vote," but incorporate into their by-laws provisions requiring a quorum for the transaction of official business. Direct elections of governmental officials approximate the collegial situation, with each literate citizen-of-age presumed to have equal competence and influence at the polls.

Governing boards of directors or trustees are also established on the collegial principle, with the requirement of a quorum in order for judgments to be binding.[12]

Decision by Compromise

On occasion there may be agreement by all parties as to the expected consequences or causes of available alternatives, but lack of consensus over preferences toward such "facts." Neither computation nor collective judgment is "appropriate" for this type of issue, for the blunt fact is that if one preference is satisfied, another is denied. An organization facing this situation may fall apart through schism, civil war, or disinterest, unless some common item or point can be found on the several extant preference scales. It can be illustrated by imagining an organization composed of two factions. For faction A, the preference scale runs 1, 2, and 3, while for faction B, the scale is 4, 5, and 6. In this case, in order for either faction to obtain at least an acceptable solution the other must be denied all satisfaction, and this presages the end of the organization. If the preference scales run 1, 2, and 3, in that order, and 3, 4, and 5, both factions can attain a modicum of satisfaction by choosing 3. The appropriate strategy where causation is conceded but preferences are in dispute thus appears to be one which will arrive at the common preference. We will refer to this strategy as decision by compromise.

A structure for compromise. Now the task is to construct an ideal organization to handle compromise types of issues economically and efficiently.

Whereas computation problems call for the smallest possible decision unit, and collective judgment for the widest possible participation, compromise seems to require a decision unit of intermediate size. What we want is a structure to facilitate bargaining, and since this involves detailed and subtle exploration of the several factional preference scales, the decision unit must be small enough to permit sustained and often delicate interchange. On the other hand, there is the requirement that all factions—or certainly all important fac-

---

[11]Max Weber discussed the "collegiality" or collegial system, but used the term more loosely than we propose to do here. See Hans Gerth and C. Wright Mills, *From Max Weber: Essays in Sociology,* New York: Oxford University Press, 1946, pp. 236-244.

[12]The typical conception of the corporation as pyramidal in form, with ultimate authority peaking in the office of the president, is thus misleading. It would be more descriptive to think of the corporation as a wigwam, with a group at the top.

tions—be involved in the decision. This leads, we think, to the *representative body* as the appropriate structure.

For this purpose, we will build rules or constraints into our organization to: (1) require that each faction hold as its *top* priority preference the desire to reach agreement, i.e., to continue the association, (2) ensure that each faction be represented in the decision unit, (3) give each faction veto power, and (4) give each faction all pertinent, available information about causation.

The United Nations Security Council approximates this type of decision unit, if we assume that the member nations represent all important blocs. Federations often provide the representative structure for boards of directors. The American Congress appears to fit this pattern, with the "veto" requirement relaxed because of the size of the body. It is possible to conceive of the Congress as an arena for bargaining and compromise, rather than judgment, with the vote considered merely a mechanical device for measuring at any point in time the current state of negotiations.[13]

The representative decision unit, operating toward compromise, is also seen, though less formally, in many loosely organized societies in the form of "consensus decision-making" by councils of tribal chiefs or elders.[14] In these instances power is relatively diffused, so that a "veto" of an alternative by any one member of the decision unit prevents the choice of that alternative. While not necessarily elected, members of the decision unit have to maintain followings and thus may be considered representatives. This is clearly brought out in the studies cited.

The American trial jury for capital cases can also be seen as an attempt to ensure bargaining or weighing of the evidence against the conflicting preferences of freeing the innocent and punishing the guilty. The jury situation differs from many other compromise situations in that each member of the unit is presumed to be an advocate of *both* of the competing values (rather than an advocate of one factional position) who "bargains with himself." The requirement of unanimity for the jury seeks to remove the decision from the area of majority judgment to one of arriving at a choice endorsable by all members of the decision unit.

Decision by Inspiration

The fourth and in our typology the final type of issue is one in which there is disagreement both as to causation and as to preferences. This is, of course, a most dangerous situation for any group to be in; certainly by definition and probably in fact the group in this situation is nearing disintegration. While this situation seems to be far removed from the usual discussions of decision-making, we believe it has empirical as well as theoretical relevance.

The most likely action in this situation, we suspect, is the decision not to face the issue. Organizations which appear to be slow to seize opportunities or

[13]This view seems consistent with the findings of Stephen A. Bailey, *Congress Makes a Law,* New York: Columbia University Press, 1950; and E. Latham, *The Group Basis of Politics,* Ithaca, N.Y.: Cornell University Press, 1952. See also Latham in Heinz Eulau, S. Eldersveld, and M. Janowitz (eds.) *Political Behavior,* Glencoe, Illinois: The Free Press, 1956.

[14]For example, see F. M. and M. M. Keesing, *Elite Communication in Samoa,* Stanford Conn.: Stanford University Press, 1956; W. B. Miller, "Two Concepts of Authority," *American Anthropologist,* April, 1955 (Chapter 7 in the present volume); and M. Nash, "Machine Age Maya: The Industrialization of a Guatemalan Community," *American Anthropologist,* Part 2, April, 1958.

to respond to environmental events may, on close inspection, be organizations which contain disagreement as to both preferences and causation. To the extent that the organization in this predicament can avoid an issue, it may at least maintain itself as an organization. If it is forced to choose, however, the organization is likely to dissolve—unless some innovation can be introduced.

Anthropologists have recorded on numerous occasions institutionalized means of gaining inspiration by referring "insoluable" problems to supernatural forces, and it is no secret that responsible public officials in "less superstitious" nations call on Divine Guidance when they must make momentous decisions for which there is no precedent and the consequences are highly uncertain. A related device is for the group to rely on a *charismatic* leader.

As Weber pointed out,[15] the charismatic leader is thought by his followers to have solutions or at least the wisdom to find them. Frequently he offers a new set of ideals or preferences which rally unity out of diversity, by shifting attention. Pointing to a real or fancied threat from outside is one ancient device for this.

The 1958 election of deGaulle and adoption of the new French communante seems to reflect the charistmatic or inspirational type of situation.[16] But it also seems possible for individuals in nominal positions of leadership to attain and articulate enough imagination to create a new vision or image and thereby pull together a disintegrating organization. This seems consistent with the conclusion of Karl Deutsch and his colleagues as to the importance of innovation and invention in bringing about political integration.[17] Whatever the particular form of leadership exercised, we believe that decisions of this type—where there has been dissensus about both causation and preferences—are *decisions by inspiration.*

A structure for inspiration. It is difficult to conceive of an ideal structure for decision by inspiration, for the thinking of the social scientist is oriented toward pattern and organization, while the situation we face here is one of randomness and disorganization. If these situations occur it probably is seldom by design. Nevertheless, an attempt to deliberately construct such a situation might be instructive for the student of organization.

What we are trying to build now has been labelled by Durkheim as a state of *anomie,* normlessness, or deregulation.[18] As a rough approximation, anomie

[15]Gerth and Mills, *op. cit.*

[16]Although nominally a choice by vote, the majority approached unanimity, and it seems that voters were not asked to judge his ability to solve such specific problems as the war in Africa, but rather were asked to impute to him and endorse qualities of omnipotence.

[17]Deutsch, et al. *Political Community and the North Atlantic Area.* Princeton, N.J.: Princeton University Press, 1957. They say: ". . . our studies of the more promising strategies of integration have left us strongly impressed with the importance of political innovation and invention. Many of the decisive advances in bringing about political integration involved the making of political decisions in a manner such that improbable or original measures were adopted rather than their more obvious or probable alternatives. Many of the central institutions of amalgamated security communities thus were original and highly improbable at the time they were adopted. The American Articles of Confederation, the Federal constitution—. . . none of these has any close counterpart in the 18th century politics or law. . . . It seems worth adding that a number of amalgamated political communities were wrecked precisely as a consequence of decisions which were highly probable at the time and place at which they were made." P. 114.

[18]Emile Durkheim, *Suicide,* transl. by J. A. Spaulding and George Simpson, Glencoe, Ill.: The Free Press, 1951. See also Robert K. Merton, *Social Theory and Social Structure,* Glencoe, Ill.: The Free Press, 1957. Chapters 4 and 5.

occurs when former goals or values have lost their meaning or significance or when such goals appear unobtainable with the means available. Thus, our problem is to create a situation of chaos, but to do so with an aggregation of persons who in some sense can be considered to constitute a group or collectivity. We will therefore call for the following constraints: (1) the individuals or groups must be interdependent and thus have some incentive for collective problem-solving,[19] (2) there must be a multiplicity of preference scales and therefore of factions, with each faction of approximately equal strength, (3) more information must be introduced that can be processed, and it must be routed through multiple communication channels,[20] and (4) each member must have access to the major communication networks, in case inspiration strikes.

While it is doubtful if empirical cases of organizational anomie are deliberately created, there seems to be evidence that the more carefully structured organizations do sometimes find themselves in a state of anomie. The routed military organization, for example, is characterized by de-emphasis of military values and an abundance of rumors, contradictory information, and loss of contact or faith in nominal leaders.

Anomie and inspiration probably appear in less stark form in formal organizations, for the most part. Befuddled administrators of organizations caught up in forces which are not understood may and sometimes do rely on decision by inspiration in one of two forms: (a) imitation of more prestigeful and successful organizations, or (b) importation of prestigeful and authoritative management consultants to tell them what they should want and how to go after it.

In each of these illustrations the effect is to convert the *anomie* situation into something resembling a computational situation, and to rely upon a decision unit composed of one individual, as in the case of bureaucracy. The basis for designating the "expert" differs, of course. But the production of a new vision, image, or belief is basically a creative kind of activity and it is doubtful if either voting or bargaining structures are likely to produce it.

Designation of Decision Units

Our argument to this point, regarding types of pure issues, pure strategies, and pure structures, can be diagrammed thus:

| | | Preferences about Possible Outcomes | |
		Agreement	Nonagreement
Beliefs about Causation	Agreement	Computation in Bureaucratic Structure	Bargaining in Representative Structure
	Nonagreement	Majority Judgment in Collegial Structure	Inspiration in "Anomic Structure"

[19]This does not guarantee, of course, that the various factions will remain members of the organization, for we have not ruled out the possibility that they will exploit other resources as substitutes for those provided by the organizations.

[20]Dissensus over causation might be achieved by *withholding* pertinent information about cause and effect, but this is not foolproof because organization members can invent *fictions* to fill in the missing gaps. Dubin describes organization fictions as ways of dealing with the unknown, and suggests that fictions can provide the ideological goals and purposes necessary to an organization, as well as beliefs regarding the efficacy of available means. See "Organization Fictions" in Robert Dubin (ed.) *Human Relations in Administration.* Englewood Cliffs, N.J.: Prentice-Hall, 1951.

Note what this suggests about differences in composition of decision units. For a computation issue, the "ideal" decision unit consists of an individual, acting on behalf of the entire organization. For the voting type of issue, the decision unit is made up of the entire membership. In the compromise situation, a group of representatives or delegates constitute the ideal decision unit. In the inspiration situation, the individual again becomes the most appropriate decision unit.

This typology has some distinct parallels to the work of March, Simon and Guetzkow who discuss four major processes: (1) problem-solving, (2) persuasion, (3) bargaining, and (4) "politics." These four processes are treated, however, simply as processes whereby organizations resolve conflict, which seems to us to be only one aspect of organizational decision phenomena. Moreover, they quickly collapse the four process categories into two: analytic and bargaining.[21]

It seems ironic that the only discipline whose focus has traditionally spanned all four types of situations has been the least productive of decision models.[22] Political science typically has dealt with three branches of government—executive (or bureaucratic); legislative (or bargaining); and judiciary (or collegial). Its interest in statesmen, great men, and leaders seems to cover the fourth (anomic or inspirational) situation.

Mixed Situations

There are a variety of reasons why the purity of our illustrations may be relatively infrequent.[23] A major proposition of this essay is that usually an organization adopts one of the four strategies—computation, collective judgment, compromise, or inspiration—as its dominant strategy, and bases its structure on that strategy.

To the extent that this is true, we can expect or predict several kinds of organizational difficulties which will be presented to administrators when the organization faces issues or problems which do not fit the formal neatness of our pure types.[24] We can also expect difficulties if the appropriate constraints are not present within the particular decision unit. Finally, we can predict that problems will arise if an issue calling for one strategy is presented to a decision unit built to exercise a different kind of strategy.

Confusion of Issues

The difficulties of means–ends distinctions are as real for operating organizations as for scientific observers. Psychological time perspectives have much to do with whether a particular issue is seen as one of means or ends. Despite

[21]See James G. March and Herbert A. Simon, with the collaboration of Harold Guetzkow, *Organizations,* New York: John Wiley, 1958.

[22]Recent exceptions to this generalization include Snyder, *op. cit.,* and Morton Kaplan, *System and Process in International Relations,* New York: John Wiley, 1957. Kaplan identified chain-of-command decision-making units; persuasive decision-making units; and veto decision-making units.

[23]On the other hand we have no proof that the pure examples are rare. Millions of organizational decisions of a computational nature, for example, probably are made every day in bureaucracies. The mixed situations may be more noticeable and memorable because of the difficulties they pose rather than because they are more frequent.

[24]It also has implications for personnel recruitment processes, but we will not deal with that matter in this paper.

the fact that social systems of various kinds generally are expected by members to persist through time, their members may attach different valences to varying periods of the future. The holder of the short-run viewpoint may see an issue as one of preferences, while the long-run adherent sees the issue as one of causation.

In a dynamic and complex organization, moreover, the range of possible outcomes widens rapidly as the time-span is extended.[25] If this is true, then members of an organization probably are less inclined to grant the competence of experts for long-run decisions, even when they would grant the ability of the same experts for short-run matters.

Thus different members of an organization or of its decision unit may respond to the same stimulus in varying ways, some seeing it as a matter for computation, others as a judgment matter, and still others as requiring bargaining.

Absence of Structural Constraints

One constraint common to all of the pure structures described earlier, except for the case where the decision unit is an individual, was that each judge, each bargainer, each faction, had equal power to influence the choice. While this usually is a formal specification for such units as trial juries, legislatures, or boards, we know that such units in fact exhibit inequality of membership. Strodtbeck, for example, reports that sex and social status affect the amount of participation of jury members in the decision process, the perceptions that fellow jurors have of their competence as jurors, and the degree to which they influence the outcome.[26] Such factors as party loyalty and party discipline, seniority, political skills, and the endorsement of pressure groups may affect the legislator's ability to make his voice heard as loudly as the next one. Within bureaucracies there are well-known inequalities between offices and divisions which formally are equal, and such scholars as Dalton have documented some of the reasons why computational experts may temper their computations with other considerations.[27]

Another constraint common to all but the anomic structure was that each participant in the decision unit have access to all available, pertinent information about causation. In fact, despite all of the attention given to communication in modern organizations, the condition called for by this constraint is at best approximated but seldom achieved. Colleagues of the expert in a bureaucracy, then, may grant the competence and good intentions of an official, but refuse to honor his decision on grounds that he did not know the local or "real" situation. Well informed minorities may control the collegial body

[25]This is suggested by the decision trees of decision theorists. See Luce and Raiffa, *Games and Decisions, op. cit.*

[26]F. L. Strodtbeck, Rita M. James and C. Hawkins, "Social Status in Jury Deliberations," *American Sociological Review,* December, 1957. Similar observations have been made in the hospital setting by A. H. Stanton and M. S. Schwartz, *The Mental Hospital,* New York: Basic Books, 1954.

[27]Melville Dalton, "Conflicts Between Staff and Line Managerial Officers," in *American Sociological Review,* June, 1950.

whose other members are ill-informed, and "private information" obtained by one faction may make a mockery of the compromise situation.

This listing is intended to be illustrative rather than exhaustive. Relaxation of other constraints, particular to peculiar structures, will be discussed below.

Inappropriate Decision Units

If organizations were completely pliable, it would be a relatively simple thing to assign each problem to a decision unit designed especially for it. But, of course, organizations would cease to be organizations if they were completely pliable. Regularity, pattern and structure are inescapable.

Presumably the basic structures which prescribe the standing or regular decision units of organizations are established because they are expected to be appropriate for the *typical* problems those organizations will face. In some organizations, at least, precedent and tradition lead members to expect that *all* decisions will be made by the decision units and processes established for typical decisions. This undoubtedly will vary with the history of the organization and with the social and cultural attitudes surrounding it. In our own society and decade, it is not unusual to hear officials of bureaucracies complain that committee participation (on judgment problems) interferes with their work—by which they seem to mean expert computation in their own offices. On the other hand, we frequently hear university faculty members, conditioned to expect collegial decisions, complain when department heads or deans make purely computational decisions.[28] There are also situations, particularly in certain types of military units, when members are dismayed if leaders so much as ask their opinions. For some in the military organization, the commander must be an expert and every issue must be a computational one.

Thus the attitudes and expectations of members may make it difficult for organizations to create *ad hoc* or alternative decision units to deal with problems for which basic, traditional structures are ill-suited.

Another important source of structural rigidity is the shifting nature of human knowledge. Types of problems which at one time are identified by members of a group as appropriate for judgment may at another time be defined as computational problems, as the group changes its beliefs about cause-and-effect relations. We will have more to say about an opposite trend below, but the dominant "scientific" trend on the American scene in recent years has been to remove more and more items from the sphere of opinion to demonstrable "certainty."

Thus problems which once called for voting or inspirational strategies have become problems for computation or bargaining, and traditional structures are threatened. The city manager movement threatens both the party organization and the council by redefining certain types of problems as no longer subject to bargaining or voting but as appropriate for expert computation. The increasing scope of required expertise forces the American Congress to establish bureaucratic agencies to make decisions which once were prerogatives of the legislature—the Congress then becomes jealous of its own creations.

[28]This often is *expressed* by questioning their competence.

Decision issues appear to be broader, more complex, and more time-consuming as we move from computation issues to voting to bargaining issues. There is reason to believe that, left to their own devices, members of social systems tend to expand decision issues. In a revealing summary of community issues and the course of their disposition, Coleman[29] notes a tendency for transformation of issues from specific to general, and from disagreement to antagonism. Bales also notes in small problem-solving groups that interpersonal tensions mount as the decision process moves from orientation to evaluation to control.[30]

As knowledge becomes increasingly pluralistic, in the sense that new specialized logics are developed, the bureaucracy encompasses not one but several sets of beliefs about appropriate means to organizational ends. Thus the competence of the single expert becomes doubted and members define issues as calling for judgment rather than computation. If, for example, the expert can be forced to admit that his is but a professional opinion—a tactic in jury trials—the way is cleared to insist that others be consulted in communities where public health experts have decided to introduce fluoride into the public water supply.[31]

It is clear that in the past several decades, American corporations have shown a proliferation of specialized staff agencies, each with its own logic for maximizing a particular function or procedure. As the beliefs about causation have thus become increasingly pluralistic, there has been a plea for the development of "generalists," but also there seems to have been a corresponding increase in the use of decision units appropriate to judgmental issues.[32] Committees, conferences, staff meetings, and "clearance" procedures have not only proliferated but have been dignified on wall charts—at least to the extent of dotted lines.

With problems which appear to call for judgment, the heat of debate can lead proponents of the several alternatives to overstate their cases and discount missing information; often it also leads them to refer to more general but extraneous organization preferences as a means of finding moral justification for the selection of the alternative they endorse. When this occurs, the issue is no longer one of judgment regarding causation, but becomes one of dispute over (relevant) ends and thus subject to compromise.

The issue which seems a natural for bargaining may verge on the anomic, since it frequently generates difficulties in the identification and exploration of causation. Inherently emphasizing preference conflict, the bargaining structure leads its members to discount causation theories endorsed by opponents and to overemphasize their own. This hampers the effort to get the "facts"

[29]James S. Coleman, *Community Conflict,* Glencoe, Ill.: The Free Press, 1957.

[30]Robert F. Bales, "The Equilibrium Problem in Small Groups," in Talcott Parsons, Robert F. Bales, and Edward A. Shils, *Working Papers in the Theory of Action,* Glencoe, Ill.: The Free Press, 1953.

[31]See Coleman, *op. cit.*

[32]For a report on the increasing use of committees for key decisions on new products, on personnel policy, production volume, and long-range planning, see "Committees: Their Role in Management Today," *Management Review,* October, 1957.

and where preferences already are at issue, disputes over facts create anomic situations. Moreover, if one faction is adamant or unwilling to "bargain fairly," there is a tendency for the other faction or factions to seek to expand the issue into a larger more general category, and to threaten the adamant faction with trouble on unrelated matters. This, too, tends toward anomie.

Administration and Decision-Making

We can now offer the general proposition that an important role for administration is to *manage* the decision *process,* as distinct from *making the decision.* We are not suggesting that administrators do one to the exclusion of the other, but if issues are not automatically crystallized, the ideal structural constraints are not automatically present, or appropriate decision units are not automatically selected, it may fall to administrators to take action which will facilitate decisions.

The following discussion is not offered as exhaustive, but as illustrative of the potential utility of considering administrative roles with respect to the decision process.[33]

Where a time dimension is not clearly implied by the nature of the issue, one role of administration is to delineate, by fiction or otherwise, such a time dimension. This facilitates the sorting out of means from ends, by the decision unit, and thus tends to contain the issue from expanding into a more complex one.

When there are many alternatives available, a role of administration is to provide machinery for elimination of all but a few. This can be particularly important when an issue is assigned to a voting unit, which seems to be able to operate effectively only on binary problems. At one level of generality this is an important role for Congressional committees.[34] At a more general level of analysis this is the function of political parties in the two party system; the necessary compromises of platform and candidates are achieved before the issue is put to the electorate. By way of contrast, in multi-party France the function of compromising a plurality of interests devolved on the legislature more than on intraparty processes, and was an important factor in the lack of effectiveness of the Fourth Republic.[35]

In the bargaining situation the important role of administration may be to obtain initial mutual commitment to reaching agreement, and to maintain this commitment as taking priority over factional preferences. This approach may guard the issue from expanding into one of anomie, for as Dubin points out, mutual commitment to the necessity for reaching agreement in effect moves

[33]For a similar conclusion, though approached differently, see Philip Selznick, *Leadership in Administration,* Evanston, Ill.: Row, Peterson and Co., 1957.

N. W. Chamberlain, in a study of the corporate decision-making process as applied to the transfer of employees, notes the distinction between deciding and managing the decision process, and offers a number of stimulating hypotheses. See Chamberlain, *Management in Motion,* New Haven, Conn.: Labor and Management Center, Yale University, 1950.

[34]See Latham, *Group Basis of Politics, op. cit.*

[35]For an analysis of this see Duncan MacRae, "Factors in the French Vote," *American Journal of Sociology,* November, 1958.

the issue in the direction of judgment and voting.[36] One method of handling the bargaining issue, and seemingly an indispensable one when the preference scales do not contain common items, is to place the particular issue in a larger context. This can be done by "horse-trading," thus assuring the losing faction on the present issue of priority treatment on a future issue.[37]

Another role of administration which seems to be important under certain conditions is that of crystallizing consensus about preferences. Ambiguity in a decision situation may result in lack of knowledge, on the part of members of a decision unit, of the similarities of their preferences. When this is the case, an administrator who can sense the agreement and articulate it may play a vital part in organizational decision. In this connection it appears that timing may be as important as sensitivity to cues. Keesing and Keesing, observing formal group deliberation in Samoa, note that a senior elite person may choose to speak early if he wants to give guidance to the discussion *or knows that prior informal consultations have made clear a unanimous stand,* but that usually he will let others carry the active roles, making his pronouncements after the debate has pretty well run its course.[38]

A final suggestion regarding possible roles of administrators in facilitating organizational decision-making concerns the extremely complicated kinds of issues that frequently face administrators of "loose" organizations. We have in mind such social systems as the community (as viewed by a mayor, council, or manager); the school district (as viewed by the superintendent or board), or the bloc of nations (as viewed by their diplomats and officials). We refer to these as "loose" organizations because only a portion of the relevant "members" are directly subject to the hierarchy of authority. In the legal sense, that is, some of the groups are not "members," although in the behavioral sense they are.[39]

When such organizations face important and complicated issues, we believe, it may become necessary for administrators to redefine the issue into a series of issues, each assigned to an appropriate decision unit. It may also be that there are patterns in the sequence in which the series is handled. For example, in order to achieve a "community decision" on a fluoridation or school bond issue, it may be necessary to *first* get agreement and commitment of the powerful elements on preferences. This might be done "informally" in the smoke-

---

[36]Suggested by his analysis of union–management relations. See "Power and Union-Management Relations," *Administrative Science Quarterly,* June, 1957.

Bernard Berelson makes a related point. Surveying political voting research he writes, ". . . it would seem to be at least likely that the *same* avowed principles underlie political positions at every point on the continuum from left to right. . . . Democratic theorists have pointed out what is so often overlooked because too visible, namely, that an effective democracy must rest upon a body of political and moral consensus. . . . In this circumstance, a seeming consensus which is accepted at its face value is far better than no consensus—and a seeming consensus is sometimes reflected in loyalty to the same symbols even though they carry different meanings. A sense of homogeneity is often an efficient substitute for the fact of homogeneity. . . . What this means, then, is that the selection of means to reach agreed-upon ends is more likely to divide the electorate than the selection of the ends themselves." See Berelson in Heinz Eulau, S. J. Eldersveld, and M. Janowitz (eds.) *Political Behavior,* Glencoe, Ill.: The Free Press, 1956, p. 110.

[37]The important role of the larger context in facilitating decisions was suggested to us by Professor Bela Gold, School of Business Administration, University of Pittsburgh.

[38]*Elite Communication in Samoa, op. cit.*

[39]Such "loose" organizations are found in industry, too. For an instructive analysis of this, see Valentine F. Ridgway, "Administration of Manufacturer-Dealer Systems," *Administrative Science Quarterly,* March, 1957.

filled room, by compromise, and it might include the important choice as to whether to tackle the issue at all. After that decision is made, the *second* step might be to frame a judgmental issue for presentation to an electorate. Finally, within the limits of the majority decision, specialists can be presented with such issues as the proper equipment for fluoridation or the most appropriate timing for bond issues.

We feel rather safe in predicting that there is a cumulative effect in this sequence. Weakness in the first step probably forecasts trouble in succeeding steps, and so on.

Administrative Tendencies to Narrow Issues

It seems apparent that in terms of time and effort, issues increase in "cost" in the same order in which they increase in breadth; computation is the quickest and simplest and involves the fewest members; judgment by voting membership is slower and diverts the energies of many; and bargaining usually is a drawn out energy-consuming process.

Organizations operate in environmental contexts and hence cannot always take a leisurely approach in making decisions. The actions of competitors or of potential collaborators and clientele frequently place time deadlines on issues. Moreover, the interrelatedness of the parts of large organizations may mean that delay at one point suspends activities at others, and when costs must be reckoned closely this fact exerts serious pressures to have issues settled promptly.[40]

Thus if an issue can be defined in more than one way, responsible officials may be tempted to define it in an easier, faster and less frustrating way, i.e., as calling for computation rather than judgment, or as appropriate for voting rather than bargaining.[41] In some cases the pressures of time, or habit, may lead administrators to force issues into molds which are patently inappropriate.

Timing of Choice and Consensus

Except in situations where force can be brought to bear on members, it appears that consensus or acceptance of both means and ends is necessary for effective organizational action.

The four types of issues posited above are successively "broader" in the

[40]Rose Laub Coser, comparing medical and surgical wards in a hospital, finds that the emergency nature of the surgical setting results in decision-making by fiat, whereas the more tentative, diagnostic atmosphere in the medical ward results in decision-making by deliberation and consensus. See Coser, "Authority and Decision-Making in a Hospital: A Comparative Analysis," *American Sociological Review,* February, 1958 (Chapter 8 in the present volume).

[41]March, Simon, and Guetzkow see this tendency. They write: "Because of these consequences of bargaining, we predict that the organizational hierarchy will perceive (and react to) all conflict as though it were in fact individual rather than intergroup conflict. More specifically, we predict that almost all disputes in the organization will be defined as problems in analysis, that the initial reaction to conflict will be problem-solving and persuasion, that such reactions will persist even when they appear to be inappropriate, that there will be a greater explicit emphasis on common goals where they do not exist than where they do, and that bargaining (when it occurs) will frequently be concealed within an analytic framework." (In *Organizations, op. cit.,* p. 131.)

Lipset, surveying political sociology, writes: "Inherent in bureaucratic structures is a tendency to reduce conflicts to administrative decisions by experts; and thus over time bureaucratization facilitates the removing of issues from the political arena." In Robert K. Merton, Leonard Broom, and Leonard S. Cottrell, Jr. (eds.) *Sociology Today,* New York: Basic Books, 1958, p. 102.

sense that they incorporate into the issue itself the necessity of finding or building consensus. It is only in the simplest type—computation—that consensus on means and ends exists prior to the decision. The judgment issue involves finding a cause and effect hypothesis about which a majority can agree. The bargaining issue involves finding a preference on which consensus can be established. The anomic situation requires the creation of both preferences and causation-beliefs acceptable to a majority.

If the fact or the fiction of consensus is not present at the time a choice is made—and this may frequently be the case when rapid decisions are necessary—the required consensus must be achieved following choice. The hypothesis here is that for organizational decisions to be implemented effectively both consensus and choice are necessary. If, for reasons of expediency, choice is made *before* consensus is achieved, the burden of achieving consensus *following* choice remains.

This hypothesis, if accurate, has important implications not only for decision-making but for the larger administrative process of which decision is a part.

Conclusion

We have attempted to develop a format for studying decision processes in organizations, by identifying four major types of decision issues and pairing them with four major strategies for arriving at decisions. For each strategy we have suggested, there is an appropriate structure. Obviously there are many combinations and permutations of issues, strategies, and structures, but we believe that the format suggested points to a limited number of such arrangements, and that patterns can be found in them. We hope we have shown that this approach to organizational decision processes has important implications for theory and application.

What has been presented here can be considered no more than a first approximation. The empirical evidence along these lines has not been collected systematically, and further conceptual development undoubtedly will be necessary. It is possible, for example, that added leverage can be gained by distinguishing between "lack of agreement" and "disagreement," and thus developing a nine-fold typology of issues.[42] This format could also be extended into an analysis of how decisions are blocked or prevented. Such an extension should tell us something about the important area of belligerent behavior in or between organizations, and it should also provide a useful test of the models presented here.

Whatever the eventual results, we hope we have made the case for development of sociological models of decision processes, which can be joined with the psychological "satisficing" model to their mutual advantage.

---

[42]Suggested by Professor Frederick L. Bates, Department of Sociology, Louisiana State University, in private communication.

13 leadership: the effective exercise of power and influence

LEADERSHIP: A BELEAGUERED SPECIES?

WARREN BENNIS

Something's happened—something that bewilders, something turbulent, convulsive, and spastic. What appears is a panorama going in and out of focus like a faulty TV tube; its flickering bluish images, pulsing to a strobe-light cadence, express the chaos of our times. Although our technology is so advanced and precise that it brings together in New York—at 600 m.p.h. speeds—people who left Los Angeles, San Francisco, Denver, Chicago, and Atlanta shortly before, it delivers them just in time to be blown to smithereens by a bomb in a baggage locker.

It's as if mankind, to paraphrase Teilhard de Chardin, is *falling suddenly out of control of its own destiny.* Perhaps only a new Homer or Herodotus would be able, later on, to show us its patterns and designs, its coherences and contours. What we hear and discern now is not one voice or signal, but a jimjangle of chords: an *a capella* choir here, a closely harmonized brass quintet there, a raucous, atonal gang in the balcony blowing on kazoos and holding up placards.

All we know for sure is that we cannot wait a generation for the historian to tell us what happened; we have to try to make sense out of the jumble of voices, dare to order the dissonant chorus of kazoos. Indeed we must try, for the first test of any leader today is to discover just what he or she *does* confront; only then will it be possible to devise the best ways of making that reality—the multiple realities—potentially manageable.

The Erosion of Institutional Autonomy

The most serious threat to our institutions and the cause of our diminishing sense of able leadership is the steady erosion of institutional autonomy. This

---

Reprinted with permission of the author and the publisher from *Organization Dynamics* (New York: American Management Association, Summer 1976).

erosion results from forces in both the external and the internal environment.

The External Environment: Multiple Dependencies

Time was when the leader could decide—period. A Henry Ford, an Andrew Carnegie, a Nicholas Murray Butler could issue a ukase—and all would automatically obey. Their successors' hands are now tied in innumerable ways—by governmental requirements, by various agencies, by union rules, by the moral and sometimes legal pressures of organized consumers and environmentalists. When David Mathews was president of the University of Alabama, before he became Secretary of Health, Education and Welfare, he characterized federal regulations (in *Science,* Vol. 190, 1975, p. 445) as threatening to

> . . . bind the body of higher education in a Lilliputian nightmare of forms and formulas. The constraints emanate from various accrediting agencies, federal bureaucracies, and state boards, but their effects are the same . . . a loss of institutional autonomy, and a serious threat to diversity, creativity, and reform. Most seriously, that injection of more regulations may even work against the accountability it seeks to foster, because it so dangerously diffuses responsibility.

Dr. Mathews will often be reminded of those words and the deadly hidden costs of compliance.

The external forces that impinge and impose upon the perimeter of our institutions—the incessant concatenation of often contrary requirements—are the basic reasons for the loss of their self-determination. Fifty years ago this external environment was fairly placid, like an ocean on a calm day. Now that ocean is turbulent and highly interdependent—and it makes tidal waves. In my own institution right now, the key people for me to reckon with are not only the students, the faculty, and my own management group, but people external to the university—the city manager, city council members, state legislature, accrediting and professional associations, federal government, alumni, alumnae, and parents. There is an incessant, dissonant clamor out there. The institution that proliferates its dependence on these "external patronage structures" blunts and diffuses its main purposes. A brilliant example of such an institution is the university; indeed, the boundaries of its autonomy resemble Swiss cheese. To cope with these pressures, every leader must create a department of "external affairs"—a secretary of state, as it were, to deal with external constituencies. (Ironically, our real Secretary of State Kissinger often finds foreign affairs thwarted by *internal* constituencies that undo his long, laborious, and precarious negotiations.)

In an analysis of my own time allocation, a research analyst determined that "50 percent of the university president's contacts were with external people, 43 percent with internal constituents, 4 percent with trustees, and 3 percent with personal or undetermined contacts. Sixty-seven percent of phone calls, 43.7 percent of mail, and 38.9 percent of meetings were with external groups." (Drea Zigarmi, "The Role of the University President as a Boundary Person," Dissertation at the University of Massachusetts, Amherst, 1974.) The study was done in the second year of my incumbency; I suspect that my involuntary orientation toward external audiences has increased year by year since then.

Accompanying all this is a new kind of populism—not the "free silver" of Bryanism, but the fragmentation of constituencies. On my own campus, which is typical, we have over 500 organized pressure groups. We have a coalition of women's groups, a gay society, black organizations for both students and faculty, a veterans' group, a continuing education group for women (late returnees to the university), a handicapped group, a Jewish faculty caucus, a faculty union organized by the American Association of University Professors, an organization for staff members who are neither faculty nor administrators, an organization of middle-management staff members, an association of women administrators, and a small, elite group of graduate fellows.

This fragmentation, which exists more or less in all organizations, marks the end not only of community, a sense of shared values, and symbols; but of consensus, an agreement reached despite differences. It was Lyndon Johnson's tragedy to plead, "Come, let us reason together," at a time when all these groups scarcely wanted to *be* together, much less reason together.

These pressure groups are intentionally fragmented. Going their separate and often conflicting ways, they say: "No, we don't want to be part of the mainstream of America—we just want to be us," whether they're blacks, Chicanos, women, the third sex, or Menominee Indians seizing an empty Catholic monastery. They tell us that the old dream of "the melting pot," of assimilation, does not work. They have never been "*beyond* the melting pot" (as Glazer and Moynihan wrote about it); they have been *behind* it.

So what we have now is a new form of politics—King Caucus, who has more heads than Cerberus, and Contending Queens who cry, "Off with their heads!" as they play croquet with flamingos. It is *the politics of multiple advocacies.* They represent people who are fed up with being ignored, neglected, excluded, denied, subordinated. No longer, however, do they march on cities, on bureaus, or on organizations that they view as sexist, racist, anti-Semitic, and so on. Now, they file suit. The law has suddenly emerged as the court of first resort.

A Litigious Society: "Is the Wool Worth the Cry?"

And so we have become a litigious society in which individuals and groups—in spectacularly increasing numbers—bring suit to resolve issues that previously might have been settled privately. An injured hockey player bypasses institutional procedures to bring formal suit. The club owners are outraged that "one of their own" took the case "outside." College students, too, unhappy with what they are learning on campus, are turning to the courts. A lawsuit against the University of Bridgeport may produce the first clear legal precedent. It was filed last spring by a woman seeking $150 in tuition, the cost of her books, and legal fees because a course required of secondary education majors was "worthless" and she "didn't learn anything." My own university faces a suit from a black woman because she lost the administrative position I had mistakenly thought she could fill. A law review has been sued for rejecting an article. In New Jersey, a federal judge has ordered 28 state Senators to stand trial for violating the constitutional rights of the 29th member, a woman, by excluding her from their party caucus. They did so, they claimed, because she was "leaking" their deliberations to the press. In a test case in Columbus, Ohio, the U.S. Supreme Court recently ruled that secondary-school students may not be suspended, disciplinarily, without formal charges and a hearing—that the loss of a single day's education is a deprivation of property. A federal court in Washington has just awarded $10,000 to each of the thousands of May 1970 antiwar demonstrators who, it found, had been illegally arrested and confined at the behest of former Attorney General Mitchell.

Aside from the merits of any particular case, the overriding fact is clear: The hands of all administrators are increasingly tied by real or potential legal issues. I must consult our lawyers in advance before making trivial decisions. The university has so many suits against it (40 at last count) that my mother now calls me "My son, the defendant."

The courts and the law are, of course, necessary to protect individual rights and to provide recourse for negligence, breach of contract, and fraud. But a "litigious society" presents consequences that no one foresaw, not least of which are the visible expense of legal preparation and the invisible cost of wasted time.

Far more serious than the expense, however, are the confusion, ambiguity, and lack of subtlety of the law and what that does to institutional autonomy and leadership. To take the example of consumer protection, we see that lawsuits are forcing universities to insert a railroad-timetable disclaimer in their catalogues—for example, "Courses in this catalogue are subject to change without notice"—in order to head off possible lawsuits. At the same time, the Federal Trade Commission is putting pressure on doctors, architects, lawyers, and other professionals to revise their codes of ethics forbidding advertising. The Buckley Amendment, which permits any student to examine his own file, tends to exclude from it any qualitative judgments that could provide even the flimsiest basis for a suit. (Ironically, Senator Buckley himself refuses to make a "full financial disclosure" of his personal wealth because he finds "the mood of suspicion . . . has created almost a presumption that public officials are corrupt or corruptible unless proven innocent.")

The confusion, ambiguity, and complexity of the law—augmented by conflicting court interpretations—tend toward institutional paralysis. Equally forbidding is the fact that the courts are substituting their judgments for the expertise of the institution. Justice may prevail, but at a price to institutional leadership so expensive, as we shall see later on, that one has to ask if the "wool is worth the cry."

A Cat's Cradle

Many of our institutions are careening (or catatonic) because of an invasion and overstimulation by external forces. We know what that does to an individual: A total reliance on external cues, stimuli, rewards, and punishments leads to an inability to control one's own destiny. People in this state tend to avoid any behavior for which there is no external cue. Without signals, they vegetate. With contrary signals, either they become catatonic—literally too paralyzed by fear of risk to choose, let alone *act* on a choice—or, conversely, they lunge at anything and everything.

The same is true of organizations and their leadership; under the influence of coercive political and legal regulations, they exhibit the same effects. Although these regulations are more pronounced in the public sector than in the private sector, in the latter area the market mechanism has heretofore been the linking pin between firm and environment—providing feedback in terms of rewards and punishments and reflecting the success or failure of decisions. Whether the organization is private or public, whether the controls are legitimate or not, there is only one natural conclusion: An excess of (even well-intended) controls will lead inexorably to lobotomized institutions.

What neither lawmakers nor politicians seem to realize is that laws and regulations deal primarily with sins of commission. Sins of omission are more difficult to deal with—partly, as Kenneth Boulding points out, because it is just damned hard in practice to distinguish between honest mistakes and deliberate evil. Legitimate risk-taking can land you in jail. On the other hand, by "playing it safe," by living up to the inverted expression, "Don't just do something, sit there," an institution, a leader, a person can avoid error; and if they keep it up long enough, they can *almost* avoid living.

As legal and political systems become increasingly concerned with sins of commission—an event exemplified in the dramatic switch from *caveat emptor* to *caveat vendor,* in the deluge of consumer protection legislation, in malpractice suits, in the environmental protection movement, in the court decisions awarding damages to purchasers of faulty products—we can get to a point where, like the California surgeons who quit operating on any but emergency patients, no producer or organization will do anything at all. Why should they? The costs of uncertainty and honest mistakes are now far too costly to bear.

At my own and many other universities, for example, we are now in the process of rewriting our catalogues so carefully that it will be virtually impossible for any student (read: *consumer*) to claim that we haven't fulfilled our end of the bargain. At the same time, because we have to be so careful, we can never express our hopes, our dreams, and our bold ideas of what a university experience could provide for the prospective student. I suspect that in ten years or so, college catalogues (rarely a publication that faculty, students, or administrators are wild about in any case) will devolve into statements that resemble nothing more than the finely printed cautions and disclaimers on the back of airline tickets—just the opposite of what education is all about: an adventurous odyssey of the mind.

All this—all the litigation, legislation, and *caveat vendor*—not only diminishes the potency of our institutions, but leads to something more pernicious and possibly irrecoverable. We seek comfort in the delusion that all our troubles—our failures, our losses, our insecurities, our "hang-ups," our missed opportunities, our incompetence—can be blamed on "someone else," can be relegated to the seamless, suffocating, and invisible "system." How convenient, dear Brutus.

Just think: At a certain point, following our current practices and national mood, all sense of individual responsibility will rapidly erode. And along with that, the volume of "belly-aching" and vacuous preaching about "the system" will grow more strident. The result: Leaders who *are* around either will be too weak or will avoid the inevitable risks involved in doing *anything*—whether good, bad, or indifferent.

I am *not* arguing the case against all regulations and controls; I am painfully conscious that some have been too long in coming—that, indeed, some are imperative for the great body of citizens and necessary if we are to realize our nation's values (for example, equality of opportunity for all); without them, I fear, our basic heritage would long ago have become indelibly corrupted. (And, of course, it is not hard to understand why campaign finances have come under control recently. How do we excuse or deal with Gulf's $12 million bribes?)

All the same, when it comes to protecting people from their exploiters, we have an extra responsibility to be so vigilant that we don't end up in a situation where everyone is enmeshed in a cat's cradle of regulations erratically intertwined with the filaments of "good intentions."

As Justice Brandeis put it many years ago:

> Experience should teach us to be most on guard to protect liberty when the governments' purposes are beneficient. Men born to freedom are naturally alert to repel invasion of their liberty by evil minded rulers. The greatest dangers to liberty lurk in insidious encroachments by men of zeal, well-meaning, but without understanding.

Variations on a Theme

The basic problem is that leaders are facing a set of conditions that seemed to take shape suddenly, like an unscheduled express train looming out of the night. Who would ever have forecast the post-Depression development in the public sector of welfare, social service, health and education? Who, save a Lord Keynes, could have predicted the scale and range of the multinational corporations? Prophetically, he wrote:

> Progress lies in the growth and the recognition of semi-autonomous bodies within the states. Large business corporations, when they have reached a certain age and size, approximate the status of public corporations rather than that of the individualistic private enterprise.

The Keynesian prophecy is upon us. When David Rockefeller goes to London, he is greeted as if he were a chief of state (and some of his empires *are* bigger than many states). But in addition to the growth of semi-autonomous, often global corporations that rival governments, we have public-sector institutions that Keynes could not have imagined. Our society's biggest employer, and the one with the fastest growth rate, is local and state government. Higher education, which less than twenty years ago was 50 percent private and 50 percent public, is now about 85 percent public and is expected to be 90 percent public by 1980. And whereas a century ago 90 percent of all Americans were self-employed, today 90 percent work in what I would call bureaucracies, as members of some kind of corporate family. They might be called "juristic" persons who work for a legal entity called a corporation or agency. Being juristic persons, they are not masters of their own actions, they cannot place the same faith in themselves that self-employed persons can.

These are the problems of leadership today. We have the important emergence of a Roosevelt-Keynes revolution, the new politics of multiple advocacy, new dependencies, new constituencies, new regulatory controls, new values. And how does our endangered species, the leaders, cope with these new complications and entanglements?

Memorandum of the People of Ohio's
13th Congressional District:

Summary: Being the Congressman is rigorous servitude, ceaseless enslavement to a peculiar mix of everyone else's needs, demands and whims, plus one's own sense of sense of duty, ambition or vanity. It is that from which Mrs. Mosher and I now declare our personal independence, to seek our freedom, as of January 3, 1977. . . .
It is a Congressman's inescapable lot, his or her enslavement, to be never alone, never free from incessant buffeting by people, events, problems, decisions. . . . It is a grueling experience, often frustrating, discouraging, sometimes very disillusioning. . . . House debates, caucuses, briefings, working breakfasts, working lunches, receptions, dinners, homework study, and even midnight collect calls from drunks. . . . you name it!
I am for opting out. I shall not be a candidate for reelection in 1976.

Charles A Mosher
Representative
13th Congressional District
State of Ohio
December 19, 1975

Managing, Not Leading

For the most part, the leaders are neither coping nor leading. One reason, I fear, is that many of us misconceive what leadership is all about. *Leading* does not mean *managing:* The difference between the two is crucial. I am acquainted with many institutions that are very well *managed* and very poorly *led.* They may excel in the ability to handle daily routines and yet never ask whether the particular routines should exist at all. To lead, so the dictionary tells us, is to go in advance of, to show the way, to influence or induce, to guide in direction, course, action, opinion. To manage means to bring about, to accomplish, to have charge of or responsibility for, to conduct. The difference may be summarized as activities of vision and judgment versus activities of efficiency.

In his decision making, the leader today is a multidirectional broker who must deal with four estates—his immediate management team, constituencies within his organization, forces outside his organization, and the media. While his decisions and actions affect the people of these four estates, their decisions and actions, too, affect him. The fact is that the concept of "movers and shakers"—a leadership elite that determines the major decisions—is an outdated notion. Leaders are as much the "shook" as the shakers. Whether the four estates force too many problems on the leader or whether the leader takes on too much in an attempt to prove himself, the result is what I call "Bennis's First Law of Pseudodynamics," which is that routine work will always drive out the innovational.

Securing the certainty of routine can be detected in the following example:

I noticed that frequently my most enthusiastic deputies were unwittingly keeping me from working any fundamental change in our institution. My own moment of truth came toward the end of my first ten months as head of the university. It was one of those nights in the office. The clock was moving toward three in the morning, and still I was not through with the incredible mess of paper stacked before me. Bone weary and soul weary, I found myself muttering, "Either I can't manage this place or it is unmanageable." I reached for my daily appointments calendar and ran my eye down each hour, each half-hour, each quarter-hour, to see where my time had gone that day, the day before, the month before.

I had become the victim of an amorphous, unintentional conspiracy to prevent me from *doing anything whatever to change the university's status quo.* Even those of my associates who fully shared my hopes to set new goals and work toward creative change were unconsciously doing the most to ensure that I would never find the time to begin. People play the old army game. They do not want to take responsibility for or bear the consequences of decisions that they should properly make. Everybody dumps his "wet babies" (as old hands in the State Department call them) on my desk even though I have neither the diapers nor the information to take care of them.

"Copping Out"

Today's leader is often baffled and frustrated by a new kind of politics—not following traditional party lines, but arising from significant interaction with various governmental agencies, the courts, and consumers, and other factions. It is the politics of maintaining institutional self-determination and mastery in times of environmental turbulence. Many leaders do not want to recognize these forces, let alone face the new politics. In 1974, the director of the New York Health Corporation resigned saying, "I already see indications that the corporation and its cause are being made a political football in the current campaign. I'm not a politician. I do not wish to become involved in the political issues here." Yet he had earlier said that he found himself "at the center of a series of ferocious struggles for money, power, and jobs among the combatants, political leaders, labor leaders, minority groups, medical militants, medical school deans, doctors and nurses, and many of my own administrative subordinates." His corporation had an $800 million budget, was responsible for capital construction of more than $1 billion, and employed 40,000 people, including 7,500 doctors and almost 15,000 nurses and nurses' aides. It embraced 19 hospitals which, with 15,000 beds, numerous out-patient clinics, and emergency rooms, treated 2,000,000 New Yorkers a year. And he was *surprised* that he was into politics—and didn't like it.

Leading Through Limits

We are now experiencing a transition period that may aptly be called an "era of limits." After the Club of Rome warned us of this in *The Limits of Growth,* the Arab petroleum boycott, soaring fuel costs, and the continuing energy crisis confirmed the brutal fact that our national goals have outrun our current means. Some political and institutional leaders exploit the situation by turning the public's disenchantment with growth into a political asset. They want to follow the popular mood rather than lead it.

The National Observer (November 29, 1975, pp. 1 and 16) calls California's young Governor Edmund G. Brown "the hottest politician in America," and quotes him thus:

Growth in California has slowed down . . . the feeling is strongly anti-growth. Once, people seemed to think there were no limits to the growth of California. Now Californians are moving to Oregon and Colorado. . . . There are limits to everything—limits to this planet, limits to government mechanisms, limits to any philosophy or idea. And that's a concept we have to get used to. Someone called it the Europeanization of America. That's part right. You take an empty piece of land and you fill it up with houses and soon the land is more scarce and the air is more polluted and things are more complicated. That's where we are today. . . .

The National Observer says his rhetoric works: "Over 90 percent of the people in California applaud his performance."

Leading by Diminuendo

Compared with the grandiose rhetoric of the past quarter-century about the ability of size and scale plus technological "know-how" to solve all of society's basic problems, the management of decline sounds at least respectably sane—especially when compared with a pronunciamento by a leader of the European Economic Community, Dr. Sicco Mansholt: "*More, further, quicker, richer* are the watchwords of present-day society. We must adapt to this for there is no alternative." *That* kind of rhetoric, especially when at brutal odds with current reality, denies the very nature of the human condition.

Thus it is understandable that a new movement, growing in popularity and becoming more sophisticated in its approach, has arisen. I call it "cameo leadership," which aspires to carve things well, but smaller. It preaches a less complicated time, a communal life—a return to Walden before the Pond was polluted, before the Coke stand made its appearance, before *Walden* itself was required reading . . . when most things were compassable.

A chief spokesman for this counter-technology movement is E. F. Schumacher, a former top economist and planner for England's National Coal Board. In his book, *Small Is Beautiful,* Schumacher writes that:

—We are poor, not demigods.

—We have plenty to be sorrowful about, and are not emerging into a golden age.

—we need a gentle approach, a nonviolent spirit, and small is beautifull. . . .

Governor Brown of California is an avid disciple of Dr. Schumacher's "Buddhist economics." Small *is* beautiful. Sometimes. Perhaps it is beautiful more often than big is beautiful. When big gets ugly, we see human waste, depersonalization, alienation, possibly disruption. When small gets ugly, something that never crosses Schumacher's mind, it leads to a decentralization bordering on anarchy—and to poverty, famine, and disease as well.

Small is beautiful. The era of limits is upon us. Who can argue? Nevertheless, these slogans are as empty as they are appealing and timely. Because they are appealing, we fail to see that they represent no specific programs for change. In fact, instead of opening up possibilities for solutions, they close them. Basically, they reflect the symptoms now afflicting us by setting rhetorical opposites against each other. Small is beautiful, so big must be ugly.

A grain of sand may be more beautiful than a pane of glass. But must we trade the glass for the sand?

The real point is not one of beauty. The real point is whether leaders can face up to and cope with our present crises, worries, and imperatives. The real problem is how we can lead institutions in a world of over two billion people, millions of whom will starve while other millions can't find work. Even those whose work is exciting and meaningful often live with quiet desperation in fear of "the others." The real question: How do we provide the needed jobs and, after that, how do we learn to lead so that people can work more cooperatively, more sensibly, more humanely with one another? How can we lead in such a way that the requisite interdependence—so crucial for human survival and economic resilience—can be realized in a humane and gentle spirit?

Sweeping and Dusting

They won't provide the answers, either, the leaders who are custodians and bookkeepers. And they don't use slogans, they positively hate them—as they do poetry, or beauty, or politics. But then, they're not running for office; instead, they run offices.

T. S. Eliot was right; the world does end with a whimper. How else, when we have bookkeepers and custodians silently tidying things up, when we have input/output without even a throughput?

Recently, an acting president of one of our most august private universities was appointed its president. He had been "acting" for about eighteen months. One of the local newspapers, in an editorial written after he was made the official president, rhapsodized about the "acting's" performance. "Dr. (X)," the editor wrote, "put the budget first in his message (*State of the University*). He acknowledged that 'a budget is merely a means to an end,' but he also knows that budgetary success is required 'to enable the continued existence of a university with ends that have characterized this University from its beginning."

I can no more argue with that—of course we must live within our means!— than I can with the aesthetics of size. "Small is beautiful" and "balanced budgets" somehow emerge as epochally captivating phrases. Shortly before his appointment, the acting president wrote a *State of the University* report in which he said, "I do not have a personal academic agenda to propose, nor one against which progress might be assessed. That must await the new president." After eighteen months, no "personal academic agenda. . . ."

Coda

Where have all the leaders gone? They're consulting, pleading, trotting here and there, temporizing, putting out fires, either avoiding or (more often) taking too much heat, and spending too much energy in doing both. They are peering at a landscape of "bottom lines" and ostentatiously taking the bus to work (with four bodyguards rather than the one chauffeur they might need if they drove) to demonstrate their commitment to energy conservation. They are money changers lost in a narrow orbit. They resign. They burn out. They decide not to run or serve. They read Buddhist economics, listen to prophets of decentralization, and then proceed to create new bureaucracies to stamp out old ones. (Nixon's "Anti-Big Government" one was bigger than Johnson's.) They are motivating people through fear or by cautiously following the "trends" or adopting a "Let's face it" cynicism. They are all characters set in a dreamless society—groping in the dark and learning how to "retrench," as if that were an art like playing the violin. And they are all scared.

And who can blame them? Sweaty palms are understandable. That is the final irony. Precisely at the time when the credibility of our leaders is at an all-time low, and when the surviving leaders feel most inhibited in realizing the potentiality of power, we most need individuals who can lead. We need people who can shape the future, not just barely manage to get through the day.

There is no simple solution. But there are things we must recognize:

1. *Leaders must develop the vision and strength to call the shots.* There are risks in taking the initiative—But the greater risk is to wait for orders. We need leaders at every level who can lead, not just manage. This means that institutions (and followers) have to recognize that they *need* leadership, that their need is for vision, energy, and drive rather than blandness and safety.

2. *The leader must be a "conceptualist" (not just someone to tinker with the "nuts and bolts").* A conceptualist is more than an "idea man"; he must have an entrepreneurial vision, a sense of perspective, the time and the inclination to think about the forces and raise the fundamental questions that will affect the destiny of both the institution and the society within which it is embedded.

3. *He must have a sense of continuity and significance in order, to paraphrase the words of Shelley, to see the present in the past and the future in the present.* He must, in the compelling moments of the present, be able to clarify problems—elevate them into understandable choices for the constituents—rather than exploit them; to define issues, not aggravate them. In this respect, leaders are essentially educators. Our great political leaders, such as Jefferson, Lincoln, and Wilson, tried to educate the people about problems by studying the messy existential groaning of the people and transforming murky problems into understandable issues. A leader who responds to a drought by attacking the lack of rainfall is not likely to inspire a great deal of confidence. What we see today is sometimes worse: leaving the problem as a problem (for example, "the economy" or "the energy crisis") or allowing the problem to stay out of control until it becomes a "crisis." What is essential, instead, are leaders who will get at the underlying issues and present a clear alternative. Dr. Martin Luther King, Jr. provided this perspective for black people. We sorely need the same leadership for the whole nation.

4. *Leaders must get their heads above the grass and risk the possibility, familiar to any rooster, of getting hit by a rock.* If a leader has the vision, takes the time, and makes the effort to lead the way by presenting a perspective, an alternative, a choice, he will need courage. He must be allowed to take risks, to embrace error, to "create dangerously" (as Camus put it in his last formal lecture—before a university audience), to use his creativity to the hilt and encourage others to do the same.

5. *The leader must get at the truth and learn how to filter the unwieldy flow of information into coherent patterns.* He must prevent the distortion of that information by overeager aides who will tailor it to satisfy what they consider to be his prejudices or vanities. The biggest problem of a leader—any leader—

is getting at the truth. Pierre du Pont put it well in a long-ago note to his brother Iréné, "One cannot expect to know what will happen, one can only consider himself fortunate if he can know what *has* happened." The politics of bureaucracy tend to interfere with rather than facilitate truth gathering.

That's mainly true because the huge size of our organizations and the enormous overload burdening every leader make it impossible for him to verify all his own information, analyze all his own problems, or always decide who should or should not have his ear or time. Since he must rely for much of this upon his key assistants and officers, he would not feel comfortable in so close and vital a relationship with men (women, unfortunately, would not even be considered!) who were not at least of kindred minds and compatible personalities.

Of course, this is perfectly human and, up to a point, understandable. But the consequences can be devastating because the leader is likely to see only that highly selective information or those carefully screened people that his key assistants decide he should see. And he may discover too late that he acted on information that was inadequate or inaccurate, or that he has been shielded from "troublesome" visitors who wanted to tell him what he should have known, or that he has been protected from some problem that should have been his primary concern.

In too many institutions, a very few people are filtering the facts— implicitly skewing reality and selecting information that provides an inaccurate picture on which decisions may be based. Such skewing can affect history: Barbara Tuchman in her recent book on China tells how, in the 1940s, Mao Tse-tung wanted very much to visit Roosevelt, but Roosevelt cancelled the proposed meeting on the basis of incredibly biased information from Ambassador Pat Hurley. It was nearly thirty years later that another President sought out the meeting with Mao that, earlier, could conceivably have averted many subsequent disasters.

So the leader cannot rely exclusively on his palace guards for information. Hard as it is to do, he must have multiple information sources and must remain accessible—despite the fact that accessibility in modern times seems one of the most underrated political virtues. The Romans, who were the greatest politicians of antiquity and probably also the busiest men, valued that quality highly in their leaders. Cicero, in praising Pompey, commented on his ready availability not only to his subordinates, but also to the ordinary soldiers in his command.

A later Roman historian recounted this even more telling anecdote about the Emperor Hadrian. The emperor, who at that time ruled almost the entire civilized world, was riding into Rome in his chariot when an old woman blocked his path and asked him to hear a grievance. Hadrian brushed her aside, saying he was too busy. "Then you're too busy to be emperor," she called after him. Whereupon he halted his chariot and heard her out.

6. *The leader must be a social architect who studies and shapes what is called the "culture of work"—those intangibles that are so hard to discern but are so terribly important in governing the way people act, the values and norms that are subtly transmitted to individuals and groups and that tend to create binding and bonding.* Whatever goals and values the leader pursues, he must proceed toward their implementation by designing a social architecture that encourages understanding, participation and ownership of the goals. He must,

of course, learn about and be influenced by those who will be affected by the decisions that permit the day-to-day realization of goals. At the very least, he must be forever conscious that the culture can facilitate or subvert "the best laid plans. . . ."

The culture of an organization dictates the mechanisms by which conflict can be resolved and the degree to which the outcomes will be costly, humane, fair, and reasonable. It can influence whether, on the one hand, there is a "zero-sum" mentality that insists upon an absolute winner or an absolute loser or, on the other, there is a climate of hope. There can be no progress without hope, and there can be no hope if our organizations view conflict as a football game, a win–lose (or possibly tie) situation. While zero-sum situations are extremely rare, most leaders, (and followers) tend to respond to most conflicts as if there can be only one winner and only one loser. In reality, organizations and nations are involved in a much different kind of contest, resembling not so much football as the remarkable Swedish game, Vasa Run; in the latter many take part, some reaching the finish line earlier than others and being rewarded for it, but all get there in the end.

Lots of things go into producing a culture: the particular technology of the institution, its peculiar history and geography, the characteristics of its people, and its social architecture. The leader must understand these things. He must have the capacities of an amateur social anthropologist so that he can understand the culture within which he works and which he himself can have some part in creating and maintaining.

7. *To lead others, the leader must first know himself.* His ultimate rest is the wise use of power. As Sophocles says in *Antigone:* "But it is hard to learn the mind of any mortal, or the heart, till he be tried in chief authority. Power shows the man."

He must learn to listen to himself. He must integrate his ideals with his actions and, even when a crackling discrepancy exists, learn to tolerate ambiguity between the desirable and the necessary—not, however, with so much tolerance that the margins between them become undiscernible. When that happens, the leader can unwittingly substitute an evasion of convenience for an authentic ideal. Soon he'll forget about the goal—and even feel "comfortable" with an illusion of progress. He must learn how to listen to understand, not to evaluate. He must learn to play, to live with ambiguity and inconsistency. Most of all, the test of any leader is whether he can ride and direct the process of change and, in the process, build new strengths.

Finale

The virtues I have just discussed may strike the reader as majestically useless —like textbook moralities, unconscionably demanding—and, worse, far too abstract to help the leader execute the complex political decisions he confronts. Moreover, the concepts of leadership I have emphasized diverge somewhat from the conventional roles assigned to the leader. Leadership has appeared in an array of more familiar metaphoric guises: the leader as judge (he pronounces verdicts and metes out punishments and rewards), the leader as manager (he conducts the routine), the leader as negotiator (he facilitates agreement or compromise), the leader as communal delegate (he presides over a town meeting), the leader as ruler (he governs despotically or democratically).

None of these appears to be the right metaphoric embodiment for organizational leadership. "Politics" might do it, if we think of the term as the arrangement of human life, relationships, and organizations in comfortable and rational modes. The leader engaged in such politics will need all the skills—of vision, conceptualization, issue definition, social architecture, and more—necessary to clarify and arrange the conduct of organized human endeavor.

All formulations of leadership, including those I have set forth here, can be dangerously misleading. For the world changes and the particulars change, and the most serious reader should apply my counsel with great caution. More important than the right metaphor in the years ahead is the capacity to be open to the unprecedented, not to get ready for *some*thing, but for *any*thing. We must learn nothing more than the value of examining—of focusing attention on the conditions of life, the particular circumstances that emerge unexpectedly—and develop an alertness in adapting to them.

We inevitably impose the order or disorder that seems inherent in things, both natural and social. Once we find the right metaphor for articulating leadership, the right conceptual framework—and as long as we realize that the metaphor must be altered as the world is altered—then we may begin to lead.

LEADERSHIP
AND ORGANIZATIONAL EXCITEMENT

David E. Berlew

Introduction

In the last several years, an increasing number of individuals—often new graduates and professionals—have rejected secure positions in apparently well-managed organizations in favor of working alone or joining up with a few friends in a new organization. Usually they do not leave in protest, but in search of "something more." The nature of this "something more" is the subject of this paper.

Many executives have blamed this disenchantment with established organizations on changes in Western society which have made an increasing number of people unsuited for organizational life. They often express the view that changes in child-rearing practices and the breakdown of discipline in the family and in our schools have produced a generation which cannot or will not exercise the self-discipline and acceptance of legitimate authority required for bureaucratic organizations as we know them to function.

Reprinted with permission of the author.

Because it has been so acceptable to fault society, the leadership of most organizations has felt little need to look inward for the source of the problem and to analyze their own and their organization's failure to attract and hold some of the best-trained people our society produces.

Those organizations which have tried to change to keep pace with society have often been frustrated. In analyzing our failure to stem the tide of increasing alienation in the workplace, Walton (1972) describes "a parade of organization development, personnel, and labor relations programs that promised to revitalize organizations," such as job enrichment, participative decision making, management by objectives, sensitivity training or encounter groups, and productivity bargaining. He argues that while each application is often based on a correct diagnosis, it is only a partial remedy, and therefore the organizational system soon returns to an earlier equilibrium. His prescription is a systematic approach leading to comprehensive organization design or redesign.

Whether we are concerned with organizations which have viewed the problem as outside of their control or those which have been frustrated in their attempts to change, one factor which has not been adequately explored and understood is that of effective organization leadership. Only an organization with strong leadership will look within itself for causes of problems which can be blamed easily on outside forces. Exceptional leadership is required to plan and initiate significant change in organizations, whether it is one of Walton's partial remedies or comprehensive organization redesign. Short-term benefits from change projects often result from leadership behavior which excites members of an organization about the *potential* for change rather than from actual change introduced.

Current Leadership Models

Almost without exception, theories of managerial leadership currently in vogue postulate two major dimensions of leadership behavior (House, 1971, Korman, 1966). One dimension concerns the manager's or leader's efforts to accomplish organizational tasks. Various writers have given this dimension different names, including task or instrumental leadership behavior, job-centered leadership, initiating structure and concern for production. The second dimension is concerned with the leader's relations with his subordinates; it has been labelled social-emotional leadership behavior, consideration, concern for people, and employee-centered leadership. Measures of the effects of leadership also usually fall into two categories: indices of productivity and of worker satisfaction. A leader or manager who is good at organizing to get work done, and who relates well to his subordinates, should have a highly productive group and satisfied workers.

There is nothing wrong with two-factor models of managerial leadership as far as they go, but they are incomplete. They grew out of a period in history when the goal was to combine the task efficiency associated with scientific management with the respect for human dignity emphasized by the human relations movement. They did not anticipate a point in time when people would not be fulfilled even when they were treated with respect, were productive, and derived achievement satisfaction from their jobs.

As a result, two-factor theories of managerial leadership tell us more about management than about leadership. They deal with relationships between man and his work, and between men and other men, but they do not tell us why some organizations are excited or "turned-on" and others are not. They do not help us understand that quality of leadership which can ". . . lift people out of their petty pre-occupations . . . and unify them in pursuit of objectives worthy of their best efforts" (Gardner, 1965).

Leadership and Emotion in Organizations

In an effort to help fill that void, the outline of a model relating types of leadership to the emotional tone in organizations is presented in Figure 1. Stages 1 and 2 of the model are derived from familiar theories of work motivation (Herzberg, 1966; Maslow, 1968; McGregor, 1967) and the two-factor models of leadership discussed earlier. Angry or resentful workers (Stage 1) are primarily concerned with satisfying basic needs for food, shelter, security, safety, and respect as human beings. Organizations in Stage 1 try to improve their situations by eliminating "dissatisfiers" through improved working conditions, compensation and fringe benefits, and by providing fair or "decent" supervision. The type of leadership associated with a change from an angry or resentful emotional tone to one of neutrality, or from Stage 1 to Stage 2, has been labelled *custodial*. These leaders are neutral, lacking either strong positive or negative feelings about their work or the organization. In the absence of "dissatisfiers," they tend to become increasingly concerned with group membership or "belonging" and opportunities to do inherently satisfying work and to receive recognition. In order to increase employee satisfaction organizations at Stage 2 introduce improvements such as job enrichment, job enlargement, job rotation, participative management, and effective (as opposed to decent) supervision. Changes are oriented toward providing work that is less routine and more interesting or challenging, building cohesive work teams, and giving employees more say in decisions that directly affect them. The type of leadership associated with this movement from neutral to satisfied workers, or from Stage 2 to Stage 3, has been labelled *managerial*.

Most of the advances in organization theory and management practice in the last few dacades have related to Stage 2: defining and controlling the elements of supervision and the organizational environment which result in high productivity with high satisfaction. While these advances have been substantial, and have led, in most cases, to healthier, more effective organizations, they have not prevented the increasing alienation of professional employees.

The addition of Stage 3 to the model to extend the emotional tone continuum to include *organizational excitement* is an attempt to deal with this phenomenon of the 1970's—the increasing number of professionals and new graduates who are rejecting secure positions in established organizations. The model suggests that for this small but growing element of the population, the satisfaction of needs for membership, achievement, and recognition is no longer enough. The meaning they seek has less to do with the specific tasks they perform as individuals than the impact of their individual and collective efforts—channelled through the organization—on their environment. The feelings of potency which accompany "shaping" rather than being shaped or

FIGURE 1

Organizational Emotions and Modes of Leadership

	Stage 1	Stage 2	Stage 3
EMOTIONAL TONE:	Anger or Resentment	Neutrality	Satisfaction	Excitement
LEADERSHIP MODE:	CUSTODIAL	MANAGERIAL	CHARISMATIC
FOCAL NEEDS OR VALUES:	Food Shelter Security Fair treatment Human dignity	Membership Achievement Recognition	Meaningful work Self-reliance Community Excellence Service Social Responsibility
FOCAL CHANGES OR IMPROVEMENTS:	Working conditions Compensation Fringe benefits Equal opportunity Decent supervision Grievance procedures	Job enrichment Job enlargement Job rotation Participative management Management by objectives Effective supervision	Common vision Value-related opportunities and activities Supervision which strengthens subordinates

giving up (and dropping out) are a source of excitement. So, too, are the feelings which stem from commitment to an organization which has a value-related mission and thus takes on some of the characteristics of a cause or a movement. At the extreme, this can lead to total involvement or total *identification*—the breaking down of boundaries between the "self" and the organization so that the "individual becomes the organization" and the "organization becomes the individual."

Stage 3 Leadership

Although Stage 3 leadership must involve elements of both custodial and managerial leadership, the dominant mode is charismatic leadership. The word "charisma" has been used in many ways with many meanings. Here we will define it in terms of three different types or classes of leadership behavior which provide meaning to work and generate organizational excitement. These are:

1. The development of a "common vision" for the organization related to values shared by the organization's members,
2. the discovery or creation of value-related opportunities and activities within the framework of the mission and goals of the organization, and
3. making organization members feel stronger and more in control of their own destinies, both individually and collectively.

Developing a Common Vision

The first requirement for Stage 3 or charismatic leadership is a common or shared vision of what the future *could be*. To provide meaning and generate excitement, such a common vision must reflect goals or a future state of affairs that is valued by the organization's members and thus important to them to bring about.

The notion that men do not live by bread alone has been recognized for centuries by religious and political leaders. All inspirational speeches or writings have the common element of some vision or dream of a better existence which will inspire or excite those who share the author's values. This basic wisdom too often has been ignored by managers.

A vision, no matter how well articulated, will not excite or provide meaning for individuals whose values are different from those implied by the vision. Thus, the corporate executive who dreams only of higher return on investment and earnings per share may find his vision of the future rejected and even resented by members of his organization. Indeed, he may even find his vision of a profitable corporate future questioned by stockholders concerned with the social responsibility of corporations. Progressive military leaders may articulate a vision or mission congruent with the needs and values of the young people they are trying to attract to an all volunteer service, only to discover that the same vision conflicts with the values of their senior officers.

An important learning from group theory and research is that informal groups tend to select as leader the individual who is most representative of the group's needs and values. Thus his hopes and aspirations, and the goals toward which he will lead the group, are automatically shared by the group's members.

One problem for heads of complex organizations is that if they are to function as leaders (as opposed to custodians or managers) they must represent and articulate the hopes and goals of many different groups, the young and the old, the unskilled and the professional, the employee and the stockholder, the minority and the majority, union and management. Only the exceptional leader can instinctively identify and articulate the common vision relevant to such diverse groups. But to fail to provide some kind of vision of the future, particularly for employees who demand meaning and excitement in their work, is to make the fatal assumption that man can and will live by bread alone.

There are dangers as well as advantages to a common vision. If top management does not sincerely believe in the desirability of the vision they articulate, they are involved in an attempt to manipulate which will probably backfire. Another danger might be called the "Camelot phenomenon": the articulation of a shared vision that is both meaningful and exciting, but so unrealistic that people must inevitably be disillusioned and disappointed. Whether the responsibility in such cases lies with the seducer or the seduced is difficult to say, but the end result is a step backward into cynicism.

Finally, the effectiveness of the common vision depends upon the leader's ability to "walk the talk": to behave in ways both small and large that are consistent with the values and goals he is articulating. In this regard, my experience in the Peace Corps taught me that the quickest way to destroy or erode the power of a common vision is for the leader to allow himself to be sidetracked into bargaining over details instead of concentrating all of his attention on identifying, tracking, and talking to the value issue involved. For example, at a meeting where Volunteers are reacting negatively to a proposed reduction in their living allowance, the Peace Corps Director or leader cannot afford to get involved in a discussion of whether or not female Volunteers will be able to afford pantyhose with their reduced allowance. The role of the leader is to keep alive the common vision which attracted Volunteers to the Peace Corps in the first place: in this case, the idea of a group of Americans whose help will be more readily accepted if they live at about the same standard as their local coworkers.

Value-Related Opportunities and Activities

It is a mistake to assume that individuals who desert or reject established organizations are basically loners. In fact, many start or join new organizations, often at considerable personal sacrifice in terms of income, security, and working conditions. It is revealing to analyze these "new" organizations for sources of meaning or excitement which may be lacking in more mature organizations. A list of opportunities present in many of the younger organizations in our society are presented in Figure 2, along with values related to those opportunities.

FIGURE 2

Sources of Meaning in Organizations:
Opportunities and Related Values

Type of Opportunity	Related Need or Value
1. A chance to be tested; to make it on one's own	Self-reliance Self-actualization
2. A social experiment, to combine work, family, and play in some new way	Community Integration of life
3. A chance to do something *well*—e.g., return to real craftsmanship; to be really creative	Excellence Unique accomplishment
4. A chance to do something *good*—e.g., run an honest, no rip-off business, or a youth counselling center	Consideration Service
5. A chance to change the way things are—e.g., from Republican to Democrat or Socialist, from war to peace, from unjust to just.	Activism Social responsibility Citizenship

A Chance to Be Tested

Many of us go through life wondering what we could accomplish if given the opportunity. Our Walter Mitty fantasies place us in situations of extreme challenge and we come through gloriously. Few of us, however, have an opportunity to test the reality of our fantasies, as society increasingly protects us from getting in over our heads where we might fail and thus hurt the organization or ourselves. This is especially true of corporations where managers are moved along slowly, and only after they have had sufficient training and experience to practically insure that they will not have too much difficulty with their next assignment.

As a Peace Corps Country Director in the mid-sixties, I was struck by the necessity of having to place many Volunteers without adequate training or experience in extremely difficult situations, and the readiness—even eagerness—of most Volunteers to be tested in this way. Some Volunteers rose to the challenge in remarkable ways, others held their own, and some could not handle the stress. Volunteers who were severely tested and succeeded were spoiled for the lock-step progression from challenge to slightly more difficult challenge which most established organizations favor to protect both themselves and the individual from failure. The same thing happens in wars and other emergency situations where planned development and promotion systems break down.

The point is that many (not all) people want an opportunity to be tested by an extraordinary challenge, and such opportunities rarely exist in established organizations. As a result, some who are most able and most confident leave the shelter of the established organization to measure themselves against a value of independence and self-reliance.

Social Experimentation

A great deal has been written about the increasing superficiality of personal relationships in our society and the resulting loneliness and alienation.

Organizations have responded with efforts to build cohesive work teams and to provide individuals doing routine, independent work with opportunities to talk with coworkers on the job. These gestures have not begun to meet the needs of persons who have been influenced by the counter-culture's emphasis on authentic relationships as opposed to role-regulated relationships, and the need to reduce social fragmentation by carrying out more of life's functions—working, child-rearing, playing, loving—with the same group of people.

Established organizations do not provide these kinds of opportunities. Many prohibit husbands and wives from working together. Child-care centers, if they exist, are separate from the parents' workplace, and the workplace is geographically and psychologically separated from the home. As a result, individuals who desire more integrated lives often leave established organizations and form new organizations, such as businesses in which wives and children can play a role and professional firms whose members live as well as work together.

A Chance to Do Something Well

Established organizations fight a continual battle between controlling costs and maintaining standards of excellence, and standards are usually compromised. This is not cynicism: A group of skilled metal workers, machinists and mechanics can nearly always produce a better automobile than General Motors if cost is no object. The opportunity to seek true excellence, to produce the very best of something, is a strong attraction, even though the market may be extremely limited and economic viability of the venture questionable. Individuals frustrated by the need to cut corners in established organizations find the alternative of a new organization committed to excellence an attractive one, and they will work long hours at low pay to make it financially viable.

A Chance to Do Good

Still others desert established organizations in the belief that they are compromising standards of honesty and consideration in their struggle to survive in "the capitalistic jungle." They form organizations to do *good:* to provide honest, no rip-off services or products, or services which they believe a "good" community should have such as free schools, legal, medical, and counselling services for the deprived, or low-income housing.

A Chance to Change the Way Things Are

Finally, many thoughtful individuals leave established organizations because they view them as too interwoven with or dependent upon the system to be effective force for change. So they form new organizations as vehicles for bringing about change, whether it is to increase our appreciation of art, to eliminate discrimination, or to protect the environment.

The critical difference between these new organizations and established organizations is that the newer ones provide oppportunities and activities closely related to the values of their members and also within the framework of the mission and goals of the organization. This is true even when the organization is as intent on making money as any established corporation (as they often are), and when they resemble a modern version of a nineteenth-century sweatshop (as they often do). Members of these organizations are not against profit making *per se* or hard work, or putting the organization before the individual. But there must be a reason for doing these things; they are not ends in themselves. The reason comes from a common vision of what they are trying to create together, as well as opportunities to behave in a value-congruent manner. These factors justify and even make desirable those characteristics of organizations which otherwise would be rejected as unnecessary or exploitative.

Few, if any, progressive executives will find the types of opportunities and values noted above distasteful or undesirable. Many, however, will conclude that it is simply unrealistic to expect to find such opportunities in a large corporation or government agency under pressure from stockholders or the voting public to maximize profits or minimize expenditures.

However, such opportunities *do* exist in large, established organizations, and where they do not, they can often be created. For example, established organizations do not have to be tied to a step-by-careful-step advancement ladder. AT&T, for example, has experimented with a system whereby potential new hires for management positions are offered exceptionally challenging year-long assignments, and are told that depending on their performance, they will either leapfrog ahead or be asked to leave the company. It provides confident individuals with a series of opportunities to test themselves. If implemented successfully, it benefits the organization by attracting and developing self-reliant managers while quickly weeding out security seekers and poor performers.

While it takes managerial leadership to introduce such changes, it takes charismatic leadership to recognize the value relevance of such a program and to integrate it with the organization's mission in such a way that it creates and sustains excitement. Too often such programs go unrecognized or unexploited as sources of increased organizational excitement simply because of a limited conception of leadership.

There are many other things that established organizations are doing or could do which qualify the right type of leadership. Our organizations and institutions have, for the most part, been quite uncreative about countering or controlling the increasing fragmentation of work and family life, and the many problems which result. I know from my own experience the extreme differences in the quality of my relationships with my wife and children now that I work at home a few days a week compared to when I spent fifty to eighty hours at the office or out of town and came home tired and irritable, often with homework. I doubt if I am much different from most other professionals in this regard. Why not actively recruit husbands and wives, as work teams when possible, and with child-care facilities nearby? Or, where possible, encourage employees to work at home on individual projects when they may have fewer interruptions than at the office?

Many organizations have a manifest commitment to excellence in their products and services, and to carrying out their corporate responsibilities toward the community. Occasionally they are in a position to spearhead social change. Too frequently, however, the value-relevant message seems directed toward customers or stockholders and only secondarily toward organization members. When it is directed toward members, it usually comes from a staff department such as corporate relations or the house organ rather than directly from the senior-line officers.This is public relations, not leadership, and whereas charisma might substitute for public relations, public relations, no matter how good, cannot substitute for charisma.

Making Others Feel Stronger

The effective Stage 3 leader must lead in such a way as to make members of his organization feel stronger rather than weaker. To achieve the organization's goals as well as to meet the needs of his more confident and able employees, his leadership must encourage or enable employees to be Origins rather than Pawns.

Richard deCharms (1968; 1969) has described Origins and Pawns in the following terms:.

> An Origin is a person who feels that he is director of his life. He feels that what he is doing is the result of his own free choice; he is doing it because he wants to do it, and the consequences of his activity will be valuable to him. He thinks carefully about what he wants in this world, now and in the future, and chooses the most important goals ruling out those that are for him too easy or too risky . . . he is genuinely self-confident because he has determined how to reach his goals through his own efforts . . . he is aware of his abilities and limitations. In short, an Origin is master of his own fate.

> A Pawn is a person who feels that someone, or something else, is in control of his fate. He feels that what he is doing has been imposed on him by others. He is doing it because he is forced to, and the consequences of his activity will not be a source of pride to him. Since he feels that external factors determine his fate, the Pawn does not consider carefully his goals in life, nor does he concern himself about what he himself can do to further his cause. Rather he hopes for Lady Luck to smile on him.

Clearly, there may only be a few people in the real world of human beings who are *always* guiding their own fate, checking their own skill, and choosing their own goals, but some people act and feel like Origins more of the time than do other people. Similarly, there are only a few people who *always* feel pushed around like Pawns.

Some individuals—parents, teachers, managers—have the ability to relate on a one-on-one basis in many ways that make another person feel and behave more like an Origin and less like a Pawn. Certain types of leaders can apparently affect entire groups of people the same way.

In an experiment conducted at Harvard University (Winter, 1967), a group of business-school students were shown a film of John F. Kennedy delivering his inaugural address. After viewing the film, samples of students' thoughts or fantasies were collected by asking them to write short imaginative stories to a series of somewhat ambiguous pictures. The thoughts of students exposed to the Kennedy film reflected more concern with having an impact on others and being able to influence their future and their environment than the thought samples of students exposed to a neutral control film. J.F.K. made them feel like Origins.

Replicating this experiment in a number of leadership training sessions, I have found the same thing: Exposure to a certain type of leader—such as John F. Kennedy—leaves people feeling stronger, more confident of being able to determine their own destinies and have an impact on the world. It was this type of reaction to J.F.K. that attracted many young people to the Peace Corps to "change the world" during the early and mid-sixties.

It is difficult to assess precisely what it was about Kennedy's leadership that had this strengthening effect. We do know that he articulated a vision of what should be which struck a resonant chord, particularly in young people and citizens of developing nations. He also projected extremely high expectations of what young people could do to remake their country, if not the world, in terms of their own values.

Although most organization leaders cannot count on such dramatic moments as a presidential inauguration, or perhaps on their oratorical powers, they nonetheless do have a powerful effect on whether those around them feel and behave like Origins or Pawns. A number of factors determine the effect they have on others in this critical area.

Beliefs about Human Nature

One important factor is the manager's beliefs or assumptions about human nature. If he believes that the average human being has an inherent dislike of work and will avoid it if he can, that most people must be coerced or controlled to get them to put forth effort toward the achievement of organizational objectives, and that he wishes to avoid responsibility, has relatively little ambition and wants security above all, then the manager will organize and manage people as if they were Pawns, and they will tend to behave as Pawns. If, on the other hand, the manager believes that the expenditure of physical and mental effort in work is as natural as play or rest, that individuals will exercise self-direction and self-control in the service of objectives to which they are committed, and that commitment to objectives is a function of the rewards associated with their achievement, including psychological rewards, then he will organize and manage people in quite a different way, with the result that they will tend to behave more like Origins than like Pawns (McGregor, 1960).

High Expectations

Another important factor is the expectations a manager has about the performance of his subordinates. To some extent, all of us are what others expect us to be, particularly if the others in question are people we respect or love. A dramatic demonstration of this phenomenon is the strong positive relationship between a teacher's expectations of how well a student will do and the student's actual performance, a relationship which persists even when the teacher's positive expectations are based on invalid information (Rosenthal and Jacobson, 1968). A second study, done in a corporate setting, demonstrated that new managers who were challenged by their initial assignments were better performers after five years than new managers who were initially assigned to relatively unchallenging tasks, despite the fact that the potential of the two groups was about the same (Berlew and Hall, 1966).

Reward versus Punishment

Some managers tend to focus their attention on mistakes: to intervene when there are problems, and to remain uninvolved when things are going well. Other managers look for opportunities to reward good performance. An overbalance in the direction of punishing mistakes as opposed to rewarding excellence lowers self-confidence and is relatively ineffective in improving performance. Rewarding examples of effective action, however, both increases self-confidence and improves performance.

Encouraging Collaboration

Americans have a tendency to compete when the situation does not demand it, and even sometimes when competition is self-defeating (as when individuals or units within the same organization compete). Diagnosing a situation as win–lose, and competing, insures that there are losers; and losing is a weakening process. If a situation is, *in fact,* win–lose in the sense that the more reward one party gets the less the other gets, competition and the use of competitive strategies is appropriate. This is usually the situation that exists between athletic teams or different companies operating in the same market. Diagnosing a situation as win–win and collaborating is a strengthening process because it allows both parties to win. A situation is *in fact,* win–win when both parties may win, or one can win only if the other succeeds, as is usually the case *within* a company or a team.

The leader who is effective in making people feel stronger recognizes collaborative opportunities where they exist and does not allow them to be misdiagnosed as competitive. When he identifies instances of unncessary competition within his organization, he uses his influence to change the reward system to induce collaborative rather than competitive behavior. If confronted with a competitive situation which he cannot or does not want to alter, however, he does not hesitate to use competitive strategies.

Helping Only When Asked

It is extremely difficult to help someone without making them feel weaker, since the act of helping makes evident the fact that you are more knowledgeable, powerful, wiser, or richer than the person you are trying to help. Those familiar with this dynamic are not surprised that some of the nations that the U.S. has most "helped" through our foreign aid resent us the greatest, particularly if we have rubbed their nose in their dependence by placing plaques on all the buildings we have helped them build, the vehicles we have provided, and the public works projects we have sponsored.

Yet the fact remains that there are real differences between individuals and groups in an organization, and help-giving is a real requirement. The effective Stage 3 leader gives his subordinates as much control over the type and amount of help they want as he can without taking untenable risks. He makes his help readily available to those who might come looking for it, and he gives it in such a way as to minimize their dependence upon him. Perhaps most important, he is sensitive to situations where he himself can use help and he asks for it, knowing that giving help will will strenghten the other person and make him better able to receive help.

Creating Success Experiences

A leader can make others feel stronger, more like Origins, by attempting to design situations where people can succeed, and where they can feel responsible and receive full credit for their success. People, whether as individuals or organizations, come to believe in their ability to control their destiny only as they accumulate successful experiences in making future events occur—in setting and reaching goals. The leader's role is to help individuals and units within his organization accumulate such experiences.

When an organization, through its leadership, can create an environment which has a strengthening effect on its members, it leads to the belief that, collectively, through the organization, they can determine or change the course of events. This, in turn, generates organizational excitement. It also becomes an *organization* which has all the characteristics of an Origin.

Some Unanswered Questions

In this paper, I have tried to analyze one aspect of the problem of alienation in the workplace: the increasing attrition of professionals and new graduates from established organizations. I have tried to suggest the nature and source of the meaning and excitement they are seeking in their work, and the type of organizational leadership required to meet their needs. However, a number of questions have been left unasked which must be explored before any conclusions can be drawn.

One such question has to do with the relationship between organizational excitement and productivity. We know there are many productive organizations—some of our major corporations, for example—which cannot be called excited or "turned-on." We have also seen excited organizations expending tremendous amounts of energy accomplishing very little. In the case of excited but unproductive organizations, it is clear that they are overbalanced in the direction of Stage 3 leadership and need effective *custodial* and *managerial leadership* to get organized and production-oriented rather than solely impact-oriented. The case of efficient and productive organizations that are not excited is more complex. Would General Motors or ITT be better off if they could create a higher level of organizational excitement? Would they attract or hold better people, or are they better off without those who would be attracted by the change? Are such corporations headed for problems which can only be dealt with by an emphasis on Stage 3 leadership, or have we overstated the magnitude of the social change that is taking place?

A second question concerns the relevance of the model to different types of organizations. There is little question of the relevance of charismatic leadership and organizational excitement to such as the Peace Corps, the United Nations, religious organizations, political groups, community action organizations, unions, and the military. The same is true of start ups where new industrial or business organizations are competing against heavy odds to carve out a piece of the market. What is not so clear is whether it is any less relevant to large, established corporations and government bureaucracies. Quite possibly, it is precisely the element which is missing from some government agencies, and one of the key elements which give one great corporation the edge over another.

While more questions have been raised than answered, there should be no confusion about one point. Just as man cannot live by bread alone, neither can he live by spirit alone. Organizations must have elements of custodial and managerial leadership to achieve the necessary level of efficiency to survive. It is not proposed that Stage 3 or charismatic leadership increases efficiency; indeed, it may reduce the orderly, professional, totally rational approach to work which managerial leadership tries to foster. However, it does not affect motivation and commitment, and organizations will face heavy challenges in these areas in the coming decade.

References

David E. Berlew, and Douglas T. Hall, "The Socialization of Managers: Effects of Expectations on Performance," *Administrative Science Quarterly,* 11, No. 2 (1966), 207–223.

Richard deCharms, *Personal Causation* (New York: Academic Press, 1968).

Richard deCharms, "Origins, Pawns, and Educational Practice," in G. S. Lessor (ed.) *Psychology and the Educational Process* (Glenview, Ill.: Scott, Foresman and Co., 1969).

John W. Gardner, "The Antileadership Vaccine," *Annual Report of the Carnegie Corporation of New York,* 1965.

Frederick Herzberg, *Work and the Nature of Man* (Cleveland: The World Publishing Company, 1966).

Robert J. House, "A Path Goal Theory of Leader Effectiveness," *Administrative Science Quarterly,* 16, No. 3 (1971), 321–338.

Abraham K. Korman, "Consideration, Initiating Structure, and Organizational Criteria—A Review," *Personnel Psychology,* 1966, Vol. 19, 349–361.

Douglas McGregor, *The Human Side of Enterprise* (New York: McGraw-Hill Book Company, 1960).

Douglas McGregor, *The Professional Manager* (New York: McGraw-Hill Book Company, 1967).

Robert Rosenthal, and Lenore Jacobson, *Pygmalion in the Classroom* (New York: Holt, Rinehart and Winston, Inc., 1968).

Richard E. Walton, "How to Counter Alienation in the Plant," *Harvard Business Review,* Nov.-Dec., 1972.

David G. Winter, *Power Motivation in Thought and Action* (Ph.D. dissertation, Harvard University, Department of Social Relations, January, 1967.)

MANAGING WORK RELATIONSHIPS IN THE 80's

DAVID E. BERLEW

There are major changes taking place in organizations which require managers to acquire skills they have never needed before. Product diversity and technical specialization are splintering organizations into smaller and smaller parts, making coordination and integration more difficult. New, more complex organization structures require managers to orchestrate the activities of individual contributors and work units over whom they have little or no formal authority. Decision making is being pushed downward to make organizations more flexible and responsive, making it necessary for peers to resolve differences and work together smoothly, often without recourse to a common superior.

We have failed in large part to prepare managers to deal with these changes in the task of managing work relationships. We have focused our attention on providing them with up-to-date analytical tools and planning methods, and keeping them abreast of changes in technology. But we teach the basics of supervision and management and rational problem solving and decision making just as we did in the sixties and early seventies. Even in those organizations which have switched their emphasis from participative to situational management (i.e., different situations require different management styles; there is "no one best way"), the focus is still on superior-subordinate relationships, the traditional management hierarchy.

The most common, and serious, skill deficit among managers today is in managing lateral relationships, that is, relationships with peers over whom they have no direct authority, and with whom they often do not share a common superior. These relationships become extremely *important* when "independent" managers are in fact dependent upon each other to carry out the tasks assigned to their separate units. They become extremely *difficult* to manage where there is a conflict in goals or priorities, that is, when maximizing productivity or efficiency in one group reduces it in the other. Despite the best efforts of organizational design experts, this type of structural conflict persists. Who among us has not been in a situation where for the good of the organization we wanted to help another manager achieve his or her goals, knowing that it will reflect negatively on our own performance to do so? The benefits of more innovative forms of organization can be realized only if managers become skilled in managing these important and difficult relationships.

The failure to manage lateral relationships shows up in a variety of familiar ways:

- Meetings proliferate and take longer, involve more key contributors, and produce fewer results.

- People deal with colleagues as if they were outside competitors.
- Unresolved issues are passed on to higher management, which must use valuable time to become familiar enough with the details of the problem to make a decision which it should not have to make in the first place.
- Agreements are reached, but not carried out.
- Units which need to coordinate their efforts end up competing or acting independently of each other.
- Coordinating committees spin their wheels and frustrate well-meaning members.
- Tough issues are not dealt with because they are too hot to handle.

The key to effective lateral relationships lies in the ability of managers to negotiate. The potential of negotiation as a powerful tool for improving coordination and resolving conflict *within* organizations has not been recognized. Most managers view negotiation as something you do with competitors, not colleagues, with the single objective of getting as much as you can while giving up as little as possible. In fact, negotiation, if done positively and creatively, is the most effective process known for resolving differences and reaching quality agreements in a way that builds rather than disrupts working relationships. To achieve these results, however, managers must learn to negotiate *positively,* and discover how negotiation can be used to manage difficult and important work relationships.

Recently my colleagues and I have been training managers (and others) in positive negotiation with considerable success. The remainder of this article highlights some of the keys to positive negotiation which managers have found to be important in using it within their organization.

Recognize Opportunities to Negotiate

Negotiation is simply a way to resolve a conflict when it is in the interest of both parties to do so. Stated more formally, negotiation is a process in which two or more parties with common and conflicting interests come together temporarily and voluntarily to put forth and discuss explicit proposals for the purpose of reaching agreement on the division of resources or the resolution of intangible issues.

Many times we simply fail to recognize the relevance of negotiation when we are dealing with problem situations within our own organization. This can be due to a traditional view of negotiation as something you do with adversaries and competitors, not with friends and colleagues. It can also result from our failure to recognize the structural basis for conflicting priorities and vested interests within organizations, which leads us to try to resolve conflicts through a rational problem solving process or by managerial fiat. In either case, the failure to negotiate when there are both conflicting and common interests increases the probability of low commitment to a decision and disrupted work relationships. Few managers will help another reach his or her goals at the expense of achieving their own, appeals to friendship and loyalty, and direct orders from a shared superior notwithstanding. People just don't work against their own self-interests, at least not for very long. However, most will go out of their way to help a colleague reach his or her goals if that colleague will reciprocate. Positive negotiation facilitates these kinds of exchanges.

Negotiation is just one strategy for dealing with situations involving both common and conflicting interests; bargaining is another. ("Take it or leave it" is a third strategic alternative, but since it has little utility for resolving conflict *within* organizations it will not be discussed here.) A key difference is that bargaining involves the exchange of one, or at most two, currencies, whereas negotiation always involves the exchange of multiple currencies. Let's look at an example of each strategy.

> *Bargaining:* An Operations Manager asks the Maintenance Manager for 1000 hours of maintenance in the next month to keep his machinery operating. The Maintenance Manager, who must also service other areas, offers 800 hours. After a short discussion they agree on 900 hours.

> *Negotiation:* The same two managers talk at length about the problems they each have and what they need to solve them. The Operations Manager learns that the Maintenance Manager has extra manpower available during the day shifts when the machines are most heavily used, but is short of help at night when they are available for maintenance. He also learns that because of the craft union work rules, the Maintenance Manager has to assign two skilled mechanics to certain jobs, even though one of them only pushes a button to stop and start the machine. For his part, the Maintenance Manager learns that the Operations Manager always has apprentice machine operators who are not fully occupied and who need to learn as much as possible about the machinery they will be operating. On the basis of this information, the two managers reach an agreement whereby the Operations Manager reschedules his production so that more machines are available for maintenace during daytime shifts, and he provides an apprentice operator to start and stop machines that maintenance mechanics are working on. Thus the Operations Manager gets all of his maintenance done (1000 hours worth) and the Maintenance Manager can complete the work in 800 hours.

In the *bargaining* example, both parties may be satisfied with their agreement, but unless they misrepresented their needs and available resources, both had to compromise. The exchange did little to strengthen their working relationship; more likely it weakened it. There is probably little commitment to the agreement: if the Maintenance Manager can get by with fewer than 900 hours in order to service other areas where he is under pressure, he will probably do it.

As a result of *negotiation,* both managers will feel committed to the agreement they have worked out, and their working relationship will probably be strengthened. They have achieved this more creative and positive solution by exploring multiple needs, and identifying alternative currencies of exchange which they can use to satisfy each other's needs. It is worth noting that it took the Managers considerably more time to negotiate than to bargain. If they were at odds over 10 rather than several hundred maintenance hours they might be wise to bargain and resolve the issue quickly.

The result of positive negotiation is an agreement that meets the needs of both (or all) parties *and* an improved working relationship. Managers who bargain when they should negotiate do not achieve this result.

Identify Alternative Currencies

Most of us are so concerned with getting what we need that we fail to explore carefully the needs of the other person. In a negotiation most of our power stems from the other party's perception that we can satisfy their needs. If you believe that you need something I can give you (a currency) more than I need what you can give me, then you have placed yourself in a low power position. Your power, and the possibility of a positive result, increases with your ability to discover other needs that I may have and to identify currencies you have to meet those needs.

The best currencies are those that are valuable to the other party but relatively inexpensive to you, or conversely, valuable to you and relatively inexpensive to the other party. In adversary negotiations, negotiators will often try to gain concessions with "future promises." How many times have you heard someone say, "I know it isn't quite what you want, but let's try it out. If you are unhappy after six months, we'll work out something different," or words to that effect? Trick currencies have no place in positive negotiation where one objective is always to strengthen a working relationship. A much better example of a currency is contained in the negotiation example above: the time of the apprentice operators was valuable to the Maintenance Manager and relatively inexpensive for the Operations Manager to provide because they had extra time and needed to learn about the machinery.

Salespersons are trained in the skills of exploring needs and relating their product to those needs. Managers, on the other hand, have had little need or opportunity to develop these skills. This part of the positive negotiation process is therefore unnatural behavior for most managers until they come to understand its importance and learn the skills required to carry it out.

Don't Confuse Needs with Objectives

The failure to distinguish clearly between needs and objectives blocks creativity and is a major contributor to deadlock in negotiations. A simple example will illustrate the point.

> Martin and Smith are section heads in the data processing department of a large corporation. Each has asked the Department Head for an additional supervisor. In support of their request both have cited an increased work load and an hourly work force declining in competence because of a tight market in the area for experienced programmers.
>
> A week later the Department Head tells Martin and Smith that due to budget constraints he can authorize only one additional supervisor, and since they are closest to the problem he wants them to decide how to best use the new position.
>
> Martin and Smith meet, each intent on having the new supervisor report to him. After a few hours they give up, take their cases to the Department Head and ask him to make a decision.

Both Martin and Smith wanted the new supervisor. Was this a need or an objective? If each of them entered the meeting convinced that they had to get the new supervisor, then they had classified it as a need. Since needs don't change or go away until they are satisfied, and only one of the two could get his need satisfied, it is not surprising that they deadlocked.

The discussion between Martin and Smith would have gone very differently if they had asked themselves two simple questions to clarify their needs and objectives:

1. What does having another supervisor do for me? Answer: It gives me increased supervisory capability. (underlying need)
2. How will I know when I've got it? Answer: When I have a new supervisor reporting to me. (negotiating objective)

If the need is for more supervisory capability, then getting the new supervisor is a satisfactory negotiating objective because it is a currency that will satisfy the need. If either Martin or Smith is offered the new supervisor, he can end the negotiation confident that by achieving his objective he will have satisfied his need.

In this example as in most cases, however, what is an obvious solution to one party is not acceptable to the other. Martin and Smith must now find alternative ways to solve the problem, and thus resolve their conflict. This means finding alternative ways of increasing supervisory capability, or ways to reduce the need for supervision. For example, Martin might agree to give Smith the supervisor and several inexperienced programmers in return for several experienced programmers who need less supervision. Or Smith might give Martin the supervisor if Martin will take responsibility for training newcomers in both sections. It is also quite possible that Smith or Martin might decide to live with his supervision problem in order to meet some other priority need. This could happen, for example, if Smith gave Martin the new supervisor in return for some of Martin's scheduled computer time.

To summarize, carefully clarifying needs and objectives before beginning a negotiation, and viewing negotiating objectives as just one (preferred) way to satisfy priority needs, will both prevent breakdowns in negotiation and help to unfreeze the creativity needed to reach a high quality settlement which all parties can embrace.

Adjust Your Tactics to Match Your Trust Level

An important criterion for selecting tactics in a negotiation is the degree to which you trust the other party. This may seem obvious, but many people behave the same way whether they are negotiating with family members, colleagues, vendors, or competitors.

Some people take the position that one should trust until the other person proves to be untrustworthy. This may be true in some situations, but not in negotiations. Naive trust is very seductive; who among us has not been tempted by the possibility of getting something for nothing. Once a negotiator has allowed himself or herself to be taken advantage of by another, intentionally or unintentionally, it creates a situation in which it is very difficult, if not impossible, to *build* trust. The person who was exploited may be able to forgive and forget, but the person who took advantage of them carries forever the fear that the person someday will pay them back.

When the trust level is very high, negotiation becomes a type of problem solving. It differs from what we normally think of as problem solving only in that there is an exchange of currencies involved. If Martin and Smith from our example trusted each other and were skilled at positive negotiation, they would have stated their requirements in terms of needs rather than objectives, and then explored alternative needs and the currencies which might be exchanged to arrive at a mutually satisfactory solution.

If there is a moderate degree of trust, it is usually advisable to state negotiation objectives as preferred solutions for meeting your needs, but not the only solution, thus showing a willingness to negotiate around objectives. You should reveal needs, but only if the other party does also. The reason is that revealing your needs when the other person does not creates the perception that you need them more than they need you, thus tilting the power balance in their favor. At the very least this will raise their settlement expectations, and if they sense they can win, may even seduce them into competitive behavior. If both parties reveal underlying needs on a *quid pro quo* basis, you will encourage exploration of alternative currencies, that is, other ways in which you can satisfy each other's needs.

When the trust level is low, caution is essential, even within your own organization. You can anticipate that the other party will state their objectives as inflexible demands, that their opening demands will be considerably above the level at which they expect to settle, that they will be reluctant to reveal underlying needs, and that they may threaten deadlock and try to put you under the pressure of a time deadline.

You can respond to these tactics in two ways. You can counter with the same tactics, at the same time not overreacting to their tactics. Or you can point out what you see happening and say that you would prefer to negotiate on the basis of a higher trust level because you believe it will lead to a more satisfactory settlement for everyone. If this doesn't work, you can either refuse to negotiate further (a "take it or leave it" strategy) or revert to the low trust, adversary tactics described above.

As organizations become more complex there are more and more conflicting interests and priorities within the context of shared organizational goals. New management philosophies push decision making down and require individuals and groups at the same level who share no immediate superior to coordinate. Negotiation has the potential to become a powerful tool for improving coordination and resolving conflict in organizations. However, the popular view of negotiation as something that tough and clever people do in adversary situations must be modified. Managers must come to understand how the process of negotiation can be used as an important tool for solving everyday problems. Moreover, they must master the range of skills required to implement a positive negotiation strategy.

⅂⅃ supervision and employee development

PARTICIPATIVE MANAGEMENT: QUALITY VERSUS QUANTITY

RAYMOND E. MILES
J. B. RITCHIE

In our view, a prime source of confusion surrounding the concept of participation is its *purpose.* We noted this confusion a few years ago,[1] drawing from our research the conclusion that most managers appeared to hold at least two different "theories" of participation. One of these, which we labeled the *Human Relations* model, viewed participation primarily as a means of obtaining cooperation—a technique which the manager could use to improve morale and reduce subordinate resistance to his policies and decisions. The second, which we labeled the *Human Resources* model, recognized the untapped potential of most organizational members and advocated participation as a means of achieving direct improvement in individual and organizational performance. Predictably, managers viewed the *Human Relations* model as appropriate for their subordinates while wanting their superior to follow the *Human Resources* logic.

Our recent research draws attention to a closely related, and probably equally important, source of confusion involving the *process* of participation. Our earlier descriptions of the purpose of participation under the Human Relations and Human Resources models implied that it is not only the degree of participation which is important, but also the nature of the superior-subordinate interaction. Upon reflection, the notion that both the quality and quantity of participation must be considered seems patently obvious. Rather surprisingly, however, the quality variable in the participative process has been infrequently specified in management theory, and even more rarely researched.

The lack of specific focus in theory or research on the quality aspect of the participative process has led, in our view, to the promulgation of a simple

Reprinted from *California Management Review,* Vol. 13, No. 4, 1971, pp. 48–56, by permission of the Regents of the University of California.

"quantity theory of participation," a theory which implies only that some participation is better than none and that more is better than a little. Clearly, a concept which, whether intended or not, appears to lump all participative acts together in a common category ignores individual and situational differences and is therefore open to a variety of justified criticisms. It is just such a simplified view that allows its more vitriolic critics to draw caricatures extending the participative process to include a chairman of the board consulting with a janitor concerning issues of capital budgeting—the sort of criticism which brings humor to journal pages but contributes little to our understanding of participation.

Recognizing these key sources of confusion, our current studies have been aimed at increasing our understanding of the process of participation under the Human Relations and Human Resources models. Specifically, we have attempted, within a large sample of management teams, to identify and measure the amount of superior-subordinate consultation and a dimension of the quality of this interaction—the superior's attitude which reflects the degree to which he has confidence in his subordinates' capabilities. (Our research approach and findings are described in a later section.) As indicated, in our theoretical framework both the quantity and quality of participation are important determinants of subordinate satisfaction and performance. For these analyses, we have focused on the impact of these variables, both separately and jointly, on the subordinate's satisfaction with his immediate superior. Our findings, we believe, clarify the role which quality plays in the participative process and add substance to the Human Relations-Human Resources differentiation.

In the following sections we explore further the concepts of quantity and quality of participation, integrate these into existing theories of participative management, and examine the implications of our research for these theories and for management practice.

The Quality Concept and Management Theory

A simple, and we believe familiar, example should assist us in firmly integrating the quantity-quality variables into the major theories of participative management and perhaps demonstrate, in part at least, why we are concerned with this dimension. Most of us have had the following experience:

> An invitation is received to attend an important meeting (we know it is important because it is carefully specified as such in the call). A crucial policy decision is to be made and our views and those of our colleagues are, according to the invitation, vital to the decision.
>
> Having done our homework, we arrive at the meeting and begin serious and perhaps even heated discussion. Before too long, however, a light begins to dawn, and illuminated in that dawning light is the fact that the crucial decision we had been called together to decide . . .

With a cynical, knowing smile, the typical organization member completes the sentence by saying "had already been made." It is helpful, however, to push aside the well-remembered frustration of such situations and examine the logic of the executive who called the meeting and the nature of the participative process flowing from his logic.

We can easily imagine (perhaps because we have frequently employed the same logic) the executive in our example saying to himself, "I've got this matter pretty well firmed, but it may require a bit of selling—I'd better call the troops in and at least let them express their views." He may even be willing to allow some minor revisions in the policy to overcome resistance and generate among his subordinates a feeling of being a part of the decision.

Purposes of Participation

Clearly defined in our example and discussion is the tight bond between the purpose of participation and the quality of ensuing involvement. And, underlying the purpose of participation is the executive's set of assumptions about people—particularly his attitudes concerning the capabilities of his subordinates.

Three theoretical frameworks describe this linkage between the manager's basic attitudes toward people and the amount and kind of consultation in which he is likely to engage with his subordinates. It is worth a few lines to compare these theory systems and to apply them to our example. Listed chronologically, these frameworks are:

- The Theory X-Theory Y dichotomy described by the late Douglas McGregor,[2]
- The System I, II, III, IV continuum defined by Rensis Likert,[3]
- Our own Traditional, Human Relations, Human Resources classification.[4]

Terminology

We have been criticized for referring to an essentially autocratic (non-participatory) style of management as traditional. Such a style is no longer traditional in the sense that it is prescribed, taught, or openly advocated by a majority of modern managers. Our research suggests that most managers consider such a style to be socially undesirable and few will admit adherence to it in concept or practice.

Nevertheless, we would argue that many if not most of our institutions and organizations are still so structured and operated that this style is alive and well today in our society. Many schools, hospitals, labor unions, political parties, and a substantial number of business enterprises frequently behave, particularly at the lower levels, in a manner which can only be described as autocratic. Thus even though their policy statements have been revised and some participative trappings have been hung about, the main thrust of their activity is not greatly changed from what it was 20, 30, perhaps even 50 years ago—they behave in a traditional manner toward the structure and direction of work. Further, the assumptions of the Traditional model are, in our view, still widely held and espoused in our society—the rhetoric has improved, but the intent is the same. These assumptions seem to us still to be part of our "traditional" approach to life. If our views are accurate, Traditional model is therefore still an appropriate tag.

McGregor's Theory X, Likert's System I, and our Traditional model describe autocratic leadership behavior coupled with tight, unilateral control, and little or no subordinate participation in the decision process. Theory X and the Traditional model explicitly delineate the superior's assumptions that most people, including subordinates, are basically indolent, self-centered, gullible, and resistant to change and thus have little to contribute to the decision-making or control process. Focusing more on descriptive characteristics and less on an explicit set of assumptions, Likert's System I manager is pictured only as having no confidence or trust in his subordinates. At the other extreme, Theory Y, system IV, and our Human Resources model define a style of behavior which involves subordinates deeply in the decision process and emphasizes high levels of self-direction and self-control. Again, both Theory Y and the Human Resources model make the logic underlying such behavior explicit—that most organization members are capable of contributing more than demanded by their present jobs and thus represent untapped potential for the organization, potential which the capable manager develops and invests in improved performance. A System IV superior is described simply as one having complete confidence and trust in subordinates in all matters. In between these extremes fall Likert's Systems II and III and our Human Relations model. Systems II and III describe increasing amounts of subordinate participation and self-control, as their superior's attitudes toward them move from "condescending" to "substantial, but not complete" confidence and trust. Our Human Relations model views the superior as recognizing his subordinates' desire for involvement but doubting their ability to make meaningful contributions.

**Theory and Management
Practice**

Comparing these frameworks with our example, it is clear that the executive calling the meeting was not operating at the Theory X, System I, Traditional end of the participative continuum. Had he followed the assumptions of these models, he would simply have announced his decision, and if a meeting were called, use it openly to explain his views. Similarly, it seems doubtful that our executive was following the Theory Y, System IV, or Human Resources models. Had he been, he would have called the meeting in the belief that his subordinates might make important contributions to the decision process and that their participation would possibly result in constructing a better overall policy. He would have had confidence and trust in their ability and willingness to generate and examine alternatives and take action in the best interest of the organization.

Instead, the meeting in the example and those from our own experience seem to be defined almost to the letter by our Human Relations logic and the behavior described in Likert's Systems II and III. The casual observer, and perhaps even the more naive participant, unaware of the reasoning of the executive calling the meeting, might well record a high level of involvement during the session—participation high both in quantity and quality. Most of the participants, however, would be much less charitable, particularly about the meaningfulness of the exercise. They would sense, although the guidance was subtle, that at least the depth of their participation was carefully controlled, just as they would be equally alert to the logic underlying the meeting strategy.

Alternative Theories

Having described varying degrees of quantity and quality participation flowing from alternative theories of management, and having attempted to link to a common experience through our meeting example, it is not difficult to conjecture about the relationships between these variables and subordinate satisfaction. We would expect subordinate satisfaction to move up and down with both the quantity and the quality of participation, and there is already some evidence, with regard to the amount of participation, at least, that it does. Thus we would expect, particularly within the managerial hierarchy, that their satisfaction would be lowest when both quantity and quality of participation were lowest—as the Traditional model is approached—and highest when both quantity and quality are high—when participation moves toward the type described in the Human Resources model.

Predicting satisfaction under the Human Relations model is less easy. If the superior's behavior is blatantly manipulative, we might expect satisfaction to be quite low despite high participation. But, if the superior's logic were less obvious, even to himself, we might expect his subordinates to be somewhat pleased to be involved in the decision process, even if their involvement is frequently peripheral.

We cannot precisely test the impact of these models on subordinate satisfaction, but our recent research does provide some evidence with regard to these conjectures, and it is therefore appropriate that we briefly describe the method of our investigation and look at some of our findings.

Research Approach

The findings reported here were drawn from a broader research project conducted among management teams (a superior and his immediate subordinates) from five levels in six geographically separated operating divisions of a West Coast firm.[5] The 381 managers involved in the study ranged from the chief executive of each of the six divisions down through department supervisors.

From extensive questionnaire responses we were able to develop measures of the three variables important to these analyses: *quantity of participation, quality of participation, and satisfaction with immediate superiors.* Our measure of quantity of participation was drawn from managers' responses to questions concerning how frequently they felt they were consulted by their superior on a number of typical department issues and decisions.[6] This information allowed us to classify managers as high or low in terms of the amount of participation they felt they were allowed. For a measure of the quality of this participation, we turned to the responses given by each manager's superior. The superior's attitudes toward his subordinates—his evaluation of their capabilities with regard to such traits as judgment, creativity, responsibility, perspective, and the like—were analyzed and categorized as high or low compared to the attitudes of other managers at the same level. Finally, our satisfaction measure was taken from a question on which managers indicated, on a scale from very satisfied to very dissatisfied, their reactions to their own immediate superiors.

Findings

The first thing apparent in our findings, as shown in each of the accompanying figures, is that virtually all the subjects in our study appear reasonably well satisfied with their immediate superiors. This is not surprising, particularly since all subjects, both superiors and subordinates, are in managerial positions. Managers generally respond positive (compared to other organization members) on satisfaction scales. Moreover, supporting the organization's reputation for being forward looking and well managed, most participants reported generally high levels of consultation, and superiors' scores on confidence in their subordinates were typically higher than the average scores in our broader research.

Nevertheless, differences do exist, differences which, given the restricted range of scores, are in most instances highly significant in statistical terms. Moreover, they demonstrate that both the quantity and the quality of participation are related to managers' feelings of satisfaction with their immediate superiors.

As shown in Figure 1, the quantity of participation achieved is apparently related to managers' feelings of satisfaction with their superiors. (The taller the figure—and the smaller the numerical score—the more satisfied is that group of managers.) Managers classified as low (relative to the scores of their peers) in terms of the extent to which they are consulted by their superiors are less well satisfied than those classified as high on this dimension. The difference in the average satisfaction score for these groups is statistically significant. The average satisfaction score for the low consultation group (2.13) falls between the satisfied and the so-so (somewhat satisfied-somewhat dissatisfied) categories. For the high consultation group, the score (1.79) falls between the satisfied and the highly satisfied categories.

A slightly stronger pattern of results is apparent when managers are regrouped in terms of the amount of confidence which their superiors have in them (Figure 2). Managers whose superiors have relatively high trust and confidence scores are significantly more satisfied (1.72) than are their colleagues (2.16) whose superiors have relatively lower scores on this dimension.

Finally, our results take on their most interesting form when managers are cross-classified on both the quantity and quality dimensions of participation. As shown in Figure 3, the progression in satisfaction is consistent with our theoretical formulation. Especially obvious is the comparison between managers classified as low both in amount of consultation received and the extent to which their superior has confidence in them (2.26) and managers who are rated high on both variables (1.55). Of interest, and relevant to our later discussion, managers whose superiors have high confidence in them but who are low in amount of participation appear slightly more satisfied (1.95) than their counterparts who are high in amount of participation but whose superiors are low in terms of confidence in their subordinates (2.05).

Linking Findings to Theory

The bulk of our findings, particularly as illustrated in Figure 3, thus appears to support our conjectures. Managers who least value their subordinates'

FIGURE 1.

Amount of Superior Consultation and
Subordinate Satisfaction

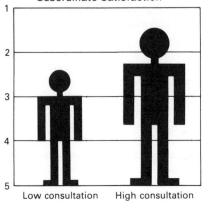

1 Very satisfied
2 Satisfied
3 Somewhat satisfied
  Somewhat dissatisfied
4 Dissatisfied
5 Very dissatisfied

FIGURE 2.

Superior's Confidence in Subordinates
and Subordinate Satisfaction

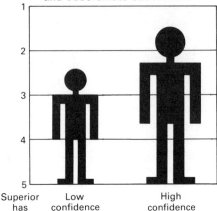

1 Very satisfied
2 Satisfied
3 Somewhat satisfied
  Somewhat dissatisfied
4 Dissatisfied
5 Very dissatisfied

capabilities and who least often seek their contributions on department issues have the least well satisfied subordinates in our study. It would probably be incorrect to place the Traditional (Theory X, System I) label on any of the managers in our sample, yet those who, relative to their peers, lean closest to these views do so with predictable results in terms of subordinate satisfaction.

FIGURE 3.

Effects of Amount of Consultation and Superior's Confidence
in Subordinates on Subordinate Satisfaction

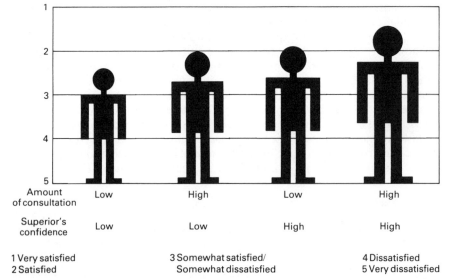

| 1 Very satisfied | 3 Somewhat satisfied/ | 4 Dissatisfied |
| 2 Satisfied | Somewhat dissatisfied | 5 Very dissatisfied |

Similarly, managers who, relative to their peers, are both high in their respect for their subordinates' capabilities and who consult them regularly on departmental issues also achieve the expected results. Precise labeling is again probably inappropriate, yet managers whose attitudes and behavior are closest to the Human Resources (Theory Y, System IV) model do in fact have the most satisfied subordinates.

Further, those managers who consult their subordinates frequently but who have little confidence in their ability to make a positive contribution to department decision making, and who thus fall nearest to our Human Relations model, have subordinates who are more satisfied than those under the more Traditional managers but are significantly less satisfied than the subordinates of Human Resources managers.

The majority of our findings support the major formulations of participative management theory, but they also suggest the need for elaboration and clarification. This need is brought to attention by the total pattern of our findings, and particularly by the results for one of our categories of managers—those high in superiors' confidence but relatively low in participation. Recall that, while the differences were not large, this group had the second highest average satisfaction score in our sample—the score falling between that of the Human Relations (high participation, low superior confidence) group and that of the Human Resources (high on each) group. Moreover, for the two groups characterized by high participation, there is substantially higher satisfaction for those whose superior reflects high confidence in his subordinates. Clearly, any theory which focused on the amount of participation would not predict these results. Rather, for these managers at least, the quality of their relationship with their superiors as indicated by their superiors' attitude of trust and confidence in them appears to modify the effects of the amount of participation.

Implications for Theory

The quality dimension of the theory of participative management has not been fully developed, but its outlines are suggested in our own Human Resources model and in McGregor's Theory Y framework. McGregor stressed heavily the importance of managers' basic attitudes and assumptions about their subordinates. In expanding on this point,[7] he suggested that a manager's assumptions about his subordinates' traits and abilities do not bind him to a single course of action. Rather, he argued that a range of possible behaviors is appropriate under Theory Y or Human Resources assumptions—a manager with high trust and confidence in his subordinates could and should take into account a variety of situational and personality factors in deciding, among other things, when and how to consult with them. Extending this reasoning, one can even imagine a Theory Y or Human Resources manager actually consulting with his subordinates less often than some of his colleagues. Nevertheless, the nature and quality of participation employed by such a manager, when it occurs, would presumably be deeper and more meaningful, which would be reflected in high levels of subordinate satisfaction and performance.

This view of the superior-subordinate interaction process, emphasizing as it does the quality of the interaction rather than only the amount, can be employed to answer three of the more pervasive criticisms of participative management. These criticisms—each of which is probably most accurately aimed at the simple quantity theory of participation—focus on the inappropriateness of extensive consultation when the superior is constrained by time, technology, and his own or his subordinates' temperament.

The Time Constraint

"In a crisis, you simply do not have time to run around consulting people." This familiar explication is difficult to debate, and in fact, would receive no challenge from a sophisticated theory of participation. In a real building-burning crisis, consultation is inappropriate, and unnecessary. A crisis of this nature is recognized as such by any well-informed subordinate and his self-controlled cooperation is willingly supplied. The behavior of both superior and subordinate in such a situation is guided by the situation and each may turn freely and without question to the other or to any available source of expertise for direction or assistance in solving the problem at hand.

Many crises, however, do not fit the building-burning category, and may be much more real to one person, or to one level of management, than to those below him. Our experience suggests that managers may not be nearly as bound by their constraints as they frequently claim to be, or if they are constrained, these limits are either known in advance or are open to modification if circumstances demand. Rather, in many instances it appears that managers employ the "time won't permit" argument primarily to justify autocratic, and at least partially risk free, behavior. If he succeeds, the credit is his, if he fails, he can defend his actions by pointing out that he had no time to explore alternatives.

Such self-defined, or at least self-sustaining, crises are most frequently employed by the manager with a Human Relations concept of participation—one who views participation primarily as a means of obtaining subordinate cooperation and who focuses mainly on the amount of formal involvement required. The crisis itself can be employed in place of participation as the lever to obtain cooperation and there is clearly no time for the sort of routine, frequently peripheral consultation in which he most often indulges.

Conversely, the manager with high trust and confidence in his subordinates' capabilities, the Human Resources manager, is less likely to employ time constraints as a managerial tactic. In real crises he moves as rapidly as the situation demands. He is, however, more likely, because of his normal practices of sharing information with his subordinates, to have a group which is prepared to join him in a rapid review of alternatives. He is unconcerned with involvement for the sake of involvement and thus his consultation activities are penetrating and to the point. His subordinates share his trust and feel free to challenge his views, just as he feels free to question their advice and suggestions openly.

The Technology Barrier

"Look, I've got fifteen subordinates scattered all over the building. What do you expect me to do—shut down the plant and call a meeting every time something happens?" This argument is obviously closely linked to the time constraint argument—technology is a major factor in determining the flow and timing of decisions. Similarly, it too flows from a Human Relations-quantity oriented view of participation.

438

A good manager obviously does not regularly "stop the presses" and call a conference. He has confidence in his subordinates' abilities to handle problems as they appear and to call him in when the problem demands his attention. This confidence is, however, reinforced by joint planning, both one-to-one and across his group of subordinates, before the operation gets under way. Having agreed in advance on objectives, schedules, priorities, and procedures, involvement on a day-to-day basis may be minimal. The manager in this instance does not seek participation to obtain cooperation with his views. Both the manager and his subordinates view the regularly scheduled work-planning and review sessions as important because they result in well-considered solutions to real problems.

The Temperament Barrier

"I'm simply not the sort who can run around to his subordinates asking them how things are going—it's just not my style." The manager who made this statement did so somewhat apologetically, but there was little for him to be apologetic about. He had a high-performing group of subordinates, in whom he placed high trust and confidence, who were in turn highly satisfied with their boss. Further, while he did not seek their views on a variety of routine departmental matters, and his subordinates did not drop in to his office to chat, he freely shared all departmental information with them and on a regular basis worked with his subordinates in coordinating department plans and schedules. In addition, he practiced a somewhat formal but effective form of management by objectives with each of his subordinates.

This manager and, unfortunately, many of the more outspoken critics of participative management, tend to feel that consultation must be carried out in a gregarious, back-slapping manner. Joint planning is a decision-making technique, and not a personality attribute. Extreme shyness or reserve may be an inhibiting factor, but is not an absolute barrier. Trust and confidence in subordinates can be demonstrated as effectively, if not more effectively, by action as by words.

Similarly, as suggested earlier, the manager who holds a Human Resources view of participation acknowledges personality and capability differences among his subordinates. He feels a responsibility to the organization and to his subordinates to assist *each* to develop continuously his potential for making important contributions to department performance. He recognizes that individuals move toward the free interchange of ideas, suggestions, and criticisms at different paces. However, by demonstrating his own confidence in his subordinates' capabilities and in their potential, he tends to encourage more rapid growth than other managers.

Concluding Comments

Our continuing research on the purpose and process of participative management has, in our view, contributed additional support for the Human Resources theory of participation. It has emphasized that when the impact on subordinates is considered, the superior's attitude toward the traits and abilities of his subordinates is equally as important as the amount of consultation in which he engages.

This not-so-startling finding allows expansions and interpretation of modern theories of participation to counter criticisms which may be properly leveled at a simple quantity theory of participation. However, although our findings have obvious implications for both theory and management behavior, they too are open to possible misinterpretation. It is possible to read into our findings, as some surely will, that subordinate consultation may be neglected, that all that matters is that the superior respect his subordinates.

Such a philosophy—tried, found wanting, and not supported by our findings—is embodied in the frequent statement that "all you need to do to be a good manager is hire a good subordinate and turn him loose to do the job as he sees fit." Such a philosophy, in our view, abdicates the superior's responsibility to guide, develop, and support his subordinates. The most satisfied managers in our sample were those who received high levels of consultation from superiors who valued their capabilities. It is our view that effective participation involves neither "selling" the superior's ideas nor blanket approval of all subordinate suggestions. Rather, it is most clearly embodied in the notion of joint planning where the skills of both superior and subordinate are used to their fullest.

Our findings emphasize the importance of attitudes of trust and confidence in subordinates, but they do not indicate their source. It is possible, but unlikely, that those superiors in our sample who reported the highest levels of trust and confidence in their subordinates did so because their subordinates were in fact of higher caliber than those of their colleagues. Within our large sample of managers, several indicators—education, age, experience, for example—suggest that managers' capabilities are roughly evenly distributed across levels and divisions within the organization.

Another possible reason for differences in superiors' attitudes on this dimension is that they are caused by interaction with subordinates, rather than being a determinant of the nature of this interaction. That is, the manager who attempts consultation which is highly successful increases his confidence in his subordinates and thus develops broader involvement. This seems to be a highly plausible explanation which has implications for management development. In fact, there is growing evidence that managers who experiment with participative techniques over lengthy periods do develop both a commitment to such practices and additional trust in their subordinates.

Notes

1. See Raymond E. Miles, "Human Relations or Human Resources?" *Harvard Business Review* (July–August 1965), p. 149.
2. See Douglas McGregor, *The Human Side of Enterprise* (New York: McGraw-Hill) 1960; and *The Professional Manager* (New York: McGraw-Hill) 1967.
3. See Rensis Likert, *New Patterns of Management* (New York: McGraw-Hill) 1961; and *The Human Organization* (New York: McGraw-Hill) 1967.
4. See Raymond E. Miles, "The Affluent Organization," *Harvard Business Review* (May–June 1966), p. 106; and Raymond E. Miles, Lyman W. Porter, and James A. Craft, "Leadership Attitudes Among Public Health Officials," *American Journal of Public Health* (Dec. 1966), p. 1990.
5. Other findings from this research are reported in L. V. Blankenship and Raymond E. Miles, "Organization Structure and Management Decision Behavior," *Administrative Science Quarterly* (June 1968), p. 106 and in Karlene Roberts, L. V. Blankenship, and R. E. Miles, "Organizational Leadership, Satisfaction,

and Productivity: A Comparative Analysis,'' *Academy of Management Journal* (Dec. 1968), p. 401.

6. For more detailed analysis of these data see J. B. Ritchie and Raymond E. Miles, ''An Analysis of Quantity and Quality of Participation as Mediating Variables in the Participative Decision Making Process,'' *Personnel Psychology.*

7. Douglas McGregor, *The Professional Manager* (New York: McGraw-Hill) 1967, p. 79.

OVERCOMING THE DYSFUNCTIONS OF MbO

STEVEN KERR

Despite tremendous interest in Management by Objectives (MbO), and its extensive use in industry as a developmental tool, ''research examining the planning, implementation and evaluation of MbO systems has been surprisingly scarce.''[1] When the very natural tendency for change agents to write about and for journals to publish successes rather than failures is taken into account, it is even more clear that little is really known about the dysfunctions which often plague MbO introductions and implementations.

There are two major problems with trying to evaluate MbO. One is that ''Management by Objectives'' is really a catch-all title for several different, if related, approaches.[2] The other is that, when introduced as a total system of management, MbO constitutes a simultaneous assault upon the organization's authority, reward communications and control systems, changing so many variables at once that careful study is all but impossible.

I am not prepared to claim without definitive data that Management by Objectives is or is not working in organizations today. Based on a review of the MbO literature and on related research, however, and aided by personal contact with MbO in four organizations (twice as an employee, twice as a consultant), I am prepared to suggest that most MbO efforts are accompanied by a number of dysfunctions, dysfunctions serious enough in many cases to keep the system from performing efficiently.

MbO is often sold as a total managerial system. I hope to show that MbO is *not* likely to be effective when employed as a total system. I hope to show also that the typical MbO process contains logical inconsistencies and makes implicit assumptions which are contrary to things we know about organizations and about people.

The purposes of this article are (1) to discuss the weaknesses underlying the MbO process, and (2) to suggest how MbO can be modified so as to permit its successful use in organizations.

Reprinted with permission of the author and publisher from *Management by Objectives,* Vol. 5, No. 1, 1976.

[1] Henry L. Tosi and William J. Bigoness, ''MbO and Personality: A Search for Comparability,'' *Management by Objectives,* 3, Number 4, 1974, p. 44.

[2] Harry Levinson, ''Management by Whose Objectives?'' *Harvard Business Review,* July–August 1970, p. 125.

Although there are several varieties of "Management by Objectives," in general MbO features "joint goal-setting between those at each level of management and those at the next higher level, the expression of objectives whenever possible in quantifiable terms such as dollars, units, and percentages, and the subsequent measurement and comparison of actual performance with the agreed-upon objectives."[3]

MbO is certainly intuitively appealing; why else would so many firms incur the heavy costs of its adoption in the absence of conclusive evidence of its worth? However, its intuitive appeal masks several important shortcomings and deficiencies. Some of the explicit claims and implicit assumptions that have been made on behalf of MbO are presented below.

Assumption 1: "Joint" Goal-Setting
among Hierarchical Unequals Is Possible

This premise lies at the heart of the MbO philosophy, and presumes that the superior can comfortably go from his "boss-judge" role to one of "friend-helper" (and, presumably, back again). It is claimed of one participative system, for example, that evaluation meetings between the boss and his subordinates can be "strictly man-to-man in character . . . In listening to the subordinate's review of performance, problems, and failings, the manager is automatically cast in the role of *counselor*. This role for the manager, in turn, results naturally in a problem-solving discussion."[4]

The assumption that such schizoid behaviour can be induced on any kind of regular basis is naive. The research literature[5] provides abundant evidence that hierarchical status differences produce some very predictable effects upon interaction patterns, subordinate defensiveness, and quantity and quality of communications, and these effects "stack the deck" against joint goal-setting by unequals. Bennis has summarized some of the difficulties involved:

> Two factors seem to be involved. . . The superior as a helper, trainer, consultant, and co-ordinator; and the superior as an instrument and arm of reality, a man with power over the subordinate. . . For each actor in the relationship, a *double reference* is needed. . . The double reference approach requires a degree of maturity, more precisely a commitment to maturity, on the part of both the superior and subordinate that exceeds that of any other organizational approach . . . It is suggestive that psychiatric patients find it most difficult to see the psychiatrist both as a human being and helper and an individual with certain perceived powers. The same difficulty exists in the superior–subordinate relationship.[6]

Assumption 2: MbO Can Be Effective at the Lowest Managerial Levels

Proponents have contended that successful implementation will enable MbO to permeate the entire organization, and be effective even at the lowest

[3]Alan C. Filley, Robert J. House and Steven Kerr, *Managerial Process and Organizational Behavior.* (Glenview, Ill., Scott, Foresman, 1976) (2nd edition, in press).

[4]Herbert H. Meyer, Emanuel Kay, and John R. P. French, Jr., "Split Roles in Performance Appraisal," *Harvard Business Review,* January–February 1965, p. 129.

[5]See for example Peter M. Blau and W. Richard Scott, *Formal Organizations* (San Francisco, Chandler, 1962), pp. 121–124 and 242–244.

[6]Warren G. Bennis, "Leadership Theory and Administrative Behavior: The Problem of Authority," *Administrative Science Quarterly,* 1960, pp. 285–287.

level of management. However, several studies have concluded that this filtering-down process very often fails to occur, and that the lower the hierarchical status of the manager the less influence he can exert, and the less he is likely to be a genuine participant in the goal-setting process.[7] In part this reflects the inherent problems of attempting joint goal-setting among hierarchical unequals.

Another reason for the failure of MbO to be effective at the lower managerial levels is an illogicality in the process itself. It is that even if we assume truly democratic, participative goal-setting at the very top of the firm (say, between the president and his divisional vice-presidents), their meetings must still ultimately produce firm, hard goals for the months ahead. The most collegial atmosphere in the world cannot keep these goals, once agreed upon, from being perceived as commitments by the parties concerned. These commitments must then serve as lower limits, as monkeys on the back of any vice-president who then seeks to establish democratic, participative goal-setting with his own subordinates. Having agreed with the president that 12 per cent growth in sales is a fair goal for the coming year, the marketing vice-president is unlikely to accept his sales manager's carefully-worded argument that 9 per cent is better. While lower-level managers may enjoy the fiction of participation, they will probably soon realize that most of their objectives have already been "locked in" by meetings held at higher levels. They of course retain the freedom to set objectives even more challenging than those agreed upon higher up; they will seldom be able to set objectives less challenging.

Varying the goal-setting sequence can serve to alter this chain of events, but will seldom improve upon it. For example, some MbO proponents claim that "simultaneous goal-setting" at all managerial levels produces genuine participation. However, the ensuing problems of coordination and communications border on the unreal. The marketing vice-president might under these conditions meet with the president, and agree "tentatively" that 12 per cent sales growth sounded pretty good for the next year. After meeting with his sales manager, who preferred 9 per cent, he would again meet with the president to renegotiate. If 10 per cent were now agreed on he would once more meet with the sales manager, to democratically explain why 9 per cent was too low. Meanwhile, however, the sales manager would have held meetings with his district managers, and perhaps become convinced that 9 per cent was too high. At this point the marketing vice-president would presumably return to his "friend-helper" the president for another round of "joint" goal-setting.

The only way to insure that low-level managers have influence is for them to initiate the process, by communicating to their superior the goals they wish to pursue during the coming period. Their superior would then set his objectives based upon their objectives, and so on up the line. This gain in low-level influence may be costly, however, since the firm's goals are essentially being set by those at the bottom of the hierarchy, who (usually) are less educated, trained, and experienced, and who may possess inadequate information. Technical drawbacks aside, this alternative is likely to be politically unacceptable to managers at the top. It is therefore no surprise that many studies have shown MbO to be increasingly ineffective at successively lower levels.

[7]See for example John M. Ivancevich, "A Longitudinal Assessment of Management by Objectives," *Administrative Science Quarterly,* 1972, pp. 126–138. More recently, Raia, and Tosi and Carroll have published results which agree.

Management by Objectives is often used in conjunction with management appraisal programmes. Some writers recommend linking it directly to the compensation programme, under the assumption that MbO provides "a means of measuring the true contribution of managerial and professional personnel."[8] However, this assumption calls to mind some impossible-to-answer questions, and very often leads to information suppression and risk-avoidance behaviour, particularly in highly uncertain and rapidly changing organizational units.

The impossible-to-answer questions include:

1. How do you tell whether the goals whose accomplishment you are rewarding are challenging?

Padding by subordinates of time it will take or money it will cost may be detectable when the superior has technical expertise in the area for which the objective is being set, and when the task depends on technology which is stable and predictable. There are numerous instances, however, in engineering, marketing, product development and other areas, when even the most astute superior will be unable to determine whether target dates have a built-in safety factor.

2. How do you insure that all your subordinates have goals which are of equal difficulty?

If MbO is to be useful as an evaluation-compensation tool, subordinates must perceive that they have a fair chance to obtain organizational rewards. Yet it is virtually impossible to devise any system which will provide for goals which are equally challenging.

3. What do you do when conditions change?

Suppose that a new competitor or a new credit rating comes along, and what formerly were challenging goals suddenly become easy goals, or impossible goals. In a truly stable environment this may not be a daily concern, but in our age of continuous "future shock" stable environments are becoming unusual. Even a modest technological development or a small change in company policy can eliminate the challenge from objectives previously set. Do we now reward for goal-attainment when a ten-year-old could also have been successful? Do we punish non-attainment of objectives which have become herculean in difficulty? Or do we spend the better part of every afternoon negotiating?

4. Is exceeding the objective good?

Even aside from the fact that conditions continually change, this question is more difficult than it may seem. In one firm I am familiar with, the completion of a task in seven weeks when it was forecasted to take ten weeks brings mild *disapproval* rather than praise. The rationale is credible enough; it is that others with whom the goal-setter interacts are not expecting the guidebook, product, software package or whatever to be ready, and so cannot take advantage of the fact that it is ready. This organization takes a position that deviations from standard *in either direction* are usually undesirable. While this may or may not be the best approach, the point is that it is seldom possible to determine whether early completion of a task is an indication of good performance

[8]George S. Odiorne, *Management by Objectives—A System of Managerial Leadership* (New York, Pitman, 1965), p. 55.

or of bad planning. That the individual worked like the dickens is seldom sufficient to resolve this dilemma.

5. How do you "objectively" reward performance under MbO?

Proponents of Management by Objectives takes special pains to avoid this question, since it is obviously one for which there is no answer. Odiorne, for example, asserts that MbO "determines who should get the *pay* increases. . . The increases are allocated on the basis of the results achieved against agreed-upon goals at the beginning of the period."[9] The problem with this, however, is that no formula for comparing "results achieved against agreed-upon goals" exists. Researchers have correctly cautioned that "evaluations should rarely be based on whether or not the objective is accomplished or on the sheer number accomplished. . .", and have listed other factors that must be taken into account, including:

—proper allocation of time to given objectives
—type and difficulty of objectives
—creativity in overcoming obstacles
—efficient use of resources
—use of good management practices in accomplishing objectives (cost reduction, delegation, good planning, etc.)
—avoidance of conflict-inducing or unethical practices[10]

Certainly it is necessary to consider these and other factors; otherwise subordinates could better themselves by taking shortcuts which negatively affect total organizational effectiveness. But take another look at the above list of "other factors" to be considered. Have you seen a list which calls for greater *subjectivity?* Could you possibly establish *objective* measures of whether "proper" time was allocated to given objectives, whether "creativity" was used to overcome obstacles, or whether "good" management practices were used? In short, MbO leaves you as dependent on subjectivity as you were before, only with the additional problem that expectations of "fair" and "objective" evaluation and reward systems have been created, making employee dissatisfaction more likely.

If the added objectivity promised by Management by Objectives typically turns out to be illusory, the information suppression and risk-avoidance behaviour often brought on by linking MbO to rewards is certainly no illusion. Common sense suggests that many employees will build margins for error into their cost estimates and target dates, and in this case common sense is supported by research.[11] Even workers high in need for Achievement will often create safety cushions, while privately setting moderate-risk objectives against which they can compete. I have seen or heard of many cases where employees set objectives on projects which were virtually or actually completed. You may be quick to brand such actions unethical; can you as quickly deny that they are rational responses to a system which requests of employees that they voluntarily set challenging, risky goals, only to face smaller paychecks and possibly damaged careers if these goals are not accomplished?

[9]Ibid., p. 66.
[10]Stephen J. Carroll and Henry L. Tosi, Jr., *Management by Objectives: Applications and Research,* (New York: Macmillan, 1973), p. 83.
[11]See for example Stephen J. Carroll and Henry L. Tosi, "Goal Characteristics and Personality Factors in a Management-by-Objectives Program," *Administrative Science Quarterly,* 1970, pp. 295–305.

MbO encourages goal-setting in extremely quantitative fashion, with intermediate and final results all expressed in dollars, dates, or percentages. While such quantification is often possible and desirable, MbO encourages it to the extent that goal displacement and inefficiency sometimes result. Studies indicate that the MbO process can cause employees to over-concentrate their efforts in areas for which objectives have been written, to the virtual exclusion of other activities.[12] Since it is seldom possible to write quantifiable objectives about innovation, creativity, and interpersonal-relations, employees under MbO are seldom evaluated in these areas, and may consequently worry little about coming up with new ideas or improving relations with other organizational units.

Even in areas for which objectives do exist, excessive emphasis on quantifiable objectives encourages (and, when linked to compensation, rewards) performance in accordance with the *letter,* not the *spirit,* of the objective. Attempting to measure and reward accuracy in paying surgical claims, for example, one insurance firm requires that managers set objectives about the number of returned checks and letters of complaint received from policyholders. However, underpayments are likely to provoke cries of outrage from the insured, while overpayments are often accepted in courteous silence. Since it is often impossible to tell from the physician's statement which of two surgical procedures, with different allowable benefits, was performed, and since writing for clarification will interfere with other objectives concerning "percentage of claims paid within two days of receipt," the new hire in more than one claims section is soon acquainted with the informal norm: "When in doubt, pay it out!"[13] The managers of these sections regularly meet or exceed their objectives in the areas of both quality (accuracy) and quantity. But at what cost to the organization?

Certainly, the dynamic environment is where new systems of planning, evaluation and communications are most needed. We already know quite a bit about managing the stable, highly-certain segments of business, and a variety of techniques such as PERT are available to us and work particularly well when parameters are known. MbO, however, is less useful when conditions are changing and the future is uncertain. We have already suggested that risk-avoidance by subordinates will most often occur under conditions of uncertainty, and we have also pointed out that under such circumstances goal difficulty is so likely to change that systematic reward and punishment under MbO is impossible.

One reviewer of the MbO literature found that "the most striking result is the emphasis on the need for goal clarity (low role conflict and ambiguity) if Management by Objectives is to be an effective planning procedure."[14] Low

[12]See for example Anthony P. Raia, "A Second Look at Management Goals and Controls," *California Management Review,* 1966, pp. 49–58.

[13]Steven Kerr, "On the Folly of Rewarding A, While Hoping for B," *Academy of Management of Journal,* 1975, in press.

[14]John B. Miner, *The Management Process: Theory, Research and Practice,* (New York, Macmillan, 1973).

role conflict and ambiguity can be fairly well established by SOPs and job descriptions in the stable, highly-certain parts of most firms; they are nearly impossible to come by in uncertain areas. MbO, after all, attempts to produce a mutually-acceptable job description, and "no matter how detailed the job description, it is essentially static—that is, a series of statements. . . The more complex the task and the more flexible a man must be in it, the less any fixed statement of job elements will fit what he does. . ."[15]

I have to this point tried to demonstrate that Management by Objectives is a sometimes overrated, flawed system which may introduce more problems than it solves. Rather than join those who attribute its failures to "errors in implementation," "not enough time," or "lack of top management support," I believe its difficulties stem from the fact that it depends upon assumptions which are contrary to what we think we know about organizations and about people.

Of course, if you are *not* knee-deep in pseudoparticipation, caution-crazy subordinates and make-believe objectivity, don't let me convince you you're sick when you're not. In this age of situational theories it is no more possible to state that something will not work than to claim it always will. However, if you *are* having problems of the kind I have described, and if you buy my argument that MbO is at least partially responsible, you may still feel that sunk cost and political realities argue against trying to quit cold turkey. The remainder of this article is therefore aimed at separating those parts of MbO worth keeping from those which ought to be discarded.

Features Worth Keeping

1. Conscious emphasis on goal-setting. Considerable research suggests that systematic, periodic goal-setting positively affects performance, and can alter an organization's activities-oriented approach in favour of one that is more results-oriented.

2. Frequent interaction and feedback between superior and subordinates. These have been found to be related to "higher goal success, improvement in relationships with the boss, goal clarity, a feeling of supportiveness and interest from one's superior, a feeling that one can participate in matters affecting him, and satisfaction with the superior."[16] Feedback frequency is particularly important "to managers low in self-assurance, cautious in decision making, and with jobs involving frequent change."[17]

3. Opportunities for participation. Although it is erroneous to assume that hierarchically-unequal individuals can comfortably engage in joint goal-setting, this does not mean that all forms of participation are impossible. Even chances to give advice about matters which will ultimately be decided higher up often have favourable effects upon subordinate attitudes. While not all workers respond positively to participation, studies indicate that performance will seldom suffer merely because of such opportunities.

One way to improve participation under MbO might be for the peer group

[15]Levinson, *op. cit.* p. 126.

[16]Stephen J. Carroll, Jr. and Henry L. Tosi, "The Relation of Characteristics of the Review Process as Moderated by Personality and Situational Factors to the Success of the 'Management by Objectives' Approach," *Academy of Management Proceedings,* 1969, p. 141.

[17]Tosi and Bigoness, *op. cit.,* p. 46.

to develop their objectives as a group. Status differentials are likely to be less important, freeing individuals of the need to be cautious and deferential.[18] Peer-group goal-setting should serve to minimize duplication of objectives and reduce paperwork. Successful negotiation with the boss should be easier, since group support would tend to offset the boss's higher rank. Communications would be facilitated and the present weakness of MbO to reward for *individual* goals accomplished, even at the expense of overall harmony or efficiency, would be resolved.

Another way to improve participation under MbO is for the organization to provide training to all subordinates and, especially, to all managers who will be required to operate under the system. The skills and attitudes necessary for MbO to be effective are neither intuitive nor "natural" to individuals brought up in traditionally bureaucratic organizations. Both book learning and simulated experiences will probably be necessary before those who will be living with the system become competent even to try it. This point should be obvious as to be unworthy of mention; yet comparatively few MbO change agents include systematic skills and attitude training as part of their programmes.

Features to Discard

1. Linking MbO to the compensation system. The only areas where tying MbO to rewards will not tend to induce risk-avoidance and goal displacement are those where conditions are so predictable that no deceit is possible. In these areas, however, incentive plans and piecework, commission, and bonus systems are already available.

2. Using MbO as an "objective" way to measure performance. While requesting that managers in their feedback sessions with subordinates totally suppress consideration of whether agreed-upon objectives have been met is probably futile, formal comparison of goals accomplished against goals set should definitely be avoided. Such comparisons *will not* enable performance reviews to be carried out on a more objective basis, but *will* cause the risk-avoidance and goal-displacement behaviour described above.

3. Focusing attention upon only those objectives which can easily be quantified. Objectives should be written "in every area where performance and results directly and vitally affect the survival and prosperity of the business."[19] This is true *whether or not* quantification is possible! Numerous instances could be cited where performance suffered either because non-quantifiable objectives were ignored altogether or because some simple-minded number (e.g., patents as *the* measure of creativity) was substituted for them.[20] Conversely, performance may be improved by keeping in mind that "although in many areas the qualitative aspects of output may have to be assessed largely in terms of value judgments, the discipline of prescribing standards of performance and of testing results against them can improve the control process."[21]

[18]Levinson, *op. cit.,* makes this point, as does Robert A. Howell, "A Fresh Look at Management by Objectives," *Business Horizons,* 1967, p. 55.

[19]Peter F. Drucker, *The Practice of Management,* (New York: Harper & Row, 1954).

[20]For examples see Kerr, *op. cit.*

[21]C. J. Hancock, "MbO Raises Management Effectiveness in Government Service," *Management by Objectives,* 3, Number 4, 1974, p. 12.

4. Making Personnel Division responsible for maintenance. Once it is decided that MbO will not be used as an instrument of evaluation and reward, the rationale for active involvement by Personnel largely vanishes. Such involvement will serve mainly to increase both the volume of required paperwork and the level of threat perceived by lower-level participants.

5. Forms, forms, and more forms. The problem of excessive paperwork has been found to be a major impediment to the effective use of MbO.[22] Once the notion of utilizing MbO for evaluation and control is abandoned, surprisingly few forms are really necessary.

6. Pre-packaged programmes and costly consultants. Although these may (or may not) be necessary for successful introduction and maintenance of the change-everything-at-once-and-see-what-happens king-sized version of MbO, they are probably unnecessary for the "mini-MbO" that will remain once "features to discard" one to four are followed.

Conclusions

In sum:
1. Management by Objectives is at present a high-cost long-run package whose success is by no means guaranteed, which generates many side effects impossible to predict or control. Two competent researchers speak of MbO as a "complex organizational change process which may be painful and time-consuming,"[23] and another points out that "it will take four to five years to achieve a fully effective Management by Objectives system."[24]

2. Management by Objectives is yet another technique that requires friendly, helpful superiors, honest and mature subordinates, and a climate of mutual trust. Carvalho has cautioned that "successful implementation of MbO requires, even demands, that all managers have a fundamental results-oriented attitude," as well as "an attitude which accepts collaboration, co-operation, and joint sharing of responsibilities as the norm rather than the exception." He goes on to state that such attitudes are hardly commonplace in most organizations today, and that to develop them a "mini-cultural revolution" will probably be needed.[25] And we have already taken note of Bennis' opinion that the double reference approach necessary for MbO to work "requires a degree of maturity, more precisely a commitment to maturity, on the part of both the superior and subordinate that exceeds that of any other organizational approach."[26] In short, *MbO often works best for those individuals who need it least.*

3. Management by Objectives is best suited to those static environments in which we already have sufficient technology to manage competently. Rapidly changing conditions and high role conflict and ambiguity seriously impair its

[22]See for example Anthony P. Raia, *Managing by Objectives* (Glenview, Ill.: Scott, Foresman, 1974.)

[23]Henry L. Tosi and Stephen J. Carroll, "Some Structural Factors Related to Goal Influence in the Management by Objectives Process," *Business Topics,* Spring, 1969, p. 50.

[24]Robert A. Howell, "Managing by Objectives—A Three Stage System," *Business Horizons,* February 1970, p. 45. See also F. D. Barrett, "The MbO Time Trip," *Business Quarterly,* Autumn 1972.

[25]G. F. Carvalho, "Installing MbO: A New Perspective on Organizational Change," *Human Resources Management,* Spring, 1972, pp. 23-30.

[26]Bennis, *op. cit.,* p. 286.

usefulness. *MbO often works best in those situations where we need it least.*

4. We must stop pretending that MbO adds much to our ability to reward and evaluate. It is unlikely to be effective when employed as a "total" management system. Its strength lies in its emphasis on goal-setting, its provision for feedback and interaction, and its opportunities for participation. These features can and should be maintained, but not at a cost of jolting the organization with massive and simultaneous changes. A good illustration of the point is given by Lasagna, who described the problems which afflicted his organization as a result of attempting to use MbO for too many purposes. He reports that they had much better success when they substituted a mini-MbO which was not tied to evaluation and compensation.[27]

The advantages that would accrue to users of a "mini-system" of MbO are due to the fact that such an approach would introduce fewer new variables, require less time to take effect, cost far less and minimize unpredictable side effects. It would be particularly effective in combating the increase in employee anxiety and defensiveness which so often accompanies MbO introduction. Furthermore, a mini-MbO would be less likely to cause management to forget that the system is in no sense a cure-all, but is rather just another tool in the managerial kit. Finally, a "mini-system" of MbO would for the first time enable scientific study of costs and benefits to be conducted, so that we may at last discover whether or not Management by Objectives is worth its cost.

[27]John B. Lasagna, "Make Your MbO Pragmatic," *Harvard Business Review,* November–December 1971, pp. 64–69.

JAPANESE MANAGEMENT:
PRACTICES AND PRODUCTIVITY

NINA HATVANY
VLADIMIR PUCIK

> The [United States] is the most technically advanced country and the most affluent one. But capital investment alone will not make the difference. In any country the quality of products and the productivity of workers depend on management. When Detroit changes its management system we'll see more powerful American competitors.
> —Hideo Sugiura, Executive Vice-President.
> Honda Motor Co.

Productivity—or output per worker—is a key measure of economic health. When it increases, the economy grows in real terms and so do standards of living. When it declines, real economic growth slows or stagnates. Productivity is the result of many factors, including investment in capital goods, technological innovation, and workers' motivation.*

After a number of years of sluggish productivity growth, the United States now trails most other major industrial nations in the rise in output per worker, although it still enjoys the best overall rate. This state of affairs is increasingly bemoaned by many critics in both academic and business circles. Some reasons suggested to "explain" the U.S. decline in productivity rankings include excessive government regulation, tax policies discouraging investment, increases in energy costs, uncooperative unions, and various other factors in the business environment.

Some observers, however—among them Harvard professors Robert Hayes and William J. Abernathy—put the blame squarely on American managers. They argue that U.S. firms prefer to service existing markets rather than create new ones, imitate rather than innovate, acquire existing companies rather than develop a superior product or process technology, and, perhaps most important, focus on short-run returns on investment rather than long-term growth and research and development strategy. Too many managers are setting and meeting short-term, market-driven objectives instead of adopting the appropriate time-horizon needed to plan and execute the successful product innovations needed to sustain worldwide competitiveness.

The performance of the American manufacturing sector is often contrasted with progress achieved by other industrialized countries—particularly Japan. Japan's productivity growth in manufacturing has been nearly three times the U.S. rate over the past two decades—the average annual growth rate between 1960 and 1978 was 7.8 percent. In the last five years alone, the produc-

*The authors would like to thank Mitsuyo Hanada, Blair McDonald, William Newman, William Ouchi, Thomas Rochl, Michael Tushman, and others for their helpful comments on earlier drafts of this paper. We are grateful to Citibank, New York, and the Japan Foundation, Tokyo, for their financial support of the work in the preparation of this paper.

tivity index has increased by more than 40 percent and most economists forecast similar rates for the 1980s. Such impressive results deserve careful examination.

Students of the Japanese economy generally point out that Japanese investment outlays as a proportion of gross national product are nearly twice as large as those in the United States, and this factor is backed by a high personal savings ratio and the availability of relatively cheap investment funds. Also, a massive infusion of imported technology contributed significantly to the growth of productivity in Japan. Among noneconomic factors, the Japanese political environment seems to support business needs, especially those of advanced industries. In addition, the "unique" psychological and cultural characteristics of the Japanese people are frequently cited as the key reason for Japan's success.

It is indeed a well-known fact that absenteeism in most Japanese companies is low, turnover rates are about half the U.S. figures, and employee commitment to the company is generally high. But although cultural factors are important in any context, we doubt that any peculiarities of Japanese people (if they exist) have much impact on their commitment or productivity. In fact, several recent research studies indicate that Japanese and American workers show little or no difference in the personality attributes related to performance. Rather, we join Robert Hayes and William Abernathy in believing that, in this context, productivity stems from the superior management systems of many Japanese firms. But the focus of our analysis is not on such areas as corporate marketing and production stategies. Instead, we will examine management practices in Japan as they affect one key company asset: human resources.

Our analysis is guided by our experience with subsidiaries of Japanese firms in the United States. Typically, these companies are staffed by a small group of Japanese managers with varying levels of autonomy relative to the company's parent. The rest of the employees are American. Although they operate in an alien culture, many of these subsidiaries are surprisingly successful. While it is often very difficult to measure the performance of newly established operations, it is no secret that production lines in several Japanese subsidiaries operate at the same productivity rate as those in Japan (for example, the Sony plant in San Diego).

This example—as well as others—serves to demonstrate that what works in Japan can often work in the United States. The techniques used by the management of Japanese subsidiaries to motivate their American workers seem to play an important part in the effort to increase productivity. Therefore, a careful examination of management practices in Japan is useful not only for a specialist interested in cross-cultural organization development, but also for the management practitioner who is losing to foreign competition even on his or her homeground. What is it that the Japanese do better?

Our discussion attempts to answer this question by presenting a model of the Japanese management system that rests on a few elements that can be examined in different cultural settings. The model will be used to highlight the relationship between the management strategies and techniques observed in Japan and positive work outcomes, such as commitment and productivity. Our review is not intended to be exhaustive, but rather to suggest the feasibility of integrating findings from Japan with more general concepts and theories. We will therefore focus on relationships that may be verified by observations of behavior in non-Japanese, especially U.S., settings.

We propose that positive work outcomes emanate from a complex set of behavioral patterns that are not limited to any specific culture. The emphasis is on management practices as a system and on the integration of various strategies and techniques to achieve desired results. We hope thus to provide an alternative to statements—often cited but never empirically supported—that the high commitment and productivity of Japanese employees is primarily traceable to their cultural characteristics.

A Management System Focused on Human Resources

Most managers will probably agree that management's key concern is the optimal utilization of a firm's various assets. These assets may vary—financial, technological, human, and so on. Tradeoffs are necessary because utilization of any one asset may result in underutilization of another. We propose that in most Japanese companies, *human assets are considered to be the firm's most important and profitable assets in the long run.* Although the phrase itself sounds familiar, even hollow, to many American managers and OD consultants, it is important to recognize that this management orientation is backed up by a well-integrated system of strategies and techniques that translate this abstract concept into reality.

First, long-term and secure employment is provided, which attracts employees of the desired quality and induces them to remain with the firm. Second, a company philosophy is articulated that shows concern for employee needs and stresses cooperation and teamwork in a unique environment. Third, close attention is given both to hiring people who will fit well with the particular company's values and to integrating employees into the company at all stages of their working life. These general strategies are expressed in specific management techniques. Emphasis is placed on continuous development of employee skills; formal promotion is of secondary importance, at least during the early career stages. Employees are evaluated on a multitude of criteria—often including group performance results—rather than on individual bottomline contribution. The work is structured in such a way that it may be carried out by groups operating with a great deal of autonomy. Open communication is encouraged, supported, and rewarded. Information about pending decisions is circulated to all concerned before the decisions are actually made. Active observable concern for each and every employee is expressed by supervisory personnel (Figure 1). Each of these management practices, either alone or in combination with the others, is known to have a positive influence on commitment to the organization and its effectiveness.

We will discuss these practices as we have observed them in large and medium-size firms in Japan and in several of their subsidiaries in the United States. Although similar practices are often also in evidence in small Japanese companies, the long-term employment policies in these firms are more vulnerable to drops in economic activity and the system's impact is necessarily limited.

FIGURE 1

Japanese management paradigm

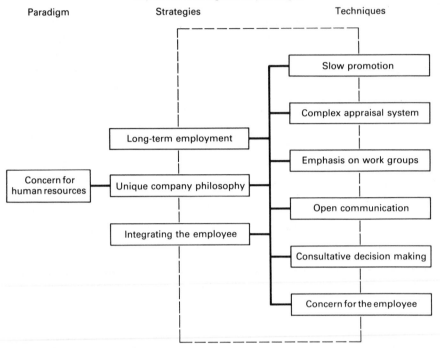

Strategies

Once management adopts the view that utilizing human assets is what matters most in the organization's success, several strategies have to be pursued to secure these assets in the desired quality and quantity. These strategies involve the following:

Provide secure employment. Although Japanese companies typically provide stable and long-term employment, many smaller firms find it difficult to do so in times of recession. The policy calls for hiring relatively unskilled employees (often directly from high schools or universities), training them on the job, promoting from within, and recognizing seniority.

The implicit guarantee of the employee's job, under all but the most severe economic circumstances, is a marked departure from conventional managerial thinking about the need to retain flexibility in work force size in order to respond efficiently to cyclical variations in demand. However, this employment system, at least as practiced in large corporations in Japan, is far from being inflexible. Several techniques can be applied to ride out recession with a minimum burden of labor cost while keeping a maximum number of regular workers on their jobs—a freeze on new hiring, solicitation of voluntary retirement sweetened by extra benefits, use of core employees to replace temporaries and subcontractors doing nonessential work, and so forth. Thus a labor force cut of approximately 10 to 15 percent in a short time period is not an unusual phenomenon. In addition, across-the-board salary and bonus cuts for all employees, including management, would follow if necessary.

Japanese managers believe that job security has a positive impact on morale and productivity, limits turnover and training costs, and increases the organization's cohesiveness. For that reason, they are willing to accept its temporary negative effect in a period of reduced demand. Long-term employment security is also characteristic of all the U.S. subsidiaries that we have visited. Layoffs and terminations occur extremely rarely. For example, the Kikkoman Company instituted across-the-board wage cuts in an attempt to preserve employment during the last recession. Murata instituted a four-day workweek, and at Matsushita's Quasar plant, a number of employees were shifted from their regular work to functions such as repairs, maintenance, and service. It should be noted that there are several well-known U.S. corporations—for example, IBM and Hewlett-Packard—that follow similar practices when the alternative would be layoff.

In Japanese companies, even poor performers are either retrained or transferred, instead of simply being dismissed. The plant manager in an electronics component factory explained how the company copes with personal failures: "We give a change to improve even if there has been a big mistake. For example, the quality control manager didn't fit, so we transferred him to sales engineering and now he is doing fine."

Research on behavior in organizations suggests that the assumptions of Japanese managers and some of their U.S. colleagues about the positive impact of job security are, at least to some degree, justified. It has been shown that long tenure is positively associated with commitment to the organization, which in turn reduces turnover. High commitment in conjunction with a binding choice (employees of large firms in Japan have difficulty finding jobs of the same quality elsewhere, given the relatively stable labor market) also leads to high satisfaction, but whether this contributes to high productivity still remains to be proved. It is, however, necessary to view the policy of secure employment as a key condition for the implementation of other management strategies and techniques that have a more immediate impact on the organization's effectiveness.

Articulate a unique company philosophy. A philosophy that is both articulated and carried through presents a clear picture of the organization's objectives, norms, and values—and thus helps transform commitment into productive effort. Familiarity with organizational goals gives direction to employees' actions, sets constraints on their behavior, and enhances their motivation. The understanding of shared meanings and beliefs expressed in the company philosophy binds the individual to the organization and, at the same time, stimulates the emergence of goals shared with others, as well as the stories, myths, and symbols that form the fabric of a company philosophy. William Ouchi and Raymond Price suggest that an organizational philosophy is an elegant informational device that provides a form of control at once pervasive and effective; at the same time it provides guidance for managers by presenting a basic theory of how the firm should be managed.

An explicit management philosophy of how work should be done can be found in many successful corporations in both Japan and the United States; examples in the United States include IBM, Texas Instruments, and U.S. Homes. Nevertheless, it is fair to say that the typical Japanese firm's management philosophy has a distinct flavor. It usually puts a heavy emphasis on cooperation and teamwork within a corporate "family" that is unique and distinct from that of any other firm. In return for an employee's effort, the family's commitment to the employee is translated into company determination to avoid layoffs and to provide a whole range of supplementary welfare benefits for the employee and his or her family. Naturally, without reasonable employment security, the fostering of team spirit and cooperation would be impossible. The ideal is thus to reconcile two objectives: pursuit of profits and perpetuation of the company as a group.

In a number of cases, a particular management philosophy that originated within the parent company in Japan is also being actively disseminated in its U.S. subsidiaries. Typically, claims of uniqueness range from the extent of the company's concern for employees' work lives to the quality of service to the customer. We quote from the in-house literature issued by one of the fastest growing Japanese-owned electronics component makers in California:

> *Management Philosophy:* Our goal is to strive toward both the material and the spiritual fulfillment of all employees in the Company, and through this successful fulfillment, serve mankind in its progress and prosperity.

> *Management Policy:* Our purpose is to fully satisfy the needs of our customers and in return gain a just profit for ourselves. We are a family united in common bonds and singular goals. One of these bonds is the respect and support we feel for our fellow family co-workers.

Integrate employees into the company. The benefits of an articulated company philosophy are lost, however, if it's not properly communicated to employees or if it's not visibly supported by management's behavior. A primary function of the company's socialization effort, therefore, is to ensure that employees have understood the philosophy and seen it in action. Close attention is given to hiring people who are willing to endorse the values of the particular company and to the employees' integration into the organization at all stages of their working life. The development of cohesiveness within the firm, based on the acceptance of goals and values, is a major focus of personnel policies in many Japanese firms.

Because employees are expected to remain in the company for a major part of their careers, careful selection is necessary to ensure that they fit well into the company climate. In many U.S.-based Japanese firms also, new hires at all levels are carefully screened with this aspect in mind. As in Japan, basic criteria for hiring are moderate views and a harmonious personality, and for that reason a large proportion of new hires come from employee referrals. In general, "virgin" workforces are preferred, since they can readily be assimilated into each company's unique environment as a community.

The intensive socialization process starts with the hiring decision and the initial training program and continues in various forms thereafter. Over time, the employee internalizes the various values and objectives of the firm, becomes increasingly committed to them, and learns the formal and informal rules and preocedures, particularly through job rotation. That process usually includes two related types of job transfers. First, employees are transferred to new positions to learn additional skills in on-the-job training programs. These job changes are planned well in advance for all regular employees, including blue-collar workers. Second, transfers are part of a long-range, experience-building program through which the organization develops its future managers; such programs involve movement across departmental boundaries at any stage of an employee's career.

While employees rotate semilaterally from job to job, they become increasingly socialized into the organization, immersed in the company philosophy and culture, and bound to a set of shared goals. Even in the absence of specific internal regulations that might be too constraining in a rapidly changing environment, a well-socialized manager who has held positions in various functions and locations within the firm has a feel for the organization's needs.

Techniques

The basic management orientation and strategies that we have just discussed are closely interrelated with specific management techniques used in Japanese firms and in their subsidiaries in the United States. The whole system is composed of a set of interdependent employment practices in which the presence of one technique complements as well as influences the effectiveness of others. This interdependence, rather than a simple cause-effect relationship, is the key factor that helps maintain the organization's stability and effectiveness. Additional environmental variables may determine which of the strategies or techniques will require most attention from top management, but in their impact on the organization no single technique listed below is of prime importance.

Slow promotion, job rotation, and internal training. All Japanese subsidiaries that we have visited have seniority-based promotion systems. At one of them, a medium-sized motorcycle plant, a seniority-based promotion system has been reinstituted after an experiment with a merit-based system proved highly unpopular with employees. Training is conducted, as expected, mostly on the job, and as one textile company executive noted, career paths are flexible: "You can get involved in what you want to do." Hiring from outside into upper-level positions is rare. According to another Japanese plant manager: "We want someone who understands the management system of the company. We want to keep the employees with us; we want to keep them happy."

Although promotion is slow, early informal identification of the elite is not unusual and carefully planned lateral job transfers add substantial flexibility to job assignments. Not all jobs are equally central to the workflow in an organization, so employees—even those with the same status and salary—can be rewarded or punished by providing or withholding positions in which they could acquire the skills needed for future formal promotions.

Job rotation in U.S.-based Japanese firms seems less planned or structured than in Japan and more an ad hoc reaction to organizational needs—but in general, the emphasis on slow promotion and job rotation creates an environment in which an employee becomes a generalist rather than a specialist in a particular functional area. For the most part, however, these general skills are unique to the organization. Several of the Japanese manufacturers that invested in the United States were forced to simplify their product technology because they were not able to recruit qualified operators versatile enough to meet their needs, and there was not enough time to train them internally.

In Japan, well-planned job rotation is the key to the success of an in-company training program that generally encompasses all the firm's employees. For some categories of highly skilled blue-collar workers training plans for a period of up to ten years are not unusual. Off-the-job training is often included, again for managers and nonmanagers alike. However, whether such an extensive training system will be transferred to U.S. subsidiaries remains to be seen.

In addition to its impact on promotion and training, job rotation also promotes the development of informal communication networks that help in coordinating work activities across functional areas and in resolving problems speedily. This aspect of job rotation is especially important for managerial personnel. Finally, timely job rotation relieves an employee who has become unresponsive to, or bored with, the demands of his or her job.

Some observers argue that deferred promotion may frustrate highly promising, ambitious employees. However, the personnel director of a major trading company has commented: "The secret of Japanese management, if there is any, is to make everybody feel as long as possible that he is slated for the top position in the firm—thereby increasing his motivation during the most productive period of his employment." The public identification of "losers," who of course far outnumber "winners" in any hierarchical organization, is postponed in the belief that the increased output of the losers, who are striving hard to do well and still hoping to beat the odds, more than compensates for any lags in the motivation of the impatient winners. By contrast, top management in many American organizations is preoccupied with identifying rising stars as soon as possible and is less concerned about the impact on the losers' morale.

Complex appraisal system.   In addition to emphasizing the long-term perspective, Japanese companies often establish a complex appraisal system that includes not only individual performance measures tied to the bottom line, but also measures of various desirable personality traits and behaviors—such as creativity, emotional maturity, and cooperation with others as well as team performance results. In most such companies, potential, personality, and behavior, rather than current output, are the key criteria, yet the difference is often merely symbolic. Output measures may easily be "translated" into such attributes as leadership skills, technical competence, relations with others, and judgment. This approach avoids making the employee feel that the bottom line, which may be beyond his or her control, in part or in whole, is the key dimension of evaluation. Occasional mistakes, particularly those made by lower-level employees, are considered part of the learning process.

At the same time, evaluations do clearly discriminate among employees because each employee is compared with other members of an appropriate group (in age and status) and ranked accordingly. The ranking within the cohort is generally not disclosed to the employees, but of course it can be partially inferred from small salary differentials and a comparison of job assignments. At least in theory, the slow promotion system should allow for careful judgments to be made even on such subjective criteria as the personality traits of honesty and seriousness. However, the authors' observations suggest that ranking within the cohort is usually established rather early in one's career and is generally not very flexible thereafter.

Employees are not formally separated according to their ability until later in their tenure; ambitious workers who seek immediate recognition must engage in activities that will get them noticed. Bottom-line performance is not an adequate criterion because, as noted, it is not the only focus of managerial evaluation. This situation encourages easily observable behavior, such as voluntary overtime, that appears to demonstrate willingness to exert substantial effort on the organization's behalf. The evaluation process becomes to a large degree self-selective.

Several other facets of this kind of appraisal system deserve our attention. Because evaluations are based on managerial observations during frequent, regular interactions with subordinates, the cost of such an evaluation system is relatively low. When behavior rather than bottom-line performance is the focus of evaluation, means as well as ends may be assessed. This very likely leads to a better match between the direction of employee efforts and company objectives, and it encourages a long-term perspective. Finally, since group performance is also a focus of evaluation, peer pressure on an employee to contribute his or her share to the group's performance becomes an important mechanism of performance control. Long tenure, friendship ties, and informal communication networks enable both superiors and peers to get a very clear sense of the employee's performance and potential relative to others.

Among the management techniques characteristic of large Japanese enterprises, the introduction of a complex appraisal system is probably the least visible in their U.S. subsidiaries. Most of their U.S.-based affiliates are relatively young; thus long-term evaluation of employees, the key point in personnel appraisal as practiced in Japan, is not yet practicable. Furthermore, the different expectations of American workers and managers about what constitutes a fair and equitable appraisal system might hinder acceptance of the parent company's system.

Emphasis on work groups. Acknowledging the enormous impact of groups on their members—both directly, through the enforcement of norms, and indirectly, by affecting the beliefs and values of members—Japanese organizations devote far greater attention to structural factors that enhance group motivation and cooperation than to the motivation of individual employees. Tasks are assigned to groups, not to individual employees, and group cohesion is stimulated by delegating responsibility to the group not only for getting the tasks performed, but also for designing the way in which they get performed. The group-based performance evaluation has already been discussed.

Similarly, in the U.S.-based Japanese firms that we have visited, the group rather than an individual forms the basic work unit for all practical purposes. Quality of work and speed of job execution are key concerns in group production meetings that are held at least monthly, and even daily in some companies. The design function, however, is not yet very well developed; many workers are still relative newcomers unfamiliar with all aspects of the advanced technology. Intergroup rivalry is also encouraged. In one capacitor company, a group on a shift that performs well consistently is rewarded regularly. Sometimes news of a highly productive group from another shift or even from the Japanese parent is passed around the shop floor to stimulate the competition.

In Japan, group autonomy is encouraged by avoiding any reliance on experts to solve operational problems. One widely used group-based technique for dealing with such problems is quality control (QC) circles. A QC circle's major task is to pinpoint and solve a particular workshop's problem. Outside experts are called in only to educate group members in the analytical tools for problem solving or to provide a specialized technical service. Otherwise, the team working on the problem operates autonomously, with additional emphasis on self-improvement activities that will help achieve group goals. Fostering motivation through direct employee participation in the work process design is a major consideration in the introduction of QC circles and similar activities to the factory floor.

Nevertheless, work-group autonomy in most work settings is bound by clearly defined limits, with the company carefully coordinating team activities by controlling the training and evaluation of members, the size of the team, and the scope and amount of production. Yet within these limits, teamwork is not only part of a company's articulated philosophy, it actually forms the basic fabric of the work process. Job rotation is encouraged both to develop each employee's skills and to fit the work group's needs.

From another perspective, the group can also assist in developing job-relevant knowledge by direct instruction and by serving as a model of appropriate behavior. The results of empirical studies suggest that structuring tasks around work groups not only may improve performance, but also may contribute to increased esteem and a sense of identity among group members. Furthermore, this process of translating organizational membership into membership in a small group seems, in general, to result in higher job satisfaction, lower absenteeism, lower turnover rates, and fewer labor disputes.

Open and extensive communication. Even in the Japanese-owned U.S. companies, plant managers typically spend at least two hours a day on the shop floor and are readily available for the rest of the day. Often, foremen are deliberately deprived of offices so they can be with their subordinates on the floor throughout the whole day, instructing and helping whenever necessary. The same policy applies to personnel specialists. The American personnel manager of a Japanese motorcycle plant, for example, spends between two and four hours a day on the shop floor discussing issues that concern employees. The large number of employees he is able to greet by their first name testifies to the amount of time he spends on the floor. "We have an open-door policy—but it's their door, not management's" was his explanation of the company's emphasis on the quality of face-to-face vertical communication.

Open communication is also inherent in the Japanese work setting. Open work spaces are crowded with individuals at different hierarchical levels. Even high-ranking office managers seldom have separate private offices. Partitions, cubicles, and small side rooms are used to set off special areas for conferences with visitors or small discussions among the staff. In one Japanese-owned TV plant on the West Coast, the top manager's office is next to the receptionist—open and visible to everybody who walks into the building, whether employee, supplier, or customer.

Open communication is not limited to vertical exchanges. Both the emphasis on team spirit in work groups and the network of friendships that employees develop during their long tenure in the organization encourage the extensive face-to-face communication so often reported in studies involving Japanese companies. Moreover, job rotation is instrumental in building informal lateral networks across departmental boundaries. Without these networks, the transfer of much job-related information would be impossible. These informal networks are not included in written work manuals; thus they are invisible to a newcomer; but their use as a legitimate tool to get things done is implicitly authorized by the formal contact system. Communication skills and related factors are often the focus of yearly evaluations. Frequently, foreign observers put too much emphasis on vertical ties and other hierarchical aspects of Japanese organizations. In fact, the ability to manage lateral communication is perhaps even more important to effective performance, particularly at the middle-management level.

Consultative decision making. Few Japanese management practices are so misunderstood by outsiders as is the decision-making process. The image is quite entrenched in Western literature on Japanese organizations: Scores of managers huddle together in endless discussion until consensus on every detail is reached, after which a symbolic document, "ringi," is passed around so they can affix their seals of approval on it. This image negates the considerable degree of decentralization for most types of decisions that is characteristic in most subsidiaries we have visited. In fact, when time is short, decisions are routinely made by the manager in charge.

Under the usual procedure for top-management decision making, a proposal is initiated by a middle manager (but often under the directive of top management). This middle manager engages in informal discussion and consultation with peers and supervisors. When all are familiar with the proposal, a formal request for a decision is made and, because of earlier discussions, is almost inevitably ratified—often in a ceremonial group meeting or through the "ringi" procedure. This implies not unanimous approval, but unanimous consent to its implementation.

This kind of decision making is not participative in the Western sense of the word, which encompasses negotiation and bargaining between a manager and subordinates. In the Japanese context, negotiations are primarily lateral between the departments concerned with the decision. Within the work group, the emphasis is on including all group members in the process of decision making, not on achieving consensus on the alternatives. Opposing parties are willing to go along, with the consolation that their viewpoint may carry the day the next time around.

However, the manager will usually not implement his or her decision "until others who will be affected have had sufficient time to offer their views, feel that they have been fairly heard, and are willing to support the decision even though they may not feel that it is the best one," according to Thomas P. Rohlen. Those outside the core of the decision-making group merely express their acknowledgment of the proposed course of action. They do not participate; they do not feel ownership of the decision. On the other hand, the early communication of the proposed changes helps reduce uncertainty in the organization. In addition, prior information on upcoming decisions gives employees an opportunity to rationalize and accept the outcomes.

Japanese managers we have interviewed often expressed the opinion that it is their American partners who insist on examining every aspect and contingency of proposed alternatives, while they themselves prefer a relatively general agreement on the direction to follow, leaving the details to be solved on the run. Accordingly, the refinement of a proposal occurs during its early implementation stage.

Although the level of face-to-face communication in Japanese organizations is relatively high, it should not be confused with participation in decision making. Most communication concerns routine tasks; thus it is not surprising that research on Japanese companies indicates no relationship between the extent of face-to-face communication and employees' perceptions of how much they participate in decision making.

Moreover, consultation with lower-ranking employees does not automatically imply that the decision process is "bottom up," as suggested by Peter Drucker and others. Especially in the case of long-term planning and strategy, the initiative comes mostly from the top. Furthermore, consultative decision making does not diminish top management's responsibility for a decision's consequences. Although the ambiguities of status and centrality may make it difficult for outsiders to pinpoint responsibility, it is actually quite clear within the organization. Heads still roll to pay for mistakes, albeit in a somewhat more subtle manner than is customary in Western organizations: Departure to the second- or third-ranking subsidiary is the most common punishment.

Concern for the employee. It is established practice for managers to spend a lot of time talking to employees about everyday matters. Thus they develop a feeling for employees' personal needs and problems, as well as for their performance. Obviously, gaining this intimate knowledge of each employee is easier when an employee has long tenure, but managers do consciously attempt to get to know their employees, and they place a premium on providing time to talk. The quality of relationships developed with subordinates is also an important factor on which a manager is evaluated.

Various company-sponsored cultural, athletic, and other recreational activities further deepen involvement in employees' lives. The heavy schedule of company social affairs is ostensibly voluntary, but virtually all employees participate. Typically, an annual calendar of office events might include two overnight trips, monthly Saturday afternoon recreation, and an average of six office parties—all at company expense. A great deal of drinking goes on at these events and much good fellowship is expressed among the employees.

Finally, in Japan the company allocates substantial financial resources to pay for benefits for all employees, such as a family allowance and various commuting and housing allowances. In addition, many firms provide a whole range of welfare services ranging from subsidized company housing for families and dormitories for unmarried employees, through company nurseries and company scholarships for employees' children, to mortgage loans, credit facilities, savings plans, and insurance. Thus employees often perceive a close relationship between their own welfare and the company's financial welfare. Accordingly, behavior for the company's benefit that may appear self-sacrificing is not at all so; rather, it is in the employee's own interest.

Managers in U.S.-based companies generally also voiced a desire to make life in the company a pleasant experience for their subordinates. As in Japan, managers at all levels show concern for employees by sponsoring various recreational activities or even taking them out to dinner to talk problems over. Again, continuous open communication gets special emphasis. However, company benefits are not as extensive as in Japan because of a feeling that American employees prefer rewards in the form of salary rather than the "golden handcuff" of benefits. Furthermore, the comprehensive government welfare system in the United States apparently renders such extensive company benefits superfluous.

In summary, what we observed in many Japanese companies is an integrated system of management strategies and techniques that reinforce one another because of systemic management orientation to the quality of human resources. In addition to this system's behavioral consequences, which we have already discussed, a number of other positive outcomes have also been reported in research studies on Japanese organizations.

For example, when the company offers desirable employment conditions designed to provide job security and reduce voluntary turnover, the company benefits not only from the increased loyalty of the workforce, but also from a reduction in hiring, training, and other costs associated with turnover and replacement. Because employees enjoy job security, they do not fear technical innovation and may, in fact, welcome it—especially if it relieves them of tedious or exhausting manual tasks. In such an atmosphere, concern for long-term growth, rather than a focus on immediate profits, is also expected to flourish.

An articulated philosophy that expresses the company's family atmosphere as well as its uniqueness enables the employee to justify loyalty to the company and stimulates healthy competition with other companies. The management goals symbolized in company philosophy can give clear guidance to the employee who's trying to make the best decision in a situation that is uncertain.

Careful attention to selection and the employee's fit into the company results in a homogeneous workforce, easily able to develop the friendship ties that form the basis of information networks. The lack of conflict among functional divisions and the ability to communicate informally across divisions allow for rapid interdivisional coordination and the rapid implementation of various company goals and policies.

The other techniques we've outlined reinforce these positive outcomes. Slow promotion reinforces a long-range perspective. High earnings in this quarter need not earn an employee an immediate promotion. Less reliance on the bottom line means that an employee's capabilities and behaviors over the long term become more important in their evaluations. Groups are another vehicle by which the company's goals, norms, and values are communicated to each employee. Open communication is the most visible vehicle for demonstrating concern for employees and willingness to benefit from their experience, regardless of rank. Open communication is thus a key technique that supports consultative decision making and affects the quality of any implementation process. Finally, caring about employees' social needs encourages identification with the firm and limits the impact of personal troubles on performance.

What we have described is a system based on the understanding that in return for the employee's contribution to company growth and well-being, the profitable firm will provide a stable and secure work environment and protect the individual employee's welfare even during a period of economic slowdown.

The Transferability of Japanese Management Practices

As in Japan, a key managerial concern in all U.S.-based Japanese companies we have investigated was the quality of human resources. As one executive put it, "We adapt the organization to the people because you can't adapt people to the organization." A number of specific instances of how Japanese management techniques are being applied in the United States were previously cited. Most personnel policies we've observed were similar to those in Japan, although evaluation systems and job-rotation planning are still somewhat different, probably because of the youth of the subsidiary companies. Less institutionalized concern for employee welfare was also pointed out.

The experience of many Japanese firms that have established U.S. subsidiaries suggests that the U.S. workers are receptive to many management practices introduced by Japanese managers. During our interviews, many Japanese executives pointed out that the productivity level in their U.S. plants is on a level similar to that in Japan—and occasionally even higher. Other research data indicate that American workers in Japanese-owned plants are even more satisfied with their work conditions than are their Japanese or Japanese-American colleagues.

The relative success of U.S.-based Japanese companies in transferring their employment and management practices to cover the great majority of their U.S. workers is not surprising when we consider that a number of large U.S. corporations have created management systems that use some typical Japanese techniques. Several of these firms have an outstanding record of innovation and rapid growth. A few examples are Procter & Gamble, Hewlett-Packard, and Cummins Engine.

William Ouchi and his colleagues call these firms Theory Z organizations. Seven key characteristics of Theory Z organizations are the following:

1. Long-term employment.
2. Slow evaluation and promotion.
3. Moderately specialized careers.
4. Consensual decision making.
5. Individual responsibility.
6. Implicit, informal control (but with explicit measures).
7. Wholistic concern for the employee.

The Theory Z organization shares several features with the Japanese organization, but there are differences: In the former, responsibility is definitely individual, measures of performance are explicit, and careers are actually moderately specialized. However, Ouchi tells us little about communication patterns in these organizations, the role of the work group, and some other features important in Japanese settings.

Here's an example of a standard practice in the Theory Z organization that Ouchi studied in depth:

> [The Theory Z organization] calculated the profitability of each of its divisions, but it did not operate a strict profit center or other marketlike mechanism. Rather, decisions were frequently made by division managers who were guided by broader corporate concerns, even though their own divisional earnings may have suffered as a result.

A survey by Ouchi and Jerry Johnson showed that within the electronics industry perceived corporate prestige, managerial ability, and reported corporate earnings were all strongly positively correlated with the "Z-ness" of the organization.

It is also significant that examples of successful implementation of the Japanese system can be found even in Britain, a country notorious for labor-management conflict. In our interpretation, good labor-management relations—even the emergence of a so-called company union—is an effect, rather than a cause, of the mutually beneficial, reciprocal relationship enjoyed by the employees and the firm. Thus we see the co-existence of our management paradigm with productivity in companies in Japan, in Japanese companies in the United States and Europe, and in a number of indigenous U.S. companies. Although correlation does not imply cause, such a causal connection would be well supported by psychological theories. Douglas McGregor summarizes a great deal of research in saying: "Effective performance results when conditions are created such that the members of the organization can achieve their own goals best by directing their efforts toward the success of the enterprise."

Conclusion

Many cultural differences exist, of course, between people in Japan and those in Western countries. However, this should not distract our attention from the fact that human beings in all countries also have a great deal in common. In the workplace, all people value decent treatment, security, and an opportunity for emotional fulfillment. It is to the credit of Japanese managers that they have developed organizational systems that, even though far from perfect, do respond to these needs to a great extent. Also to their credit is the fact that high motivation and productivity result at the same time.

The strategies and techniques we have reviewed constitute a remarkably well-integrated system. The management practices are highly congruent with the way in which tasks are structured, with individual members' goals, and with the organization's climate. Such a fit is expected to result in a high degree of organizational effectiveness or productivity. We believe that the management paradigm of concern for human resources blends the hopes of humanistic thinkers with the pragmatism of those who need to show a return on investment. The evidence strongly suggests that this paradigm is both desirable and feasible in Western countries and that the key elements of Japanese management practices are not unique to Japan and can be successfully transplanted to other cultures. The linkage between human needs and productivity is nothing new in Western management theory. It required the Japanese, however, to translate the idea into a successful reality.

Selected Bibliography

Robert Hayes and William Abernathy brought the lack of U.S. innovation to public attention in their article, "Managing Our Way to Economic Decline" (*Harvard Business Review,* July–August 1980).

Thomas P. Rohlen's book, *For Harmony and Strength: Japanese White-Collar Organization in Anthropological Perspective* (Berkeley: University of California Press. 1974), is a captivating description of the Japanese management system as seen in a regional bank. Peter Drucker has written several articles on the system, including "What We Can Learn from Japanese Management" (*Harvard Business Review,* March–April 1971). His thoughts are extended to the United States by the empirical work of Richard Pascale, "Employment Practices and Employee

Attitudes: A Study of Japanese and American Managed Firms in the U.S."
(*Human Relations,* July 1978).

For further information on the Theory Z organization see "Type Z Organization: Stability in the Midst of Mobility" by William Ouchi and Alfred Jaeger (*Academy of Management Review,* April 1978), "Types of Organizational Control and Their Relationship to Emotional Well-Being" by William Ouchi and Jerry Johnson (*Administrative Science Quarterly,* Spring 1978), and "Hierarchies, Clans, and Theory Z: A New Perspective on Organization Development" by William Ouchi and Raymond Price (*Organizational Dynamics,* Autumn 1978).

Douglas McGregor explains the importance of a fit between employee and organizational goals in *The Human Side of Enterprise* (New York: McGraw-Hill, 1960).

15 leadership and organization climate

CLIMATE AND MOTIVATION: AN EXPERIMENTAL STUDY

GEORGE H. LITWIN

The experimental study described here was designed to test certain hypotheses regarding the influence of leadership style and organizational climate on the motivation and behavior of organization members. The study involved the creation of several simulated business organizations. Three research objectives were established: first, to study the relationship of leadership style and organizational climate; second, to study the effects of organizational climate on individual motivation, measured through content analysis of imaginative thought; third, to identify the effects of organizational climate on such traditional variables as personal satisfaction and organizational performance.

An important methodological objective was the development of an experimental design consistent with the molar conception of organizational climate. The experimental design allowed only one variable input, leadership style, and measured the climate and motivation that were produced. Rather than focusing on the series of organizational and psychological occurrences following from various "natural" leadership styles, an attempt was made to create three distinct styles, and to measure their effects. Less emphasis was placed on the mechanism through which leadership style influences climate than on the specific nature of the climates produced and their effects on motivation.

Author's Note: The concepts and research presented in this paper are developed more fully in *Motivation and Organizational Climate* by George H. Litwin and Robert A. Stringer, Jr. (Boston: Harvard University, Graduate School of Business Administration, Division of Research, 1968).

Reprinted, with permission of author, from *Organization Climate: Explorations of a Concept*, Renato Tagiuri and George H. Litwin, eds. (Boston: Harvard University, Graduate School of Business Administration, Division of Research, 1968), pp. 169–90.

This study draws on recent systematic research and theory-building in the field of human motivation carried on by McClelland (1961), Atkinson (1968, 1964), and others. Atkinson (1964, pp. 240-314) has developed a formal model of motivational behavior which puts considerable emphasis on environmental determinants of motivation. The assumptions underlying the Atkinson model can be roughly restated as follows:

1. All individuals have certain basic motives or needs. These motives represent behavior potentials and influence behavior only when aroused.
2. Whether or not these motives are aroused depends upon the situation or environment perceived by the individual.
3. Particular environmental properties serve to stimulate or arouse various motives. In other words, a specific motive will not influence behavior until the motive is aroused by an appropriate enrivonmental influence.
4. Changes in the perceived environment result in changes in the pattern of aroused motivation.
5. Each kind of motivation is directed to the satisfaction of a different kind of need. The pattern of aroused motivation determines behavior, and a change in the pattern of aroused motivation will result in a change of behavior.

Several motives have been identified and studied (see Atkinson, 1958). Among the most significant of these are: the *need for achievement* (*n* Achievement), defined as the need for success in relation to an internalized standard of excellence; the *need for affiliation* (*n* Affiliation), defined as the need for close interpersonal relationships and friendships with other people; and the *need for power* (*n* Power), defined as the need to control or influence others and to control the means of influencing others. Systematic methods for measuring the strength of these motives through content analysis of thematic apperceptive stories have been developed and validated (Atkinson, 1958).

It is useful to think that each kind of motivation (achievement, affiliation, power) has a "characteristic" kind of behavior associated with it. Achievement-motivated individuals set high but realistic goals, are likely to plan ahead, enjoy taking personal responsibility, and are desirous of prompt and concrete feedback on the results of their actions. Affiliation-motivated individuals seek warm relationships and friendship. They are not concerned with getting ahead but enjoy jobs where they can be with people and help people. Power-motivated individuals tend to seek positions of power or influence; they are politicians, executives, military officers, and teachers.

In the Atkinson model, two situational or environmental determinants of motivation are described, expectancy and incentive value. Expectancy refers to the subjective probability or likelihood of need satisfaction (or frustration). Incentive value is the amount of satisfaction or frustration the person attaches to the outcome of a behavior sequence. These variables are rather particularistic and molecular—in any real life situation, many hundreds of expectancies and incentive values might be generated. The assessment of expectancies and incentive values has proven feasible in the controlled laboratory studies that have been conducted by Atkinson and his associates (see Atkinson and Feather, 1966), but such assessment is extremely difficult, if not impossible, in complex social situations. . . .

The concept of organizational climate fits the need for a broader, more molar framework for describing the environmental influence on motivation. As defined earlier in this volume, organizational climate is the quality or property of the organizational environment that (a) is perceived or experienced by organization members and (b) influences their behavior. In this study, the term organizational climate refers specifically to the motivational properties of the organizational environment; that is, to those aspects of climate that lead to the arousal of different kinds of motivation. In Atkinson's terms, organizational climate is the summary of the *total pattern of expectancies and incentive values that exist in a given organizational setting.*

Through a series of theoretical analyses and empirical studies, a climate measurement instrument with reasonable reliability and validity was developed (see Litwin and Stringer, 1968). The instrument is a 31-item questionnaire which provides scores on the following six dimensions:[1]

1. *Structure:* the feeling the workers have about the constraints in their work situation; how many rules, regulations, and procedures there are.
2. *Responsibility:* the feeling of being your own boss; not having to double-check all your decisions.
3. *Risk:* the sense of riskiness and challenge in the job and in the work situation.
4. *Reward:* the feeling of being rewarded for a job well done; the emphasis on reward versus criticism and punishment.
5. *Warmth and Support:* the feeling of general "good fellowship" and helpfulness that prevails in the organization.
6. *Conflict:* the feeling that management isn't afraid of different opinions or conflict; the emphasis placed on settling differences here and now.

Methodology

Experimental Design

Three simulated business organizations were created, each with 15 members plus a president, who was a member of the research staff. The presidents were instructed regarding the leadership style they were to maintain. The particular leadership styles, and hypotheses regarding their effects, are described below.

Leadership style was the major variable input. All other factors were controlled as carefully as possible. The physical locations were identical, the technology and essential tasks were the same, and the members of the organizations were matched with respect to age, sex, background, motive patterns, and personality characteristics. The design represents a refinement of a classic study conducted by Lewin, Lippitt, and White (1939).

Each simulated business operated in a 100-seat classroom. The work involved the production of miniature construction models of radar towers and radar-

[1]Dr. Herbert H. Meyer of the General Electric Company collaborated in the development of this questionnaire. The development of two later forms of this questionnaire and their respective scoring dimensions are described in more detail in Dr. Meyer's paper, "Achievement Motivation and Industrial Climates," in *Organizational Climate: Explorations of a Concept,* Renato Tagiuri and George H. Litwin, eds. (Boston: Harvard University, Graduate School of Business Administration, Division of Research, 1968).

controlled guns of various kinds from "Erector Set" parts. A typical product was comprised of from 30 to 50 parts. The businesses had three major tasks and three corresponding functional departments—production, product development, and control (or accounting). The president appointed people to each department, selected department managers, and was responsible for establishing job specifications and operating procedures.

The businesses were responsible to a simulated government agency, which released specifications for new products and product changes and requested bids on product orders of various sizes. Although each business started with the same product line, additions to and shifts in the product line were required. The simulated agency utilized a cost-plus control procedure, and the presidents were responsible for the preparation of detailed accounting statements showing material usage, labor efficiency, productivity, and contract by contract performance.

The 15 subjects assigned to each business included 13 men and 2 women. The subjects ranged in age from 18 to 29 years. All were hired (at an average hourly wage of $1.40) to participate in a study of "competitive business organizations." The 45 subjects were selected from an initial subject pool of 78 because they composed the "best" matched groups. The dimensions along which the groups were matched were: age, college major, business or other work experience, n Achievement, n Affiliation, and n Power scores, and California Psychological Inventory personality profiles (particularly overall elevation, and elevation in the major areas). Attention was given to careful matching with respect to initial motive scores, since aroused motivation was a major output measure.

The experiment was conducted over a two-week period, comprising eight actual days of organizational life. The work day averaged about six hours. During the course of the experiment, daily observations were made and periodic readings were taken using questionnaires and psychological tests. These data were used to provide feedback to the presidents indicating to what extent they were achieving the intended leadership styles.

Organization A: British Radar

The president placed strong emphasis on the maintenance of a formal structure. Members of the organization were assigned roles, their spheres of operation were tightly defined, and they were held responsible for the strict performance of their duties. Seriousness, order, and relative status were heavily stressed. All levels of management were encouraged to exercise position-based authority, and deviation from explicit organizational rules was punished. Communication was allowed only through strict vertical channels, was formal in nature, and was only permitted to cover matters directly related to the task. A conservative policy was maintained toward the task, the managerial credo being that reliable and consistent quality was more important than product innovation.

It was expected that in the climate thus produced the workers or participants would react against the formal structure and that boredom and aggression against the symbols of authority would be high. General job satisfaction was expected to be low.

A loose, informal structure was endorsed by the president of Organization B. He stressed friendly, cooperative behavior, group loyalty, and teamwork, and he tried to reflect these values in his own behavior. Group decision making was encouraged at every level. Punishment was dispensed with and was replaced with a relaxed atmosphere of encouragement and assistance. To insure the absence of conflict and frustration, managers were encouraged to pay special attention to the self-development and personal well-being of the workers. Group meetings were established in which the workers could get to know one another better.

It was expected that the climate of Organization B would lead to a feeling of group unity among the members. It was assumed that this unity, being born out of affiliative norms, would be more focused on interpersonal relationships than on task excellence. Thus, it was felt that, while job satisfaction would be high, efficiency would be only moderate.

Organization C: Blazer Radar

High productivity was valued by the president of Organization C. Each participant was encouraged to set his own goals and to take personal responsibility for results. Efforts to be innovative and creative were suported and reinforced by management. Competitive feedback was given frequently so that progress toward goals could be easily evaluated. Rewards for excellent performance were given in the form of recognition and approval, as well as in promotions and pay raises. An attempt was made to create a feeling of pride and teamwork in the organization through emphasis on competition against an external standard. Members were encouraged to seek each other's help around task issues, and no formal system of communications was instituted.

The researchers expected that worker enthusiasm would be high, along with personal commitment and involvement. While productivity would therefore be high, it was felt that the emphasis on improved performance would induce the workers to report that even better performance could be achieved.

Summary and Hypotheses

Exhibit 1 is a summary representation of the leadership style inputs for the three simulated business organizations. It represents, in generic terms, the directives given by the researchers to the presidents. The vertical divisions are a rough attempt to correlate the leadership style inputs with the dimensions of climate to which they seem most clearly related.

The researchers formulated a series of hypotheses regarding the experimental effects of climate on aroused motivation. The hypotheses, as originally stated for each organization, are set forth below:

1. The climate created in Organization A will stimulate or arouse *need for power* relative to the other two climates, and the strength of the aroused *need for achievement* and *need for affiliation* will be correspondingly reduced.

EXHIBIT 1
Summary of Leadership Style Inputs

Climate Dimension	Organization A (British)	Organization B (Balance)	Organization C (Blazer)
1. Structure	maintain order exercise authority and control	maintain informality	maintain informality
2. Standards, Responsibility			set high standards for individuals and organization encourage innovation
3. Reward and Punishment	criticize poor performance criticize deviation from rules	avoid individual punishment give general, positive rewards (unconditional) positive regard)	give individual and organizational rewards, praise, promotion reward excellent performance
4. Warmth and Support		create warm, friendly relationships create relaxed, easygoing atmosphere	give individual and organizational support
5. Cooperation and Conflict		stress cooperation avoid conflicts create warm, personal relationships with subordinates	stress cooperation in work tolerate personal and task-related conflict
6. Risk and Involvement	stress conservatism avoid deep involvement		stress moderate risks, create pride in organization, stress challenge, fun and excitement of work

2. Relative to the other two climates, the climate of Organization B will arouse the *need for affiliation*. The *need for power* will be correspondingly reduced, and the *need for achievement* will be relatively unaffected.

3. The climate of Organization C will arouse the *need for achievement* relative to the other two climates, and the *need for affiliation* and *need for power* will not be affected.

Exhibit 2 summarizes the hypotheses concerning the motive arousal effects of the three experimentally induced climates. It should be noted that each leadership style was intended to create a climate that would make one motive more salient. Thus, the climates, and the leadership styles designed to create them, can be characterized as power-related (Organization A), affiliative (Organization B), and achieving (Organization C).

The connection between leadership style and motivation can be analyzed through a comparison of Exhibits 1 and 2. The leadership style inputs for the president of Organization A, for example, are meant to discourage behavior which would lead to the fulfillment of either the *need for achievement* or the *need for affiliation*. Each directive reduces either the incentive value or expectancy (or both) of satisfaction associated with these needs. Similarly, the leadership directives of Organization B generally increase the expectancy and incentive value of feelings associated with the members' *need for affiliation*.

EXHIBIT 2

Summary of Hypotheses Concerning
the Motivational Effects[a] of Climate

Motive	Organization A (British)	Organization B (Balance)	Organization C (Blazer)
n Achievement	reduction effect	no effect	arousal effect
n Affiliation	reduction effect	arousal effect	no effect
n Power	arousal effect	reduction effect	no effect

[a]Effects are statements of change relative to other business groups, as measured by thematic apperceptive measures of motivation.

Applying the Atkinson model, one would expect a need to be aroused when the incentive and expectancy of success are high and to be reduced when they are low.

The climate model affords a level of generalization and collectivity which greatly simplifies the task of identifying motivational determinants. Rather than dealing with individual incentives and expectancies, it tries to measure the total situational influence. As previously stated, climate represents some sort of sum of the expectancies and incentive values generated in a situation. The present experiment was intended to demonstrate the relationship between climate and three specific kinds of aroused motivation. The design was an attempt to study the arousal effects of climate on one motive at a time, in order to provide clear demonstration of these relationships.

Results and Discussion

Effects of Leadership Style on Climate

Observation, interview, and questionnaire data revealed three distinct social and work environments emerging during the course of the experiment. Exhibit 3 summarizes the climate questionnaire data collected for each week. Statis-

EXHIBIT 3

Mean Climate Dimension Scores in the Three Simulated
Organizations (Measured in Week I and Week II)

Climate Dimension	Organization A (British)		Organization B (Balance)		Organization C (Blazer)		F-Ratios	
	Week I	Week II	Week I	Week II	Week I	Week II	Week I	Week II
Structure	19.8	21.4	13.4	15.1	14.3	16.0	16.1**	20.4**
Responsibility	12.6	11.6	13.9	15.3	15.6	16.3	3.0*	15.0**
Risk	9.7	8.5	10.3	10.3	11.8	12.4	4.7*	17.8**
Reward	18.0	15.7	29.4	27.2	27.7	22.5	39.7**	58.4**
Warmth and Support	15.8	14.6	26.8	24.8	22.7	24.2	62.1**	82.2**
Conflict	9.2	9.6	5.0	5.8	7.1	6.6	23.6**	23.3**

$^*p < .05.$
$^{**}p < .01.$

tically significant differences among the three organizations are demonstrated for all the climate dimensions.

Observation data indicate that Organization A was characterized by isolation, organizational formality, and an avoidance of conflict. The climate data indicate high scores on the Structure dimension, and low scores on Responsibility, Reward, and Warmth and Support. These data seem to reflect the feelings of the members about the climate, as indicated in responses to open-ended questions and in post-study interviews. They reported that the climate was highly constraining, conservative, cold, and formal. Conflicts (between managers and workers) were reported to be widespread but suppressed. High scores on the Conflict dimension, intended to measure the capacity to confront conflict openly, were apparently generated by the presence of considerable unresolved conflict.

Organization B developed norms of friendliness and equality. These characteristics are demonstrated in the consistently high scores on the dimensions of Warmth and Support and Reward. The data are supported by statements of the members that the climate was relaxed, friendly, very loosely structured, and personally satisfying.

Organization C was characterized by activity, teamwork, competitiveness, and an enjoyment of work. The climate data in Exhibit 3 indicate high scores on Responsibility, Risk, Reward, and Warmth and Support. The members described the climate as loosely structured and high in rewards for individual initiative.

Effects of Climate on Motivation

Immediate Effects. On the second, fifth, and seventh days of the eight-day simulation, the participants were asked to complete an individual report describing in several paragraphs their thoughts, feelings, concerns, and actions during the past several days. These descriptions were scored for *n* Achievement, *n* Affiliation, and *n* Power, using standardized content analysis procedures (see Atkinson, 1958). The scores thus derived represent measures of aroused motivation, and differences among the three organizations in these motivation scores can be assumed to describe the arousal effects of the induced climates.

Exhibit 4 graphically depicts the levels of aroused motivation in the three climates. Exhibit 5 shows the results of a series of One-way Analyses of Variance of the data presented in Exhibit 4. Almost all the differences in aroused motivation among the three climates are statistically significant (as can be seen from the F-Ratios). *All the hypotheses regarding the arousal effects of the experimental climates are confirmed.* Organization A created a high level of power motivation; Organization B created a high level of affiliation motivation; and Organization C created a high level of achievement motivation.

The hypotheses regarding the reduction effects of the experimental climates are not generally confirmed. While Organization A did create the lowest average level of achievement motivation, as was hypothesized, there was no difference between the level of aroused affiliation motivation in Organizations A and C. Furthermore, Organization B created, by the seventh day, a moderate but significant arousal of power motivation.

EXHIBIT 4

EXHIBIT 4
The Effects of Climate on Situationally Aroused Motivation

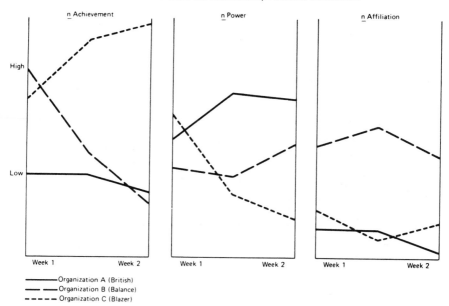

n Achievement n Power n Affiliation

Organization A (British)
Organization B (Balance)
Organization C (Blazer)

EXHIBIT 5
Results of One-Way Analyses of Variance
for Aroused Motivation Scores Derived from the
Individual Reports for Three Simulated Organizations

Data Collected [a]	Motivation Content	F-Ratio [b]	Significance Level
First Testing (Day 2)	n Achievement	3.87	.05
	n Affiliation	3.49	.05
	n Power	.89	—
Second Testing (Day 5)	n Achievement	6.39	.01
	n Affiliation	13.86	.01
	n Power	3.74	.05
Third Testing (Day 7)	n Achievement	9.98	.01
	n Affiliation	11.11	.01
	n Power	3.27	.05

[a]The simulated business organizations were run for 8 days, and individual reports were collected on three occasions, on Day 2, Day 5, and Day 7. The aroused motivation scores were derived from several open-ended questions requiring description of the person's thoughts, feelings, concerns, and actions.
[b]Based on One-Way Analyses of Variance of differences between the three organizations ($N = 15$ in each).

Long-Term Effects. A standardized thematic apperception instrument[2] was used to measure the overall change in *n* Achievement, *n* Affiliation, and *n* Power. These tests were administered several days "before" and "after" the simulation experience. The bar graphs in Exhibits 6, 7, and 8 outline the results. A One-way Analysis of Variance of the *change scores* for each of the

[2]The Test of Imagination, developed by McClelland and used extensively in his studies (McClelland, 1961).

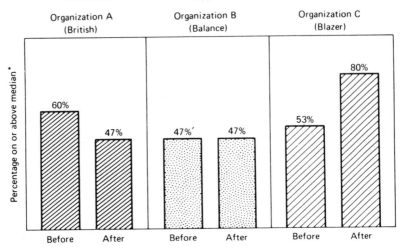

EXHIBIT 6

The Effects of Climate on Changes in Need for Achievement

Organization A (British)

Organization B (Balance)

Organization C (Blazer)

Percentage on or above median*

60% 47% 47%' 47% 53% 80%

Before After Before After Before After

*Median for all climates BEFORE = 10
Median for all climates AFTER = 7

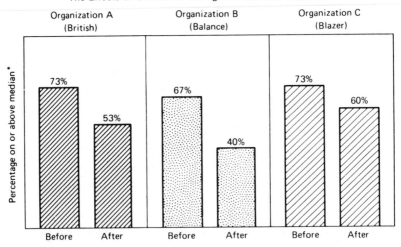

EXHIBIT 7

The Effects of Climate on Changes in Need for Affiliation

Organization A (British)

Organization B (Balance)

Organization C (Blazer)

Percentage on or above median*

73% 53% 67% 40% 73% 60%

Before After Before After Before After

*Median for all climates BEFORE = 4
Median for all climates AFTER = 5

climates showed that none of the changes was significant. All *n* Achievement scores declined, while *n* Affiliation and *n* Power showed some increase.

The general decline in *n* Achievement was anticipated. In hiring the subjects, the researchers introduced an array of "arousal" cues. For example, subjects were told that the simulation would be competitive, and that there were a

476

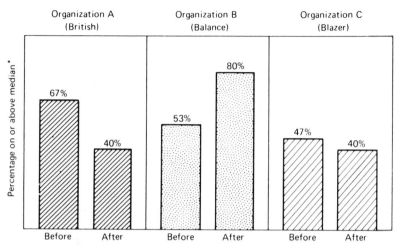

EXHIBIT 8
The Effects of Climate on Changes in Need for Power

Organization A (British)   Organization B (Balance)   Organization C (Blazer)

*Median for all climates BEFORE = -11
Median for all climates AFTER = 13

limited number of positions available. In other words, when the subjects took the initial tests, they were excited and tended to score high in *n* Achievement.

The fact that none of the motive changes was statistically significant suggests that the climate conditions did not affect the more generalized (and stable) patterns of expectancy and thematic response elicited by the standardized instrument. The situationally specific cues in the individual report questionnaire did elicit the varying patterns of thematic response that were hypothesized. The more general cues in the standardized instrument did not elicit such patterns of varying thematic response. The length of time the participants lived and worked in the experimentally generated climates may have been the critical factor in determining the extent to which more general and stable behavior tendencies were affected. The eight-day climate experience in this study does not appear to have created lasting changes in motive strength.

Though the motive scores did not change significantly, the trend, for *n* Achievement, was in the direction that was hypothesized. Relative to the other businesses, *n* Achievement scores in Organization C showed some gain. For *n* Affiliation, there were no differences among the three businesses. For *n* Power, Organization B showed some gain.

Although the hypotheses concerning the effects of climate on before–after measures of motivation were not confirmed, other measures of personality did reveal significant before–after changes. Three scales on the California Psychological Inventory (CPI) showed significant before–after changes. These scales were: Self-Acceptance, Responsibility, and Communality. Without going into the detailed definitions of these scales, the results indicate that the members of Organization A became less content with themselves, less accepting of others, and more anxious and impatient. Members of Organization B changed little on these dimensions, and members of Organization C tended to grow in responsibility, patience, and resourcefulness.

Effects of Climate on Satisfaction and Performance

The researchers were interested in measuring the effects of climate on job satisfaction and performance. Exhibit 9 summarizes the immediate effect of climate on these two measures.

EXHIBIT 9
Effects of Climate on Performance and Satisfaction

	Organization A (British)	Organization B (Balance)	Organization C (Blazer)
Performance			
Profit; ( ) = Loss	$7.70	$(5.30)	$72.30
% Profit; ( ) = Loss	81%	(.80%)	11.7%
No. of new products developed	4	6	8
Materials-Saving Innovations (estimates)	$0.00[a]	$25.10	$43.80
Units Rejected by Government	0	1	4
Satisfaction[b]	low (3.2)*	high (6.4)	high (5.8)

[a]British never deviated from government specifications, and their material charges were used as a base figure.

[b]Satisfaction as described here was measured in response to the question, "How satisfying has your job and your participation been?" on a 9-point rating scale, after 7 days of work in the organization. The numbers shown are the mean scores for the 15 people in each organization.

*An Analysis of Variance shows that the means are significantly different from each other ($p < .05$), and further analysis shows that the Balance mean is significantly different from the other two.

Satisfaction. Measures of satisfaction were collected at three points during the two-week simulation.[3] Satisfaction was reported to be high in Organizations B and C, and consistently low in Organization A. The sources of satisfaction in Organizations B and C may be quite different. Organization B aroused affiliation motivation, and the suggestion is that members are reporting satisfaction with the warm, friendly, relaxed atmosphere. Organization C aroused achievement motivation, and the suggestion is that members are reporting satisfaction with the challenging goals and the rewards for excellent performance.

Performance. Organization C significantly outperformed its two competitors. This company was able to introduce more new products, enjoyed the highest profits, and cut material costs substantially. This last factor probably contributed to the relatively high number of rejects.

Organization A enjoyed the best "quality" reputation. This is because it never attempted to "cut corners," and was very conservative in its bidding. It was not able to innovate and generally showed a marked degree of inflexibility in the changing marketplace.

Organization B, with the poorest profit showing, did enjoy a good "quality" image. It also was able to encourage innovation. Its bids were generally competitive with those of Organization A, but Organization B was unprofitable because it supported an extremely high (unfavorable) labor variance.

[3]Responses to the question, "How satisfying has your job and your participation been?"

It should be noted that the members of Organization A repeatedly stated that if they had been "allowed" to maintain a stable one or two product line, their efficiency and productivity would have been much improved. The structured climate prohibited organizational adaptability in this simulated marketplace.

A summary of the data on satisfaction and performance in relation to motive arousal follows:

Organization	Motive Aroused	Satisfaction	Performance
A	n Power	Low	Low
B	n Affiliation	High	Low
C	n Achievement	High	High

Conclusions

1. A major conclusion of this experimental study is that distinct organizational climates can be created by varying leadership style. Such climates can be created in a short period of time, and their characteristics are quite stable.

2. Once created, these climates seem to have significant, often dramatic, effects on motivation, and correspondingly on performance and job satisfaction. Each of the three experimentally induced climates aroused a different motivational pattern.

3. Organizational climates may effect changes in seemingly stable personality traits. This conclusion is somewhat tentative. Motive strength, as measured by a standardized thematic apperceptive instrument, was not significantly affected, but certain personality dispositions, measured through a standardized empirically validated personality test, were affected by the climate.

4. These findings suggest that organizational climate is an important variable in the study of human organizations. The climate concept should aid, first, in understanding the impact of organizations on the person and the personality. If significant changes in relatively stable personality factors can be created in *less than two weeks*, then we can imagine how living in a given climate for a *period of years* could dramatically affect many aspects of personal functioning, capacity for productive effort, commitment to long-term relationships (such as friendships and marriage), etc. An understanding of climate will aid in the study of the management process, particularly with regard to the effects different styles of management have on people, on organizational performance, and on organizational health.

References

Atkinson, J. W., ed. (1958) *Motives in Fantasy, Action, and Society.* Princeton: Van Nostrand.

Atkinson, J. W. (1964) *An Introduction to Motivation.* Princeton: Van Nostrand.

Atkinson, J. W., and N. T. Feather, eds. (1966) A *Theory of Achievement Motivation.* New York: Wiley.

Lewin, K., R. Lippitt, and R. K. White (1939) "Patterns of Aggressive Behavior in Experimentally Created 'Social Climates,' " *Journal of Social Psychology*, 10: 271–299.

Litwin, G. H., and R. A. Stringer, Jr. (1968) *Motivation and Organizational Climate.* Boston: Division of Research, Harvard Business School.

McClelland, D. C. (1961) *The Achieving Society.* Princeton: Van Nostrand.

MOTIVATION OF RESEARCH AND DEVELOPMENT ENTREPRENEURS: DETERMINANTS OF COMPANY SUCCESS

HERBERT A. WAINER

IRWIN M. RUBIN

In an attempt to associate need for achievement (*n* Ach) and economic development, McClelland (1961) looks to the entrepreneur as the one who translates *n* Ach into economic development. The entrepreneur in McClelland's scheme is "the man who organizes the firm (the business unit) and/or increases its productive capacity [p. 205]."

The present authors' aim was to test McClelland's macro theory of economic growth at the micro level of organizational performance. The principal interest in considering McClelland's work stems from his discussions of who entrepreneurs are and of their different behavioral styles predicted from differences in need patterns. McClelland's underlying assumption is that entrepreneurs have a high *n* Ach and that in business situations this high *n* Ach will lead them to behave in certain ways and have certain tendencies.

Based on McClelland's discussion, the present authors raised the proposition that the degree to which an entrepreneur is motivated by *n* Ach directly influences his skill as an entrepreneur and consequently his enterprise's performance. The major hypothesis to be tested concerns the relationship between an entrepreneur's level of *n* Ach and his company's performance.

Schrage (1965), in testing the relationship between the entrepreneur's *n* Ach and company performance, reported that companies run by entrepreneurs who have a high *n* Ach tend to have either high profits or losses ($\pm 3\%$ of

Abridged from the *Journal of Applied Psychology*, Vol. 53, No. 3 (1969) by permission of the publisher and authors.

The research presented in this paper was supported in part by grants from the Massachusetts Institute of Technology Center for Space Research and by the National Aeronautics and Space Administration (NsG-235 and NsG-496). However the findings and views reported are those of the authors and do not necessarily reflect those of the supporting agencies. This work was done in part at the Massachusetts Institute of Technology Computation Center.

The authors wish to acknowledge the work done by Charles W. McLaughlin, a master's degree candidate in the Massachusetts Institute of Technology, Sloan School of Management, in the collection of data for this paper.

sales), while those run by low n Ach entrepreneurs tend to have low profits or losses ($\leq 3\%$ of sales). Reanalysis of his data by the present authors sheds considerable doubt on the validity of his findings. The primary source of doubt was a discrepancy between the scores Schrage used for n Ach and those subsequently derived when the same protocols were rescored by the Motivation Research Group at Harvard. The fact that his results departed markedly from established theory further substantiates this concern.

In addition to the relationship between n Ach and company performance, the authors were interested in the interrelationships among three needs, n Ach, need for power (n Pow), and the need for affiliation (n Aff), with respect to company performance. n Pow is defined by Atkinson (1958) as "that disposition, directing behavior toward satisfactions contingent upon the control of the means of influencing another person [p. 105]."

n Aff is concerned with the establishment, maintenance, or restoration of positive affective relationships with other people, that is, friendships. Statements of liking or desire to be liked, accepted, or forgiven are manifestations of this motive (Atkinson, 1958). McClelland's (1961) discussion of the joint product of n Pow and n Aff in relation to dictatorship stimulated this aspect of the inquiry. He found that n Pow was not related to economic growth but was related to style of leadership. More specifically, the combination of a high n Pow and a low n Aff was associated with the tendency of a country to resort to totalitarian methods as a style of leadership.

The present authors propose that n Ach has behavioral manifestations different than either n Pow or n Aff in terms of the individual's relationships with people. n Pow and n Aff are interpersonally oriented needs. Implicit in their definitions is the existence of other human beings whom the n Pow or n Aff motivated individual can influence and control, or with whom he can be friends. n Ach, on the other hand, seems to be a more internalized need. The n Ach motivated individual may need other people to help him satisfy his n Ach, but the nature of his relationship with them, or more appropriately his effectiveness with them, will be determined by other needs. The authors suggest that n Ach is a primary consideration determining noninterpersonally related behavior that leads to high company performance. n Pow and n Aff are primary considerations determining interpersonal behavior that affects company performance. n Pow and n Aff, then, can be looked upon as having strong implications as determinants of management style.

Numerous other attempts have been made to identify those personality traits which differentiate leaders from nonleaders or effective leaders from ineffective leaders. These studies have, in general, failed to find any consistent pattern of differentiating traits. In a broad sense, the present research is analogous to these prior efforts in that it seeks to explain company performance on the basis of certain personality characteristics of the president. Steps were taken, however, in anticipation of two potential problem areas: (*a*) that personality description and measurement themselves are not yet adequate; (*b*) that the groups studied have usually been markedly different from one another and this may have concealed a relation between personality and the exercise of leadership that would have appeared within a more homogeneous set of groups or situations.

The major personality variable of interest in the present study is the need for achievement. On the basis of the existing body of research, McClelland's version of the Thematic Apperception Test (TAT) was deemed a reliable means of measuring n Ach (Atkinson, 1958; McClelland, 1961). With respect to the second problem area, a very homogeneous set of groups has been examined, thus mitigating the potential influence of the "situation."

For these reasons, the focus in this study was upon the new, small, technically based enterprise. The entrepreneur president of such a company has placed himself in a situation where his n Ach, to the extent that it exists, can readily be translated into concrete behavior. He starts the company, hires the people, and motivates them, sells, plans, takes risks, and so on. It is his personality and motivation that mold the company in its every aspect. Furthermore, in such situations, the entrepreneur's efforts and decisions are likely to be very important in determining the initial success of the venture.

Method

Fifty-one small technically based companies in the Boston area comprised the sample. All were at least 4 but less than 10 years old at the time of the study and all were "spin-offs" from one of the Massachusetts Institute of Technology research laboratories or industrial laboratories around the Boston area. They ranged in business activities from service, such as computer software development, to manufacturing, such as special purpose computers and welded modules. Company and entrepreneurial personality information were gathered from the entrepreneur president. The typical entrepreneur, based on the central tendencies for the total sample of entrepreneurs, was approximately 36 years of age when he started his new enterprise, was educated to the master's degree level, and had considerable experience at a technically advanced research laboratory prior to starting his new enterprise. Among the information gathered were company yearly sales figures and scores on McClelland's version of the TAT for each entrepreneur. The yearly sales figures were used as the basis for determining the growth rate, defined in detail below. The index of performance was derived from the growth rate. The TATs were scored for n Ach, n Pow, and n Aff by the Motivation Research Group at Harvard University. The resulting scores were the basis for analysis of the strength of various needs in relation to performance.[1]

TABLE 1

Means, Medians, and Ranges of Variables Measured

Variable	M	Mdn	Range
n Ach	5.9	5.0	− 5 to18
n Pow	9.7	9.5	0 to 19
n Aff	3.5	3.0	0 to 16
Growth rate	.40	.375	0.0 to 2.10

Growth rate is defined as follows: *annual increase in the logarithm of sales volume between the second and most recent year reported.* For example, Com-

[1]Average intercoder reliabilities of scores from the Motivation Research Group are in the high .80 range.

pany A is 7 yr. old. Its second-year sales were $100,000 and its last year (seventh) sales were $950,000. These two sales values are plotted on semilog paper. The growth rate is indicated by the percent rate of change from year to year. This is, of course, constant over the 7 years. The growth rate in this case would be approximately .56. Table 1 summarizes the general characteristics of the four variables with which this paper is concerned. The method of analysis in all cases was a comparison of high, moderate, and low groups.

Results

Need Strength versus Company Performance

The major hypothesis in this study predicts a direct and positive relationship between an entrepreneur's n Ach and the performance of his company. No directional hypotheses were specified concerning the relationships between n Pow, n Aff, and company performance.[2]

Referring to Table 2, it can be seen that, within the range of moderate to high n Ach, a very marked positive relationship exists between n Ach and company performance. The growth rate of those companies led by entrepreneurs with a high n Ach was almost 250% higher (.73 versus .21) than those companies led by entrepreneurs with a moderate n Ach. Here again, however, the relationship is not purely linear since the low n Ach group has a mean performance score slightly *higher* than the moderate n Ach group but still significantly lower than the high n Ach group.

n Pow, as can be seen from Table 2, is completely unrelated to company performance. n Aff, on the other hand, exhibits a mildly negative, nonlinear, relationship to company performance. The data were then examined to see if the observed relationship between n Ach and n Aff influenced the relationship found between n Ach and performance.[3] No such contamination was found. Of those who were classified in the low n Aff group ($n = 13$), only six fell into the high n Ach group. n Ach, in other words, directly affects company performance, independent of its relationship to n Aff.

The results of this section are summarized graphically in Figure 1 (see p. 165). The percentage of companies within each subgroup (high, moderate, low), whose performance is above that of the median for the total sample of entrepreneurs, is plotted for each of the needs. Seventy-nine percent of those companies led by entrepreneurs whose n Ach was high had a growth rate which was above the median for the total sample of entrepreneurs.

Joint Products of Needs versus Performance

The previous section focused on variations in company performance resulting from each of the three needs (n Ach, n Pow, and n Aff) taken singularly. The aim in this section is to explore the question of whether or not any *pattern*

[2]The following are the Kendall Tau correlations between the three needs and company performance (growth rate). n Ach versus performance: $T = .15, p < .08. N = 51$ (one tailed). n Pow versus performance: $T = .05, p < .64, N = .51$. n Aff versus performance: $T = -.11, p < .28, N = 51$.

[3]The three needs were found to be related: n Ach was positively related to n Pow and negatively related to n Aff; n Pow was negatively related to n Aff.

of need strengths appears to be associated with high company performance. In examining the data, it was noticed that, in addition to the very wide differences in company performance noted *between* high, moderate, and low n Ach groups, there existed substantial variations in company performance *within* each of these three groups. In other words, although the high n Ach group exhibited very high performance in comparison with the moderate and low n Ach groups, the range of performance scores *within* the high n Ach group was from .14 to 2.10. Similar within-group ranges were observed in the other two n Ach groupings.

An attempt was made, therefore, to determine whether these within-group variations could be attributed to variations in the strengths of the other two needs being investigated, n Pow and n Aff. The authors have further split the samples into high versus low performers (at the median performance score *within* each n Ach group) and compared levels of n Pow and n Aff within each of these new subgroups.

TABLE 2
Relationship between n Ach, n Pow, and n Aff
and Growth Rate

Need	Code for Mann–Whitney U Results [a]	Strength	Mean Growth Rate
n Ach	A	High ($\geqslant$ 9) $N = 14$	.73
	B	Moderate (4 $\geqslant$ x $\leqslant$ 8) $N = 19$	.21
	C	Low ($\leqslant$ 3) $N = 18$	.36
n Pow	A	High ($\geqslant$ 13) $N = 15$	.38
	B	Moderate (8 $\geqslant$ x $\leqslant$ 12) $N = 19$	.47
	C	Low ($\leqslant$ 7) $N = 17$	.36
n Aff	A	High ($\geqslant$ 4) $N = 20$	.33
	B	Moderate (2 $\geqslant$ x $\leqslant$ 3) $N = 18$	.30
	C	Low ($\leqslant$ 1) $N = 13$	.67

[a]Results of Mann–Whitney U tests: n Ach versus growth rate: A versus B. $p < .0001$; A versus C, $p < .006$; B versus C, $p < .08$, one tailed. n Pow versus growth rate: A versus B, $p < .80$; A versus C, $p < .90$; B versus C, $p < .80$, two-tailed. n Aff versus growth rate; A versus B, $p < .81$; A versus C, $p < 16$; B versus C, $p < .10$, two-tailed.

The following patterns emerge from the data. . . . Within the low n Ach group, variations in performance are unaffected by variations in n Pow or n Aff. Within the moderate n Ach group, n Pow is identical for high versus low performers, while high performers within this group have a significantly higher n Aff. Finally, within the high n Ach group, n Aff is identical for high versus low performers, while high performers within this group have a significantly lower n Pow.

In summary, the *highest performing companies* in this sample were led by entrepreneurs who exhibited a high n Ach and a moderate n Pow. Those en-

FIGURE 1

Percentage of Companies Above Median Growth Rates as a Function
of the President's Achievement, Power, and Affiliation Motivation

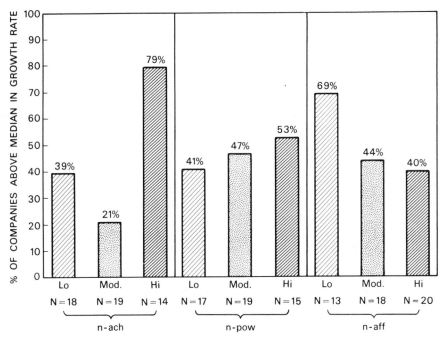

COMPANY PRESIDENT'S MOTIVATION

trepreneurs who had a high *n* Ach coupled with a high *n* Pow performed less
well than their high *n* Ach counterparts who exhibited only a moderate level of
n Pow.[4] Within the moderate *n* Ach group, higher performing companies were
led by entrepreneurs who had a high *n* Aff.

Discussion

The major hypothesis tested in this study predicted a positive relationship
between an entrepreneur's level of *n* Ach and his company's performance. The
authors' findings strongly support the conclusion that high *n* Ach is associated
with high company performance, but the relationship between *n* Ach and performance is not linear across the entire range of *n* Ach scores. The relationship
is markedly linear for the entrepreneurs whose *n* Ach is moderate to high.
However, these entrepreneurs who scored low in *n* Ach were not significantly
lower performers than those whose *n* Ach was moderate.

In an attempt to explain this nonlinearity it seems reasonable to assume that

---

[4]When the authors use the phrases "moderate *n* Pow" or "high *n* Pow," they are using as their
reference point the distribution of scores observed in this study sample. Their specification, for example, of *high n* Pow as being ⩾ 13.0 was made *prior* to the analyses under discussion in this section. Consequently, classification of a mean *n* Pow of 13.1 as high and a mean *n* Pow of 9.4 as
moderate is consistent with their a priori definitions.

other needs or factors are influencing the entrepreneurial behavior of individuals who are not moderate to high in their level of n Ach. It is extremely likely that some threshold level of n Ach is necessary before one could assume that the strength of the need is significantly affecting the individual's behavior. In addition, it is obvious that the authors do not see n Ach as being the only (or for that matter the most important) factor that influences company performance. They are arguing, however, that where the need exists in sufficient strength to influence entrepreneurial behavior significantly, company performance in general will improve.

A secondary aim in this study was to explore the question of whether a certain pattern or combination of needs was most often associated with high performance. In the introduction to this paper, it was suggested that n Pow and n Aff were needs whose behavioral manifestations were interpersonal in character. Satisfaction of these two needs, by definition, involves relationships with other people. n Ach, on the other hand, is much more individualistic in character. Satisfaction of one's n Ach, although often involving contact with other people, has behavioral manifestations which are qualitatively different in nature than either n Pow or n Aff.

The results of this study suggest that the combination of a high n Ach and a moderate n Pow characterizes the highest performing companies in the sample. In other words, a high (as opposed to moderate) level of n Pow appeared to counterbalance to some extent the positive benefits of a high level of n Ach.

One possible explanation for this finding lies in the relationship between n Pow and various styles of leadership. the lower an individual's n Pow, the more permissive or laissez-faire his style of leadership, the higher his n Pow, the more autocratic or authoritarian his style of leadership. The middle of the n Pow spectrum represents a mixed influence of the two extreme styles which is best described as democratic.[5] Prior research (Lippitt and White, 1958) has suggested that in certain situations the most effective leadership style is democratic and that performance of groups controlled in this manner is better than that of groups controlled by either of the other two styles.

Somewhat more difficult to explain is the finding concerning the positive differential effect on company performance, within the moderate n Ach group, of a high versus low n Aff level. It may be that for those individuals who have only a moderate level of n Ach, a high level of n Aff enables them to form close interpersonal relationships with their colleagues. In this way, the moderate n Ach individual may be able to acquire the assistance he needs from his colleagues, some of whom may well have a higher level of n Ach than he himself has.

Interpretations in this area of need combinations must be viewed, at this point, as speculative and suggestive of further research. Analysis of the results of this study indicates that more complex relationships do have to be examined if a realistic view of performance determined by personality is to be gained. Future research should include replications of this study and the use of larger samples for the investigation of these hypotheses.

---

[5]The authors have assumed, of course, that high n Pow leaders are more likely to exercise an autocratic style of leadership and low n Pow leaders a laissez-faire style.

References

Atkinson, J. W. *Motives in Fantasy, Action and Society.* Princeton, N.J.: Van Nostrand, 1958.

Lippitt, R., and R. K. White. "An Experimental Study of Leadership and Group Life." In *Readings in Social Psychology.* New York: Holt, Rinehart & Winston, 1958.

McClelland, D. C. *The Achieving Society.* Princeton, N.J.: Van Nostrand, 1961.

Schrage, H. "The R & D Entrepreneur: Profile of Success." *Harvard Business Review,* 1965.

EVOLUTION AND REVOLUTION AS ORGANIZATIONS GROW

LARRY E. GREINER

A small research company chooses too complicated and formalized an organization structure for its young age and limited size. It flounders in rigidity and bureaucracy for several years and is finally acquired by a larger company.

Key executives of a retail store chain hold on to an organization structure long after it has served its purpose, because their power is derived from this structure. The company eventually goes into bankruptcy.

A large bank disciplines a "rebellious" manager who is blamed for current control problems, when the underlying cause is centralized procedures that are holding back expansion into new markets. Many younger managers subsequently leave the bank, competition moves in, and profits are still declining.

The problems of these companies, like those of many others, are rooted more in past decisions than in present events or outside market dynamics. Historical forces do indeed shape the future growth of organizations. Yet management, in its haste to grow, often overlooks such critical developmental questions as: Where has our organization been? Where is it now? And what do the answers to these questions mean for where we are going? Instead, its gaze is fixed outward toward the environment and the future—as if more precise market projections will provide a new organizational identity.

Companies fail to see that many clues to their future success lie within their own organizations and their evolving states of development. Moreover, the inability of management to understand its organization development problems can result in a company becoming "frozen" in its present stage of evolution or, ultimately, in failure, regardless of market opportunities.

My position in this article is that the future of an organization may be less determined by outside forces than it is by the organization's history. In stressing the force of history on an organization, I have drawn from the legacies of European psychologists (their thesis being that individual behavior is determined primarily by previous events and experiences, not by what lies ahead). Extending this analogy of individual development to the problems of organization development, I shall discuss a series of developmental phases through which growing companies tend to pass. But, first, let me provide two definitions.

1. The term *evolution* is used to describe prolonged periods of growth where no major upheaval occurs in organization practices.
2. The term *revolution* is used to describe those periods of substantial turmoil in organizational life.

As a company progresses through developmental phases, each evolutionary period creates its own revolution. For instance, centralized practices eventually lead to demands for decentralization. Moreover, the nature of management's solution to each revolutionary period determines whether a company will move forward into its next stage of evolutionary growth. As I shall show later, there are at least five phases of organization development, each characterized by both an evolution and a revolution.

Key Forces in Development

During the past few years a small amount of research knowledge about the phases of organization development has been building. Some of this research is very quantitative, such as time-series analyses that reveal patterns of economic performance over time.[1] The majority of studies, however, are case-oriented and use company records and interviews to reconstruct a rich picture of corporate development.[2] Yet both types of research tend to be heavily empirical without attempting more generalized statements about the overall process of development.

A notable exception is the historical work of Alfred D. Chandler, Jr., in his book *Strategy and Structure*.[3] This study depicts four very broad and general phases in the lives of four large U.S. companies. It proposes that outside market opportunities determine a company's strategy, which in turn, determines the company's organization structure. This thesis has a valid ring for the four companies examined by Chandler, largely because they developed in a time of explosive markets and technological advances. But more recent evidence suggests that organization structure may be less malleable than Chandler assumed; in fact, structure can play a critical role in influencing corporate strategy. It is this reverse emphasis on how organization structure affects future growth which is highlighted in the model presented in this article.

From an analysis of recent studies,[4] five key dimensions emerge as essential for building a model of organization development:

1. Age of the organization.
2. Size of the organization.
3. Stages of evolution.
4. Stages of revolution.
5. Growth rate of the industry.

I shall describe each of these elements separately, but first note their combined effect as illustrated in Exhibit 1. Note especially how each dimension influences the other over time; when all five elements begin to interact, a more complete and dynamic picture of organizational growth emerges.

After describing these dimensions and their interconnections, I shall discuss each evolutionary revolutionary phase of development and show (a) how each stage of evolution breeds its own revolution, and (b) how management solutions to each revolution determine the next stage of evolution.

Age of the Organization

The most obvious and essential dimension for any model of development is the life span of an organization (represented as the horizontal axis in Exhibit 1). All historical studies gather data from various points in time and then make comparisons. From these observations, it is evident that the same organization practices are not maintained throughout a long time span. This makes a most basic point: management problems and principles are rooted in time. The concept of decentralization, for example, can have meaning for describing corporate practices at one time period but loses its descriptive power at another.

The passage of time also contributes to the institutionalization of managerial attitudes. As a result, employee behavior becomes not only more predictable but also more difficult to change when attitudes are outdated.

Size of the Organization

This dimension is depicted as the vertical axis in Exhibit 1. A company's problems and solutions tend to change markedly as the number of employees

EXHIBIT 1

Model of Organization Development

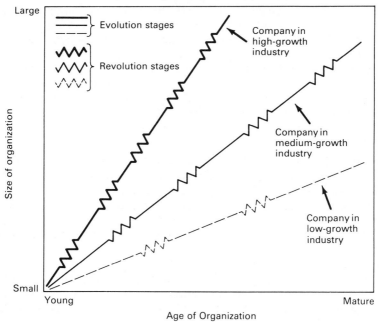

and sales volume increase. Thus, time is not the only determinant of structure; in fact, organizations that do not grow in size can retain many of the same management issues and practices over lengthy periods. In addition to increased size, however, problems of coordination and communication magnify, new functions emerge, levels in the management hierarchy multiply, and jobs become more interrelated.

Stages of Evolution

As both age and size increase, another phenomenon becomes evident: the prolonged growth that I have termed the evolutionary period. Most growing organizations do not expand for two years and then retreat for one year; rather, those that survive a crisis usually enjoy four to eight years of continuous growth without a major economic setback or severe internal disruption. The term evolution seems appropriate for describing these quieter periods because only modest adjustments appear necessary for maintaining growth under the same overall pattern of management.

Stages of Revolution

Smooth evolution is not inevitable; it cannot be assumed that organization growth is linear. *Fortune's* "500" list, for example, has had significant turnover during the last 50 years. Thus we find evidence from numerous case histories which reveals periods of substantial turbulence spaced between smoother periods of evolution.

I have termed these turbulent times the periods of revolution because they typically exhibit a serious upheaval of management practices. Traditional management practices, which were appropriate for a smaller size and earlier time, are brought under scrutiny by frustrated top managers and disillusioned lower-level managers. During such periods of crisis, a number of companies fail—those unable to abandon past practices and effect major organization changes are likely either to fold or to level off in their growth rates.

The critical task for management in each revolutionary period is to find a new set of organization practices that will become the basis for managing the next period of evolutionary growth. Interestingly enough, these new practices eventually sow their own seeds of decay and lead to another period of revolution. Companies therefore experience the irony of seeing a major solution in one time period become a major problem at a latter date.

Growth Rate of the Industry

The speed at which an organization experiences phases of evolution and revolution is closely related to the market environment of its industry. For example, a company in a rapidly expanding market will have to add employees rapidly; hence, the need for new organization structures to accommodate large staff increases is accelerated. While evolutionary periods tend to be relatively short in fast-growing industries, much longer evolutionary periods occur in mature or slowly growing industries.

Evolution can also be prolonged, and revolutions delayed, when profits come easily. For instance, companies that make grievous errors in a rewarding industry can still look good on their profit and loss statements; thus they can avoid a change in management practices for a longer period. The aerospace industry in its infancy is an example. Yet revolutionary periods still occur, as one did in aerospace when profit opportunities began to dry up. Revolutions seem to be much more severe and difficult to resolve when the market environment is poor.

Phases of Growth

With the foregoing framework in mind, let us now examine in depth the five specific phases of evolution and revolution. As shown in Exhibit 2, each evolutionary period is characterized by the dominant *management style* used to achieve growth, while each revolutionary period is characterized by the dominant *management problem* that must be solved before growth can continue. The patterns presented in Exhibit 2 seem to be typical for companies in industries with moderate growth over a long time period; companies in faster growing industries tend to experience all five phases more rapidly, while those in slower growing industries encounter only two or three phases over many years.

It is important to note that *each phase is both an effect of the previous phase and a cause for the next phase.* For example, the evolutionary management style in Phase 3 of the exhibit is "delegation," which grows out of, and becomes the solution to, demands for greater "autonomy" in the preceding

EXHIBIT 2

The Five Phases of Growth

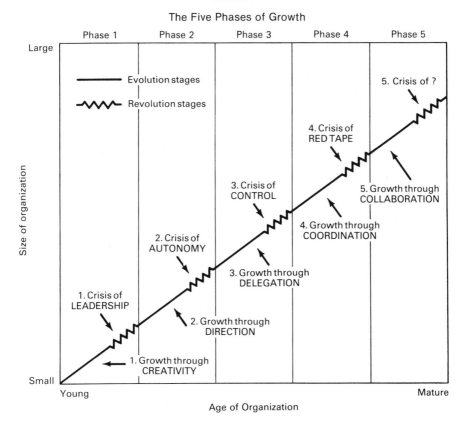

Phase 2 revolution. The style of delegation used in Phase 3, however, eventually provokes a major revolutionary crisis that is characterized by attempts to regain control over the diversity created through increased delegation.

The principal implication of each phase is that management actions are narrowly prescribed if growth is to occur. For example, a company experiencing an autonomy crisis in Phase 2 cannot return to directive management for a solution—it must adopt a new style of delegation in order to move ahead.

Phase 1: Creativity . . .

In the birth stage of an organization, the emphasis is on creating both a product and a market. Here are the characteristics of the period of creative evolution:

- The company's founders are usually technically or entrepreneurially oriented, and they disdain management activities; their physical and mental energies are absorbed entirely in making and selling a new product.
- Communication among employees is frequent and informal.
- Long hours of work are rewarded by modest salaries and the promise of ownership benefits.
- Control of activities comes from immediate marketplace feedback; the management acts as the customers react.

. . . *& the leadership crisis:* All of the foregoing individualistic and creative activities are essential for the company to get off the ground. But therein lies the problem. As the company grows, larger production runs require knowledge about the efficiencies of manufacturing. Increased numbers of employees cannot be managed exclusively through informal communication; new employees are not motivated by an intense dedication to the product or organization. Additional capital must be secured, and new accounting procedures are needed for financial control.

Thus the founders find themselves burdened with unwanted management responsibilities. So they long for the "good old days," still trying to act as they did in the past. And conflicts between the harried leaders grow more intense.

At this point a crisis of leadership occurs, which is the onset of the first revolution. Who is to lead the company out of confusion and solve the managerial problems confronting it? Quite obviously, a strong manager is needed who has the necessary knowledge and skill to introduce new business techniques. But this is easier said than done. The founders often hate to step aside even though they are probably temperamentally unsuited to be managers. So here is the first critical developmental choice—to locate and install a strong business manager who is acceptable to the founders and who can pull the organization together.

Phase 2: Direction . . .

Those companies that survive the first phase by installing a capable business manager usually embark on a period of sustained growth under able and directive leadership. Here are the characteristics of this evolutionary period:

- A functional organization structure is introduced to separate manufacturing from marketing activities, and job assignments become more specialized.
- Accounting systems for inventory and purchasing are introduced.
- Incentives, budgets, and work standards are adopted.
- Communication becomes more formal and impersonal as a hierarchy of titles and positions builds.
- The new manager and his key supervisors take most of the responsibility for instituting direction, while lower-level supervisors are treated more as functional specialists than as autonomous decision-making managers.

. . . *& the autonomy crisis:* Although the new directive techniques channel employee energy more efficiently into growth, they eventually become inappropriate for controlling a larger, more diverse and complex organization. Lower-level employees find themselves restricted by a cumbersome and centralized hierarchy. They have come to possess more direct knowledge about markets and machinery than do the leaders at the top; consequently, they feel torn between following procedures and taking initiative on their own.

Thus the second revolution is imminent as a crisis develops from demands for greater autonomy on the part of lower-level managers. The solution adopted by most companies is to move toward greater delegation. Yet it is difficult for top managers who were previously successful at being directive to give up responsibility. Moreover, lower-level managers are not accustomed to making decisions for themselves. As a result, numerous companies flounder during this revolutionary period, adhering to centralized methods while lower-level employees grow more disenchanted and leave the organization.

Phase 3: Delegation . . .

The next era of growth evolves from the successful application of a decentralized organization structure. It exhibits these characteristics:

- Much greater responsibility is given to the managers of plants and market territories.
- Profit centers and bonuses are used to stimulate motivation.
- The top executives at headquarters restrain themselves to managing by exception, based on periodic reports from the field.
- Management often concentrates on making new acquisitions which can be lined up beside other decentralized units.
- Communication from the top is infrequent, usually by correspondence, telephone, or brief visits to field locations.

The delegation stage proves useful for gaining expansion through heightened motivation at lower levels. Decentralized managers with greater authority and incentive are able to penetrate larger markets, respond faster to customers, and develop new products.

. . . *& the control crisis:* A serious problem eventually evolves, however, as top executives sense that they are losing control over a highly diversified field operation. Autonomous field managers prefer to run their own shows without coordinating plans, money, technology, and manpower with the rest of the organization. Freedom breeds a parochial attitude.

Hence, the Phase 3 revolution is under way when top management seeks to regain control over the total company. Some top managements attempt a return to centralized management, which usually fails because of the vast scope of operations. Those companies that move ahead find a new solution in the use of special coordination techniques.

Phase 4: Coordination . . .

During this phase, the evolutionary period is characterized by the use of formal systems for achieving greater coordination and by top executives taking responsibility for the initiation and administration of these new systems. For example:

- Decentralized units are merged into product groups.
- Formal planning procedures are established and intensively reviewed.
- Numerous staff personnel are hired and located at headquarters to initiate companywide programs of control and review for line managers.
- Capital expenditures are carefully weighed and parceled out across the organization.
- Each product group is treated as an investment center where return on invested capital is an important criterion used in allocating funds.
- Certain technical functions, such as data processing, are centralized at headquarters, while daily operating decisions remain decentralized.
- Stock options and companywide profit sharing are used to encourage identity with the firm as a whole.

All of these new coordination systems prove useful for achieving growth through more efficient allocation of a company's limited resources. They prompt field managers to look beyond the needs of their local units. While these managers still have much decision-making responsibility, they learn to justify their actions more carefully to a "watchdog" audience at headquarters.

. . . & the red-tape crisis: But a lack of confidence gradually builds between line and staff, and between headquarters and the field. The proliferation of systems and programs begins to exceed its utility; a red-tape crisis is created. Line managers, for example, increasingly resent heavy staff direction from those who are not familiar with local conditions. Staff people, on the other hand, complain about uncooperative and uninformed line managers. Together both groups criticize the bureaucratic paper system that has evolved. Procedures take precedence over problem solving, and innovation is dampened. In short, the organization has become too large and complex to be managed through formal programs and rigid systems. The Phase 4 revolution is under way.

Phase 5: Collaboration . . .

The last observable phase in previous studies emphasizes strong interpersonal collaboration in an attempt to overcome the red-tape crisis. Where Phase 4 was managed more through formal systems and procedures, Phase 5 emphasizes greater spontaneity in management action through teams and the skillful confrontation of interpersonal differences. Social control and self-discipline take over from formal control. This transition is especially difficult for those experts who created the old systems as well as for those line managers who relied on formal methods for answers.

The Phase 5 evolution, then, builds around a more flexible and behavioral approach to management. Here are its characteristics:

- The focus is on solving problems quickly through team action.
- Teams are combined across functions for task-group activity.
- Headquarters staff experts are reduced in number, reassigned, and combined in interdisciplinary teams to consult with, not to direct, field units.
- A matrix-type structure is frequently used to assemble the right teams for the appropriate problems.
- Previous formal systems are simplified and combined into single multipurpose systems.
- Conferences of key managers are held frequently to focus on major problem issues.
- Educational programs are utilized to train managers in behavioral skills for achieving better teamwork and conflict resolution.
- Real-time information systems are integrated into daily decision making.
- Economic rewards are geared more to team performance than to individual achievement.
- Experiments in new practices are encouraged throughout the organization.

. . . & the ? crisis: What will be the revolution in response to this stage of evolution? Many large U.S. companies are now in the Phase 5 evolutionary stage, so the answers are critical. While there is little clear evidence, I imagine the revolution will center around the "psychological saturation" of employees who grow emotionally and physically exhausted by the intensity of teamwork and the heavy pressure for innovative solutions.

My hunch is that the Phase 5 revolution will be solved through new structures and programs that allow employees to periodically rest, reflect, and revitalize themselves. We may even see companies with dual organization structures: a "habit" structure for getting the daily work done, and a "reflective" structure for stimulating perspective and personal enrichment. Employees could then move back and forth between the two structures as their energies are dissipated and refueled.

One European organization has implemented just such a structure. Five reflective groups have been established outside the regular structure for the purpose of continuously evaluating five task activities basic to the organization. They report directly to the managing director, although their reports are made public throughout the organization. Membership in each group includes all levels and functions, and employees are rotated through these groups on a six-month basis.

Other concrete examples now in practice include providing sabbaticals for employees, moving managers in and out of "hot spot" jobs, establishing a four-day workweek, assuring job security, building physical facilities for relaxation *during* the working day, making jobs more interchangeable, creating an extra team on the assembly line so that one team is always off for reeducation, and switching to longer vacations and more flexible working hours.

The Chinese practice of requiring executives to spend time periodically on lower-level jobs may also be worth a nonideological evaluation. For too long U.S. management has assumed that career progress should be equated with an upward path toward title, salary, and power. Could it be that some vice presidents of marketing might just long for, and even benefit from, temporary duty in the field sales organization?

Implications of History

Let me now summarize some important implications for practicing managers. First, the main features of this discussion are depicted in Exhibit 3, which shows the specific management actions that characterize each growth phase. These actions are also the solutions which ended each preceding revolutionary period.

In one sense, I hope that many readers will react to my model by calling it obvious and natural for depicting the growth of an organization. To me this type of reaction is a useful test of the model's validity.

But at a more reflective level I imagine some of these reactions are more hindsight than foresight. Those experienced managers who have been through a developmental sequence can empathize with it now, but how did they react when in the middle of a stage of evolution or revolution? They can probably recall the limits of their own developmental understanding at that time. Perhaps they resisted desirable changes or were even swept emotionally into a revolution without being able to propose constructive solutions. So let me offer some explicit guidelines for managers of growing organizations to keep in mind.

EXHIBIT 3

Organization Practices during Evolution in the Five Phases of Growth

Category	PHASE 1	PHASE 2	PHASE 3	PHASE 4	PHASE 5
MANAGEMENT FOCUS	Make & sell	Efficiency of operations	Expansion of market	Consolidation of organization	Problem solving & innovation
ORGANIZATION STRUCTURE	Informal	Centralized & functional	Decentralized & geographical	Line-staff & product groups	Matrix of teams
TOP MANAGEMENT STYLE	Individualistic & entrepreneurial	Directive	Delegative	Watchdog	Participative
CONTROL SYSTEM	Market results	Standards & cost centers	Reports & profit centers	Plans & investment centers	Mutual goal setting
MANAGEMENT REWARD EMPHASIS	Ownership	Salary & merit increases	Individual bonus	Profit sharing & stock options	Team bonus

Know Where You Are in the Developmental Sequence

Every organization and its component parts are at different stages of development. The task of top management is to be aware of these stages; otherwise, it may not recognize when the time for change has come, or it may act to impose the wrong solution.

Top leaders should be ready to work with the flow of the tide rather than against it; yet they should be cautious, since it is tempting to skip phases out of impatience. Each phase results in certain strengths and learning experiences in the organization that will be essential for success in subsequent phases. A child prodigy, for example, may be able to read like a teenager, but he cannot behave like one until he ages through a sequence of experiences.

I also doubt that managers can or should act to avoid revolutions. Rather, these periods of tension provide the pressure, ideas, and awareness that afford a platform for change and the introduction of new practices.

Recognize the Limited Range of Solutions

In each revolutionary stage it becomes evident that this stage can be ended only by certain specific solutions; moreover, these solutions are different from those which were applied to the problems of the preceding revolution. Too often it is tempting to choose solutions that were tried before, which makes it impossible for a new phase of growth to evolve.

Management must be prepared to dismantle current structures before the revolutionary stage becomes too turbulent. Top managers, realizing that their own managerial styles are no longer appropriate, may even have to take themselves out of leadership positions. A good Phase 2 manager facing Phase 3 might be wise to find another Phase 2 organization that better fits his talents, either outside the company or with one of its newer subsidiaries.

Finally, evolution is not an automatic affair; it is a contest for survival. To move ahead, companies must consciously introduce planned structures that not only are solutions to a current crisis but also are fitted to the *next* phase of growth. This requires considerable self-awareness on the part of top management, as well as great interpersonal skill in persuading other managers that change is needed.

Realize That Solutions Breed New Problems

Managers often fail to realize that organizational solutions create problems for the future (i.e., a decision to delegate eventually causes a problem of control). Historical actions are very much determinants of what happens to the company at a much later date.

An awareness of this effect should help managers to evaluate company problems with greater historical understanding instead of "pinning the blame" on a current development. Better yet, managers should be in a position to *predict* future problems, and thereby to prepare solutions and coping strategies before a revolution gets out of hand.

A management that is aware of the problems ahead could well decide *not* to grow. Top managers may, for instance, prefer to retain the informal practices of a small company, knowing that this way of life is inherent in the organization's limited size, not in their congenial personalities. If they choose to grow, they may do themselves out of a job and a way of life they enjoy.

And what about the managements of very large organizations? Can they find new solutions for continued phases of evolution? Or are they reaching a stage where the government will act to break them up because they are too large?

Concluding Note

Clearly, there is still much to learn about processes of development in organizations. The phases outlined here are only five in number and are still only approximations. Researchers are just beginning to study the specific developmental problems of structure, control, rewards, and management style in different industries and in a variety of cultures.

One should not, however, wait for conclusive evidence before educating managers to think and act from a developmental perspective. The critical dimension of time has been missing for too long from our management theories and practices. The intriguing paradox is that by learning more about history we may do a better job in the future.

Footnotes

1. See, for example, William H. Starbuck, "Organizational Metamorphosis," in *Promising Research Directions,* eds., R. W. Millman and M. P. Hottenstein (Tempe, Ariz., Academy of Management, 1968), p. 113.

2. See, for example, The *Grangesberg* case series, prepared by C. Roland Christensen and Bruce R. Scott, Case Clearing House, Harvard Business School.

3. *Strategy and Structure: Chapters in the History of the American Industrial Enterprise* (Cambridge, Mass., The M.I.T. Press, 1962).

4. I have drawn on many sources for evidence: (a) numerous cases collected at the Harvard Business School; (b) *Organization Growth and Development,* ed. William H. Starbuck (Middlesex, England, Penguin Books, Ltd., 1971), where several studies are cited; and (c) articles published in journals, such as Lawrence E. Fouraker and John M. Stopford, "Organization Structure and the Multinational Strategy," *Administrative Science Quarterly,* 1968, Vol. 13, No. 1, p. 47; and Malcolm S. Salter, "Management Appraisal and Reward Systems," *Journal of Business Policy,* 1971, Vol. 1, No. 4.

⒗ motivation and the design of work

TURNING PEOPLE ON TO WORK

WILLIAM A. PASMORE

It has been said that a manager's primary task is to get things done through other people. Whether or not one accepts this to be true, it is apparent that motivating people to perform well has become a major managerial task. Most business schools now require their students to take courses in the behavioral sciences, many organizations have undertaken programs to tap the potential of their human resources, and scholars have written thousands of articles on the subject. After nearly four decades of intensive study of human behavior in organizations beginning with the classic Hawthorne studies in 1939, it seems appropriate to pause for a moment to consider what we have learned.[1] This article reviews several of the most popular methods of organizational change and seeks to answer the perennial question, "What does it take to turn people on to their work?"

At the most basic level, it would appear that in this country and others, the assumption has been made that people work to satisfy various needs or desires; these needs may be for financial rewards and the things that money can buy, or they may be for less tangible rewards, such as recognition or personal development. The general motivational theory that best defines this assumption is expectancy theory.[2] Briefly, expectancy theory states that a person will perform some behavior *if* that behavior is likely to lead to some desired outcome. While this theory helps us to understand why people seek employment in the first place, it tells us little about why people sometimes cease to work toward organizational goals or even begin to work *against* them. Reports of high levels of absenteeism, turnover, and even sabotage are not uncommon; what is it that turns people off their jobs, and what can managers do to turn them back on?

Prepared specifically for this volume.

[1]Roethlisberger, F., and Dickson, W. *Management and the Worker.* Cambridge, Mass.: Harvard University Press, 1939.

[2]Mitchell, T. Expectancy Model of Sub Satisfaction, Occupational Preference and Effort: A Theoretical, Methodological and Empirical Appraisal. *Psychological Bulletin,* 1974.

Probably the best known answers to these questions have been provided by Maslow and further elaborated by Herzberg.[3,4] Their theories propose that human needs are arranged in an hierarchy, and that lower level needs (for survival and security) must be satisfied before higher-level needs (for interaction with others, recognition, and self-actualization) become important motivators of behavior. The reason why many people lose interest in their work, according to these theories, is that their jobs only offer satisfaction of lower-level needs. When satisfied, these needs no longer motivate behavior—they no longer make the employee *want* to do more than the minimum required. To tap human potential, the theories contend that opportunities must be provided for employees to satisfy their higher-level needs through work by adding more responsibility, self-direction, and developmental scope to the job. This process of building opportunities into jobs for the satisfaction of higher-level needs has been termed "job enrichment" and is one of the primary methods of organization improvement in use at the present time.

Although the theories of Maslow and Herzberg take us a step closer to an answer to our initial query, they do not help to explain why some people decide to make their livings laying bricks while others become concert pianists; nor do they help us understand why two people, doing the same job under the same conditions, may react to the job in different ways. What the need-hierarchy theories do not state explicitly is that satisfaction of higher-level needs tends to be an extremely idiosyncratic affair. What one individual desires in the way of recognition, responsibility, or achievement may be quite different from that of another, depending upon each person's background, values, culture, upbringing, prior experiences, and so forth. This may be why some people, seemingly established in secure careers, make dramatic shifts in their vocations at midlife.

In addition, an individual's decision concerning achievement of organizational goals will be impacted by his/her immediate surroundings. The norms of the work group may be for high or low productivity; the supervisor may or may not provide adequate training and assistance; the technology may facilitate goal accomplishment if it runs smoothly or may frustrate all efforts to achieve output goals if it is in a state of disrepair. All these factors and others in the immediate work context tend to influence the level of effort put forth by employees.

Codifying individual value systems, backgrounds, experiences, or immediate work situations is a complex task which applied behavioral scientists have only begun to undertake and may never complete. Because we cannot determine what each individual in an organization desires and design jobs specifically for each person, we instead develop methods of improving organizations which allow organizational members some discretion in influencing their work experiences and rewards. Naturally, limits must be imposed on individual freedom to assure that organizational goals be met; it simply would not do to have a bricklayer practicing to become a concert pianist on company time. What is important is that the individual have at least *some* desire to be engaged in the type of work being performed and that the individual somehow be able to influence the actual work being performed and the rewards received

[3]Maslow, A. H. *Motivation and Personality.* New York, Harper & Row, 1954.
[4]Herzberg, F. One more time: How do you motivate employees? *Harvard Business Review,* 1968, 46, 53–62.

for the completion of that work. If managers or consultants make assumptions about what specific opportunities turn people on to work and design jobs accordingly without employee input, the important motivation that comes from personal expression in designing one's own job will probably be lost.

Several important themes run through the preceding discussion. First, that except for lower-level needs, the satisfaction of human needs through work is an idiosyncratic affair; what is rewarding to one individual may not be to another. Therefore, if an employee is to be *internally* motivated to achieve organizational goals, there must be some latitude for *employee involvement* in work design and associated reward systems.

Second, it is apparent that the satisfaction of employee needs *must* be provided *through the work itself:* what an employee actually does from day to day. Basically, no matter how innovative an organization is in terms of its products, technology, or attitudes toward employees, a boring job will still be boring and nonmotivating. Therefore, any attempts to improve employee attitudes and performance without affecting the work itself are missing the mark, and probably will not lead to long-term motivation and productivity.

Finally, it was noted that the interaction of individualistic employee needs and the work itself takes place in an *immediate work context.* The immediate work context is the setting in which the work is performed and includes, among other things, norms of the work group concerning productivity and group-member behavior, the quality of the relationship between employees and management, the way the work is laid out, and the quality of equipment and materials. Because of these factors, every organization presents a unique work setting; but more than that, these things mediate each *individual's* reaction to the organization. Although little research has been performed on the impact of these factors, it may be assumed that in general an individual will find the immediate work context to be either supportive or *nonsupportive;* if nonsupportive, the employee will find it difficult to achieve the organization's goals. For example, the equipment and materials used may be poor, thereby making it difficult to achieve standard production rates; or, the work group may exert subtle pressures on an individual to limit the amount produced. In such cases it is unlikely that the individual will be able to satisfy important higher-order needs that come from doing a job well, being part of a successful organization, and so forth.

In summary, it is suggested here that turning people on to their work requires a combination of factors. Assuming that basic lower-level needs are met, the *work itself* must allow opportunities for employees to satisfy certain higher-order needs. At least in part, *the employee must be involved* in determining what needs are important and what opportunities should be made available for the satisfaction of those needs. Finally, the *immediate* work context must provide support for the person to take advantage of the opportunities created to satisfy through work the needs that have been identified.

What methods have been developed by applied behavioral scientists to accomplish the goals of satisfying employee needs while achieving organizational objectives? Needless to say, there have been many, and they vary in their scope and ease of application. Incentive systems have been created; educational programs have been offered; sports equipment and athletic contests have been provided; music has been piped into the plants; the list seems almost endless. At the same time, only a handful of techniques exist which are based on the principles outlined earlier in this paper: namely, that once lower-level needs are satisfied, organizations can only be successful by providing opportunities for employees to satisfy their higher-order needs while working toward organizational goals. These techniques are grouped together under the heading "organizational development" and have been described in detail by a number of authors.[5-8]

For the purposes of this paper, only three of these techniques will be reviewed in detail. These are: (1) *data feedback* methods, in which information is collected from employees concerning the state of the organization which is then used for collaborative problem solving; (2) *job enrichment* techniques, which are based on Herzberg's theory described earlier and attempt to add more responsibility, variety, autonomy, and feedback to jobs; and (3) *sociotechnical system* interventions, which adjust the technology of the organization and the way work is done to meet the needs of employees.

These techniques were chosen because of their widespread use and the difference in their scope; data feedback interventions focus almost entirely on organizational communication and problem solving; job enrichment interventions focus on individual jobs; and sociotechnical system interventions are aimed at human and technical factors throughout an organization. Each technique will be evaluated in terms of how well it meets the criteria for turning people on to work and in terms of its impact on productivity. It will be demonstrated that there are trade-offs to be considered in the use of each, and that in the ideal, some combination of these aproaches is probably best.

A number of organization development methods have been termed *human process* interventions because they seek organization improvement through increased communication and problem-solving activities.[9] Data feedback interventions fall under this heading, as do sensitivity training, team building, grid training, role clarification, management by objectives, and other techniques. While some changes in the work itself may result from the application of these methods, their primary targets are more often employee attitudes, supervisory behaviors, or company policies, rules, and procedures.

Exactly how do data feedback interventions work and how effective are they? A model of the strategy underlying data feedback interventions is shown in Figure 1. As indicated, the data feedback method calls for the completion of a survey or interview by employees at all levels of the organization. Excellent descriptions of the next steps have been provided by others, so only a brief description of the actual process will be presented here.[10-12] Once collected, data

[5]French, W., and Bell, C. *Organization Development.* Englewood Cliffs, N.J.: Prentice-Hall, 1973.

[6]Friedlander, F., and Brown, L. D. Organization development. *Annual Review of Psychology,* 1974, 25, 313–341.

[7]Bennis, W. *Organization Development: Its Nature, Origins and Prospects.* Reading, Mass.: Addison-Wesley, 1969.

[8]Fordyce, J., and Weil, R. *Managing with People.* Reading, Mass.: Addison-Wesley, 1971.

[9]Friedlander, F., and Brown, L. D., op. cit.

[10]Neff, F. Survey Research: A tool for problem diagnosis and improvement in organizations. In S. Miller, and A. Gouldner, (eds.), *Applied Sociology.* New York: Free Press, 1965, 23–38.

[11]Miles, M., Horstein, H., Callahan, D. Calder, P., and Schiavo, R. The consequences of survey feedback: Theory and evaluation. In W. Bennis, K. Benne, and R. Chin, (eds.), *The Planning of Change.* New York: Holt, Rinehart and Winston, 1969, 456–468.

[12]Bowers, D., and Franklin, J. Survey guided development: Using human resource management in organizational change. *Journal of Contemporary Business,* 1972, *1,* 43–55.

FIGURE 1
Data Feedback Change Strategy

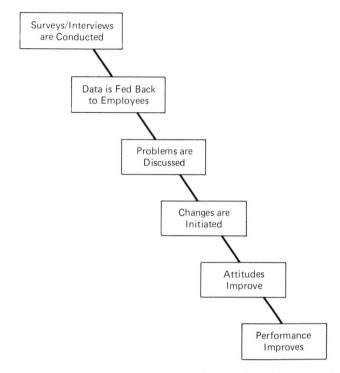

are analyzed for each organizational family, which consists of a supervisor and all those who report directly to him/her. The feedback of the information is conducted by each supervisor with the help of a consultant, typically in what is referred to as a "waterfall" pattern. Beginning at the top of the organization, each supervisor discusses the feedback with his/her subordinates, who in turn feed the information to the next lower organizational level. Through this process, each supervisor participates in two meetings and is thereby provided with increased understanding of the data. Organizational communication increases at the same time, as information flows down the hierarchy and suggestions for change travel upward.

Another survey feedback technique, developed by Tolchinsky and Pasmore, has been named "bottom-up" since information is fed back to the lowest organizational levels first.[13] This avoids any "filtering" of the data by management and therefore tends to be perceived as more participative by employees. In addition, this method allows employees to formulate action proposals to be considered by each level of management along with the data.

In either method, during the feedback sessions the consultant has the important responsibility of ensuring that the issues generated by the data are transformed into proposals for change. The consultant rarely suggests what changes are needed; rather, it is said that he/she acts as a "catalyst" or "trans-

[13]Tolchinsky, P., and Pasmore, W. *Survey Feedback from the Bottom Up.* Purdue University, Department of Administrative Sciences, 1977.

ducer" in the transformation of data to action. By assisting in the clarification of information, stimulating discussion, and focusing the energy of the group on identifying problems and working out solutions, the consultant attempts to maximize *employee involvement* in the problem-solving process.

Still referring to Figure 1, other problems are discussed and changes initiated in response to employees' suggestions. These changes should lead to improved attitudes on the part of employees, which in turn are expected to lead to improved performance.

From this introduction it should be apparent that data feedback techniques are quite participative in their approach to change, in contrast to the more unilateral work redesign methods to be discussed shortly. If one strongly endorses the Lewinian notion that participation in a change process facilitates acceptance of the change, one would expect that data feedback techniques would be quite successful in securing organizational improvement. Nevertheless, while there is evidence that survey feedback interventions in particular result in improved employee attitudes, there is little evidence that data feedback or other human process interventions affect organizational productivity.

In a large study with the Detroit Edison Company, Baumgartel was able to demonstrate improved attitudes in groups receiving survey feedback treatments, with the greatest attitudinal changes occurring in those departments which received the most intensive feedback.[14] Mann studied six accounting departments of a large firm.[15] Four of the departments engaged in extensive survey feedback activities and the other two acted as controls. Mann reported more significant positive attitude changes as well as greater perceptions of organizational change by employees in the experimental units as compared to the control units. Chase reported that the survey feedback method tended to equalize power between supervisors and emloyees, and Brown found evidence that participant involvement in an organization increased as the result of a survey feedback intervention.[16,17]

Bowers reported that the survey feedback technique was more effective than several other human process interventions in producing attitudinal and organizational climate change, although the study received some methodological criticism.[18,19] Miles and others report improved quality of interaction among group members, and improved satisfaction when decisions made were, in fact, carried out.[20] Hand, Estafen, and Sims noted that in a laboratory experiment involving business students in a simulation game, groups receiving

[14]Baumgartel, H. Using employee questionnaire results for improving organizations. *Kansas Business Review,* 1959, 2–6.

[15]Mann, F. Studying and creating change: A means to understanding social organization, in Bennis et al., op. cit. (Ref. 11).

[16]Chase, P., A survey feedback approach to organization development. In *Proceedings of the Executive Study Conference.* Princeton, N.J.: Educational Testing Service, 1968.

[17]Brown, L. D. Research action: Organizational feedback, understanding and change. *Journal of Applied Behavioral Science.* 1972, *8,* 674–697.

[18]Bowers, D. OD techniques and their results in 23 organizations: The Michigan ICL study. *Journal of Applied Behavioral Science,* 1973, *9,* 21–43.

[19]Pasmore, W. The Michigan ICL study revisited: An alternative explanation of the results. *Journal of Applied Behavioral Science,* 1976, *12,* 245–251.

[20]Miles et al., op. cit.

survey feedback interventions were more satisfied but did not outperform control groups.[21]

At least three studies report the results of organizational change efforts that utilized the survey feedback technique in conjunction with other human process interventions. Nadler and Pecorella report increased satisfaction after their interventions for employees but not for first-level supervisors.[22] Kimberly and Neilsen report improvements in employee attitudes and product quality, but no improvements in the level of productivity after their interventions.[23] Hautaluoma and Gavin report that employees perceived positive changes in the psychological meaning of their jobs as measured by the Job Descriptive Index.[24,25] This was in spite of the fact that the workers perceived no change in the work itself, a finding also reported by Nadler and Pecorella. Additionally, Hautaluoma and Gavin report that the attitudes of both employees and managers improved after the change programs, and that both absenteeism and turnover decreased. None of the change programs mentioned above combined the survey feedback technique with methods that were directly aimed at changing the work itself.

In summarizing the research performed on survey feedback and other human process interventions, it would seem safe to conclude that the methods do result consistently in improved employee attitudes. However, because most of the studies have focused exclusively on attitudinal changes, the impact of these interventions on productivity remains largely untested. In the few investigations which have considered the impact of human process interventions on productivity, the results have not been impressive. The effect on productivity of combining human process interventions with other types of interventions is just beginning to be investigated. Overall, data feedback interventions do tend to provide employee involvement in problem solving. Additionally, these techniques often focus on supervisory–subordinate relationships and may therefore have some impact on the immediate work context. However, these methods rarely, if ever, affect the work itself or the technology used to accomplish organizational tasks.

Job Enrichment Interventions

Job enrichment interventions are often less participative than the human process interventions just discussed. In one study, changes were introduced in a number of departments without informing the employees or their immediate

[21]Hand, H., Estafen, B., and Sims, H. How effective is data survey feedback as a technique of organization development? An Experiment. *Journal of Applied Behavioral Science,* 1975, *11,* 333–347.

[22]Nadler, D., and Pecorella, P. Differential effects of multiple interventions in an organization. *Journal of Applied Behavioral Science,* 1975, *11,* 348–366.

[23]Kimberly, J., and Nielsen, W. Organization development and change in organization performance. *Administrative Science Quarterly,* 1971, *16,* 497–514.

[24]Hautaluoma, J., and Gavin, J. Effects of organizational diagnosis and intervention on blue-collar blues. *Journal of Applied Behavior Science,* 1975, *11,* 475–496.

[25]Smith, P., and Cranny, C. Psychology of men at work. *Annual Review of Psychology,* 1968, *19,* 467–496.

supervisors of their purpose.[26] In job enrichment interventions, it is expected that employees will be motivated to perform their jobs well to take advantage of opportunities to satisfy their higher-level needs through the work itself. A model of the strategy underlying job enrichment interventions has been provided by Hackman, Oldham, Janson, and Purdy and is reproduced in Figure 2.[27] As shown, the first step to be taken in job enrichment interventions is to initiate changes in the content of employees' jobs. The manager should combine tasks, form natural work units, allow employees to establish relationships with clients, add responsibility and autonomy to the job, and provide immediate feedback to employees concerning their performance. These changes improve certain core dimensions present in every job, which tend to arouse what are called "critical psychological states" in the employee. If all these critical psychological states are present to at least some minimum extent, and if the employee has high growth need strength (that is, if the employee strongly desires more recognition, advancement, autonomy, achievement, personal development, and so forth), he/she will take advantage of these opportunities and perform well. The expected outcomes are therefore high internal work motivation, high-quality work performance, high satisfaction with the work, and low absenteeism and turnover.

How effective are job enrichment interventions? Several reviewers have already addressed themselves to this question. Ford reports that the results of nineteen job enrichment projects in AT&T were quite positive. Overall, eighteen of the nineteen projects yielded improvements in quality, satisfaction, and productivity.[28] Davis reviewed six early job enrichment projects which resulted in improved productivity, attitudes, quality, and cost.[29] Paul and Robertson report that the results of six job enrichment interventions in Imperial Chemical Industries Limited were generally positive, although more so in terms of performance than satisfaction.[30] The researchers concluded that changes in employee attitudes take longer than changes in productivity, based upon the observation that the greatest changes in attitudes took place in the longest of their studies.

Lawler reviewed 10 studies of job enrichment interventions and found quality improvements in all but productivity increases in only 4.[31] In reviewing 27 studies, Srivastva and others conclude that[32]

> the results were overwhelmingly positive. Sixty-seven percent (18/27) of the experiments showed totally positive results on those variables that were measured, whereas no study reported totally negative results. Taking into account only those studies which measured a particular dependent variable, the totally positive results were: quality—100% (17/17); costs—90%

[26]Ford, R. *Motivation Through the Work Itself.* New York: American Management Association, 1969.

[27]Hackman, R., Oldham, G., Janson, R., and Purdy, K. A New Strategy for Job Enrichment, *California Management Review, 27* (4), 57–71, 1975.

[28]Ford, R., op. cit.

[29]Davis, L. The design of jobs. *Industrial Relations,* 1966, *6,* 21–45.

[30]Paul, W., and Robertson, K. *Job Enrichment and Employee Motivation.* London: Gower Press, 1970.

[31]Lawler, E. Job design and employee motivation. *Personnel Psychology,* 1969, *22,* 426–435.

[32]Srivastva, S., Salipante, P., Cummings, T., Notz, W., Bigelow, J., and Waters, J. *Job Satisfaction and Productivity.* Cleveland, Ohio: Case Western Reserve University, Department of Organizational Behavior, 1975.

FIGURE 2

The Full Model: How Use of the Implementing Concepts Can Lead to Positive Outcomes

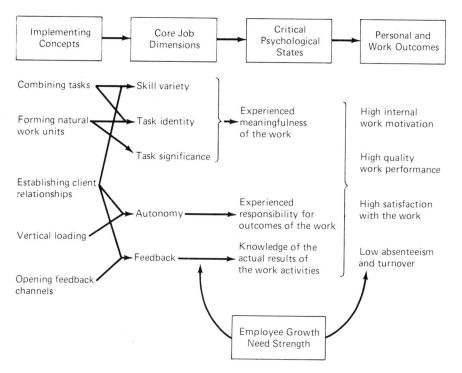

(9/10); withdrawal—86% (6/7); attitudes—76% (16/21); and productivity—75% (15/20).

Despite these optimistic reviews, some authors are more cautious in their appraisal of job enrichment efforts. Hulin and Blood noted that early studies
lacked meaningful controls or methodological rigor, and therefore conclude
that "the case for job enlargement has been drastically overstated and
overgeneralized."[33] Hackman reports his personal observations made during
15 to 20 job enrichment efforts:[34]

> In interpreting our observations and conclusions, it is important to under-
> stand that we have *not* researched the "superstar" projects. Not a single
> one of our tests has been conducted at a new plant, designed and staffed in
> accord with the freshest precepts of behavioral science. Instead, we have
> focused our attention on "regular" organizations, organizations struggling
> to figure out, sometimes with professional help, sometimes not, just how
> one goes about reaping the benefits of job enrichment.
>
> What we have seen out there in the "organizational heartland" is not very
> encouraging. If our observations are representative (and, holding aside the
> superstar projects, there are reasons to believe that we have seen some of

[33]Hulin, C., and Blood, M. Job enlargement, individual differences, and worker responses.
Psychological Bulletin, 1968, *69,* 41–55.
[34]Hackman, J. *On the Coming Demise of Job Enrichment.* Technical Report 9, Department of
Administrative Sciences, Yale University, 1974.

the more thoughtfully-done work redesign projects) job enrichment is failing at least as often as it is succeeding.

Hackman places the blame for the high failure rate he observed on a number of factors. Among these factors were the following three: (1) in some projects the work itself did not change, (2) the effects of job changes were diminished by insufficient attention to the surrounding work system, and (3) the projects were often dictated by management and bureaucratically controlled. The observant reader will note the relationship between these problems associated with some job enrichment interventions and the criteria presented earlier for successful organizational change of change in the work itself, change in the immediate work context, and employee involvement in the change process.

Other pessimistic notes concerning job enrichment interventions have also found their way into the literature. Alderfer describes the results of a three-year job enrichment project.[35] Although employees were more satisfied with their jobs and pay than workers in traditional facilities, they tended to be less satisfied with the respect they received from their superiors. Similarly, Lawler, Hackman, and Kaufman report that changes associated with a job enrichment effort in a telephone company resulted in poorer interpersonal relationships between workers and supervisors and *among the workers themselves.*[36] The same study noted no changes in the levels of job involvement, internal motivation, or desire for higher-order need satisfaction on the part of employees after the intervention. These results are inconclusive, however, as the researchers report that the jobs remained unchanged on a number of important dimensions after the intervention. These results and others have prompted several authors to comment that job enrichment interventions have been applied rather indiscriminantly. These authors argue that job enrichment is not appropriate under certain circumstances, and should only be applied after thorough diagnosis of the entire organization.[37-39]

In summarizing the literature on job enrichment, one can only conclude that job enrichment interventions can result in improved attitudes and performance if handled properly and if they take place in the proper setting. These efforts are aimed primarily at the work itself, and can run into problems due to lack of employee involvement in the change process or inadequate consideration of the immediate work context. It is interesting to note however, that some studies, like that of Paul and Robertson, report improved productivity *without* improved employee satisfaction. This suggests that changing the work itself may have the most immediate consequences for organizational productivity, at least in the short run. Overall, it seems that the best position to be taken at this time regarding the effectiveness of job enrichment interventions is one of guarded optimism.

Sociotechnical system interventions directly change the behavior required of workers to perform their tasks, and thus focus on changing the work itself. At the same time, these interventions pay particular attention to providing a

[35]Alderfer, C. Job enlargement and the organizational context. *Personnel Psychology,* 1969, *22,* 418-426.

[36]Lawler, E., Hackman, J., and Kaufman, S. Effects of job redesign: A field experiment. *Journal of Applied Social Psychology,* 1973, *3,* 49-62.

[37]Yorks, L. Key elements in implementing job enrichment. *Personnel,* 1973, 45-52.

[38]Sirota, D., and Wolfson, A. Job enrichment: What are the obstacles? *Personnel,* 1972, 8-17.

[39]Reif, W., and Monzcka, R. Job redesign: A contingency approach to implementation. *Personnel,* 1974, 18-28.

social climate to support the required behavior changes, and therefore the immediate work context.

As shown in Figure 3, sociotechnical system interventions begin with the formation of a study group composed of representatives from all parts and levels of the organization to assist in the analysis/change process. The formation of such a group is in itself an intervention into the immediate work context, which provides opportunities for involving people in important decisions regarding their work. This group, with the help of a facilitator, directs an analysis of the organization's environment, social system, and technical system. The details of how these analyses are conducted are too cumbersome to report here, but have been described elsewhere.[40] The objective of these analyses is to produce a set of system redesign proposals that take into account the unique aspects of the business situation, workforce, and technical system in creating a new work environment. The new environment, as in job enrichment interventions, generally includes greater variety, autonomy, responsi-

FIGURE 3

Sociotechnical System Change Strategy

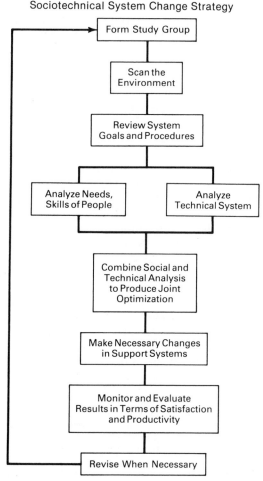

[40]Pasmore, W. *Using Sociotechnical Systems to Design Effective Organizations.* New York: Wiley, Forthcoming, 1983.

bility, and feedback for employees. Beyond this, however, supportive changes are also initiated in the immediate work context. Employees are typically formed into self-governing teams that are primarily responsible for operating major segments of the production process. The technology itself may be altered to allow human operators more control over the process; physical facilities may be altered to provide group meeting space or eliminate barriers to communication among workers and between workers and management; changes in policies and procedures are also required to provide teams with the flexibility needed to manage their own work areas; and often, changes in reward systems are undertaken to provide team incentives for performance.

In this process, attitudes and performance may change simultaneously or either may proceed the other. Over time, changes in both areas are monitored and evaluated to determine if changing conditions require revisions to system design.

The strategy of sociotechnical system intervention just outlined does include employee involvement through the representative study group. However, only a small number of employees can be involved in the group at any given time, so the majority of employees usually do not experience the process of sociotechnical system change as a participative one. In fact, some initial resistance from employees and managers not involved directly in the study group is a common problem in sociotechnical system intervention.

How effective are sociotechnical system interventions? In an early study, Trist and Bamforth discovered that individual and organizational performance was greatly affected by the way in which jobs were structured and workers interacted with machinery. Although the researchers made no interventions themselves, they noted that those settings conforming to the description of sociotechnical systems outlined above were by far the most productive and had the lowest rates of absenteeism.[41] Rice reports the results of a sociotechnical system intervention in a material weaving company in India.[42] Employees were formed into groups and held responsible for the operation of a certain number of automatic looms. The new organization reduced the number of job categories from twelve to three, and made the teams rather than supervisors responsible for coordinating the maintenance and operating efforts. Rice reports that the new system increased productivity and worker morale while significantly reducing the level of damage to equipment and material. A follow-up study conducted some 20 years later indicated that the original changes and results were still in effect.[43]

Several projects were undertaken with the Norwegian government by Emery and Thorsrud.[44] One of these studies was discontinued due to union pressure, and another, while successful, was particularly slow in its implementation. Employees were not involved in the initial sociotechnical system analysis and resented some of the changes made in the work environment.

Hill reports excellent results of a sociotechnical system intervention in a

[41]Trist, E., and Bamforth, K. Some social and psychological consequences of the longwall method of coal-getting. *Human Relations,* 1951, *4,* 3–38.

[42]Rice, A. *Productivity and Social Organization: The Ahmedabad Experiment.* London: Tavistock Publishing, 1958.

[43]Miller, E. Socio-technical systems in weaving, 1953–1970: A follow-up study. *Human Relations,* 1975, *28*(4), 349–386.

[44]Emery, F., and Thorsrud, E. *Form and Content in Industrial Democracy.* London: Tavistock Publications, 1969.

British oil refinery in terms of productivity, satisfaction, and turnover.[45] Walton reports similar results for a pet-food plant designed using sociotechnical principles.[46] Cummings and Srivastva report mixed results of sociotechnical system experiments in an aluminum manufacturing plant.[47] Srivastva and others, upon reviewing the results of sixteen sociotechnical system interventions, conclude that:[48]

> The results from socio-technical experiments are highly positive. Seventy-five percent of the experiments show totally positive results. The percentage of studies showing positive results for each dependent variable were as follows: productivity, 93%; costs, 88%; quality, 86%; withdrawal, 73%; attitudes, 70%.

In summary, the results of the sociotechnical system studies reviewed demonstrate that sociotechnical system interventions rather consistently result in both improved productivity and satisfaction. These interventions can encounter difficulties, however, if particular attention is not paid to involving employees in the change process.

A Comparison and Summary

None of the three types of interventions described above meets all the criteria for turning people on to their work; each is deficient in some respect. Figure 4 illustrates the strengths and weaknesses of each type of intervention.

Figure 4 shows that only data feedback interventions provide extensive employee involvement in the change process. Hence, only data feedback or other human process interventions provide that employees specify what opportunities for need satisfaction are important to them. Job enrichment and sociotechnical system intervention may fail to turn employees on to work because they assume that certain needs motivate all employees, when in fact need satisfaction is an idiosyncratic affair. Data feedback interventions may also provide some supportive changes in the immediate work context, as relationships between employees and their supervisor improve. Data feedback interventions do little, however, to change the nature of the work itself. Although employees may specify what needs are important to them, changes are seldom made that provide employees with opportunities to satisfy those needs through the work itself.

Job enrichment interventions do change the work itself; however, these changes are usually made unilaterally and it is assumed that all employees are motivated by the same needs. In addition, because job changes are made individually, an employee working on an enriched job may find the immediate work context nonsupportive. Others may resent the new role for various reasons, supervisory relationships may worsen, or the employee may not be provided with the training or tools needed to fulfill the new responsibilities.

Sociotechnical system interventions, like job enrichment, make changes in the work itself to allow opportunities for the satisfaction of employee needs. Because the process of sociotechnical system interventions is complex, there is

[45]Hill, P. *Towards a New Philosophy of Management.* New York: Barnes and Noble, 1971.

[46]Walton, R. How to counter alienation in the plant. *Harvard Business Review,* 1972, *50,* 70–81.

[47]Cummings, T., and Srivastva, S. *The Management of Work.* Kent, Ohio: Kent State University Press, 1977.

[48]Srivastva et al., op. cit.

FIGURE 4
Strengths and Weaknesses of Selected Interventions

Type of Intervention	Employee Involvement	Change in the Work Itself	Change in the Immediate Work Context
Data feedback	✓		✓
Job enrichment		✓	
Sociotechnical system		✓	✓

typically little employee involvement. Therefore, as in job enrichment interventions, certain assumptions have to be made concerning what needs motivate most people. Unlike job enrichment interventions, however, sociotechnical system interventions provide changes in the immediate work context that will support employees' efforts to satisfy their needs through the work itself.

Obviously, one way to overcome the difficulties inherent in each of these methods is to use a combination of interventions. Such efforts are only now beginning to take place. One such project, conducted by Pasmore and King, combined survey feedback and job enrichment interventions in one unit of a plant and survey feedback and sociotechnical system changes in another. The combined interventions resulted in improved employee attitudes in both units; however, only the combined survey feedback and sociotechnical system intervention resulted in productivity improvements and cost savings.[49]

Although more studies are needed, it is apparent that in this case, only sociotechnical system intervention was able to create an immediate work context that supported productivity improvements. This may be attributed to a number of changes that were made in the sociotechnical system unit; employees were formed into self-governing work teams that performed major portions of the production process and provided their own maintenance and quality control functions; the technology was designed to provide employees with control over the production process and rate; buffer inventories were established which allowed the work team to shut down production in their area to hold meetings on a regular basis; and supervisors were trained to educate their work teams in both technical and human relations skills.

This study also casts further doubt on the traditionally assumed satisfaction–productivity relationship. In the unit in which job enrichment and survey feedback interventions took place, attitudes improved but performance did not. In this unit the immediate work context constrained efforts to increase productivity. Although relations with supervision improved somewhat, cor-

[49]Pasmore, W., and King, D. Understanding organizational change: A comparative study of multifaceted interventions. *Journal of Applied Behavioral Sciences,* 1978, in press.

responding changes in the technology or the work relationships among employees did not take place. Increased satisfaction does *not* therefore necessarily result in improved productivity; changes must also be made in the immediate work context which provides the support and opportunity for productivity increases.

Could the satisfaction and productivity increases that took place in the unit receiving the sociotechnical system intervention have occurred without employee involvement through the data feedback intervention as well? Perhaps, but it seems unlikely. The plant studied was unionized, and the union steadfastly opposed *any* changes in work design until they were granted a role in the redesign process. The survey feedback intervention opened up channels of communication between union and management and allowed the employee-determined opportunities for need satisfaction to be incorporated into the final design. Although attempts to unilaterally change organizations in non-union settings may be successful, it is more likely that the outcome of such efforts will be compliance rather than commitment by employees.

While employees may not be able to express their concerns with redesign efforts through a union, it is likely that without their involvement in the efforts they will find more covert and possibly damaging ways to express their disapproval.

In conclusion, we know a great deal more about how to increase employee motivation and performance than we did four decades ago. Some of our major learnings can be summarized as follows:

1. There is no guarantee that increasing employee motivation will lead to improved performance. Other variables including the ability of the employee and the design of work mediate the motivation/performance relationship.
2. Turning people on to work requires their involvement in decision making regarding changes in the work itself, as well as in the creation of supportive immediate work contexts.
3. Trying to change motivation or performance by changing one thing at a time (e.g., pay) usually changes nothing. To improve an organization's performance, the whole organization needs to change. There are no shortcuts or gimmicks that produce long-term improvement.
4. Often the major problem with organizational performance is not employee motivation but rather *managerial* resistance to creating the conditions needed to allow employees to achieve success. On the other hand, given managerial backing for the creation of supportive immediate work contexts, many methods are now available that can result in improved organizational success. The level of improvement attained with these methods is directly proportionate to the willingness of managers to allow employees to become involved in significant decisions regarding the operation of the firm.

Given the preceding, it is not surprising to find researchers beginning to turn their attention away from the question of employee motivation to consider issues associated with the reduction of managerial resistance to change. Perhaps the next article in this genre should be entitled "Turning Managers on to Turning People on to Work." If one can find answers here, we will truly have taken a significant step forward in our bid to make our organizations productive, healthy environments for human existence.

ALIENATION AT THE TOP

GEERT HOFSTEDE

A large European corporation suffered the resignation of three key executives within two months. Distressed by these losses, which were totally unexpected, the president asked a consulting psychologist to conduct postexit interviews with the three men. Were the three resignations in any way related? Did they signal a serious crisis of which the president was unaware?

The three men all received the psychologist very willingly. In fact, they appeared eager to supply this kind of feedback-from-a-distance to their former employer. The interviews revealed that on a direct cause-and-effect level, their almost simultaneous resignations were a coincidence. They had not been influenced by each other, and their new jobs were with different companies.

However, in many ways their three cases were strikingly similar. All three men were in their early forties—an age that normally is the peak of a man's working life, when he has both a past to build upon and a future to look forward to. All three so far had spent virtually their entire careers with the same large employer, had liked their jobs, and had been highly successful. All three had been very well paid, and prospects of improved earnings in their new jobs were minor or nonexistent; job security was less in the new job than in the old. All three were quite positive about their former employer: "It is a great company. What I am now, I owe to them." However, all three complained about being increasingly frustrated by company bureaucracy as they had moved up, and all three moved to new positions that involved a bigger job in a smaller company.

No specific organizational crisis, then, caused these executives to resign; instead, the cause was a midcareer crisis in their personal orientations toward their work—a common feeling of frustration, meaninglessness, and powerlessness that seemed to have grown parallel to the increase in their formal power as measured by their hierarchical positions. They felt less and less able to make the impact on the company that they wanted to make, and for this they blamed not particular individuals but a conglomerate of impersonal forces generated by "company bureaucracy."

The Alienation Phenomenon

The ambition to make a meaningful impact, however modest, in one's life environment is common to most people. Many people worry nowadays about the state of mind of industrial and office workers who have to do simple, repetitive tasks devoid of any meaning to them. The word *alienation* is used to describe the effect of these jobs on people.

Alienation is a term borrowed from sociology and used by different authors to include different attributes, but it always centers on an individual's feeling

---

Reprinted by permission of the publisher from *Organization Dynamics,* Winter, 1976.
This study was supported by a grant from executive search consultants Berndtson International S. A., Brussels.

of powerlessness and meaninglessness, his inability to influence or even understand the forces upon which his life and happiness depend. This feeling is by no means limited to industrial workers. Over the past five or ten years, the term has also been used to describe the state of mind of students at American universities. Feelings of alienation may be found, though to different extents, at all levels within bureaucratic organizations.

The word *bureaucracy,* in popular parlance, has acquired a strong negative connotation—but in its original sociological context, it refers to any formal system for simplifying the management of large and complex activities. As such, it applies to public as well as private organizations, the shop floor as well as the executive suite. Bureaucracies are born of necessity; without them, large-scale human activities would be unmanageable. The paradox is that, by their very existence, they call forth forces that defeat their own ends. The main problem appears to be that the models of people on which bureaucratic structures are built are too different from real people. Bureaucracies ask people to behave in standardized ways, whereas real people are never standard. If we force them to behave as if they were, the consequence is alienation. The three executives who blamed their move on bureaucracy in the large corporation moved to escape the alienation they had begun more and more to feel.

Attitude Survey

I would now like to describe an example of employee alienation in a large multinational corporation that operates in many European countries. This corporation markets its products through a subsidiary in each country. It operates sales offices in the major cities, which are coordinated by a head office in each country. All country head offices report directly to an international headquarters located in Europe.

In 1968 and 1969, this corporation conducted a series of attitude surveys of all its employees and managers. These surveys seemed to show an alienation problem at a surprising place—within the corporation's international headquarters. Moreover, this alienation problem not only affected the headquarters' rank-and-file employees but also its managers. In fact, there were reasons to consider the problem more serious for managers at the international headquarters than for other categories of employees.

Attitude-survey results, far from being dull statistics, can reveal fascinating secrets about the functioning of organizations. I shall present some of the main corporate findings on the alienation phenomenon so that the reader can judge for himself. (Those who want to take my analysis for granted can skip Figure 1 through Figure 5 and begin reading again at "The Price of Alienation.")

In composing the survey questionnaire, we believed that one yardstick for determining the meaningfulness of a job would be a person's feeling able to make some contribution to the overall company result. We therefore asked (among other things), "How satisfied are you with your opportunity to make a real contribution to the success of the company?" In Figure 1 the distribution of answers to this question is shown for three groups of employees: managers (anyone responsible for coordinating the work of others), professional employees (college-level, specialized personnel such as salesmen, engineers, and accountants), and clerical employees (noncollege-level, administrative personnel). Results are also divided according to three kinds of work locations: sales offices (within countries), country head offices, and the international headquarters.

Figure 1 reveals that for all three categories of employees—managers, professionals, and clerks—there is a consistent decrease of satisfaction from the sales offices to the international headquarters. Also, managers are more satisfied than professionals, and professionals more than clerks, except in international headquarters, where clerks are more satisfied than professionals. In fact, the satisfaction level of managers in the international headquarters (47 percent satisfied) is almost exactly the same as for professionals in the country headquarters (48 percent) and for clerks in the sales offices (46 percent).

That managers are more satisfied with their opportunity to contribute to the company's success than clerks was to be expected because, by definition, they have a more central role in the organization. But although the international headquarters also has a central role, its satisfaction level is *lowest*. This level increases as we go to the country head offices, and from there to the sales offices. Dissatisfaction indicating alienation, therefore, is least present at the sales offices and reaches a peak at the international headquarters.

Other Survey Results

The attitude surveys also showed that satisfaction with opportunity to make a real contribution to the success of this company tended to go hand in hand with satisfaction on other aspects of job content. In a statistical analysis of the survey scores for each of the various categories of employees, a close correlation was found between satisfaction with opportunity to contribute and the answers to two other questions, "How satisfied are you with the challenge of the work you do—the extent to which you can get a personal sense of accomplishment out of it?" and "How satisfied are you with the extent to which you use your skills and abilities on your job?" The three questions together form a statistical "cluster" that indicates, in general, satisfaction with the *intrinsic nature or content of the job.* The close relationship between these three

FIGURE 1

Satisfaction with Opportunity to Contribute to Company Success

	Percent Scoring		
	Dissatisfied or Very Dissatisfied	Neither Satisfied nor Dissatisfied	Satisfied or Very Satisfied
Managers in:			
Sales offices	5	18	77
Country head offices	9	31	60
International headquarters	14	39	47
Professional employees in:			
Sales offices	6	32	62
Country head offices	16	36	48
International headquarters	24	50	26
Clerical employees in:			
Sales offices	14	40	46
Country head offices	17	42	41
International headquarters	21	46	33

questions implies that the two other questions should show differences between managers and others and between sales offices and headquarters similar to those shown by satisfaction with opportunity to contribute. Figure 2 allows us to verify this (for simplicity's sake only percent satisfied answers are shown).

Figure 2 reveals the same kind of differences between managers, professionals, and clerks and between sales offices, country head offices, and international headquarters that Figure 1 showed. However, the differences in Figure 2 tend to be smaller than in Figure 1. Especially for managers, there are greater differences between sales offices and headquarters on satisfaction with opportunity to contribute than on challenge or use of skills. This suggests that the differences in managers' feelings of challenge and use of skills may be the *consequences* of their different satisfaction with opportunity to contribute.

The Subjective Importance of Contributing to Company Success

Satisfaction with opportunity to contribute is subjectively more important to managers than it is to other organization members. This was disclosed in the above mentioned attitude surveys by a parallel set of questions to the satisfaction questions; these parallel questions tried to elicit the *importance* of various work aspects to the employee. Instead of "How satisfied are you with . . .?" the questions began with "How important is it to you to . . .?" (for example, have a job that allows you to make a real contribution to the success of your company).

All in all, there were 22 importance and 22 satisfaction questions, the 22 items covered the entire field of the relationship of a person with his job—such as earnings, impact on personal life, learning, security, interpersonal relationships, and advancement opportunities. The importance questions allowed us to rank these 22 items in order of the importance attached to them by a certain category of employees. Rank 1 would be given to the item that, on the average, received the highest importance score; rank 22, the lowest. The relative importance attached to contributing to company success by our various categories of employees is shown in Figure 3.

FIGURE 2
Intrinsic Job Interest

	Percent Scoring "Satisfied" or "Very Satisfied"	
	Challenge of the Work	Use of Skills and Abilities
Managers in:		
Sales offices	77	65
Country head offices	66	61
International headquarters	56	55
Professional employees in:		
Sales offices	71	57
Country head offices	53	48
International headquarters	39	37
Clerical employees in:		
Sales offices	53	46
Country head offices	46	42
International headquarters	34	36

FIGURE 3

Importance of Contributing to Company Success

	Average Rank Order
Managers in:	
Sales offices	5[1]
Country head offices	3
International headquarters	2
Professional employees in:	
Sales offices	14
Country head offices	15
International headquarters	12
Clerical employees in:	
Sales offices	16
Country head offices	18
International headquarters	18

[1]Rankings: 1, most important; 22, least important.

Figure 3 proves what was stated above: Managers distinguish themselves from others by attaching much higher importance to contributing to company success. Whereas for professionals and clerks this issue ranks from 12 to 18 out of 22, for managers it ranks fifth in the sales offices, third in the country head offices, and second in the international headquarters. In the international headquarters, the only work aspect managers rate more important than contributing to company success is challenging work. In the country head offices, managers view challenging work and a good working relationship with your manager as being more important than contributing to company success. In the sales offices, the four items rated more important by managers are, in order of importance, challenging work, considerable freedom to adopt your own approach to the job, an opportunity for advancement, and training opportunities.

If we compare the satisfaction percentages (Figure 1) and the importance rankings (Figure 3), we can see that the problem of alienation—not making a real contribution to the success of the company—is particularly acute for the international-headquarters managers by a combination of high attached importance (ranked second) and low satisfaction (47 percent satisfied). It is much less pressing, for example, with clerical employees who, while not very satisfied, indicate by their low importance scores that to them many other aspects of the job can compensate for the lack of satisfaction with opportunity to contribute to company success. This way out is not open to most managers.

Images of the Organization as Such

Alienation does affect one's self-image but not necessarily one's image of the organization one works for. In fact, the two may be negatively related. The surveys also contained a question about the image of the company as such (not in terms of one's personal contribution to it): "How satisfied are you with the extent to which this company is regarded as successful?"

The results for managers are shown in Figure 4. As the overall level of answering was very favorable, we have taken the cutoff point between very satisfied and satisfied. It is clear that in this case the highest success ratings come from international headquarters and the least high from the sales offices.

This is the opposite of the trend for the question about the managers' personal contribution to the company's success. It seems that the lack of satisfaction of the international-headquarters managers with their personal contribution is partly compensated by a sense of pride in the company—"Never mind my job, but it is a great company to be in."

FIGURE 4

Success of the Company as Such

	Percent Scoring		
	No Feeling or Dissatisfied	Satisfied	Very Satisfied
Managers in:			
Sales offices	18	53	29
Country head offices	15	52	33
International headquarters	11	45	44

Motivational Consequences of "Red Tape"

When they were presented with the survey data, some people were surprised; they had expected that respondents in the subsidiaries would be the *least* satisfied because they would be frustrated by the headquarters interventions. This expectation was based on the implicit assumption that bureaucratic systems ("red tape") were invented by people in headquarters who obviously should like what they were doing. Our data show this assumption to be wrong. In fact, it is a gross oversimplification of the origins of bureaucracy. The surveys did address the issues of the relationships between subsidiaries and headquarters, however. Managers and professionals in the country head offices were asked how frequently (if at all) the following problems occurred:

1. International headquarters doesn't give people in our country head offices enough support.
2. International headquarters interferes too much.

People in the sales offices were asked the same questions with regard to *both* international headquarters and the country head offices.

The answers are summarized in Figure 5:

1. Those answering *very frequently or frequently* never exceed one-third of the managers or professionals questioned.
2. Sales offices had few problems with international headquarters (these were dealt with at country-head-office level), but they had about the same level of problems with their country head office as country head offices had with international headquarters.
3. In all cases, problems were somewhat more frequently seen as not enough support rather than as too much interference.
4. In all cases, problems were somewhat more frequently felt by managers than by nonmanagers.

However, a more important finding (not visible in Figure 5) was that the answers to the questions on support and interference were statistically only weakly related to those about other aspects of the managers' or professionals' job satisfaction. Feeling a lack of support or too much interference, although frustrating, did not seem to affect too much the way people felt about their work. In the total picture of the attitude of people toward their jobs it stayed at the level of a minor irritation. The feeling of alienation that we related to not feeling able to make a real contribution to the company's success goes much deeper. There is no real adversary to blame; the system in which one is absorbed is unclear and the individual feels he is wasting his time, although working very hard.

FIGURE 5

Distribution of Responses to the "Support" and "Interference" Questions

	From Country Head Office				From International Headquarters			
	Not Enough Support		Too Much Interference		Not Enough Support		Too Much Interference	
	Very frequently or frequently	Seldom or never	Very frequently or frequently	Seldom or never	Very frequently or frequently	Seldom or never	Very frequently or frequently	Seldom or never
Managers in:								
Sales offices	32	24	27	27	13	59	7	72
Country head offices	—	—	—	—	31	29	26	42
Professional employees in:								
Sales offices	30	27	23	34	5	75	3	83
Country head offices	—	—	—	—	25	34	21	47

(Expressed in percentages. The percentages of those answering "sometimes" are not shown.)

The Price of Alienation

The price an organization pays for the alienation of its employees will vary from company to company, job to job, and individual employee to individual employee. In general, alienated employees will lower their aspirations to perform because they see their performance as meaningless anyway. They are less likely to exert effort. An illustration of this: Surveyed managers in country sales offices reported spending considerably more voluntary overtime on their jobs than did managers in country and international head offices (observation of managers in action confirms that sales office managers do spend longer hours working). In spite of this, sales office managers did not claim to be overloaded any more frequently than did head office managers; a considerably greater fraction of sales office managers would accept these long hours without feeling overloaded.

Other things being equal, employees with higher skill and education levels will expect more intrinsic satisfaction from their jobs and will want to use their skills as fully as possible. They are, therefore, more likely to quit if they feel alienated and if alternative jobs are available. People who have experienced success in the past are more frustrated by alienation than are less successful people.

This fact was demonstrated in a study within the same company in which 326 participants of an in-company executive training program were followed through their careers after training. The average time span between training and follow-up was four years. During this period, 20 participants had left the company (a very low turnover fugure). However, out of these 20, 16 had been rated by their trainers as being among the top third of their class. This means that the one-third of most successful trainees were eight times as likely to quit as the two-thirds of less successful ones.

Even if we discount the fact that trainers are not infallible in their judgment, it is still a reasonable assumption that these more successful trainees would also tend to be the better performers in their day-to-day jobs. This study therefore shows how alienation may lead to selective employee turnover: The more successful people tend to leave. The departure of the three executives mentioned in the introduction to this article upset their president because they, too, were star performers. There is a real danger that a company headquarters by this process may become stuck with a residue of disillusioned low achievers, who in turn expand the bureaucracy of which they themselves are the victims.

In the previous paragraphs we have assumed a potential need to achieve and to make a contribution to the company's success in all people; we have blamed the situation rather than the employees when this contribution was missing. We also recognize, however, that persons and even entire cultures differ in their need for achievement and their need to contribute. Jobs with a low potential to contribute to the company's success will, by a process of natural selection, attract persons for whom the need to contribute is low. Our data suggest that such people are more likely to stay in headquarters jobs than are strong achievers.

Job Enrichment for Headquarters Executives

On the shop and office floor, the danger of alienation has been recognized and efforts are being made to restore humanity to jobs that the bureaucratic process dehumanized. These efforts generally are called "job enrichment," to use Frederick Herzberg's terminology. Some approaches to job enrichment focus mainly on the structure of individual jobs, the dominant trend in the United States. In Europe, especially in Sweden and Norway, job enrichment has concentrated on changing group tasks rather than individual jobs.

Is job enrichment possible in the headquarters of large corporations? It is unlikely in this case that restructuring individual jobs will be sufficient because in the forces that lead to alienation, the entire bureaucratic system of the organization is involved. Job-enrichment approaches here should include not only individuals but also groups and the role of entire departments.

Let us first look at the kind of jobs we usually find in headquarters. There is a great variety: top executives with their personal staffs; those who deal with the outside on behalf of the corporation; those who plan ahead for the short and for the long term and those who look after the execution of these plans by the various subsidiaries; those who write policies for the corporation and those who check whether these policies are followed; those who coordinate the flow of funds, materials, people, orders, and ideas between the various subsidiaries; and those who possess unique expertise or perform unique services that the subsidiaries are not in a position to do by themselves. The bigger the headquarters becomes, the greater the number of those necessary to keep the headquarters itself running.

Why, then, in our multinational corporation would alienation be so much lower in the sales offices than in such a headquarters? What is different about jobs in sales offices? At least two differences are noteworthy:

1. Sales office jobs compared with headquarters jobs contain a much more direct feedback about results—one knows whether one has worked successfully or not.
2. Sales office jobs more than headquarters jobs involve a direct client or customer relationship—there is a visible person, the customer, who is either satisfied or not.

Now both *direct feedback* and a *client relationship* are recognized by job enrichment experts to be among the key requirements for an "enriched" job. Headquarters jobs, on the other hand, usually receive little or no feedback on their success, and it is generally less clear who their client is—the subsidiary offices, higher management . . . or do they have clients at all?

It is evident that, with headquarters containing such a mixed bag of roles, the alienation phenomenon will not be the same among all headquarters activities. In fact, the employee attitude survey recorded that among these activities, the satisfaction with "contribution to company success" varied from 70 percent to only 20 percent of personnel scoring "very satisfied" or "satisfied" (taking managers, professionals, and clerical employees together). We should, therefore, further investigate who in headquarters felt alienated and who not, and why. For this purpose, I shall first describe another study, the headquarters effectiveness study.

The Headquarters Effectiveness Study

In the same multinational corporation that supplied the alienation data, the chief headquarters executive, after the employee attitude survey, decided he wanted feedback on the effectiveness of his international headquarters operation. He asked the corporate personnel research department to carry out a study of how people in country head offices looked at the job done by their international headquarters counterparts. This survey, carried out half a year after the employee attitude survey, became known as the "Headquarters Effectiveness Study." In this study, the departments of the international headquarters were divided into seven main functions (such as market research, finance, and personnel) and then subdivided into 49 departments or activities. For each activity, the person acting as the main "customer" in each country head office was presented with a written questionnaire to be returned to the corporate personnel research department. Anonymity of answers was guaranteed unless customers expressly wanted their identity to be known. Of the more than 1100 questionnaires mailed out, more than 800 (73 percent) were returned. The questionnaire contained some forced-choice questions along with a number of write-in questions. The responses to the latter were assembled for each of the 49 international headquarters activities and sent to the person responsible for that activity.

Among other things, the forced choice questions tried to have the customers rate the headquarters activities on the two dimensions of *support* and *control.* Support was defined as "advice and counsel, help with specific problems, expert answers, and information that helps you to do a better job." Support given by the international headquarters activity in the past 12 months was evaluated by the country head office customers from the points of view of quantity and of quality. Control was defined as "staff supervision; monitoring country practices, policies, and procedures; international coordination; auditing; and so on—all aimed at ensuring a high level of overall performance." The customers were asked how they felt about the amount of control received from their international headquarters counterpart over the past 12 months.

The results revealed that quantity and quality of support generally went hand in hand, making it possible to compute a support index for each activity of the international headquarters, including both quantity and quality. Control and support were less strongly related (if at all, control was related to quantity of support but not to quality). Some headquarters activities were seen as high in both support and control and some as low in both support and control, but others were high in support and low in control or low in support and high in control.

Relationships between Perceived Support and Control and Headquarters Alienation

I have already mentioned that this headquarters effectiveness study (in which people in the country head offices rated the international headquarters) followed closely after the employee attitude survey (in which people both in the country head offices and in international headquarters rated their own jobs). The researchers wondered whether any relationship would show up between the outcome of the two surveys. In the employee attitude survey, the seven main functional groups within the international headquarters varied considerably in their satisfaction with their opportunity to make a real contribution to the success of the company. Could the satisfaction or dissatisfaction of international headquarters employees with the meaningfulness of their jobs be in any way related to the way in which their function was perceived by their customers at country headquarters?

Figure 6 shows the results of a comparison of both surveys. The seven main functional areas in international headquarters have been coded A through G according to the rank order of their employees' scores on "satisfaction with the opportunity to contribute to the company's success." Thus A is the function with the highest average satisfaction (low alienation) and G with the lowest average satisfaction (high alienation). The same functional areas have been ranked according to their ratings received on support and control in the headquarters effectiveness study—that is, in the way they are perceived by their customers.

The results in Figure 6 are remarkable. Self-ratings of headquarters employees on satisfaction with opportunity to contribute run almost perfectly parallel to the ratings received on support as perceived by their customers in the country head offices. Such a similarity in ranking is extremely unlikely to occur by chance. On the other hand, no consistent relationship is visible between satisfaction with opportunity to contribute and ratings received on control.

This gives us a clue as to why not all parts of headquarters show equal alienation: Where the function is able to establish an effective support relation with its customers in the country headquarters, alienation is less. Whether the function exercises control (that is, formal power) does *not* appear to be related to feelings of alienation.

FIGURE 6
Comparison of Outcomes of Two Surveys

Headquarters Main Functions	Employee Attitudes Survey[1]	Headquarters Effectiveness Study[2]	
		Support Index[3]	Control Score
A	1[4]	1	2
B	2	2	6
C	3	3	4
D	4	4	3
E	5	6	5
F	6	5	1
G	7	7	7

[1]Ranking of satisfaction with opportunity to contribute to company's success.
[2]Rankings of ratings by country head office counterparts.
[3]Quantity plus quality.
[4]Rankings: 1, high.

Let us look at the extremes in Figure 6 more closely. Function A, which has the highest scores on satisfaction with opportunity to contribute and support but also a high score on control, is a relatively small office (13 people) in charge of customer service. It is manned by ex-customer-service engineers who are well aware of the problems in the various countries. It maintains a tight control on the productivity of the customer-service activities in the countries because it has a say in their budgets. However, the headquarters staff has maintained the same service attitude toward the engineers in the countries that these engineers are supposed to show toward their customers: Calls for help are always honored. Most people in the countries feel that the headquarters' targets for productivity are tough but realistic.

Function G, scoring low on satisfaction with opportunity to contribute, support, and control, is the largest single functional group; it comprises 75 people. This suggests that the size of the headquarters group has something to do with both alienation and effective functioning. I will come back to the issue of size later on; size, however, does not explain all the differences between functions. For example, functions E and F in Figure 6, with relatively unfavorable alienation scores, are at the same time fairly small groups. Function G supplies support and control in the marketing area basically in the same way that Function A does to customer service. However, the marketing area is much more complex than the customer service area. Therefore, more people are needed at headquarters to deal with marketing problems; most of them are experts in their own area, but as experts they often have trouble communicating with subsidiaries. Also, the rapid growth and frequent reorganizations of this part of the headquarters staff has led to a lack of clarity as to responsibilities both in the subsidiaries and among the headquarters staff themselves. A relatively large part of the staff is new at headquarters and inexperienced at this kind of work. People in the subsidiaries, who do not think that headquarters can really help them, will not so easily take their problems to headquarters; consequently, the headquarters staff feels isolated and is uninformed about what goes on in the subsidiaries. Because of this lack of information, policies issued by the headquarters staff may not sufficiently take the reality of the subsidiaries into account; this, in turn, diminishes the subsidiaries' confidence in headquarters even more. It was remarkable that one small group within Function G, which had been unaffected by most reorganizations and whose role was clear, was not dissatisfied but, on the contrary, highly satisfied with its opportunity to contribute to company success.

In general, we may conclude that the international headquarters functions that have received favorable scores on support are comparable to the sales offices in which, as we have also seen, alienation is low. In both cases, there is a supportive relationship with the customer that, to the members of the selling department, involves a constant and natural feedback on the meaningfulness of what they are doing. If the customer really feels helped, the salesman feels rewarded. We have already seen (Figure 5) that people in the sales offices and in the country head offices have more problems with not enough support from headquarters than with too much interference—that is, an excess of control.

Support, Control, and Power

Our analysis leads to a very important conclusion for the battle against headquarters alienation. If headquarters departments get a role in which they are able to give true support (as defined by its receivers), their members are not likely to feel alienated. It is immaterial whether they simultaneously exert control. It is perfectly possible to combine control and support. Control roles without support are also possible, but they are likely to be alienating to the role incumbents.

Traditional thinking about organizations has stressed control rather than support relationships. The organization chart, for example, is a diagram of the distribution of formal control in an organization; it does *not* show support relationships. It is much easier to formalize control than support. However, in actual practice in organizations, this kind of control is often imaginary. It is common knowledge that the importance of a job is not always reflected in the organization chart. Control, as previously defined in the headquarters effectiveness study, aims at "ensuring a high level of overall performance." It can do this only if it has an influence on how things are done. But control without support is an extremely blunt weapon. It can do things like suppressing an expenditure or replacing a person. However, this in itself does not ensure high performance or solve a problem. In particular, the replacing of people—a popular solution in the case of business problems—is often no solution at all. The people may change, but the problems survive. (The case of Function G as described above shows even that the very act of shifting people around too frequently breeds new problems.) A real influence on how things are done is obtained through a process of support rather than control: supplying new know-how or tools and becoming aware of the problems at the same time.

This analysis would not be complete if we did not look at something that underlies both control and support—power. Control, as we described it, can be equated with *formal* power, but this is only one side of the coin. We owe to the French sociologist Michel Crozier a study of the phenomenon of power in bureaucratic organizations. Crozier relates power—quite independently of the formal organization chart—to *uncertainty*. Whenever events have become completely certain or predictable in an organization, a well-planned production process, or a perfect bureaucracy, no one has much power however high his position. Real power rests with those who command the sources of uncertainty. In the well-planned production process, this may be the union leader who can authorize a strike or the personnel officer who negotiates with the union leader. In our case of international headquarters Function A (customer service), the main source of uncertainty is problems with customers. These are dealt with at the local office level. However, by virtue of its support relationship with the countries, the headquarters staff is called in whenever a problem becomes really serious—a procedure that keeps them in direct contact with the source of uncertainty; this is the real source of their power. In the case of Function G (marketing), again the uncertainties arise mainly at the sales office level. In this case, however, the lack of a support relationship—in the eyes of the people in the countries—cuts the international headquarters staff off from the sources of uncertainty, which means they have no real power.

Power, in the above sense, is the opposite of alienation. This kind of power means the ability to make a meaningful contribution to what is going on. What our study has shown is that such power is scarcely related to control (formal power) at all, but that it depends on the existence of a support relationship.

Strategies for Reducing Headquarters Alienation

Effective strategies for reducing headquarters alienation will, as shown by the previous data, at the same time make the headquarters—and through it, the entire organization—more effective. The challenge is formidable, conflicting as it does with the essence of the bureaucratic tradition. I can think of four strategies, four "R's," in increasing order of difficulty, as techniques for enriching headquarters management jobs: reflecting, recruiting, rewarding, and restructuring.

1. *Reflecting* means presenting headquarters with a periodic mirror to reflect its image with the subsidiaries it coordinates. The headquarters effectiveness study described earlier in this article was such a mirror. That the company's top management conducted it at all represented a recognition that the opinion of the people in the subsidiaries about headquarters did matter. A reflecting study of this kind is to the headquarters what a study of customer satisfaction is to a sales office. The headquarters effectiveness study generated an enormous amount of qualitative feedback, which was further handled at the level of each separate headquarters activity. Unfortunately, I do not possess data on the amount of change brought about by this feedback. However, an analogy with the process of change after regular employee attitude suverys (something that has been researched rather extensively) makes me suppose that the crucial factor in determining further change is the setting of priorities by higher management. This relates the strategy of reflecting to recruiting and rewarding.

2. *Recruiting* of personnel for headquarters management jobs is obviously of key importance for the role that headquarters will fulfill in the organization. We have noted previously that, by a process of natural selection, low achievers may be the ones to stay whereas the most successful people may leave. We have also seen the importance of the recruiting policy in the headquarters Function A case, where all managerial and professional jobs were filled by expractitioners from the service field, a practice that led to an effective support role for headquarters. If headquarters has to give support, it is essential that only people knowledgeable and experienced enough to be accepted as supporters are recruited to headquarters. However, this presents a conflict with two other reasons for recruiting in headquarters: training and shelving. In

many companies, serving a term at headquarters is an essential part of a person's training. Such a trainee is usually not the ideal supporter for the subsidiaries; it is often by the blunders he makes in his dealings with these subsidiaries that he really learns. The other reason for recruiting to headquarters is shelving: Managers, especially higher managers, who have become redundant elsewhere in the organization and for whom at the time no equivalent employment is available, are conveniently stored in a headquarters position, with a job title whose length generally is inversely related to its real content.

Recruiting for a support role at headquarters means that training assignments should be well distinguished and limited to those positions where expertise is less necessary and that attempts at shelving should be vigorously resisted. Last, the length of the headquarters assignment is very important. It probably takes an average of two years for a headquarters manager to establish the necessary personal contact with his clients; thus he only starts to be fully effective after that point. The ideal duration for a headquarters assignment, therefore, is not less than four years. An upper limit is less easy to mandate; six to eight years may be the period after which the headquarters manager's experience gets stale and he/she needs to have more direct on-line exposure to problems.

3. *Rewarding* is a crucial aspect of the headquarters' role dilemma. The formal reward structure of headquarters operations often prevents the building up of a support relationship. Headquarters people typically face upward—they are magnetically drawn toward the power center of the organization, which is physically close to them and from which they expect their rewards in the form of decisions on their careers. It is important to be visible to one's headquarters boss and to the higher bosses, up to the president.

A support relationship with the subsidiaries, however, means a facing outward and mostly downward in the hierarchy. Many headquarters people believe—with ample justification—they are not rewarded for that. They are not against support but, because their rewards lie elsewhere, they accord it low priority. Top management in headquarters communicates through its reward policy the kind of behavior it considers desirable. If the way to be promoted is to serve your boss ("He needs this report before Monday") rather than serve your clients in the subsidiaries, this will be the headquarters' priority; but the price to be paid is alienation.

In a study I did of budget control systems in five Dutch companies, I compared the attitudes of lower line managers about cooperation with the budget department to the budget department's criteria for performance appraisal. The latter were determined by asking the budget people to rank ten possible criteria in the order in which they thought their boss used them when appraising their performance. It appeared that what line managers thought about the budget department was related to where the budget people placed "tactfulness" as a performance criterion. In the company where the cooperation was best, the budget people thought that their tactfulness (in dealing with the line managers) was their boss' *first* criterion in appraising their performance. In the company with the worst cooperation, tactfulness placed fourth.

The company that placed tactfulness first had an interesting policy that I would recommend for any organization that wants its personnel to give high priority to support. For staff or headquarters jobs, this company determined who the clients were whom the staff man was supposed to serve. When it was time for the yearly performance evaluation, the staff man's boss was requested to call these clients and ask their opinions about the staff man's performance. Staff/line communications in this company were the best of the five companies studied.

4. *Restructuring* is the hardest way to reduce headquarters alienation; it may also be the most effective one. It means that in any case where a headquarters role leads to alienation, it should be determined whether or not this role can be eliminated completely. If a manager thinks he does not make a meaningful contribution to the success of the company, maybe his job should not be done at all. In the cases of the headquarters functions A and G, we saw that *size* has something to do with alienation; not so much the size of the entire organization, as of the units in which people work. Making a meaningful contribution is easier in a small group with face-to-face contact than in a large one; the needs for coordination, which detract from the contribution itself, increase disproportionally with the number of people. It is therefore important to keep headquarters groups small and to reduce their coordination with other groups to the minimum necessary. From a study of organizational stress in the early sixties, Robert L. Kahn of the University of Michigan and four others drew a number of conclusions on how to limit the need for coordination in organizations:

> . . . treat every coordinative requirement as a cost, which it is. For each functional unit in the organization, ask how independent it can be of others and of top management. For each position, ask how autonomous it can be made, what is the minimum number of other positions with which it must be connected, and for what activities and purposes the connections are essential. . . . The advocacy of minimal coordination contrasts sharply with the notions of centralized leadership, with the idea that ultimate and maximum control must originate from a central source and maximum information return to that source. Coordination only when justified by functional requirements or systemic risk also points up a common fault of management, a preoccupation with organizational symmetry and aesthetics, and an emphasis on the regularities and beauties of the organization chart. The organization which follows this principle of coordinative economy would not necessarily be small, but it would not have grown haphazardly and it would not regard size as an unmixed blessing. It would be decentralized, flat and lean, a federated rather than a lofty hierarchical structure.

In such an organization, the risk of headquarters alienation would be greatly reduced.

Conclusion

This article has been based on data collected in private business enterprises. The increase in alienation when we move from the periphery to the center of such organizations makes us recognize that business and public organizations, after all, are not so different. The stereotypes of the civil servant do apply to many a headquarters executive in business. Large organizations have problems in common, regardless of who owns them. However, business organizations have a tradition of greater flexibility. It is easier to experiment with new forms of organization in business than in government.

If we do not want to adopt the pessimistic view that our entire society is doomed to increasing bureaucratization with a consequent alienation, such experimentation with less bureaucratic organization forms is essential. We cannot stop with enriching the jobs of manual and office workers; in fact, some of the failures of job enrichment projects at those levels may stem from an absence of a job enrichment philosophy in the entire organization—including its headquarters management.

INDUSTRIAL DEMOCRACY AND PARTICIPATIVE MANAGEMENT: A CASE FOR A SYNTHESIS[1]

BERNARD M. BASS
V. J. SHACKLETON

Since World War II there has been the distinct growth of two trends in management-worker relations; industrial democracy and participative management. Both of them are ways of trying to increase shared decision making between workers and management. So are they the same, and if not what is the difference? *First,* the two methods have been adopted with different fervor and with different results in different countries. Thus industrial democracy has appeared most often in Europe; participative management in the United States. But with the increasing trend toward the internationalization and "harmonization" of business methods changes may be in store for American management. Examining what has happened in other parts of the world may give us some clues as to how things might go in the future.

A *second* difference is that despite their similarity of intent, they represent fundamental differences of method. Industrial democracy is a formal, usually legally sanctioned arrangement of worker representation at various levels of management decision making. Participative management is an informal style of face-to-face leadership, but these two models for worker-management collaboration, industrial democracy, and participative management, can complement each other rather than merely compensate for each other. An integration of both approaches can be made, although nationality differences, situational factors, and occupational level must be taken into account. Industrial democracy and participative management may each be best utilized for different aspects of managing the firm or agency. Both may be contraindicated for certain kinds of problems. Some understanding of the factors affecting the use of one approach rather than the other is obviously of great importance to modern management.

First we will look at what has been happening in the United States and other parts of the world.

[1] We wish to thank Dr. Eliezer Rosenstein, Technion-Israel Institute of Technology, for his assistance.

Reprinted from the *Academy of Management Review,* Vol. 4, No. 3, 1979, 393–404.

Sweden

Sweden has made the most progress toward industrial democracy and participation, but we need to clarify how these terms are used in this particular context. People started talking about participation in Sweden 50 years ago and they called it industrial democracy. More recently, experiments of all kinds, in and outside the business world, have been tried. Worker decision making, worker decision sharing, self-governing groups, and on-the-job democracy are some examples. In 1946, employer and employee organizations agreed that in firms with over 50 employees, works councils, with representatives from both sides, would meet regularly to solve problems and exchange information. Subsequently, these organizations started a number of projects in firms of various sizes to provide channels for employee influence. Presently, Sweden, Denmark, and Norway lead the way in shop-floor democracy.

In some factories in these countries autonomous working groups have been introduced. This approach is often called direct participation because it is concerned with the actual day-to-day content of a worker's job. Its aim is to increase autonomy and decision-making discretion as much as possible. Workers often take responsibility for their own inspection and progress control and may be self-managing from receipt of orders to inspection dispatch.

A distinction can be made between industrial democracy such as the works councils and the improvements in the "quality of working life" which autonomous group working can bring. It is true that the latter is often motivated by productivity considerations. However, the experiments of Volvo in Sweden, ICI and Phillips in the United Kingdom, and other examples, have resulted in attempts to bring back something of the craftsman approach to many jobs in offices and factories (7, 12, 22).

Britain

The United Kingdom and Ireland are the only countries in the European community that do not have statutory requirements for information dissemination, consultation, or worker representation on boards. Changes are occurring in the United Kingdom in a way which may put it along with the leaders of industrial democracy in Europe. Over the last two or three years there has been considerable debate in the United Kingdom about the future shape of industrial democracy. In early 1977 some far-reaching proposals for workers' representatives to sit on the Board of Directors of companies were put forward by the government-backed Bullock Committee. The Bullock ideas are now dead, killed by both trade unions and employers. The report had three fundamental flaws: (a) it tried to impose a universal formula for participation on British industry, (b) it virtually ignored the rights of nonunion members, and (c) it recommended immediate trade union parity on the board with shareholders' representatives. But out of this false start has come a government white paper, published in May 1978, which is a distinct improvement in all three areas. It emphasizes flexibility and voluntary participation schemes negotiated company by company. However, it also proposes a legally enforceable fallback to encourage both sides of industry to negotiate seriously.

The government white paper. The new proposal includes a two-tier system of company management that would be introduced into United Kingdom company law. But the first workers are unlikely to be appointed before 1984. As a first step toward evolving a "positive partnership" between management and workers it proposes that companies employing more than 500 people should be put under a legal obligation to discuss all "major proposals" affecting the workers with their trade union representatives. To that end, trade unions in companies should form joint representation committees (JRC's) which would have the right to require the boards to discuss industrial strategy.

The government also believes that employees should have a right of representation on the boards of their companies. It intends to legislate a two-tier board structure with separate policy and management boards as an option for any company. If unions and managements cannot agree on the arrangements for worker-directors, a statutory right to have employee representatives on a policy board for all companies with more than 2,000 people is envisaged. Here again the initiative will come from the JRC, which would have the power to require a ballot of all employees to decide if they want workers on the board. After the committee has had 3 or 4 years of experience, it would be able to exercise its statutory right to ballot.

The white paper's evolutionary, voluntary, flexible approach is seen as more in the spirit of industrial democracy than the more heavy-handed Bullock report. This makes it all the more unfortunate that many of Britain's industrialists reacted to the proposals with an outburst of criticism. As many commentators quipped, Britain's management greeted the white paper with the enthusiasm of the proverbial Victorian mill-owner faced with the abolition of child labor.

Social class and societal differences have created different needs within industrial democracy. The bane of British industrial relations remains the ingrained attitude of "them and us." These attitudes are far less marked in the industries of Europe and the United States. British industrialists are probably wrong in their exaggerated fear of worker directors. To think of them as posing nothing but problems contradicts much foreign experience and plays into the hands of those who see industry as nothing but a class battlefield. It is hoped that the white paper will move Britain forward in ways that build on the traditions and patterns of British industry and society.

Many large organizations have already implemented some of the white paper's recommendations or gone beyond them. Notable among them is the Post Office Board, which has reached agreement with the unions over a proposed two-year experiment in industrial democracy. In January, 1978, the existing seven-person board was replaced by a group of 19, with seven management and seven trade union members. Two "independents" were from a list submitted by a government minister responsible for the Post Office, but they have had to be agreed on by both sides. The independent element also includes two members appointed to represent the consumers' interests. The chairman or chief executive comes from the management side.

Participatory management. Many contend that putting employees on the board will force managements and unions to create the necessary substructure. Such a step would be expected to act as a guarantee and catalyst of effective participation at lower levels. Certainly, Chrysler (UK) Ltd. seems to be an example of an attempt to make participative management and industrial democracy walk hand-in-hand. In 1976 the company encouraged trade union representatives to sit in on management discussions, allowing them to participate in management decisions where they wish. A communication exercise was instituted to inform employees about company plans and problems. This involved an extensive training program involving all employees. At the plant level, employees have been involved in discussions involving production, health, and safety at work, as well as the company's future. Worker participation even extended to two seats on the Board of Directors. There were reports that initially many employees were skeptical or resistant, claiming that management was not serious about participation, and that the reforms were only instituted because of British government demands. But worker morale has improved and the company's labor relations have been drastically transformed (3, 7, 22).

Germany

In Germany, the industrial relations structure was mainly set up with the aid of the Allies, particularly the United States and Britain, at the end of World War II. New approaches were developed with a minimum of social strife, due in part to the structure of the unions. *First,* the unions are not fragmented as they were before the war and as they still are in the United Kingdom. The Federation of German Trade Unions was formed in 1949 with 16 member unions, one for each main sector of industry or service trade.

Second, a system of co-determination, or *Mitbestimmung,* was set up under which an enterprise has two boards—a management board and a supervisory board. The supervisory board involves the directors and sets company policy. The management board involves senior management concerned with day-to-day implementation. Companies with more than 500 workers have supervisory boards composed of two-thirds shareholders' representatives and one-third worker representatives. Only in the coal and steel industries is there an even split, although this is changing. By June, 1978, all companies with more than 2,000 employees were to have equal representation on supervisory boards. Such a system seems a logical extension of the much-praised postwar model, but it is not without its critics. Employers claim that important decisions may be deadlocked. Workers fear that parity will not be achieved because one of their members must be a senior executive elected by all white-collar workers, who may prove to support the shareholders' interests rather than the employees (7, 17, 25).

The United States

Despite their general appeal and common objectives, participative management and industrial democracy have developed independently. The promotion of one is somehow associated with the neglect of the other. Thus, in the United States, worker participation is associated with the participative style of management (6, 11, 13, 16). This is due, perhaps, to the more fertile soil in the United States, with its traditions of democracy and individualism, compared to the more class-conscious Europe. In Europe, worker participation is mainly associated with industrial democracy. But there is a continuing flow of influences across the Atlantic in both directions. European management has been under the influences of American management education in the post-World War II era. This has been due to United States' multinational corporate investment in European management education. The result has been a considerable transfer of participative management practices to Europe. However, one must not overlook important indigenous examples of participative management in Europe, principally the autonomous work groups in Norway, Sweden, and Denmark.

Now, we are beginning to see the first signs of the transfer of European-style industrial democracy to the United States. After the Chrysler Corporation offered its workers in Britain two seats on the British Board of Directors, United Auto Workers' President Leonard Woodcock wondered if Chrysler was ready to make the same offer in the United States, but he regarded the matter as "a philosophical thought," not as a major demand.

Industrial democracy has not been totally absent in the United States. In the early 1920s, the government model of an elected body of worker representatives with relatively little real power appeared in paternalistic companies. The widely-used, 20-year-old Scanlon Plan (10) for planning and sharing gains from the reduction of controllable labor costs contains many elements of participation. More recently, as a counterbalance to the adversary and crisis character of labor-management collective bargaining, the steel industry formed a joint labor-management committee. It was designed to work together as a study group on a continuing basis to address problems of common interest. Rushton management and its miners are practicing a form of industrial democracy, as is Eaton Corporation. Jamestown, New York, is involved in a total community effort involving unions, management, and the local community (19, 20, 21, 22).

Implementing worker participation is not always easy. In the early 1970s General Foods opened a pet food plant in Topeka, Kansas, that was designed to be run with the minimum of supervision. Many of the traditional tasks of management such as interviewing prospective employees, making job assignments, and even deciding pay raises were to be taken over by the workers. It has had mixed results, with many of the problems arising from the threatened role of management and professionals. It will no doubt take a long time for attitudes toward the traditional role of worker and manager to adjust to innovations such as the General Foods experiment. But the evidence also suggests that commitment and satisfaction among operatives is higher than under the old system (24).

Nevertheless, in the United States the two major models of industrial democracy and participative management have been almost mutually exclusive. Labor apologists have seen participative management, and the human relations movement in general, as management ploys to avoid sharing power with employees. Only through collective bargaining, they say, can employees exert real influence. And collective bargaining is industrial democracy rather than participation as we have described it. In fact, it is a form of "disjunctive" participation. Workers form an organization counter to that of management in order to interact with it from outside. Bargaining is distinctly different in form and effect from collaboration. Collective bargaining is a formal process of accommodation to resolve conflicting interests of equal parties. Joint collaboration, or consultation, assumes management and labor share common objectives that can provide a basis for cooperation between the two (3, 18, 22).

Two Trends: the Structural and the Behavioral

So far, we have seen that there are two initially distinct major trends. One is industrial democracy; the other is participative management. The *first* is structural; the *second* is behavioral.

The structural approach is formally organized industrial democracy, increasing the equalization of power by joint decision making through direct or elected representation on ad hoc or permanent committees, councils, and boards at various levels of management decision making.

The behavioral approach is participative management. It is face-to-face, informal sharing of decision making at the workplace. It is "shop-floor democracy." It is an informal arrangement between managers and subordinates whereby managers—through indoctrination, training, organizational policy, social pressure, or other means—involve their subordinates in consensual decision making about matters of importance to all concerned.

Just how effective are these changes in terms of increased satisfaction and productivity? One problem is that reliable empirical studies have been rare. The study by Obradovic (15) of Yugoslav worker council meetings or Rosenstein's (18) examination of the Israeli system have been exceptions. Publication is expected soon of a comprehensive study in 12 nations (excluding the United States) of the relation between mandated practices for industrial democracy and their behavioral consequences (9). Currently, we have to rely on various research studies that have sought to answer three main questions:

   a. What is the incidence of participative styles of management?
   b. Which styles do people prefer?
   c. How effective is each style?

These studies have allowed us to learn the conditions under which participation is likely to improve performance or to be counterproductive. Personality, task, organization, and culture make the difference. A description of a few of these research studies follows.

Incidence of Participative Styles

PROFILE is a survey feedback process (1). A questionnaire is completed by managers. A parallel one is completed by their subordinates. Recent results with over 350 managers and their 1500 subordinates from a variety of organizations show that the most common style of relating between middle managers and subordinates in the United States is *consultation*. The manager obtains information and opinion from his or her subordinates before making a decision. In similar studies we have completed in Spain for higher level managers in smaller firms, consultation likewise is the preferred way of relating to subordinates. However, manipulation and authoritarian direction are much more frequent observances in Spain than the United States.

Preference for Styles

Cascio (4) noted that among nearly 300 managers who played subordinate roles in Exercise Supervise, whether or not participants were satisfied in decision-making meetings with participative supervisors depended on their national identity. Table 1 shows that among Europeans and Japanese, at least

TABLE 1

Reported Satisfaction of Subordinates Following Decision Making with Participative, Persuasive, and Directive Superiors

Number	Culture	Percentage of Subordinates Who Were Most Satisfied in Decision-Making Meetings with Participative Supervisor
65	Dutch-Flemish	64.7
50	Nordic: Danish, Norwegian, Swedish, Austrian, West German, German Swiss	56.4
202	Anglo-Americans: British-Northern Irish, American, Australian	53.1
179	Latin: Brazilian, Columbian, French, Italian, Spanish, French Swiss, Walloon	52.6
28	Japanese	50.0
12	Greek	44.0
37	East Indian	29.4

Adapted from W. F. Cascio, "Functional Specialization, Culture, and Preference for Participative Management," *Personnel Psychology*, Vol. 27 (1974), p. 599.

50% were most satisfied with participative supervisors. But for India, the figure dropped to 29%. Even within the European group, there were marked differences. Subordinates from the Dutch-Flemish culture were most likely to be satisfied with a participative supervisor. Almost 65% were most satisfied with this arrangement, while the figures dropped to 56% for Nordic subordinates, 53% for Anglo-Americans, and 50% for Japanese.

Similarly, 75% of Indian managers preferred uninterested, uninvolved subordinates when making decisions; while Americans, Europeans, and Japanese preferred active, involved subordinates. Function made a difference as well. While 57% of managers from personnel preferred participative supervisors, only 50% from sales and 44% from finance did so.

Effectiveness of Styles

Results from our PROFILE studies point to organizational and task elements that affect the frequency with which participative management will be employed and influence its subsequent effectiveness. According to survey data from 277 United States' subordinates, participative management is most frequent when organizational policies are clear. It is also important that the manager has long-term objectives, the climate of the organization is warm and trusting, tasks are complex, and subordinates have more information about the decision than does the manager. Effectiveness of work unit operations is enhanced by participative management when organizational policies are clear, tasks are complex, and subordinates have more discretionary opportunities on how to complete their jobs.

A study of self-planning showed similar results (2). Several reasons can be offered for this. Sense of accomplishment may be greater when executing one's own plan rather than an assigned plan. There may be more commitment to see the validity of a plan by executing it successfully and more confidence that it can be done. Understanding of the plan is likely to be greater. Human resources may be better utilized. There may be a perception of more flexibility and more room for modification and initiative to make improvements in an assigned plan. There are likely to be fewer communication problems and consequent errors and distortions in pursuing instructions. Finally, competitive feelings aroused between planners and those who must execute the plans are avoided because planners and doers are the same persons.

However, there were distinct differences between the efficiency of self-planning, depending on the nationality of the manager. Managers from the United States profited the most from self-planning, while Northern European managers seemed to gain the least. Efficiency differences favoring self-planning by nationalities were in order: North Americans, Irish, French, Colombians, British, Italians, Japanese, Belgians, Dutch, Swiss, Danes, and West Germans. Surprisingly, the West Germans implemented others' plans slightly more efficiently than their own plans. This was the only nationality where there were no efficiency differences in favor of self-planning. Although the German sample did just as well working on others' plans as their own, they were like other nationalities in preferring to work on their own plan, feeling more committed and responsible for it and thinking it to be a better plan.

Reconciling the Differences between Industrial Democracy and Participative Management

Despite the major differences between industrial democracy and participative management, the idea of worker participation, in all its forms, is widespread today in a variety of economic and political systems. However, there is a considerable gap between the ideological acceptance of the idea and its actual implementation. This gap constitutes a source of disappointment to those ardent advocates of participation who find it difficult to illustrate, on a wide scale, the positive impact of participatory programs.

We now see the prospects brightening for a merger of the two models and propose that there are three types of relationships. *First,* industrial democracy and participative management can be compensatory; if you have one, you do not need the other. *Second,* one approach can complement the other. *Third,* differential application can be used in such a way that each can be applied to different aspects of worker-management relations. Let us look at each of these alternatives.

Compensatory Relationship

With industrial democracy, properly practiced, workers can vote for policy changes through their elected representatives. They can make their feelings known by communicating with their elected representatives. The major weakness of this argument is that it is almost impossible for the shop-floor worker to participate in decisions made at the top of the hierarchy. Another weakness is the exclusion of the lower and middle management from the participatory process. These managers, often ignored and eliminated from the mechanisms of industrial democracy, disassociate themselves from the participatory process and undermine its potential effectiveness.

On the other hand, with participative management, the argument is that no formal organizational mechanisms are needed to permit workers to air their grievances and suggestions with their superiors. Regular organizational channels can be used. What they discuss is likely to be more relevant to their immediate workplace than to organization-wide matters. However, the danger of concentrating on participative management measures of all kinds while ignoring participation at the top is that when the crucial and strategic decisions are made unilaterally by management, participation at the bottom of the hierarchy will be gradually limited to marginal issues. Consequently, participative management measures will lose their meaningfulness.

Complementary Relationship

Each approach can reinforce the other. Democracy, or better yet, consensual decision making, is practiced within the immediate face-to-face work group as well as in the election of representatives to higher management councils. To have substance, industrial democracy must operate side by side with face-to-face participative management. Research has shown that in Yugoslavia, with the formalities of worker council decision making about organization-wide issues, it is the managers, bankers, technocrats, Communist party members, and other key people who initiate the decisions of consequence. Workers may feel no real ownership of decisions in an industrial democracy where immediate manager-worker relationships are traditional and authoritarian. Similarly, other writers have described the phenomenon of "double loyalty" and other internal problems of integrative mechanisms in West Germany and Israel.

A major problem of industrial democracy is how to separate union participation in top-level decision making from collective bargaining. Critics argue that unions will use what they have learned on the board about overall strategy in areas such as manpower planning and investment for furthering the interests of their members. Although the European experience has often been that these problems do not materialize, it is a sensitive area for the defenders of industrial democracy.

The key to mutual support between participative management and industrial democracy lies in the extent to which participative management results in self-planning in the organization. As technology advances, increasingly the worker becomes the regulator of an industrial process—the adjuster, monitor, and diagnostician dealing with unprogrammed, unpredictable fluctuations in the system (5). For this kind of effort, workers must have an understanding of that part of the system for which they are responsible. This understanding should be based on broad rather than narrow training. The worker should be ready to react without necessary consultation with higher authority. Self-planning is the key to the complementarity of participative management and industrial democracy.

Self-planning in different situations. The decision as to whether to operate self-planning varies according to the situation. For example, planning may require special knowledge, information, and facilities ordinarily unavailable to the doers. Time required to plan may make it impossible for those who must execute the plans to engage in developing them. There are individual as well as national differences in performance and satisfaction with self-planning.

The end objectives may have to be imposed by higher authority while the means could be left to self-planning. For example, delivery of quality service within satisfactory cost constraints may be imposed by legislative requirements on hospital board policies. Yet, much self-planning could be introduced to reach these objectives.

Let us now look at some of these situational considerations in more depth, by taking a hypothetical corporation called Fixit Corporation whose president decides that self-planning is a good idea. The president calls in a consultant. What might the consultant look for as prerequisites for effective self-planning? Since Fixit Corporation has factories and offices in many parts of the world, one important factor in self-planning might be the *nationality* of the personnel employed. The implications of the Cascio study for Fixit Corporation are that the greatest benefits from self-planning are to be gained in the United States, France, and Britain. At the West German site, plans might be developed at the United States headquarters and communicated to the German management team.

The next factor considered by the consultant is the *occupational level*. Self-planning clearly constitutes a meaningful means of participation for professionals because of their strong identification with their occupation and their expectations for job satisfaction. In most cases they expect to take part in the planning phase of their work. Self-planning by professionals may help to moderate the potential conflict between the professional and the organization. But the importance and meaningfulness of self-planning as a component of the job has also surfaced for blue-collar and white-collar employees, hand in hand with the growing interest in job enrichment. Because job enrichment work has been ongoing in all the countries in which Fixit Corporation has sites, this brings into question whether all jobs ought to be considered for greater self-planning.

Whether the work is *programmed* or *unprogrammed* also has a bearing on self-planning. There are greater efficiencies in standardized programs and plans such as blueprints or available computer routines and the conditions for self-planning are constrained by these already available procedures for getting work done. Nevertheless, in most firms, including Fixit Corporation, there remains much unprogrammed work now planned by higher authority or by staff specialists whose plans are reviewed by higher authority before they are implemented. It is in these unprogrammable areas that self-planning and self-monitoring can be used to advantage. So the consultant looks at the specific jobs in Fixit Corporation. Many of the supervisory jobs in assembly, quality control, and packaging areas involve unprogrammed activities such as personnel problems, equipment breakdowns, shortage of materials, covering for a sick workmate, etc. These are obvious areas for self-planning in small teams.

This brings in the question of *training*. Many of the skills learned by supervisors, such as planning, are skills that will be needed by operators if self-planning is to be encouraged. Special training may be provided to operators in Fixit Corporation on objective setting, scheduling, evaluating plans, and measuring progress toward achieving goals. The likely result is an upgrading of the status and general skill level of all members of the organization. Operators now plan and staff planners become teachers and consultants on how to plan. In addition, operator self-planning requires fuller understanding of organizational processes and policies outside the immediate working area of the operator. Again, broader training of operators is likely to be required. This in turn is likely to make operators more readily available for transfer and promotion, more alert to system problems, and more ready and able to communicate such discoveries to colleagues and bosses.

Self-planning goes with *self-direction* and *self-control*. It becomes necessary to do so if adequate self-direction and self-control are to be expected, for the latter will require high degrees of understanding, commitment, and felt responsibility which are most likely to develop under self-planning.

Next, the consultant considers the prerequisites in managerial attitudes and policies. A fundamental *policy change* is required if self-planning is to be encouraged. As long as planning is seen as a management prerogative, self-planning will be in conflict with the organization's authority and decision structure. Many other changes may be required also if self-planning is to be encouraged, changes more suited to an industrial democracy than a traditional top-down organization.

The allocation of more responsibility and autonomy to operating personnel requires management to take more *risks*. At the same time, organization development efforts need to be encouraged to reduce worker suspiciousness about management's motivation as opportunities for worker self-planning are increased. If self-planning is instituted, *coordination* requirements within the "doer" group are likely to increase. More attention will have to be paid to the horizontal communications—characteristic of democratic rather than autocratic management. Thus the Fixit Corporation consultant has to consider additional communications training for all employees. A most important factor to consider is whether senior managers are prepared for the terrific strain that self-planning will impose on the whole organization as it moves even further than it is already toward a democratic, participative climate.

Differential Applications

What we have seen so far is the general utility of a mutually supportive participative management within a democratically organized industry. Further examination suggests that while many issues call for both, different issues may call for one without the other, or for neither.

We can sort issues into: (a) those likely to be better handled by means of democratically elected worker representatives, (b) those better handled by face-to-face participative management, (c) those where both approaches are likely to be appropriate, and (d) those where neither is desirable and it is advisable to reserve decisions exclusively for management (assuming them to be responsible to all constituencies—including employees, shareholders, customers, and community). Table 2 illustrates these four possibilities and our reasons for the choice of approach. It also suggests some examples as a basis for further study and examination. The nature of the subject may determine the extent to which industrial democracy and/or participative management measures can be effectively used. It is dangerous to talk, though, in universal terms, because this may vary by country depending on the structure of the organization and the value system of the particular society. Fortunately, a 12-nation consortium is completing a detailed examination of what industrial democratic practices are required within their countries and what are the behavioral outcomes (9). Preliminary analyses suggest that the speculations presented here will be subject, to some extent, to confirmation or disconfirmation.

TABLE 2

Speculative Suggestions for Issues That Can Be Dealt with Best by
Industrial Democracy, Participative Management, Both, and Neither

Issues	Industrial Democracy	Participative Management	Reason
Pay and benefits	Yes	No	Principles of equity, company finances, need to avoid maximizing self-interest.
Job satisfaction	No	Yes	Participative management will directly improve.
Career development	Yes	Yes	Broad policies need to be set at higher levels, but career planning is best as self-planning.
Working conditions: sociotechnical issues	Yes	Yes	Plant-wide problems and community affairs are best dealt with by council and staff. On the other hand, changes may be instituted and implemented best through participation in the decision process at the local level.
Job security	Yes	Yes	Market conditions and finance of the firm as a whole require organization-wide attention. Yet some commitment to strategies such as sharing reductions in hours can be best accomplished at local levels via participative endeavor.
Financing/marketing	No	No	Optimal strategies here should be sought by a management responsible to its various constituencies. To the degree that best solutions are matters of mathematics, legal constraint, or market demands rather than debate, decisions should be reached without worker involvement.

Conclusions

We have examined the relationships between two models of worker participation: industrial democracy and participative management. These models have developed independently, yet from a conceptual and a practical point of view there is no need to view them as mutually exclusive. Because both models are based on the assumption that those at the bottom of an organizational hierarchy should take part in managerial decision making, they may reinforce and augment each other.

Although the two types of worker participation must be simultaneously developed and integrated, there is also an optimal division of labor between them in terms of organizational and personnel issues to be dealt with. Cultural and national differences must also be taken into account. A major factor in the effectiveness of industrial democracy will be the extent to which it fosters development and implementation of participative management styles at all levels in organizations.

It is unlikely that the trend toward industrial democracy and participative management is "a passing fad." The results of a 1975 survey of the readership of the *Harvard Business Review* give some indication (14). The question posed was whether management ideology in 1985 would be dominated by concerns for the human and social side of enterprise or by the classical economic arguments for profit maximization and survival of the fittest.

Given one extreme or the other, 73 percent of the United States respondents felt that by 1985 management ideology will be dominated by concerns for self-fulfillment and self-respect. A well-designed organization will make full use of individual capabilities. Rights to income, health, and education will be seen as more important than property rights. Regulation is necessary because community needs often differ from consumer needs. This anticipated socially responsible management world view is the antithesis of Social Darwinism—only the fit survive in an individualistic struggle in which initiative and hard work pay off. Property rights and unregulated free market are sacrosanct as the guarantees of individual liberty.

In spite of their expectations of a more socially concerned future, two-thirds of these same United States respondents preferred to be identified with Social Darwinism, even more so if they were older, senior executives. Perhaps indicative of more experience with industrial democracy by 1975 in Europe, two-thirds of the foreign readers who responded to *HBR* were in favor of the socially minded view.

A majority of United States managers today see themselves as institutional stewards trying to find optimum solutions that meet the diverse interests of their organizational sponsors, government, clients, and employees. In the coming years, we expect increasing attention to be paid to industrial democracy and participative management as ways to achieve such optimization (14).

References

1. Bass, Bernard M. "A Systems Survey Research and Feedback Procedure for Management and Organizational Development," *Journal of Applied Behavioral Science,* Vol. 12 (1976), 215–229.
2. Bass, Bernard M. "Utility of Self-Planning on a Simulated Production Task with Replications in Twelve Countries," *Journal of Applied Psychology,* Vol. 65 (1977), 506–509.
3. Bass, Bernard M., and Eliezer Rosenstein. "Integration of Industrial Democracy and Participative Management: U.S. and European Perspectives," in *Managerial Control and Organizational Democracy,* B. T. King, S. S. Streufert, and Fred E. Fiedler (eds.), (Washington, D.C.: Victor Winston & Sons, 1977).
4. Cascio, W. F. "Functional Specialization, Culture and Preference for Participative Management," *Personnel Psychology,* Vol. 27 (1974), 593–603.
5. Davis, Louis E. "The Coming Crisis for Production Management: Technology and Organization," *International Journal of Production Research,* Vol. 9 (1971), 65–82.
6. Derber, J. "Cross-Currents in Workers' Participation," *Industrial Relations,* Vol. 9 (1970), 123–136.
7. Emery, F. E., and E. Thorsrud. *The Form and Content in Industrial Democracy* (London: Tavistock, 1969).
8. Hall, R. H. *Occupations and the Social Structure* (Englewood Cliffs, N.J.: Prentice-Hall, 1975).

9. IDE International Research Group, "Industrial Democracy in Europe," *Social Science Information*, Vol. 15 (1976), 177–203.

10. Lesieur, Fred (ed.). *The Scanlon Plan* (New York: Wiley, 1958).

11. Likert, Rensis. *The Human Organization* (New York: McGraw-Hill, 1967).

12. Link, R. "Alienation," *Sweden Now*, June 1971, pp. 36–39.

13. MacGregor, Douglas. *The Human Side of Enterprise* (New York: McGraw-Hill, 1960).

14. Martin, W. F., and G. C. Lodge. "Our Society in 1985—Business May Not Like It," *Harvard Business Review*, Nov.–Dec. 1975, pp. 143–152.

15. Obradovic, J. "Workers' Participation: Who Participates?" *Industrial Relations*, Vol. 14 (1975), 32–44.

16. Patchen, M. *Participation, Achievement and Involvement on the Job* (Englewood Cliffs, N.J.: Prentice-Hall, 1972).

17. Raskin, A. H. "The Workers' Voice in German Companies," *New York Times*, June 11, 1976, section 4, p. 7.

18. Rosenstein, Eliezer. *Workers Participation in Management: Problematic Issues in the Israeli System*, Unpublished paper, School of Management, SUNY, Binghamton, N.Y., 1976.

19. Roach, John M. *Workers' Participation: New Voices in Management* (New York: The Conference Board, 1973).

20. Roach, John M. *Recent Initiatives in Labor-Management Co-operation* (Washington, D.C.: National Center for Productivity and Quality of Working Life, 1976).

21. Singer, J. N. "Participative Decision-Making About Work—An Overdue Look at Variables Which Mediate Its Effects," *Sociology of Work and Occupations*, Vol. 1 (1974), 347–371.

22. Strauss, G., and Eliezer Rosenstein. "Workers' Participation: A Critical View," *Industrial Relations*, Vol. 9 (1970), 197–214.

23. Walker, K. "Workers' Participation in Management—Problems, Practice and Prospects," *Bulletin of International Institute of Labor Studies*, Vol. 12 (1974), 3–35.

24. Walton, Richard E. "Quality of Working Life: What is It?" *Sloan Management Review*, Fall 1973, pp. 11–12.

25. Wilpert, B. "Research on Industrial Democracy: The German Case," *Industrial Relations Journal*, Vol. 6 (1975), 53–64.

17 organization design: organization structure and communication networks

DESIGNING THE INNOVATING ORGANIZATION

JAY R. GALBRAITH

Innovation is in. New workable, marketable ideas are being sought and promoted these days as never before in the effort to restore U.S. leadership in technology, in productivity growth, and in the ability to compete in the world marketplace. Innovative methods for conserving energy and adapting to new energy sources are also in demand.

The popular press uses words like *revitalization* to capture the essence of the issue. The primary culprit of our undoing, up until now, has been management's short-run earnings focus. However, even some patient managers with long-term views are finding that they cannot buy innovation. They cannot exhort their operating organizations to be more innovative and creative. Patience, money, and a supportive leadership are not enough. It takes more than these things to achieve innovation.

It is my contention that innovation requires an organization specifically designed for that purpose—that is, such an organization's structure, processes, rewards, and people must be combined in a special way to create an innovating organization, one that is designed to do something for the first time. The point to be emphasized here is that the innovating organization's components are completely different from and often contrary to those of existing organizations, which are generally operating organizations. The latter are designed to efficiently process the millionth loan, produce the millionth automobile, or serve the millionth client. An organization that is designed to do something well for the millionth time is not good at doing something for the first time. Therefore, organizations that want to innovate or revitalize themselves need two organizations, an operating organization and an innovating organization. In addition, if the ideas produced by the innovating organization are to be implemented by the operating organization, they need a transition process to transfer ideas from the innovating organization to the operating organization.

This article will describe the components of an organization geared to producing innovative ideas. Specifically, in the next section of this article, I describe a case history that illustrates the components required for successful innovation. Then I will explore the lessons to be learned from this case history by describing the role structure, the key processes, the reward systems, and the people practices that characterize an innovating organization.

The Innovating Process

Before I describe the typical process by which innovations occur in organizations, we must understand what we are discussing. What is innovation? How do we distinguish between invention and innovation? Invention is the creation of a new idea. Innovation is the process of applying a new idea to create a new process or product. Invention occurs more frequently than innovation. In addition, the kind of innovation in which we are interested here is the kind that becomes necessary to implement a new idea that is not consistent with the current concept of the organization's business. Many new ideas that are consistent with an organization's current business concept are routinely generated in some companies. Those are not our current concern; here we are concerned with implementing inventions that are good ideas but do not quite fit into the organization's current mold. Industry has a poor track record with this type of innovation. Most major technological changes come from outside an industry. The mechanical typewriter manufacturers did not introduce the electric typewriter; the electric typewriter people did not invent the electronic typewriter; vacuum tube companies did not introduce the transistor, and so on. Our objective is to describe an organization that will increase the odds that such nonroutine innovations can be made. The following case history of a nonroutine innovation presents a number of lessons that illustrate how we can design an innovating organization.

The Case History

The organization in question is a venture that was started in the early seventies. While working for one of our fairly innovative electronics firms, a group of engineers developed a new electronics product. However, they were in a division that did not have the charter for their product. The ensuing political battle caused the engineers to leave and form their own company. They successfully found venture capital and introduced their new product. Initial acceptance was good, and within several years their company was growing rapidly and had become the industry leader.

However, in the early 1970s Intel invented the microprocessor, and by the mid-to-late seventies, this innovation had spread through the electronics industries. Manufacturers of previously "dumb" products now had the capability of incorporating intelligence into their product lines. A competitor who understood computers and software introduced just such a product into our new venture firm's market, and it met with high acceptance. The firm's president responded by hiring someone who knew something about microcomputers and some software people and instructing the engineering department to respond to the need for a competing product.

The president spent most of his time raising capital to finance the venture's growth. But when he suddenly realized that the engineers had not made much progress, he instructed them to get a product out quickly. They did, but it was a half-hearted effort. The new product incorporated a microprocessor but was less than the second-generation product that was called for.

Even though the president developed markets in Europe and Singapore, he noticed that the competitor continued to grow faster than his company and had started to steal a share of his company's market. When the competitor became the industry leader, the president decided to take charge of the product-development effort. However, he found that the hardware proponents and software proponents in the engineering department were locked in a political battle. Each group felt that its "magic" was the more powerful. Unfortunately, the lead engineer (who was a co-founder of the firm) was a hardware proponent, and the hardware establishment prevailed. However, they then clashed head-on with the marketing department, which agreed with the software proponents. The conflict resulted in studies and presentations, but no new product. So here was a young, small (1,200 people) entrepreneurial firm that could not innovate even though the president wanted innovation and provided resources to produce it. The lesson is that more was needed.

As the president became more deeply involved in the problem, he received a call from his New England sales manager, who wanted him to meet a field engineer who had modified the company's product and programmed it in a way that met customer demands. The sales manager suggested, "We may have something here."

Indeed, the president was impressed with what he saw. When the engineer had wanted to use the company's product to track his own inventory, he wrote to company headquarters for programming instructions. The response had been: It's against company policy to send instructional materials to field engineers. Undaunted, the engineer bought a home computer and taught himself to program. He then modified the product in the field and programmed it to solve his problem. When the sales manager happened to see what was done, he recognized its significance and immediately called the president.

The field engineer accompanied the president back to headquarters and presented his work to the engineers who had been working on the second-generation product for so long. They brushed off his efforts as idiosyncratic, and the field engineer was thanked and returned to the field.

A couple of weeks later the sales manager called the president again. He said that the company would lose this talented guy if something wasn't done. Besides, he thought that the field engineer, not engineering, was right. While he was considering what to do with this ingenious engineer, who, on his own had produced more than the entire engineering department, the president received a request from the European sales manager to have the engineer assigned to him.

The European sales manager had heard about the field engineer when he visited headquarters, and had sought him out and listened to his story. The sales manager knew that a French bank wanted the type of application that the field engineer had created for himself; a successful application would be worth an order for several hundred machines. The president gave the go-ahead and sent the field engineer to Europe. The engineering department persisted in their view that the program wouldn't work. Three months later, the field engineer successfully developed the application, and the bank signed the order.

When the field engineer returned, the president assigned him to a trusted marketing manager who was told to protect him and get a product out. The engineers were told to support the manager and reluctantly did so. Soon they created some applications software and a printed circuit board that could easily be installed in all existing machines in the field. The addition of this board and the software temporarily saved the company and made its current product slightly superior to that of the competitor.

Elated, the president congratulated the young field engineer and gave him a good staff position working on special assignments to develop software. Then problems arose. When the president tried to get the personnel department to give the engineer a special cash award, they were reluctant. "After all," they said, "other people worked on the effort too. It will set a precedent." And so it went. The finance department wanted to withhold $500 from the engineer's pay because he had received a $1,000 advance for his European trip, but had turned in vouchers for only $500.

The engineer didn't help himself very much either; he was hard to get along with and refused to accept supervision from anyone except the European sales manager. When the president arranged to have him permanently transferred to Europe on three occasions, the engineer changed his mind about going at the last minute. The president is still wondering what to do with him.

There are a number of lessons about the needs of an innovative organization in this not uncommon story. The next section elaborates on these lessons.

The Innovating Organization

Before we can draw upon the case history's lessons, it is important to note that the basic components of the innovating organization are no different from those of an operating organization. That is, both include a task, a structure, processes, reward systems, and people, as shown in Figure 1. Table 1

FIGURE 1

Organization Design Components

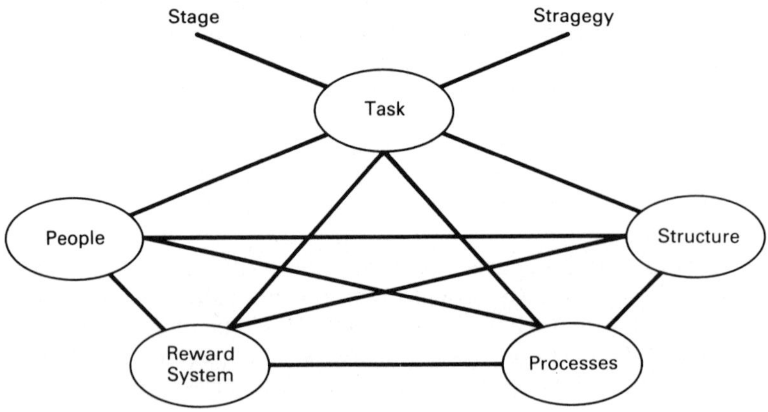

TABLE 1

Comparison of Components of Operating and Innovating Organizations

	Operating Organization	Innovating Organization

Structure	Division of labor
	Departmentalization
	Span of control
	Distribution of power
		Roles:
		  Orchestrator
		  Sponsor
		  Idea generator (champion)
		Differentiation
		Reservations

Processes	Providing information and communication Planning and budgeting Measuring performance Linking departments	Planning/funding Getting ideas Blending ideas Transitioning Managing programs
Reward systems	Compensation Promotion Leader style Job design	Opportunity/autonomy Promotion/recognition Special compensation
People	Selection/recruitment Promotion/transfer Training/development	Selection/self-selection Training/development

compares the design parameters of the operating organization's components with those of the innovating organization's components.

This figure shows that each component must fit with each of the other components and with the task. A basic premise of this article is that the task of the innovating organization is fundamentally different from that of the operating organization. The innovating task is more uncertain and risky, takes place over longer time periods, assumes that failure in the early stages may be desirable, and so on. Therefore, the organization that performs the innovative task should also be different. Obviously, a firm that wishes to innovate needs both an operating organization and an innovating organization. Let's look at the latter.

Structure of the Innovating Organization

The structure of the innovating organization encompasses these elements: (1) people to fill three vital roles—idea generators, sponsors, and orchestrators; (2) differentiation, a process that differentiates or separates the innovating organization's activities from those of the operating organization; and (3) "reservations," the means by which the separation occurs—and this may be accomplished physically, financially, or organizationally.

The part that each of these elements plays in the commercialization of a new idea can be illustrated by referring to the case history.

Roles

Like any organized phenomenon, innovation is brought about through the efforts of people who interact in a combination of roles. Innovation is not an individual phenomenon. People who must interact to produce a commercial product—that is, to innovate in the sense we are discussing—play their roles as follows:

• Every innovation starts with an *idea generator* or idea champion. In the above example, the field engineer was the person who generated the new idea—that is, the inventor, the entrepreneur, or risk taker on whom much of our attention has been focused. The case history showed that an idea champion is needed at each stage of an idea's or an invention's development into an innovation. That is, at each stage there must be a dedicated, full-time individual whose success or failure depends on developing the idea. The idea generator is usually a low-level person who experiences a problem and develops a new response to it. The lesson here is that many ideas originate down where "the rubber meets the road." The low status and authority level of the idea generator creates a need for someone to play the next role.

• Every idea needs at least one *sponsor* to promote it. To carry an idea through to implementation, someone has to discover it and fund the increasingly disruptive and expensive development and testing efforts that shape it. Thus idea generators need to find sponsors for their ideas so they can perfect them. In our example, the New England sales manager, the European sales manager, and finally the marketing manager all sponsored the field engineer's idea. Thus one of the sponsor's functions is to lend his or her authority and resources to an idea to carry the idea closer to commercialization.

The sponsor must also recognize the business significance of an idea. In any organization, there are hundreds of ideas being promoted at any one time. The sponsor must select from among these ideas those that might become marketable. Thus it is best that sponsors be generalists. (However, that is not always the case, as our case history illustrates.)

Sponsors are usually middle managers who may be anywhere in the organization and who usually work for both the operating and the innovating organization. Some sponsors run divisions or departments. They must be able to balance the operating and innovating needs of their business or function. On the other hand, when the firm can afford the creation of venture groups, new product development departments, and the like, sponsors may work full time for the innovating organization. In the case history, the two sales managers spontaneously became sponsors and the marketing manager was formally designated as a sponsor by the president. The point here is that by formally designating the role or recognizing it, funding it with monies earmarked for innovation, creating innovating incentives, and developing and selecting sponsorship skills, the organization can improve its odds of coming up with successful innovations. Not much attention has been given to sponsors, but they need equal attention because innovation will not occur unless there are people in the company who will fill all three roles.

• The third role illustrated in the case history is that of the *orchestrator*. The president played this role. An orchestrator is necessary because new ideas are never neutral. Innovative ideas are destructive; they destroy investments in capital equipment and people's careers. The management of ideas is a political process. The problem is that the political struggle is biased toward those in the establishment who have authority and control of resources. The orchestrator must balance the power to give the new idea a chance to be tested in the face of a negative establishment. The orchestrator must protect idea people, promote the opportunity to try out new ideas, and back those whose ideas prove effective. This person must legitimize the whole process. That is what the president did with the field engineer; before he became involved, the hardware establishment had prevailed. Without an orchestrator, there can be no innovation.

548

To play their roles successfully, orchestrators use the processes and rewards to be described in the following sections. That is, a person orchestrates by funding innovating activities and creating incentives for middle managers to sponsor innovating ideas. Orchestrators are the organization's top managers, and they must design the innovating organization.

The typical operating role structure of a divisional firm is shown in Figure 2. The hierarchy is one of the operating functions reporting to division general managers who are, in turn, grouped under group executives. The group executives report to the chief executive officer (CEO). Some of these people play roles in both the operating and the innovating organization.

The innovating organization's role structure is shown in Figure 3. The chief executive and a group executive function as orchestrators. Division managers are the sponsors who work in both the operating and the innovating organizations. In addition, several reservations are created in which managers of research and development (R&D), corporate development, product development, market development, and new process technology function as full-time sponsors. These reservations allow the separation of innovating activity from the operating activity. This separation is an organizing choice called differentiation. It is described next.

FIGURE 2

Typical Operating Structure of Divisionalized Firm

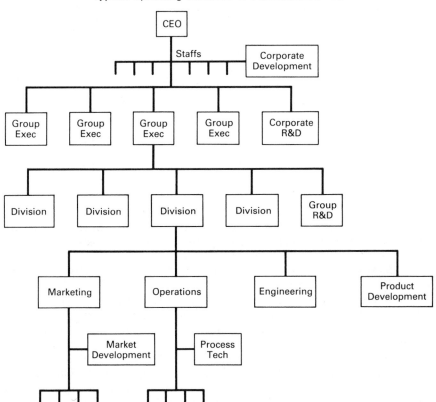

FIGURE 3

An Innovating Role Structure (differentiation)

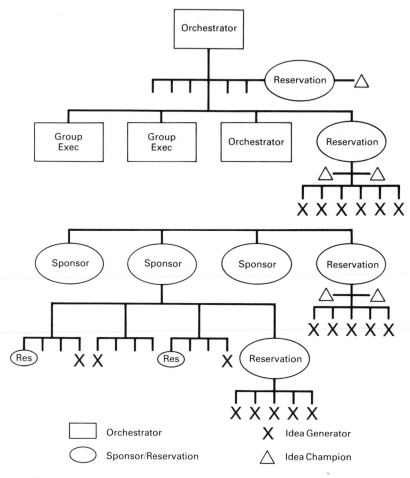

Differentiation

In the case history we saw that the innovative idea perfected at a remote site was relatively advanced before it was discovered by management. The lesson to be learned from this is that if one wants to stimulate new ideas, the odds are better if early efforts to perfect and test new "crazy" ideas are differentiated—that is, separated—from the functions of the operating organization. Such differentiation occurs when an effort is separated physically, financially, and/or organizationally from the day-to-day activities that are likely to disrupt it. If the field engineer had worked within the engineering department or at company headquarters, his idea probably would have been snuffed out prematurely.

Another kind of differentiation can be accomplished by freeing initial idea tests from staff controls designed for the operating organization. The effect of too much control is illustrated by one company in which a decision on whether to buy an oscilloscope took about 15 to 30 minutes (with a shout across the room) before the company was acquired by a larger organization. After the acquisition, that same type of decision took 12 to 18 months because the purchaser required a capital appropriation request. Controls based on operating logic reduce the innovating organization's ability to rapidly, cheaply, and frequently test and modify new ideas. Thus, the more differentiated an initial effort is, the greater the likelihood of innovation.

The problem with differentiation, however, is that it decreases the likelihood that a new proven idea will be transferred back to the operating organization. Herein lies the differentiation/transfer dilemma: The more differentiated the effort, the greater the likelihood of producing a new business idea, but the less likelihood of transferring the new idea into the operating organization for implementation. The dilemma occurs only when the organization needs both invention and transfer. That is, some organizations may not need to transfer new ideas to the operating organization. For example, when Exxon started its information systems business, there was no intention to have the petroleum company run this area of business. Exxon innovators had to grow their own operating organizations; therefore, they could maximize differentiation in the early phases. Alternatively, when Intel started work on the 64K RAM (the next generation of semiconductor memories, this random access memory holds roughly 64,000 bits of information), the effort was consistent with their current business and the transfer into fabrication and sales was critical. Therefore, the development effort was only minimally separated from the operating division that was producing the 16K RAM. The problem becomes particularly difficult when a new product or process differs from current ones, but must be implemented through the current manufacturing and sales organizations. The greater the need for invention and the greater the difference between the new idea and the existing business concept, the greater the degree of differentiation required to perfect the idea. The only way to accomplish both invention and transfer is to proceed stagewise. That is, differentiate in the early phases and then start the transition process before development is completed so that only a little differentiation is left when the product is ready for implementation. The transition process is described in the section on key processes (page 552).

In summary, invention occurs best when initial efforts are separated from the operating organization and its controls—because innovating and operating are fundamentally opposing logics. This kind of separation allows both to be performed simultaneously and prevents the establishment from prematurely snuffing out a new idea. The less the dominant culture of the organization supports innovation, the greater is the need for separation. Often this separation occurs naturally as in the case history, or clandestinely, as in "bootlegging." If a firm wants to foster innovation, it can create reservations where innovating activity can occur as a matter of course. Let us now turn to this last structural parameter.

Reservations

Reservations are organizational units, such as R&D groups, that are totally devoted to creating new ideas for future business. The intention is to reproduce a garage-like atmosphere where people can rapidly and frequently test their ideas. Reservations are havens for "safe learning." When innovating, one wants to maximize early failure to promote learning. On reservations that are separated from operations, this cheap, rapid screening can take place.

Reservations permit differentiation to occur by housing people who work solely for the innovating organization and by having a reservation manager who works full time as a sponsor. They may be located within divisions and/or at corporate headquarters to permit various degrees of differentiation.

Reservations can be internal or external. Internal reservations may include some staff and research groups, product and process development labs, and groups that are devoted to market development, new ventures, and/or corporate development. They are organizational homes where idea generators can contribute without becoming managers. Originally, this was the purpose of staff groups, but staff groups now frequently assume control responsibilities or are narrow specialists who contribute to the current business idea. Because such internal groups can be expensive, outside reservations like universities, consulting firms, and advertising agencies are often used to tap nonmanagerial idea generators.

Reservations can be permanent or temporary. The internal reservations described above, such as R&D units, are reasonably permanent entities. Others can be temporary. Members of the operating organization may be relieved of operating duties to develop a new program, a new process, or a new product. When developed, they take the idea into the operating organization and resume their operating responsibilities. But for a period of time they are differentiated from operating functions to varying degrees in order to innovate, fail, learn, and ultimately perfect a new idea.

Collectively the roles of orchestrators, sponsors, and idea generators working with and on reservations constitute the structure of the innovating organization. Some of the people, such as sponsors and orchestrators, play roles in both organizations; reservation managers and idea generators work only for the innovating organization. Virtually everyone in the organization can be an idea generator, and all middle managers are potential sponsors. However not all choose to play these roles. People vary considerably in their innovating skills. By recognizing the need for these roles, developing people to fill them, giving them opportunity to use their skills in key processes, and rewarding innovating accomplishments, the organization can do considerably better than just allowing a spontaneous process to work. Several key processes are part and parcel of this innovating organizational structure. These are described in the next section.

Key Processes

In our case history, the idea generator and the first two sponsors found each other through happenstance. The odds of such propitious match-ups can be significantly improved through the explicit design of processes that help sponsors and idea generators find each other. The chances of successful match-ups can be improved by such funding, gettings ideas, and blending ideas. In addition, the processes of transitioning and program management move ideas from reservations into operations. Each of these is described below.

Funding

A key process that increases the ability to innovate is a funding process that is explicitly earmarked for the innovating organization. A leader in this field is

Texas Instruments (TI), a company that budgets and allocates funds for both operating and innovating. In essence the orchestrators make the short-run/long-run tradeoff at this point. They then orchestrate by choosing where to place the innovating funds—with division sponsors or corporate reservations. The funding process is a key tool for orchestration.

Another lesson to be learned from the case history is that it frequently takes more than one sponsor to launch a new idea. The field engineer's idea would never have been brought to management's attention without the New England sales manager. It would never have been tested in the market without the European sales manager. Multiple sponsors keep fragile ideas alive. If engineering had been the only available sponsor for technical ideas, there would have been no innovation.

Some organizations purposely create a multiple sponsoring system and make it legitimate for an idea generator to go to any sponsor who has funding for new ideas. Multiple sponsors duplicate the market system of multiple bankers for entrepreneurs. At Minnesota Mining and Manufacturing (3M), for example, an idea generator can go to his or her division sponsor for funding. If refused, the idea generator can then go to any other division sponsor or even to corporate R&D. If the idea is outside current business lines, the idea generator can go to the new ventures group for support. If the idea is rejected by all possible sponsors, it probably isn't a very good idea. However, the idea is kept alive and given several opportunities to be tested. Multiple sponsors keep fragile young ideas alive.

Getting Ideas

The process of getting ideas occurs by happenstance as it did in the case history. The premise of this section is that the odds of match-ups between idea generators and sponsors can be improved by organization design. First, the natural process can be improved by network-building actions such as multidivision or multireservation careers or company-wide seminars and conferences. All of these practices plus a common physical location facilitate matching at 3M.

The matching process is formalized at TI, where there is an elaborate planning process called the *o*bjectives, *s*trategies and *t*actics or OST system, which is an annual harvest of new ideas. Innovating funds are distributed to managers of objectives (sponsors) who fund projects based on ideas formulated by idea generators, and these then become tactical action programs. Ideas that are not funded go into a creative backlog to be tapped throughout the year. Whether formal, as at TI, or informal, as at 3M, it is noteworthy that these are known systems for matching ideas with sponsors.

Ideas can also be acquired by aggressive sponsors. Sponsors sit at the crossroads of many ideas and often arrive at a better idea by putting two or more together. They can then pursue an idea generator to champion it. Good sponsors know where the proven idea people are located and how to attract such people to come to perfect an idea on their reservation. Sponsors can go inside or outside the organization to pursue these idea people.

And finally, formal events for matching purposes can be scheduled. At 3M, for example, there's an annual fair at which idea generators can set up booths to be viewed by shopping sponsors. Exxon Enterprises held a "shake the tree event" at which idea people could throw out ideas to be pursued by attending sponsors. The variations of such events are endless. The point is that by devoting time to ideas and making innovation legitimate, the odds that sponsors will find new ideas are increased.

Blending Ideas

An important lesson to be derived from our scenario is that it is no accident that a field engineer produced a new product idea. Why? Because the field engineer spent all day working on customer problems and also knew the technology. Therefore, one person knew the need and the means by which to satisfy that need. (An added plus: The field engineer had a personal need to design the appropriate technology.) The premise here is that innovation is more likely to occur when knowledge of technologies and user requirements are combined in the minds of as few people as possible—preferably in that of one person.

The question of whether innovations are need-stimulated or means-stimulated is debatable. Do you start with the disease and look for a cure, or start with a cure and find a disease for it? Research indicates that two-thirds of innovations are need-stimulated. But this argument misses the point. As shown in Figure 4(a), the debate is over whether use or means drives the downstream efforts. This thinking is linear and sequential. Instead, the model suggested here is shown in Figure 4(b). That is, for innovation to occur, knowledge of all key components is simultaneously coupled. And the best way to maximize communication among the components is to have the communication occur

FIGURE 4

Linear Sequential Coupling Compared With Simultaneous Coupling of Knowledge

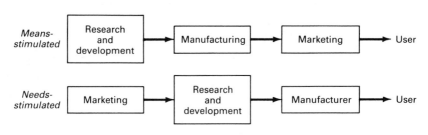

(a) *Linear Sequential Coupling*

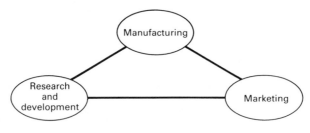

(b) *Simultaneous Coupling*

intrapersonally—that is, within one person's mind. If this is impossible, then as few people as possible should have to communicate or interact. The point is that innovative ideas occur when knowledge of the essential specialties is coupled in as few heads as possible. To encourage such coupling, the organization can grow or select individuals with the essential skills or it can encourage interaction between those with meshing skills. These practices will be discussed in a people section.

A variety of processes are employed by organizations to match knowledge of need and of means. At IBM they place marketing people directly in the R&D labs where they can readily interpret the market requirement documents for researchers. People are rotated through this unit, and a network is created. Wang holds an annual users' conference at which customers and product designers interact and discuss the use of Wang products. Lanier insists that all top managers, including R&D management, spend one day a month selling in the field. It is reported that British scientists made remarkable progress on developing radar after actually flying missions with the Royal Air Force. In all these cases there is an explicit matching of the use and the user with knowledge of a technology to meet the use. Again these processes are explicitly designed to get a user orientation among the idea generators and sponsors. They increase the likelihood that inventions will be innovations. The more complete a new idea or invention is at its inception, the greater the likelihood of its being transferred into the operating organization.

Transitioning

Perhaps the most crucial process in getting an innovative product to market is the transitioning of an idea from a reservation to an operating organization for implementation. This process occurs in stages, as illustrated in the case history. First, the idea was formulated in the field before management knew about it. Then it was tested with a customer, the French bank. And finally, at the third stage, development and full-scale implementation took place. In other cases, several additional stages of testing and scale-up may be necessary. In any case, transitioning should be planned in such stages. At each stage the orchestrator has several choices that balance the need for further invention with the need for transfer. The choices and typical stages of idea development are shown in Table 2.

At each stage these choices face the orchestrator: Who will be the sponsor? Who will be the champion? Where can staff be secured for the effort? At what

TABLE 2

Transitioning Ideas by Stages

	Stages			
Choices	I	II	Nth	Implementation
Sponsor	Corporate	Corporate	. . .	Division
Champion	Corporate	Corporate	. . .	Division
Staffing	Corporate	Corporate-division	. . .	Division
Location	Corporate	Corporate	. . .	Division
Funding	Corporate	Corporate	. . .	Division
Autonomy	Complete	Complete	. . .	Minimal

physical location will work be performed? Who will fund the effort? How much autonomy should the effort have, or how differentiated should it be? For example, at the initial new idea formulation stage the sponsor could be the corporate ventures group with the champion working on the corporate reservation. The effort could be staffed with other corporate reservation types and funded at the corporate level. The activity would be fully separate and autonomous. If the results were positive, the process could proceed to the next stage. If the idea needed further development, some division people could be brought in to round out the needed specialties. If the data were still positive after the second stage, then the effort could be transferred physically to the division, but the champion, sponsor, and funding might remain at the corporate level. In this manner, by orchestrating through choices of sponsor, champion, staff, location, funding, and autonomy, the orchestrator balances the need for innovation and protection with the need for testing against reality and transfer.

The above is an all-too-brief outline of the transition process; entire books have been written on the subject of technology transfer. The goal here is to highlight the stagewise nature of the process and the decisions to be made by the orchestrator at each stage. The process is crucial because it is the link between the two organizations. Thus to consistently innovate, the firm needs an innovating organization, an operating organization, and a process for transitioning ideas from the former to the latter.

Managing Programs

Program management is necessary to implement new products and processes within divisions. At this stage of the process, the idea generator usually hands the idea off to a product/project/program manager. The product or process is then implemented across the functional organization within the division. The systems and organizational processes for managing projects have been discussed elsewhere and will not be discussed here. The point is that a program management process and skill is needed.

In summary, several key processes—that is, funding, getting ideas, blending ideas, transitioning, and managing programs—are basic components of the innovating structure. Even though many of these occur naturally in all organizations, our implicit hypothesis is that the odds for successful innovation can be increased by explicitly designing these processes and by earmarking corporate resources for them. Hundreds of people in organizations choose to innovate voluntarily, as did the field engineer in the case history. However, if there were a reward system for people like these, more would choose to innovate, and more would choose to stay in the organization to do their innovating. The reward system is the next component to be described.

Reward System

The innovating organization, like the operating organization, needs an incentive system to motivate innovating behavior. Because the task of innovating is different from that of operating, the innovating organization needs a different reward system. The innovating task is riskier, more difficult, and takes place over longer time frames. These factors call for some adjustment of the operating organization's reward system, the amount of adjustment depending on how innovative the operating organization is and how attractive outside alternatives are.

The functions of the reward system are threefold: First, the rewards must attract idea people to the company and the reservations and retain them. Because various firms have different attraction and retention problems, their reward systems must vary. Second, the rewards provide motivation for the extra effort needed to innovate. After 19 failures, for example, something has to motivate the idea generator to make the 20th attempt. And, finally, successful performance deserves a reward. These rewards are primarily for idea generators. However, a reward-measurement system for sponsors is equally important. Various reward systems will be discussed in the next sections.

Rewards for Idea Generators

Reward systems mix several types of internal motivators, such as the opportunity to pursue one's ideas, promotions, recognition, systems, and special compensation. First, people can be attracted and motivated intrinsically by simply giving them the opportunity and autonomy to pursue their own ideas. A reservation can provide such opportunity and autonomy. Idea people—who are internally driven—such as the field engineer in our story can come to a reservation, pursue their own ideas, and be guided and evaluated by a reservation manager. This is a reward in itself, albeit a minimal reward. If that minimal level attracts and motivates idea people, the innovating organization need go no further in creating a separate reward system.

However, if necessary, motivational leverage can be obtained by promotion and recognition for innovating performance. The dual ladder—that is, a system whereby an individual contributor can be promoted and given increased salary without taking on managerial responsibilities—is the best example of such a system. At 3M a contributor can rise in both status and salary to the equivalent of a group executive without becoming a manager. The dual ladder has always existed in R&D, but it is now being extended to some other functions as well.

Some firms grant special recognition for high career performance. IBM has its IBM fellows program in which the person selected as a fellow can work on projects of his or her own choosing for five years. At 3M, there is the Carlton Award, which is described as an internal Nobel Prize. Such promotion and recognition systems reward innovation and help create an innovating culture.

When greater motivation is needed, and/or the organization wants to signal the importance of innovation, special compensation is added to the aforementioned systems. Different special compensation systems will be discussed in the order of increasing motivational impact and of increasing dysfunctional ripple effects. The implication is that the firm should use special compensation only to the degree that the need for attraction and for motivation dictate.

Some companies reward successful idea generators with one-time cash awards. For example, International Harvester's share of the combine market jumped from 12 percent to 17 percent because of the introduction of the axial flow combine. The scientist whose six patents contributed to the product development was given $10,000. If the product continues to succeed, he may be given another award. IBM uses the "Chairman's Outstanding Contribution Award." The current program manager on the 4300 series was given a $5,000 award for her breakthrough in coding. These awards are made after the idea is successful and primarily serve to reward achievement rather than to attract innovators and provide incentive for future efforts.

Programs that give a "percentage of the take" to the idea generator and early team members provide even stronger motivation. Toy and game companies give a royalty to inventors—both internal and external—of toys and games they produce. Apple Computer claims to give royalties to employees who write software programs that will run on Apple equipment. A chemical company created a pool by putting aside 4 percent of the first five years' earnings from a new business venture, which was to be distributed to the initial venture team. Other companies create pools from percentages that range from 2 to 20 percent of cost savings created by process innovations. In any case, a predetermined contract is created to motivate the idea generator and those who join a risky effort at an early stage.

The most controversial efforts to date are attempts to duplicate free-market rewards within the firm. For example, a couple of years ago, ITT bought a small company named Qume that made high-speed printers. The founder became a millionaire from the sale; he had to quit his previous employer to found the venture capital effort to start Qume. If ITT can make an outsider a millionaire, why not give the same chance to entrepreneurial insiders? Many people advocate such a system but have not found an appropriate formula to implement the idea. For example, one firm created five-year milestones for a venture, the accomplishment of which would result in a cash award of $6 million to the idea generator. However, the business climate changed after two years, and the idea generator, not surprisingly, tried to make the plan work rather than adapt to the new, unforeseen reality.

Another scheme is to give the idea generator and the initial team some phantom stock, which gets evaluated at sale time in the same way that any acquisition would be evaluated. This process duplicates the free-market process and gives internal people the same venture capital opportunities and risks as they would have on the outside.

The special compensation programs produce motivation and dysfunctions. People who contribute at later stages frequently feel like second-class citizens. Also, any program that discriminates will create perceptions of unfair treatment and possible fallout in the operating organization. If the benefits are judged to be worth the effort, however, care should be taken to manage the fallout.

Rewards for Sponsors

The case history also demonstrates that sponsors need incentives, too. In the example, because they were being beaten in the market, the sales people had an incentive to adopt a new product. The point is that sponsors will sponsor ideas, but these may not be innovating ideas unless there's something in it for them. The orchestrator's task is to create and communicate those incentives.

Sponsor incentives take many forms. At 3M, division managers have a bonus goal that is reached if 25 percent of their revenue comes from products introduced within the previous five years. When the percentage falls below the goal, and the bonus is threatened, these sponsors become amazingly receptive to new product ideas. The transfer process becomes much easier as a result.

Sales growth, revenue increase, numbers of new products, and so on, may be the bases for incentives that motivate sponsors.

Another controversy can arise if the idea generators receive phantom stock. Should the sponsors who supervise these idea people receive phantom stock, too? Some banks have created separate subsidiaries so that sponsors can receive stock in the new venture. To the degree that sponsors contribute to idea development, they will need to be given such stock options, too.

Thus, the innovating organization needs reward systems for both idea generators and sponsors. It should start with a simple reward system and move to more motivating, more complex, and possibly more upsetting types of rewards only if and when attraction and motivation problems call for them.

People

The final policy area to be considered involves people practices. The assumption is that some people who are better at innovating are not necessarily good at operating. Therefore, the ability of the innovating organization to generate new business ideas can be increased by systematically developing and selecting those people who are better at innovating than others. But first the desirable attributes must be identified. These characteristics that identify likely idea generators and sponsors are spelled out in the following sections.

Attributes of Idea Generators

The field engineer in our case history is the stereotype of the inventor. He is not mainstream. He's hard to get along with, and he wasn't afraid to break company policy to perfect his idea. Such people have strong egos that allow them to persist and swim upstream. They generally are not the type of people who get along well in an organization. However, if an organization has reservations, innovating funds, and dual ladders, these people can be attracted and retained.

The psychological attributes of successful entrepreneurs include great need to achieve and to take risks. But, to translate that need into innovation, several other attributes are needed. First, prospective innovators have an irreverence for the status quo. They often come from outcast groups or are newcomers to the company; they are less satisfied with the way things are and have less to lose if there's a change. Successful innovators also need "previous programming in the industry"—that is, an in-depth knowledge of the industry gained through either experience or formal education. Hence, the innovator needs industry knowledge, but not the religion.

Previous startup experience is also associated with successful business ventures. As are people who come from incubator firms (for example high-technology companies) and areas (such as Boston and the Silicon Valley) that are noted for creativity.

The amount of organizational effort needed to select these people varies with the ability to attract them to the organization in the first place. If idea people are attracted through reputation, then by funding reservations and employing idea-getting processes, idea people will, in effect, select themselves—they will want to work with the organization—and over time their presence will reinforce the organization's reputation for idea generation. If the firm has no reputation for innovation, then idea people must be sought out or external reservations established to encourage initial idea generation. One firm made extensive use of outside recruiting to accomplish such a goal. A sponsor would develop an idea and then attend annual conferences of key specialists to determine who was most skilled in the area of interest; he or she would then interview appropriate candidates and offer the opportunity to develop the venture to those with entrepreneurial interests.

Another key attribute of successful business innovators is varied experience, which creates the coupling of a knowledge of means and of use in a single individual's mind. It is the generalist, not the specialist, who creates an idea that differs from the firm's current business line. Specialists are inventors; generalists are innovators. These people can be selected or developed. One ceramics engineering firm selects the best and the brightest graduates from the ceramics engineering schools and places them in central engineering to learn the firm's overall system. They are then assigned to field engineering where they spend three to five years with customers and their problems and then they return to central engineering product design. Only then do they design products for those customers. This type of internal coupling can be created by role rotation. Some aerospace firms rotate engineers through manufacturing liaison.

People who have the characteristics that make them successful innovators can be retained, however, only if there are reservations for them and sponsors to guide them.

Attributes of Sponsors and Reservation Managers

The innovating organization must also attract, develop, train, and retain people to manage the idea development process. Because certain types of people and management skills are better suited to managing ideas than others, likely prospects for such positions should have a management style that enables them to handle idea people, as well as early experience in innovating, the capability to generate ideas of their own, the skills to put deals together, and generalist business skills.

One of the key skills necessary for operating an innovating organization is the skill to manage and supervise the kind of person who is likely to be an idea generator and champion—that is, people who, among other characteristics, do not take very well to being supervised. Idea generators and champions have a great deal of ownership in their ideas. They gain their satisfaction by having "done it their way." The intrinsic satisfaction comes from the ownership and autonomy. However, idea people also need help, advice, and sounding boards. The successful sponsor learns how to manage these people in the same way that a producer or publisher learns to handle the egos of their stars and writers. This style was best described by a successful sponsor:

> It's a lot like teaching your kids to ride a bike. You're there. You walk along behind. If the kid takes off, he or she never knows that they could have been helped. If they stagger a little, you lend a helping hand, undetected preferably. If they fall, you catch them. If they do something stupid, you take the bike away until they're ready.

This style is quite different from the hands-on, directive style of managers in an operating organization. Of course, the best way to learn this style is to have been managed by it and seen it practiced in an innovating organization. Therefore, experience in an innovating organization is essential.

More than the idea generators, the sponsors need to understand the logic of innovation and to have experienced the management of innovation. Its managers need to have an intuitive feel for the task and its nuances. Managers whose only experience is in operations will not have developed the managerial style, understanding, and intuitive feel that is necessary to manage innovations because the logic of operations is counterintuitive in comparison with the logic of innovations. This means that some idea generators and champions who have experienced innovation should become managers as well as individual contributors. For example, the president in our case history was the inventor of the first-generation product and therefore understood the long, agonizing process of developing a business idea. It is also rare to find an R&D manager who hasn't come through the R&D ranks.

The best idea sponsors and idea reservation managers, therefore, are people who have experienced innovation early in their careers and are comfortable with it. They will have been exposed to risk, uncertainty, parallel experiments, repeated failures that led to learning, coupling rather than assembly-line thinking, long time frames, and personal control systems based on people and ideas, not numbers and budget variances. Sponsors and reservation managers can be developed or recruited from the outside.

Sponsors and reservation managers need to be idea generators themselves. Ideas tend to come from two sources. The first is at low levels of the organization where the problem gap is experienced. The idea generator who offers a solution is the one who experienced the problem and goes to a sponsor for testing and development. One problem with these ideas is that they may offer only partial solutions because they come from specialists whose views can be

FIGURE 5
An Innovating Organization's Design Components

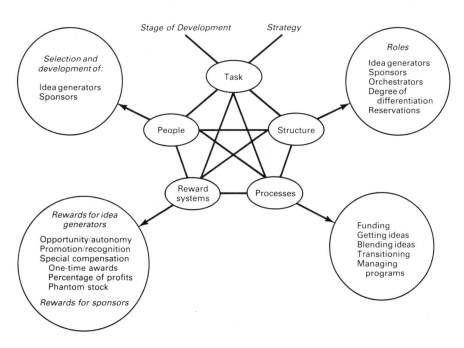

parochial and local. But sponsors are at the crossroads of many ideas. They may get a broader vision of the emerging situation as a result. These idea sponsors can themselves generate an idea that is suitable for the organization's business, or they can blend several partial ideas into a business-adaptable idea. Sponsors and reservation managers who are at the crossroads of idea flow are an important secondary source of new ideas. Therefore, they should be selected and trained for their ability to generate new ideas.

Another skill that sponsors and especially reservation managers need is the ability to make deals and broker ideas. Once an idea has emerged, a reservation manager may have to argue for the release of key people, space, resources, charters, for production time, or a customer contact. These deals all require someone who is adept at persuasion. In that sense, handling them is no different than project or product management roles. People do vary in their ability to make deals and to bargain and those who are particularly adept should be selected for these roles. However, those who have other idea management skills may well be able to be trained in negotiating and bargaining.

And, finally, sponsors and reservation managers should be generalists with general business skills. Again, the ability to recognize a business idea and to shape partial ideas into business ideas are needed. Sponsors and reservation managers must coach idea generators in specialties in which the idea generator is not schooled. Most successful research managers are those with business skills who can see the business significance in the good ideas that come from scientists.

In summary, the sponsors and reservation managers who manage the idea-development process must be recruited, selected, and developed. The skills that these people need relate to their style, experience, idea-generating ability, deal-making ability, and generalist business acumen. People with these skills can either be selected or developed.

Thus some of the attributes of successful idea generators and idea sponsors can be identified. In creating the innovating organization, people with these attributes can be recruited, selected, and/or developed. In so doing, the organization improves its odds at generating and developing new business ideas.

Summary

The innovating organization described is one that recognizes and formalizes the roles, processes, rewards, and people practices that naturally lead to innovations. The point we have emphasized throughout this article is that the organization that purposely designs these roles and processes is more likely to generate innovations than is an organization that doesn't plan for this function. Such a purposely designed organization is needed to overcome the obstacles to innovation. Because innovation is destructive to many established groups, it will be resisted. Innovation is contrary to operations and will be ignored. These and other obstacles are more likely to be overcome if the organization is designed specifically to innovate.

Managers have tried to overcome these obstacles by creating venture groups, by hiring some entrepreneurs, by creating "breakthrough funds," or by offering special incentives. These are good policies but by themselves will not accomplish the goal. Figure 1 conveyed the message that a consistent set of policies concerning structure, process, rewards, and people are needed. The innovating organization is illustrated in Figure 7. It is the combination of idea people, reservations in which they can operate, sponsors to supervise them, funding for their ideas, and rewards for their success that increase the odds in favor of innovation. Simply implementing one or two of these practices will result in failure and will only give people the impression that such practices do not work. A consistent combination of such practices will create an innovating organization that will work.

Selected Bibliography

The basic ideas of organization design and of blending structure, processes, rewards, and people practices are described in my earlier book, *Organization Design* (Addison-Wesley, 1978). The idea of differentiation comes from Paul Lawrence and Jay Lorsch's *Organization and Environment* (Harvard Business School, 1967). One can also find there the basic ideas of contingency theory.

The structure of the innovative organization and the three roles involved are similar to those identified in the investment idea and capital budgeting process. These have been identified by Joseph Bower in *The Resource Allocation Process* (Division of Research at Harvard University, 1968).

Innovation itself has been treated in various ways by many people. Some good ideas about technological innovation can be found in Lowell Steele's *Innovation in Big Business* (Elsevier, 1975).

COMMUNICATIONS IN THE RESEARCH
AND DEVELOPMENT LABORATORY

Thomas J. Allen

Ask any manager of research and development what are the most serious problems affecting the efficiency of his work, and his answer will almost certainly involve some aspect of communication. The communication of ideas is central to the research and development process, and without effective communication among its participants, the quality of the work must necessarily suffer.

Despite its importance, however, little has been known until quite recently about the manner in which scientific or technological information actually passes from one person to another. This article presents results from a series of studies conducted over the past few years in the Sloan School of Management to explore the process of information flow in research and development organizations.

Two rather general conclusions result from earlier studies at the Sloan School: First of all, surprisingly few ideas flow into the laboratory directly from the scientific or technological literature; in the case of some 19 research and development projects studied, for example, only 15 per cent of the "idea generating messages" could be attributed to the literature. And more significant for management, perhaps, is the finding that extra-organizational channels consistently perform more poorly than internal information channels in the provision of technical information; this was first seen in the case of proposal competitions where teams which relied more heavily on information sources outside of their parent organization consistently produced proposals of poor technical quality. Lack of technical capability within the laboratory was largely responsible for the decision to use outside sources, and inverse relations were found between the use of such sources and the size of the laboratory's technical staff and its ratio to the laboratory's total employment. Laboratories which do not have the necessary technical manpower resources attempted unsuccessfully to substitute through reliance upon outside technical personnel.

Reprinted from Technology Review, 70, No. 1 (October–November 1967), 31–37. Used with permission of *Technology Review* and Thomas J. Allen. Copyright by the Alumni Association of the Massachusetts Institute of Technology.

On the other hand the use of internal consultants bears a weak but consistently positive relation to performance. It is best, of course, to have the information already available among the proposal team members; but when information must be sought, as indeed it often must, then sources within the information seeker's organization seem much more capable than outside sources of fulfilling the need.

But among academic scientists, W. O. Hagstrom in his book *The Scientific Community* found a strong positive relation between performance and extra-organizational communication. In this instance, the organization (an academic department) occupies a subsidiary position to a more inclusive social system—the "invisible college" or academic discipline. While the communication process (in Hagstrom's case) is external to the academic department, it is *internal to the academic discipline.*

The concept of a shared coding scheme produces a rather simple and straightforward explanation for all of this. In industrial and governmental situations, the laboratory organization assumes an overwhelming importance, demanding loyalty and affiliation far beyond that required by academic departments. The members of such organizations acquire shared coding schemes, or common ways of ordering the world, through their common experience and organization that can be quite different from the schemes held by other members of their particular discipline. This is not true of the academic scientists, whose alignments seem to develop more strongly with others who share their peculiar research interests than with those who share a particular university or department; in other words, an "invisible college" now becomes the mediator of the coding scheme.

It is possible, of course, to hypothesize upon devices to reduce the organizational boundary impedance. One of these possibilities, which may well arise spontaneously, is a two-step process in which certain key individuals able to do so act as bridges linking the organization members to the outside world. Information then enters the organization through these individuals, operating within and transmitting between two coding schemes.

The possibility that such individuals exist, who in effect straddle the closed society of the organization and the wide open one of the outside world, function efficiently in both, and cross easily between them, holds obvious significance for their potential usefulness in information transfer. Recent studies in the Sloan School have sought to identify such people in connection with an examination of the flow of information both into and within the confines of research organizations.

But before turning directly to this particular problem, let us briefly review a body of research on the flow of information in a somewhat different context.

Public Opinion Research

Twenty years ago, P. F. Lazarsfeld, B. Berelson, and H. Gaudet, to explain a phenomenon which they observed in decision-making during the course of the 1940 election campaign, first proposed what has become known as the two-step information flow hypothesis. It appeared that ideas flow from radio and print to opinion leaders and from them to the remainder of the population. Instead of a simple direct connection between mass media and the general public, the process is more complex, involving the individual's social attachments to other people and the character of the opinions and activities which he shares with them. Thus the response of an individual to a communicated message cannot be accounted for without reference to his social environment and to the character of his interpersonal relations. This two-step flow was found to be mediated by "opinion leaders" who in every stratum of society perform a relay function: controlling the flow, for example, of political information from mass media to electorate and thus influencing the vote. The opinion leaders proved to be considerably more exposed than the rest of the population to the formal media of communication. And they were most likely to be exposed to the media appropriate to the sphere of their principal concern, and to have a greater number of interpersonal contacts outside of their own groups.

This hypothesis appears well established in the wide context of public opinion. An obvious next step is to ask whether it is relevant to the far more specific problem of communications in research and development organizations.

Our earliest studies gave some evidence that members of an engineer's immediate work group or colleagues in other parts of the organization are often instrumental in delivering information to him or making him aware of the existence of a particular source. Repeatedly we found that several sources, rather than one single one, had contributed to the discovery or formulation of a particular idea. In one case, for example, an engineer's colleague hears a paper at a conference of the Society of Automotive Engineers, associates the device described with a problem the engineer is tackling, and tells him about it. The engineer follows up the lead by searching the literature, writing the man who delivered the paper, and making arrangements with a vendor who can supply some of the hardware. Another case is quite similar. A vendor visits a particular engineer and tells him about a new piece of equipment that his company has developed. The engineer knows of a colleague to whose problems this equipment might be relevant and suggests that the vendor call on him; the application turns out to be appropriate.

These instances, stated exactly as they were related to the interviewers, are not isolated occurrences. Very frequently an intermediary directly relays information he has obtained from another source, or indirectly assists in the transaction. The early studies certainly suggest the possibility of a two-step flow in technological communication.

Networks of Communication

The evidence I have cited encouraged us to design a second series of studies, aimed at defining both the nature of the process by which information flows into the organization and the channels through which information proceeds among scientists within it.

Turning first to information exchange within the organization, we investigated the influence of two factors on the structure of the network through which technical information flows. These were the organization's formal structure—the work groups as they appear officially on the organization chart—and its informal structure—patterns of friendship and social encounters. We examined the impact of these factors on communications in two organizations; the first was a small laboratory in which 34 professionals were actively engaged in work on new materials and devices in the fields of direct energy conversion and solid state electronics, both for military and industrial applications, and the second a department of a large aerospace firm.

We asked the scientists in the two laboratories the following questions:

1. Socialization. Name the three or four persons from the laboratory with whom you meet most frequently on social occasions.
2. Work group. Name the people whom you consider to be members of your present work group.
3. Technical discussion. Name the three or four people with whom you most frequently discuss technical matters.
4. Special information. Please think back to the last technical assignment you completed and try to identify the most difficult technical obstacle or subproblem you had to resolve in the course of this job. Indicate the sources of information which were especially helpful in overcoming this obstacle.
5. Research idea. To whom in the laboratory would you first express an idea for a new research project?

Our questionnaire to the small laboratory employees also included two questions dealing with individuals' methods of gathering information. These asked the number of technical periodicals read regularly and the extent to which personal friends outside their organization and technical specialists inside were used as sources of information.

Figures 1 and 2 accompanying this article summarize our results; in compiling them we used three different criteria to measure information flow—technical discussion, information to overcome central research problems, and discussions of research ideas (from questions three, four, and five, above).

Scientists in both the laboratories we studied tended largely to discuss technical matters with the individuals with whom they also met socially. In the small laboratory this results largely, but not entirely, from the rather tight clique found among the Ph.D.'s in the group. As a matter of fact, the relation between socializing and technical discussion is not statistically significant when we consider the Ph.D.'s alone. In the larger research and development department, by contrast, the choice of individuals for technical discussion does not appear to be related to any differentiation of status.

The two other criteria of information flow show less obvious connection with the social network than does technical discussion. Only in the larger laboratory in the case of the upward flow of research ideas, in fact, is there any significant relationship. Nevertheless, since the technical discussions between colleagues are certainly an important mechanism for transferring technical information of various sorts, and even though we cannot determine from these data what is the primary impetus (that is, whether socialization brings about transfer of information or technical discussions lead on to social contacts), we conclude that the laboratory's informal structure has an important position in information transfer.

The question of the impact of the formal structure of the organization upon

FIGURE 1
Socialization-Choices

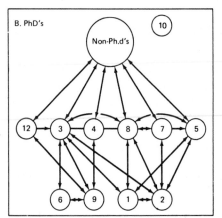

A. Non PhD's

FIGURE 2
Technical Discussion-Choices

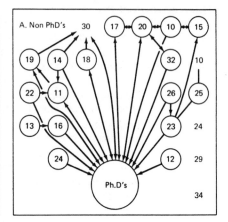

A. Non PhD's

B. PhD's

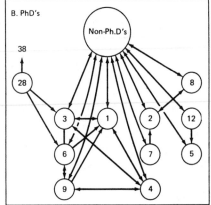

B. PhD's

These figures illustrate the pattern of relationships among the members of a small research and development laboratory.

In the left pair of charts the arrows indicate the direction of socialization choices; at the right the pattern of technical discussion choices. Since two distinct cliques were evident, those holding and not holding Ph.D. degrees are shown separately in these diagrams.

The large circle labeled "non-Ph.D." at the left, representing the Ph.D. to non-Ph.D. choices, shows practically no social intercourse between the two groups. The circle labeled "Ph.D." above gives an indication of which non-Ph.D.'s choose into the Ph.D. group. Nine non-Ph.D.'s do so but in only two cases, subjects 24 and 28, is the choice reciprocated. Reciprocal choices are indicated by the double-headed arrows. Non-respondents are represented by uncircled numbers.

communication remains. Comparison between the work groups and the social networks shows that, while much of the socialization does occur within work groups, the two networks are somewhat independent and should exert separate influences on information flow. If anything, the formal organization influences communication even more strongly than the informal network. The structure of the work groups influences not only technical discussion but also the upward flow of ideas. In fact, the part of the social network beyond the individual's work group has rather less influence on technical discussions than the complete informal network. Clearly, then, the formal organization is the more important, but by no means the sole determinant of information flow.

The Impact of Status on Communication

Several experiments by social psychologists have demonstrated that in social systems based on status hierarchies, individuals high on the status ladder will tend to like and communicate frequently with one another while those low in the hierarchy will neither like nor communicate with each other as much. In addition, the members of lower status will direct most of their communication toward those in the higher status clique, although the subjects of their attention do not generally reciprocate it.

The small laboratory provides an almost perfect example of this. Even a causal glance at the figures on page 423 shows the impact of status (exemplified) here by possession of a Ph.D. degree) on the laboratory's communication network. The Ph.D.'s form a tightly knit group; they apparently communicate quite freely among themselves but seldom meet socially or discuss technical matters with the non-Ph.D.'s.

This Ph.D. cliquism could in itself drastically disrupt the organization's performance, but an even more serious effect is evident. The non-Ph.D.'s in the laboratory scarcely socialize with one another, and they discuss technical matters among themselves far less than do their Ph.D. colleagues. Furthermore, the non-Ph.D.'s direct the majority of both their social attention (64 per cent) and technical discussions (60 per cent) to the Ph.D.'s. By contrast, the Ph.D.'s direct only 6 per cent of their social attention and 24 per cent of their technical discussion to the non-Ph.D.'s.

Some 15 years ago, H. H. Kelley, . . . explained the tendency among the lower members of a two-level hierarchy to direct their attention upward as a form of substitute promotion for those who wish to move upward in the organization. A few years later, A. R. Cohen found that one form of communication with upper members of the hierarchy (conjectures about the nature of the higher status job) increases both when "locomotion is desired but not possible and where it is possible but not desirable." We can best describe the situation in the smaller laboratory as one in which upward mobility is highly desirable but, in the short run, impossible. It is, therefore, hardly surprising that the non-Ph.D.'s should try to enhance their own status by associating with the higher status Ph.D.'s in the laboratory. An organization which employs both Ph.D.'s and non-Ph.D.'s together in the same tasks is almost certain to give the most rewarding experiences, as well as publication and recognition, predominantly to those holding the advanced degree. This state of affairs drives the non-Ph.D.'s to a strategy of gaining reflected glory as satellites of the higher status group; they therefore tend to avoid associating with their lower status colleagues in the effort to gain vicariously the kudos denied to them in reality.

Technological Gatekeepers

Thus far I have restricted myself to the problems of exchanging information between people. Just as important to research management, however, is the stage that immediately precedes this in the chain of communication—the methods and sources that individuals use to gather their information. Looking back at those individuals who were chosen most frequently by their colleagues for technical discussion, or who were cited as sources of critical incident information, we are now able to compare their behavior with that of their colleagues to see whether these "opinion leaders" display any systematic differences in their use of the information system. We compare these "opinion leaders" with their apparently less-informed colleagues in terms of their use of friends outside the laboratory, of technical staff within, and of the technical literature.

Table 1 illustrates the difference between the information gatherers and their colleagues in the small laboratory. The technological gatekeepers clearly read more of the literature and consult more with outside sources than does the average professional in the laboratory; the contrast is especially pronounced in the case of professional journals (those sponsored by scientific and engineering societies).

We also used another criterion of information flow to identify the main sources of information in the laboratory, asking the scientists to indicate the source of any information which influenced the course of their most recently completed research projects. Twelve people in the smaller laboratory cited seven colleagues as the sources of that information, and Table 2 compares these seven with the other professionals in terms of information gathering behavior. The pattern of greater outside contacts and more exposure to the literature reappears.

	TABLE 1: Comparison of Communication Behavior and Technical-Discussion Choices			TABLE 2: Comparison of Communication Behavior and Identification as the Source of Special Technical Information During One of the Lab's Projects		
Based on Mann–Whitney U-Test Performed between the Two Groups	*Number of Times Chosen on Technical-Discussion Matrix*					
	Six or More	*Four or Fewer*	*Level of Statistical Significance*	*Seven Individuals Cited*	*Others*	*Level of Statistical Significance*
Percentage who are above median in using personal friends outside the laboratory as an information source	64%	25%	0.06	67%	30%	0.10
Percentage who are above median in using technical specialists within the laboratory as an information source	50	40	0.47	57	40	0.17
Percentage who are above median in total number of technical periodicals read	88	40	0.01	100	45	0.05
Percentage who are above median in number of professional and scientific periodicals read	75	35	0.001	86	35	0.03

Thus, there appear to be two distinct classes of individuals within this laboratory. The majority have few information contacts beyond the bounds of the organization. Their internal sources are the other class—the small minority which has extensive contacts outside the laboratory. Information flow in this laboratory is a two-step process, wherein six or seven individuals act as technological gatekeepers for their colleagues. Indeed, the study showed that two of these gatekeepers were responsible for introducing all four of the "most important technical ideas" that had been introduced into the organization during the preceding year.

The individual gatekeepers vary somewhat in the actual sources of information that they use. Some rely more upon literature than discussions, while others operate in reverse manner. If a gatekeeper has a greater number of contacts outside his laboratory, he does not necessarily read the literature more, and vice versa. Therefore, since the gatekeepers do not all tend the same gate, the laboratory as a whole receives a balanced quota of information from the outside world.

The opinion leaders in the laboratory are not of a monolithic sort. Each has his own sources of information and information from each gatekeeper has its own particular function in the laboratory. The situation closely resembles that in the world of mass communication to which I referred earlier in this article. In that context, opinion leaders could be differentiated by topic: those influential in public affairs were not necessarily influential in determining fashion patterns, for example.

We can perhaps extend the analogy between the laboratory and mass communications a little further by examining the source literature of the opinion leaders in the two situations. Studies of mass communication showed that movie leaders read movie magazines more, public affairs leaders read more news magazines, fashion leaders read more fashion magazines, and so on. This background strongly suggests that we should look in more detail at the content of the messages processed by the various gatekeepers in R & D laboratories. By analogy, the selection of channels by scientific and technological gatekeepers may be based on the qualitative nature of the information in which the gatekeeper specializes, different channels varying in their ability to provide different types of information. As an example, the literature has been shown to provide information which is important for keeping abreast of the state of a technological field, while oral sources are probably better in providing more specific detailed information about particular techniques. Gatekeepers who specialize in knowledge of the state-of-the-art would thus tend to read the literature more, while those specializing in particular research techniques would interact more with individuals outside the laboratory.

The studies I have described hold two very significant implications for the managers of research and development laboratories. First, they suggest that managers should aim to understand the factors which influence the flow of technical information in the organization; some of these factors are under the management's control and can be used to improve the communication system in action. Second, they emphasize that management should recognize the value of technological gatekeepers; all too frequently rewards by-pass the individuals responsible for information transfer, and managers often fail to make effective use of these individuals.

⃞18 organizational analysis: the organization as an open system

TOWARDS AN OVERALL VIEW OF ORGANIZATIONAL DEVELOPMENT

J. V. CLARK
C. G. KRONE

Our goal in this paper is to provide an integrated overview of the changing field of organizational development, into which new concepts and new intervention processes can be placed. We start from two premises:

1. A healthy organization is one capable of integrating proactively with its physical, social and biological environment (Clark, 1963).
2. An effective organizational development practitioner is someone who enables an organization to develop the attitudes and processes which will allow it to integrate proactively with its environment.

The Individual and His Small Group — Communication

Starting from these two premises, one can think about the interpersonal communications type of interventions (task-group team meetings, management development laboratories, Blake grids, etc.) in the following way. At the outset of such small group meetings, one is aware that very little information about the present situation in which the members find themselves is being exchanged. They suppress thoughts and feelings they have about themselves and others and they are insensitive to thoughts and feelings others have about the same subject.

From the standpoint of an individual member, his "life-space" looks something like Figure 1.

As the diagram suggests, Member 1 is insensitive to many of his own feelings, nearly all the feelings and most of the thoughts of others. He sends a few

---

Reprinted by permission of the authors.

FIGURE 1

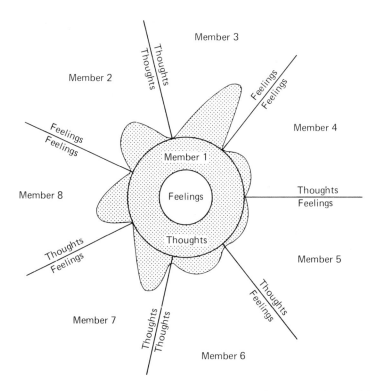

thought messages to a few members and has, but doesn't send, considerably more.

This situation exists from the very outset of a group because all the members have brought to it a set of socially acceptable rules about approprate things to see and say. So there is a structure operating which, for good or bad, consistently separates individuals one from another, since without information there can be no relation. As the group develops, a great deal more information gets exchanged, usually preceded by heated debates on whether or not it is appropriate to change the social rules which govern information exchange between people. As more information gets exchanged, an individual wants to connect with more members and with more aspects of any one member and so frequently chooses to communicate more aspects of *himself* to more people. It is this process which is so exciting to people in such groups. They are often delighted with these new choices and capacities. They speak of new-found potentialities in themselves and others and remark often of getting out of "boxes", 'ruts' and 'grooves'. At this stage, a member's life-space looks like Figure 2.

By now, this process is rather familiar, but readers wishing to delve into it further, as well as the process of enabling it to occur in task groups, can consult Clark (1963, 1970a, 1970b).

FIGURE 2

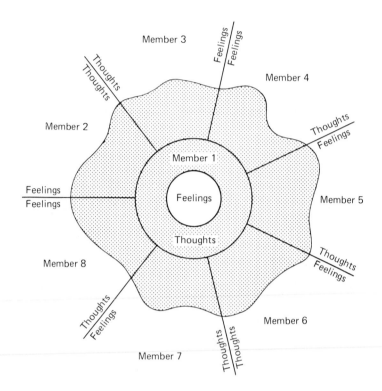

The Individual and His World—Appreciation

Another typical result of attending small group communication programs has been that, outside the group, an individual begins to feel that he understands and perhaps is even somewhat similar to many different kinds of people. If, in his group, he has gotten to know persons of different ages, colors, hierarchical positions, religions, political persuasions, etc., he has come to feel the excitement of relating more openly with them. Consequently he may feel he perceives all "young people," "blacks," "women," etc., more accurately and can therefore relate more adaptively with them. One of the most common results of organizational development programs in industry, by way of illustration, is that people feel they get along better with their wives and children. Again, to illustrate graphically, a member's life-space in regard to social groups may look something like Figure 3 before entering into the training experience.

And after, if he has been in a fairly heterogeneous group, perhaps something like Figure 4.

In moving from Figure 3 to Figure 4, several things have happened. First, new judgments about reality were made and, second, these new realities came to be *valued* in a different sort of way—new aspects of new people were, so to

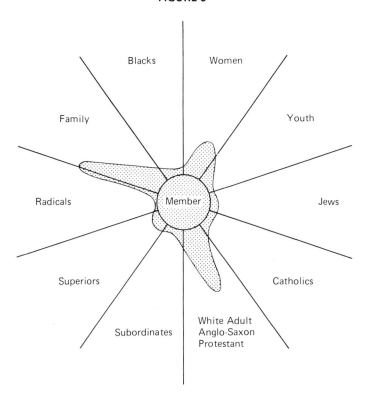

FIGURE 3

speak, "appreciated." Thus, for example, not only were another member's feelings perceived, but it became *important* to understand them. Thus what Geoffrey Vickers calls the "appreciative system" of the individual has changed (Vickers, 1969); he sees more of his environmental realities and he values them differently.

The Individual in His Turbulent World—Debilitation

We can summarize the last section by saying that under conditions of a fairly stable social and physical environment (an individual's "world"), he feels excited and growthful when his appreciative system changes. In a sense, this was the situation during the middle 1960s when our organizational development programs were focusing on interpersonal communication processes. However, in the late 1960s, people's worlds started changing much more rapidly than their appreciative systems.

The external part of this problem, the changing world itself, has been discussed by Emery and Trist (1965) in their paper on 'The causal texture of organizational environments', where they point out that environments become unpredictable and increasingly unmanageable for people when aspects within those environments interact upon one another regardless of the behavior of any single person or organization within it.

575

FIGURE 4

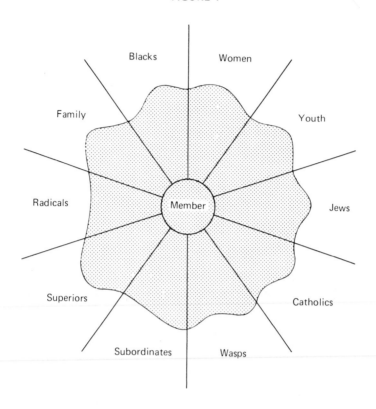

Clearly, such social–physical–biological environments are becoming typical today. And the consequences of living in that kind of world have been well described by Alvin Toffler (1970) in his book on *Future Shock*. He took the description and label "future shock" from the rather well documented experience of culture shock, which is a state of extreme anxiety, disorientation and debilitation suffered when one is unable to predict the meaning of his own or others' social actions. Toffler cites the Peace Corp's experience in this regard, which is that its members require six months or more to recover. Future shock is the same thing, only worse, because in culture shock the culture more or less stays put while the individual figures out its structure and meaning. But hardly anyone's world stays put, nowadays. And so what people in the early throes of future shock try to do is to reintroduce a sense of structure and predictability by reiterating and reinforcing the values of the sector of the world they are most familiar with. They are much like the frustrated tourist who speaks his own language slowly and loudly upon encountering someone who speaks a different one.

Toffler describes many ways of alleviating the symptoms of future shock, but the most penetrating analysis of the process of adaptation in turbulent environments has been made by Vickers (1968) in his paper on "The limits of government." He maintains bluntly that either mankind learns to develop new appreciative systems rapidly and constantly or it is caught in the 'ecological trap' of being unable to adapt to a changing environment, as was the dinosaur. In discussing this trap, Vickers observes that the conditions necessary to regulate large-scale social and political systems become increasingly difficult to obtain as the lead time needed to mount any regulative action becomes ever longer (due to the increasing complexity of most social and technical problems), while the future span over which any reliable prediction can be made grows even shorter. He sums it up, quite pessimistically, when he says, "It is quite possible for the world as we know it to become unregulable in important fields, in that it might pass the point beyond which *any* considered action might have a statistical probability of becoming worse than random."

But, he continues, "the condition which produces this unhappy result is not primarily due to exploding technology, but to the limitation of human communication (to generate) a sufficiently agreed view of the situation, a sufficient consensus on the course to pursue and sufficient common action to achieve it." By communication, he means the failure to maintain "appropriate shared ways of distinguishing the situation in which we act, the relations we want to regulate, the standards we need to apply and the repertory of actions available to us."

Graphically, the connection between Vickers's point and our discussion here can be illustrated by our Figures 3 and 4. If someone is in a real-life situation with the Figure 3 groups as its main actors (a university president comes to mind, for example), then the appreciation of that situation represented by the shaded area in Figure 3 is clearly maladaptive. His appreciation must shift toward Figure 4, as must the appreciation of *all* involved.

The Organization and Its Future in a Turbulent Environment— Open-Systems Planning

As a result of this contemporary necessity to develop appreciative skills in order to mediate between an organization's turbulent environment and the future shock of its members, Charles G. Krone, in collaboration with James V. Clark and G. K. Jayaram, has been developing a technology of so-called "open-systems planning" based on Miller's general systems behavior theory (Miller 1965). While it will be described in detail in a subsequent paper, open-systems planning is, briefly, a set of procedures whereby groups can:

1. Rapidly identify and map out the dynamic realities which are in their environment.
2. Map out how the organization represented by the members of the group presently acts toward and hence values those realities.
3. Map out how the organization wants to engage with those realities in the future (that is, to set value-goals).
4. Make plans to restructure the "architecture" of the organization in order to influence the environmental realities in the valued directions.

We have developed this method with the help of nearly a hundred client systems of many types and levels, working with industrial, religious, community, educational and governmental groups. Our experience to date has been that, while considerable discouragement and even depression are encountered along the way, such systems can, as a result of seeing more of and valuing differently the complicated texture of their environments, generate a considerably more varied range of action possibilities from which to choose directions and strategies. Moreover, they are able to visualize *alternative* futures and to take action against *them* instead of an assumed "it."

Before we proceed, we would like to draw attention to the temptation we and some of our clients have experienced to see open-systems planning as an organizational development intervention which ought to supercede team meetings which "only" change norms and styles of communication. But notice that communication is the skill necessary in order to develop common appreciative systems between individuals or groups. And it is surely large groups of people who must, *together,* develop new appreciations before organizations can survive in turbulent environments. We have learned and relearned what we should already have known, that open-systems planning is likely to be unsuccessful as an organizational intervention unless it is introduced into groups with well developed communication skills—groups, that is, whose members have learned to perceive and value one another's thoughts and feelings. It will *surely* be unsuccessful unless such groups come to value, early in the process, the necessity of special work on communication improvement. We will return to this point in a more general sense at the conclusion of this paper.

By way of illustration, we can look at the familiar situation of an organization investing huge amounts of capital to build a product which it believes to

FIGURE 5

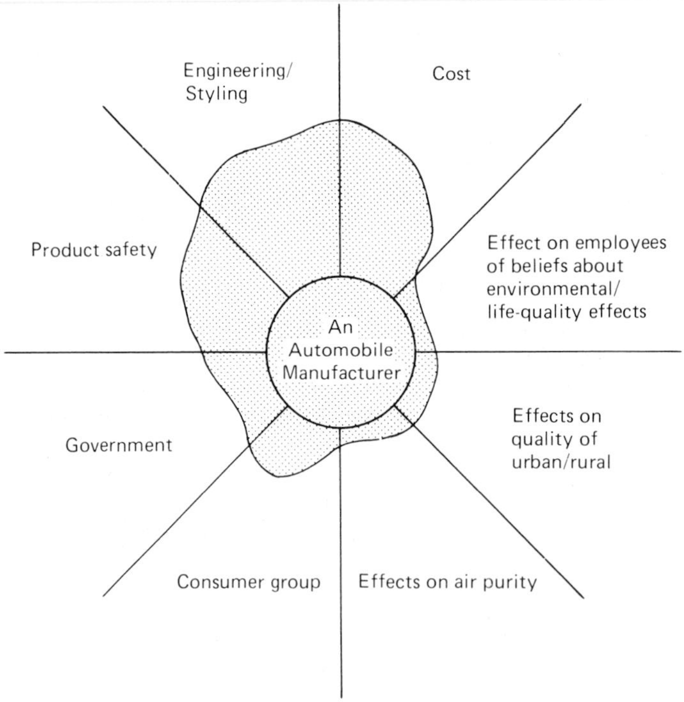

be technically superior, only to discover almost overnight that it had failed to consider the effects on the product of the rapidly changing value shifts in the society in which it is being made and sold. Had certain social and political realities been better perceived, corporations might have wished not to invest so heavily in certain market capacities. On the other hand, appreciative systems include both reality judgements and value judgements. Situation, if perceived more accurately at the outset, can be valued differently and, as a consequence, acted upon differently.

Continuing in the vein of the above example, one can appreciate what is happening in the automotive industry in different sorts of ways, depending on the scope with which they are dealt. If one is valuing only the narrow sphere of what might be called the "primary effects" of automobiles—transportation—one can say, eyeing some of the criticism one sees today, "the public does not appropriately value the transportation and beauty of my products." The appreciative map of such an hypothetical observer is seen in Figure 5. Doubtless he would consider the domains he pays attention to as primary and all the others as secondary. Moreover, he would have created organizational forms that reflect that division, placing immense resources against the primary domains and scant ones against the others.

On the other hand, if an appreciative system allowed one to deal with and positively value not only knowledge about primary but also about secondary effects, one would look at the problem of studying the effects of automotive transportation as shown in Figure 6.

FIGURE 6

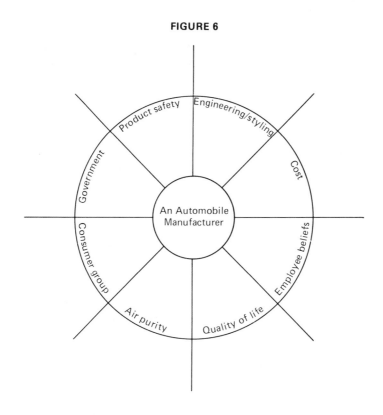

Moreover, one might put considerable organizational resources against monitoring and otherwise engaging with those parts of the organization's world from which it hears about secondary effects, be they technical, social, political, physiological or whatever.

Thus, if one were convinced of the truth of negative second level social and physiological effects, a more growthful response might be "The second level effects of my products are so great that I need to create a new form (perhaps even an earlier form) which is more effective when I take into consideration the *whole* of both the first and second level effects."

On the other hand, one can appreciate these other second-level domains of the organization's world—the social and political, for example—whether or not one were convinced that negative effects existed in the physiological domains. One could then make the statement that the public as a whole is becoming more growthful and valuing the totality of things in their worlds, and that therefore and because of this growth they might positively value something that looks like technological de-innovation, electric or steam automobiles, say. If an electric car appeared superior against the physical environment it might well be considered more effective transportation by the social and political parts of the organization's world.[1]

Another possible strategy resulting from the Figure 6 appreciation would be to create entirely new kinds of super-organizations for changing large-scale public systems such as rapid transit and the like. Such newer forms of social architecture stem from viewing all of society as an interrelated system. Such social "meta-problems" (see Chevalier, 1966) have been identified as characteristic of a society at the "post-industrial" level (see Trist, 1970).

Whether or not a single organization can influence total societies toward such an appreciation or such super-organizational forms is difficult to say since it hasn't been tried very much. However, redesigning internal organizational structures to meet newly appreciated environmental facts at any level is the final area of organizational development we wished to discuss in his paper, and so we will turn to it now.

**The Organization and Its Presence in a Turbulent Environment—
Open-Systems Designing**

Briefly stated, open-systems organizational redesigning is the practice of creating organizational processes such that members are allowed to make dynamic responses to the dynamic environments of the technologies that form the core of their work. While no one has exactly elaborated this concept in the literature, a good basic first approximation is contained in *A System Approach to the Design of a Descriptive Model of Organizational Structure* by Driggers (1966).

We will try to illustrate, however, by taking some examples from some open-systems design projects on which we are working (see Krone, 1970, for a discussion of one of these projects). Consider, first off, the usual manufacturing organization in which everyone is given instructions to play roles which

[1]The above examples are genuinely hypothetical for two reasons: (a) the authors have considerable hindsight about the physical and political domains of the automotive industry and, (b) very little technical knowledge of the secondary effects on social and physiological environments. We don't feel particularly lonely along either dimension.

focus their attention on some aspect of their technology. Jobs are prescribed such that nearly everyone is assigned a particular part of the internal operation to "run" (line) or "audit" (staff) or "improve" (often uncertain). A typical linear technology (assembly line, packing line, etc.) then, would look like Figure 7.

FIGURE 7

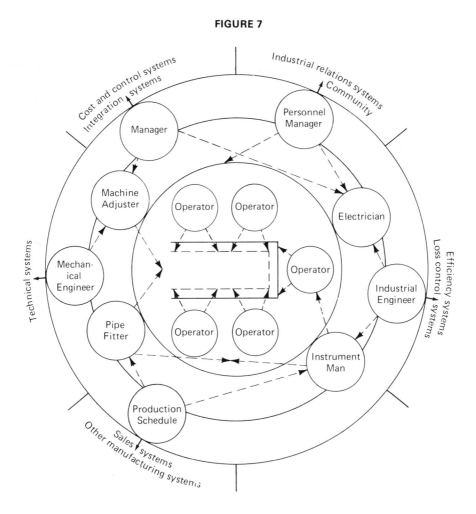

In the center can be seen five 'operators' who have been planned for by the five management personnel seen in the outside circle and maintained by the four maintenance personnel seen in the middle circle. The arrows going out from each person indicate the areas he is to appreciate and attend to, according to his job description and the other prescribed behaviors coming in from the different environmental domains attended to by the managers (illustrated in Figure 7 by the outward arrows).

Such a system is familiar to all of us and requires no elaboration here, although Drigger's discussion of the assumptions underlying it is interesting.

Before passing on to an open-system design, however, we would like to call attention to the fact that the organizational structure depicted in Figure 7 is designed to produce the constricted appreciation patterns we have seen throughout our discussion in Figures 1, 3 and 5. In fact, members attempting wider appreciation patterns such as those seen in Figure 2, 4 and 6 above and 8 below are typically punished for such offenses as "rate-busting," "crossing craft-lines," "usurping management prerogatives," or just plain "sticking your nose in where it doesn't belong."

In some of the open-systems redesign projects in which the authors are involved, this form of organization is abandoned in favor of a system in which the people who have direct responsibility for maintaining the flow of product of one form or another (a product concept can be the product of an information processing system, for example) also have direct responsibility for identifying and proactively engaging with the environments of that production flow. For example, in the project described in Krone's paper, packing line workers identify, ahead of time, changes in sales volume, product formulation, social processes in the community, and so forth, and restructure their system so as to appropriately engage it with those forthcoming environmental changes.

In graphic form, such an organization might appear as in Figure 8.

FIGURE 8

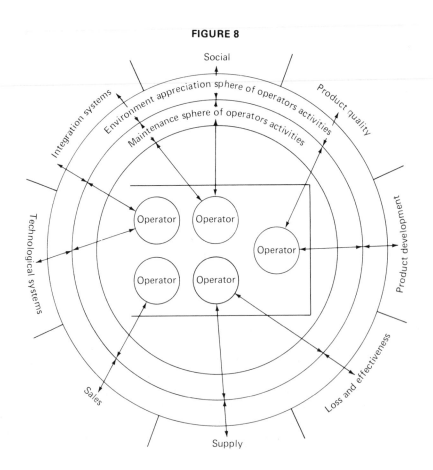

One aspect of this organizational form is difficult to depict graphically, and that is the portion of the world around the core technology to which particular operators often attend shifts, by common consent. It may shift during a day, or over a period of weeks or months.

In any case, as we mentioned earlier, an operator moves from an appreciative map such as seen in Figure 9 towards one similar to Figure 10.

FIGURE 9

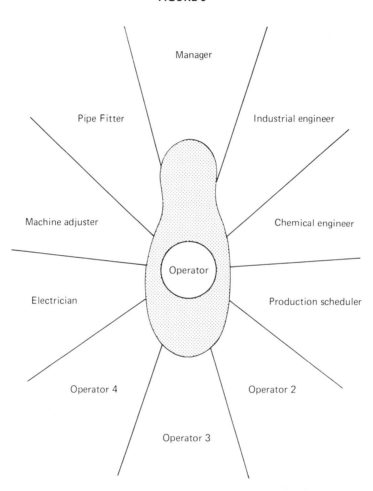

As mentioned earlier, a particular operator may have a somewhat differently shaped appreciative "profile," but he surely will have a considerably larger lifespace within which to operate than he did when his appreciative map was similar to Figure 9.

Under such an organizational design, the role of management moves away from identifying environmental changes and directing the system's responses to them, toward identifying changes in the capacity of the work force itself to engage in that process. Management then, in fulfilling its functions asks ques-

FIGURE 10

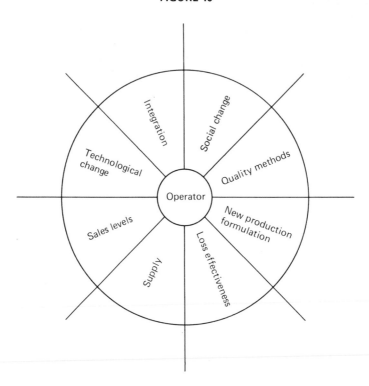

tions such as, "Does the system have enough information about the environment?" "Does it have enough information about its responses to the environment?" "Are its members helping one another to more effectively engage in appreciative acts?" etc. It monitors, that is, whether or not people who directly engage with the technology have the appropriate capacities, information and organizational forms to engage directly with the environment of that technology.

When the manager shifts to these kinds of concerns, his map, from our point of view, shifts from a narrow one where he is directly concerned with cost and control of the technological processes towards a broader one where he is concerned directly with the processes that result in effective costs and control of the technology. These new concerns are with the growth of people, with his own ability to create systems which allow for the identification and linkage between appropriate people and appropriate environmental domains, his own ability to create systems which allow for appropriate "links" with the future, his own ability to create systems that can generate values, and even valued values (although that gets a little tricky), and the like.

It is clear, then, that the new life-space of the new manager is larger only to the extent that he appreciates those aspects of this world that have to do with the growth of people and the growth of his own capacity to facilitate the growth of people. Recall here that excitement around one's own and others' personal growth was a central outcome of the small group meetings described at the beginning of this paper. From the standpoint of organizational development as a field, therefore, we ourselves have not moved away from where we started in our appreciation, but have simply expanded from it, trying to take a dose of our own medicine.

Organizational Developing

Our experience has led us to value, as steps in our practice, the headings of this paper. Recall that when we were talking about organizational development interventions we had four categories: (a) the individual and his small group—communication, (b) the individual and his world—appreciation, (c) the organization and its future in a turbulent environment—open-systems planning, and (d) the organization and its present in a turbulent environment—open-systems designing.

It was only when we introduced a symptom we hadn't anticipated along the way that we inserted another category between (b) and (c); the individual in his turbulent world—debilitation.

Our categories form a map which looks like this:

Aspects of Organizational Developing

	Intervention Structures	Intervention Processes
Internal to a system	Open-systems designing 4	Communication 1
External to a system	Open-systems planning 3	Appreciation 2

Our own view is that an organizational development program is not complete until activities occur spontaneously and continuously in all boxes, without professional outside intervention.

Our experience with several such programs has been that, while they are developing, they need to proceed clockwise and also that they tend to fade out if they fail to proceed onward until all four steps have been covered. Neither proposition has been tested in the experimental sense, of course, but our best clinical judgement supports them both at the present time, and so we pass them on to our clients and colleagues. Where you start on the circle, by the way, seems to depend on a number of situational factors, including the culture in which the organization is embedded. In most American projects with which we are acquainted, projects start with communication (1), but we have been involved in varying degrees with a large-scale project in England which started with a version of open-system planning (3).

However, as implied earlier, our experience is also indicating that, regardless of where you start, the Figure 11 process is iterative, primarily because of the difficulties encountered by the manager who is fostering open-systems redesign activities. If he has started with (1) and proceeded on through (2) and (3) he has experienced, so far, largely the delight of enlarged appreciations of and within his own personal world. But, in open-systems redesign, it is the system as a whole which enlarges its potentialities,[2] and, as we stated before, it is often difficult for managers to conceive of their own individual worlds as expanding under those conditions. We repeat this point because it is troublesome to us, troublesome both as consultants to, and as friends of, our clients. At the present time it is difficult to know ahead of time which managers will, and which will not, enlarge their appreciative systems to include the growth-monitoring and growth-inducing aspects central to the open-systems manager's "core technology." In our framework, of course, which might at this point be called "open-systems consultation," this problem must be identified and shared with managers as soon as it is perceived. We hope very much to participate in its resolution whenever we can, but it would be presumptuous and inaccurate to imply, in a closed-system sense, that we can "solve" it. This paper was generated, in large part, by the desire to enlist the help of our clients with this extraordinarily difficult problem.

References

Chevalier, M. (1966), "Towards an action framework for the control of pollution," *Canadian Council of Resource Ministers' Conference on Pollution,* Montreal.

Clark, J. V. (1962), "A healthy organization," *California Management Review,* vol. 4, no. 4, Summer, pp. 16–30.

Clark, J. V. (1963), "Authentic interaction and personal growth in sensitivity training groups," *Journal of Humanistic Psychology,* Spring, pp. 1–13.

Clark, J. V. (1970a), "Task group therapy 1: goals and the client system," *Human Relations,* vol. 23, no. 4, pp. 263–77.

Clark, J. V. (1970b), "Task group therapy 2: intervention and problems of practice," *Human Relations,* vol. 23, no. 5, pp. 383–403.

Driggers, P. F. (1966), *A System Approach to the Design of a Descriptive Model of Organizational Structure,* unpublished Ph.D. dissertation, University of Illinois.

Emery, F. E., and Trist, E. (1965), "The causal texture of organizational environments," *Human Relations,* vol. 18, February, pp. 21–32.

Krone, C. G. (1970), "Organizational response to technological change," the Procter and Gamble Company, unpublished mimeo; paper presented to the 1970 meetings of the Institute for Management Sciences, U.C.L.A.

Miller, J. G. (1965), "Living systems: basic concepts," *Behavioral Science,* vol. 10, nos. 3, 4, July and October, pp. 337 *et seq.*

Toffler, A. (1970), *Future Shock,* Random House.

Trist, E. (1970), "Urban North America in the next 30 years," in W. Schmidt (ed.), *Organizational Frontiers,* Wadsworth.

Vickers, G. (1968), "The limits of government," ch. 4, pp. 73–95, in *Value Systems and Social Process,* Basic Books.

[2] A point clarified for us during a conversation with our colleague, W. H. McWhinney of U.C.L.A.

A CONGRUENCE MODEL FOR DIAGNOSING
ORGANIZATIONAL BEHAVIOR

DAVID A. NADLER
MICHAEL TUSHMAN

Managers perform their jobs within complex social systems called organizations. In many senses, the task of the manager is to influence behavior in a desired direction, usually toward the accomplishment of a specific task or performance goal. Given this definition of the managerial role, skills in the diagnosis of patterns of organizational behavior become vital. Specifically, the manager needs to be able to *understand* the patterns of behavior that are observed, to *predict* in what direction behavior will move (particularly in the light of managerial action), and to use this knowledge to *control* behavior over the course of time.

The understanding, prediction, and control of behavior by managers occurs, of course, in organizations every day. The problem with managerial control of behavior as frequently practiced is that the understanding–prediction–control sequence is based on the intuition of the individual manager. This intuitive approach is usually based on models of behavior or organization which the manager carries around in his/her head—models that are often naive and simplistic. One of the aims of this paper will be to develop a model of organizations, based on behavioral science research, that is both systematic and useful.

The model to be discussed in this paper will serve two ends. It will provide a way of systematically thinking about behavior in organizations as well as provide a framework within which the results of research on organizational behavior can be expressed.

Effective managerial action requires that the manager be able to diagnose the system s/he is working in. Since all elements of social behavior cannot be dealt with at once, the manager facing this "blooming-buzzing" confusion must simplify reality—that is, develop a model of organizational functioning. The diagnostic model will present one way of simplifying social reality that still retains the dynamic nature of organizations. The model will focus on a set of key organizational components (or variables) and their relationships as the primary determinants of behavior. The diagnosis of these key components will provide a concise snapshot of the organization. However, organizations do not stand still. The diagnositc model will preserve the changing nature of

---

This is an unpublished manuscript, printed here with the permission of the authors.

organizations by evaluating the effects of feedback on the nature of the key components and their relationships. In all, the diagnostic model will provide a way of thinking about organizations by focusing on a set of key variables and their relationships over time. The model will therefore not consider all the complexity of organizational behavior. To be useful in real settings, insight from the model must be supplemented with clinical data and managerial insight.

Besides as a way of thinking about organizational behavior, the diagnostic model can also serve as a vehicle to organize a substantial portion of research on organizational behavior. An increased awareness of the research results concerning the relationships between the key components should help the manager make the link between diagnosing the situation and making decisions for future action. The model, then, cannot only help the manager to diagnose and describe organizational behavior, but it can provide an effective way to organize and discuss behavioral science research results that may be of use to managers.

While the diagnostic model is a potentially powerful managerial tool, it must be seen as a developing tool. Parts of the model are less well developed than others (e.g., the informal organization). As research in organizational behavior advances, so, too, should the development of this diagnostic model. Finally, no claim is made that this model is the most effective way of organizing reality. It is suggested, however, that models of organizational behavior are important and that they ought to (1) deal with several variables and their relationships, and (2) take into account the dynamic nature of organizations.

In conclusion, the premise of this article is that effective management requires that the manager be able to systematically diagnose, predict, and control behavior. The purpose of this paper is to present a research-based (as opposed to intuitive) model of organizational behavior that can be used to diagnose organizations as well as to integrate behavioral science research results. The model should therefore be of use to practitioners in organizations as well as to students in the classroom.

Basic Assumptions of the Model

The diagnostic model that will be discussed here is based on a number of assumptions about organizational life. These assumptions are as follows:

1. *Organizations are dynamic entities.* Organizations exist over time and space, and the activities that make up organizations are dynamic. There are many definitions of organizations, such as Schein's (1970) statement that

> an organization is the rational coordination of the activities of a number of people for the achievement of some common explicit purpose or goal, through division of labor and function, and through a hierarchy of authority and responsibility.

While definitions like this are adequate to define what an organization is, they are static in nature and do not enable one to grasp how the different components of organization interact with each other over time. An adequate model of organizations must reflect the dynamic nature of organizational behavior.

2. *Organizational behavior exists at multiple levels.* There are different levels of abstraction at which organizational behavior can be examined. Specifically, behavior occurs at the *individual,* the *group,* and the *organizational systems* levels. Behavior that is attributable to each of these levels can be identified and isolated (that is, one can see the behavior of individuals as different from the behavior of groups or of organizations themselves). At the same time, these three levels interact with each other, organizational-level behavior being affected by the behavior of individuals, group-level behavior being affected by the organizational-level phenomena, and so on.

3. *Organizational behavior does not occur in a vacuum.* Organizations are made up of both social and technical components and thus have been characterized as sociotechnical systems (Emery and Trist, 1960). The implication of this is that any approach to looking at behavior must also take into account the technical components of the organization—such issues as the nature of the task and the technology. Since the organization is dependent on inputs, knowledge, and feedback from the environment, our model must also take into account the constraints of the organization's task environment (e.g., to what extent the market is changing).

4. *Organizations have the characteristics of open social systems.* Organizations have the characteristics of systems that are composed of interrelated components and conduct transactions with a larger environment. Systems have a number of unique behavioral characteristics, and thus a model of organizational behavior must take into account the systemic nature of organizations.

Open-Systems Theory

The point made above about open-systems theory is a crucial one which needs to be explored in more depth. The basic premise is the characteristics of systems that are seen in both the physical and social sciences (Von Bertalanffy, 1962; Buckley, 1967) are particularly valuable when looking at organizations. Social organizations, it is claimed, can be viewed as systems (Katz and Kahn, 1966) with a number of key systems characteristics.

What is a system and what are systems characteristics? In the simplest of terms, a system is a "set of interrelated elements." These elements are interdependent such that changes in the nature of one component may lead to changes in the nature of the other components. Further, because the system is embedded with larger systems, it is dependent on the larger environment for resources, information, and feedback. Another way of looking at a system is to define it as a mechanism that imports some form of energy input from the environment, which submits that input to some kind of transformation process, and which produces some kind of energy output back to the environment (Katz and Kahn, 1966). The notion of open systems also implies the existence of some boundary differentiating the system from the larger environment in which it is embedded. These system boundaries are usually not rigid. This familiar view of a system can be seen in Figure 1. Closed systems, on the other hand, are not dependent on the environment and are more deterministic in nature. Closed systems tend to have more rigid boundaries and all transactions take place within the system, guided by unitary goals and rationality. (An example approaching a closed system would be a terrarium, completely self-contained and insulated from the larger environment.)

FIGURE 1
The Elementary Systems Model

A more extensive definition of open systems has been presented by Katz and Kahn (1966) in the form of a listing of characteristics of open social systems. An adapted list of these characteristics is as follows:

1. *Importation of energy.* A system functions by importing energy (information, products, materials, etc.) from the larger environment.
2. *Throughput.* Systems move energy through them, largely in the form of transformation processes. These are often multiple processes (i.e., decisions, material manipulation, etc.)
3. *Output.* Systems send energy back to the larger environment in the form of products, services, and other kinds of outcomes which may or may not be intended.
4. *Cycles of events over time.* Systems function over time and thus are dynamic in nature. Events tend to occur in natural repetitive cycles of input, throughput, and output, with events in sequence occurring over and over again.
5. *Equilibrium seeking.* Systems tend to move toward the state where all components are in equilibrium—where a steady state exists. When changes are made that result in an imbalance, different components of the system move to restore the balance.
6. *Feedback.* Systems use information about their output to regulate their input and transformation processes. These informational connections also exist between system components, and thus changes in the functioning of one component will lead to changes in other system components (second-order effects).
7. *Increasing differentiation.* As systems grow, they also tend to increase their differentiation; more components are added, more feedback loops, more transformation processes. Thus, as systems get larger, they also get more complex.
8. *Equifinality.* Different system configurations may lead to the same end point, or conversely, the same end state may be reached by a variety of different processes.
9. *System survival requirements.* Because of the inherent tendency of systems to "run down" or dissipate their energy, certain functions must be performed (at least at minimal levels) over time. These requirements include (a) goal achievement, and (b) adaptation (the ability to maintain balanced successful transactions with the environment).

Open-systems theory is a general framework for conceptualizing organizational behavior over time. It sensitizes the manager to a basic model of organizations (i.e., input–throughput–output–feedback) as well as to a set of basic organizational processes (e.g., equilibrium, differentiation, equifinality). While systems concepts are useful as an overall perspective, they do not help the manager systematically diagnose specific situations or help him/her apply research results to specific problems. A more concrete model must be developed that takes into account system-theory concepts and processes and helps the manager deal with organizational reality.

According to Figure 1, organizations (or some other unit of interest, e.g., a department or factory) take some set of inputs, work on these inputs through some sort of transformation process, and produce output that is evaluated and responded to by the environment. While managers must attend to the environment and input considerations, they must specifically focus on what the organization does to produce output. That is, managers are intimately involved in what systems theory terms the *transformation processes*. It is the transformation processes, then, that the model will specifically focus on. Given the cycle of processes from input to feedback, the model will focus on the more specific variables and processes that affect how the organization takes a given set of inputs and produces a set of organizational outputs (e.g., productivity, innovation, satisfaction). While the diagnostic model will specifically focus on the determinants of the transformation processes and their relationships to outputs, it must be remembered that these processes are part of a more general model of organizational behavior that takes inputs, outputs, and the environment into account (see Figure 1).

The model focuses on the critical system characteristic of dependence. Organizations are made up of components or parts that interact with each other. These components exist in states of relative balance, consistency, or "fit" with each other. The different parts of the organization can fit well together and thus function effectively; or fit poorly, leading to problems. Given the central nature of fit in the model, we shall talk about it as a *congruence model* of organizational behavior, since effectiveness is a function of the congruence of the various components.

This concept of congruence between organizational components is not a new one. Leavitt (1965), for example, identifies four major components of organization as being people, tasks, technology, and structure. The model presented here builds on this view and also draws from models developed and used by Seiler (1967), Lawrence and Lorsch (1969), and Lorsch and Sheldon (1972).

What we are concerned about is modeling the *behavioral* system of the organization—the system of elements that ultimately produce patterns of behavior. In its simplest form, what inputs does the system have to work with, what are the major components of the system and the nature of their interactions, and what is the nature of the system output?

The congruence model is based on the system's assumptions outlined above. The inputs to the system (see Figure 2) are those factors that at any one point in time are relatively fixed or given. Three major classes of inputs can be identified: (1) the environment of the system, (2) the resources available to the

FIGURE 2
The Systems Model as Applied to Organizational Behavior

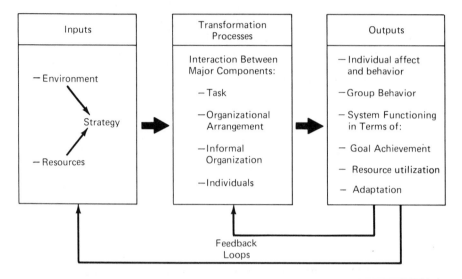

system, and (3) the organizational strategies that are developed over time.

The transformation process of the system is seen as the interaction between four major components of the organizational system. These components are (1) the tasks of the organization, (2) the individuals in the organizational system, (3) the organizational arrangements, and (4) the informal organization.

The outputs are the results of the interactions among the components, given the inputs. Several major outputs can be identified, including individual affect and behavior, group behavior, and the effectiveness of total system functioning. Looking at the total system, particular attention is paid to the system's ability to attain its goals, to utilize available resources, and to successfully adapt over time. Explicit in the model are feedback loops running from the outputs and the transformation process. The loops represent information flow about the nature of the system output and the interaction of system components. The information is available for use to make modifications in the nature of systems inputs or components.

In understanding the model, it is therefore important to understand what makes up the system inputs, components, and outputs and how they relate to each other. In particular, it is important for the manager to understand how system components relate to each other since these relationships are particularly critical for influencing behavior.

The Nature of Inputs

Inputs are important since at any point in time they are the fixed or given factors that influence organizational behavior. The inputs provide both constraints and opportunities for managerial action. While the diagnosis of organizational behavior is focused primarily on the understanding of the interactions among system components, an understanding of the nature of the inputs is still important. The major classes of inputs that constrain organizational behavior are listed in Table 1. A brief description of these inputs is as follows:

1. *Environmental inputs.* Organizations as open systems carry on constant transactions with the environment. Specifically, three factors in the environment of the specific organization are important. First, there are the various groups, organizations, and events that make up the external environment. This includes the functioning of product, service, and capital markets; the behavior of competitors and suppliers; governmental regulation; and the effect of the larger culture. Second, the organization may be embedded within another larger formal system. For example, a factory that is being considered may be part of a larger multinational corporation or of a larger corporate division. These larger "supra-systems" form an important part of the environment of the organization. Third, both the internal and external environment can be described according to a number of dimensions that appear to impact the functioning of organizations (Emery and Trist, 1965). Specifically, the issues of stability and homogeneity of the environment are important.

TABLE 1
Dimensions of System Inputs

Environment	Resources	Strategy
External environment Markets Government Financial institutions Competitors Suppliers Labor unions The larger culture, etc. Internal environment Immediate supra-systems Environmental characteristics Stability Homogeneity	Capital Raw materials Technologies People Intangibles	Critical decisions in the past Identification of environmental opportunities and distinctive competences Organizational mission Long-range and short-range goals Plans

2. *Resources.* Another important input is composed of the resources that are available to the organization. Any organization has a range of resources available as inputs. Major categories for classifying resources would include capital resources (including liquid capital, physical plant, property, etc.), raw materials (the material on which the organization will perform the transformation process), technologies (approaches or procedures for performing the transformation), people, and various intangible resources.

3. *Strategy.* Over time, organizations develop ways of utilizing their resources that deal effectively with the constraints, demands, and opportunities of the environment. They develop plans of action that centrally define what the organization will attempt to do in relation to the larger systems in which it is embedded. These plans of action are called strategies and are another major input.

While all three inputs are important, one, however, has a very critical primary effect upon the nature of one of the components, and therefore it ultimately affects all the components and their interactions. This input is strategy.

As has been said, an organization as an open system functions within a larger environment. That environment provides opportunities for action, it provides constraints on activities, and it makes demands upon the organization's capacities. The organization faces the environment with a given set of resources of various kinds: human, technological, managerial, and so on. The process of determining how those resources can best be used to function within the environment is generally called strategy determination (see Newman and Logan, 1976, or Andrews, 1971). The organization identifies opportunities in the environment where its distinctive competence or unique set of resources will provide it with a competitive advantage.

Some organizations develop strategies through formalized and complex processes of long-range strategic planning, while other organizations may give no or little conscious attention to strategy at all. Further, the process of strategy formulation can itself be seen as the output of intraorganizational processes (e.g., Bower, 1970; Mintzberg, 1973). The point is, however, that organizations have strategies, whether they be implicit or explicit, formal or informal. The point for organizational behavior is that the strategy of an organization is probably the single most important input (or constraint set) to the behavioral system. The strategy and the elements of that strategy (goals or plans) essentially define the *task* of the organization, one of the major components of the behavioral system (see Figure 3). From one perspective, all organizational

FIGURE 3

The Role of Strategy as the Primary Input to the Model

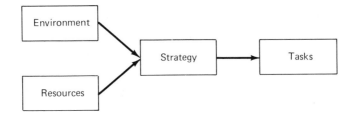

behavior is concerned with implementation of strategies through the performance of tasks. Individuals, formal organizational arrangements, and informal organizational arrangements are all important because of their relationship to the tasks that need to be performed.

The inputs listed above therefore provide opportunities, provide constraints, and may even make demands upon the organization. Given these inputs, the issue of how the organization functions to make use of the opportunities and constraints provided by the inputs is perhaps the most central issue of managerial and organizational behavior.

The Nature of Organizational Components

Assuming a set of inputs, the transformation process occurs through the interaction of a number of basic components of organization. The major components (listed with their subdimensions in Table 2) are as follows:

1. *Task component.* This component concerns the nature of the tasks or jobs that must be performed by the organization, by groups, and by individuals. Major dimensions of tasks include the extent and nature of interdependence between task performers, the level of required skill, the degree of autonomy, the extent of feedback, the variability of the task, the potential meaningfulness of the task, and the types of information needed to adequately perform the task.

2. *Individuals component.* This component obviously refers to the individuals who are members of the organization. The major dimensions of this

TABLE 2
Basic Characteristics of Behavioral System Components

Task	Individuals	Organizational Arrangements	Informal Organization
Organizational tasks	Response capabilities	Subunits	Small-group functioning
Complexity	Intelligence	Grouping of tasks and roles	Norms
Predictability	Skills and abilities	Unit composition	Informal goals
Required interdependence	Experience	Unit design	Communication patterns
	Training	Formal leadership in the unit	Cohesiveness
		Physical arrangements, etc.	Informal group structures
Subunit and individual tasks	Psychological differences	Coordination and control	Intergroup relations
Complexity	Need strength	Goals	Conflict/cooperation
Predictability	Attitudes	Plans	Information flows
Required interdependence	Perceptual biases	Hierarchy	Perceptions
Autonomy	Expectations	Reward systems	Organizational level
Feedback	Background differences	Personnel systems	Networks, cliques, and
Task variety		Control systems	coalitions
Task identity		Integrator roles	Conflicting interest groups
Task meaningfulness		and groups	Power distribution
Task skill demands			Ideology and values

component relate to the systematic differences in individuals which have relevance for organizational behavior. Such dimensions include background or demographic variables such as skill levels, levels of education, and so on, and individual differences in need strength, personality, or perceptual biases.

3. *Organizational arrangements.* This includes all the formal mechanisms used by the organization to direct structure or control behavior. Major dimensions include leadership practices, microstructure (how specific jobs, systems, or subcomponents are structured), and macrostructure (how whole units, departments, and organizations are structured).

4. *Informal organization.* In addition to the formal prescribed structure that exists in the system, there is an informal social structure that tends to emerge over time. Relevant dimensions of the informal organization include the functioning of informal group structures, the quality of intergroup relations, and the operation of various political processes throughout the organization.

Organizations can therefore be looked at as a set of components, including the task, the individuals, the organizational arrangements, and the informal organization. (For the complete model, see Figure 4.) To be useful, however, the model must go beyond the simple listing and description of these components and describe the dynamic relationship that exists among the various components.

The concept of fit. Between each pair of inputs there exists a degree of congruence, or "fit." Specifically, the congruence between two components is defined as follows:

> the degree to which the needs, demands, goals, objectives and/or structures of one component are consistent with the needs, demands, goals, objectives and/or structures of another component.

Thus fit (indicated by the double-headed arrows in Figure 4) is a measure of the congruence between pairs of components. Because components cover a range of different types of phenomena, however, fit can be more clearly defined only by referring to specific fits between specific pairs of components. In each case research results can be used as a guide to evaluate whether the components are in a state of high consistency or high inconsistency. An awareness of these fits is critical since inconsistent fits will be related to dysfunctional behavior.

FIGURE 4

A Congruence Model for Diagnosing Organizational Behavior

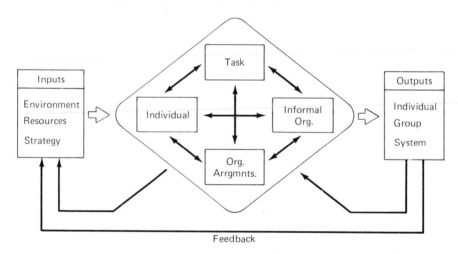

Specific definitions of congruence and examples of research on the nature of these fits is presented in Table 3. For each of the six fits among the components, more information is provided about the specific issues that need to be examined to determine the level of consistency between the components. Citations are given for examples of the research relevant to each of these relationships.

The congruence hypothesis. Just as each pair of components has a degree of high or low congruence, so does the aggregate model display a relatively high or low total system congruence. Underlying the model is a basic hypothesis about the nature of its and their relationship to behavior. This hypothesis is as follows:

> other things being equal, the greater the total degree of congruence or fit between the various components, the more effective will be organizational behavior at multiple levels. Effective organizational behavior is

TABLE 3
Definitions of Fits and Examples of Research

Fit	The Issues	Examples of Research on the Fits
Individual-organization	To what extent individual needs are met by the organizational arrangements; to what extent individuals hold clear or distorted perceptions of organizational structures; the convergence of individual and organizational goals.	Argyris (1957), Vroom (1959), Tannenbaum and Allport (1956), Schein (1970)
Individual–task	To what extent the needs of individuals are met by the tasks; to what extent individuals have skills and abilities to meet task demands.	Turner and Lawrence (1965), Hackman and Lawler (1971), Hackman and Oldham (1975)
Individual-informal organization	To what extent individual needs are met by the informal organization; to what extent the informal organization makes use of individual resources, consistent with informal goals.	Whyte (1955), Hackman and Morris (1976), Gouldner (1954), Crozier (1964), Trist and Bamforth (1951)
Task–organization	Whether the organizational arrangements are adequate to meet the demands of the task; whether organizational arrangements tend to motivate behavior consistent with task demands.	Burns and Stalker (1961), Woodward (1965), Lawrence and Lorsch (1969), Vroom and Yetton (1973)
Task–informal organization	Whether the informal organization structure facilitates task performance or not; whether it hinders or promotes meeting the demands of the task.	Blake, Shephard and Mouton, (1964), Blau (1955), Trist and Bamforth (1951), Burns and Stalker (1961), Gouldner (1954)
Organization-informal organization	Whether the goals, rewards, and structures of the informal organization are consistent with those of the formal organization.	Roethlisberger and Dickson (1939), Dalton (1959), Likert (1967), Crozier (1964), Strauss (1962)

defined as behavior which leads to higher levels of goal attainment, utilization of resources, and adaptation.

The implications of the congruence hypothesis in this model is that the manager needs to adequately diagnose the system, determine the location and nature of inconsistent fits, and plan courses of action to change the nature of those fits without bringing about dysfunctional second-order effects. The model also implies that different configurations of the key components can lead to effective behavior (consistent with the systems characteristic of equifinality). Therefore, the question is not finding the "one best way" of managing, but of determining effective combinations of inputs that will lead to congruent fits.

This process of diagnosing fit and identifying combinations of inputs to produce congruence is not necessarily an intuitive process. A number of situations that lead to consistent fits have been defined in the research literature (for example, see some of the research cited in Table 3). Thus, in many cases fit is something that can be defined, measured, and quantified in many organizational systems. The basic point is that goodness of fit is based upon theory and research rather than intuition. In most cases, the theory provides considerable guidance about what leads to congruence relationships (although in some areas the research is more abundant than others; the research on informal organization, for example, has been sparse in recent years). The implication is that the manager who is attempting to diagnose behavior needs to become familiar with critical findings of the relevant research so that s/he can evaluate the nature of fits in a particular system.

The model indicates that the outputs flow out of the interaction of the various components. Any organizational system produces a number of different outputs. For general diagnostic purposes, however, four major classes of outputs are particularly important:

1. *Individual behavior and effect.* A crucial issue is how individuals behave, specifically with regard to their organizational membership behavior (for example, absenteeism, lateness, turnover) and with regard to performance of designated tasks. Individuals also have effective responses to the work environment (levels of satisfaction, for example) which also are of consequence. Other individual behavior such as nonproductive behavior, drug usage, off-the-job activities, and so on, are also outputs of the organization in many cases.

2. *Group and intergroup behavior.* Beyond the behavior of individuals, the organization is also concerned with the performance of groups or departments. Important considerations would include intergroup conflict or collaboration and the quality of intergroup communication.

3. *System functioning.* At the highest level of abstraction is the question of how well the system as a whole is functioning. The key issues here include (1) how well is the system attaining its desired goals of production, output, return on investment, etc.; (2) how well the organization is utilizing available resources; and (3) how well is the organization adapting (i.e., maintaining favorable transactions with the environment over time).

Using the Diagnostic Model

Given the diagnostic model, the final question to be addressed here is how the model can be put to use. A number of authors have observed that the conditions facing organizations are always changing and that managers must therefore continually engage in problem identification and problem-solving activities (e.g., Shein, 1970). These authors suggest that managers must gather data on the performance of their organization, compare the ideal to the actual performance levels, develop and choose action plans, and then implement and evaluate these action plans. These problem-solving phases link together to form a *problem-solving process* if the evaluation phase is seen as the beginning of the next diagnostic phase. For long-term organizational viability, this problem-solving process must be continually reaccomplished (Schein, 1970; Weick, 1969). The basic phases of this problem-solving process are outlined in Figure 5.

How does the diagnostic model relate to this problem-solving process? The problem-solving process requires diagnosis, the generation of action plans, and the evaluation of the action plans. *Each of these steps requires a way of looking at organizations to guide the analysis.* To the extent that the diagnostic model integrates system-theory concepts and presents a specific model of organizations, the model can be used as the core of the problem-solving process. The model can therefore be used as a framework to guide the diagnosis, the evaluation of alternative actions, and the evaluation and feedback of the results of a managerial action. Further, to the extent that the manager is familiar with the research results bearing on the different fits in the model, s/he will be better able to both diagnose the situation and evaluate alternative

FIGURE 5
Basic Phases of Using the Diagnostic Model

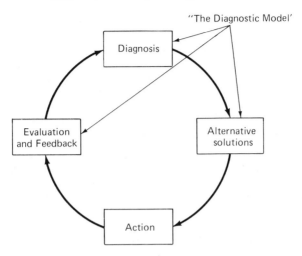

action plans. In short, the problem-solving process, along with the research-based use of the diagnostic model, can be used as an effective managerial tool.

Given the problem-solving process and the diagnostic model, it is possible to identify and describe a number of discrete steps in the problem-solving cycle. These steps can be organized into three phases: (1) diagnosis, (2) alternative solutions–action, and (3) evaluation–feedback. The basic phases and their component steps will be outlined here.

The Diagnostic Phase

This phase is premised on the idea that any managerial action must be preceded by a systematic diagnosis of the system under investigation. This phase can be broken into four distinct, but related, steps.

1. *Identify the system.* Before any detailed analysis can begin it is important to identify the system being considered. The unit of analysis must be clearly specified (i.e., project, division, organization). The boundaries of the focal unit, its membership, and what other units constitute the layer system should be considered.

2. *Determine the nature of the key variables.* Having defined the system, the next step is to use the data in the situation (or case) to determine the nature of the inputs and the four key components. The analyst should focus on the underlying dimensions of each variable. The diagnosis should focus not on an exhaustive description of each component but on the dimensions the analyst considers most important in the particular situation. The question could be phrased: In this situation, what are the most salient characteristics of the key components that are affecting the observed behavior?

3. *Diagnose the state of fits and their relationship to behaviors (i.e., out-puts).* This step is the most critical in the diagnosis phase. It really involves two related stages: (a) diagnosing fits between the components, and (b) considering the link between the fits and system output.

a. Using experience, observations, and relevant research knowledge, the manager must evaluate each of the fit lines in the model. The analyst must focus on the extent to which the key components are consistent (or fit) with each other. For instance, to what extent are the organizational arrangements consistent with the demands of the task?

b. Fits (or lack of fits) between the key components have consequences in terms of system behavior. This step makes the fit-to-behavior link explicit. That is, given the diagnoses of the various fits, the analyst must then relate the fits to behaviors observed in the system (e.g., conflict, performance, stress, satisfaction). This is a particularly key step since managerial action will be directed at the inconsistent fits to improve some aspect of the organization's behavior.

4. *Identifying critical system problems.* Based on the diagnosis of fits and their behavioral consequences, the final diagnostic step is to relate the set of behaviors to system outputs (goal achievement, resource utilization, and adaptation). Given these outputs, the manager must then evaluate which system behaviors require managerial attention and action.

The diagnostic phase forces the analyst to make a set of decisions. The anlayst must decide the unit of analysis, make decisions as to the most salient characteristics of each of the key variables, make decisions as to the relationships between the key components and their effects on behavior, and relate the observed behaviors to system outputs and decide on the system's most pressing problems. None of these decisions are clear cut—each involves managerial discretion. It follows that there is no one best diagnosis of any set of organizational conditions. The final point to be made in the diagnosis phase is that diagnosis makes a difference. The manager's diagnosis must lead to a set of actions. Different diagnoses will therefore usually lead to different actions.

Alternative Solutions—Action Plan Phase

Diagnosis leads to a consideration of potential managerial actions. This alternative action phase can be separated into three stages.

5. *Generate alternative solutions.* Having identified critical problems and the relationship between fits and behavior, the next step is to generate a range of possible managerial actions. These actions or interventions will be directed at the inconsistent fits, which will in turn affect the behaviors under consideration.

Action plans for a particular situation may differ. There may be different diagnoses or there may be a number of interventions or organizational arrangements leading to the same end point (following from the system characteristic of equifinality). In short, there is not likely to be one most appropriate set of managerial actions to deal with a particular set of conditions.

6. *Evaluating alternative strategies.* While there usually is not one single most appropriate managerial action to deal with a particular situation, the various alternatives can be evaluated for their relative merits. To what extent do the solutions deal with the inconsistent fits? Does one solution deal with the inconsistent fits more comprehensively? Are there dysfunctional second-order (i.e., latent) consequences of the action—for instance, will changing the task dimensions deal with an inconsistent task–informal organization fit but adversely affect the task–individual fit? In short, given the highly interdepen-

dent nature of open systems, the manager must systematically evaluate the alternative actions. Based on theory, research, and experience, the manager must make predictions about the possible effects of different strategies. The manager should therefore focus on the extent to which the intervention deals with the critical system problem *as well as* with the possibilities of latent consequences of the intervention. This exercise of prediction should provide a way of evaluating the relative strengths and weaknesses of the alternative actions.

7. *Choice of strategies to be implemented.* Given the explicit evaluation of the different approaches, the final step in this phase is to weigh the various advantages and disadvantages of the aternative actions and choose an action plan to be implemented.

Evaluation and Feedback Phase

The diagnosis and alternative solution–action phases leave the manager with an action plan to deal with the critical system problem(s). The final phase in using the diagnostic model deals with the implementation of the action plan and with the importance of evaluation, feedback, and adjustment of strategy to meet emergent system requirements.

8. *Implementation of strategies.* This step deals explicitly with issues that arise in introducing change into an ongoing system. This step recognizes the need to deal with the response of organizations to change. To what extent will the intervention be accepted and worked on as opposed to resisted and sabotaged? There is an extensive literature dealing with the implementation of change programs (e.g., Walton, 1975; Rogers and Shoemaker, 1971; French and Bell, 1973). While these considerations cannot be dealt with here, it is important to highlight the potential problems of translating plans and strategies into effective action.

9. *Evaluation and feedback.* After implementing a strategy, it is important to continue the diagnostic activity and to explicitly evaluate the actual vs. the ideal (or predicted) impact of the intervention on the system. Feedback concerning the organization's or the environment's response to the action can then be used to adjust the intervention to better fit the system's requirements and/or deal with any unanticipated consequences of the change. In a sense, then, step 9 closes the loop and starts the diagnosis–alternatives–action–evaluation cycle again (See Figure 5).

In conclusion, we have discussed a number of discrete, though related, steps for using the diagnostic model. The model provides a way of systematically diagnosing organizations. This diagnosis can then be used as an integral part of a problem-solving strategy for the organization. Further, the model can assist the manager in evaluating alternative solutions (i.e., what fits are dealt with) as well as evaluating the effects of the managerial actions (i.e., what fits were affected). Since organizations are made up of processes that must recur over time, the manager must continuously go through the kind of problem-solving strategy indicated in Figure 5. If this adaptive-coping kind of scheme is critical for organizational viability over time (see Schein, 1970), the diagnostic model can be seen as a concrete research-based tool to facilitate the diagnosis of the system *and* to provide a base for evaluating alternative actions and the consequences of those actions.

The diagnostic model and the problem-solving cycle are ways of structuring and dealing with the complex reality of organizations. Given the indeterminate nature of social systems, there is no one best way of handling a particular situation. The model and problem-solving cycle do, however, force the manager to make a number of decisions and to think about the consequences of those decisions. If the diagnostic model and problem-solving process have merit, it is up to the manager to use these tools along with his/her experiences to make the appropriate set of diagnostic, evaluative, and action decisions over time.

Summary

This article has attempted to briefly outline a model for diagnosing organizational behavior. The model is based on the assumption that organizations are open social systems and that an interaction of inputs leads to behavior and various outputs. The model presented is one based on the theory and research literature in organizational behavior and thus assumes that the manager using the model has some familiarity with the concepts coming out of this literature. Together with a process for its use, the model provides managers with a potentially valuable tool in the creation of more effective organizations.

References

Andrews, K. R. *The concept of corporate strategy.* Homewood, Ill.: Dow Jones-Irwin, 1971.

Argyris, C. *Personality and organization: The conflict between system and the individual.* New York: Harper & Row, 1957.

Blake, R. R., Shephard, H. A., and Mouton, J. S. *Managing intergroup conflict in industry.* Houston, Tex.: Gulf, 1964.

Blau, P. M. *The dynamics of bureaucracy.* Chicago: University of Chicago Press, 1955.

Bower, J. L. *Managing the resource allocation process.* Cambridge, Mass.: Harvard University Graduate School of Business Administration, Division of Research, 1970.

Buckley, W. *Sociology and modern systems theory.* Englewood Cliffs, N.J.: Prentice-Hall, 1967.

Burns, T., and Stalker, G. M. *The management of innovation.* London: Tavistock Publications, 1961.

Crozier, R. *The bureaucratic phenomenon.* Chicago: University of Chicago Press, 1964.

Dalton, M. *Men who manage.* New York: Wiley, 1959.

Duncan, R. Characteristics of organizational environments. *Administrative Science Quarterly,* 1972, *17,* 313–327.

Emery, F. E., and Trist, E. L. Socio-technical systems. In *Management sciences models and techniques,* Vol. II. London: Pergamon Press, 1960.

Emery, F. E., and Trist, E. L. The causal texture of organizational environments, *Human Relations,* 1965, *18,* 21–32.

French, W. L., and Bell, C. H. *Organization development.* Englewood Cliffs, N.J.: Prentice-Hall, 1973.

Gouldner, A. *Patterns of industrial bureaucracy.* New York: Free Press, 1954.

Katz, D., and Kahn, R. L. *The social psychology of organizations.* New York: John Wiley & Sons, 1966.

Hackman, J. R., and Lawler, E. E. Employee reactions to job characteristics, *Journal of Applied Psychology*, 1971, *55*, 259–286.

Hackman, J. R., and Morris, C. G. Group tasks, group interaction process and group performance effectiveness: A review and proposed integration. In L. Berkowitz (ed.), *Advances in experimental social psychology*. New York: Adademic Press, 1976.

Hackman, J. R., and Oldham, G. R. Development of the job diagnostic survey. *Journal of Applied Psychology*, 1975, *60*, 159–170.

Lawrence, P. R., and Lorsch, J. W. *Organization and environment: Managing differentiation and integration*. Homewood, Ill.: Richard D. Irwin, 1969.

Leavitt, H. J. Applied organizational change in industry. In J. G. March (ed.), *Handbook of organizations*. Chicago: Rand McNally, 1965, 1144–1170.

Likert, R. *The human organization: Its management and value*. New York: McGraw-Hill, 1967.

Lorsch, J. W., and Sheldon, A. The individual in the organization: A systems view. In J. W. Lorsch and P. R. Lawrence (eds.), *Managing group and intergroup relations*. Homewood, Ill.: Irwin–Dorsey, 1972.

Mintzberg, H. *The nature of managerial work*. New York: Harper & Row, 1973.

Newman, W. H., and Logan, J. P. *Strategy, policy, and central management*, 7th ed. Cincinnati, Ohio: South-Western Publishing Co., 1976.

Roethlisberger, F. J., and Dickson, W. J. *Management and the worker*. Cambridge, Mass.: Harvard University Press, 1939 (also New York: Wiley, 1964).

Rogers, E. M., and Shoemaker, F. F. *Communication of innovations: A cross-cultural approach*. New York: Free Press, 1971.

Schein, E. H. *Organizational psychology*. Englewood Cliffs, N.J.: Prentice-Hall, 1970.

Seiler, J. A. *Systems analysis in organizational behavior*. Homewood, Ill.: Irwin–Dorsey, 1967.

Strauss, G. Tactics of lateral relationships. *Administrative Science Quarterly*, 1962, *7*, 161–186.

Tannenbaum, A. S., and Allport, F. H. Personality structure, and group structure: An interpretive study of their relationship through an event structure hypothesis, *Journal of Abnormal and Social Psychology*, 1956, *53*, 272–280.

Trist, E. L., and Bamforth, R. Some social and psychological consequences of the long wall method of coal-getting. *Human Relations*, 1951, *4*, 3–38.

Turner, A. N., and Lawrence, P. R. *Industrial jobs and the worker*. Boston: Harvard University School of Business Administration, 1965.

Von Bertalanffy, L. *General systems theory: Foundations, development, applications*, rev. ed. New York: Braziller, 1968.

Vroom, V. H. Some personality determinants of the effects of participation. *Journal of Abnormal and Social Psychology*, 1959, *59*, 322–327,

Vroom, V. H., and Yetton, P. W. *Leadership and decision making*. Pittsburgh, Pa.: University of Pittsburgh Press, 1973.

Walton, R. E. The diffusion of new work structures: Explaining why success didn't take. *Organizational Dynamics*, 1975 (Winter), 3–22.

Weick, K. E. *The social psychology of organizing*. Reading, Mass.: Addison-Wesley, 1969.

Whyte, W. F. (ed.) *Money and motivation: An analysis of incentives in industry*. New York: Harper & Row, 1955.

Woodward, J. *Industrial organization: Theory and practice*. New York: Oxford University Press, 1965.

19 planned change and organization development

STRATEGIES FOR LARGE SYSTEM CHANGE

RICHARD BECKHARD

Introduction

The focus of this article is on assisting large organization change through consultative or training interventions. As used below, "client" refers to an organization's leader(s) and "consultant" refers to the intervenor or change facilitator. Note that the consultant can come from within or from outside the organization.

Intervention is defined here as behavior which affects the *ongoing social processes* of a system. These processes include:

1. Interaction between individuals.
2. Interaction between groups.
3. The procedures used for transmitting information, making decisions, planning actions, and setting goals.
4. The strategies and policies guiding the system, the norms, or the unwritten ground rules or values of the system.
5. The attitudes of people toward work, the organization, authority, and social values.
6. The distribution of effort within the system. Interventions can affect any one or several of these processes.

The first part of this article describes a model of diagnosis and strategy planning which has had high utility for the author during the past several years. The second part examines a number of actual strategies in organization and

Reprinted by permission of the author and publisher from *Sloan Management Review*, Winter 1975.

This article is adapted from a chapter by the author in *Laboratory Method of Changing and Learning*, Benne, Bradford, Gibb, and Lippitt, editors, forthcoming Spring 1975 from Science and Behavior Books, Palo Alto, California.

large system change and the issues of where to begin change and how to maintain change.[1]

A Model for Change Planning

The following model is far from perfect. However, its use seems to enable one to ask the "right" questions and to obtain answers that yield a basis for relatively trustworthy judgment on early interventions into the large system. For convenience the model will be discussed under four headings.

Defining the Change Problem

When a change effort is initiated, either the client and/or the consultant, or some other part of the system has determined that there is some need for change. An initial diagnostic step concerns analyzing what these needs are and whether they are shared in different parts of the system. For example, let us suppose top management in an organization sees as a major need the improvement of the supervisory behavior of middle management and, simultaneously, the personnel staff in the organization sees as a *prior* need a change in the behavior of the top management and a change in the reward system. These are two very different perceptions of the priority of need for initial change, but a common perception that there is a need for change in the organization does exist. As a part of determining the need for change, it is also useful to collect some information from various parts of the system in order to determine the strength of the need.

There are two distinct ways of defining the change problem. The first considers the *organization* change needed or desired. For example, does the need concern changing the state of morale, the way work is done, the communication system, the reporting system, the structure or location of the decision making, the effectiveness of the top team, the relationships between levels, the way goals are set, or something else? The second considers what *type* of change is desired and what the hierarchy or rank-ordering of these types is. One should ask whether the primary initial change requires a change:

1. Of attitudes? Whose?
2. Of behavior? By whom and to what?
3. Of knowledge and understanding? Where?
4. Of organization procedures? Where?
5. Of practices and ways of work?

Rank-ordering the various types of change helps to determine which early interventions are most appropriate.

Having defined the change problem or problems from the viewpoint of both organizational change and change process, one can look at the organization system and subsystems to determine which are primarily related to the particular problem. The appropriate systems may be the organizational hierarchy, may be pieces of it, may be systems both inside and outside of the formal structure, or may be some parts of the formal structure and not other

---

[1]For a more detailed explanation of the author's views concerning organization development and intervention, see Beckhard [1].

parts. A conscious identification of those parts of the total system which primarily affect or are affected by the particular change helps to reduce the number of subsystems to be considered and also helps to clarify directions for early intervention.

Determining Readiness and Capability for Change

Readiness as stated here means either attitudinal or motivational energy concerning the change. Capability means the physical, financial, or organizational capacity to make the change. These are separate but interdependent variables.

In determining readiness for change, there is a formula developed by David Gleicher of Arthur D. Little that is particularly helpful. The formula can be described mathematically as $C = (abd) > x$, where C = change, a = level of dissatisfaction with the status quo, b = clear or understood desired state, d = practical first steps toward a desired state, and x = "cost" of changing. In other words, for change to be possible and for commitment to occur there has to be enough dissatisfaction with the current state of affairs to mobilize energy toward change. There also has to be some fairly clear conception of what the state of affairs would be if and when the change were successful. Of course, a desired state needs to be consistent with the values and priorities of the client system. There also needs to be some client awareness of practical first steps, or starting points, toward the desired state.

An early diagnosis by the consultant of which of these conditions does not exist, or does not exist in high strength, may provide direct clues concerning where to put early intervention energy. For example, if most of the system is not really dissatisfied with the present state of things, then early interventions may well need to aim toward increasing the level of dissatisfaction. On the other hand, there may be plenty of dissatisfaction with the present state, but no clear picture of what a desired state might be. In this case, early interventions might be aimed at getting strategic parts of the organization to define the ideal or desired state. If both of these conditions exist but practical first steps are missing, then early intervention strategy may well be to pick some subsystem, e.g., the top unit or a couple of experimental groups, and to begin improvement activities.

The following case illustrates these ideas. A general manager was concerned that the line managers were not making good use of the resources of the staff specialists. He felt that the specialists were not aggressive enough in offering their help. He had a desired state in mind of what good use of staff by line would be. He also had a practical first step in mind: send the staff out to visit the units on a systematic basis and have them report to him after their visits. The manager sent a memo to all staff and line heads announcing the plan. Staff went to the field and had a variety of experiences, mostly frustrating. The general manager got very busy on other priorities and did not hold his planned follow-up meetings. After one round of visits, the staff stopped its visits except in rare cases. Things returned to normal. An analysis showed that the general manager's real level of dissatisfaction with the previous state of affairs was not high enough to cause him to invest personal energy in follow-up reporting, so the change did not last.

Capability as defined here is frequently but not always outside of personal control. For example, a personnel or training manager may be ready to initiate a management development program but have low capability for doing it because he has no funds or support. The president of an organization may have only moderate or low readiness to start a management development program but may have very high capability because he can allocate the necessary resources. Two subordinates in an organization may be equally ready and motivated towards some change in their own functioning or leadership skills. One may have reached the ceiling of his capabilities and the other may not. Looking at this variable is an important guideline in determining interventions.

Identifying the Consultant's Own Resources and Motivations for the Change

In addition to defining the client and system status, and determining with the client the rank-ordering of change priorities, it is necessary for the consultant to be clear with himself and with the client about what knowledge and skills he brings to the problems and what knowledge and skills he does not have. One of the results of the early dependency on a consultant, particularly if the first interventions are seen as helpful or if his reputation is good, is to transfer the expertise of the consultant in a particular field to others in which his competence to help just is not there.

Concerning motivations, one of the fundamental choices that the consultant must make in intervening in any system is when to be an advocate and when to be a methodologist. The values of the consultant and the values of the system and their congruence or incongruence come together around this point. The choice of whether to work with the client, whether to try to influence the client toward the consultant's value system, or whether to take an active or passive role is a function of the decision that is made concerning advocacy vs. methodology.

This is not an absolute decision that, once made at the beginning of a relationship, holds firm throughout a change effort. Rather, it is a choice that is made daily around the multitude of interventions throughout a change effort. The choice is not always the same. It is helpful to the relationship and to the change effort if the results of the choice are known to the client as well as to the consultant.

Determining the Intermediate Change Strategy and Goals

Once change problems and change goals are defined, it is important to look at intermediate objectives if enough positive tension and energy toward change are to be maintained. For example, let us suppose that a change goal is to have all of the work teams in an organization consciously looking at their own functioning and systematically setting work priorities and improvement priorities on a regular basis. An intermediate goal might be to have developed within the various divisions or sections of the organization at least one team per unit by a certain time. These *intermediate* change goals provide a target and a measuring point en route to a larger change objective.

One other set of diagnostic questions concerns looking at the subsystems again in terms of:

1. Readiness of each system to be influenced by the consultant and/or entry client.
2. Accessibility of each of the subsystems to the consultant or entry client.
3. Linkage of each of the subsystems to the total system or organization.

To return to the earlier illustration concerning a management development program, let us suppose that the personnel director was highly vulnerable to influence by the consultant and highly accessible to the consultant but had low linkage to the organization, and that the president was much less vulnerable to influence by the consultant and the entry client, here the training manager. Then the question would be who should sign the announcement of the program to line management. The correct answer is not necessarily the president with his higher linkage nor the personnel man with his accessibility and commitment. The point is that weighing these three variables helps the consultant and client to make an operational decision based on data. Whether one uses this model or some other, the concept of systematic analysis of a change problem helps develop realistic, practical, and attainable strategy and goals.

Intervention Strategies in Large Systems

The kinds of conditions in organizations that tend to need large system interventions will now be examined.

Change in the Relationship of the Organization to the Environment

The number and complexity of outside demands on organization leaders are increasing at a rapid pace. Environmental organizations, minorities, youth, governments, and consumers exert strong demands on the organization's effort and require organization leaders to focus on creative adaptation to these pressures. The autonomy of organizations is fast becoming a myth. Organization leaders are increasingly recognizing that the institutions they manage are truly *open* systems. Improvement strategies based on looking at the internal structure, decision making, or intergroup relationships exclusively are an incomplete method of organization diagnosis and change strategy. A more relevant method for today's environment is to start by examining how the organization and its key subsystems relate to the different environments with which the organization interfaces. One can then determine what kinds of organization structures, procedures and practices will allow each of the units in the organization to optimize the interface with its different environment. Having identified these, management can turn its energy toward the problems of integration (of standards, rewards, communications systems, etc.) which are consequences of the multiple interfaces.

The concept of differentiation and integration has been developed by Paul Lawrence and Jay Lorsch.[2] In essence, their theory states that within any organization there are very different types of environments and very different types of interfaces. In an industrial organization, for example, the sales department interfaces with a relatively volatile environment: the market. The production department, on the other hand, interfaces with a relatively stable environment: the technology of production. The kind of organization structure, rewards, work schedules and skills necessary to perform optimally in these two departments is very different. From a definition of what is appropriate for each of these departments, one can organize an ideal, independent structure. Only then can one look at the problems of interface and communication.

Clark, Krone and McWhinney[3] have developed a technology called "Open

[2]See Lawrence and Lorsch [4].
[3]See Krone [3].

608

Systems Planning" which, when used as an intervention, helps the management of an organization to systematically sharpen its mission goals; to look objectively at its present response pattern to demands; to project the likely demand system if no pro-active actions are taken by the organization leadership; to project an "ideal" demand system; to define what activities and behavior would have to be developed for the desired state to exist; and finally to analyze the cost effectiveness of undertaking these activities. Such a planning method serves several purposes:

1. It forces systematic thinking.
2. It forces people to think from outside-in (environment to organization).
3. It forces empathy with other parts of the environment.
4. It forces the facing of today's realities.
5. It forces a systematic plan for priorities in the medium-term future.

This is one example of large system intervention dealing with the organization and its environment. Another type of intervention is a survey of organization structure, work, attitudes and environmental requirements. From this an optimum organization design is developed.

There is an increasing demand for assistance in helping organization leaders with these macro-organization issues. Much current change agent training almost ignores this market need. Major changes in training are called for if OD specialists are to stay organizationally relevant.

Change in Managerial Strategy

Another change program involving behavioral science oriented interventions is a change in the *style* of managing the human resources of the organization. This can occur when top management is changing their assumptions and/or values about people and their motivations. It can occur as a result of new inputs from the environment, such as the loss of a number of key executives or difficulty in recruiting top young people. It can occur as females in the organization demand equal treatment or as the government requires new employment practices. Whatever the causes, once such a change is planned, help is likely to be needed in:

1. Working with the top leaders.
2. Assessing middle management attitudes.
3. Unfreezing old attitudes.
4. Developing credibility down the line.
5. Dealing with interfacing organizations, unions, regulatory agencies, etc.

Help can be provided in organization diagnosis, job design, goal setting, team building, and planning. Style changes particularly need considerable time and patience since perspective is essential and is often lost by the client. Both internal and outside consultants can provide significant leadership in providing perspectives to operating management. Some of the questions about key managers that need answers in planning a change in managerial strategy are:

1. To what degree does the top management encourage influence from other parts of the organization?
2. How do they manage conflict?
3. To what degree do they locate decision making based on where information is located rather than on hierarchical roles?
4. How do they handle the rewards that they control?
5. What kind of feedback systems do they have for getting information about the state of things?

Change in the Organization Structures

One key aspect of healthy and effective organizations is that the structures, the formal ways that work is organized, follow and relate to the actual work to be done. In many organizations the structure relates to the authority system: who reports to whom. Most organizations are designed to simplify the structure in order to get clear reporting lines which define the power relationships.

As work becomes more complex, it becomes impossible in any large system to have *one* organization structure that is relevant to all of the kinds of work to be done. The basic organization chart rarely describes the way even the basic work gets done. More and more organization leaders recognize and endorse the reality that organizations actually operate through a variety of structures. In addition to the permanent organization chart, there are project organizations, task forces, and other temporary systems.

To clarify this concept, we examine a case where a firmly fixed organizational structure was a major resistance to getting the required work done. In this particular consumer-based organization there was a marketing organization that was primarily concerned with competing in the market, and a technical subsystem that was primarily concerned with getting packages designed with high quality. Market demands required that the organization get some sample packages of new products into supermarkets as sales promotions. The "rules of the game" were that for a package to be produced it had to go through a very thorough preparation including design and considerable field testing. These standards had been developed for products which were marketed extensively in markets where the company had a very high share. The problem developed around a market in which the company had a very low share and was competing desperately with a number of other strong companies. Because of the overall company rules about packages, the marketing people were unable to get the promotion packages into the stores on time. The result was the loss of an even greater share of the market. The frustration was tremendous and was felt right up to the president.

Within the marketing organization there was a very bright, technically oriented, skilled, abrasive entrepreneurial person, who kept very heavy pressure on the package technical people. He was convinced the he could produce the packages himself within a matter of weeks as opposed to the months that the technical people required. Because of his abrasiveness he produced much tension within the technical department and the tensions between the two departments also increased. At one point the heads of the two departments were on a very "cool" basis. The president of the company was quite concerned at the loss of markets. He had attempted to do something earlier about the situation by giving the marketing entrepreneur a little back room shop in which he could prove his assertions of being able to produce a package in a short time. The man did produce them, but when he took them to the technical people for reproduction, they called up all the traditional ground rules and policies to demonstrate that the package would not work and could not be used.

The client, here the president, had diagnosed the problem as one of non-cooperation between departments and particularly between individuals. Based on this diagnosis he asked for some consultative help with the interpersonal problem between the marketing entrepreneur and the people in the technical department. He also thought that an intergroup intervention might be appropriate to increase collaboration between the groups.

The consultant's diagnosis was that although either of these interventions was possible and might, in fact, produce some temporary change in the sense of lowering the heat in the situation, there was little possibility of either event producing more packages. Rather, the change problem was one of an inappropriate structure for managing work.

The consultant suggested that the leaders of marketing and technical development together develop a flow chart of the steps involved in moving from an idea to a finished promotion package. Then they were to isolate those items which clearly fitted within the organization structure, such as the last few steps in the process which were handled by the buying and production department. The remaining steps, it was suggested, needed to be managed by a temporary organization created for just that purpose. The consultant proposed that for each new promotion a temporary management organization be set up consisting of one person from packaging, one from marketing, one from purchasing, and one from manufacturing. This organization would have, as its charter, the management of the flow of that product from idea to manufacturing. They would analyze the problem, set a timetable, set the resource requirements and control the flow of work. The resources that they needed were back in the permanent structures, of which they were also members. This task force would report weekly and jointly to the heads of both the technical and marketing departments. The president would withdraw from the problem.

The intervention produced the targeted result: promotion packages became available in one-fifth of the time previously required. The interpersonal difficulties remained for some time but gradually decreased as people were forced to collaborate in getting the job done.

Change in the Ways Work Is Done

This condition is one where there is a special effort to improve the meaningfulness as well as the efficiency of work. Job enrichment programs, work analysis programs, and development of criteria for effectiveness can all be included here. To give an example, an intervention might be to work with a management group helping them examine their recent meeting agendas in order to improve the allocation of work tasks. Specifically, one can get them to make an initial list of those activities and functions that absolutely have to be done by that group functioning as a group. Next, a list can be made of things that are not being done but need to be. A third list can be made of those things that the group is now doing that could be done, even if not so well, by either the same people wearing their functional or other hats, or by other people. Experience has shown that the second two lists tend to balance each other and tend to represent somewhere around 25-30 percent of the total work of such a group. Based on this analysis a replan of work can emerge. It can have significant effects on both attitudes and behavior. The output of such an activity by a group at the top means that work gets reallocated to the next level, and thus a domino effect is set in motion which can result in significant change.

Another illustration concerns an organization-wide change effort to improve both the way work is done and the management of the work. The total staff of this very large organization was about forty thousand people. During a six month period, the total organization met in their work teams with the task of developing the criteria against which that team wanted the performance of their work unit to be measured. They then located their current performance against those criteria and projected their performance at a date about six months in the future against the same criteria. These criteria and projections were checked with senior management committees in each subsystem. If approved they became the work plan and basis for performance appraisal for that group.

With this one intervention the top management distributed the responsibility for managing the work to the people who were doing the work throughout the organization. The results of this program were a significant increase in productivity, significant cost reductions, and a significant change in attitudes and feelings of ownership among large numbers of employees, many of whom were previously quite dissatisfied with the state of things. Given this participative mode, it is most unlikely that any future management could successfully return to overcentralized control. Much latent energy was released and continues to be used by people all over the organization who feel responsible and appreciated for *their* management of *their* work.

Change in the Reward System

One significant organization problem concerns making the reward system consistent with the work. How often we see organizations in which someone in a staff department spends 90 percent of his time in assisting some line department; yet for his annual review his performance is evaluated solely by the head of his staff department, probably on 10 percent of his work. One result of this is that any smart person behaves in ways that please the individual who most influences his career and other rewards rather than those with whom he is working. Inappropriate reward systems do much to sabotage effective work as well as organization health.

An example of an intervention in this area follows. The vice president of one of the major groups in a very large company was concerned about the lack of motivation by his divison general managers toward working with him on planning for the future of the business as a whole. He was equally concerned that the managers were not fully developing their own subordinates. In his opinion, this was blocking the managers' promotions. The vice president had spoken of these concerns many times. His staff had agreed that it was important to change, but their behavior was heavily directed toward maintaining the old priorities: meeting short-term profit goals. This group existed in an organization where the reward system was very clear. The chief executives in any sub-enterprise were accountable for their short-term profits. This was their most important assignment. Division managers knew that if they did not participate actively in future business planning, or if they did not invest energy in the development of subordinates, they would incur the group vice president's displeasure. They also knew, however, that if they did not meet their short-term profit objectives, they probably would not be around. The company had an executive incentive plan in which considerable amounts of bonus money were available to people in the upper ranks for good performance. In trying to find a method for changing his divison managers' priorities, the group vice president looked, with consultant help, at the reward system. As a result of this he called his colleagues together and told them, "I thought you'd like to know that in determining your bonus at the next review, I will be using the following formula. You are still 100 percent accountable for your short-term profit goals, but that represents 60 percent of the bonus. Another 25 percent will be my evaluation of your performance as members of this top management planning team. The other 15 percent will be your discernible efforts toward the development of your subordinates." Executive behavior changed dramatically. The reality of the reward system and the desired state were now consistent.

We have examined briefly several types of organization phenomena which need large system oriented interventions. We will now look at initial interventions and examine some of the choices facing the intervenor.

Early Interventions

There are a number of choices about where to intervene. Several are listed here with the objective of creating a map of possibilities. The list includes:

1. The top team or the top of a system.
2. A pilot project which can have a linkage to the larger system.
3. Ready subsystems: those whose leaders and members are known to be ready for a change.
4. Hurting systems. This is one class of ready system where the environment has caused some acute discomfort in a generally unready system.
5. The rewards system.
6. Experiments: a series of experiments on new ways of organizing or new ways of handling communications.
7. Educational interventions: training programs, outside courses, etc.
8. An organization-wide confrontation meeting, bringing together a variety of parts of the organization, to examine the state of affairs and to make first step plans for improvement.[4]
9. The creation of a critical mass.

The last concept requires some elaboration. It is most difficult for a stable organization to change itself, that is, for the regular structures of the organization to be used for change. Temporary systems are frequently created to accomplish this. As an example, in one very large system, a country, there were a number of agencies involved in training and development for organization leaders. The government provided grants to the agencies for training acitivities. These grants also provided funds to support the agency staffs for other purposes. Because of this condition each agency was developing programs for the same small clientele. Each agency kept innovations secret from its competitors.

[4]For one view of this, see Beckhard [2].

In an attempt to move this competitive state toward a more collaborative one, a small group of people developed a "nonorganization" called the Association for Commercial and Industrial Education. It was a luncheon club. Its rules were the opposite of an ordinary organization's. It could make no group decisions, it distributed no minutes, no one was allowed to take anyone else to lunch, there were no dues, and there were no officers or hierarchy.

In this context it was possible for individuals from the various competing agencies to sit down and talk together about matters of mutual interest. After a couple of years it even became possible to develop a national organization development training project in the form of a four week course which was attended by top line managers and personnel people from all the major economic and social institutions in the country. Only this nonorganization could sponsor such a program. From this program a great many other linkages were developed. Today there is an entire professional association of collaborating change agents with bases in a variety of institutions, but with the capacity to collaborate around larger national problems.

Maintaining Change

To maintain change in a large system it is necessary to have conscious procedures and commitment. Organization change will not be maintained simply because there has been early success. There are a number of interventions which are possible, and many are necessary if a change is to be maintained. Many organizations are living with the effects of successful short-term change results which have not been maintained.

Perhaps the most important single requirement for continued change is a continued feedback and information system that lets people in the organization know the system status in relation to the desired states. Some feedback systems that are used fairly frequently are:

1. Periodic team meetings to review a team's functioning and what its next goal priorities should be.
2. Organization sensing meetings in which the top of an organization meets, on a systematic planned basis, with a sample of employees from a variety of different organizational centers in order to keep apprised of the state of the system.
3. Periodic meetings between interdependent units of an organization.
4. Renewal conferences. For example, one company has an annual five-year planning meeting with its top management. Three weeks prior to that meeting the same management group and their wives go to a retreat for two or three days to take a look at themselves, their personal and company priorities, the new forces in the environment, what they need to keep in mind in their upcoming planning, and what has happened in the way they work and in their relationships that needs review before the planning meeting.
5. Performance review on a systematic, goal-directed basis.
6. Periodic visits from outside consultants to keep the organization leaders thinking about the organization's renewal.

There are other possible techniques but this list includes the most commonly used methods of maintaining a change effort in a complex organization.

Summary

In order to help organizations improve their operational effectiveness and system health, we have examined:

1. A model for determining early organization interventions.
2. Some choices of change strategies.
3. Some choices of early interventions.
4. Some choices of strategies for maintaining change.

The focus of this article has been on what the third party, facilitator, consultant, etc., can do as either a consultant, expert, trainer, or coach in helping organization leaders diagnose their own system and plan strategies for development toward a better state. This focus includes process intervention but is not exclusively that. It also includes the skills of system diagnosis, of determining change strategies, of understanding the relationship of organizations to external environments, and of understanding such organization processes as power, reward systems, organizational decision making, information systems, structural designs and planning.

It is the author's experience that the demand for assistance in organizational interventions and large system organization change is increasing at a very fast rate, certainly faster than the growth of resources to meet the demand. As the world shrinks, as there are more multinational organizations, as the interfaces between government and the private sector and the social sector become more blurred and more overlapping, large system interventions and the technology and skill available to facilitate these will be in increasingly greater demand.

References

1. Beckhard, R. *Organization Development: Strategies and Models.* Reading, Mass.: Addison-Wesley, 1969.
2. Beckhard, R. "The Confrontation Meeting." *Harvard Business Review*, March–April 1967.
3. Krone, C. "Open Systems Redesign." In *Theory and Method in Organization Development: An Evolutionary Process*, edited by John Adams. Rosslyn, Va.: NTL Institute, 1974.
4. Lawrence, P. R., and Lorsch, J. W. *Organization and Environment: Managing Differentiation and Integration.* Boston: Harvard Business School, Divison of Research, 1967.

INFLUENCE AND ORGANIZATIONAL CHANGE

GENE W. DALTON[1]

During the last few years a new term, "organization development," has been rapidly finding its way into the organization charts of American corporations. Because of the recency of this phenomenon it is sometimes difficult to ascertain the extent to which the activities carried out under this title are old activities being carried out under a new name or a new set of activities aimed at an old but increasingly urgent problem. But one fact does emerge: there is an increasing number of men in these organizations whose primary function is to foster change. This has always been part of the job of a manager, and often a significant part; but now there is an increasing number of men in the organizations who are essentially specialists in the process of organizational change.

Almost inevitably, a part of the requirement of this new role will be an ability to be explicit about the change process itself, for the O.D. specialist will be an adviser and helper more often than an initiator. In this role of counselor, he will need a framework or model for both thinking and talking about the means by which individuals and groups are influenced to change their behavior in organizations. A model has a number of uses. It can help order the available data and clarify discussion. It can provide some much-needed categories so that similarities between similar acts can be highlighted. It can point out the multiple functions which some act performs without forcing us to talk about everything at once.

For several years my colleagues and I have been studying an organization in which a new director of a research and development center set out to change the behavior of a substantial number of managers and engineers. We observed his efforts over time and attempted to measure their effects. Over a period of a year and a half it became increasingly evident that he had been successful in influencing one group of the men but had had little effect on the others. This result both baffled and challenged us. In our attempt to understand the differ-

---

First presented and published as a paper at a Conference on Organizational Behavior Models, Kent State University, May 1969, and reprinted here by permission. The central ideas of the paper were developed in G. W. Dalton, L. B. Barnes, and A. Zaleznik, *The Distribution of Authority in Formal Organizations* (Boston: Division of Research, Harvard Business School, 1968). The research was generously supported by the B. F. Goodrich Endowment and the Ford Foundation Research in Organizational Behavior and Administration.

[1]Professor of Management, Brigham Young University.

ence, we examined the studies we could find which described instances where someone had successfully influenced others to change their behavior. From the analysis of these studies and of our own data we constructed an elementary model of the influence process in organizational change. I am proposing that it may serve as a useful point of departure for those engaged in organization development, as well as for those of us who study organizational life.

Organizational and Individual Change

First I should clarify what I mean by organizational change. As used here, the term refers to any significant alteration of the behavior patterns of a large number of the individuals who constitute that organization. I make a point of this because students of organizations, in their efforts to characterize an organization as a system or organism, too often lose sight of the fact that the "behavior" of an organization is made up of the actions and interactions of the individuals in it. We read so frequently about an organization "adapting" to market shifts, economic conditions, and scientific discoveries that we slide over the internal processes by which an organization does that adapting. The biological analogy of an organism adapting to its environment can be dramatic and conceptually helpful, but students of organizations typically make only partial use of the analogy. They stop at this generalized level of explanation and fail to follow their biologist colleagues, whose concepts they have borrowed, to the next step of examining the internal processes by which the system adapts.

Our focus will be on the response within the organization to factors in its environment. Typically, one or more individuals in the organization see something in the environment which calls for different behavior on the part of the members of the organization. He (or they) then tries to move others in the organization to make this change in their behavior. This is fundamentally an influence process, and it is the process I shall be representing here. The primary data chosen for illustration come from our own study plus studies of change in organizational settings by Guest,[2] Seashore and Bowers,[3] Jaques,[4] and Blake, Mouton, Barnes, and Greiner.[5] These all focused on the internal change process.

Some of the best reported studies of the influence process, however, were made in nonorganizational settings: experimental studies of attitude change, individual and group psychotherapy, religious conversion, and so-called thought reform. In deciding whether to draw from these, I was faced with the question as to whether studies of individual change can materially aid our understanding of organizational change, and my answer was affirmative. Certainly, membership in a formal organization places the individual within a potent influence network, and any explanation of changes in his behavior and attitudes must take this network into account. But we must not allow ourselves to presume that behavior in formal organizations is discontinuous from human behavior

[2]Robert H. Guest, *Organization Change: The Effect of Successful Leadership* (Homewood, Ill.: Richard D. Irwin, Inc. and The Dorsey Press, 1962).

[3]S. E. Seashore and D. G. Bowers, *Changing the Structure and Functioning of an Organization* (Ann Arbor: University of Michigan, Survey Research Center, Monograph No. 33, 1963).

[4]Elliott Jaques, *The Changing Culture of a Factory* (London: Tavistock Publications, Ltd., 1951).

[5]Robert R. Blake, Jane S. Mouton, Louis B. Barnes, and Larry E. Greiner, "Breakthrough in Organization Development," *Harvard Business Review*, November–December 1964.

elsewhere. The object of change in planned change programs is the behavior and attitudes of individuals. Within an organization, those attitudes and actions form an inextricable part of larger formal and informal systems, but the workings of social processes ultimately take place as intrapersonal and interpersonal processes.

Sequencing

In our study of the events at the Nampa Development Center, one of the first things we noted was the importance of time. Often the most significant fact about a given event was that it followed other events or that it created a condition which influenced subsequent events. This is also the one point on which other students of change agree—that behavioral and attitudinal change takes place in sequential steps or phases.

. Probably the most fruitful conception of the change process, judging from the frequency of its use by others and by the research it has stimulated, is the three-step model advanced by Kurt Lewin:[6] unfreezing the system which is operating in a given pattern, moving to a new pattern, and refreezing into this new pattern. Lewin postulated that systems tend to operate in a given pattern or at a given level as there is a relative balance of forces acting on the system.

A sequential model achieves a number of functions. It provides a dimension along which to order events and draws attention to events and conditions at the boundaries of the phenomena under examination. Too often, I think, those of us managing or studying organizations tend to be ahistorical in our approach.[7] For example, in our own study, when we conceived of "unfreezing" broadly, we were led to examine not only the unsettling effects of the director's changes in the organizational structure, but also the conditions in the organization at the time he became director and the events leading up to them. Using this one dimension, time, we could characterize the change process at the center, where successful, as shown in Figure 1.

FIGURE 1

Unfreezing		Change	Refreezing
Tension and the need for change was experienced within the organization.	Change was advocated by the new director.	Individuals within the organization tested out the proposed changes.	New behavior and attitudes were either reinforced and internalized, or rejected and abandoned.

Subprocesses

So far, so good. Time is important, and a sequential model such as Lewin's is useful in pointing to the tendency toward orderly movement related to prior events. But, as we compared the successful and unsuccessful attempts to exert influence, it also became obvious that there was not one process at work but

[6] Kurt Lewin, "Group Decision and Social Change," in T. M. Newcomb and E. L. Hartley (eds.), *Readings in Social Psychology* (New York: Holt, Rinehart & Winston, Inc., 1958).
[7] For a notable exception, see L. E. Greiner, "Antecedents of Planned Organizational Change," *Journal of Applied Behavioral Science*, Vol. 3, No. 1 (1967).

several, all moving simultaneously. Where influence was successful, changes occurred not only in the way an individual related to the influencing agent, but also to his co-worker and to himself. As interaction patterns were dissolving and reforming, changes were taking place within the individuals involved, changes in their feelings about themselves and in the objectives they sought.

We identified four major subprocesses that tended to characterize successful change in our own study and in the other empirical studies of change we examined.

The four subprocesses are characterized by movement:

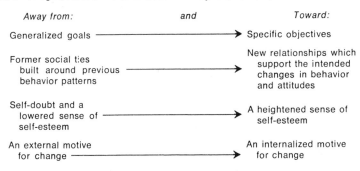

A Model for Induced Change

If we combine these four subprocesses with our notion of sequencing, we arrive at the diagram in Figure 2. Following this diagram, we shall look at the two antecedent conditions which were present in each case of successful planned change examined. Then we shall look separately at each of the four subprocesses pictured.

Internal Tension as an Antecedent Condition

At the risk of stating a truism, let me point out that one of the most important conditions necessary for the successful initiation of change is a sense of tension or a felt need for change among those who are the targets of influence. In nearly every instance, in the studies reviewed, where one person or group successfully influenced the behavior of others, those influenced were experiencing a more-than-usual amount of tension or stress.

In our own study, a major project on which many of the men had worked for years had just been discontinued and the technology sold to a competitor. The decision by top management not to manufacture or market the product, which had been announced just prior to the new director's appointment, had generated a sense of disappointment and frustration at the center, since many had come to identify their own future with the success of the project. The men were also concerned about the falling prices of their division's major product and at the center's apparent lack of success in recent years at translating their technical capabilities into dramatic new products.

Guest, in his three-year study of leadership and organizational change in an automobile assembly plant, reported that before the arrival of the new production manager, who succeeded in "turning the plant around" from the least to the most efficient plant in the division, there was great tension. Labor griev-

FIGURE 2
A Model of Induced Change

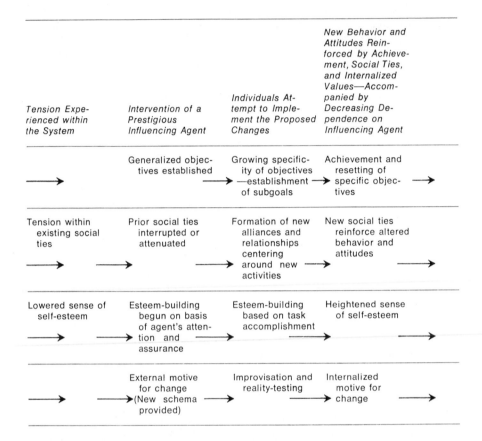

Tension Experienced within the System	Intervention of a Prestigious Influencing Agent	Individuals Attempt to Implement the Proposed Changes	New Behavior and Attitudes Reinforced by Achievement, Social Ties, and Internalized Values—Accompanied by Decreasing Dependence on Influencing Agent
→	Generalized objectives established	Growing specificity of objectives —establishment → of subgoals	Achievement and resetting of specific objectives →
Tension within existing social ties →	Prior social ties interrupted or attenuated →	Formation of new alliances and relationships centering around new → activities	New social ties reinforce altered behavior and attitudes →
Lowered sense of self-esteem →	Esteem-building begun on basis of agent's atten- → tion and assurance	Esteem-building based on task accomplishment →	Heightened sense of self-esteem →
→	External motive for change →(New schema provided)	Improvisation and reality-testing →	Internalized motive for → change →

ances were high, turnover was twice that in other plants and the plant was under constant pressure from division headquarters.[8]

Seashore and Bowers, in their study of an ultimately successful change effort by a consulting-research team from the University of Michigan, reported that in the year prior to the interventions of the team, "Banner [the company] dropped to a very marginal profit position. . . . Waste, service, and quality problems arose. . . . There was a sense of things getting out of control, a feeling shared and expressed by many non-managerial people."[9]

Elliot Jaques, in his pioneering study of social and technical change in the Glacier Metal Company, reported the impact of a crisis which resulted in a large number of layoffs and "great anxiety about job security. The procedure adopted [to handle the layoffs] had lessened some of the morale problems— but it did not and could not remove everyone's anxiety about job security."[10] Jaques, in fact, concluded that a necessary factor in allowing for a working

[8]Guest, *op. cit.*
[9]Seashore and Bowers, *op cit.*
[10]Jaques, *op. cit.*

through of group problems was a "problem severe and painful enough for its members to wish to do something about it."

Blake, Mouton, Barnes, and Greiner, describing a major organizational change effort featuring a training program, noted the presence of great tension in the Sigma plant prior to the training consultant's arrival at the plant. A merger had taken place, bringing the plant under a new headquarters staff, and a serious problem arose over the "use of Sigma manpower on construction work of new projects." When the headquarters staff began to "prod Sigma," the plant management "became defensive" and according to one of the managers at headquarters, "some of our later sessions became emotional. Strained relations between different departments and levels within the plant began to develop."[11] Greiner reported that "plant morale slipped badly, insecurity arose and performance slumped," while a manager within the plant reported that "everything seemed to get out of control."[12]

This uniformity was also evident in other settings where there was a successful attempt to influence attitudes and behavior. The religious convert usually is experiencing self-doubt and guilt before he gives careful heed to the missionary or revivalist. A need for change is already felt by the person who walks into the Christian Science reading room or the revivalist tent. Certain organizations, such as Alcoholics Anonymous, whose central aim is to induce specific behavioral change, refuse to admit anyone unless he is consciously experiencing distress. An applicant to A.A. must openly admit the failure of previous individual efforts and his need for help.[13] Jerome Frank suggests that in psychotherapy the presence of prior emotional distress is closely related to the results of the treatment. He argues as follows:

> The importance of emotional distress in the establishment of a fruitful psychotherapeutic relationship is suggested by the facts that the greater the over-all degree of expressed distress, as measured by a symptom check list, the more likely the patient is to remain in treatment, while conversely two of the most difficult categories of patients to treat have nothing in common except lack of distress.[14]

Even in Chinese "thought-reform" prisons, where the interrogator had the power to induce new stress, the presence of internal tension prior to imprisonment appears to have been a crucial factor in the prisoner's susceptibility to influence and attitude change. Schein and his associates, who studied the Chinese thought-reform program as it was reported by American civilian prisoners in Chinese prisons, assigned a crucial role to the sense of guilt experienced by the individual. They reported that "if the prisoner-to-be was susceptible to social guilt, he was particularly vulnerable to the pressure of the cellmates in a group cell."[15]

It is important to note that these are qualitatively different situations, in many ways, from industrial settings; alcoholics, Communist prisoners, and psychiatric patients share an emotional distress and lack of control over their own actions which differentiate them from men working in industrial organiza-

[11] Blake *et al., op. cit.*
[12] *Ibid.*
[13] O. H. Mowrer, *The New Group Therapy* (Princeton, N.J.: D. Van Nostrand Co., 1964).
[14] Jerome Frank, *Persuasion and Healing* (New York: Schocken Books, 1963).
[15] Edgar H. Schein *et al., Coercive Persuasion* (New York: W. W. Norton & Co., 1961).

tions. But as in the industrial studies, attempts to influence behavior have a high probability of success only when the individuals have been experiencing internal stress.

In an organization, of course, the need for change isn't experienced uniformly throughout the organization and its locus helps determine the methods used to effect change. If the tension is felt primarily by those at the top of the authority structure but not by those below, change efforts will be exerted through the existing authority structure. Resistance usually takes the form of circumvention and token compliance. If, on the other hand, the tension exists at the bottom of the legitimate power structure, but not at the top, attempts to change the organization take the form of a revolt and an attack on the existing authority structure, as in campus riots and wildcat strikes. The extent and locus of tension also help determine outcomes. In our own study, two groups, the senior scientists and junior managers, were relatively more frustrated than others at the center and it was among the men in these groups that the new director found the greatest acceptance of the changes he proposed.

Authority and Prestige of the Influencer

The forces for change represented by tension and the desire for change must be mobilized, however, and given direction, while forces acting to resist change in a given direction must be overcome, neutralized, or enlisted. In an organization, unless there is to be protracted resistance, someone must gain the acceptance and possible support of individuals not seeking change and even those who feel threatened by it.

A second prerequisite for successfully induced change, therefore, appears to be that the initiation comes from a respected and, ideally, a trusted source. The persons being influenced need confidence that the change can, in fact, be effected and a large part of this confidence comes initially from their confidence in the power and judgment of the influencing agent. When men are unsure of their capacity to cope effectively with the situation, they identify with someone whom they perceive as having the knowledge or power to successfully cope with it and who states *where* they need to change. As such, he is then placed in a position where his expectations can become "self-fulfilling prophecies."[16]

In the organizational studies reviewed, successful attempts of change were either initiated by the formal head of the organizational unit involved or were given his strong support. In Guest's study, the initiator was the new plant manager, who brought with him a strong reputation for success in his previous position. Furthermore, it quickly became obvious to the other employees that he had the support of the district management.[17] (Pelz reported that upward influence with one's own superior was a necessary condition for influence with subordinates.[18]) Jaques also had the active support of the managing director of Glacier Metals.[19]

The changes at the "Banner Corporation"[20] were initiated by the highest

[16]R. Rosenthall and L. F. Jacobsen, "Teacher Expectations for the Disadvantaged," *Scientific American*, April 1968.

[17]Guest, *op. cit.*

[18]D. C. Pelz, "Influence: A Key to Effective Leadership in the First-Line Supervisor," *Personnel*, Vol. 29 (1952).

[19]Jaques, *op. cit.*

[20]Seashore and Bowers, *op. cit.*

official at the plant. He gained support from Rensis Likert and brought in an agent from the Survey Research Center who carried with him the prestige of the university as well as the authority of an experienced manager. The change effort at the Sigma plant had a similar dual sponsorship, receiving active support from the plant manager and a consultant, Robert Blake, who "had an impressive reputation with the management in other parts of [the headquarters company]."[21] (As a contrast to these successful change efforts, consider for a moment the many ineffectual training programs for first- and second-line supervisors in which the top management group did not participate and therefore never fully understood or supported.)

Nonorganizational studies show the same link between prestige and influence: individuals tend to believe and do those things suggested by authoritative, prestigeful sources.[22] Goal-setting studies reported by Mace indicated that setting goals for individuals and associating these goals with prestigeful authorities like "scientific progress" or "the advancement of research" tended to have a favorable effect on performance.[23]

Studies of operant conditioning of verbal behavior, where one person reinforces certain verbal signals emitted by another person, indicate that when the conditioner has some prestige or power in the subject's eyes, the influence tends to be stronger and more consistent. Students were more consistently influenced by their instructors, for example, than by fellow students. (Of course, this was several years ago. Perhaps today instructors over 30 may not enjoy the same influence.)

Another area of study focusing on the persuasive influence of a prestigeful figure is faith-healing and the so-called "placebo effect" in medicine. Jerome Frank reports that even healers regarded by the community as charlatans or quacks, were able, in some instances, to bring about change and symptom relief among persons who regarded them as sources of authority and power. Their success appeared to rest on their ability to evoke the patient's expectancy of help. In medical treatment, the fact that relief and healing can be brought about solely by the patient's expectation of help from the physician, is demonstrated by experiments verifying the so-called "placebo effect." In these studies, the doctor administers a pharmacologically inert substance to the patient rather than an active medication. Since the placebo is inert, its beneficial effects derive from the patient's confidence in the doctor's prescription and in the institutions of science and medicine which he represents. There is evidence that placebos can have marked physiological effects. Studies have shown that their use has been accompanied by healing of tissue damage ranging from warts to peptic ulcers. A similar effect is the "hello-goodbye" effect in psychotherapy. Patients who merely had contact with a prestigeful (in their eyes) psychiatrist improved significantly over the individuals in a control group who were placed on a waiting list and did not see a psychiatrist. In fact, these minimal contact patients showed almost as much improvement of certain kinds as a third group who underwent prolonged treatment.[24]

[21]Blake, Mouton, Barnes, and Greiner, *op. cit.*

[22]C. J. Hovland, I. L. Janis, and H. Kelley, *Communication and Persuasion: Psychological Studies of Opinion Change* (New Haven, Conn.: Yale University Press, 1953).

[23]C. A. Mace, "Satisfaction in Work," *Occupational Psychology*, Vol. 22 (1948), pp. 5–12.

[24]Frank, *op. cit.*

Even in thought-reform prisons, there is some suggestion that interrogators or cellmates with higher education and intelligence, as this was perceived by the prisoner, were more likely to be able to influence the prisoner than were those whom he "looked down on."[25] Statistical evidence on American prisoners of war in Korea show the small proportion (about 15 percent) of the prisoners who were classified as collaborators came primarily from low-status positions in American society,[26] and were therefore among the group most likely to see their interrogators and discussion leaders as prestigeful persons. In one of the most graphic accounts by a prisoner who successfully resisted influence by his interrogators, Gonzales reports that he never came to think of his interrogators as authorities in any real sense nor in any way superior to himself except that they were more numerous than he.[27] There is, of course, abundant evidence in our own study and elsewhere to refute a claim that any change initiated by a high status person will be successful. The process of change is more complex than that. But prestige and power on the part of the initiator seem to be a necessary, if not sufficient, condition for introducing large-scale change in any system. Where the person planning to initiate change does not already possess prestige and power in the organization, as Loomis has pointed out, it is his first task to develop "social capital" for himself, i.e., to build his reputation and power in the social system he intends to change.[28]

The Subprocesses

Now let us turn from the conditions which precede and facilitate change to an examination of the change process itself. The subtleties and interdependencies of the process, of course, are difficult and, in many ways, impossible to represent or describe because the phenomena occur simultaneously and are "of a piece." But as is shown in the diagram, we were able to distinguish four major subprocesses, all of which seemed to proceed simultaneously in those instances where individuals and groups were influenced to change their behavior and where these new behavior patterns persisted. Movement along each of these four streams characterized the junior managers and senior scientists at Nampa, but were either absent or restricted among the other men at the center whose behavior and attitude changed least.

Movement along each of these streams, where present, appeared to follow a consistent pattern or direction, and while each seemed distinct and separable, movement along all four appeared to occur simultaneously. The first two deal with changes in shared objectives and relationships, while the last two concern changes within the individual.

[25]Schein *et. al., op. cit.*

[26]J. Segal, "Correlates of Collaboration and Resistance Behavior among U.S. Army's POW's in Korea," *Journal of Social Issues,* Vol. 13, pp. 31–40.

[27]V. Gonzales and J. Gorkin, *El Campesino: Life and Death in Soviet Russia* (New York: G. P. Putnam's Sons, 1952).

[28]C. P. Loomis, "Tentative Types of Directed Social Change Involving Systematic Linkage," *Rural Sociology*, Vol. 24, No. 4 (December 1959).

The first pattern which consistently seems to characterize successful attempts to bring about behavioral and attitudinal change is a movement from generalized goals toward specific and concrete objectives. As the change progresses, the targets take on greater immediacy and concreteness; one of the clearest signals that a new pattern of behavior will not be established and maintained is the objectives remaining general and nonspecific. In the Nampa Center the changes outlined for all the groups began at a very general level. The junior managers, for example, were told that they were to take on more responsibility for the administration of their groups and to "plan the technical work" for their groups. The senior managers were told to spend at least half their time doing long-range planning. Soon afterward, the junior managers were asked to prepare budget requests for their groups. Later they were given responsibility for performing a specific technical objective and a target date was set for completion, and soon they were working out a week-by-week projected schedule. The assignment given the senior managers to do long-range planning, however, remained essentially at that level of generality, with neither the director nor the senior managers working out intermediate or subobjectives. Fifteen months later, of course, it was the junior and not the senior managers whose attitudes and behavior had changed in the intended direction.

In each of the other studies, whenever someone successfully influenced another person or group of persons to change their behavior or attitudes, movement toward greater specificity of goals was a prominent feature. Sometimes the person initiating the change set the subgoals, sometimes those being influenced set them; most often it was a joint or alternating arrangement. But the consistent element was that someone set concrete subgoals and the behavior change moved along step by step. Guest reported that the new manager at Plant Y began by outlining a "few general goals," such as better planning. He set up meetings for discussing general problems, but attention was steadily brought to focus on improving specific areas, such as accounting methods and inspection procedures.[29] Jaques' report of a three-year period of change in the Glacier Metal Company described how the project team worked successfully with councils and management groups at various levels and departments throughout the organizations. The process followed in their work, with each group showing remarkable consistency, began with the general goals of "understanding their difficulties," moved to a goal of understanding their own "here-and-now" relationships, and finally headed toward the resolution of specific problems or the writing of a new constitution.[30]

The plant manager's initially announced objective at "Banner Corporation" was to introduce "participation management" into the organization. After several months, four subgoals were explicitly stated as a way of implementing the overall goal:

1. Increased emphasis on the work group as a functioning unit.
2. More supportive behavior from supervisors.
3. Greater employee participation in decision making.
4. Increased interaction and influence among work group members.

[29]Guest, *op. cit.*
[30]Jaques, *op. cit.*

A series of meetings with all the supervisors in the experimental department followed, in which the objective became more and more operational in the minds of the supervisors. Finally, these intermediate goals were translated into more specific goals, such as bringing the employees into the decisions about a new shift rotation scheme.[31] The changes reported by Blake *et al.* at the Sigma refinery followed an identical pattern,[32] beginning with a training program in which the objectives for the participants were the general goals of understanding the concepts and assessing their own present management style. Other meetings followed in which the objectives were to explore ways to transfer the new concepts and personal learning of the seminars to the operation of their own group. The objective became even more concrete as the men consciously tried to use some of their new problem-solving methods in working out a program for reducing utility costs and in negotiating a difficult union-management contract.

Outside organizational settings, the most carefully conceptualized example of this aspect of the change process is found in the descriptions of the therapeutic process.[33] At the beginning of the relationship between the patient and the therapist, the mutually understood objective is usually relatively general in character: to help the patient to operate more effectively in his environment, to find relief from serious distress, or to achieve an understanding of the patient's problems and their causes. Explorations may begin by looking at the patient's past behavior, his relationships outside therapy, and his feelings about these. But nearly all schools of therapy agree that as the relationship continues, the patient comes to show feelings and behavior toward the therapist similar to those making trouble for him outside therapy. The examination of these concrete specific events acted out in their own relationship is undertaken as a means of achieving the more general objective. Religious conversion begins with goals of total repentance and "casting off the old man for the new," but where the conversion has lasting effects, this general goal moves toward the specific objectives of giving up certain practices, making contributions or proselyting others. Then as an individual makes small behavioral commitments in a certain direction, he justifies and rationalizes these acts by accepting values and explanations which reduce dissonance between these acts and his self-image. He becomes his own socializing agent. Even in the thought-reform prisons, the early demand of the interrogator for confession of guilt narrows and focuses to the objective of producing a written document confessing specific "criminal acts" which the interrogator will accept.

Altering Old Relationships and Establishing New Social Ties

The second pattern which seemed to characterize successful change was the loosening of old relationships and the establishment of new social ties which support the intended changes in attitude and behavior. Old behavior and attitudes are often deeply imbedded in the relationships which have been built up over the years, and as long as the individuals involved maintain these relationships unaltered, changes are unlikely to occur. By the same token, new behavior

[31]Seashore and Bowers, *op. cit.*
[32]*Op cit.*
[33]M. I. Stein, *Contemporary Psychotherapies* (Glencoe, Ill.: Free Press, 1961).

patterns are most readily and firmly established when they are conditions of regular membership in a new group, for group members exercise the most powerful tool for shaping behavior: selective reinforcement of responses with immediate rewards.

In other studies this is the dimension of the change process that has been most explicitly recognized: the beliefs, attitudes, and activities of a person are closely related to those of his reference groups. New attitudes and new activity patterns are most likely to be established when an individual becomes associated with a new reference group.[34] Certainly, not all of an individual's former associations will counteract an intended change, nor will new groups formed in a change situation always work in the direction that the influencing agent intends; but, in general, any significant changes in activities or attitudes include some movement from old object relationships toward new ones.

Behavioral scientists did not originate the idea that an alteration of old relationships facilitates change in individuals or groups. Most influencing institutions in our society separate the individual whom they wish to influence from his regular social contacts and routines. Convents, monasteries, and prisons tend to make this a total separation, and educational institutions make the same separation to a lesser degree by their physical distance from home and a demanding work load. Perhaps the best reported study of this is the work done by Newcomb at Bennington College. During their four years at the college, the girls tended to take on the attitudes of the faculty and student leaders, and to relinquish those of their parents.[35] The individual's greater susceptibility to influence when he is separated from social contacts which support his current beliefs was ingeniously demonstrated by the famous Asch experiments: when subjects were placed in a situation where no other person agreed with the subject's own judgments, a third of the subjects came to doubt their own perceptions to the extent that they reported seeing what the others reported in over half the trials. Yet, if only one person in the group confirmed a subject's own perception, his resistance to social pressure was significantly increased.[36] Rice, in his study of change in a textile weaving mill in India, found some confirmation for his argument that this need for removal from previous contacts applied also to groups where the group was the focus of change. Otherwise the prior social relationships continued to support the behavior patterns and attitudes which the change program was trying to alter.[37]

Breaking up or loosening former social ties may act to unfreeze an individual or group, but this alone provides no assurance that any resulting changes will be in a given direction or that they will have any permanency. Establishing new relationships which reward the desired behaviors and confirm the modified attitudes also seems to be essential. Otherwise, there will be an active seeking to return to former activities and attitudes and to the relationships which supported and reinforced them.

[34]B. Berelson and G. A. Steiner, *Human Behavior: An Inventory of Scientific Findings* (New York: Harcourt, Brace & Co., 1964).

[35]T. M. Newcomb, "Attitude Development as a Function of Reference Groups: The Bennington Study," in E. E. Maccoby, T. T. Newcomb, and E. L. Hartley (eds.), *Readings in Social Psychology* (New York: Holt, Rinehart & Winston, Inc., 1958).

[36]S. E. Asch, "Effects of Group Pressure upon the Modification and Distortion of Judgments," in H. Guetzkow (ed.), *Groups, Leadership, and Men* (Pittsburgh: Carnegie Press, 1951).

[37]A. K. Rice, *Productivity and Social Organization: The Ahmedabad Experiment* (London: Tavistock Publications, Ltd., 1958).

In our study of the Nampa Center, all the men in the experimental sections reported some disruption of their former relationships. Changes in job requirements and work schedules broke up former important interaction patterns in all the groups, but there was a sharp difference among the groups in the extent to which new relations were established. The men in the groups which eventually changed most were assigned to new decision-making committees with their peers from other parts of the company. When decisions were made in the groups there were strong pressures from the other members of the group to defend these decisions, even in dealings with the senior managers. The men who eventually changed least, on the other hand, established no new relationships. Their previous ties were attenuated, but they formed no new relationships which might have pulled them more closely into new patterns of activities and beliefs.

One of the most interesting studies illustrating this phenomenon was the follow-up study of an International Harvester Company training program emphasizing human relations skills which the investigators categorized as "consideration." Tested before and after the two-week training program, the foremen's attitude test scores shifted until these foremen actually scored lower in consideration than did a control group who had not been trained. Only those foremen whose immediate superiors scored high on consideration continued to score high themselves. The other foremen, whose superiors did not place a high value on consideration, returned to a pattern very close to that of their chiefs. Daily interaction completely negated the effect of the training program. The foremen's ties had been interrupted only during the two weeks' training period. Then they returned to a situation where the most significant relationship was with their own supervisors. No continuing new relationships had been established which would act to confirm and reinforce any attitude changes begun in the training program.[38]

A study which differs in important ways from the International Harvester study, yet confirms its findings, is the Barnes and Greiner investigation of the effects of Blake's organization development program at the Sigma oil refinery. At Sigma the management and staff members at all levels of the plant went through an initial training program during which men were taken out of their regular work groups and placed among relative strangers. They then returned to their old work groups, as in the International Harvester program, but with the difference that their superiors and colleagues had also been through the same training experience. In addition, a second series of meetings was held in which the teams who worked together jointly examined their own operations and made mutual commitments to change. A follow-up study revealed that the program had had an impact on the plant's operations and on the behavior and attitudes of some of the men but, again, not all. In this case, 92 percent of the supervisors who were rated as most changed by their subordinates worked in groups where a majority of their colleagues were also rated as "most improved" by their subordinates, while only 26 percent of the supervisors rated as "least improved" worked in such groups. In fact, it appeared to the investigators that even the presence of only one "least improved" cynic was enough to have a strong dampening effect, since 60 percent of the "most improved" supervisors worked in settings where there were no "least improved" colleagues whatso-

[38]E. A. Fleishman, E. F. Harris, and H. E. Burtt, *Leadership and Supervision in Industry* (Columbus, Ohio: Personnel Research Board, Ohio State University, 1945).

ever.[39] As in the Nampa and International Harvester studies, there was no behavioral change unless relationships changed to support the new behavior. The Sigma study, however, differs in one significant way: the major reinforcing relationships in the refinery study were with the *same* people with whom they had worked before. The parties to the relationship had not changed, but the relationships had. This, of course, has important implications for an administrator who wishes to maintain his work teams intact, but hopes to alter behavior and attitudes in these groups. Still, the major point to be made here is that unless the relationships change, behavioral change is more difficult.

Some of the other studies involved an actual breakup of former associations, while in others the parties did not change but the relationships between those parties did. Guest, in his study of a successful change, reported a high incidence of personnel shifts' breaking up old social ties and establishing new relationships which supported the new behavior patterns. There were few discharges, but a program of planned and deliberate lateral transfers and promotions was instituted. Only 25 percent of the plant's supervisors held the same job throughout the period studied. Moreover, the plant manager set up a new pattern of interactions through an increased use of meetings.

> The scope and function of the meetings established by the new manager stood in marked contrast to those of the earlier period: there were more of them, they were regularly scheduled, they covered a wider range of activities, more people took part in them. . . .[40]

Relationships in these meetings were established around new attitudes and behaviors, and support and reinforcement for the new behavior patterns came from these ties.

The studies reported by Jaques and by Seashore and Bowers, however, focused on changes in the nature of the existing relationships. Jaques found that at Glacier Metals a number of new relationships had been established around the new activities (new worker-management committees, etc.), but the primary thrust of the research team's efforts was to alter the expectations and the reinforcement patterns in the existing relationships. This came primarily through what they termed "role clarification" and "working through." Role clarification consisted of a joint examination of the several roles members were expected to play in the group and in the organization as well as the achievement of a common set of expectations about the new ways in which those roles were to be filled. Jaques described "working through" as a serious attempt to voice the unrecognized difficulties, often socially taboo, which had been preventing the group from going ahead with whatever task it may have had. The research team's focus on "working through" was not to aid in the solution of any one problem but to alter the relationship and the manner of working together. Jaques' underlying thesis was that, "Once a group has developed insight and skill in recognizing forces related to status, prestige, security, [etc.] . . . these forces no longer colour subsequent discussion nor impede progress to the same extent as before."[41]

The most vivid example of new social interactions acting to bring about the intended change itself is in the "struggle sessions" in thought-reform prisons.

[39]Blake *et al., op. cit.*
[40]Guest, *op. cit.*
[41]Jaques, *op. cit.*

In some reform prisons on the Chinese mainland, Western prisoners were placed in cells with a group of "advanced" prisoners, who had already made confessions or were in the process. These prisoners, who themselves were taking on the reformed attitudes, and who were given to know that the progress of the entire cell was dependent on the performance of the least-reformed member, exerted strong pressures (accusations, browbeating) on their new member. The potency of this pressure from fellow prisoners was so pronounced that Schein concluded it was the single most effective device used to influence the prisoners to confess and change attitudes.[42] The Communist prison struggle groups are an extreme form of a group influencing a new member to assume new behaviors and attitudes, but the same process goes on in all groups with lowered intensity. The entering member is required to demonstrate adherence to the norms and values of the group to a greater extent, even, than established members.[43]

The establishment of new social ties for confirmation and reinforcement of changes already begun has also traditionally been a part of evangelistic programs. John Wesley organized his converts into small units of 12 or less. This small group, with a chosen leader, met together weekly to tell of their experiences. The leader visited a member each week to collect dues and to verify the sincerity of his conversion. Quarterly, each member was reissued a ticket of membership admitting him to sacrament meetings. Backsliding was watched carefully, and even three or four absences could bring the loss of one's ticket and expulsion from the Society.[44] The importance of the establishment of new social relationships which confirm and support change begun is probably best illustrated by examining change attempts where new ties are not established. Following a Billy Graham crusade in New York City, an informal survey of individuals who came forward and converted during the crusade found that only those who were subsequently integrated into local churches maintained their faith. For others, the conversion became merely a temporary and lapsed reponse.[45]

There are those who lay complete stress on group membership and social pressure in explaining the change process. Such explanations seem incomplete, and that is obviously not our position here, but movement along this dimension appears to be a necessary if not sufficient condition for inducing significant and lasting behavioral change.

Heightening Self-Esteem

Changes in self-esteem on the part of the person being influenced also appear to be an integral part of the process. Interestingly, a movement toward greater self-esteem seems to be a facilitating factor, not only in the establishment of new patterns of thought and action, but also in the unfreezing of old patterns. The abandonment of previous patterns of behavior and thought is easier when an individual is moving toward an increased sense of his own worth. The movement along this continuum is away from a sense of self-doubt toward a feeling of positive worth—from a feeling of partial inadequacy toward a confirmed sense of personal capacity. The increased sense of one's own po-

[42]Schein et al., op. cit.
[43]George C. Homans, *The Human Group* (New York: Harcourt, Brace & Co., 1950).
[44]W. Sargent, *Battle for the Mind* (Garden City, N.Y.: Doubleday & Co., 1957).
[45]Schein et al., op. cit.

tential is evident throughout this continuum, not merely at the end. This may seem a paradox, but the contradiction is more apparent than real.

As noted earlier, one of the preconditions for successful change is the experience of stress within the system. Though stress is usually present even before the intervention of the change agent, the agent himself can play an extremely important role in challenging the individual's sense of adequacy. His means of doing this may be explicit or implicit. The negative diagnosis may be openly stated, as when the religious revivalist points to the prospective proselyte's indulgent life and calls him to repentance. The older members at an A.A. meeting may confront the alcoholic with the fact that he is destroying himself and his family. The Communist prison interrogator may insist on the prisoner's "criminal acts against the people." On the other hand, the negative diagnosis may be communicated implicitly by the agent's acting to introduce change in the object system, such as a psychotherapist embarking on a program of treatment after he has had exploratory talks with the patient.

In organizational change, we also find both patterns. A new executive may confront the members of the organization with the inconsistencies and inefficiencies in their operations, as he did in the Nampa case. An outside consultant, however, will more often seek a confrontation among the members of the organization. For example, Robert Blake, in working with the management of the Sigma plant, suggested an initial meeting between plant managers and the headquarters staff, at which the problems uncovered "shocked" the plant management. From this meeting came the impetus to design a development program in which each of the members of the supervisory group were likewise confronted by others' perceptions of his behavior.[46] Jaques and the research team at Glacier Metals worked with the staff in their meetings and helped them to "express feelings which they had been suppressing sometimes for years." Many, for the first time, were able to assess the consequences of some of their behavior.[47]

On the other hand, the manager of the plant sudied by Guest entered into a situation where the men had already had abundant evidence of the unsatisfactory consequences of their behavior He felt it necessary only to acknowledge this evidence.

> In the first meeting with all supervision he put forward what he called "a few basic goals" for the organization in terms of expected efficiency and quality. He stated candidly to the group that Plant Y had a bad reputation. He said he had heard that many members of the group were not capable of doing their jobs. He said he was "willing to prove that this was not so, and until shown otherwise, I personally have confidence in the group."[48]

In each of these instances, the manager or consultant signaled that the men needed to change; that their former performance was not adequate or appropriate. How, then, does this kind of action foster a heightened sense of worth? The men cannot help feeling they are of some worth, receiving this much attention from someone whom they respect. He is making an investment in them. Even though he is communicating a negative evaluation of their present behavior or attitudes, he is also indicating that he has higher expectations. He

[46]Blake *et al., op. cit.*
[47]Jaques, *op. cit.*
[48]Guest, *op. cit.*

is saying, in effect, that he respects their potential. Finally, when he communicates his negative diagnosis he also offers hope, implying that there is a better way and that he knows that better way. The effect on self-esteem is negative at this point in that the attention received derives from their past inadequacy—their need to change. But it is positive in that it lays a foundation for a new beginning, and promise of better results in the future.

In instances of successful change, there is a movement toward increased self-regard as the person finds himself capable of making the changes in behavior. He experiences a sense of accomplishment, a relief from tension, and a reintegration around a new pattern of activity and thought. The junior managers at Nampa, for example, had the opportunity to assume new roles and take on new tasks. As they accomplished these tasks, which had been previously performed by their superiors, they gained a new confidence rooted in their own achievements.

This gain in self-esteem was evident in each of the studies. Early in each of the organizational studies, managers began listening to their subordinates and responding to them. In each case subordinates began taking on responsibilities and participating in decisions that had been withheld from them in the past. The confidence gained from success in these early attempts led to further steps. In Guest's study, men expressed an increasing feeling of competence ("Just gradually we learned how to do the job") and confidence in their future ("The foreman knows that he's got the stuff, he's going to be recognized and promoted"). Toward the end of the period studied, the "promotion" theme was mentioned often in the interviews, while only three years earlier none had expressed the hope of advancing.[49] At the Sigma Refinery, studied by Barnes and Greiner, a new set of programs for increasing productivity and improving costs were confidently and successfully carried out.[50] At Glacier, Jaques reported that increased confidence and self-esteem was demonstrated in a capacity to tackle formerly taboo problems with considerably less anxiety.

The study of the "Banner Corporation," conducted by Seashore and Bowers, is perhaps the most interesting of the four concerning this factor, in that managers and consultants were explicit about the need for increased self-esteem. The consultants set a goal to build "supportive supervisory behavior," which they defined as increasing "the extent to which subordinates (at all levels) experienced positive, ego-sustaining relations with superiors and peers whenever they undertook to act in ways which would promote their common goals."[51] Paradoxically, it was at "Banner" that increased confidence was most difficult to attain; the early attempts at supervisory support became the focus of misunderstanding and ill-will. The supervisors attempted in good faith to be "supportive" but often found no way to link this up to accomplishment. Indiscriminate support not only failed to build self-esteem but actually undermined it. This factor, plus a deteriorating economic situation and some formal organizational blocks controlled by higher management, retarded progress to the point where the representative from the Survey Research Center proposed a suspension of the field work. It was only after a reorganization, allowing the plant greater freedom, that the latent gains from the early change efforts began

[49] *Ibid.*
[50] Blake *et al., op. cit.*
[51] Seashore and Bowers, *op. cit.*

to produce the spiraling achievement and confidence that increased plant productivity.

The best known study demonstrating that a heightening of self-worth is an integral part of the influence process comes from the Relay Assembly Test Room Experiments begun in 1924 by the Western Electric Company at their Hawthorne works. The tests, of course, were initially designed to examine the "relation of quality and quantity of illumination to efficiency in industry," but the baffled experimenters found that productivity increased in their "test groups" and "control groups" in almost equal magnitude. They were obtaining greater efficiency, but it apparently was not "illumination that was making the difference!" Further study, this time experimentally varying rest pauses and working hours, again revealed no simple correlation between the experimentally imposed changes and rate of output. Production rose steadily even when the experimental conditions were returned to their original condition. This time, however, the experimenters took careful note of other factors, one of which was the experimenters' influence on the girls to increase productivity. Ostensibly, the experiment had not been an attempt to change behavior, and the experimenters disclaimed any conscious desire to influence the girls toward increased production. The superintendent's notes concerning the first meeting held with the girls indicated that great care was taken to convince them that the purpose of the test was not to boost production:

> The group were assured that the test was not being set up to determine the maximum output, and they were asked to work along at a comfortable pace and particularly not to attempt to see how much they could possibly do.[52]

But in fact the girls received signals which conveyed an exactly opposite message.[53] The superintendent's next words were:

> If increased output resulted from better or more satisfactory working conditions, both parties would be the gainers.[54]

Increased productivity *was* what interested the experimenters! The girls could see that it was the production output which was being recorded so meticulously and subjected to such careful scrutiny.[55]

In retrospect, the treatment the girls were given seems almost perfectly designed to increase their sense of self-esteem. A new supervisor who was promoted to department chief became the test observer and he treated them very differently from their previous superior. The observer and the experimenters made every effort to obtain the girls' whole-hearted cooperation for each change, consulting them about each change and even canceling some changes

---

[52]F. J. Roethlisberger and W. J. Dickson, *Management and the Worker* (Cambridge, Mass.: Harvard University Press, 1939).

[53]Committee on Work in Industry. National Research Council, *Fatigue of Workers: Its Relation to Industrial Production* (New York: Reinhold Publishing Corp. 1941), pp. 56–66.

[54]Roethlisberger and Dickson, *op. cit.*

[55]There seems little doubt that the girls received this message whether the experimenters were consciously trying to convey it or not. Studies have shown that even when one person in a close interpersonal relationship is trying to be "nondirective," the other person's behavior can still be strongly influenced by the subtle signals of approval and disapproval which the first person unintentionally gives. E. J. Murray, "A Content Analysis Method for Studying Psychotherapy," *Psychological Monographs*, Vol. 70 (1956).

which did not meet with their approval. The girls' health, well-being, and opinions were the subject of genuine concern. Investigators spent full time recording and analyzing their output and the superintendent of the inspection branch visited the room frequently, accompanied by an intermittent stream of industrial psychologists and university professors. Each of the girls became a valued member of a cohesive and cooperative group, and as their efficiency increased, so did their sense of confidence.

The experimenters had sought to hold all factors constant except those which were explicitly manipulated in each period. In their attempts to provide an optimal climate for objective research, however, the things which were changed most were the very factors most likely to facilitate change. Each of the conditions and processes so far described was present: (1) the girls, in a new and unfamiliar situation, were initially tense and unsure; (2) persons holding great prestige in the girls' eyes introduced the change; (3) initially the objective which the researchers sought was vague and unclear to the girls, but, judging from the reports, it became increasingly clear to the girls that the research had a specific objective—to find ways to increase productivity; (4) the girls were separated from their former associates and formed a new group built around new activities and attitudes; and finally, (5) the experimenters created conditions which gave the girls a greater sense of importance and worth. The Relay Assembly Test Room Experiment Series has been cited by many writers to illustrate many things, but whatever else it demonstrates, it provides us with carefully reported instance of influence and induced change—with increasing self-esteem an integral part of that process.

Internalization

Internalization of the motive for change was the fourth part of the influence process. The motivating force toward a particular change originates outside the individuals to be influenced. They may be actively searching for more adequate behavior, but the actual kind or direction of the change originates outside. Someone else introduces the plan, the scheme, the interpretation, the suggestion, or the idea. Where the new behavior patterns are to become lasting, however, the individuals involved must internalize or come to "own" the rationale for the change.

Internalization occurs as an individual finds the ideas and the prescribed behavior intrinsically rewarding in helping him to cope with external and internal stresses. He adopts the new behavior because he sees it as useful for the solution of a problem or because it is congenial to his own orientation.[56] In

[56]We are very close here to Kelman's formulation of identification. (See "Processes of Opinion Change," *Public Opinion Quarterly*, Spring, 1961; and "Compliance, Identification and Internalization, Through Processes of Attitude Change," *Journal of Conflict Resolution*, Vol. 2. No. 1 (March 1958). Kelman, however, argues that internalization is not a necessary part of the influence process. An individual, he reasons, may adopt a new behavior pattern through *compliance*, not because he believes in the content, but in order to gain a specific reward or avoid some anticipated punishment. Or he may, through identification, accept influences in order to establish or maintain a relationship with another person or group. This distinction between compliance, identification, and internalization may be made conceptually, but in complex interpersonal relations, in which social influence is being exerted over an extended period of time, neither compliance to external demands nor identification with new reference groups appears to operate successfully without internalization of content on the part of the persons being influenced. Certainly in the Nampa situation, it would be difficult to explain the changes we have noted in terms of compliance or identification alone.

the Nampa Center as well as in the historical and experimental settings mentioned earlier, internalization seemed to consist of three elements:

1. Provision of a new cognitive structure.
2. Application and improvisation.
3. Verification through experience.

Provision of a new cognitive structure. To judge from the studies examined, the first step in the internalization process is the influencing agent's introduction of a new conceptual framework. The new framework may be restricted to a way of conceiving of a limited set of phenomena or it may be far-reaching in its attempt to explain the totality of a person's experience. In either case, the individual is given a new means for reordering the information he has about himself and his environment. Implicit in the framework are relationships of acts to outcomes so that certain ends call for certain behavior. The framework also provides a language which not only communicates the cognitive structure, but creates an "associative net"[57] by which the individual can relate the events in his own life to the new scheme. Once an idea has been acquired, it serves as a discriminative stimulus and increases the probability that a wide range of relevant behaviors will occur.[58]

This provision of a new cognitive structure by the person seeking to exert influence was a part of all the organizational change studies examined. The new director in our study spent a considerable amount of time differentiating his views of authority from that which underlay the manner in which the Nampa Center had been administered before. At the "Banner Corporation," the plant manager and the consultants agreed that the first step was to "provide the plant management group of 14 people with a thorough grounding in the concepts and research basis for participation management." A series of seminars were agreed upon partly "to explore the concepts" and to "outline a conceptual scheme."[59] At the Piedmont Oil Refinery, a training program which emphasized a conceptual scheme developed by Robert Blake, called the Management Grid, initiated the change, providing the managers at the plant with new ways of conceiving of their experiences and actions.[60] In other instances, such as the automobile assembly plant studied by Guest, the new scheme was not presented as formally. The new manager met with the plant in various meetings and told them "what he believed in." He outlined in writing a long-range program and he set up a series of regular meetings to examine their operations. Gradually, the men were brought to "a greater awareness of how the total organization fitted together."[61]

The introduction of a new conception of experience as a part of the internalization process is even more apparent in nonorganizational settings. The religious evangelist presents a world view which explains events in terms of spiritual force and points to the relationships of man's actions to this force. The Communistic prison interrogator advances a world view which interprets events

[57]David C. McClelland, "Toward a Theory of Motive Acquisition," *American Psychologist*, May 1965.

[58]A. H. Brayfield, "Human Resources Development," *American Psychologist*, Vol. 23, No. 7 (July 1968).

[59]Seashore and Bowers, *op. cit.*

[60]Blake *et al., op. cit.*

[61]Guest, *op. cit.*

as part of a struggle between "progress" and "reaction." From this world view proceeds a prescription of "progressive" and "reactionary" behavior. Different forms of psychotherapy provide a conception of health and sickness that enables the patient to reconceive of his life and supplies him with a consistent way of interpreting his experiences.

Application and improvisation. Introduction of a new cognitive structure is not sufficient for internalizing to take place, however. The individual must in some way "make it his own." Our data suggest that he must actively participate in trying to understand the scheme and apply it to his own problems. Where internalization occurs, typically the guidelines are general enough that the person being influenced is forced to improvise. Thus the new cognitive structure has to be amplified and integrated into the individual's existing thought patterns. King and Janis demonstrated the effectiveness of improvisation for inducing opinion change in an experiment with college students.[62] Three groups of male students were presented with a written document concerning the induction of graduating college students into the military service, a topic of personal importance to them. Men in one group were asked only to study the statement. Men in a second group were asked to read it aloud with as much affect as possible so that the statement could be tape-recorded and played to judges. Those in the third group were asked to read the statement, then to role-play the part of an advocate of the views stated in the paper. Results of questionnaires filled out several months before and immediately after the experiment showed that only the group who had had to improvise showed a significant opinion change. Moreover, the experimenters' analysis showed that the difference between the groups could not be attributed to closer attention to the written statement nor higher satisfaction with their performance.

In the studies at "Banner," Piedmont, and Guest's auto assembly plant, the supervisor had to improvise to make the suggested ideas operational in their own department. At "Banner," the managers and supervisors had to build on their own ideas in order to implement "participation management" in their own part of the plant. At Piedmont, the men had an idea at the end of the training session about the aims of "9,9" management, but they had to improvise to apply the ideas to their own unique situation. At the auto assembly plant studied by Guest the supervisors were impressed by the way the new manager treated them and by his use of meetings to gather the relevant information and to plan the work. But they had to take his pattern, modify it, and improvise to make the new approach work for them.

Schein and his associates reported that in the Chinese thought-reform prisons, the prisoners were kept under extreme pressure to make a confession of their guilt.[63] But they were not told what the content of the confession was to be. The prisoner had to supply the material for the confession himself. He was only told repeatedly to stop holding back and to make a complete confession. Only then would there be any promise that the pressure would cease. His task was to produce a confession which would demonstrate to the satisfaction of his captors his complete and unequalified acceptance of the Communist scheme of

[62]B. King and I. Janis, "Comparison of the Effectiveness of Improvised vs. Non-Improvised Role Playing in Producing Opinion Change," *Human Relations.* Vol. 9, pp. 177–86.
[63]Schein *et al., op. cit.*

things. To do this he had to improvise with material from his own experience. Usually, completely fabricated confessions were condemned and rejected. For an acceptable selection and interpretation of this material he had to look for cues from his interrogator, his fellow prisoners who had successfully confessed, and from the controlled mass media. The prisoner had to try repeatedly to demonstrate that he had come to interpret the events in his life in terms of the constructs of his captors. Having had to use these constructs to analyze his own life experiences, the prisoner found the Communistic world view less implausible and foreign.

Verification through experience. Testing a new scheme through one's own experience is probably the most important of the three elements of internalization, and it is too often overlooked in the rush to examine the irrational aspects of the influence process. The individual adopts the attitude or behavior and gives it meaning independent of the original source only as he finds it valid in working with his own problems. He must test it against the world as he perceives that world.

At Nampa the junior managers were told that they would be the contact men for their projects with research and sales, and before long they were assigned to committees with important and urgent tasks with these men. In approximately the same manner, the senior scientists were given an openended assignment: to make themselves more useful to the line projects. Soon afterward they were assigned to committees where the task was to plan and execute line projects. Specific organizationl mechanisms were provided by the director to help both groups achieve their objectives, and thus they consistently found their experience coinciding with their expectations.

For the other two groups the situation was very different. The senior managers' assignment to do long-range technical planning was no more openended than the assignments given the two groups just discussed, but no mechanisms were established to implement this difficult assignment. Moreover, the senior managers could see that the director was not in the same power position to support them in their role as long-range planners as he was for the junior managers and senior scientists in their new roles.

Though the situation for the junior scientists was different, the net result was the same. The director did have the power to support his assertion that the changes would give the junior scientists more responsibility and autonomy, but he provided no specific organizational mechanisms to help bring this about.

At "Banner," experimenters first introduced participative management in an industrial engineering project; efficiency rose and morale remained high. So later they set up an experimental department, and again the early results were close enough to those anticipated that the superintendents in the plant chose to extend the new management methods to other departments. At Plant Y the supervisors tried new methods of running their departments and produced better results. Following the new manager's lead in holding regular meetings, they found it possible to coordinate their efforts better. They took chances, made mistakes, and were not fired. In recommending technical changes they found each change gave them "that much more chance to think ahead so we won't get in the hole next time." At Sigma the management at the plant drew heavily on the approaches developed in the Grid Laboratory sessions in deciding how to handle a manpower reduction, and the results were so encouraging that they sought to use the approach on more of their operating problems.

In each of the above instances, the new scheme found confirmation in the individual's experience, but there is also the other side of the coin. One of the striking outcomes of the Chinese thought-reform program among Western prisoners is that among most returned prisoners, it did *not* produce long-range ideological changes independent of the external support provided in the prison setting. Only a very few former prisoners maintained an espousal of the ideological position "taught" in the prison after they had had time to reevaluate the prison experience and had new sources of information which they could check. What would have happened to these prisoners had they returned to a Communist society is impossible to say, but where the viewpoint of his captors failed to find validation in the prisoner's experience after the prison experience, it was not internalized. Of course, in those areas where the Chinese captors' schema *did* continue to be congruent with their experience, the change in the ex-prisoners' attitudes and behavior continued to be effected.[64]

In one sense, this part of the internalization process may be termed reality-testing, but this is not to say that uniform views of reality prevail. Indeed, an individual's perception of reality may be distorted, but for an individual to integrate the new construct into his system of beliefs he must validate it through his perception of reality.

Implications

So much for the model itself, what are its implications? For those who have a major interest in organizational change, a model such as this raises three kinds of issues:

1. Technical
2. Moral.
3. Social.

By the term "technical," I refer simply to the issues concerning how someone can do his task more effectively. In this vein, even an elementary paradigm like this shows the utility of such a device to a practitioner. If nothing else, it serves as a check list, forcing him to ask himself what he has neglected. For example, the importance of tension and the recognition by those involved that some change is required would seem to be nothing beyond common sense. But how often is it ignored by the managers, or by the organizational development staff man who is eager to demonstrate the utility of his methods? It is my hope that better models will keep the organizational development specialist from becoming a victim of the "law of the instrument" (i.e., if you give a boy a hammer, he'll find things to hit) and push him toward an improvement of his diagnostic skills.

The near-necessity that the change be introduced or supported by those with power and respect has been learned many times, the hard way, by those in management training. Although a chief executive's actual participation may not be necessary or in some cases even desirable, his understanding and support can

[64]*Ibid.*

be vital. A full recognition of this feature of organization change processes may lead the O.D. staff man to spend more time as a counselor to the line executive and less time in training sessions. The line manager may accomplish more using means available to him than the staff specialist can with many times the effort. But this will require those engaged in organizational development work to educate themselves, not only in training methods, but also in the creative design of formal structures and in the behavioral effects of information and measurement systems.

Movement toward increasingly specific goals, while seeming the most obvious, is, from my observation, probably the dimension on which most change efforts flounder. General goals, often widely and genuinely shared, too frequently die for the lack of the crucial idea as to how the first few concrete steps can be taken. Laboratory training often provides a first useful step, but the steps which can help an individual or a group translate the goal from there into daily job performance arise only from planning and creative collaboration of the parties involved.

The use of laboratory training methods has made a major contribution to organizational change in providing a means, however imperfect, of changing relationships without requiring that work teams be broken up or that change wait upon shifts in personnel. But more needs to be learned about the use of groups to support and reinforce change and experimentation. Work by Schein[65] and others suggests that there is much to be learned about helping individuals enter and exit from organizational units with greater understanding in order to maximize their own effectiveness and freedom.

At an intuitive level, we all understand the part self-esteem plays in change, but the message from the learning theorists about the superior effectiveness of positive reinforcements as a teaching strategy has yet to be fully utilized. Concerning internalization, it is my opinion that as we improve our models of behavioral change, we will become even more impressed with the importance of the cognitive constructs. The constructs used more widely now by those in industry (such as McGregor's X and Y) benefit from the impact which a dichotomy provides, but they also suffer from the polarization it induces. In my opinion, we need new constructs and have been living on the conceptual capital of a prior decade for some time.

The moral issues raised by the use of some explicit representation of the influence process are probably heightened by citing examples drawn from clearly coercive instances of influence as I have done here. In one sense, this is a semantic issue. "Influence" as a descriptive term may cause concern, while "leadership" would have an opposite effect. But there is more here than semantics. Manipulation does occur. Anyone who deals with others in a responsible position is in danger of becoming manipulative. His only effective means of coping with this danger is an intelligent awareness of his own actions and motives and an openness in his dealings with others. A refusal to examine his aims and the processes in which his actions play a part can do no more than serve as a psychological defense against some guilt he may feel. We are all in the business of influencing others. It is not our understanding or consciousness which presents the real moral issues, but our motives and methods. These can be better scrutinized when made explicit.

[65]Edgar H. Schein, "Organizational Socialization and the Profession of Management," *Industrial Management Review*, Winter, 1968.